A Serious Character

A Serious Character

The Life of Ezra Pound

Humphrey Carpenter

Houghton Mifflin Company

Boston / 1988

First American edition 1988

Copyright © 1988 by Humphrey Carpenter.

ALL RIGHTS RESERVED.

For information about permission to reproduce selections from
this book, write to Permissions, Houghton Mifflin Company,
2 Park Street, Boston, Massachusetts 02108.

Library of Congress Cataloging-in-Publication Data

Carpenter, Humphrey.
A serious character.

Bibliography: p.
Includes index.
1. Pound, Ezra, 1885–1972—Biography. 2. Poets,
American—20th century—Biography. I. Title.
PS3531.082Z5526 1988 811'.52 [B] 87-37836
ISBN 0-395-41678-7

Printed in the United States of America

Q 10 9 8 7 6 5 4 3 2 1

'are you or are you not, a serious character?'
Ezra Pound, 1913, quoted by Charles Olson

'a seereeyus kerakter'
Ezra Pound to James Laughlin,
27 September 1936

Contents

Preface

If Ezra Pound had not existed, it would be hard to invent him. On the other hand, somebody stumbling across the facts of his life for the first time might suppose him to be an exotic character in fiction or drama, rather than a real historical person.

But he did exist, and not surprisingly he has been the subject of numerous pieces of biography. Indeed one author coming fresh to the field in 1982 threw up his hands and observed: 'The biographical literature on Pound is staggering.' So it is, at least in quantity. His extraordinary personality inspired his literary friends to try to make sense of him on paper from the outset, while for every William Carlos Williams, W. B. Yeats, Ford Madox Ford or Ernest Hemingway who took up a pen to describe an Ezra they had known for years, there has been a multitude of journalists or academics writing about him at one remove – the shelves are now cluttered with seemingly endless recapitulations of his 'life and contacts', examined from any number of angles. Yet only one full biography has previously been attempted, which of necessity had to be provisional and limited.

In the late 1960s, while Ezra Pound was still alive, Noel Stock, an Australian who had edited a magazine dedicated to propagating Poundian ideas, was staying at Ezra's daughter's home in the Italian Tyrol. While sorting family papers which were then stored there, Stock put together an account which was published in 1970 as *The Life of Ezra Pound*. Stock's book was scrupulously accurate as far as it went, but besides being based on limited sources it had to be approved by Ezra's wife Dorothy, who (since Ezra had been judged insane in 1946) had legal control of his affairs. Stock thus felt himself unable to discuss the intricacies of Ezra's private life and character in much detail. He chose in general to restrict himself to a plain and where necessary discreet statement of facts, though he did now and then voice his own increasing disillusion with Ezra's ideas and poetry.

There had earlier (1960) been an imaginatively researched but rather impressionistic and selective account of his life by an American journalist, Charles Norman, while since his death two books, *The Last Rower* (1976) by C. David Heymann and *The Roots of Treason* (1984) by E. Fuller Torrey, have enquired particularly into his wartime broadcasts and his subsequent indictment for treason and detention in a mental hospital. Heymann and Torrey both unearthed fresh material, but both were motivated by a strong dislike, which naturally affected their handling of the facts. There have also been more limited and partisan studies of his life by enthusiasts for his ideas, not to mention a mass of critical and analytical works on his poetry.

Quite apart from the question of scope, most of the biographical nets so far for Ezra Pound have been too rigid. So agile and slippery a creature cannot be caught by predetermined methods. Again and again one seems to have him by the tail, only to find that he has merely cast off another skin and slipped away, leaving one clutching just a persona or mask. I make no claims for this book other than that I have tried to avoid that particular mistake.

Ezra Pound's relatives and friends have behaved towards me with great kindness, but it is not in any way an 'authorized' biography. However, I must express my considerable gratitude to his literary estate for granting permission to quote without restriction from his letters and other unpublished papers. Proper acknowledgement of this and other kindnesses will be found at the end of the book.

Part One

1885–1908
'Ra'

1

It Might Go Off And Hurt Someone

'Ezra Loomis Pound was born . . . in a pioneer shack.' He wasn't, and it is typical of Ezra that one of his biographers should muddle fact with myth from the very beginning. Sorting out sheer history, indeed, proves almost impossible with him from start to finish. Almost better, perhaps, to swallow legend whole; for example Ford Madox Ford's splendid spoof of Ezra's entry into the world: 'Born in the blizzard, his first meal consisted of kerosene. That . . . accounted . . . for the glory of his hair.' Amiable nonsense of this sort is not always very far from the truth.

Nevertheless the facts must be disentangled, and the reality appears to be that he was born at about 3 p.m. on 30 October 1885 – a date he afterwards labelled as 'Ole EZ HIZ Birthday' – not in any pioneer shack, but in something that Ford Madox Ford's very European eye might have mistaken for one: a simple white-painted two-storey wooden house in the remote mining community of Hailey, Idaho, in the American West.

Thirty-five years later, sitting in a Venice hotel, Ezra began to write about his own origins and birth, devoting a mocking little prose narrative, *Indiscretions*, to demonstrating how, over the generations, his family had managed to personify almost everything of consequence that had happened in America since the arrival of the *Mayflower*. It was possible, he said, 'to feel that one could write the whole social history of the United States from one's family annals'.

The West has to feature somewhere in any chronicle that claims pan-Americanism. Yet it was only a set of curious chances that took Homer Loomis Pound, Ezra's father, to what, even in American eyes, was the edge of civilization.

*

Recording his semi-mythical family history with Henry Jamesian mock-solemnity in *Indiscretions*, Ezra carefully distances himself from it, disguising the family name as 'Weight', thereby shunning the other meanings of 'pound', which we, with hindsight, might regard as prophesying both economics and imprisonment. Nor does he allude to the entry in the *Dictionary of American Biography* for one Thomas Pound, who flourished in the second half of the seventeenth century, and was a pirate. Born in England, this Pound turned buccaneer on the American coast, was reprieved from hanging by the exertions of certain worthy contemporaries, and afterwards sailed back to Europe and respectability. No connection with Ezra's family can be proved, but, remembering the shape of Ezra's own career, and Wyndham Lewis's characterization of Ezra as 'a bombastic galleon' with 'a skull and crossbones' flying from its mast, one wonders.

Throughout *Indiscretions*, Ezra casts a sceptical eye on family legend. He doubts whether – as his grandmother had told him – a maternal ancestor had really set foot on the American continent as respectably early as 1632. He hardly seems to believe that the Pounds (his own branch of them) were descended from a seventeenth-century New Jersey whaler, or that this John Pound, who died in Piscataway in 1691, was the patriarch of six Quaker generations of Pounds – in which no less than three successive eldest sons were baptized Elijah. Only with his grandfather, Thaddeus Coleman Pound, does Ezra begin to treat family history as fact rather than myth. And only with Thaddeus does he begin to express any admiration.

*

Thaddeus Coleman Pound had already lost two fortunes by the time his grandson Ezra was born. His vanished riches had been amassed from a lumbering business and a railway company. By 1883 he was merely a farmer, if still a fairly wealthy one, but he retained among his assets a few silver mines of doubtful worth near Hailey, Idaho, in the Rockies; and it seemed a good idea to dispatch his only son Homer out there, to see if the men working the mines on his behalf were honest (which was improbable).

Thaddeus had a little influence in Washington, which he used to ensure Homer a Government salary when he arrived. Thus Homer, to his great astonishment, received an official wire that the President had appointed him 'Register' of the Hailey Land Office. He was unable to find Hailey on the map.

It was a convenient method of dealing not only with the family mines, but also with Homer, who so far had shown no determination to do anything other than run away from school. Having achieved distinction in 1858 as supposedly the first white child to be born in northern Wisconsin, Homer made no other effort to mark himself out, and was content to remain under the shadow of his energetic father. Thaddeus's taste for setting the world to rights would in time be passed on to Ezra, but his son, a freewheeler by nature, was never touched by it. Despite his name – a tribute to a great-uncle who was said to have read the adventures of Odysseus in their original language – Homer was untroubled by education. He remembered four words of the Chippewa speech, taught to him in infancy by his Indian nurse, but bothered to learn little else. He was sent to military academy in Minnesota, but did not care for it and rode home at once on the cow-catcher of a train. Later, West Point was tried with similar results, Homer descending from the train even before it arrived there, and returning home on another. In *Indiscretions*, Ezra regards this behaviour with admiration.

By the time Homer reached his mid-twenties it was felt that he should contribute to his upkeep, especially since Thaddeus was now losing his third fortune as determinedly as he had depleted the first two – this time by adjusting (with the aid of a saw) the length of the cows' horns on the family farm at Chippewa Falls, Wisconsin, in the fervent but mistaken belief that it would improve their milk yield, and by executing extravagant plans to bottle a local spring water that he hoped would make him 'millions' (but which, said Ezra, tasted only like water).

On his arrival, in Idaho, Homer saw why Hailey had attracted the attention of few cartographers. Surrounded by the fastnesses of the Saw-Tooth Range (in Ezra's words 'miles of real estate, most of it up on end'), the town consisted of one hotel, one street, forty-seven saloons, and a newspaper. There was also a minister, whose salary was collected in the forty-seven bars by a couple of church elders, each taking one side of the street. The more sheepish of the bar proprietors advertised their liquor under such euphemisms as 'Kentucky Hardware'. Homer Pound, a teetotaller by inclination, is reputed to have drunk 'a certain amount of lemonade' in these establishments.

Later, he communicated to his son Ezra vignettes of certain Hailey 'characters': Horace Morgan the gambler, in a long black coat; 'Blue' Dick, who owed his name to an accident with blasting powder; and miners with names like Curley and Poison, who 'were known to carry sticks of dynamite in their boots'. It was not a genteel society; the local paper would announce the recent activities of horse-thieves much as if it were chronicling the proceedings of a ladies' sewing circle. Fortunes were made abruptly: a man who sawed logs for Homer one week declined the next invitation to do so because he now had 'ten thousand' in the bank, and would Homer care to go East for him and sell a mine?

Homer had been called by the President to establish a Government Land Office, to which miners from several hundred miles around would come to file their claims. The law permitted prospectors to 'stake out' a certain number of acres, providing that they 'worked' them in person, and took from them a minimum amount of precious metals each year. Failure to do so allowed another miner to 'jump' the claim (declare it his own) if he worked it himself. Under this system, tempers often became heated. Homer described how one claimant grabbed a ·42 calibre six-shooter off the Land Office wall in order to avenge a friend. Precisely whose six-shooter is not clear: Homer had packed a firearm in his bag when leaving Wisconsin, 'but his cousin, Harve, took it away saying he'd "Better not 'cause it might go off and hurt someone."'

Off the main street of Hailey, with its boardwalks and horse-dirt, the land had been marked out; and in June 1884 Homer paid $500 for a plot and the new house that stood on it, a solid-looking frame-and-clapboard building, containing a 'music room' as well as three bedrooms and quite substantial eating and living quarters. It was reputedly the first house in Idaho Territory to display plaster on its inside walls; it stood at the corner of Second and Pine Streets. So spacious a residence had been selected by the young Land Register because he was about to marry.

*

Some two or three years earlier, drifting between various forms of temporary employment, Homer had travelled to Washington in the wake of his father, hoping to see the sights and perhaps improve himself. Such trips were common among the fashionable, who liked, as Ezra noted in his Canto 83, 'to sit in the Senate gallery / or even in that of the House / to hear the fireworks'. Among these *aficionados* of Capitol Hill was a Mrs Frances Amelia Weston of New York, who journeyed regularly to Washington to shake hands with each newly elected President – even with Grover Cleveland, though he 'drank' – and to dance at every Inaugural, 'for a vast period of years'. In 1881 there were no less than two Inaugurals to draw her there from New York City, where she resided with her husband, Ezra Brown Weston, and her niece Isabel. The installation of President Garfield was swiftly followed by an assassin's bullet, so that a few months later the procedure was repeated for President Arthur. At one of these occasions, perhaps on the dance floor itself, Mrs Frances Amelia Weston made the acquaintance of Mr Homer Pound.

Frances Weston, soon to be known to the Pound family as Aunt Frank, could have stepped from the pages of Henry James. At first sight she seemed comfortably situated in the fashionable classes, attending regularly at such 'smart' New York churches as Dr Parkhurst's or St Bartholomew's, and, with comparable regularity, journeying to Europe in June 'with a vast collection of valises, suit-cases, hold-alls, band-boxes, and heterogeneous parcels'. However, doubts about the security of her niche in society might be engendered by a glimpse of her husband, Ezra Brown Weston, distinguished by cubical side-whiskers, who would explode with 'prodigious pop-guns of good humour' that displayed a cheerful non-metropolitan sense of comedy. Witness his narrative of Cleveland's electoral victory: 'An' I bet . . . a dollar an' the first thing I knew in the morning was a fellah yelling hurrah for Grover, and running off with my ash-barrel'; this followed by 'bubbles and gurgles of merriment'. The anecdotal style was carefully noted by great-nephew Ezra Pound.

Like the Pounds, the Westons claimed an impeccable American pedigree; but also like them, they were now perceptibly descending in the world. Ezra Brown Weston traced his ancestry, a little imaginatively, to a rich London merchant who had helped transport settlers across the Atlantic in the earliest days of colonization. This Ezra had worked as a bank broker and in cattle-feed. A brother, James, ran a Metallic Artificial Arms and Legs business on Broadway that prospered gruesomely during the Civil War. Another brother, Harding, for a time sold newspaper advertising. Then, in a voluminous wooden mansion at Nyack, on the Hudson River near New York City, Ezra Weston established what he intended as a refuge from city life for the 'artistic', over which he would preside in the manner of a country gentleman, fostering talents. (Great-nephew Ezra planned a similar venture: the Ezuversity.) The scheme was not a startling success; Ezra Weston quickly acquired a curious band of dependants, including a maiden lady who occasionally 'made small and neat sketches in lead pencil' but otherwise 'pursued a career of masterly inactivity', her only contribution to the household being to 'do the accounts'. Sometimes the guests 'paid' for their upkeep with half-painted pictures; more frequently they did not; and Ezra Weston was also handing out money to his brother Harding, who had become a professional wastrel.

Harding Weston possessed a small military pension earned from a few months' service in the Civil War, and this and his temperament disinclined him to sustained employment. After his spell in the newspaper business, he lived precariously as (at different times) a broker, a clerk, a seller of patent medicines, and a pedlar of 'Shakers' Toothache Pellets'. He was possibly in prison for a while. In 1858 he married Mary Parker, whose mother was a Wadsworth. This connection was her only asset, for Harding soon ceased to support either her or their daughter Isabella, generally known as Isabel, born in 1860 – who was to become Ezra Pound's mother.

By the time Isabel had reached her teens, she and her mother were dependent on Uncle Ezra and Aunt Frank, with whom they were virtually resident. Family legend has it that some time after he had abandoned his wife and daughter, Harding Weston came to Nyack to beg money once more. The request being refused, Harding punched his brother's head and was not seen again by the family. Indeed, until he was twelve Ezra Pound believed his maternal grandfather to be dead, though by the time he wrote *Indiscretions* he knew better: 'A Sixth Avenue barber once asked me if I had seen him . . . He was at last report still remaining, invisible.' Ezra never learnt much about Harding's career and character, but remembered his mother remarking of her father, in condemning tones: 'He had ideas.' Harding eventually ended his life in a veterans' hospital, where he was reported to be suffering from 'attacks of viciousness', and was described as 'very quarrelsome' and requiring 'a great deal of care'. Another hospital report spoke of him as someone who 'seemed to have visionary powers that had gone astray'.

By 1880 Ezra Weston's artistic colony at Nyack had failed, and the building had been surrendered to the mortgage company; but the Westons, always survivors, somehow had enough money left to open a boarding-house in New York City, at 24 East Forty-Seventh Street, a reasonable address in mid-Manhattan near the Grand Central rail depot. It was to this establishment that the young Homer Pound travelled a year or two later 'in my great-aunt's somewhat voluminous wake,' wrote Ezra Pound, 'and upon a possibly somewhat sketchy invitation'. No doubt Homer was attracted there by New York 'life'. Perhaps also his eye was already on Harding's daughter Isabel.

Isabel's mother, Mary, made a living as the chatelaine of a rooming-house for shop and office girls on Lexington Avenue, but retained a precise sense of status, often reminding Isabel that she had been born in a porched house on Fourteenth Street and Second Avenue 'when it was the thing to be born there'. Isabel, said her son, 'was an only child, spoiled, and "liked pretty things"', who grew into a good-natured, good-looking, but some-what affected and distant personality. William Carlos Williams, meeting her about twenty years after her marriage to Homer Pound, thought her 'a remote, even bewildered woman, erect and rather beautiful in an indiffer-ent middle-aged way'. She and Homer made an oddly assorted pair, he with his slow Midwestern drawl, she very upright, with a 'high society' voice. The poet Louis Zukofsky, staying with them both in Rapallo in 1933, noticed that Isabel held herself like Queen Mary. Ezra Pound described his parents' courtship as the meeting between the city girl and the country boy.

Isabel's mother did not regard Homer as the perfect match for a young lady with Wadsworth blood. It appeared, indeed, that Isabel had 'drawn a dud in the conjugal struggle'; but Homer, aware of these feelings, tactfully conducted the opening negotiations in writing, and by 1884 he had a respectable job, which was more than could be said for most of the Westons. Active opposition soon melted away, Homer made the journey eastwards from Hailey, and on 26 November 1884, in the big parlour of Aunt Frank and Uncle Ezra's boarding-house on Forty-Seventh, with a Presbyterian pastor presiding, he and Isabel were married.

The couple made the obligatory honeymoon visit to Niagara Falls, called upon Homer's father in Wisconsin, then continued their journey to Idaho Territory. Their son Ezra was afterwards much amused to contemplate this westward trek, which seemed to him to have the quality of a burlesque show. In their retinue was Mary Beaton, termed by him a 'stylish New York nigger', a maid who had been with Uncle Ezra and Aunt Frank for many years, 'and always havin' been gaoin' with her Miss when she mahr'd'. The township of Hailey until now had possessed only one black face, that of the barber, and on her arrival Mary Beaton made a considerable impression, not least because of the finery of her wardrobe. But Hailey and its uncouth manners soon proved too much for her, and she departed one midnight, 'without her variegated assortment of clothing'. Isabel's next maid left almost as suddenly, marrying a rich prospector and going to live at the Hailey hotel. Thereafter, the Pounds 'had a Chinaman to do the cooking and he was a model of virtue'. It was into this household, eleven months after his parents' marriage, that Ezra Pound was born.

It was indeed an all-American ancestry, ranging from whaler to New England blue blood and patent-medicine pedlar, from pioneer, lumberman, and railway builder to failed hotel proprietor. There were even supposed to be horse-thieves in the family: Ezra himself liked to think of them as relatives, though the claim was unproven. But, he alleged, such all-American stock rarely breeds what is popularly supposed to be the 'American type': the go-getter determined to improve his material condition. According to Ezra, such a seeker after riches is more likely to be of recent immigrant descent. What he called 'the more deeply rooted population', the Anglo-Saxon colonial Americans from which he himself sprang, seemed to him unlikely to give birth to that species. Rather, he said, 'it produces now and again an individual'.

2

The Infant Gargantua

Legends again. 'Violet Hunt, who always had a fine gift for invention, announced once in a moment of irritation that Ezra was really the offspring of wandering Red Indians who had abandoned the child, which contrived, however, to keep itself alive (until handily rescued by a delightful old gentleman from the Middle West who never loses any opportunity of referring with amused pride to his strange foundling) by sucking the kerosene from a tin that this strange babe found lying somewhere in the vast American deserts.'

But then Ezra himself, in *Indiscretions* (1923), narrates his own birth in almost equally fantastic fashion, citing a simultaneous event from the Hailey annals of which his father had told him, and which seemed a portent – though in 1920 when he wrote *Indiscretions* he could not know how accurate a portent – for his own life:

> Before the birth of the infant Gargantua, the great elephant Sampson broke loose from the travelling circus, and upset the lion cages and chased his keeper out of the tent; and his keeper jumped on his cayoos and put for the railroad siding, and you could have seen the cowboys out after it, letting off their six-shooters into its rear.
>
> I heard it all . . . twenty times over, before the trainer wrote his reminiscences (illustrated, *Saturday Evening Post*). The trainer omits the detail of the cowboys, his attention having been fixed on the narrow opening between the two ore cars, because an elephant 'never goes round anything'. It was undoubtedly very clever of the trainer to get the mad animal wedged in between the angle of those cars where it could be

dealt with. And they tied down the elephant Sampson and beat him with hot iron bars, and he grit 'on them with his teeth', and they couldn't make him trumpet. And his keeper begged them not to kill him, but they had to anyhow, only a few months later.

And as the inhabitants weren't uncontaminated savages, and as Fraser's *Golden Bough* was not in their list of reading, they none of them realized what it meant . . .

And the infant Gargantua was born . . .

He was born on 30 October 1885 in the clapboard house on Second and Pine, not far from the forty-seven saloons of Hailey, and 'I believe I came out bouncing'. They named him Ezra after his great-uncle, and Loomis after his father's mother's family; but for daily use they called him 'Ra', pronounced 'Ray'.

In childhood Ezra showed no sign of preferring his full name, and it seemed likely that he would go through life as Ra Pound. The association with the Egyptian sun god did not escape him: during the 1940s, when attacking the supposed international Jewish conspiracy, he wrote to a German acquaintance on the subject of his first name: 'My present position is that the name was Egyptian, Ez (rising) and Raa, proper divine honorific, and that the goddam yitts pinched it as they did everything else.'

*

'Nothing so boring as trype re/ infancy, especially second-hand,' he warned one of his biographers (Patricia Hutchins). But it is surely not altogether 'trype' to try to establish why he remained an only child. Neither parent came from a large family: Homer had one sister, Isabel no siblings. Not until Ezra was nearly four years old did Homer again find a dependable job with good prospects in a part of the country suitable for the civilized upbringing of children. Perhaps Isabel found one infant more than enough outlet for her own hopes and ambitions. She became pregnant once more after Ezra's birth, but miscarried and did not try again. Thus Ezra had the assurance of his parents' unwavering faith and support. 'A man,' wrote Wyndham Lewis paraphrasing Freud, 'who has been the indisputable favourite of his mother keeps for life the feeling of a conqueror.' In Ezra's case read also 'father', as exemplified in Homer's remark to Max Beerbohm at Rapallo in the 1930s: 'You know, Mr Beerbohm, there isn't a darn thing that boy of mine don't know.'

Of the two parents, Homer's enthusiasm for 'Son', as they called him was more obvious. Ezra was grateful to his father for having provided 'continuous sympathy', but in *Indiscretions* he called Homer 'the naïvest man who ever possessed sound sense . . . whose virtues have more than once served him as well as, or possibly better than, other men are served by intellectual ability'. Similarly, Ezra once labelled his father 'my best and most faithful reader, but . . . no intellectual by a long shot'. Actually, Homer's only completely naïve characteristic was his blind admiration for Ezra, and there were more resemblances between father and son than might at first appear. Samuel Putnam, a literary friend of Ezra's who received letters from Homer during the 1920s, observed that they read very much like Ezra's own, even the spelling. Homer wrote to Ezra in 1924, after Yeats had invited the Pounds to Ireland:

> Dear Son,
> Now for the Oirshish invitation – do you *accept?* . . . You may remember Tyson the plumber at Wyncote – well . . . one of his daughters has become quite a pinanist – How about the de-lux edition – is it in process – Want to read that poem of yours on WAR;;;;&&&. Mother reading Havilock Ellis – The Dance of Life. *Warm* weather here today . . .
> > Lovingly
> > Dad.

The letter is typed; Homer was not inspired to such oddities with the pen. Yet in his few pieces of published prose there are similarities to Ezra's writing: in 1898 he gave advice to readers of his local newspaper on 'Where to Find Gold':

> I send you a few facts that show how we are 'forging' ahead of other countries, also a few words of warning against the rush for the Klondike . . . My answer is to try it first nearer home. Well, where? Colorado, Idaho, Montana, California. If you are determined to go into the mining business, but if you are doing fairly well where you are better stick to it . . . What is our own country doing? The best answer is to give you some facts . . .

Ezra, writing on economics, on 'international Jewry', on anything, was always offering to 'give you some facts'.

Ezra was never contemptuous towards Homer, usually enthusiastic, always affectionate. In 1919 he even suggested that Homer himself become a writer. There was a prospect of a new weekly magazine starting in London, and 'there might be an opening for a sober and energetic American . . . someone who will be really honest'. Yet despite his considerable filial loyalty, he knew that there was something essentially comic about his father, and about the American type of which Homer was representative – slow, easygoing, philosophical in a homespun way, difficult to shock out of his gentle pace – 'That boy is always springing some surprises,' Homer would say of the outrageous Ezra – yet obstinate, immovable, and self-willed. If Ezra quite involuntarily took on some of Homer's characteristics – and his disarming simplicity of approach to any task or issue surely came from Homer – there was also an element of satirical impersonation of his father in his own performance. Certainly he mimicked Homer's type when, in his own middle age, he adopted for public pronouncements the species of American personality that Samuel Putnam describes as

> the philosopher of the crossroads grocery and the cracker-barrel, a type that has existed and still exists from Maine to the state of Idaho, where Pound was born. It is a type that, as I know from my own boyhood, is almost invariably 'agin the Government' and addicted to 'cussing out' things as they are.

Ezra was not the only American writer or performer to observe the comic potential in this character. Mark Twain often portrayed it in his fiction, and himself took on some of its qualities. (Ezra affected to despise Twain: 'buncombe . . . a third-rate writer, intellectually a coward'.) Something of the cracker-barrel sage may be found, too, in the stage and screen personally created by W.C. Fields, born in Philadelphia, where Ezra spent most of his youth. There are echoes of Fields' absurd drawl in Ezra's wartime broadcasts, even in his readings of the Cantos.* And if we are looking for non-literary models for elements in Ezra's performance, we are likely to be struck by his remark, made in 1919, that the showman P.T. Barnum was 'the real Murkhn [American] expression'.

*

If questioned about his father, Ezra would usually emphasize their closeness to each other, at the expense of his mother. 'My harmony with my father was unusual,' he told a psychiatrist at St Elizabeths† Hospital in 1946. 'I was my father's son in opposition to my mother . . . My own case is the farthest removed from the Oedipus complex.' Yet it was not quite so simple. Ezra's affection for Homer was tempered by a readiness to use him whenever possible as a drudge. He was impatient with his father's failings; once when Homer sent a manuscript of Ezra's to the wrong editor, Ezra addressed him in mock-bullying tones as 'UNFORtunate Man'. His relationship with his mother was more subtle.

'I never appreciated her until she was dead,' he told the same psychiatrist, but this was nonsense. Certainly he took her no more seriously than he did Homer – 'Looking more like a presbyterian peacock than ever,'

---

*I owe this observation to Roger Lewis.

†The hospital spells its name without an apostrophe, pedantically reproducing an early error.

he wrote to her in 1908 after she had sent him a photograph of herself – but the tone of his letters to her is playful almost to the point of flirtation, in contrast with the plain, direct line he took with Homer. (He rarely wrote to both parents at once: each seemed to require a different manner.)

There was much in Isabel to amuse him. He laughed at her *Ladies' Home Journal* mind, her fondness for 'Art' of the chocolate-box variety, her upright carriage and social nuances. There is something undeniably comic about one of her letters that survives, written in 1925 from America to Ezra's wife Dorothy in Italy, in a formal, upright, rather cramped hand, very different from Homer's easy-flowing copperplate:

> My dear Dorothy,
>   By way of Holiday greeting I have sent an antique [?] arranged as an addition to a negligee. Your approval of the old shawl led me to think you might find use for this article.
>   We were very pleased to have a view of the terraza and the family. The portraits indicating sporting attire looked comfortable . . .
>   Occasionally there are intimations of winter's approach mostly just autumn weather out of doors. A good furnace keeps the interior above seventy. Mr Pound provided attractive feeding – [illegible] & seed – for our winter birds - Cardinals, Woodpecker, Nuthatcher Chickadees & squirrels are numerous and very intimate . . .
>   Holiday greetings to you both.

Yet there are touches of Ezra here too, in the almost Jamesian periphrasis of certain expressions. And if Ezra often chose to laugh at his mother, he could also be strikingly sympathetic. While admitting to his father that 'mother approves convention' and that in this respect 'our view point is different', he was always anxious not to 'excite' or upset her, and would break any alarming news to his father alone, asking him not to pass it on. His letters to Isabel are effete and amused, almost dandified, suggesting a considerable affection. The women he took up with throughout his life tended to resemble her – slightly aloof, socially conscious, restrained, not given to demonstrations of feeling.

Indeed, though he often played the revolutionary or iconoclast, he never experienced any break with his parents. To the end, Homer and Isabel remained his special confidants, so that his letters to 'Dear Dad' and 'Dear Mother', while certainly not short on posing, seem far nearer his 'real' character than do, say, his letters to his future wife during their courtship. Possibly his running away from America to Europe at the age of twenty-three was some substitute for adolescent rebellion. Yet it was to his parents, after arriving in Europe, that he gave the most detailed and honest account of his situation, while to friends of his own generation he chose to remain enigmatic and boastful. His parents were the nearest he had to allies, the only people with whom pretence was unnecessary, to whom he could display, at least now and then, the vulnerability that no one else must see.

*

'And the infant Gargantua was born, and was photographed, and Maria Easton [Mary Weston, Isabel's mother; the family names are changed in *Indiscretions*] came out to see if he looked like his pictures. And the cowboys . . . shot up the town of Cheyenne, where she had to change cars and spend the night. Forty of 'em came down the main street on their ponies, yelling and letting off their six-shooters . . . And she didn't understand what it meant . . . And the hotel had only wooden partitions, and you could hear everything that went on in the next room. And there wasn't any lock on her door . . . And Maria Easton got on the train next morning and came to Hailey, and she said, "Oh! . . . How could you bring my daughter to *such* a place?"'

Isabel felt much the same. She quarrelled with the Chinese cook, found the 'servant problem' altogether too much for her, and moved into Hailey's only hotel, taking the infant Gargantua with her. (Ezra, in times of stress, always liked to live in hotels.) Meanwhile Thaddeus came out to inspect his silver mines and his son's competence in overseeing them. What he found did not please him, 'Dick, Curley & Co' had been engaged to work the mines on his behalf, but, as Ezra puts it, they began to feel that 'their own personal ownership had advantages', so they dug up a quantity of rock that they knew to contain no ore, and announced that the vein was played out. Homer went up to the mine to argue with them. 'By the time the boulder collided with him,' writes Ezra, 'he had already the proofs in his various bags and pockets.' He 'appreciated Dick's delicacy in not having shot him', and understood that 'accidents in mines were unavoidable, and that the next one would be somewhat worse'. The courts decided in Thaddeus's favour, but took eighteen years to reach this decision, by which time 'Dick, Curley & Co' were no doubt living in luxury in the East.

There seemed, then, to be several reasons why the Pounds might consider leaving Hailey. Isabel finally declared that she could stand the altitude no longer – the town was some 5,000 feet above sea level – so Homer agreed to pack up and go. On 15 September 1886, not quite eleven months after Ezra's birth, the house was sold to Homer's successor at the Land Office, and soon afterwards, the family set off east again.

And Hermy [Isabel] couldn't stand the high altitude any longer, and had to be taken back east in the blizzard, behind the First

Rotary Snow-plough. And the infant Gargantua had the croup, and woke all the people in the 'sleeper'. And the inventor of the First Rotary Snow-plough was on board, and he said, 'Madame, if you will give that child a little kerosene oil it will cure it.' And Hermy was indignant. And Gargantua barked for an hour longer; and no one got any sleep in the sleeper. And the inventor of the First Rotary Snow-plough said again to Hermione: 'Madame, I have reared seven myself, and they have all had croup. And I have cured all their croups with a few drops of kerosene oil, dripped onto a lump of sugar.' And Hermione, at last, consented; and the Infant Gargantua slumbered until the train pulled into Chicago.

Ezra never returned to Hailey. As a young man he felt that he had been drawn east by 'the love of adventure & metropolitan life'; moreover, 'it will be observed that I smother if I move westward or inland in the U.S.A. . . . have had literally a sense of drowning or gasping for breath – west of the Alleghenies'. In most respects, that he had been born in Idaho meant nothing to him. He had left the place far too young to have even the faintest memory of it. Yet this early departure itself had a significance, for throughout his life he never lived anywhere that was unarguably 'home', a place where his family belonged and had a personal history.

*

The family went to Homer's father's home at Chippewa Falls, Wisconsin, but did not stay there long. Thaddeus was suffering fresh financial troubles, and he and his daughter-in-law, with her grand city airs, did not get on. There was, however, a welcome for them at Aunt Frank and Uncle Ezra's boarding-house in New York City, so here they stayed for quite some time, while Homer, in a somewhat leisurely fashion, contemplated the future. There was plenty of room alongside the 'paying guests' in the big brownstone house; Ezra remembered it as endlessly accommodating, with an army of folding beds, which eventually surfaced in Canto 80: 'does any museum / contain one of the folding beds of that era?'

And the infant Gargantua spoke the English tongue and used syntax and eschewed the muliebria of diminutives. And at the age of two years, less two months, he gave a correct medical diagnosis of his ailments, to the great amazement of old Dr Dowling, who had expected him to say 'goo-ah' . . . And at the age of two years and four months he denounced Mary Beaton (in error) for wasting his talcum, when she spilt the baking-powder for the biscuits (*anglicè*: scones) . . . And at the age of two years and five months he said: 'Ma Easton is a steer.'

He was a handsome child, with his mother's rather haughty looks, and a fine head of hair that Isabel made him wear in curls as late as the age of four. He remembered voicing a 'masculine protest' at this continuing effort to 'make me an object of beauty'.

At the age of two years and six months, he was taken to Newport, Rhode Island, 'for the spring season'. At three, he went with his parents for another visit to grandfather Thaddeus in Wisconsin; he afterwards retained a memory of the house – a mansion of some grandeur – but of his grandfather he had no recollection 'of anything save his beard'. The household still included great-grandfather Elijah, residing with his son, as was great-great-uncle Joel, who claimed to have ridden on the first railroad train in America.

> And Gargantua walked in the footsteps of his great-grandfather . . . and he made for himself a cane and leant heavily upon it in walking, in the manner of his great-grandfather . . . and he spent as much time as possible in the large double kennel of the sheepdogs.

Thaddeus, unlike his grandson, *had* been born in a pioneer shack, a log cabin in Elk, Pennsylvania. Brought up as a Quaker,* he had been a high-school teacher for a time, but had also gone in for less conventional forms of knowledge – phrenology, spiritualism, and 'magnetic healing', which he and his brother Albert had demonstrated to eager small-town crowds. There seems indeed to have been something of the travelling mountebank about Thaddeus. A Wisconsin journalist described him in 1870 as having, in conversation, 'a sort of magnetic power little less than fascinating'.

The young Thaddeus had married Susan Angevine Loomis, a tight-lipped lady descended from a family of lawyers, and settled in Chippewa Falls where he became a bookkeeper in a lumbering firm, quickly rising to a partnership in the Union Lumbering Co. He immersed himself in politics, was elected Lieutenant Governor of Winsconsin in 1870, and six years later entered Congress as a Republican. An enthusiast for public works of every kind, he soon turned his attention to railway building. 'Whenever he discovers a great public need he hastens to find a way to supply it,' declared a newspaper. Ezra later noticed a marked similarity of style between his own writing and his grandfather's speeches, a 'certain lack of beating about the bushes'.

---

*Ezra on his grandfather's sect: 'If I could believe the Quakers banned music because church music is so damn bad, I should view them with approval.' He suspected that their asceticism might be largely fake, but thought they had some admirable Confucian-style ideas, and wondered whether 'Quakerism tempered with classic mythology would give one a working hypothesis'.

Almost single-handedly Thaddeus had established the Chippewa Falls Northern & Eastern Railway Company, by the simple if unusual method of printing his own money. His lumbering company paid its employees in its own 'banknotes' – credit slips redeemable only at the company store (a dubious but common practice among big firms at this period) – and Thaddeus, spurning the idea of bank loans for his railway, used this home-made currency to raise credit, thereby anticipating and partly inspiring a segment of his grandson's economic philosophy in the 1930s. The big companies responded by ganging up and refusing to sell him rails, so, said Ezra, he went 'up to the north of New York State, and found some rails on an abandoned road up there . . . and had them shipped out'. This achievement is celebrated in Canto 28: 'And that man sweat blood to put through that railway, / And what he ever got out of it?'

What Thaddeus did get, for a brief period, was his name on the front of a locomotive. But he was soon pushed out of business by a monopolist named Weyerhauser, who absorbed the Chippewa Falls line into his own Northern Pacific – a clear case, in Ezra's mind, of an unscrupulous 'immigrant' doing down a 'native' Pound. Then came a bank panic. The Union Lumbering Co. (whose 'banknotes' were not favourably regarded by the US Treasury) went into the hands of a receiver, and the firm was sold to none other than the Weyerhauser Logging Company.

'This is my war all right, I have been in it for twenty years, my Grandad was in it before me,' said Ezra recalling these events at the microphone in 1942. 'My Grand Dad . . . fighting the kikefied usurers.' Thaddeus seemed to represent 'all that is decent in America . . . the total American heritage'.

Some of Thaddeus's contemporaries would have disagreed with this portrait. In Congress he demonstrated a high moral character, originating bills to promote female suffrage and the 'civilizing' of the Indians; but his matrimonial conduct caused a stir. He separated from his wife, whose laconic nature had proved a mismatch with so exuberant a husband, and 'took to himself a second feminine adjunct, without sanction of clergy'. This lady, said to have been of an 'amiable' nature, Thaddeus rashly allowed to accompany him to Washington, where she ruined his political chances. Thaddeus was promised a seat in President Garfield's cabinet, but another nominee, J. G. Blaine, declined 'to sit in the same cabinet with a man who was not living with his wife', and since Blaine was the more powerful, Thaddeus bowed out. Four years later, when Blaine was running for President, Thaddeus pamphleteered against him, accusing him of corruption, and played a significant part in his defeat.

Susan, Thaddeus's estranged wife, adopted for the remainder of her days a *modus vivendi* that delighted Ezra: 'At the age of 160 she and *her* mother, who must have been by that time 180 (exactitude is no matter when one reaches these legendary numbers), lived in Montana, not together, but each alone in her cabin with a good two miles of veldt between them. From her presumably I derive my respect for the human being as an individual, my dislike of herding, and of the encroachment of one personality upon another in the sty of the family.' A letter from Ezra to his mother from around 1907 describes his grandmother telling him 'she believed in letting people be as happy as they could without interference'. He quoted this with marked approval.

*

Before his marriage, Homer had worked for a few months at the United States Mint in Philadelphia, where he received training in the assaying of precious metals, a necessary qualification for running the Land Office in Hailey. A little more than two years after leaving Idaho, finally picking up the traces of a career again, Homer applied for a job with the Bureau of Engraving & Printing (where paper money was manufactured) in Washington; but nothing was available, so he turned again to Philadelphia, and found a job there in the Assayer's department of the Mint at $5 a day. In June 1889, when Ezra was nearly four, the Pounds moved to Philadelphia.

It was a lowly job, but the work appealed to Homer, and there was in theory some prospect of promotion, though he never managed to improve his position very much. In 1891 he became a salaried assistant at $2,000 per annum, but although his local newspaper loyally spread the rumour in 1902 that he was 'a candidate for superintendent of the Mint' and called him 'chief assayer', he had actually remained a rank-and-file member of the Assayer's department. At his retirement in 1928, he was second-in-command, but his annual income was only $500 over its 1891 level. Ezra spoke angrily of his father's 'miserable salary'. The job was so lacking in status that from 1910 Homer had to 'clock in' and 'clock out', which also offended Ezra deeply.

However, both as a child and a grown man, Ezra could be moved to excitement by contemplating the actual work his father did, and its significance. He concludes *Indiscretions* with a vivid account of a childhood visit to the Mint, in those days a formidable building on Chestnut Street, just south of Philadelphia's ornate City Hall, its Palladian architecture grotesquely marred by a tall furnace chimney. Ascending the steps and walking through the rotunda, past a lounging group of tobacco-chewing Civil War veterans, the young Ezra would be taken up the staircase to the Assaying Office. There, he and his mother would discover Homer using a gold balance so sensitive that it could register the weight of a signature on a visiting card, or squinting through a bottle of silver in solution, then writing figures on a blackboard. It seemed to Ezra that his father's skill in thus measuring the quality of silver, merely by eye, was 'an aesthetic perception, like the critical sense'. Ezra was also attracted by the notion of judging 'the *fineness* of the metal', and by the business of detecting fraud or false hopes. The Mint was often sent specimens of so-called gold by fortune hunters – either lumps of iron pyrites, which looked like gold-bearing ore, or objects sold as gold bricks, which, beneath a thin veneer of the real thing, were made of lead. It was Homer's job to write reports on these. Later, Ezra could see the similarity between this and detecting the fake in other people's poetry.

A cheerful informality ruled at the Mint, and Homer, always the soul of geniality, was allowed to take visitors into the vaults to see the gold bars and sacks of silver dollars. He and the custodians – it was an old joke – would indicate the $20,000-bags, and say: 'You can have that sack if you can carry it out.' Ezra remembered seeing a recount of the silver coinage, when he was eight years old in 1893. The bags containing the dollars had almost rotted away, and Ezra watched while 'the men half-naked with open gas flares, shovelled it into the counting-machines, with a gleam on tarnished discs'. It was a sight to make a child wonder greatly about the meaning and nature of money.

3

Suburban Prejudice

Homer rented a house at 208 South Forty-Third Street, West Philadelphia, not far from the University of Pennsylvania, and in those days at the edge of the city. It was one of a row built of brick, with a small front lawn and steps up to the front door: three storeys high, quite substantial. The district was respectable and remained so until the Depression; but Isabel's social ambitions could not be satisfied within a city that by 1889 was becoming, as Ezra put it in his own fashion, 'flooded with "inferior races", with the "off-scourings of Europe"'. This immigrant takeover of urban life, well under way when the Pounds arrived in Philadelphia, was driving many middle-class families out to the suburbs in an attempt to preserve the 'native' culture from the hopeful hordes of European refugees. It was a rearguard action, for in the long run many of the immigrants would come out on top, relegating families like the Pounds to 'nouveau poor'. But it was a movement which, in March 1890, Homer, Isabel, and Ezra found themselves joining.

They went eleven miles north of downtown Philadelphia, to the borough of Jenkintown, and took a lease on what the local newspaper called 'George W. Tomlinson's new house', 417 Walnut Street. Jenkintown lay in the ribbon development that had grown up alongside the Philadelphia & Reading Railway, built northwards out of the city through Chelten Hills and towards New York in 1855. Jenkintown itself was a rail junction and small shopping town for the local farming community, though by the 1890s agriculture was giving way to 'dormitory' housing for families where the husband, like Homer Pound, must travel daily into the city to work. Trains ran into the city every fifteen minutes or so, with a journey time of only half an hour. Automobiles were still virtually unknown; the dirt tracks were mainly used by buggies and farm carts, and close by the

Jenkintown Station a 'Boarding & Livery Stable' was kept by Levi Bean. Boardwalks of planking protected dresses and trouser-legs from the dust, mud, and horse droppings.

Electric light came to Jenkintown just after the Pounds, in July 1890. Gas arrived eight years later, being manufactured in a plant alongside the railroad. There were still occasional rural intrusions: the local paper reported in May 1890 that 'A bear passed through the streets on Wednesday evening, but Officer York escorted him quietly beyond the borough limits.' The standard of living was high. Admittedly a small group of poorish rental houses stood by the tracks, occupied by Italian immigrant railroad labourers, and a few Negroes who worked as domestic servants dwelt in an alley behind the larger mansions; but the main population was of the white middle class, an expanding, fairly prosperous community. The children were well dressed, healthy, and well fed, families usually small, infant mortality low. The district voted solidly Republican.

The atmosphere was quintessentially small-town. Early in 1892 the local newspaper, the *Hatboro Public Spirit*, recorded that a Negro, George Newman, caught *in flagrante* with Mrs Benjamin Washington, had been given 'a severe pummelling' and was only allowed to leave the town provided he did not return. Gossip was tremendous; by the mid-1890s the *Public Spirit* had acquired a rival, the *Jenkintown Times–Chronicle*, and both chiefly filled their pages with tittle-tattle. In consequence the activities of the Pounds, like other Jenkintown families, were recorded in some detail.

The house they rented was in one of the principal side-roads, not far from the station: semi-detached, the lower storey built of brick, the upper two of timber. Low fences divided the narrow backyards from each other, engendering an easy atmosphere. Two fences away, 'ole man Comley', who lived 'next the Coulters', would amuse the four-year-old Ra Pound by warning against the very habit in which he was himself indulging at that moment:

> . . . ole man Comley wd. say: Boys! –
> Never cherr terbakker! Hrwwkke tth!
> Never cherr terbakker!

This, recorded in Canto 28, was 'a very early and treasured memory'. Ra began to make friends with other children. Further up Walnut Street lived the Schwarz family – a surname which indicates that Jenkintown was not quite free of immigrant blood. Their daughter Lula, aged twelve, was 'friendly and protective' towards him. Down the hill in West Street were the Schivelys, engaged in the coal and lumber business, whose daughter Nan he 'adored'. Ra was 'still in loathed kilts', with his hair in curls, which perhaps encouraged the maternal affection of older girls.

At the age of five, he joined a gang led by a lad named Sheridan, 'the dashing and heroic and all-competent builder, who put tin roof on hen house etc.' Such hero figures became Ra's favourite type, and he liked to operate in gangs, preferring this to friendship with individuals.

Homer Pound's easygoing manner ensured that he was quickly welcomed into Jenkintown society. Though grandfather Thaddeus had abandoned the Quaker practices of his own upbringing, and had given his son no religious training, Homer now adopted the Presbyterianism in which his wife had been reared, and he, Isabel and Ezra began to attend the Grace Presbyterian Church, one of the social hubs of the community. After only a year in the congregation, Homer was elected one of the three Trustees of the church. He was also chosen as president of the Jenkintown Lyceum Association – the Lyceum being a hall next to the Presbyterian church, used for plays and recitals. Soon after he had taken presidential office, an embarrassing incident occurred. It was the custom now and then to give entertainment for the benefit of the church and other good causes. On 21 March 1892 the Lyceum Association issued a public apology in the columns of the *Public Spirit* for announcing one such event as a 'Banjo Club', whereas it had proved to be 'a minstrel performance, which was highly distasteful'. Vulgarity, in this case the impersonation of Negro minstrels, could not be tolerated in such a correct community.

A month later, the same newspaper reported that the new proprietors of the Beechwood Inn, by the railroad station, 'announce that hereafter no Jews will be taken to board there. In previous years the Hebrews have been plentiful.' A Jenkintown contemporary of Ezra's, Edward Hicks Parry, has described this as the most blatant expression of a prejudice that was found 'always round-about, to be likened best, perhaps, to a thin, barely perceptible dust that would be kicked up'. Parry emphasizes that anti-Semitism was not practised in his own home, nor in Ezra's. But its presence in the community he could not deny.

It was part of the general resentment towards all immigrants. 'No foreign labor on our streets,' declared the *Public Spirit* on 26 November 1892. 'Give our citizens a chance.' And the *Jenkintown Times–Chronicle* wrote on 30 May 1896: 'Just no more Italians . . . Is our budding hope that this place will be entirely aristocratic squelched?' It is notable that, when Ezra Pound talked regretfully of his own anti-Semitism to Allen Ginsberg in 1967, he spoke of it as a 'suburban prejudice'.

*

Isabel gave Ra a little desultory education before he began school, reading to him from classic authors after lunch each day. When his grandmother Mary Weston visited the family, she too liked to administer doses of Scott and Dickens. He was also introduced to Kipling, whose 'bustuous noises' he afterwards regarded with mild affection, though he preferred the stories to the verse. American poets featured in the diet too, Longfellow in particular, since Mary Weston with her Wadsworth descent could proudly claim family connection; also the more vulgar but eminently popular James Whitcomb Riley. This accomplished imitator of the Hoosier dialect of Midwestern America was best known for 'Little Orphant Annie' (1885), with its warning that

> The Gobble-uns'll git you
> Ef you
>   Don't
>   Watch
>   Out!

In 1945 Ezra found some verses by Riley in a popular anthology he picked up in the communal lavatories of the Pisa prison camp, and wondered 'wd/ Whitcomb Riley be still found in a highbrow anthology?' The answer is no, for Riley is almost forgotten now; but he is certainly one of the ancestors of Ezra's own eccentric spellings, impersonations of dialect, and idiosyncratic layout on the page.

Looking back on his childhood, Ezra recalled his vague impression that American poetry 'wasn't quite as good as the English at any point'. Yet no such qualification needed to be made for the best American prose, such as *Uncle Remus*, first published five years before Ezra's birth, with sequels appearing at frequent intervals during his childhood. In 1958, staying with his daughter's family in Italy, he took delight in reading to his grand-children Joel Chandler Harris's tales of Brer Fox and Brer Rabbit. From childhood they were an intimate part of his mental world, from which in the 1920s he drew nicknames for certain literary friends ('Possum' and others). Like James Whitcomb Riley's poems, the Uncle Remus stories, with their impersonation of Negro speech, showed what could be achieved by distorting the written language until the reader has to struggle to disentangle meaning: 'Brer Fox ain't never kotch him yet, en w'at's mo', honey, he ain't gwinter . . . Dat's all de fur de tale goes.'

Brer Rabbit is a perennial trickster, especially resourceful in adversity, a specialist in trapping the trapper in his own devices. When Ezra played the Uncle Remus game with T. S. Eliot in the 1920s, he gave the name 'Brer Rabbit' to himself.

*

In Jenkintown, Ra received the beginnings of a formal education at a dame school, in an old colonial house next to the Presbyterian church, run by a Miss Elliott. He irritated his first schoolmates with evidence of precocious-ness: 'I . . . used polysyllables, in the wake of my mother.' Though gradually he established a *modus operandi* with other children, and joined gangs, his schooldays were not marked by any warm friendships. Generally reticent about the earliest period of his life, he would occasionally drop some remark which hinted at deep discomfort: 'A man judges his own age according to . . . whether or not, as a small boy in school, he encountered more skunks than decent fellows.'

In April 1892, two years after the Pounds had arrived in Jenkintown, the *Public Spirit* announced another move: from Walnut Street 'to Mr Burrough's house on Hillside Avenue'. Only a few months later they packed up again, 'emigrating', as Ezra put it, a quarter-mile across the railroad tracks to a new area of housing, adjacent to Jenkintown and calling itself Wyncote.

At first Wyncote could boast a more rural appearance than Jenkintown proper; but the arrival of the gasworks and of an ice-making plant next to the railroad freightyard soon diminished this, and the few colonial houses scattered about the district were fast swamped by the 'infilling' of speculative builders. New streets were given determinedly rustic names – Greenwood Avenue, Fernbrook Avenue, Glenside – and the rows of big glasshouses at the Heacock family's floral business together with Levi Bean's livery stable ('Hoss an buggy $1 fer the afternoon,' remembered Ezra), showed that the community was certainly not urban. But the backbone of Wyncote, as of Jenkintown, was the commuter railroad, and one advantage of the Pounds' new house was its proximity to the station – a mere five minutes' walk away. Each weekday evening in fine weather, Isabel, elegantly dressed, would be seen along with other Wyncote wives setting out to meet her husband as he returned from work.

The Pound house, at 166 Fernbrook Avenue, near the bend in an L-shaped road that led off Greenwood Avenue (the main station approach), was purchased on a mortgage for $6,000 in the name of Isabel Pound. According to Ezra, the necessary cash had been provided by Isabel's mother, though one also suspects the hand of Aunt Frank and Uncle Ezra. It was a handsome, wooden, three-storeyed detached house, about twice the size of that on Walnut Street, as splendid and respectable a home as Isabel could have desired, and a good deal grander than Homer's job at the Mint would be expected to provide. Here at last the Pounds remained, Ezra until he went away to college, Homer and Isabel until their retirement. The unsettled period of their lives was ostensibly over. Yet Ezra never felt much sense of home there. 'I was,' he wrote in 1920, 'brought up in a district and city with which my forebears had no connection, and I am therefore accustomed to being an alien, and it is just as homelike for me to be an alien in one place as in another.' And he told Thomas Hardy: 'I come from an American suburb – where I was not born – where both parents are really foreigners.'

*

The new house was considerably larger than the Pounds' immediate needs and the capacity of their pocket, so Isabel was obliged to take in lodgers (though she preferred the euphemism 'paying guests') who generally came through the local Presbyterian church. When they and the living-in maid had been accommodated, there still remained a generous amount of space for Ezra and his parents, at least on the upper floors – more than half a dozen bedrooms, no less than three bathrooms, and a Tower Room, occupying a turret that perched strikingly alongside the top-floor gables, hinting at castellation. Downstairs, Isabel furnished the front and back parlours with such indications of status as a grandfather clock, celebrated for having stood in the Wayside Inn of Longfellow's poem, and family portraits hung, as Ezra put it, at 'strategic points'. The back parlour was referred to as the 'library', and the staircase windows, in the best possible taste, were of stained glass.

In this large house it was possible to be a nomad, and Ra tended to move his own quarters from one room to another. At various times he slept in all three bedrooms on the top floor, and in the Tower Room. Now, as in later life, he showed no inclination to create any kind of comfortable nest or habitat for himself.

The living-in maid was always a Negro. In later years Ezra recalled that there had always been 'good food . . . in my young times, the black cook could make a brown stew. No second-rate cookin' entered my face till I got . . . to college.'

Fernbrook Avenue, where the Pound house stood, lay in a rising neighbourhood. Local residents included George H. Lorimer, an up-and-coming Philadelphia journalist soon to make his name and fortune as editor of the *Saturday Evening Post*. Lorimer would sometimes take short-cuts through the Pounds' yard and chat to Homer about the tricks of his trade, 'and my ole man went on hoein' corn / while George was a-tellin' him,' Ezra writes in Canto 81. Ezra later picked on Lorimer, with his fondness for 'Get Rich Quick' feature articles, as 'vulgar . . . without even the natural American gusto and genuine unconsciousness of all civil values'. Cyrus Curtis, the Philadelphia publisher who founded the *Ladies' Home Journal* and who would be Lorimer's proprietor on the *Post*, was another neighbour on Fernbrook; Ra peered over the banisters at Curtis's square-cut beard when he came to dinner. There was indeed much emphasis in the community on 'culture' and 'refinement', promoted by lantern shows, reading groups, recitals; but Ezra later dismissed the rationale governing such activities as 'that lolly pop & sugar candy philosophy which rots so much american art'. He regarded his mother as especially prone to this, remarking of her taste, at the end of her life: 'She doesn't know a good book from a bad one.' In 1913 he wrote to her: 'I am profoundly pained to hear that you prefer Marie Corelli to Stendhal but I cannot help it.' And a year later, when she had encouraged him to write the kind of 'poetry' that would be to her taste:

> I don't know when I am likely to write molasses and sugar, I should say vaguely 'never'. However there are plenty of people doing it so you won't lack for verses, pretty pretty verses like the sitting-in-the-tree birds
>
> > tell me not in mournful wish-wash
> > life's a sort of sugared dish-wash
> > and all that sort of thing.
>
> My soul's nose is scratching itself on the stars
> I use the clouds as a hanky
> > Blow ye winds heighō.

And in a letter of 1919, to his father, he delivered his final dismissal of the type of society found in Wyncote, and its supposed interest and discrimination in literature:

> Quite a number of 'nice' amiable people, but passive and mostly illiterate, utterly unorganized. At any rate no use so far as supporting the arts or permitting discrimination is concerned. Ought to be left in peace, like other placid cattle, and not bothered about altitude of their perceptivity.

The attack was, of course, richly deserved; yet Ezra himself was not entirely immune from those failings he criticized so vituperatively. Throughout his life he retained, in his intellectual attitudes, something of the American suburban, seeking out the erudite and the obscure because it seemed to him 'refined' and remote from the common herd. His promotion of other writers and artists, invaluable as its results sometimes were, smacked a little of the small-town showman – the huckster peddling his toothache pills or giving demonstrations of 'magnetic healing'. Even more typically American was his belief, retained throughout his life, that the earthly paradise could really be built, the Utopian society genuinely achieved, through the efforts of determined individuals.

4

The Way Poundie Felt

In Wyncote he transferred to another dame school, known grandly as the Chelten Hills School, but really just the Heacock (pronounced 'Haycock') family house, up the hill from the railroad tracks. 'The Haycocks [*sic*], quakers, certainly did NOT approve of yr/ correspondent,' he wrote in the 1950s. 'E.P. attended their dames school from the age of 6–7.' The Heacocks' Quaker principles led them to include the small son of their black maid Dorcas among the otherwise all-white pupils. Ezra described this child, a cheerful lad named Rushton, as 'an abolitionist horror who was exhibited, much as a convert from the far Isles, but who rather gave out, I think, about the age of puberty'. Rushton's presence in the school caused a stir in the community.

The first reference to Ezra in print is in a doggerel poem published in the school magazine in the spring of 1894:

> Rushton was sucking his finger,
> And laughing at Ra Pound.

The cause of the laughter is not specified, but it may have been Ra's polysyllables – he remembered being called 'Professor' by schoolfellows. In his first school photograph we see a child small for his age, rather withdrawn and uncommunicative in appearance, sitting at the back of the group between two distinctly tough-looking boys. One of them, Tommy Cochran, became a particular friend. On the other side is Jimmy Luskin, son of a local grocer, a tall lout with a shifty expression. Ra liked the company of the muscular: another schoolfriend was Ned Heacock, the family's 'kid bro/', who became 'a pal till he went canoein' on some wild river out Oregon way & drowned very young'.

In September 1894, Wyncote opened its first public elementary school, and Ra was among the thirty-seven children enrolled there. Public education was generally regarded as the social inferior of private schools, but in Wyncote it was agreed, in Ezra's words, 'that no social taint shd/ attach to "public" instruction'. Several non-white children were taught in the school; Ezra remembered them as 'the good Miners, of colour', a 'desegregated 12 year old lanky high yaller sister and 2 smaller darker'. He says nothing further about them.

The public school was at first held in a temporary building, with Miss Florence Ridpath as sole teacher, but she 'made life too pleasant for the children, and faded after one year'. Ra was very fond of her, and wrote to her when she was an old lady, reminding her how she had 'wept after keeping me in after school one day . . . probably from despair at being unable to controll the uncontrollable'. With her departure in September 1895 when he was almost ten, a new permanent school building was opened – Homer Pound was one of those who had worked for its establishment – and the size of the staff was increased. Ra was, at first, taught by the strict Blanche Summers – 'the indestructible Blanche S/' who 'reigned in severity'. He did not care for the grim new stone building, and his nose was offended by the 'smell of the basement' where the boys' lavatories were situated.

Out of school, he and friends roamed the lanes around Wyncote in search of adventure. One day Ra and Ned Heacock 'almost drowned' rescuing Ned's dog from a flash flood. Another time Ra wrote to his mother (who was away from home) describing a day spent sledging with Tommy Cochran through the snow-covered roads. Ra learned to skate, and taught himself tennis by knocking a ball against the side of the house, cracking the stained-glass window.

His earliest surviving letter was written to his mother just before his tenth birthday, when Isabel was visiting her family in New York. He writes in a very clear adult hand.

Wyncote
Oct 1. 1895

Dear Ma,

I went to a ball game on Saturday between our school and the Heacocks. the score was thirty-five to thirty-seven our favor, it was a hard fight in which wee were victorise. They put in a colored man for first base and then to pitcher but he soon was knock out as he gave two many men laces on balls,* as it did not do any good they chucked him off, the umpire cheated until pa come and then he quit he was accused of being bulyed into it by the heacocks who it is sed paid him but he denies it.

*To 'lace' a ball is to drive it hard and straight.

Wee spent a pleasant sunday. Monday I went after wlnuts
and picked for Dayton and Fousty as I could not cary hom all I
picked up and so I now have a flourbag full. To day I went for
chestnuts, but got not enough to speak of (I went with Tom and
Pud) then went up to Puds where wee met Joe and then wee
played fussy untill I had to go hom. Wee are well and happy
give my love to aunt Frank and Cousin Sady. As nobody has
looked over this pleas excuse mistakes.
                Love from all
                Your loving son
                E. L. Pound

His spelling remained uneven until, in his late teens, he began to invent
eccentric word forms of his own. Quite apart from the amusement these
caused him, they had the advantage of cloaking his often genuine ignorance
as to the correct form.

His early letters to his parents give the impression of an ordinary
cheerful boy with plenty to do. He mentions a cream tea at Wanamaker's
store in Philadelphia, a sprained finger resulting from a football game with
friends, and his hope that his father will bring him stamps from New York.
If the polysyllabic 'Professor' was not entirely at ease among his schoolfellows, no hint of this comes out in the letter.

                                    ❋

He often went to visit Aunt Frank and Uncle Ezra in Manhattan, and these
trips gave him considerable entertainment. He liked to play checkers with
Jim, the black manservant, out on the apple barrel in the backyard of the
boarding-house, and to listen to the lodgers arguing politics over their
meal. He describes them in Canto 74:

> . . . the voice of Monsieur Fouquet or the Napoleon 3rd
> barbiche of Mr Quackenbos, or Quackenbush
> as I supposed it,
> and Mrs Chittenden's lofty air

In New York, he began to gain experience of distinctively European
food, for Aunt Frank would sometimes treat him at Mouquin's French
restaurant off Sixth Avenue. But he was more struck by the excellent
American dishes, prepared by black cooks. 'I mean at cookin' we were
second to no man,' he wrote fifty years later. 'The ice cream made of
CREAM, all cream and peaches, solid peaches.' Ice cream remained his
favourite dish even into old age.

He liked the New York street life: the jingling bells of the horse-cars on
Madison Avenue as they rolled down to the Crosstown Tunnel at

Forty-Second, with its cool whitewashed interior; the mystery of the open gulch along Park Avenue, through which the trains hooted out of Grand Central; Lexington Avenue and its cable cars. He recollects such scenes in Canto 74, concluding with the words 'refinement, pride of tradition'.

These qualities were particularly conveyed to him by his grandmother Mary Weston, who after Uncle Ezra's death in 1894 gave up her own lodging-house for girls on Lexington Avenue and moved in with Aunt Frank, occupying a room crammed with bric-à-brac from Aunt Frank's European travels and Mary Weston's own family history: 'alabaster / Towers of Pisa . . . / coloured photographs of Europa / carved wood from Venice venetian glass and the samovar / and the fire bucket, 1806 Barre Mass'chusetts'.

Barre was the town where certain Weston ancestors had settled in the early nineteenth century. Grandmother Weston would show Ra the bucket, along with coats of arms, indian ink drawings by long-dead relatives, and other objects from the family archives. As a Wadsworth on her mother's side she could claim descent from the William Wadsworth who had arrived from England on the *Lion* in 1632; she also cherished the belief that she was related to the Captain Joseph Wadsworth who in 1687, under the very nose of James II's representative, had snatched the Connecticut Charter and hidden it in an oak tree on the lawn of the Governor's mansion, to protect the state from British tyranny. Ezra describes this legend humorously in *Indiscretions* as an example of his grandmother's passion for stuffing him full of 'romantic Colonial history'; yet he was genuinely impressed by his supposed ancestor's blow for freedom, and in Canto 97 he asks: 'Will they get rid of the Rooseveltian dung-hill / And put Capn. Wadsworth back in the school books?'

In adult life Ezra's inclination was to mock his grandmother's 'elaborate misrepresentations of descent', and to imply that he had been deterred from swallowing this kind of 'bait' through her 'elderly garrulity'. Yet in 1946 he told a St Elizabeths psychiatrist that it was essential to view his character against the 'backdrop' of romanticized American colonial history which she had supplied, and he described her death, which happened when he was twelve years old, as his 'first sorrow'. It was largely owing to her that he came to regard himself, in adult life, as a 'native' American of old and distinguished stock, far superior to the newcomers.

*

At the age of eleven, in March 1897, he made a formal profession of faith at the Calvary Presbyterian Church in Wyncote. During childhood he was, in his own words, 'an earnest Christian' who read the Bible 'daily' and took religion 'with great seriousness'.

Until he was in his mid-teens, the Calvary Church was in the charge of the Reverend Carlos Tracy Chester, an ebullient man with literary interests (he was co-editor of the Philadelphia *Book News Monthly*). Ra became friends with his son, Hawley, with whom at the age of eleven he

> invented, not a god, but a djinn, posessed of nearly all the divine attributes . . . We used this djinn solely for the annoyance and mystification of a third and younger small boy who bored us and who persisted in lending us his company . . . He spent at least a year in the state of a man who sends for the priest on his death-bed. The enjoyment of this sort of hoax lasts into mature states of society.

In 1901 a new minister arrived, the Reverend William Barnes Lower, a rather hearty individual who organized Bible classes for the young. Ra, then sixteen, did not care for this, and afterwards dated his move away from religion from Lower's arrival, although he continued to attend church well into his college days.

In September 1897, shortly before his twelfth birthday, he was sent, along with Tommy Cochran and two other Wyncote boys, to Cheltenham Military Academy. This was a private school for about sixty boys, near enough to Wyncote for Ra to walk there daily at first, though later he became a boarder. Known as CMA, it was one of the many small military-style schools then in vogue. Its pupils wore Civil-War-style uniform, and there was drilling, rifle shooting, and a bugle and drum band.

Ra found the military element irritating – 'I could stand everything but the drilling' – and he looks uncomfortable and rather lost in a photograph of the CMA boys in their uniform. However, his expression may owe something to difficulties with eyesight. He suffered from a severe astigmatism, and was prescribed glasses – he is wearing them in this picture. (Later he abandoned them when not reading or writing, probably from vanity.)

Everything apart from this photograph suggests that he enjoyed life at CMA and found the drill and other military activities absurd rather than distressing. A cartoon drawn by him for his parents a year or so after he had arrived shows a comic figure labelled POUND enduring cannon-fire and under attack by '6 hundred' soldiers; it is captioned

THE WAY POUNDIE
FELT.

And his letters to his parents from the CMA give no indication that he underwent anything worse than the usual tribulations of a not-very-conscientious schoolboy.

His inclinations were towards open-air activities rather than reading or study. He afterwards said he had been 'rejected for most sports' because he was 'too young and light', but this only seems to mean that he was kept out of the CMA football team. (He eventually reached the height of 5 feet 10 inches, and remained lightweight until his middle years.) He played plenty of tennis, and took up fencing, at which he proved quite a success. 'Reed & I went over home & got the foils,' he wrote to his parents in January 1899. 'We fenced that afternoon & in the evening went into the city to show off our grand act as a "Picked Corps of Cadets: from C.M.A." We did ourselves proud & have been excused from all drill since.'

He played chess too; the same letter mentions that 'Reed & I have used up our spare time in contending over the Chess board', and that he has a 'challenge' at chess 'from the Major for tomorrow night & one from Mr Doolittle'. This was Frederick J. Doolittle who taught Latin and Greek at the CMA and was known as Cassius because of his lean and hungry appearance. Ra liked him, but was himself no more than adequate at classical languages. He left school reasonably competent in Latin but with little skill in Greek. (In 1955 he admitted that he was 'too god damn iggurunt of Greek' to translate Homer.) Nevertheless he became excited by the Homeric epics while at the CMA, and vividly remembered hearing, aged thirteen, a passage from Homer declaimed by someone after a game of tennis.

As he reached his mid-teens he became known as a local beau; Edward Hicks Parry remembers how 'on a Sunday afternoon . . . with his gloves and hat and cane . . . he came a-courting'. His attention was particularly taken by a Wyncote girl named Adele Polk, whom a photograph shows to have been handsome in a slightly masculine way. Sixty years later he wrote to a Wyncote correspondent: 'Give my regards to Adele Polk, surprised that she still has that name. Why she shouldn't have ben taken to wife beats me. Mebbe she was choosey. I think there was english ancestry.'

*

During Ezra's childhood and adolescence Wyncote grew rapidly and the more successful neighbours built grand mansions. Cyrus Curtis, having bought the *Saturday Evening Post* and made a fortune from it, moved from Fernbrook Avenue into a pseudo-Renaissance pile nearby, while George H. Lorimer, now editing the *Post* for Curtis, J. B. Stetson the hat manufacturer, and John Wanamaker the Philadelphia merchant prince, were among others who created palaces for themselves within a mile or two of the Pound residence. A correspondent to the Jenkintown paper in 1897 observed complacently: 'This place reminds us of a fairy garden, and . . . the fairies are not lacking. Some of the best known and wealthiest Philadelphia business people live in these elegant mansions.'

In fact the Wanamaker mansion, Lyndenhurst, looked more like an ogre's castle than a fairy residence, with its heavyweight mock-Norman turrets and castellations. By the time Ra Pound had seen Europe he understood the absurdity of it. He wrote in 1912: 'There are, within a mile or two of my home, a castle something like Hawarden, and one something like Blenheim, and a great manor house (Elizabethan) and none of this is architecture.' In February 1907 Lyndenhurst caught fire, and Ra and Homer were among those who rushed over to help save Wanamaker's 'old masters'. Ra, who by then knew his way around the Prado museum in Madrid, got much amusement from what followed:

> When Mr Wanamaker's picture gallery burned in the dead of winter I was able to observe the destruction of faked Van Dykes etc., *comme spectacle*, the muffler'd lads of the village tearing down gold frames in the light of the conflagration, the onyx-topped tables against the blackness were still more 'tableau', and one cd. think detachedly of the French Revolution. Mr Wanamaker was nothing to me, he paid his employees badly, and I knew the actual spectacle was all I shd. ever get out of him.

The Wanamaker fire came towards the end of Ra's time in America, and sowed the seeds of his contempt for rich Americans who could afford to patronize living artists but instead bought faked old masters – a not inconsiderable element in his coming feud with his native country.

Meanwhile, the Wyncote middle classes continued their struggles against those lower in the pecking order. 'All Italians but two families have moved away,' reported the *Times–Chronicle* with approval on 5 June 1897. Providing they kept in the ghettos, the immigrants could be sure of benevolent treatment from at least some of the WASP Wyncotians; Homer and Isabel Pound began to undertake Presbyterian mission work in the slums of Philadelphia, travelling in on Sundays to hold classes and services for poor Italian children. Ra sometimes went with them. He remembered his mother playing the organ and his father 'dividing a shell collection among the urchins'.

*

He might never have learned the difference between a faked and a real old master if Aunt Frank had not decided, when he was twelve in the summer of 1898, to take him on a trip to Europe. His account in *Indiscretions* does not mention that his mother came too. The *Times–Chronicle* reported on 27 August 1898: 'Mrs Homer L. Pound and son are spending the summer in Europe.'

For three months' travel Aunt Frank took an enormous quantity of assorted baggage, including 'ninety-seven little tissue-papers of green tea prepared in advance'. They sailed from New York, and Ra quickly found that the ocean did not agree with him. In England they visited the London sights, Kenilworth, Warwick Castle, and Stratford. From Brussels on 5 July, Ra wrote to his father that he had 'celebrated the 4th (yesterday) by being overcome by the English Chanel and depositing both breakfast & lunch in its depth'. Thence they went to Germany (Cologne, Mainz, Nuremberg), to Paris, Lucerne, and the Alps, and to Genoa, Como, Florence, Rome, Naples, and north again to Venice. Even in such a crowded trip, 'Venice struck me as an agreeable place – as, in fact, more agreeable than Wyncote, Pa., or "47th" and Madison Avenue. I announced an intention to return.'

Aunt Frank's grand tour continued into Spain, where the party visited Granada and Seville, and they crossed the Straits of Gibraltar to Tangier, where Ra was amused by his great-aunt's 'wide and white-bodiced figure . . . perching on a very narrow mule'. By early September they were on their way home, and in mid-Atlantic Ra wrote some doggerel to amuse his father, who had just sent him a present of a knife:

> Though not among the famous bards
> I send to you my kind regards
> > For knives galore
> > And for kind wishes for more
> > > Be it in Lucerne, Como or Naples
> > > Or be it in Rome and the state of the Papals . . .

Naturally the European trip opened his eyes. 'Comin' from a duck-board country,' he said in a broadcast many years later, 'I was interested in LATIN order. Order in stone work, in paintin' . . . I liked Quattrocento paintin'. P. Uccello. First freshman theme I wrote was on Paolo Uccello, picture in Louvre I reckon.' And he wrote to Aunt Frank in 1912:

> Every now and again, when I compare my advantage of training
> to those of people about me, it comes over me, how much I owe
> you for starting me globe-trotting at an early age. I think my
> thanks were rather inadequate at the time, and, in fact, it is only
> later that I have come to realize how much work those
> preliminary tours have saved me.

But he is giving the game away here. Though the trip genuinely widened his horizon, it also made him feel superior to those who had been given no such advantage. He felt that it 'saved' him the necessity of studying European art and culture in any great depth, since he had glimpsed them at first hand. It is the first example of a characteristic cutting of corners.

*

His movements during the school year 1900 to 1901, when he was fifteen, are mysterious. He apparently did not graduate at the CMA, so presumably he left early and went to some other school before entering university. During the 1950s when Carl Gatter was collecting memories of Ezra in Wyncote, he heard a rumour that Ra had left the CMA early after he had been led into a homosexual experience by an older student. There is no other evidence of this.

Ra emerges from this mysterious period in August 1901, when the *Times–Chronicle* reports him vacationing with his parents at Ocean City, New Jersey. A month later he began classes at the University of Pennsylvania.

Lily Pound In The Frog Pond

He said he 'got into college on my Latin; it was the only reason they *did* take me in'. He gave his mother credit for having 'stirred him up to get into college at the age of fifteen', which he afterwards regarded as 'a tremendous saving of time'. One might wonder why, if he was a prodigy, his family did not send him to Harvard or some other distinguished East Coast university, rather than to the indifferent University of Pennsylvania, just down the railroad line – but, of course, it *was* just down the line. Ra continued to live at home at first, commuting to college daily, which helped to cut down expense. Indeed, it is to their credit that Homer and Isabel sent him to university at all. None of his near relatives had had a college education, and many of his schoolfellows were given no such chance but had to begin earning a living straight away. Ezra rightly remained grateful to his father for drudging in the Mint to support his continuing education.

In 1901 the University of Pennsylvania had no campus, but was merely a group of buildings in the western part of Philadelphia, standing on busy streets through which trolley-cars ran. The undergraduate intake was small, the teaching undistinguished; most alumni became Philadelphia businessmen. In the glass door of the solid brownstone Fine Arts Library were set the words 'TALKERS ARE NO GREAT DOERS'.

In the photograph of his 1901 freshman class at 'Penn', Ra Pound has clearly chosen to stand out from the herd. He has placed himself at the back in the corner. The others wear ties or bow-ties and are hatless while he sports a floppy beret and a big white cravat. He looks determinedly isolated. Such detachment was understandable, for he was under a double handicap – two years younger than most of his class, and living at home. Earliest impressions of him by fellow freshmen were of 'a person aloof from his classmates and indifferent to them', of someone who 'didn't appear to have or care to have any particular friends'.

Freshmen at Penn were given a thoroughly mixed curriculum. During 1901 to 1902 Ra studied English composition, English language, public speaking, algebra, solid geometry, trigonometry, German grammar and texts, Livy and Horace, American colonial history, and the principles of United States government. The lack of specialization did not disturb him; he was beginning to develop a mind that liked varied diet rather than the thorough study of one subject. He preferred to pick up titbits of information and synthesize them, rather than to become expert in one conventionally accepted subject. 'Does any really good mind ever "get a kick" out of studying stuff that has been put into water-tight compartments and hermetically sealed?' he asks in *Guide to Kulchur* (1938). The Cantos are his chief exemplification of this mental collage principle. On the other hand he had to admit that the defect of American education, with its fear of specialization, was that it discouraged real thinking and gave rise instead to what he called an 'omnimurkn diarhoea' of sloppy mental habits.

If he planned to protect himself at Penn by a stance of intellectual detachment and aloofness, he would have to develop mental interests beyond the hotchpotch of the official curriculum. He decided to become a poet. 'I knew at fifteen pretty much what I wanted to do,' he wrote twelve years later. 'I resolved that at thirty I would know more about poetry than any man living, that I would know the dynamic content from the shell, that I would know what was accounted poetry everywhere.'

In fact there is no clear evidence of his having composed much serious poetry until he was eighteen,* and when he did start, he wrote chiefly about the idea of being a poet:

> I have heard a wee wind searching
> Through still forests for me,
> I have seen a wee wind searching
>   O'er still sea.
>
> Thru woodlands dim
>   Have I taken my way,
> And o'er silent waters, night and day
> Have I sought the wee wind.

---

*His first published poem was a limerick, printed in the *Jenkintown Times–Chronicle* of 7 November 1896 (when he was eleven), on the defeat of William Jennings Bryan:

> There was a young man from the West,
> He did what he could for what he thought best;
>   But election came round;
>   He found himself downed,
> And the papers will tell you the rest.
> Aged 11 years   E.L. Pound, Wyncote

He may also have been the author of 'Ezra on the Strike', a doggerel about current events published in the same paper on 8 November 1902.

The wee wind presumably stands for poetic inspiration. Another poem from these early days shows him with an exalted view of the poet's calling, though now he is beginning to pay serious attention to rhythm (the scansion marks are his own):

> Ī ăm thĕ tŏngue ănd thĕ brain
> Ī ăm thĕ sŏng ănd thĕ thŏught
> Ī ăm thĕ vŏice ŏf thĕ pĕople
> ănd Ī ăs mysēlf ăm not
>
> Ī ăm ă hŏllŏw rĕed
> Bŭt thĕ sŏng ĭs blŏwn thrŭ mē
> Ī ăm thĕ bĕatĕn strĭngs ŏf thĕ lūte
> ănd thĕ lēaf ŏf thĕ Āspĕn trēe . . .

Technique concerned him seriously from the start. He said, a few years later, that, he believed 'the "Impulse" is with the gods', but that 'technique is a man's own responsibility', with the result that even his earliest surviving poems have a sureness of rhythm which makes up for much of their jejuneness.

In 1930 he alleged that he had 'entered U. Penn at 15 with intention of studying comparative values in literature (poetry) and began doing so unbeknown to the faculty'. He repeated this statement in various forms throughout his life, so often that one has to take note of it.

> I began an examination of comparative European literature in or about 1901; with the definite intention of finding out what had been written, and how.

> Started in U. Penn. at 15 to FIND out what had been written, and what was the BEST of it, in as many languages as I could git under my occiput; to KNOW what the real thing was.

> I did have the idea, at fifteen, of making a general survey. Of course whether I was or wasn't a poet was a matter for the Gods to decide, but at least it was up to me to find out what had been done.

However, there is little evidence that as yet he had any special interest in literature. The only Distinction of his freshman year was in solid geometry. He had a quick eye for geometric shapes, and said he had once managed to pass a geometry test 'on sheer intuition'; he 'saw clearly where the line *had* to go, as clearly as I ever saw an image'.

He studied English under Professor Felix Schelling, but did very little work. A contemporary recalled how, while Schelling lectured on Shakespeare, Ra Pound 'would take out an immense tin watch and wind it with elaborate deliberation'. Ezra himself admitted that during his freshman year he did 'little more than play chess'. He was given a place on the university team, but his game was erratic, intuitive rather than calculating.

Though he had decided to preserve himself from the herd at Penn by cultivating an intellectual manner, he had no objection to being noticed. The *Jenkintown Times–Chronicle* reported on 19 April 1902, towards the end of his freshman year:

> The U. of P. students haven't any use for loudness in half-hose. They compelled one of their number to adopt Nature's own 'flesh color' en route to our village. The temperature registered about forty degrees. He is doing well.

Ezra recalled this incident in 1955: 'Haven't been in a frog pond since my freshman year.' He explained that freshmen were forbidden to 'wear red sox', but he took this as a personal challenge. According to another student, the dousing was in 'the lily pond in the botanical garden'. Ezra claimed he wore the offending socks again the next day.

The incident, semi-mythical as it may be, signifies a stage in the disappearance of the nondescript Ra Pound and the emergence of the distinctive Ezra. It seems indeed the baptism of this new persona. 'Ezra Pound's crazy', one of his friends was warned by schoolfellows. 'He wanted them to throw him in the pond.' At Penn they called him 'Lily' Pound. Enjoying the attention, he cultivated the dandy image.

*

In his freshman year he made only one male friend, who was not at the university. Will Brooke Smith, aged seventeen, was studying at the Philadelphia School of Industrial Art. His parents were dead; he lived with an aunt and uncle in the fashionable northern part of the city. To Ezra, he preached the doctrine of a life for art's sake, and expounded the ideas of the effete 1890s. Ezra was not altogether ready for this: when Brooke Smith gave him a copy of Oscar Wilde's *Salome* with the Beardsley illustrations, he 'cut 'em out, they were so ugly'. But the relationship stirred him, and its effect was sealed by Brooke Smith's death from tuberculosis in 1908. Ezra afterwards wrote of him:

> Will Smith . . . avoided a very unpleasant era of American life by dying of consumption to the intimate grief of his friends. How in Christ's name he came to be in Phila. – and to know what he did know at the age of 17–25 – I don't know. At any rate, thirteen years are gone; I haven't replaced him and shan't and no longer hope to.

The friendship was crucial enough for Ezra to dedicate his first book of poetry to Brooke Smith, calling him his 'first friend'.

In memoriam eius mihi caritate primus William Brooke Smith,
Painter, Dreamer of Dreams.

*

At the end of his freshman year it was clear that he was not doing well at
his studies. The Distinction in solid geometry was his single peak, and he
only achieved passes in other subjects, including English composition, with
a few B grades (meaning 'good') here and there. Dr Schelling of the English
department said eighteen years later that he had found him 'a remarkably
idle student'.

Homer and Isabel took him on another trip to Europe in the summer
vacation following his freshman year, from June to September 1902. The
journey included return visits to London and Venice. That autumn his
parents let their Wyncote house and moved temporarily into Philadelphia,
while Ezra, beginning his sophomore year at Penn, took up residence in a
dormitory, visiting his parents at weekends. He immediately became the
butt of a whole series of pranks by his student neighbours in the building,
who decided that he must be 'a sort of screwball, very easily duped'. But
the jokes tended to backfire.

One night two seniors staged a mock fight in his room, during which (by
prearrangement) one of them threw a bucket of water over the other,
deliberately soaking Ezra's bed. Ezra, however, never 'caught on' that he
was the real target. The next morning one of the protagonists 'asked him
how he managed to sleep in that wet bed. "Oh," said he, "I didn't sleep in
the bed, I slept on the floor." And then with a laugh – "But I will never
forget the look on your face when he threw that water on you."' On
another occasion the same seniors woke Ezra in the middle of a freezing
night, and told him to run for a doctor as another student was dangerously
ill. Ezra was given a non-existent address, 3990 Walnut Street. When he
had gone they all sat up in glee waiting for him to return disgruntled, but
no Ezra. Finally they went to bed. Then, 'about an hour later,' says one of
them, 'there was a knock on my door and there stood Pound and a man
with a black bag . . . "You gave me a wrong address. I had to wake up three
doctors before I could get one to come . . ."' It was the same in later life.
He would naïvely take everything at face value, occasionally to his
disadvantage, but more often scoring over those who thought to trip him
up.

He was not elected to any fraternity at Penn, though according to one
story he was invited to join one but 'bit one of the brothers during an
undignified part of his initiation and left the fraternity house in a huff,
never to return'. However, fraternity membership was not a *sine qua non*
of Penn life, and his exclusion seems to have meant nothing to him.

He began to make acquaintances through sport. He acted as usher for football games, played tennis, and took fencing lessons from the university coach, an Italian named Leonardo Terrone. He did not get into the fencing team, but was accepted as part of the 'gang' at the fencing club. In 1908 he sent Terrone a copy of his first book of poems, and reported to his father that it seemed 'to have made a hit . . . several of the gang according to him are interested'. One of the poems in it, 'For E. McC.', is addressed to 'my counter-blade' in the fencing club, and begins

> Gone while your tastes were keen to you,
> Gone where the grey winds call to you,
> By that high fencer, even Death,
> Struck of the blade that no man parrieth . . .

The poem has often been supposed to be addressed to an undergraduate called Eugene McCartney, but he was alive when it was written. It may have been about an imaginary death, an imaginary friend.*

Ezra kept his fencing foils for the rest of his life, and loved the sport, explaining that this was because it involved matching oneself against a single opponent's skill rather than battling in a crowd. It was an exercise in 'thinking the other man's thought & muscular coordination'. He was not well co-ordinated, and he fenced with wild, unconventional strokes. Another member of the club, looking back half a century later, describes his technique:

> I remember once we were fencing with walking sticks or umbrellas in his poppa's front hall. I happened to be on the squad at the university, which he wasn't good enough to make . . . He greeted me with an offer for a friendly bout with two of his father's walking sticks. I took one, made a few formal flourishes and placed myself *en garde* . . . [I] could have shoved the stick through his mouth and out his asshole, if it had been important enough to do so, but [I was] holding back, kidding . . . Before I could do more than laughingly provoke him, [he] came plunging wildly in without restraint, and hit me with the point of the cane above my right eye to fairly lay me out . . . He damned near put my eye out . . . I . . . told him what I thought of him and threw down my stick. He felt triumphant that he had put the whole team of the University of Pennsylvania behind him with that single stroke . . . Served me damn well right. I should have knocked the hell out of him . . . You can't trust a guy like that!

---

*A. Walton Litz suggests that the poem is '*for* McCartney but *about* William Brooke Smith'.

The words are those of William Carlos Williams, in 1902 a nineteen-year-old freshman in the medical school of Penn, living a rather homesick existence in a single room in a dormitory building near Ezra's. When he heard a sophomore music major playing the piano in the next room, Williams took out his own violin and struck up, hoping to make friends. The musician was not particularly interested, but thought Williams might be odd enough to get on with one of his classmates, the peculiar Ezra Pound, whom he went and fetched. 'Old Ez staggered up the stairs,' said Williams. 'I don't remember that though. I don't remember the first meeting at all. But it just took one look and I knew he was it.'

At first they had little in common other than loneliness and a desire to show off their sophistication. Williams came from an ordinary middle-class home in Rutherford, New Jersey, but, thanks to his father's job in the rum trade, he had visited Europe and had spent a year at a finishing school in Geneva. Besides fencing, he acted, played the violin and sang. A student publication described him as a 'dark Spanish beauty'. (His mother was half Spanish.) He was determined to make a career in medicine, but he had 'started to write and was putting down . . . little poems, pretty bad poems'. He let Ezra see them; Ezra 'was not impressed. He was impressed with his own poetry; but then, I was impressed with my own poetry, too, so we got along all right.'

Ezra was glad to find someone who would show any serious sympathy with his poetic ambitions. He once tried reading a poem to the captain of the fencing team, '& he assuming a grave & terible air said ponderously . . . "*that* is a *ver-ry* darn foolish thought"'. Williams was critical, but he understood.

Ezra was still doing no work. During his sophomore year his courses included the nineteenth-century English novelists, ethics, logic, and more Latin texts, including Sextus Propertius, but he paid little attention. However, on his own initiative (and probably following suggestions from Brooke Smith) he began to read widely in modern poetry – Browning, and such 1890s figures as Arthur Symons and Ernest Dowson. Williams was still discovering the Romantics, so he was excited by the wider horizons Ezra could show him. Williams told his mother that they were talking together about 'subjects that I love yet have not had time to study and which he is making a life work of. That is literature, and the drama and the classics, also a little philosophy.' He judged Ezra 'the livest, most intelligent and unexplainable thing' he had yet come across, and afterwards felt that 'before meeting Ezra Pound is like B.C. and A.D.'

It was equally important for Ezra too. His first intellectual friendship, with Brooke Smith, had been a case of mentor and acolyte; now the roles could be reversed, which was what he preferred. He started to treat Williams with comic condescension, as a not-very-bright pupil who, nevertheless, had promise, a creature of good intentions but limited intelligence who needed the guidance of Ezra's more subtle mind. His letters to Williams are lofty and elder-brotherish, and he claimed to derive much amusement from the spectacle of 'pore old Bill Carlos trundling along'. He realized however that Williams's attempts at poetry were a great deal less artificial and embellished than his own.

Williams was not taken in by Ezra's airs. He wrote to his mother about his friend's effect on his fellow students at Penn, saying,

> not one person in a thousand likes him, and why? Because he is so darned full of conceits and affectation. He is really a brilliant talker and thinker but delights in making himself just exactly what he is not: a laughing boor. His friends must be all patience in order to find him out and even then you must not let him know it, for he will immediately put on some artificial mood and be really unbearable. It is too bad, for he loves to be liked, yet there is some quality in him which makes him too proud to please people.

'A laughing boor' does not sound much like the later Ezra. But another observation of Williams's shows that he was already developing a characteristic that would become familiar. He was learning to hide any symptoms of self-doubt beneath the surface. 'If he ever does get blue,' wrote Williams to his mother, 'nobody knows it . . . he is the essence of optimism . . .'

*

Williams was in the audience in April 1903 when Euripides' *Iphigenia in Tauris* was staged in an English translation by undergraduates at Penn, with Ezra among the chorus of women. Williams remembered the hilarious sight of him in 'a great blonde wig at which he tore as he waved his arms about and heaved his massive breasts in ecstasies of extreme emotion'. Various members of Ezra's family came to witness this spectacle, including Aunt Frank from New York. His parents cannot, however, have been pleased with the results he was showing at the end of his sophomore year. This time he had earned no distinctions, only a few Bs and mostly plain passes, and had failed entirely in one history course. Williams afterwards felt that Ezra's wish at this time to 'impress everyone about him with the profundity of his wit' had been a disguise for the fact that 'generally speaking his head was fairly empty'.

Though he liked to give the impression of being widely read, he once admitted, at the end of his life: 'I've read too little and I read very slowly.' Partly in compensation for this, he began to persuade himself that knowledge consisted of nuggets, of items that could be picked up at random wherever they happened to catch the eye. 'It is not necessary,' he said to Williams one day, 'to read everything in a book in order to speak intelligently of it.' He added: 'Don't tell everybody I said so.'

It was in itself no very damaging admission, but Ezra carried it to extremes, sometimes judging a book on the most superficial grounds. Samuel Putnam once handed him a couple of Italian dictionaries and asked which was the better. 'In place of opening them or even so much as glancing at the names on the covers, he balanced one in each hand. "This seems to be the weightier of the two," he announced. I thought he must be jesting; but he was not.'

Occasionally his ignorance was laid bare. When Ernest Hemingway asked him what he really thought about Dostoyevsky, 'To tell you the truth, Hem,' Ezra said, 'I've never read the Rooshians.' But usually, if cornered, he would produce the most vehement self-justification: 'Tolstoi, russian therefore a mess.' But had he read Tolstoy? 'Have I got to *read* the god damn thing, despite its being by the mess TolsthOIK? Balony!'

His more perceptive friends were aware of his reading habits. 'He has tasted an enormous number of books,' wrote Richard Aldington, (who became a friend in 1912), 'yet I doubt if he has ever read one with concentration from cover to cover.' T. S. Eliot derived enormous amusement from the spectacle of Ezra posing as scholar. He wrote to him in 1934 after spotting some howlers in Ezra's quotations from Mallarmé in *Make It New*: 'I always said now didnt I theres some subjects on which the Duck Rabbit is touchinly ignorant such as French literature, drama, philosophy and theology *exceptin* Lope de Vega etc. Japanese drama, Javanese hip dancing, some French literature in the middle ages and some scholastic or pre-scholastic works . . .' But most people were fooled most of the time. 'With one day's reading a man may have the key in his hands,' Ezra wrote in the Pisan Cantos, and he usually worked on this principle of judicious selection, deploying his limited knowledge with considerable agility.

Eliot made another dig in the same 1934 letter: 'As for your general thinkin ability . . . the less said about that the Better especially as thats my weak Point too and we mustnt let down the Union.' Behind Eliot's teasing there is serious comment. 'He doesn't have a great mind and never did,' wrote Williams of Ezra in 1945, 'but that doesn't make him any the less a good poet.' Ezra once spoke of his mind as having 'the desultory faculties of a lyric poet'. He suggested that while the prose writer is expected to 'describe precisely the nature of the engine, the position and relation of its wheels', the poet is 'a sort of steam-gauge, voltometer, a set of pipes for thermometric and barometric divination. He is not even compelled to be logical.' He believed that good prose arises 'from an instinct of negation; is the detailed analysis of something detestable; of something which one wants to eliminate. Poetry is the assertion of a positive, i.e. of desire, and endures for a longer period.' He felt that his own mind was made for the poetic process, and that this excused its shortcomings in logical thought and analysis.

*

At the age of seventeen, staying in New York, Ezra wrote this letter to his father, on a typewriter:

> Lieber Vater.
> Noddings egzitemendz didding. Odervise dings vas az dey vas. I send this epistle that thou mayst have cognizance of the aforesaid fact.
> We are all able to imbibe nurrishment. I am writing this by bum gass light. Dont forget to send over my bathing suit. und quq. did it. This wassing chewsday you having left moon days there is not much to write . . .
>
> > with love
> >
> > Son

Spelling like this mock-German had featured widely in jokes and comic strips since America was first overrun by immigrants. Other misspellings in such letters were sometimes a consequence of Ezra's over-hastiness with the typewriter; for example, in February 1905 he wrote from Hamilton College to his father:

> Killing time before Dutch with George Day8s type writer /
> Dont know that there is any thing in in particular that I think of just now only I might as weel write to you as do anything else . . .

This was one of his earliest uses of the diagonal line, which became a favourite punctuation mark and increasingly adorned his letters. He may have originally used it in error – on many keyboards it is placed next to the full stop – but its idiosyncratic appearance soon made him adopt it deliberately.

He typed with immense energy, banging away so hard that in later years he sometimes broke 'the main back spring' of the machine. He usually hit the space bar twice between each word, and allowed generous gaps between lines. 'In typing leave good triple space between the lines,' he told his mother in 1908 when she was making a fair copy for him. 'It is much easier on the editorial eye & consequently on the temper.' In fact the eye is disconcerted by so much space on the page, and one wonders whether there was some deeper attraction to him in this extra spacing. The later parts of the Cantos depend on empty space (gaps between lines, indentations) almost as much as on words.

Until he was about thirty he continued to use a pen for much of the time, preferring a simple nib and holder to the fountain variety, which never produced ink fast enough for him. In September 1903 he signed a letter to his parents for the first time not as 'Son' or 'E.L. Pound' but with a flourishing, bold *Ezra Pound*.

6

Just So The Mask Shall Fit

In the summer of 1903, at the end of his sophomore year, it was agreed that Ezra should leave the University of Pennsylvania and complete his undergraduate studies elsewhere, at Hamilton College, Clinton, in New York State. Given his increasingly determined character and Homer's and Isabel's pliability in accepting his wishes, it is likely that Ezra originated the idea. Hamilton could offer him a wider choice of courses and would therefore (he may have argued) give him a chance to do better. Regulations at Penn laid down that he could only study for credit those languages (Latin and German) which he had offered at enrolment; at Hamilton he would be allowed to add Italian and Spanish, to which he was now attracted. He may also have told his parents, with justice, that his poor results at Penn were largely the result of bad teaching and an atmosphere that discouraged real academic study. Hamilton had a much better reputation.

He probably heard something about Hamilton from the Reverend Carlos Tracy Chester, who had been a student there. (Although no longer at the Calvary church, Mr Chester was still in the Philadelphia area, running the *Book News Monthly* and keeping in touch with Ezra.) On 11 June 1903, while spending part of his vacation in New York with Aunt Frank, Ezra went to look at the college.

Hamilton was a complete contrast to the dehumanized atmosphere of Penn. Standing on a hilltop near the town of Clinton in upstate New York, it boasted an ivied quadrangle resembling Harvard, and had only a small number of students – a mere forty or so in each year's class. Ezra took to it at once, and reported to his father that he had had a successful interview: 'Saw Dr Stryker this P.M. & I arranged my course. I shall graduate with "05" O.K.' (In other words he would study at Hamilton for only two years before graduation; his two years at Penn would be allowed for credit.) 'Am delighted much about everything. The college is set way up in the hills & there is a fine view down the valley to Utica & beyond. There seems to be a dandy crowd of fellows here.'

The President of Hamilton was the rotundly named Dr Melanchthon Woolsey Stryker, a vigorous lion of a clergyman with a talent for insulting the famous in his pulpit – he labelled Theodore Roosevelt 'the Idol of Mediocrity', and poured scorn on President Eliot of 'mighty Harvard' for allowing students to choose their own courses. Ezra derived amusement and inspiration from these performances.

*

His first letter to his parents from Hamilton, dated 30 September 1903, reports that he is determined to join a fraternity, Delta Kappa Epsilon, and has, apparently, already done so – he is 'pledged' to it, and tells them 'I dont believe I could have made a better choice'. He explains that he can now go and live in the fraternity house, instead of in a dormitory. He tells his father there will be very little extra expense – a crucial point, for Homer's resources were fully stretched – and adds:

> . . . as fellows here must join a fraternity or be out in the cold I
> dont know I can explicitly name advantages but you ought to
> be able to understand. If you dont I dont know what you can
> do about it. Talk frats with someone who has been in one.

Then something went wrong. It is said that the Delta Kappa Epsilon fraternity heard word from Penn in a telegram: 'UNDER NO CONSIDERATION PLEDGE EZRA POUND', and the invitation to membership was withdrawn. At all events he did not move into the fraternity house, and – unlike the majority of Hamilton undergraduates – there is no mention of a fraternity after his name in the college yearbook.

We know nothing of his immediate reaction, but the next surviving letter home shows that by his second semester he had decided that the move from Penn had been a complete mistake. It was written on 29 April 1904. In it, he asks his father to see the Penn authorities and ask if, supposing he returned there, he would be credited for work done at Hamilton. He continues:

> I guess I'd better come back where I belong . . . I get more tired
> of the place every day & if it is as bad as it is now it will be
> worse next year . . . I suppose I could have decent quarters next
> year but all the rooms in the new dormitories are for two or
> three men, and as all the fraternity men room with their own
> men. And as all the fellows fit to room with are in the frats. I

cant get a room without paying double . . . You neednt tell mother I'm feeling this way about things . . . Anyway I guess it runs in the family to keep cheerful.

    Good Bye

In a postscript he contemplates coming back to live at home again while completing his studies at Penn: 'there are only three of us & we might as well get acquainted while we have the chance'.

We do not have Homer's reply, but Ezra did not leave Hamilton. His next letters show him carrying on there much as usual, pushing unhappiness beneath the surface and displaying that family inclination to 'keep cheerful', though there are moments when his loneliness shows clearly through.

*

It took him most of the summer vacation of 1904 to come to the final decision that he must carry on at Hamilton – continuing doubts are apparent in his letters to his father – but by August he had made up his mind, and was able to contemplate the situation with some equanimity. While staying with friends on Long Island he wrote to his mother of his academic work that after a year more he 'should be able to speak French German & Spanish fairly well & have my reading knowledge of Italian in reserve . . . And Hamilton will be better next year & I will not be an outsider . . . I think I'll be more a man at the end of it.'

So he was back at Hamilton in September, occupying rooms that he called 'Buzzards Roost', roosting there alone. Now and then he would wander down into Clinton to do some shopping; mostly when not attending classes he sat by himself, working. 'Essay on early poetry of Wm Morris,' he reported to his mother on a typical day. 'Down into Clinton to get socks, garters etc. Otherwise nothing doing.' He made no further attempt to ingratiate himself with his fellow students. For their part they were guarded towards him rather than mocking; afterwards they described him in such terms as 'not popular but interesting', 'kept strictly to himself', 'lived his own life, and it had very little connection with the College'. There is one unsubstantiated story of his room being wrecked by rowdies in search of sport, but on the whole he seems to have been left alone. He joined the chess team, and played some tennis. Afterwards he spoke to William Carlos Williams of two years of 'hell' at Hamilton, but most of the time he was careful to present his parents with a calm façade.

'Everything here o.k.,' he told his mother at the beginning of the new academic year, in September 1904. 'I am reading & doing odd jobs for the joint, & occasionally hearing Miss Heyman play. It is a comfort to find a person with brains & sense. once & a while.' Katherine Ruth Heyman here receives her first mention, so casually that one might assume Homer and

Isabel were already acquainted with her. In fact it was Ezra's habit all his life to allude to people – in letters and in print – without necessary explanations.

Eleven years older than Ezra, Katherine Ruth (Kitty) Heyman was a concert pianist who had been born in California of a Jewish musician father and a 'colonial' mother. She was an interpreter of Scriabin, and appeared at least once as a soloist with the Boston Symphony Orchestra, but she never became well known. She was no beauty: a musician friend, Faubion Bowers, describes how

> Kitty's hair had very early turned grey . . . [but] she made herself up as a younger woman . . . Bright red lipstick. Eyeshadow that made her eyes more enormous than they already were, as if to swallow the beak of her shamed nose . . . Lamé housegowns of pastel and glint . . . and there was one suggestive, heavily metallic brocade of rioting colors with a diamanté butterfly over the most pubic pelvis. Yet . . . she was fanatically moral. She had never married. She told me she had 'never given myself to a man', or woman for that matter, although some of her best friends et cetera . . . She also sported a wedding ring, occasionally, which made her 'a bride of Christ', she said.

Ezra seems to have run across her in the environs of Hamilton. Thereafter she began to play an ambiguous part in his life, rather as Will Brooke Smith had done in Philadelphia, turning up at unpredictable moments and breathing an air of excitement. It was with Brooke Smith that he placed her a few years later when summarizing his friendships of early days: 'My first friend was a painter, now dead. 2nd a Pyanist, naturally 15 years plus agée que moi,' Does 'naturally' mean that he thought it inevitable he would be attracted to an older woman? Certainly there was something maternal in the relationship; he sometimes referred to her as 'the Kitty-mama'. But he also called her plain 'Kitty' or 'Katie', and she gave him a ring that had belonged to her mother, which he was to keep 'till we are both very old'.

She was a devotee of the occult, enthusing over theosophy, ectoplasms, and tarot cards; she told a friend that she had met Scriabin on the moon and made love with him. Ezra expresses something of their relationship in a 1906 poem, 'Scriptor Ignotus', dedicated to her. In it, he speaks in the persona of Bertold Lomax, an English scholar of Dante who died in Ferrara in 1723 with his own 'great epic' unwritten; the lady organist of Ferrara to whom the poem is ostensibly addressed is obviously meant to represent Miss Heyman. He declares that if his 'great forty-year epic' is ever written, then everyone will say of her that 'she 'twas that played him power at life's morn . . . And God's peace dwelt in the mingled chords /

She drew from out the shadows of the past.' There is however, a degree of irony in the note at the end that Lomax died with the epic unwritten.

*

After Ezra's mention in September 1904 of Kitty Heyman to his parents, we hear nothing of her for a while, and letters show him making the best of his situation at Hamilton. In October he found 'a freshman who is respectable for a room mate', and in consequence he moved out of Buzzard's Roost into 'the New Dorm'. It is striking that, although he was now a senior, only a freshman would share with him.

The freshman, Claudius A. Hand, one of the only other two Hamilton students who did not belong to a fraternity, had to put up with being woken in the middle of the night when Ezra had finished a poem that he wanted to read aloud. Ezra would ask if he could make anything of it, Hand would invariably say 'No', whereupon Ezra would show signs of despair, and sometimes tear up the poem.

He read his poetry very badly at this stage of his life. William Carlos Williams claimed that listening to it was 'a painful experience' because 'it was often impossible to hear the lines . . . His voice would trail off . . . until they were inaudible – from his intensity. I seldom let on except, occasionally, to explode with the comment that unless I could *hear* the lines how could he expect me to have an opinion of them.'

Though he had decided to become a poet, he assumed that some other way of making a living would be necessary. He told Hand he wanted to live abroad and might get a job in the Consular Service. His mother, he said, would like 'to see me in the Diplomatic Corps – "Ambassadour to the Ct. of St James"'. He also contemplated the law or Wall Street, but wrote to his father that 'the consular service would be more enjoyable'; he might start as '14th assistant secretary to the ministers office boy at Berlin'. He was still doing some German, and this and his courses in Romance languages should provide him with some of the qualifications.

For the first time since entering college he began to benefit from one of the professors. William Pierce ('Bill') Shepard taught Romance languages and literature at Hamilton, and was a withdrawn, aggressive man, 'a formidable and awesome creature,' writes a Hamilton alumnus, 'whose squinting glance and sunken cheeks caused thrills to run up and down spines'. Shepard's refusal to run with the herd no doubt appealed to the outcast Ezra, who enjoyed his classes, though at first he spurned Shepard's offer of extra teaching. 'Got more mediaeval philosophy in one canto of Dante's Paradise than I ever expect to get again,' he wrote to his mother after one of Shepard's classes. 'He told me if I wanted any more I could go to Thomas Aquinas & the other mediaeval latin writers. I said "No thanks this is enough" so we go on to Canto X.'

Besides Romance languages, he was studying Anglo-Saxon and English literature, and was still doing mathematics, as well as enduring 'hot air about Parliamentary law' from Dr Stryker. He found Anglo-Saxon 'very fascinating', but had no time to make more than a superficial acquaintance with it. Even his Romance courses had a great deal crammed into them. Within a week or two of each other he was reading Corneille's *Le Cid*, the *Lais* of Marie de France, Pascal's *Pensées*, and Flaubert's *Salammbô*, not to mention trying to get a grounding in Spanish. Yet success was often a matter simply of clocking up a certain number of hours in class rather than demonstrating achievement. 'Am not expected to continue it beyond required time,' he writes of one of his courses.

As the autumn semester of 1904 progressed, he began to spend some spare time discussing literature with Professor Joseph Darling Ibbotson, known as 'Bib', who taught English and Anglo-Saxon. 'Went down & talked books etc with Bib,' Ezra reported to his mother. And again: 'Going my homeward way at 10pm, I noticed Bib's lights ablaze and knowing that he is still mostly college boy despite his family and professorship I dropped in and we smoked and talked for an hour or two longer.' Ibbotson was faintly taken aback by these night visitations; he has described how Ezra once dropped in at 11.40 p.m., staying until nearly 3 a.m., talking about Ossian, which (typically) he had discovered not in the original but in an obscure German translation.

At one of these night-time sessions, or perhaps in class, Ibbotson made a casual remark that had a striking effect on Ezra. 'It is nigh on to 43 years,' Ezra wrote to him in 1946, 'since you sd: "a man who has spent 40 years on an epic" – re/ Bentley.' Ibbotson was actually referring not to poetic composition, but to the enormous labours of Richard Bentley of Cambridge in 'editing' *Paradise Lost* during the early eighteenth century – a ridiculous enterprise based on the notion that Milton's original text had been corrupted by an amanuensis and needed to be restored. Ezra seems to have been struck by the remark that the work took Bentley forty years. It sowed the idea of writing an epic poem so huge that it would require a similar time span. In 1936 he offered the Hamilton alumni magazine the suggestion that they 'might record that the CANTOS started in a talk with "BIB", and Bib's remarks on Bentley's attempt to "edit" Milton'. But at first he thought of writing not a long poem but a play: 'I was in them days contemplatin a jejune trilogy on Merozia. Which Bib was naive enough to agree wd/ be a man's magnum opus if he pulled it off.'

In a letter to Ibbotson, he recalled that the original project had been 'a play about Marozia'. The choice of subject was typically recondite: Marozia, a tenth-century noblewoman, married three powerful Italians in turn, was the mistress of one Pope and the mother of another. Ezra observed that she was 'the sort [of woman] I admire very much', and mentioned how she had made her husbands successful through her wiles. Nothing is known about his projected play.

He would later claim that he 'began the Cantos about 1904 . . . I had various schemes . . . The problem was to get a form – something elastic enough to take the necessary material.' Elsewhere: 'Cantos started in 1904 or '5 but didn't get onto paper.' But the only contemporary evidence that he was contemplating a major work at such an early date is the mention in 'Scriptor Ignotus' of a 'great forty-year epic' – presumably an allusion to Ibbotson's remark about Bentley. In the event the writing of the Cantos, which did not begin until 1915, was to occupy about five years longer than this estimate.

*

During his second year at Hamilton, he gradually moved beyond the poetry of 'I have heard a wee wind searching', and began to adopt different characters or masks in his verse, through which he spoke. Sometimes he chose the voice of an 1890s decadent poet like Dowson: 'Memory faileth, as the lotus-loved chimes / Sink into fluttering of wind . . . / The strange night-wonder of your eyes / Dies not . . .' Another time the voice was hearty and masculine: 'For God, our God, is a gallant foe . . . / Whom God deigns not to overthrow / Hath need of triple mail.' Neither of these masks was convincing; he had not yet found an identity that fitted snugly. More striking is the simple piece entitled 'On His Own Face in a Glass', which puzzles over this whole question of who is one's 'real' self:

> O strange face there in the glass!
>
> O ribald company, O saintly host!
> O sorrow-swept my fool,
> What answer?
>   O ye myriad
> That strive and play and pass,
> Jest, challenge, counterlie,
>
> I ? I ? I ?
>   And ye?

The last line ingeniously throws the question back to the reader, but the self-doubt is plain to see. As Ezra wrote in 1913, 'The real meditation is . . . the meditation on one's *identity*. Ah, voilà une chose!! You try it. You try finding out why you're you & not somebody else. And who in the blazes are you anyhow. Ah voilà une chose.'

It was a legitimate question. Was he the retiring intellectual who shunned the company of fellow students in the pursuit of learning? Was he a 'character' who did not mind being thrown into frog ponds? Was he

Homer and Isabel's cheery optimistic 'Son'? Was he Kitty Heyman's soul mate? Was he 'Bib's' aspiring poet, about to take up his pen for a forty-year epic? The answer seemed to be that each of these personalities felt like the true one at the moment it was being worn, but could swiftly be succeeded by another that appeared just as genuine. As he wrote in 1915: 'In the "search for oneself", in the search for "sincere self-expression", one gropes . . . One says "I am" this, that, or the other, and with the words scarcely uttered one ceases to be that thing.'

Another poem, written in 1905 during his time at Hamilton, says much the same thing but more metaphysically. Entitled 'Plotinus' after the most celebrated of the Neoplatonist philosophers, it expresses the wish to undergo some kind of mystical-intellectual experience, to be drawn 'thru the node of things/Back sweeping to the vortex of the cone' (this is his earliest use of the term 'vortex'). But he hesitates to undergo the experience because he feels himself to be merely 'an atom on creation's throne', 'lonely as a lonely child'. So he decides to make 'New thoughts as crescent images of *me*', new personalities or masks for himself. 'And with them was my essence reconciled / While fear went forth from mine eternity.' The poem says rather self-consciously that he feels more comfortable when he is not trying to expose his real self to the world, but can hide behind a variety of images.

He raised this personal matter again in another poem, two years later, where he speaks of it in plainer terms. Evidently in the interval he has grown accustomed to the idea:

> . . . 'tis not need we *know* our every thought
> Or see the work shop where each mask is wrought
> Wherefrom we view the world . . .
> . . . just so the mask shall fit.

Wyndham Lewis once remarked on Ezra's habit of donning masks. He wrote: 'Pound is that curious thing, a person without a trace of originality of any sort . . . Yet when he can get into the skin of somebody else . . . he becomes a lion or a lynx on the spot.'

7

Not Yet Lost Virginity

His letters to his parents from Hamilton showed further signs of uneasiness. 'Am at peace with the world,' he told Homer on his nineteenth birthday, 30 October 1904, but he added rather pathetically: 'Penn–Harvard victory gave me a chance to celebrate without anyone catching on the fact it was a birthday.'

He was writing to his mother or father almost daily now, simply for someone to talk to. He admitted to feeling 'absolute isolation from all "humanity"', though 'there are a few white folks even up here'. He and his room-mate Hand had nothing to say to one another, and he continued this letter:

> I dont suppose anyone can live in books steadily & not get grouched occasionally. Have seen & heard nothing outside this cramped narrow lopsided hole except last Saturday. I'm not grouching only it gets monotonous.

A few days later he ran away from Hamilton.

He travelled south-west across New York State to Ithaca, where he wrote to his father on the stationery of the Ithaca Hotel:

> Dear Dad,
>   As you see I have broke out. I'd been bottled on that desolate mountain top about as long as I could stand it. so I'm taking a little vacation. Break it gently to mother. she wanted me to get shoes instead of enjoying life. I think you'll understand the situation better yourself, you left on the front of an engine once yourself, guess it runs in the family . . .

I shall probably be back in Hamilton when you get this as I
am not long on either cuts or coin . . .
          Your wayward son
               Ezry

He was indeed back at Hamilton within a few days; he reported to his
mother: 'Had a rather enjoyable time . . . everything o.k.'

He had to go back, for there was nothing to run away from but himself,
and he was developing more sophisticated techniques than this for coping
with his difficulties. Nevertheless in later years, at occasional moments of
crisis, there would be other runnings-away.

*

For the rest of the 1904 autumn semester he occupied himself 'plugging
away' at Greek, at Browning's *Sordello* (which in time would provide a
setting-off point for the Cantos), and at 'Dago Lit.' He spoke of this as
'getting on the job'. The Hamilton courses were little more than a hasty
tour of the various languages and their literatures, but, far from regretting
the absence of challenge to original thought and real scholarship, he
delighted in cutting corners, and swiftly developed an ability to get by in
subjects of which he was ignorant. 'Passed Analyt.,' he told his mother in
January 1905. 'The faculty of mathematics in consultation could not
fathom my method but the key problem demanded an equation & I wrote
it despite the formulae etc. supposed to be necessary there to & which I
didn't know.'

His method might be summarized as, first, to have plenty of self
confidence; next, to lay his work out with a dash so that it *looked* plausible
(for example, in his early attempts at musical notation he disguises his
ignorance by the sheer flourish with which he jabs notes on the paper); and
last, to get the 'feel' of a subject, picking up its jargon and the kind of
questions that would interest real experts, thereby giving an impression of
genuine knowledge. Occasionally he would lift the mask of erudition
enough to reveal this technique, to make such remarks as 'Really one
DON'T need to know a language. One NEEDS, damn well needs, to
know the few hundred words in the few really good poems that any
language has in it.' His performance was backed by an excellent memory,
so that he retained, almost involuntarily, anything that had happened to
catch his attention.

In January 1905 he stumbled across a group of Hamilton freshmen who
had been set Emerson's essay on 'Self-Reliance' as an assignment, and were
trying to discuss it. 'I butted in & helped 'em tear it out.' Freshmen had to
put up with him because of his seniority, and he decided to capitalize on
this. A few days later: 'Have gathered a very decent gang of freshmen who
have begun to meet here decently & in order on Tuesday evenings.' This

was the first of a series of groups at which he would expound to what was intended to be an admiring audience. 'Tuesday . . . have had my kindergarten this evening,' he reports from Hamilton in April 1905, though he does not say what diet he fed to the 'children'.

At the time that he started this freshman group, the Romance professor Bill Shepard lent him 'a book of french translations of O[ld] F[rench] & Provencal'. He immediately announced to his parents that he would be doing 'studies in Provencal & extended works in old F.' He gave them no reason for this decision: perhaps at first it was the esoteric nature of the subject that appealed, for no other students were doing it and it was chiefly his own idea. 'I was NOT directed to Provençal,' he emphasized with pride years later. 'Shepard kindly gave me some when I asked for it.'

Once he had made contact with the subject, he quickly became excited by the troubadour poets. 'I suppose "Peire Cardinal" will be the particular troubadour that I shall study for the next couple of years,' he told his mother in the letter in which he first mentions Provençal. And a month later he has done 'about two hundred pages of french on Raimon de Miraval troubadour of Provence'. The troubadours appealed to him because they accorded with his view of the nature and character of a poet: it was attractive to think of oneself as a combative, aggressive wandering minstrel, an outcast who nevertheless commanded the attention of a cultured audience. In his book *The Spirit of Romance* (1910) he admits to a 'temperamental sympathy' with these figures and their age.

*

During his time at Hamilton he made some acquaintances through a church social group, among them a girl named Viola Baxter. To his parents he mentions getting 'rash' and hiring 'a hoss an wagin fer to go aout driving in. P.S. I didn't went alone also. etc. she is pretty nice also. her face looks more like a face than a coal scuttle.'

Two years later he described her to William Carlos Williams as 'one of the few girls I have fallen in love with', but if that was really so, he does not seem to have felt it very seriously. He exchanged letters with her, and continued to do so long after her marriage, in a way that does not suggest a genuine love affair in the past. It became typical of him to keep in touch with former girlfriends like this. He never broke off with a quarrel, but allowed any romantic element – if there was one – to shade off into the cheerful camaraderie which seemed to suit him better. This suggests an admirable loyalty and affection, but also an absence of strong feeling.

Even in his earliest days, when he was trying out all kinds of masks and voices as a poet, he wrote almost nothing that can be called love poetry. Sexuality was eventually allowed to have its place in certain cantos and in *Homage to Sextus Propertius*, and here and there he meditates on the nature of love itself, but very little, throughout his life, seems to record or reflect personal feelings. He once admitted that there was 'personal love poetry neither in Cantos nor in any Epos'.

Perhaps it is foolish to look for it, as he once suggested in a letter to the novelist May Sinclair:

> Wotcher mean by 'great pash. human theem'??
>   'She was pore butt she wuz honest
>   Victim OF!!
>   luh village crime'???

But it is hard to escape the suspicion that its absence is an indication of a failure to engage in love. An undated early poem, 'The Summons', seems to suggest that this was the case. It tells the beloved: 'I cannot bow to woo thee /With honey words and flower kisses.' Instead he is

> . . . ever swept upward
> To the centre of all truth
> So must I bear thee with me
> Rapt into this great involving flame . . .
> And in the glory of our meeting
> Shall the power be reborn.

Love affairs had to be converted into a source of mental power. Love in itself was not attractive.

His attitude to women was apparently, as his daughter Mary has observed, one of 'respect above all' rather than of romantic love or desire. She adds that his understanding of sexuality was 'naïve'. This was one reason why all the women to whom he was attracted remained loyal to him: he made no demands upon them. Williams, who had as close a knowledge of Ezra's early love affairs as anyone, observed: 'If he ever got under a gal's skirts it must have been mainly with his imagination.'

*

In May 1905, shortly before the end of his time at Hamilton, a poem of Ezra's was published for the first time in the college literary magazine. It was a translation of what he described to his parents as 'the Belengual Alba or Dawn song. it is in Mediaeval Latin with Provencal refrain. Oldest Provencal written MSS of 10th century & song probably older.' His translation was in archaic English:

> Dawn light, o'er sea and height, riseth bright,
> Passeth vigil, clear shineth on the night . . .

He told his parents he was also trying to translate a poem by the troubadour Giraut de Bornelh, which used only five rhymes in sixty-eight lines.

With graduation from Hamilton very near, he considered the future, and thought of a teaching post at the CMA: 'Guess I'll take a job in C.M.A. Latin or English dept (or Fr & German if necessary) . . . I could hold down Latin at Cheltenham with less trouble than any other job I could get . . . Anybody desiring a tutor . . . can have me at special rates.'

He took his final exams in June 1905. He had already done much better at Hamilton than at Penn, achieving Distinctions in Anglo-Saxon, Bible study, bibliography, orations, parliamentary law, and advanced French, with Bs in German, Italian, and elementary Provençal; and now he had no trouble with the examinations. At the end of June 1905 he was awarded the degree of Bachelor of Philosophy, and was also given the college second prize in French. 'I am graduating the youngest in my class & with the rep. of being the best read man therein,' he wrote home. And as the final days approached: 'Commencement foomalities tomorrow & then this chapter is ended. Two letters from mother & some wild idea about my being vice consul in sibolulia. all right. I'd just as soon go if theres anything in it.' No job at the CMA materialized, so his thoughts turned to graduate studies at Penn. By the end of the summer he had decided to return there full time, for a one-year Master's course in Romance languages, during which he would live at home.

He was able to start with a clean slate back at Penn, since the Department of Romance languages had no previous experience of him. He enrolled for every course they offered: Old Spanish, Spanish drama, Spanish literature, Old French, Provençal, and Italian, plus three credits of special work in Latin. His tutor for everything except the Latin was Dr Hugo A. Rennert, Professor of Romance Languages and Literature, a dandy in appearance and ironical in manner. In Canto 28 Ezra recalls how 'old Rennert wd. sigh heavily / And look over the top of his lenses' when some latecomer hurried in. He was amused by Rennert's strictures, in his Midwestern drawl, on an 'editor' who had attempted to 'correct' the Old Spanish *El Cid* on the supposition that it required ten syllables in every line: 'Naow effa man had sense enough to write a beautiful poem like this, wudn't yeow think he wudda had sense enough to be able to keount ep to ten on his fingers *ef he'da wanted tew*?'

Ezra benefited greatly from his self-elected special seminars in Latin, with an Assistant Professor, McDaniel, whose elucidations of Catullus and Martial gave him his first sense of the need for 'clarity and hardness' in language. On the other hand, when he suggested to McDaniel that he might do 'a thesis on some reading matter OUTSIDE the list of classic authors included in the curriculum', he was told: 'Mr Pound, we shd. have to do so much work ourselves to verify your results.' The work he wanted to do was on Latin writers of the Italian Renaissance, whom he was beginning to discover for himself. Their appeal to him resided largely in their obscurity. He began to plan to do doctoral work, after his Master's year, on some aspect of Romance literature.

William Carlos Williams was still at Penn, patiently working his way through medical school, and once again listened to Ezra reading new poems. He noticed that 'Ezra never explained or joked about his writing as I might have done, but was always cryptic, unwavering and serious in his attitude toward it. He joked, crudely, about anything but that.' More seriously, Williams was disturbed by what he calls the 'side' (vanity) that 'went with all his posturings as a poet. To me that was the emptiest sort of old hat . . . a silly and unnecessary thing . . . My upbringing assumed rather the humility and caution of the scientist.' But others were more impressed.

*

During his freshman year at Penn, Ezra had been to a Hallowe'en party in Philadelphia. Among the guests was the daughter of the Professor of Astronomy, Hilda Doolittle. 'I was 15 and he was 16,' she writes. 'He was dressed in a green robe. He said it was not Chinese. He had got it on a trip he had made with his cousin or aunt some years before. In Tunis, I think . . . Ezra . . . had Gozzoli bronze-gold hair and the coat caught up with his hair and odd eyes.'

The Tangier robe – Aunt Frank never took him as far as Tunis – was a manifestation of his increasing interest in his own appearance. In particular he had begun to realize that his hair had possibilities. Hilda Doolittle calls it bronze-gold, but no two descriptions of it are quite the same. Others spoke of it as 'gold-red', 'brown', 'sandy', even 'peroxide blonde'. During college years he began to brush it vertically above his forehead, so that it became a startling headpiece. Even Williams had to take note of it: 'He had a beautifully heavy head of blond hair of which he was tremendously proud. Leonine. It was really very beautiful hair, wavy. And he held his head high. I wasn't impressed but I imagine the ladies were.'

As late as the First World War, when he was turning thirty, this is how one of his ladyfriends (Stella Bowen) regarded him:

> He was not unbeautiful. His face, shaped like the ace of
> spades, . . . was topped by a big bank of light-coloured crinkly
> hair which went straight on up, continuing the line of the
> sloping forehead and the long, straight nose. Under the nose
> was an equally long, straight mouth with flexible corners.

But it was not his physical appearance that appealed to Hilda Doolittle when she first met him at the 1901 Hallowe'en party, dressed in the green robe; it was a gesture of kindness. 'I had a friend whose favourite sister was suffering from stupid nerve-specialists . . . [Ezra] said: "Don't you think

Matilda might like that green coat?"' He gave it to her, 'just to cheer her up'.

Hilda lived in Upper Darby, a couple of miles beyond the western edge of Philadelphia, not very far from the university. When Ezra met her at the party she was still a schoolgirl. By 1905 when he came back to Penn from Hamilton she had become a freshman at nearby Bryn Mawr, but she dropped out after failing in English. Ezra started seeing her regularly; indeed he had kept in touch with her while he was away at Hamilton. In April 1905 William Carlos Williams was invited out to a supper organized by Ezra, who was paying a short visit home from Hamilton, and Hilda was in the party. Williams described her to his brother:

> She is tall, about as tall as I am, young, about eighteen and, well, not round and willowy, but rather bony, no that doesn't express it, just a little clumsy but all to the mustard. She is a girl that's full of fun, bright, but never telling you all she knows, doesn't care if her hair is a little mussed, and wears good solid shoes. She is frank and loves music and flowers and I got along with her pretty well. Now can you see what she's like? Anyway, she is the daughter of the professor of astronomy at U. of P. and lives out in the country on the grounds where the observatory is.

Forty-five years later, in his autobiography, Williams was more coolly analytical of Hilda, describing her as

> . . . tall, blond and with long jaw but gay blue eyes . . . There was about her that which is found in wild animals at times, a breathless impatience, almost a silly unwillingness to come to the point. She had a young girl's giggle and shrug which somehow in one so tall and angular seemed a little absurd. She fascinated me, not for her beauty, which was unquestioned if bizarre to my sense, but for a provocative indifference to rule and order which I liked. She dressed indifferently, almost sloppily and looked to a young man, not inviting – she had nothing of that – but irritating, with a smile.

Williams, Ezra, Hilda and others of their 'gang' would go for country walks near her father's observatory, or they would take the train out to Wyncote where Ezra's mother would feed them, and they would gather round the piano in the front parlour and sing, with Williams playing his violin. 'No one had a voice,' says Williams. 'We'd do our best to please Mrs Pound. Ezra himself couldn't even carry a tune as far as I ever heard.' Lack of skill never deterred Ezra, however. Isabel's attempts to teach him to play the piano had failed, but he would lose no opportunity to sit down at the key 'and let fly for us – seriously', writes Williams. 'Everything, you might say, resulted except music. He took mastership at one leap: played Liszt, Chopin – or anyone else you could name – up and down the scales, coherently to his own mind, any old sequence. It was part of his confidence in himself.'

Hilda Doolittle was impressed by this self-confident front. She thought Ezra 'immensely sophisticated, immensely superior', far above her brothers and their friends with whom she danced at parties. She had to admit that Ezra 'danced badly', but 'one would dance with him for what he might say'.

Isabel Pound approved of Hilda: the father's professorship and the rather grand family house at Upper Darby seemed to indicate a quite satisfactory match for 'Son', if he ever got round to proposing, and she would sometimes invite Hilda to musical gatherings at Wyncote. To Williams, Ezra seemed to be 'wonderfully in love' with Hilda; he 'exaggerated her beauty ridiculously' when he talked about her. As for Hilda herself, 'First kisses?' she wrote more than fifty years later. 'In the woods, in the winter – what did one expect? Not this. Electric, magnetic, they do not so much warm, they magnetize, vitalize. We need never go back. Lie down under the trees . . .' But nothing more than kisses, as Ezra himself emphasized long after, in a letter to an English correspondent:

> The america of 1900 will sound . . . like lost arcadia . . . The young trusted to enjoy themselves and stop just short of copulation . . . Emotional refinement, and couples when the female consented slipping from the dance floor for further but wholly unfecundative caresses in the night air . . . And not till yr/ correspondent got to england, where the males were scarce, did he pass beyond these Idyllic raptures.

Hilda, looking back on those early caresses, could speak of her 'not yet lost virginity'; yet her memories were of a passionate intensity:

> There was a crow's nest that my younger brother had built – bench boards and a sort of platform. The house is hidden by the great branches. There is an occasional cart or carriage from the highway or turnpike, beyond the hedge. At half-hour intervals a tram or trolley jolts past. He must not miss the last 'car' and the train to Wyncote, on the Main Line. 'There is another trolley in half an hour,' I say, preparing to slide out of the crow's nest.

'No, Dryad,' he says. He snatches me back. We sway with
the wind. There is no wind. We sway with the stars. They are
not far.

We slide, slip, fly down through the branches, leap together
to the ground. 'No,' I say, breaking from his arms, 'No,'
drawing back from his kisses. 'I'll run ahead and stop the
trolley, no – quick – get your things – books – whatever you left
in the hall.' 'I'll get them next time,' he says. 'Run,' I say, 'run.'
He just catches the trolley . . . Now, I must face them in the
house . . . Why had I ever come down out of that tree?

'Dryad' was his chosen name for her; he said she looked like a
tree-nymph, even like a tree. She loved the name, far more euphonious
than 'Hilda Doolittle'; it made her feel something other than a professor's
daughter who had just failed at Bryn Mawr. She signed her letters to him
'Dryad' for the rest of their lives. It was his first but by no means last
invention of a mask for someone else, which stuck, and changed their
perception of themselves.

He began to write poems about her:

> She hath some tree-born spirit of the wood
> About her . . .
> The moss-grown kindly trees, meseems, she could
> As kindred claim . . .

Soon he was reading William Morris to her in the tree-house. She describes
how he 'literally shouted' Morris's 'The Gilliflower of Gold' across the
orchard, and read her 'The Haystack in the Floods' with 'passionate
emotion'.

Pre-Raphaelitism was the language in which almost any 'artistic' young
man would conduct an affair in those days. It was also easier to address her
as 'Is-hilda' than to say, even to himself, what he really felt about her. 'He
brought me [a] reprint of the Iseult and Tristram story,' she writes. 'He
called me Is-hilda and wrote a sonnet a day; he bound them in a parchment
folder.' He called it 'Hilda's Book'; the poems in it talk of Hilda (just as,
elsewhere, simultaneously, he talked of Kitty Heyman) as a source of
enlightenment and secret knowledge, as if she were some figure in a
Gnostic heresy of the early Church rather than a real girl he had kissed in a
tree-house. In the poems she is a 'Soul / Caught in the rose-hued mesh / Of
o'er fair earthly flesh' who is 'Rare light to me, gold-white / In the
shadowy path I tread'. He experiences her thoughts passing through him
like the wind bearing the smell of roses. Thanks to her he has 'many new
things understood' and knows 'the truth of things unseen'. In another
poem the two of them dwell in a high castle, reminiscent of some

troubadour knight's stronghold, which has been built by gods and Druids far 'above the hum of life' at a height where the activities of ordinary mortals sound like 'faint murmuring'.

By 1905 he had read the early Yeats, as well as Morris; there is an echo of Yeats's 'I have been a hazel-tree' (in 'He Thinks of His Past Greatness' published in *The Wind among the Reeds* in 1899) in one of the tree poems in 'Hilda's Book':

> . . . I have been a tree amid the wood
> And many new things understood
> That were rank folly to my head before.

There are touches of Rossetti too (Hilda describes how he brought her 'The Blessed Damozel' and the Rossetti version of Dante's *Vita Nuova*) and plenty of Swinburne, who still seemed the most modern voice in poetry. Ezra later made no secret of his early admiration for Swinburne, whom he claimed was almost the only Victorian to keep alive some 'pagan' notion of poetry as a pure art. As late as 1926 he was recommending Swinburne to young poets for sheer rhythm and sound: 'Damn it all Swinburne beats us all.'

Swinburne was among the 'armloads of books' he would bring to Upper Darby. He was educating Hilda, giving her the literature courses she had failed at Bryn Mawr. He signed his poems to her with a gadfly, explaining that this was an imitation of the butterfly used by Whistler as signature on his paintings. Whistler was 'our only great [American] artist'. He, Ezra Pound, was going to 'carry into our American poetry the same sort of life and intensity which [Whistler] infused into modern painting'. Whistler seemed a sort of modern troubadour, an outcast for Art's sake, a Bohemian dandy whose clothes Ezra began to copy – the best model he could think of at present.

The Hilda experience was intense – the poems make that clear – but it was the intensity of somebody who felt his mind illuminated by new ideas, rather than that of a young man in love with a girl. Long afterwards he described the period of his life from sixteen to twenty-four (1901–09) as coloured by 'mysticism', and said that the poems written then showed he had received a 'mystic illumination' (shades of Kitty Heyman and her occult enthusiasms), even that some of them, in which he described taking on another shape ('I have been a tree amid the wood'), were really 'Poems of Madness' which genuinely 'questioned his sanity'. If so, it was a rather self-conscious and self-induced madness. And he allowed little to survive from all this. He recalled that although at this period he wrote a Petrarchan sonnet 'every morning before breakfast', he soon tore them all up.

8

The Athens Of The West

His first year of postgraduate studies went smoothly enough, and at its conclusion in mid-1906 he was awarded his Master of Arts degree at Penn. He marked the occasion by writing a comic poem for his parents about the necessity of now earning his living – though it suggests that he may after all choose to be a penurious poet:

> Go little verse
>   Go forth and be damned
> Throughout your limited sphere
>   But prithee tell
>   To the bards of hell
> Who live on nothing a year
>   That a Master of Arts
>   And a man of parts
> Is trying the same thing here.

The end of the academic year was celebrated by Ezra's 'gang', including William Carlos Williams and Hilda Doolittle, who gathered for a seaside party at Point Pleasant, New Jersey, where one of them had a family cottage. A storm blew up: Hilda, walking on the shore, was knocked down by huge waves and nearly drowned, while Williams was nearly struck by lightning. They chose not to regard it as an augury.

Williams was leaving Penn for a hospital internship in New York; Ezra was coming back to do a doctorate, on a George Lieb Harrison Foundation Fellowship for the year 1906 to 1907, worth $500. He called it 'a pittance from Sugar Trust money', but it was actually no insubstantial sum (a quarter of his father's annual salary); and it now provided enough for him to make his first solo trip to Europe, in the summer of 1906.

His chosen thesis subject was 'The *Gracioso* in the plays of Lope de Vega'. The *gracioso* is the comedian or buffoon in sixteenth-century Spanish drama, often the servant or squire of a knight, who comments satirically on the action, like Sancho Panza in *Don Quixote*. The choice of the great Spanish playwright was obviously influenced by Professor Rennert, who had himself written a life of Lope. But that Ezra should be willing to study any form of drama seems a little odd in view of his contempt for the theatre as art: already he was forming the view that drama is limited as an art form by having to entertain a crowd, whereas poetry can speak to the minds of the elect. Lope held little interest for him; in his book *The Spirit of Romance* he dutifully mentions Lope's plays and the *gracioso*, but has very little to say about either and gives not the slightest evidence of affinity with the subject. He already strongly preferred Provençal and Italian to Spanish, but Professor Rennert was a specialist in neither.

Ezra landed at Gibraltar and went at once to Madrid, where the American consulate arranged permission for him to work on Lope in the royal library. But he found it had been a mistake to start work so near to the heart of it all; better to have got the feel from a distance first, 'in the Brit. Museum or in some subsequent American what-not'. After a few days he gave up and explored the Prado museum instead.

The *Jenkintown Times–Chronicle* took note that a local resident was abroad: 'Wyncote has been represented, at Madrid, Spain, during the wedding of the young king, by Ezra, son of Homer L. Pound, who expects to be there several weeks.' But then Ezra found himself in a crowd outside the palace when an assassination attempt was made against King Alfonso and his bride. The consequence was that 'the anarchist suspects and uncatalogued foreigners began to be confused in the eyes of the law'; so he decided to be on his way. For all his excitement over history in the Cantos, he never wanted to witness crises at first hand. In this sense there was nothing of the journalist about him, no interest in reportage.

At some point during his Spanish travels he became acquainted with a pair of middle-aged American spinsters, Miss Adah and Miss Ida Lee Mapel, who took a liking to him. (They would play a part later in his life.) He explored Burgos and the surrounding countryside, the setting of *El Cid*. In October the *Book News Monthly* in Philadelphia printed his account of this, under the heading 'Burgos, a Dream City of Old Castile' – perhaps the Hollywood title was devised by Mr Chester:

> Although of the Cid's house there remains nothing but a 'Solar' . . . there are still many doorways in Burgos to which he might have come, as in the old 'Poema', battering with his lance butt at the door closed *por miedo del Rey Alfonso* – for fear of the king Alfonso, who had sent letters saying that 'none should

open to Ruy Diaz, and that whoso open to Ruy Diaz would
lose his possessions, and the eyes of his head to boot.' The only
one of all Burgos that dared tell these tidings to the Cid was a
little maid of nine; and there are yet in Burgos window and
balcony from which she might have leaned, with her black eyes
wonder wide . . . The little girl is still in the capital of 'Castilla'.
I saw her . . . a pair of very big black eyes, and a very small girl
tugging at the gate latch; and I knew of a surety that she had
sent away the Campeador at the king's bidding.

One of the first pieces of his prose to be published, it shows what a
Pre-Raphaelite he had temporarily become.

He told his mother he had 'got a cheap ticket to Paris', and would go
there in mid-June for two weeks of Sorbonne lectures. Arriving in the
French capital, he went 'exploring' with a young Frenchman who was
studying at Penn. Then off to London, where he stayed in a boarding-
house in Duchess Street off Portland Place and spent a week in the British
Museum Reading Room: he found the chairs 'very slippery, thoroughly
uncomfortable', and was mesmerized by the tiers of volumes and false
doors covered with imitation book-backs 'which surround that focus of
learning'. He tried to work out how long it would take to read everything
stored there, and decided against it. 'There must be some other way for a
human being to make use of that vast cultural heritage.' Much of his life
was spent trying to find a solution to this problem, to decide what it was
necessary, and unnecessary, to read.

*

Back at Wyncote in August 1906, he wrote a review of *Le Secret des
Troubadours* by Josephin (*sic*) Péladan for the *Book News Monthly*. It says
much for the tolerance of Mr Chester that he accepted a piece on such an
outré subject, and it is rather odd that Ezra should have thought the topic
worth airing to an unsophisticated Philadelphia readership. But all his life
he never discriminated between suitable and unsuitable places in which to
publish his discoveries, often rushing into print at a moment's notice,
claiming that he had the 'lowdown' on some new topic.

The book on the 'secret of the troubadours' which he reviewed for Mr
Chester was a prime example of 'lowdown'. (This was a favourite term of
Ezra's: he once announced suddenly to an acquaintance, after he had been
working in various Italian archives, researching for the Cantos: 'I've found
the lowdown on Elizabethan drama', and waved an old leatherbound
volume: 'It's all in here . . . The whole business is cribbed from these
Italian state papers.') He found *Le Secret des Troubadours* during his two
weeks in Paris, in what he called 'that nervy little bookshop of E. Sansot,

which lucky wanderers in Paris will fall upon in the Rue St André des Arts'. Josephin Péladan, was, though Ezra's review did not say so, a French Rosicrucian, and the book is a typically Rosicrucian hotchpotch of Gnostic religion, occultism, and vague sexuality. Even Ezra admitted that it 'invades the realm of uncertainty', but he said he found it 'filled with the snap of brilliant conclusions'. Péladan's idea was that a 'mystic extra-church philosophy or religion' had been secretly handed down from the Mysteries of Eleusis in ancient Greece to the Albigensian heretics and the troubadours of medieval Europe. The book pictures the troubadours as the last guardians and practitioners of this supposed secret religion, in which sex, or rather the mental enlightenment supposedly achieved through sex, was worshipped rather than repressed. Ezra only hints at this in the review: he seems to be too deeply excited about it to be able to explain.

*

His own poetry was still wrestling with the question of identity, trying out a wide variety of masks and voices. In 'La Fraisne' ('The Ash Tree'), written around 1906, he experiments in a Yeatsian manner with the story of a troubadour who runs mad in the forest for unrequited love and chooses a tree as his bride.

> Once there was a woman . . .
> . . . but I forgot . . . she was . . .
> . . . I hope she will not come again.
>
> . . . I do not remember . . .
> I think she hurt me once but . . .
> That was very long ago.
>
> I do not like to remember things any more.

It was his first exercise in fractured narrative, which later became a characteristic device in his poetry.

As well as Yeats, he tried his hand at Browning. He produced a comic little piece called 'Mesmerism' which is both a tribute to Browning and a parody of his style:

> You wheeze as a head-cold long-tonsilled Calliope,
> But God! what a sight you ha' got o' our innards,
> Mad as a hatter but surely no Myope,
> Broad as all ocean and leanin' man-kin'ards.

Technically this was the most skilful thing he had written so far, exactly catching the Browning manner. As 'Mesmerism' tries to suggest, there was a deep appeal to Ezra in Browning's idiosyncratic word-twisting, which seemed to offer more possibilities for honest portrayal of feelings than did plainer speech. Also, he saw a kindred spirit in Browning's assumption of different personae in dramatic monologues. Finding that the Browning voice fitted him so well, he took to using it frequently over the next few years.

*

He was back at Penn in the autumn of 1906, not only trying to progress with his doctoral work on the *gracioso* but also taking every available course in Romance languages. He put his name down for classes in Provençal, Sicilian poetry, the *Chanson de Roland*, Boccaccio, Dante, the Old Spanish *Poema de Fernán González*, and plays by Lope de Vega and his contemporaries. He also enrolled for English department courses in Chaucer, drama, literary criticism, current criticism, and contemporary poetry. Having voluntarily taken on so much – he was only required to attend twenty-four hours of classes during the entire academic year – he abandoned it all almost at once, scarcely turning up for anything.

Just as bad, he managed to quarrel with a key member of the English department. 'In 1907 I achieved the distinction of being the only student flunked in J.P.'s course in the history of literary criticism. So far as I know I was the only student who was making any attempt to understand the subject of literary criticism and the only student with any interest in the subject.' ('J.P.' was Josiah Penniman, a careerist who later became Provost of the university; Ezra later castigated him as one of 'those professors who regard their "subject" as a drill manual', thereby rising 'most rapidly to positions of executive responsibility'.) On top of this, he again convinced Dr Schelling that he was thoroughly lazy. His attitude may be surmised from the languid tone of a note he wrote to Schelling during this year:

> I have already begun work on 'Il Candelaio' which is eminently germain to my other Romance work – and in which I have considerable interest.
>
> On the other hand, since the study of Martial there is nothing I approach with such nausea and disgust as Roman life (Das Privatleben). Of course if you consider the latter of some importance, I shall endeavor to make my hate do as good work as my interest.

Such a superior air must have infuriated, and when he walked out of Schelling's course on Elizabethan drama, Schelling understandably concluded that Ezra was taking 'no interest in the graduate work'. To which, when he read it some years later, Ezra responded: 'He is in error. I – and I was almost the only student who did – took sufficient interest in the system of instruction to protest against it with as much vigour as I was then able.'

This fracas set Ezra's face permanently against the American academic establishment, yet oddly he never levelled specific charges, never said precisely what it was that had led to his protest. Perhaps he had lost direction in his work, now that it was no longer merely a question of attending courses and bamboozling examiners. His thesis on the *gracioso* was petering out, and this must altogether have disheartened him. 'I have spatted with nearly everybody,' he wrote in the summer of 1907, but in reality some of the fight was with himself.

William Carlos Williams agreed with Ezra about the failings of Penn. Such colleges, he said, were merely 'a stronghold of privilege, of dyed in the wool conservatism'. Yet he himself thought the best thing to do was 'work for what you can get out of it'. Perhaps if Williams had still been around, Ezra would not have thrown in the towel; but he was in New York, and Ezra had no one else to listen to. At the end of the academic year he did not even bother to submit his official record book for signature to any instructor other than Professor Rennert in the Romance languages department. His research fellowship was not renewed, and in the summer he left Penn, never to return.

In later years he attacked his alma mater unreservedly. 'NO American University has ever tried to be a centre of thought,' he wrote to Schelling in 1916. When the alumni secretary wrote to him soliciting a contribution to funds, he replied describing Penn as an 'otiose institution' which perpetuated 'routine and stupidity'. He concluded: 'All the U. of P. . . . or any other god damn American college does or will do for a man of letters is to ask him to go away without breaking the silence.' To Schelling he also spoke, in terms bordering on paranoia, of 'the university's personal loathing of me'. On the other hand, at intervals over more than twenty years after leaving Penn, Ezra was still trying to acquire his doctorate from the university, asking if he could submit various pieces of work that he had completed.

*

During the summer of 1907, while looking around for a more permanent job, he worked as a private tutor for a wealthy family at Scudders Falls near Trenton, New Jersey, preparing the son, John Scudder, for college entrance. One day young Scudder came back to the house accompanied by a girl of twenty-three named Mary Moore, daughter of a Trenton streetcar company owner and bank president. She saw Ezra lounging in a hammock on the front porch and asked: 'Who is that curly mop?' She began an amiable flirtation with him.

A little older than Ezra (who was now twenty-one), Mary Moore was pretty and brisk, an emancipated New Woman with an independent spirit and a disregard of convention. There was nothing intellectual about her and she had no literary interests, but Ezra liked her gaiety and energy.

They went for long walks, picnics, and canoe trips together. It was very different from the intensity with 'Dryad' (who was not told about a rival). He chose to address Mary, in his letters, in a languid 1890s manner, writing in green or violet ink in a spindly hand very different from the plain penmanship he used for his parents. The actual content of the letters, however, was not quite as effete as their appearance. His main purpose was to cover the page without committing himself, as he admits in one of them:

> Look at the scandalous long way I write your letters – it is positively shocking I write so much that I dont realy write I just make copy letters [*sic*] so that they will be legible – writing looks like this only it takes longer to do.

He addressed her by a variety of pet names – 'Grey Eyes', 'Your Ladyship', 'Maridhu', 'Beloved Your Grace'. But the most commonly used, variations on 'Rabbit' ('Dear Furry Little Rabbit', 'O Rabbit most fur' and so on), were as much her invention as his. 'In those days,' she explains, 'my pet name was Bunny, and I signed letters, etc., with a Japanese rabbit.' At the end of her life, she said: 'People ask me if Ezra and I were engaged. I don't remember. It's none of their business . . . We were warm, loving friends . . . A kiss on the forehead was as far & as passionate as our love-life went.'

The persona that he displayed to Mary Moore – dandified, self-consciously 'arty' – was one he would often use again with ladyfriends. Sometimes it led him into unusual paths. He told Mary that he had been browsing through the Arthur Rackham edition of *Peter Pan* (there was a Barrie-like whimsy in his affair with Mary), and wrote to her:

> Also it was this evening a very lovely rainyness that was cold &
> nice to walk in & made me start things like
> > 'Breathing my love out to the rain,
> > Because you lack me & my Soul
> >
> > > my Soul'
> which I can not finish after comeing into the house.

He introduced her to his mother, and Mary said she found Isabel as 'pixyish' as Ezra – an epithet which seems unbelievable until one realizes how contrived a character he was showing her.

His letters to her leave it a mystery as to whether he really wanted to marry her. Probably he was uncertain himself. Occasionally a serious romantic note seems to creep in: ' . . . it would take us all of five years to get caught up with all the things we want to do together & haven't got started – or only just barely started on yet.' Then he lapses again into his 1890s pose, or scribbles some lightweight nonsense about his daily life:

Among the vulgah dinner is considered as a meal. mother brought me up to regard it rather in the light of a ceremony. But chez moi ici it is neither one is neither bored nor does one have the table – one sits on a sofa & pounds nuts . . . while there ariseth incense unto the goddess Caffine.

Yet there were moments when he evidently felt he was exposing his 'real' self to her. When the flirtation finally petered out some months later, he wrote her a letter that hints at some genuine pain, as well as admitting his habit of hiding behind poses:

While spiritually I have shown myself naked & been mocked – because – & because you have very furry fur – that was no reason why I should – against my rule-general make display of the rather repulsive mechanism of my mental in'nards – mais chose faite one returns to the state of begarbment which I should not have abandoned.

*

While he was teaching at Scudders Falls and dallying with Mary Moore, he heard, through the graduate school at Penn, of a job at Wabash College, a not-very-flourishing Presbyterian institution at Crawfordsville in Western Indiana. The job was advertised very grandly as 'Chairman of the Department of Romance Languages', but there was no such department. The President of Wabash had merely decided to divide the modern languages teaching into two sections, Germanic and Romance, and thought he would get a better class of applicant for a lowly instructor's job if he described it in this fashion.

Ezra was interviewed for the job in Philadelphia in early August 1907 by the President himself, Dr George Lewes Mackintosh. Afterwards he wrote exultantly to his mother: 'Wabash nailed & everything most delightful . . . French Spanish & Italian to run as I hang please. 1½hr. with Dr MacKintosh & twas did. & Blessed of most blessed jokes on you dear. I did it without those essentials of all life a coat, a collar, a neck tie. Also my shoes were not shined. After 21 years . . . I can retire to Venice on half pay & live & loaf as I please. probably full profeship in 2 yrs. I couldn't have hit a neater job if I had made it myself (barring pay for 1st 2 yrs. which is a very small matter).'

But by the time he set off for Wabash, he was having qualms about leaving the Eastern states for the unknown interior. 'Gee. talk about "Rure", he wrote to his parents during the long train journey to Indiana. '1 stone house (i.e. part stone) for last nine hours . . . corn, corn, corn, or terbakky . . . And to think we pity the pore ignorunt furriner!' Gawsh. I wont be near as caustic about Yourupeen decadence the next time I see it.'

Crawfordsville was a quiet, slow-moving, inoffensive Indiana town, small in every sense of the word. It contained a couple of theatres, but almost the only other feature was the seventy-five-year-old college, whose presence led the citizens to claim the title – or so said Ezra – 'the Athens of the West'. (He added sarcastically that it was a town with 'literary traditions', for General Lew Wallace the author of *Ben Hur* had died there.) Academically the college was negligible. Its only distinguishing mark was its Little Titans football team, who had beaten Harvard.

At first Ezra was firmly disposed to make the best of everything. 'I guess I will make out pretty well,' he wrote to Isabel from the Crawford House Hotel where he was staying while looking for lodgings; 'everyone seems kindly disposed & town is not so worse.' He rented a room in Milligan Terrace, with a bath, facilities for cooking, and a private entrance. 'It is so strange to get a house that was good stile when most everything wasn't,' he wrote to Mary Moore, 'a brick, white paint, gothic . . . The only jangle is the red cloth they left on my table & that is easily eliminated . . . I am not at all afraid that you will be disappointed when I bring you here.'

She was not sure she wanted to be brought there. 'From letters written in Crawfordsville,' she recalls, 'I gathered that he was making plans for our marrying.' He wondered about wedding presents as a source of furnishings: could one 'trust to extract from ones friends at the nuptial hold-up'? He must leave off writing this and 'get acquainted with the faculty, so that your Ladyship shall have reception ready'. He was also corresponding with the Dryad, in the particular language which *that* affair required.

On inspection the college seemed reasonably pleasant, though some things astonished him: 'This God forsaken state has a law against the sale of cigarettes – wherefor one can buy only poor ones' (he had taken to smoking): so would 'Grey Eyes' please 'procure me des Bourbons Rouges'? She did, whereupon he thanked her in green ink as 'a veree nice rabbit-kitten' and enclosed 'the two Villonades which you once thought you wanted'.

These were two poems celebrating the poet Villon, who had spent much of his time fleeing from the law. 'Drink ye a skoal for the gallows tree!' cries Ezra's Villon in 'A Villonaud: Ballad of the Gibbet',

> François and Margot and thee and me,
> Drink we the comrades merrily
> That said us, 'Till then' for the gallows tree!

The other poem, 'Villonaud for this Yule', was a Christmas piece in similar style. He explained to his parents: 'Villonaud is a compound on name Villon. for one Francois Villon a french poet of the XIII century or the XII or XIV I'm no good at dates.' (Villon actually lived in the fifteenth

century.) He said he had been 'trying & think succeeded in expressing the
Villon spirit'; he thought that Robert Louis Stevenson's essay on Villon
caught it too, and the poems really have more of Stevenson about them
than of fifteenth-century France. (And of Rossetti: Ezra said he had
modelled the 'Villonaud for this Yule' on Rossetti's translation of Villon's
'Ballad of Dead Ladies'.) He sent the two poems to *Atlantic* magazine,
which returned them with a polite note; he told Mary Moore he did not
'give one highly damaged under done dam' about this rejection. This was
his Villon voice. 'Villon never forgets his fascinating, revolting self . . .
Villon is shameless,' he wrote in *The Spirit of Romance*, two years later.
'Villon's greatness is that he unconsciously proclaims man's divine right to
be himself.' In fact Villon is not much like that, but Ezra was writing about
himself, or what he wanted to be when in his Villon mood.

The Villon persona was not one that particularly suited him. He was not
yet very good at playing the rebellious Bohemian. He smoked a lot at
Crawfordsville, chiefly because the college forbade it, but in later years he
would only very rarely be seen with a cigarette. About alcohol, also
forbidden at Wabash, he was more certain: he did not like it. The writer
Robert McAlmon, who observed him moving among the American literary
drunkards of Paris in 1923, recorded bluntly: 'Ezra doesn't drink.' Left to
himself he would indeed rarely have touched a drop. His preference was
for a great quantity of fresh water, uncontaminated by 'purifying' chemi-
cals. He greatly disliked the idea of finding inspiration in one's cups
('booze is not river of enlightenment'). In Europe he would usually be seen
with a token glass of wine accompanying his meal, but said in 1946 that he
had only been drunk three times in his life. On the whole he was, in
William Carlos Williams's words, 'gingerly and temperate' where liquor
was concerned, very much a product of his Presbyterian American
upbringing. Indeed no physical stimulus seemed to hold much attraction
for him. Ford Madox Ford suggested that, whereas 'most poets take to
drink, narcotics, lechery', Ezra chose instead to indulge in 'abuse of fools'.

*

The autumn term of 1907 at Wabash College began on 16 September, and
Ezra wrote to Mary Moore: 'In general the stew dents are of a more
civilized variety than I had expected.' The business of teaching did not
worry him, since he was so fresh from being a pupil himself: 'I am so
familiar with all available methods of bluff that I insist on work.   all the
work & no substitute for work except intelligence – which is rare.'

The students were unsure what to make of him. After a few weeks 'one
delegation of about-to-flunks ave awaited on the president to complain erbout me orful langwidge and the number of cigarillos I consume'.
One of them recalls him as 'exhibitionist, egotistic, self-centred and

self-indulgent', but another thought him a breath of air, and there is an eloquent tribute from a student, Robert Winter, who afterwards taught Romance languages at Northwestern University and in China: 'Without Pound I probably would now be an idiot crawling about in Crawfordsville.'

There were the same mixed reactions among the faculty. He made friends with a young instructor in English named Stevens with whom he thought of rooming – 'a very sane & joyous companion we eat ensemble a good part of the time'. But he wore out one of the professors, Rollo Walter Brown, who writes:

> The trace of the showman and charlatan in him was very strong . . . He was half a brilliant – at least superficially brilliant – and interesting man. Sometimes when he came to our house I was exceedingly glad to see him. But by the time he had stayed from four on Sunday afternoon till twelve or one at night, and had crawled all over the sofa and stuck his feet up against the wall and otherwise engaged in unnecessary contortions, I was at least glad to see him go.

He spent most of his spare time by himself, feeding in his room ('4 boiled potatoes,' he told Mary Moore, 'cream, nuts, rye bread, coffee, apricots a la patent process') and arranging the ornaments and drapery with special care: 'I hemmed me this day a green burlap cover for this little table and a curtain for some ugly little shelves.' His father wrote to ask if he felt he was really 'on the right track' as far as a career was concerned. Ezra answered that 'there seems to be plenty to be done here', though certainly he would 'skidoo to parts more plush lined' back in 'the effete east' if something better came along. But when Isabel suggested they ask their *Saturday Evening Post* neighbour in Wyncote, George H. Lorimer, for a job, Ezra did not fancy the idea at all: 'no vacation from June to Sept. no being thru your set work by 11 a.m. no pension.'

He had acquired his own typewriter, and was 'trying in what spare time I get to do some writing'. Browning was very much his master still. The narrator of 'Cino', a Browning-style dramatic monologue he wrote around now, is Cino da Pistoia, friend of Dante and womanizer, who feels he has wasted his life serenading 'women in three cities' and wants to turn to a better kind of poetry. But it is too late to change, and Cino's hymn to the sun ('Pollo Phoibee, old tin pan you') comes out as absurd and trite, a warning to poets not to waste their best years on women. 'Cino' was easily the best thing Ezra had written yet, many-layered (himself impersonating Browning, Browning impersonating Cino, Cino mimicking his audience and singing his ridiculous song to Phoebus) and perhaps autobiographical, for Cino's women 'mostly had grey eyes' – recalling one of Mary Moore's pet names. The dramatic monologue appealed hugely to Ezra – he explained to William Carlos Williams that he intended it to seem like 'the poetic part of a drama the rest of which . . . is left to the reader's imagination'; the trick was 'to make ones characters live'.

Another monologue written by Ezra at Crawfordsville, 'Na Audiart', is spoken by the twelfth-century knight and troubadour Bertran de Born, who pretends to himself that he can manufacture an ideal woman from all the ladies he desires. He particularly wants the torso of the incomparable Lady Audiart, though he knows she hates him. Ezra may have first encountered the story in the original Provençal, but he also read it in a modern American book, *The Troubadours at Home* (1899) by Justin H. Smith, whose text is romantic and popular in style, with touches of Sir Walter Scott. It deals gushingly with such matters as Bertran's love for Audiart and his invention of the composite lady: 'The castle was a bright and lively abode, for there lived here a young, fair, and clever lady named Audiart . . . The languishing poet nearly lost his senses for joy . . .'

Bertran in 'Na Audiart' does what Ezra himself preferred doing with his own women, constructing a romantic ideal out of touch with reality. It was easy for Ezra to be flirtatious with Mary Moore when they were separated by several hundred miles. He sent her the ring given him by Kitty Heyman, telling her it would do until they could buy one together. Like Bertran, he preferred to dally in imagination with a whole series of women rather than commit himself to one. He was still writing to the Dryad, and in Crawfordsville he was amused to come across another Mary Moore, a good-looking young widow whose full name was Mary Moore Shipman Young. He asked his own Mary Moore if they were related. If so, 'I can go to Indianapolis to football games & feeding – without having it supposed that there is anything pronouncedly sudden in the habit of wasting our spare time together which we have naturally fallen into because we are the only two people here who think London & Paris are nearer the hole the earth goes round about than this [illegible] of the West.'

His courtship of this new Mary Moore caused certain local problems. Dr Mackintosh, the President, a widower, was rumoured to be interested in her himself, and Ezra's habit of entertaining her in the family-parlour-cum-music-room at Milligan Terrace began to irritate the landlord and his wife, who were already aggrieved by his inviting students to his rooms late at night. In mid-October he was obliged to find new lodgings on South Washington Street, in a rather spartan rooming-house used by travelling actors and vaudevillians who performed at the town's two theatres, the Majestic and the Music Hall ('High-Class Vaudeville: No Drinking'). He began to take an interest in his fellow lodgers – such characters as 'Maudie Minerva, Novelty Act', 'Burk & Erline, Automobile Girls', 'Annette Link, Soubrette', and 'Alice B. Hamilton, Character Singing Comedienne'. This led quickly to trouble, as Ezra explained in a letter written on 11 November to an acquaintance from Penn days named Hessler, who was teaching in Michigan:

> Two stewdents found me sharing my meagre repast with the lady–gent impersonator in my privut apartments.
>
> keep it dark and find me a soft immoral place to light in when the she-faculty wives git hold of that jewcy morsel. Don't write home to me folks. I can prove an alibi from 8 to 12 p.m. and am at present looking for rooms with a minister or some well established member of the facultate. For to this house come all the travelling show folk and I must hie me to a nunnery ere I disrupt the college.

He added a note of explanation that the 'lady–gent impersonator' had been 'stranded hungry and it not being convenient to carry a dinner across the hall as I had done coffee and toast'.

He mentioned the incident in a letter to the first Mary Moore explaining that the 'impersonator' was a British girl who did a 'toff' act in a monocle, but that her English accent and jokes made her incomprehensible to the Indiana audiences, and she was out of work and penniless. He had been feeding her regularly, usually carrying coffee and toast to her room, but on this occasion had cooked up a 'repast' for her and invited her to join him. She was 'quite english, quite appreciative of my ability to make coffee & salad – the only person here besides your name sake who understands that this is not the mid-axis of the universe'. The incident amused him greatly; it had 'yielded material for half a novel', though he doubted he had 'the energy to compose it'.

He says nothing further about the lady impersonator for the time being, but she may have been the inspiration of 'Fifine Answers', another Browning-style monologue, in which the speaker is a prostitute who can 'Drink all of life and quaffing lustily / Take bitter with the sweet without complain' – a pleasant way for Ezra to think of himself, indeed, when in his Villon-Bohemian mood.

To leave the theatrical boarding-house and look for rooms in a minister's or professor's house may have seemed a logical way of re-establishing his dented respectability, but it led him into more trouble. He now took lodgings at 412 South Grant Avenue, a house facing the campus belonging to the Misses Ida and Belle Hall, who regularly let rooms to bachelor teaching staff. It was an injudicious choice. Ezra's rooms had last been occupied by an irreproachable elderly bachelor, Professor Henry Z. McLain (always referred to by the Misses Hall as 'dear Zwingli'), who had dropped dead in chapel a few months earlier; the rooms had remained empty as a memorial ever since. In came Ezra, delighting in such aphorisms as: 'Religion, oh, just another of those numerous failures resulting from an attempt to popularize art.'

It is surprising that the Misses Hall tolerated him for a single week, let alone the two months for which he remained there, but around the time he arrived, his ebullience was somewhat dampened. Mary Moore of Trenton announced in a letter that she had become engaged to a young gentleman named Oscar Macpherson. 'Dear Furry Little Rabbit,' Ezra replied to her,

> I do not love you at all except as I love all beautiful things that run around in the sunlight and are happy.
>
> As soon as my Mat Arnoldesque high seriousness invaded my letters you abandoned me. Got engaged to Oscar. Besides the plumbing in Crawfordsville is beneath your exquisiteness.
>
> You don't like geniuses. I'm sorry but they are nice toys at times.

He was not quite suffering from a broken heart. Indeed, it seemed to suit him almost better to carry on his flirtatious correspondence with her unburdened by any consideration of marriage. He saw 'no reason why our friendship should not be as simple – as purely decorative – as & perhaps a shade more delightful than Oscar . . . would approve . . . We are both charming (at times) and I shall eat muffins in your parlour.' He continued to address her as Rabbit. The trouble was not that he had been in love with her, rather that he liked flirting with so many girls at once. 'Mary Moore, why the devil do I love so many people *so much*!?! . . . It would be so much simpler just to particularly love one Bug or something.' This problem, if it really was one, did not resolve itself.

Latin Quarter Type

Having lost the pretence that he was shortly going to marry Mary Moore and bring her there, be began to get bored with Crawfordsville. He wrote a poem called 'In Durance' in which he complained of being 'homesick after mine own kind'; certainly there were 'friendly faces' all around him, but he wanted the company of those who 'have some breath for beauty and the arts'. The homesickness was not for the good folk of Wyncote – 'ordinary people touch me not,' he said – but for 'my kin of the spirit', soul mates who could share some spiritual 'surging of power', someone like Katherine Ruth Heyman who would 'come mewards bearing old magic'. Not surprisingly, Crawfordsville did not seem able to supply that need. He now felt in 'the sixth circle of desolation' out there in remotest Indiana.

He briefly entertained hopes when, towards Christmas, he heard of a young man in the town, Fred Vance, who had recently 'had an atelier on the Rue Notre Dames des Champs' in Paris. 'I haven't met him yet – saw one of his oils this p.m., & think he may be human.' When Ezra finally ran across him, he 'almost felt alive' because Vance greeted him in French.

Vance had studied art in Rome and Chicago as well as Paris, and was working on the staff of the *Crawfordsville Journal*. Ezra persuaded him to make some drawings for a long poem or story he was working on called 'Abbeville' (it does not survive). But his admiration for Vance began to evaporate when he discovered that the painter was using his completed canvases as Christmas presents; this was not the high seriousness of a true artist. Some years later in a draft for an early canto, Ezra gave a pitying, condescending portrait of Vance as an example of the cultural barrenness of Middle America:

> . . . in middle Indiana,
> Acting as usher in the theatre,

Painting the local drug-shop and soda bars,
The local doctor's fancy for the mantel-piece.

Nevertheless, Vance and one or two others, mostly Wabash students, seemed adequate fodder for a regular *soirée* in Ezra's lodgings, a descendant of the freshman group he had organized at Hamilton. One of those who attended, an undergraduate named Fred H. Rhodes, has left this caustic description of the proceedings:

> Ezra gathered around himself a small group of advanced thinkers in the arts . . . to which a very few privileged disciples were invited . . . After the preliminary formalities, Pound seated himself on a chair, while his disciples and satellites disposed themselves gracefully, but somewhat uncomfortably, cross-legged on the floor, at the feet of the master. The leader then began a spirited but disconnected discourse on many topics, leaping from subject to subject with the agility of a mountain goat. His dissertation was, at appropriate intervals, broken (but not interrupted) by sage interjections of agreement from the artist [Vance] and by the hearty applause of the undertaker [possibly Vance's father, actually a bookstore employee]. The subordinate satellites listened with rapt attention . . . [Ezra] was disdainfully critical of the current trends in social and political life, in economics, in art, in education, and in other fields in which he was equally an authority.

The malicious tone of this memoir might lead one to discount it were it not for the striking similarity between this *soirée* and later ones held by Ezra.

*

Returning to Crawfordsville in January 1908 after a Christmas visit home, he mentioned to his mother that she could 'send me the saphire if you wish, or simply give it to Hilda some time when you and she are alone'. With Mary Moore bespoke to 'Oscar', he might as well turn his attentions back rather more fully to the Dryad, and make moves towards an engagement of sorts, preferably as casual and undefined as that with Mary had been.

Then, out of the blue, to Homer, on about 14 February:

> Dear Dad
> Have had a bust up. but come out with enough to take me to Europe. Home Saturday or Sunday. Dont let mother get excited.
>   Ez.

And on the back:

> I guess something that one does not see but something very big
> & white back of the destinies. has the turning & the loading of
> things & this thing & I breath again.
>   lovingly
>   E.P.

In fact you need say nothing to mother till I come.

The 'bust up' was a repetition, with frills, of the incident at his previous lodgings with the lady–gent impersonator, Indeed the same girl was probably involved, since Ezra afterwards referred to the earlier incident and the final row as if they were one and the same. This is the story as recorded many years later in the centenary history of Wabash College, based on recollections gathered from students and faculty:

> The end came on a bitterly cold night . . . After reading late into
> the night he walked downtown through a blizzard to mail a
> letter. On the street he met a girl from a stranded burlesque
> show, penniless and suffering from the cold. He took her to his
> warm rooms. She spent the night in his bed, he on the floor of
> his study. He went off to his eight o'clock recitation in the
> morning. The ladies from whom he rented the rooms, the
> Misses Hall, went upstairs to make the bed and found in it the
> girl . . . They telephoned the President, and a trustee or two.
> Shortly after there was a discussion between these gentlemen
> and Mr Pound, a discussion at distinctly cross purposes . . .
> And they were content to use the occasion to make an
> arrangement about their contract that encouraged Mr Pound to
> shake the dust of a small middle-western Presbyterian college
> forever from his feet.

Ezra told much the same story to the Dryad when he next saw her: 'I found her in the snow, when I went to post a letter. She was stranded from a travelling variety company. She had nowhere to go. I asked her to my room. She slept in my bed. I slept on the floor.' To a Crawfordsville girl named Viola Baylis, whom he had dated once or twice, he added that he had 'heated water for tea over his gas-light flame, "to bring warmth to her frozen body", [and] gave her his bed, where she slept "safe as in her mother's arms", while he lay, fully clothed on the floor, wrapped in his topcoat.' He ever afterwards proclaimed his innocence, writing years later to James Joyce: 'She wouldn't have "tempted" Caliban in the height of his first spring rut, ma che! at any rate my innocence of that period was not excited.'

The bust-up with the Wabash authorities was spread over several days, and had not yet concluded when Ezra first reported the crisis to his father. He told a student that he had challenged the President and the Trustees to prove immorality; they eventually admitted that they could not, and consequently offered to reinstate him. At this point he wrote to his father: 'Have been recalled', but 'think I should rather go to ze sunny Italia.' The Trustees had already promised him financial compensation for dismissal, and this would provide enough for a European trip, so when they offered him his job back he 'told the board "To go to Hell" and resigned'.

Dr Mackintosh and the Trustees had other reasons besides the actress for wishing to see the back of him. The college magazine had pointed out his repeated absences from chapel, and there was his constant smoking and his language, even a horrid rumour that he put rum in his tea, all adding up to the conclusion that he was, as he put it, 'the Latin Quarter type' and not Wabash material at all. He would receive his entire salary up to the end of the academic year – an admission that they had no right to sack him – if he departed promptly. Some of his colleagues were extremely jealous. His friend Stevens observed: 'Gee!! wish I wuz fired.'

For the moment, Ezra himself could feel nothing but delight. 'Have had more fun out of the fracasso than there is in a dog fight, & hope I have taught 'em how to run a college.' A few months later his chief emotion was still relief at having escaped. 'If ever anybody shuts *you* up in Indiana for four months,' he told William Carlos Williams, 'you will probably rise up and bless the present and sacred name of Madame Grundy for all her holy hypocrisy.' But he had not really been in any hurry to get out, and (as he admitted to Williams) he was sore at having been 'degraded, branded with infamy, etc., for feeding a person who needs food'. The fact that his 'k-rear as a prof in the corn belt' had 'ended in smoak' naturally led to a certain 'DEEspair of the future. etc.' Underneath the brash reaction to his dismissal he suffered a real crisis of self-confidence, hinted at in a poem a few months later, in which he remembers that

> Cold, ah a-cold
> > Was my soul in the caves
> > Of ill-fearing.

Back at home the incident provided splendid fuel for scandalmongers. Ezra was delighted by all the rumours: 'They say in Wyncote that I am bi-sexual and given to unnatural lust,' he told the Dryad. Hilda now definitely believed herself engaged to him. There was the sapphire that Isabel had given her on his behalf, and she wrote to William Carlos Williams that she was prepared to spend the rest of her life with Ezra, who was even trying to persuade her to join his flight to Italy: '"You must come away with me, Dryad." "How can I? How can I?" His father would scrape up enough for him to live on.' But there was still Doolittle *père* to contend with.

'Pound went one day to the observatory to ask for her hand, and Professor Doolittle, a tall, gaunt man who spoke with deliberate slowness said . . . "Why, you're nothing but a nomad!"' This is legend (from Charles Norman's life of Ezra); at least, the Dryad herself makes no mention of it in her exotic, wistful memoir of the affair, *End to Torment*. But her own version is just as highly coloured:

> We were curled up together in an armchair when my father found us. I was 'gone'. I wasn't there. I disentangled myself. I stood up; Ezra stood beside me. It seems we must have swayed, trembling . . . 'Mr Pound, I don't say there was anything wrong *this* time. I will not forbid you the house, but I will ask you not to come so often.'

Her father burnt (so she says) Ezra's letters to her, now or later. And then an old schoolfriend told her Ezra had just been 'engaged to Mary Moore, anyhow. Bessie Elliot could have had him for the asking. There was Louise Skidmore, before that.' And Kitty Heyman, and Viola Baxter, and Mary Moore Shipman Young, and Viola Baylis; all quite innocent, and getting engaged in those days was a frequent pastime. Nevertheless poor Hilda had thought herself the only one.

'The engagement, such as it was,' she writes, 'was shattered like a Venetian glass goblet, flung on the floor.' On 7 March 1908 she wrote to Williams saying that the betrothal had been called off and Ezra was about to depart for Gibraltar.

*

The more he considered it, the less seemed to hold him to America, at least at present: no job, and a bad time of year for finding one in the academic field; a broken 'engagement', for what it had been worth; no publisher interested in his poetry. He had put together a collection of about forty poems and offered it to Thomas Bird Mosher, publisher of de luxe reprints, but Mosher would not take it. The only poem he managed to get into print was an effete piece about the medieval Latinists beginning 'Ye fellowship that sing the woods and spring', which Mr Chester good-naturedly published in the *Book News Monthly* in January 1908. Ezra was probably rather dubious about it himself, since he signed it 'Weston Llewmys', a variation of two family names that he sometimes used for promulgations demanding a particularly 'aesthetic' persona. He afterwards remarked that during his first five years as a poet 'I had exactly one brief poem accepted by one American magazine'.

He knew that Kitty Heyman would be on a European tour during the spring and summer. Perhaps he could get his poems printed over there, and come back something of a celebrity before restarting a career in the academic field. He was not considering any sort of permanent emigration; on the other hand he set no date for his return.

Around the second week in March he called on William Carlos Williams to say goodbye. In New York he also picked up some money that Aunt Frank had offered him towards the ticket to Gibraltar. Now that the Dryad was out of the picture, he turned again to Mary Moore to provide a suitable quayside farewell, which she obligingly did, on St Patrick's Day, 17 March 1908. He gave her a hug, she promised to come and see him in Europe, and the RMS *Slavonia* carried him out from harbour to the open sea.

Part Two

1908–20
'Ezra'

1

An Excellent Place To Come To From Crawfordsville

The Cantos begin with a solemn departure by sea:

> And then went down to the ship,
> Set keel to breakers, forth on the godly sea . . .

Ezra's Atlantic crossing in March 1908 was not quite so Homeric, 'the passage over' (he told Mary Moore) 'being divided between hellish weather & consequences. & a desperate poker game that netted me enough for Stewards tips but not quite enough for my cigarettes as well'.

At the time, he had every expectation of returning within a matter of weeks. Later, when he knew that the 1908 voyage had been one of exile, he spoke as if a permanent departure at that age was inevitable, scarcely worth discussion. 'I dunno what my twenty-three infantile years in America signify. I left as soon as motion was autarchic.' But this is misleading. He knew perfectly well that, whatever had driven him to Europe, he was an American through and through, without any choice in the matter. 'It would be about as easy', he wrote in 1912, 'for an American to become a Chinaman or a Hindoo as for him to acquire an Englishness or a Frenchness or a European-ness that is more than half skin deep.' And in 1939, as his attacks on the US Government were approaching their height: 'I don't have to try to be American . . . Am I American? Yes, and buggar the present state of the country.'

William Carlos Williams eventually came to see Ezra's departure from the USA in 1908 as something approaching an act of treason: 'Ezra is one of a well recognized group of Americans who can't take the democratic virus . . . I for one believe that had they remained nearer to the fountain which gave them originally their power . . . their work would have assumed more impressive proportions.' Williams himself chose not merely to stay in the USA but to settle in his birthplace of Rutherford, New Jersey, where he practised as a doctor all his working life and where most of his poetry is set. Ezra replied to his taunt: 'Don't expect the world to revolve about Rutherford. If you had any confidence in America you wouldn't be so touchy about it.'

Though he remained deeply American, Ezra suffered no nostalgia for scenes of childhood. A letter to his mother written in 1920 is exceptional in that it looks back with amused affection to Wyncote as he remembered it:

> . . . Solomon Jerome Levi Sheip   Cigar boxes. Is Mr Kunkle still opposite, and Lower's bedroom still lined with pink satin, and Miss Annie Hacock still waving suffrage banners, and Bean still at the livery stable and Chris Myers shoeing horses, and the Luskins increasing . . .

*

Legends again: Ford Madox Ford liked to tell how 'Mr Pound had come over to Europe as a cattle-hand.' In fact it was a very spruce young passenger who gave his final tip to the steward and disembarked from the *Slavonia* at Gibraltar on 23 March 1908. 'I am landed right side up with care,' he wrote to his father. He found a room for a few nights in King Edward's Institute for Soldiers and Sailors, 'I being of that quality in the ranks of H. M. Fortuna.' Afterwards, in Canto 80, he said he had 'brought with me $80' on leaving America, implying that this was not a large sum. It kept him going for some time, however, and there was, too, his Wabash salary to come in instalments. Also, he had arranged to act as a guide around Spain for an American family named Dunlap, for which he would receive $15 a day. He hoped for further work of this sort during the summer, and described himself as 'Ezra Pound, Conductor'.

He moved to the London Hotel in Gibraltar. Walking through the streets he heard a voice behind him: 'Meestair Freer! Meestair!' Freer had been Aunt Frank's surname before her marriage to Uncle Ezra, and she still travelled under it. Ezra was being hailed by a courier, a Jew named Yusuf Benemore who recognized him from his visit to Gibraltar with his great-aunt ten years earlier. He wrote to his father that Benemore had kindly 'posted me at his club so I can have people to talk Spanish with when I feel like it'.

'Club' was a euphemism. Ezra describes it in Canto 22:

> And a chap in a red fez came in, and grinned at Mohamed
> Who spat across four metres of table
> At Mustafa. That was all there was
> To that greeting; and three nights later
> Ginger came back as a customer, and took it out of Mohamed . . .

And Yusuf said: Vairy foolish, it will
    Be sefen an' seex for the summons.

Yusuf also took Ezra to a synagogue; the proceedings are described in this canto: 'And in came the levite and six little choir kids / And began yowling the ritual / . . . and the rabbi / . . . grinned, and pulled out his snuff-box . . .' Ezra recalled the synagogue scene again in Canto 76, written in 1945 not long after his virulently anti-Jewish wartime broadcasts, observing that 'in the synagogue in Gibraltar / the sense of humour seemed to prevail'. The memory seemed set apart from all his attacks on 'kikery'.

The Dunlaps arrived in Gibraltar on 10 April, and, to his alarm, Ezra found that his duties were to include looking after four children. He set off around Spain, taking the family to Seville and Granada, but ten days of this was enough. He returned to Gibraltar and took a boat to Genoa, then travelled for a few days by train among the northern Italian cities, reaching Venice at the end of the month. 'Venice arrived OK & comfortably fixed,' he told his father. 'Tea at Dr Robertson's yesterday.'

Dr Sandy Robertson was the Scottish Presbyterian minister in Venice, a castigator of the Church of Rome who would hand out such tracts as *The Harlot of the Seven Hills*. Ezra gives a comic glimpse of him in Canto 76. He told his parents he had also run across 'some pleasant folks at hotel Milan who feed & gondole me now & then'. These were a couple of American spinsters, 'a certain Miss Wells, well along in the afternoon of life, & [a] "plain Massachusetts person" Norton by name, whose papa happens to be Charles Elliot [*sic*] Norton'. Being 'gondoled' was far beyond his own pocket; in Canto 3 he relates how he 'sat on the Dogana's steps' (the custom-house, overlooking the entrance to the Grand Canal) because 'the gondolas cost too much'. While it was true, as he says in *Indiscretions*, that Venice was 'an excellent place to come to from Crawfordsville, Indiana', he rather hoped to find some sort of work to keep himself going through the summer.

It was advisable to stay in a cheap part of the city away from San Marco and the tourist traps. In Canto 26 he describes how, by the statue of St Theodore and the crocodile on its column opposite the Doge's Palace, he considered his plans:

> I came here in my young youth
>   and lay there under the crocodile
> By the column, looking East on the Friday,
> And I said: Tomorrow I will lie on the South side
> And the day after, south west.

South and south-west of the Grand Canal lay the small artisan houses and shops of Dorsoduro, and here he found a cheap room over a bakery, at 861

Ponte San Vio, 'by the soap-smooth stone posts where San Vio / meets with il Canal Grande.'

He considered getting a job as a gondolier – 'I think I could gondola for a few weeks without any detriment to my health' – not realizing that the profession was rigidly closed to outsiders. (But he persuaded a gondolier to give him a lesson for a few minutes one day.) He went to an employment office in search of part-time work, but found nothing suitable, and the clerk, discovering that he wanted to write poetry, laughed at his aspirations. In any case money was not yet a major concern. 'Things O.K.,' Ezra wrote to his father in early May, 'guess I can hold out on present stores till June 20th or 30th.' For lunch he usually bought sweet potatoes from cook-stalls, for supper a plate of barley soup.

Though his letters from Gibraltar and Spain had been cheerful enough, underneath he was still shaken by his dismissal from Wabash. Poems written in March and April include an exhortation to pull himself together ('O heart o'me . . . / Beat again'), and some lines entitled 'Narcotic Alcohol' in which, very uncharacteristically, he decides to turn to drink to ease his misery – 'heart-slain, / Head-tortured, wracked of the endless strain'. But Venice quickly revived him. 'Alma Sol Veneziae', written in his room at San Vio, describes how the Venetian sunlight has 'given me back / Heart for the Tourney'. Another poem, headed simply 'San Vio, June', says much the same: 'Old powers rise and do return to me / Grace to thy bounty, O Venetian sun.'

The thing now was to get his poems into print, and it seemed simplest to do it at his own expense. Dr Robertson, the minister, recommended him to a printer named Antonini in the Cannaregio quarter, who agreed to set them up and produce a paper-bound book of about seventy pages. Ezra decided to have only 150 copies printed, partly to save money, partly so that the book would 'be a rarity'. He told his father he hoped before long to be able to announce "First edition" exhausted', thereby giving 'the impression of a larger circulation'.

He wrote to Mary Moore:

> O Sanctissima Rabbitarum: . . . I am about to be published here in Venice . . . Of course I am not rash enough to expect any-one to buy the book after finding out what is in it . . . altho' I myself feel that there is an occasional dab of that recherché quality on some of the pages . . . Of course I shall love you just the same even if you don't succeed in laying pipe for review.

And: 'If I can pick up enough row of reviews,' he wrote to Homer, 'I'll make somebody reprint on the strength of having sold the first edition very quickly.' He told his father to try the book on Ella Wheeler Wilcox, whom

Homer had known as a boy in Wisconsin. Any sort of publicity would have its value.

He named the book *A Lume Spento*, 'With Tapers Quenched', a phrase from the *Purgatorio* (Canto 3, line 132) describing how Manfred, who died excommunicate, had his corpse carried without the usual lighted candles. A note on the back of the title page explained that the book was to have been called 'La Fraisne' after the first poem in it, and would have been

> dedicated to such as love this same beauty that I love, somewhat after mine own fashion. But sith one of them has gone out very quickly from amongst us it [is] given A Lume Spento (With Tapers Quenched) in memoriam eius mihi caritate primus William Brooke Smith Painter, Dreamer of dreams.

Why Ezra should have thought the passage from Dante about Manfred applicable to Brooke Smith is not clear; but it suited the thoroughly 1890s mood in which he had chosen to introduce the poems (the 'Note Precedent to 'La Fraisne'' which opens the book is in the same languid mock-archaic style as the dedication). In any case, foreign phrases and titles tended to appeal to him simply because they were foreign, as Richard Aldington has pointed out:

> Ezra liked foreign titles. His own include *A Lume Spento, Personae, Ripostes, Quia Pauper Amavi*; and where other people wrote a preface, Ezra pretentiously indicted prolegomena. It was rumoured later that he was responsible for making T. S. Eliot use the title *Ara Vos Prec*, a snippet of medieval Provençal which I imagine is unintelligible to most people. It seems a rather childish form of high-hatting, especially since Ezra was apt to get into ludicrous difficulties with his languages.

A Lume Spento did not represent the full range of what he had written. He told William Carlos Williams that he had omitted from it 'one tremendously gloomy series of ten sonnets' and also some 'mild, pretty verses' which would scarcely 'convince any publisher or critic that *I* happen to be a genius and deserve audience'. Occasionally he had moments of feeling that there was no point in trying to interest the public at large – he 'came very near telling the first man who ordered a copy that he didnt realy want it & that he wouldn't be able to understand it & that I therefore didnt want to sell it to him'. But his predominant instinct was that of the showman. He wrote to his father:

> Sound trumpet. Let rip the drum & swatt the big bassoon. It pays to advertise . . . What we want is <u>one big</u> hoorah of fore announcements, & one <u>more</u> big hoorah of reviews.

And, as a mark of his about-to-be-achieved importance in the world of letters, he had some stationery printed:

EZRA POUND
861 PONTE S VIO – VENICE

*

Antonini needed several weeks to assemble the book, so Ezra, with an eye to earning his living by the pen, got on with some prose. He worked at two short stories, 'La Dogesa's Necklace' and 'Genoa', which he told his mother he would send to her for typing, and for offering to *Smart Set*, the New York magazine. She could try them on other editors if they were rejected. From now on he treated his parents as if they were drudges in the office of his literary agent or publicist, giving them constant orders and requests for action. They were delighted to comply.

The short stories (which have not survived) were done in the spirit of the Browning-style verse monologues such as 'Cino'. 'I write them in the first person of any character that comes into my head,' Ezra told Homer, '& say anything I can think of that might make 'em sell.' He did not think he had any vocation to fiction: he wrote it to make money, and he was bored by the 'purely mechanical side' of it. He told his parents not to let American editors soften up what he had said about Tangier, and his mother must not censor the word 'spat' in the Genoa story, though he knew she would much prefer 'expectorated'.

Isabel assumed that he was coming back to another university job in America. He had indeed put in for a couple, in Vermont and far west in his native Idaho, but he did not count on getting either, and was rather hoping that his applications might have been sent in too late. He was now certain that, at least in a year or so, he ought to 'establish my self in London'. Maybe he should get on with that right away. 'As events have always shaped themselves to hurry me along a bit faster than I should have moved my self, it may be that I am not to wait.'

Meanwhile, Venice seemed very homely, 'nothing but a rather small wet village'. He was introduced to the composer Wolf-Ferrari, and was offered what he grandly described as 'a $ contract to teach the Italian tongue'. It cannot have been a very lucrative arrangement, for by mid-June he was running out of money. Wabash College had failed to send the balance of what they owed him, *Smart Set* was not interested in his short stories, and his hopes of guiding Americans round Italy had not materialized. He wrote to Homer that the only thing left seemed to be the pawn-shop, after which 'I could, I trust, starve like a gentleman. Its listed as part of the poetic training, you know.' Homer sent off some money.

The rejection of the stories did not crush his hopes of earning money in this way. He contemplated 'a novel on Spain' and some more short stories. He told Homer that in the press notice of *A Lume Spento* for the Hailey newspaper he might hint 'that there is a vague chance of the Univ. of Idaho securing my services if they try hard enough. Personally I am not dazzled by the job, but it would do if nothing better turned up.' The summer was passing; he would have to 'dynamite Antonini' if the book of poems were to appear in time for him to get to England. 'Want to have a month up the thames somewhere & meet Bill Yeats & one or two other humans if convenient.'

Afterwards he said that W. B. Yeats had been the magnet that drew him to London, because in those days 'Yeats knew more about poetry than anybody else'; he wanted 'to sit at Yeats's feet, and learn what he knew'. Yeats had 'ripped away the rhetoric of English verse' so that 'for the first time in English there were lyrics that read from one end to the other, in a straight simple sentence, with no deflection of word-order'. But there were other things he might do in England. He wrote to Balliol College, Oxford, asking whether he could complete his doctorate there. Meanwhile he was still planning the launch of *A Lume Spento* and thinking about reviews. 'I shall write a few myself & get some one to sign 'em . . . these remarks are strictly en famille – I am to figure always as the modest violet.'

In the last week in June he found new lodgings, 'more airy quarters overlooking 3 canals'. Miss Wells and Miss Norton had rented the rooms for a year, paying in advance, but had then left them, so Ezra took over the new accommodation rent free. The lodging was on the corner of the Fondamenta Nani and the Calle dei Frati, only a few hundred yards from Ponte San Vio. One of his windows overlooked the canal and church of San Trovaso; the other had a view of the Ognissanti side canal and of the big Giudecca waterway beyond. Opposite was a gondola repair yard and boatshed which, said Ezra, 'is probably an exact replica of what it was in the sixth century, etc.' There was hardly a tourist voice to be heard in this out-of-the-way corner, while just visible from his windows were the masts of a schooner moored on the Zattere, 'a real live one'. Moreover, he was still only ten minutes from San Marco, 'where there flows all the shame of the world'. It was, as he remarked to Mary Moore, 'a fit abode for a poet. Stage setting at least correct.' But *A Lume Spento* took an age to appear. 'The "Tapers" seem indefinitely quenched in printer's ink,' Ezra wrote to Mary Moore a little after midsummer. And when the proofs turned up he was suddenly depressed to contemplate his work in cold print. He considered whether to 'chuck the lot into the tide-water'.

During June, Kitty Heyman arrived in Venice on her European tour, surrounded by various American hangers-on. Ezra was glad, he said, to feel 'one of the gang' for a bit, and he immediately appointed himself Kitty's manager, holding a press conference about her, helping to arrange a

Venetian performance, and writing to the New York papers that her next American recital would be 'the event of the coming piano season'. He considered accompanying her to Paris and London before she went back to the States. Kitty was the 'greatest livin' she pyanist', and he could shepherd her all round the States and make their fortunes.

On a little further consideration *A Lume Spento* did not seem to deserve a watery grave, so he sent the proofs back to Antonini. After Kitty had given her Venetian concert he wrote a poem about it ('"Her" dreaming fingers lay between the tunes') which was quoted in a Venice newspaper. The poem called her 'the West's fore-dawn'. Elsewhere he spoke of her as 'The Aube of the West Dawn' – an 'Aube' or 'Alba' being the dawn song of a troubadour after a night of adulterous love. His relationship with Kitty, however, seems to have remained as chaste as ever.

When he was not with Kitty's gang, eating ices at Florian's or bathing on the Lido, he worked at a collection of new poems that he intended should follow *A Lume Spento* speedily into print, copying them into an exercise book labelled 'San Trovaso'. He described this project to Homer as '"San Trovaso" – my Venetian work' and said it was 'painted on ivory' where *A Lume Spento* had been 'on canvass'. It included several poems about Venice itself, most notably 'Night Litany':

> . . . Yea the lines hast thou laid unto me
> in pleasant places,
> And the beauty of this thy Venice
> hast thou shewn unto me
> Until is its loveliness become unto me
> a thing of tears . . .

He was very excited by this poem, afterwards saying that 'for days the "Night Litany" seemed a thing so little my own that I could not bring myself to sign it'.

A Lume Spento finally emerged from Antonini's print shop in the third week of July. Ezra was upset by the appearance of the first copies: 'they are not finished right . . . the damn fool printer has cut off a good half inch of margin & rough edge & made the thing look like a Sunday School hymn book . . . If Venice were not the most beautiful face on earth I should have the doleful dumps.' In fact only about twenty copies were spoiled – he had the rest trimmed to his liking – and fifteen of these went off at once to Homer for the American press. In due course presentation copies were parcelled up for Mary Moore, the Dryad, and William Carlos Williams.

Williams sent some strong criticisms of the poems; he was upset by what he called 'bitter, personal notes' and an air of 'poetic anarchy'. Hilda Doolittle was equally unenthusiastic. Ezra wrote back jauntily, praising Williams for being 'sincere'. A copy was also mailed to W. B. Yeats, who in reply tactfully communicated that he found the verses 'charming'. Ezra was delighted. 'I have been praised by the greatest living poet,' he told Williams.

The reviews did not exactly flood in – for a long time there were none at all – but eventually Ella Wheeler Wilcox obliged Homer with this notice in a New York paper:

> A LUME SPENTO ('With Tapers Quenched') is the title of a slender little booklet of verse which came to me from Venice, Italy, the other day . . . The name of the poet is 'Ezra Pound' and when I realize that this poet is grown to the age of manhood it makes my own youth seem far and far away; for somewhere among my souvenirs of a Springtime of life there is a little tintype picture of several youths and maidens: and the father of this poet is among the number and so am I.
>
> And when I stop and remember that my own wee son, who tarried so short a time on earth, would be also mangrown were he here: and he too might be writing verses, even as the son of my friend of long ago . . . Success to you, young singer of Venice! Success to 'With Tapers Quenched'.

It was at least a public notice of the book. 'I guess dad can live it down,' Ezra wrote to Isabel, 'she evidently wanted to be kind.'

The Philadelphia *Book News Monthly*, from which Ezra might have expected some loyalty, let him down. No review appeared for nearly a year, and when it finally came it was very short and very unenthusiastic: 'Mr Pound is talented, but he is very young . . . He affects obscurity and loves the abstruse . . . though a certain underlying force gives promise of simplicity to come.' There was, however, a third review, in the *Evening Standard & St James's Gazette* in London. It has been described as the work of 'a Venetian critic', but it is more than possible, in view of his determination (expressed to Homer) to 'write a few [reviews] myself', that this critic was Ezra:

> Wild and haunting stuff, absolutely poetic, original, imaginative, passionate, and spiritual. Those who do not consider it crazy may well consider it inspired. Coming after the trite and decorous verse of most of our decorous poets, this poet seems like a minstrel of Provence at a Suburban musical evening . . . words are no good in describing it.

Ezra did not feel that way about *A Lume Spento* for the rest of his life. By 1965 it seemed to him 'stale creampuffs'. This was unfair: stale is precisely what the poems are not. Despite the wealth of self-consciously literary references and frameworks, ranging from Provençal to the Celtic

Twilight via Browning, the book is full of intense feeling, and has more conviction than much of what was to follow. Though it appears at first glance to be a jumble of subject matter and dramatic monologues – Cino, Fifine, Villon, who come and go in an 1890s mist – any suggestion that the poems are the product of a desultory and faintly decadent mind is thoroughly misleading. They are a series of passionate statements on the matters that concern him most, cast in this form only because he had to use masks.

*

'Am going up to London about the first of Aug.,' he told his father. 'Venice is still as charming as when I arrived, but I suppose I'll get back here again before forever & I can probably find more congenial work in London, besides Venice is no winter resort.' Kitty Heyman had now left Venice, and Ezra had lost interest in the notion of being her manager. No American university job had come up, so he felt he might as well drift to London for a few weeks and see what he could achieve there. A Philadelphia travel agent had given him a contact at the London Polytechnic, and he hoped to pick up some lecturing work.

He remained in Venice for another ten days – it was difficult to tear himself away from such a lotus-eating life. In his later poetry Venice would often stand as a representation of the Perfect City; in the Pisan Cantos he simply recites the names of three canals beside which he lived at different times, as if they were talismans: 'Trovaso, Gregorio, Vio'. And elsewhere in the same section of the Cantos, in a passage omitted from the published text, he admits to downright nostalgia:

> San Giorgio, San Trovaso . . .
> Will I ever see the Giudecca again?
>   or the lights against it or Ca Foscari
>   or Ca Giustinian . . .
>   or the boats moored off le Zattere . . .

The summer of 1908 in Venice had been a crucial pause for him in the headlong events of recent months, a stocktaking, a chance not just to get his poems into print but to reassure himself about his own mission, to build up the self-confidence that would be essential if he were to make any kind of splash in London. There had been a few moments of self-doubt, but they were now behind him for good. The make-up was complete for the British performance. On 11 August he left Venice 'with pleasant introductions in Paris which I shan't have time to use . . . I go to London on divers chances . . . Here goes . . .'

2

Deah Old Lunnon

'I came to London with £3 knowing no one.' He wrote this five years later in 1913; it may have been a little more than £3, but he was usually accurate in such details, and there was almost certainly nothing left after the summer in Venice and the rail journey through Italy and France. He knew no one in the British capital. To make a mark in the short time he felt he had at his disposal, at the age of not quite twenty-three, with no previous experience of England other than a few days as an adolescent tourist and a week reading in the British Museum, would be a test of all his powers.

He chose London as his stage not only because of his admiration for Yeats, who lived there during much of the year, but because London in 1908 seemed to him indubitably 'the *centre* of at least anglo-Saxon letters, and presumably of intellectual action . . . There was *more* going on, and what went on went on *sooner* than in New York.' Actually there was remarkably little going on in literary London in 1908; it was one of the dead periods in English writing. But the London literary world, enfeebled as it might be, had for Ezra the immense advantage of being small and close-knit, so that if reputations were to be made at all, they could be achieved almost overnight – a very different matter from the diffuse American literary community, if any such community could really be said to exist.

He arrived at Victoria Station on 14 August 1908 and made his way to the boarding-house in Duchess Street where he had stayed two years earlier. Once settled in, he wrote a cheery note to Mary Moore:

> Deah old Lunnon. Seeking what giants & dragons I may devour . . . This is about the first breathing space I've taken since a 72 hour stretch sans bunk from Venice here – except this a.m. waiting to get a lady hung at Steinway Hall.

The lady – whatever he was doing with or for her – was a London contralto named Elizabeth Granger Kerr, to whom Kitty Heyman had recommended him. He called on her when he arrived and got her to referee his re-application for a reader's ticket at the British Museum. The meagreness of these beginnings was not conveyed to the folks at home. 'I think if I stay here long enough I may meet several people of the kind one reads about,' he told Mary Moore, while to Homer he was even more optimistic:

> Dear Dad:
> I've got a fool idea that I'm going to make good in this bloomin village. You'll have to stand to the guns for a month or so.
> The remittance I suggested as a greeting for my arrival here has not arrived. & my assets are something under 1 £ but my name is good here [8 Duchess Street] and so is the board . . . I suppose it'll take a good six weeks to get realy under way . . .

The first step towards recognition was to get *A Lume Spento* read by all the important people. He went down to Vigo Street just off Piccadilly Circus where Elkin Mathews's bookshop was much frequented by poets and critics. Mathews had been a key figure in the 1890s; he and John Lane had published *The Yellow Book* and were, in Ezra's words, 'the two peaks of Parnassus', the hub of 'the buggars' gang'. Lane then started his own business, taking several authors with him, but Mathews – though by 1908 no longer a fashionable figure in the literary world – retained Wilde, Yeats, Arthur Symons, Lionel Johnson, and John Addington Symonds on his list. He was sympathetic to young unknowns, and had just published James Joyce's collection of verse, *Chamber Music*.

Mathews told Ezra he was willing to give *A Lume Spento* some space in his shop, and seemed to take quite a liking to the young American. When Ezra started enthusing about W. M. Rossetti's translation of the *Convivio* of Dante and said he should publish it, Mathews agreed to look at it, and sure enough he brought it out a few months later. Ezra described this as his 'first little job in London'. It was the start of his innumerable campaigns to get other people's work into print.

He also asked Mathews if he would be willing to publish the 'San Trovaso' poems he had been writing in Venice. Mathews replied diplomatically that it was a busy time of year, better wait a few months. On 26 August, a couple of weeks after his arrival in London, Ezra wrote to his father that he was 'down to 1s 5d. but in no danger of starvation . . . Elkin Mathews cant use anything before Xmas. nothing definite at Polytechnique yet.' He owed £1 11s 6d weekly for full board at Duchess Street, but Miss Withey the landlady seemed willing to wait for the money, and continued to feed him. The Polytechnic was rather a disappointment; he had hoped to start some regular lecturing in September, but there was nothing firm on offer.

Another possible way of earning a living was to work again as a courier or guide. The Philadelphia travel agent who had given him the Polytechnic contact wrote that there would probably be a group he could conduct round Spain in the spring. Meanwhile 'if I can hang on here in London I can get literary position that would take ten years at home . . . I don't think I'll need more than one London season. – I'd have to have it sometime, & this looks as if it were it. - & I have the two books to push. – A. L. Spento and "San Trovaso".' In fact if 'San Trovaso' got into print quickly there was more stuff back in the drawers at Wyncote, enough 'to make a third volume . . . enough as far as bulk goes to make a 4th & 5th – but I object to turning out mediocre material'. Homer must announce the publication of 'San Trovaso' as imminent. 'Lord knows when it'll get into print – but announce it.'

He sent 'San Trovaso' off to J. M. Dent for consideration. After the usual delay they rejected it. He went round London bookshops making himself known. 'Told John Lewis's manager yesterday that I was quite competent to sell an edition of blank paper. – that line of talk seems more effective than the "great literary merit" stunt.' Self-assurance was an absolute essential, even to the point of brashness. 'Directions: for life in the capital,' he told a young writer a few years later: 'NOT to use the competent and defensive air . . . it is no use. People here haven't time.'

By 14 September a little money had trickled through from Homer, though not enough to keep him going. He filled up spare time with 'rakeings from the Renaissance stuff' in the Reading Room of the British Museum, where he registered his subject of research as the Latin poets of the Renaissance. He told Homer he was sure his work on them would 'attract a lot of notice. later or sooner.'

An American publisher seemed interested in printing an edition of *A Lume Spento*, but then wrote that he would not do it after all. 'I dont much mind. Had had all the fun of expecting his edition without the bother of correcting it.' By mid-September it seemed that Elkin Mathews might do an edition – at least, that was how Ezra chose to interpret Mathews's suggestion that the book needed an introduction. Meanwhile, the six weeks that Ezra had thought it would require to get under way in London were running out, and so was his credit at Miss Withey's. The day came when she indicated that a non-paying lodger was no longer welcome, and Ezra found himself and his belongings on the pavement.

He borrowed 10s from Miss Kerr the contralto, went to Islington where he had been told he could live for very little, and raised a further 10s at a pawnbroker's ('G.L. Lawrence, Loan Agent'). On the strength of this he took a room in a grubby lodging-house 'complete with billiard table (no cushions), bath (out of order), h. and c. (geyser not working), pink, frilly paper decorations: complete board and lodging 12/6 per week . . . Foods, unthinkable and unimaginable, odours, etc!' Even so he knew that this glimpse of the 'viscera' of London was not taking him 'anywhere near the bottom'. All he told his parents was: 'I have survived the week. I think when I get home, whenever t'ell that is, I will know a h-l-l-l-l of a lot of things wot I didn't us' t'er.' He was deeply relieved to receive money from Homer: '4 £ thank Gawd it has come.'

This cash arrived on 27 September. The next day he moved back to 'a respectable part of London'. He found a cheap but clean boarding-house kept by a Mrs Joy at 48 Langham Street, very near Miss Withey's. He would only have to pay '7s a week for room' and could eat 'where I like. guess I'll be able to run it at that.' He moved in at the beginning of October, shortly before his twenty-third birthday, and from then on Homer sent him £4 a month, enough to cover the rent and with some left over for modest food. When necessary, Ezra wrote to ask for more.

*

His new digs amused him. They were next door to a pub called The Yorkshire Grey, and he could overhear 'old Kate', one of the regulars, as he relates in Canto 80, 'stewing with rage / concerning the landlady's *doings* / with a lodger unnamed . . . / "married wumman, you couldn't fool *her*" . . .' His experiences in Islington made him study the faces of the working classes in the London streets, and he wrote a poem about them, 'Piccadilly', rather like a Victorian drawing-room ballad:

> Beautiful, tragical faces,
> Ye that were whole, and are so sunken;
> And, O ye vile, ye that might have been loved,
> That are so sodden and drunken,
>   Who hath forgotten you?

On 11 October he told Homer he had 'put out some new lines and am trying to keep in motion', but London still resolutely refused to pay attention to him, and he spent most of his time sitting in the British Museum writing poems. Among them was 'Marvoil', another Browning-style monologue, this time spoken by a troubadour; 'And Thus In Nineveh' ('I / Am here a Poet, that doth drink of life/ As lesser men drink wine'); and 'The White Stag', which expressed his present situation crisply enough:

> 'Tis the white stag, Fame, we're a-hunting,
> Bid the world's hounds come to horn!

During October a small crack appeared in London's resistance. The

Evening Standard & St James's Gazette published his two-stanza poem 'Histrion', a rather embarrassing piece about his fondness for assuming the personalities of other poets ('Thus am I Dante for a space and am / One François Villon, ballad-lord and thief'). Elkin Mathews, however, made no further moves towards reprinting *A Lume Spento* or accepting the 'San Trovaso' poems, so Ezra took matters into his own hands, selected fifteen pieces from the 'San Trovaso' manuscript, took them to a printer in Mortimer Street near his digs, and said he would pay to have them printed in a booklet. He decided to call it *A Quinzaine for this Yule* ('quinzaine' sounded better than 'fifteen') and subtitled it 'From a Venetian sketch-book'. He ordered 100 copies, added a dedication to Kitty Heyman ('To the Aube of the West Dawn'), and made up an epigraph on the subject of Beauty, Marvel and Wonder, supposedly by 'Weston St Llewmys' (though the printers accidentally rendered the last word 'Llewmy'). He kept it dark that publication was again at his own expense, giving the impression that the printers themselves, Pollock & Co, were publishing the book.

The poems were thin stuff after *A Lume Spento*. They had all been written in a few weeks, whereas the first book contained gleanings from about five years. Ezra was aware of the collection's limitations. 'It lacks, on the surface, the virility. & vitality of A.L.S. but it lacks several faults of A.L.S. also,' he told Homer. 'The workmanship is perhaps finer.' One of the few attractive pieces was 'Night Litany' with its naïve but rather touching delight in Venice.

At the end of November he ate his Thanksgiving dinner 'solus' in Pagani's restaurant, 'which has the best feed in London & where the waiters hang round me for the sake of a few words of Italian'. It was no worse than celebrating his birthday surreptitiously at Hamilton. 'Saw Yeats at a matinee of his "Deirdre" yesterday,' he reported, 'but he was in one part of the house & I in another there was nothing more than seeing.'

※

A Quinzaine for this Yule was finished by the printer in good time for Christmas, and once again Elkin Mathews made vaguely encouraging remarks about reprinting it some time or other at his own expense. And this time it really happened.

Perhaps the copies printed for Ezra sold well because 'Yule' was in the title; perhaps Mathews was beginning to feel sorry for the endlessly hopeful young American. At all events he decided to order 100 more copies from Pollock's, and by the end of December they were in his shop, bearing the words 'Printed for Elkin Mathews, Vigo Street, London W.' Ezra was still (as he himself said) the 'undiscovered author' of two books of 'unintelligible worse'. But one of the books had been taken on by a real literary publisher. The White Stag would be hunted down yet.

3

The Most Charming Woman in London

The Polytechnic decided it could fit in a few lectures by him after all. On 21 January 1909 he began to deliver a series of six, entitled 'A Short Introductory Course of Lectures on the Development of Literature in Southern Europe'. He said that he was now the 'loudly advertised lecturer on "the Devil upment of Literachoor in Southern Yourup"', and told his father to describe him in future press releases as 'Lecturer on Romance Literature for the London Polytechnique'.

Thirty-five people turned up for the first lecture, which was entitled 'The Search for the Essential Qualities of Literature'. Fewer came back next week, when Ezra began an exposition of the troubadours. He blamed the London fog, which he said was reducing other lecturers' audiences too, 'so I dont stand badly with the management'.

Even with the lectures to write there was still plenty of time to be filled. At the beginning of February he began work on a prose critique of Walt Whitman. 'From this side of the Atlantic I am for the first time able to read Whitman,' he wrote, 'and from the vantage of my education and – if it be permitted a man of my scant years – my world-citizenship: I see him America's poet . . . He *is* America. His crudity is an exceeding great stench, but it *is* America.' But Whitman never really appealed to him, though sometimes he felt he should be interested. Two years later he wrote: 'I never have owned a copy of Whitman. I have to all purposes never read him.' What somebody took for Whitman's voice in his own work was (he said) merely the influence of America, 'the feel of the air, the geomorphic rhythm force'. By 1919 he was prepared to allow that Whitman 'wrote badly a good deal of the time but ultimately got a technique . . . Bill Williams much nearer him, really, than I am.'

Elkin Mathews must have sold some of the 100 copies of *A Quinzaine for this Yule* that he had ordered from the printer, for during January 1909 he agreed to issue under his own name, and at his own expense, a selection from *A Lume Spento* to which Ezra would add some new poems – though according to Ezra's account of it, four years later, the financial arrangements were only agreed upon after negotiation:

> So far as I can remember our only discussion of business was as follows:-
> *Mr E.M.:* 'Ah, eh, do you care to contribute to the costs of publishing?'
> *Mr E.P.:* 'I've got a shilling in my clothes, if that's any use to you.'
> *Mr E.M.:* 'Oh well, I rather want to publish 'em anyhow.'

The new book was to be called *Personae*. Ezra wrote to Isabel on 19 January 1909: 'Well mother mine: We appear to be working out of the amateur class. Mathews is using the "Personae" in his best series. – real fine book with ornamentation & whiskers i.e. binding.'

Mathews was a fund of stories about the previous literary generation, and liked to tell how when he went to tea with Swinburne and his keeper Watts-Dunton there were 'three teacups / two for Watts-Dunton who liked to let his tea cool'. Ezra asked if he might presume to call on the household himself, but was warned that Swinburne was stone deaf with a bad temper, so he told Homer 'I haven't continued investigation in that direction'. By the end of the year Swinburne was dead. Ezra afterwards called this his 'only miss' in his attempts to pay homage to celebrated literary survivors.

By hanging around Mathews's bookshop he began to get to know a sprinkling of contemporary *literati*. He announced to William Carlos Williams on 3 February 1909 that he was 'by way of falling into the crowd that does things here. London, deah old London, is the place for poesy.' Some of Mathews's introductions were merely to other young unknowns, such as an Oxford poet named James Gryffyth Fairfax, who lent Ezra an enormous poem in manuscript which had touches of Tennyson and Swinburne but became terribly boring after forty pages. However, Fairfax had some society contacts and introduced Ezra to a Knightsbridge hostess, Mrs Alfred Fowler, whose salon sometimes included Robert Bridges and Max Beerbohm. Ezra began to take tea there. He met neither of these celebrities, but did make the acquaintance of the interestingly named Mrs Shakespear, who gave him an invitation to tea at her own Kensington house in Brunswick Gardens. He went there with a young Australian poet, Frederic Manning, and on Sunday 1 February 1909 reported to his mother: 'The week has been fairly full . . . Tea with Manning and a certain Mrs Shakespeare who is undoubtedly the most charming woman in London.'

Olivia Shakespear, then in her mid-forties, was the daughter of an Indian Army major-general and a first cousin of the 1890s poet Lionel Johnson. She was married to a London solicitor, Henry Hope Shakespear, whose family claimed no connection with William Shakespeare (they had been rope-makers in the East End in the seventeenth century), though Olivia thought a relationship could be hinted at, since she liked to spell the playwright's name 'Shakespear', a habit she passed on to Ezra.

Ten years after her marriage to Mr Shakespear and the birth of their only child Dorothy, Olivia had a secret affair with her cousin Lionel's friend W. B. Yeats. In his posthumously published *Memoirs*, where he calls her 'Diana Vernon', Yeats writes of her:

> She had a profound culture, a knowledge of French, English, and Italian literature, and seemed always at leisure. Her nature was gentle and contemplative, and she was content, it seems, to have no more of life than leisure and the talk of her friends. Her husband, whom I saw but once, was much older and seemed a little heavy, a little without life. As yet I did not know how utterly estranged they were.

The affair between Mrs Shakespear and Yeats began (in 1895) with a 'long passionate kiss' on a train. For nearly a year they exchanged further kisses 'in railway carriages and at picture galleries and occasionally at her house', and Yeats 'thought I was once more in love' (he had loved, and been rejected by, Maud Gonne). He took rooms in Woburn Buildings off the Euston Road so they could became lovers; Olivia accompanied him to a shop in Tottenham Court Road to buy a double bed, and Yeats describes 'an embarrassed conversation upon the width . . . every inch increased the expense'. When the bed was installed Yeats found himself 'impotent from nervous excitement'. They tried again a week later, but 'my nervous excitement was so painful that this time it seemed best but to sit over tea and talk'. However 'my nervousness did not return again, and we had many days of happiness'.

The love affair flourished for a while, but then Maud Gonne came to London and Olivia realized that Yeats was still in thrall to her. They separated for many years, but by the time Ezra met Olivia in January 1909 she and Yeats were once again friends, though not lovers. In the poem 'Friends' published five years later, Yeats praises Olivia for not allowing anything to intervene between 'Mind and delighted mind'.

Shortly before the affair with Yeats, Olivia had begun writing novels. By the time Ezra met her she had published five, all of them dealing with impossible marriages and the strains on women who wanted sexual liberty but found themselves trapped by Victorian convention. The first, *Love on a Mortal Lease* (1894), attempts to assert that 'any union that is sanctified by love' is 'a real marriage', but Olivia lacked the nerve to put this proposition to the test in her books, and usually took refuge in melodrama rather than letting her heroines practise any sustained liberation. Ezra read the latest of her books, *The Devotees* (1904), and recommended it to Mary Moore, though he remarked, 'it is not nearly so enjoyable as she is'.

By the time he met Olivia he had cooled towards Kitty Heyman. He told Mary Moore that 'her bally highness & I have been on terms of most frigid politeness for some time'. He had seen Kitty in London and attended a piano recital by her, but now only as a 'disinterested spectator' whose enjoyment of Kitty's playing was merely 'impersonal'. However he 'had tea afterwards with the most charming woman in London. The enjoyment is not always impersonal.'

Olivia was twenty-one years older than Ezra – compared with Kitty's fifteen – and was a classic late Victorian beauty who had splendidly retained her looks. She was also, as Ezra so frequently said, charming. 'Everybody confides in her,' wrote one of her cousins. 'You will, before you've known her twelve hours. Oh, she never asks for confidences; she'd much rather not be bothered with them; but people will tell her things, – especially when their lives are – shall we say – tangled?'

Romantic friendship with such a woman was very much to Ezra's taste, far more than the notion of marriage to somebody nearer his own age. 'As for wives?' he wrote to his mother. 'It ought to be illegal for an artist to marry, or nearly that . . . If the artist must marry let him find someone more interested in art, or his art, or the artist part of him, than in him. After which let them take tea together three times a week. The ceremony may be undergone to prevent gossip, if necessary.'

His second visit to the Shakespears was on 16 February 1909. Afterwards, he told Mary Moore he had been 'sitting on the same hearth rug' where Yeats had often sat. Olivia's friendship with the great man (though Ezra had no idea how intimate it had been) was an additional attraction; surely now he would get the long-awaited introduction?

During the tea-party 'he began to talk – He talked of Yeats, as one of the Twenty of the world who have added to the World's poetical matter – He read a short piece of Yeats, in a voice dropping with emotion, in a voice like Yeats' own – He spoke of his interest in all the Arts, in that he might find things of use in them for his own – which is the Highest of them all.'

It was slightly risky to give this performance on the hearth rug of one of Yeats's friends. But the act went down extremely well, especially with the Shakespears' daughter, Dorothy, a year younger than Ezra, who wrote this account in her notebook. Dorothy had been educated at a Hampshire boarding school, with a year of 'finishing' at Geneva, since when she had had nothing to do but accompany her mother on social engagements, paint watercolours, read, and write letters to cousins and schoolfriends. Her father took no interest in her and her mother was over-protective. She had fully inherited her mother's looks, but from her father she had acquired a considerable reserve that glazed over her porcelain-shepherdess features. Her mother's social round took her almost exclusively among female cousins and aunts, and there had been no romance in her life, though she was already twenty-two.

The visitor's name excited her.

> Listen to it – Ezra! Ezra! [she wrote in her notebook]. And a third time – Ezra! He has a wonderful, beautiful face, a high forehead, prominent over the eyes; a long, delicate nose, with little, red nostrils; a strange mouth, never still, & quite elusive; a square chin, slightly cleft in the middle – the whole face pale; the eyes gray-blue; the hair golden-brown, and curling in soft wavy crinkles. Large hands, with long, well-shaped fingers, and beautiful nails.

Her mother complained mildly of his 'untidy boots', but Dorothy protested in her notebook that one could not notice such a thing 'when there is his moving, beautiful face to watch . . . I do not think he knows he is beautiful.'

Sitting on a low stool near the hearth rug, listening to his pronouncements on Yeats and the poetic calling, she dared to interrupt for a moment, asking if he had ever 'seen things in a crystal?' (She herself liked consulting palmists.) Ezra answered with smiling condescension: 'I see things without a crystal.' Wilde or Bunthorne could not have done better. Dorothy did not feel snubbed; she listened eagerly as he declared that he was waiting for 'the Great Inspiration'. He wished above all to be 'in readiness, open-minded and waiting' for 'the Great Day' whenever it should come.

Dorothy was deeply moved. But she wrote of him afterwards in her notebook: 'Are you a genius? or are you only an artist in Life?'

*

Ezra went home to Langham Street, carrying away no notion of the impression he had made on the daughter, but himself still more enraptured with the 'charming' mother. He began to write to Olivia, using the gallant, courtly tone he had employed for Mary Moore and other ladyfriends. He opened one letter 'Salve', and referred to Olivia as 'her highness'. After a few weeks he celebrated 'the anniversary of his landing in Europe' by taking her to Kitty Heyman's recital. Dorothy came too, but Ezra did not mention this to Mary Moore when describing the afternoon.

In letters to his parents he listed his friendship with the Shakespears as if it were another of his literary contacts: 'I think the Shakespears & Selwyn Image are about the most worth while out of the lot I have come across.'

Selwyn Image, to whom he was introduced by Elkin Mathews, was one of the old Rhymers' Club set, a painter of stained glass as well as a poet. Another Mathews introduction was to Laurence Binyon, a keeper of prints and drawings at the British Museum and an occasional poet. Things seemed to be moving at last.

Ernest Rhys, founder of the Everyman series for J. M. Dent, was yet one more Mathews habitué who took the young American under his wing. At Rhys's Hampstead house Ezra met Miss May Sinclair, novelist and fringe member of the H. G. Wells circle. She invited him to tea, and he responded with gallant letters. Mathews also fixed him up with an invitation to a dinner of the newly established Poets' Club, where Hilaire Belloc would be one of the attractions. When the evening came round, George Bernard Shaw was there too; Ezra found the whole affair frightfully boring, but it led to a lunch with the novelist Maurice Hewlett, so that they could grumble together about it.

Mary Moore wrote to ask if London was fun. Ezra replied: 'Sometimes. 6 months ago it was decidedly not. Lately it has been.' And to his parents: 'I seem to fit better here in London than anywhere else.' But literary introductions did not provide an income, and it still seemed sensible to continue looking for a job in an American university. He booked a provisional passage back to the USA on 10 March. Then he changed his mind – 'I thought I was going to sail home come Wednesday but I ain't.'

*

One excuse for not going home was that the printer was taking an age over *Personae*, and he ought to be in London when it was published. Another was his hope of meeting Yeats, still unfulfilled. 'Yeats is coming over from Ireland soon,' he told Homer in early March 1909, '& I dont think such chances of acquaintance should be lost . . . this being in the gang & being known by the right people ought to mean a lot better introduction of "Personae" reviewing etc.' Suddenly Yeats was expected the next Friday, 'and the most charming woman in London has invited him to meet me'. But in the event 'Yeats . . . couldn't or didn't get here', though 'Mrs Shakespear has him nailed to meet me when he does come'.

Meanwhile Dorothy Shakespear continued to write about Ezra in her notebook:

> He (Ezra) has passed by the way, where most men have only dreamed of passing. He . . . has learned to live beside his body. I see him as a double person – just held together by the flesh . . . He can starve . . . that his spirit may bring forth the 'highest of arts' – poetry . . . 'It is worth starving for' he said one day.

Ezra saw himself in much the same terms. In a poem written for *Personae* he projected himself into the predicament of Glaucus, the mortal who eats a magic herb and becomes a sea-god, estranging himself from the woman who loves him. Ezra told his mother that the poem ('Idyl for Glaucus') was meant to describe a case like his own, 'where the mans further or subtler development of mind puts a barrier between him & a woman to whom he has become incomprehensible'.

The Glaucus poem was one of the few successful new pieces in the book, which was largely made up of reprints from *A Lume Spento*. Too many of the others were hopelessly leaden in style and subject matter. The supposedly iconoclastic 'Revolt against the Crepuscular Spirit in Modern Poetry', which began 'I would shake off the lethargy of this our time', was written in exactly the lethargic post-1890s diction it claimed to mock.

Personae came out on 16 April 1909, with the dedication: 'This book is for Mary Moore of Trenton, if she wants it.' Ezra did not draw Mary's attention to this when he sent a copy to her, though on the dedication page he had added: 'In attestation whereof I do set and sign EP.' She failed to notice, and it was some months before a friend pointed out to her that she was the dedicatee.

The first reviews appeared within a matter of days. The *Evening Standard & St James's Gazette* had now abandoned the services of the 'Venetian critic' for another anonymous reviewer, who thought the book 'queer' and often 'incoherent' but was 'attracted occasionally by lines which are almost, if not quite, nonsense. Our conclusion is that Mr Pound is a poet, though a fantastic one.' A day later another anonymous reviewer in the *Daily Telegraph* remarked that the name Ezra Pound sounded rather comic, but thought that the book contained 'a thread of true beauty'. Ezra was told that the *Telegraph* critic was W. L. Courtney, editor of the *Fortnightly Review*. He remarked of Courtney's piece that at least it was lengthy – a new book by Maurice Hewlett had got about half the space – and was really 'not so rotten'.

*

During March, a little before the publication of *Personae* but too late for inclusion in it, he wrote his best poem to date: 'Sestina: Altaforte', another Browning-style dramatic monologue, spoken by Bertran de Born. This troubadour–knight (whom Ezra had already impersonated in 'Na Audiart', the poem about the perfect lady manufactured from various women) was put in hell by Dante because he was a notorious 'stirrer up of strife'. Now it was Bertran's irascibility and love of battle that Ezra mimicked. This is his account of how 'Sestina: Altaforte' came to be written:

I had had de Born on my mind. I had found him untranslatable. Then it occurred to me that I might present him in this manner.

I wanted the curious involution and recurrence of the Sestina.*
I knew more or less of the arrangement. I wrote the first
strophe and then went to the [British] Museum to make sure of
the right order of permutations, for I was then living in
Langham Street, next door to the 'pub', and had hardly any
books with me. I did the rest of the poem at a sitting.
Technically it is one of my best, though a poem on such a theme
could never be very important.

The last remark is sheer snobbery, a reaction to the deserved popularity of
'Sestina: Altaforte'. The poem, a loose rendition of one of Bertran's war
songs (there is a more literal version in the 'Proença' chapter of Ezra's *The
Spirit of Romance*), erupts splendidly out of the languor he had recently
begun to affect in his poetry:

> Damn it all! this our South stinks peace.
> You whoreson dog, Papiols, come! Let's to music!
> I have no life save when the swords clash.
> But ah! when I see the standards gold, vair, purple, opposing
> And the broad fields beneath them turn crimson,
> Then howl I my heart nigh mad with rejoicing.

This was how Ezra liked to think of himself when in his aggressive,
anti-received-opinions mood. It was a mask that fitted him very well, as
T. S. Eliot later observed, singling the poem out for special praise among all
Ezra's early work: 'A complete success in a most difficult form. There is no
false antiquity here, in either word or phrase.'

    After writing 'Sestina: Altaforte' Ezra told May Sinclair that he had just
composed 'a most blood-curdling sestina, which I think I have divested of
the air of artificiality supposed to haunt that form'. Miss Sinclair thought
that it should be offered to a newly established magazine, the *English
Review*, so she took Ezra down to Holland Park Road in West London
where the magazine was being run from a flat above a fishmonger's shop.

    Its editor, the man whose name Ezra was soon delighting to render in
such forms as 'Forty Mad-Dogs Whoofer', was then in his mid-thirties and
was trying to set himself up as a person of influence in the literary world.
Ford Madox Hueffer, who renamed himself Ford Madox Ford during the
First World War, was the son of a German-born music critic and an
English mother, daughter of the Pre-Raphaelite painter Ford Madox

---

*In which the same six end-words conclude the six lines of each stanza, but in a different
order every time.

Brown. Up to now, Ford had written about twenty-five books, mostly ephemeral and ranging from children's fairy tales to historical fiction, though he had collaborated on two novels with the then almost unknown Joseph Conrad. He hoped that his new *English Review*, to which Conrad and H. G. Wells had given their support, would give him better standing in the world of letters.

May Sinclair told him that she wanted to introduce 'the greatest poet to the greatest editor in the world' (or so, typically, said Ford). Ezra found himself facing a person of thoroughly unprepossessing appearance. 'This ex-collaborator with Joseph Conrad', remarked Wyndham Lewis some years later,

> was himself, it always occurred to me, a typical figure out of a Conrad book – a caterer, or corn-factor, coming on board – blowing like a porpoise with the exertion – at some Eastern port . . . a flabby lemon and pink giant, who hung his mouth open as though he were an animal at the Zoo inviting buns – especially when ladies were present. Over the gaping mouth damply depended the ragged ends of a pale lemon moustache.

But though Ford Madox Hueffer and Ezra Pound could scarcely have been more different in appearance and manner, there was a certain similarity in character, Ford being given to boastful exaggeration to the point of absurdity. In one mood he 'boomed through endless anecdotes of Great Victorians, Great Pre-Raphaelites, Henry James, and somebody no one else had ever heard of'. In another he might recall 'his year's service in an aristocratic German regiment', or begin an anecdote with 'When I was last with the Kaiser . . .', talking voluble German and remarking 'Of course, you English . . .' After 1914 he 'discovered that he was and always had been a patriotic English gentleman'.

These last acid observations are by Richard Aldington, who characterizes Ford as 'a sort of literary Falstaff', and gives this example of his flexible treatment of truth, at a dinner party at the Aldington family home:

> The food and wine were good, and Ford, ever susceptible to the genial influences of the table and good fellowship, opened the flood-gates of his discourse and babbled o' green fields – I should say, of celebrities – in his most imaginative strain. A scholarly recluse like my father . . . was an ideal subject for Ford's experiments. He sensed the virgin sucker at once. So we had the stories about Ruskin, and my uncle Gabriel and my Aunt Christina [Hueffer claimed to be related to the Rossettis]; the Conrad and James stories; the story of the abbé Liszt's concert and how Queen Alexandra took the beautiful infant

Ford on her knees and kissed him; the 'old Browning' stories, and the Swinburne stories; gradually working back through the 19th century. My father was swimming in bliss, although once or twice he looked a little puzzled. And then Ford began telling how he met Byron. I saw my father stiffen . . .

In the years that followed his first visit to the Holland Park flat, Ezra often played Hal to this Falstaff, egging on to many a literary Gadshill the man whom he nicknamed 'Fat Ford'. Ford himself was entertained and spurred on by the young madcap. He took little serious interest in Ezra's writing ('Said he never could understand a goddamned thing,' remarked Ezra), but was delighted to have found someone as splendidly absurd as himself. His reminiscences are full of comic vignettes of Ezra, most of them drawn entirely from his imagination.

Ezra was equally uninterested in what Ford actually wrote. He delighted in Ford's brisk off-the-cuff literary judgements, which were nearly always right, and in his ability as an editor to detect the quality of a manuscript almost by its smell ('I don't read manuscripts,' Ford would say, 'I know what's in 'em'). He thought Ford's conversation first-rate ('Fordie / never dented an idea for a phrase's sake') but was impatient with most of his fiction, or such of it as he bothered to read, finding it full of 'semblable clots of ancient furniture sentimental, traditional, purely decorative et bloody cetera'. This was true enough of Ford's early work, but Ezra similarly dismissed Ford's one-time collaborator Conrad, whom he thought of 'very considerably lower category' and 'less intelligent' than Ford himself. He also failed to distinguish out of Ford's mass of books – more than eighty in all – his real achievements, *The Good Soldier* and the *Parade's End* series of novels. Probably he scarcely looked at them. In a moment of honesty he once admitted that he 'never did read novels apart from Flaubert and H. James for specific purposes', and to Ford himself he wrote: 'I never did like NOVELS just as such.'

For all his nonsense, Ford was just the friend and supporter Ezra needed in his attempts to make a name for himself in London in 1909. He afterwards judged that Ford 'had all his faults, like his moustache, out in front where everyone cd/ see,' and was 'au fond a serious character as J. J. [Joyce] the Reverend Eliot and even ole Unc Wm/ the yeAT were NOT'. (Actually quite the opposite was true: Ford markedly lacked seriousness, which was why he and Ezra got on.) Wyndham Lewis, looking back over this period in Ezra's life, thought that Ford was an essential buffer between Ezra and the British literary establishment. He could not 'see him stopping here very long without some such go-between as Ford Madox Hueffer'.

It was Ezra's sheer Americanism that first amused Ford. 'When I first knew him,' he writes in his memoirs,

his Philadelphian accent was comprehensible if disconcerting . . . he was astonishingly meagre and agile. He threw
himself alarmingly into frail chairs, devoured enormous quantities of your pastry, fixed his pince-nez firmly on his nose, drew
out a manuscript from his pocket, threw his head back, closed
his eyes to the point of invisibility and looking down his nose
would chuckle like Mephistopheles and read you a translation . . . The only part of that *albade* that you would understand would be the refrain:
    'Ah me, the darn, the darn it comes toe sune.'

Ford is remembering Ezra's 'Alba Innominata: from the Provençal',
written around the time he met Ford, with its refrain 'Ah God! Ah God!
That dawn should come so soon.'

Ezra found Ford equally comic from the outset. David Garnett recalls
how during the months when Ford was running the *English Review* he
would array himself 'in a magnificent fur coat; wore a glassy topper; drove
about in hired carriages; and his fresh features, the colour of raw veal, his
prominent blue eyes and rabbit teeth smiled benevolently and patroniz-
ingly upon all gatherings of literary lions'. But the magazine was a startling
success, thanks to Ford's simple expedient of printing (in the first
half-dozen issues) new work by such established names as Hardy, James,
Galsworthy and Wells. Ezra soon joined them, and his ruling emotion was
gratitude to be in such company: 'Have just received proofs of my
"Sestina: Altaforte" from the English Review . . . probably the best
magazine in the country. I suppose the sestina is about the most blood
curdling thing the good city has seen since dear Kit Marlowe's day but it
seems to have affected an entrance.'

4

Yeats Has At Last Arrived

The dreariness of the Poets' Club accurately reflected the state of English writing at this time. The excitements of the 1890s, for what they had been worth, were dead and gone; even the Georgians had not yet identified themselves as a group. Recollecting the London literary world of 1909 thirty years later, Ezra spoke of it as an 'arthritic milieu', picking out the names of Henry Newbolt and Edmund Gosse as especially deplorable *éminences grises* behind the Edwardian uncertainties. 'Gosse's generation,' he wrote, 'was contemptible, mingy, they were carrots not animals. Born under the Victorian fugg, insularity, a meagreness, a dwindling.'

Even allowing for the usual Poundian exaggeration, it was a dull period. Vague memories of the Decadents and the Celtic Twilight predominated in the fashionable poetic style, producing something that Ezra rightly called 'a horrible agglomerate compost . . . a doughy mess of third-hand Keats, Wordsworth, heaven knows what, fourth-rate Elizabethan sonority blunted, half-melted, lumpy'. Yeats had set a certain example, but that had been obscured, said Ezra, by 'Mr (early) Yeats's so very poetic language'. The only alternative to the doughy mess seemed to be the seafaring heartiness of Newbolt's 'Drake's Drum' and John Masefield's *Salt-Water Ballads*, spoofed thus by Ezra in a letter to May Sinclair:

> Hear Masefiled [*sic*] sung by a gent in a white waistcoat,
> 'They bold burly sailormen abaft the Round Pond . . .'

Prose was rather more lively, being dominated by such figures as Arnold Bennett, Galsworthy, Wells, Shaw, Chesterton and Belloc. Ezra disliked (and was jealous of) the Bennett–Wells type of popular-successful novelist, and later took the opportunity to snarl at both men. He quite liked such Galsworthy as he looked at, paid no attention to Belloc (though the two later rubbed shoulders in certain journals and had anti-Semitism in common), and dubbed Chesterton 'a yahoo', though he and Chesterton had certain similarities, as both of them eventually realized. (Chesterton, reviewing Ezra in 1935, observed that each was characterized by 'furious likes and dislikes', though Ezra's fury seemed to him the greater.) Ezra was ambiguous, too, towards Shaw. In 1916 he called him an 'intellectual cheese-mite' and attacked him for trivializing Ibsen, yet four years later he allowed that 'Dear old Shaw has amused us'. In 1917 he was glad of the support of 'old G.B.S.' for an exhibition of Vorticist photography. They got on well when they met.

But though the ogres might prove thoroughly human if encountered individually at close quarters, collectively and from a distance they seemed a bad régime in need of dethroning. Certainly a young man named T. E. Hulme and his friends, who met in Soho on Thursday evenings in secession from the Poets' Club, felt that there was room for improvement, though they themselves could hardly be called literary revolutionaries. Ezra describes them in a letter to his father in August 1909, three months after he had begun to keep their company:

> The crowd I meet on Thursdays consists of Storer. whose poems I'll send you in the dim future, Hulme who writes poetry – so so. (did review of me in the New Age) Fitzgerald who journalizes & poetizes somewhat – occasionally Tancred. (stock exchange) who does epigrams. & admires my sonnet – Th' Amphora, above the rest of my works.

T. E. Hulme was the son of a Staffordshire businessman who played country squire. He went to Newcastle-under-Lyme High School, where he won an exhibition to St John's College, Cambridge, but was sent down from the university in 1904 for misbehaviour during a Boat Race rag. (According to J. C. Squire he had the 'longest mock funeral' ever seen at Cambridge.) He went off to Canada, where legend has it that he worked as a lumberjack. In 1908 he came back to Cambridge, where he attended philosophy lectures without enrolling again as an official student. He then drifted to London, and was drawn into the radical group who contributed to the weekly magazine the *New Age*, among whom he gained a reputation as a philosopher, though his 'philosophical' ideas amounted to little more than a rejection of liberal humanism in favour of a vigorously pessimistic outlook. Later he became interested in the writings of Bergson. None of this remotely concerned Ezra, who once remarked that he thought Hulme's philosophical studies merely 'crap'. He added : 'DAMN Bergson and frog diarhoea.'

Indeed, it is not obvious what did attract him to Hulme. He was mildly amused by what he called Hulme's 'outward image of a Yorkshire farmer –

the Pickwickian Englishman who starts a club'. No doubt Hulme's sheer
brawn and physical toughness appealed to him – Hulme was big and bony
and once picked up Wyndham Lewis and held him upside down. He also
had plenty of nerve. Legend relates that one day he was apprehended by a
policeman while urinating in Soho Square in broad daylight: 'You can't do
that here.' Hulme replied: 'Do you realize you're addressing a member of
the middle class?' The policeman withdrew apologetically.

David Garnett relates another Hulme anecdote:

> Hulme would suddenly pull out his watch while a group of his
> acquaintances sat talking with him at a table in the Café Royal.
> 'I've a pressing engagement in five minutes' time,' he would say
> and stride out of the building. Twenty minutes later he would
> return, wipe his brow, and complain that the steel staircase of
> the emergency exit at Piccadilly Circus Tube Station was the
> most uncomfortable place in which he had ever copulated.

When asked whether he remembered Hulme relating such amatory
adventures, Ezra snorted: 'Can't recall T.E.H. ever divagating from ideas
to personal tosh.' Nevertheless Hulme as tough guy appealed to him more
than Hulme as philosopher, perhaps even more than Hulme as theoretician
of literature.

The Poets' Club was started in 1908 as a monthly gathering (at the
United Arts' Club) for dinner, readings and a paper. Rather surprisingly,
considering that Edmund Gosse and Henry Newbolt were among the
founders, and that he did not regard himself as a poet, Hulme was asked to
be its secretary. He cared little for its meetings, and was delighted when a
young poet named F. S. Flint attacked it in the *New Age* for its 'suave
tea-parties', comparing it unfavourably with Verlaine and his contemporaries 'conning feverishly and excitedly the mysteries of their craft'. Flint
concluded: 'The Poets' Club is Death.' Hulme's response was to gather
Flint and others of like mind for Thursday evening sessions which might
capture some of the feverish excitement for which Flint pined.

Flint, born in the same year as Ezra, was the son of a London
commercial traveller. He left school at thirteen, but educated himself in ten
languages and rose to be a senior statistician in the Ministry of Labour. In
1909, the year that Ezra met him and the Hulme group, Flint had his first
poetry printed privately – a set of love lyrics to his wife. He admired and
was well informed about the French Symbolists. A contemporary describes
him as 'Frank Flint, bespectacled, shy, apologetic . . . ashamed of his own
Cockney antecedents . . . doomed perpetually to follow, and never to lead'.
Ezra himself spoke of Flint as 'never at best distinguished for energy and
initiative', but said that he 'ought to get his due, whether that wd/ content
or even please him is another matter . . . You can quote me as saying "the

last really Keatsian mind in England, or at any rate a pure specimen of that kind of mind" . . . Victim of milieu, or at any rate sunk.' Of the other poet members of the Thursday group, Ezra thought that F. W. Tancred was 'a perfect museum piece'. Edward Storer had published a couple of books of verse, one of which contained an attack on current poetic conventions. Ezra said he himself preferred Desmond FitzGerald's verse to either Storer's or Flint's, 'but they didn't get a bullet proof cover to it, any of 'em'.

The group first met on the last Thursday in March 1909, at the Tour Eiffel restaurant in Percy Street, just north of Soho. According to Flint, 'Mr Pound did not join us until the third evening, and he may have forgotten or been unaware of the excitement with which the diners on the other side of our screen heard him declaim the "Sestina: Altaforte" . . . how the table shook and cutlery vibrated in resonance with his voice!' This was on Thursday 22 April, six days after the publication of *Personae*.

Ezra himself certainly knew the effect that 'Sestina: Altaforte' could have, given enough volume. 'I can hardly read it aloud ' he remarked to his father soon after writing it, 'because an accurate rendition would require a 54 inch chest.' On the Thursday following his recitation at the Tour Eiffel, the manager placed a screen around the Hulme table so that the group could conduct future business without causing so much disturbance to other diners.

Frank Flint allowed that Ezra was a 'picturesque' addition to the group, and that 'his habit of declaiming so that the whole place resounded' was splendidly disconcerting to the other customers, but he was emphatic that Ezra 'added nothing to the discussion' when they all talked poetry. Rather, 'he took very much. He took away the whole doctrine of what he later called Imagisme.'

Flint was exaggerating: no such doctrine existed among the Hulme group in 1909 (nor, arguably, did it have much existence later). What Ezra chiefly gained from Hulme and the others was his first experience of being welcomed into a contemporary literary movement or clique, rather than remaining an outsider, a loner. The group was much more kindly disposed towards him than Flint's remarks suggest. Flint himself reviewed *Personae* in the *New Age* (not Hulme, as Ezra told his father) and made some encouraging remarks:

> Mr Pound is a poet with a distinct personality. Essentially, he is
> a rebel against all conventions except sanity; there is something
> robustly impish and elfish about him . . . Mr Pound writes in a
> free form of verse that will not, I hope, lead him into the wastes.
> He is working towards a form that other English poets might
> study.

The Hulme group was certainly interested in the kind of metrical experiments Ezra was making, as yet very tentatively, in his poems. Flint afterwards recalled how, in their dissatisfaction with the poetry that was then being generally written in England, they 'proposed at various times to replace it by pure *vers libre*; by the Japanese *tanka* and *haikai*; we all wrote dozens of the latter as an amusement'. Hulme as 'ringleader' insisted on 'absolutely accurate presentation and no verbiage'. There was also much talk about 'French theory' – the experiments in free verse of the Symbolists, Mallarmé, Rimbaud and Verlaine chief among them. During all this, says Flint, Ezra 'listened' but 'could not be made to believe that there was any French poetry after Ronsard. He was full of his troubadours but I do not remember that he did more than attempt to illustrate (or refute) our theories occasionally with their example.'

Ezra's comparative non-participation was largely due to his dislike of other people's enthusiasms. He had not discovered the Symbolists for himself, and consequently he was in no hurry to allow their importance. He was also a bad conversationalist. 'If there IZ anything qui ne m'interesse pas,' he wrote in 1935, 'c'est de la CONversation. especially yawpin' 'bout licherchoor.' He could be a consummate verbal performer if he had the chance to construct his aphorisms in advance, or was allowed to pursue paths he knew well already, but throughout his life he was unable to respond quick-wittedly to unexpected verbal challenges. Letters were his preferred means of communication. When in the company of others, he had to have free rein to say everything he wanted, in his own time, or he could contribute next to nothing to the proceedings.

So he brought comparatively little to the Hulme group, and for the moment learnt almost nothing from it that advanced his poetry. He did not even enjoy himself very much at the Tour Eiffel on Thursday nights; two years later he called the weekly gatherings 'dull enough at the time, but rather pleasant to look back upon'. However, he found among Hulme's friends an audience that would listen to his recitations, and he began to realize the value of such coteries as a way of trying out and advancing one's work. 'If young men funk that sort of thing,' he said to an apprentice poet thirty years later, 'I don't see what resonance they can expect; it is sting without sounding board.'

*

The success of 'Sestina: Altaforte' spurred him to write something else in a popular idiom. He told his father in the third week of April 1909, just after he had been introduced to the Hulme group: 'I have this morning written a Ballad of Simon Zelotes, which is probably the strongest thing in english since "Reading Gaol". and a thing that any one can understand.' The poem was called 'Ballad of the Goodly Fere', and four years later Ezra described its beginnings:

> I had been the evening before in the 'Turkish Coffee' café in Soho. I had been made very angry by a certain sort of cheap irreverence which was new to me. I had lain awake most of the night. I got up rather late in the morning and started for the Museum with the first four lines in my head . . .
>
>> Ha' we lost the goodliest fere o' all
>> For the priests and the gallows tree?
>> Aye lover he was of brawny men,
>> O' ships and the open sea.

The speaker is Simon the Zealot, and he is talking of Jesus. Ezra continues the reminiscence:

> I wrote the rest of the poem at a sitting, on the left side of the reading-room, with scarcely any erasures. I lunched at the Vienna Café, and later in the afternoon, being unable to study, I peddled the poem about Fleet Street, for I began to realize that for the first time in my life I had written something that 'everyone could understand', and I wanted it to go to the people.
>
> The poem was not accepted. I think the *Evening Standard* was the only office where it was even considered. Mr Ford Madox Hueffer first printed the poem in his review some three months afterwards.

'Fere' means mate or companion, and the poem portrays Christ as a ballad hero, a lover of 'brawny men', 'the open sea', and 'good red wine', who curses his captors: 'I'll see ye damned!' Like 'Sestina: Altaforte' it is an exercise in the expression of masculinity, superficially convincing, but under close examination a pastiche of the Chesterton or even Newbolt–Masefield manner. Fleet Street rejected it because its portrait of Jesus seemed too daring. Later, T. S. Eliot disliked it heartily (and excluded it from his 1928 selection of Ezra's poems for Faber and Gwyer) on different grounds. Eliot would only say that it 'has a much greater popularity than it deserves', but he must have found the Christ in it thoroughly antipathetic to his own religious feelings. Perhaps he was also made uneasy by the faintly homosexual overtones.

It is striking that Ezra wrote it after being shocked by somebody's irreverence. He had not really moved very far away from his Presbyterian upbringing. During this part of his life he had ambiguous feelings towards Christianity; he said he objected to what he called the 'British Empire' aspect of it, but he distinguished modern religion from the teachings of

Christ himself, of whom he approved for not speaking against the pagan gods.

'Ballad of the Goodly Fere' was published by Ford Madox Hueffer in the *English Review* in October 1909, and it caused a stir that delighted Ezra. 'The Simon Zelotes ballad,' he told his father, 'seems to have moved things. Letters complimentary from one of the cabinet . . . & about 150 subscriptions stopped by the horrified.' He told his father to offer it to American periodicals; Homer was to say that the 'American serial rights were available. It occurred to Ezra that he could 'become popular by doing Ballades of Goodly Peter, Paul, John, Judas Iscariot Masefield, etc.'

*

'I shall not go to Venice,' he told his father at the end of April 1909, contemplating his summer plans. 'The London game seems to have too many chances in it to risk missing them by absence.' He said he knew there were more 'unhatched eggs' of reviews of *Personae* on the way. Moreover, 'Yeats has at last arrived and I had about five hours of him yesterday.'

It was Olivia and Dorothy Shakespear who took him to Yeats's London lodgings at 18 Woburn Buildings, where Yeats held regular Monday evening salons for his admirers and literary friends. In Canto 82 Ezra describes one of the admirers, F. W. Tancred of the Hulme group, asking Yeats in absurdly respectful tones if he 'would read us one of your own choice / and / perfect / lyrics'. Ezra could scarcely hope to progress as yet beyond this outer circle of acolytes, but Yeats took notice of him from the outset, and only a week after their first meeting wrote him this note:

> Dear Mr Pound
>   Can you come & see me on Monday evening next? I expect
> Antonio Cipicco an italian poet of note, & Florence Farr with a
> Psaltery & some other friends. I have to thank you for a kind
> thought about Italy & will do so when we meet.
>   Yr ev
>   W. B. Yeats

Ezra was soon lecturing his parents on which of Yeats's works to read: ' "The Wind among the reeds" "Red Hanrahans song for Ireland" & one or two of the short lyrics in some of the other collections.' He reported that Yeats seemed 'inclined to be decent to me', and as he is 'the greatest poet of our time I thought you might like the autograph'. He enclosed it for his parents.

*

He decided to move out of central London for the summer, into the suburb of Hammersmith, 'where a friend will lend me a garden & a hammock'. He told Homer not to 'send me more than $20 at a time. and I am going to try to draw not more than $250 between now & a year from now.' But when Homer misunderstood, and said he would send $10 rather than $20 as the next payment, Ezra wrote back: 'Please, what am I to eat?'

The garden and hammock were at 10 Rowan Road, off Brook Green in Hammersmith. Possibly Ford Madox Hueffer had something to do with the arrangement, for his mother lived in the neighbourhood. The room cost only 3s 6d a week, and the surroundings were pleasant, although Ezra had to pay bus fares to and from the British Museum which 'destroyed profit'. However, he was now earning a little money: 'Eng. Rev. sends £3 for the Sestina. so if Dad only sent $10 on June 15 it will be OK,' he told Isabel. He began to spend Sunday evenings at Eldon Road in Kensington at the home of Victor Plarr, Librarian of King's College, London, a minor 1890s poet and member of the Rhymers' Club. He went there largely to hear Plarr's anecdotes of such Decadents as Ernest Dowson and Lionel Johnson; there is a vignette of this in *Hugh Selwyn Mauberley* (1920), where Plarr appears as 'Monsieur Verog . . . last scion of the / Senatorial families of Strasbourg' (Plarr was born near Strasbourg):

> For two hours he talked . . .
> Of Dowson; of the Rhymers' Club;
> Told me how Johnson (Lionel) died
> By falling from a high stool in a pub . . .

Plarr was not an appealing character – cynical and uncommunicative, with a smoker's cough and the habit of borrowing money from juniors at work. Ezra did not especially care for him, describing him in a 1911 letter as 'that dignified official'; but he valued him for antiquarian reasons, and found Plarr's isolation from the literary world ('Detached from his contemporaries, / Neglected by the young') rather admirable.

He was grateful for what Plarr could tell him about previous generations of poets, just as he had appreciated Elkin Mathews's stories about Swinburne. 'I have enjoyed meeting Victorians and Pre-Raphaelites and men of the nineties through their friends,' he wrote in 1913. 'I have seen Keats' proof-sheets. I have had personal tradition of his time at second-hand. This, perhaps, means little to a Londoner, but it is good fun if you have grown up regarding such things as about as distant as Ghengis Khan or the days of Lope de Vega.' Ezra's rebelliousness never took the form of rejecting the work of earlier generations *in toto*. Quite apart from his admiration for nineteenth-century figures such as Browning and Swinburne for what they had achieved as poets, he was attracted, with the mind of a random collector rather than a literary historian, to the slightly *outré* details of celebrated lives that Plarr delighted in providing: the sort of details that would eventually build up the texture of the Cantos.

*

His London life began to develop a pattern. 'Victor Plarr . . . Sunday supper-&-evenings. Yeats. Monday evenings, & . . . a set of new Rhymers gang [the Hulme group] on Thursdays.' Reviews of *Personae* continued to appear; Edward Thomas, then a writer of miscellaneous prose and not yet a poet, discussed it in the *Daily Chronicle* on 7 June, praising it at length and observing that Pound 'is only just getting under sail, that he will reach we know not where'. Thomas followed this with a much longer piece in Ford Madox Hueffer's *English Review* the same month, in which he called the book 'admirable'. Other reviews appeared during the summer; Rupert Brooke, a latecomer in the December *Cambridge Review*, expressed himself irritated by Ezra's 'foolish archaisms' but thought he had 'great talents' and might one day be 'a great poet'. And in July the *Bookman* printed a gossipy little paragraph about Ezra, complete with studio photograph by Elliott & Fry of Baker Street, in which, with hair swept back over his still beardless profile, he looked very much the American student, younger than his twenty-three years. He told the reporter he had 'a very much greater liking for the English people than for their climate', and that thanks to a 'faculty of self-criticism' he had 'burned two novels and three hundred sonnets'. The *Bookman* remarked that *Personae* had 'met with an unusually appreciative reception'.

But the prime accolade, the recognition that the young Philadelphian who had arrived in London as a complete unknown less than eleven months earlier was now a public figure, came in a paragraph in the 23 June 1909 issue of *Punch*, which announced that 'Mr Welkin Mark (exactly opposite Long Jane's)' (that is, Elkin Mathews, opposite John Lane's)

> begs to announce that he has secured for the English market the palpitating works of the new Montana (U.S.A.) poet, Mr Ezekiel Ton, who is the most remarkable thing in poetry since Robert Browning. Mr Ton, who has left America to reside for a while in London and impress his personality on English editors, publishers and readers, is by far the newest poet going, whatever other advertisements may say. He has succeeded, where all others have failed, in evolving a blend of the imagery of the unfettered West, the vocabulary of Wardour Street, and the sinister abandon of Borgiac Italy.

Ezra wrote to his mother: 'London has finally offered to me its ultimate laurel . . . "Punch" has taken cognizance of my existence.' And to William Carlos Williams: 'I am, after eight years' hammering against impenetrable adamant, become suddenly somewhat some of a success.' He delivered some sharp reproofs against Williams's own *Poems* (1909) which Williams had sent him: 'Your book would not even attract passing attention here . . . You are out of touch . . . And remember a man's real work is *what he is going to do*, not what is behind him.'

5

Ezra! Ezra!

The pages in Dorothy Shakespear's notebook were still being filled with meditations about him:

> 2 June 1909
> It is not friendship & love that I am wanting – it is that something beyond the horizon . . .

> 10 July
> Ezra called me a name that made me smile for joy – 'You are Triste, Little Brother?' he asked three days ago. And again yesterday he said 'Little Brother' – and it touches & shows me that I have something after all, hidden though it be, where my soul was – once.

By now Ezra was not unaware of Dorothy's interest in him. It was still Olivia whose company he sought principally, but he could not be unresponsive to the daughter's silent but obvious adoration. During July he wrote her a poem, addressing her as 'White Poppy, heavy with dreams' and telling her 'I am come for peace, yea from the hunting / Am I come to thee for peace.' She copied it into her notebook, though she did not know what it meant. Ezra meanwhile received from his mother 'certain commendations of matrimony   a state which I should find highly impractical at the moment.'

The popular success of *Personae* meant nothing in financial terms – Elkin Mathews never cleared the expenses of printing the book, nor did Ezra receive a farthing from it – but Mathews expressed himself willing to consider another collection of poems in the autumn, and Ezra treated his own continuing penury as material for a romp in the style of Burns, written for the Thursday evening Hulme group:

... My name but mocks the guinea stamp,
And Pound's dead broke for a' that.

Although my linen still is clean,
My socks fine silk and a' that,
Although I dine and drink good wine –
Say, twice a week, and a' that ...

Ye see this birkie ca'ed a bard,
Wi' cryptic eyes and a' that,
Aesthetic phrases by the yard;
It's but E.P. for a' that.

In fact cash was not in particularly short supply. The printing of the 'Ballad of the Goodly Fere' and two other poems in the *English Review* in October 1909 brought him enough money to order a £5 suit, and the dollars from Homer continued to trickle in. Though in the Burns poem he vowed to 'stick to rhyme for a' that', privately he continued in his attempts to get an income from prose, and wrote 'an interminable beginning of a novel', telling May Sinclair that he had abandoned it because 'I am man and mortal, the feminine power of endurance is beyond me.' Fifty years later he recalled that the novel had been 'damn bad ... based more or less on experience ... I wrote myself into a state of exhaustion doing five chapters at one sitting, arose the next day, filled reams and then stuck.' He burnt the manuscript.

His mother sent the suggestion that he should write a verse epic about the Wild West. Ezra answered: 'My Gawd!! What has the west done to deserve it.' Seriously, he told her, an epic required a 'beautiful tradition' with a firm, narrative outline (such as the *Odyssey*); also a hero and 'a dam long time for the story to lose its gharish detail & get encrusted with a bunch of beautiful lies'. Contemporary subjects were therefore out of the question, and the USA could not produce an epic until it engendered a hero on the Don Quixote scale. He went on:

> The american who has any suspicion that he may write poetry. will walk very much alone. with his eyes on the beauty of the past of the old world, or on the glory of a spiritual kingdom, or on some earthly new Jerusalem, & which might as well be upon Mr Shackleton's antarctic ice fields as in Omaha for all the West has to do with it ... Epic of the West. it is [as] if I asked some one to write my biography. – it is more as if I had asked them to do it 12 years ago. It is truly American –, a promoters scheme.

His mother had suggested that a Western epic would make him famous throughout America, but he scorned that goal. If he genuinely achieved something in poetry 'america would never realy find it out. They'd hear a lecture about it. & swallow somebody elses opinion. & persist in their ignorance of the original.' What he valued was 'praise from Yeats, or appreciation from a circle that have listened to Swinburne reading his own verse'. By comparison, celebrity in America would be like making one's name manufacturing Beecham's Pills.

One evening in September he went to dine at the Square Club, a literary gathering founded by Chesterton and including such solid figures as Masefield and Galsworthy, though younger men went there too. At the club, Ezra met Edward Thomas, whom he described to his father as one of 'the fellows who have reviewed me to advantage'. But now Thomas had changed his mind; almost as soon as he sent off his two reviews of *Personae* he suffered a violent reversal of opinion. 'Oh I do humble myself over Ezra Pound,' he wrote to a friend on 12 June. 'He is not & cannot ever be very good. Certainly he is not what I mesmerized myself – out of pure love of praising the new poetry! – into saying he was & I am very much ashamed & only hope I shall never meet the man.' Possibly the Square Club itself was responsible for the change of opinion. Edgar Jepson, another member, recalled 'the pale, shocked, contorted glances of the poet-makers' after Thomas had dared print his praise of the *arriviste* young American. 'How could he have liked the verse of a man whom none of them had discovered, much less made!' However, talking to Walter de la Mare, Thomas made no mention of the opinion of the club; he said he had simply been seduced by Pound's verbal pyrotechnics into believing, erroneously, that this was the new poetry for which many of his generation were waiting.

*

During the summer the London Polytechnic told Ezra they would like him to give a full course on Romance literature in the coming lecture season. 'I am to give 21 be d——d lectures for the Polytec. & I wish I wuz ded.' However, Ernest Rhys managed to persuade J. M. Dent to print the lectures as a book. The subject, Ezra told his mother, would be 'Short history of everything from the beginning of creation until day after yesterday next, or some such.'

The contract with Dent (who proved to be 'an interesting old scoundrel') was actually for a study of medieval southern European literature up to Lope de Vega, and Ezra asked his father to send over the books he needed. To his mother he grumbled about all the work that would be involved: 'You know I have never made any pretense of loving labour or believing in its dignity. I never voluntarily do anything but write lyrics & talk to my friends.' He admitted that he might quite enjoy composing music, 'if I were not tone deaf', or painting or sculpture 'if I were not so damned clumsy'. As it was, he tried to participate in these arts 'by proxy & stimulation'. Nothing else was of the slightest interest to him.

He worked very fast at the book-cum-lectures, and had reached the end of the third chapter by early September. Olivia Shakespear 'has angelicaly offered to do emanuensis work,' he told Homer, but it was still dreadfully hard going. He wanted it all to be 'diabolically clever' and to 'cauterize' the German scholars, but at the same time it must seem 'careless'. Also he needed to develop 'a prose style as concise as Stevenson's', which would be a challenge, since he knew that up to now he had had 'absolutely no prose style at all. or a d—— bad one which is worse'.

Although his letters were, in their eccentric way, small masterpieces of allusive, colloquial prose, formal writing was a different matter. So far, his few published prose pieces had been in the Pre-Raphaelite manner, only suitable for churning out (as he put it in the pseudo-Burns poem) 'Aesthetic phrases by the yard'. He would have to find something better for *The Spirit of Romance*, as the book was to be called. Part of the trouble was that he had such a poor opinion of prose as a means of communication. 'I should never think of prose as anything but stop-gap,' he told his mother. 'If anything is not sufficiently interesting to be put into poetry . . . it is hardly worth saying at all.'

His lack of pleasure in reading novels, and his ignorance (at this period) of most fiction apart from Henry James, deprived him of models. Yet he could be almost as good a judge and editor of other people's prose as of their verse. Certainly he had a keen ear for prose rhythm. What concerned him in his own prose – at least in the early years, when he cared about it – was his lack of ability to explicate. By nature he always went at a subject sideways or upside down, assuming that the reader already shared his own knowledge of it and wanted observations and aphorisms rather than explanation. Indeed his prose was often not prose at all. For example a 1928 article on Guido Cavalcanti makes minimal sense if read for information, but if broken up into lines becomes almost plausible as poetry:

> It is not maiming, it is not curtailment.
> The senses at first seem to project for a few yards beyond the
> > body,
> Effect of a decent climate where a man leaves his nerve-set
> > open . . .

The Spirit of Romance does not suffer from this failure to explicate anything like as markedly as do his later prose writings. There are passages in the book – for example his description of Dante's life – which are lucid and conventional narrative, though they lack the true Ezra fire and are merely lecture-room stuff. However, the preface to the book is typical of him, both in its dismissive attitude to conventional scholarship and as a statement of his own attitude to the literature of past eras, and for these reasons it is well worth reading.

In it, he boldly condemns 'philology', this being his (incorrect) term for Germanic-style nineteenth-century literary scholarship. He maintains that 'the poetry of a certain period' does not require a scientific approach if it is to be studied fruitfully, for to the truly imaginative mind

> all ages are contemporaneous. It is B.C., let us say, in Morocco. The Middle Ages are in Russia. The future stirs already in the minds of the few . . . The real time is independent of the apparent . . . many dead are our grandchildren's contemporaries, while many of our contemporaries have already been gathered into Abraham's bosom, or some more fitting receptacle.

This may be meaningless as an introduction to a literary history, but as a statement of values it anticipates the principles – inasmuch as there were any – on which the Cantos were written.

He goes on to explain that in *The Spirit of Romance* he has selected for discussion only such medieval works as 'still possess an interest other than archaeological', and has aimed at 'selection rather than . . . presentation of opinion' – that is, description rather than analysis or critical commentary. All his statements, he says, will be based on his personal reaction to the texts 'and not upon commentaries'. This was a lie. In his 1929 revision of the book he confessed that a passage comparing Gothic architecture to the writings of Apuleius was a 'mere parroting' of a passage in J. W. Mackail's *Latin Literature* (1895). 'I did not *know*; but I had to get through my introduction and . . . at the subject of the book I was trying to write.'

Much of *The Spirit of Romance* is, as he admitted in this revision, 'an aimless picking up of tidbits' not governed by any discernible plan. This is certainly true of his opening chapter on the 'Phantom Dawn' of the troubadour age, and of those on Arnaut Daniel, 'Proença' (the troubadours themselves), and 'Geste and Romance', all of which chiefly consist of his own translations from the writers mentioned; the chief attraction of the project at this stage seems to have been the chance to make these translations. They are not, however, very polished or accomplished, and were done in a hurry. He usually uses free verse without much internal rhythm, and frequently drops into prose. It is also evident that he cares little for some of the material he is describing – he admits to a lack of sympathy for the long medieval romances that form the subject of his fourth chapter – and the book only comes alive with the chapter 'Psychology and Troubadours', which was not in the original edition and was first given as a separate lecture in 1912. The chapter on Dante is particularly disappointing; on the *Divine Comedy* he can only offer a potted plot summary with some undergraduate-style comment: 'There is grim humor through these canti . . . It is possible that the figures in the *Purgatorio* are less vigorous than those in the *Inferno* . . .'

Yet even in the duller chapters of *The Spirit of Romance* his flashes of insight can be startling. For example, he observes of Lope de Vega: 'I think his thoughts outran even his pen's celerity, so that often he writes only their beginnings' (he is describing himself here); and the chapter on Villon is a vivid, energetic, lucid assessment and panegyric of its subject, the most readable and inspired part of the book.

*

He decided to move closer to central London. 'My adress hence forth is to be. 10 Church Walk. Kens. W. London. nearer town & with old Kensington church yard under my windows. also nearer most of my friends.' Church Walk is a quiet alley that meanders secretively between the beaten track of Kensington High Street and the parish church of St Mary Abbots, opening out into a pleasant courtyard at the end of which stands number ten, a modest three-storey corner house. It was the sort of spot, secluded and charming but very near the main arteries, that Ezra would afterwards choose to occupy in Paris, Rapallo, and Venice.

'Am luxuriating in a new sizable room,' he told Homer in August 1909, just after he had moved in. He was the tenant of a Mrs Langley and her husband, who rented him a bed-sitting room on the top floor for 8s a week, and provided meals at extra charge when he wanted them. He described the Langleys as 'positively the best England can produce at ANY level'. Sam Langley managed a branch of a chain grocery; his wife was 'a yeoman's darter from the farms to narth somewhere'. They kept a pair of hens in the tiny yard behind the house.

Ezra's new home was a moment's stroll from the Underground railway station, handy for shops and cafés and the Kensington public library. The only snag was the noise of the bells of St Mary Abbots, which he found infuriating. He protested to the vicar, a Mr Pennefeather, telling him that the ringers (a crack team) were a 'foul nuisance'. It was said, indeed, that he wrote a letter of complaint in Latin, and that it was prominently displayed in the vestry. His campaign had no effect except on himself: he developed a violent prejudice against 'campanolatry', asserting that 'the act of bell-ringing is symbolical of all proselytizing religions. It implies the pointless interference with the quiet of other people.' In *Guide to Kulchur* he seriously asserts that the nuisance of the bells contributed to the destruction of his sympathies with religion:

> Questionings aroused by the truly filthy racket imposed on denizens of Kensington, W.8. by a particular parson. It appeared to me impossible that any clean form of teaching cd. lead a man, or group, to cause that damnable and hideous noise and inflict it on helpless humanity in the vicinage . . . Vigorous anticlerical phase ensued.

Certainly he had turned anti-church by February 1910, a few months after moving into Church Walk. 'When I go to church I usualy wish I hadn't,' he told his mother. 'The carols I heard on Xmas were disgusting profanity and the trial of [being] "preached to death by wild curates" does not appeal. The catholics are no better as they dont stick to their ritual but try to talk. I shall wait until I find myself in some southern climate. where they understand religion.'

Apart from the bells, Church Walk was ideal. Mrs Langley's meals proved edible – which Ezra found 'remarkable for a british female' – though in any case he now received frequent dinner invitations. His room was small but pleasantly furnished, with 'a very nice mahogany wash stand that folded down to look like a desk'. Admittedly there was 'no h & c'; Ford Madox Hueffer remembered coming to the room and finding Ezra 'in tub' – a tin bath filled with cans of hot water from the kitchen below – and the only lavatory was situated in the yard near the hen coop. Richard Aldington noticed that the house was pervaded by 'an extraordinary odour . . . imperfect drainage, a slight escape of gas, years of insufficient cleaning . . . and the memory of unnumerable meals'. But Ezra was perfectly content: 'I find a bath can be dispensed with PROVIDED one have a geyser that will make the liquid for dumpable detached bath really hot. Whereas the damp coolish hot bath of a boarding house is disgusting.'

He liked to get up late in the morning and begin work slowly, unless he was in one of the bursts of furious activity in which his writing was sometimes produced. In his younger days he usually felt that the morning 'should be devoted to that deep & profound form of meditation which the vulgar have termed "sleep"'. He admitted that he had been glad to 'rapturously scribble' in the early morning in America and Venice, but in London 'it is impossible because there is no sun to rise'. Once awake he would begin the day with a ritual of coffee-making, using powdered Dutch coffee and a home-made filter (a piece of cloth stretched over the cup) through which he would pour the water carefully drop by drop. Then came his toilet. Richard Aldington, who observed this ritual once or twice when living nearby, describes it in his novel *Death of a Hero* (1929), where Ezra appears as the painter, Mr Upjohn:

> He washed and rinsed his face thoroughly, brushed his teeth until [one] apprehended lest the bristles be worn to the bone, gargled and spat freely. He soaped and pumiced his hands, which were large, yellow, and slightly spatulate; and excavated his nails with singular industry and pertinacity. He then . . . combed and brushed and re-brushed and re-combed his coarse hay-like hair until it crackled with induced electricity . . . He arrayed himself in a clean collar, a tie of remarkable lustre and

size, and a narrow-waisted rather long coat . . . This singular
scene, which occupied the best part of an hour, was conducted . . . with great gravity, varied by the emission of a singular
and discordant chant or hum, and wild petulant oaths whenever
any object of the toilet or of his apparel did not instantly
present itself to his hand.

The 'chant or hum' was also emitted when he was composing poetry. It
was as if he had a perpetual tune or rhythm in his head; perhaps it was the
interruption of this that made him so angry with the church bells.

The elaborate preparations when dressing were partly on account of his
fastidious nature (some years later Yeats remarked on his 'dread of
infections'), but they also had something about them of an actor dressing
and making up for a character role. When he was not venturing into the
public eye he took much less trouble. 'I did think of shaving but decided
against it,' he told his mother one day when he had no engagements.
'Beauty lies in the eye of the beholder & I shall not go forth to get beheld.'

He possessed 'two remnants of suits in which I do not venture out.
except in the immediate neighbourhood for morning errands', there was
also a rather elderly dinner jacket (he had just stopped saying 'tux' or
'tuxedo') in which he often chose to lecture at the Polytechnic, hoping to
give the occasion even more tone. And there was the new suit, purchased
with the £5 earned from the 'Ballad of the Goodly Fere'. Ezra told his
mother on 4 November: 'The Zelotes suit of clothes is a success.' It was not
a suit in the conventional sense, but the characteristic 'poet's outfit' in
which he now took care to be seen.

It consisted of a shirt (preferably of a striking colour) worn with its very
large collar half open and a broad tie knotted loosely as if it were a cravat.
Spats were added over the shoes, and the whole was topped with a velvet
jacket, or sometimes with a grey overcoat whose buttons had been replaced
by squares of lapis lazuli. When he required glasses (as he still did for
reading) he now used a pair of pince-nez. Most significant of all, he
abandoned his clean-shaven features for a thin moustache, swept outwards,
and a small goatee beard.

Gone was the rather juvenile-looking American (he was now twenty-
four); the image became that of the classic Bohemian, the popular idea of
the Artist. There were daily variations: sometimes he would wear a
sombrero ('my luxurious hat'); another time the tie might be discarded for
a black satin stock purloined from the wardrobe of his great-grandfather;
or there might be 'a dark blue cotton shirt . . . and a Panama hat'. Out of
doors an ebony cane was added; he wielded it with some flourish, so that
he passed down the street with a 'perpetual air of majestic flowing and
billowing'.

The costume was modelled on that of Whistler, who had worn similar clothes thirty years earlier. Ezra's appearance also had Biblical overtones, which did not escape his friends. When the photographer Alvin Langdon Coburn took some portraits of Ezra at his Church Walk digs arrayed in a dressing-gown (Ezra alleged that he was recovering from an attack of jaundice, but the garment probably appealed for its own sake), Mrs Langley observed of the results: 'I hope you won't be offended, sir, but it is rather like the good man of Nazareth.' A friend similarly suggested that 'Leonardo da Vinci might have used him equally well as a model for a cynical Christ with his eyes open; or for a spiritual and not wholly covetous Judas.' And Frederic Manning remarked that Ezra was becoming 'more like Kh-r-ist and the late James McNeill Whistler every year'.

Once toilet and costume were complete, Ezra would saunter out into Kensington. Years later he wrote affectionately of 'the pale grey light in Kensington Gardens, and the gulls floatin' over the round pond, and the so very quiet demeanour of the nicely dressed females that used to float up the broadwalk'. For a light luncheon he would step up to Holland Street, where Miss Ella Abbott, an exile from the Middle West of America, kept a tea-shop. Ezra describes how she 'wanted to feed only artists . . . at 1/3 per scrambled eggs on one slice of toast'. She became a great admirer of his, buying his books for Christmas presents and taking out subscriptions to magazines that printed his work. There were plenty of other customers to her taste, for at this period Kensington was, as Ezra put it, 'SWARming' with artistic types. Ford Madox Hueffer described the district as 'a high class Greenwich Village, with the difference that its denizens were expected to be 'wealthy, refined, delicate and well-born'.

Ford himself could be found virtually in residence just round the corner from Miss Abbott's tea-shop, though not at his own house, for 80 Campden Hill was the home of a Mrs Hunt, widow of the Pre-Raphaelite painter Alfred William Hunt, and South Lodge, as the villa was somewhat grandiosely named, also housed her daughter Violet, with whom Ford was having an affair.

Violet Hunt, eleven years older than Ford, wrote bad romantic novels with such titles as *The Maiden's Progress*. They were widely gossiped about as *romans à clef*, for as Douglas Goldring (Ford's editorial assistant on the *English Review*) remarked, Violet had already 'wept copiously on several famous shoulders'. H. G. Wells was among Ford's predecessors in her bed; Wells smugly described their affair as a series of mutually gratifying embraces which caused no 'disturbance of our literary work'. Violet created far more trouble for poor Ford; she is the original of the tormenting *femme fatale*, Sylvia, in his *Parade's End*.

She had met Ford years earlier, but paid no attention to him until he printed a short story by her in an early number of the *English Review*, whereupon his life was swiftly taken over, and he found himself living at South Lodge. Ford had a wife who refused to divorce him, so he tried to carry on as if his marriage did not exist. Miss Hunt was by no means to the liking of all his friends; even as a girl she had been known as 'Immodest Violet', and now several of his social circle melted away. He and Violet consequently set out to create a new clique for themselves, and Ezra, arriving in Kensington just at this moment, eagerly appointed himself a principal figure in it.

During his days above the fishmonger, Ford had not managed to control Ezra, even supposing that he wanted to. 'To the right of me,' he writes of that era,

> lived a most beautiful lady . . . Almost as soon as I stood on my doorstep Fate would send that Beautiful Lady bearing down on me. At the same moment from the left Ezra would bear down. Ezra had a forked red beard, luxuriant chestnut hair . . . He wore a purple hat, a green shirt, a black velvet jacket, vermilion socks, openwork, brilliant tanned sandals, trousers of green billiard cloth, in addition to an immense flowing tie that had been hand-painted by a Japanese Futurist poet.
>
> So, with the Beautiful Lady on my left and Ezra on my right, Ezra scowling at the world and making at it fencer's passes with his cane, we would proceed up Holland Park Avenue . . .

There was even less escape at South Lodge; Ezra would come up the hill from Church Walk at the faintest suggestion of an invitation. On a typical afternoon he reports that Ford and Violet 'have just come into the "Pyatzaa"' (the courtyard at Church Walk) 'and summoned me to tea. And I've already had 5 cups of my own. Natheless I think I will go up.' Another day he was off to 'Violet Hunt's garden party'. (He warned his mother that Violet's fiction was 'full of horrors — you'd better leave it alone'.) Things took a little time to warm up; in November 1909 he was still writing to Ford as 'Dear Mr Hueffer' but four months later was regularly going for walks with him. 'In a very short time,' writes Ford, 'he had taken charge of me.'

At first, Douglas Goldring of the *English Review* was a little suspicious of Ezra:

> He struck me as a bit of a charlatan, and I disliked the showy blue glass buttons on his coat; indeed, his whole operatic outfit of 'stage poet', stemming from Mürger [author of the book on which *La Bohème* was based] and Puccini . . . I failed to appreciate Ezra's cosmopolitan Yankee Muse, and thought much of his verse pretentious. But one day I happened to see

round Ezra's pince-nez, and noticed that he had curiously kind, affectionate eyes. This chance discovery affected my whole conception of him. Perhaps it reveals part of the secret of his hold over Ford.

Goldring felt it was Ezra far more than Ford himself who brought about 'the transformation of South Lodge from a rather stuffy and conventional Campden Hill villa, into a stamping ground for *les jeunes*'. Goldring continues:

> He not only subjugated Ford by his American exuberance, but quickly established himself at South Lodge as a kind of social master of ceremonies. Opposite the house there was a communal garden containing tennis courts, which the Hunts and other local residents were accustomed to hire for their annual garden parties. Ezra immediately grasped its possibilities and having a liking for tennis . . . insisted that the tennis courts should be made available. Ford and Violet, both of whom adored every form of entertaining and loved to be surrounded by crowds of friends, were delighted. The garden was taken over and every afternoon a motley collection of people, in the oddest costumes, invaded it at Ezra's instigation, and afterwards repaired to South Lodge . . . to discuss *vers libre*, the prosody of Arnaut Daniel and, as Ford records, 'the villainy of contributors to the front page of *The Times Literary Supplement*'.

Tennis games between Ezra and Ford were a very curious affair. Brigit Patmore, another of the South Lodge circle, describes how the two looked 'readier to spring at each other's throats than the ball . . . It seemed to matter little how often they served fault after fault. They just went on till the ball was where they wanted, then one or other cried "game" or "Hard luck", "My set" or "That's love-all" or "Six sets to one!" It was beyond anyone to umpire or score.' Violet Hunt recalls Ezra 'sitting down composedly in his square and jumping up in time to receive his adversary's ball . . . the flaps of his polychrome shirt flying out like the petals of some flower', and Ford himself remarked that a game of tennis against Ezra was 'like playing against an inebriated kangaroo'. Another South Lodge regular, Kathleen Cannell, adds that 'Violet Hunt had a parrot that screamed "Ezra! Ezra!" when we came in from tennis.' (They had all carefully coached it.)

Indoors at South Lodge, Ezra would never sit still, and was always 'jumping and twisting' in his chair with a 'backward jerk of the head, as he emphasized each point'. This naturally 'endangered every chair he sat on', and Violet was furious when one day he tipped a delicate cane and gilt affair back on its legs and broke it. Thereafter, she and Ford carefully provided him with one from the kitchen. (He did similar damage to a chair of Gertrude Stein's about a dozen years later.) When talking, says one of his acquaintances of this period, he had 'a most irritating staccato voice, and a short unnecessary cough which he wielded like a weapon'; 'a slight cough', says another, 'which came between every other word'. Brigit Patmore describes his habit of 'half swallowing short sentences or speaking through closed teeth', which made him 'almost unintelligible' until one got used to it. Some, Ford among them, claimed to find him even less comprehensible because of his Philadelphia accent, though Brigit Patmore thought he had 'no American accent – or just the slightest'. At her first meeting with Ezra, Dorothy Shakespear had thought the accent 'odd . . . half American, half Irish'.

Soon after his irruption into the Hunt–Ford household, he acquired an extra item of costume which caused some talk. He had been at the Shakespears' one day when the veteran Decadent poet Arthur Symons called, accompanied by his American friend Alice Tobin. Symons presented Olivia with a single red rose, and Tobin, not to be outdone, plucked from her ear a turquoise earring and gave it to Ezra. For some months he wore it in public, feeling that it gave the final Whistlerian touch. Edgar Jepson describes him turning up at the ultra-conservative Square Club wearing 'a velvet coat and one turquoise ear-ring'.

*

In mid-November 1909 Violet Hunt gave an At Home at the Reform Club. Ezra was there, and so was a young schoolmaster from Croydon, David Herbert Lawrence, whose poems Ford was publishing in the *English Review*. He was introduced to Ezra. 'He is 24, like me,' Lawrence wrote a day or two later, 'but his god is beauty, mine life. He is jolly nice: took me to supper at Pagani's, and afterwards we went down to his room at Kensington. He lives in an attic, like a traditional poet, but the attic is a comfortable well furnished one . . . He is rather remarkable, a good bit of a genius, & with not the least self-consciousness. This afternoon I am going to tea with him & we are going out after to some friends . . . He knows W. B. Yeats & all the Swells.'

Ford had been anxious about meeting this 'discovery', whom he knew was the son of a Nottinghamshire miner – 'How exactly was I to approach him in conversation?' – and at a lunch given by Violet, Ezra deliberately made a nuisance of himself by asking Ford, in front of Lawrence, 'How would *you* speak to a working man?' Ezra was inclined to patronize Lawrence, 'but this was always a failure,' reports a mutual acquaintance, 'for Lawrence would seem quite unaware until the moment came when he could insert a neat and unexpected little barb into Ezra's ego'. The relationship was therefore an odd and uneasy one, but a friendship of sorts existed, at least for a few months. Ezra recalled Lawrence once missing the train to his home in Croydon and spending the night at 10 Church Walk on a 'sort of armchair convertible to cot'. When, years later, someone suggested he had disliked Lawrence, he replied that he had 'disagreed' with but 'never disliked' him.

After Lawrence's fiction began to be published, Ezra showed a predictable distaste for the emphasis on physical sexuality. 'Though I have often enjoyed him,' he wrote, two years after *Sons and Lovers* (1913) had come out, 'I do not want to write, even good stories, in a loaded ornate style, heavy with sex, fruity with a certain sort of emotion.' And elsewhere he suggested that acceptance of the Lawrentian world view would exclude 'an awful lot of FIRST cat/ values'. But Lawrence's poetry impressed him: 'I think he learned the proper treatment of modern subjects before I did.'

His behaviour at the lunch for Lawrence was typical of the way he drew attention to himself on such occasions. Ernest Rhys describes him at a supper party which included Lawrence, Ford and Yeats, who was holding forth at such length that Ezra

> may have felt he was not getting a fair share of the festivity. So . . . seeing the supper table dressed with red tulips in glasses, he presently took one of the flowers and proceeded to munch it up. As Yeats, absorbed in his monologue, did not notice this strange behaviour, and the rest of us were too well-bred to take any notice, Ezra, having found the tulip to his taste, did the same with a second flower.

Ezra labelled the story 'apocryphal' when it was repeated to him, adding: 'Ford – W.B.Y. NEVER at same dinner' (he always emphasized that they did not get on). Yet F. S. Flint, who was not given to exaggeration, said he had sat next to Ezra when it happened, and 'wondered whether tulips were poisonous and that would have been the end of him!' Moreover the Italian scholar Arundel del Re said he was there too, only in his version it was roses, not tulips, and Ezra himself was holding forth while munching the petals. After they had been consumed, Mrs Rhys 'turned to him and said: "Would you like another rose, Mr Pound?" '*

Whatever the origin of the tale, he liked to display a brash disregard for Hampstead and Kensington convention. At the dinner table of May Sinclair, who for all the mild feminism of her fiction kept a very Edwardian household, he could be seen (said Richard Aldington) 'alternately leaning

---

*Yeats did not claim to have seen it happen, but reported to Lady Gregory that 'Mrs Fowler & her sister . . . had asked him [Ezra] to dinner soon after he came from America & he had not been able to eat anything owing to his having "eaten the table-orniments before the dinner began".' (Letter of 21 April 1914; text kindly supplied by John Kelly.)

forward to spear potatoes with his fork from a dish in the middle of the table, and then lolling back to munch his capture'. This was partly sheer appetite: he relied on such occasions to make up for his rather meagre diet when not dining out. One evening at Miss Sinclair's he 'whistled downstairs to Nellie [the maid] and then yelled at her to bring him a second helping'. Nellie, who dominated the household, 'would *not*', and Miss Sinclair 'abided by Nellie's decision'.

The uncouth behaviour was also the result of his lack of social experience, and of any instinct as to how he was expected to conduct himself. Certainly his mother had coached him in mechanical pieces of courtesy; he wrote to her: 'Of course the term "social sense" can not be applied to anything I possess, but the substitute which serves me very well in place of it is presumably due to you.' But the standard of good manners that served in Wyncote did not take him far in the drawing rooms of Kensington or Hampstead in 1909, certainly not without that sensitivity to the feelings of others which might have made up the deficiency – a sensitivity that he entirely lacked. Like the hero of Wyndham Lewis's novel *Tarr* (1918) he 'had no social machinery at all at his disposal and was compelled to get along as well as he could with the cumbrous one of the intellect. With this he danced about it is true: but it was full of sinister piston-rods, organ-like shapes, heavy drills.'

*

A little verse was now going the rounds in London under the title 'The Virgin's Prayer':

> Ezra Pound
> And Augustus John
> Bless the bed
> That I lie on.

Ezra quoted it to Wyndham Lewis nine years later: 'Authorship unrecognized, I first heard it in 1909. It is emphatically NOT my own, I believe it to have come from an elder generation.' He said that nobody else had ever coupled his name with the sexually predatory and much gossiped about Augustus John. He made no comment on the rhyme's implications.

It is true that he was indulging in mild flirtations with the slightly 'fast' young ladies he met at South Lodge. There was Brigit Patmore, unhappily married to Coventry Patmore's grandson, herself beautiful and rich; Ezra called her 'charming'. Another member of the Ford–Violet Hunt circle, Phyllis Bottome, who had written a novel at the age of twenty-one, writes of Ezra: 'He introduced me to the first really good meal I ever tasted. He knew where the best things in London, gastronomic or artistic, were to be found . . . [He] gave me the first unbiased and objective literary criticism I had ever known.' She was a year older than him; possibly the relationship was intimate, since she also writes that 'the biology of sex was to the young Ezra a joyous discovery', but elsewhere she characterizes their friendship as one of her purely 'intellectual intimacies'.

There is some evidence that he had an affair with Ione de Forest, this being the stage name of a very young French dancer, Jeanne Heyse, also known as Joan Hayes, who was a member of the *New Freewoman* circle – Ezra soon became a contributor to that magazine. She is apparently the subject of his poem 'Dance Figure', written in 1912:

> Dark eyed,
> O woman of my dreams,
> Ivory sandaled,
> There is none like thee among the dancers,
> None with swift feet . . .

Ione de Forest committed suicide in August 1912 at her home in Chelsea, at the age of nineteen. Ezra refers to her in the poem 'Ione, Dead the Long Year:

> . . . Empty are the ways of this land
>   Where Ione
> Walked once, and now does not walk
> But seems like a person just gone.

She reappears in Canto 7:

>   Ione, dead the long year . . .
> But *is* she dead as Tyro? In seven years?

This was written seven years after Ione de Forest's death. Nothing more is known about her or what Ezra may have had to do with her.

By 1912 he had formulated a doctrine of sex as a Mystery or secret cult that revealed great truths to its enlightened practitioners. He was moving towards this idea – derived from the French Rosicrucian book on the troubadour 'secrets' he had reviewed in 1906 – during his first two years in London, and one day he worked himself round to divulging it to D. H. Lawrence. 'He discussed, with much pursing of lips and removing of frown-shaken eyeglasses,' writes Lawrence in a letter, 'his projection of writing an account of the mystic cult of love – the Dionysian rites, and so on – from earlier days to the present. The great difficulty was that no damned publisher in London dare publish it. It would have to be published in Paris.'

Richard Aldington believed Ezra to be a sexual *naïf* posing as a man of experience. In his short story 'Nobody's Baby' (1932), Aldington gives one of his wickedly funny portraits of Ezra in the character of Charlemagne

Cox, a mountebank musician from the USA who loves to talk about

the (alleged) extent of his conquests. Apparently it was impossible for any woman to resist a siege by Mr Cox . . . He was positively worn out by the pursuit of numerous wealthy and lovely females . . . Not that he didn't sometimes take pity on them . . . but he had his a't [art] to consider. A't must come first. So long as a woman was a stimulus to his a't, he didn't mind obliging – otherwise, he cut it out.

Aldington also describes Cox claiming that he has exceptional sexual potency, that he models his seductions on Stendhal's *De l'Amour*, and that because his infatuated women will not take precautions he is already the father of many illegitimate children. This, however, proves to be a complete *blague*, and it is implied that Cox is impotent.

Aldington meted out the same treatment to another of his fictional characters modelled on Ezra, Mr Upjohn in *Death of a Hero*, of whom he writes: 'While gallantly and probably necessarily discreet as to his conquests, he was always prepared to talk about love, and to give subtle erotic advice, which led any man who had actually lain with a woman to suspect that Mr Upjohn was at best a fumbler and probably still a virgin.'

*

'Yeats left this morning for Dublin,' Ezra wrote to his mother on New Year's Day 1910. 'He is the only living man whose work has anything more than a most temporary interest.' He was still considerably in awe of Yeats, to the extent that he could only gauge Yeats's opinion of him and his work through remarks that the great man made to other people. Ezra told Mary Moore that 'W.B.Y. says behind my back that I'm one of the few that count.' And to his mother in February 1910: 'It is rumored that Yeats intends to say something decent about me in one of his lectures next week. but as he has never been known to do anything he intended to, I shall take some stock in the rumor, after it has been verified by fact.' Sure enough, when it came to the lecture the remark was not made; but rumour continued benevolent. Ezra told Homer in March 1910 that the latest report was of Yeats saying something 'to the effect that "there is no younger generation (of poets). E.P. is a solitary volcano." "If he writes rhyme like an amateur he writes rhythm like a master." – Well he hasn't seen the later work where we begin to consider whether [it] will rhyme or not.' And just in case Homer felt like using these remarks for publicity, Ezra reminded him 'this is private conversation' and 'can not be used on reporters or publishers'.

Yeats had recently written to Lady Gregory:

This queer creature Ezra Pound . . . has become really a great authority on the troubadours, has I think got closer to the right sort of music for poetry than Mrs Emery [Florence Farr] – it is more definitely music with strongly marked time and yet it is effective speech. However he can't sing as he has no voice. It is like something on a very bad phonograph.

Ezra would have agreed with this last remark. 'I have the organ of a tree toad,' he once observed of his vocal cords to James Joyce, adding that this was fortunate, for if he had really been able to sing 'I shd. have warbled & done no bloomin' thing else'. William Carlos Williams thought Ezra's attempts to perform music were sheer conceit, part of his would-be omniscience in the arts. But the remark to Joyce suggests (and other things, such as the humming while he worked, confirm it) that he could not get music out of his head and wanted to sing in order to express it.

Florence Farr had developed a method of speaking Yeats's verse to music, accompanying herself on a psaltery made by Arnold Dolmetsch; Yeats found Ezra's attempts at chanting, crude as they were, more effective and less pretentious. But if he gave Yeats any ideas about the performance of poetry, Ezra learnt a great deal more here from Yeats than he taught the great man. Soon, he was reciting his own poetry in a highly stylized manner that was undoubtedly borrowed from Yeats's own distinctive chant – though Ezra does not seem to have been conscious of this himself. In 1938 he entertained Ronald Duncan by

> giving an imitation of Yeats reading his own poems. Then a few minutes later . . . he . . . began to read some of his own poems . . . in the extraordinary sing-song voice which he always affected whenever he read poetry. When he had finished reading, Rose Marie gaily congratulated him on his 'hilarious imitation of Yeats' . . . Her mistake was understandable: there was no difference in the style of the reading.

When Ezra first heard his own recorded voice he was startled by what he called the 'Irish brogue'.

*

'"Exultations" has gone to the printer,' he told his father in September 1909 announcing the imminence of his next collection of poems less than six months since *Personae* had been published. Meanwhile on Monday evenings at eight thirty he began to deliver the Polytechnic lectures that were to be published as *The Spirit of Romance*. Olivia and Dorothy Shakespear attended faithfully, but there were only about twenty in the audience on the first night (about half what Ezra had expected) and the numbers did not pick up. Dorothy afterwards recalled that the whole thing had been 'dismal': Ezra had totally failed to get through to his 'very small' audience and had overestimated their knowledge. Ezra himself admitted that the series had not 'caught hold'.

Exultations appeared on 25 October 1909, Elkin Mathews having had 1,000 sets of sheets printed, the same as for *Personae*. The book was dedicated to the Reverend Carlos Tracy Chester and, like *Personae*, consisted largely of reprints – thirteen of its twenty-seven poems came from *A Lume Spento* or *A Quinzaine for this Yule*. The new pieces included 'Sestina: Altaforte' and 'Ballad of the Goodly Fere', but the majority of them were dreary stuff, such as 'Sestina for Ysolt', 'Planh for the Young English King', the 'White Poppy' poem he had written for Dorothy, and the 'Alba' whose refrain ('Ah God! Ah God! That dawn should come so soon!') had made Ford chortle so much. However, there was one fine poem not published before, 'Piere Vidal Old', in which the speaker is a famous Provençal troubadour who is supposed to have 'run mad, as a wolf, because of his love for Loba of Panautier'. Vidal's first name is more usually spelt 'Peire' – Ezra himself gives it that way in *The Spirit of Romance*, published only a few months after *Exultations* – and the 'Piere' spelling in the title of the poem was probably an error: it is the sort of casual mistake found throughout his correspondence. He retained it for all later printings of the poem. This was typical: he would rarely change anything, however mistaken, once it had appeared in print. That something had been published seemed to give it an automatic authority for him.

Exultations shows how he was slipping into an 1890s languor in his poetry. The prevailing tone of the new pieces was distinctly Decadent:

> I am aweary with the utter and beautiful weariness
> And with the ultimate wisdom and with things terrene . . .

> I would that the cool waves might flow over my mind,
> And that the world should dry as a dead leaf . . .

> White Poppy, heavy with dreams,
> O White Poppy, who art wiser than love . . .
> I am come for peace, yea from the hunting . . .

T. S. Eliot, at this time studying at Harvard, was shown 'those little things of Elkin Mathews, *Exultations* and *Personae*' by an undergraduate friend, who told him: 'This is up your street, you ought to like this.' But, says Eliot, 'I didn't really. It seemed to me rather fancy old-fashioned romantic stuff, cloak-and-dagger kind of stuff. I wasn't very impressed by it.'

Reviews of *Exultations* were perceptibly more cautious than those of *Personae* had been. The 'Ballad of the Goodly Fere', about which Elkin

Mathews had been rather nervous, received enthusiastic notices, but in general the feeling was that 'if Mr Pound could only forget his literature' (his literary influences) 'he would exult to more purpose'. This was F. S. Flint writing in the *New Age*. Edward Thomas in the *Daily Chronicle* suggested that under the 'turbulent opacity of his peculiarities' there was 'very nearly nothing at all', and judged Pound's present state to be 'still interesting – perhaps promising – certainly distressing'. At Christmas 1909 Ezra reported to his father a 'colourless notice' in the *Observer*, but added: 'I am however past the point where the reviews make much difference.'

During November 1909 he went up to Lincolnshire with Frederic Manning, to stay with Arthur Galton, an unmarried high-church clergyman and belletrist with whom Manning shared a house. 'Galton is an old friend of Mathew Arnold,' Ezra told his father, '& has known about everyone since the flood.' He wrote enthusiastically of Manning's new poem 'Persephone' and quoted some to Homer; it was languid, Decadent stuff, but Ezra in his present mood loved it, just as he delighted in the Galton–Manning bachelor ménage with its bitchy gossip about ecclesiastical goings-on (Galton had spent a period as a Roman Catholic before being, exceptionally, readmitted into Anglican holy orders). Galton told Ezra how much he loved the 'Ballad of the Goodly Fere', while Manning wrote Ezra letters in a minute, delicate hand, beginning 'My dear Ezra' – an unusually intimate form of salutation in those days – and concluding 'yours always, Fred'.

Ezra told his parents he thought Manning a more interesting poet than William Carlos Williams. 'He is rather intelligent . . . We disagree upon most matters   are pretty well in accord in the belief that we are the genuinest or at least the only significant writers under thirty. In which faith we write parodies of each other. compose poems upon each others frailties & vanities, abuse each other in public with a violence which terrifies the bystanders. In fact our friendship is as firmly founded as could possibly be desired.' This was written in March 1910. Later he and Manning fell out – a letter from Manning in 1914 mentions 'a good deal of ill feeling' – though after Manning's death in 1935 Ezra spoke of friendship with him as having been the 'first licherary ComPanionship in Eng/ of Ez'.

*

Just before Christmas 1909 he asked his father to find out if he might qualify for a Rhodes Scholarship to Oxford to finish his doctorate – 'I could use £300 a year quite nicely.' He was making a little cash by giving literary classes for society ladies: 'I teach Mrs Fowler, Lady Antonia Maude, Mrs Baker & Mrs Bon. mostly read the *mss.* of the book [*The Spirit of Romance*] or translate from the Poema del Cid & other mediaeval stuff; for their delectation.' This proved 'lucrative', but he still depended chiefly on Homer for income: 'Please fire up again on March 1st unless you hear anything to the contrary. I don't think you will hear to the contrary.' And when March came he admitted that his financial state 'appears precarious'. Could he please have a further £4 in the middle of the month?

Homer and Isabel asked repeatedly when he would return home – it was now two years since they had seen him – and he supposed he had better apply for a job at the University of Pennsylvania 'or something of that sort'. The idea of living permanently in America 'is of course most revolting', but it might be useful to come back for a time and find 'an american publisher & certain american outlets for ones stuff'. He duly applied for a job at Penn, and also made enquiries at Princeton. Neither university wished to acquire his services. He next suggested that his mother might like to insert the following advertisement 'in some reputable daily':

POET
Out of a job.

Specialities: incisive speech, sarcasm, meditation, irony
(at special rates), ze grande manair (to order)
will do to travel, or stand unhitched while being fed.
Price £1 per hr. – special rates for steady consumers.

He finished writing *The Spirit of Romance* in mid-February 1910, saying he hoped never to have to do another book in prose, 'except perhaps for introductions to certain things' such as some of Lope's plays and *El Cid*, which he wanted to translate. 'My mind, such as I have, works by a sort of fusion, and sudden crystalization, and the effort to tie that kind of action to the dray work of prose is very exhausting. One should have a vegetable sort of mind for prose. I mean the thought formation should go on consecutively and gradualy, with order rather than epigrams.' It was an accurate summary of his limitations.

He applied for one more American job – a professorship at Hobart College, Geneva, NY – observing that the publication of *The Spirit of Romance* 'ought to make that sort of thing easier'. He decided to sail for the USA in June, whether or not he had found a job there. Meanwhile he would take the proofs of the book to Verona for Easter, where he would have 'sunlight and quiet for my final revision'. He chose Verona because it was 'perhaps the most beautiful city in north Italy. The church of San Zeno is the ultimate perfection.' Also Dante had written much of the *Divine Comedy* there. 'Ergo Verona.'

Before Ezra left London, William Carlos Williams turned up on a visit from Leipzig where he was pursuing his medical studies. 'Bill has arrived & I am attempting to broaden his mind,' Ezra told his mother on 6 March

1910. 'We dine at the Shakespears & probably go on to Yeats' at home.'
Williams had hoped to get outside London and see some countryside, but
Ezra would have none of that: 'Did you come to see me or the sheep in
Hyde Park?' He himself almost never left the capital; the Lincolnshire visit
to Galton and Manning had been an exception. 'I know hardly any
England save London,' he admitted in 1912. He argued that 'all great art is
born of the metropolis', that 'all civilization has proceeded from cities and
cenacles'. One of America's reasons for failing to produce great art was, he
said, her lack of a real capital city.

Williams found him an infuriating host, not least because he would
always walk several paces in front in the street; and it was embarrassing
when Ezra made an ostentatious pass at a woman in the National Gallery.
Ezra made sure that Williams's mind should be 'duly benefited' by the
visit: he 'crammed' him with 'Turner & other such' in the Gallery, and sent
him to the Elgin Marbles and the Tower. At Yeats's Monday evening they
heard Yeats himself reading Ernest Dowson by candlelight – 'Not my
dish', said Williams – but despite Ezra's build-up about how much Yeats
admired him, nobody paid the slightest attention to them at first. It was not
until they were leaving that Yeats called Ezra back and said a few words to
him. Williams found the 'intense literary atmosphere' of all this 'fatiguing
in the extreme. I don't know how Ezra stood it, it would have killed me in
a month. It seemed completely foreign to anything I desired.'

6

Sediment

Ezra set off for Italy on 22 March 1910. 'Ezra has gone – to Italy,' Dorothy wrote in her notebook. 'Ezra! Ezra! beautiful face . . . when you made yourself ugly by shaving off your joyous hair, I was miserable . . . When you are gone away, I shall hardly dare to speak of you.' Olivia had promised that she and Dorothy would try to join him in Italy in a few weeks.

He planned to pass swiftly through Paris, stopping only to have breakfast with a musician named Walter Rummel, who took a special interest in the song settings of the troubadours. He and Rummel took such a liking to each other that Ezra decided to spend the night at his home – in the event, two nights. Afterwards, he reported that he had had a 'charming' time.

Walter Morse Rummel, two years younger than Ezra, owed his second name to his maternal grandfather, inventor of the magnetic telegraph and its code. His father Franz Rummel was a concert pianist of some reputation in Europe and the USA, and thanks to the Morse fortunes young Walter had been provided with an extensive musical training on both continents. At present he was studying in Paris, and was a hanger-on in the Debussy circle. Isadora Duncan, who fell in love with him in 1918, describes him as 'the picture of the youthful Liszt', but she told a friend that he 'preferred to make love to himself behind the closed doors of his room'.

In Canto 80 Ezra describes Rummel living in chilly Paris bohemianism:

> - and dear Walter was sitting amid the spoils of Finlandia
> a good deal of polar white
>   but the gas cut off.
> Debussy preferred his playing.

Elsewhere he called Rummel 'that eminently proper young man'; but in 1910 he took to the young pianist at sight, and after this first Paris meeting always referred to him as 'Walter' in letters to his parents – most unusually, for apart from 'Bill' Williams, he would almost invariably label males by their surnames. 'I suppose he means to music about what I do to poetry,' he told his parents.

From Rummel's Paris flat he went on to Verona, where he revisited San Zeno, which he described as 'pure magic . . . its toned brown-pink outside & the inside is proportion lifted into a sort of divinity'. He failed to rent an apartment in a 'pink marble palace' and could find no other suitable 'lodgement' to match his present effete mood, so he took a train to Lake Garda and settled at Sirmione, in the Hotel Eden. 'Ecco mi. in a real hotel. 3 meals a day "tutto compreso" on "Lago di Garda" . . . I shall stay here and absorb sunlight for a month or two.'

Sirmione lies on a narrow promontory which projects into Garda, the most eastward and the largest of the Italian lakes. At its northern extremity the Alps begin; at the southern end, Sirmione is almost an island, once a quiet fishing village but by 1910 already a thriving spa – 'a favourite German resort in spring and autumn', says the 1906 Baedeker. Ezra knew of the place from Catullus, who wrote his poetry there, and from the sixteenth-century Renaissance Latin versifier Marcus Antonius Flaminius, whose lines he quotes (in his own translation) in *The Spirit of Romance:*

> O pleasing shore of Sirmio,
> White-shining hill of Catullus!
> O Muse, teach me to sing the praise
> Of the blest sylvan ways
> Citrus laden . . .

The Eden was cheap (7 lire per day full board) and 'miles of lago di Garda' lay under Ezra's window. Despite the tourists (there were six other hotels in the village) it was really still 'the same old Sirmio that Catullus raved over a few years back and M. A. Flaminius more recently'. Moreover, 'there are, thank god, no americans here'. The place seemed 'predestined' for him, and here (he said) he would stay for the summer, 'bar running up to Venice'. He expected the Shakespears to turn up somewhere in the vicinity fairly soon.

Sirmione is among the Italian scenes invoked in the Cantos to represent what Ezra called 'the original world of gods', the pagan pre-Christian dawn in which the classical deities walked the earth. Now, during his first visit, he praised the place in a short poem that describes how 'the sun / Lets drift in on us through the olive leaves / A liquid glory'. He was not by nature a landscape enthusiast. 'Scenery . . . bores me,' he wrote to his mother in 1908 when contemplating organizing a tour for Americans around the Italian lakes. But he could not shut his eyes to the backdrop at Garda. 'Just at present,' he wrote to Mary Moore,

> I am . . . living in great luxury on the edge of a very large sapphire which certain damn fools think is water. the gods reside on Mt Riva at the other end of it . . . I ocasionaly correct the proofs of my scholarly work about to be printed in London. & I spend the rest of the time in sun baths or similarly strenuous pursuits.

To his parents he added that for preference he would 'live in Italy most of the time', urging them to buy a plot of land beside Garda to 'save me the pain of crossing the Atlantic'. And to Hilda Doolittle: 'I've been about a bit and I know paradise when I see it.'

With the proofs of *The Spirit of Romance* out of the way, he considered beginning a new work. He told his father that if he had found somewhere to stay in Verona 'I might have written a book on Can Grande de la Scala' (the dedicatee of Dante's *Paradiso*), but now 'I'm going to write about Guido Cavalcanti in stead'. Actually he did not write very much at this time about the thirteenth-century Tuscan poet who was one of Dante's most accomplished predecessors, but translated him instead. His *Sonnets and Ballate of Guido Cavalcanti* was eventually published in 1912.

He was drawn to Cavalcanti because he believed that the Tuscan had managed to say, very accurately, some of those things about sex and love that he himself was struggling to express. In a 1911 article he praises Cavalcanti for 'exact psychology . . . an attempt to render emotions precisely', and he says this again in his introduction to the translations: 'Than Guido Cavalcanti, no psychologist of the emotions is more keen in his understanding, more precise in his expression; we have in him no rhetoric, but always a true description.' However, a reader of Ezra's translation of the *Sonnets and Ballate* may well be moved to ask 'Description of what?', for in it he conveys no psychological exactitude, but merely indulges in a neo-Elizabethan (or perhaps ersatz-Metaphysical) woolliness of expression, encrusted with archaisms:

> Because a lady asks me, I would tell
> Of an affect that comes often and is fell
> And is so overweening: Love by name.
>
> E'en its deniers can now hear the truth,
> I for the nonce to them that know it call,
> Having no hope at all
>   that man who is base in heart
> Can bear his part of wit
>   into the light of it . . .

Part of the fault lay with Dante Gabriel Rossetti, who had translated a selection from Cavalcanti's sonnets in his *Early Italian Poets* (1861). In Ezra's introduction to his own versions he says that Rossetti has been 'my father and my mother', though Rossetti had not managed to 'see everything', and Ezra claimed to be bringing out greater significance in certain lines. He called his own method with the poems 'scholastic' as opposed to Rossetti's 'aesthetic' approach, but this was an unfortunate claim in view of the critical censure that his translations attracted when they were published in 1912. 'Either Mr Pound knows very little about the Italian language, or he is totally lacking in that critical judgment necessary to the translator,' wrote Arundel del Re in *Poetry Review*. Ezra had printed Cavalcanti's original Italian alongside his own versions, but, said del Re, had used an 'obsolete and untrustworthy' text, had introduced 'amendments' which had no textual justification, and was incapable of spelling names correctly – del Re cited 'Cherchi for Cerchi, Bundelmonti for Buondelmonti, Oderesi for Oderisi, - and with Dante before him – Cristofore Landiano for Cristoforo Landino'. Even the opening line of the canzone quoted above, which Ezra considered by far the most important of Cavalcanti's poems (it turns up in a new translation as Canto 36), had been given by him, ludicrously, as 'Donna mi pregna' instead of 'Donna mi prega', thereby rendering it not 'A lady entreats me' but 'A lady impregnates me'. Understandably, del Re felt that 'these slips . . . are sufficient to condemn him as a serious student', though he was kind enough to allow that Ezra was 'earnestly striving after a vital idea of which one sometimes catches a glimpse amid the general tangle and disorder'.

Ezra was angry about the review. 'A. de R. got a good deal out of six misprints. The rest is malignant buncomb.' But only a few years later he was saying to James Joyce: 'I once did a bad translation of Guido Cavalcanti.' (The book had by then virtually vanished; only a few copies were sold, and the remaining stock was eventually destroyed in a fire at the binder's.) Eventually he could see that what had 'obfuscated' the translation was 'not the Italian . . . difficult as it then was for me to read . . . but the crust of dead English, the sediment present in my own available vocabulary'.

Some of the spelling mistakes in the Italian text may have been Dorothy Shakespear's, since she made some transcriptions for Ezra from the early nineteenth-century edition of Cavalcanti he was using in the British Museum. When writing to her from Sirmione to ask for them, he told her: 'I have written ten more lines of my canzone.' He explained to his father that he had 'resurrected a beautiful Canzon form from the Provençal which has never been used in English.' So began the poems that went into his *Canzoni* (1911), a collection that suffered from the same faults of 'obfuscation' and 'sediment' that spoilt the Cavalcanti translations. Meanwhile, to his mother, he was humorously envisaging the composition of 'a bombastic, rhetorical epic wherethrough will move Marconi, Pierpont Morgan, Bleriot, Levavasour, Latham, Peary, Dr Cook, etc. clothed in the heroic manner of greek imitation'. This would, he said, prove to be the last major work of poetry before literature went into 'a sort of artistic dark ages' around AD 2000. 'I shall write it myself if threatened with actual starvation.'

*

Olivia and Dorothy Shakespear arrived at Sirmione during April. Dorothy afterwards recalled the time she and her mother spent there as 'those exquisite days . . . Truly my life was lived then.' Her perception of Lake Garda and the mountains 'was the first time I ever saw colour', and she spent a lot of time painting watercolours. Ezra was at his most serene; he declared that he 'would much rather lie on what is left of Catullus' parlour floor and speculate the azure beneath it and the hills off to Salo and Riva with their forgotten gods moving unhindered amongst them, than discuss any processes and theories of art whatsoever'. The three of them travelled to Venice, which Ezra found 'rather like a machine shop after Sirmione'. But the Shakespears did not return with him to Garda, and by the time Ezra returned to London at the end of May he had been forbidden by Olivia to come to their house, or to write to Dorothy.

It is impossible to say for certain what had happened, but it seems that during their time together at Sirmione he had at last reciprocated Dorothy's romantic interest in him, and that this took Olivia by surprise. After all, it had definitely been to her that Ezra paid court in London. But now he had written a poem, set at Sirmione and indubitably addressed to Dorothy, in which he declared that he had no use for the concept of paradise; rather, after death, his soul would meet Dorothy's 'at Sirmio' and no rumour of 'havens more high and courts desirable' could lure them beyond 'the cloudy peak of Riva' which overlooks the lake.

If Olivia had known him better, she might have realized that the attention he was paying to Dorothy did not exclude anyone else from his affections. Her ostensible reason for the ban, as Dorothy put it, was that Ezra could not find '£5,000 a year . . . in a fortnight', could not quickly produce evidence of his capability of supporting her should they marry and therefore could not qualify as a suitor. But Olivia (which seems far more remarkable) also told Ezra that Dorothy was not good enough for him. 'What distresses me,' she wrote to him (in the summer of 1911, a year after forbidding him the house),

> is that I see her becoming always more fundamentally selfish and self-absorbed. Of course this does not show on the surface,

as her manners are too good – but I really don't believe she would stir a finger to help her dearest friend if it cost her a moment's trouble or inconvenience . . .

You will probably think all I say very brutal, because you are in love with her; but you are quite intelligent enough to get outside that if you choose, & see that she is not perfection.

This extraordinary letter becomes more explicable if one accepts that Olivia greatly resented Ezra (as she supposed) having transferred his affections from her. Perhaps she had hoped that the ex-mistress of Yeats would become the mistress of Ezra Pound. Richard Aldington contemplated this possibility in his story 'Nobody's Baby', in which Dorothy is portrayed as Ophelia Dawson:

> Obviously the girl was in love with that lanoline Hermes profile, and couldn't see the fool for the god. But the mother? Was she trying to put the girl off, to save her from an utterly foolish match? Or, improbably, was she . . . trying to snatch him for herself?

*

The ban proved scarcely necessary, for almost as soon as Ezra got back to London from Sirmione he set off for the USA, sailing on 15 June 1910. It was the return home that he had been putting off for more than a year, and he had no notion when he would be back in England. Dorothy wrote to him that she was determined he should 'come back next summer', by which time she would 'surely be strong enough' to tell her mother she could choose her own friends. She thanked him 'eternally, for you have given me Life in a way which I had no idea existed'.

Ezra himself showed no signs of the pangs of disappointed love. 'I hope to occupy myself with some profitable & commercial enterprise immediately on my arrival on the U.S.,' he told his father. He had said much the same to D. H. Lawrence when they met at Violet Hunt's just before his departure. 'Having had all the experiences possible for a poor man, he will now proceed to conquer riches, and explore the other hemisphere.' Lawrence wrote to a friend. 'He will sell boots – there is nothing in that blown egg literature. I ventured to suggest that he should run a Cinematograph: a dazzling picture palace: for which valuable suggestion he tendered me a frown.'

Lawrence would have agreed with an article on Ezra in the *Boston Evening Transcript* which appeared shortly after their conversation. It was a review of *The Spirit of Romance*, just published in London by Dent and in New York by Dutton. The reviewer judged that Ezra's 'clear insight' was weakened by 'a hunger for publicity'. Another American review, in the *Nation*, was downright contemptuous: 'The few bits of really good comment are too rare to be worth hunting for.' In Britain, Edward Thomas in the *Morning Post* praised the translations which were peppered throughout the book but attacked its idiosyncrasies (for example a snarl against Whitman) and said he felt Ezra was essentially 'negative', a destroyer, and lacked the 'strong personality' to bring off this sort of performance successfully.

Arriving in New York, Ezra immediately set to work to explore the possibilities of commerce. He contacted a shady businessman, Frank 'Baldy' Bacon, whom he had met some years ago at Aunt Frank's boarding-house. This gentleman had an office in Nassau Street in the financial district, where he sold 'odd sorts of insurance', operating by private intelligence as to which shipping companies were the most careless and likely to cause accidents, or 'where a man was most likely / To lose a leg in bad hoisting machinery' (this is from Ezra's cryptic biography of him in Canto 12). Bacon told Ezra that he had once saved his employers $11,000 by buying up 'all the little copper pennies in Cuba', though it had required certain precautions such as 'Sleeping with two buck niggers chained to him'. Money, he emphasized to Ezra, actual hard currency, was the only thing worth dealing in – '"No interest in any other kind uv bisnis," / Said Baldy.' He shared his office with a colourful-looking person named Mons Quade, who 'wore a monocle on a wide sable ribbon'; Ezra thought Quade a 'damn good fellow'.

'Had Bacon go over financial end of the game,' Ezra wrote to his father from New York. 'He says its very straight & conservative.' By this time he had evidently seen his parents and explained to them what 'the game' was, so we have no record of what he was up to. He told Homer he was to 'have a shy at a job with the concern when it gets under weigh. Shares per $10. now 5.50 – you can't have mine just yet.' He said it was a pity Homer could not spare any 'shekels' to invest: he had written to Aunt Frank, who was now out of the boarding-house business, to see if she was interested, and suggested that Homer should try to raise money from his friends in the Mint, since he was drawing a commission on any shares he could sell. He also contacted two wealthy cousins on his mother's side, Charles and William Wadsworth, pillars of the New York Stock Exchange, in whom he had previously taken no interest. He visited their country homes and tried to extract some money from them for his scheme.

The only possible evidence as to what it was all about has been left by William Carlos Williams, who was back at home in New Jersey by the time Ezra reached the American shore. Ezra went to see him and

made the proposal . . . that we get a big supply of '606', the new anti-syphilitic arsenical which Ehrlich had just announced to the world, and go at once with it to the north coast of Africa and there set up shop. Between us, I with my medical certificate and experience, he with his social proclivities, we might, he thought, clean up a million treating all the wealthy old nabobs there – presumably rotten with the disease – and retire to our literary enjoyments within, at most, a year.

Williams thought there might be something in it, but his father, an experienced businessman, would only 'shake his head' at the idea. Thereafter Ezra seems to have parted company with Baldy Bacon and the business world, though he was delighted to run across Baldy again in Paris in the 1920s, just after writing about him somewhat libellously in the Cantos.

*

In New York, Ezra met up with Walter Rummel, who was also visiting the USA, and they spent a couple of weeks together at a small house in Swarthmore, just outside Philadelphia, which Homer and Isabel were renting for the summer while leasing their Wyncote mansion. (Homer was no doubt trying to recoup the considerable sums he was having to disburse to Ezra). 'Walter & I had two weeks at Swarthmore that mattered,' Ezra wrote a year later, 'but he has doubted my sanity or respectability or both ever since I took him to New York & housed him in a flat I'd borrowed from a mad lady from Colorado.' Hilda Doolittle came over to Swarthmore to see Ezra and to hear Walter play, and nearly forty years later recalled the 'sheer bliss' of 'that concert at your summer home'. She knew nothing of Dorothy Shakespear, and wanted to go to Europe with Ezra, despite her family's continuing opposition.

The New York apartment belonging to the 'mad lady' was at 270 Fourth Avenue (now Park Avenue South), and Ezra made it his base for the remaining months of 1910. Still supported financially by his father, he spent part of his time in a not-too-energetic attempt to improve his contacts with American literary circles. As a base for operations he used a bookshop on Twenty-Ninth Street run by an Englishman, Laurence Gomme, which was the nearest thing he could find to Elkin Mathews's establishment. He hung about there in the hope of discovering interesting faces and names, but could find no man of more note than Joyce Kilmer, the author of 'I think that I shall never see / A poem lovely as a tree'. He concluded that among contemporary North American poets Bliss Carman was 'about the only one of the lot that wouldn't improve by drowning'.

He called on Witter Bynner, poetry editor of *McClure's* and himself a poet and translator, who had seen Ezra and his work before he left for

Europe in 1908 and had recently played a part in persuading Small, Maynard & Co. of Boston (publisher of Bynner's own poetry) to issue *Provença*. This was a selection from *Personae* and *Exultations* together with a few new poems, which was to come out shortly. Bynner was amused by Ezra's 'happily cuckoo troubadour' appearance, which on this occasion included one tan and one blue shoe, and a 'shiny straw hat' with a ribbon adorned with 'red polka dots'. *McClure's*, however, did not have a readership with strong stomachs, and Bynner could offer nothing. When *Provença* appeared there were some predictable grumblings from the more staid quarters: 'We began the examination of this book of poems with great expectations and we lay it down with considerable contempt for the bulk of English criticism that has pretended to discover in these erratic utterances the voice of a poet,' wrote the critic of the *Boston Evening Transcript*, who thought Ezra had been awarded his English laurels 'prematurely' and suggested that he should pay attention to his distant maternal cousin Longfellow, from whom he could 'learn a great deal'.

Better reviews were to appear: H. L. Mencken in *Smart Set* thought the poems 'uncouth, hairy, barbarous' but liked their 'stark, heathenish music', and Floyd Dell in the *Chicago Evening Post* said that Ezra knew what he was doing and was a 'true poet'. But Mencken's review was not printed until the following April, by which time Ezra was out of the country again, so he left the USA in the belief that Dell was the only critic with 'any worthy conception of poetry'.

While in New York he was invited to attend one of the first meetings of the newly formed Poetry Society of America. But formal gatherings of this sort were no substitute for the literary cliques of London. Moreover a conversation with one poet in particular convinced him that any genuine American talent was certain to be stifled at birth:

> I met a man in New York . . . I liked some of his lyrics. I said, 'Give me some more and I'll take 'em to London and have 'em published.' I found the rest of his work, poem after poem, spoiled. I said: 'Why do you do this and this?' He said: 'They told me to.' I said: 'Why have you utterly ruined this cadence, and used this stultifying inversion to maintain a worn-out metre that everyone is tired of?' Same answer.

Not surprisingly, given his tendency towards such inquisitions, the general feeling among the younger New York poets was that the twenty-five-year-old returned exile was 'surly, supercilious and grumpy'. For his part Ezra concluded that 'there is no man now living in America whose work is of the slightest interest to any serious artist'. He thought the best remedy would be a 'college of the arts' in New York, and drafted a constitution for it – the first of many such schemes that he would attempt to promote:

a college of one hundred members, chosen from all the arts, sculptors, painters, dramatists, musical composers, architects, scholars of the art of verse, engravers, etc., and they should be fed there during the impossible years of the artist's life – i.e., the beginning of his career.

But no one in New York was even interested in publishing this prospectus.

During his time there, he worked at 'my new collection of poems for London', to be published once again by Elkin Mathews – there was no question of transferring this crucial part of the operation to an unsympathetic New York. He had dinner with Aunt Frank, now married to a doctor; her boarding-house had been demolished by a property speculator who had erected the Ritz-Carlton Hotel on the site, since when she herself had run the grandly named New Weston Hotel on the corner of Madison and Forty-Ninth. True to Weston form, this had just failed financially and the creditors were suing. Ezra showed little sympathy with his great-aunt's misfortunes. 'From the way mother wrote,' he remarked to his father, 'one would have expected to find the good lady selling matches on the street.'

Without the old family boarding-house on East Forty-Seventh as a base, he drifted about Manhattan, looking dispassionately at the 'surging crowd on Seventh Avenue' with eyes made more sophisticated by Europe. Beginning to write down his impressions with the hope of publication, he thought the people 'eager, careless, with an animal vigour unlike that of any European crowd that I have ever looked at. There is none of the melancholy, the sullenness, the unhealth of the London mass, none of the worn vivacity of Paris.' He also thought he detected the first stirrings of a true American art in the New York architecture: 'The city has put forth its own expression. The first of the arts arrives.' The Pennsylvania Railroad Station and the Metropolitan Life tower (one of the earliest skyscrapers) seemed to him a 'real achievement' comparable to 'the palaces of the Renaissance'. On the other hand the neo-classical Public Library, recently built, was 'botch . . . false . . . hideous'. He went to the firm of architects responsible for it and told them so, but 'found it impossible' to make them 'understand any of this'. Preferable to the Library's pomposity was the entrepreneurial fashion in which one speculator had stuck 'the façade of a Gothic cathedral' on an apartment building overlooking Central Park. 'The result is bad, but the spirit which tries this sort of thing is bound to win to some better ending.'

This analysis of New York was written up eighteen months later, in London, for a series of articles entitled 'Patria Mia'. Through them rises a crescendo of praise for the sheer uncompromising urbanness of the city:

And New York is the most beautiful city in the world? It is not far from it. No urban night is like the night there . . . Squares after squares of flame, set up and cut into the aether. Here is our poetry, for we have pulled down the stars to our will.

This is the Ezra who thought he could not write prose.

W. B. Yeats's elderly father, the painter J. B. Yeats, had settled in New York. Ezra called on him, and during August the two of them went on a jaunt to Coney Island accompanied by John Quinn, a New York Irish lawyer and art collector who was patron and financial godfather to old Yeats. Ezra loved the 'sham fairyland' of the amusement park, and later wrote to Quinn recalling the happy vision of 'Yeats père on an elephant . . . smiling like Elijah . . . and of you plugging away in the shooting gallery'. Yeats senior wrote to his poet son that young Ezra was 'quoting quantities of your verse . . . I liked his look and air.'

Hilda Doolittle came up to New York to see Ezra again, and once more he encouraged her to visit Europe. She still did not appreciate the unreliability of any pledge he might seem to be making, and persuaded herself that they were once again unofficially engaged. In fact, he was also spending time again with Kitty Heyman, who was in New York, and with Viola Baxter, his girlfriend from Hamilton College days, who was in the city. Moreover he did not draw Hilda's attention to the final section of *Provença*, which had just been published. Headed 'Canzionere: Studies in Form', it was dedicated 'To Olivia and Dorothy Shakespear'.

On 22 February 1911 Ezra boarded the *Mauretania* for the voyage back to London. His parents were distressed to see him depart again; he told them it had 'not been particularly easy' to make the decision to go. Apart from anything else, life in America could offer 'considerably more comfort' than that in London – in other words, he was getting better value there from Homer's monthly allowance of dollars. But, he explained, the USA seemed to have 'nothing so new or so different' to build into his poetry.

The trip had fired him with an enthusiasm for certain things American, in particular the brash urban style of New York, and he had begun to take an interest in the literary welfare of contemporary American poets. Yet this was something he could conduct just as well, perhaps more effectively, from the other side of the Atlantic, while it would take more than the New York night sky to convince him he was living in the best place for his own literary needs. From now on in letters to his parents there were far fewer remarks about the possibility of coming 'home' to the USA again. Home indeed was now really Europe.

But not necessarily London. Arriving there, he wrote to his mother that it was splendid to be back – 'Have seen Yeats, Plarr, Hueffer, May Sinclair, all of whom are revivifying' – but he was not yet 'fit for the eight hours conversation day' (he had been slightly unwell towards the end of his

American visit), so he was now 'off to Paris this a.m.' after a mere three days in England. As T. S. Eliot observed many years later:

> He seemed always to be a temporary squatter . . . [with] a kind of resistance against growing into any environment. In America he would no doubt always have seemed on the point of going abroad; in London, he always seemed on the point of crossing the Channel. -

Ezra himself admitted in *Guide to Kulchur* that his predisposition, at least in youth, was 'nomadic', and he expatiated on this in a 1936 letter:

> Ownership is often a damnd nuisance, and anchor. It was my parents owning a house that put me wise, and I struggled for years to own nothing that I can't pack in a suitcase. Never really got it down to less than *two* suitcases. Which is a *nuisance* and really a stigma of poverty. Given adequate purchasing power one cd. *own* less.

He would travel about Europe with a minimum of premeditation and an absolute disregard for bother about tickets or currency, rarely troubling to supply his intimates with more than the barest details of his next address, if known. He often assumed that some such address as 'Ezra Pound, Sirmione' would do – which, given his prominent appearance, it usually did. He treated the world as if he belonged everywhere, or nowhere in particular. When Mary Moore asked in 1909 when he was coming home, he replied: 'Ain't got no home.' Richard Aldington noticed that 'he went off to Paris or Venice with vastly less fuss than a Georgian affronting the perils of the Cotswolds.'

*

He arrived in Paris and reported 'I'm very comfortable in a big pension by the Odeon. but shall go out to Walters place in a week or so. – about as soon as I shall be fit for musical activity.' London had been 'quite delightful but much too active for my present tastes'. His letters to his parents were growing short and languid. A few days later he reported that he had 'encamped' for a week or so with Walter Rummel, and that they had attended an 'exhausting concert' together. The only foreseeable 'disturbance' to his languor would be dinner next Tuesday with Arnold Bennett. After the dinner he reported that Bennett had seemed dull 'but might have interested me more if I had been feeling more vigorous'. He was a little more animated when mentioning the doings of Yeats, who had also turned up in Paris. However, when Yeats tried to introduce him to 'the crop of poets' who hung around the offices of the symbolist review *Le Mercure de France* he thought them 'a rather gutless lot', and made no attempt to understand what was going on in modern French poetry. Symbolism made him laugh. In Canto 83 he describes his amusement at Yeats's sympathy for it:

and Uncle William dawdling around Notre Dame
in search of whatever
                              paused to admire the symbol
with Notre Dame standing inside it.

The serious business for him at the moment was working with Walter Rummel on the music of the troubadours, which they now decided to reconstruct. Ezra dictated melodies out of his own head to fit three of his own poems in Provençal metre, to which Walter wrote accompaniments (the results were published by Augener of London a few months later).

He drifted pleasantly about Paris. 'I've seen a number of Cézanne pictures . . . have met Walter's brother who paints & plays the cello, & diverts me more or less. Walter goes to London in June & I guess I'll go to Italy about then.' He finished the short introduction to the Cavalcanti translations, noting that the last touches were put to it in 'Margaret Craven's [sic] apartment in Paris'. Margaret Cravens, four years older than Ezra, was an American pianist to whom he had been introduced by Walter. She came from Indiana and was in Paris for a year to study with Ravel. She commissioned a portrait of Ezra, painted by another American émigré, Eugene Paul Ullman, whose wife 'deplored' the amount of time Ezra spent in Margaret Cravens's apartment and believed they were lovers, though this was mere speculation.

As the Cavalcanti book was finished, he turned to translating Arnaut Daniel, the troubadour whom Dante had generously called *il miglior fabbro*, 'the greater craftsman', and who, said Ezra, 'used more different rhyme sounds than any other troubadour'. Ezra was not very interested in rhyme, and he later admitted to Dorothy that 'Arnaut is not so important as poetry but the eagle was interested & I've writ a monstrous long introduction'. 'The Eagle' was their private nickname for Yeats, suggested by his frequent use of the printed writing paper of the Royal Societies Club, whose telegraphic address was 'Aquilae, London'. It seemed appropriate to his grand manner.

The Arnaut Daniel translations, finished around midsummer 1911, were dispatched to a Chicago publisher, Ralph Fletcher Seymour, who issued a prospectus for the book; but Seymour's list was then taken over by another firm, who did not care for Ezra or Arnaut and returned the manuscript. Later, Ezra said he was 'profoundly glad' that the translations had not come out in their original form, which was as clouded by Victorian language as the Cavalcanti had been.

He was still contemplating a job at the University of Pennsylvania or some other American university, though now only half-heartedly. 'Don't bother too much about the U. of P.,' he wrote to his father from Paris. 'I've got my eye on something better.' He did not say what it was. He briefly thought he might 'come home in June', but felt it would be more pleasant to drift to Italy. At the moment he was not asking for any extra money from Homer over and above his regular allowance. Yet somehow (for reasons that would eventually become apparent) he had enough money in his pocket to contemplate an indefinite stay in Italy: 'Bill Williams brother is in Rome & I may winter there.' He set off from Paris, at the end of May 1911, for Sirmione.

He now had 'another prose book' in his head; he thought it might be about 'philosophy from Richard St Victor to Pico della Mirandola, or more or less so, but I'm casting about for something more lucrative'. The only 'philosophy' from this period that remotely interested him was Neoplatonism, which he felt to be related to his still developing theories about the troubadours. A little later he told his parents he was 'working on a book about the Renaissance. and I think in my mild way that it will give me a chance for a little straight hitting.' Meanwhile he went 'Veronizing' with Edgar Williams, younger brother of William Carlos, who was in Italy on a travelling scholarship to study architecture. 'He and I were examining Italy,' Ezra wrote a few months later. In his beloved San Zeno at Verona they spotted a column 'with the artisan's signature . . . Thus: "Me Mateus fecit." That is what we [in America] have not, where columns are ordered by the gross.' He remembered this again in Canto 45, where he attacks 'Usury' for corrupting the arts, and cites the signed column as an example of an artistic golden age.

During this summer at Sirmione he made a modern English version of the Anglo-Saxon poem *The Seafarer* which he published a few months later. Those who assumed he was simply trying to translate the original were as contemptuous of the results as Arundel del Re had been of his Cavalcanti. An Oxford scholar of Anglo-Saxon, Kenneth Sisam, complained that his *Seafarer* was riddled with 'careless ignorance or misunderstanding'. On the other hand, unlike the Cavalcanti translations, it was full of energy, and communicated the character of the original if not its details:

> He hath not heart for harping, nor in ring-having
> Nor winsomeness to wife, nor world's delight
> Nor any whit else save the wave's slash,
> Yet longing comes upon him to fare forth on the water.

Clearly the figure of the rootless, homeless Seafarer was a persona Ezra enjoyed – though since he himself invariably suffered from seasickness it must have required some effort of imagination – but he rejected without comment a whole moralizing section of the original poem, and also cut out all the Christian references. Nor was he any more accurate with individual words of Anglo-Saxon than he had been with medieval Italian, translating *englum* as 'English' instead of 'angels', and rendering *Eorpan rices* as 'earthen riches' rather than 'kingdoms of the earth'.

Canzoni, his new collection of poems, was now ready. Elkin Mathews published it in July 1911 while Ezra was at Sirmione. Like the section of *Provença* which had anticipated it, the book was dedicated to Olivia and Dorothy Shakespear. Though Ezra was still having no direct contact with Dorothy, Olivia permitted her to write to him to thank him for her copy. In it, she found his poem on their souls being united at Sirmione after death. She answered that she would 'surely meet you at Sirmio' in spirit, if it were not possible in the body.

This poem was actually one of the few digestible serious pieces in *Canzoni.* Most of the book suffered from a terrible languor, and was encrusted with a 'sediment' of Victorian language like the Cavalcanti and Arnaut Daniel translations. The chief purpose of those poems which gave the book its title was to demonstrate the viability in English of the Provençal *canzone* form, but the effect was not of an experiment so much as of the last twitch of a poetic corpse, the body being recognizably that of the Pre-Raphaelites:

> Korè my heart is, let it stand sans gloze!
> Love's pain is long, and lo, love's joy is brief!
> My heart erst alway sweet is bitter grown;
> As crimson ruleth in the good green's stead,
> So grief hath taken all mine old joy's share
> And driven forth by solace and all ease
> Where pleasure bows to all-usurping pain.

Reviews were justifiably abusive: 'lamentable failure . . . the result of mere reading . . . the personal touch is entirely wanting . . . affectation combined with pedantry' (this last phrase is Walter de la Mare, unsigned, in the *Westminster Gazette*), 'the heavy incrustations of verbiage are very tiring' (J. C. Squire in the *New Age*), 'so much of his inspiration seems bookish' (F. S. Flint in *Poetry Review*). Yet if Ezra had taken reviews to heart – which he said he no longer did – he would have found almost as much to encourage him as to depress. Most of the critics sugared their pills, de la Mare allowing that he was a true poet underneath, Squire that his artistry was 'excellent . . . within the limits that he has imposed on himself', Flint that he could 'write prettily in the regular metres'. It would take a more candid voice than theirs to persuade him that he was on the wrong track.

He himself explained years later of *Canzoni* that he intended it to be 'a sort of Purgatorio with the connecting links left out', a progress through the poetic ages:

> Artistically speaking its supposed to be a sort of chronological
> table of emotions: Provence; Tuscany, the Renaissance, the
> XVIII, the XIX, centuries, external modernity (cut out), sub-
> jective modernity. finis . . . I dont suppose any body'll see
> it . . . in this light but when my biographers unearth this missive
> it will be recorded as an astounding proof of my genius.

He said that his original scheme had been partly destroyed because he had
lost his nerve over the poems that were intended to express 'external
modernity'. At proof stage he had cut out 'Redondillas, or Something of
that Sort', a loosely written piece of over 100 lines summarizing his own
experiences and opinions in a manner that is occasionally amusing, more
often embarrassing:

> I would sing the American people,
>   God send them some civilization;
> I would sing of the nations of Europe,
>   God grant them some method of cleansing . . .
> I don't like this hobbledy metre
>   but find it easy to write in . . .

He omitted it because, he said, he had been 'affected by hyper-aesthesia or
over-squeamishness'; quite rightly, for though the 'I' in it is for a change
indubitably himself, its face is curiously blank. By trying to be natural he
had managed to be no one in particular.

The omission of 'Redondillas' together with a couple of other vaguely
modern and satirical pieces left *Canzoni* heavily weighted in favour of the
archaic poems. Nevertheless an attempt at contemporary speech did
remain, in the closing sequence of the book, entitled 'Und Drang', where
some fragments hint at a desire for a modern style:

> I have gone seeking for you in the twilight,
> Here in the flurry of Fifth Avenue,
> Here where they pass between their teas and teas.

The voice was uncertain, tending to lapse into archaism and inversion. This
same passage concludes:

> Yet I am fed with faces, is there one
> That even in the half-light mindeth me.

Looking back on these 1911 experiments, Ezra dismissed them as 'false
starts'.

In later years he was inclined to label the whole of *Canzoni* as
'moribund', and almost nothing from it appears in his own selections from

his early work, nor in T. S. Eliot's 1928 selection. It is easy to dismiss it as the final sticking in the mud of Ezra's attempt to revive troubadour poetry, which he afterwards realized had been completely useless. 'There is,' he wrote in 1922, 'a beauty in the troubadour work which I have tried to convey. I have failed almost without exception.' Yet *Canzoni* was also an effort, however uncertain, towards a modern voice, and he now sensed that modernity was demanded of him. He only wanted reassurance.

7

New Age

He left Sirmione at the end of July 1911 and stopped off at Milan, spending a morning in the Ambrosian Library, where he inspected a manuscript of Arnaut Daniel's poetry which contained musical notation. To his delight, it accorded exactly with his theory as to how the troubadours had used music. He copied it out, and it was published in a collection of troubadour songs, with accompaniment by Walter Rummel, during 1912. Ezra's search for troubadour music was not simply antiquarian, but was motivated by a feeling that he could push his own poetry forward if only he could discover the proper 'music' in it. The troubadours had a special importance for him because they had used their own 'tunes' consciously, but their original melodies, once discovered, were not altogether satisfactory. Trying out one tune he had discovered with a set of Arnaut Daniel words, he and Rummel were unable to find a musical interpretation that had the 'force' Ezra believed the words naturally possessed. A desire to solve this problem eventually led him to write his own musical accompaniments for medieval poetry.

'My address after Aug. 1st.,' he told Dorothy, 'is c/o F. M. Hueffer, 15 Friedrichs Strasse, Giessen, a/L, Germany.' Ford Madox Hueffer was spending the summer in Giessen, a small university town north of Frankfurt, in the hope of being able to qualify for German citizenship (on account of having a German father) and thereby getting a divorce from his English wife, who was still refusing to free him to marry Violet Hunt. He asked Ezra to come and act as his secretary for a few weeks. Ezra was perfectly happy to do this – Violet describes how he would willingly use up 'his intense and feverish energy taking down winged words' for Ford – but it was presumably amusement and some stimulating Ezraic talk that Ford also wanted. He certainly got them.

'I had very little time to myself while with Hueffer,' Ezra wrote to his mother. 'Not that there was much work done, but we disagree diametrically on art, religion, politics & all therein implied; & besides he's being married.' (This proved otherwise: Ford's attempt at the divorce failed, though Violet, who had accompanied him to Giessen, took to calling herself 'Mrs Hueffer' until Ford's wife objected.) 'I was dragged about to a number of castles, etc.', Ezra continued, 'which were interesting & about which I persistently refused to enthuse.' Violet recalls one of these expeditions, in which they discovered, still standing in a ruined church, a medieval wooden stage on which miracle plays had been performed. Ezra clambered on to it and declaimed his own verse 'in a sort of medieval chant . . . And then with an insidious crash, he disappeared and made his descent into hell . . .'

He had nothing much to say in favour of Germany. 'I don't approve of it. tho' Giessen is a "model town".' Ford took him to Nauheim, which Ezra thought 'a springs & baths hell' (it was to be the principal setting of Ford's masterpiece *The Good Soldier*). One day Ezra went to Freiburg by train, where he spent an afternoon with a Provençal scholar, Dr Émil Lévy, compiler of an eight-volume dictionary of that language, who (so Professor Rennert at Penn had told him) was the only man who 'knows anything about Provençal'. Ezra showed Dr Lévy the transcriptions of Arnaut's notation he had brought with him from Milan – 'Not that I could sing him the music.' Canto 20 contains an account of their conversation:

> And he said: 'Now is there anything I can tell you?'
> And I said: I dunno, sir, or
> 'Yes, Doctor, what do they mean by *noigandres*?'

This was a crux in the edition Ezra had been using of Arnaut's *canzoni*: '*E jois lo grans, e l'olors de noigandres*.' Other texts have '*nuo gaindres*', '*nul grandes*', or '*notz grandres*', and probably '*noigandres*' was an editorial misreading. However, Dr Lévy took the question with gratifying seriousness:

> And he said: 'Noigandres! NOIgandres!
> 'You know for seex mon's of my life
> 'Effery night when I go to bett, I say to myself:
> 'Noigandres, eh, *noigandres*,
> 'Now what the DEFFIL can that mean!'

It was exactly the sort of esoteric detail that delighted Ezra, who set great store by the wisdom of experts, expecially if they lived in places not easily accessible to his friends.

He brought copies of his own *Canzoni* to Giessen and gave one to Ford, hoping for approval of the new poems. What he got instead was a vivid demonstration of disgust. Almost thirty years later, he still vividly recalled how Ford had showed his contempt for the book by quite literally rolling about on the floor in simulated agony.

> Ford . . . felt the errors [in *Canzoni*] . . . to the point of rolling (physically, and if you look at is as mere superficial snob, ridiculously) on the floor of his temporary quarters at Giessen when my third volume displayed me trapped . . . in . . . the stilted language that then passed for 'good' English.

Ezra, said Ford, was not merely 'trapped' in his 'jejune provincial effort' to adopt the manner of an outworn poetry. He was 'fly-papered, gummed, and strapped down', and must tear himself free at once.

'That roll,' Ezra wrote later, 'saved me at least two years, perhaps more. It sent me back to my own proper effort, namely, toward using the living tongue.' At the time he can scarcely have been very pleased, for though Ford himself wrote a certain amount of minor verse, he was no Yeats. Ezra would not have listened if he did not find Ford such congenial company, was not still grateful to him for early support in the *English Review*, and did not value him as a link with the older generation. And, of course, Ford spoke thoughts that were already forming in his own mind.

Ford put his case eloquently, to judge by the way he argued the issue in a 1913 article on the need to write contemporary-style poetry. 'For myself,' he says of his own verse,

> I have been unable to do it: I am too old perhaps or was born too late – anything you like. But there it is – I would rather read a picture in verse of the emotions and environment of a Goodge Street anarchist than recapture what songs the syrens sang. That after all was what François Villon was doing for the life of his day, and I should feel that our day was doing its duty by posterity much more surely if it were doing something of the sort.

A year or so later, Ezra could not praise Ford too highly for the mauling he had administered to *Canzoni*. 'I would rather talk about poetry with Ford Madox Hueffer than with any man in London . . . Mr Hueffer's beliefs about the art may be best explained by saying that they are in diametric opposition to those of Mr Yeats.' (Yeats had not yet endured Ezra's repetition to him of Ford's lecture on the need to modernize one's language.) 'Mr Hueffer believes in an exact rendering of things. He would strip words of all "association" for the sake of getting a precise meaning.' And in May 1913 Ezra remarked to Dorothy: 'Verily the more people I meet the more respect I have for F.M.H. – When I think of how he struggled with me in germany!'

*

Ford started to put his own precepts into practice soon after their conversation. In December 1911 Ezra noted that he was 'making some sort of experiments in modernity'. It was by no means Ford's first work in poetry – he had already written sufficient for his *Collected Poems* to appear at the end of 1913 – but it was his first attempt at the contemporary; Ezra called his earlier stuff 'Pre-Raphaelite practices'. The most striking result of these experiments was Ford's long poem 'On Heaven', published in 1914, in which paradise is pictured as an idyllic life with Violet Hunt in the South of France. Rambling and rather touching, it was written after she had challenged him to produce a definition of 'a working heaven'. When it first appeared Ezra called it 'the best poem yet written in the "twentieth-century fashion"', but Ford was doing no more than putting into a nominal verse form (for 'On Heaven' is not very far from prose) the impressionistic narrative style he was developing in his fiction.

This would not be Ezra's way of finding a modern voice. He felt that impressionism was not good enough because 'ANY dud bread dough' was 'capable of receiving an impression'. He wanted something more objective and hard. He also observed how Ford 'fills in the lacunae between his occasional passages of poetry with doggerel instead of with dullness', and this was a questionable advance over Victorian practice. 'Mr Hueffer is so obsessed with the idea that the language of poetry should not be a dead language, that he forgets it must be . . . dignified, more intense, more dynamic, than to-day's speech as spoken.' And when reviewing Ford's *Collected Poems* he described him quite rightly as 'not a poet but merely a very distinguished amateur stepping into verse from the sister art'.

So he had to find his own modern style in his own way, and for some months he did not know how to begin. How, he asked in an article shortly after getting back from Giessen, 'shall the poet in this dreary day attain universality, how write what will be understood of "the many" and lauded of "the few"?' He was inclined from habit to resort to his old attitude of aestheticism:

> The only way to escape from rhetoric and frilled paper decoration is through beauty . . . I mean by that that one must call a spade a spade in form so exactly adjusted, in a metric in itself so seductive, that the statement will not bore the auditor . . . We must have a simplicity and directness of utterance, which is different from the simplicity and directness of daily speech, which is more 'curial', more dignified . . . There are few fallacies more common than the opinion that poetry should mimic the daily speech . . . Colloquial poetry is to the real art as the barber's wax dummy is to sculpture.

Cautious stuff: he was not going to take any plunges yet.

But if the matter of diction was still unresolved, he already sensed which path would prove the right one in the question of rhythm and metre. Only a few weeks after Ford had rolled on the floor, Ezra wrote to Dorothy:

> Surely all systems of metric . . . have been a vulgarity & a barbarism, and their beautiful results have been due to genius & accident & not to any virtue inherent in the 'system'. *Melos* is compounded out of . . . speech, music & rhythm . . . And unless you write in quantity (by intent or accident) those three things mean mess (with little, very little love in it).

*

He was back in London at the end of August 1911. As his old Church Walk room was not available, and as Walter Rummel had appeared, they took a flat together, first at 39 Addison Road North, in a remote part of Kensington, then at 2a Granville Place off Oxford Street.

Ezra called on Olivia Shakespear – Dorothy was away from home – hoping to obtain permission to visit Dorothy regularly. Olivia did not agree to this, but she was still willing to be courted herself by Ezra ('I will write again,' she told him, '& fix a day for you to come next week'). When Dorothy got home, she and Ezra took to meeting clandestinely in the Elgin Marbles room of the British Museum – a trysting place in Olivia's novel *Love on a Mortal Lease* – but neither of them felt very comfortable about the deception, and Dorothy advised Ezra to have a straight talk with her father, recommending him to make 'plain, businesslike statements' about his financial situation and prospects.

Ezra completely misunderstood the tone of voice required for such things. On 11 October he went without appointment to Mr Shakespear's office (Shakespear & Parkyn, solicitors) and took him by storm with 'statements' about his finances, pulling out a handful of banknotes from his pocket as proof that he had money. He also told Mr Shakespear that he received a regular income of £200 a year quite apart from his literary work. Mr Shakespear was not unimpressed by this but asked for proof. Ezra's answer was to tell him to write to Homer, who would confirm that he was financially secure. He then rushed home and mailed a letter to Homer telling him what to say. Homer was not to alter 'jot nor tittle' of the following draft, upon pain of Ezra's wrath:

> Dear Mr Shakespear,
>   Naturaly [*sic*] my son has not mentioned this matter to me, but if he wants anything he is very likely to get it. Any items he may have given you about his finances are presumably correct. He is no longer in bonds of necessity. My home is at his

disposal and I only wish he would make more use of it than he does.

He seemed rather preoccupied when he was last with us but it might have been Guido Cavalcanti.

If there is anything else I can do for you in the matter please let me know.

Believe me, yours very sincerely.

To which Ezra added: 'I think that will be about all. I realize I am a remarkable child . . . You might add in a PS . . . "His work is rather remarkable."'

Nowhere did he give any explanation to his father of what all this was about – there was no mention of Dorothy, nor of marriage. (This was merely his habitually secretive way.) But he told Homer what he had already told Mr Shakespear, that he was now receiving a regular non-literary income of £200 a year, equivalent to $1,000: 'I get $1,000 a year apart from what I make at royalties, poems sold to magazines, lectures etc.'

Homer must have wondered where Ezra was obtaining this mysterious income, which explained his air of affluence in the last few months. An answer of a sort came from Ezra a day later:

I have received orders to do my *own* work & not to worry about the immediate returns. But that is no body's business except my own. and the less said about it the better.

I am, as you may have surmised from my epistle of yesterday, attempting to marry the gentleman's daughter. I shall do so in any case but dont want to disturb the sepulchral calm of that english household more than need be.

She'll have about the same ammount of her own so we shall do very nicely . . .

You may remember what a poor photograph of the lady looks like. I shall not indulge in further comment – apart from the evidence of my published works – which are very inade-quate.

If Ezra really wanted to marry Dorothy – more than he had wanted to marry either the Dryad or Mary Moore, to both of whom he had been 'engaged' – one cannot help feeling that it was largely because Dorothy's parents were trying to stop him, and he did not like being opposed. As to 'the evidence of my published works', there was only the one recent poem about his affection for her. He seemed perfectly happy living with Walter.

Homer, as always, obeyed Ezra's instructions, writing to Henry Hope Shakespear that to the best of his knowledge Ezra had an income of $1,000 a year in addition to royalties. (Ezra had changed his mind about the draft and had said that his father could write in more mild terms.) Mr Shakespear replied rather dubiously that he had 'never for a moment doubted the accuracy' of Ezra's statement about his non-literary income, but Ezra had given 'no information as to the source' and was not 'prepared to say that it was of a permanent nature'. He explained that he and Olivia 'like him very much, & consider he has great abilities; but until he has some regular income in addition to a permanently secured £200 a year, it is obvious that he is not in a position to marry.'

Ezra now tried to ignore the subject in letters home, but Homer naturally pressed him for some further explanation of the mysterious income. Ezra would only say that 'the source is anonymous & the donation voluntary'. He added that yet more money was in sight, from a London publisher, Swift & Co., who were taking his Cavalcanti translations and were offering terms for future books that seemed to 'guarantee my continuing existence'.

Hilda Doolittle now arrived in London, travelling with a girlfriend, Frances Gregg, who 'had filled the gap in my Philadelphia life after Ezra was gone'. She and Frances stayed, on Ezra's recommendation, at his former digs in Duchess Street, while he moved back into Church Walk because the room had become available and Walter Rummel had left for Paris. Just before Walter went, Hilda (who remembered him from Swarthmore in the summer of 1910) met him; Rummel said to her: 'I think I ought to tell you, though I promised Mrs Shakespear not to . . . there is an understanding. Ezra is to marry Dorothy Shakespear.'

It was a malevolent thing to do – it hints at complex feelings between Ezra and Walter – and for Hilda 'a chasm opened'. Yet she knew enough of Ezra to realize how little the word 'engagement' might mean, and she stayed on in London. 'Drifting. Drifting. Meeting with him alone or with others at the Museum tea room . . . I had my allowance now. Drifting . . .' And sure enough Ezra strung her along, just the same as ever: 'I remember how he said to me in London . . . "Let's be engaged – don't tell – ".'

Olivia Shakespear, understanding that she could never have Ezra for herself, now began gradually to give way, and agreed that he might visit Dorothy now and then until his finances clarified themselves. So he began to call regularly again at the Shakespear house. He also introduced Olivia and Dorothy to Hilda. Similarly when Mary Moore came to London a few months later, Dorothy was told by Ezra to invite her to tea. Ezra still displayed not the slightest inclination towards monogamy. The more numerous the 'charming' ladies and the less he was seriously committed to any of them, the better.

As if to provide an explanation, during this autumn he wrote a lecture in which he discussed romance and sexuality as he saw them. Entitled 'Psychology and Troubadours', it had been commissioned by one of

Yeats's occult-minded friends, G. R. S. Mead, and was delivered by Ezra to Mead's Quest Society. (Eventually it was included as an extra chapter in the revised *Spirit of Romance*.) The chief source of its ideas was the Rosicrucian book *Le Secret des Troubadours* which he had reviewed five years earlier.

The lecture asserts that the *canzoni* of the troubadours are not just vague expressions of romantic feelings, but allusions to a specific 'love code' or 'love cult' which, he asserts, was descended from 'pagan rites of May Day' and owed much to the Eleusinian Mysteries of ancient Greece. Of what, then, did the cult consist? Ezra says it was 'stricter, or more subtle, than that of the celibate ascetics', and that it involved a sublimation of sexuality into something more refined and intellectual; that it was 'a cult for the purgation of the soul by a refinement of, and lordship over, the senses.' It was a religion or philosophy in which 'a sheer love of beauty and a delight in the perception of it' was cultivated in place of 'all heavier emotion'. It led not to the 'whirl or madness of the senses' which results from actual sexual involvement, but to 'a glow arising from the exact nature of the perception', an intense pleasure derived from the intellectual contemplation of physical beauty.

He speaks of the cult in an intense and mysterious fashion, which leaves one in no doubt that he regarded himself as a latter-day practitioner. One must conclude, then – and the nature of his romantic entanglements supports this – that at present he was not in search of actual sexual experience at all, but was trying to practise and perfect the dispassionate contemplation of beauty that he describes in the lecture. Whether he may have done so from nervousness of sex, from private feelings of sexual inadequacy, or from an unconscious doubt as to whether he had any sexual desire for women at all, one can only conjecture.

While writing the lecture in 1911 he told Dorothy he found the whole subject very difficult to put into words. 'Don't *you* be "nebulous to the Nth" about yr. Troubadour psychology,' she told him. 'Say you're a reincarnation so you *know*. Are you? do you?'

*

In February 1912 Ford Madox Hueffer, who was back in London, introduced him to Henry James. Ezra told his mother that he and James had 'glared at each other across the same carpet'. They both attended the same lunch party a month later, and this time Ezra found James 'quite delightful'. At a third meeting he liked him still more. Eighteen months later he was proudly reporting 'James saying decent things about me, I dont know precisely what, but the news is consoling, as he is one of the six intelligent people on the island'. There is a memory of one of his encounters with James in Canto 7: 'the great domed head . . . Moves before me . . . And the old voice lifts itself / weaving an endless sentence'.

James mattered to Ezra as the great example of the American exile sitting in judgement on two continents. He was particularly admiring of what James had said about America, asserting that without him 'whole decades of American life . . . would have been utterly lost'. But by 1918, when he wrote a long obituary study of James's work (the most substantial piece he ever produced on any prose writer) he was more obsessed with James's achievement as *the* author who captures the sensations of the 'American who has come abroad'. Though the convolutions of James's prose style might seem very far from his own determination to achieve poetic statements 'close to the thing', he felt a verbal affinity, a shared national characteristic:

> Old Henry James worried his European readers to death by his parentheses. They are an American habit, they mean something to us and for us as Americans. They mean something more than the one track mind. But they do NOT imply deviation or lack of direction. They are a desperate attempt, no not an attempt, a DEVICE, to avoid leaving out something NEEDED, some part of the statement needed to set down, to register the direction, and meaning.

James gradually became one of his own personae. His style in his early letters, especially to women friends, tended to show James's influence; he admitted this to May Sinclair in 1909, describing it as 'my reminiscence of H. James, his style'. The reason was partly his need for a courteous, elegant model, but also (as he admitted to Dorothy) that he had an 'unconquerable aversion to simple statement'.

*

Despite his mysterious annual income of $1,000 and the agreement with his new publisher, Swift & Co., Ezra wanted to provide himself with regular literary journalism. Through the T. E. Hulme group he made contact with A. R. Orage, editor of the weekly *New Age*, for which F. S. Flint and other members of the group often wrote. Orage took a liking to Ezra's manner and offered him a regular column, beginning in November 1911.

Alfred Richard Orage, twelve years Ezra's senior, was a former elementary-school teacher from Leeds who had come to London in 1906 as a free-lance journalist and had bought the moribund *New Age* and begun to edit it. He subscribed to Guild Socialism, but the paper was not limited to this political viewpoint; Chesterton, Wells, and Bennett were among the contributors, and Orage, besides writing political commentary, had his own literary column, though Ezra thought he showed an 'unconscious antipathy to art'. Certainly the dull pages of the *New Age* were an unlikely stamping ground for Ezra, but during the next decade Orage proved an 'excellent friend' to him, publishing nearly 300 of his articles and proving the most reliable of all his literary employers to date.

The fee was small – Orage himself said someone had nicknamed the paper the *No Wage* – but the guinea a week he paid Ezra was better than nothing, and Ezra once said that Orage 'did more to feed me than anyone else in England'. Ezra paid no attention whatever to the rest of the paper ('I hope you don't think I *read* the periodicals I appear in') and could not imagine who would wish to subscribe to so dreary and vaguely bad-tempered a journal. 'To this day I haven't the faintest idea who *read* that paper,' he said in 1935. 'The only man I ever met who had seen my stuff in the *New Age* was an admiral.' However almost any regular outlet was better than none, and the very unfashionableness of the paper appealed to him and made it easier to spread himself within its pages. He told T. S. Eliot in 1922 that he had 'found it less interruption to my work to write for the New Age at £1/1 an article, than to keep up ones intercourse with Mayfair.'

Orage and his contributors gathered weekly over tea and buns in a café near the magazine's offices, which were in Cursitor Street off Chancery Lane, and Ezra could sometimes be seen there; he described how the *New Age* occupied '2 VERY small cells in print shoppe'. He made no new friends in the group. Paul Selver, a schoolmaster who often contributed to the magazine, recalled how 'with his clipped beard . . . and his velveteen appearance, Ezra flaunted his aestheticism in a manner which jarred upon some of the less aesthetic *New Age* ites. Behind his back they passed more or less rude remarks.'

His first series of articles for the magazine had a thoroughly 'aesthetic' title, 'I Gather the Limbs of Osiris'. An editorial note explained: 'Under this heading Mr Pound will contribute expositions and translations in illustration of "The New Method" in scholarship.' Ezra's first piece, published on 20 November 1911, was his translation of *The Seafarer*, which, fine as it was in many respects, may have prompted readers who knew Anglo-Saxon to wonder whether the 'New Method' made a virtue of inaccuracy. Next week, under the subtitle 'A Rather Dull Introduction', he explained that the Method actually consisted of the selection of what he called Luminous Detail. This meant choosing something that would truly illuminate a work of art or a historical event, rather than offering mere 'multitudinous detail'. He asserted: 'The artist seeks out the luminous detail and presents it. He does not comment.'

This apparently casual statement was his first reference to the system of 'thought' which would dominate his mature years. He found reassurance for using it a little later when he discovered Ernest Fenollosa's writings on the Chinese ideogram, and thereafter labelled it the Ideogramic Method, but essentially he developed it before he read Fenollosa. It consisted simply of *selection* rather than *analysis*. He would pick out items – works of art, lines in a poem, pieces of music, snippets of news, whatever happened to catch his attention and seemed to relate to his current obsession – and hold them up for attention as if their significance were self-evident. This principle would govern both the Cantos and his economic–political activities of the 1930s and 1940s.

The next set of Luminous Details presented to readers of the *New Age* were some of his translations from Cavalcanti and Arnaut Daniel, interspersed in alternate weeks with a discussion of the relation of the present-day artist to tradition. At its conclusion he described the series, quite rightly, as 'these rambling discourses', but he conveyed in them his current preoccupation with searching for a modern poetic voice.

He began to find another way in which he might pursue that search when, with Dorothy, he attended a series of lectures by T. E. Hulme on Henri Bergson. Ezra had no interest in Bergson – Dorothy had to drag him there – but he woke up when he heard Hulme saying that the artist does not *create* a truth but *discovers* it, picks out 'something which we, owing to a hardening of our perceptions, have been unable to see ourselves'. The real challenge to a poet, said Hulme, was to satisfy this 'passionate desire for accuracy'.

Ezra thought about this all winter, and in February 1912 discussed it in an article which he contributed to *Poetry Review* under the mis-spelt title 'Prologomena' (for 'Prolegomena'). He said he believed in the need for 'poetry which corresponds exactly to the emotion or shade of emotion to be expressed', and he made a forecast that twentieth-century poetry, at least during the next decade or so, would 'move against poppy-cock', would be 'harder and saner', would become 'austere, direct, free from emotional slither'.

This reflected Ford Madox Hueffer's influence as much as Hulme's. Ezra was saying, in effect, that he was ready for contemporary speech in his poetry – for 'the trampling down of every convention that impedes or obscures'. He accepted that 'a vast number of subjects cannot be . . . properly rendered in symmetrical forms'. Moreover 'no good poetry is ever written in a manner twenty years old, for to write in such a manner shows conclusively that the writer thinks from books, convention and cliché, not from real life'. This sounds like a hostile review of his own *Canzoni* – it was much what the actual reviewers of it had said. He concluded by prophesying the coming of a new poetry that will be 'like granite'.

His own most determined attempt at modernity was 'Portrait d'une Femme', sent to the *North American Review* in January 1912. The title and subject matter were obviously derived from Henry James; the portrait itself may be of Olivia Shakespear, since the line 'Great minds have sought you – lacking someone else' seems to hint at her substitution for Maud Gonne in Yeats's affections. But the poem is also a very accurate description of Ezra's own mind, of his preference for Luminous Detail rather than systematic thought, though such self-portraiture can hardly have been intended:

> Your mind and you are our Sargasso Sea,
> London has swept about you this score years
> And bright ships left you this or that in fee:
> Ideas, old gossip, oddments of all things,
> Strange spars of knowledge and dimmed wares of price . . .
> Trophies fished up; some curious suggestion;
> Fact that leads nowhere; and a tale or two,
> Pregnant with mandrakes, or with something else
> That might prove useful and yet never proves . . .

As a poem – and it was the best he had written since 'Sestina: Altaforte' – it was not granite hard, more an exercise in Ford Madox Hueffer-style impressionism with overtones of James. Even so it was too rough for the *North American Review*, which rejected it outright (though it had previously accepted some of his poems) on the absurd ground that the opening line contained too many 'r' sounds. The rejection still rankled six years later, when Ezra wrote in the iconoclastic *Little Review*: 'As we are no longer governed by the *North American Review* we need not condemn poems merely because they do not fit some stock phrase of rhetorical criticism.'

He saw a lot of Yeats during this winter of 1911-12, and was now 'taking charge', as Douglas Goldring puts it, of Yeats's Monday evening salons at Woburn Buildings, at times almost reducing Yeats himself from master to disciple. Goldring recalls how

> when Ezra took me for the first time to one of Yeats's 'Mondays' . . . he dominated the room, distributed Yeats's cigarettes and Chianti, and laid down the law about poetry. Poor golden-bearded Sturge Moore, who sat in a corner with a large musical instrument by his side (on which he was never given a chance of performing) endeavoured to join in the discussion on prosody, a subject on which he believed himself not entirely ignorant, but Ezra promptly reduced him to a glum silence.

Yeats's notes to Ezra were now almost chummy. 'My dear Ezra, will you dine with me on Monday at 7 (at the Hotel)?' He made no pretence of sharing Ezra's views on anything, least of all poetry, describing him some years later as 'Ezra Pound, whose art is the opposite of mine, whose criticism commends what I most condemn, a man with whom I should quarrel more than with anyone else if we were not united by affection'. Quite apart from anything else, Yeats found Ezra of practical use. His letters to him were scattered with requests for errands when he was out of town. Would Ezra go round to Woburn Buildings to look for a parcel that Yeats had forgotten about, and deliver it to a London address? 'Charge me with taxi . . . I do not want to feel I am using up your time.' And when during the winter of 1912-13 Yeats felt thoroughly seedy, with a bad digestion and headaches, he engaged Ezra not merely to read to him in the evenings but to teach him fencing:

> I thought no more was needed
> Youth to prolong
> Than dumbbell and foil
> To keep the body young

– so Yeats writes in *The Wild Swans at Coole* (1919), but the reality was less elegant than the poem suggests: Ezra recalled how Yeats would 'thrash around with the foils like a whale'.

He continued to respect Yeats hugely for his past achievements, but felt on closer acquaintance that the mind of 'the greatest living poet' was 'a bit wooly at the edges', and said that Yeats sometimes 'gave the impression of being even a worse idiot than I am'. Elsewhere he wrote: 'Yeats on VERY rare occasions would make an intelligent remark / the MORE so, the more violently he wd/ deny it a year or six years later.' And in print twenty-five years after they had met, he described Yeats as 'now muddled, now profound, now merely celtic'.

*

Early in 1912 his arrangement with Swift & Co. was formalized. They were to pay him £100 a year for ten years as an advance on royalties against forthcoming books, in return for which they would become his sole British publisher. On the strength of this, Ezra wrote to Henry Hope Shakespear to say he was now earning 'about £400 per. year, with reasonable chance of increase. This would not go very far in England but Dorothy seems to think she could live abroad for a year or so . . . I dare say you think it a rather mad-cap scheme but there is a chance she might enjoy it.' Of Swift & Co., who had an office in Covent Garden, he observed: 'The son of some fairly solid people has just gone in as junior partner, so I feel fairly confident about the firm.'

Mr Shakespear still did not consider this a sufficient financial basis for marriage; as Dorothy put it, 'Father "won't recognize" our engagement'. But 'engagement' was definitely the light in which she herself now regarded it, and she took to wearing a ring, though not on her finger ('I wore the Ring round my neck last night!') Such a settled state of affairs was not much to Ezra's taste, and he wrote a poem, 'Middle-Aged', which suggests that the 'fires' of young love are 'over and spent' – he was now twenty-six. But the poem was carefully placed within quotation marks, as a monologue by some unidentified speaker.

Towards the end of February 1912 he handed in the typescript of a new collection of poems to Swift & Co. Dedicated to William Carlos Williams, it was called *Ripostes*. The book had been finished too soon after Ford's strictures on *Canzoni* to show many major changes of style. It included 'Portrait d'une Femme' and 'The Seafarer', both of them far better than anything in *Canzoni*, but there was still a strong flavour of the Pre-Raphaelites and the 1890s:

> No, no! Go from me. I have left her lately.
> I will not spoil my sheath with lesser brightness,
> For my surrounding air has a new lightness;
> Slight are her arms, yet they have bound me straitly
> And left me cloaked as with a gauze of aether.

On the other hand in a poem called 'The Return' the diction was certainly not contemporary but the metrical scheme was a remarkable departure:

> See, they return; ah, see the tentative
>   Movements, and the slow feet,
>   The trouble in the pace and the uncertain
>   Wavering!
>
> See, they return, one, and by one,
> With fear, as half-awakened;
> As if the snow should hesitate
> And murmur in the wind,
>   and half turn back;
> These were the 'Wing'd-with-Awe',
>   Inviolable.
>
> Gods of the wingèd shoe!
> With them the silver hounds,
>   sniffing the trace of air!
>
> Haie! Haie!
>   These were the swift to harry;
> These the keen-scented;
> These were the souls of blood.
>
> Slow on the leash,
>   pallid the leash-men!

Ezra said he had written this poem in a quarter of an hour. Yeats saw it as soon as it was published in the *English Review* in June 1912, and Dorothy describes him reading it aloud at the Shakespears 'with due music' and saying he was 'very pleased' with it, calling it 'distinguished'. A few days later she told Ezra: 'W.B.Y. says The Return is "flawless".' Later, Yeats called it 'the most beautiful poem that has been written in the free form, one of the few in which I find real organic rhythm'. (In America, E. E. Cummings read it as an undergraduate and always remembered the 'thrill' it first gave him.)

To Dorothy, Ezra described it as an exercise in 'Sapphics', but it is not in the strict sapphic metre, and he seems to have meant that he was returning to the Greek and Latin method of determining metre by quantity – that is, by the length of time required to pronounce each syllable, rather than by fitting the words into a predetermined stress pattern. Yeats recognized this, and said that the poem seemed as if Ezra were 'translating at sight from an unknown Greek masterpiece'. Clearly he wrote 'The Return' without any predetermined metrical pattern in mind, since he describes, in a letter to Dorothy, how he analysed its rhythm *after* composition:

> I was very bucked on analyzing 'The Return' – which I did straight away – that it is in almost uniform feet (systema graeca, – – ◡ –) as to quantity – if one counts certain pauses after the unit is determined, etc.

Then he laughed at himself and suggested he was getting 'a little too *much* ear'. However, William Carlos Williams once said that Ezra was 'possessed of the most acute ear for metrical sequences, to the point of genius, that we have ever known'; and 'The Return' is the first poem that demonstrates this.

The subject of the poem seems to be the pagan – presumably Greek – gods, and their tenuous, uncertain relationship with the modern age. But it is also 'about' its own technique. The 'tentative / Movements' and the 'uncertain / Wavering' are both Ezra's own hesitation as he experiments very cautiously with a new metrical system, and a demonstration that he can express irregular, uncertain, faltering rhythms with a degree of realism that would be almost impossible in most regular metrical schemes. There is, then, really no 'meaning' detachable from the poem at all. (Ezra hinted at this in a 1935 letter to Carlos Izzo, who was trying to translate it into Italian: 'The TOTAL effect shd. be aimed at, and LOCAL equivalence, of word or rhythm, melted out of the translation.') In 1914 he said of the poem that it had an 'objective reality' like a piece of sculpture (he cited works by Jacob Epstein and Henri Gaudier-Brzeska). It was an object to be contemplated rather than a statement containing a detachable meaning.

Though Yeats described 'The Return' as free verse, it is unlikely that

Ezra himself would have so labelled it. He believed, both then and later, that there is 'anarchy' in true *vers libre* 'which may be vastly overdone', and that the genre suffers from 'a monotony of bad usage as tiresome as any typical eighteenth or nineteenth century flatness'. In 1917 he quoted with approval a dictum of T. S. Eliot, 'No *vers* is *libre* for the man who wants to do a good job', and observed that as many traps lie in free verse as in regular metrical schemes. 'Beware of the rocking cradle,' he wrote to the young poet Archibald MacLeish in 1926, 'the balanced sentence, the swing of rhythm that makes one go and stick in a word for the sake of syllables, or something to fill out. It is more insidious in "free verse" than in fixed, because less obvious.'

*

To the more casual observer the most striking thing about *Ripostes* was not 'The Return' but the inclusion of an appendix entitled 'The Complete Poetical Works of T. E. Hulme'. In a facetious preface to this, Ezra explained that he was printing Hulme's poems because Hulme, enviably, had completed his entire *oeuvre* at the age of thirty (to which the twenty-nine-year-old Hulme added a footnote: 'Mr Pound has greatly exaggerated my age'). The Complete Works consisted of five very short poems.

Behind this cliquish little joke, and an allusion by Ezra to 'certain evenings and meetings of two years gone', there was a real wish to gain some attention for Hulme's brief experiments in poetry. F. S. Flint explains that though Hulme never regarded himself as a serious poet, he wrote a piece that the Thursday group called 'The Red-Faced Farmer', and would recite it as his standing contribution. Ezra printed it in 'The Complete Poetical Works', under the title 'Autumn':

> A touch of cold in the Autumn night –
> I walked abroad,
> And saw the ruddy moon lean over a hedge
> Like a red-faced farmer.
> I did not stop to speak, but nodded,
> And round about were the wistful stars
> With white faces like town children.

Then one evening, says Flint, 'to our enormous astonishment' Hulme produced four more short pieces – the remaining Poetical Works – which Flint describes as 'little Japanese pictures'. There are certainly touches of the *haiku* about them. They are none of them very skilful, and they scarcely justify Flint's wish that Hulme had stuck to verse rather than taking to philosophy, but evidently Ezra now thought their almost childlike use of imagery suggested a possible way forward for his own work. He hints, in his preface to the Poetical Works, that Hulme was really setting up a 'School of Images', though he discusses this in the satirical tone appropriate for the occasion:

> As for the 'School of Images', which may or may not have existed, its principles were not so interesting as those of the 'inherent dynamists' or of *Les Unamistes*, yet they were probably sounder than those of a certain French school which attempted to dispense with verbs altogether; or of the Impressionists who brought forth
>> 'Pink pigs blossoming upon the hillside';
> or of the Post-Impressionists who beseech their ladies to let down slate-blue hair over their raspberry-coloured flanks . . .
>> As for the future, *Les Imagistes*, the descendants of the forgotten school of 1909, have that in their keeping.

Readers of *Ripostes* must have wondered who the mysterious *Imagistes* might be.

None of Ezra's friends could have enlightened them, nor even Ezra himself, for no such group or school of poetry yet existed. Richard Aldington guesses that Ezra coined the name *Les Imagistes* while writing the preface to Hulme's poems, without having more than the vaguest idea of what it might mean. 'My own belief,' he writes, 'is that the name took Ezra's fancy, and that he kept it *in petto* for the right occasion. If there were no Imagists, obviously they would have to be invented.'

8

Foreign Correspondent

'Whenever Ezra has launched a new movement,' Aldington goes on, 'he has never had any difficulty about finding members. He just calls on his friends.' In this case the first of the friends Ezra turned to, to create *Les Imagistes*, were Aldington himself and Hilda Doolittle.

Hilda was still in London, living on her allowance and torn between the rather stifling affections of her American girlfriend Frances Gregg (whom Ezra named 'The Egg' and sneered at as a second-rate 'she-poet') and her slender hopes of not losing Ezra to Dorothy Shakespear. Early in 1912 Richard Aldington was introduced to Ezra, and Ezra immediately passed him on to Hilda.

Brigit Patmore had brought Aldington into Ezra's orbit. She had been asked by friends to look after 'a clever boy' who was in London 'because he won't go into his father's law business'. Not quite twenty, Aldington was the son of a Portsmouth solicitor. He had been given the thorough classical education of an English public schoolboy, and had visited Italy. His father had a large library of the English poets, and by his mid-teens Richard was widely read in them. He turned to intense classicism as a way of escaping a stuffy home and finding a style for himself in poetry. While at University College, London, he started to write *vers libre*, though not under the influence of the French Symbolists; he 'got the idea from a chorus in the *Hippolytus* of Euripides'. At this point he met Ezra.

Paul Selver of the *New Age* describes Aldington as 'a brawnyish, blond, good-looking young man who . . . affected a coat of stagey cut. He had about him something which Ezra, I fancy, would have called *panache*, and a plain speaker . . . I fear, blasted swank.' He also had a very English sense of irony, somewhat lost on Ezra. Over the years to come he played a dual role in Ezra's life: chiefly Sancho Panza to Ezra's Quixote, but with touches too of Iago, the latter gradually dominating the relationship. His delight in mocking Ezra was largely that of the cultivated Englishman laughing at the brash American, whom he supposes to be at least partially a mountebank. He sketched something of this ambiguous relationship in his war novel *Death of a Hero*, where the hero George Winterbourne makes the acquaintance of the painter Mr Upjohn:

> In the case of George and Mr Upjohn there was at least a truce to the instinctive hostility and grudging which human beings almost invariably feel for one another. Ties of mutual self-interest bound them. George made jokes and Mr Upjohn laughed at them: and vice versa. Mr Upjohn desired to make George a disciple, and George was not averse from making use of Mr Upjohn . . . They ate together, and even lent each other small sums of money without security. The word 'friend' is therefore justified *à peu près*.

But despite Aldington's frequent gibes at Ezra's expense, he admired a lot about him. In 1913 he took it upon himself to write to an editor who was quarrelling with Ezra:

> Of course it's no business of mine, but you know Ezra Pound does actually *know* more about poetry than any person in these islands, Yeats not excepted. Of course, he will insult you; he insults me; he insults Mr Hueffer; he insults everybody; most of us overlook it because he is American, and probably doesn't know any better. On the other hand he is certainly the cleverest man writing poetry today, so you'd better do what he says.

Aldington was particularly impressed by Ezra when he compared him to the Georgian poets, who were beginning to identify themselves as a group. Aldington had no time for them. 'The Georgians were regional in their outlook and in love with littleness,' he writes. 'They took a little trip for a week-end to a little cottage where they wrote a little poem on a little theme. Ezra was a citizen of the world, both mentally and in fact.' At a Soho dinner organized by Harold Monro, publisher of *Georgian Poetry*, everyone (says Aldington) 'was deploring Ezra and running him down. Finally I could stand it no longer. I stood up and said: "Ezra Pound has more vitality in his little finger than the whole lot of you put together," and walked out. That queered my pitch with a large and powerful clique, but I have never regretted it.'

Georgian Poetry was edited by Edward Marsh, cultured Englishman and civil servant; he and Ezra had little time for each other. Marsh asked if he could include 'Ballad of the Goodly Fere' and 'Portrait d'une Femme' in the first Georgian volume (1912), but Ezra refused, because the 'Goodly

Fere' did not seem to him to 'illustrate any *modern* tendency' (it was pastiche), and he wanted to reserve 'Portrait d'une Femme' for *Ripostes*, which was due to appear at about the same time as *Georgian Poetry*. He offered Marsh anything from *Canzoni*, but understandably Marsh did not care to take this up. By the time of the second *Georgian Poetry*, Marsh had decided to exclude any non-British poets. Being a classical scholar, he was understandably infuriated when Ezra, sitting next to him at a dinner, lectured him about quantitative verse and sapphics, and would not listen to Marsh's correction of his mistakes.

Ezra had some respect for Harold Monro, who published *Georgian Poetry* from his Poetry Bookshop and edited *Poetry Review*, to which Ezra sometimes contributed, but he thought the magazine generally 'rotten', and his obituary of Monro in the *Criterion* in 1932 delivered its few compliments very back-handedly: 'We used to distinguish him from most of his circle . . . by saying that he alone among them suffered from his stupidity. The rest were unconscious and unsuspicious, but Harold . . . was pervaded by a vague uneasiness . . .'

When the first *Georgian Poetry* came out, Ezra was very caustic about it, comparing it to a fatuous American anthology just published, *The Lyric Year*. Among the poets represented in it he exempted from abuse only D. H. Lawrence and Lascelles Abercrombie. By 1915 he was referring to the Georgians as 'the stupidest set of Blockheads to be found in any country', and was calling the no longer admired Abercrombie a 'literary hen-coop'. Only Rupert Brooke now seemed tolerable to him – 'the best of the younger English'.

Abercrombie soon became a *bête noire* with Ezra, to the extent that a legend grew up (narrated here by Forrest Reid) that he had

> challenged Abercrombie to a duel for advising young poets to abandon realism and study Wordsworth (some versions say Milton). Abercrombie, it is said, took the challenge seriously and became frightened when told Pound was an expert fencer . . . But Abercrombie took advantage of the challenged party's right to choose the weapons and proposed that they bombard each other with copies of their unsold books. Soon thereafter, the story goes, Abercrombie paid a visit to Yeats; greeted by Pound at the door, he fled. That apparently closed the menacing incident, and two bards were preserved.

*

As soon as he had introduced them to each other, Ezra began to treat Aldington and Hilda Doolittle as a couple of pet dogs, describing them to Dorothy as 'the two people who in all decency ought to regard it as their sole duty to stand present & keep me amused'. He said he had 'reared them with such persistent solicitude'. Since Hilda was the Dryad, Aldington quickly became the Faun, an allusion to his own poems 'The Faun Sees Snow for the First Time' and 'The Faun Captive', as well as to his youth and innocence. 'The Dryad has arrived with its faun,' Ezra writes in a typical letter to Dorothy. So Hilda, once Is-Hilda and the inspiration of 'Hilda's Book', was reduced to the status of a rather comic disciple.

In the spring of 1912 Ezra went off to Paris with the Faun and the Dryad in tow. He stayed with Walter Rummel in rue Raynouard ('I'm making a few small translations from Provençal for some tunes which Walter is resurrecting'), and also spent time with Margaret Cravens, the young American pianist he had met in Paris a year earlier. Margaret now learnt from Walter Rummel (another indiscretion on his part) of Ezra's unofficial betrothal to Dorothy, and Ezra wrote to Dorothy that Margaret would like her to come and stay. Dorothy regretted that this was not possible as there was no official engagement between them – which no doubt was the answer Ezra wanted her to give, a proof to Margaret of the looseness of his attachment. But if Margaret had thought herself a woman of some importance to Ezra, she must now have realized she was only part of a crowd – he also introduced her to Mary Moore, who was in Paris.

He went browsing among the bookstalls along the Left Bank. 'I've turned up several ancient tomes on the quais that I may be able to use in my work.' Among them was a Latin version of the *Odyssey* by Andreas Divus Justinopolitanus, an obscure poet of the early sixteenth century, or possibly rather earlier. The text excited Ezra, and eventually he used a passage from it, translated into English, as the opening of the Cantos. It was typical that his interest in the *Odyssey*, never much aroused in school or university days, should suddenly spring to life through finding an obscure medieval version. It is hard to perceive that the Andreas Divus text adds anything of significance to Homer; Ezra called it 'singable', but was more honest when he admitted that he found it easier to read than the Greek: 'It is very simple Latin, after all, and a crib of this sort may make just the difference of permitting a man to read fast enough to get the swing and mood of the subject, instead of losing both in a dictionary.'

He spent some of his Paris time working in the Bibliothèque Nationale on a projected book about the troubadours, to be called 'Gironde', for which he intended to collect material during a walking tour through southern France. He set off on the tour at the beginning of June, arriving in Limoges, but had scarcely got off the train when he heard from Dorothy – the only person who knew his address – that Margaret Cravens had committed suicide. He immediately returned to Paris.

'Sadness and nobility and so many things are in the web,' he wrote to Dorothy, 'Write to me, dear, and I will answer as best I can. I won't say, "don't write me trivial things", but write . . . gravely for a little.' This was a self-aware reaction, and he gives no indication of how deeply the news had affected him, or whether he felt he had been a cause of the suicide.

It has been suggested that Margaret Cravens killed herself because Walter Rummel, whom she knew well, had just announced his sudden marriage to another musician, Thérèse Chaigneau. Others have supposed the cause to be the news of Ezra's engagement to Dorothy. Margaret, whose father had taken his own life a year earlier, left a letter to Ezra (Dorothy mentions it), but it is not known what it contained. The only account of the circumstances surrounding her death has been given by Martha Ullman West, granddaughter of the American who had painted Ezra's portrait for Margaret in Paris the year before. She writes that Margaret

> had seemed increasingly withdrawn and had almost glorified her father's suicide the year before. She had been under a doctor's care for what in those days was called neurasthenia. [She] calmly shot herself through the heart, leaving no note to explain her reasons . . . The penultimate act of her life was to play on her piano a song by Pound and Rummel that they had dedicated to her.

To which can only be added Ezra's brief mention of her in Canto 77: 'O Margaret of the seven griefs / who hast entered the lotus.'

*

He resumed his walking tour. On 26 June he wrote to Dorothy from Paris: 'Tomorrow it's Uzerche & then the road for a week.' His purpose was to 'cover the ground of the chief troubadours', and he had plotted a route after studying Justin H. Smith's *The Troubadours at Home*. He wanted not only to see such castles as Bertran de Born's Altaforte but to trace the old roads that connected them, to be able to say (as he puts it in a 1915 poem): 'The old roads have lain here. / Men have gone by such and such valleys / Where the great halls were closer together . . . / I have walked over these roads; / I have thought of them living.'

He took a train from Paris to Uzerche, near Poitiers, and first traced the steps of de Born, visiting his castle – now named Hautefort – as well as Montaignac, where had lived the Lady Maent whom Bertran loved. He also inspected Poitiers; in Canto 45 he cites the church of St-Hilaire there as one of the great achievements of medieval architecture. He walked between twenty and twenty-five miles each day, on one occasion using a borrowed Touring Club de France card (the only kind of *carte d'identité* or passport that he had bothered to take, so regulation-free was the pre-1914 world) to get himself a bed in a small inn when 'covered with twenty miles of mud'. Another time, visiting Marueil, the birthplace of 'Arnaut of Marvoil' about whom he had written a poem, he found 'an old woman, glad to hear Arnaut, / Glad to lend one dry clothing'. He went to Châlus, where Richard Coeur de Lion had been killed by an arrow, and to Périgueux, where he watched festivities in the street: 'I have seen the torch-flames, high-leaping, / Painting the front of that church; / Heard, under the dark, whirling laughter.' Afterwards he described that country-side as 'the world's best . . . In every town a romanesque church or château . . . Food every ten miles or fifteen or twenty. When I say food, I mean food . . . With fit track to walk on.'

Going gradually southwards, by the beginning of July he had arrived at Sarlat, just above the Dordogne, where he 'climbed rickety stairs' in the old bishop's palace. He wrote to Dorothy telling her he had 'arrived here via Uzerche, Brive, Souillac. – I am sick of names ending in – ac, the first 50 are interesting but after that it becomes a bore.' He went on through Gourdon – which features in Canto 4: 'Blue agate casing the sky (as at Gourdon that time) . . .' – stopped at the post office in Cahors to collect letters, then went a long stretch over the hills to Rodez with its fine Gothic cathedral. 'This Rodez is really good but I your humble serviteur am also a-weary,' he wrote to Dorothy. 'One is finally, here, in what I presume are mountains.' Rodez was associated with several troubadours, but what drew him there was the story in *The Troubadours at Home* about Sordello's love for the Lady Guida of Rodez and his rivalry for her hand with Peire Vidal.

Ezra then pursued the old route between Rodez and Albi ('90 pedes-trated miles in last four days'), took a train to Foix, south of Toulouse, whence he walked to the old walled city of Carcassonne, then went to the coast at Narbonne. *The Troubadours at Home* devotes much space to Peire Vidal's association with this area, and calls a walk through it 'a journey from star to star past the wall of heaven'. From Narbonne he went on by train again to Arles, where he 'corrected Mead's proof' (the proof of 'Psychology and Troubadours' for Mead's Quest Society magazine) and examined the Church of St Trophime, which appears in Canto 45 as another example of achievement before the rise of 'Usura'. Then he visited Beaucaire with its ruined thirteenth-century castle – 'Aucassin's Beaucaire which is *really* charming. I nearly sat down for a week there.' Reaching Nîmes, he went to 'a very amusing bloodless bull fight in the blooming roman arena'. There remained only 'the little stretch between Le Puy & Clermont', a journey across the hills of the Auvergne. Up to now the weather had been generally hot, but on this final stretch

> The wind came, and the rain,
> And mist clotted about the trees in the valley,
> And I'd the long ways behind me.

He met a gypsy, who asked him 'Have you seen any others, any of our lot, / With apes or bears?' This delighted Ezra, since Le Puy had been the scene of an annual fair in the troubadour age.

He was back in Paris by the last week in July, having gained some feeling of 'what the country meant to the wandering singers . . . why so many canzos open with speech of the weather'. In 1945 during his imprisonment at Pisa, the landscape of the walking tour kept recurring to him as a vision of the earthly paradise:

> to set here the roads of France,
> > of Cahors, of Chalus,
> > > the inn low by the river's edge,
> the poplars . . .
>
> we will see those old roads again, question,
> > > > possibly
> but nothing appears much less likely.

*

When he got back from the walking tour, he was his usual cool self about Dorothy. 'I'll be over in a day or so,' he wrote to her from Paris, 'but don't bother to have me in until it's convenient.' A few weeks later, Olivia made one of her periodic attempts to put an end to the affair, reminding Ezra that he had said he was 'prepared to see less of Dorothy this winter', and asking him to keep this promise. She wrote:

> I don't know if she still considers herself engaged to you – but as she obviously can't marry you, she must be made [to] realize that she can't go on as though you were her accepted lover – it's hardly *decent*! . . . She can't . . . 'transfer her affections' to anyone else whilst you are always about – & you'll be doing her a great injury if you stand in the way of her marrying – She & I can't possibly go on living this feminine life practically à deux for ever . . . You *ought* to go away – Englishmen dont understand yr American ways, & any man who wanted to marry her wd be put off by the fact of yr friendship (or whatever you call it) with her.
>
> If you had £500 a year I should be delighted for *you* to marry her . . . but as you haven't, I'm obliged to say all this . . . I shouldn't mind yr coming to see her once a week, but she can't go about with you American fashion – not till she is 35 & has lost her looks. Tomorrow is her [twenty-sixth] birthday, & all I can feel is that I wish she had never been born.

Ezra merely reported to Dorothy: 'I'm to be let in *once* a week', to which

Dorothy replied 'Once a week be hanged', and they carried on just as before.

'Gironde', his projected book about the troubadours, based on the walking tour, now began to seem 'a dam'd nuisance'. Part of the trouble as usual was his prose style. He went over what he had written with Ford, who told him it was as bad as Robert Louis Stevenson – 'and that is very violent for him,' said Ezra (though he himself liked Stevenson, and in 'Gironde' was bound to be influenced by *Travels with a Donkey*). Also he was bored with the subject. His mind was now on the contemporary. For a while he thought of combining 'Gironde' with his observations on present-day America (based on what he had seen in New York eighteen months earlier), and using them as the two halves of one book, showing the troubadours and modern Americans as contrasting examples of 'medievalism'. But the plan faded away, taking 'Gironde' with it, as he became absorbed in the American part of the project.

He started to write up his American notes in the *New Age* under the title 'Patria Mia', a series of articles characterizing America as a medieval society about to emerge into its Renaissance. At present (he said) New York was in the Dark Ages, and he himself was a product of 'the American mediaeval system', but he announced 'the imminence of an American Risorgimento', and said that when that event came it would make the Italian Renaissance 'look like a tempest in a teapot!'

Later, he realized that his hope for an American Renaissance was in itself an essentially American trait – 'Damned mania for reforming things, due to my presbyterian training' – and that he was externalizing his own situation. Having long enthused for things medieval, he was now determined to emerge into a feeling of contemporaneity, accompanied by a rebirth of his artistic powers. Typically, while so preoccupied, he decided not to reform just himself but the whole of America.

He wrote a poem, 'To Whistler, American', in which he described himself as one of those 'Who bear the brunt of our America / And try to wrench our impulse into art'. America as a whole was 'a mass of dolts', but an American artist such as Whistler could 'Show us there's chance at least of winning through'.

Almost at once, he found what seemed a perfect tool for his American Renaissance. While he was still writing 'Patria Mia' in August 1912, he had a letter from a lady in Chicago, Harriet Monroe, asking him to contribute to a new magazine she was about to launch under the title *Poetry*. Ezra decided on the spot that *Poetry* would be the wagon on which American poets would roll across the plains into their Renaissance.

Harriet Monroe was a fifty-two-year-old spinster, the daughter of a lawyer. For nearly a quarter of a century she had been writing bland, mediocre verse, which she was now having difficulty in getting published, so she decided to start her own poetry magazine. She raised money from a hundred patrons and sent a circular to possible contributors. Ezra was on her list because, when she had visited London two years earlier, Elkin Mathews had drawn him to her attention.

'Dear Madam,' Ezra replied at once, 'I *am* interested.' Since she was proposing (so she said) to start the only serious poetry magazine in America, he was prepared to offer her a favour: 'You may announce . . . that for the present such of my work as appears in America . . . will appear exclusively in your magazine.' And more; he himself, he said, had been 'on the verge of starting a quarterly', but now he would transfer his editorial energies to *Poetry*, 'keeping you or the magazine in touch with whatever is most dynamic in artistic thought, either here or in Paris'. There could, he told her, be nobody better for the job – 'I *do* see nearly everyone that matters' – and with a Renaissance around the corner it was no time to hide one's light. 'Any agonizing that tends to hurry what I believe in the end to be inevitable, our American Risorgimento, is dear to me.'

So Harriet Monroe, who had hoped for a contributor, acquired a self-appointed overseas editor. She wrote back to say that she would be delighted, and could she announce it in the first issue of the magazine? 'All right,' answered Ezra, 'you can put me down as "foreign correspondent" or foreign editor if you like, and pay me whatever and whenever is convenient.' The first number of *Poetry* in October 1912 duly gave his name as 'Foreign Correspondent', and added: 'Mr Ezra Pound . . . authorizes the statement that at present such of his poetic work as receives magazine publication in America will appear exclusively in *Poetry*.'

However, at the moment he did not have much poetic work to offer, exclusively or otherwise. He sent Harriet Monroe 'all that I have on my desk', but this consisted solely of 'To Whistler, American' and 'Middle-Aged', the poem about the cooling of love. She printed them both, and he was gratified when the description in the Whistler poem of the American people as a 'mass of dolts' aroused what Miss Monroe termed 'emphatic resentment' among readers. She defended him and the poem energetically in the magazine's pages.

If he had not yet very much to offer *Poetry* himself, he could drum up material from others. He told Richard Aldington to provide something for the magazine, which Aldington did, but then 'departed with dampened spirits' after Ezra had told him what was wrong with it. A more productive approach might be to imitate Yeats and hold a weekly salon, so Ezra made it known that anyone would be welcome at Church Walk on Tuesday evenings, and told his mother he would be 'conducting a literary kindergarten for the aspiring etc etc'. It was the same description (and the same evening of the week) that he had used for his freshman group at Hamilton ten years earlier. The Faun and the Dryad dutifully turned up on the first

Tuesday, and F. S. Flint came along out of curiosity. Also present was Paul Selver of the *New Age*, who was annoyed by the 'flippant and knowing manner' in which Ezra conducted the conversation, and the 'cabbalistic argot' of Aldington's and Hilda's replies. 'I assumed that deep was answering unto deep. But gradually I reached the conclusion that I failed to fathom the meaning of these exchanges because there was little if any meaning to fathom.'

Another Tuesday, Florence Farr came along and read from the works of the Bengali poet Rabindranath Tagore, whom Yeats had just discovered for himself and for the British literary world, and who arrived in London a week or two later to promote his own English translations of his songs, about to be published with an introduction by Yeats. Ezra told Harriet Monroe that he would definitely try to get some of Tagore's verses for *Poetry* – 'They are going to be *the* sensation of the winter' – and sure enough the December issue contained six Tagore poems with a two-page note by Ezra, saying he found in them 'a quiet proclamation of the fellowship between man and nature'. Actually he had tried to 'improve' a few details in the poems before publication, but Tagore put a stop to that.

Ezra told readers of *Poetry* that 'world-fellowship' was 'nearer' thanks to Tagore's visit to London, and said to Dorothy that Tagore made him feel 'like a painted pict with a stone war club'. Aldington was tickled by this new enthusiasm: 'I wasn't allowed to see Tagore, as being too profane; but I could always tell when Ezra had been seeing him, because he was so infernally smug.' In fact after Tagore had left London and gone on to America, Ezra lost interest, dismissing the Bengali's mysticism as an 'oriental beetle with 46 arms' and saying that all Indian art was mushy.

Apart from Tagore, it was difficult at first to find anything worth sending to Miss Monroe in Chicago. He would not touch the mainstream Georgians, but he tried Walter de la Mare, whom he had met at the Square Club and whose poems mildly intrigued him. But though de la Mare had had one or two good things to say about *Canzoni* in print, privately he thought Ezra 'unspeakable . . . with his patchoulied fallalaries', and he declined the invitation.

The Tuesday evenings were not achieving much. One week the gathering listened to Marjorie Kennedy Fraser performing Celtic folk songs, but this was run-of-the-mill Celtic Twilight, and there seemed nothing left after all but to use the Faun. Ezra told Harriet Monroe he would send along 'some of young Aldington's stuff'. He did not hold out much hope – 'Richard sends me some bad poems,' he said to Dorothy – and he wrote in *Poetry*: 'Among the very young men, there seems to be gleam of hope in the work of Richard Aldington, but it is too early to make predictions.' (A vast gap of seven years separated Ezra from the 'very young' Aldington.) However, there were ways of promoting even such minor stuff, and when the first

Aldington poem appeared in *Poetry* in November 1912 Ezra provided an explanatory note that it was the work of 'one of the "Imagistes", a group of ardent Hellenists who are pursuing interesting experiments in *vers libre*; trying to attain in English certain subtleties of cadence of the kind which Mallarmé and his followers have studied in French'.

This came as a surprise to Aldington, who had scarcely heard of Mallarmé, let alone read or tried to copy him, and was not aware that he was 'one of the "Imagistes"'. And if the Imagistes were 'a group of ardent Hellenists', then Hilda must be one of them too, though Ezra had never thought of her as a potential poet. But then one day at the British Museum she showed him a page of manuscript. This is how she tells the story:

> 'But Dryad,' (in the Museum tea room), 'this is poetry.' He slashed with a pencil. 'Cut this out, shorten this line. "Hermes of the Ways" is a good title. I'll send this to Harriet Monroe of *Poetry*. Have you a copy? Yes? Then we can send this, or I'll type it when we get back. Will this do?' And he scrawled 'H.D.   Imagiste' at the bottom of the page.

Aldington similarly describes how 'Ezra was so much worked up by these poems of H.D.'s that he removed his pince-nez and informed us that we were Imagists. Was this the first time I had heard that Pickwickian word?' He did not remember, but rather thought it was.

Ezra afterwards rewrote history and pretended that the Imagist movement had all been planned in advance. 'In the spring or early summer of 1912, "H.D.", Richard Aldington and myself decided that we were agreed upon the [Imagist] principles.' But neither Aldington nor Hilda remembered any such conversation, and in a more honest moment Ezra admitted that 'the name was invented to launch H.D. and Aldington before either had enough stuff for a volume'.

Neither Aldington nor Hilda was very keen on the label, nor on the invention of a new name for Hilda. 'I didn't like his insistence that the poems should be signed: "H.D. Imagist",' writes Aldington, 'because it sounded a little ridiculous. And I think [she] disliked it too. But . . . it was only through him that we could get our poems into . . . *Poetry*.' Perhaps Ezra thought Doolittle too ridiculous a name for a poet, though Shaw's *Pygmalion*, which ever afterwards made it seem a little absurd, did not receive its first performance until the next year, 1913.

'I've had luck again,' Ezra wrote to Harriet Monroe early in October 1912, 'and am sending you some *modern* stuff by an American. I say modern, for it is in the laconic speech of the Imagistes, even if the subject is classic . . . This is the sort of American stuff that I can show here and in Paris without its being ridiculed. Objective – no slither; direct – no excessive use of adjectives, no metaphors that won't permit examination.

It's straight talk, straight as the Greek! And it was only by persistence that I got to see it at all.'

So it appeared that the Imagistes were not necessarily 'ardent Hellenists' after all. 'H.D.' was an Imagiste in spite of, rather than because of, writing about Greek subjects. She and her fellows (whoever they might be) were attempting to be 'laconic', 'objective', and 'direct'; were supposed to be writing 'straight talk'. Actually Ezra was merely describing the poem Hilda had written (and he had rewritten), 'Hermes of the Ways':

> The hard sand breaks,
> and the grains of it
> are clear as wine.
>
> Far off over the leagues of it,
> the wind,
> playing in the wide shore,
> piles little ridges,
> and the great waves
> break over it.
>
> But more than the many-foamed ways
> of the sea,
> I know him
> of the triple path-ways
> Hermes
> who awaits.

This appeared in *Poetry* in January 1913, along with two others by Hilda in similar style, 'Priapus, Keeper-of-Orchards' and 'Epigram (After the Greek)', duly signed 'H.D., Imagiste'. An editorial note stated that they were the work of 'an American lady resident abroad, whose identity is unknown to the editor'. Ezra perceived the publicity value in a mysterious pseudonym. He was getting into his stride in a new role, that which Wyndham Lewis later called 'a poet and an impresario, at that time an unexpected combination'.

In private Ezra was amused by the idea of 'H.D.' the poet. In August 1913 he told Dorothy: 'The Dryad – with no sense of modernity – has writ a poem to Tycho the god of little things. That in an age of "Tatcho" [a patent remedy for baldness] & "Little Titch" [a music-hall performer] and with all the decent names in the classical dictionary to choose from.' Some while later Ezra remarked to his father, 'Hilda had a flash in her first poems,' implying that he thought little of what she had written since.

Now that the Imagistes were launched, it was time Ezra himself turned into one. 'I've been writing some new stuff in an utterly modern manner,' he told his father, referring to 'Contemporania', a sequence of self-consciously modern poems that he sent off to Harriet Monroe in mid-October 1912. 'I don't know that America is ready to be diverted by the ultra-modern, ultra-effete tenuity of Contemporania,' he observed to her. 'You must use your own discretion about printing this batch of verse. At any rate, don't use them till you've used "H.D." and Aldington, s.v.p.' The poems were about the idea of being a modern poet who caused outrage simply through his modernity – a rather inverted subject.

The sequence began with 'Tenzone', a prologue:

> Will people accept them?
>   (i.e. these songs).
> As a timorous wench from a centaur
>   (or a centurion),
> Already they flee, howling in terror.

The modern poet then announces that he does not suffer from the 'virgin stupidity' of his audience, nor is he one of 'the nerve-wracked' or 'the enslaved-by-convention', and he expresses his contempt for the outworn values that crush such people. He is scornful towards his own earlier work, which he says only appealed to people because it was 'twenty years behind the time', and now he will throw such stuff to the wind:

> Come, my songs, let us express our baser passions,
> Let us express our envy of the man with a steady
>   job and no worry about the future.
> You are very idle, my songs.
> I fear you will come to a bad end.

Of course none of this was Imagisme, according to his various definitions of that somewhat elusive poetic movement. It was just a clearing of the ground, a blast to announce the appearance of a new circus-act. It was not even one of Ezra's more convincing personae. But buried in the 'Contemporania' sequence were several more serious pieces that invited closer inspection – especially the last poem of all, a mere two lines in length, headed 'In a Station of the Metro':

> The apparition of these faces in the crowd:
> Petals on a wet, black bough.

Just after finishing 'Contemporania', Ezra explained how he wrote this little piece:

> I got out of a train at, I think, La Concorde and in the jostle I
> saw a beautiful face, and then, turning suddenly, another and
> another, and then a beautiful child's face, and then another
> beautiful face. All that day I tried to find words for what this

made me feel. That night as I went home along the rue
Raynouard I was still trying. I could get nothing but spots of
colour. I remember thinking that if I had been a painter I might
have started a whole new school of painting. I tried to write the
poem weeks after in Italy, but found it useless. Then only the
other night, wondering how I should tell the adventure, it
struck me that in Japan, where a work of art is not estimated by
its acreage and where sixteen syllables are counted enough for a
poem if you arrange and punctuate them properly, one might
make a very little poem . . . And there, or in some other very
old, very quiet civilisation, some one else might understand the
significance.

Despite his initial hesitation in sending 'Contemporania' to Harriet
Monroe, he now felt thoroughly modern. 'God knows I wallowed in
archaisms in my vealish youth,' he wrote to her. In fact the supposed
modernity of 'Contemporania' would soon look fairly rusty to him.
Neither now nor later could he achieve natural modernity by writing about
the present day. Wyndham Lewis felt this acutely: 'When he tries to be
up-to-date it is a very uncomfortable business . . . Life is not his true
concern . . . his field is purely that of *the dead* . . . whose life is preserved
for us in books and pictures.'
    Of course 'Contemporania', written in a hurry and to fill a gap, was not
a serious attempt at anything more than baiting. He told Harriet Monroe
that to publish it would give her 'your chance to be modern . . . to produce
as many green bilious attacks throughout the length and breadth of the
U.S.A. as there are fungoid members of the American academy'. She felt
fairly bilious herself when confronted by such lines in 'Contemporania' as
'Speak well of amateur harlots' or 'Dance the dance of the phallus', and she
protested to Ezra. He replied: 'Morte de Christo! . . . You can't expect
modern work to even look in the direction of Greek drama until we can
again treat actual things in a simple and direct manner.' Miss Monroe was
far from convinced, and would have turned the sequence down altogether
but for the intervention of Rabindranath Tagore, then in Chicago, who
(alleged Ezra) told Miss Monroe that 'Contemporania' was the only real
poetry he had seen since setting foot in the United States. But she insisted
on some cuts, and Ezra reluctantly agreed to them.
    When 'Contemporania' appeared as the leading item in the April 1913
issue of *Poetry*, Ezra got the public reaction he wanted. Raymond
Macdonald Alden in the *Nation* mumbled about 'indecencies', and claimed
that the verses would appeal to the 'frankly lascivious'; while the *Dial*
critic, Wallace Rice, complained that '*Poetry* is being turned into a thing for
laughter', and rejected all *vers libre* as formless. Harriet Monroe sent a

spirited reply to the *Dial*, in which she pointed out that Mr Rice's own poetic experience consisted chiefly of editing *The Little Book of Brides* and *The Little Book of Kisses*. On the other hand, which Ezra had presumably not expected, 'Contemporania' also inspired a number of parodies, two in the *Chicago Tribune*, others – of which this is an example – the work of Richard Aldington, printed during 1914:

> Come my songs
> (For we have not 'come' during three of these our delectable
> canzoni)
>
> Come, my songs, let us go to America.
> Let us move the thumbs on our left hands
> And the middle fingers of our right hands
> With the delicate impressive gestures
> Of Rabindranath Tagore.

Ezra claimed that he had virtually commissioned the Aldington versions himself – 'No one whom I hadn't had under my own jurisdiction could have done the job so well' – but they are virtually indistinguishable from the originals, which seems to say something about 'Contemporania'. Even 'In a Station of the Metro' submitted all too easily to Aldington's mocking pen:

> The apparition of these poems in a crowd:
> White faces in a black dead faint.

*

If Ezra was modest about 'Contemporania' when first sending the poems to Miss Monroe, he was all too confident of how to treat other people's work submitted to him as Foreign Correspondent of *Poetry*. Emboldened by his successful pruning of the 'H.D.' poem, he began to attack anything that landed on his desk. One of the first victims was Yeats.

On soliciting contributions for *Poetry* from Yeats, Ezra was rewarded by five poems in manuscript, with a request to check the pronunciation. This he did, making some alterations. Then, which he had not been asked to do, he went on to 'improve' the wording in three places. In the poem 'Fallen Majesty' he cut 'as it were' from the final line ' . . . that seemed, as it were, a burning cloud'. In 'To a Child Dancing in the Wind' he altered Yeats's 'Nor he, the best warrior, dead' to 'Nor him, the best labourer, dead'. And in 'The Mountain Tomb' he changed the line 'Nor mouth with kissing or the wine unwet' to 'Nor mouth with kissing nor with wine unwet'.

Yeats was furious; Ezra told Harriet Monroe that he was like an outraged monarch – 'Oh la la, ce que le roi desire'. But gradually Yeats began to think that the changes made some sense, and by the time the texts had achieved finality in his *Collected Poems* he had adopted something very close to Ezra's versions.

Sending on the Yeats poems to Harriet Monroe, Ezra observed: 'I don't think they're his absolute best, but they show a little of the new Yeats, as in "Child Dancing" . . . "Fallen Majesty" is just where he was two years ago.' He had now determined to take the master in hand. 'Although he is the greatest of living poets,' he wrote in *Poetry* in January 1913, 'his art has not broadened much in scope during the past decade.' Just after this was written and sent off to Chicago, Yeats himself experienced 'a fortnight of gloom over my work – I felt something wrong with it. However on Monday night I got Sturge Moore in and last night Ezra Pound and we went at it line by line and now I know what is wrong and am in good spirits again. I am starting the poem about the King of Tara and his wife ["The Two Kings"] again, to get rid of Miltonic generalizations.'

A letter from Ezra to Harriet Monroe at this juncture explains what he said to Yeats. It was actually much what he had heard from Ford in Germany:

> Objectivity and again objectivity, and expression; no hind-side-beforeness, no straddled adjectives (as 'addled mosses dank'), no Tennysonianness of speech: *nothing* that you couldn't in some circumstance, in the stress of some emotion, *actually say*. Every *literaryism*, every book word, fritters away a scrap of the reader's patience, a scrap of his sense of your sincerity.

Yeats reported to Lady Gregory of these sessions with Ezra and Sturge Moore: 'Ezra is the best critic of the two.' (To which Ezra remarked 'I should *hope* so!!!') Yeats went on: 'He . . . helps me to get back to the definite and concrete.'

While all this was going on Ezra told Dorothy that 'the Eagle' had 'done two more poems to Mabel Beardsley' (part of the sequence 'Upon a Dying Lady') and 'I object to his having rimed "mother" immediately with brother and I wish he wouldn't ask me for criticism except when we're alone. *One* of [the] lyrics is rather nice, but he cant expect me to like stale riming, even if he does say its an imitation of an Elizabethan form. Elizabeefan . . . Its just moulting eagle.' And four months later: 'I think the Eagle's "Grey Rock" is very fine – but his syntax is getting obscurer than Browning's.'

Though Yeats was appreciative of the criticism, he was doubtful about Ezra's own poetry. 'In his own work,' he wrote to Lady Gregory, 'he is very uncertain, often very bad though very interesting sometimes. He spoils himself by too many experiments and has more sound principles than taste.'

The re-education of Yeats, coming on top of the successful creation of

'H.D.', encouraged Ezra to feel he had an automatic right to 'edit' everyone's poetry, published or unpublished. He was still doing it in the 1930s, when Daniel Cory, a neighbour in Rapallo, handed him a Petrarchan sonnet that he had already had printed in *Poetry*. Ezra asked if Cory wanted a 'detailed criticism', and on being told yes, 'picked up a large crayon and started to make substantial incisions in the flesh of my sonnet'. Cory immediately snatched the poem back.

Cutting was the critical tool that came most readily to Ezra's hand. He defended the practice to Archibald MacLeish in 1926:

> I find people often can NOT rewrite, they get a thing down, and then get paralysis, and imagine it wont go any other way. And as ce cher Ford has so well said: there are always forty ways to say ANYTHING and the first one is usually wrong. I dont mean my slashes are definite improvements, merely a suggested possible elimination or change, and a queery as to whether certain words really function.

He despised most people for not being strong enough to stand up to his slashings, saying (to a young poet) that they came to him for advice as if he were 'a chartered accountant' – they were happy when he gave them 'statements of assets', but were upset by 'my statement of liabilities'. Indeed, 'practically no one save Yeats & Eliot' had really been able to take it on the chin, and had 'stood up to my criticism for a protracted period'.* Yet though he had an acute ear for weak lines in other people's work, it is striking that he did not apply it to much of his own. 'The ideal way to edit,' he wrote, 'is to sit down at a man's desk and rifle it. (Ethics be damned.)' But the desk that was constantly accessible remained almost unrifled. Once he had finished a poem he almost never altered it. The impatience that made him want to set other poets' houses in order did not allow him to pay more than cursory attention to his own.

*

Ripostes was published by Swift & Co. at the beginning of October 1912, to generally enthusiastic reviews. F. S. Flint, writing in Harold Monro's poetry magazine, had nothing but praise for Ezra's 'determination towards a mastery of his medium', and singled out 'The Return' for special praise. It was now widely felt that Ezra was very near finding his mature voice. This was stated explicitly by John Cournos, a Russian-American poet and journalist who had just arrived in England. Writing in the *Philadelphia Record*, Cournos remarked that 'no one need be astonished if, having passed through the various stages of his wide-ranged development and

---

*His editing of Eliot began several years later.

manifold experiment, he shall achieve something altogether new and distinctly his own'.

In London, Ezra took Cournos under his wing, introducing him to Yeats and Ford and selling some of his work for him when he needed money. Cournos afterwards called him 'one of the kindest men' he had ever met. In fact, just as this was going on Ezra was in financial difficulties. 'Dear Dad,' he wrote to his father on 10 October 1912, just after the publication of *Ripostes*:

> I am in my 'last ditch' and I want you, if you can, to stand to the guns. My patron is dead – has been for some months – Swift decamped & the firm is in liquidation. None of this bothers *me* much as I can by now look out for myself. But Dorothy's family is making a row and the whole brunt of the thing seems to fall on her.

He and Dorothy had had to 'break the engagement', but he did not propose to sit back and see her 'sold off in society fashion'. Could Homer and Isabel give them a home for a while 'if we bolted'? But Dorothy wouldn't come without a formal invitation: his parents were to cable a reply, 'simply "Come" or "Dont"', and 'mother must sign'.

Even now, after the death of the mysterious patron who had been providing him with $1,000 a year, Ezra did not tell his parents who it had been, nor ever mention the subject to anyone else. But since he says that the patron died 'some months' before this letter, it may well have been Margaret Cravens, who had killed herself in June – a likely enough person to give Ezra a regular allowance so that he could get on with his work without financial worries (she first met him just before the allowance began to be paid). She was not rich – to save money she had shared a small apartment in Paris with two other girls – but she was being financed by an affluent aunt in Madison, Indiana, and she may have scraped up enough to give to Ezra, no doubt depriving herself of many comforts in the process. Very likely he exaggerated the degree of support he was getting from her.

More is known about the collapse of Swift & Co. In Ezra's own words 'a beautiful and human chapter is to be writ re/ the rise and jailing of Granville, Napoleon of Publishing'. Charles Granville, *littérateur* and manager of Swift, ran off to Morocco – 'They caught the *mgr.* in Tangier with *some* of the goods,' Ezra told his father – and the firm, which had specialized in free-thinkers and mystics, though it did have Katherine Mansfield on the list, went into the hands of a liquidator. Granville was put in prison. 'A man of infinite humanity,' wrote Ezra. 'And three women waited on the jail steps.' (His own position was much the same when he emerged from St Elizabeths forty-five years later.) After his time in prison Granville started the magazine *Future*, to which Ezra sometimes contributed. Meanwhile 'Swift's liquidator has paid up,' Ezra told his father in December 1912. He would receive £25 a quarter for one year, then a lump settlement of £65 – a good bargain considering that all he had given Swift was the Cavalcanti translations and *Ripostes*.

As it turned out, he did not need to call on his father for financial assistance after all. His needs at present were very slight – fees from *Poetry* (which sent him $100 at regular intervals), and the guinea a week from the *New Age*, easily covered his upkeep when bulked out by the allowance from Homer – and the row at the Shakespears blew over as his finances improved. Olivia and her husband subsided into resigned passivity, and Ezra and Dorothy were left to carry on much as before. Isabel Pound had wired 'COME' in reply to Ezra's request, but the elopement proved unnecessary. Ezra reassured his parents: 'Naturally I should have arrived duly and legally united. You needn't have been alarmed on that score.' Dorothy passed her twenty-sixth birthday, and became perceptibly less of a marriageable asset to her family. 'So we procede as heretofore,' wrote Ezra to his father, 'with due placidity and decorum.'

9

Our Little Gang

Ezra decided it was time for a public unveiling of the Imagistes, so he engaged F. S. Flint to write a piece about them for *Poetry*. 'Flint is doing an intelligent article . . . chiefly at my own dictation.' Flint describes how Ezra arrived one day with an 'interview with himself' already written, but Flint would not sign it without being allowed to rewrite it a bit (though not very much). The finished version, published in March 1913, began as follows:

IMAGISME

> In response to many requests for information regarding *Imagism* and the *Imagistes*, we publish this note by Mr Flint, supplementing it with further exemplification by Mr Pound. It will be seen from these that *Imagism* is not necessarily associated with Hellenic subjects, or with *vers libre* as a prescribed form.

The article explained that Mr Flint had 'sought out an *imagiste*' (who from what followed could be seen to bear a strong resemblance to Mr Pound) and was able to glean this information from him:

> The *imagistes* admitted that they were contemporaries of the Post Impressionists and the Futurists; but they had nothing in common with these schools. They had not published a manifesto. They were not a revolutionary school; their only endeavor was to write in accordance with the best tradition, as they found it in the best writers of all time, – in Sappho, Catullus, Villon. They seemed to be absolutely intolerant of all poetry that was not written in such endeavor, ignorance of the

best tradition forming no excuse. They had a few rules, drawn up for their own satisfaction only, and they had not published them. They were:

1. Direct treatment of the 'thing', whether subjective or objective.

2. To use absolutely no word that did not contribute to the presentation.

3. As regarding rhythm: to compose in sequence of the musical phrase, not in sequence of a metronome.

The first and second 'rules' were simply what Ezra had been trying to practise since Ford's attack on *Canzoni*, and what he had been trying to persuade Yeats to do. The third was the principle on which 'The Return' had been written. None of the three bore the slightest resemblance to his earlier description of Imagisme as *vers libre* written by 'ardent Hellenists'.

The Flint interview with the mysterious Imagiste went on to quote this individual as saying that 'by these standards' he and his fellow practitioners 'judged all poetry, and found most of it wanting'. They also held among themselves 'a certain "Doctrine of the Image", which they had not committed to writing; they said that it did not concern the public, and would provoke useless discussion.' This was Ezra belatedly realizing that if the movement was called Imagisme, it would have to have some sort of dogma about imagery and images; he was also exploiting the publicity value of mystery.

A reader of *Poetry* might well have judged from this that London was swarming with Imagistes; and there now followed six pages headed 'A Few Don'ts by an Imagist', this time openly signed by Ezra, and described by him to Harriet Monroe as 'instructions to neophytes' which might 'enable our contributors to solve some of their troubles at home'. Now at last he had something to say about imagery itself.

> An 'Image' [he wrote] is that which presents an intellectual and emotional complex in an instant of time . . . It is the presentation of such a 'complex' instantaneously which gives that sudden sense of liberation . . . which we experience in the presence of the greatest works of art.
>
> It is better to present one Image in a lifetime than to produce voluminous works.

He then gave his list of 'don'ts', most of which were fairly self-evident ('Use no superfluous words . . . Go in fear of abstractions . . .') though among them was one other observation about images:

> Don't use such an expression as 'dim lands of *peace*'. It dulls the image. It mixes an abstraction with the concrete. It comes from

the writer's not realizing that the natural object is always the *adequate* symbol.

In the midst of all the tomfoolery, all the air of a 'promoter's scheme' with which Imagisme was launched, there was one real step forward by Ezra. It was not very far from the method of the French Symbolists, but while they used images to stand specifically for something else ('The symbolist's *symbols* have a fixed value, like numbers in arithmetic,' wrote Ezra), an Imagiste would employ them *for their own sake*, not intending that they should have any detachable abstract meaning. An obvious example was his own poem 'The Return'.

The idea that an image should present an 'intellectual and emotional complex' in a single 'instant of time' comes very near to the core of his own practice as a poet. He was postulating something not dissimilar to T. S. Eliot's celebrated assertion, six years later, that the only way of 'expressing emotion in the form of art' was to discover 'an "objective correlative" . . . a set of objects, a situation, a chain of events which shall be the formula of that *particular* emotion'. The only difference is that Eliot assumes that a set or chain of objects or events is required to achieve the effect, while Ezra speaks of it being done in a single 'instant of time', 'instantaneously'. According to him, a single image is enough.

Though the idea of being 'modern' for its own sake played no part in the supposed doctrines of Imagisme, his insistence on allowing images to stand by themselves as objective realities without abstract meaning was bound to lead to the poetry now called modernist. If a poet writes by means of unexplained and detached images, rather than by using simile, metaphor, or symbolism, then the images themselves become the poetry, and the reader is left to do all the work of explanation, is expected to make all the effort necessary to establish a coherent narrative. So, though Imagisme was not supposed to be 'a revolutionary school' in itself, it was likely, if taken seriously, to lead to revolution.

*

Having set himself up as the head of a poetic school, Ezra began to hand out headmasterly reproofs. Among those reprimanded was Harriet Monroe herself, the editor of *Poetry*: 'You know as well as I do that you could have written the "Nogi" [one of her own poems, printed in the magazine] in four lines if you'd had time to do so.' Needless to say, the often very bad American poetry which took up many of the magazine's pages infuriated him: 'Good god! Isn't there one of them that can write natural speech without copying clichés out of every Eighteenth Century poet still in the public libraries?' Soon the *Poetry* office files were bulging with outbursts from him: 'I'm sick to loathing of people who don't care for the

master-work . . . what is the use of printing 'em?' Harriet Monroe took all
this very amiably. In her autobiography she speaks of Ezra's 'rather
violent, but on the whole salutary, discipline', and says she found herself
being 'rapidly educated' by him.

These letters to Miss Monroe have a hysterical edge not found before in
his correspondence. Of a popular magazine that had 'taken up' Rabindranath Tagore, he wrote to her in March 1913:

> These fools don't KNOW anything and at the bottom of their
> wormy souls they know they don't and their name is legion and
> if once they learn that we do know and that we are 'in' first,
> they'll come to us to get all their thinking done for them and in
> the end the greasy vulgus will be directed by us.

More and more he was inclined to brand the public as a 'mass of dolts', a
view he had held since undergraduate days at Hamilton, when it had been
necessary for him to take refuge in solitary erudition; but until now there
had been no point in saying so publicly.

In an article in *Poetry* during 1913, he asserted that his aim in England
had been to make friends with as many as possible of 'the two hundred
most interesting people' in the island. As for the remainder, 'I do not see
that we need to say the rest live under them, but it is certain that what these
[200] people say comes to pass.' America, he said, resembled England with
'the two hundred most interesting people removed'. Much of this was
motivated by sheer impish delight in annoying the staid American readers
of *Poetry*, but like all his performances it began to take hold of him. He was
soon asserting that the artist would be dictator of the future:

> The modern artist . . . knows he is born to rule but he has no
> intention of trying to rule by general franchise. He at least is
> born to the purple . . . Modern civilisation has bred a race with
> brains like those of rabbits and we who are the heirs of the
> witch-doctor and the voodoo, we artists who have been so long
> the despised are about to take over control.

Of course this was pure *blague*, but the joke grew out of his very real
feeling that the artist is a superman. He particularly hated the motto, taken
from Whitman, which adorned the front of *Poetry*: 'To have great poets
there must be great audiences too.' Ezra fumed about this in *Poetry* in
1914: 'The artist is not dependent upon the multitude of his listeners.
Humanity is the rich effluvium, it is the waste and the manure and the soil,
and from it grows the tree of the arts . . . This rabble, this multitude – does
not create the great artist. They are aimless and drifting without him.' And
soon he began to associate the triumph of great art with the rejection of
democracy: 'The voice of the majority is powerless to make me enjoy, or

disenjoy, the lines of Catullus. I dispense with a vote without inconvenience; Villon I would not dispense with.'

Yet Ezra had, at present, no political dogma to preach, nor any interest in public affairs. For now, he confined his performance as the castigator of the 'mass of dolts' to purely literary and artistic matters. His only positive credo at this period was that good artists, of whatever kind, must be recognized and encouraged. Moreover, despite all his furious declarations about the superiority of great artists, he remained strikingly modest about his own work. 'No poet,' wrote T. S. Eliot on the young Ezra, 'was, without self-depreciation, more unassuming about his own achievement in poetry. The arrogance which some people have found in him, is really something else; and whatever it is, it has not expressed itself in an undue emphasis on the value of his own poems.' Wyndham Lewis spotted this too: 'In his attitude towards other people's work Pound has been superlatively generous . . . He does not in the least mind being in service to somebody (as do other people it is usually found) if they have great talent. No envy of the individual is attached to the work. I have never known a person less troubled with personal feelings.' And in 1925 Ernest Hemingway commented on the spectacle of 'Pound the major poet devoting, say, one fifth of his time to poetry. With the rest of his time he tries to advance the fortunes, both material and artistic, of his friends . . . And in the end few of them refrain from knifing him at the first opportunity.'

*

Hemingway's comment exactly describes Ezra's activities during the early months of 1913. He began to look for talent for *Poetry* outside his own circle, unearthing writers whose work did not much appeal to him, but whose qualities he perceived and whom he tried to promote. In March he wrote to one of the *Poetry* staff: 'Have just discovered another Amur'kn. VURRY Amur'k'n, with, I think, the seeds of grace. Have reviewed an advance copy of his book.'

This was Robert Frost, nine years Ezra's senior, who had just arrived in England after a long period of farming in America. F. S. Flint ran across him and introduced him to Ezra, who immediately acquired an advance copy of Frost's first book of poems, *A Boy's Will* (Frost grumbled that Ezra had taken the only copy then in existence) and wrote a review of it. The extent of his acquaintance with Frost at this period (friendship would scarcely be the word for it) is hard to determine. There is a story of a quarrel over lunch, and of a 'ju jitsu demonstration Pound made on Frost's person in a restaurant'. At all events neither made a favourable impression on the other. Nor did Ezra much enjoy the poems in *A Boy's Will*, but he decided that here was someone who really did 'care for the master work', and wrote to Harriet Monroe: 'I admit he's as dull as ditch water, as dull as

Wordsworth. But he is trying almost the hardest job of all and he is set to be "literchure" some day.'

He remained scathing about Frost's New England poetry. In 1931 he called it

> Sincere, very dull, without tragedy, without emotion, without metrical interest, a faithful record of life without intellectual interest or any desire for anything not in it . . . inferior to Crabbe, but infinitely better than fake. A great deal of New England life is presumably as Frost records it. It is difficult to see how such life differs greatly from that of horses and sheep.

In 1913 he tried to 'improve' Frost's poems for *Poetry*, just as he had Yeats's and Tagore's. Frost describes how 'Pound . . . took a poem of mine, said: "You've done it in fifty words. I've shortened it to forty-eight." I answered: 'And spoiled my metre, my idiom, and idea."'

Ezra's review of *A Boy's Will* appeared in *Poetry* in May 1913. Suppressing virtually all his dislikes of Frost's idiom, and concentrating on what he admired, he called it 'a little raw' but emphasized its strength: 'This man has the good sense to speak naturally and to paint the thing, the thing as he sees it . . . He is without sham and without affectation.' He also reviewed the book in London, in the *New Freewoman*, speaking of Frost's 'feel of some sober local wood god, innocent for the most part of our language, half indifferent to, and half dismayed at our customs'.

Harriet Monroe did not care for Frost's poetry, and told Ezra so. He replied. 'I don't doubt that the things Frost sent you were very bad. But he has done good things and whoever rejected 'em will go to hell along with *Harper's* and *The Atlantic*.' When he read Frost's 'Death of the Hired Man', he told his father it was 'better than anything' in *A Boy's Will*, and without asking Frost he sent it straight off to *Smart Set* in New York. Frost angrily demanded it back – it is not clear why – and, for the time being, that was the end of their association. Ezra took no further interest in Frost's progress. Thirteen years later he wrote: 'Mr Frost . . . hzas prebebly gawt the gnasty gnoyse of gnu inglend in his bloody dull meritoria. I dont know, haven't red enny fer a glong time.'

Some lines in Frost's poem 'The Code – Heroics', published by a reluctant Harriet Monroe in *Poetry* in February 1914, exactly describe Ezra's way of encouraging poets he had discovered:

> What he liked was someone to encourage.
> Them that he couldn't lead he'd get behind
> And drive, the way you can, you know, in mowing
> Keep at their heels and threaten to mow their legs off.

This was the technique he normally employed with William Carlos

Williams. Now he put Williams in touch with Harriet Monroe, who agreed to print some of his poems; and he persuaded Elkin Mathews to publish a collection by Williams, *The Tempers*, reviewing it himself in December 1913:

> He makes a bold effort to express himself directly and convinces one that the emotions expressed are veritably his own . . . He is for the most part content to present his image, or the bare speech of his protagonist, without border or comment . . . One is disappointed that Mr Williams has not given a larger volume, and one hopes for more to come.

In private he retained his usual condescending attitude to Williams's work, observing to Dorothy that 'Bill's mental processes' (his poems) were 'quite iluminating', and usually referring to him as 'Little Bill'. Yet though he would always treat Williams as irredeemably parochial, he allowed that this had great virtues. In the 1919 letter to his father in which he praises P. T. Barnum as the true expression of the American spirit, he goes on: 'Other "best thing in the country", Bill Williams, half inarticulate, but solid.' And to Margaret Anderson of the *Little Review* in 1918, comparing Williams with Amy Lowell: 'Bill Wms. is *the* most bloody inarticulate animal that ever gargled. BUT it's better than Amy's bloody ten-cent repetitive gramophone.' To Williams himself he wrote in December 1913: 'I still think as always that in the end your work will hold. After all you have the rest of a lifetime . . . You may get something slogging away by yourself . . .'

A third 'discovery' dispatched to Harriet Monroe during 1913 was D. H. Lawrence. Ezra told her in March: 'Lawrence has brought out a vol. He is clever; I don't know whether to send in a review or not.' He had previously seen, and grudgingly admired, poems by Lawrence in the *English Review* and in *Georgian Poetry*. Now he wrote in *Poetry* (July 1913) of Lawrence's new book *Love Poems and Others*:

> The *Love Poems*, if by that Mr Lawrence means the middling-sensual erotic verses in this collection, are a sort of pre-raphaelitish slush, disgusting or very nearly so . . . [But] when Mr Lawrence ceases to discuss his own disagreeable sensations . . . there is no English poet under forty who can get within shot of him . . . Mr Lawrence has attempted realism and attained it. He has brought contemporary verse up to the level of contemporary prose, and that is no mean achievement.

To Harriet Monroe, who was printing Lawrence's poems on his recommendation, he wrote in September 1913: 'Lawrence, as you know, gives me no particular pleasure. Nevertheless we are lucky to get him . . . I *recognize* certain qualities of his work. If I were an editor I should probably accept his work without reading it.'

It was in this spirit of recognizing true distinction in work for which he did not personally care that he began, at last, to pay some attention to modern French poetry. Motivated by his claim to be able to let Harriet Monroe know what was going on in Paris as well as in London, during his next visit to the French capital in April 1913, he took some trouble to survey its contemporary poetic scene. 'Have met lot of the younger french poets. on my way thru' Paris,' he wrote to his father. 'Romains, Vildrac, Duhamel, Arios, etc.' He afterwards described his adventures in an article in the *New Age*:

> I fetched up in the cellar of the 'Chatelet' . . . I found about twenty men in an alcove. They were rather tense and laconic. The brains of to-morrow's Paris were holding a council of war; it was not a plot against the State but only against the general stupidity . . . For three satiric hours I watched the little flame of free intelligence at strife for its very existence.

This introduction to the Chatelet group was probably effected by John Gould Fletcher, a prickly exile from Arkansas whom Ezra met in Paris along with a Philadelphian, Skipwith Cannell, both of them poets. Fletcher recalls how he himself was 'able, by quotation and example' to show Ezra 'that my favorite French symbolists were using my own devices of internal rhyme, vowel assonance, and the like . . . [This] seemed to impress him with the thought that there might be something in the symbolists after all, whom he had never actually read.'

Ezra ran across Fletcher again, and (says Fletcher) 'borrowed an armful of my French books and departed. When I next saw him . . . he told me that he was hoping to do an article for Orage of the *New Age* on these poets.' Fletcher was 'somewhat aggrieved at his taking credit, thus blithely, for introducing these poets to the English public, when I . . . had discussed them with him minutely.'

The articles for the *New Age* were entitled 'The Approach to Paris' and ran during the autumn of 1913. Realizing, as Ezra put it in *Poetry* in October that year, that he had 'spent about four years puddling about on the edges of modern French poetry without getting anywhere near it', he now identified and described the contemporary or recent Frenchmen whom the experts considered important, and attempted an introduction to their work. His principal choices were Remy de Gourmont, Jules Romains, Charles Vildrac, François Jammes, Tristan Corbière, and Rimbaud. It was quite a lengthy list, but he had not been much excited nor learnt anything radical in Paris. He concluded the articles rather cautiously, saying only that 'Paris is rather better off for poets than London', though in *Poetry* he kept up his performance as scourge of the poetasters: 'If our writers would keep their eye on Paris instead of on London . . . there might be some chance of their doing work that would not be *démodé* before it gets to the press.'

F. S. Flint had spent some years unsuccessfully trying to convince Ezra of the importance of modern French poetry, and was understandably scornful of this sudden assumption of the mantle of omniscience in this subject: 'In his eagerness to be the first guide along that delectable road – which I had made – he cut such strange capers and said such strange things that the prudent have been suspicious ever since.' In a more honest moment during his current display of enthusiasm for the French, Ezra admitted (in the *New Freewoman*) that he was not very well equipped linguistically to appreciate the French: 'Of course you never know where you are, in treating a foreign work of your own day . . . You know what moves and what pleases you, the rest is approximation. The finer shades may escape you.'

*

From Paris he went on as usual to Sirmione, where he told Dorothy that he was writing 'some more minute poems – a few of them proper'. These were more pieces resembling 'Contemporania', published in *Poetry* and *Smart Set* towards the end of 1913. Most were in the by now familiar facetious hortatory tone – 'Good God! They say you are *risqué*, / O canzonetti!' – and one, 'The Rest', was a complacent address to his fellow American poets:

> O helpless few in my country,
> O remnant enslaved! . . .
>
> Take thought:
> I have weathered the storm,
> I have beaten out my exile.

In May he was in Venice, awaiting the arrival of Aldington and Hilda. 'The Dryad has some slight affiliation with Verona, but the pair of 'em, wholly Hellenized . . . are going to be very much [out] of place in bella Venezia.' He gathered that they were 'falling in love with each other somewhere en route from Napoli. I suppose I'll have to be ready with a pontifical sanction.' When they arrived there was less comedy than he had anticipated: 'The Dryad . . . doesn't seem much more in love with it than when she left london.' However, Hilda married Aldington the following October, with Ezra among the witnesses. Hilda afterwards felt it had happened on the rebound of her feelings for Ezra.

There was yet another hiccup in his own engagement to Dorothy when he got back to London in June 1913. It arose out of his trying to bully the

Shakespears over their guest list for a private recital by Walter Rummel. Dorothy wrote to him angrily: 'Don't you know by this time that one of the things it is *pas permis* to do, is to interfere with other people's drawing rooms? ... You affect not to care about other people – but you try to interfere a good deal with their doings when they affect yourself.' Ezra's only reply was to send a poem, 'The Choice':

> It is odd that you should be changing your face
>> and resembling some other women to plague
>> me;
> It is odd that you should be hiding yourself in the cloud
>> of beautiful women, who do not concern me.

Dorothy wrote back to him:

> My very dear.
>> I cannot marry you. (I can but hope it's not
> mere cowardice, but a true instinct.)
>> I am sorry, sorry, sorry
>> and send my
>
>
>> Love

To which Ezra replied enigmatically:

> you can not
>> you can not
> you can not.

After a few days there was a reconciliation, but some of his friends, including Yeats, believed the 'engagement' to have been broken off, not least on the evidence of a poem Ezra had just written:

> As a bathtub lined with white porcelain,
> When the hot water gives out or goes tepid,
> So is the slow cooling of our chivalrous passion,
> O my much praised but-not-altogether-satisfactory lady.

In August they had another small disagreement. Dorothy mentioned that she was 'doing some new early Vict. wool work – which is half Italian & quite pretty', to which Ezra replied: 'I am not in the least sure that you ought to embroider. It kills time but it also draws off a lot of little particles of energy, that ought to be dammed up until they burst out into painting.' She answered: 'I think one wastes more energy doing nothing & feeling miserable about it, than in embroidery.' He: 'It is not as if embroidery *exercised* any faculty ... Its not much better than smoking.' At which point she gave up.

*

During the summer of 1913, Ford and Violet Hunt recommended him for the post of literary editor of the *New Freewoman*, a fortnightly with which their friend Rebecca West had just become involved. The paper, founded two years earlier by Dora Marsden of the Women's Social and Political Union, represented a mildly feminist–suffragist viewpoint, and was also concerned with such aspects of emancipation as the freedom to discuss sex in literature. 'The Freewoman has turned over three columns to me,' Ezra told his mother in August 1913, 'so I'm a sort of editor. I buy the poetry and do the notices. Which means to say I can amuse myself by drawing comparisons between the intelligence of my friends and the utter imbecility of my enemies.'

He was warned by Henry James, from whom he tried unsuccessfully to get a contribution to the paper, that he might become a 'Bondsman' to these New Freewomen, but in reality the job gave him a British outlet comparable (except in remuneration) to *Poetry*. At first he had no money with which to pay his contributors, but then John Gould Fletcher agreed to put up some cash in return for having his own poems printed in the magazine. (Typically, Ezra did not reveal Fletcher's identity to Dora Marsden and her colleagues, describing him mysteriously as his 'Sanctus Patronus'.) Ezra's mark quickly became visible on the paper: he printed an article on Imagisme, supposedly by Rebecca West but in fact lifted wholesale from the Flint–Pound pieces in *Poetry*, and this was followed by his own entire 'Contemporania' sequence.

Rebecca West was only briefly associated with the paper, and Ezra scarcely got to know her, though he had the impression she admired his poetry. Of the other *New Freewoman* ladies, Dora Marsden and her colleague Harriet Shaw Weaver, he afterwards observed that if either of them had reservations about him, 'no sign appeared', though the very correct-seeming Miss Weaver 'must have considered me rather like an unpredictable hippo'. He was left to get on with things as he saw fit, and there was 'little or no communcation' between him and Miss Marsden. Miss Weaver rather impressed him; he said that in any company she radiated an almost visible feeling of silence, 'a sudden stopping of all noise'. Iris Barry, a member of Ezra's entourage during the First World War, describes her as 'the lady sitting up so very straight with her severe hat and nervous air – she might have been a bishop's daughter, perhaps? *That* was the lion-hearted Miss Harriet Weaver.' Ezra was later to metamorphose this unlikely lady into James Joyce's publisher.

It quickly became evident that he was going to lead the Misses Weaver and Marsden and their paper by the nose, in whatever direction he happened currently to fancy. He immediately secured as a serial an English translation of *The Horses of Diomedes*, an overwritten and effete piece of soft erotica by Remy de Gourmont, the elderly Decadent poet and novelist whose writings he had just stumbled across in Paris. Yeats justifiably scorned this interminable serial ('Pink sensuality'), but Ezra claimed that de Gourmont displayed a 'gracious wisdom of the senses', whatever that might mean. More familiar Poundian names began to appear in the *New Freewoman* over the next few weeks: there was an article by Ford, reviews by Ezra of D. H. Lawrence's and Frost's poetry, and sequences of poems by 'H.D.' and Aldington, under the heading 'The Newer School'. By the autumn, Ezra was turning out a series of his own articles under the title 'The Serious Artist', in which he defined art as a science, a process of collecting 'lasting and unassailable data'.

The title of the *New Freewoman* began to seem highly inappropriate for such material, and after Ezra and others had put pressure on Miss Weaver and Miss Marsden it was changed to the *Egoist*, which was supposed to imply its character as 'an organ of individualists of both sexes', though a less charitable interpretation might have been made. By the autumn of 1913 Dora Marsden felt that Ezra was treating the journal as entirely his property, while his promise that the literary section would increase sales had proved an empty one. Squabbles about who was really in charge led Rebecca West to resign, whereupon Ezra slipped Richard Aldington into her sub-editorial chair almost before Miss Marsden had time to notice. However, once Aldington was installed he turned on his mentor, and to Ezra's irritation made it abundantly clear that he would not take orders from him.

Just as he was making the *Egoist* a centre of operations, Ezra also began to contribute regularly to *Smart Set*, an up-and-coming New York society journal whose editor Willard Huntington Wright called on him in London and asked him to become a 'finder' for the magazine, just as he was for *Poetry*, though on a more modest scale. Consequently Ford, D. H. Lawrence, and others from Ezra's stable could soon be seen showing their paces in its pages. Shortly afterwards H. L. Mencken, *enfant terrible* of American letters, became joint editor in New York – a man whose noisy performances had something in common with certain aspects of Ezra. On one occasion Ezra described Mencken, deadpan, as 'very tiresome to a serious character like the undersigned, but simpatico'.

Ezra began to send his own poems to *Smart Set* rather than to *Poetry*, thereby breaking his promise of exclusive American magazine rights to Harriet Monroe. He told her candidly that *Smart Set* paid better. Also its editor 'has the good sense to divide all of the poets . . . into two classes: Yeats and I in one class, and everybody else in the other. Such illumination can not pass without reward.'

However, he still let Miss Monroe have a good deal of his work. By the beginning of August 1913 he had typed out a new collection of poems, called *Lustra*, and he told her to select 'ten or a dozen pages in some way that will establish the tone . . . the force behind this new and amazing state of affairs'. (A *lustrum* is an offering for the sins of a people or nation, but Ezra seems to have thought the word meant 'obsequy' or 'funeral rite', since he described the poems as the '*last* obsequies of the Victorian period'.) There was actually nothing in *Lustra* likely to 'amaze' anyone who had read 'Contemporania', because poems from that sequence made up a large part of the collection as it stood in the summer of 1913, and the new pieces were in much the same style. The impression given by *Ripostes*, that he was about to find his mature voice and would soon cease experimenting, was not borne out. There were plenty of squibs in the 'Contemporania' style, plenty of dry little epigrams, but despite occasional moments of what might be thought of as Imagisme, the prevailing mood was cynical and shallow:

> She had a pig-shaped face, with beautiful colouring,
> She wore a bright, dark-blue cloak,
> Her hair was a brilliant deep orange-colour,
> So the effect was charming
> As long as she looked away.

There was also, for the first time in his work, a superior, cliquish air:

> I join these words for four people,
> Some others may overhear them,
> O world, I am sorry for you,
> You do not know these four people.

Yeats had now begun to feel that Ezra was getting nowhere in his poetry. In a lecture in Chicago in March 1914 he observed tactfully: 'Much of his work is experimental; his work will come slowly; he will make many an experiment before he comes into his own.'

Harriet Monroe published selections from *Lustra* in *Poetry* in November 1913, obeying orders, and by this time the full typescript (said Ezra) had 'gone off to shock publishers readers'. Evidently they were shocked, or at least made discouraging noises, for Ezra reported nothing more of the book for many months. By the time it re-emerged, his poetry had gone through another major change.

*

Amy Lowell arrived in London in mid-July 1913, wanting to meet Ezra and learn how to be an Imagiste. She had submitted poems to Harriet Monroe, who had accepted but not yet printed them. During the early months of 1913 Miss Lowell had scanned *Poetry* eagerly, hoping to see them, and so could not help observing the dawn of Imagisme and the mystery surrounding it. She decided that she must become an initiate.

Eleven years older than Ezra, Amy Lowell was a scion of the celebrated Massachusetts literary and academic family; her brother was President of Harvard. Scarcely five feet tall and almost as broad, she dressed in mannish clothes, wore her hair in a bun, carried a pair of pince-nez on her nose, and smoked small cigars – she lived with an actress, and would shock people as she removed the silver wrappers by declaring: 'It's just like undressing a woman.' Ferris Greenslet of Houghton Mifflin, her first publisher, thought she could have passed for the President of Harvard himself.

Her social position and considerable wealth (from family textile mills) had been an obstacle to establishing herself as a poet. Her stilted first collection, *A Dome of Many-Coloured Glass* (1912), was greeted with indifference, and she felt the need to make alliances with other poets and learn from them. So she came to London, took a suite in the Berkeley Hotel and, armed with a letter of introduction from Harriet Monroe, sent out dinner invitations to Ezra, 'H.D.', Aldington, and John Gould Fletcher.

Aldington and Hilda read her book, and thought it 'the fluid, fruity, facile stuff we most wanted to avoid'. On the other hand they were charmed by Amy in person: 'It would have been difficult to resist that vivacious intelligence.' Ezra felt the same: 'Miss Lowell gives me hopes for the future of America,' he told his mother, though he said it would take time and his own blue pencil to sort her out. 'When I get through with that girl she'll think she was born in free verse.' Amy, meanwhile, had taken a hard look at Ezra. She wrote to a friend back home that he was 'the oddest youth, clever, fearfully conceited, &, at the same time, excessively thin-skinned; & I imagine that never, since the days of Wilde, have such garments been seen in the streets of London. He arrays himself like the traditional "poet" of the theatre.'

She gave Ezra plenty of 'fat dinners' and drove him around in a hired motor car. In return he 'launched her on Ford & the Eagle', then sent her off to Paris with 'one or two introductions'. She was 'pleasingly intelligent' about what she saw and heard there. By the time she returned to New England in September she had begun to write the sort of thing he wanted. Aldington rather cynically observed 'a sudden conversion to free verse and (probably owing to Ezra's blue pencil) a more austere style'.

Ezra thought she had possibilities as a patron. The *Egoist* had encountered financial difficulties, so he tried to arrange for her to buy it and install him as editor. But its lady directors agreed that 'the Egoist spark of intelligence is not to be extinguished under Miss Lowell's respectable bulk', and Harriet Shaw Weaver decided to finance and take over the sole editorship of the paper herself.

'Am thinking of publishing a small anthology of *les jeunes*,' Ezra told his mother in early September 1913, and two months later he was asking Amy Lowell if he could use one of her new free verse poems in 'a brief anthology *Des Imagistes* that I am cogitating'. Aldington and 'H.D.' were to be represented, of course, along with F. S. Flint, Ford Madox Hueffer (scarcely a *jeune*, more a benevolent uncle), William Carlos Williams, and the American émigrés John Cournos and Skipwith Cannell. Another of the expatriates, John Gould Fletcher, afterwards pretended that he had been offered a place in the book too, but had refused because he knew that the Imagistes had 'no particular poetic program'. Through pique at being left out, he warned Amy Lowell not to participate in the anthology, alleging that it would really be edited by Aldington 'to give him . . . a send-off in the United States'. Fletcher concluded melodramatically: 'My relations with Pound are at an end.' Amy paid no attention.

Des Imagistes was supposed to be a counter-operation to the alarmingly popular *Georgian Poetry*, of which a second volume was about to appear. Aldington regarded Ezra's title for his anthology as utterly absurd: 'What Ezra thought *Des Imagistes* meant remains a mystery, unless the word *Anthologie* was assumed to precede it. Amy's [later] anthologies were called *Some Imagist Poets*, so she may have supposed that Ezra thought *Des Imagistes* meant *Quelques Imagistes*. But why a French title for a collection of poems by young American and English authors? Search me.'

Aldington's first guess was right – a letter from Ezra to Dorothy refers to the book as 'Antologie des Imagistes' – while the French title was simply a hang-over from the original publicity operation in *Ripostes* and *Poetry*, though from this time on the movement was generally referred to by the English form of its name, Imagism. But Aldington was not the only person to laugh at the book's title. F. S. Flint called it 'stupid', and though he participated in *Des Imagistes* he soon quarrelled with Ezra, objecting to Ezra's implied claim to have invented the whole movement, and alleging that the principal tenets had been stolen from the Hulme group. Ezra called Flint's version of history (published in the *Egoist* in 1915) simply 'bullshit'.

Des Imagistes quickly found an American publisher. A young New York poet, Alfred Kreymborg, was starting a periodical called the *Glebe* together with the painter and photographer Man Ray, and Ezra offered them the anthology in its entirety to make up a complete number of the magazine. Kreymborg accepted enthusiastically, and Harold Monro, who was publishing *Georgian Poetry* in London, was persuaded by Ezra to import some sheets and issue *Des Imagistes* under his own imprint.

'We are getting our little gang after five years of waiting,' Ezra wrote to William Carlos Williams in December 1913, while in the *New Freewoman* he spoke of 'my school' of poetry , thereby confirming Flint's impression that he was claiming total credit for the operation. He also failed to acknowledge that thirty-one of the forty-seven poems in the book had first appeared in *Poetry*, and Harriet Monroe threatened legal action, withdrawing only on condition that printed stickers of acknowledgement were added to copies.

Ezra had long felt that Miss Monroe was failing to make the best of *Poetry*, and he and Amy Lowell now became united in contempt for her. 'I agree with you,' he wrote to Amy, 'that "Harriet" is a bloody fool.' Her chief sin was the printing of masses of vapid American 'rotten poetasters'. Joyce Kilmer's 'Trees' was among the 1913 contributions, and there were plenty even below that level, such as 'A Day for Wandering' by 'Clinton Scollard', supposedly the pseudonym of a retired professor from Ezra's own Hamilton College – or could this have been Ezra himself in jest?

> For me were all the smiles
> Of the sequestered blossoms there abloom (etc.)

Ezra soon decided he could not associate himself with rubbish, and in November 1913 wrote to Ford: 'Will you please take over the foreign correspondence of "Poetry" & communicate with them to the effect that I have turned it over to you.' The bemused Ford, who had had no warning of this, wrote to Harriet Monroe:

> I don't know whether he has the literary advisership of your organ to dispose of, but I am perfectly certain that I could not do his job half so well as he has done. Could you not make it up with him or reinstate him . . .? Besides, if I tried to help you that energetic poet would sit on my head and hammer me till I did exactly what he wanted and the result would be exactly the same except that I should be like the green baize office door that every one kicks in going in or out.

Miss Monroe communicated these sentiments to Ezra, who replied:

> All right, but I do not see that there was anything for me to have done save resign at the time I did so. I don't think you have yet tried to see the magazine from my viewpoint . . . If I stay on the magazine it has got to improve . . . I am willing to reconsider my resignation pending a general improvement of the magazine, and I will not have my name associated with it unless it does improve.

He told Amy Lowell he was sure the improvement 'won't happen – so I shall be compelled to resign permanently some time or other', and by the end of March 1914 he was screaming once more at Miss Monroe that she seemed to be 'trying to run an ambulance corps for the incapable'.

His attack on *Poetry* was short-sighted. The magazine certainly published a good deal of tripe, but the proportion of Ella Wheeler Wilcox-style verse was steadily diminishing as Harriet Monroe allowed Ezra to instil better taste in her, and there were two notable discoveries that had nothing to do with him. Vachel Lindsay's 'General William Booth Enters into Heaven' appeared in the magazine during 1913, and Carl Sandburg had a sequence of his 'Chicago poems' printed in the issue for March 1914. Ezra did not notice either for some time, and when he eventually observed Lindsay he simply said, 'Oh gawd!!!' Later, he admitted that Lindsay was unusual in paying so much attention to sound, but he thought the result was 'interesting only as Kipling's was. Believe me one can write it by the hour as fast as one scribbles.' To prove this he published, in the *Little Review* in 1918, a forty-eight-line 'poem' in imitation of Lindsay's 'General William Booth', written (he said) in precisely four minutes and thirty-one seconds:

> Whoop golly-ip Zopp, bob BIP!!
> I'm Mr Lindsay with the new sheep-dip,
> I'm a loud-voiced yeller, I'm a prancing preacher,
> Gawd's in his heaven! I'm the *real* High Reacher.

By February 1916 he could not fail to take notice of Carl Sandburg, since that month *Poetry* published a lengthy article by Sandburg on Ezra, in which he called Ezra 'the best man writing poetry today'. In consequence Ezra proposed Sandburg for a 'Fellowship given for creative ability' when suggesting such a project to the University of Pennsylvania that year: 'Sandburg is a lumberjack who has taught himself all that he knows. He is on the way toward simplicity.' The Lindsay–Sandburg school of new American poetry might have seemed to him evidence of the Renaissance he had been calling for when *Poetry* opened shop. Harriet Monroe certainly thought so; she wrote in *Poetry* that Lindsay 'represents a tendency much richer and more indigenous than the imagists . . . His roots run deep into the past of American literature: Mark Twain and [James Whitcomb] Riley and Brer-Rabbit Harris were his collateral relatives.' But Ezra had not unearthed Lindsay himself, and he set himself in opposition to all he represented.

During 1918 he persuaded the *Little Review* to publish an article by Edgar Jepson (of the Square Club in London) damning the 'Western School' of American poetry, specifically Lindsay, Edgar Lee Masters of *Spoon River Anthology*, and Robert Frost; Sandburg was omitted presumably because he had flattered Ezra. Jepson called Lindsay's poetry 'rank bad workmanship' and Frost's 'a maundering dribble'. Ezra appended a note that he respected Jepson's 'fitness as a judge'.

Jepson's fatuous piece needled William Carlos Williams into writing, in the prologue to his *Kora in Hell* (1920), an attack on another school of

American poets – the exiles. Williams gave them ironical praise for having 'the wit and courage and the conventionality' to go to London 'where the signposts are already marked', and condemned them to his particular hell for their 'assumption that there is no alternative but their own groove'. Ezra replied to this, admitting that Jepson was not 'a fountain of wisdom', but he had been the best person available 'to penetrate Harriet's crust'. He grumbled that Williams and others had sat back and let him have 'the whole stinking sweat of providing the mechanical means for letting through the new movement . . . the mot juste, for honest clear statement in verse. Then you punk out, cursing me for not being in two places at once.'

10

Orient From All Quarters

At about the time of Ezra's attempted resignation from the staff of *Poetry* in the autumn of 1913, the magazine awarded its first annual prize for the best poem printed in its pages during the year. Miss Monroe wanted Vachel Lindsay to win it for 'General William Booth', but Ezra called this an 'insult', and insisted that the award (of $250) should go to Yeats for 'The Grey Rock'. Yeats wrote thanking *Poetry* for the money, and adding: 'I will keep £10, and with that I will get Mr Sturge Moore to make me a book-plate', but the rest he intended to give to 'some American young writer'. So Ezra himself walked off with £40 of the prize, Yeats having chosen him 'because, although I do not really like with my whole soul the metrical experiments he has made for you, I think those experiments show a vigorous creative mind'. Ezra spent the money on a new typewriter and 'two statuettes from *the* coming sculptor, Gaudier-Brzeska'.

In July 1913 he had gone to the Albert Hall with Olivia Shakespear for an exhibition by a group called Allied Artists. 'We wandered about the upper galleries,' he writes of that occasion,

> hunting for new work and trying to find some good amid much bad, and a young man came after us, like a well-made young wolf or some soft-moving, bright-eyed wild thing. I noted him carefully because he reminded me a little of my friend Carlos Williams.
>
> He also took note of us, partly because we paused only before new work, and partly because there were few people in the gallery, and partly because I was playing the fool and he was willing to be amused by the performance. It was a warm, lazy day, there was a little serious criticism mixed in with our

nonsense. On the ground floor we stopped before a figure with bunchy muscles done in clay painted green. It was one of a group of interesting things. I turned to the catalogue and began to take liberties with the appalling assemblage of consonants: 'Brzxjk – ' I began. I tried again, 'Burrzisskzk – ' I drew back' breathed deeply, and took another run at the hurdle, sneezed, coughed, rumbled, got as far as 'Burdidis –' when there was a dart from behind the pedestal and I heard a voice speaking with the gentlest fury in the world: 'Cela s'appelle tout simplement Jaersh-ka. C'est moi qui les ai sculptés.'

And he disappeared like a Greek god in a vision.

Henri Gaudier, who called himself Gaudier-Brzeska, was twenty-one years old when he met the twenty-eight-year-old Ezra Pound. He had been born in mid-France, the son of a joiner; his ancestors were stone-carvers, and he claimed to be able to find an almost exact portrait of himself on the west front of a certain cathedral. He had studied art here and there, and in Paris had met and taken up with Sophie Brzeska, a neurotic Polishwoman twenty years older than he who was threatening to kill herself. They began a strange ménage together, he adding her surname to his. He addressed her as 'Mamus', 'Little Maman', even 'Mumsie', and called himself 'Little Pik'. To the outside world they announced themselves as brother and sister.

They drifted to London, living off her savings, and when these ran out Sophie went to Suffolk to work for a while as a governess, while Henri got various poorly paid jobs and studied in museums in spare moments. Up to this time he had painted, but now he took up sculpture. Legend has it that this began when he met Jacob Epstein, who somehow assumed from Gaudier's intelligent interest that the young Frenchman was a sculptor too, and asked him if he cut direct in stone, rather than working in plaster?

'Most certainly!' said Gaudier, who had never yet done anything of the sort.

'That's right,' said Epstein: 'I will come around to your place on Sunday.'

So Gaudier at once went out, got three small blocks, and by working more or less night and day had something ready by Sunday.

(This story is told by Ezra in his book on Gaudier.)

At first influenced by Rodin, Gaudier soon began to feel representational art to be unsatisfactory. During 1911 he wrote to Sophie that great classical sculpture was beautiful because 'the masses of which it is composed have sufficient truth in their disposition to give the sensation of many rhythms', but line in itself, the accurate representation of the human body or other subjects, was 'nothing but a decoy' and had 'nothing essentially to do with beauty'. He began to experiment with non-representational forms in which 'energy' could be conveyed by the relationship between 'masses', and emotions expressed through 'the arrangement of surfaces'. On these principles he sculpted works that had a certain resemblance to Cubism, but also a strong flavour of ancient Egyptian statuary and African totems.

His early days in London were a saga of friendships and useful connections made only to be destroyed by his and Sophie's strange behaviour. Middleton Murry and Katherine Mansfield met and liked him, but soon kept away because Mansfield could not endure Sophie's presence. Frank Harris, another potential patron, commissioned a portrait bust but then found Gaudier intolerable at close quarters (he was, said Richard Aldington, 'probably the dirtiest human being ever known, and gave off horrid effluvia in hot weather'). Gaudier was given a little work by Roger Fry's Omega Workshop, but until he met Ezra there had still been no enduring or really productive contacts.

Following their brief encounter at the Albert Hall, Ezra took pains to discover Gaudier-Brzeska's address, and wrote to him inviting him to supper. There was no reply, and on the day suggested, the sculptor did not appear. 'I had over-prepared the event,' writes Ezra in an uncharacteristically personal poem. 'Villanelle: the Psychological Hour',

> With middle-ageing care
> I had laid out just the right books . . .
> And now I watch, from the window,
> the rain, the wandering buses . . .

Gaudier intended to come, but at the last moment he had a row with Sophie. The next day, said Ezra, 'I received a letter addressed to me as "Madame".' Feeling that things were somewhat on the wrong footing, he persuaded John Cournos, who knew Gaudier, to arrange a reintroduction. He then went to Putney where the Frenchman worked.

His 'studio' was a dark, mud-floored, smelly cavern under half a railway arch, from which, it was said, the penurious Gaudier would emerge at night to raid a mason's yard for suitable pieces of stone. He let Ezra see some of his work, which at first Ezra made no pretence of comprehending. 'The jargon of these sculptors is beyond me,' he wrote in the *Egoist* a little later. 'I do not know precisely why I admire a green granite, female, apparently pregnant monster with one eye going around a square corner.' But he was captivated by what he called the 'general combat' and 'emotional condemnation' of Gaudier-Brzeska's style, and believed it was an accurate representation of 'the present condition of things'. He bought two pieces, a marble group and a torso, at 'what would have been a ridiculous figure had it not been that he had next to no market and that I have next to no income'. In fact it had been only 'a bit of unforeseen and unrepeatable luck' – that enabled him to find any cash for them at all.

Since he was interested in Gaudier-Brzeska, he determined that the young sculptor should take notice in return of him and his own work. 'I therefore opened fire with "Altaforte", "Piere Vidal", and such poems as I had written when about his own age. And I think it was the "Altaforte" that convinced him I would do to be sculpted.' In fact, according to John Cournos, Gaudier was really impressed by the 'Bloody Sestina' because as Ezra roared out the first line, 'Damn it all! all this our South stinks peace!' Gaudier misheard the last word as 'piss'. (When Cournos told Ezra, he was delighted.)

Ezra described Gaudier, who looked to him 'exactly like some artist out of the Italian renaissance', as 'the only person with whom I can really be "Altaforte"'. He continued to seek out the sculptor's company – and still derived some amusement from his name. 'Brzx. came in & watched me grill a chop last evening,' he told Dorothy. The two men had 'long, gay, electrified arguments', Gaudier preaching anarchy and Ezra declaring himself a middle-aged sceptic. Gaudier, speaking in a staccato that came 'partly from his nature, partly from the foreignness of his accent and the habit of pronouncing each syllable', would tell Ezra anecdotes of his European wanderings, cheerfully accepting Ezra's designation of him as 'a sort of modern Cellini'.

Sometimes he would arrive at Church Walk with 'four small statues in his various "pockets" and three more of considerable weight slung on his back in a workman's straw basket', and would lend half of them to Ezra for a week almost without a thought, so that the room became for the duration 'rich as a palace'. Ezra began to try to understand them, comparing his friend's work at first with Epstein. 'Of course G.B. isn't Epstein – not yet,' he wrote to Dorothy. 'Epsteins stuff throws him into the shadow, but then Epstein is 20 years older.' Ezra himself admired Epstein as 'the first person who came talking about form, not the *form of* anything'. But when he eventually met him he cared little for him personally – 'Jacob is a fool when he hasn't got a chisel in his hand and a rock before him.'

It was some time before Ezra became able to talk convincingly about sculpture. There was an embarrassing moment when he and Gaudier-Brzeska visited Epstein's studio, and Ezra began to hold forth about one of the works on display; Gaudier hissed at him to be quiet and told him he knew nothing. In the *Egoist* in March 1914, Ezra struggled to find the vocabulary to compare the two men: 'It is no use saying that Epstein is Egyptian and that Brzeska is Chinese. Nor would I say that the younger man is a follower of the elder. They approach life in different manners.'

Quite apart from his difficulty in analysing non-naturalistic visual art, he had no natural taste for it. In 1917 he told J. B. Yeats that he thought most modern art 'damn bad' (though he added, 'a man of genius has a right to any mode of expression'), and said that on the whole he would 'go on believing in realism'. He was contemptuous towards Picasso, who he said had once had 'serious intentions' but then took to painting rubbish because he could command a high price for anything.

*

The September 1913 issue of *Poetry* contained a sequence of verses entitled 'Scented Leaves – from a Chinese Jar'. They were the work of Allen Upward, an English barrister and traveller who sometimes contributed to the *New Age*. As well as securing these Chinese-style poems for *Poetry*, Ezra persuaded Upward to let him print them in the *Egoist*. He told Dorothy: 'Upward of the chinese poemae is quite an addition.'

He was attracted by Upward's esoteric knowledge of folklore and anthropology, and at the end of September 1913 he went down to Upward's family home in the Isle of Wight to soak some of it up. 'He seems to [know] things that ain't in Frazer,' Ezra told Dorothy, 'at least he talked sense about sun-worship & the siege of Troy, and he has been "resident" in Nigeria, & diverse other adventures.' Upward was the type of anthropologist who liked to reject all conventional views of religion and culture, and synthesize his knowledge into something more exotic. 'He has derived the word God from the word Goat,' wrote Ezra of Upward's book *The Divine Mystery* (1907). 'He has related prophecy to astrology . . . Modern marriage is, apparently . . . derived from the laws of slave concubinage . . . The lovely belief in a durable hot hell dates back to the Parsee who squatted over a naptha vocano . . . It is a great book for liberations.'

Upward explained to Ezra that his 'Scented Leaves' sequence of poems was not a translation from the Chinese, nor even a paraphrase, 'but that he made it up out of his head, using a certain amount of Chinese reminiscence'. He showed Ezra the standard work on the subject, H. A. Giles's *History of Chinese Literature* (1901), which Ezra found 'a very interesting book. Upward has sort of started me off in that direction.' At Upward's instigation he also looked at 'a french translation of Confucius and Mencius' – Pauthier's 1841 *Les Quatres Livres de Philosophie Morale et Politique de la Chine*.

In the same letter to his parents in which he describes this visit to Upward (written at the end of September 1913), he goes on: 'Have seen Mrs Fenollosa (relict of the Fenollosa who has written on Chinese Art, and who had so much to do with the Freer collection) and Sarogini Naidu (of Hyderabad, authoress of divers poems).' And to Dorothy on 2 October: 'Dined on Monday with Sarojini Naidu and Mrs Fenolosa, relict of the writer on chinese art, selector of a lot of Freer's stuff, etc.* I seem to be getting orient from all quarters . . . I'm stocked up with K'ung fu Tsze, and Men Tsze, etc. I suppose they'll keep me calm for a week or so.' Sarojini Naidu was a distinguished Bengali poetess living in London, whom Ezra knew through his contact with Tagore. The meeting with her proved of no importance, but Mrs Fenollosa changed the course of his work.

Ernest Fenollosa, her late husband, was a Spanish-American really named Alvarez, born in 1853 in Salem, Massachusetts. After studying at Harvard, he taught political economy and philosophy at Tokyo University, this being the period when the Japanese were letting in foreign trade and culture for the first time since the seventeenth century. Alvarez/Fenollosa acquired all kinds of titles from the Japanese – 'Professor of Logic', 'Professor of Aesthetics', 'Commissioner of Fine Arts to the Japanese Government' – and soon abandoned the subjects he had been teaching, realizing that he could make a reputation by preserving and popularizing oriental culture just as the Japanese themselves were being attracted by the west. He came back to New England in 1890 as Curator of Oriental Art at Boston Museum, having already sold his own collection of Japanese painting to that institution, and became a popular lecturer in the United States. His knowledge of oriental culture was fairly hazy: he could only understand the Chinese language and its poetry with the help of Japanese interpreters, and while his 'expertise' was good enough for American lecture tours, he probably sensed that it would look thin on paper. He compiled a mass of notes for a projected book, but died in London in 1908 without having written any of it in a completed form.

With the aid of Laurence Binyon of the British Museum and two Japanese scholars, his widow managed to use his notes as the basis of a two-volume book, *Epochs of Chinese and Japanese Art* (1912), but the result was more redolent of the drawing room than the library, and showed strikingly little scholarship or even sympathy with its subject. 'How a great practical people,' reads a typical passage

> like those healthy shoots of the Altaic race, the Chinese and the Japanese, could ever have taken up with such a negative, pessimistic, and non-political religion as the Buddhist renunci- ation, may seem fairly questionable.

A good deal of material remained unused in notebooks after Mrs Fenollosa and her helpers had finished the book – chiefly translations from Chinese poetry and Japanese Noh plays – but by this time the widow had had enough (the work had taken her three years), and probably also doubted the commercial value of what was left, though she was vaguely

* The Freer Collection of oriental art is in the Smithsonian.

looking for someone who might make use of it. Not surprisingly, she was distrustful of academic experts, and she thought that it would have to be someone with her husband's unconventional spirit and enthusiasm rather than an accredited scholar. Meanwhile Ezra, after his visit to Upward, had been reading Giles's *History of Chinese Literature*, 'and I wasn't content with the translations' (Giles's versions were very stilted and unexciting). 'I wanted to know how I could get some more Chinese.'

When they met at Sarojini Naidu's house, Ezra thought Mary Fenollosa 'the lightest possible, apparently frivolous society woman'. So he was rather surprised when 'after a couple of weeks I got a note', an invitation to a hotel off Trafalgar Square. 'There she was . . . and she merely said, "You're the only person who can finish this stuff the way Ernest wanted it done." Then she sent me the manuscript.'

That was how he remembered it half a century later. Actually the second meeting was in the Café Royal on 6 October 1913. 'I dined last night with Heinemann, Sarojini & Mrs Fenollosa – good food – café Royal – mild memories of Whistler,' Ezra reported to Dorothy. Possibly Mrs Fenollosa summoned him to the hotel a few days later. When she made her proposal she 'said that Fenollosa had been in opposition to all the Profs. and academes, and she had seen some of my stuff and said I was the only person who could finish up these notes as Ernest would have wanted them done'. She told him she would give him £40 to cover his expenses, after which he was on his own financially, but he could keep any profit he might make. 'There *are* some white folks in the world,' he observed.

He accepted on the spot, feeling that the Chinese stuff might help the development of Imagism: 'There is *no* long poem in chinese. They hold if a man can't say what he wants to in 12 lines, he'd better leave it unsaid.' He thought one of the poets might be described as 'Chu Yüan, Imagiste.'

Mrs Fenollosa gave him another dinner with William Heinemann, the publisher, whom she was determined should 'support' Ezra after the £40 had run out, though Heinemann did not oblige. Eight weeks later Ezra had been handed 'all old Fenollosa's treasures in mss.' and by that time was already hard at work on the material.

*

He began looking through it while staying in Sussex with Yeats. The idea was that he should act as Yeats's secretary for the winter. 'My stay in Stone Cottage will not be in the least profitable,' he told his mother. 'I detest the country. Yeats will amuse me part of the time and bore me to death with psychical research the rest. I regard the visit as a duty to posterity.' It did not actually prove so bad.

Yeats had recently been staying in Sussex with Olivia Shakespear's brother, his wife, and her daughter by a previous marriage, Georgie

Hyde-Lees, in their cottage at Coleman's Hatch in Ashdown Forest. Yeats enjoyed himself so much that he decided to winter in the same village, and found that rooms could be rented from the Misses Welfare who kept the nearby Stone Cottage. He did not wish to pass a winter alone, so he engaged Ezra. 'I am taking a secretary though I shrink from the expense,' Yeats told his father, 'believing that I shall be able to bear the expense because I shall be able to write . . . He will answer the business letters.' Yeats was still rather wary of Ezra. 'He is certainly a creative personality of some sort,' he wrote to Harriet Monroe, 'though it is too soon to say yet of what sort.'

Dorothy knew Coleman's Hatch from visits to her uncle, and warned Ezra: 'You really must have a pair of very thick boots, or shoes, and warm socks. Its a drippy kind of place.' The cottage overlooked the open heath, 'out in the dampish bosom of nature', wrote Ezra to May Sinclair after he had arrived early in November 1913; 'by the waste moor (or whatever) and the holly bush', he adds in Canto 83. 'We have four rooms of a cottage on the edge of a heath and our back is to the woods,' Yeats told his father.

It was as much a scene from Hardy as from the Celtic Twilight; Ezra took to it. 'It is fine wild country here,' he reported to his own father, 'and I suppose I will benefit accordingly. London seems reasonably far off and one is glad of the quiet . . . W.B.Y. is just starting for the post so I conclude this.' Yeats, an indefatigable correspondent, spent much of his time *en route* for the village post office. Ezra found he was expected to earn his keep at the typewriter, and complained one Sunday that they had done '21 letters on the holy sabbath' and he must rush to the post because the Eagle was 'beginning to fuss'. The Misses Welfare recalled their astonishment when one morning Yeats 'came back from the post office and said, "Why, there's nothing doing; all shut up." "But Mr Yeats," I said, "didn't you know, it's Christmas Day!"'

The cooking of the Misses Welfare was beyond reproach – 'The first evening, Mr Pound said to me, "I haven't had a meal like that for a long time"' – though Ezra recalls in Canto 83 how Yeats

> would not eat ham for dinner
> because peasants eat ham for dinner
>   despite the excellent quality
> and the pleasure of having it hot.

Yeats liked to go out in the evening for long walks, and when the landladies expressed anxiety about the effects of the damp weather on his health, Olivia Shakespear reassured them: 'Don't worry, if he can stand the Irish weather in the bogs he can bear anything you get there.' Ezra reported to Dorothy of these walks: 'It rains. I have not yet got lost in the wild, tho' the eagle tried to go the wrong way once, with amazing persistence.'

'When breakfast was over,' says Miss Welfare, 'they would get to work as if life depended on it. "Don't disturb him," Mr Pound used to say, if I wanted to dust, and Mr Yeats would be humming over his poetry to himself in the little room.' Ezra remembered this humming sound – not unlike his own when writing – in the Pisan Cantos:

> the noise in the chimney
> as it were the wind in the chimney
> but was in reality Uncle William
> downstairs composing . . .

When they were not working or going for damp walks, Yeats made Ezra read aloud to him. 'Did we ever get to the end of Doughty: *The Dawn in Britain*?' Ezra asks in Canto 83, remembering also Yeats 'hearing nearly all Wordsworth / for the sake of his conscience but / preferring Ennemosor on Witches'. This was Joseph Ennemoser's *The History of Magic* (1854), which even Ezra preferred to Wordsworth, whom he regarded with almost as much loathing as Milton: 'Wordsworth . . . was a silly old sheep with a genius . . . for imagisme, for a presentation of natural detail, wild-fowl bathing in a hole in the ice, etc., and this talent . . . he buried in a desert of bleatings.'

Ezra's feeling after they had been at Stone Cottage for ten days was that Yeats 'improves on acquaintance . . . We conversed all last evening – a pastime preferable to labour.' A month later he wrote to William Carlos Williams: 'Yeats is much finer *intime* than seen spasmodically in the midst of the whirl. We are both, I think, very contented in Sussex.' From Ennemoser on Witches they turned to *Le Comte de Gabalis*, a seventeenth-century book on the Rosicrucian Philosophy, and also took some indoor exercise. 'We find we have room to fence in the study when the weather is bad,' Ezra told his mother. 'We read mss. plays for the Abbey, and sources for Yeats' ghost book, and I am deciphering Fenollosa's hieroglyphics.'

*

He had brought Fenollosa's notebooks with him, and before he began work on them he wrote some short Chinese-style poems of his own. Based on translations in Giles's *History of Chinese Literature*, they were experiments with images, much like 'In a Station of the Metro':

> O fan of white silk,
>   clear as frost on the grass-blade,
> You also are laid aside.

He included them in *Des Imagistes*.

By Christmas he was deep into the Fenollosa notebooks. On 16

December he wrote to Dorothy: 'I have cribbed part of a Noh (dramatic eclogue) out of Fenollosa's notes. The Eagle calls it charming.' On 31 January 1914 he sent the completed text off to Harriet Monroe, who published it in *Poetry* in May. Entitled *Nishikigi*, it was the work of Zeami Motokiyo, the outstanding fourteenth-century actor–playwright of Noh theatre. It tells the story of two lovers, never united during their lives, whose ghosts wander on a mountainside; a priest meets them and brings about their union through his goodwill. In his accompanying note to Harriet Monroe, Ezra claimed that printing it in *Poetry* 'will give us some reason for existing'. He called its discovery 'about the best bit of luck we've had since the starting of the magazine'.

When *Nishikigi* led off the May 1914 issue of *Poetry* it was printed, at Ezra's request, with no mention of his name, but simply as 'translated from the Japanese of Motokiyo by Ernest Fenollosa'. It was in free verse with some prose passages. In polishing Fenollosa's rendering, Ezra had let a suggestion of Yeats's verse-dramas creep in, as in this final chorus:

> We ask you, do not awake,
> We all will wither away.
> The wands and this cloth of a dream.
> Now you will come out of sleep,
> You will tread the border and nothing
> Awaits you; no, all this will wither away.
> There is nothing here but this cave in the field's midst.
> To-day's wind moves in the pines;
> A wild place, unlit, and unfilled.

This infection of style worked both ways. Yeats recorded that while Ezra was working on the Noh plays at Stone Cottage he 'read me a great deal of what he was doing'. Yeats was deeply struck by what he called 'these strange and poignant fables'; he singled out *Nishikigi*, saying it reminded him of an Irish folk tale. A few months later, when he wrote the first of his own 'Plays for Dancers', *At the Hawk's Well*, there were marked traces of Noh in it. Designed to be played to the accompaniment of zither and flute, the Yeats play has a mountainside setting resembling *Nishikigi*, and an old man who recalls the priest of the Noh play. 'With the help of Japanese plays "translated by Ernest Fenollosa and finished by Ezra Pound",' Yeats wrote in April 1916, 'I have invented a form of drama, distinguished, indirect, and symbolic, and having no need of mob or Press to pay its way – an aristocratic form.'

The first performance of *At the Hawk's Well*, in a London drawing room in April 1916, with Ezra among the audience, was given partly under the guidance of Michio Itow, a young Japanese dancer then staying in London whom Ezra had drawn into his orbit – he calls him 'one of the few interesting japs I ever met'. Itow was no expert in the Noh traditions, but, realizing what was wanted, he quickly read up the subject in libraries and became one. He could be seen daily at London Zoo, flapping and prancing as he imitated the movements of hawks, with Yeats watching him in rapt admiration. Inspired by Itow, during the autumn of 1915 Ezra worked out a dance sequence entitled 'The Birth of the Dragon, a choreograph'.

While polishing *Nishikigi* Ezra was filled with enthusiasm for the orient, and even contemplated emigrating there. In London he met an official of the Chinese Mint, who seemed confident that he could provide a job for Homer Pound in Peking, and was optimistic about finding something for Ezra himself. 'We may yet be a united family,' Ezra wrote to his father in January 1914. He noted that there would have been a difficulty in nomenclature if he had chosen Japan: 'The phonetic translation of my name into the Japanese tongue [means] "This picture of a phallus costs ten yen."'

*

At Stone Cottage he was still seeking material for *Des Imagistes*, and asked Yeats if there was anything in Ireland. Yeats said he thought an Irishman named Joyce had written some good lyric poetry – one piece in particular, 'I Hear an Army Charging upon the Land' – but he could not find Joyce's poems among his books. Ezra decided the matter was worth pursuing, and discovered (probably through Elkin Mathews, who had published him) that Joyce was living in Trieste. Ezra wrote to him on 15 December 1913.

> James Joyce ESq.
> Dear Sir: Mr Yeats has been speaking to me of your writing. I am informally connected with a couple of new and impecunious papers ("The Egoist" . . . and the "Cerebrilist" . . .)* . . . I also collect for two American magazines which pay top rates . . . This is the first time I have written to any one outside of my own circle of acquaintance (save in the case of French authors). These matters can be better dealt with in conversation, but as that is impossible, I write.
>
> 'The Smart Set' wants top notch stories. 'Poetry' wants top notch poetry . . . As I dont in the least know what your present stuff is like, I can only offer to read what you send . . .
>
> I am bonae voluntatis, – don't in the least know that I can be of any use to you – or you to me. From what W.B.Y. says I imagine we have a hate or two in common – but thats a very problematical bond on introduction.
>
>   Yours sincerely,
>   Ezra Pound

* He had just contributed his first piece to the *Cerebralist*, but it closed after one issue.

It was an uncharacteristically diffident letter. When it arrived in Trieste it intrigued Joyce and gave him a little hope, for his fortunes were very low. He had left Ireland ten years earlier, at the age of twenty-two, but *Chamber Music*, his collection of poems published by Elkin Mathews in 1907, was still his only book in print. Since 1905 he had been trying to get his short stories *Dubliners* through the press without expurgation, but all efforts had failed, and this had seriously frustrated his work on a novel, originally called 'Stephen Hero'. During his ten years in Trieste he had tried to support himself, his wife Nora, and their two children by various schemes, including giving English lessons, but money was a rarity in the Joyce household. Joyce wrote to his wife's uncle a few months after he heard from Ezra: 'If I could find out . . . who is the patron of men of letters I should try to remind him that I exist: but I understand that the last saint who held that position resigned in despair and no other will take the portfolio.' He did not yet know that Ezra had appointed himself to the post.

Before Joyce had replied to Ezra's first letter, Yeats managed to unearth a copy of *Chamber Music*, and Ezra wrote again to Joyce to say that he and Yeats were 'both much impressed' by the poem 'I Hear an Army', and could he have permission to use it in 'my anthology of Imagists'? He offered a guinea down and a share in the profits if there should be any – 'this is not the usual graft anthology, the contributors are to share proportionately, if the book earns anything' (Edward Marsh was offering the same share of royalties for contributors to *Georgian Poetry*).

Ezra had not spotted any modern tendencies in Joyce's poem; some years later he referred to *Chamber Music* rather disparagingly as 'thirty-odd pages of conventional, sensitive verse'. But it was 'the only Irish verse which had sufficient severity for me to consider it relative to "our own" imagiste . . . ambitions in 1912 and '13'.

Joyce wrote back giving Ezra permission to print the poem, and telling him something about his present situation. He enclosed a detailed account of his misadventures over *Dubliners*. Two publishers, Grant Richards of London and Maunsel of Dublin, had signed contracts but then backed out because Joyce would not let them censor the book. Joyce also sent Ezra a copy of *Dubliners* and the first chapter of the rewritten 'Stephen Hero', now entitled *A Portrait of the Artist as a Young Man*.

Ezra was immediately attracted by the fact that Joyce had been hampered by narrow-minded publishers. Possibly this interested him more than Joyce's writing, which for all his coming championship of Joyce was never altogether to his taste. From now until the publication of *Ulysses* in book form, he pursued the Joyce cause tirelessly, but very largely because Joyce's status as a literary outlaw aroused his vehement fellow feeling. Joyce seemed to him the perfect example of the selfless artist who had 'weathered the storm' and 'beaten out his exile' to produce the 'master work', the isolated and rejected genius abandoned by an uncaring world.

With this is mind, he set himself to praise Joyce, though at first he had to struggle to find words in which to do it. This is apparent from the letter he wrote to Joyce in mid-January 1914, just after receiving *Dubliners* and the first chapter of *A Portrait of the Artist as a Young Man*:

> I'm not supposed to know much about prose but I think your novel is damn fine stuff – I dare say you know it as well as I do – clear and direct like Merimée.
>
> I am sending it off at once to THE EGOIST . . . Confound it all, I can't usually read prose at all not anybody's in English except James and [W. H.] Hudson and a little Conrad . . .
>
> I think the stories good – possibly too thorough, too psychological or subjective in treatment to suit that brute in New York [the editor of *Smart Set*] . . . Anyhow we'll have a go at him and see what can be done.

The praise sounds rather forced, and further difficulties are evident in a review he wrote of *Dubliners* when it finally got into print some months later:

> Mr Joyce writes clear and hard prose. He deals with subjective things, but he presents them with such clarity of outline that he might be dealing with locomotives or with builders' specifications . . . He gives us things as they are . . . It is surprising that Mr Joyce is Irish. One is so tired of the Irish or 'Celtic' imagination . . . flopping about. Mr Joyce does not flop about. He defines . . . I think there is a new phase [of Irish literature] in the works of Mr Joyce. He writes as a contemporary of continental writers.

He is defining Joyce by what he is not – not subjective, not Celtic – rather than praising him in positive terms. He does not even say what the stories are about.

Smart Set rejected the three *Dubliners* stories Ezra sent them; he called their reaction 'a prime example of bull shit'. He also showed H. L. Mencken, then just taking over the co-editorship, excerpts from *A Portrait of the Artist as a Young Man*, but Mencken declined the book as 'too long and diffuse'. However, Harriet Shaw Weaver immediately accepted the novel for serialization in the *Egoist*: the first instalment appeared immediately in the issue dated 2 February 1914 – Joyce's thirty-second birthday. Ezra had warned Joyce that 'the Egoist cant pay'; its only value was therefore as a medium of publicity, which proved highly effective. On the strength of the serialization Joyce persuaded Grant Richards, the London publisher who had let him down over *Dubliners*, to reconsider that book. Richards brought it out in June 1914.

Miss Weaver and her colleague Dora Marsden accepted *A Portrait of the Artist as a Young Man* for the *Egoist* without realizing what they were in for. Ezra wrote to Joyce that he hoped they would not 'jibe [sic] at one or two of your phrases', and in fact they seem to have let the book through after merely glancing at the opening paragraphs of the first chapter, which looked innocent enough, and were certainly more attractive than the interminable *Horses of Diomedes* with which Ezra had been burdening them. But trouble was not long in coming.

Joyce sent the manuscript chapter by chapter to Ezra, but during the summer of 1914 the printers of the *Egoist*, who were liable to prosecution in instances of obscenity, objected to Stephen Dedalus's daydreams about the prostitutes of Nighttown. Miss Weaver was by now aware of the nature of the book, but she stood by it and was reluctant to agree to cuts, though she had to allow the omission of one paragraph. Soon there were further objections, whereupon she changed printers; the successors, co-operative at first, eventually objected to the words 'fart' and 'ballocks', and nothing could be done to prevent further censorship. Ezra had almost anticipated this crisis a year earlier, arguing in the course of his *Egoist* series 'The Serious Artist' that 'good art however "immoral" is wholly a thing of virtue . . . Good art can NOT be immoral. By good art I mean art that bears true witness, I mean the art that is most precise.'

Despite these snags, *A Portrait of the Artist as a Young Man* attracted the reaction for which Ezra hoped. After it had been running for two months he told Joyce it was 'getting you a "Gloire de cenacle" . . . Hueffer and every one with whom I have spoken of the novel have all called it good stuff.' Yeats wrote to Ezra to say he thought it 'very great' and was 'absorbed' in it. By this time Ezra had chosen a provisional place for Joyce in his pantheon alongside D. H. Lawrence as 'the two strongest prose writers among les jeunes, and all the rest are about played out'. Eighteen months later Joyce had been promoted by him to '*without exception* . . . the best of the younger prose writers . . . His style has the hard clarity of a Stendhal or a Flaubert.' To Joyce himself he made a favourable comparison with Hardy and Henry James, but these constant comparisons with other writers — something he never needed to do when discussing poetry — suggest continuing uneasiness and a lack of real feeling for Joyce's work. Ezra never discussed the actual content of *A Portrait of the Artist as a Young Man*, except to say in a letter to his father: 'MY GAWD how he wipes the floor with the Sainte Foi Catolique in that sermon!!!' But in any case Joyce did not need a critic, and he was immensely grateful for what Ezra had done. 'I can never thank you enough,' he wrote to Yeats, 'for having brought me into relation with your friend Ezra Pound who is indeed a miracle worker.'

*

While Ezra was still beating out his exile from London at Stone Cottage over Christmas and New Year 1913–14, he helped to organize a visit by a 'committee' of poets to Wilfred Scawen Blunt, who lived about twelve miles away in the village of Crabbet. Indeed judging from the composition of the 'committee' – Ezra, Yeats, F. S. Flint, Richard Aldington, Victor Plarr and Sturge Moore – the whole thing was undoubtedly Ezra's own idea.

Wilfred Scawen Blunt was in his seventy-fifth year, and seemed to Ezra like a Victorian version of himself: irascible, widely travelled, anti-imperialist (Blunt had been to prison for his support of Irish Home Rule), a Byronic amorist (he had married Byron's granddaughter), bearded and formidable, a neglected poet. Ezra had known about him for at least a year; in *Poetry* in January 1913 he praised him as 'the grandest of old men, the last of the great Victorians, great by reason of his double sonnet, beginning "He who has once been happy is for aye / Out of destruction's double reach . . ."' Yeats suggested they should honour Blunt by holding a public dinner for him in London, but Blunt said he would much rather they all came to him, so the visit was arranged for Sunday 18 January 1914. 'The Eagle says he is going to hire a motor car to take us to Blunt,' Ezra told Dorothy. 'If it is as dammmmM cold sunday next as it is now we'll arrive like a box of marrons glacés.'

Rather at the last minute, Ezra ordered a 'sarcophagus' from Gaudier-Brzeska, a small marble box in the style of a reliquary, carved with a modernistic reclining female nude on one side and the words 'Homage to W. S. BLVNT' on the other. In this were placed manuscripts by each of the 'committee', including a presentation verse by Ezra which praised Blunt for having

> gone your individual gait,
> Written fine verses, made mock of the world,
> Swung the grand style, not made a trade of art,
> Upheld Mazzini and detested institutions.

When they arrived and the presentation was made, Blunt showed some annoyance at this verse, for Ezra had confused Mazzini, leader of the 1848 revolutionary government in Italy (with whom Blunt had no connection whatever), with the Egyptian rebel Ahmed Arabi, whom Blunt had actively supported. Nor did Blunt care for the reliquary itself, which he afterwards described as 'terribly post-futurist'. In his speech of thanks, remembers Aldington, he told the 'committee' that 'he wasn't sure at first whether we were a deputation of poets or horse-breeders'.

However, he entertained them royally. Ezra described for the benefit of readers of *Poetry* how they had been regaled 'with the roast flesh of peacocks at Newbuildings, a sixteenth-century defensible grange' (the house actually dates from 1683). To his mother, Ezra wrote: 'We were fed upon roast peacock in feathers which went very well with the iron-studded barricades on the stairway and other mediaeval relics and Burne-jones tapestry.' Blunt's granddaughter has written: 'Regarding the roasted peacock – The one appearing in full plumage was in fact the skin of the whole bird arranged over a dummy to look realistic – the roasted bird followed on a separate dish.'

Frederic Manning and John Masefield were to have been there too and had contributed poems to the reliquary, but Manning had to go back to Lincolnshire and, said Ezra, 'Masefield's wife wouldn't let him out.' After lunch they all posed for a photograph, Ezra and Yeats rivalling each other's endeavours to look the stage poet (Yeats won easily). 'Yeats disguised by influenza and glasses,' said Ezra of the picture when he saw it. 'The rest quite recognizable.' Hilaire Belloc who lived quite near came in for tea, 'which in his case', said Aldington, 'consisted of a pint of claret in a large crystal goblet'. Blunt had delayed Belloc's arrival lest he should deflect the entire day's conversation to 'Marconis and Jews'.

Blunt was touched by the tribute, but thought the whole occasion somewhat ridiculous, and was not impressed by Ezra, whom he described to a friend as 'an American . . . Europeanized [who] has contracted all the absurdities of the day, and is now a cubist . . . He makes himself a sort of understudy of Yeats, repeating Yeats' voice with Yeats' brogue, an odd nervous little man with a mop of reddish hair looking as if dyed and a jerky manner as if afflicted with St Vitus' dance.' Nevertheless he agreed to let Ezra call again two months later, accompanied by Aldington, on which occasion Blunt appeared at dinner in the full regalia of an Arab sheikh, with a brace of gold-mounted pistols in his sash, and lifting his glass cried 'Damnation to the British Government' – 'which treasonable toast', says Aldington, 'we were forced to accept'.

In the most celebrated passage of the Cantos, the 'Pull down thy vanity' lines of Canto 81, written in the prison camp at Pisa, Ezra turns to the example of Blunt:

> To have, with decency, knocked
> That a Blunt should open
>   To have gathered from the air a live tradition
> or from a fine old eye the unconquered flame
> This is not vanity.

But Blunt was more important to him as a figurehead than as an actual poet. On this second visit to Newbuildings, Ezra got Blunt to agree to send some manuscripts to *Poetry*, and told Harriet Monroe that 'the Blunt stuff, glory of the name etc. ought to build up our position . . . Besides it is good of its kind.' Blunt failed to deliver, whereupon Ezra lost interest: 'I won't stir him up . . . I don't care about giving people the sort of stuff they want, or using stuff in the old manner.'

*

On their return to Stone Cottage from the first visit to Newbuildings, Yeats wrote a poem suggested by the occasion, 'The Peacock', which begins

> What's riches to him
> That has made a great peacock
> With the pride of his eye?

It was printed in *Poetry* in April 1914, and in Yeats's new collection, *Responsibilities*, which came out that spring. In Canto 83 Ezra recalls Yeats at work on it in the cottage, trying each line over to himself:

> Uncle William
> downstairs composing
> that had made a great Peeeeacock
>   in the proide ov his oiye
>   had made a great peeeeeeecock in the
> made a great peacock
>   in the proide of his oyyee
>
> proide ov his oy-ee
> as indeed he had

Yeats's new book *Responsibilities* showed the results of Ezra's strictures on his verse a year earlier. He would, no doubt, have developed his new, harder, more rigorous style without Ezra's help, but the process had been speeded up. There is some evidence that Ezra helped to choose the new book's rather severe title. When *Responsibilities* was published, Ezra reviewed it in *Poetry* (May 1914). He said that Yeats was 'so assuredly an immortal' that there was no need for him to 'recast his style to suit our winds of doctrine'; nevertheless, there was 'a manifestly new note' which had been sporadically apparent for the last four years. Ezra called this new note 'direct . . . and free of the "glamour". I've not a word against the glamour as it appears in Yeats' early poems, but we have had so many other pseudo-glamours . . . since the nineties that one is about ready for hard light.'

*

When Ezra finally returned to London from Stone Cottage, Gaudier-Brzeska began work on a carved stone head of him. There were sittings during February 1914, Gaudier making a number of sketches of Ezra in Indian ink: Ezra afterwards estimated them as 'a hundred . . . many of which could be recognized as portraiture, and any one of which might serve as sculptural education'. Executed with a brisk boldness, these preliminary studies of head and neck were entirely realistic, with no hint of what was to come in the carving, though it has often been noticed that some of them bear a resemblance to the shape of the intertwined E and P in Ezra's signature, as he sometimes executed it:

Gaudier-Brzeska could not usually afford marble – when he and Ezra rode on top of a bus past a cemetery he would curse the 'waste of good stone' – and he had intended to create the bust in plaster. But Ezra thought this a pity, and himself purchased a very substantial block, several feet in dimension, having no idea how much work this would mean for Gaudier. Two months of solid cutting were only interrupted when Gaudier had to reforge his worn-out chisels. Partly to save money but also on principle, Gaudier made all his own tools. Similarly he disliked the 'softness' of castings made from plaster, and preferred to cut direct in brass. In this fashion he made a knuckle-duster for T. E. Hulme, who said he would use it to 'tame' his women.

'Brzeska is using up a ton of Pentilicon for my head,' Ezra told his father on 28 February 1914. As he cut, Gaudier would mutter to Ezra: 'You understand it will not look like you, it *will – not – look* – like you. It will be the expression of certain emotions which I get from your character.' Really the head was scarcely inspired by Ezra at all: the arrangement of beard and hair are just recognizably his, but the 'emotions' expressed are the precise opposite of the nervous energy conveyed by the man himself – an energy that Gaudier's preliminary drawings exactly capture, so it must have been a conscious decision, dictated maybe by the medium of marble, not to pursue that line of interpretation. Ezra himself observed that the bust was 'eternally calm – which I ain't'.

Gaudier chose to create what looked like a religious monument or totem from some ancient ritual, an austere priestly figure (he called it 'Hieratic Head of Ezra Pound') that seems to have been suggested by a gigantic

Easter Island cult figure in the British Museum. Nevertheless, Ezra sat as model, and loved it. 'Some of my best days,' he wrote a few months afterwards, 'the happiest and the most interesting, were spent in his uncomfortable mud-floored studio when he was doing my bust . . . There was I on a shilling wooden chair in a not over-heated studio with the railroad trains rushing overhead, and there was the half-ton block of marble on its stand, and bobbing about it was this head "out of the renaissance". I have now and again had the lark of escaping the present, and this was one of those expeditions.'

Jacob Epstein came to see what was going on; and Gaudier explained to him that the head had a 'virile . . . biological significance'. Seen from the front or side, it had begun to resemble a phallus in outline, while from the top there projected a forelock with its own phallic prominence. At the rear, the top part took on the appearance of scrotum. 'Brzx's column gets more gravely beautiful & more phallic each week,' Ezra told Dorothy on 10 March 1914. However as work progressed the bust became somewhat less outrageous – 'it will be no use to the police,' Ezra said – and in its final state it emphasized inscrutable calm rather than virility. Ezra said that if he had really looked like that himself, 'I should have had the firmness of Hotep-hotep, the strength of the gods of Egypt.' He had found it more impressive two weeks before it was finished. 'I do not mean to say it was better, it was perhaps a *kinesis*, whereas it is now a *stasis*; but before the back was cut out, and before the middle lock was cut down, there was in the marble a titanic energy, it was a great stubby catapult, the two masses bent for a blow . . . But in sculpture there is no turning back.'

The bust was immediately displayed at the Whitechapel Gallery; Ezra and Gaudier joked of the time when Ezra would sell it to the Metropolitan Museum for $5,000 and they would both 'live at ease for a year'. After it had been exhibited in Whitechapel, he had it placed in Violet Hunt's front garden on Campden Hill, where it sat for many years, as Richard Aldington said, 'much to Violet's distress'. No one could afford a pedestal, so it stood on the grass, a prey to mud, moss, snails, and the lawn-mower. Ezra would sometimes go and clean it up, borrowing a brush and pail from Violet's elderly maid, who on being asked Mr Pound's whereabouts would reply that he could be found 'a-scrubbin' his MONUMENT'.

11

Almost As Intelligent . . . !

Des Imagistes was published in the United States at the beginning of March 1914 and in London the next month. In its final state it contained poems by Richard Aldington, 'H.D.', F. S. Flint, Skipwith Cannell, Amy Lowell, William Carlos Williams, James Joyce, Ford Madox Hueffer, Allen Upward and John Cournos, as well as six by Ezra, four of which were in the Chinese style. There was no preface or notes to explain the nature and beliefs of the Imagists, so that the book seemed excessively cryptic (not to say dull), though Ezra gave a newspaper interview at the time of publication in which he announced that 'The Anthology does not represent the personalities of those included, nor does it represent their differences, but the line where they come together, their agreement that the cake-icing on the top of poetry – the useless adjectives and the unnecessary similes which burden verse like cumbrous ornaments – should be avoided.'

Des Imagistes received a wide press in America, though mostly of an abusive nature; Aldington remembered how 'columnists parodied the poems, or reproduced them (without payment) accompanied by derisive remarks'. In England there was less interest, most of it hostile; a number of copies were grumpily returned to Harold Monro's Poetry Bookshop, which was selling the book. Ezra did not care: the anthology was the obsequy of the Imagist movement as far as he was concerned. He was by now leaping on to other projects and enthusiasms.

After coming back to Church Walk from Stone Cottage he wrote to Dorothy on 21 January 1914:

> Dearest
> I perceive that this week will be unduly elongated. I think you'd better perhaps marry me and live in one room more than the dryad.
>   E.

Dorothy was now only two and a half years away from her thirtieth birthday, Ezra a year nearer his. Both parties had assumed for some time that they would eventually marry, and her parents' opposition had faded stage by stage into inertia. Yet in the past Ezra had expressed a determination to keep marriage at bay lest it interfere with his art. He was always ready to scoff at it as an institution; he did not want to be 'looked after' – he was self-sufficient domestically and knew that Dorothy, brought up by a dominating mother and surrounded by servants, possessed almost no household skills; and he was not short of female companionship in his bachelor state. The only positive benefit from marriage would be Dorothy's private income, but there were less drastic methods than marriage of acquiring a subsidy.

Sophie Brzeska asked him why he was bothering to get married. 'It doesn't matter,' he told her. 'It's just a question of a few procedures for the sake of convenience.' (He did not specify what convenience.) She persisted, asking 'What if one wishes to separate? Look what terrible chores you'll have to go through.' Ezra replied: 'Why get a divorce? One lives in mutual tolerance.'

Probably his and Dorothy's ages had something to do with it. He may have felt it was time for a change in lifestyle. Perhaps, however improbably, the example of Aldington and Hilda, who had married the previous autumn, influenced him; or perhaps it was not a careful decision at all, rather, as the letter to Dorothy suggests, a casual notion, a spur-of-the-moment reaction to a temporary lull in his affairs. After all, he did not usually take much trouble over the major choices in his life.

Dorothy's reply made no reference to the proposal, but evidently she agreed, pending the consent of her parents. This took time to acquire. She wrote to him on 13 February 1914: 'O. S. said, that she thought it would be more diplomatic if she were to talk to H.H.S. [Dorothy's father] herself first. So she is doing so now – this minute – & I am feeling glad it isn't me – and very jumpy . . . *Later*. Consent appears to be given – with some reluctance.'

Shortly after this, Ezra wrote to his mother: 'I dare say I *am* going to be married. The family has ordered the invitations and stuff for curtains etc. In which case I shall *not* come to America and if you want to inspect us you will have to come over here.' To his father he added: 'There will be no fuss.'

There was however a certain amount of disagreement between Ezra and Dorothy's father, who wanted them to be married in church. 'Unless you feel very strongly on this point,' Ezra wrote to Mr Shakespear, 'I should much rather go through the simple and dignified service at the Registry.' He went on to discuss his religious feeling at expansive length: what he chiefly objected to was the clergy – 'thousands of prim, soaped little

Tertullians', as he called them in the *Egoist*, 'opposing enlightenment, entrenched in their bigotry'. The Mass rather appealed to him as an ancient, even pagan cult that was not widely understood. As for the Deity, he thought it valid to use the term 'God' for 'the intimate essence of the universe', something outside oneself and '*not* of the same nature as our own consciousness', but any attempt to construct religious dogma was merely 'bluff based on ignorance'. Christ seemed to him a 'heroic figure' who was 'not wholly to blame for the religion that's been foisted on him'. .

Henry Hope Shakespear was a little taken aback by Ezra's lecture on religion. He replied that it was not his suggestion that they should be married in church; he had simply assumed it. He said that he would not try to force his views, and they could use the registry office if they wanted to, but 'it will be more distressing to me than perhaps you can understand'. Even before Mr Shakespear had sent his letter, he heard from Dorothy 'that you have both decided to defer to my wishes & I heartily thank you'. Mr Shakespear became quite friendly as the wedding approached, writing to his future son-in-law as 'Dear Ezra'. But some of Dorothy's friends were dubious about what the future held for her. Mrs Eva Fowler observed to Ezra that she could understand how Dorothy might fall in love with him, but to *marry* him – 'well she *might* have done it herself,' said Ezra, 'but she wouldn't have let anybody belonging to her attempt it'. Yeats was in the USA, and expressed no such reservations, writing to Homer Pound that Ezra had 'found for himself a very clever, a very charming and a very beautiful wife. I shall be back in time for the marriage.'

It was arranged that Dorothy should have an annuity of £150 a year, quite adequate to support her, indeed enough to keep them both above the poverty line. In 1922 Ezra told John Quinn that he had only kept afloat since his marriage thanks to Dorothy's income, which her parents had regularly augmented; and in 1946 he explained to a doctor at St Elizabeths that Dorothy had had 'enough to keep us going', which had given him the freedom to write as he pleased. 'I was not writing for money, so they had no means of crushing me.' On top of Dorothy's funds, Homer Pound, instead of continuing to pay an allowance, deposited a capital sum with the Jenkintown Bank & Trust Company, on the interest of which Ezra could draw without explanation, provided that no withdrawal exceeded $100.

Ezra's access to Dorothy's income inevitably affected the nature of his literary work in the years following the marriage. It freed him not only from the necessity of earning his living but even of considering his audience. He could operate entirely as he wished, with publication and sales as only a secondary consideration. His and Dorothy's private means also made him behave, at least some of the time, like a languorous gentleman of leisure who had no particular end in view. 'You subsidized drifters,' he sneered at his old professor, Felix Schelling, in 1933, referring

to the academic profession; but the epithet could have been justly applied
to himself. More damaging than the absence of a need to earn was his belief
that, because he was not driven by a commercial motive, his work was *de
facto* of importance: 'Nothing written for pay is worth printing. ONLY
what has been written AGAINST the market.'

*

As soon as the wedding was arranged, he took a flat at 5 Holland Place
Chambers, just around the corner from Church Walk, and moved in at
once. He told Dorothy that it suited him 'like an old glove, & seems about
as convenient as my new typewriter'. Holland Place Chambers was an
oppressive late-Victorian block of flats with *art nouveau* trimmings and
inadequate daylight; Ezra's apartment was small and dark, and the main
room was pentagonal. The rent was apparently paid by Olivia, who was
the legal tenant.

The Aldingtons were already living in the block, on the same floor as the
flat Ezra chose, and Hilda had little warning of the new tenants: 'I found
the door open one day . . . and Ezra there . . . "What are you doing?" I
asked . . . I was rather taken aback when they actually moved in. It was so
near.'

Ezra was still getting fun from mocking her. She appears in a poem in his
Lustra:

> The Dryad stands in my court-yard
> with plaintive querulous crying . . .
> She says, 'May my poems be printed this week?
> The god Pan is afraid to ask you,
> May my poems be printed this week?'

She and Aldington soon found his proximity too much for them. They
moved out of their flat and went, said Ezra, 'to Cape Hampstead and now
reside there beyond the reach of any known form of transport'. Hilda had a
stillbirth ('Hilda's infant died, so dont send it a christening spoon,' Ezra
told his mother), the marriage foundered, and when she became pregnant
again, in 1918, it was by a man named Cecil Gray. Ezra visited her in the
London nursing home where the baby, Perdita, was born, and told her:
'My only real criticism is that this is not my child.' He seemed in any case
to regard Perdita as his property: in 1940 he suggested to his American
publisher, the young James Laughlin, that Laughlin might marry her:
'I think mebbe H.D.'s darter is in Svizzera if she ain't in Lunnon with her
Ma/ a fine well grown gal wot might keep you from messy / liance.'

After the collapse of her marriage to Aldington, Hilda virtually abandoned men and took up with the writer 'Bryher' (Winifred Ellerman), who
had considerable private means derived from a wealthy Jewish financier

and shipowner father. Ezra and Bryher quickly developed a strong mutual dislike, Ezra writing in 1956 that Bryher had 'systematicly obstructed, like many of her race, as much of my activity as possible'. (He had once asked Bryher for help, and she had refused.)

Shortly before his own wedding Ezra determined to teach himself to cook. He told his mother: 'I shall have a gas range to play with, and hope thereby to free myself from part of the necessity of restaurants. Please send me the receipts and specifications and directions for pancakes, waffles, fried chicken *à la Lucy*, that brown hard fry with gravy. Also cream-soups, tomato and potato. and any other of the simple pleasures. When you come over I shall probably insist on your bringing an American ice cream freezer, unless by some miracle I find that they can be obtained here.' In fact, after marriage he and Dorothy ate out almost as often as he had in bachelor days, frequently at Belotti's in Old Compton Street, 'the cheapest clean restaurant with a real cook', Ezra called it. Dorothy made no attempt to learn to cook – 'Remember, I can't do a thing myself,' she warned him soon before the marriage – and Ezra accepted this philosophically. 'Some cook some do not cook, / some things can not be changed,' he writes in Canto 54. Wyndham Lewis has recorded that Ezra was 'an excellent cook'.

Ezra gave his parents virtually no information about the wedding. Homer publicized the event, as he did all his son's doings, in the Philadelphia newspapers, but gave Dorothy's age as twenty and admitted that he did not know the name of the officiating clergyman, nor any other details of the ceremony. He and Isabel were sent an invitation, but purely as a formality. On the day itself, Monday 20 April 1914, a postcard went off to them from 12 Brunswick Gardens, Dorothy's home:

Salutations.
Ceremony legalized

love
D.P.
E.P.

The service was held quite early in the morning at St Mary Abbots.* Dorothy was quietly dressed in a coat and skirt, and there were only about half a dozen guests. After lunch the Shakespears gave a small reception at Brunswick Gardens. For their honeymoon Ezra and Dorothy went to Stone Cottage, where the Misses Welfare looked after them. Ezra spent most of his time working on Noh dramas. 'We have been down here for a little over a fortnight,' Ezra told his father, 'and I have been plugging into the Fenollosa mss. at a great rate . . . We were married on the twentieth, I think I wrote but dont remember.' They drove over to visit Wilfred

* Yeats was back in London, but it is not clear whether he attended. To Lady Gregory he merely says: 'Ezra Pound was married yesterday.' (21 April 1914.)

Scawen Blunt, who welcomed them in his Arab robes; afterwards Blunt judged that Dorothy had somewhat 'deodorized' Ezra's character, 'and he needed deodorizing'. Dorothy, meanwhile, as she put it years later, was 'trying to make out what sort of creature I was going to be living with'.

*

Ezra had begun by being attracted to Olivia; that much is abundantly clear. But 'the most charming woman in London' had proved something of a disappointment; Olivia once told him she 'never understood anything he said'. Dorothy had originally been intended by him for the role of disciple rather than confidante or lover. In one of his earliest letters to her he set her to write out some sonnets of Cavalcanti, apparently as a penance or as part of her education. He also remarks that he hopes she is 'the Griselda type' rather than the Ibsen-Shaw species of New Woman. He liked to address her in the plural: 'Personally we think you fulfill your destiny most admirably.' He was not concerned to have a love affair with her, but to expedite his art; he reminds her in a 1910 letter that 'the ultimate aim is poesia'.

Though a disciple was what he got, Dorothy was never negligible as a personality. Her letters to Ezra before their marriage show her as a sardonic judge of character, far from naïve in her observations. For example, at a *pension* in Malvern in the spring of 1912 she reports to Ezra that 'A horrid man has come for Sunday & so we have had to give up the smoking room . . . He has a bad face & his wife a very "tight" one: I suppose he tries her severely: & there is a swarm of their offspring, all red-headed & sickly-looking.' And on another occasion in Sherborne: 'There is an engaged couple in the house – HE seems colonial and horribly shy – SHE is given to hunting & good works in due seasons.'

According to the fashions of the time, Dorothy was thoroughly emancipated, at least in superficial matters. She called her mother 'Olivia' or 'O.S.', and used 'damn' and 'bloody' in her letters. She was widely read; in the spring of 1912 she reported that she was enjoying W. P. Ker's history of medieval English literature, Bacon's Essays, the Dialogues of St Gregory, and Renan's romanticized *Vie de Jésus*. Of these, possibly the St Gregory was Ezra's suggestion, but the rest seem to have been her own choice. In later years she could be found poring over Voltaire in the original (she regarded herself as a Voltairean free-thinker) and the complete works of Henry James.

She took a close interest in Ezra's poetry, and before publication he would sometimes ask her opinion as to whether a particular effect 'worked'. (On the other hand she said that he 'never spoke about his work while it was still being composed. Only after he had got it down into reasonable shape.') She also paid attention to the writings of people Ezra was championing: he told Joyce in the summer of 1915 that she was re-reading *Dubliners* and making appreciative comments. Above all she absorbed herself deeply in the Cantos. 'I got all entangled with the Cantos,' she said at the end of her life. 'Ezra quite spoils anything else for me.'

She continued to draw and paint, designing covers for several of Ezra's books. These show an intelligent absorption of modern abstract painting, while her line drawings have a remarkable similarity – too accomplished to be altogether imitation – to those of Gaudier-Brzeska. Her admiration for him is clear from the amount of his work (drawings and sculpture) that she bought with her own money. Ezra sometimes mentioned her paintings and cover designs to his parents, but he took no trouble to encourage her ambitions. He wrote to John Quinn in 1917: 'I distrust the "female artist" as much as even you can.' And in the *New Age* a year later: 'Not wildly anti-feminist we are yet to be convinced that any woman ever invented anything in the arts.' His attitude to Dorothy's intellect was, on the whole, condescending. To Wilfred Scawen Blunt, in a letter of March 1914, he describes her as 'much more charming and decorative than I am – and almost as intelligent . . .!'

Ezra's friends chiefly observed her silence: their memoirs of him in London, Paris, and Rapallo often refer to her 'just sitting there like a beautiful ornament, silent most of the time.' One of them described her as 'carrying herself delicately with the air, always, of a young Victorian lady out skating'.

She had had an exceptionally happy childhood – she told Yeats she would not have altered anything in it – but the long period in her twenties of living almost in purdah with her mother had given her little stimulus, and she did not possess sufficient independence of spirit to break free from the parental fold until time and Ezra had worn down its walls.

'There is this strong English side,' someone who knew her well has said of her. 'You don't write about what you feel. You don't put your emotions on the written page. I can hear [her] saying "It doesn't *matter* what I feel."' That had not always been the case, as her notebook entries show at the time she first met Ezra. But most of her vitality gradually went underground, or disintegrated.

After the Pounds had been married for ten years, one of Ezra's girlfriends from college days asked Hilda Doolittle for news of Ezra. 'Yes, Ez is "married",' answered Hilda, 'but there seems to be a pretty general consensus of opinion that Mrs E. has not been "awakened" . . . She is very English and "cold" . . . and has never been known to make a warm friend with a man or woman. She loathes (she says) children! . . . I don't think she can be poignantly sensitive or she would never have stuck Ezra.'

Hilda seems to be hinting at a lack of sexual awakening. Dorothy had first been attracted to Ezra by his glamorous appearance as the stage poet, but later, during the seemingly endless years of their courtship, this initial passion evidently cooled, so that little more than friendly feelings seem to have remained. His lack of physical response apparently discouraged her from giving him what she called in her notebook, in the early days of their friendship, 'the hot-coloured passion which dying leaves a blackness of Hell'. Instead, as she wrote in the notebook in these early weeks, he seemed to want only 'an exquisite delicate love'.

By nature Dorothy seems to have been quite highly sexed. In a letter to Ezra before marriage she mentions a dream of embracing a friend of theirs, Jim Fairfax, and another of a statue of a mother and child 'warm & alive – nude & grouped Rodinesquely'. On another occasion she admits that 'really when I "think" I only get into tangles & make myself miserable . . . *not* about my soul! but about my body'. At a hotel in Ilfracombe, before marriage, she admitted to being disturbed by 'the engaged & honeymooning couples . . . leaning towards each other'. The impression is of somebody hankering for physical love.

There is some evidence that Ezra and Dorothy did not sleep in the same room. Describing a visit to Holland Place Chambers by Conrad Aiken in the summer of 1914, just after the marriage, Ezra wrote that 'a Harvard man entered my hall bedroom, if you could call it HALL', which seems to indicate separate sleeping quarters, even in the cramped space of the tiny flat. James Laughlin, who spent a great deal of time in the Pounds' apartment in Rapallo in the 1930s, had the impression that Dorothy was sleeping in her 'studio' rather than sharing the double bed in Ezra's room – though by this time much had happened that may have changed the relationship.

In 1914 Ezra had no intention of begetting a child. He wrote three years later in the *Little Review*:

> I am, with qualifications, Malthusian. I should consent to breed under pressure, if I were convinced in any way of the reasonableness of reproducing the species. But my nerves and the nerves of any woman I could live with three months, would produce only a victim . . . lacking in impulse, a mere bundle of discriminations. If I were wealthy I might subsidize a stud of young peasants, or a tribal group in Tahiti.

He took much the same line when writing to his mother in 1920: 'When I am really opulent . . . I shall set up a stud farm.' And of a cousin who had just produced a male heir, the same year: 'I hope [he] can afford it; and that he derives pleasure from the presence of it, its bottles, its diapers, its damp pieces of biscuit . . .'

In his poetry he liked to give the impression of casual virility, with allusions to 'the dance of the phallus'. The month before his marriage he published a poem entitled 'Coitus', which begins: 'The gilded phaloi of the crocuses are thrusting at the spring air.' But it seems doubtful that sexuality played any part in his marriage. When a psychiatrist questioned him about this at St Elizabeths in 1946 he showed 'considerable reluctance' to discuss it, and became 'evasive'. When pressed for details he would only say: 'You may state that my sexual and marital adjustments were perfectly compatible'; to which it may be objected that he naturally found such questioning deeply offensive, and was likely to hold back any information. Yet he went on to tell the same doctor quite freely about a 'wet dream' he had experienced in Pisa.

There could be a buried reference to his own condition in the squib 'Mr Styrax', one of the 'Moeurs Contemporaines' sequence of poems written three years after his marriage:

> Mr Hecatomb Styrax . . .
>
>   . . . has married at the age of 28,
> He being at that age a virgin.

Ezra himself was twenty-eight at the time of his marriage.

In Rapallo in the 1930s, Daniel Cory said to Ezra one day when they were alone together that Dorothy 'must have been a lovely girl when he had first met her in England. He was silent for a moment before replying: "Yes, she was. I fell in love with a beautiful picture that never came alive."'

12

Youth Racket

On 1 March 1914 Ezra wrote to his mother: 'Wyndham Lewis is starting a new quarterly "Blast" which will be the sole intelligent publication in England. You will thoroughly detest it.' His parent asked who Lewis was. 'I dont know that I have written of him,' replied Ezra, 'but he is more or less one of the gang here at least he is the most "advanced" of the painters and very clever and thoroughly enigmatic.'

Percy Wyndham Lewis was the son of an American who had led a cavalry charge in the Civil War, and had escaped from imprisonment in the South. Technically a lawyer, Lewis's father lived as a romancer and professional idler, sponging off the family wealth. He married a sixteen-year-old English girl, half his own age; she eventually left him because of his infidelities, and brought up her son, born in 1882, in genteel poverty in England. Lewis described himself as 'an only child of a selfish vigorous little mother'.

Lewis went to Rugby School, where he detested the system and was despised by its members, but was allowed to study drawing. He left after only two years, and at the age of fifteen entered the Slade School of Art, where he was regarded as the best draughtsman since Augustus John, but once again disliked the system. He then had seven years of Bohemian adventuring on the Continent, during which he became a friend and rival of Augustus John himself, whose seductions he attempted to ape. His own first illegitimate child (of several) was born to a German mistress; he disowned it and in 1909 returned to England, where he called on Ford Madox Hueffer at the *English Review*. Finding Ford in the bath, he told him (said Ford) 'in the most matter-of-fact way that he was a man of genius', and read a piece of prose aloud. Ford accepted it, and took other pieces by Lewis, who rather wanted to write a popular novel.

Ford describes Lewis as he was around 1914 in the persona of George Heimann in his novel *The Marsden Case* (1922):

> A face . . . alabaster white and aquiline; intent under a slouch hat . . . The foreignness of his aspect, his high-crowned hat, his coat, black and buttoned-up round his neck, like a uniform – always a startling effect, his immense black Inverness cloak, his young beard and his long black hair drooping over his ears, all these things were the products of a sojourn in Bohemia, not of foreign birth.

Lewis remarked of his own appearance:

> Outwardly, I have been told, I looked like a *moujik*: but if so it was a *moujik* who bought his clothes in Savile Row or Brook Street and his most eccentric shirts in the Burlington Arcade. I had the tarnished polish of the English Public School, of the most gilded cafés of five or six continental capitals.

Ernest Hemingway, who disliked him, added that he had the eyes 'of an unsuccessful rapist'.

In London, Lewis began to receive commissions as a painter. Ford and Violet Hunt paid him to do an abstract panel for the study at South Lodge, described by Rebecca West as 'very violent and explosive' (it was a brilliant red). She remembered Ford saying he 'found it extremely restful'. In the spring of 1912, along with Epstein and two other artists, Lewis was commissioned by Frida Strindberg, the playwright's third wife, to decorate the Cave of the Golden Calf, London's first 'arty' night club. She contracted to pay him £60 but then quarrelled with him, so he got his money by taking it from the till. Ezra was amused by Madame Strindberg, a volatile Viennese: he alleged that he once heard her say to a Guards officer in the club: 'Yes, I vil sleep vit you. It is nossing. But talk to you half an hour. Neffair! Vun must traw de line SOMMEFERE!!'

By 1911 Lewis had begun to paint in the Cubist style, finding a congenial subject in a set of near-abstract illustrations to *Timon of Athens*, with whose hero he closely identified. Ezra judged these drawings 'a great work' on the theme of 'the fury of intelligence baffled and shut in by circumjacent stupidity' (he, too, saw himself as a Timon).

The *Timon* drawings were exhibited at the second Post-Impressionist show in 1912, and Lewis was asked by its organizer Roger Fry to join his Omega Workshops when they opened in Fitzroy Square the next year. For Omega, Lewis painted some screens and candle-shades, but he soon quarrelled with Fry and left, taking Gaudier-Brzeska, Edward Wadsworth, and others with him. This quarrel was certainly one to draw Ezra's sympathy; in 1917 he wrote to his father: 'I may have met Clive Bell, but there are a lot of those washed-out Fry-ites, and I cant tell one from the other. A sort of male Dorcas-society.' The 'Bloomsbuggars', as he liked to call them, never attracted the faintest admiration from him. Writing to Henry Miller in 1934 he spoke contemptuously of 'the weak minded Woolf female'.

Following the break with Omega, Wyndham Lewis founded a 'Rebel Art Centre' in a London house, 38 Great Ormond Street. Financed by one of his woman friends, it started rather tamely with Saturday tea-parties and work not unlike that of the Omega, though he kept an empty room to represent the impending arrival of great art. A lecture was given at the Centre by Ford Madox Hueffer who alleged that during it he sustained 'a sharp blow from one of Lewis's largest paintings', which fell off the wall on to his head.

Ford played some part in introducing Lewis to Ezra, but their first meeting was immediately due to Laurence Binyon of the British Museum. It took place in the Vienna Café, a triangular coffee-house favoured by readers in the Museum, which occupied the corner of New Oxford Street and Bloomsbury Street. Lewis dated the encounter as probably 'in 1910 though I have no calendar, engagement book, old letters'. More likely it took place a year earlier, soon after Ezra had arrived in London, judging from his description of the occasion in Canto 80, where he says that 'Mr Lewis had been to Spain' – Lewis's visit to Spain took place in the summer of 1908.

Binyon, says Ezra, thought of it as a meeting between 'his bull-dog, me' and 'Mr P. Wyndham Lewis . . . Mr T. Sturge Moore's bull-dog', Lewis being known to Sturge Moore too. Lewis, also, used an animal metaphor for that first encounter beneath the mirrored ceiling of the Vienna Café, saying that Ezra approached him 'as one might a panther, or any other dangerous quadruped – tense and wary, without speaking or smiling: showing one is not afraid of it, inwardly awaiting hostile action'.

The two men were at that time strikingly similar in appearance. Augustus John's 1905 portrait of Lewis shows a lean, dark-haired young man with a moustache that functions much like Ezra's 'poet' beard, and a sharp, tense face. By 1914 he had fattened a bit (he later became portly) but there was still the guarded, combative look in the eyes. Douglas Goldring of the *English Review* noticed the resemblance between Ezra and Lewis, observing that 'in clothes, hairdressing and manner' neither made a 'secret of their calling'.

Lewis remembered that at the first meeting with Ezra

> I did not speak to him: on the second occasion he addressed a few remarks to me, but I did not reply. I did not consider it necessary to do so, he seemed in fact to be addressing some-

body else. I mean that what he said did not appear to be appropriate, or to have any relevance – as a remark addressed to *me* . . . There had been some question of the whereabouts of a kidnapped or absconding prostitute . . . 'This young man could probably tell you!' was I think what he said, with great archness . . . He had been told that I was a 'rebel' . . . but it did not occur to him that I might not be a *conventional* rebel.

At the third meeting Lewis finally 'answered the hail' from Ezra's pirate galleon, 'and going on board, I discovered beneath its skull and crossbones . . . a heart of gold'.

For a time the two had nothing to say to each other. Ezra had 'discovered' Lewis as an *alter ego* of himself, a force equally to be recognized in London artistic circles, but at first he neither knew Lewis's writings nor had much idea of his work as a painter. Soon, however, he began to perceive the 'gold' in Lewis's character. 'Lewis *can* at moments be extremely irritating,' he wrote in 1916. 'But then, damn it all, he is quite apt to be in the right.' It was almost a matter of seeing himself in a mirror: 'A volcanic and disordered mind like Wyndham Lewis's,' he wrote after they had known each other many years, 'is of great value, especially in a dead, and for the most part rotted, milieu.' Lewis was also as nomadic as himself: Ezra summed him up as 'Wyndham L/ "I'll give you an address when I get one."'

By 1914 they knew each other well enough for Lewis to invite Ezra to hold an Imagist Evening at the Rebel Art Centre (though it never took place), and when early that year Lewis decided to start a magazine it was natural to turn to Ezra. They had some talk about it in restaurants during February and early March, and after one of those meetings Lewis (said Ezra) went off 'with eleven nice blasty poems of mine. At last there's to be a magazine one can appear in without a feeling of degradation.'

To Dorothy, Ezra initially described *BLAST* as a 'revue cubiste'. To James Joyce, who he suggested might contribute, he spoke of it as 'a new Futurist, Cubist, Imagiste Quarterly'. In fact it was simply a Rebel Centre on paper, intended to incorporate anyone from the modern artistic 'isms' who would join in a 'blast' against the stale ends of Victorianism which Lewis believed still dominated British life. Ezra was particularly ready for the venture, feeling himself now in need of something more aggressive than the delicate cadences of Imagism. 'The modern artist,' he wrote in the *Egoist* in February 1914, just as Lewis was beginning to get his team together, 'must live by craft and violence. His gods are violent gods . . . Those artists, so called, whose work does not show this strife, are uninteresting.'

Lewis took the idea for *BLAST* from the Italian Futurists, who had held an exhibition in London in 1912, and whose leader, the poet F. T. Marinetti, was there again in November 1913 when Lewis attended a dinner for him. On this occasion, said Lewis, Marinetti boomed out his poem 'The Siege of Adrianople' in a voice that afterwards made 'a day of attack upon the Western Front' seem 'nothing to it'. Marinetti's Futurism, with its aggression, its cult of machinery and violence, and its contempt for 'cultural heritage', anticipated certain aspects of Fascism. Marinetti also turned up at one of Yeats's salons at Woburn Buildings, where, says Richard Aldington, he bawled a poem about the Automobile at such a level that 'Yeats had to ask him to stop because neighbours were knocking in protest on the floor, ceiling and party walls'.

If Futurism supplied the aggression of *BLAST*, the name that the magazine's perpetrators chose for themselves was dreamt up by Ezra. The word 'vortex' had appeared once in his poetry and several times in his letters since 1908, either as a term for the artist's mental process – 'Energy depends on ones ability to make a vortex, genius *même*' – or as a way of describing the intense cultural life of London; he wrote to William Carlos Williams in December 1913: 'You may get something slogging away by yourself that you would miss in the Vortex.' Now, he and Lewis decided to give their new 'movement' the name 'Vorticism'.

'It was Pound who invented the word "vorticist",' writes Lewis. In the first issue of *BLAST*, in June 1914, Ezra could be found expounding this new 'ism' in the tones of P. T. Barnum:

> The vortex is the point of maximum energy. It represents, in mechanics, the greatest efficiency . . . The vorticist relies . . . on the primary pigment of his art, nothing else. Every conception, every emotion presents itself to the vivid consciousness in some primary form. It is the picture that means a hundred poems, the music that means a hundred pictures, the most highly energized statement, the statement that has not yet SPENT itself in expression, but which is the most capable of expressing THE TURBINE.

None of these assertions has anything to do with the actual meaning of 'vortex' (which the *Oxford English Dictionary* glosses as, in modern parlance, 'a rapid movement of particles of matter round an axis; a whirl of atoms, fluid or vapour; an eddying or whirling mass of fire or flame; a state or condition of human affairs comparable to a whirl or eddy by reason of rush or excitement'). Ezra's definition is a hang-over from Imagism, with its emphasis on 'primary' forms of expression, though he has broadened it to bring in painting and music, and gives a sidelong glance at Futurism with the reference to turbines.

The choice of name for the movement was not, however, arbitrary. It appealed to Ezra because it expressed the inexorable haste of his own mind, which, whirlpool-like, was constantly hungry for matter to suck up and expel. More immediately, his selection of the 'Vortex' image for the new movement was due to Allen Upward's new book *The New Word*, which he reviewed for the *New Age* in April 1914. In this book, Upward dismissed the usual view of the physical universe as Matter and Power, and argued the existence of a 'whirl-swirl' which is both matter and power at the same time: 'The ideal whirl-swirl . . . is the true beat of strength . . . which we feel in all things . . . in ourselves, and in our starry world, the beat that is called Action and Reaction.'

Ezra had set himself up as the head of Imagism, but he made no such claim for the new venture, and wrote: 'I am not the "head of the vorticist movement"'. Lewis was the leading force; Ezra took something of a back seat. Vorticism drew comparatively little from his typewriter, and was for him more in the nature of an amusing diversion than a development of his work. On the other hand Lewis felt that the whole thing would never have happened without Ezra's love of battle. 'It was scarcely our fault that we were a youth racket,' he writes. 'It was Ezra who in the first place organized us willy nilly into that. For he was never satisfied until everything was *organized* . . . He had a streak of Baden Powell in him, had Ezra, perhaps more than a streak.'

*

Vorticism was born when Ezra and Dorothy called at the Rebel Art Centre at tea-time one Saturday, and Lewis showed his confidence in Ezra by inviting them into the back room to see his paintings, which were kept locked there for fear of imitators. Dorothy had the impression that Ezra was virtually the only 'fellow artist' Lewis was then allowing to see them *en masse*.

Ezra did not find it easy to digest them. In print two years later he was still floundering in vague assertions that Lewis's talent was 'a matter of almost speech in form', and that his 'general surge' was 'toward the restitution of the proper value of *conception*'. Similarly when he tried to discuss the pictures of Edward Wadsworth, one of Lewis's fellow-secessionists from the Omega, he talked about 'brilliant and interesting refractions' and said vaguely that 'Cubism is an art of patterns . . . a pattern of solids'; he admitted that it was 'difficult' for him to find words to describe it.

The Rebel Art Centre collapsed almost before Vorticism had got going. In June 1914 its patron, Kate Lechmere, was stolen from Lewis's bed by T. E. Hulme. Lewis threatened to kill Hulme, and pursued him to his Soho lodgings, whereupon Hulme dragged Lewis downstairs, and the conflict began in earnest. 'I seized Hulme by the throat,' Lewis writes nostalgically in *Blasting and Bombardiering*, 'but he transfixed me upon the railings of Soho Square. I never see the summer house in its centre without remembering how I saw it upside down.'

The Vorticists' first public action was to separate themselves from the Futurists. This arose out of the publication in the *Observer* on 7 June 1914 of a Futurist Manifesto, written by a British disciple of Marinetti, Christopher Nevinson, who was a member of the Rebel Art Centre and used its address for the manifesto. Nevinson claimed in the manifesto that Lewis and his associates were part of the Futurist movment. Lewis refused to accept this. 'You Wops,' he told Marinetti, 'insist too much upon the Machine . . . We've had machines in England for a donkey's years. They're no novelty to *us*.' A week later the *Observer* carried a statement by the 'Director of the Rebel Art Centre' that he and his colleagues wished to 'dissociate' themselves from the manifesto. Meanwhile Lewis, with what he called 'a determined band of miscellaneous anti-futurists' including Gaudier-Brzeska, infiltrated a lecture by Marinetti at the Doré Galleries in Bond Street. Gaudier-Brzeska led the disruption, subjecting Marinetti to ceaseless verbal sniping, while (says Lewis) 'the remainder of our party maintained a confused uproar'.

Behind the undergraduate-style joking was a serious artistic issue. Gaudier, writing of Nevinson's paintings, called Futurism 'impressionism using false weapons. The emotions are of a superficial character, merging on the vulgar . . . union jacks, lace stockings and other tommy rot.' Ezra said Futurism was 'propaganda that could get along by itself without any painting whatever'.

The first appearance of the Vorticists in full regalia was with the opening issue of their magazine *BLAST*. During April 1914 the *Egoist* carried a full-page advertisement stating that *BLAST* would be published quarterly; the first number would contain

> Story by Wyndham Lewis. Poems by Ezra Pound. Reproductions of Drawings, Paintings, and Sculpture by Etchells, Nevinson, Lewis, Hamilton, Brzeska, Wadsworth, Epstein, Roberts, etc. etc . . . NO Pornography. NO Old Pulp. END OF THE CHRISTIAN ERA.

The money for *BLAST* was mostly put up by Lewis's mother, though Kate Lechmere (before she walked out on Lewis) donated £100. John Lane agreed to publish it, and Lewis found a jobbing printer in Harlesden who was prepared to set up some eccentric typography.

'I am sure BLAST will be horrible,' Dorothy wrote to Ezra not long before their wedding. (She added that she thought Lewis's pictures 'filthy'.) When the first copies appeared, Ezra was greatly tickled by the shocking pink paper and the shrieking black capitals. 'Delicate sensitive work,' he told his mother. Official publication day was 20 June 1914.

BLAST was subtitled *A REVIEW OF THE GREAT ENGLISH VORTEX*. It opened with the cry 'Long Live the Vortex!' and declared that

> great artists in England are always revolutionary . . . Blast sets out to be an avenue for all those vivid and violent ideas that could reach the Public in no other way . . . WE ONLY WANT THE WORLD TO LIVE, and to feel its crude energy flowing through us.

The first item was a series of 'Blasts' and 'Blesses', lists of persons or institutions deemed worthy either of curses or praise – an idea lifted from the '*merde à*' and '*rose à*' lists in Marinetti's magazine *Lacerba*. In *BLAST*, England itself was blasted for 'its climate . . . dismal symbol of effeminate lout within . . . the flabby sky that can manufacture no snow, but can only drop the sea on us in a drizzle like a poem by Mr Robert Bridges'. There were also blasts against many individuals, including Galsworthy, Dean Inge, Elgar, St Loe Strachey the editor of the *Spectator*, and Ezra's bell-ringing vicar of St Mary Abbots, while the 'Bless' list included Madame Strindberg, James Joyce, and Kate Lechmere, but also (less predictably) J. M. Barrie, Henry Newbolt, and the Pope. Douglas Goldring recalls that these lists were put together at a tea-party: 'Lewis and Ezra Pound presided over it jointly, and the guests were the oddest collection of *rapins* in black hats, girls from the Slade, poets and journalists.'

Next came a Manifesto, signed by Aldington, Gaudier-Brzeska, Ezra, Wadsworth, Lewis, and others; then some poems by Ezra. These were in his familiar 'Contemporania' style ('Let us deride the smugness of *The Times*: GUFFAW! / So much for the gagged reviewers . . .'), though the context drew out of him a new note of hysteria:

> You slut-bellied obstructionist,
> You sworn foe to free speech and good letters,
> You fungus, you continuous gangrene.

Aldington thought this poor stuff. 'Mr Pound cannot write satire,' he observed in the *Egoist*. 'All this enormous arrogance and petulance and fierceness are a pose. And it is a wearisome pose.' However, one of Ezra's *BLAST* poems, as Lewis put it, 'cheered things up a little' with printer, publisher, and public. This was 'Fratres Minores':

> With minds still hovering above their testicles
>   Certain poets here and in France
>   Still sigh over established and natural fact
> Long since fully discussed by Ovid.

> They howl. They complain in delicate and exhausted metres
> That the twitching of three abdominal nerves
> Is incapable of producing a lasting Nirvana.

John Lane, though he had stomached the more subtle outrages of the *Yellow Book* when he published it in the 1890s, summoned Lewis to see him and demanded that the first and penultimate lines of this should be deleted. According to Iris Barry, a team of 'young maidens' was thereupon employed by Lewis to score them out with black ink, though this proved transparent, which helped the sales.

Two other lines in a *BLAST* poem by Ezra were not deleted:

> Let us be done with Jews and Jobbery,
> Let us SPIT upon those who fawn on the JEWS for their
> money.

This early instance of his railing against Jewish financiers was changed in his collected *Personae* (1926) so that the target for abuse became 'panders' and 'big-bellies'. However, in the society into which *BLAST* first erupted, the original lines raised few eyebrows.

Next after his poems in the first *BLAST* came reproductions of paintings by Edward Wadsworth (a very remote cousin on Ezra's mother's side); Ezra described him as 'not nearly so important as Lewis, but good'. Then followed the centrepiece of the first issue, Lewis's highly eccentric play *Enemy of the Stars*. Next, by comparison very low key but actually the most enduring item in the magazine, came what was announced as the first part of a serial, 'The Saddest Story' by Ford Madox Hueffer – the novel Ford eventually published as *The Good Soldier*. The remaining contributions included a rather lurid story about a marriage by Rebecca West, and two statements about art headed 'Vortex', the work of Gaudier-Brzeska and Ezra respectively.

A. R. Orage reviewed *BLAST* in the *New Age* a month after it had appeared, judging it 'not unintelligible . . . but not worthy the understanding', and really without significance. On the whole, though, *BLAST* stirred up the outrage for which Lewis and the others had hoped: G. W. Prothero, editor of the 'heavy' *Quarterly Review*, wrote to Ezra saying he could not publish anything by a contributor to 'such a publication as *BLAST*. It stamps a man too disadvantageously.' (Prothero had previously printed an article by Ezra on the troubadours.) A woman wrote to Violet Hunt asking if her copy of *BLAST* could not be resold to 'someone who hadn't daughters'? Richard Aldington noted that there was 'a dismal howl of protest' from most of the reviewers, and that everyone was talking about it. 'On two occasions', wrote Aldington a month after publication, 'I have seen copies of *BLAST* brought into crowded rooms . . . and from that moment *BLAST* has been the sole topic of conversation.'

Despite its appearance, *BLAST* was not revolutionary. Partly a jest at the expense of convention, it was also a celebration of the diverse and contradictory facets of English cultural life – hence the double appearance of certain names in both the 'Blast' and 'Bless' lists. Itself thoroughly English in character, it had no particular target other than a vague aim of destroying what Lewis called 'the Royal Academy tradition' – a painter's *bête noire* rather than a writer's. Indeed, *BLAST* had the air of a wild party given by art students rather than that of a serious attempt to found a new artistic movement or overthrow existing ones.

13

An American Called Eliot

The publication of *BLAST* was celebrated on 15 July 1914 with a dinner at the Dieudonné restaurant in Soho, organized by Ezra, as 'Lewis has gone to Paris for the interim and left me to run the thing. Vorticism is sweeping the land,' Ezra's letter to his father continued. 'Blast is positively the largest periodical ever printed. etc. come on over and dont expect me to stand here talkin.' (His parents were about to visit him.)

Just before the dinner, Amy Lowell arrived in London again. She was looking forward to catching up with all the latest news of Imagism, and to consolidating her position within that movement. This time she brought her actress lover, 'Peter', and her maroon Pierce-Arrow motor car with liveried chauffeur to match. She settled into her suite at the Berkeley – and was then taken aback to discover that Imagism had faded from the picture, and that Ezra was now involved in running a new clique. Not wishing to be left out, she asked for introductions to the 'Vorticists'. Ezra good-naturedly put her and 'Peter' on the guest list for the Dieudonné dinner.

The evening was not a success for her. Gaudier-Brzeska, seated within eye range, could not keep his sculptor's glance off Amy's extensive proportions; in Canto 77 Ezra recalls 'Gaudier's eye on the telluric mass of Miss Lowell'. Amy was nettled by the perky, grubby little Frenchman. Nor was the situation improved when she attempted a conversation with Ford Madox Hueffer, who had contributed to *Des Imagistes* but now strenuously denied being an Imagist, a Vorticist, or any other kind of -ist.

Retiring temporarily hurt, Amy then rallied and announced that she would give her own dinner at the Dieudonné in belated celebration of the publication of *Des Imagistes*. All the contributors to that book who were in London accepted her invitation, and she persuaded Harold Monro to supply complimentary copies (there were plenty left, for the edition had not proved a sell-out) to be set at everyone's place. She was still hoping to unearth the secret 'Doctrine of the Image' to which Ezra and F. S. Flint had alluded so mysteriously in the original articles on Imagism, no one having explained to her that it did not exist, or that if it did, nobody could now remember what it was.

The evening proved even more upsetting for her than the *BLAST* dinner, for none of the guests would listen to her questions about Imagism or conduct a serious conversation. When she asked Ezra about the 'secret doctrine', he disappeared into the kitchen and came back with a large galvanized tub. Reminding Miss Lowell about the line 'not the water, but you in your whiteness, bathing' in her poem in *Des Imagistes*, he said that the movement had not really been *Imagistes* after all but *Nagistes*, and suggested that Amy might like to display her own whiteness by bathing in this vessel.

The dinner broke up in hilarity, and the enraged Amy began to plan her revenge. She would once more hold a dinner, but this time in her hotel suite, and Ezra would not be invited. She chose only four guests: Hilda and Richard Aldington, and D. H. Lawrence from the *Imagistes* anthology, and John Gould Fletcher who resented having been left out of the book and had now a paranoid dislike of Ezra. This dinner, on 30 July, was the first gathering of what Amy had decided would be a rival Imagist movement. She planned to put together her own anthology.

The Aldingtons accepted the invitation, being glad of a Mayfair meal and the prospect of getting into print in America; and neither Lawrence nor Fletcher (both of whom turned up) minded upsetting Ezra in the least. The morning after this cabal, Amy drafted and sent out a prospectus to F. S. Flint, Ford Madox Hueffer, and – not wishing to leave him in ignorance of her offensive – to Ezra himself.

He wrote back quite courteously, saying he would not try to stand in the way of her project, but he could scarcely believe that a 'probably incompetent committee' (the poets themselves, who would select from their own work) would be 'my critical and creative equals'. He would also prefer there to be a definite distinction made between this enterprise and the original Imagist group, 'in which case the new group would find its name automatically'. He soon had his own name for it: *Amygisme*.

He might have continued to be fairly good-natured in his response to Amy's pirate operation if her current publisher, Macmillan, had not advertised her new collection *Sword Blades and Poppy Seed* as the work of 'the foremost member of the Imagists, a group of poets that includes William Butler Yeats, Ezra Pound, Ford Madox Hueffer'. Ezra contemplated legal action in response to this. Meanwhile Flint and Ford had agreed to participate in the Amygist anthology, and Ezra warned Aldington and Hilda (according to Amy) that 'they had to choose between him and her . . . They told Ezra . . . that they felt it only fair to let the poets choose their own contributions . . . He then tried to bribe them, by asking them to get up an Anthology with him, and leave me out. This they absolutely refused to do . . . We all agreed that Ezra could not expect to run us all his own way forever.'

When Ford discovered the row that was brewing, he pulled out of Amy's group, but the others stayed, and plans went ahead for *Some Imagist Poets* (for Amy had ignored Ezra's plea that the Imagist name should not be used) to be published in America. One result of the scrap was that Ezra hardened his attitude towards Hilda Doolittle. In 1920, writing to William Carlos Williams, he called her 'that refined, charming, and utterly narrow-minded she-bard "H.D."', as if the pseudonym itself now seemed ridiculous to him.

Hilda thought equally poorly of him. She wrote of him in 1924: 'Ezra is kind but blustering and really stupid. He is adolescent. He seems almost "arrested" in development.' Richard Aldington was just as resentful of Ezra's behaviour over Amygisme, and responded by using his deputy editorship of the *Egoist* to keep Ezra out of the regular columns of that magazine.

Amy's *Some Imagist Poets* sold very well – far better than *Des Imagistes* – and two further volumes came out under her management in 1916 and 1917. Ezra's chief objection to Amygisme was sloppiness – he said she had turned the movement into 'a democratic beer-garden' – and he complained that she was willing to allow any kind of *vers libre* into the books, whether it could be justly called Imagist or not. He was right on both counts. On the other hand her contributors printed many of their best poems in the three volumes of her anthology, the first of which (at least) reads far better than the ditchwater-dull *Des Imagistes*.

*

During the summer of 1914 Homer and Isabel Pound came to London for a brief visit. War broke out. Neither event interested Ezra very much. The beginning of hostilities was chiefly memorable to him for the occasion on which

> a navvy rolls up to me in Church St. (Kensington End) with:
> Yurra Jurrmun!
> To which I replied: I am *not*.
> 'Well yurr szum kind ov a furriner.'

He was, indeed, technically an alien, and at one point during the war the police intervened. Early in 1916, he and Dorothy were staying with Yeats at Stone Cottage, when the local policeman paid a visit and pointed out that since Coleman's Hatch was within reach of the sea, Ezra was, strictly speaking, an 'Alien in a Prohibited Area', and must report regularly to the nearest police station (as must Dorothy, now an American by marriage). Ezra was furious, and he and Yeats attempted to influence the authorities. 'Yeats took a few shots at it,' Ezra told his father, '[and] got a letter from the poet laureate which would have hanged all three of us in any country in Europe, a perfect extacy of timidity on old Bridges part, derived from reading Conan Doyle.'

Ezra's attitude to the war was as far as possible to pay no attention to it. He suggested that it was 'possibly a conflict between two forces almost equally detestable', though he added: 'One does not know; the thing is too involved.' Probably it was 'only a stop gap. Only a symptom of the real disease.' After it was over, in *Hugh Selwyn Mauberley* (written in 1920), he judged it to have been a pitiful and pointless waste, a struggle to defend a 'botched civilization'. Yet he admitted to a certain admiration for the British achievement, the way that 'groggy old England' had somehow got 'up onto her feet', which in 1914 had seemed hardly possible given 'the state of decadence and comfort and general incompetence'.

From 1914 through to 1918 he contemplated doing some 'war work', but never gave serious attention to the matter. 'True they wont have Americans in the English Army yet,' he wrote to his mother in the spring of 1915, 'and that I am unlikely therefore to enter active service, but it is still possible that I may find some indirect work to do.' In 1916 he enquired if 'in view of the National Service activity' – conscription, recently introduced – 'perhaps the time has come when I might be given something to do . . . I believe my French, Italian, and Spanish are not too dilapidated, and have some memory of mathematics, and german, for what these graces are worth.' But he did not pursue the idea.

In *Death of a Hero* Aldington makes Mr Upjohn observe of the conflict: 'What I mean to say is that the most important thing is that the process of civilization shouldn't be interrupted by all this war business': and this was only a slight caricature of Ezra's attitude. Indeed, he resembled the intellectual in the popular anecdote of the day – again related by Aldington – who, when presented with a white feather by a militant lady asserting that 'men are dying for civilization', replies, 'Madam, *I* am that civilization.'

At first the only visible result of the onset of hostilities for Ezra was Gaudier-Brzeska's disappearance from London. He had previously evaded his statutory military service in France, but in August 1914 wanted to fight, and was told by his embassy that he could return without penalty. He took a ferry to Boulogne and presented himself to an officer, who immediately accused him of desertion and threatened 'Ten years in Africa!' He was arrested and locked in a guard house in Calais, from which he promptly escaped, returning to England that night. 'He was back here for about three weeks,' writes Ezra, 'undertook to make two huge garden vases for Lady Hamilton, got very much bored with it . . . The bombardment of Rheims was too much for him, his disgust with the boches was too great to let him "stay idle". He got some better guarantee of safe-conduct from his Embassy and went back.'

Gaudier behaved characteristically at the front. From the trenches he sent Ezra another 'Vortex' essay for the next number of *BLAST*, postponed by the war, in which he wrote:

> Two days ago I pinched from the enemy a mauser rifle. Its heavy unwieldy shape swamped me with a powerful IMAGE of brutality . . . I found that I did not like it. I broke the butt off and with my knife I carved it in a design, through which I tried to express a gentler order of feeling, which I preferred. BUT I WILL EMPHASIZE that MY DESIGN *got its effect* (just as the gun had) FROM A VERY SIMPLE COMPOSITION OF LINES AND PLANES.

Gaudier was soon promoted to sergeant and selected for training as an officer. Ezra reported to his father during November 1914 that, though 'slightly wounded', the sculptor was 'having the time of his life apparently'.

Ezra had now 'stopped taking in the paper . . . War losing interest.' He rather wished that President Wilson would send over the American navy – 'it would be exhillerating but very imprudent. Besides I dont know that a german conquest would do any real harm. However it ought to have been swifter in its progress if it was to be painless.' Later in the war, his mother began to worry as to whether he and Dorothy were getting enough to eat – there was publicity about food shortages in Britain – but Ezra told her not to be alarmed. Any increase in food prices could 'easily be made up by dining "in" one more night per week instead of going down town to Bellotti'. In any case 'I have never seen such chops as the two now in the kitchen. I think it must have been an Amy Lowell among sheep.'

In the spring of 1915 Zeppelins began to raid London. 'We have hopes that they'll get the church at the corner,' wrote Ezra to his father; and in another letter: 'I offer five shillings to the first german who will bust up that damn bellfry or murder the vicar.'

*

His next scheme after the outbreak of war was to propose the foundation in London of a College of Arts. The war, he said, would deprive young Americans of a chance to study on the Continent, so he proposed to offer a set of 'contacts with artists of established position'. The 'faculty' would include himself, Gaudier-Brzeska if he could be prised away from the front, Wyndham Lewis, and the musician Arnold Dolmetsch, whom Ezra had just met. The idea was publicized in the *Egoist* during the autumn of 1914, but nothing came of it.

Ezra was taken to the Dolmetsch home at Haslemere by Alvin Langdon Coburn, who was a friend of the Dolmetsch family. 'Find Dolmetsch very interesting,' Ezra wrote to his father in October 1914, 'and have commissioned a clavicord. Hope to be able to pay for it by the time it is finished.' He wrote enthusiastically about the Dolmetsch revival of early music in the *New Age*, describing the bearded musician with his bright eyes as a manifestation of 'the God Pan'. The clavichord duly arrived in Holland Place Chambers, where Wyndham Lewis regarded it as 'a strange unaccountable sort of mouse-trap'. Ezra could barely play it at first, but as the years passed he learnt, said Louis Zukofsky, to perform 'very fluidly'.

He had also become acquainted with Conrad Aiken, a Harvard graduate four years younger than himself who was living in London and writing poetry. Ezra cared little for Aiken – 'that rather poor fish' – and Aiken, though at first an admirer of Ezra's poetry, gradually became hostile. In his autobiographical monologue *Ushant* (1952) he mocks 'Rabbi Ben Ezra', though this joke (from the Browning monologue of that title) had occurred to Ezra years earlier. 'Ben Ezra' had been his name for himself in one of his letters to Mary Moore.

Whatever he felt about Ezra personally, Aiken perceived that he had influence, and in September 1914 he went to Holland Place Chambers to talk to him about certain American poets whose work he admired, and who he thought deserved more attention in *Poetry* and other magazines where Ezra had contacts. He 'told me about American writing', said Ezra scornfully, 'but I declined to eat it'. Aiken's particular favourite was Edwin Arlington Robinson, whose sober New England verse was beginning to make a reputation; but Ezra did not care for it, any more than he liked Frost's. Aiken was on his way out of the flat when Ezra asked him if there was nobody genuinely *modern* he could recommend? Maybe someone at Harvard, 'something DIFFERENT'? Aiken thought for a moment, and answered: 'Oh well, there is Eliot.' Ezra asked who Eliot was, and was told: 'A guy at Harvard doing funny stuff.' Actually, added Aiken, Eliot was in England at the moment, so Ezra could meet him if he wanted to. Ezra told Aiken to arrange it.

That was how Ezra remembered the conversation, but according to Aiken's own version he had been trying to interest Ezra in Eliot all along. He describes how he had already hawked Eliot's 'The Love Song of J. Alfred Prufrock' around London, showing it to Harold Monro in the hope that he would print it in his magazine *Poetry & Drama*, but Monro called it 'absolutely insane' and 'practically threw it back' at him. 'Later,' continues Aiken, as I was walking back to my boarding house on Bedford Place I began to wonder if Monro hadn't thought it was mine, so I mailed it to him with a note which said, 'It's really by Mr T. S. Eliot.' It was again turned down. So I went to see Pound.

On 22 September Ezra wrote to Harriet Monroe at *Poetry*: 'An American called Eliot called this p.m. I think he has some sense tho' he has not yet sent me any verse.' Then on 30 September, after Eliot had let him see 'Prufrock':

> I was jolly well right about Eliot. He has sent in the best poem I have yet had or seen from an American. PRAY GOD IT BE NOT A SINGLE AND UNIQUE SUCCESS. He has taken it back to get it ready for the press and you shall have it in a few days.
>
> He is the only American I know of who has made what I can call adequate preparation for writing. He has actually trained himself *and* modernized himself *on his own*. The rest of the *promising young* have done one or the other but never both (most of the swine neither). It is such a comfort to meet a man and not have to tell him to wash his face, wipe his feet, and remember the date (1914) on the calendar.

Eliot returned the corrected 'Prufrock' to Ezra some time during October, and Ezra sent it off to *Poetry*: 'Here is the Eliot poem. The most interesting contribution I've had from an American. P.S. Hope you'll get it in soon.' He also offered H. L. Mencken at *Smart Set* another poem Eliot had given him, 'Portrait of a Lady': 'I enclose a poem by the last intelligent man I've found – a young American, T. S. Eliot (you can write to him direct, Merton College, Oxford). I think him worth watching – mind "not primitive".'

Thomas Stearns Eliot, born three years later than Ezra, had certain similarities to him. He had progressed from a birthplace in the Midwest (St Louis, Missouri) to the East Coast (high school at Milton Academy near Boston, then undergraduate and graduate studies at Harvard), though, unlike Ezra, his character owed far more to New England than to Middle America. He now felt an outsider to his upbringing, as did Ezra, both in credo and personality. Raised in a severe inherited Unitarianism – his ancestors included the Reverend Andrew Eliot, an eighteenth-century Boston minister who had declined the presidency of Harvard because of religious duties, and William Greenleaf Eliot (his grandfather), a celebrated Unitarian divine – he had been unable to shake off an early training in self-denial. Yet for some years now he had felt completely estranged from the arid religion of his childhood. He was in search of religious experience, but not of that sort.

Eliot had found Harvard scarcely more congenial than Ezra had discovered Penn to be, hardly entering its social life and acquiring little from his English and philosophy courses. But, again like Ezra, he had encountered one or two professors who helped to put him on exciting paths, notably Irving Babbitt, whose lectures in French literary criticism led him to the French Symbolists at the age of twenty. Particularly captivated by the mannered, self-mocking poetry of Jules Laforgue, he learned from it the value of a varied set of voices or personae, just as Ezra had from Browning.

Eliot was by nature homeless. He spent a year in Paris (1910–11) after completing his undergraduate studies – it was there that 'Prufrock' had been mainly written – and then, after a year's postgraduate work in philosophy at Harvard, he went to Oxford for further study towards a Harvard doctorate in that subject. However, he was acutely sensitive to place. His early poetry derived much from his exploration of the Boston slums and vacant lots, which both horrified and engaged his imagination. He was wary of emotional contacts and their complexities, which was very obvious even to his casual acquaintances. Far less obvious was the vast and at times scarcely repressible sense of humour that lay beneath the hesitant, cautious surface of Eliot's personality.

The most dramatic difference between Ezra and Eliot was the one that Ezra had spotted at once on first reading 'Prufrock'. Ezra had 'modernized' his own poetry by several awkward, public stages (not yet complete when he met Eliot), in response to criticism by Ford and his concern for his reputation. At a deeper level, he remained unenthusiastic about most forms of modern art and literature. Eliot, however, had painfully and privately, but steadily and thoroughly, etched out a modern style for urgent personal reasons, seeking some method of expressing his own detached sensibilities.

In the autumn of 1914 Oxford was almost lifeless; most undergraduates had enlisted as soon as war broke out, and Eliot, trying to settle in to a half-closed Merton College, was doubly glad to make contact with Ezra and receive his encouragement. His own impressions of Ezra's poetry (he had only seen *Personae* and *Exultations*) were far from favourable, and he had made some rather caustic remarks to Conrad Aiken about it; but he found a certain attraction in the sheer vigour of Ezra's work. Fourteen years after they had first met, Eliot wrote of Ezra's early poetry:

> I confess that I am seldom interested in what he is saying, but only in the way he says it. That does not mean he is saying nothing . . . But Pound's philosophy, I suspect, is just a little antiquated. He began as the last disciple of the Nineties, and was much influenced by Mr Yeats and Mr Ford Madox Ford. He added his own extensive erudition, and proceeded to a

curious syncretism which I do not think he has ever set in order.

But what he thought of Ezra's poetry did not really matter during the autumn of 1914. He was affected only by the encouragement Ezra gave him to stick to poetry, and not – as Eliot had intended – to resign himself to an academic career in philosophy. 'I had kept my early poems (including "Prufrock" and others eventually published) in my desk from 1911,' writes Eliot. Ezra made him get them out again.

Harriet Monroe received 'Prufrock' from Ezra towards the end of October 1914, and was disappointed. She assumed that a 'new' American poet, as Ezra had described Eliot, would write like Vachel Lindsay, Carl Sandburg, or Frost, and she was unprepared for the very European world-weariness of Eliot's Laforgue-derived voice in 'Prufrock'. She wrote critically to Ezra about it.

He answered twice on the same day. His first letter said that her objection to Eliot was 'the most dreary and discouraging document that I have been called upon to read for a very long time'. In the second he wrote: 'No, most emphatically I will not ask Eliot to write down to any audience whatsoever . . . Neither will I send you Eliot's address in order that he may be insulted.'

Her objections to 'Prufrock' naturally increased his commitment to getting the poem into print. If she had accepted it without demur he might have grown less passionately attached to it, for – as is clear from his attempts to explain it to her – he did not altogether understand it. When she continued to complain, he wrote to her:

> 'Mr Prufrock' does not 'go off at the end'. It is a portrait of failure, or of a character which fails, and it would be false art to make it end on a note of triumph. I dislike the paragraph about Hamlet, but it is an early and cherished bit and T. E. [*sic*] won't give it up, and as it is the only portion of the poem that most readers will like at first reading, I don't see that it will do much harm.
>
> For the rest: a portrait satire on futility can't end by turning that quintessence of futility, Mr P. into a reformed character breathing out fire and ozone.

He concluded by asking her to 'get on' with printing the poem 'in a nice quiet and orderly manner', assuring her that it was better than 'the other poems of Eliot' that he had seen, and also that Eliot was 'quite *intelligent* (an adjective which is seldom in my mouth)'.

The 'other poems of Eliot' that he mentioned to Harriet Monroe were probably a set of intensely religious pieces (never published), which show

Eliot expressing an imaginary commitment to faith. Eliot's religious inclinations, still inchoate, did not please Ezra. Convinced that Eliot was a satirist, he tried to persuade him to perform as one. The results, written during Eliot's months at Oxford, were several poems in which the voice approaches the genuinely satirical, such as 'The Boston Evening Transcript' and 'Aunt Helen'. Ezra was prepared to countenance what he called 'that unitarian upbringing' if it could be turned to this kind of mockery of its own social ambience.

When making Eliot ransack his desk, Ezra discovered that the creator of 'Prufrock' was fond of bawdry. Eliot had written a series of mildly scurrilous rhymes which seemed ideal for the next *BLAST*, and Ezra told Wyndham Lewis about them. 'Eliot has sent me Bullshit & the Ballad for Big Louise', Lewis wrote to Ezra in January 1915. 'They are excellent bits of scholarly ribaldry. I am longing to print them in *Blast*; but stick to my naïve determination to have no "Words ending in -Uck, -Unt and -Ugger."' Eliot communicated his mild disappointment about this to Ezra:

> I have corresponded with Lewis, but his Puritanical Principles seem to bar my way to Publicity. I fear that King Bolo and his Big Black Kween will never burst into print. I understand that Priapism, Narcicism etc are not approved of, and even so innocent a rhyme as
>
> > – pulled her stockings off
> > With a frightful cry of 'Hauptbahnhof!'
>
> is considered decadent.

Eliot added that he was sending a small poem, with the apology for it that 'I am constipated & have a cold on the chest. Burn it.' Ezra did. It was called 'Suppressed Complex'.

'King Bolo and his Big Black Kween' featured in a series of rhymes that Eliot showed to certain friends over the years. He sent one of them – a rather tame example – to Ezra in 1922:

> King Bolo's big black basstart Kuwheen,
> > That plastic & elastic one,
> Would frisk it on the village green,
> > Enjoying her fantastikon.

Ezra was no doubt amused by this, which fitted his image of Eliot the satirist rather better than did Eliot's inclinations towards religious conversion. Without Ezra to keep him on the 'satire' rails, Eliot might have gone on more quickly towards actual religious commitment. As it was, Dorothy Pound said she and Ezra always felt Eliot was 'wrestling with a devil or an angel', which they found most uncomfortable.

Harriet Monroe finally published 'Prufrock' in the June 1915 *Poetry*, but tucked it away inconspicuously at the back of the 'new verse' section. Ezra nevertheless tried to bully her into giving Eliot the annual *Poetry* prize: 'If your committee don't make the award to Eliot, God only knows what slough of ignominy they will fall into . . . !!!!!!!!' In spite of this she only allowed Eliot an honourable mention; the prize went to Vachel Lindsay for 'The Chinese Nightingale'. However, Ezra managed to include 'The Boston Evening Transcript', 'Aunt Helen', and another new poem by Eliot, 'Cousin Nancy', in the October 1915 *Poetry*, and though 'Portrait of a Lady' was turned down by *Smart Set* he managed to place it with Alfred Kreymborg for his magazine *Others*. Further Eliot poems, 'Preludes' and 'Rhapsody on a Windy Night', appeared in the second and final *BLAST* (published in July 1915).

'Eliot has done a few amusing poems,' Ezra wrote to his father when some new manuscripts arrived. And to his mother: 'Eliot down from Oxford yesterday, very intelligent.' Harriet Monroe, though, continued unenthusiastic, and without Eliot's permission deleted an entire line from his 'Mr Apollinax' when publishing it in *Poetry* because it contained the word 'foetus'.

After a year of their acquaintance, Ezra was speaking of Eliot with some pride. 'I have more or less discovered him,' he wrote to John Quinn in August 1915. 'He has more entrails than might appear from his quiet exterior, I think.'

*

Ezra began to introduce Eliot to London literary and artistic circles, taking him, on Thursday evenings when Eliot was in London, to Belotti's or, when that closed because of Zeppelin raids, to a Chinese restaurant in Regent Street, where he would gather his own clique together for weekly sessions. Iris Barry, an apprentice member of this group from 1915, describes its meetings:

> Into the restaurant with his clothes always seeming to fly round him, letting his ebony stick clatter to the floor, came Pound himself with his exuberant hair, pale cat-like face with the greenish cat-eyes, clearing his throat, making strange sounds and cries in his talking, but otherwise always quite formal . . . Semi-monstrous . . . pendulous lower lip drooping under sandy moustache as he boomed through endless anecdotes of Great Victorians, Great Pre-Raphaelites . . . was Ford Madox Hueffer . . . Tall, lean and hollow cheeked . . . was T. S. Eliot, generally silent but with a smile that was as shy as it was friendly, and rather passionately but mutely adored by the three

or four young females who had been allowed in because of some crumb of promise in painting or verse . . . Now and then Yeats appeared.

Eliot did not take to Ford in the least; he told Ezra he was bored by Ford's 'egotistical meanderings about his own services to English literature'. Nor was he comfortable in the Yeats circle. Ezra sometimes brought him to the Monday evenings at Woburn Buildings, but though Eliot quickly learnt from Ezra to regard Yeats 'rather as a more eminent contemporary than an elder', he observed to Ezra (in 1922) 'Yeats does not particularly like me, I believe.' In 1957 Ezra wrote to Yeats's widow speculating 'whether TSE and Uncle Wm/ didn't tend to bring out the worst of each other, or at least neglected to develop a mutual illumination.'

Not surprisingly, Eliot felt a little ambivalent about all these attentions from Ezra, as he afterwards suggested. He recalled how Ezra would, in their early days together,

> go to any lengths of generosity and kindness; from inviting constantly to dinner a struggling author whom he suspected of being under-fed, or giving away clothing (though his shoes and underwear were almost the only garments which resembled those of other men sufficiently to be worn by them), to trying to find jobs, collect subsidies, get work published and then get it criticised and praised . . . a degree of direction which not all the beneficiaries deserved, and which was sometimes an embarrassment. Yet, though the object of his beneficence might come to chafe against it, only a man of the meanest spirit could have come to resent it.

Eliot spoke also of Ezra's 'restless energy', in which it was 'difficult to distinguish the energy from the restlessness and the fidgets'. Being championed by such an individual was not necessarily an indication of one's worth, since Ezra quite clearly needed a constant supply of causes, whether or not they were valid.

Ezra did not immediately feel that Eliot was his best discovery yet. To Harriet Monroe he kept on calling him 'intelligent', but qualified this with 'I don't know him well enough to make predictions'. Early in 1915 he was prepared to say 'that young chap will go quite a long way', but he ranked Edgar Lee Masters, whose *Spoon River Anthology* came out that year, as Eliot's equal: 'He and Masters are the best of the bilin'.' By 1917 he had begun to feel he was dealing with someone of the very top rank: 'Eliot has thought of things I had not thought of, and I'm damned if many of the others have done so.'

Eliot finished his year at Oxford and, while he completed his doctoral dissertation for Harvard, worked as a schoolmaster, first for a term at High Wycombe Grammar School, then in North London at Highgate Junior School. 'Thank God he has got a job in London after Christmas,' Ezra remarked to Harriet Monroe in December 1915. Throughout this time, he was trying to persuade Eliot not to return to Harvard to take his *viva voce* and complete the formalities for his doctorate, but to stay in England and get on with his poetry, as he himself had in 1908. He tried to school Eliot in his own methods of self-advertisement:* in June 1915 he wrote to Eliot's father (at Eliot's request), substantiating Eliot's claim to be making a mark in the London literary world – though, typically, the letter was chiefly taken up with Ezra presenting his own credentials as a figure of importance in that world.

Eliot's inclination to stay in England was reinforced when he married – perhaps again a little in imitation of Ezra – an Englishwoman, Vivien Haigh-Wood, just after leaving Oxford in June 1915. ('Eliot has suddenly married a very charming young woman,' Ezra told Homer.) Ezra was a fairly close observer of the eccentricities of this marriage, though in the early days they chiefly took a comic form. Eliot and Vivien were both present at the seaside in 1916, and Ezra reported that Eliot had just 'walked into his landlady's bedroom, "quite by mistake", said he was looking for his wife. Landlady unconvinced. Wife believes in the innocence of his intentions. Landlady sympathetic with wife . . . Landlady (in parenthesis) unmarried but under fifty.'

From the beginning, Eliot wrote to Ezra in a florid, self-amused manner utterly unlike the serious character seen by most of his acquaintances. Yet it would be wrong to suppose that he was necessarily being more 'natural', more himself, in his letters to Ezra. Rather, he adopted Poundian mannerisms, sometimes parodying Ezra's own languor, sometimes his aggression. Ezra in consequence grew increasingly puzzled by Eliot, perhaps sensing that here was someone whose manipulation of personae was even more accomplished than his own. And he was quite unable to decide which way Eliot would jump. 'I have known Eliot for thirty years, and you are never sure,' he told Charles Olson in 1946. 'You know when he says "No", he won't do a thing, but when he says "Yes", you are never sure he will.'

---

* But he was aware that their approaches must be different. According to Hugh Kenner, he told Eliot: 'You let *me* throw the bricks through the front window. You go in at the back door and take the swag.'

14

Demon Pantechnicon Driver

Ezra and Dorothy spent part of the winter of 1914–15 with Yeats at Stone
Cottage. 'We are reading Doughty's "Arabia Deserta" a fine book. and also
a lot of damn'd translations of icelandic sagas. W.B.Y. has done some
poems & is beginning a dam'd play.' Meanwhile Ezra himself had 'busted
into Fenollosa's chinese notes – (not Japanese) & found some fine stuff.
that has kept me going for the past ten days . . . Have sent some to
"Poetry".' This was in November. By Christmas he could report: 'Have
got a good little book out from Fenollosa's Chinese notes.' Elkin Mathews
immediately agreed to publish the book, under the title *Cathay*.

Ezra did much of the work on it in London, before going to the cottage.
Hilda Doolittle, at that time still living across the hallway in Holland Place
Chambers, reported that 'Ezra is doing Chinese translations – and some are
very beautiful! He comes running in four or five times a day now with new
versions for us to read.' But at moments *Cathay* suggests the view from
Stone Cottage in the Sussex rain:

> The clouds have gathered, and gathered,
>   and the rain falls and falls,
> The eight ply of the heavens
>   are all folded into one darkness,
> And the wide, flat road stretches out.

Ezra did not wish he had known Fenollosa personally. 'I have constantly
to thank god that Fenollosa is dead,' he wrote to Yeats's father. 'I should
have had "*the* hell of a time" trying to edit him living.' Yet he had reason to
be grateful for Fenollosa's thoroughness. In order to record the Chinese
poems which Ezra worked into *Cathay*, Fenollosa had first copied down
the original Chinese characters, then written out a phonetic transcription

(using the Japanese pronunciation of his helpers in Tokyo, where the work was done), then made a character-by-character translation into English, and finally given a line-by-line rendering, with interpretative notes where necessary. Ezra worked all this into modern English free verse, often making surprisingly few changes from Fenollosa's line-by-line versions. Fenollosa's method had the advantage that – unlike his translations of the Noh plays – the original text was recorded (as near as possible) exactly as it stood, without more than minimal translator's interpretation. Ezra was therefore able to get very close to the Chinese, if he wanted to.

The Chinese poems had a far deeper appeal to him than the Noh plays. Not only did they seem to be thoroughly Imagist in their flat presentation of landscape and personal observation – and Imagist on a larger scale than he had thought possible, for some of the poems in *Cathay* are of more than fifty lines – but they were also untainted by any of that supernatural element so marked in the Noh plays, which Ezra thought almost as silly as Yeats's Celtic fancies. In a 1916 commentary on one of his Noh translations he wrote that the Noh authors inclined towards 'a form of psychology which is, in the West, relegated to spiristic séances . . . If the Japanese authors had not combined the psychology of such matters with what to me is a very fine sort of poetry, I would not bother about it.' The Noh dramas seemed all faintly Symbolist or Impressionist, neither very clear nor hard. 'China is fundamental, Japan is not,' he wrote to John Quinn in 1917. He claimed that you could not go 'back of' the best poems he had chosen for *Cathay*: they were pure element.

He chose to publish only a very small selection of poems from Fenollosa's Chinese transcriptions, those that he called 'unquestionable' in their excellence, excluding any that required to be broken up with 'a tedium of notes'. The most widely represented poet in *Cathay* was Li T'ai Po, who lived in the eighth century AD, though in the original printing of the book, following Fenollosa, Ezra gave his name solely in its Japanese form, 'Rihaku'. Despite Ezra's assertion that Chinese poetry is 'fundamental', Li T'ai Po had in fact adapted older verses; Arthur Waley writes that often, when he appears to be communicating some personal experience, he is really 'skilfully utilizing some poem by T'ao Ch'ien or Hsieh T'iao'. His real distinction in his day was much the same as Ezra's: 'he represents', writes Waley, 'a reaction against the formal prosody of his immediate period'. By 1918 (three years after the publication of *Cathay*) Ezra had come to realize that Li T'ai Po was not an original poet but, as he put it, 'a great compiler', whose work consisted largely of 'old themes rewritten, of a sort of summary of the poetry which had been before him'.

Fenollosa's translations, literal as they tried to be, were inevitably coloured by his Japanese helpers' readings of the Chinese, which among other things produced completely different sounds from the original language (hence 'Rihaku' for Li T'ai Po). Ezra adhered to this system hereafter when working on Chinese texts. He wrote of it, to a Japanese friend, in 1940:

> Several half-wits in a state of half-education have sniffed at my going on with Fenollosa's use of the Japanese sounds for reading ideogram[s]. I propose to continue. As sheer sound Dai Gaku is better than Ta Tsü. When it comes to the question of transmitting from the East to the West, a great part of the Chinese sound is no use at all. We don't hear parts of it, and much of the rest is a hiss or mumble. Fenollosa wrote, I think justly, that Japan had kept the old sounds . . . long after the various invasions from the north had ruined them in China.

Partly because of these idiosyncrasies, partly because of his own supremely careless attitude to texts, Ezra's *Cathay* is in no sense a work of scholarship. Not only were the Chinese names filtered through Japanese versions, but he then proceeded to miscopy some of them. Sometimes he also confused Fenollosa's explanatory notes with the actual text. And in 'The River Song' the lines beginning 'And I have moped in the Emperor's garden' are actually a different poem which he has stuck on to the first one by mistake. Again and again, he departs from Fenollosa's translation and creates a new poem of his own. After *Cathay* had been published, he claimed that his versions had been 'approved by one or two people who know some of the originals', and said they were 'closer than the *Rubaiyat*' to their texts, but really they are never close at all. Even a predominantly sympathetic Chinese scholar, Wai-Lim Yip, author of a 1959 study of *Cathay*, has to allow that 'anybody who has some sense of the syntax of the Chinese language will be ready . . . to denounce Pound'. Although Ezra tried to justify his liberties by claiming that 'the ideographs leave one wholly free as to phrasing', and said it was impossible to convey the Chinese 'art of sound and metric' in English, the plain fact is that very often he tampered with the meaning of the original quite wilfully.

Given that he allowed himself complete freedom with the material, it is striking how very little of his own voice is recognizable in *Cathay*. Or rather, one is astonished by the ease with which he has found a new persona for the task:

> While my hair was still cut straight across my forehead
> I played about the front gate, pulling flowers.
> You came by on bamboo stilts, playing horse,
> You walked about my seat, playing with blue plums.
> And we went on living in the village of Chōkan:
> Two small people, without dislike or suspicion.

At fourteen I married My Lord you.
I never laughed, being bashful.
Lowering my head, I looked at the wall.
Called to, a thousand times, I never looked back.

At fifteen I stopped scowling,
I desired my dust to be mingled with yours
Forever and forever and forever.
Why should I climb the look out?

At sixteen you departed,
You went into far Ku-tō-en, by the river of swirling eddies,
And you have been gone five months.
The monkeys make sorrowful noise overhead.

You dragged your feet when you went out.
By the gate now, the moss is grown, the different mosses,
Too deep to clear them away!
The leaves fall early this autumn, in wind.
The paired butterflies are already yellow with August
Over the grass in the West garden;
They hurt me. I grow older.
If you are coming down through the narrows of the river
    Kiang,
Please let me know beforehand,
And I will come out to meet you
        As far as Chō-fū-Sa.

This poem, 'The River-Merchant's Wife: A Letter', the most celebrated
piece in *Cathay* – indeed the most appealing poem of Ezra's whole career –
is a vision through female eyes. For all the aggressive masculinity of
'Sestina: Altaforte' and the would-be satirical snarls of *BLAST*, it is the
River-Merchant's Wife, the quiet Chinese girl, who seems the most
convincing.

*

It is fortunate that the Fenollosa material came into Ezra's hands in 1913
rather than a few years earlier, when he was still using Victorian and 1890s
voices for his translations. Nor could he have been genuinely attracted to
the Chinese verses, which again and again celebrate limitation and self-
effacement – usually very un-Poundian emotions – had he not happened to
be in a period of calm after the mock-explosions of *BLAST*, with no urgent
campaigns to conduct, no pressing battles to fight.
    The success of *Cathay* is largely an achievement of diction. Fenollosa's

line-by-line translation of 'The River-Merchant's Wife', in the notebooks, has no confidence of style:

> My hair was at first covering my brows [*child's method of*
> *wearing hair*]
> Breaking flowers I was frolicking in front of our gate
> When you came riding on bamboo stilts [*you – ride on –*
> *bamboo-horse – come*]
> And going about my seat you played with the blue plums
> Together we dwelt in the same Chokan village
> And we two little ones had neither mutual dislike nor suspicion.

(The words in italics were supplied by Fenollosa as explanation.) Ezra picks up the awkwardness of the Fenollosa literal rendering, and chooses to emphasize it, repeating the word 'playing' so as to sound like a child, eliminating anything that a small girl might not actually say. Arthur Waley, though an accomplished Chinese scholar, was not able to equal this effect when, in his own version of the same poem, he smoothed the rough edges, missing the deliberately childlike cadences of Ezra's rendering:

> Soon after I wore my hair covering my forehead
> I was plucking flowers and playing in front of the gate,
> When you came by, walking on bamboo-stilts
> Along the trellis, playing with green plums.
> We both lived in the village of Ch'ang-kan,
> Two children, without hate or suspicion.

Waley's *One Hundred and Seventy Chinese Poems* (1918), his first collection of Chinese translations, came out three years after *Cathay*. He had taught himself Chinese and Japanese, in spare time from his work with Laurence Binyon in the Oriental division of the British Museum Print Room; but though his linguistic expertise far exceeded Ezra's, his book could not help showing the influence (somewhat watered) of *Cathay*. As Yeats put it eighteen years later in *The Oxford Book of Modern Verse*, 'Ezra Pound's *Cathay* created the manner followed with more learning but less subtlety of rhythm by Arthur Waley.' In private Waley is said to have been contemptuous of Ezra's sinology, but he helped him with Noh translations – in Ezra's collection of them published in 1916 an introductory note thanks Waley for his help with orthography, and for assisting him 'out of various impasses where my own ignorance would have left me' – and in his 1950 edition of Li T'ai Po, Waley calls Ezra's 'Exile's Letter' in *Cathay* a 'brilliantly paraphrased' version.

Ezra reviewed Waley's *One Hundred and Seventy Chinese Poems* when the book first appeared:

I find it somewhat heavy going, but Mr Waley has an excellent
eye for subject matter, and has indubitably provided a valuable
interpretation of the verbal meaning of the originals . . . The
style of his versions is simple, not by any means free of dead
and lifeless phrases, not always swung with emotional cadences,
but at any rate free of the trivialities and frivolities of his
predecessor Dr Giles.

By the mid-1930s, however, Ezra was vehemently anti-Waley, perhaps
because he thought Waley had jumped on the *Cathay* bandwagon. When
Daniel Cory mentioned Waley's name to him, the result was 'a fusillade of
expletives'.

*

Cathay was published in April 1915. *The Times Literary Supplement* called
it 'sharp and precise' and hoped for more in the same vein. Ford Madox
Hueffer praised the poems in *Outlook* as 'things of supreme beauty',
commending them for 'rendering concrete objects that the emotions
produced' – which sounds like a quotation from the Imagiste manifesto –
and he, and A. R. Orage in the *New Age*, both judged *Cathay* easily the
best work Ezra had yet published. (Orage phrased this in barbed fashion:
'the best and only good work Mr Ezra Pound has yet done'.) Amy Lowell
wrote to Harriet Monroe: 'Ezra's new book *Cathay* is full of the most
beautiful things. I have seldom read anything finer. What a pity the boy
does not confine himself to working and leave strictures on other people's
work alone.' As a result of reading it, Amy began her own Chinese
translations in a style which, despite occasional Hollywoodisms, owes
much to *Cathay* without remotely equalling its poise.

Although over the years there has been a powerful chorus of disapproval
from sinologists, some of whom would reject the whole of *Cathay* outright
because of its inaccuracies and inadequacies as translation, many critics go
to the opposite extreme and ignore the question of accuracy, treating the
book as original poetry that happens to have a Chinese flavour. A more
judicious view was expressed by T. S. Eliot in his introduction to Ezra's
Selected Poems (1928), where he spoke of Ezra as 'the inventor of Chinese
poetry for our time', observing that 'each generation must translate for
itself'. This is surely the point: however accurate *Cathay* may or may not
be as pure translation, it precisely answered a certain need of Ezra's own
generation; its real achievement was to provide that generation with a new
voice for poetry. George Steiner is scarcely exaggerating when he writes, in
After Babel (1975), that the *Cathay* poems 'altered the feel of the language
and set the pattern of cadence for modern verse' – though Wyndham Lewis
assessed Ezra's achievement in *Cathay* a touch more ironically in the
second number of *BLAST*, which appeared a few weeks after *Cathay* had

been published: 'Demon pantechnicon driver, busy with removal of old world into new quarters. In his steel net of impeccable technique he has lately caught Li Po. Energy of a discriminating element.'

*

Ezra liked this remark. In 1917, when busy about everybody's literary affairs, he wrote to Joyce: 'I feel Lewis' definition of me as a "pantechnicon" becoming daily more apt.' And the next year he signed a letter to Joyce: 'ye complete journaliste and pantechnicon patent attachment, E.P.'

After finishing *Cathay*, he regarded himself as something of a proven expert in Chinese; he suggested that it should replace Greek in the academic curricula, since China had a 'good past' rather than a 'fifth rate imitation'. He began to try to read Chinese texts in the original, with the aid of a dictionary, though he did not find it easy; Dorothy, who drew the ideograms for the Cantos, said that she eventually 'learned to look them up' in the dictionary, but 'Ezra never quite did, though he learned many of the simpler radicals'. Ezra himself told a Japanese correspondent in 1936: 'You really must not run away with the idea that . . . I can do more than spell out ideograms *very* slowly with a dictionary.' On the other hand, he came to believe that he had an intuitive understanding of many of the characters – a notion he seems to have acquired from Gaudier-Brzeska, who, writes Ezra in his book on the sculptor,

> was so accustomed to observe the dominant line in objects that, after he had spent what could not have been more than a few days studying the subject at the museum, he could understand the primitive Chinese ideographs (not the later more sophisticated forms), and he was very much disgusted with the lexicographers who 'hadn't sense enough to see that *that* was a horse', or a cow or a tree or whatever it might be, 'what the — else could it be! The — fools!'

Ezra tried to practise this himself, and came to believe that he could instinctively spot mistakes or inadequacies in a translation of Confucius, without the dictionary – 'I had only the look of the characters and the radicals to go on from.'

He was encouraged to study the ideograms themselves by an essay he found among the Fenollosa papers. Entitled 'The Chinese Written Character as a Medium for Poetry', it excited him just as much as the *Cathay* poems, and he immediately tried to get it published, 'but the adamantine stupidity of all magazine editors delays its appearance,' he wrote in June 1915. The essay was no mere piece of philology but, claimed Ezra, 'a study of the fundamentals of all aesthetics'. Certainly it was to have a major influence on his own thought and poetry.

Fenollosa worked on the assumption that Chinese characters are almost entirely pictorial in their origins – which is not strictly true, there being a large proportion of phonetic representations as well – and asserted that the ideograms give their readers a 'vivid shorthand picture of the operations of nature'. Combining the techniques of painting and language, the ideograms, he felt, could convey a picture of the world that was more objective and more dramatic than either painters or writers could manage on their own. Fenollosa concluded that, because of this highly charged nature of the Chinese characters, if two or more ideograms are placed side by side, a particularly resonant effect is produced. In this process of 'compounding' the ideograms, he said, 'two things added together do not produce a third thing *but suggest some fundamental relation between them*'.

These last words (not italicized in Fenollosa's text) deserve considerable emphasis, because they describe precisely the principle on which Ezra allowed his own mind to work during the middle years of his life, the principle on which he wrote the Cantos.

The essay goes on to attack what it calls 'the tyranny of medieval logic', by which Fenollosa simply means conventional rational argument using deduction and proof. This method of thinking, he claims, is based on the fallacy that

> thought is a kind of brickyard . . . baked into little hard units or concepts. These are piled in rows according to size and then labelled with words for future use. This use consists in picking out a few bricks, each by its convenient label, and sticking them together into a sort of wall called a sentence . . . The sheer loss and weakness of this method are apparent and flagrant. Even in its own sphere it can not think half of what it wants to think. It has no way of bringing together any two concepts which do not happen to stand one under the other and in the same pyramid.

Fenollosa concludes by suggesting that this distinctively European 'process of abstraction' is really such poor stuff that it should be abandoned for the Chinese 'pictorial method' of representing ideas, which would be 'the ideal language of the world'.

The essay appealed deeply to Ezra because it expressed and justified what he already knew about his own mental processes, and powerfully reinforced his tendency towards certain non-rational habits of mind. 'A new mode of thought was foreseen,' he wrote of the essay, and it was a mode towards which he himself had always been inclined. In 1911, in his first series of articles for the *New Age*, where he had described the artist's instinctive preference for Luminous Detail over abstract argument, he had argued that an artist must not try to analyse a phenomenon or explain it in abstract terms, but should merely present it in a series of pictures or plain statements – which is what Imagism had been trying to achieve. Fenollosa stated it more powerfully than Ezra felt he could have managed alone.

Hereafter, he labelled this Fenollosa school of thinking 'The Ideogramic Method'. The 'method' consisted of doing away with abstract argument, or any other obviously rational process, and instead, 'presenting first one facet and then another' for the reader to contemplate and meditate on – lining up ideas or images side by side, but not linking them by any stated theory. Ezra once enlarged upon this in an article:

> The so-called 'logical' method permitted the methodist to proceed from inadequate cognizance to a specious and useless conclusion; these methodists then took great pleasure in thinking that they had moved in a straight line instead of a crooked line between these unfortunate states.

By contrast, the Ideogramic Method seemed to him much more 'scientific'. As he put it, 'the scientist to-day heaps together his facts and has to find organizations that fit them'.

The Ideogramic Method would perhaps have been highly productive had he followed this last rubric to the full – if, having 'heaped together' his facts, he had then troubled to find 'organizations' to fit and explain them. Unfortunately he generally stopped at the first stage, judging that the facts themselves, without any kind of organization or interpretation being imposed on them, were self-evident of some larger truth; feeling that, in Fenollosa's words, the mere setting of concept A alongside concept B immediately suggested 'some fundamental relation between them'.

His affection for the Method was not in itself absurd. Like many intellectuals of his generation, he wanted to get away from the heavy, ponderous logic of the nineteenth-century German school of scholarship (which he always characterized as 'philology'). He was trying to achieve some clarity and sense after an academic fog, and at the best moments of his work he captured it – nowhere better than in *Cathay*, which is simply the cool presentation of certain facets of experience. The Ideogramic Method is in some ways, too, a very real principle of modernism, for it rejects a coherent line of argument in favour of implied mental relationships. Ezra also wanted to get away from the nineteenth-century insistence on specialized knowledge; he felt that anyone has a right to survey the whole field of human thought and experience: 'The error of philology in the XIX century was to split everything into slivers, get a man concentrated on a small enough microscopic area, and mebbe you can prevent him seeing what it has to do with the next field.'

But while at its best the Ideogramic Method could genuinely illuminate – as in, for example, the finest passages in the Pisan Cantos, where the juxtaposition of apparently disparate memories and notions produces a feeling of enlightenment and intuitive understanding of the world – at other times the result was just a muddle. Donald Hall, interviewing Ezra for the *Paris Review* in 1960, observed him practising the Method impromptu. Hall noticed how he would very often answer a question with an apparent irrelevance:

> I would ask him . . . perhaps about coming to Italy in 1908, and his answer would begin with an anecdote about the first rotary snowplow, or about assayers in the Philadelphia mint. At first I thought he misunderstood my questions. Then when he persisted . . . from initial anecdote to finished answer, I would see the . . . analogical relevance . . . the ideogramic method . . . by which differing items, juxtaposed, yield a generality nowhere stated. But often he could not persist or develop – he forgot, he lost himself – and I sat in silence across from him, with the fragment of an answer hanging in the air between us.

A less sympathetic observer, one of the psychiatrists who interviewed Ezra in Washington in 1945, told the jury who were considering his mental health: 'His [mental] production has been unusually hard to follow. He speaks in bunches of ideas.'

15

Get On With Our Renaissance

The beginning of 1915 saw him back with a vengeance on his modern Renaissance trail. It could no longer be an exclusively American Renaissance, since it now contained such figures as Wyndham Lewis and Gaudier-Brzeska, but that did not lessen his commitment, and it was to an American collector, John Quinn, that he now turned, urging him to buy works by these and other living artists and thereby single-handedly set such a Renaissance in motion. His argument was concise and dramatic. 'If a patron buys from an artist who needs money,' he wrote to Quinn in March 1915, 'the patron then makes himself equal to the artist: he is building art into the world; he creates.' He commended Quinn for doing this to some extent already: 'If there were more like you we should get on with our renaissance.'

This was his first contact with Quinn since they had met in New York in 1910. Quinn was not a rich man by American standards, but he lived modestly and spent all his surplus income on the arts. Born in 1870 of Irish parents, he had studied law at Harvard and become a partner in a New York legal firm. Visiting Ireland and England in 1902, he bought paintings from J. B. Yeats and his son Jack, and the next year arranged for W. B. Yeats to go on his first American lecture tour. Quinn also helped Yeats *père* to set himself up in America for the last years of his life, and became a patron of Augustus John and a friend of Joseph Conrad, whose manuscripts he bought. He took an interest in Ezra's progress after their meeting in 1910, and was therefore offended when he read an article by him in the *New Age* in January 1915 which appeared to be partly an attack on himself. Writing of Jacob Epstein, Ezra complained that the sculptor was short of patronage, yet there were 'American collectors buying autograph MSS. of William Morris, faked Rembrandts and faked Van Dykes'. Since Quinn had recently purchased Morris manuscripts from the poet's daughter May he assumed that Ezra had him in mind – though when Quinn protested by letter, Ezra replied that he was chiefly thinking of the fake old masters at the Wanamaker mansion in Wyncote.

The consequence was that Quinn immediately began to buy works from Epstein, with Ezra as adviser. 'If you are still getting Jacob's "Birds",' Ezra wrote to him, 'for God's sake get the two that are stuck together, not the pair in which one is standing up on its two legs.' (Epstein told Quinn that Ezra ought to mind his own business.) Ezra soon diverted Quinn to his own protégés, encouraging him to take an interest in Gaudier-Brzeska and Wyndham Lewis. Quinn's response was to offer to buy anything of Gaudier's that Ezra cared to choose on his behalf.

Though Ezra encouraged Quinn to believe that patronage was a branch of the arts, he himself displayed a disarming tendency to treat the paintings and sculptures he was buying for Quinn merely as commodities with a market value. For example, he wrote to Quinn of Wyndham Lewis: 'I think his prices will soar like Matisse's when once they start.' He reminded Quinn that he should treat the purchases as an investment. 'You must not corner the market against yourself,' he warned him – that is, must not buy up all the Gaudiers and Lewises and thereby reduce their prices. This attitude led him to make some rather surprising statements. 'Roughly speaking Brzeska's drawings are all the same,' he wrote to Quinn. '30, 40, or even 50 ought to be enough for any single collection.'

He never took money from Quinn for these services – 'I am not looking for a soft job, at least not in that way,' he told a friend – but hoped to use Quinn's backing to acquire control of a magazine, which he could use as an outlet for his and his protégés' work, and he wrote various prospectuses 'designed to entrap American dollars'. In the spring of 1915 he tried to take over an 'ancient weekly' called *The Academy*, and a little later the same year he considered founding a new fortnightly on the lines of *Le Mercure de France*. At one point, Quinn offered him a personal subsidy of just over £100 a year, if he could get an editorial post once again on the *Egoist* and 'make something of that paper'. Harriet Shaw Weaver was in favour of the idea, but her colleague Dora Marsden was not – she thought Ezra would reduce their editorial powers 'to zero'. All this, together with instructions to Quinn about buying works of art, and organizing a Vorticist show in New York, meant a constant flood of letters from Ezra to Quinn. Indeed Quinn eventually became so overwhelmed that he asked Ezra to write him a separate letter on each topic, so that they could be filed under the proper headings. Ezra replied that the best name for a Pound file would be 'Ezra Pound, MESS'.

James Joyce was still under Ezra's wing. Ezra persuaded H. L. Mencken to print two of the *Dubliners* stories in *Smart Set* in May 1915, fixed Joyce up with a London literary agent (J. B. Pinker), and offered to write the *Egoist* a series of twelve articles free of charge on condition that they would pay £50 each to Joyce and Wyndham Lewis. The scheme was not carried out, but Miss Weaver sent Joyce that sum out of her own pocket in belated payment for the serialization of *A Portrait of the Artist as a Young Man.* Ezra also devoted much energy to trying to raise money for Joyce from the Royal Literary Fund, writing on this subject to H. G. Wells, and persuading Yeats to approach the even more influential Edmund Gosse, whom Ezra did not scruple to bombard with criticism – 'It seems to me ridiculous that your government pensions should go for the most part to saving wrecks rather than in the fostering of letters.' In the event the Fund granted Joyce £75.

This was the first time Ezra had had much contact with Wells, whom he called 'a sloppy sort of animal, would decorate a butcher's shop to advantage. Mixture of vulgarity and vigorous intellect, which sometimes works, and equally often does NOT.' Yet he told Joyce after lunching with Wells in 1918: 'I think you would like [him] . . . His remarks on Q. Victorias monument before Buckingham palace I shall reserve for some future work of my own.' They were eventually recorded in Canto 42: ' "And how this people CAN in this the fifth / et cetera year of the war, leave that old etcetera up / there on that monument!" H.G. to E.P. 1918.' (Much later, in 1940, Wells sent Ezra a copy of his book *The Work, Wealth and Happiness of Mankind,* keen to solicit praise. Ezra replied abusively, complaining that Wells had not defined his terms: 'No. Damn it, you use a good phrase and then you flop; you muff.')

Edmund Gosse both infuriated and amused Ezra as an example of the literary stuffed shirt. In *Poetry* (March 1918) he was very rude about Gosse's *Life of Swinburne,* calling it 'merely the attempt of a silly and pompous old man to present a man of genius'. He did admit – thinking of the Joyce business – that Gosse had fulfilled his public duties 'with great credit and fairness', but said he had the 'cant and fustiness' of 'many literary figures of about his age and generation'. Gosse rejoined to this impertinence that Ezra was a 'preposterous American filibuster and Provençal charlatan', and recalled how when Ezra had come to Hanover Terrace for one of Gosse's hallowed At Homes, he had had the temerity to 'PUSH PAST PARKER', the formidable parlourmaid who opened the front door. Ezra's last word on their differences, in a 1920 letter to May Sinclair, was: 'Foetid corpse Edmund of the house of Gosse.'

Ezra's efforts on behalf of Joyce steadily bore fruit. In June 1916 he secured a grant of £2 a week for him from the Society of Authors. Another grant, a lump sum of £100, was extracted from the Civil List of the Asquith Government, and Yeats's friend and patron, Lady Maud Cunard, agreed to send Joyce £20, providing it was given anonymously. Nancy Cunard describes Ezra as at this time calling 'almost daily' on her mother to promote the causes of Joyce and Wyndham Lewis. Most important of all, it was due to Ezra's enthusiasm for Joyce – though he knew nothing about it at the time – that Harriet Shaw Weaver began anonymously, in February 1917, to send £50 to Joyce four times a year. When he eventually discovered this, Ezra was not altogether pleased: 'Miss W/ dumped it all onto Joyce, rather to my annoyance, as it cd/ have been spread and a few MORE supplied with necessities.' (But this was written many years later, after he had turned against Joyce.)

'But for you I should have been derelict,' Joyce wrote to Ezra in 1917, though usually he accepted Ezra's help without surprise, regarding it as no more than his due. However, he taught his son and daughter, both Italian-speaking, to call Ezra 'Signore Sterlina'. Not that Ezra's concern for Joyce ended with finance: learning in 1916 that Joyce was having eye trouble, he made him send photographs, on the basis of which he made his own diagnosis: 'I suspect your oculist of believing that your astigmatism is harmonic and not inharmonic . . . I'd like to see your glasses prescription.' He tried to put Joyce in touch with his own eye specialist in Philadelphia, but, not surprisingly, Joyce preferred to be treated on the spot in Zurich, where he was then living. (Ezra turned doctor again the following year, when Wyndham Lewis wrote to him to say he thought he had gonorrhoea; Ezra replied at some length, analysing the symptoms Lewis had reported, and saying he thought it improbable that there was any infection.)

Ezra's efforts for Joyce included trying to find a producer for his play *Exiles* – 'I will see that your play is read by the agent of one very practical American dramatic company, which does a big business,' he wrote to Joyce. This project was more or less on the boil for two years; at one stage he convinced John Quinn to contact a New York theatrical agent who, to Joyce's delight, was named L. Bloom. However Ezra eventually realized the play's limitations as a piece of theatre: 'When you are a recognized classic people will read it because you wrote it and be duly interested and duly instructed – but until then I'm hang'd if I can see what's to be done with it.'

He soon added Wyndham Lewis's first novel *Tarr* to the fight. The book, based on Lewis's experiences as a young painter in Paris, was completed in 1915 but failed to find a commercial publisher; Ezra told Harriet Shaw Weaver that the *Egoist* had better 'lead off once again'. She obligingly began to serialize it in the following January, and later, at Ezra's behest, Quinn arranged for American publication. Unlike Joyce's writings, *Tarr* required a certain amount of apology; Ezra had to admit that Lewis's prose was 'uncouth' and 'confused', but he said it was the confusion of 'an over-abundant source that has not yet got itself sorted out', the uncouthness of a 'man with a leaping mind'. He thought a comparison with

Dostoevsky was valid. Actually *Tarr* was more to his taste than Joyce's
work. He said some years later that it seemed to him the product of a mind
'far more fecund and original' than Joyce's. This judgement (given after he
had read *Ulysses*) may owe something to the resemblance of the book's
hero, Frederick Tarr, to Ezra himself as well as to Lewis. Tarr is
ferociously energetic in pursuit of his art, is awkward in conversation, lacks
any social graces, enters into 'engagements' with women without seriously
intending to marry them, and is delighted when they break them off. He is
also described as having a hidden inner personality, a 'crafty daimon'
which, 'aghast at its nakedness, would manage to borrow or purloin some
shape or covering' from certain more 'elegantly draped' acquaintances.

*

'Gaudier is getting tired of the trenches,' Ezra told his mother in early June
1915, 'its time someone came in and hurried matters.' He had speculated in
February in the *New Age* what a loss would result if Gaudier-Brzeska were
destroyed: 'the uncreated forms of a man of genius cannot be set forth by
another.' But when the news came a few weeks later, he reacted very
calmly: 'Brzeska has been killed, which is pretty disgusting, though I
suppose it is a marvel it hasn't happened before.' This letter to his father,
written just after he had heard the news, continues with mere gossip:
'Walter [Rummel] is over, vide enclosed. He goes to Paris after a final show
on Friday. Hueffer in this morning, has done another book on France . . .
Chap, named Waley, from Museum, in last night to see Fenollosa mss. . . . .
Lewis flourishing. Why do you spend money on such rot as Century
magazine ???????? gosh!!!' There was no further reference to Gaudier-
Brzeska.

Writing to Harriet Monroe, he passed on the news chiefly as a piece of
journalistic copy that she could use for the next issue of *Poetry*: 'I went out
this A.M. and all that offers is the ghost of a ghoul's article on Brzeska. He
was killed at Neuville St Vaast, early this month, but the news is just in.'
He appeared to be more upset five months later when he heard that Remy
de Gourmont had just died: 'His death is a great loss to everybody, and a
particular loss to me as he had been so interested in the projected
magazine.'

In due course, the extinction of Gaudier drew from him the expected
obituary phrases: 'A great spirit has been among us, and a great artist is
gone. Neither the man nor the artist had shown any trace of failure.' (This
was in the second and final *BLAST*. In the spring of 1918 he was speaking
of Gaudier's death as 'the gravest individual loss which the arts have
suffered during the war'. And in 1934: 'For eighteen years the death of
Henri Gaudier has been unremedied . . . There is no reason to pardon this
either to the central powers or to the allies or to ourselves.' It has been

suggested that the direction his own life took in the decades following Gaudier-Brzeska's death owed much to the loss of the sculptor, that his rage against the Government of the United States and his support for Mussolini were somehow a product of his feelings about Gaudier. This idea may have originated with Charles Olson, who after talking to Ezra in 1946 wondered whether 'Gaudier's death is the source of his hate for contemporary England and America', whether 'in 1915, his attack on democracy got mixed up with Gaudier's death, and all his turn since has been revenge for the boy's death'. But it is hard to perceive much connection, and the evidence is that by the time Gaudier died Ezra was already beginning to modify his idolatry for him.

Certainly he spent considerable time immediately following Gaudier's death in assembling a book about him, which was accepted for publication by John Lane in early September 1915. But the very haste of this seems faintly ruthless, and *Gaudier-Brzeska: a Memoir* (1916) is largely composed of articles that Ezra (and Gaudier himself) had already written for *BLAST*, the *New Age*, and the *Egoist*; much of the rest is taken up by Gaudier's own letters from the trenches. Ezra's chief original contribution to the book was his reminiscence of the man, rather than the artist, and at one point in it he admits: 'There are few things more difficult than to appraise the work of a man suddenly dead in his youth; to disentangle "promise" from achievement; to save him from that sentimentalizing which confuses the tragedy of the interruption with the merit of the work actually performed.'

The Gaudier book did much to establish its subject's reputation: Henry Moore has spoken of its importance in directing his own attention to African and pre-Columbian carving, and has said that Gaudier's writings on sculpture, quoted in it, 'made me feel certain that in seeking to create along paths other than those of traditional sculpture, it was possible to achieve beauty'. But while, thanks to the admiration of Moore and other sculptors, Gaudier-Brzeska's fame steadily grew following his death, Ezra himself was increasingly inclined to devalue him. In Paris in the 1920s he became a great admirer of Brancusi, whom he said he regarded as Gaudier grown up; consequently he treated his memories of Gaudier rather lightly, perhaps feeling a little cynical about his youthful enthusiasm for him. 'And Henry Gaudier went to it,' he writes in Canto 16, 'and they killed him, / And killed a great deal of sculpture' – which is scarcely the tone of somebody describing an unforgivable wrong. As early as 1916 he was inclined to set Epstein higher than Gaudier. 'Epstein hasn't Gaudier's intelligence,' he wrote to John Quinn, 'but in that flenite [a sculpture Quinn had bought] and in the *Sun-God* he has got more intensity than Gaudier had managed to put into any one piece of work.' It is hard to believe that if Gaudier had lived Ezra would have gone on unremittingly

championing, idolizing, and supporting him. His three great protégés who
survived, Joyce, Eliot, and Lewis, all eventually lost his concentrated
favour. Such permanent place as Gaudier did acquire in Ezra's pantheon is
largely due, one suspects, to his being a Peter Pan who could not grow up
and disappoint.

T. E. Hulme was killed in action in September 1917, and here again there
is no indication that Ezra took the loss very seriously, for he treats
Hulme's war experiences flippantly in Canto 16:

> And ole T.E.H. he went to it,
> With a lot of books from the library,
> London Library, and a shell buried 'em in a dug-out,
> And the Library expressed its annoyance.

Wyndham Lewis enlisted shortly after Gaudier was killed; Ezra was
indignant that he should have to do this while America persisted in keeping
out of the war – 'When is our disgusting country going to send the fleet to
Trieste or Fiume or the Dardanelles?' he asked his father. 'Uncle Sam is
cutting a damn rotten figure.' But he expressed no particular anxiety about
Lewis's safety, and their correspondence while Lewis was in the army was
chiefly concerned with raising money for Lewis from John Quinn and
other sources.

When news of Gaudier's death came through, Quinn told Ezra to buy
everything of his he could get his hands on, and also promised to
underwrite the cost of a Vorticist exhibition in New York which would
chiefly feature Gaudier and Lewis. Ezra replied to these instructions: 'It's
a man's letter and I thank you for it.' He immediately contacted Sophie
Brzeska and bought drawings from her, also depositing £30 with the
Omega Workshops to 'hold down' anything of Gaudier's that they had.
All this, added to his efforts on behalf of Joyce, Lewis, and now and then
Eliot, made him feel, he said, like a 'universal committee for the arts'.
Besides Lewis, the Vorticist painters Edward Wadsworth, Frederick
Etchells and William Roberts had entered the army, and Ezra was trying to
sell their pictures in New York too. The arrangements for the New York
exhibition were complicated by the ever-difficult Sophie Brzeska, who was
unwilling to do anything that Ezra wanted; and when the New York show
was finally mounted in August 1916, Quinn's art friends were not
impressed by the paintings, which one of them described as 'too literary'.
Quinn himself was almost the only buyer; he purchased thirty-two works
by Lewis for £375 as well as drawings by the other Vorticist painters.

Ezra himself was meanwhile becoming a Vorticist of the visual arts. He
and Alvin Langdon Coburn invented a 'Vortoscope', which would take
Vorticist-style photographs. Its chief component was Ezra's shaving
mirror, with the aid of which they managed to create some mildly unusual

pictures in which the human face (often Ezra's own) was broken into a series of abstract shapes. Ezra described the invention in his best Barnum tones:

> Coburn and I have invented the vortoscope, a simple device which frees the camera from reality and lets one take Picassos direct from nature . . . Select the unit of design, cut out everything we don't want, and build the result . . . It would be perfectly possible to pretend that we'd discovered a new painter.

This brand of instant modernism continued to appeal to him intermittently for several years, and in Paris in the 1920s he and a movie-photographer named Murphy tried it with cinematograph film. However, they were soon overtaken by the more sophisticated experiments of Man Ray and Léger.

*

Manuscripts and endless correspondence about all these concerns poured into Ezra's flat at Holland Place Chambers. In the middle of dealing with the Gaudier-Brzeska estate, Joyce's fortunes, and Wyndham Lewis's income, he thought of a way in which to introduce Eliot's poetry to an English audience in book form. As there was not yet enough of it to fill a book by itself, Ezra planned an anthology in which Eliot's verse would be the principal feature. Elkin Mathews agreed to publish it, and because the book exemplified no particular school of poetry Ezra decided to call it *Catholic Anthology*, using 'catholic' in the sense of 'universal'. When the book appeared in November 1915 Elkin Mathews received protests about the title from Francis Meynell and other Roman Catholic figures in the literary Establishment; Ezra complained that Mathews's 'funk' over this had deterred him from sending out review copies, so that the book was ignored. In fact, *Catholic Anthology* vanished almost without trace simply because it was a hotchpotch of widely varying quality. Eliot's contributions were 'Prufrock', 'Portrait of a Lady', 'The Boston Evening Transcript', 'Aunt Helen', and 'Hysteria', but unfortunately his 'Preludes' and 'Rhapsody on a Windy Night', just published in the second *BLAST*, were not included. There were poems by Yeats and William Carlos Williams, but the rest of the space was filled with such banalities as 'Letter from Peking' by Harriet Monroe, which Ezra said he had put into the book in order to cajole her permission for the reprinting of poems that had first appeared in *Poetry*.

The *Catholic Anthology* had, none the less, a sufficiently modern look for Arthur Waugh (father of Evelyn) to single it out in the *Quarterly Review* as a target for abuse. Judging the volume to be the work of 'literary Cubists' who threatened 'anarchy' and 'red ruin', Waugh continued:

It was a classic custom in the family hall, when the feast was at its height, to display a drunken slave among the sons of the household, to the end that they, being ashamed at the ignominious folly of his gesticulations, might determine never to be tempted into such a pitiable condition themselves.

This, said Waugh, was the only conceivable value of such poets as T. S. Eliot. Ezra alluded to this in an *Egoist* article entitled 'Drunken Helots and Mr Eliot', where he wrote: 'All I can find out, by asking questions concerning Mr Waugh, is that he is "a very old chap", "a reviewer".'

Ezra himself contributed his now distinctly outworn 'Contemporania' sequence of poems to the *Catholic Anthology* – an admission that he had nothing new to offer at present after *Cathay*, no revolutionary programme other than to champion and promote certain artists and writers. Such new poetry of his that appeared in magazines during these months – and it was strikingly sparse – was usually rather trivial, a return yet again to the 'Contemporania' note, an indication that *Cathay* had been merely a passing phase, a one-off enterprise. For example, there was the squib 'Our Contemporaries' which appeared in *BLAST* of July 1915:

When the Taihaitian princess
Heard that he had decided,
She rushed into the sunlight and swarmed up a cocoanut
                    palm tree,

But he returned to this island
And wrote ninety Petrarchan sonnets.

This was an allusion to Rupert Brooke, who had visited Tahiti shortly before the war, and had written a poem to a native girl with whom he had an affair. Brooke had died shortly before Ezra's poem was published, so it was thought to be in bad taste. Ezra defended it to Harriet Monroe, saying it had been written 'months before his death' (*BLAST* was supposed to have gone to press in December, while Brooke was still alive), and that it contained 'nothing derogatory', being merely a 'complaint against a literary method' – Brooke had experienced some 'vivid poetry' in his life, but then went off to associate with the unspeakable Georgians.

At the moment, Ezra understandably had little intellectual energy to spare for anything more ambitious. 'My head is a squeezed rag,' he wrote to Joyce in September 1915, saying he had done 'nothing but write 15 page letters to New York'. Occasionally his patience snapped. In August 1917 he found himself in the middle of simultaneous and equally incomprehensible cables from both Quinn and Joyce on the matter of Joyce's play *Exiles* and his financial situation. Thanks to the Post Office, the Joyce telegram read like something out of the future *Finnegans Wake*: 'CABLE QUINN

CONFRIN OR REMIT YOU TELEGRAPHICALLY NOTHING HERE REMITTING JOYCE.' Ezra exploded to Joyce: 'WHAT????'

Such energies as he was left with after his campaigns tended to direct themselves more and more towards matters of public concern, rather than to his own writing. In May 1915 he told H. L. Mencken that he wanted the tariff taken off books imported into America, and was concerned about the censorship of literature sent through the mail. He was still calling for his Renaissance, but now tended to see it in terms of measures like these rather than artistic advances. A typical 'Renaissance' article by him, in *Poetry* for March 1917, contained these exhortations, under the heading 'Things to Be Done':

> First, *we should get the tariff off books* . . . Second, *we should get a good copyright law* . . . Third, *let us learn more languages* . . . Fourth, *we should multiply translations* . . . Fifth, *we must try to think, at least a little, about civilization.*

Yet at the very moment that he was complaining of being grotesquely overloaded, seeming concerned only with the fortunes of other writers and with public matters rather than his own work, he was making his first attempt to begin the Cantos.

16

Endless Poem

A change of direction became perceptible in his poetry in March 1915, when he published 'Provincia Deserta' in *Poetry*. A poem of about eighty lines, it is a loose, relaxed, and therefore uncharacteristic piece of free verse describing his 1912 French walking tour. In it, he claims that he managed to experience something of history at first hand by visiting these places: 'I have walked over these roads; / I have thought of them living.'

During the next month, he made an even more untypical venture into Byronic rhymed satiric verse, sending *Smart Set* 200 lines entitled 'L'Homme Moyen Sensuel', in the hope that he might be asked to contribute such stuff regularly. He suggested modestly that they 'boom it as THE SATIRE, "best since Byron" . . . It is not such an awful lie, if one considers that nobody has written satire, in the best English iambic tradition, since God knows when.' But *Smart Set* turned the poem down, for it was a dismal piece of work. 'Byron's technique is rotten,' Ezra wrote later that year, but his own in this poem rarely measured up to that of *Don Juan*. There were occasional good couplets ('Some men will live as prudes in their own village / And make the tour abroad for their wild tillage'), but mostly the metre and rhyme were very laboured; for example: 'And timorous love of the innocuous / Brought from Gt. Britain and dumped down a' top of us.' Yet the poem was an attempt to break new ground.

Its hero, Radway, is a young American growing up in the cultural milieu Ezra himself had known, and the poem begins: ''Tis of my country that I would endite, / In hope to set some misconceptions right.' No doubt if it had continued beyond the first instalment, Radway would have crossed the Atlantic and had similar experiences to Ezra. As it is, the story comes abruptly to an end when he joines 'the Baptist Broadway Temple' because he 'found it profitable'. The mistake was to cast such a journey in the form of satire, a medium for which Ezra had absolutely no talent. He was a dab hand at schoolboy mockery, and could produce some extremely funny if rather crude parodies, but the restraint and measured irony of the true satirist were not in his repertoire. Also, he was not sure enough of his own beliefs to have a firm base from which to mount a satirical operation. He admitted to Yeats's father in 1917 that 'my satires . . . are not in themselves a full expression of my poetic beliefs, but only a rest'.

A third and final stage in this ground-clearing was published in *Poetry* in December 1915: 'Near Périgord', in which, again drawing on memories of his 1912 walking tour, he puzzles over what might be the secret meaning of Bertran de Born's *canzone* about his ideal lady made up from different elements of real women (the inspiration of Ezra's own early poem 'Na Audiart'). He suggests that it may have had a local, political significance, for all the ladies mentioned in it were married to powerful local rulers: 'for every lady a castle, / Each place strong'.

'Near Périgord' is less interesting for its subject matter than its method. For a start, Ezra has chosen to revive his Browning voice, not used for some years, this apparently being the tone he still prefers for a detached discussion of historical characters and events. He begins with a plain narrative of the facts of the case, then proceeds to a fictionalized incident in which, after de Born's death, the troubadour Arnaut Daniel wonders whether Bertran really loved the Lady Maent or whether his poetic address to her was just a strategic ruse. In the final section, we learn from Bertran himself that he did love her, and he believes that without him she is merely 'A broken bundle of mirrors', a jumble of incomplete perceptions.

'Glad you like the Perigord poem,' Ezra wrote to his father in December 1915. But he himself was not satisfied with it: 'I think I have missed fire. I wanted to convey the *"sense & the feel" that something critical is happening to someone else at a distance* . . . We must have another try at it.' This letter does not really make clear what he was after (nor does the poem). On the other hand the poem's final line, 'A broken bundle of mirrors', serves admirably as a description of the technique towards which his poetry now moved.

In 'Near Périgord' the Browning voice slips away after the first few stanzas, and we hear something rather rare: Ezra immersed in the description of scenery, intent on conveying setting and atmosphere:

> Chalais is high, a-level with the poplars.
> Its lowest stones just meet the valley tips
> Where the low Dronne is filled with water-lilies.
> And Rochecouart can match it, stronger yet,
> The very spur's end, built on sheerest cliff . . .

And again:

> Bewildering spring, and by the Auvezere
> Poppies and day's eyes in the green émail
> Rose over us; and we knew all that stream,
> And our two horses had traced out the valleys;
> Knew the low flooded lands squared out with poplars . . .

'If you like the "Perigord",' he told Homer, 'you would probably like Browning's "Sordello"' – though he added: 'It takes a bit of reading.' He himself had recently been looking through *Sordello* again. 'It is a great work & worth the trouble of hacking it out,' he told his father. 'I began to get it on about the 6th reading – though individual passages come up all right on the first reading. It is probably the greatest poem in English.' The re-reading (he explained) had been to help him with his work on 'a longish new poem'. It would be 'two months at least before I can send it. – I suppose – as I dont want to muddle my mind now in the Vth canto – by typing the first three cantos. and I don't want to leave the only copy with a typist while I'm out of town. Besides you may as well have a shot at "Sordello" first.'

This letter, written during December 1915, contains the first reference to his 'cantos' under that name, but work had started some months earlier, since in mid-September he told a correspondent he was 'at work on a cryselephantine poem of immeasurable length which will occupy me for the next four decades unless it becomes a bore'. He informed John Quinn that he was writing his 'life work in verse'; rather later he mentioned to Quinn his 'work on a new long poem (really L O N G, endless, leviathanic)'. Sending a poem for *Poetry* in June 1916 he told Harriet Monroe: 'My next contribution will probably be a 40 page fragment from a more important opus.' Sure enough 'Three Cantos', the first three of the five he said he had written by that time (though there is no trace of a Canto 4 or 5 from this period) appeared in *Poetry* during the summer of 1917, starting in June.

Three months before these 'Three Cantos' were printed, Ezra wrote to Joyce:

> I have begun an endless poem, of no known category. Phano-
> poeia or something or other, all about everything . . . I wonder
> what you will make of it. Probably too sprawling and unmusi-
> cal to find favour in your ears. Will try to get some melody into
> it further on.

'Phanopoeia' means 'light- or image-making', and Ezra used it in exactly that sense in a sequence of short imagistic poems entitled 'Phanopoeia', first published in 1918. Indeed, it became one of the three principal categories in his definition of poetry. On the other hand in the letter to Joyce about 'Three Cantos' he implies that 'Phanopoeia' means 'all about everything', in which case it should be 'Panopoeia'. Given his shaky knowledge of Greek, the mistake seems quite likely.

Certainly his intention from the very outset of work on the Cantos was to create a poem that could deal quite literally with everything – everything of importance in human experience which did not seem to him to have been adequately recorded elsewhere. The presumption in this may seem appalling; yet having decided to write a long poem it was natural for him, given his character and the lack of any current preoccupation, to want to make it all-embracing, a pantechnicon (with himself as driver) into which anything and everything could be stuffed. 'You had six centuries that hadn't been packaged,' he remarked in his 1960 *Paris Review* interview, looking back at the original idea behind the Cantos. 'It was a question of dealing with material that wasn't in the *Divina Commedia*.'

There was no plan of composition as such: he would strike out with no expectations and see what happened. Rather more than thirty years later, he cited the following limerick in a letter:

There once was a brainy baboon
Who always breathed down a bassoon,
    For he said, 'It appears
    That in billions of years
I shall certainly hit on a tune.'

*

A recent editor of Browning's poetry has remarked that Ezra Pound 'is probably the only person who has ever seriously claimed to have understood *Sordello*'. Because of its convoluted obscurity, G. K. Chesterton judged it 'the most glorious compliment that has ever been paid to the average man'. Ezra turned to it, hoping that it would give a push-start to his great enterprise, not merely because of his affection for Browning, and because almost nobody else could claim to have read it, but because in it Browning had set out to extend the bounds of narrative technique on an extreme scale – hence its incomprehensibility.

Sordello has an ostensibly historical subject, the life of the medieval Provençal poet of that name who is mentioned in the *Purgatorio*, but is really an experiment in narration, for Browning himself is the real 'hero' of the poem, and constantly stands back from the story to draw attention to himself and his role as creator. For example, in the opening lines he talks of himself as a comic lecturer or clownish narrator, standing on the stage next to Sordello, 'Motley on back and pointing-pole in hand / Beside him'.

The first of Ezra's 'Three Cantos' – his 1915 attempt at a beginning, very

different from the finished article – starts by trying to analyse this quality
in *Sordello*, and contemplates copying it. Ezra imagines how his own poem
might, like Browning's, be a peepshow booth with a showman standing in
front of it. This is how he starts the first of these earliest Cantos:

> Hang it all, there can be but one *Sordello!*
> But say I want to, say I take your whole bag of tricks,
> Let in your quirks and tweeks, and say the thing's an art-form,
> Your *Sordello*, and that the modern world
> Needs such a rag-bag to stuff all its thought in;
> Say that I dump my catch, shiny and silvery
> As fresh sardines flapping and slipping on the marginal cobbles?
> (I stand before the booth, the speech; but the truth
> Is inside this discourse – this booth is full of the marrow of
>   wisdom.)
> Give up th' intaglio method . . .
> Does it matter?

The role of Browningesque showman was a natural, plausible one for him,
one in which he could assume all kinds of personae, could introduce
allusions to other poets (Browning included). It was an extension of his
current work as impresario of a twentieth-century Renaissance. There was
no need to hide himself in a Prufrock, even a Stephen Dedalus or a
Frederick Tarr; he, after all, was the most vigorous character in his own
world, and his use of *Sordello* as a model for the opening of the poem
suggested that he would be taking due account of that.

The remainder of the first of these experimental 'Three Cantos' explores
the relationship to each other of the three layers of narration: Sordello
himself, Browning, and Ezra. The 'rag-bag' method of *Sordello* – the
jumbling together of different historical periods and poetic styles – is
compared to Ezra's own multi-faceted historical consciousness: 'Ghosts
move about me,' he writes, 'Patched with histories.' Like Browning, he has
the facility for entering into a dead age: 'I walk Verona . . . I see Can
Grande' (allusions to Dante). If anyone questions the worth of the
fragments he is going to present, his justification is that he lives in an age
that has no agreed belief or philosophy, so that it is necessary to resort to
this technique. 'You had one whole man?' he asks Browning.

> And I have many fragments, less worth? Less worth?
> Ah, had you quite my age, quite such a beastly and
>   cantankerous age?
> You had some basis, had some set belief.
> Am I let preach? Has it a place in music?

All this has taken up nearly fifty lines. He now goes on to describe himself at Sirmione on Corpus Christi day – the 'great day' in Book III of *Sordello*. He sees it not as a Christian saint's day but as a pagan, pre-Christian festival. This passage, the nearest Ezra can come to religious feeling, emphasizes that for him the pagan gods are living now:

> . . . the place is full of spirits,
> Not *lemures*, not dark and shadowy ghosts,
> But the ancient living, wood-white,
> Smooth as the inner bark, and firm of aspect . . .
> Glaukopos, clothed like the poppies . . .

The word 'Glaukopos' is the first example of a certain kind of multi-layered allusion that would appear often in the Cantos. 'Glaukopis' (*sic*) is one of the epithets of Athene in the *Odyssey*, and Allen Upward picked it up in *The New Word*, citing a dispute among scholars as to its precise meaning. They wondered, says Upward, whether it could mean 'blue-eyed' or 'grey-eyed' or 'glare-eyed' when 'all the time they had not only the word *glaux* staring them in the face, as the Athenian name for owl . . . but they had the owl itself cut at the foot of every statue of Athene . . . to tell them that she was the owl-eyed goddess'. Ezra is alluding to this crux when he uses the word for his pagan spirits.

And yet this vision of the gods leaves him still uncertain. 'How shall we start hence, how begin the progress?' he asks after nearly 150 lines of this first experimental canto, and for a moment he denies that he can really perceive antiquity: 'No, take it all for lies. / I have but smelt this life, a whiff of it . . .' Then he reassures himself, in the closing lines, that with 'worlds enough' available from past ages, and with 'new form' suggested by 'Picasso or Lewis', he ought to be able to 'guess a soul for man', or at least dedicate himself to Imagist poetry ('If for a year a man write to paint . . .') and see what that will achieve.

Though Ezra later discarded this opening canto entirely from the finished work, it does, as he observed in the Foreword to the *Selected Cantos* (1967), form the 'best introduction' to the whole poem as it was to emerge, being the nearest approach he ever made to a clear statement of method and purpose. Too derivatively Browningesque to represent quite all the facets of Ezra as he was by 1915, it nevertheless conveys (sometimes with disarming honesty) his ambitions and hopes for the poem. One can see why he repudiated its voice, but that voice was an honest one.

*

The second of the 'Three Cantos', which appeared in *Poetry* a month after the first in July 1917, continues his exploration of fragments of the past, through which he is evidently still searching in order to find a beginning and a method for his enterprise. He recalls the bars of troubadour music he found in Milan ('There's the one stave, and all the rest forgotten. / I've lost the copy I had of it in Paris'), and hopes that Arnold Dolmetsch can bewitch modern listeners back into that age ('Dolmetsch will build our age in witching music'). Then, in the idiom of *Cathay*, a lute-girl appears out of nowhere, rather like a spirit in the *Inferno*, and tells a tale of love wearing out: 'Many a one / Brought me rich presents; my hair was full of jade . . . / And then one year I faded out and married.' She is echoed by Catullus's expressions of disgust for his old love, Lesbia, and by the failure of *amour courtois* in the story of Vincent St Antoni, whose beloved abandoned 'the whole convention' of adulterous courtly love when she believed her husband to be dead. These allusions are loosely connected to each other by a stream of consciousness; through this method Ezra hopes to present what he calls 'Ply over ply of life'. The mere mention of the name 'Gordon' in the lines 'Lady of Montfort, / Wife of William à Gordon' is enough to recall Gourdon, one of the villages through which he walked in 1912, and into the poem comes the St John's Eve festival he witnessed there. This in turn suggests that he might write 'a tale of lances' – and up on the screen of his mind comes 'My cid rode up to Burgos', an image from *El Cid* and his own 1906 explorations of Spain, closely followed by 'Kumasaka's ghost' from a Japanese Noh play with a warrior hero. Further allusions of this sort follow, but the second of the 'Three Cantos' ends in contemplation of the fall of medieval Europe and of the failure of Fred Vance, the painter whom Ezra had known at Crawfordsville: over-educated and utterly out of touch with the 'animate' life of the pagan world, knowing no better than to adore the tepid mythology of nineteenth-century French art and to use it, watered still further, as material for adorning the local doctor's mantelpiece.

The third and final canto of this 1915 experiment, published in *Poetry* in August 1917, suggests other methods of examining the 'ply over ply of life'. After a brief vision of 'a half-cracked fellow' – the seventeenth-century visionary writer John Heydon, whom Ezra briefly contemplates using as a guide to the underworld of the past – he turns to the medieval Latin version of the *Odyssey* by Andreas Divus that he had found on a Left Bank bookstall, and begins to quote from it in an English translation intended (he said) to be 'an approximation of the metre of the Anglo-Saxon "Sea-farer"'. The passage chosen is the 'Nekyia', often regarded as earlier and more primitive in origin than the rest of the *Odyssey* (Ezra wrote that it 'shouts aloud that it is *older* than the rest'), in which Odysseus describes his escape from Circe and the libations with which he and his men summon up the dead from Avernus. It is this passage, slightly altered, that Ezra eventually shifted to the opening of Canto 1 and hence of the entire Cantos.

He finally chose the 'Nekyia' for this prominent place in the whole work because it was a perfect example of the 'ply over ply' method. It is a reworking of medieval Latin (itself a reworking of ancient Greek) into English that is at once modern and a re-creation of Anglo-Saxon. We therefore observe (by implication) Ezra discovering Andreas Divus for himself, Andreas Divus rediscovering Homer for a medieval audience, Homer 'discovering' Odysseus and his experiences, and finally Odysseus himself summoning up the dead – which is what Ezra had been trying to do in different ways throughout the 'Three Cantos'.

Ezra regretted that the 'Three Cantos' had to be published one by one in consecutive issues of *Poetry* rather than together, but told Harriet Monroe to 'string it out into three numbers if that's the best you can do'. They were printed without preamble, notes, or any other form of explanation. Not surprisingly, they made a poor impression on most readers, for they only become interesting when read with the hindsight of the finished Cantos; if encountered in isolation they seem muddled and muddling, disturbingly loose in form, and for the most part tiresomely echoing Browning. A typical reaction at the time was that of the *New Age* reviewer, Adrian Collins, who wrote: 'After these fireworks one may be glad to turn for relief to the simple prattle of *Sordello*.' Harriet Monroe did not care for them, nor did Carl Sandburg. Ezra wrote to her that he was 'sorry' to hear of these reactions, but 'I can't see how anyone can see the thing in such small sections . . . Eliot is the only person who proffered criticism instead of general objection . . . One can't stop merely because some people haven't read Latin.' However, to James Joyce he admitted that the 'Three Cantos' were 'very shaggy', and when reprinting them in book form not long after they had appeared in *Poetry* he made various cuts and changes in phrasing and word order, without substantially altering anything.

In his correspondence with Joyce he referred to 'Three Cantos' so often that is clear he wanted Joyce to read them, and to take account of the fact that 'Signore Sterlina' could produce a major work himself: '*Poetry* is serializing the first 3 cantos of my long poem – *but* I have since revised and cut out . . . so would rather you judged it from the forthcoming £ volume . . . *if* you can wade through it all.' (Conceivably the 'serial' method by which he chose to produce Cantos, both now and later, had something to do with the way in which *A Portrait of the Artist as a Young Man* and *Ulysses* appeared in print chapter by chapter.) And a month later, to Joyce: 'I hope to God you wont try to read my beastly long poem in *Poetry*, I have revised the whole thing, and it is at least better than it was, and will appear in my American edition [of *Lustra*] . . .'

Joyce took no more than a distant and polite interest in Ezra's poetry – or, for that matter, in anyone else's work at this stage of his life; he later admitted that while *Ulysses* was running in the *Little Review* he had never read anything in that magazine 'except for my own installments'. He did tell Ezra he was 'looking forward' to reading 'Three Cantos', but he made no comment if he ever did, though he remarked that *Cathay* had given him 'much pleasure' and said he hoped *Lustra* would contain 'one or two sweet lines for my oldfashioned ear'. This sort of thing was no more than a sop, as Ezra eventually realized. In 1955 he wrote that 'to the best of my recollection' Joyce had 'never alluded to any of his eng/ & am/ contemporaries as writers'. He said that Joyce had maintained a 'discrete silence' (*sic*) about all his poetry except *Hugh Selwyn Mauberley*, and there had been only 'one discrete sentence re/ that'. (Ezra told Charles Olson that this sentence, describing and alluding to the deliberately over-polished 'Medallion' in *Hugh Selwyn Mauberley*, ran as follows: 'The sleek head of verse, Mr Pound, emerges in your work.')

When in 1925 Joyce was asked to write a tribute to Ezra for a Pound number of the magazine *This Quarter*, he produced what sounded like a formal testimonial intended to accompany a job application, making no reference to Ezra's writings but praising him for his 'friendly help, encouragement and generous interest'. Joyce once dreamt that he saw Ezra as the leader of 'some American journalists', which was perhaps how he really thought of him. Ezra judged that 'J.J. regarded me, so far as I know, as a useful member of the bourgeoisie with a bee in his bonnet' – acceptable because that bee was, for a time, a determination to help Joyce.

But by 1925 Joyce was not entirely ignorant of the Cantos, for in that year he parodied them:

> Is it dreadfully necessary
> > AND
> (I mean that I pose etc) is it useful, I ask
> this
> > > HEAT!?
> We all know Mercury will know *when*
> > he Kan!
> > but as Dante saith:
> > 1 Inferno is enough. *Basta*, he said, *un'inferno,*
> *perbacca!*
> And that bird –
> > Well!
> HE   oughter know!
> > (With apologies to Mr Ezra Pound)

17

Baser Passions

Ezra himself was far from confident about the direction he had taken in
'Three Cantos', judging by remarks he made in print at the time of working
on them. In the first of these cantos themselves he asks whether the idea of
writing a poem on the grand scale is not absurd, and whether he should not
'sulk and leave the word to novelists'. In *Poetry* in April 1916 it worried
him that 'James Joyce, by far the most significant writer of our decade, is
confining himself to prose'. He showed no serious commitment to the
'endless poem', telling Harriet Monroe in August 1917, just as she had
finished serializing 'Three Cantos': 'Anyway my next batch of stuff will be
short poems, which, let us hope, someone will enjoy. Also one should not
do the same thing all the time. The long poem is at least a change.'

He was now making strenuous efforts to find a publisher for *A Portrait
of the Artist as a Young Man* in book form. As the months passed Joyce's
novel was rejected by Heinemann, and John Lane. Duckworth said Joyce
had ability but should try his hand at something else. The book had been
submitted by Joyce's agent J. B. Pinker, and Edward Garnett, reading
manuscripts for Duckworth, recommended that it be 'pulled into shape'
and be made less 'sordid'. Ezra's response to Pinker, on 30 January 1916,
was apoplectic:

> These vermin crawl over and be-slime our literature with their
> pulings, and nothing but the day of judgement can, I suppose,
> exterminate 'em . . . It is with difficulty that I manage to write
> to you at all on being presented with the Duckworthian muck,
> the dungminded dungbearded, penny a line, please the
> mediocre-at-all-cost doctrine. You English will get no prose till
> you exterminate this breed . . .
>   Canting, supercilious, blockhead . . .

Really, Mr Pinker, it is too insulting, even to be forwarded to
Joyce's friend, let alone to Joyce.
   And the end – also found fault with – again, Oh God, O
Montreal –
   Why can't you send the publishers readers to the serbian
front, and get some good out of the war . . .

This letter marks the beginning of a new period in his correspondence, in
which righteous anger would stir him again and again to vehemence, abuse,
harangues, and disjointed expression.

   These outbursts were at present usually directed towards such issues as
the mishandling by others of Joyce's works, and were rarely prompted by
any notion that he, Ezra Pound, had been maltreated by others. (Indeed
even in later days, when he was attacking a far wider range of targets, the
suggestion that he himself had suffered ill-treatment rarely came into it.)
Nevertheless, it began to be rumoured that he had a persecution complex.
Typically, Richard Aldington was the first to suggest it. Just after Ezra's
row with Amy Lowell had broken out in the summer of 1914, Aldington
told her that Ezra 'looks terribly ill . . . He lies on a couch and says he has
"cerebral gout".' Aldington wondered if he might be 'a little cracked. He
doesn't seem to be able to talk of anything except himself and his work.'

   There does indeed seem to be a touch of paranoia in a note appended to
Cathay, in which Ezra speaks of 'the personal hatred in which I am held by
many, and the *invidia* which is directed against me because I have dared
openly to declare my belief in certain young artists'. There is a suggestion
of a persecution complex, too, in a letter he wrote in the summer of 1915 to
the *Boston Evening Transcript*, complaining about a statement there that
Robert Frost was the first American poet to make a reputation in London.
Ezra's reply – that he had done it himself several years before Frost –
accused the paper of the 'twistings of malice', and suggested that its staff
'detested' him.

   Yet if these were real moments of paranoia, and not just a pose, they
were temporary and uncharacteristic. On the whole, he enjoyed hostile
reviews of his own work. 'Can dad send on the *Transcript* attack?' he asked
his mother in June 1916. 'Specimens of assininity not rare but nearly
always diverting.' In the same letter he mentioned that a 'prominent
London ass' had 'confessed two weeks ago that he had been trying to ruin
my career for sometime and here I was "more like a rock than ever". Poor
chap! The only compliment he could have paid me.'

   It is often hard to believe that his anger in letters is real. It sounds much
more like someone pretending to be angry, a caricature of rage: 'God
buggarin DAMN it . . . krrrrist . . . god dry up her pancreas . . .' (this was
of Harriet Monroe). Such real fury as the letters manifest stemmed mostly

from a desire to deal thoroughly and honestly with issues that pained him. He did not want to descend into what he called 'mere conversation and politesse'. He said he believed that in important issues there 'arent any short cuts', and that it was essential to display a 'degree of intolerance' simply in order 'to get the job done'.

The anger, or mock-anger, began to seduce him away from wiser courses of action. He undoubtedly enjoyed it, or else he would not have continued with it, for inevitably it was often unproductive – for example, the furious letter to Pinker about Garnett's report on *A Portrait of the Artist as a Young Man* produced no result whatever. His anger also had the serious drawback in that it became a validation of the causes he espoused. By 1917 he was prepared to praise irascibility as a virtue: 'I have never known anyone worth a damn who wasn't irascible.' This attitude was hardened by camaraderie with Wyndham Lewis, to whom anger was even more of a credo; Lewis wrote, in a series of 'Imaginary Letters' that he and Ezra exchanged in the *Little Review*: 'It is more *comfortable* for me, in the long run, to be rude than polite.' Yet as early as 1912, before he had come to know Lewis properly, Ezra was proud of his aggression, portraying himself, in a letter to Harriet Monroe, as a Bertran de Born glorying in the attacks of his foes: 'I've got a right to be severe. For one man I strike there are ten to strike back at me. I stand exposed. It hits me in my dinner invitations, in my weekends, in reviews of my own work. Nevertheless it's a good fight.' He added: 'I don't love my fellow man, and I don't propose to pretend to.'

The gentler-minded, when they were given the right of reply, were puzzled. 'Why, why will you needlessly irritate people?' Elkin Mathews asked him in 1916 during the grumbles about the title of *Catholic Anthology*. Ezra's response was complacent: 'I AM annoying. There is no gittin' round that.' John Gould Fletcher suspected that he had derived the habit, like his costume, from Whistler, who loved to infuriate in just this fashion. The English tended to assume that it was merely American impatience, a transatlantic desire to get things done without wasting time, and Ezra seems to have held this view up to a point. In 1920 he wrote to Joyce: 'The curse of me & my nation is that we always think things can be bettered by immediate action of some sort, *any* sort rather than no sort.' Wyndham Lewis, too, thought of Ezra as an American bull in an English china shop: 'He had rushed with all the raw solemnity of the classic Middle West into a sophisticated post-Nineties society . . . for whom the spectacle of American "strenuousness" – the Bull Moose tradition – was something that hardly any longer deserved a smile.' Yet when a fellow American, Margaret Anderson, met Ezra for the first time, she observed:

Ezra's agitation was not of the type to which we were

accustomed in America – excitement, pressure, life too high-geared. It gave me the sensation of watching a large baby perform its repertoire of physical antics gravely, diffidently, without human responsibility for the performance.

If the performance was not essentially American, how did it originate? Wyndham Lewis thought its roots lay in Ezra's desire to prove himself 'superior to all other intellectuals . . . and all poets'. Yet, as Lewis himself often pointed out, the greater part of Ezra's energy was devoted to promoting causes other than his own work. Moreover the tactlessness and irritability were almost exclusively limited to his correspondence. Those who knew him personally perceived an essential kindness beneath the aggressive surface – 'a rugged and headstrong nature, and he is always hurting people's feelings,' said Yeats, 'but he has I think . . . great goodwill'. Wyndham Lewis had to admit, in the middle of a blast against Ezra in *Time and Western Man* (1927), that 'a kinder heart never lurked beneath a portentous exterior than is to be found in Ezra Pound'.

So why the irascibility, why the pose – which increased greatly in middle age – of Bertran de Born crying for the sound of battle? It began with Ezra's natural and justifiable impatience with the sluggishness of Edwardian and Georgian literary London, and with the failings of Harriet Monroe in Chicago. Then came the difficulty of getting Joyce's work into print and of raising money for him, with Gaudier's death and Wyndham Lewis's perpetual shortage of funds added to give Ezra an almost impossible workload. When overloaded, he blew off steam noisily – and rather enjoyed the sound he was making. He was far better at criticizing, mocking, and tearing down than at constructing his own positive systems of thought, and during his years in London there was much in English cultural life that deserved mockery. But, as with everything in his life, he did not know when to stop, and when this performance evoked a lively (albeit aggrieved) response from his audience, he settled even more firmly into the role, taking no account of where it might eventually lead him.

In his 1915 attack on the *Boston Evening Transcript* for supposedly neglecting himself when praising Frost, Ezra suggested that the offending article was the work of 'your (? negro) reviewer', a reference to William S. Braithwaite, one of the first black authors to win public attention in America, who had written a rude review of *Provença* for the *Transcript* in 1910. And during 1917 he observed in the *Little Review* on the subject of Ford Madox Hueffer and the *English Review*: 'As its glory was literary, not commercial, it was bought by certain Jews, who thought Mr Hueffer a damn fool'; he spoke of them as 'manufacturing, political hebrews'. The *English Review* had been purchased, when Ford needed funds in 1910, by Sir Alfred Mond, chemical manufacturer and politician, who had promptly sacked Ford from the editorship. When writing of the struggle of the artist in America in the *Little Review* in 1917 Ezra again brought Jews into the issue:

> Unfortunately the turmoil of yidds [*sic*], letts, finns, esthonians [*sic*], cravats, niberians, algerians, sweeping along Eighth Avenue in the splendour of their vigorous unwashed animality will not help us. They are the America of tomorrow . . . The turmoil of Yidds, Letts, etc. is 'full of promise' . . . But our job is to turn out good art.

After this had been printed, the magazine reported that it had received 'countless letters from Jews, Letts, Greeks, Finns, Irish, etc., protesting'.

A poem by Ezra, 'Upon the Harps of Judea', published in the *Little Review* in November 1918, was never reprinted:

> The noble sentiments
> Which fill the form of this unbearable Jew
>   (four ft. 9 in. by 3 ft.)
> Overflow into his countenance
> and out of his countenance
> and into his gestures
> and into his carriage
> to the devastation of everyone.

The poem goes on to describe the embarrassment the Jew causes to a Chinaman, a 'wounded Tommy of an inferior class', and others, among them a shy 'younger semite'. It ends:

> *In ripis Babiloniis, in ripis Babiloniis,*
> *In ripis Babiloniis, planga-a-a-a-avimus.*

It appears that part of this growing obsession with race sprang from a schoolboyish love of guying comic foreigners. By 1915 he had begun to adopt a series of mimicked accents into his talk. Iris Barry was taken by him on a walk across Wimbledon Common in 1916, and writes of that occasion:

> His is almost a wholly original accent, the base of American mingled with a dozen assorted 'English society' and Cockney accents inserted in mockery, French, Spanish and Greek exclamations, strange cries and catcalls, the whole very oddly inflected, with dramatic pauses and *diminuendos*.

*

The friendship with Iris Barry, begun in the summer of 1916, was the first of Ezra's many teacher–pupil relationships. In a series of letters, he gave her his course of 'KOMPLEAT KULTURE', including a quick guide to classical literature: 'Virgil is a second-rater, a Tennysonianized version of Homer . . . There is no history of Greek poetry that is worth ANYthing.' He also dealt with English poetry: 'Perhaps one shouldn't read it at all. Chaucer has in him all that has ever got into English.' He persuaded Iris to leave her home in Birmingham and come to London to study, which she did in 1917. Similarly he took in hand the education of Stella Bowen, a young Australian studying painting with Sickert at the Westminster School of Art, who with her drama student friend Phyllis Reid had met him at a party. Stella writes of these months:

> Ezra took the trouble to occupy himself with our joint education. I expect it was fun for him to harangue two girls who took him so very seriously, and it was certainly fine for us. But it was all rather difficult for there were so many things we were forbidden to admire, and so few exponents of the arts he recommended . . . The public was an imbecile, and the artist was to make no compromise with popular taste. 'Getting across' was the last thing he should consider.

Already, as in *Guide to Kulchur* twenty years later, he was finding it far easier to condemn than to praise.

He introduced Stella Bowen to Ford Madox Hueffer, who had broken with Violet Hunt, and Stella became Ford's next mistress. Similarly, when Wyndham Lewis came back from the war he took up with Iris Barry (whose real surname was Crump), who bore him two children. Their relationship proved brief, and after it ended she became a film critic and novelist, was twice married, and had a stormy but successful life. She said she had 'no contact' with Ezra after 1918, and told one of his biographers that 'relations were severely severed and I hope we don't have to go into *that* . . . I just simply had reasons and some of them extremely personal for not wanting to see him.' Ezra did not seem to share this attitude, since in 1934 he wrote to her asking for help with various projects, and also called on her in New York in 1939. It would perhaps be wrong to read too much into her remarks; his pupil–teacher relationships seem to have been innocent, and though some of his friends took advantage of these young ladies, he himself probably did not.

*

Ezra and Dorothy spent the winter of 1915–16 once again at Stone Cottage with Yeats. 'I am down here in the country because I can't afford London,' Ezra told Joyce after Christmas. Yeats reported to John Quinn that Dorothy was doing 'the housekeeping', and that both Pounds 'treat me with the respect due to my years and so make me feel that it is agreeable to grow old.' Yeats had in fact just reached the age of fifty; two years later he married Dorothy's 'cousin' Georgie Hyde-Lees, stepdaughter of Olivia Shakespear's brother. It was apparently Ezra who first remarked on the squareness of 'George' Yeats (as she liked to be called after marriage); Dorothy wrote to him in 1911: 'Georgie's face *is* square: but she is very handsome . . . She is awfully intelligent, & I believe admires yr. poems – what more can be said?' But thereafter George was always designated in the Ezra–Dorothy correspondence by a drawing of a square.

Ezra was best man at the Yeats wedding, at the Harrow Road Register Office in London in October 1917, and afterwards was instructed by Yeats to send a telegram announcing the event to Lady Gregory at Coole Park – though, knowing Ezra's epistolary tendencies, Yeats added: 'NOT one that will be talked about in Coole for the next generation.' Ezra remarked to John Quinn that the new Mrs Yeats seemed attractive and sensible, and at least would not be a 'flaming nuissance'. He and George actually got on very well, and she often took him into her confidence.

At Stone Cottage in the winter of 1915–16, taking turns to read aloud, Yeats and Ezra worked their way through much of Walter Savage Landor's nine volumes of *Imaginary Conversations* (1824–29), in which historical characters down the ages dispute amiably with each other. The enormous length of the work, together with Landor's quarrelsome character, immediately calls to mind the Cantos. There is no doubt that Landor's individualism and his personal history – he had considerable difficulties in finding a publisher for his works, and, in the words of the *Dictionary of National Biography*, 'repudiated all sympathy with popular feeling' – increased his appeal to Ezra. Writing to J. B. Pinker in January 1916, he called Landor 'the best mind in your literature' and compared Landor's troubles with his own in getting Joyce into print. He told Iris Barry to read Landor, and was still going on about him in *ABC of Reading* (1934), where he praises him as 'a figure to put against Voltaire . . . so far ahead of his British times that the country couldn't contain him'.

Though he was not interested in Landor as a model for poetry (he told Iris Barry he 'isn't very good as a poet save in a few places . . . no use as a model'), he wondered if the *Imaginary Conversations* might not themselves suggest a way forward for his own work. As a first venture into this genre he translated a similar book, the *Dialogues des Morts* (1687) by Bernard de Fontenelle, in which celebrated figures from past ages converse in Paradise. The result is a witty attack on received attitudes and values, and Ezra produced some serviceable translations of twelve of the dialogues, which were printed in the *Egoist* and then issued as a small book by Harriet Shaw Weaver. Ezra told his mother that 'the Fontanelle [*sic*] was great fun to do – and most sane & charming'. He then began to produce some original work in this genre, contributing to the *Little Review* (June 1917)

'An Anachronism at Chinon', a conversation between a modern American (himself) and the ghost of Rabelais. The two compare notes and agree that in such matters as the suppression of learning and the censorship of literature, their eras are roughly the same.

He was exploring the possibilities of prose, as if to assure himself, before embarking seriously on the 'endless poem', that he was not a prose writer by vocation. He tried his hand at a short story, 'Jodindranath Mawhwor's Occupation', which describes the life of a wealthy and lascivious Indian who follows the rubrics of the Kama Sutra and gives advice to his son, telling him with which women he should or should not enter into connection. A stilted, self-conscious piece of work, it perhaps aimed at something of Wyndham Lewis's cold-bloodedness in talking about sex. Another prose venture was to make a volume, in discussion with Yeats, out of 'the high and mountainous parts of old Pop Yeats' letters. Some of which arc quite fine.' These *Passages from the Letters of John Butler Yeats*, published in 1917 by W. B. Yeats's sisters at their Cuala Press, were arranged by Ezra as a series of aphorisms or *pensées*, some of which he probably felt had a bearing on the contemplated 'endless poem'. For example: 'Man never has changed and never will change, the same yesterday, to-day and for ever.' And: 'I am haunted by single lines, plucked here and there by infallible instinct; there is no critic like the memory.' Reviewing it himself in *Poetry*, Ezra wrote: 'I know of no modern book which contains so much good sense about poetry.'

For a brief period it seemed as if W. B. Yeats would draw him into the theatre. 'Yeats thinks he is going to startle the elect with a performance of his own celtic noh [*At the Hawk's Well*] and a farce of mine in a month or so . . . I dare say it will end in a riot of mask makers and musicians.' This was from Stone Cottage to his parents at the end of February 1916. Another letter, written to them at about the same period, says that because *At the Hawk's Well* is so simple to stage, it will help to lessen the 'dominion' of the 'chews' (Jews) in the professional theatre. Ezra's own play was a short farce, which Yeats encouraged him to expand in the hope that the Abbey Theatre in Dublin might perform it, but the management there rejected it as indecent. * A little later in 1916 there was a scheme for

* The play has been unearthed from the Pound Archive at Yale by Donald Gallup, and published in Ezra Pound, *Plays Modelled on the Noh (1916)*, Friends of the University of Toledo Libraries (Toledo, Ohio), 1987. Entitled 'The Protagonist', it is a very short piece set outside an Irish jail; a burly, mysterious prisoner stands silent while all around speculate on what his crimes may have been. There is a great deal of comic stage Irish – passably well done – but no real dénouement. Gallup points out that it is modelled on the Japanese *kyogen* or comic interlude. The other plays in Gallup's edition are another comic Irish piece, in which a womanizer and a virtuous man compare notes about marriage, and a version of the Tristan story, along the lines of *Nishikigi*, in which the characters include a sculptor who resembles Gaudier-Brzeska.

Ezra himself to stand in for the Abbey's manager, but this too was vetoed in Dublin. It was the year of the Easter Rising; Ezra wrote to his parents in late May that Yeats had been 'very much surprised' by the outbreak, and said he had 'found both John Quinn and James Joyce sentenced to five years imprisonment in the same list, however they seem to have been duplicate . . . Waley even heard a rumour that Yeats himself had been shot – but having just seen him in Museum St, was able to contradict it.' Ezra teased Yeats by pretending to believe that he had played a crucial part in the Rising. Yeats's Irish nationalism did not claim his respect, nor was he impressed by Maud Gonne when she appeared in London in 1917. To Quinn he called her 'fanatic' if not actually 'lunatic', and said he regarded the wartime threat to England from Irish treachery as all too real. In 1920 he wrote in the *New Age*: 'There is no topic . . . more soporific and generally boring than the topic of Ireland *as Ireland, as a nation.*' And in his book *Jefferson and/or Mussolini*, written in 1933, he calls Ireland an 'unspeakable and reactionary island'.

Early in 1916 he was still making efforts to have *A Portrait of the Artist as a Young Man* issued as a book. Harriet Shaw Weaver was willing for the *Egoist* itself to act as publisher, but was worried about a repetition of trouble with the printers over censorship. Ezra suggested that if she could find no one to take on the unexpurgated text, 'largish blank spaces' be left where passages had to be cut out. Then the missing portions could be 'manifolded . . . by typewriter on good paper, and if necessary I will paste them in myself . . . And damn the censors.' Such measures proved unnecessary: *A Portrait of the Artist as a Young Man* was published in December 1916 by Huebsch in New York (largely thanks to the efforts of John Quinn) and by The Egoist Ltd in London three months later, using imported American copies. Ezra reviewed it in the *Egoist*, offering it as a cure-all for Ireland: 'If more people had read *The Portrait* [sic] and certain stories in Mr Joyce's *Dubliners* there might have been less recent trouble in Ireland.'

Meanwhile his own work had run into trouble with censors. By May 1916 he had sent Elkin Mathews the typescript of an expanded *Lustra*, the collection he had originally assembled in the autumn of 1913, when it chiefly consisted of 'Contemporania'-style squibs. To these he had now added all the *Cathay* poems, as well as other serious pieces, among them 'Provincia Deserta' and 'Near Périgord'. (The 'Three Cantos' would have been included had not Ezra been waiting for them to appear in *Poetry* first; they were eventually printed in the American edition of *Lustra*.) Though Elkin Mathews had not been enthusiastic about the book when it was first submitted, Ezra did not expect any trouble this time. But when the book was already set up in type Mathews 'got a panic' and (wrote Ezra to Iris Barry) marked 25 poems for deletion. Most of them have already been printed in magazines without causing any scandal whatever, and some of them are among the best in the book . . . The scrape is both serious and ludicrous. Some of the poems will have to go, but in other cases the objections are too stupid for words. It is part printer and part Mathews.

The suppression of D. H. Lawrence's *The Rainbow* the previous year had made printers nervous about possible prosecution for obscenity, but it seems to have been Mathews's own anonymous reader rather than the printer (Clowes) who raised the most vocal objections to *Lustra*. His report is scattered with such comments as 'Sorry stuff . . . An impudent piece . . . silly nonsense . . . Better keep his *baser passions* to himself . . . Smelly like its subject.' He was outraged by this little masterpiece:

> Winter is icummen in,
> Lhude sing Goddamm,
> Raineth drop and staineth slop,
> And how the wind doth ramm!
>   Sing: Goddamm.
> Skiddeth bus and sloppeth us,
> An ague hath my ham.
> Freezeth river, turneth liver,
>   Damn you, sing: Goddamm.
> Goddamm, Goddamm, 'tis why I am, Goddamm,
>   So 'gainst the winter's balm,
> Sing goddamm, damm, sing Goddamm,
> Sing goddamm, sing goddamm, DAMM.

Mathews himself wrote to Ezra that this was 'Blasted blasphemy & a damned parody' and 'must be omitted'. The reader was also upset by what he called a 'Pitiful Parody' of an all-too-well-known Yeats poem:

> THE LAKE ISLE
> O God, O Venus, O Mercury, patron of thieves,
> Give me in due time, I beseech you, a little tobacco-shop,
> With the little bright boxes
>   piled up neatly upon the shelves
> And the loose fragrant cavendish
>   and the shag
> And the bright Virginia
>   loose under the bright glass cases,
> And a pair of scales not too greasy,
> And the whores dropping in for a word or two in passing,
> For a flip word, and to tidy their hair a bit.

O God, O Venus, O Mercury, patron of thieves,
Lend me a little tobacco-shop,
    or install me in any profession
Save this damn'd profession of writing,
    where one needs one's brains all the time.

Yeats himself obviously enjoyed the parody; many years later he wanted to include it in his *Oxford Book of Modern Verse*, and it may not be too fanciful to detect a faint echo of it in one of his own most famous late poems, 'The Circus Animals' Desertion', where the last stanza refers to 'the foul rag-and-bone shop of the heart'.

Most of Elkin Mathews's *Lustra* objections were to Ezra's Catullus-style epigrams (there were several in the collection), which allude in ironical tones to the irregular sexual lives of apparently respectable citizens. For example: 'Erinna is a model parent. / Her children have never discovered her adulteries . . .' and 'Bastidides . . . / Has become the father of twins; / But he accomplished this feat at some cost; / He had to be four times cuckolded.' Mathews judged poems such as this 'very nasty'. He sent Ezra a list of proposed deletions and alterations. Ezra's response to this attitude is typified in a letter to H. L. Mencken a few weeks later: 'Christianity has become a sort of Prussianism, and will have to go. All the bloody moral attacks are based on superstition, religion, or whatever it is to be called.' In an article written this year (1916), he said he made 'no plea for smuttiness, for an unnecessary erotic glamour', but if one could not write 'with the scientist's freedom and privilege' than 'what is the use of anything, *anything*?'

He tried to enlist the help of Yeats in combating Elkin Mathews. Yeats said he did not mind any of the indecencies, but disliked some of the 'violent' poems. Ezra also turned to J. B. Pinker, and to Augustine Birrell, the Liberal MP and cabinet minister, both of whom tried to persuade Mathews that there was no resemblance between *Lustra* and the prose of D. H. Lawrence. Ezra told Mathews that 'four perfectly well-bred women' (he did not identify them) had thought the book acceptable.

Eventually a compromise was reached. The public edition of *Lustra* would be pruned along the lines Mathews suggested – with the consequence, said Ezra, that 'the pretty poems and the Chinese softness' somewhat predominated, and 'debilitated the tone'. In return for what Ezra called the 'tacit hypocrisy' of this, Mathews agreed to order 200 unexpurgated copies from the printer, which he would sell to anyone specifically requesting one – though Clowes refused to print 'in any form whatever' four of the poems. These were 'Winter is iccumen in'; the poem about the cuckolding of Bastidides (apparently because it began 'Nine adulteries, 12 liaisons, 64 fornications / and something approaching a rape /

Rest nightly upon the soul of our delicate friend Florialis'); 'The Lake Isle', because of its reference to 'whores'; and a two-line poem entitled 'Pagani's, November 8':

> Suddenly discovering in the eyes of the very beautiful
> Normande cocotte
> The eyes of the very learned British Museum assistant.

It was therefore the 'castrato' edition of *Lustra*, as Ezra called it, that the London reviewers considered in October 1916. The critics' reaction was summed up by *The Times Literary Supplement*, which, after reminding readers that it had already praised the *Cathay* poems, judged of the rest of the book that Ezra had merely chosen to express 'any chance whim of his own', usually mere snorts of 'indifference and impatience'; Catullus, obviously his model, had done this better. 'Why should he so constantly be ironical about nothing in particular?' asked the reviewer.

There was no repetition of the censorship of *Lustra* in America, where eventually, thanks to the efforts of John Quinn, Alfred A. Knopf agreed to publish the book as it stood, with the sole exception of the Bastidides poem – and even this was included in a private edition distributed by Quinn. The Knopf printing, which did not appear until October 1917, also included a selection of 'Poems Published before 1911' (a reprint of *Ripostes*) and 'Three Cantos', though these were in a different order from the serialization in *Poetry*, the sequence now running II, III, I, an indication that Ezra was already repenting of his candid opening. Babette Deutsch wrote a eulogy of his expanded *Lustra* in *Reedy's Mirror*, but Louis Untermeyer in the *Dial* thought the book 'a confused jumble and smattering of erudition', and G. W. Cronin in *New York Call Magazine* felt Ezra had 'no real joy in anything . . . his sensations are secondary, aesthetic, not . . . primary and direct'.

John Quinn thought the American publication of *Lustra* would attract more notice if it were accompanied by an introduction to Ezra's work. Knopf agreed, providing Quinn subsidized it, and Ezra immediately nominated T. S. Eliot to write a pamphlet about him, though he said Eliot must do it anonymously: 'I want to boom Eliot, and one cant have too obvious a ping-pong match at that sort of thing.' He also thought it might 'bitch' Eliot's chances with the 'elder reviews' and the more 'godly' publishers if he were identified as a promoter of Ezra and *Lustra*. Eliot took his time over the task – one reason that the American *Lustra* appeared a year after the British – but finally delivered the text of *Ezra Pound: his metric and poetry* in September 1917, Ezra himself passing it on to Quinn with the comment that it was sound and unsentimental. He had made a few alterations in it where he thought necessary; indeed, were it not for Eliot's own testimony that he 'wrote it under considerable pressure of time' and the existence of the manuscript (at Harvard), one might suppose Ezra himself to have been the author, so Poundian are many of its cadences – or was this meant by Eliot as a subtle parody?

> Though Mr Pound is well known, even having been the victim of interviews for Sunday papers, it does not follow that his work is thoroughly known. There are twenty people who have their opinion of him for every one who has read his writings with any care ... This essay is not written for the first twenty ... but for the admirer of a poem here or there, whose appreciation is capable of yielding him a larger return. If the reader is already at the stage where he can maintain at once the two propositions, 'Pound is merely a scholar' and 'Pound is merely a yellow journalist' ... there is very little hope. But there are readers of poetry who have not yet reached this hypertrophy of the logical faculty ...

Similarly early in 1917 the *Egoist* ran a series of three articles praising Ezra as a poet and 'a great scholar', written by Jean de Bosschère, a French artist, illustrator and poet living in London. The English translation was probably by the 'great scholar' himself, who described the articles as 'altogether the most lengthy treatment I have had yet from any critic'. Eliot, in an undated note, wrote to Ezra:

> Ezzum Pound, Sir, what I forgot to say was, as well as I can reclect, I don't believe anybody worth noticing learned anything from Bosschère. Not that that's anything against him; it's just a Fact, I was a Green & Bitter Child etc.

18

Mr Atheling And Mr Dias

'I am bubbling at my Jap plays for MacM,' Ezra told Wyndham Lewis. This was *'Noh' or Accomplishment*, a study of Noh drama written up by him from Fenollosa's notes, together with the texts of a number of Noh plays, published by Macmillan in January 1917 and by Knopf in New York six months later. 'Getting placed with MacMillan *here*, is quite a step onward,' Ezra told his mother. 'I dont suppose it will begin to be remunerative for some time, but still it is a sort of Bank of England firm.' Four of the Noh plays, in Fenollosa/Pound translations, were also published by the Cuala Press in Ireland ('Cuala weird sisters, smeary type very HARWtistik press,' said Ezra).

The Macmillan edition attracted a good press. Ezra had learnt a lot about translating Noh since 1913, and the new versions were energetic and colloquial. But later he became aware of the shortcomings of Fenollosa's material as an authoritative introduction to the plays. In 1927 he wrote that it was merely 'scattered fragments left by a dead man, edited by a man ignorant of Japanese. Naturally any sonvbitch who knows a little Nipponese can jump on it.' Even as early as 1916 he was rather impatient with the Noh plays. 'I don't like them so well as the Chinese stuff in *Lustra*,' he wrote to Joyce. And to Quinn: 'It's all too damn soft. Like Pater, Fiona Macleod and James Matthew Barrie, not good enough.' Meanwhile he began to wonder 'if there is a decent translation of Confucius . . . He was certainly a much nicer man than St Paul.'

He began to plan a book on Wyndham Lewis, similar to that on Gaudier-Brzeska but shorter, and also a monograph on early Greek sculpture, which would trace 'the development of forms (Vortistically)' and would direct a good deal of ridicule at the *Encyclopaedia Britannica* article on the subject. He thought of taking as collaborator on this book the popular illustrator and painter Edmund Dulac, a neighbour in Kensington, who had designed the costumes and masks for Yeats's *At the Hawk's Well*. 'Dulac,' Ezra told his mother, 'will probably burst out as THE portrait painter before very long.' And to Quinn: 'Dulac . . . is much more interesting than his published works. I wish to God he would get uncoiled from . . . illustrations in batches of fifty.' But Dulac was earning too much from books to be lured into great art; the projected collaboration on Greek sculpture faded away, and the study of Lewis had to be abandoned because it would cost too much to print the plates.

Ezra's frantic activity on behalf of Lewis and Joyce started to subside into a period of doldrum. No project seemed to lead anywhere. His income, reduced by the wartime slump in book and magazine publication, hit a 'low water mark' in the year ending 30 October 1916 (his thirty-first birthday) during which he grossed, he said, only £48. A few months later he was blaming this on unpopularity – it was 'because I dared to say that Gaudier-Brzeska was a good sculptor and that Wyndham Lewis was a great master of design' – but really he had nothing new to offer editors and publishers. He could never have lived off his literary income (when T. S. Eliot began work with Lloyds Bank in March 1917 he was paid £130 per annum, so Ezra's earnings were well below subsistence level), but Dorothy's money kept them both going, and there was no real anxiety. Nevertheless, Ezra liked to have some income of his own. 'All life's blessings except loose change seem to have been showered upon me,' he told Joyce in September 1916, and said he hoped 'to remedy that deficiency AT ONCE', though he admitted to having written 'nothing of importance for ages'.

Nothing major occupied his mind: his days, he said, were 'dotted with reviews'. Editors would profess themselves 'delighted' and promise more work, but then did 'NOT send it'. The reviewing itself 'amuses me' but was probably not 'of much interest to anyone else'. Much of it consisted, as he admitted, of repeating the same things about his protégés over and over again: 'Joyce is a writer, GODDAMN your eyes. Joyce is a writer, I tell you Joyce etc . . . Lewis can paint, Gaudier knows a stone from a milk-pudding.' Almost the only new idea was that he should translate opera libretti for Sir Thomas Beecham's Opera Company. This immediately brought him 'sponged stalls' at the Aldwych opera season, where he thought Beecham conducted 'very finely' (and judged Wagner 'a bum artist'), and he was paid about 40 guineas by Beecham for translating Massenet's *Cendrillon*. The work was not performed and no further commissions were forthcoming.

Even when good ideas came his way, he could kill them off with a characteristic display. During 1916 he offered another project to Macmillan, a ten-volume anthology of world poetry, for which he composed a thoroughly impressive scenario in the office of the literary agent A. P. Watt. Unfortunately he included in it the statement 'It is time we had something to replace that doddard Palgrave.' As the Macmillan fortunes were founded on the success of Palgrave's *Golden Treasury*, they turned down the proposal. Ezra responded by regarding it as a plot. He told John Quinn: 'Macmillan affair very much as I should have expected'; an 'anonymous blackmailer' in the firm had 'warned them that I was myself', and one could recognize the signs of 'hatred and terror'. In 1936 he was still muttering about 'that stinking sugar teat Palgrave'. Eventually he began to hint that Macmillan's rejection had marked the start of a conspiracy among British publishers to exclude his work. 'From that day onward,' he wrote in the late 1920s, 'no book of mine received a British imprimatur . . .' The truth was that for many years he offered nothing further of consequence to any established British publishing house.

'I have absolutely no connections in England that are any use,' he told Joyce in January 1916. There is no editor whom I wouldn't cheerfully fry in oil and none who wouldn't as cheerfully do the same by me.' This was nonsense. A. R. Orage of the *New Age* and Harriet Shaw Weaver of the *Egoist* stood loyally by him, and even more august doors were sometimes opened to him. In the autumn of 1916 Bruce Richmond, editor of *The Times Literary Supplement*, commissioned him to review a book attacking America's isolationism in the First World War; it was published in the issue of 19 October. 'Had my first article in the "Times" (Literary Supplement) this a.m.,' wrote Ezra to his father with obvious pride. 'It would be considerable help if they should decide to give me any sort of regular allotment.' It was a good article, lively and coherent, but Richmond did not repeat the invitation.

Despite the lack of remunerative work and his increasing feelings of hostility towards publishers and editors, Ezra did not yet contemplate leaving London. 'It seems very difficult to get it into your head,' he wrote to his mother in November 1916, 'that I earn my living, or such living as I do earn, by being in London. AND that to go to America would be to lose all I have gained or at least set me back two or three years . . . Add to it the fact that I loathe the American state of mind . . . Europe at present is much too interesting to leave.'

*

He continued to negotiate for control of a magazine. After a while he and John Quinn conceived the idea of taking over a section of an existing American periodical, the *Little Review*. Early in 1917 Ezra wrote to its co-editor Margaret Anderson: 'I want a place where I and T. S. Eliot can appear once a month . . . and where Joyce can appear when he likes, and where Wyndham Lewis can appear if he comes back from the war . . .

I must have a steady place for my best stuff (apart from original poetry, which must go to *Poetry* . . .).'

The *Little Review* had been founded in Chicago in 1914 by Margaret Anderson, then only twenty-one but already an experienced literary editor and reviewer. Though run on a shoestring, it soon began to attract most of the leading modern American writers and poets. In 1916 Anderson was joined by the equally resourceful Jane Heap (or 'Jh' as she signed herself in print). Anderson had corresponded with Ezra since the magazine's early days, and when the idea came up that the *Little Review* should employ him as 'foreign editor', she and Heap hailed it enthusiastically. Ezra approved of what the magazine had done so far, but was a little condescending; he described it to Harriet Monroe as 'a jolly place for people who aren't quite up to our level'. He greatly liked the editors' decision to leave half the pages of one issue completely blank because they had not found enough good contributions, but he wanted to be sure that they were serious characters and not just a couple of would-be Bohemians. Quinn thought them unbusinesslike, but admitted that he found Anderson 'a damned attractive young woman' (he was a rather bottled-up bachelor). He agreed to give Ezra $750 a year for two years to finance his part of the magazine, $300 to be kept in return for editorial duties, the remainder to be used for paying contributors.

Ezra intended his work for the *Little Review* to be part of a two-pronged operation. With Aldington now away at war, he would secure for Eliot the assistant editorship of the *Egoist*, and would print Joyce's work in both magazines at once, distributing other items as he thought fit. Harriet Shaw Weaver duly agreed to employ Eliot at £9 per quarter (partly backed by Ezra, using Quinn's money, though Eliot did not know this), in such time as Eliot could spare from his job at Lloyds Bank.

Ezra's arrival at the *Little Review* was announced in the issue for May 1917, where he explained to readers that he had 'accepted the post of Foreign Editor' chiefly because he wanted

> a place where the current prose writings of James Joyce, Wyndham Lewis, T. S. Eliot, and myself might appear regularly, promptly, and together, rather than irregularly, sporadically, and after useless delays.
>
> My connection with the *Little Review* does not imply a severance of my relations with *Poetry* . . . But [*Poetry*] has never been 'the instrument' of my 'radicalism'. I respect Miss Monroe . . . but in the conduct of her magazine my voice and vote have always been the vote and voice of a minority . . . *Poetry* has shown an unflagging courtesy to a lot of old fools and fogies whom I should have told to go to hell tout pleinement and bonnement.

There followed Eliot's first contribution to the *Little Review*, 'Eeldrop and Appleplex', a prose fable about two personages bearing faint resemblance to Eliot and Ezra. They rent 'two small rooms in a disreputable part of town', one of the 'evil neighbourhoods of silence', where each pursues 'his own line of enquiry', Appleplex questioning the 'lower classes of both sexes' closely about their lives, while Eeldrop preserves 'a more passive demeanor' and eavesdrops – as his name suggests – on 'the conversation of the people among themselves'. This rather arid little joke was followed by Ezra's short story 'Jodindranath Mawhwor's Occupation', and six 'Imaginary Letters' of 'William Bland Burn to his Wife' by Wyndham Lewis – the beginning of a series of aphorisms in epistolary form, in which, in later issues, Ezra also participated. The next *Little Review*, in June 1917, included Yeats's 'The Wild Swans at Coole' and six other of his poems while the July issue had poems by Eliot. Other contributions marshalled by Ezra during his early months with the magazine were plays by Lady Gregory and Arthur Symons, a prose piece by William Carlos Williams, and translations from Chinese by the man whom Ezra was now describing to Lewis as 'the corpse-like Waley'.

Ezra complacently told Lewis that this standard of material 'ought to announce to the desert places that the magazine is reel, refined litterchure'. Yet there was a rather incestuous, claustrophobic air about the operation. Such pieces as 'Eeldrop and Appleplex' and the 'Imaginary Letters' seemed to address a very select circle (chiefly composed of their own authors), and there was nothing in prose remotely comparable to the serialization of *A Portrait of the Artist as a Young Man* in the *Egoist*. After only a couple of months, Margaret Anderson and Jane Heap began to receive readers' letters protesting about the influence of Ezra and his gang. One correspondent claimed that since he had arrived, the magazine had been 'filled with pointless eccentricities and gargoyles – with once in a while a very beautiful thing in it'.

Part of the trouble was that Ezra was not discovering new writers for the *Little Review* as he had for *Poetry* – a rare exception being Marianne Moore, whose work he would have printed had he not run out of money. To his father in January 1919 he described her as 'almost unintelligible, lesser Eliot', and he was saying much the same fifteen years later: 'DAMN hard to read, especially in the first time; but if the reader CAN get thru it, the registration is, I believe, rather more accurate than that in the current magzzeenz.' He wrote to Miss Moore in December 1918: 'Your stuff holds my eye. Most verse I merely slide off of.' Thanks to his efforts, her first book, *Poems* (1921), was published by the 'Egoist Press'.

The October 1917 issue of the *Little Review* was suppressed by the United States Post Office, because it included Wyndham Lewis's short story 'Cantleman's Spring Mate', in which a soldier (closely resembling

Lewis) seduces a country girl before setting off for the trenches. Margaret Anderson expressed no regrets about publishing it, and in the March 1918 issue Ezra ridiculed the opinion, given by the judge who had ordered the suppression, that while indecency can be allowed in the classics as they have few readers, modern fiction might be read by the undiscriminating and thus cause corruption. Ezra's reply took the form of the poem 'Cantico del Sole', which repeats the words

> The thought of what America would be like
> If the Classics had a wide circulation
>   Troubles my sleep.

Harriet Monroe commented rather icily in *Poetry* that the *Little Review* was now 'under the dictatorship of Ezra Pound', and privately she complained bitterly to him that he had sent Margaret Anderson poems by Yeats which ought to have gone to *Poetry*. Ezra replied that he would sell verse to whoever paid the best and could get it into print the fastest.

*

Eliot had now written enough poems of which Ezra approved to fill a small book. Ezra went to Elkin Mathews and discussed publication, but their relations had been poor since the row over the censorship of *Lustra*, and Mathews muttered about cost and risk, and demanded an advance payment. Ezra decided to publish the book himself, telling Harriet Shaw Weaver that if the *Egoist* would lend its imprint he would raise the money. She agreed, and Quinn offered a financial guarantee, but Ezra thought this unnecessary. Eliot did not know that Ezra was the backer (Dorothy had agreed to provide funds), though in fact all that proved necessary was a loan to the *Egoist* of £5 towards expenses, later repaid.

Prufrock and Other Observations, a forty-page booklet in pale yellow cardboard covers, was published by 'The Egoist Ltd' in June 1917, 500 copies being priced at 1s each. It sold very slowly and received a terse and unenthusiastic response from most reviewers, although Ezra himself did everything in his power to promote it. His first review of it was in the *Egoist* during the month of publication:

> Mr Eliot has made an advance on Browning. He has also made his dramatis personae contemporary and convincing. He has been an individual in his poems. I have read the contents of this book over and over, and with continued joy in the freshness, the humanity, the deep quiet culture . . . Mr Eliot at once takes rank with the five or six living poets whose English one can read with enjoyment . . . The *Egoist* has published the best prose writer of my generation. It follows the publication of Joyce by

the publication of a 'new' poet who is at least unsurpassed by
any of his contemporaries, either of his own age or his
elders . . .

This read more like a publisher's blurb than a review, but Ezra tackled
Prufrock more seriously and at greater length in *Poetry* (August 1917),
commending Eliot's completeness at depicting 'our contemporary condition', hinting at the presence of 'two sorts of metaphor: his wholly
unrealizable, always apt, half ironic suggestion, and his precise realizable
picture', and speaking of the 'personal rhythm' of Eliot's free verse as 'an
identifiable quality of sound as well as of style'. He concluded that the
book was 'the best thing in poetry since — (for the sake of peace I will
leave that date to the imagination)'.

It was a generous review, but it left the faint impression that he still did
not understand or enjoy Eliot's poetry. He said nothing about individual
poems, and anyone not already familiar with Eliot's work would scarcely
have gained any idea of its nature from the review.

*

America's entry into the First World War in the spring of 1917 pleased
Ezra – he ascribed it to the effect of Wyndham Lewis's pictures on New
York – and he wrote to John Quinn to see if he could 'get me a war job', as
the American Embassy in London said it had 'no instructions' for making
use of expatriates. He suggested to Quinn that he might be of use in
France, where 'my profession will not be against me, with the French, nor
even my appearance'. Nothing resulted; by mid-July 1917 Ezra claimed to
have been told that 'those employed by our government will be selected
from the inhabitants of Missouri and on the basis of complete ignorance of
all Europe'. He thought it ironical that two of his male cousins should be
able to join the army, while 'I who care something for civilization should
be left at my typewriter', though he agreed that 'an intelligent government
would of course preserve people like Lewis and myself'.

Despite his new outlet in the *Little Review*, he continued to drift. He
wrote a series of articles for the *New Age* entitled 'Studies of Contemporary Mentality', which he described accurately to Lewis as 'entertaining . . . unimportant'. They consisted of contemptuous and often vitriolic
observations on current British journals and magazines, based not on any
very close study but simply on his assumptions about their stupidity. For
example: 'Never till now . . . have I read a copy of *Blackwood's*, never has
my eye performed the Gargantuan feat of penetrating its double-columns',
after which he goes on to cull random examples of what he considers its
fatuities. Even the *Spectator*, whose 'mentality' he had often abused before,
was not, it appeared, very well known to him: 'Save that it has given me

one, or perhaps it is two, favourable reviews, I know absolutely nothing about it.' Many years later he said that the series had been 'a *sottisier*, trying to make a few people see why the printed matter on sale in [London] . . . would finally kill off the inhabitants', but he admitted that it did 'NOT arouse interest'.

His next contributions to the *New Age* were more remarkable. During November 1917 he began to write art criticism for the paper under the name 'B. H. Dias', and a month later opened a series of music reviews as 'William Atheling'. He told his father: 'Am doing art and music critiques under pseudonyms, paying the rent. rather entertaining work. NOT to be *mentioned*. It may be I have at last found a moderately easy way to earn my daily. Bloody queer what a man will do for money. MUSIC!!!!'

A. R. Orage, who was short of regular contributors because of the war, had engaged him to work under these pseudonyms, as well as continuing to accept a weekly column from him on literary topics. This meant that Ezra now earned 4 guineas a month from the *New Age*. He afterwards described this as 'the SINEWS' of his income during this period. He explained that he used the pseudonyms partly because 'no one writer should publicly appear to know about everything', and because his own name would lead to suspicions (in the art criticisms) of 'Vorticist Propaganda'. But there was more than convenience in the ruse. For the first time he was creating personae which had almost a fleshly existence.

He described 'William Atheling', the music critic, as 'more a secondary personality than a nom de plume, that is to say he had a definite appearance (baldheaded) and a definite script (crabbed with an old fashioned slant)'. Similarly he once wrote to the *New Age* under his own name to complain about the 'B. H. Dias' art column, then made Dias reply to Pound.

Mr Atheling made his bow on 6 December 1917, introducing himself to readers as 'a musician . . . one who has for long watched the opera with a sort of despairing hope'. In this first review he praised Beecham's production of *Figaro*. On his next appearance he admitted that there had been a 'ten years' lapse' in his regular concert-going (Ezra had sometimes attended recitals in Philadelphia as a young man), and said he approached the London concert scene with a 'mixture of curiosity and trepidation'. He then held forth, while reviewing a piano recital, on his theory that every piece of music has only one correct tempo, 'the time for sound, the real rhythm' – an idea Ezra derived from his quantitative experiments in poetry – but then somewhat spoilt the solemnity of this harangue by remarking that 'the piano . . . depends for its effects so much on the sound of a lot of notes stuck together'.

It soon appeared that Mr Atheling was not possessed of a standard musical terminology. He sometimes resorted to curious expressions, referring to a Frank Bridge composition as 'a sort of pee-wee-pee-wee sound, with a hang and drag in it', telling readers that César Franck 'believed that if you could only keep up some sort of bim-bim-bim-ation long enough you would end by exciting the auditor', and remarking that Brahms 'suggests a back parlour with heavy curtains, probably puce-coloured'. The Kreutzer Sonata included (according to Atheling) a passage where 'the piano jabs in, and jerks on the violin, tum, tum, ti, ump, tum tump, ti ump . . . It is the great fight of solar plexus versus ear'; and he said he regarded Beethoven as of interest chiefly because of his deafness, a 'symbol of the suffering or decadence of the European ear, and the general triumph of loudness'.

It also seemed that Atheling did not care for orchestral concerts, but spent most of his time at the small recital halls – probably because free press tickets were more readily available there – and sometimes attended private musical soirées. Atheling's *alter ego* complained later that he had had to put up with 'an unending series of rag-bag programs' at such places, but he could have made more effort to hear performances by high-calibre international singers and instrumentalists. Not that details of actual performance meant much to him, since by his own admission he was almost tone deaf. However, he was not above telling performers how to do it. A contemporary remembers how at concerts he would cough critically with 'a frightfully sharp cough', and could be found during the interval 'explaining expansively . . . how the compositions should have been performed by blocking the air vigorously with his arms and hands'.

He took almost no interest in modern music. Schoenberg, Ravel and Bartók could be heard in London at this period, but they did not feature in his column, and though after listening to Stravinsky's *Three Pieces for String Quartet* he judged him 'a composer of the first order', he said this with little conviction and seemed to be deterred by Stravinsky's modernism. He remarked of one of the pieces that 'it might . . . stop at various places where it does not', and so doubted whether 'its structure is very good'. In 1924 he remarked that Stravinsky had 'arrived as a comfort, but one could not say definitely that his composition was the new music; he had a refreshing robustness; he was a relief from Debussy; but this might have been merely the heritage of polish [*sic*] folk music manifest in the work of an instinctive genius . . . Stravinsky's merit lies very largely in taking hard bits of rhythm, and noting them with great care.'

Despite 'Atheling's' limitations and idiosyncrasies – indeed, because of them – these studies of 'musicians on the hoof' (as Ezra called them some years later) are vigorous and often very funny, refreshingly without the flag-waving and floor-thumping of his literary articles of the time. His 'B. H. Dias' Art Notes for the *New Age* had a more conventional character. Ezra had already gained some experience in writing about painting and sculpture. But there are still many passages which no professional art critic would have dared to write.

For example, 'Dias' says of the Serbo-Croatian sculptor Mestrovic: 'His pièce-de-résistance is a crucifix . . . The crucifix at best is a displeasing and eminently (and, I dare say, intentionally) unaesthetic object. As a fetich it lacks notably the energy, the horrific energy, of African and Mexican fetiches . . . Mestrovic's crucifix . . . in a reproduction . . . made me slightly ill. I had a definite qualm in the stomach. Any sheep in a butcher's-shop might have so yawed at the mouth.' Mr Dias possessed all Ezra's usual qualities, suggesting, for example, that exhibitors at the Pastel Society showed signs of 'decay . . . mortality and corruption', and 'the sooner the process completes itself the better for all concerned'.

Despite a great deal of literary journalism, Ezra had never yet done any regular reviewing of new books. This was remedied between April 1918 and June 1919, when he contributed a 'Books Current' series to the monthly magazine *Future*. He was allowed to select his own titles, and among these he reviewed Lytton Strachey's *Eminent Victorians* (about which he was very enthusiastic); he also picked deliberately on writers he disliked – for example: 'The protuberance of Mr L. Housman into the world of printed books has always seemed to me one of those actualities which we may deplore, but can not ameliorate.' Despite this regular column, he did not begin to develop into a 'critic' as such (as contrasted with Eliot), and had no wish to. 'I consider criticism merely a preliminary excitement,' he once wrote, 'a statement of things a writer has to clear up in his own head sometime or other, probably antecedent to writing; of no value unless it come to fruit in the created work later.'

The music, art, and 'Books Current' reviews kept him working at top speed. 'Really !!!! when the hell am I supposed to write letters – eat – sleep – etc.' he asked his parents, and he said he shuddered to think of 'the number of words I have slapped thru this machine during the past two weeks'. But none of it was leading to 'the loftiest literature', and he admitted to his father that a typical article turned out during this period was 'written AT LENGTH to fill space, only you neednt say that'.

In the summer of 1918, in order to cope with this workload he took on 'a typist three days a week so that I shall have less mechanical waste of time. & can use my lofty intelligence for more intelligent matters than swatting a Corona'. This was Iseult, daughter of Yeats's beloved Maud Gonne. Maud was in prison for breaking a ban on re-entering Ireland, and the twenty-three-old Iseult was in London trying to make a life for herself. Though Ezra had no sympathy with the Gonne politics, he was greatly attracted to Iseult. He told Yeats that he did not altogether like to refer to her as his secretary – 'my poems are much too ithyphallic for any secretary of her years to be officially in my possession' – and said he could not afford to pay her more than £5 a month. His concern that the association with Iseult might cause scandal seems to have been justified. According to one of Maud Gonne's biographers, some years after Iseult had married she confessed to her husband that 'her relationship with Ezra Pound had been more than friendly', though another biographer says that there were only 'rumours' of an affair. *

* Francis Stuart, Iseult's husband, remains convinced that an affair with Ezra did take place, and that it was Iseult's first sexual experience. He alludes to it in his book *Black List, Section H* (Penguin edition, 1982, pp. 26-7): 'Iseult told him that while alone in Yeats's house [in London] ... she had become the mistress of the poet Ezra Pound.' (Information from Geoffrey Elborn.)

19

Obscene, As Life

Ezra's first attempts to persuade Joyce to contribute to the *Little Review* were not successful. Joyce's eyes were giving him trouble, and in any case (as he told Ezra) he felt unsuited to 'magazine' demands: 'I am quite sure that, with your usual friendliness, you exaggerate the value of my poor signature as a "draw",' he wrote in April 1917. 'I have very little imagination. I am also a very bad critic. For instance, some time ago a person gave me a two-volume novel to read . . . I read it at intervals for some time, till I discovered that I had been reading the second volume instead of the first. And if I am a bad reader, I am a most tiresome writer – to myself, at least. It exhausts me before I end it. I wonder if you will like the book I am writing? . . . Strange to say, in spite of my illness I have written enough lately.'

Ulysses had been begun in Trieste not long after Ezra had 'discovered' Joyce, though its conception had occurred ten years earlier. The first Ezra seems to have heard of its title was in a letter from Joyce's wife Nora at the beginning of September 1917. On the tenth of that month he replied to her: 'the Egoist is going to serialize Ulysses, that much you can tell James.' The *Little Review* would 'print to synchronize with Egoist', for which he could promise at least '£25 extra'. This he expected to be able to double; indeed he thought that Joyce could probably make '£100 altogether' out of serial rights to the book, 'or as much of it as printers will print' – for although he had seen nothing of the text he naturally anticipated the same sort of difficulties as had occurred with *A Portrait of the Artist as a Young Man*.

On 19 December 1917 he wrote again to Joyce, acknowledging the receipt of 'Pages 1–17' of *Ulysses*, praising it both seriously (he said most of it was too good for him to 'prattle into criticism') and also in a comic voice: 'Wall, Mr Joice, I recon your a damn fine writer, that's what I recon'. And

I recon' this here work o' yourn is some concarn'd litterchure. You can take it from me, an' I'm a jedge.'

This cracker-barrel persona soon became familiar in his correspondence. It was derived partly from childhood memories of Wyncote characters, partly from such figures in popular American literature as Artemus Ward, a backwoodsman turned itinerant showman, whose *Sayings* (written by Charles F. Browne in the mid-nineteenth century) are full of comic misspellings, and the Irish-American saloon keeper, Mr Dooley, in the books of F. P. Dunne, who speaks rather like this. Few people, though, found Ezra's adoption of the character very funny – Wyndham Lewis writes that it 'can never have illumined anything but the most half-hearted smile (however kindly)'. Ezra used it more and more in his middle years, and took the performance seriously. When giving instructions about the transcription of his letters, he said that while there was 'no need to preserve ALL the simple errors of typing', such words as 'Waal' (for 'Well') SHOULD read Waal (not wall) even with three aaa to give the varnakular'.

His use of this voice to Joyce on receiving the beginning of *Ulysses* seems to betray a certain unease. In *Guide to Kulchur* he recalls his 'joyous satisfaction' as the first chapters 'rolled' into Holland Place Chambers, but he immediately goes on to speak of the book, as he had of 'Prufrock', as if it were satire. He says he felt from his first reading that 'the diagnosis and cure' of society's evils were in the book; that it seemed to him that 'the sticky, molasses-covered filth of current print, all the fuggs, all the foetors, the whole boil of the European mind, had been lanced'. With this one may contrast Yeats's reaction when he began to read the complete *Ulysses* in 1922. He wrote to Ezra: 'I read a few pages of Ulysses at a time as if he [*sic*] were a poem. Some passages have great beauty, lyric beauty, even in the fashion of my generation, and the whole book incites to philosophy.' Each found in it what he brought to it.

Ezra's overriding feeling was that *Ulysses* was 'obscene, as life itself is obscene', and thus was 'an impassioned meditation on life'. This sophistry did not disguise that he found Bloom, with his lavatorial and sexual musings, quite unpalatable. The most he could say to Joyce was that 'Bloom is a great man' who had proved that, despite readers' fears, Joyce was capable of creating a 'second character' alongside Stephen Dedalus. But to make Bloom acceptable to his own fastidious tastes, he had to regard him as a satirical creation into whom Joyce had put his supposed disgust of humanity, rather than (as is really the case) a celebration of human frailties, intended to engage the reader's sympathy and affection. '*Ulysses* is a summary of pre-war Europe,' wrote Ezra in 1933, 'the blackness and mess and muddle of a "civilization" led by disguised forces and a bought press, the general sloppiness, the plight of the individual intelligence in that mess! Bloom very much *is* the mess.'

The earliest pages, where Buck Mulligan uses such epithets as 'snotgreen' and 'scrotumtightening', confirmed his expectations that Joyce would once again lead the *Egoist* into trouble. 'I suppose we'll be damn well suppressed if we print the text as it stands,' he told Joyce. 'BUT it is damn wellworth it.' And he told H. L. Mencken that 'Joyce's new novel has a corking 1st Chap. (which will get us suppressed).' Sure enough the *Egoist* printer refused to set the very first episode of the book, and Harriet Shaw Weaver decided that serialization was impossible. She managed to print only small selections from the text during 1919. However, Margaret Anderson and Jane Heap engaged a Serbo-Croat printer who understood scarcely any English, and the first instalment of the novel appeared in the *Little Review* in March 1918.

Ezra wrote to Joyce that he did not mind the prospect of suppression if everything was as good as the first chapter – 'Its worth it'. But he told Mencken that the second section for serialization (Stephen Dedalus at the boys' school) was not so good, and to Joyce himself he raised objections to the fourth, which introduced Bloom and described him 'easing' himself on the 'jakes' at the bottom of his garden:

> Section 4. has excellent things in it; but you overdo the matter. Leave the stool to Geo. Robey. He has been doing 'down where the asparagus grows' for some time. *
>
> I think certain things simply bad writing, in this section . . . The contrast between Blooms interior poetry and his outward surroundings is excellent, but it will come up without such detailed treatment of the dropping feces . . .
>
> I'm not even sure 'urine' is necessary in the opening pages.†
> The idea could be conveyed just as definitely.

He supposed that eventually an unexpurgated text might be published ('in a greek or bulgarian translation'), but at present there was 'risk enough' without such details of bodily processes. If the *Little Review* were suppressed too often the closure might be final, 'to the damn'd stoppage of all our stipends'. Nor was he prepared to contemplate the jailing of Margaret Anderson 'for a passage which I do not think written with utter maestria'.

Joyce must have felt that if Ezra did not care for this passage – very mild by the standard of much that was to come – he would be out of tune with the entire enterprise. No reply from him survives. Meanwhile, without waiting for Joyce's reaction (for time was short), Ezra deleted about

* The music hall comedian George Robey sang a song about an outdoor privy.

† 'Mr Leopold Bloom . . . liked grilled mutton kidneys which gave to his palate a fine tang of faintly scented urine.'

twenty lines from the text before sending it off to Margaret Anderson, removing all reference to Bloom entering the privy, let alone defecating. He told Quinn he had cut some lines, but said nothing about it to Joyce. However, Joyce noticed the cuts when he received the printed text, and wrote to Harriet Shaw Weaver (who was still hoping to print the book) saying that he could not countenance this kind of alteration.

The matter was never discussed between Ezra and Joyce (who may not have been aware that Ezra himself was the censor), but in a letter to Joyce of July 1918 Ezra compared his own form of 'indecency' to Joyce's: 'I am much milder and far less indecent – au moins – je suis peut etre un peu plus phallique, mais mi interessent moins les excremens et les feces humains et des bestiaux . . .' (The adoption of French suggests embarrassment at the whole topic.) Actually the opposite was true: Ezra inclined strongly towards excremental imagery. His Hell Cantos, written about four years later, condemn their victims not to an inferno but to a stinking mire of human faeces, and give the impression that he was much more genuinely obsessed with excretion than was Joyce, who alludes to Bloom's morning defecation quite lightheartedly, making it one of the more pleasant moments of Bloomsday. Ezra may have liked to think of himself as 'phallic', but there was little in his work (especially before 1918) to justify the epithet. Of the two, as Molly Bloom's soliloquy in *Ulysses* demonstrates, Joyce was the writer more deeply drawn to sexuality.

Though his reactions to the first chapters of *Ulysses* were mixed, Ezra was prompted by reading them to reconsider his own 'endless poem', which had lain neglected for about two years. However, he felt unable to write any new cantos before he had made up his mind about the form of the opening. In the American printing of *Lustra* he had altered the order of the 'Three Cantos', and now, in February, March and April 1918, he published a new and drastically reduced version of them in *Future*. The first section, headed 'Passages from the Opening Address in a Long Poem', consisted of excerpts from the first of the 'Three Cantos', beginning 'Ghosts move about me patched with histories'. Then came other fragments, ending with the Nekyia passage from Andreas Divus, shorn of almost all preliminary matter. In this truncated condition the 'Three Cantos' convey much less to the reader than in their original version. Yet Ezra had discarded his self-conscious musings about method and purpose and, if the result was far less attractive as poetry, it did suggest an increased confidence that the enterprise was viable.

*

He still seemed to be drifting. In June 1918 Knopf in New York published *Pavannes and Divisions*, a collection of mostly prose pieces reprinted from journals to which he had contributed in recent years. There was no British edition, and Knopf was only willing to issue the book because Quinn had provided $150 backing. It was not an attractive volume, including such oddments as 'Jodindranath Mawhwor's Occupation', a dreary series of articles from the *New Age* on 'Elizabethan Classicists', and the failed Byronic experiment 'L'Homme Moyen Sensuel'. Eliot reviewed it tactfully in the *Egoist* ('Whether we agree or not with his opinions, we may be always sure that . . . he is not to be diverted . . . from the essential literary problem'); but Louis Untermeyer in *New Republic* called it 'a carefully enshrined series of trivialities', Conrad Aiken in the *Dial* said that its outstanding feature was 'dullness', and Emanuel Carnevali in *Poetry* thought it 'a sequence of false steps made by its author in his effort to gain a recognition that he misses and longs for'.

If Ezra read the Untermeyer and Aiken reviews, he must have found them the more stinging, since they were by men up to now reasonably enthusiastic about his work and aims, who felt he had gone into a decline. Untermeyer looked back to *Provença* (the American edition of Ezra's early poems) and recalled it as 'a highly personal and distinctive collection'; he felt Ezra had descended from that height into 'querulous dogmatizing'. Aiken recalled *Cathay* with affection, and spoke of Ezra's talent in the past for 'finding the latest procession and leading it attired in the most dazzling of colours'; all the worse, he felt, that he had now declined into a noisy and indifferent literary journalist. (H. L. Mencken wrote approvingly to Untermeyer: 'Your piece on Pound is capital. I have a feeling you are right about him.')

Although *Pavannes and Divisions* certainly indicated his limitations as a critic, soon after its appearance he published his first sustained critical examination of one writer, which was much better than anything in the book. 'Have at last finished my long scrawl on James,' he told his mother at the end of June 1918, 'and sent off same. Feeling the weight off my boozom.' This was an extended commentary on Henry James for the August 1918 number of the *Little Review*, which was to be devoted to James's work (the novelist had died in 1916). Ezra called his James study a 'Baedeker to a continent', and it gave him a new sense of direction.

'When he isn't being a great and magnificent author,' Ezra wrote to Quinn while he was at work on the study of James, 'he certainly can be a very fussy and tiresome one. I think the main function of my essay is to get the really good stuff disentangled from the inferior.' He saw James in terms of his own character, as a 'hater of tyranny' who wrote against 'oppression' and supported 'the rights of the individual against all sorts of intangible bondage'. Since Ezra was not capable of a sustained critical argument, the essay sprawled over some 20,000 words, tackling the books one by one in an 'ideogramic' rather than a connected manner. Yet it was full of vigorous, spontaneous judgements.

What especially attracted him about James's style was precisely that discursiveness in the later writings which alienates so many readers. He wrote admiringly of James's 'atmospheres, nuances, impressions of personal tone and quality', and argued that these, rather than the narrative, were really the 'subject' of the books: 'In these he gets certain things that almost no one else had done before him'. When he resumed work on the Cantos a year or so later, he tried to find some comparable technique himself.

But enterprises like the James assessment did not attract him for long. He told Margaret Anderson he did not 'want to sink wholly into criticism to the utter stoppage of creation', and at the beginning of January 1918, he informed Harriet Monroe that he had 'nearly finished completely rewriting' the translations of Arnaut Daniel that he had originally made in 1912. The new versions were sent off to a private press in Ohio, but never arrived, thanks either to wartime censorship or the sinking of a boat. Some were eventually published in Ezra's *Instigations* (1920). Though they paid a good deal of attention to rhythm, and communicated a certain easy delight in love –

> . . . for with no food or slender
> Ration, I'd have joy's profusion
> To hold her kissed . . .
>
> Arnaut hers from foot to face is . . .

– they were still predominantly archaic, full of such forms as 'drinketh' and 'becometh', and they failed to bring Arnaut alive for a modern reader in the way that Li T'ai Po had been brilliantly revitalized in *Cathay*.

Ezra made translations from other Provençal poets, and sent them to Harriet Monroe in January 1918 under the title 'Langue d'Oc'. Written in the same archaic style as the Arnaut versions, they attempted to catch the troubadours' amused delight in adulterous love. He delivered them to *Poetry* along with a second short sequence, 'Moeurs Contemporaines', which he told Harriet Monroe should accompany the Provençal pieces. The 'moeurs' were a set of dry little character sketches in a restrained version of the *Lustra* epigram style, laced with Henry James. Among them, as Ezra mentioned to Joyce, was a brief sketch of James himself:

> They will come no more,
> The old men with beautiful manners . . .
>
> And he said:
>   'Oh! Abelard!' as if the topic
> Were much too abstruse for his comprehension . . .

Ezra had written of James that his 'drawing of *moeurs contemporaines* was so circumstantial, so concerned with the setting, with detail, nuance, social aroma'. (The actual French phrase came from Remy de Gourmont, who said that Flaubert's subject was 'les moeurs de ses contemporains'.)

Harriet Monroe would not print either 'Langue d'Oc' or 'Moeurs Contemporaines' because of their innuendoes about sexual *mores*. In consequence Ezra handed both sequences over to Margaret Anderson, and they appeared in the *Little Review* in May 1918. With hindsight, each can be seen as a step towards his next two major poems. 'Moeurs Contemporaines' anticipates some of the method and matter of *Hugh Selwyn Mauberley*, while 'Langue d'Oc' was a first sketch for a major work that he completed in the autumn of 1918. 'Also done a new *oeuvre* on Propertius,' he told his father on 3 November of that year. 'Have sent it to that imbecile Harriet . . . She will probably die in spasms.'

20

Devirginated Young Ladies

The idea of putting Sextus Propertius into modern English grew from Ezra's 'KOMPLEAT KULTURE' programme that he had drawn up for the education of Iris Barry in 1916. In the 'Latin' section of his curriculum he told Iris: 'Catullus, Propertius, Horace and Ovid are the people who matter. Catullus most . . . Propertius for beautiful cadence though he uses only one metre.' And in another letter: 'If you CAN'T find *any* decent translations of Catullus and Propertius, I suppose I shall have to rig up something.'

Propertius lived in the first century BC and wrote four books of elegiacs, of which the principal subject is his infatuation for his mistress, Cynthia. He describes this in terms of feverish passion, humiliation and anxiety. Ezra could discover no satisfactory English translation, and remarked to his father that the Victorian classicist J. W. Mackail, whose *Latin Litera-ture* he often used, had been 'a complete ASS, seen no irony in Propertius, read him entirely through Burne-Jones, Vita Nuova, Victorian slosh and Xtn sentimentality'. He suspected that most readers gained little from Propertius save a 'charming cadence' or two, and had not 'observed him twisting the tails of official versifiers, Horace and Virgil, Augustus living split of [Woodrow] Wilson'. He saw Propertius as very much a rebellious artist like himself, 'really up against things very much as one is now', and he set out to resuscitate this true Propertius for modern readers, hoping he could 'give as much Rome as *Cathay* gave China'.

His *Homage to Sextus Propertius* was based on selected passages from the second and third books of Propertius' *Elegies* (Loeb numbering). The first book of the original (not translated by Ezra) describes the beginning of Propertius's liaison with Cynthia. After its publication Propertius became acquainted with Maecenas, literary patron and powerful political figure, who asked him to write fewer love poems and turn to political and military matters. But Propertius went on writing what he wanted. Ezra therefore saw him as 'the spirit of the young man of the Augustan Age, hating rhetoric and undeceived by imperial hog-wash' – exactly his view of himself in relation to 'imperial' Britain and America. 'I have perhaps overemphasized the correspondence between Augustan Rome and the present,' he wrote when *Homage to Sextus Propertius* was finished, 'but there is still a great deal unchanged.'

He did not translate the elegies in the order of the originals, and indeed left out the greater part of them altogether, presenting the reader with a series of rearranged excerpts on a scheme which is in no respect Propertius' own. He described *Homage to Sextus Propertius* as 'a rendering in contemporary speech of certain passages in Books II and III', and justified his general adoption of colloquialism (far more marked than in *Cathay*) with the claim that Propertius 'is colloquial in the sense that his elegant elegiacs run in simple and normal order of words, by contrast to Horace's jig-saw method. He is tying blue ribbons in Horace's and Virgil's respective tails, by the *tone* in which he uses his erudition.' He admitted that Propertius' early poems partly justified Mackail's view of him as a 'Victorian sentimentalist', but said that he himself was taking the best bits of the later work, 'the "Immortal Part" of S.P.', and isolating it 'as far as I can'.

Homage to Sextus Propertius begins with a poem about the artist's need to turn his back on the platitudes of Empire and write inspired lyric verse, even though he will not be praised for it until long after his death. Ezra's Propertius recalls the function of lyric poetry in mythology (for example, Orpheus taming the beasts with his songs), and claims that time will settle his reputation, however ill the present age may treat him:

> And I also among the later nephews of this city
> > shall have my dog's day,
> With no stone upon my contemptible sepulchre . . .
> And in the mean time my songs will travel,
> And the devirginated young ladies will enjoy them
> > when they have got over the strangeness . . .
> There will be a crowd of young women doing homage to my
> > palaver,
> Though my house is not propped up by Taenarian columns . . .
> Nor are my caverns stuffed stiff with a Marcian vintage,
> My cellar does not date from Numa Pompilius,
> Nor bristle with wine jars,
> Nor is it equipped with a frigidaire patent;
> Yet the companions of the Muses
> > will keep their collective noses in my books,
> And weary with historical data, they will turn to my dance tune.

The lines about the cellar are entirely Ezra's interpolation.

The second poem in the sequence has Phoebus Apollo and Calliope (muse of epic poetry) reminding Propertius that his talent is not for Virgilian epic – 'Who has ordered a book about heroes?' – but for love poetry. The third describes a midnight summons to Cynthia, and Propertius' reflections on the dangers attendant both on acceptance and refusal:

> Midnight, and a letter comes to me from our mistress:
> Telling me to come to Tibur:
> >   *At* once!!
> 'Bright tips reach up from twin towers,
> 'Anienan spring water falls into flat-spread pools.'
>
> What *is* to be done about it?
> >   Shall I entrust myself to entangled shadows,
> Where bold hands may do violence to my person?
> Yet if I postpone my obedience
> >   because of this respectable terror,
> I shall be prey to lamentations worse than a nocturnal assailant.
> *And* I shall be in the wrong,
> >   *and* it will last a twelve month,
> For her hands have no kindness me-ward.

In the fourth poem, having refused to make the journey, he asks his slave for a report of Cynthia's reaction: 'Tell me the truths which you hear of our constant young lady, Lygdamus.' Turning back to the subject of war poetry in the fifth, he attempts to write like Virgil and produces a ridiculous parody: 'Now if ever it is time to cleanse Helicon . . . / O august Pierides! Now for a large-mouthed product . . .' He then explains to his patron Maecenas that 'My genius is no more than a girl', and there follows one of the most delightful passages in the sequence:

> If she with ivory fingers drive a tune through the lyre,
> >   We look at the process.
> How easy the moving fingers; if hair is mussed on her forehead,
> If she goes in a gleam of Cos, in a slither of dyed stuff,
> There is a volume in the matter; if her eyelids sink into sleep,
> There are new jobs for the author;
> And if she plays with me with her shirt off,
> >   We shall construct many Iliads.
> And whatever she does or says
> >   We shall spin long yarns out of nothing.

This is altogether a new voice in Ezra's poetry.

In the sixth poem Propertius contemplates his death, his modest funeral, and the 'not unworthy' verses he will leave behind. In the seventh there is an account of a night spent with Cynthia – again in a manner difficult to imagine in Ezra's earlier poetry:

> Me happy, night, night full of brightness;
> Oh couch made happy by my long delectations;
> How many words talked out with abundant candles;
> Struggles when the lights were taken away;
> Now with bared breasts she wrestled against me,
>   Tunic spread in delay;
> And she then opening my eyelids fallen in sleep,
> Her lips upon them; and it was her mouth saying: Sluggard!

The eighth poem describes Cynthia's arrival on Olympus after her death; the ninth asks that she shall be spared from dying of illness – and when she is, Propertius demands from her 'the ten nights of your company you have promised me'. Next comes Propertius' imaginary kidnap by a band of Cupids while he is wandering drunkenly on a visit to another woman. He is taken to Cynthia's room, where she upbraids him for faithlessness. All this is narrated in a drunken but also ironic tone:

> And a minute crowd of small boys came from opposite,
>   I do not know what boys,
> And I am afraid of numerical estimate . . .
>   . . . And the noose was over my neck.
>   And another said 'Get him plumb in the
>   middle!
> 'Shove along there, shove along!' . . .
> And Cynthia was alone in her bed.
>   I was stupefied.
> I had never seen her looking so beautiful . . .
> You will observe that pure form has its value.

(The last line, another interpolation, is an in-joke for Vorticists.) Propertius is thrown out by Cynthia and in the twelfth poem finds himself replaced in her bed by a minor poet named Lynceus. He concludes the sequence by placing himself hopefully in the ranks of the great love-poets: 'Propertius of Cynthia, taking his stand among these.'

At the end of 1918, Ezra told Marianne Moore that *Homage to Sextus Propertius*, just completed, was his 'best work' to date. In fact *Cathay* deserves to be rated slightly higher as poetry for its precision and almost faultless diction; by comparison *Propertius* is a rambling, discursive, and sometimes rather muddled piece of work. But in terms of rhythm it was a very considerable technical advance. 'It is too late to prevent vers libre,'

Ezra wrote in the *Egoist* during 1917, 'but, conceivably, one might improve
it.' The sequence uses loose rhythms, apparently bound to no set scheme,
which are in fact strictly regulated by a musical beat or implied time
signature that varies in each poem. There is also considerable use of implied
pauses or caesuras, achieved partly through indentations and line breaks.*

While he was working on *Propertius*, Ezra began to promulgate in some
detail his belief that:

> . . . there are three 'kinds of poetry':
> *Melopoeia*, wherein the words are charged, over and above
> their plain meaning, with some musical property, which directs
> the bearing or trend of that meaning.
> *Phanopoeia*, which is a casting of images upon the visual
> imagination.
> *Logopoeia*, 'the dance of the intellect among words' . . .
> [which] employs words not only for their direct meaning,
> but . . . takes count in a special way of habits of usage, of the
> context we *expect* to find with the word . . . and of ironical
> play . . . It is the latest come, and perhaps most tricky and
> undependable mode.

While its application to all poets' work is doubtful, this is a good
exposition of how Ezra's own verse operates and what it aims to do.
Cathay, for example, is chiefly an exercise in phanopoeia. The epigram-
matic poems in *Lustra* are pieces of logopoeia with little concern for image
or sound. *Homage to Sextus Propertius* was his first 'modern' work of any
length that aimed for and often achieved success in all three categories.

It did not worry him in the least that *Propertius*, like *Cathay*, was an
exercise in translation rather than an original poem. He wrote in the *Egoist*
in October 1917, when the sequence was probably already in his mind if
not actually begun:

> A great age of literature is perhaps always a great age of
> translations . . . We have long since fallen under the blight of
> the Miltonic . . . stilted dialect in translating the classics, a
> dialect which imitates the idiom of the ancients rather than
> seeking their meaning . . . Is a fine poet ever translated until
> another his equal invents a new style in a later language? . . . Is
> not a new beauty created, an old beauty doubled, when the
> overchange is well done?

At its best moments, *Homage to Sextus Propertius* justifies this claim,

---

* James Laughlin says that Basil Bunting told him that Yeats admired the sixth *Homage to
Sextus Propertius* poem ('Me happy, night, night full of brightness') as 'the best *vers libre* yet
written, the way Ez found out how to modulate one line into another'.

but from the beginning even a reader ignorant of the original Latin may feel uneasy about some aspects of the sequence. At one moment Ezra introduces a refrigerator, and later there is a comic reference to Wordsworth, yet at other times he sticks almost pedantically to Propertius' words, and includes undigested mythological allusions that seriously impede the flow and have echoes of a plodding schoolboy 'crib':

> Neither would I warble of Titans, nor of Ossa
> > spiked onto Olympus,
> Nor of causeways over Pelion,
> Nor of Thebes in its ancient respectability,
> > nor of Homer's reputation in Pergamus,
> Nor of Xerxes' two-barreled kingdom, nor of Remus and his
> > royal family,
> Nor of dignified Carthaginian characters . . .

Originally he seems to have intended to produce a reasonably close translation as in *Cathay*, but Propertius evidently became a more modern figure than he had expected. After he had finished, he said that with hindsight he would have preferred to create a 'composite character' containing 'something of Ovid', not just a portrait of Propertius but 'inclusive of the spirit of the young man of the Augustan age'. Typically, he did not trouble to go back to do this.

He explained his title, *Homage to Sextus Propertius*, by saying that he meant it in the sense of Debussy's *Hommage à Rameau*. In fact the title is rather inappropriate to the work. Thomas Hardy suggested to Ezra in a 1921 letter that the sequence might better have been called 'Sextus Propertius Soliloquizes'. This is not an enlightening suggestion (no one title would be likely to encapsulate all the aspects of the sequence), but Ezra made a great deal of it. He had written to Hardy asking for a contribution to a magazine and sending him a copy of his *Quia Pauper Amavi*, which included *Propertius*, asking for comments and criticism – he revered Hardy as a giant of a past age. When he received Hardy's comment he said it was 'infinitely valuable' and claimed (without explaining what he meant) that it identified 'the weak spot in most writing of the last 30 years'. He had no further communication from Hardy, but by 1934 he was saying of the old man's remark: 'Nobody has taught me anything about writing since Thomas Hardy died.'

*

Viewed biographically rather than in a critical vacuum, the most striking thing about *Homage to Sextus Propertius* is that it is very erotic, and seems to convey a real delight in sex. Ezra had reacted with distaste to the eroticism of D. H. Lawrence, and during 1912 in the *New Age* he had sneered at the 'virility' school of literature which 'seems to imagine that man is differentiated from the lower animals by possession of the phallus'. He said much the same in 'Fratres Minores' in the first number of *BLAST*. Though there had been phallic allusions in his own verse since 'Contemporania' in 1912, these were no more than a minor manifestation of his desire to flout convention and stir up outrage, and they did not seem to reflect a real interest in sexuality. *Homage to Sextus Propertius* is a very different matter.

The change is noticeable in the first poem of the sequence, where the Eleusinian Mysteries, which Ezra supposed to be the origin of the troubadours' love-cult, are referred to very casually as 'the Grecian orgies'. The sexual imagery in the lines 'Bright tips reach up from twin towers, / Anienan spring water falls into flat-spread pools' (which is not in the original Latin) seems to be the relaxed imagining of someone really at ease with sexuality, very different from the vague references to spiritual power derived from the contemplation of beauty in the early poems to the Dryad and Kitty Heyman. There is also a pleasant absence of either coyness or boasting in the descriptions of love-making with Cynthia.

In his 1956 letter to Ingrid Davies, Ezra said he did not 'pass beyond' the 'wholly unfecundative caresses' of his youth in America until he 'got to england, where the males were scarce'. Men were not in short supply in England when he arrived in 1908, but by 1917, with conscription taking away those few eligible males who had not already enlisted voluntarily, there was almost no one left except the wounded and those on leave. Richard Aldington's account of London during the First World War in *Death of a Hero* confirms this picture, and even suggests that women were more aroused than usual:

> The war . . . all the dying and wounds and mud and bloodiness – at a safe distance – gave them a great kick, and excited them to an almost unbearable pitch of amorousness. Of course, in that eternity of 1914–18 they must have come to feel that men alone were mortal, and they immortals; wherefore they tried to behave like houris with all available sheiks . . . And then there was the deep primitive physiological instinct – men to kill and be killed; women to produce more men to continue the process. (This, however, was often frustrated by the march of Science, viz. anti-conceptives; for which, much thanks.)

It was this ambience which led Ezra (in 1926) to write to William Carlos Williams of London as having 'a greater proportion of females above that of males [which] makes it THE land for the male with phallus erectus. London THE cunt of the world.'

The second poem of the second section of his *Hugh Selwyn Mauberley*, written in 1920, further suggests that the innocent Ezra was 'devirginated' around 1917. In it, Mauberley, the dilettante, dithering aesthete who represents aspects of Ezra himself, experiences 'bewilderment' when he first encounters sexuality. He cannot 'designate' – explain the importance of – his 'new found orchid' (an image for sexual potency, from the Greek *orchis*, meaning testicle). Mauberley never emerges from this bewilderment, but languishes in an attempt to interpret sex in terms of artistic endeavour – 'This urge to convey the relation / Of eye-lid and cheek-bone / By verbal manifestation', lines that seem to mock Ezra's own earlier inclination, in his love-cult musings, to sublimate sexual feelings into the purely intellectual worship of beauty. Through this, Mauberley loses the chance of real sex, represented in the poem by 'wide-banded irides' (that is, irises, implying vaginas) and 'botticellian sprays', which he had 'passed' in a state of 'anaesthesis', only waking up to what he was missing too late. Moreover, since at the opening of the *Hugh Selwyn Mauberley* sequence Mauberley is said to have 'passed from men's memory' in the thirty-first year of his age, it may not be too fanciful to date a major change in Ezra's life and character as coming after the autumn of 1916, when he had his thirty-first birthday.

'After years of continence / he hurled himself into a sea of six women,' Ezra wrote in one of the 'Moeurs Contemporaines' poems, completed in the autumn of 1917 not long before he began work on *Propertius*. Is there autobiography concealed in this? Had the sexual abstinence which may have marked Ezra's marriage now been broken – and not with Dorothy? *Propertius* and other fragments seem to suggest so.

One amorous exploit – though perhaps it scarcely deserves that title – seems to have involved both Ezra and Eliot. Canto 77, written at Pisa in 1945, includes a glimpse of

> Grishkin's photo refound years after
>   with the feeling that Mr Eliot may have
> missed something, after all, in composing his vignette.

Grishkin appears in Eliot's 'Whispers of Immortality', first published in his 1920 *Poems*:

> Grishkin is nice: her Russian eye
> Is underlined for emphasis;
> Uncorseted, her friendly bust
> Gives promise of pneumatic bliss.

'Grishkin' was Serafima Astafieva (1876–1934), a Russian dancer with the Diaghilev company who opened her own ballet school in London. Ezra was evidently attracted to her, but he told Charles Olson that she would 'have nothing to do' with him, saying it would be 'robbing the cradle'.

However, says Olson, 'Eliot he brought together with her'.
Ezra wrote to Henry Bamford Parkes in 1933:

> I led Eliot up to her wot posterity now knows as 'Grishkin'
> with the firm intuito that a poem wd. result, & intention that it
> should.
>   But that is an UNIQUE experiment in my annals.

He recorded nothing further about the nature of Eliot's relationship with
'Grishkin', but told Olson of

> a dance of Astafieva, spermatopyros, done in her studio, come
> down from Byzantium, the making of the seed of life, it turning
> into fire, and then the drinking of it. Maybe I was the only one
> to understand it. The female equivalent of sperm, whatever that
> is. Yes, the little English girl next to me did, she got excited.

There is an allusion to this in Canto 79: 'So Astafieva had conserved the
tradition / From Byzance and before then / Manitou remember this fire.'
('Manitou' is the Algonquin Indian name for the creative power in all
things.) The same incident is alluded to at the end of Canto 39:

> Dark shoulders have stirred the lightning
> A girl's arms have nested the fire,
> Not I but the handmaid kindled
>   Cantat sic nupta
> I have eaten the flame.

If we continue the search for the 'six women' – or however many or few
there may have been – responsible for Ezra's sexual awakening around
1917, we rarely find more than fragments to go on. One of them may have
been a singer whom Ezra met in London around the end of 1917. 'The new
diseuse, Raymonde Collignon is, I think, going to do Walter's setting of the
troubadour songs,' he wrote to his father on 24 January 1918. He reviewed
her performances several times in the warmest terms; the first was in the
March 1918 *Little Review*, where he did not normally write on musical
topics:

> There is a new diseuse loose on London . . . She is singing
> folk-song without the vegetarian and simple life element. She is
> the first singer to work on Walter Rummel's reconstructions of
> XIIth century Provençal music. Her name is Raymonde Col-
> lignon . . . She is really a consummate artist.

Two months later, as 'William Atheling' in the *New Age*, he was speaking
of 'Raymonde Collignon's delicate and exquisite art . . . It is nearly
impossible to get this old music sung with due precision and delicacy

and . . . she is equipped for it.' For a time her singing revived all his old enthusiasm for the troubadour music. He told his mother that having at last found 'the right singer' he had been 'down to the museum' with Mademoiselle Collignon, 'digging at mss'.

It has been plausibly suggested that Raymonde Collignon is the subject of the two poems which close the two sections of *Hugh Selwyn Mauberley*, 'Envoi' and 'Medallion'. The description in 'Medallion' of the female singer as a porcelain figure seems to recall a *New Age* review written at about the same time as *Mauberley*, which describes Collignon as 'non-human . . . a china image'. And 'Envoi' is certainly addressed to a singer, either human or metaphorical, who is described as having sung 'that song of Lawes' – though in most respects the poem seems to be about England. But even if these two poems do refer to Collignon, we glean nothing from them about her or Ezra's possible feelings for her, beyond a glimpse of her 'sleek head' emerging from 'the gold-yellow frock', her hair 'A basket-work of braids which seem as if they were / Spun in King Minos' Hall'.

No other individual woman seems to be alluded to in Ezra's poetry from this period. However in the late 1950s when Patricia Hutchins, who was writing a book about his London years, corresponded with him about his life at this period, he sent her (in a series of cryptic letters) quite a substantial list of what he called 'people of chaRRm as of 1917' whom he suggested she might try to meet before writing her book. For example: 'Gladys Hines (*sic*), after 1914 / vid Capitals/ Cantos 17/27/ Rodker folio/'. Gladys Hynes, a painter, drew the initial letters for *A Draft of the Cantos 17–27*, a folio printed by John Rodker in 1928, and she signed the copies together with Ezra. In another letter to Patricia Hutchins, Ezra writes: 'Heaven knows what Sheila Hynes [Gladys's sister] can tell you of the period, whereof she and Gladys were as stars in the firmament, a gentle light amid nebulae.'

Another letter mentions 'Daphne Bishop, early Hammersmith Brook Green studio/ friend of Florence Farr, married C. Bax.' Ezra lived near Brook Green, Hammersmith, for a few weeks in the summer of 1909, soon after he had arrived in London. 'Daphne Bishop' was actually Gwen Bishop, née Bernhard Smith, who married the playwright Clifford Bax and died in 1926, though it seems possible that she was known as 'Daphne' among her friends, since that name appears in what is thought* to be a list of Ezra's supposed girlfriends given by Yeats in his poem 'His Phoenix', published in *The Wild Swans at Coole* (1919):

> There's Margaret and Marjorie and Dorothy and Nan,
> A Daphne and a Mary who live in privacy . . .

---

* By Richard Ellmann, in his *Eminent Domain*.

If this refers to Ezra's private life, then 'Dorothy' is clearly identifiable. 'Mary' might be Mary Butts, since she features in one of Ezra's lists sent to Patricia Hutchins: 'Edw/ Sq/ Studios, Stella Bowen, Phyllis Read [*sic*], later Vallence/ Mary Butts m/ Rodker / friend of Yeats. N.W. novelist etc.' Mary Butts came from a well-off Dorset family. She had studied at the London School of Economics and, at the time she met Ezra, was working in the East End slums. She later married John Rodker, poet and printer of some of Ezra's work, and achieved some reputation as a novelist and short-story writer before her early death.

Edwardes Square, mentioned in this list, was half a mile from Ezra's and Dorothy's flat in Holland Place Chambers, and was the home of an artists' colony. The tenants included Stella Bowen and Phyllis Reid. In her memoirs, Stella describes how they first met Ezra. The pair of them gave a party in Pembroke Studios

> to say good-bye to some artist going to the front, and to it came Ezra Pound . . . [He] decided that two personable young women who lived in a large studio, danced to a gramophone, and longed to be sociable, were fit and proper persons to be cultivated, especially as one of them (Phyllis) had an insatiable appetite for poetry. To me, he was at first an alarming phenomenon. His movements, though not uncontrolled, were sudden and angular, and his droning American voice, breaking into bomb-shells of emphasis, was rather incomprehensible as he enlightened us on the Way, the Truth, and the Light, in Art. He desired us to teach him to dance, and quickly evolved a highly personal and very violent style . . . which caused him the greatest satisfaction . . .
>
> Ezra was a dear, as we soon discovered. But when he first came to call after the party, with the proposal that we should join his weekly dinner club at Bellotti's in Soho, I was too alarmed by his wild man's aspect to accept. I decreed that Margaret Postgate should go with Phyllis in my place, and if their report were favourable, I would go next time!

Margaret Postgate, known as 'Mop' because of her mop of hair, had been at Roedean with Phyllis. When Ezra knew her she was junior classics mistress at St Paul's Girls' School in Hammersmith. She and her brother Raymond were both eventually disinherited by their father (author of *Postgate's Latin Primer*), he for being a conscientious objector, she for marrying the socialist G. D. H. Cole. She ended her life as Dame Margaret Cole; in her biography of her husband she mentions her friendship with Ezra without giving details, and says that before her marriage she was living in a room in Mecklenburgh Square 'rented from the Imagist poet

H. D. through the medium of Ezra Pound'. Ezra recalled that one of his very rare experiences of being drunk happened when he visited 'Mop' Postgate's father, who lived in retirement in Cambridge: 'I [have] had a few hysteric drunks . . . One was whether Oxford or Cambridge gave a better education, and I surreptitiously puked – this was with Postgate, whom I remember on my last visit to him, sitting up in bed, quoting Aeschylus.'

He included Mop in Patricia Hutchins's list: 'MOP, Mrs G. D. H. Cole, friend of Stella's.' It seems likely that she was the Margaret in Yeats's list of Ezra's girlfriends. Stella Bowen describes her in those days as 'shy, untidy, and wild, with a little square face under an immense mop of dark hair, small shoulders hunched, long arms held in at the elbows, and narrow hands with long gesticulating fingers . . . She [would] edge away from strangers, and despise the small change of mannerly greetings, [but] no bushel capable of hiding her light has ever been discovered!'

The Marjorie and Nan of Yeats's list defy identification, but other names are scattered suggestively through Ezra's letters to Patricia Hutchins, such as 'Brigit Patmore, V. Hunt circle.' His friendship with Brigit Patmore began in 1909. That it may have been more than friendship is suggested by Dorothy Pound's resentment of her – Noel Stock remembers that she would refer scathingly to 'Patmore' – and also by the dedication of *Lustra* (1916) to Brigit, disguised under the troubadour name 'Vail de Lencour' (merely 'V. de L.' in the book). Indeed, if one had to pick any particular name as the Cynthia of Ezra's *Homage to Sextus Propertius* it would be her – beautiful, rich, sophisticated, unhappily married, restless.

Another entry in the Hutchins list reads: 'Annette Hullah / fotostats provencal music / that Holland Lane or whatever, running down from Keng/High St, to other main st/'. Annette Hullah was the author of *A Little History of Music* (1911), a book for children, which includes a chapter on the troubadours that seems to suggest the influence of Ezra. The list continues:

> A Moseby-Stark, who got hitched to an artist named Lipscomb or Luscomb / and whom I didn't remember by that name (i.e. her husb/) when Jepson brot her to a party in 1927.* to MY regret, cause she wuz a nice gal/ whom I met only a few times.
>
> 2. Kitty Carr-Gom, whom Violet [Hunt] couldn't locate in 1938/.†   3. P. G. Konody's second spouse who let us use studio in 1927. I think she was ill, at any rate didn't see her in 38 . . .

---

*More probably 1929, when Ezra paid a brief visit to London from Rapallo.

†The year of his next visit to England.

And dear Marquesita, of Beggars Opry etc. later Mrs Chif-
feyley or however he spelled it.

Raymonde Collignon, was thinking of immagratin to her
orfspring now in U.S.

and Powys Mathers relict.

London was inhabited pre-1914 [sic] AND of course
Atheling got round.

It seems that he did. The list is still not exhausted: 'Ethel Mayne, G. R. S.
Mead, district SWARming with 'em. Evelyn Underhill, not that she was
MY dish of tea. Phyllis Bottome, Brunswick Gdns. 14.' Evelyn Underhill,
scarcely anyone's 'dish of tea' in the sense that Ezra implies, was a
well-known Christian mystical writer and 'spiritual director', ten years
Ezra's senior. She seems a very odd inclusion in this list, though their
circles certainly overlapped, since she lived on Campden Hill near Violet
Hunt and her friends included May Sinclair and Maurice Hewlett. Phyllis
Bottome was one of the Violet Hunt circle at South Lodge, and it was she
who remarked in her memoirs on the young Ezra's growing delight in 'the
biology of sex'.

*

Just as Ezra expected, Harriet Monroe was shocked by a good deal of
Homage to Sextus Propertius, and decided to publish only four of the
twelve poems, afterwards explaining that to print the whole sequence
would probably have 'agitated the censor'. Ezra took this fairly calmly.
'Harriet has bust up my Propertius sequence,' he wrote to his mother, 'but
is paying a decent price for the four things she is printing.' Her selection
naturally excluded the erotic pieces, and most of the vigorous passages too,
and gave a very poor idea of the nature of the sequence.

The war came to an end. Ezra told John Quinn he had caught a cold
wandering about in the rain 'to observe effect of armistice on the populace'.
And to Joyce he remarked: 'We will now have the competition of all the
returning troops to contend with.' Richard Aldington had come back 'with
a surface of modesty'. But Aldington did not feel the same way about Ezra.
'For some reason,' he writes, 'Ezra had become violently hostile to
England . . . At any rate he kept tapping his Adam's apple and assuring me
that the English stopped short there. I thought at first he meant that he had
been menaced by the returning troops as a slacker . . .'

For the first few weeks after the Armistice, Ezra seemed content to be
sitting in London, watching things get back to normal; but a change of a
not altogether favourable nature soon became perceptible to him. Among
other things, the next few years were to see the swift ascent of T. S. Eliot to
the celebrity that Ezra himself had enjoyed until recently – and which Eliot
was able to maintain much less precariously. Aldington writes:

Ezra started out in a time of peace and prosperity with everything in his favour, and muffed his chances to become literary dictator of London – to which he undoubtedly aspired – by his own conceit, folly and bad manners. Eliot started in the enormous confusion of war and post-war England, handicapped in every way. Yet by merit, tact, prudence, and pertinacity he succeeded in doing what no other American has ever done – imposing his personality, taste, and even many of his opinions on literary England.

In a 1933 letter Ezra made a rueful comparison between his own and Eliot's ascendancy, saying he himself was one of those who when young had been tempted to 'state views which are based on what one happens to know, and not on the available data' – he had trodden the thin ice of opinions not backed up by proper knowledge. Another and 'cannier' line was to 'stick to what one knows'. This technique, he said, explained the 'rise to the heights of T. S. E. as an authority'.

In the autumn 1921 issue of the *Little Review* he was already sarcastically calling Eliot 'the Dean of English criticism' and was ridiculing one of his *dicta*, that 'the greatest poets have been concerned with moral values'. A few months later Eliot succeeded in doing what Ezra had often tried, and started his own influential literary magazine. The *Criterion* did not make Eliot an Establishment figure overnight: Daniel Cory records that as late as 1932 there was a 'formidable body of settled opinion' that regarded the author of *The Waste Land* as an 'eccentric fraud'. Nevertheless the rather *louche* poet of the First World War years swiftly disappeared behind the façade that Ezra began to call 'the Reverend Eliot', only revealing his more mobile features to a highly select audience – in which Ezra, it is true, was always included.

It took Ezra some time to become aware of his loss of supremacy in his quarter of London intellectual life. Nevertheless there are signs of unease in his correspondence soon after the Armistice. In a letter to Marianne Moore in February 1919 he said he must give up his hope of an American Renaissance: 'Must let it alone . . . Must return to the unconcern with U.S.A. that I had before 1911–12.' Writing to Joyce he wondered whether he was not 'perhaps better at digging up corpses of Li Po, or more lately Sextus Propertius, than in preserving this bitched mess of modernity'. And it was at this juncture that *Homage to Sextus Propertius* was published and was violently attacked.

*

The four *Propertius* poems chosen by Harriet Monroe were printed in the March 1919 *Poetry*, and in the next number Miss Monroe published a letter from Professor William Gardner Hale of the University of Chicago criticizing Ezra's handling of the Latin text. 'If Mr Pound were a professor of Latin,' declared Hale, 'there would be nothing left for him but suicide.'

Hale said that he found the four poems he had seen to contain about sixty errors. 'Mr Pound,' he judged, 'is incredibly ignorant of Latin.' For a start there was the stylistic question. If, as appeared from many phrases, Ezra was aiming at colloquialism, how could he perpetrate such expressions as 'Her hands have no kindness me-ward'? Then again, said Hale, for a colloquial rendering it was oddly burdened with 'Baedekeresque explanations' of proper names, as in

> Though my house is not propped up by Taenarian columns
> From Laconia (associated with Neptune and Cerberus)

– the second line of which, Hale continued, was added apparently after looking up '*Taenarus*' in *Harper's Latin Dictionary*.

Hale then came to his prize catch. The lines

> *Quippe coronatos alienum ad limen amantes*
> *Nocturnaeque canes ebria signa fugae*

should read, according to the Loeb translation: 'For thou shalt sing of garlanded lovers watching before another's threshold, and the tokens of drunken flight through the dark.' Ezra had rendered them

> Obviously crowned lovers at unknown doors,
> Night dogs, the marks of a drunken scurry.

Among the errors here Ezra, as Hale put it,

> mistakes the verb *canes*, 'thou shalt sing', for the noun *canes* (in the nominative plural masculine) and translates by 'dogs'. Looking around then for something to tack this to, he fixes upon *nocturnae* (genitive singular feminine) and gives us 'night dogs'! . . . For sheer magnificence of blundering this is unsurpassable.

Hale's remaining crop did not include anything quite as spectacular as this – he quibbled about Ezra's having rendered *punica rostra*, 'purple beaks', as 'their Punic faces', which he said was about as nonsensical as translating 'crockery' by 'China' – but he expressed himself shocked by 'one peculiarly unpleasant passage in Mr Pound's translation', of which there was 'no suggestion in the original':

> And in the meantime my songs will travel,
> And the devirginated young ladies will enjoy them
> 　　　when they have got over the strangeness.

Propertius' text, said Hale, here reads: 'Meanwhile let me resume the wonted round of my singing; let my lady, touched (by my words), find pleasure in the familiar music.' He agreed that 'just possibly' Propertius meant 'young ladies' rather than 'my lady' (the Latin is *puella*); but he said that the words '*Gaudeat in solito tacta puella*' could not possibly give Ezra's 'decadent meaning', which had been reached by supposing *tacta*, 'touched (by the music)', to be the opposite of *intacta*, 'virgin', and by reading *in solito*, 'in the familiar (music)', as a negative, *insolito*, 'by the unfamiliar'.

Hale concluded by saying that while he did not actually think Ezra need do away with himself, he begged him to 'lay aside the mask of erudition. And, if he must deal with Latin, I suggest that he paraphrase some accurate translation.'

As soon as he had seen Hale's letter, Ezra wrote to his father: 'Hale is a bleating ass and Harriet Monroe is another.' He disagreed with two of Hale's criticisms, saying that 'Punic' was a perfectly acceptable translation of *punica*, and that *insolito* was not an error, and went on: 'He is probably wrong, in other matters, on which argument wd. be possible.' He accused Hale of 'utter insensitiveness' in the 'relation of latin to english', said that 'my poem never for a moment pretends to translate', felt that Hale could be pardoned for part of his attitude because 'the fragment which that stick Harriet has printed is unintelligible', and concluded: 'I wont propose to argue with the monkey house.'

His next reaction was to write a reply to *Poetry* intended for publication. Addressed to 'Editor, *Poetry*' and dated 14 April 1919, it reads as follows:

> Cat-piss and porcupines! The thing is no more a translation than my 'Altaforte' is a translation.
>   Poor brute naturally can't make much of the fragment of the poem you have used; but he misses a number of avoidances of literal meaning, including that unfortunate (from his presumable ? point of view) misstatement about Thebes.
>   In final commiseration,
>   E. Pound

(The 'misstatement about Thebes' may have been the line: 'And Citharaon shook up the rocks by Thebes', in the first poem in the sequence.) Harriet Monroe received the letter, but she did not print it; quite apart from its opening sentence, it must have seemed to her a very poor defence.

Ezra drafted another much more substantial reply to Hale, and showed it to May Sinclair a year later, describing it as 'a letter I did *not* send to Hale'. It begins:

> Allow me to say that I would long since have committed suicide had desisting made me a professor of latin. I am told that these

luxuries come high in your august city, as high as '$12,000 and a house' per year, and that the position is therefore of some eminence; yet even with this there is no guarantee of utter infallibility.

He goes on to defend *insolito* and 'Punic', and continues: 'I never for one moment presented my poem as a translation, let alone an *ad verbum* translation.' This would have been more apparent, he says, if the whole sequence had been printed, and not just 'mangled fragments'.

> At no time had I attempted more than a portrait, or a presentation of a certain spirit. If I have forced the meaning . . . (which I do not grant without queery) I have not forced it beyond the character of the author . . . Hale, however, is a perfect example of the spirit which keeps the classics 'uninteresting'. We all know that Propertius went to mid-week prayer meeting . . . As for the 'mask of erudition' it is precisely what I have *not* assumed in my 'Homage', it is precisely what I have thrown on the dust heap; and for 'sheer magnificence' I would rather attain it even blundering than write of the 'Marcian flow' [Hale's correction of another error] . . . My respect for my author would not only lead me to put a dog in place of a serenade, but . . . willingly I would have inserted whole passages out of Ovid.

Another reply to Hale by Ezra comes in a letter he sent to A. R. Orage at the *New Age*, who liked the sequence while being aware of the errors, and said so in his own paper. To Orage, Ezra wrote:

> As a Prof. of Latin . . . Hale should be impeccable and without error. He has NO claim to refrain from suicide if he errs in any point . . . If I were . . . a professor of Latin in Chicago, I should probably have to resign on divulging the fact that Propertius occasionally copulavit, i.e. rogered the lady to whom he was not legally wedded.

But he made no further attempt to refute Hale in public, and Harriet Monroe wrote that it was clear he had felt Hale's attack to be 'unanswerable'. She added that Ezra had 'never forgiven it'. When Ezra saw her remarks, which were printed in the *English Journal* in 1931, he wrote to its editor: 'I did not at the time reply to Hale because I could not assume that he had seen the entire poem.' And he went on to defend again his method with Propertius.

Despite this belated attempt to make it seem otherwise, Hale's attack had clearly nettled him deeply, and his silence in print was undoubtedly due to his extreme discomfiture. His already considerable suspicion and resentment of the professional academic world – and hence his dislike and rejection of conventional logical processes of thought – must have been deepened considerably by the experience.

His first letter to Harriet Monroe after reading Hale's comments hints that he himself was now aware of further errors in the sequence; perhaps he feared exposure of these, and further mockery, if he attempted a public reply. In fact if the entire *Homage to Sextus Propertius* is examined – as Ezra demanded that it should be before criticisms were made – it becomes clear that the 'night dogs' stand on the tip of a very considerable iceberg of howlers.

Ezra pointed out in a 1922 letter that if he had simply wanted to translate Propertius correctly it would have been 'perfectly easy to correct one's divergencies from Bohn crib. Price 5 shillings.' The striking thing is that clearly he made no such effort. At no point did he compare his own rendering with a literal translation, so that he was completely unaware of his 'divergencies' until he read Hale. And though there was then still time to remove the errors in the rest of the sequence before it was all published, he did not do so, even though he must now have guessed how erroneous was much of his rendering of Propertius' words.

The non-use of a 'crib' in *Homage to Sextus Propertius* is strikingly different from the method of *Cathay*, where he worked from a literal translation. In his rational moments he must have known that his Latin was not up to the job, but obviously he did not care. Or rather, he went about the translation as if he felt he had an instinctive, intuitive knowledge of the language that was quite different from a scholar's competence in the rudiments of grammar and syntax – it corresponded to his belief that he could understand certain Chinese ideograms merely by staring at them. Indeed, he once argued in an article on 'Elizabethan Classicists' for the *Egoist* that an accurate knowledge of Latin grammar and syntax were not necessary to a proper understanding of the language. He suggested that the teaching of grammar by rules was 'largely a hoax' since Latin has 'certain case feelings' rather than absolutely precise rules. He went on: 'When the classics were a new beauty and ecstasy people cared a damn sight more about the meaning of the authors, and a damn sight less about their grammar and philology.' The nature of the howlers in *Homage to Sextus Propertius* shows this nonsensical belief in action. What we see is not someone making mistakes through ignorance so much as rushing on regardless because he thinks that he, and perhaps he alone, has the key to what the poem is really about.

The howlers are chiefly governed by Ezra's refusal to consider grammatical relationships, and his continuing to work as though Latin were an uninflected language whose meaning was governed mainly by word order – or at times not even by that, for occasionally he treats the Latin words as if they were capable of meaning anything he wanted them to. An example of this is his handling of Propertius' lines

Multi, Roma, tuas laudes annalibus addent,
  Qui finem imperii Bactra futura canent

('Many, O Rome, shall add fresh glories to your annals, singing that Bactra shall be the limit of your empire'.) Bactra – which lay beyond the borders of the Roman Empire – is treated by Ezra as if it were the (plural) subject of *canent*; he also transposes it geographically (it is nowhere near the Caucasus):

  Celebrities from the Trans-Caucasus [i.e. *Bactra*] will belaud
             Roman celebrities
  And expound the distentions of Empire.

Ezra's comment, in a letter to his father, on such detail was: 're names in Propertius, I dont see that one need know anything about any of them to get the general sense of any passage . . . Place names dont hold up the sense much.' In a letter to May Sinclair he said he had 'blurred' the use of names and details of Roman history and mythology 'as one blurs, or refrains from painting, a background of a picture with the distinctness of the foreground'. But this was precisely what he did not do with any consistency; too often he left the details in the picture, and got them wrong.

Some of the best moments in the sequence come when he has indeed 'blurred', abandoning any pretence of translating, and interpolating modern equivalents – such as the 'frigidaire patent' that Propertius' cellar cannot boast, and the use in the final poem of the adjective 'Wordsworthian' to describe a certain kind of boring landscape poetry. He came to believe that it was for this that Hale and Harriet Monroe had attacked him: 'I am unable to imagine a depth of stupidity so great as to lead either Miss Monroe or the late Hale into believing that I supposed I had found an allusion to Wordsworth . . . [in] Propertius.' But Hale never mentioned the Wordsworth line (which in any case did not appear in the *Poetry* printing), and merely complained mildly that 'Mr Pound is often undignified or flippant'. He would, no doubt, have been able to understand and perhaps even enjoy a wholesale transposition of Propertius into the modern age, had Ezra attempted it. What he could not stomach, and what it is quite impossible to explain away, is the sheer quantity of error where the translation is supposed to be accurate. As Ezra's publisher James Laughlin wrote to Ezra in 1935, 'I didn't think it was a translation, but where a line was translated I thought it ought to be translated right.'

The *Propertius* row has bubbled on ever since. Six sections of the poem were printed in the *New Age* during the summer of 1919; in October the whole sequence finally appeared in print (in Ezra's *Quia Pauper Amavi*)

and received some good reviews as well as bad. These included one from a classical scholar, Adrian Collins, who admitted the presence of 'major blunders' but said that people who knew no Latin could and should read it 'with the speed and gusto with which it was evidently written'. However, in 1941 Logan Pearsall Smith could be found grumbling (in a book on Milton) about Ezra's 'veritable snowstorm of howlers'; Robert Graves, himself an eccentric translator, took Ezra to task for it in *The Crowning Privilege* (1955); and as late as 1961 the classicist Professor Gilbert Highet wrote of *Homage to Sextus Propertius* as 'an insult both to poetry and to scholarship'. Throughout all this, T. S. Eliot sat on a characteristic fence, omitting *Propertius* from his 1928 selection of Ezra's poems for Faber and Gwyer on the grounds that, while classicists would be outraged, those who knew no Latin would make nothing of it, but remarking in the 1948 edition of the same book that he would now 'write with less cautious admiration of it'.

Ezra remained utterly unrepentant. 'Be assured,' he told May Sinclair in March 1920, 'that wherever an initial mistranslation pleased me it has been left sacred.' This letter provides also the most revealing account of his method in the 'translation': 'I don't think I have consciously paid *any* attention to grammar anywhere in the "Homage". Rendering is purely ideographic, i.e. whole thing rendered into Chinese and then into English.' Such candour makes it absurd to try to explain away the faults of *Homage to Sextus Propertius*. Rather, one should be amazed that he got any of it right. He had behaved like a lazy and ignorant schoolboy faced with a Latin text that he has not prepared, who has forgotten to bring his 'crib' with him into the classroom but trusts to his own luck and inspiration. And it is precisely this cheeky method that makes *Homage to Sextus Propertius*, at its best, such fun, night dogs, devirginated young ladies, and all.

21

Try This On Your Piano

Ezra's first note to *Poetry* about Hale's criticisms was signed 'In final commiseration.' Harriet Monroe told him she would interpret this, 'as you doubtless intended', as his resignation from the staff of *Poetry*. Perhaps he had not intended that at all; but there it was, and he had to accept the situation, though he told Yeats it would cut out a large part of his income. At about the same time – it is not clear why – he ceased to be Foreign Editor of the *Little Review* (though he still contributed) and the job passed to John Rodker. Meanwhile his next book of poems, *Quia Pauper Amavi*, was turned down by Elkin Mathews, who objected to *Homage to Sextus Propertius* and 'Moeurs Contemporaines'. The book was taken over by the *Egoist* – in effect Ezra himself. On top of this Knopf in New York backed out of his promise to publish *Instigations*, another collection of Ezra's prose pieces; the book was eventually issued in America by the small firm of Boni & Liveright.

In May 1919 Ezra told Joyce he felt conscious of 'stasis or constipation' in his affairs. Perhaps it was simply a desire to get things moving again that made him write a new canto – the first for more than three years. 'Here is a draft of Fourth Canto,' Ezra told his father during the spring. 'Fifth is begun.' The same letter mentioned that he and Dorothy had 'some hope of getting South' for the first time since the war. 'At least we have our passports.'

He had not needed a passport before 1914, and he was now infuriated by the bureaucratic 'imbecilities', the 'godblasted red tape' which had appeared since the Armistice. Though his grumble about the 'brute stupidity of the gentleman behind the partition in an American passport bureau in Paris' in 1919 only arose from a small incident,* it added to his accumulation of aggression towards his native country. In 1924 he asked Yeats, then a senator of the Irish Republic, if he could get him an Irish passport 'and thus free me from degrading contact with the sons of bitches who represent the infamous [Woodrow] Wilsonian tyranny and red tape'.

He and Dorothy were in France from late April until September 1919. They stayed briefly in Paris with the Misses Ida and Adah Lee Mapel, the American spinsters whom Ezra had met in Spain in 1906, then went down to Toulouse. 'Have been resting a month,' Ezra wrote to his father from that city at the end of May. 'Old Dulac, father of Edmund Dulac, painter, very hospitable to us here.' From Toulouse the Pounds made an expedition to Nîmes, Arles and Avignon, so that Ezra could 'renew my retina with certain outlines'; he reported to Olivia that Dorothy was 'industriously painting'. They also went north into troubadour country; early in August they were at Altaforte. Another trip was south to Montségur in the Pyrenees, where Ezra examined the ruins of a castle destroyed at the time of the suppression of the Albigensians; Ezra believed it to have been a temple of his love-cult, and it appears fleetingly in Cantos 23 and 76.

In Toulouse in June he received the typescript of a new chapter of *Ulysses* – and was disconcerted by its scarcely comprehensible impressionistic opening ('Bronze by gold heard the hoofirons, steelyringing Imperthnthnthnthnthn . . .'). He wrote to Joyce suggesting that 'perhaps twenty words coherent' would 'not only clarify but even improve'. Joyce paid no attention. Meanwhile, *Ulysses* was running into serious trouble in New York: the January and May 1919 episodes in the *Little Review* led to the confiscation and burning of both issues by the postal authorities. So far there had been no judicial hearing, but the threat of a prosecution for obscenity grew nearer, and Ezra, as well as worrying about incomprehensibility, reproved Joyce for the conclusion of the new chapter, which described Bloom slowly farting. He told Joyce: 'One *can* farht with less pomp and circumstance.' He also suggested that Bloom had been 'disproportionately' on stage; 'where in hell' was Stephen?

From Toulouse, Ezra contributed a series of articles to the *New Age* on the subject of provincialism, entitled 'The Regional', written in a languid manner as befitted an extended summer holiday, but which contained some very precise thoughts about the method he was beginning to practise in his new cantos. 'A man may try,' he wrote, 'without rhetoric, without hankering after grandiose utterances, to straighten out his ideas on history,

---

* Telling the story to D. G. Bridson at St Elizabeths, Ezra claimed that the passport official had tried to refuse him re-entry to Britain on the grounds that the US Government wanted all citizens to return home. This scarcely seems likely; he may have been confusing whatever happened in 1919 with a row he had at the American Consulate in Rome during the Second World War, when this was indeed official policy.

the rise of nations, the developments and atrophies of civilization.' He said that he disliked general theories about history that were not anchored 'in particular and known objects'. He mentioned two detailed pieces of local history he had picked up in Provence: the burning of the city of Béziers by a band of tinkers who had been driven out by Simon de Montfort's knights, and the fall of Montségur, which had outlasted the attacks on the Albigensians but was then destroyed by special order of the King. 'Snippets of this kind,' he wrote,

> build up our concept of wrong, of right, of history. I put down these pellets in this manner, not merely as a confession of how I catch myself thinking, but because other people think no better, because the burnt-in detail is tied by no more visible cords to the next detail, and is founded no more demonstrably into the underlying conviction-plus-passion.

It was the Ideogramic Method applied to history, and it seemed to suggest a way forward for the Cantos.

Canto 4, begun just before the journey to Toulouse, was the first in which he practised this method of approaching and 'bottling' history and human experience. Gone now were the Browningisms and the confiding narrator of 'Three Cantos'. The new canto, though dense and difficult to read, was an enormous advance on the self-conscious narrative technique of the earlier attempt. Shifts from one image to another, 'ply over ply', now happened of their own accord without any emphasis on Ezra the observer. Thematically the choice of material was less eccentric, more schematic, the whole following a stream of consciousness but also related to a careful plan.

The canto is largely a tracing of the theme of seduction and slaughter consequent upon sexual entanglements. Its technique is to place before the reader first one and then immediately another image of this, from classical or medieval literature, superimposed or set in montage without any connective tissue. We jump immediately from Itys, who was killed and fed to his father after raping his mother's sister Philomela, to Cabestan, a troubadour murdered by his mistress's husband who then served his heart to her; the same woman is mourning for both deaths:

>   Ityn!
> Et ter flebiliter, Ityn, Ityn!
> And she went toward the window and cast her down,
>   All the while, the while, swallows crying:
> Ityn!
>   'It is Cabestan's heart in the dish.
>   'It is Cabestan's heart in the dish?
>   'No other taste shall change this.'

Philomela was changed into a nightingale, and Procne, mother and killer of Itys, into a swallow, which provides the implied link to the next passage, which simultaneously presents Actaeon and Peire Vidal, both of whom became wild animals in pursuit of their loves and were thus the prey of their own hounds. The theme of metamorphosis is picked up in allusions in the second half of the canto to 'The pine at Takasago' (in the Noh play *Takasago* an old couple are changed, like Philemon and Baucis, into a pair of trees), and to the notion from a Chinese poet of there being a male and female wind. Then comes a glance at the story of Danaë, 'the god's bride', who lies at the top of a gilded tower where Zeus visits her in a 'golden rain' and begets Perseus. Canto 4 ends with a glimpse of a procession in honour of the Virgin seen by Ezra during his stay at Toulouse, which seemed to him 'like a worm, in the crowd' – words similar to those he used in a letter to his father describing it: 'this vermiform object . . . the worm of the procession . . . No merely medieval but black central African superstition . . .'

The classical and medieval allusions within Canto 4 are reasonably within the grasp of an educated reader, though the unexplained references to Japanese and Chinese texts would scarcely have been accessible when the canto was first published, not least because they were partly derived from mistranslations by Fenollosa and Ezra. Certainly no one outside Ezra's circle could have been expected altogether to understand the purely personal memories – 'the wind out of Rhodez', 'the church roof in Poitiers', 'at Gourdon that time' – which derive from his travels in France in 1912. But it is these as much as the thematic linkings that give Canto 4 its sureness of touch. We are being presented with a 'thin film of images' (words from this canto) from the retina of an individual eye, and the very personal nature of these, even their near-incomprehensibility, gives verisimilitude to the stream of consciousness technique.

The new narrative method of Canto 4 was developed from a number of models and influences. Ezra's 1918 study of Henry James taught him something about nuance; he had learnt a little from the impressionism of the later chapters of *Ulysses*; and he was becoming enthusiastic about the narrative precision of Flaubert, whom he praised wildly in the 'Regional' articles, saying that 'nineteenth century thought' consisted simply of Stendhal and Flaubert. The text of Canto 4 underwent no such major changes as 'Three Cantos' suffered, and there are only minor differences between its first printing (by John Rodker in a pamphlet a few months after it was written) and the eventual text in the finished Cantos. It seemed that the method of the 'endless poem' had been found.

*

Eliot joined the Pounds briefly in France in mid-August, spending a week with them in the Dordogne. Together, he and Ezra examined the castle of Excideuil, associated with the troubadour Giraut de Bornelh, where, according to Canto 29, Eliot told Ezra: 'I am afraid of the life after death' – and, after a pause, 'Now, at last, I have shocked him.'

Eliot relaxed enough by the end of the holiday to grow a beard – Richard Aldington said it looked awful. Ezra and Eliot left Dorothy sketching at Excideuil and walked together to Thiviers and Brantôme. Ezra reported to Dorothy by postcard: 'T. has 7 blisters.' Eliot then departed to examine the Dordogne prehistoric cave paintings by himself before returning to London.

Ezra continued to take the closest interest in Eliot's work. The poems that Eliot was now writing – among them 'Sweeney among the Nightingales', 'Whispers of Immortality', 'Gerontion' and others that eventually appeared in his 1920 *Poems* – were, according to Ezra, mainly the result of his and Eliot's conviction that the 'dilutation' of *vers libre* by such pernicious influences as Amygisme had produced a 'general floppiness' among contemporary poets, and that some 'counter-current' must be set in motion, some new element of discipline introduced. Ezra prescribed as tonic for them both Théophile Gautier's *Émaux et Camées* (1852), the *Bay Psalm Book* (a collection of metrical psalms used by the Massachusetts Bay Colony in the mid-seventeenth century), and the use of 'rhyme and regular strophes'. The result, said Ezra in 1932, was 'poems in Mr Eliot's *second* volume' and also his own *Hugh Selwyn Mauberley*.

Ezra had discovered the strict quatrains of Gautier in 1912, and had praised his capacity for 'perfectly plain statements'. In a 1918 essay on French poetry he spoke of Gautier as a sculptor cutting in 'hard substance'. Eliot said he and Ezra had 'studied Gautier's poems, and then we thought, "Have I anything to say in this form which will be useful?"' The consequence for Eliot was the discovery of an almost absurdly regular form, which could provide an ironic counterpoint to the eccentricities of a poem's subject matter.

Eliot did not arrive at this new form without difficulties. The various typescripts of his poems from this period (now in the Berg Collection of the New York Public Library) have many queries and suggestions on them in Ezra's handwriting. He attacked the opening of 'Gerontion' (one of the more irregular poems in the collection):

> Here I am, an old man in a dry month,
> Being read to by a boy . . .

Ezra crossed out 'Here I am' and 'Being read to by' and wrote:

> b – b - b *Bd* + *bb* consonants and 2 prepositions
> ? *to by*

Eliot left these lines unchanged, but elsewhere he followed Ezra's suggestions, changing (for example) the opening of the poem 'Burbank with a Baedeker: Bleistein with a Cigar' at Ezra's instigation, so as to tighten up the rhythm.

There are scattered comments and queries by Ezra, mostly dealing with minutiae, in several other poems. But Ezra's most substantial contribution was to Eliot's 'Whispers of Immortality'. Perhaps because he himself had introduced the original of 'Grishkin', subject of the second half of the poem, to Eliot, he felt a special interest in it. At all events he worked closely on it, so closely that the finished poem is almost a collaboration.

The earliest of the typescripts shows Eliot in considerable doubt as to whether anything could be made of the poem at all. At the end he added a note asking whether it was worth attempting another version; it seemed minor, and failed to convey anything of Grishkin's sexuality. Ezra duly crossed out most of it, though he also picked out the best lines, marking his approval. For example he put a pair of brackets around 'But I must crawl between dry ribs / To keep my metaphysics warm'. The poem was at first untitled; at this stage Ezra suggested calling it 'Night thoughts on immortality' or 'Night thoughts on Gautier' (it is markedly in the Gautier manner), and he wrote on the back of an early version:

Webster
    "
Don[n]e
    "
Gautier

He suggested to Eliot that the poem, somewhat formless in the first version, be constructed as a 'general statement & conclusion', and he advised 'no pipit' – in the first version the final stanza refers to Pipit, who also appears in Eliot's 'A Cooking Egg'.

A later version of the poem shows him attacking the stanza on Donne, slashing out two lines vigorously, and suggesting as a substitute for the second line:

Who found no substitute for sense

– words that, after trying an alternative of his own, Eliot eventually adopted.

The end of the poem gave Eliot great trouble. At the middle stage of composition it had two dreary concluding stanzas about the Sons of God and the Sons of Men. Ezra slashed out one of these and queried the position of the other. To a pair of lines describing the Sons of God entertaining the wives of men he added the comment: 'What angel hath cuckolded thee?'

The poem went through several versions, including one to which Eliot gave the heading

TRY THIS ON YOUR PIANO
WHISPERS OF IMMORTALITY

before it emerged as we now have it. There are no less than eight different typescripts in the Berg folder, and other drafts evidently existed. As well as these and other suggestions made alongside the actual text, Ezra wrote Eliot the following note about the poem, roughly half-way through the various stages of composition:

'SODOMY!' said the Duchess, approaching the Ormulu clock.
If at A. you shift to 'my' i.e. *your* 'experience' you would conceivably reach Grishkin's Dunlop tyre boozum by the line of greatest directness.
If at B. you should then leap from the bloody, boozy and Barzeelyan Jag-U-ARRR to the Abstracter entities who would not have resisted either the boozum or the 'smell of baked meats', you could thence entauthenexelaunai to the earlier termine.
But I must crawl, etc. metaphysics warm having in the lines precedent used your extant rhyme in 'charm', applying same to either boozum, odour, or enticement of the toutensemble.
Omitting fourth stanza of the present Nth. variant [a second stanza about Donne, which Eliot indeed rejected]. wash the whole with virol and leave in hypo.
At any rate, I think this would bring us nearer the desired epithalamium of force, clearness and bewtie.

Given that the two could work together so closely on one poem, it is surprising that they did not collaborate more fully, though of course, by letting Ezra criticize like this, Eliot was getting the best out of him, employing his almost faultless ear for rhythm gone wrong or an effect misplaced. He never made any public acknowledgement of the fine tuning that Ezra had given the poems, but then Ezra never mentioned it either. Perhaps he thought it all in the day's work.

*

By now Ezra felt it 'a crime against literature' to let Eliot 'waste eight hours vitality per diem' in the bank. He told John Quinn he was contemplating raising funds 'to get him out of it', and he decided that £400 per annum needed to be raised 'from four or five people who wd. keep their mouths shut'. He said he would contribute £50 as long as he could afford to, though Eliot would not be told about this. Quinn responded with only moderate enthusiasm. He said he would give another £50, but was unwilling to ask anyone else for money. A few months later, Ezra's financial position no longer allowed him to help.

Similarly, Eliot was becoming concerned about what he perceived as a change in Ezra's fortunes. In January 1920 he wrote to Quinn that there was now no 'organ of importance' in which Ezra could get his work published, 'and he is becoming forgotten . . . I know that Pound's lack of tact has done him great harm. But I am worried as to what is to become of him.'

22

Douglas The Real Mind

The Pounds came back to London in September 1919, and Ezra once again began to look for a means of supporting himself – an all-too-familiar process. In October he managed to get himself appointed drama critic of a journal called the *Outlook*, for which he would be well paid. It was the sort of job for which he had been searching for years. He published two reviews under the pseudonym 'Marius David Adkins' and was then 'fired in the most caddish manner possible' (he supplied no details).

The following spring he held down for rather longer a job as drama critic of the moribund *Athenaeum*, which was then being edited by John Middleton Murry. His reviews, signed 'T.J.V.', were predictably caustic about West End theatre; he wrote of Barrie's *Mary Rose* that it was 'a fine example of what is wrong with the English stage'. He admitted to Joyce that he had nothing to offer his readers 'save a general dislike of the modern English theatre'. However, the job paid him £10 a month, and thus restored what he had earned from *Poetry*. Meanwhile he continued to write for the *New Age*, but Orage could still only pay very little, and this was a discouragement to quality. 'One simply can't afford to rewrite and properly compress stuff for his rates,' observed Ezra to Quinn.

His new collection of poems, *Quia Pauper Amavi* (the title, from Ovid, seemed to have no relevance to the contents*), was published by the *Egoist* in October 1919. Though strikingly different from its predecessors – it consisted of the four sequences 'Langue d'Oc', 'Moeurs Contemporaines', 'Three Cantos' (in their original form), and 'Homage to Sextus Propertius' – it produced little interested reaction, most reviewers contenting themselves with berating Ezra for the inaccuracies of the Propertius (which they

---

*Ezra translated it for James Laughlin as 'Love on the Dole'.

might not have seen but for Professor Hale). John Gould Fletcher in the monthly *Chapbook* described the book as 'the patchwork and debris of a mind which has never quite been able to find the living, vivid beauty it set out to seek'. Critics were now expected to make such comments about Ezra's work. If he was not exactly forgotten, as Eliot had suggested, he was certainly no longer in the ascendancy.

Even Eliot himself, reviewing the book in the *Athenaeum*, produced a piece that Ezra called 'granite wreaths, leaden laurels, no sign of exhilaration'. Only May Sinclair observed in print that anything very different was happening to his poetry. In the *North American Review* she wrote admiringly of *Homage to Sextus Propertius*: 'You know that it is right because you feel that it is alive.' And she had this to say of 'Three Cantos':

> The form gives scope to his worst qualities and his best; his obscurity, his inconsequence, his caprice, his directness, his ease in the attack; his quickness . . . Anything may happen in this art-form . . . There are as yet but three Cantos published; there may be three hundred before Mr Pound has done, and no reason beyond the reader's convenience why the endless rhapsody should be divided into Cantos at all.

*

'Have done cantos 5, 6, and 7, each more incomprehensible than the one preceding it; dont know whats to be done about it,' Ezra wrote to his father on 13 December 1919. The 'endless rhapsody' was suddenly steaming ahead, though he told Quinn that he felt the whole work was getting 'too too too abstruse and obscure for human consumption'.

This was no exaggeration. The three new cantos were far more opaque than anything before. Like Canto 4 they exemplified Ezra's belief that 'snippets' build up our concept of right and wrong in history, and his theory that 'the method of Luminous Detail' should be pursued in the study of historical events. Unfortunately, in most parts of these new cantos the snippets were much less comprehensible and the details far less luminous than in Canto 4.

Canto 5 deals with fratricides or near-fratricides in ruling families. Its central images are the murder of John Borgia by his elder brother Cesare and the killing of Alessandro Medici by his cousin Lorenzo. Borgia is thrown into the Tiber ('John Borgia is bathed at last') and the canto describes Lorenzo contemplating his cousin's murder by pushing him off a wall. The sixteenth-century Italian historian Varchi is seen pondering the motives behind these actions, and Ezra seems to be condemning writers who conceal or ignore facts about such crimes. But the canto is so full of allusions and half-illusions, so lacking in any kind of luminosity of its own, that almost nothing can be extracted from it without elaborate exegesis, which in the end seems scarcely worth the effort.

Canto 6 recounts the history of Louis VII of France, his wife Eleanor of Aquitaine, and her second marriage to Henry II of England. Writing in his 'Regional' series, Ezra said that relationships between figures like these were as intriguing as anything in a Henry James novel. But his cullings from the historical sources are so eclectic and apparently arbitrary that the canto is opaque and unrewarding. Only in Canto 7 does he recapture something of the real 'ply over ply' feel, as he slips almost imperceptibly from the Trojan elders ('The old men's voices, beneath the columns of false marble') to Henry James in a drawing room ('the great domed head . . . the old voice lifts itself / weaving an endless sentence'). For the first time the present day makes itself firmly apparent; there is a glimpse of Ezra himself in contemporary Paris: 'And the bus behind me gives me a date for peg: / Low ceiling and the Erard and the silver' (Walter Rummel's apartment).

Though his letters to his father and Quinn show that he was worried about the incomprehensibility of the new cantos, he implicitly defended obscurity in the *New Age* in November 1919, while he was writing them, saying that it was not necessary for an artist to 'bring up his knowledge into the mint of consciousness' before transmitting it to his public. Yet he did not like obscurity for its own sake: while reading William Carlos Williams's *Kora in Hell* during 1920 he wrote to him that he was 'inclined to think it is probably most effective when comprehensible'. And to Thomas Hardy in March 1921 he declared:

> I don't want to be obscure – the young poet of 25 who excuses an incoherence on the ground that the people 'never read all the words on a page but merely get a general impression', lifts my hair in horror.
> I am perfectly willing to demand that the reader should read as carefully as he would a difficult latin or greek text.

But the obscurity of Cantos 5, 6 and 7 does not recall a classical text which will finally reward patient unravelling. Rather, the reader encounters an imagination that has not left sufficient clues as to its activities.

The question of obscurity continued to worry him. He wrote hopefully to his old professor from Penn, Felix Schelling: 'In the cantos, as yet? I have managed to make certain passages intelligible in themselves, even though the whole is still unintelligible???? Or perhaps I haven't.' In the spring of 1920 he had told a magazine editor he could produce at least two cantos a year, but no further composition took place until 1922, and this hiatus may have been the result of his worries about incomprehensibility.

*

Only a few weeks after writing the new cantos he stumbled across the dogma that eventually became the driving force behind much of the work. On 22 February 1920 he wrote to his father: 'Have a shot at C. H. Douglas' *Economic Democracy*.'

He reviewed this book two months later in the *Little Review*, where he said he welcomed Douglas's ideas as a much-needed counterblast to the Fabian notion of 'man as a social unit', to 'German philology' with its 'sacrifice of individual intelligence to the Moloch of "Scholarship"' (no doubt he was thinking of Professor Hale), and to George Bernard Shaw's assertion that man is inferior to ideas. Alongside these, Douglas seemed 'a Don Quixote desiring to *"Make democracy safe for the individual"*'.

What was this panacea that could restore individualism to the modern world? It was a little difficult to discover; Ezra's review (like most of his later writings on the subject) hardly indicated what Douglas's book was about. He described it as written in 'rugged and unpolished but clean hitting prose' and said it was 'almost impossible to prove the validity' of Douglas's ideas through quotation. It is doubtful that he fully understood Douglas's theory, for he said repeatedly that Douglas's arguments could not be summed up in a review, although he had plenty of space at his disposal had he chosen to try.

Clifford Hugh Douglas (1879–1952) was a Cheshire draper's son who went to Stockport Grammar School and worked, before the First World War, for the Westinghouse engineering company in India. During 1914–18, as a major in the Royal Flying Corps, he was stationed at the Royal Aircraft Factory in Farnborough in order to reorganize its production and cost accounting. He was already puzzled by the nature of the money supply in Britain and the Empire, and while at Farnborough he developed a theory, which he called 'Social Credit', that seemed to explain everything and suggested remedies for the deficiencies of the system. Douglas found an enthusiastic disciple in A. R. Orage (who helped to improve his prose style), and his *Economic Democracy* was serialized in the *New Age* during 1919.

Ezra met Douglas at the *New Age* office and visited him at his rooms in the Temple. Paul Selver describes Douglas as 'squat and bald, with a foghorn voice, and somewhat Jewish in appearance', which 'imparted a touch of burlesque irony' since Social Credit soon became implicitly anti-Semitic. Selver adds that when Douglas was present nobody else could get a word in. 'Nor was there the remotest likelihood that anything else but Social Credit would discussed, or rather expounded.' Another contemporary describes Douglas as 'absurd' in appearance, short and tubby, resembling a penguin.

Douglas came to Orage because other editors had turned him down. His visionary manner appealed to the quixotic Orage, who described Douglas as 'the Einstein of economics; and in my judgement as little likely to be comprehended practically'. Douglas took Orage as collaborator for his second book, *Credit-Power and Democracy* (1920), and the *New Age* soon bristled with Social Credit slogans.

Douglas had originally been struck by the fact that just before the First World War it had been 'very difficult to get on with various sorts of work in which I was engaged because there was always some question of scarcity of money', but the moment war broke out 'there was no difficulty about getting money for anything, however wild cat the proposal seemed to be'. He considered the problem, and swiftly concluded that the production of goods by manufacturers does not of itself provide sufficient employment or pay sufficient wages to generate enough purchasing power for all manufactured goods to find a market. There is a gap, which is normally filled by exporting the surplus goods and by borrowing money to finance production and create further employment. But, said Douglas, exports lead to competition between countries, which leads to war, while borrowing leads to the accumulation of an unrepayable debt.

Ezra believed that Douglas had discovered the 'great defect' of capitalism; but he had oversimplified the problem, treating production of goods and retail purchasing as if they were the only components in the economic chain, whereas there exists a number of layers between producer and consumer (wholesaler, distributor, et al.) which themselves generate employment and create further purchasing power. Nor was Douglas correct in suggesting that loans automatically accumulate and become unrepayable. In practice, manufacturers' borrowings from banks fluctuate continually, while the amount of credit available to industry does not, as Douglas believed, steadily diminish, but alters as the result of other market factors.

Yet Douglas was by no means a crank or totally wrong-headed in his analysis of the failings of the capitalist system. J. M. Keynes's 'General Theory' of economics, first published in book form in 1935, resembles Douglas's analysis in that it argues that a *laissez-faire* economy without Government intervention will find equilibrium only at a high level of unemployment – a theory that the twentieth century has steadily proved correct.

In the early stage of his acquaintance with Douglas, Ezra tried to get Keynes to take note of Douglas's ideas. He told his father in February 1920 that he had 'managed a meeting between Douglas and Keynes on Thursday last. Douglas the real mind. Keynes fairly courageous in his book [*The Economic Consequences of the Peace* (1919)], but has invented whole Roman Apostolica Church of economics, just as bad as the old Whore of Babylon.' Keynes's real sin in Ezra's eyes was that he belonged to the despicable tribe of 'pseudorasts and Bloomsbuggars' and could therefore be dismissed as 'a fake, a typical Bloomsbury figure who has attained prominence by loose expression and by the persistent peddling of bunk'.

Douglas's remedy for the flaw he had perceived in the economy was that 'the State should lend, not borrow': that there should be Government intervention in the form of 'Social Credit', a new 'money', the closely controlled circulation of which would enable manufacturers to lower their prices, and allow consumers to buy freely. This would dispense with bank loans, destroy the power of the money-lenders, and inaugurate a new era of personal freedom and prosperity. If the scheme were adopted, wrote Douglas in *Economic Democracy*, then 'out of threatened chaos might the Dawn break; a dawn which at the best must show the ravages of storm, but which holds clear for all to see the promise of a better Day'. The language indicates the fanaticism which infected Social Credit from the start.

The new 'money' was not to be created by taxation. Indeed it was not to be 'money' in the old sense at all, simply 'certificates of work done', based on the Government's careful estimate of actual production – a 'National Dividend' and a 'Compensated Price' rather than the inflationary printing of currency. If prices began to rise then the subsidy would be withheld. It was to be based, as Ezra put it, on 'the nation's real profits', on 'what the whole people produce' rather than on the whim of bankers. It was thus, he said, 'REAL' money.

This was where more orthodox economists parted company with Douglas. Keynes argued that while there was 'no valid reply' to much of Douglas's criticism of the *laissez-faire* system, the Social Credit remedy was mere 'mystification'. He added that the withholding of dividends if prices went up would not differ from the banks' refusal to renew loans or overdrafts. F. S. Flint, a trained statistician as well as a poet, examined Social Credit in print and similarly asserted that Douglas's system did not bear inspection. He explained:

> The national dividend is nothing more than the printing of money disguised under a metaphor . . . [It] is difficult to see how . . . [it] could be prevented from raising prices . . . To superimpose a National Dividend or a Compensated Price, or both, such as Major Douglas advocates . . . would lead to continuous inflation and collapse through too much money, instead of through too little.

Ezra answered this by asserting that Social Credit was 'not inflationist and can *not* lead to inflation'; but his only argument was that inflation 'has always meant a depreciation of the value of the monetary unit' and this was not technically possible under Social Credit. He offered no mathematical or other proof, and refused to recognize that Flint had any authority in the subject or that he was more than a minor Imagist.

He was not beyond seeing faults in Douglas: he observed that there was an 'absence of practicality' in Social Credit, an 'absence of consideration of *means* whereby state wd. arrange to compensate, etc.' But in general he refused to discuss challenges to Douglas's ideas, treating them as self-evident.

*

Ezra's first trumpeting of Social Credit as something that could 'make democracy safe for the individual' was soon replaced by another, more disturbing emphasis. As early as March 1920 the *New Age* carried a piece by him which mentioned approvingly 'Major C. H. Douglas' profound attack on usury.'

It was true that in *Economic Democracy* Douglas made some vague remarks about money-lenders. For example: 'Positions of power fall to men whose very habit of mind . . . must quite inevitably force them to consider the individual as mere material for a policy.' But there was nothing stronger than this, and it is possible that Ezra came to Douglas hoping to find an anti-Semitism in his attack on money-lending which was not really there. On the other hand, his own writing had already shown definite elements of it.

In November 1919 in the *New Age* he alleged that while an African savage uses his tribal god merely as an excuse to 'bash' his neighbour, 'the Jew, however, received a sort of roving commission from his "Jhv" [Jehovah] to bash all and sundry'. Moreover, 'since the lions of the Tribe of Judah gave up the sword, "beat it" metaphorically into the pawn-shop, their power has steadily increased; no such suave and uninterrupted extension of power is to be attributed to any "world-conquering bellicose nation"'. There were, apparently, complaints about this from *New Age* readers, for in the next issue he wrote:

> My last antithesis sprang from no antisemitism. I point out
> simply the practicality of avoiding needless coercions, strifes,
> and combustions. Inasmuch as the Jew has conducted no holy
> war for nearly two millennia, he is preferable to the Christian
> and the Mahomedan.

But this was just a sop. He had always enjoyed expressing, when it amused him, the anti-Semitism typical of many white middle-class Americans.

A major acceleration of anti-Jewish feeling had begun in the United States in the 1870s. Jewish settlers had faced difficulties in America ever since they had started to arrive there in the seventeenth century, but a new note of suspicion and hatred appeared with the mass immigration from Eastern Europe during the last quarter of the nineteenth. Jews began to be identified widely with petty crime – in 1908 the New York City police commissioner claimed that 50 per cent of the city's criminal class were Russian Jews – and Fagin-like Jews were depicted with vehement hostility in popular literature such as the rags-to-riches novels of Horatio Alger. The verb 'to Jew', meaning to cheat by sharp practices, entered the American slang vocabulary as early as the 1840s. The Civil War earned Jews the reputation for exploitation and profiteering at the expense of both sides (General Grant issued an infamous Order in 1862 expelling all Jews from Tennessee for violating trade regulations), and one newspaper declared that 'Hooked-nose wretches speculate on disasters, and a battle lost to our army is chuckled over by them, as it puts money in their purse.' Even the novels of Henry James reflect these attitudes, with their frequent inclusion of unpleasant Jewish money-lenders and other unflattering portraits of the race. Intolerance was widespread among the patricians of the eastern American seaboard. James Russell Lowell, though a Hebrew scholar and devotee of Old Testament Jewry, developed a terrible repugnance for the modern Jews of Europe which grew into an insane obsession. The descendants of John Quincy Adams, Henry and Brooks Adams, blamed the Jews for the iniquities of modern American society. Until the end of the 1920s – after which the picture was complicated by a reaction against reports of Nazi anti-Semitism in Germany – in quarters such as these there was an almost ubiquitous interpretation of Jewish solidarity as a conspiratorial desire to seize power. It was in this climate that the Harvard-educated T. S. Eliot could write in 'Gerontion'

> My house is a decayed house,
> And the Jew squats on the window-sill, the owner,
> Spawned in some estaminet of Antwerp,
> Blistered in Brussels, patched and peeled in London

– could speak in 'Burbank with a Baedeker' of Bleistein as a 'Chicago Semite Viennese' with 'A lustreless protrusive eye'; could observe indeed that

> The rats are underneath the piles.
> The Jew is underneath the lot.

Anti-Semitism often found a populist platform. In May 1920, just as Ezra was praising C. H. Douglas in the *Little Review*, Henry Ford began to write a series of rabidly anti-Semitic articles in his American journal the *Dearborn Independent*, blaming all society's ills, from Tammany Hall corruption and bootlegging to the 'sensuousness' of jazz music, on the influence of the Jews. Ford was eventually persuaded to apologize, but the episode did not harm his reputation. Even an intelligent, well-educated man like John Quinn could write in 1923 to Lady Gregory: 'I don't believe that . . . anything ever came out of the Jews or Jerusalem except filth and stench. We have two million seven hundred thousand Jews in New York City and they are awful.' (Quinn, it should be remembered, was an Irishman.)

Ezra, then, brought a good deal of experience of anti-Semitism with him to London, and he found plenty of it there when he arrived. Suspicion and fear of Jewish financiers was such a commonplace of Edwardian society that Ford Madox Hueffer could write casually in his novel *A Call* (1910) that a Harley Street doctor was 'heavily indebted to the Jews'. Dorothy Pound had been brought up in this climate: in a 1913 letter to Ezra she observes that 'rich, stockbroking Jews are *not* nice company', and James Laughlin remembers that when the conversation got round to the Jews there would be 'a gleam in her eye'.

'I am racially fifteen parts English and the remaining sixteenth part Celtic,' Ezra wrote in the *New Age* in January 1920, 'and I was born in a country where the Anglo-Saxon stock is now said to be in a minority.' At moments he seemed quite unambiguously anti-Semitic. Around 1916 he wrote to a correspondent: 'Hueffer is damn well no jew, and no man ever had less of the jew in him.' Yet the next moment he might attack racial prejudice as a symptom of mental inadequacy. 'Jews!!!! ooo sez I ates the jews?' he asked his father in 1927. 'I hate SOME JEWS, but I have greater contempt for Christians. Look wot they dun to america; Bryan, Wilson, Volstead,* all goyim, horrible goyim. Curtis, Lorimer,† american womens clubs, all the tripe, all goyim. Of course some jews are unpleasant, ask any jew if they aint.' He was similarly eloquent in October 1920 when his father made some adverse remark about 'niggers', remarking: 'My recollections of nearly all the niggers I have ever known are quite pleasant; I can't say as much or anything like for whites . . . frankly after 35 years among anglo-saxons I am not in the least convinced that they are superior to any race whatsoever.'

Throughout his adult life he was friendly with a number of Jews, and he seemed to see no contradiction between this and his expression of anti-Jewish attitudes. In December 1921 he wrote in a letter about some unidentified acquaintance:

> I will say this at least for Gracie, she isn't a jew. (Sauf les Cohens, les chers Cohens. Give them my best regards, with affectionate greetings to Mrs C. and respectful salutations to Judith, and cordial poignee de main to Father.)

---

*William Jennings Bryan, fanatical defender of religious fundamentalism; Woodrow Wilson; and Congressman Volstead who introduced Prohibition.

†Cyrus Curtis and George H. Lorimer, respectively owner and editor of the *Saturday Evening Post*, figures from Ezra's Wyncote childhood.

One may try from all this to draw some consistent picture of his attitudes: to say he had imbibed a certain amount of prejudice in his childhood and never shook it off; that he was inclined to air it whenever he wanted to tease or be outrageous, but was never blindly anti-Semitic in the way that (say) Henry Ford or John Quinn were; and that at more sober moments he did not dream of suggesting that the Jews were more responsible for the world's ills than was any other race. But to argue consistency would be misleading. On this issue more than anything else he was completely unpredictable, impossible to pin down, delighting in making anti-Semitic statements on inappropriate occasions, and equally pleased to annoy anti-Semites by saying that he had plenty of Jewish friends. A naughty schoolboy might do as much, and really there seems something essentially childish about his whole interest in Jews and Jewry.

Like a schoolboy, he was perpetually interested in circumcision and its effects (he himself had not been circumcised). He told Charles Olson in 1946:

> There was a Jew, in London, Obermeyer, a doctor . . . of the endocrines, and I used to ask him what is the effect of circumcision. That's the question that gets them sore . . . that sends them right up the pole. Try it, don't take my word, try it . . . It must do something, after all these years and years, where the most sensitive nerves in the body are, rubbing them off, over and over again.

Olson noted that when he said this he looked 'impish as hell'.

23

Atmospheres, Nuances

Early in 1920 T. S. Eliot, worrying about Ezra's future, asked John Quinn to persuade the *Dial* to take him on as its representative in London. Founded in Chicago in 1880 as a monthly journal of literary criticism with a conservative tone, the *Dial* was now based in New York and being edited by Eliot's old school and college acquaintance Scofield Thayer. As Eliot himself admitted, it was still 'second-rate and exceedingly solemn'. He hoped that Ezra might be able to liven it up.

Thayer agreed that Ezra should receive $750 for an experimental year, during which he would perform the sort of services he had for *Poetry* and the *Little Review*; but there was no question of publishing inflammatory material like *Ulysses*, and he would have no say in editorial policy. Ezra made the best of this, ordering impressive printed stationery with the *Dial* name at the top and a list of well-known contributors he hoped to commission, but he found it rather a come-down. Thayer was inclined to behave like the curator of an over-endowed American picture gallery, wanting 'European celebrities' at any cost and spending 'vast sums getting their left-overs'. Ezra himself succeeded in printing nothing of note by anyone else in the *Dial*'s pages but the magazine was prepared to publish his own work, and it became the current testing ground for fresh cantos. Also, in September 1920, it printed six poems from the first part of his new sequence *Hugh Selwyn Mauberley*.

'Am sending you "Mauberley", my new poems, advance sheets,' Ezra wrote to his father during the spring of 1920. The entire sequence was printed in London by John Rodker in June 1920 under the title *Hugh Selwyn Mauberley by E. P.* in an edition of 200 copies with initial letters drawn by Edward Wadsworth. It was reprinted in Ezra's *Poems 1918–21* (Boni & Liveright, 1921) and in *Personae* (1926).

The anonymous *Times Literary Supplement* reviewer of the Rodker edition thought *Hugh Selwyn Mauberley* 'needlessly obscure . . . an esoteric volume'. However, in the autumn of 1920 Ezra told his father that 'Yeats appears to approve rather vigorously of parts of Mauberley';* Eliot wrote of it in 1928 as 'much the finest poem, I believe, before the Cantos'; and it was the first piece of Ezra's work really to impress F. R. Leavis. In *New Bearings in English Poetry* (1932) Leavis writes:

> In *Mauberley* we feel a pressure of experience, an impulsion from deep within. The verse is extraordinarily subtle, and its subtletly is the subtlety of the sensibility that it expresses. No one would think here of distinguishing the way of saying from the thing said.

One day in a garden in Cambridge Leavis read *Hugh Selwyn Mauberley* to one of his pupils, Ronald Duncan. 'The superb restraint of *Mauberley*, its urbane flexibility,' writes Duncan, 'the way the verse is handled so that the meaning runs against the verse-structure, impressed me deeply. I had never read anything like this before. All the romantic outpourings seemed tame compared to the tough irony of Pound.'

Ezra himself said that *Hugh Selwyn Mauberley* originated as an attempt to repeat the 'message' of *Homage to Sextus Propertius*. 'Propertius/ is related to ANY empire declining onto the shit pile. When even tolerably intelligent people couldnt understand THAT, I did the Mauberley, all on the top; or at least with external details modern.' He thought on the whole it was an 'advance' on *Propertius*, 'by no means as rich . . . but has form, hell yes, structure, and is in strictly modern décor.'

Hugh Selwyn Mauberley,† the implicit subject of the whole sequence and the explicit central figure of the second half, is another of Ezra's masks or personae, but more consciously artificial than those he had previously

---

*Ezra sent Yeats a copy of the Rodker printing of the poem, and Yeats wrote back on 22 August 1920 that the first section had 'an extraordinary distinction, & an utterly new music'. Some of the second section had 'lovely lines' but 'I have not mastered the poem yet'. He continued: 'But those first 14 pages, there I am certain, there certainly you have discovered yourself – a melancholy full of wisdom & self knowledge that is full of beauty – style which is always neighbour to nobility when it is neighbour to beauty, a proud humility, that quality that makes ones hair stand up on end as though one saw a spirit. You have gripped all that now.'

†His name seems to have been derived from several people. 'Selwyn' may have came from Selwyn Image, one of the 1890s figures whom Ezra knew in London. The critic J. J. Espey, who has studied the poem at length, suggests that 'Hugh' may have something to do with a character in Henry James's short story 'The Figure in the Carpet', Hugh Vereker, a novelist pursued by a young scholar who hopes to discover the great uniting theme that runs through his work. Espey has also discovered the existence of a Brigadier Hugh Stephenson Moberley (1873–1943), though there is no evidence that Ezra knew him.

adopted, a pose that he did not wish for a moment to be confused with his real self. 'Of course I'm no more Mauberley than Eliot is Prufrock,' he wrote in 1922. Mauberley is a refined, effete, exclusively 'aesthetic' and dilettante version of certain aspects of Ezra, and is mocked by him for making the wrong choices. Mauberley lets himself become the victim of the society in which he moves, and so fails to be a great artist. The poem is thus a kind of cautionary tale, a warning to its own author.

But only at particular moments. At other times it is simply a set of vignettes of certain of Ezra's contemporaries in thin disguise, the theme disappearing behind a series of accomplished experiments in rhythm and sound. Leavis rightly judged it Ezra's technical masterpiece, but it is a triumph of versification and verbal dexterity that frequently fails to communicate discernible meaning, and Ezra's claim that it has structure can scarcely be justified. A plan exists, but it is very loosely executed.

*

The full title and subtitle, *Hugh Selwyn Mauberley (Life and Contacts)* announces the work as if it were a piece of pompous literary biography such as Gosse's *Life of Swinburne*, which Ezra thought so ridiculous. The first poem, 'E. P. Ode Pour l'Election de Son Sepulchre', was suggested by Ronsard's 'De l'Election de son Sepulchre', and is an ironic epitaph on Ezra himself by his critics:

> For three years, out of key with his time,
> He strove to resuscitate the dead art
> Of poetry; to maintain 'the sublime'
> In the old sense. Wrong from the start . . .

The 'three years', if we are to treat this as strict autobiography, would be 1909–1911, during which Ezra had devoted himself to the resuscitation of the troubadours, Cavalcanti, and other practitioners of the 'sublime'. He goes on to excuse (with heavy irony) his absurd determination to 'wring . . . lilies from the acorn' by observing that he was 'born / In a half savage country' and was simply 'out of date'. He then portrays himself as a Ulysses fishing by 'obstinate isles' (his studies in Provençal and other erudite literature) rather than paying attention to 'the march of events'.

In the second poem (untitled, as are many in the sequence) he replies to this ironic self-denunciation, saying he lives in an age which prefers 'mendacities' to 'the classics in paraphrase' (a reference to the attacks on *Propertius*). 'The age demanded' such artistic short-cuts as 'a mould in plaster / Made with no loss of time', an image recalling Gaudier-Brzeska's struggle to use stone and metal rather than plaster. The third poem contrasts modern trivialities with the classical ideals, in a verse form taken from Gautier:

> The tea-rose tea-gown, etc.
> Supplants the mousseline of Cos,
> The pianola 'replaces'
> Sappho's barbitos.

'Barbitos' means 'lyre', and the opening line alludes to Gautier's poems 'La Rose-thé' and 'A une robe rose'. The 'mousseline of Cos' again recalls *Propertius* ('If she goes in a gleam of Cos, in a slither of dyed stuff, / There is a volume in the matter').

The fourth poem describes the sacrifices of the First World War, which seem pointless in view of the 'many deceits' of the civilization they were meant to defend, though the poem praises heroism in the trenches:

> . . . Died some, pro patria,
> non 'dulce' non 'et decor' –
> walked eye-deep in hell
> believing old men's lies, then unbelieving
> came home, home to a lie . . .
>
> Daring as never before, wastage as never before,
> Young blood and high blood,
> fair cheeks, and fine bodies;
>
> fortitude as never before
> frankness as never before,
> disillusions as never told in the old days,
> hysterias, trench confessions,
> laughter out of dead bellies.

This is fine stuff, but one cannot help remembering that Ezra had spent the war at his typewriter in Kensington and at Stone Cottage. The fifth poem is more honestly expressive of his feelings that the war dead had wasted their lives defending 'an old bitch gone in the teeth, / . . . a botched civilization'.

The remainder of the first half of *Mauberley* is made up of a series of portraits of eras or individuals intended to epitomize what Ezra believes to be the decayed intellectual–artistic state of England. The poem 'Yeux Glauques' (an expression from Gautier, also recalling *glaukopos* in 'Three Cantos') describes the Pre-Raphaelite era, during which Gladstone and Ruskin were 'respected', Swinburne and Rossetti 'abused', and the prevailing image was of Lizzie Siddal's 'vacant gaze' in Burne-Jones's pictures. Ezra then turns to one man as representative of the 1890s – Victor Plarr, whose reminiscences of the Rhymers' Club had so intrigued him, and whom he disguises as 'Monsieur Verog . . . out of step with the decade / . . . Neglected by the young', but by implication a representative of a better era than the present. In contrast are two portraits of successful contemporary *littérateurs*, first Max Beerbohm ('Brennbaum') who is described as hiding his supposedly Jewish race beneath a mask of English correctness (Beerbohm was not in fact Jewish)*, and 'Mr Nixon', the literary go-getter interested only in cash – a caricature of Arnold Bennett, to whom Ezra often referred as a symbol of the age's degeneracy. Mr Nixon's concluding piece of advice, given 'In the cream gilded cabin of his steam yacht', is 'give up verse, my boy / There's nothing in it.'

In contrast, the tenth poem of the sequence describes an impecunious 'stylist' who has taken shelter from an unappreciative world in a ramshackle cottage. This is Ford Madox Hueffer, who had served in the war (though over age) and who was now living penuriously in Sussex. He changed his surname to Ford by deed poll in June 1919, saying it was 'partly to oblige a relative & partly because a Teutonic name is in these days disagreeable'. The relative was his wife, who had objected to Violet Hunt calling herself 'Mrs Hueffer'. Though Ford and Violet had now parted company, Ezra continued to socialize with both, observing 'These things do happen – one receives the parties on alternate days.' Ford was now living with Ezra's friend Stella Bowen – he told her he was 'a lonely and very tired person who wanted to dig potatoes and raise pigs and never write another book'. Ezra visited them; Ford describes how 'Mr Pound appeared, aloft on the seat of an immense high dog-cart, like a bewildered Stuart pretender visiting a repellent portion of his realms. For Mr Pound hated the country, though I will put it on record that he can carve a sucking pig as few others can.' During this period of country life Ford bought an Angora goat which he named Penny, 'because he facially resembled (but was not) POUND, Ezra'.

Next, *Mauberley* considers two female types, the 'educated' middle-class Englishwoman in whom 'No instinct has survived . . . / Older than those her grandmother / Told her would fit her station', and the fashionable literary hostess to whom poetry is merely a device for social manipulation. This poem, with Ezra/Mauberley's uncertainties about his clothes and the value of his hostess's 'approbation', has a certain resemblance to 'Prufrock':

> . . . In the stuffed-satin drawing-room
> I await the Lady Valentine's commands,
>
> Knowing my coat has never been
> Of precisely the fashion
> To stimulate, in her,
> A durable passion;

---

*Ezra wrote to his father in March 1914 that Beerbohm was going to draw a caricature of him, but it does not seem to have happened. He did not say how or where he met him.

Doubtful, somewhat, of the value
Of well-gowned approbation
Of literary effort . . .

The first section of *Mauberley* concludes with an 'Envoi' in imitation of Waller's 'Go, Lovely Rose', which was set to music by Henry Lawes – a recollection of the last age in England when poetry was still closely allied with music. If (says Ezra) England could still have a feeling for 'song' it would condone and understand his own faults and recognize his virtues. Instead it cares only for transient, trivial things, while he himself wants great art that will survive. He seems finally to be warning England that 'some other mouth' (perhaps another country) might be 'as fair as hers', might provide a worthy home for a poet such as himself. But this is a rather conjectural interpretation, and 'Envoi' remains enigmatic. Is an actual singer, perhaps Raymonde Collignon, being addressed?

Tell her that goes
With song upon her lips
But sings not out the song, nor knows
The maker of it, some other mouth,
May be as fair as hers,
Might, in new ages, gain her worshippers,
When our two dusts with Waller's shall be laid,
Siftings on siftings in oblivion,
Till change hath broken down
All things save Beauty alone.

The poem is an elegant pastiche of a seventeenth-century lyric, but it seems an odd stylistic conclusion to a sequence in 'strictly modern décor'. Ezra afterwards (1926) described *Mauberley* as 'distinctly a farewell to London', but at the time he wrote it he does not seem to have begun seriously to consider leaving England. Perhaps, with its condemnation of so much in English artistic life, the sequence itself may have prompted him to leave.

*

The second half of *Hugh Selwyn Mauberley* seems to begin the whole enterprise again, for it is headed 'Mauberley (1920)' as if it were an entirely different work. In fact this second section is almost a mirror image of the first, revisiting it and sometimes quoting directly from it. However, instead of merely presenting a series of detached pictures of British artistic life, with Ezra himself as implied observer, it now gives a connected biographical portrait of the invented Mauberley. We have had the milieu; now we have the story.

The most significant difference between the two halves is that, whereas by implication Part I criticizes and rejects the milieu it describes, in Part II Mauberley himself accepts it and tries to survive in it without combating its faults. He therefore falls prey to it, producing only insignificant art before fading away into obscurity or perhaps an early death. The date '1920' at the head of the section seems intended to emphasize that all this is taking place at the present time.

The first poem in the second section describes Mauberley abandoning worthy artistic endeavours for trivial public tasks. He is here presented as an engraver or painter (he is never specifically stated to be a poet), and the poem shows him turning aside from fine etching ('the "eau forte / Par Jacquemart"' – a reference to an engraving of Gautier which appears as the frontispiece to *Émaux et Camées*) in order to make 'medallions' of the famous. The result is merely 'an art / In profile; / Colourless . . .' In the second poem, having drifted for years in his own illusory notions about beauty, Mauberley becomes aware of sexual love as something he could have experienced – but it is already too late:

> Given that is his 'fundamental passion',
> This urge to convey the relation
> Of eye-lid and cheek-bone
> By verbal manifestation . . .
>
> He had passed, inconscient, full gaze,
> The wide-banded irides
> And botticellian sprays implied
> In their diastasis;
>
> Which anaesthesis, noted a year late,
> And weighed, revealed his great affect,
> (Orchid), mandate
> Of Eros, a retrospect.

'The Age Demanded' (the next poem) seems to show Mauberley retreating from its demands into isolation, which strengthens him against its gibes but leads to his 'final / Exclusion from the world of letters'. But this is a difficult and needlessly obscure passage, all nuance and no statement, and Ezra seems once again to be talking about himself rather than Mauberley – the 'Exclusion from the world of letters' is certainly what he believed he had experienced.

In the fourth poem Mauberley drifts, a mere hedonist, to his demise on some 'unforecasted beach'. The final poem, 'Medallion', is perhaps meant to be Mauberley's own work, a highly mannered porcelain portrait of the singer (therefore, presumably, England herself) of the 'Envoi' of Part I. Yet it is hard to believe that there is meant to be parody in its muted tones:

> The face-oval beneath the glaze,
> Bright in its suave bounding-line, as,
> Beneath half-watt rays,
> The eyes turn topaz.

Could the drifting, hedonist Mauberley really have created this? Does Ezra want us to take it as a piece of failed minor art?

One is left with the final impression that *Hugh Selwyn Mauberley*, for all its apparent scheme and its frequent concern – at least in Part I – with the literary world that Ezra knew, is in the end a chiefly abstract work, which takes care of the sounds in the hope that the sense will take care of itself: a game with language, rhythm, and metre, in its own words

> A consciousness disjunct,
> Being but this overblotted
> Series
> Of intermittences

which is scarcely meant to yield more than the most impressionistic narrative, nor to picture anything other than itself. Like Ezra's 1912 poem 'The Return' it is not so much a poem about its ostensible subject as an object with an independent reality of its own, a piece of abstract sculpture.

On two occasions, Ezra compared it to a work of fiction. He said it had been a 'definite attempt to get the novel cut down to the size of verse'; and he called it 'a study in form, an attempt to condense the James novel'. The clue here is 'James'. We should not look for plot but for manner of narrative, and remember Ezra's remark, in his *Little Review* study of James, that James's real 'subject' was 'atmospheres, nuances, impressions of personal tone and quality'.

The weakness of *Mauberley* is that comprehension has too often been sacrificed to nuance. Its strength is the advance in verse technique. When prescribing that he and Eliot should study Gautier and metrical psalms, Ezra was not advocating the abandonment of *vers libre* and a return to strictly metrical forms. During 1920 he explained to Ford Madox Ford that any element of regularity must be balanced by an equal irregularity in some other aspect: 'In verse one can take any damn constant one likes, one can alliterate, or assone, or rhyme, or quant, or smack, only one MUST leave the other elements irregular.' This is the principle on which *Mauberley* is constructed. It is, as Ezra put it elsewhere, 'regular verse' with 'an irregular movement underlying'. The regularity was derived from Gautier; the broken rhythms, which deliberately obtrude and work against the urbanity of the form, were learnt (as Ezra explained to Felix Schelling in 1922) partly from Bion, the first century BC Greek poet, particularly his *Adonis*: 'Syncopation from the Greek, and a general distaste for the slushiness and

The house built for Homer in Hailey, Idaho, where Ezra was born. *(University of Texas)*

Ezra aged three, still in pinafore and ringlets, on the knee of his grandfather Thaddeus. Homer stands behind; opposite sits great-grandfather Elijah. *(Mary de Rachewiltz)*

Grandfather Thaddeus Pound: 'Wherever he discovers a great public need he hastens to supply it.' *(Mary de Rachewiltz)*

Ezra and his classmates at the Wyncote Public School, probably in the spring of 1895, when he was nine. He is second from the right in the back row, with Tommy Cochran on his left and the tall Jimmy Luskin on his right. *(University of Pennsylvania)*

Homer and Ezra in Homer's office at the Mint. *(Mary de Rachewiltz)*

Ezra, aged twelve, wearing glasses, looking very much the new boy at Cheltenham Military Academy. *(University of Pennsylvania)*

Ezra, aged about thirteen, perches on the arm of his mother's chair (wearing his CMA uniform) in a photographer's studio; Isabel is now in her late thirties. *(Mary de Rachewiltz)*

Commencement ceremony at the University of Pennsylvania during Ezra's freshman year. *(University of Pennsylvania)*

Freshman group photograph, University of Pennsylvania, 1901–2. Ezra stands at the left-hand end of the back row, in beret and white scarf. *(University of Pennsylvania)*

William Carlos Williams as Ezra first knew him. *(New Directions Publishing Corp.)*

Ezra *(second from left)* as a maiden in Euripides' *Iphigenia in Tauris*, University of Pennsylvania, April 1903: 'He . . . heaved his massive breasts in ecstasies of extreme emotion.' *(University of Pennsylvania)*

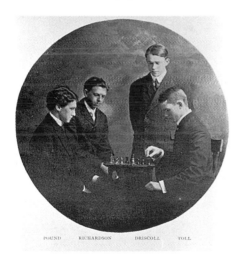

POUND   RICHARDSON   DRISCOLL   TOLL

Chess team at Hamilton College; Ezra is now aged eighteen. *(University of Pennsylvania)*

Hilda Doolittle around the time Ezra
began to court her, in 1905, when she was
nineteen. *(Perdita Schaffner and New
Directions Publishing Corp.)*

Another portrait of Hilda Doolittle: 'Is-
hilda . . . Dryad . . .'
(Mary de Rachewiltz)

Mary Moore of Trenton: 'Dear Furry
Little Rabbit'. *(University of
Pennsylvania)*

Venice: junction of the Canal San Vio with the Canal Grande, a few yards from Ezra's first lodging in 1908: 'By the soap-smooth stone posts where San Vio / meets with Il Canal Grande.' *(Photo by Humphrey Carpenter)*

This Book was

LA FRAISNE

(THE ASH TREE)

dedicated

to such as love this same
beauty that I love, somewhat
after mine own fashion.

But sith one of them has gone out very quickly from amongst us it is given

A LUME SPENTO

(WITH TAPERS QUENCHED)

in memoriam eius mihi caritate primus

William Brooke Smith

Painter, Dreamer of dreams.

Dedication page of *A Lume Spento* (1908), Ezra's first printed collection of poems. *(Bodleian Library)*

Two portraits of Dorothy Shakespear:
'With the air, always, of a young Victorian
lady out skating.' *(Mary de Rachewiltz)*

A portrait photograph of Ezra taken by
Elliott and Fry of Baker Street and printed
in *Bookman* in July 1909, just as London
was starting to notice him.
(Yale University)

10 Church Walk, Kensington. The 'X'
marks Ezra's room. *(University of Texas)*

Ezra in his dressing gown at Church Walk, photographed by Alvin Langdon Coburn. 'More like Kh-r-ist and the late James McNeill Whistler every year,' said Frederic Manning. *(Bodleian Library)*

'H. D., Imagiste.' Hilda Doolittle around the time (1912) that Ezra enrolled her into his 'little gang'. *(Yale University and New Directions Publishing Corp.)*

Richard Aldington, the other pioneer Imagist: 'Whenever Ezra has launched a new movement . . . he just calls on his friends.' *(Photo by Howard Coster, National Portrait Gallery)*

The poets' outing to Wilfred Scawen Blunt, 18 January 1914: 'He wasn't sure at first whether we were a deputation of poets or horse-breeders.' *Left to right:* Victor Plarr, Sturge Moore, W. B. Yeats ('disguised by influenza and glasses'), Blunt, Ezra, Richard Aldington (with hair, moustache and beard copied from Ezra), and F. S. Flint. *(University of Texas)*

Henri Gaudier-Brzeska at work on the head of Ezra, under the railway arches at Putney, February 1914: 'It *will – not – look* – like you.' *(Bodleian Library)*

One of Gaudier-Brzeska's preliminary drawings for the head. *(Kettle's Yard, University of Cambridge)*

Gaudier-Brzeska's *Hieratic Head of Ezra Pound. (Kettle's Yard, University of Cambridge; Anthony d'Offay)*

Wyndham Lewis in 1914, the year in which he and Ezra joined forces on *BLAST*. *(BBC Hulton Picture Library)*

'An American called Eliot', at about the time Ezra met him, in the autumn of 1914.
(BBC Hulton Picture Library)

Passport photograph of Ezra, *c.* 1919. *(Yale University)*

swishness of the post-Swinburnian British line.' But really, as Ezra wrote elsewhere of the *Mauberley* style of verse, 'There aren't any *rules*. Thing is to cut a shape in time. Sounds that stop the flow, and durations, either of syllables, or implied between them.'

Shifting To Paris

Soon after *Mauberley* was finished, around the end of April 1920, Ezra and Dorothy left London for another Continental holiday, going via Paris to Venice, which Ezra had not visited since before the war. The intention was to continue to Trieste where James Joyce was again living, but Dorothy became unwell and they decided to retreat to Sirmione instead. However, before they left Venice, Ezra began to write his next series for the *New Age*. This was *Indiscretions*, his Jamesian exercise in autobiography, published in the magazine in twelve instalments beginning at the end of May. The use of James's voice was partly dictated by his wish to distance himself from the highly personal subject matter, to set himself above this potentially trivial chronicle of family matters. It was also to remind the reader that, like a James novel, it was supposed to be a representative account of a certain ambience of American life.

The writing of an autobiography, however restricted and mannered, together with the publication at about the same time of *Umbra*, all that he wished to 'preserve' from his early poetry (issued by Elkin Mathews in the summer of 1920), hints at a consciousness in Ezra of some imminent change in his life. It was partly an awareness of the closing of his youth: he would be thirty-five in October. There was, however, no suggestion in *Indiscretions* that he might leave London. Indeed he spoke of that city as an outstanding place in which to collect specimens of human behaviour, a locality where 'one has so much better a chance of finding a "good one", a higher demarcation, a wider divergence from human cliché'. By contrast Paris seemed merely 'parenthetical', an 'occasional watch-tower'; Venice was certainly capable of administering 'the old kick to the senses', but not perhaps of offering any new perception about humanity.

By mid-May they were at Sirmione, at the Hotel Eden. Life by Lake

Garda was still astonishingly cheap: Ezra wrote to Joyce – whom he had never yet met – asking him to spend a week there at his and Dorothy's expense. Joyce sent back a tentative 'yes' and made plans to travel from Trieste, but, typically, failed to appear on account of railway strikes, accidents, and timetables that did not appeal to him. He wrote to Ezra about this at enormous length, mentioning in passing that he could not afford to buy clothes in Trieste, 'so I think I ought to go to Dublin to buy them'. He added 'This is a very poetical epistle. Do not imagine that it is a subtly worded request for secondhand clothing. It should be read in the evening when the lakewater is lapping and very rhythmically.'

Ezra had been awaiting Joyce's arrival on the evening originally agreed. Joyce's non-appearance was accompanied by a huge thunderstorm, 'as I thought cd. portend only the arrival of Vulcan Dedalus,' Ezra wrote to him. When he learnt of all Joyce's complications with regard to travel, not to mention clothes, he replied: 'Christ, what can I advise you to do.' He tried to persuade Joyce to 'come here with family – regarding it as 1st stage of journey to Ireland', and said 'I shall be glad to contribute 1000 lire' which 'wd. break the back of a fortnights expenses here . . . With your reputation you should be able to live – oh christ, I don't know how anyone lives. I live but haven't offspring.'

A fine farce now ensued, with Ezra rushing around Sirmione making arrangements for the arrival of the entire Joyce family, and sending complicated instructions to Joyce, who was meanwhile in an agony of indecision, suggesting that Ezra should come to Trieste, and putting off the journey because of his dread of thunderstorms. Then abruptly on 8 June he made up his mind, bringing his lanky son Giorgio with him 'to act as a lightning conductor'.

In the Pisan prison camp in 1945 'a small rain storm' brought to Ezra's mind

> the arrival of Joyce et fils
> at the haunt of Catullus
> with Jim's veneration of thunder and the Gardasee in
> magnificence.

He went over to Desenzano, the nearest railway station, and brought Joyce back to the Hotel Eden.

Ezra's first impression of Joyce was not good: he afterwards remembered encountering a 'shell of cantankerous Irishman'. Joyce sensed this and thought Ezra found him disappointing. But the reaction was only superficial; a couple of weeks later Ezra wrote to Quinn: 'I got the impression that the real man is the author of *Chamber Music*, the sensitive. The rest is the genius; the registration of realities on the temperament, the delicate temperament of the early poems. A concentration and absorption passing Yeats . . . Also great exhaustion, but more constitution than I had expected, and apparently good recovery from eye operation.' Joyce's first impression of Ezra, meanwhile, was of 'a large bundle of unpredictable electricity', 'a miracle of ebulliency, gusto, and help'.

One of their first topics on the drive back to the Hotel Eden was the identity of Joyce's mysterious patron – in fact Harriet Shaw Weaver – who had been making regular payments to him since 1915. Ezra asked Joyce if he thought it might be Quinn; Joyce afterwards recalled that 'My high tenor shout of "Who?" must have been heard in Milan.' Joyce stayed in Sirmione for two days, and after talking to Ezra decided he would take his family experimentally to Paris, for reasons that Ezra had already put to him by letter, namely that 'France *was* the cheapest place last year' and 'the Portrait ought to be translated into french'. Ezra himself planned to go on to Paris from Sirmione and would be 'seeing people' there who 'shd. or might be useful to you'.

Despite Joyce's disclaimer that he was not begging for clothes, he seems to have accepted some from Ezra, and money too, judging from a limerick he wrote on his return to Trieste:

> A bard once in lakelapped Sermione [*sic*]
> Lived in peace, eating locusts & honey,
>   Till a son of a bitch
>   Left him dry on the beach
> Without clothes, boots, time, quiet, or money.

'Left Italy on tram, *causa sciopero* [because of a strike],' Ezra wrote to a friend from Paris on 19 June. 'Very lucky to get out . . . reckon the next man will come out in a cab.' In Paris he and Dorothy stayed in a hotel in the rue de Beaune. Ezra noted that the capital was trying to maintain the 'illusion' that it was still the hub of the universe. He immediately busied himself with preparing the way for Joyce, distributing copies of *A Portrait of the Artist as a Young Man* and finding a translator – Madame Ludmila Bloch-Savitsky – whose version appeared in 1924 as *Daedalus*. He also arranged temporary lodgings for the Joyces and described 'a day's hell' partly spent on 'a question of sheets and truckle-beds for the errors J.J.'s his misspent premalthusian youth' – in other words, providing for Giorgio and Joyce's daughter Lucia. Early in July the Joyces arrived for what was meant to be a week or so. They stayed for twenty years.

Ezra arranged a large number of introductions for Joyce, one of which proved more than useful. He took the Joyces to a Sunday afternoon gathering at the Neuilly home of the poet André Spire. The guests included a Left-Bank bookseller named Adrienne Monnier who was accompanied by her close friend Sylvia Beach, daughter of a Princeton Presbyterian minister. A few months earlier Miss Beach had opened her own English-language bookshop in Paris under the name 'Shakespeare and Company'. She now approached and asked 'Is this the great James Joyce?' An association began of immense importance for *Ulysses*.

Ezra and Dorothy returned to London at the end of July 1920, whereupon Ezra discovered to his disgust that Middleton Murry had sacked him from his job as drama critic of the *Athenaeum*. The cause was Ezra's review in April of a production of *The Government Inspector*, in which he had written:

> It is difficult to stifle all one's inner inquiries, and not wonder what the play would be like if acted as a scathing realist satire; not, of course, that it would . . . be possible for Mary Grey to act anything.

The following issue brought a lengthy apology to Miss Grey from Middleton Murry, who explained that one of his assistants had let the passage through in his absence, and that he would never have allowed it himself.

Ezra was seriously put out by the sacking. He told Joyce that the £10 a month from the *Athenaeum* had been 'my chief local asset . . . my chief cash reason for return to this brass-bound clay-hummock'. Moreover, as he reported to Quinn, Orage at the *New Age* was 'killing off "B. H. Dias"'. No art criticisms by Ezra under this pseudonym were printed after he got back to London, though he continued his music notes as 'William Atheling'. He said to Quinn that he was 'grateful' for the chance to bury Dias, but it was a further reduction in his income.

Despite his own near-insolvency he remembered that Joyce still needed a pair of shoes. He acquired some second-hand brogues, wrapped them in brown paper, and sent them to Paris in the care of Wyndham Lewis and Eliot, who were calling on Joyce before embarking on a French walking tour. It seemed not inappropriate that their first meeting with Joyce should have been much occupied with their attempts to undo what Lewis called 'the crafty housewifely knots of the cunning old Ezra'. Joyce was not pleased in such company to find that the parcel contained old shoes, and restored his dignity by taking Eliot and Lewis out to a lavish dinner at his own expense. (In 1953 Ezra wrote: 'Jas J/ and W.L./ together were more fun than a guignol, a pair of very cagey Kilkenny kats, or hyenas.')

Not long after, Ezra had to inform Joyce that the issue of the *Little Review* containing the 'Nausikaa' episode of *Ulysses*, in which Bloom masturbates while watching Gerty MacDowell on the beach, had been 'pinched by the PO-lice'. A prosecution was begun by the New York Society for the Prevention of Vice, and the case was heard in February 1921. Despite energetic defences of the book and its author by Quinn and others, the *Little Review* was found guilty of obscenity and was fined – though only minimally, on the understanding that no more of the book would be serialized, which it was not.

In September 1920, a little over a month after returning from Paris, Ezra began to show signs of radical discontent with living in London. 'There is no longer any intellectual *life* in England,' he wrote to William Carlos Williams, 'save what centres in this eight by ten pentagonal room' (his own flat) 'and NO literary publication whatever extant in England, save what "we" print (*Egoist* and Ovid Press)' – the latter was John Rodker's imprint. In contrast, he expressed enthusiasm for the French capital in his series 'The Island of Paris', which ran in the *Dial* from September to December 1920.

He began this by admitting that it was hard to take up any kind of 'critical attitude' to Paris, thanks to such seductive features as 'gardens . . . within two stones-throw of the river . . . fifteenth-century stairs and remnants of sixteenth-century classic ornament'. He now saw the absurdity of searching hastily there, as he usually had on his Paris visits, for 'the triple extract of literature for export purposes . . . a poetic serum for English letters'. He was the first to admit that Paris was insular – hence the title of the series – and that French literary society knew even less of the outside world than did 'the elder generation of English'. No French writer in particular attracted his admiration; in a rather abrupt survey of current practitioners he mentioned Apollinaire, Aragon, Breton, and Valéry, but had nothing much to say about them. Proust seemed to him 'the nearest the French can get to Henry James' but he had 'yet to be convinced' that he had 'the centre and weight of James Joyce'. On the other hand 'they are, these Parisians, more serious in experiment and more thorough than other people. If there is a dearth of great authors there is . . . a far greater number of groups, *unanime* or *polyanime*, in a state of pleasing and possibly pregnant fermentation.' He still had only the most superficial knowledge of French literary life, but his very ignorance of it made him hopeful.

Throughout the autumn of 1920 he was uncertain about the future, speculating as to whether the time had come for him to return to America. He thought he might be able to support himself by lecturing, perhaps at Columbia or at the City College of New York – he did not fancy 'HAAvud'. But really he knew, as he wrote to William Carlos Williams, that New York 'wants me as little now as it did ten and fifteen years ago'. Moreover, the prospect of living there was as unattractive as ever. It would mean giving up 'every shred of comfort, every scrap of my personal life'. Yet it might be mere 'masochism' to remain in London. For the first time, in this letter to Williams of 11 September, he mentioned the notion of 'shifting to Paris'.

He aired the idea of an American lecture tour when talking during the autumn to the American writer Ben Hecht, who was reporting on 'Lit'ry London' for a New York magazine. Wyndham Lewis was also present, and according to Hecht the conversation went like this:

Mr Lewis: Do you think, Hecht, I could make any money by lecturing in America?

Mr Pound: Nonsense, Lewis. You'd be a dismal sort of failure. Unless you went in your soldier suit and –

Mr Lewis: I would like to deliver some lectures on painting and make enough money to live on for several years. Do you think it's possible, Hecht?

Mr Pound: Absolutely no. I am the sort of person who could make a fortune at the trick. You see, I am deliciously disliked in the States and would therefore attract a crowd. If I could get a good manager to advertise me and spread broadcast the information that I will appear in blue earrings and that I own the only overcoat that has four lapis lazuli buttons I would really be an astounding success.

Mr Lewis: If I could clean up enough cash in a year it would be just the thing I want.

Mr Pound: Hecht will tell you that you've no chance. You remember the time you spoke at Hulme's lecture? The audience left to a man right in the midst of your eloquence. You're utterly incoherent, Lewis, as a talker, and your intelligence unfits you absolutely as a lecturer. By the way, Hecht, what sort of man is Knopf?

Mr Lewis: Is Margaret Anderson light or dark?

Mr Pound: I could bring my Dolmetsch clavichord along and deliver the lectures sitting down, or in fact from a recumbent position . . .

Despite this facetious notion of a lecture tour *à la* Wilde, he was half inclined to remain in London. He wrote to Ford Madox Ford: 'it seems to me one will have to try to start a magazine here.' On 8 November, writing to Quinn again, he pictured himself as a Mauberley remaining in London: 'Only question of whether living in hot house smelling orchids so exclusively, hearing one's own divisions on the clavichord, etc. IS best for one's work . . . I don't want to go soft, or get to producing merely "objets d'art" instead of "oeuvres".' Yet in his letter to Ford he asked 'Whether twere better in the jettison of noncombustibles to treck for Paris, and forget the natural idiom of this island, or in the face of all too damn tumultuous seas and boat-rates emigrate, and on the quayed and basket-covered banks of bleak Manhattan, chase the trade of letters!!!'

The indecision of a Hamlet did not suit him. Gradually he abandoned the American notion, saying he had envisaged it as 'a descent into the inferno', and just before Christmas he and Dorothy decided to go on holiday in January to the South of France, then to try an extended spell of Paris life from the spring. 'Scheduled to leave for Avignon via Paris in Jan.,' he told his mother on 20 December. 'Expect to be in Paris from Apr 20 onwards till further notice.' To his father he added a few days later: 'Think it is about time you began to read french in your off hours . . . Certainly France is the only remaining country where your pension wd. be of much use.'

He did not announce his departure from London as necessarily being permanent. A. R. Orage reported in the *New Age* that Ezra was going abroad 'perhaps for one year, perhaps for two, perhaps for good'. (One of Ezra's last contributions to that journal, on 25 November 1920, as 'William Atheling', was his review of a recital by a violinist named Olga Rudge, who he said had 'charmed one by the delicate firmness of her fiddling'.) After arriving in France he would commit himself no further than by saying, in a letter to William Carlos Williams, 'I rather want to take a solid year in Paris'. He retained the London flat in Holland Place Chambers, subletting it to Agnes Bedford, a professional musician and one of Wyndham Lewis's mistresses, who had helped Ezra with work on troubadour songs. He left most of his books there, and would often write asking her to send over some item or other, using her as secretary–courier–agent in exchange for the flat. He told Miss Bedford to 'open any letters that come for me; throw away the bores; answer any that you think worth it'.

Orage wrote in the *New Age* of Ezra's departure that he himself could well understand the motives, but found the gesture 'difficult to approve'. He accepted that, like 'others who have striven for the advancement of intelligence and culture in England', Ezra had made enemies, and so found it difficult to earn a proper living. 'But, all the same, it is here or nowhere that the most advanced trenches of the spirit are to be found; and it is here, I believe, that the enemy will have to be defeated.' He called Ezra's belief that Paris was a place of importance in cultural matters 'a delusion and an illusion! . . . France has long ceased to be in the van of culture . . . Even with Mr Pound in it, I expect nothing from Paris for the next quarter of a century.'

Briefly passing through Paris early in January 1921 on his way south with Dorothy, Ezra gave an interview to the Paris edition of the *New York Herald*. He said he had left England because he found 'the decay of the British Empire too depressing a spectacle to witness at close range'. He told the reporter he would 'keep clear of England and devote himself to his study of 12th-century music . . . He is also writing a long poem.'

A little over a year later he wrote: 'I daily ask myself why the hell I stayed in Eng. so long; and then comfort myself with the reflection that one cdnt/ have left during the war, and that I probably escaped as soon as possible, or very nearly so.' In Paris he told Sylvia Beach that he and Dorothy had felt 'obliged to flee . . . because the water was creeping up, and they might wake up some morning to find they had web feet'. But was it really England he was trying to escape, or himself? If the English intellectual scene was waterlogged, was that not exactly the state in which he had found it in 1908? In those days, as a young man, he had felt able, if not to drain the marsh single-handed, then at least to reclaim some firm ground on which he and a few allies could live. If he was now despairing, that despair must reflect his own loss of certainty – not a loss of energy or vitality but of a sense of plan or direction.

Once he had gone, he showed not the slightest regret or desire to return. Dorothy often crossed the Channel and spent weeks at a time with her family, but Ezra rarely accompanied her, and made only very occasional and fleeting trips to London. He clearly felt that it was a piece of his past. 'I have an absolute mistrust of anything English,' he wrote to Eliot during 1922, 'particularly of any "upper class" interest in literature . . . I don't want to appear [in print] in England. I have no belief in their capacity to understand anything. They still want what I was doing in 1908. They want imitations and dilutations.' The same year he was claiming, in a letter to someone planning to start a magazine, that 'the history of English literature' was solely 'as shown in her exiles: Landor in Italy, Keats, Shelley, Byron, Beddoes out of England, Browning in Italy'. It was now up to him to prove that he belonged in that company.

Part Three

1921–45
'E. P.'

1

'I Have Made An Opera'

'Mental life reduced to a minimum. five hours on tennis court,' Ezra wrote to Agnes Bedford from the Côte d'Azur in March 1921. In a tennis tournament on Saturday he had 'earned 11 francs . . . about enough to pay for 2 tennis balls. Otherwise life uneventful.' And to his family he reported a Riviera winter of 'sun and sea, and tennis'.

He and Dorothy were staying at the Hôtel Terminus in St-Raphael, while for three months Ezra enjoyed one of his periodic phases of doing absolutely nothing – phases which now and then would intervene between his more characteristic stretches of furious activity. It was no doubt a simple need for occasional recuperation, but he also liked to remind himself that he was essentially frivolous by nature, was not driven by a conscience or ethic which demanded that he labour eight hours a day at his typewriter for work's own sake. He had a wife with a private income; why should not he and Dorothy sometimes live the leisured life?

From their base in St-Raphael, the Pounds contemplated adopting the Riviera mode with some regularity. They looked at Cannes, which Ezra thought 'rubbish', but Nice had 'more guts' than he expected, and seemed 'quite a possible place to live for a season'. Meanwhile he was reminded of the iniquities of the *laissez-faire* economic system by the fluctuations of the currency market. '*If* I'd turned all my £ into francs 3½ weeks ago,' he wrote to his father, '& turned it all back ten days ago I'd have made 1000 fr.' As it was he had probably lost some money: 'It is no job for an amateur.' Nevertheless he was leading a good life, as good as the lives of 'Rockefeller & Morgan & various other pods who *have* large sums written down on paper to their credit'; and unlike them he had no responsibilities. It seemed 'proof that I know something about economics'.

He told Ford Madox Ford he was doing no writing at all, and that the

Riviera seascape reminded him of 'the unrealities of the musical comedy stage'. At the local tennis club he had won a silver ashtray. Ford expanded this into Ezra's having won 'the tennis championship of the south of France', and in his memoirs he describes Ezra riding in triumph alongside the mayor with 'an immense silver shield' on his knees.

Ezra told Ford on 6 April 1921 that he and Dorothy would shortly be setting off for Paris, where he would 'plunge into gawd knows wot. – certainly a change of life'. Just before they left St-Raphael there was a local fête, where Ezra's attention was caught by some medieval-style music played on 'four Tambour & small flutes. – tambour about 3 feet deep' (he sent his father a sketch of it and its player). It planted an idea in his head.

Arriving in Paris, he and Dorothy took a garret room in the Hôtel du Pas-de-Calais in the rue des Saints-Pères, off the boulevard Saint-Germain. 'I perceive that chaos begins again,' Ezra wrote to Agnes Bedford. 'Have only seen 17 people since my arrival here & have not yet found what walk of life I am to perambulate . . . If you have any suggestions as how I should employ my remaining years do envoy them.' The seventeen included Jean Cocteau and the Impressionist–Dadaist painter Francis Picabia, both of whom Ezra found 'intelligent', but for the moment he said he was doing nothing but 'refrain from superfluous actions' and get plenty of sleep. He made contact with James Joyce and read the latest *Ulysses* chapter, which was 'enormous – megaloscrumptious – mastodonic'.

On closer acquaintance he judged Cocteau 'the BEST poet and best prose writer' in Paris. As for Picabia, the painter's Sunday salons seemed to him the most brilliant gatherings he had ever attended. Picabia amused him by scrawling a parody of a Picasso drawing, and on the strength of this Ezra would say for years: 'Picabia is the man who ties the knots in Picasso's tail.'

Making literary and artistic contacts provided sufficient amusement for the moment. The Pounds' hotel was adequate for their needs, slightly too expensive, 'but hardly worth the trouble to move'; there was 'a very pleasant high balcony'. They were both hotel dwellers by nature rather than home makers. Scofield Thayer (editor of the *Dial*) turned up in Paris and ran Ezra to earth. 'When one arrives at his hotel,' he reported, 'one usually learns from the young lady that Mr Pound is *au bain*. But the young lady consents to go upstairs to see Mr Pound and to inquire if Mr Pound will see guests. Mr Pound receives, beaming and incisive.'

Thayer agreed that Ezra should take over the regular 'Paris Letter' column in the *Dial*, but he was not prepared to renew Ezra's tenure of the foreign editorship, which had just completed its experimental year. Ezra wrote to John Quinn to see if he could help replace it with a similar job on *Century* magazine, but for once Quinn rebelled and told him 'go to hell'. Quinn increasingly believed that Ezra had sold him a dud in the form of the Wyndham Lewis paintings and Gaudier-Brzeska sculptures he had bought, but which no one else in New York seemed to value. He subsequently recovered his temper and approached *Century* on Ezra's behalf, but with no result.

Thus, during his Paris sojourn Ezra had no steady income of his own, apart from the comparatively small sums he received for the *Dial* 'Paris Letter'. A fellow Hamilton College alumnus, named Saunders, visiting Paris with his wife and meeting Ezra, formed the impression that he was on the brink of poverty and gave him a handsome cheque. Ezra accepted it but passed it on to someone in serious need. Dorothy's income could just about keep them both, thanks to a favourable exchange rate, although they had to live simply. When Thayer's *Dial* colleague Gilbert Seldes fed Ezra at 'a very good restaurant near the Odéon', Ezra 'ate as if he'd never had a meal before'. Quinn came to Paris during the summer of 1921 and perceived that Ezra was 'rather on his uppers'. He discreetly offered a loan of $200, which Ezra declined, saying that things would pick up; but when Quinn got back to New York, Ezra wrote saying he would like the money after all. Quinn sent it with the message that it was not to be repaid – 'just forget it'.

The only new form of paid literary work Paris brought him was translation. Boni & Liveright, who were now publishing his poetry in New York, gave him a contract advancing him $500 annually for translating from the French, the books to be chosen by the publisher, though Ezra could reject anything he did not like. He produced an English text of Remy de Gourmont's *Physique de l'Amour* and translated a thriller by Édouard Estaunié, the translator's name here being given as 'Hiram Janus'. After this the arrangement lapsed.

His loss of influence with the *Dial* led him to look for a sympathetic magazine that would publish his own stable of writers, and he turned his attention once more to the *Little Review*, which had suspended publication since the *Ulysses* trial but would be resuming in the autumn of 1921 as a quarterly. Ezra tried to take some control over it. 'Am taking up the *Little Review* again, as a quarterly,' he wrote to Wyndham Lewis in April 1921. 'Some of the best here in Paris' (he said) had agreed to contribute to the opening number as a protest against the suppression of *Ulysses*. He himself was writing on the sculptor Brancusi. When the first issue of the new *Little Review* appeared it had Ezra's name on the front page once more, under the heading 'Administration'. However, the attempted takeover came to nothing. The front page continued to carry his name, but after this the magazine only appeared sporadically.

He commended Brancusi elsewhere in print, as energetically as he had ever praised Gaudier-Brzeska, and told Ford he wanted to write a book on 'Brancusi (the beautiful genius). He is doing what Gaudier might have done in thirty years time.' Brancusi himself was rather condescending about Gaudier, saying that sculpture wasn't a job for the young, and that Gaudier had had plenty of talent but no time to achieve results. Ezra disloyally drank this in while 'knocking about' in Brancusi's Paris studio. He could also see that Brancusi's existing reputation made a Pound-style promotion quite unnecessary. But watching Brancusi encouraged him to try his own hand at sculpture. 'I have spent two days chipping a block of marble myself,' he told his father. 'It will not be a chef d'oeuvre, but I have even less respect for bad sculpture than I had before I tried stone cutting.' According to Ford, he 'acquired pieces of stone as nearly eggshaped as possible, hit them with hammers and then laid them about on the floor'. At about this time he also tried painting. Long ago he had dabbled about with oils – 'I couldn't draw a pig,' he once told Dorothy, 'but it was entertaining just the trying to prepare a palette.' He took it up again while in Paris. And only a few weeks after arriving there, he began to compose the music for an opera.

*

It was to be called *Le Testament de Villon*, and the libretto would be drawn from Villon's lengthy poem *Le Grand Testament*, a burlesque catalogue of bequests in the poet's supposed will, punctuated by lyrical *ballades* and *rondeaux*. Ezra arranged excerpts from this to create an implied plot, the sung text to remain in medieval French but with some spoken dialogue, partly translated from Villon and partly invented, delivered in English.

The desire to write an opera was immediately inspired by the folk musicians at St-Raphael, whose style he hoped to capture in his orchestration. His first idea was to get Walter Rummel to write down the music from his dictation, but he soon decided that Rummel 'isn't going to be of any use . . . the last time I heard him his playing had every possible skill and no interest'. In any case 'it will probably be more satisfactory to do it myself, ourself, our selves or however it works out'.

These observations were in a letter to Agnes Bedford. It had occurred to Ezra that as a trained musician she would be able to correct his technical defects in music. On 5 May 1921, as a start, he asked her to

send me the Dolmetsch book . . . ALSO, if convenient, a statement of what notes come aisy on the oneth, twoth, threeth and fourth strings of A. cello, B. Basss viol. If you can obtain said information without arousing suspicion.

Will probably send you my first scrawls sprawls, for criticism in a few days. or weeks or months . . .

Cello is I believe written in same clef as the troubadour stuff in original mss. ??? No. ? That clef is only half tone lower than mod. treble?? It don't in the least matter for the moment, but might save time starting to write stuff in something vaguely resembling some known form of notation.

He contemplated trying to get hold of a book on orchestration, 'if it weren't immorally certain that the damn thing wd. be wholly wrong'.

In his eyes the opera was not a particularly daring enterprise. He had now been researching into troubadour music for a decade, and had composed his own setting for troubadour poems with Rummel's assistance. The only new departure was that he would attempt to notate the music himself and to compose and orchestrate the accompaniment. Without a keyboard (his clavichord was still in London) this would certainly be a challenge, but he told Agnes Bedford that he had some ideas:

> I have a vague suspicion that cello ought to be about three notes lower than voice to sustain it, and that bass viol ought to be about an octave below (below voice), running onto nine below on occasion. BUTT this is extremely vague, possibly it shd. be two octaves, save that I want to use that cellarage for definite purposes.

When he got on to such technical matters his complete ignorance of musical theory revealed itself, and the enterprise indeed appeared absurd and presumptuous. He lacked not only a theoretical training but any real experience of performance, not to mention that by his own admission he was virtually tone deaf – could scarcely distinguish between the pitches of individual notes, further than to identify that some were high and others low. His friends received the news of the project with disbelief. 'Pound writing an opera?' said William Carlos Williams. 'Why, he doesn't know one note from another.'

And yet music, or at least one aspect of it, was an integral part of him. Brigit Patmore called on the Pounds one day and at the door heard 'the puzzling sound of a typewriter and what seemed the yowling of a bass Siamese cat'. Dorothy explained: 'Yes, it's Ezra. He always does that when he's working.' She added that he had 'a *wonderful* sense of rhythm', which Brigit greatly doubted, since when dancing he moved 'according to no rules I understood . . . with extremely odd steps . . . to unearthly beats'. But he danced whenever an opportunity presented itself. In the summer of 1921 he delightedly reported 'dancing the tango for first time last sabath eve. shall have another try tomorrow'. Someone else describes him as having a passionate if eccentric sense of rhythm like that of a jazz drummer. It was closely related to the rhythmical subtlety of his experiments in quantitative verse, and the way in *Mauberley* in which the rhythm of individual words goes against the rhythmic structure of the stanzas – just as a jazz drummer uses a 4:4 time signature as the basis for elaborate improvisation.

What Brigit Patmore heard at the door of the flat – and many others noticed it over the years – was the 'music' in his head, to which the words of his poems were set. His delving into the relationship between music and poetry – particularly his investigation into the troubadours' original tunes – was therefore not a dispassionate piece of academic research, but seems to have grown from a desire to see if other poets had shared his own way of writing.

It was only a very short step from this to composing the opera. The rhythms of Villon's fifteenth-century French – a very un-operatic language, with its host of short syllables and consonants, and few mellifluous vowels – offered a challenge to discover the 'tunes' that Ezra believed undoubtedly lay behind the poems, and to write down and perform them. 'The HOLE point of my moozik,' he wrote of the opera, was that 'the moozik fits the WORDS and not some OTHER WORDS.'

Le Testament de Villon was planned in one act, to last about an hour. Set chiefly in a brothel next to a cathedral, it opens with Villon, who is wanted by the authorities for his many supposed crimes, reviewing the transience of life and love in a song with the celebrated refrain 'Mais où sont les neiges d'antan?' He also sings of his premonition of death, to the ironic comments of his friend Ythier. An old prostitute, La Hëaulmière, enters and laments her vanished charms in the harsh 'Ha, vieillesse felonne et fière'. A foppish gallant stumbles in to visit one of the girls; the voice of Villon's mother is heard from the cathedral praying for her own salvation; and a priest, attempting to come into the brothel to buy the services of a girl, has his way barred by the boozy brothel-keeper Bozo, who boasts of the delights of his profession, 'En ce bordeau ou tenons notre estat'. Villon and his companions sing a drinking-song, 'Père Noé, qui plantastes la vigne', at the end of which they collapse drunkenly. They are arrested and carried off for execution, and in the second and final scene they hang on the gallows and sing the motet 'Frères humains qui après nous vivez'.

Soon after revealing his first plans for the opera to Agnes Bedford, Ezra asked his mother to send over 'my Hamilton College hymnal', or at least to detach and mail the pages he wanted – 'one of Luthers "Ein Fest Burg" and one or two others of plain songs (Draw nigh Emanuel)'. Two months later, in July 1921, he acquired 'a five hundred page volume on musical history'. By then he had already 'pounded out' (his own term for it) the score of the opera, at high speed, without any professional assistance or books to guide him – on 16 May, a mere matter of days after deciding to begin work, he told Agnes Bedford: 'I have done 116 pages of something that looks, at 1st glance, like an orchestral score.' And about a couple of days later: 'I dont see that it is so bloody difficult, though it cant be done in ten days.'

In a sense he was employing the method that he had used successfully in examinations at Hamilton College when he knew almost nothing about the subject. The earliest surviving drafts of *Le Testament de Villon* (now at Yale) have about them the dash and bold penmanship of a Mozart or a Beethoven, though a closer look reveals that the details are often vague. Ezra admitted to Agnes Bedford that in certain places it still remained 'to decide on bloomin pitch intervals between notes'.

He alleged that he was using a restricted scale with only '7 possible' notes, omitting B flat and employing 'sharps only for asperity', except in one place 'where the 5 sharp motif runs against pumppapummm pupupam-pupumpuh'. Agnes Bedford must have wondered what she was being let in for. The opera actually uses the simplest possible scale, that of C major, the white notes of the piano, with only the rarest excursions on to the black. Its oddity and 'medievalism' come not from any unorthodoxy of scale or tonality, but from Ezra's refusal to use conventional harmony or counter-point, or even to write structured melodies with beginnings, middles, and ends. He simply set each phrase of the poem on its own merits, giving it the rhythm and changes of pitch he believed were implicit in the words, and then going on to the next phrase with little or no backward glance at any earlier melodic passage. *Le Testament* is thus almost entirely unthematic and nearly tuneless, although there is a slight symmetry between some of the phrases in each song (rather like the symmetrical line lengths, or implied line lengths, in *Mauberley*) which gives a little coherence. More-over, each song seems positively hectic in the way that one phrase rushes on to the next, with scarcely a chance for the singer to breathe. Nor are there orchestral interludes or preludes, and the opera begins and ends with great abruptness.

Ezra explained to Agnes Bedford at the outset that he was 'striving for archaism', and therefore rejected not only harmony but even the idea of 'a continuous contrapounto'. The accompaniment consists chiefly of a doub-ling of the voice (usually in unison or at the octave, but occasionally in thirds or some less conventional interval) by a number of instruments, each of which joins with the singer only for a short phrase before being replaced by another. The effect is percussive, disjointed and arbitrary. Any instru-ments would serve this purpose providing there was a sufficient variety of tone colour, but from the outset Ezra envisaged quite a rich palette – 'Saxophone, Cello, Bass Viol . . . oboe, flute, horn', as well as some higher strings. Bozo's song required 'trombone, traditional sign of boracchios [drinking]', and he also fancied 'about four brace of mandolins at one place, and possibly a couple of guitars'. The orchestra was beginning to assume Wagnerian proportions, but Ezra said he wanted to keep each instrument 'to its half dozen or dozen best notes'. The point was to avoid 'all that has been considered the chiefest of necessities since the death of Mozart', and in particular to 'get the charm of . . . the fife and tambour-de-provence corps of four, who played the same tune for three hours one evening at St Raph.'

He pressed on by himself, finding it 'a damnd nuisance' not having Agnes Bedford there to check over and criticize his work, nor any instrument on which to try it out. He found musical notation very tiresome – 'the damndest thing to get simple facts *from* ever invented. Perfectly simple AFTER the fact, but impenetrable before it.' By 25 May 1921, apparently in no more than three weeks after beginning work, he had written the greater part of the opera. He told Agnes Bedford there remained 'only the booze song' to be written, and he had run out of manuscript paper. He sent her some of the score, asking whether she could 'make anything' of it. Meanwhile he had been sitting through a performance of Debussy's *Pelléas et Mélisande*, which encouraged him to jettison 'the whole bloomin' era of harmony' and orchestrate *Le Testament* for 'two tins and wash board, anything rather than that mush of hysteria'. His ignorance of music, he said, would hold 'no further terrors' for him 'if that DAMN thing is the result of what is called musical knowledge'.

Agnes Bedford's comments on what he sent her do not survive, but she seems to have offered him little encouragement. However, given his determined nature, this pushed him into a more trenchant defence of his position. He told her that his 'premier principe' was 'RIEN that interferes with the words, or with the utmost possible clarity of impact of words on audience'. He wanted her to make fair copies from his original notation, no easy task given the limitations of his rough draft; he admitted that he had only managed to write down 'an aid to memory', a mere reminder of the tunes and rhythms he had in mind rather than an accurate record, though he believed this was what the troubadours themselves had done. 'I can read it, but nobody else can without hearing it first.'

During August 1921, Agnes Bedford came over to Paris and, on a borrowed piano, went through the music with him, transcribing what he sang more accurately than he had managed. Ezra afterwards apologized for exhausting her, describing it as 'the fortnight I nearly killed you'. But he was evidently not satisfied with the achievements of these sessions, since three years later he enlisted another musician, George Antheil, to 'edit' the score.

The first trained musician other than Agnes Bedford to comment on *Le Testament* was Yves Tinayre, a singer, to whom Ezra showed the score a year or so after it had been written. Tinayre was astonished by the lack of perceptible melody, let alone harmony. 'The conception was entirely novel to me,' he recalled. 'The music was longitudinal and linear.' Ezra drew his attention to the importance of rhythm, saying it mattered far more than pitch. Indeed in 1911 he had argued, in the introduction to his Cavalcanti translations, that pitch and harmony are only branches of rhythm:

> Rhythm is perhaps the most primal thing known to us . . .
> music is . . . pure rhythm, rhythm and nothing else, for the
> variation of pitch is the variation of rhythms of the individual
> notes, and harmony the blending of these various rhythms.

This is nonsense as a general statement about music, for the pitch of an individual note has no generic connection with the rhythm of a piece, but it is an accurate enough explanation of the nature of the 'music' in his own poetry, and also of the role of pitch in the very unconventional *Le Testament de Villon*.

Although the songs in the earlier part of the opera are within a small vocal compass (usually an octave or less) and little occurs in the orchestral score other than the doubling of the voice, as the work progresses it begins to develop more sophisticated techniques. Villon's mother, praying to the Virgin, is provided with an urgent counterpoint of low bell and other percussion. The priest's short song is a vivacious piece in strict dance rhythm with harmonized accompaniment on double-stopped violin (this accompaniment may have been the work of Olga Rudge, who played the violin in the first performance). The drinking song of Villon and his companions contains quite elaborate choral and orchestral writing, both harmonic and contrapuntal, and the final gallows motet, 'Frères humains', is an extraordinary achievement, cool and assured, harmonically sophisticated, with suggestions of Stravinsky, for whose work it could pass – indeed almost any post-Romantic composer would be proud of it. The Stravinsky colouring perhaps comes from George Antheil, the score's 'editor', but some of the best effects are too unconventional by Stravinskyan standards not to be Ezra's own.

Though *Le Testament* is thoroughly idiosyncratic, it anticipated the style of a number of modern composers who chose to learn from medieval music. Ezra worked in ignorance of any such tendency among musical modernists, which was then in its infancy. The modernism of his opera was unselfconscious, almost accidental. He had set out, as in his poetry, to resuscitate a dead art that had been practised in the medieval period. He achieved strikingly modern effects chiefly by straining towards revivalism.

If *Le Testament de Villon* shows signs of the amateur it is not in the music, but in his failure to write satisfactorily for the stage. The work scarcely qualifies as 'opera', having more affinity to such medieval French folk-song fables as *Aucassin et Nicolette*. Possibly it would have been best conceived for concert performance. Ezra claimed he had constructed the libretto on the 'greek model', but the result is too compressed and too static to achieve much theatrical impact (unless of course a producer injects a good deal of 'business'), and is more satisfactory on record.

'I have made an opera out of Villon's text,' Ezra wrote to Yeats. 'It ought ultimately to be a french national fete; as Villon is their only possible substitute for Homer.' He read the libretto aloud to Jean Cocteau, who giggled all the time, since he found anything medieval quite ridiculous. Ezra also decided to buy a wind instrument to help him gain some sense of how the work should be orchestrated. 'Was it you who stimulated Pound to the purchase of a BASSOON?' Wyndham Lewis wrote to Agnes Bedford. 'And if so, do you think that is an action justified by the facts of existence, as you understand them?' Ernest Hemingway later recalled with horror the sound of 'Ezra learning to play the bassoon'. At first, Ezra told his mother that he was finding the instrument 'good for the lungs'; but a month later: 'The bassoon slumbers.'

After *Le Testament de Villon* was finished he waited patiently for a chance for it to be performed. He wrote to Agnes Bedford: 'Do you advise me to revise that OP. or take to painting??? Or literature? OR – ?'

2

Great Clot Of Genital Fluid

'Have been doing translation of Gourmont's *Physique de l'Amour*,' Ezra told Agnes Bedford on 21 June 1921, while still at work on the first draft of the opera. He explained that it was a 'rush order' for Boni & Liveright in New York, a case of '25 pages per diem . . . pornography for pastors of U.S.' When it was published in 1922, booksellers were warned that 'discretion' should be used in its distribution; in London it was issued by the Casanova Society.

Remy de Gourmont's book is an essay, presented as scientific but mostly based on folklore, in support of the pleasure principle in sexuality. De Gourmont speaks out in favour of promiscuity, arguing that civilized man only endures monogamy if he can 'leave it and return at will', a solution 'more elegant' than divorce, which usually leads to 'the same thing over again'. There is nothing of interest in the book itself, but Ezra supplied a Translator's Postscript which set out his own theory about sexuality – a theory far more exotic than anything de Gourmont had to say.

He had changed his attitude to the subject since 1914, when he wrote contemptuously of those poets whose minds could scarcely be distinguished from their testicles. Indeed, he now considered the mental and sexual organs to be closely related. 'It is more than likely,' he wrote,

> that the brain itself is, in origin and development, only a sort of great clot of genital fluid held in suspense or reserved . . . This hypothesis . . . would explain the enormous content of the brain as a maker or presenter of images . . . I offer an idea rather than an argument, yet if we consider that the power of the spermatozoide is precisely the power of exteriorizing a form; and if we consider the lack of any other known substance in

nature capable of growing into brain, we are left with . . . one conclusion . . . that the spermatozoic substance must have greatly atrophied in its change from lactic to coagulated . . . condition.

He went on to suggest that there were traces of this brain-as-spermatozoa theory 'in the symbolism of phallic religions, man really the phallus or spermatozoide charging, head-on, the female chaos . . . Even oneself has felt it, driving any new idea into the great passive vulva of London, a sensation analogous to the male feeling in copulation.' He had said something like this when writing in 1916 to John Quinn on the subject of Vorticism, calling it 'every kind of geyser from jism [semen] bursting up white as ivory, to hate or a storm at sea. Spermatozoon, enough to populate the island with active and vigorous animals.'

He did not make the suggestion, either in the de Gourmont book or elsewhere, that geniuses require constant sexual outlet, or that virility means higher thought. 'In no case,' he wrote, could mental ability 'be a question of mere animal quantity of sperm.' But he expressed no dissent from de Gourmont's argument in favour of promiscuity, and he suggested that there might possibly be 'some correlation between complete and profound copulation and cerebral development'. Woman was relegated to the role of 'the conservator, the inheritor'; was perhaps 'clever, practical', but emphatically 'not inventive, always the best disciple of any inventor'.

During the mid-1930s, James Laughlin, Ezra's American publisher, listened to him expounding these theories. He had the impression that Ezra believed that the brain acquires ideas, or the raw material for them, at the moment of orgasm, and he suggests that the way in which Ezra liked to sit from his middle years onwards may have had something to do with this. Ezra would almost lie flat in a chair – or better still, recline on a sofa – with his head as far back as possible, as near as he could manage to the horizontal. 'Fluids don't run uphill,' observes Laughlin. 'The poet reclined as much as possible to facilitate and increase the flow of spermatozoa from his balls to his bean.'

The period following the spread of Freud's ideas produced a crop of eccentric theories about the relation between sex and mental activity, such as D. H. Lawrence's *Fantasia of the Unconscious* (1922), which argues that humanity should trust the impulses of the 'spontaneous centres' (chiefly the sexual instincts) rather than rely on purely cerebral judgements. Women usually played a minor part in such male-originated theories, being generally regarded as mere passive receptors. Nevertheless Ezra's notion, even by the fashion of the time, seems particularly male-oriented, and there appears to be no reason why, according to his theory, mental enlightenment should not be achieved by masturbation or homosexual activity as well as through heterosexual copulation.

Ezra did not care for Freud's ideas. In 1933 he summed them up as

> the flower of a deliquescent society going to pot. The average
> human head is less in need of having something removed from
> it, than of having something inserted . . . The general results of
> Freud are Dostoievskian duds, worrying about their own
> unimportant innards with the deep attention of Jim drunk
> occupied with the crumb on his weskit.

He also spoke of the 'germy epoch of Freud', and observed to Wyndham
Lewis that Freud's teaching was 'unmitigated shit . . . laid out in most
elegant arabesques'. In due course his anti-Semitism became entangled with
his hatred of psychology, so that he wrote of 'the vienese poison . . . whole
pewk of kiketry, aimed at destroying the will / introspective idiocy / non
objective'. Practitioners of Freud's profession were labelled 'kikietrists'.
(This had little to do with his experiences in St Elizabeths, where he was
subjected to almost no Freudian or any other analysis.)

His attitude to Freud, which of course Freudians would ascribe to fear of
his own unconscious, deprived him of one of the major influences on
modernism. Freud's anti-paternalistic, radical attitude to human personality did much to liberate the arts from nineteenth-century convention, and
Ezra's rejection of Freudianism shows once again how he worked in
isolation from the mainstream of modern artists. To be fair, though, T. S.
Eliot was just as anti-Freud. In one of his essays he compared the age of
Dante, in which 'men still saw visions', with the present day in which we
merely believe that 'our dreams spring from below'. In 'The Dry Salvages'
he speaks of the exploration of dreams as among 'the usual / Pastimes and
drugs', and he wrote to James Strachey that he had read very little of Freud,
believing it 'undesirable' for a poet to know too much about the workings
of the mind. On the other hand, at least in his unregenerate days, Eliot was
amused by Ezra's supposed amorous adventures (which he may have
suspected took place largely in his friend's mind), judging by a remark at
the end of a 1922 letter to him: 'O student of the Kama-Sutra, grow fat and
libidinous.' Another letter to Ezra from Eliot in the same years ends:
'Good fucking, brother.'

*

It is not clear how much Ezra followed this exhortation during his Paris
sojourn. He was often seen enjoying night life without Dorothy. Kathleen
Cannell, estranged wife of Skipwith, describes him dropping in 'at all
hours, even midnight' to take her to 'a dive in the rue du Lappe, to the Bal
Bullier, or to a party'. He now liked to give the impression that he
considered extramarital affairs *de rigueur*; during 1921 he wrote to Picabia

that he had been in Paris three months 'without finding a congenial mistress'.

During this period his name was linked with that of Bride Adams, née Scratton, a married woman a few years older than himself whom he had met in London. He recalled her as one of the 'two charrming females with accurate eyes still left . . . the lass wid. a delicate air. nuances . . .' He gave her the troubadour name 'Thiy', under which she is mentioned in Canto 78. In 1923 he arranged for the publication, under the title *England* (and with the author's name given as B. M. G.-Adams), of a set of her prose sketches of English country-house and provincial life; they are in a neat sardonic manner which demonstrates considerable talent as a writer. She contributed further pieces of this nature to the *transatlantic review* while Ezra was associated with it. In 1923 when she was divorced for adultery by her husband, Ezra was named as co-respondent; but Ezra's family and Noel Stock are of the opinion that, as Stock puts it, 'by the time of the divorce Ezra was simply being gallant and getting Bride out of a ghastly marriage'. Ezra may have been referring to this episode when he wrote in *Guide to Kulchur* that the divorce laws of England were 'immoral'.

There is nothing in Bride Scratton's letters to Ezra – many of which survive – to suggest either that they were having an affair, or that they had had one. In 1928 she told him she was 'desperately in need of money' to help bring up her two younger children, of whom she had been given custody; she signed her letter 'Bride Scratton'. Ezra sent her a loan for which she expressed much gratitude. A later letter addresses him rather familiarly as 'Dear Ra' – an indication that the acquaintance went back many years – but when their correspondence resumed during his St Elizabeths days there was no hint of anything other than friendship; her letters then were signed in such formal style as 'With best New Years wishes, B. Scratton.' She often sent greetings to Dorothy.

There may have been other women: a letter to Agnes Bedford from Ezra in December 1921 mentions Raymonde Collignon conspiratorially: 'Raymonde had not been delivered when I last saw her, but was looking ENORmous. That is of course, nNot public property. neither is it my domestic affair.' Anything, or nothing, might be made of this. Agnes Bedford herself, whose affair with Wyndham Lewis did not begin until rather later, may have been involved with him; his letters to her become progressively more affectionate, ending with such expressions as 'love' or 'ever' and addressing her as 'Dearest Agnes' or 'Chere Agnes' – though they do not show the coy gallantry that usually accompanied his romances.

Margaret Anderson, who came to Paris while Ezra was there, observed that he had 'become fairly patriarchal in his attitude to women. He kissed them upon the forehead or drew them upon his knee with perfect obliviousness to their distaste for these mannerisms.' Richard Aldington, however, noted a change in Dorothy: 'Where he had waxed fat she had shrunk. Hers was not merely the fashionable skeleton silhouette. It was a kind of premature withering, like an apple left too long on a fruit-dish. There was a virginal pathos in her fragility, in the thin hands and wrists, and the legs which seemed too long for so tiny a trunk.' Aldington's epithet 'virginal' seems to hint that he knew a good deal about the marriage.

> There were little wrinkles round her eyes, [he continues] a sharp line on either side of her mouth, and she had cut her long dark hair to an Eton crop, which gave her the appearance of a prematurely-aged and nervous schoolboy. I noticed with pain that she repelled even the gentlest and most friendly approach with a neurasthenic hostility, and that she had unconsciously adopted some of [Ezra's] habits of speech, including a pathetic echo of his rasping laugh . . . She seemed so emptied of life, so devoid of any interest or ambition.

This description of Dorothy appears in Aldington's story 'Nobody's Baby', but a glance at any photograph of Dorothy taken during this period shows how true to life was the description, though Aldington is a little unfair in suggesting that she has lost her looks. Rather, the porcelain innocence of the pretty young Edwardian has given way to something sadder but also more striking. Ernest Hemingway, who met her for the first time in Paris in 1922, thought her 'very beautiful'.

3

70 *bis*

Dorothy did not fit into her Paris surroundings. William Carlos Williams, visiting the city, noted that 'the erectness of the British walk, the shoes, but especially the design of the hat she had on, could never have originated in the French capital'. She told him she 'intensely disliked' it there, 'as much because of its people as its winter weather, neither fish nor flesh. Italy, as with all Englishmen and Germans, she adored.'

Ezra, however, was thoroughly at home. Margaret Anderson observed that he had now adopted 'the large velvet beret and flowing tie of the Latin Quarter artist of the 1830s'. He soon became a familiar figure striding the streets, his head thrown back, beard thrust out. There were touches of grey in the beard now, hints at thirty-six of middle age. He made a virtue of this, beginning to adopt the persona of an older man, a little condescendingly concerning himself with the juveniles.

He was often seen at the Paris salon of Natalie Clifford Barney, an American exile who inhabited an ancient mansion in the rue Jacob, complete with a temple in the garden, and cultivated the acquaintance of the older French intellectuals. She introduced Ezra to Anatole France, Gide, and Valéry. She was also a notorious lesbian seductress who had allegedly lured the most beautiful women in Paris into her bed. Even the discreet (and herself lesbian) Sylvia Beach comments in her autobiography on 'the ladies with high collars and monocles' whom one would meet on Friday evenings at 20 rue Jacob, strolling through the garden and lingering among the Doric columns of Natalie's Temple à l'Amitié. But Natalie enjoyed male company too, and had inspired the ageing Remy de Gourmont's *Letters to an Amazon*. Ezra had corresponded with her since 1913 when he began to translate de Gourmont for the *Egoist*, and in 1919 she submitted to him for criticism a bilingual volume of her own poems.

He gave the criticism unstintingly, but was more admiring of her epigrams, *Pensées d'une Amazone*, which he reviewed with tempered enthusiasm for the *Dial*. William Carlos Williams, taken to the rue Jacob by Ezra, found the Amazon herself 'hardy' but 'extremely gracious and no fool, far less so than Ezra under the circumstances'.

Ezra mixed with Dadaists, Surrealists, and other fashionable groups of younger Paris intellectuals. In a photograph of the opening of the Jockey night club in Montparnasse he stands alongside Tristan Tzara, Man Ray, and Cocteau. He once contributed to the Dadaist journal *391*. The movement afforded him some mild amusement, but he thought them an insular bunch. 'The Dadaists,' he wrote in the *Dial*, 'converse solely with dadaists, and seek that small scattered tribe throughout the nations . . . which hardly commits them to great catholicity'. He described himself as 'provisionally pro-Surrealist', and went on:

> Naturally, at my age, I think I could have brought up most of these young men better than they have been brought up, but when I look at their *elders*, the French *literati* of my own age, I am damn well pro-Surrealist and nothing they do causes me any regret or astonishment.

Yet he never became wholly enamoured of the movement, and eventually judged of it that 'The mere flight . . . from defined words and historic fact is not sur but SUBrealism; it is no more revolutionary than the dim dithering of the aesthetes in 1888.'

He could often be seen in one of the Left-Bank cafés that were fashionable with artists and intellectuals, such as the Deux Magots or the Dôme. Alfred Kreymborg, who had published *Des Imagistes* in America a decade earlier, spotted him on the terrace of one of these, looking 'like one of Trilby's companions'. Kreymborg talked to him about a possible list of contributors to a new magazine, whereupon Ezra took out a pencil and slashed out name after name on Kreymborg's list, 'usually with some cutting remark'. He addressed Kreymborg and his companion as 'you Americans'. Similarly, writing to Marianne Moore, he spoke of 'your young fellow citizens'. Most of them, he observed to her, now appeared to be on their way to Paris.

When Margaret Anderson and Jane Heap of the *Little Review* arrived in Paris, Ezra invited James and Nora Joyce to meet them. 'It was one of those gatherings of people who have a great deal to say to each other,' writes Anderson, 'in which the very interest of the things to be said imposes a doubt in advance that they can or will be said.' Great literary conversations did not usually take place when Joyce was guest of honour. Ezra describes a supper party arranged to introduce him to Proust (the host was Sydney Schiff):

Recollection of JJ's account dinner at the loathsome Schiff's vurry amusin/ . . . the phoney S/ trying to get conversation between two stars/ J/ mentioning book Pr/ hadn't read, and the little squirt [Proust] running thru list of 'vous connaisses la Duchesse de Twittlewatte'. responsus. No, monsieur, Squirt/ vous connaisses la Marquise de Bouggleswache? JJ 'No, Monsieur.'

Ezra also supplies a glimpse of Joyce on top form. He suggested to somebody who wished to organize a Joyce celebration in the 1950s that they

start contest as to who can kick a chandelier apparently 6 to 10 inches higher than head of the person attempting to kick it.

IN MEMoriam of Jim's Xmas Expression of relief at departure of bores AFTER a dinner party, dedicated if I recall to Xmas celebration.

Mr J's talent for comedy shd/ NOT be underestimated, none of you will be able to rival his singing of BLaRRRney Castle me DaRRling, y'r nothing nowe butta STOWNE.

> Or: they got that t'ilet
>   from Pontius Pilate.
>   lines that follow:
> 'That judges on the bench aRRe forced to wear
> A nightgown and a bag-wig made
>   Of someone else's hair,
>   They got that t'ilet etc.'
> tune 'Mr Dooley'
>   and re/ pumflisticators and talwaggers,
>   and the telepopsical interrrpreters of Ulysses:
> 'If ONLY some one had said that the book is
>   so damn funny!!.'

There is a brief glimpse in Canto 74 of 'Jim the comedian singing'.

Ezra met Gertrude Stein at her Paris home. She records in *The Autobiography of Alice B. Toklas* that she 'liked him but did not find him amusing. She said he was a village explainer, excellent if you were a village, but if you were not, not.' Ezra had no better opinion of Miss Stein. In a 1927 letter he wrote: 'Gertie Stein is supposed to haff a stdyle pecause she writes yittish wit englisch wordts. That is not the way to did it but it shows how effektif it iss yess.' Their mutual irritation seems to have grown largely from the occasion when Ezra took Scofield Thayer to meet her. She records that this time 'Ezra fell out of Gertrude Stein's favourite little armchair . . . and Gertrude Stein was furious. Finally Ezra and the editor of

The Dial left, nobody too well pleased. Gertrude Stein did not want to see Ezra again. Ezra did not quite see why.'

William Carlos Williams says Miss Stein told him she had warned Ezra that the chair was not strong, but he 'sprawled in it in his usual fashion and broke one of the back legs'. Thayer suggests another motive for Ezra's hostility to her – that 'In conversation she put it all over Ezra, who got back by saying all sorts of things on the way home.' Gertrude Stein herself claims he wished to continue the acquaintance, and, meeting her in the Luxembourg Gardens, said he would like to call. She replied: 'I am sorry, but Miss Toklas has a bad tooth and besides we are busy picking wild flowers.' She adds: 'All of which was literally true, like all of Gertrude Stein's literature, but it upset Ezra and we never saw him again.' He countered by referring to her as 'an old tub of guts', and ascribed to her the statement: 'The Jews have produced only three originative geniuses: Christ, Spinoza, and myself.' Possibly she reminded him of Amy Lowell.

*

He had not been long in Paris when he observed to Ford Madox Ford that American writers and editors were arriving there 'like leaves in autumn'. To his parents, he reported having 'heard more of the yank language in six months here than in six years of London', and indeed it was in Paris that he met for the first time a number of Americans with whom he had corresponded for years, Margaret Anderson, Harriet Monroe, Alfred Kreymborg among them. Strikingly, nothing of consequence came of any of these encounters. They proved the closing of old chapters.

Ezra cared little for the drunken antics in which some of his fellow countrymen conspicuously indulged in the cafés and night clubs of Montparnasse. 'Booze in literature is a pest,' he wrote of this manifestation; 'we owe its resurgence in contemporary letters to our autochthonous imbecility and to its expression in one of the worst legal outrages of all time' (Prohibition). However, he made some experiments with intoxication around this time, which he described in 1946: 'The first time I took absinthe I urinated about four gallons and woke up like a new man. I took it two or three more times and finally gave it up.' Artificial stimulants appealed to him little more now than they had in his youth.

What he resented most about the American invasion was that Paris was swiftly becoming too fashionable. Afterwards he spoke harshly of 'every man's Paris', with 'Picabia gone to hell, Brancusi recognized by the cognoscenti, Cocteau in *Vogue*'. He disliked being part of any crowd unless he was its acknowledged leader.

Most young American writers in Paris regarded him, if not as a leader, then with a certain awe. Scofield Thayer introduced him to the twenty-seven-year-old E. E. Cummings, whose poems the *Dial* had published.

Cummings had admired Ezra's poetry for some time, and he took to the man at once. He describes how during a walk through the Paris streets at night 'Ezra was more than wonderfully entertaining: he was magically gentle, as only a great man can be towards some shyest child.' To one of his own biographers Cummings emphasized in 1957: 'Please let me make something onceforall clear: from my standpoint, not EEC but EP is the authentic "innovator", the true trailblazer of an epoch.' On his side Ezra spoke of Cummings's 'bright inimitable, but with difficulty saleable verses'.

Despite the American onrush into Paris, he felt that fools were 'less in one's way here, or at least for the moment', and that there was 'the intelligent nucleus for a movement here, which there bloody well isn't in England'. But he showed no sign of knowing what the movement, when and if it got going, would be, or of being certain in which direction his own work would go.

*

In December 1921, some eight months after arriving in Paris, he and Dorothy began to rent a studio apartment at 70 *bis*, rue Notre Dame des Champs, a quiet side-street in Montparnasse favoured by artists,* only a couple of minutes' walk from the Dôme and Coupole cafés. The studio, one of a dozen or so in the building, was reached by a dark alley leading down into a shady courtyard. It was a 'find' even by Parisian standards. Stella Bowen observed it with a painter's eye:

> The courtyard of 70 *bis* . . . was one of those quiet and secret corners tucked away behind the street façade, whose narrow entrance you might pass in ignorance a thousand times. It was adorable, with tall, damp, black-boughed trees, a mouldering plaster statue, a grubby goldfish pond, and not so much as a dab of paint or a visible sign of repair upon any of the ancient studios surrounding it. I think that any foreigner who has lived in Montparnasse leaves a little piece of his heart behind him, buried in a courtyard such as this. His mind cherishes a vision of summer greenery drooping down across the windows, dusty ivy on a tattered trellis, some ornamental shrubs, a stone bench, a few bulbs and the dark-stained façade of a shabby *pavillon*. He will remember a stucco wall with rows of pale grey shutters, some shut, some open, and some at half-cock, with a peeping concierge within and a row of stockings drying on a string.

*It is sometimes stated that Whistler lived there as a young man, but he was only a visitor, calling sometimes on George du Maurier and other English artists who rented a studio at no. 53.

The Pounds' studio was on the ground floor, facing the alley from the street. 'We are up the hill from the river here, and the air good,' Ezra told his parents. It was 'more like Kensington' than he would have thought possible. Besides the main living room, the apartment contained a tiny lean-to kitchen and a small bedroom reached up an open staircase. The rent was low. There were only two disadvantages: that (as Stella Bowen says) 'being on the ground floor, they were at the mercy of anybody who chose to stroll in and knock; hordes came'; and the cold in winter, the single stove being quite inadequate. One October day Ezra wrote to Agnes Bedford:

> The rain ploppeth, the slop sloppeth
> The cold stoppeth
> $\qquad\qquad$ my circulation.
> The stove wheezeth, my nose not breezeth,
> $\quad$ O Jheezeth!
> $\qquad$ Flu and Damnation.

Ernest Hemingway observed that the studio 'was as poor as Gertrude Stein's studio was rich'.

Ezra reported to his parents that eating at home was a change 'after 9 months of restaurants'. He was still the cook in the ménage: William Carlos Williams describes him operating 'over an alcohol lamp on a shaky-looking table'. Wyndham Lewis believed he 'actually . . . cooked better in Paris than he did in London'.

Just before moving into the studio the Pounds went to London and brought back the greater part of their books and paintings, the Gaudier-Brzeska sculptures, and even Ezra's fencing foils, which were propped in a corner of the studio above adjoining bookcases. Ezra was soon using the studio for an exhibition: 'Am having a show of Koumé's paintings in this studio on Tuesday,' he wrote in July 1922, 'large canvases, some of them.' This was Tami Koumé, a Japanese abstract painter he had befriended and who was eventually killed in a Tokyo earthquake, thereby automatically becoming for Ezra someone who would undoubtedly have reached tremendous heights.

After moving into 70 *bis*, Ezra reported that he was busy 'cleaning, building furniture, having *cheminee* in back room rebuilt at landlords expense'. He made two tables out of old packing cases and rough boards, painted bright scarlet, and also several armchairs with canvas seats. They were put together with hammer and nails, but he planned them well and they held firm. Ford Madox Ford describes one of the chairs:

> It was enormous, compounded of balks of white pine, and had a slung canvas seat so large that, once you sat down, there you lay

until someone pulled you out . . . I struggled on that chair-
bottom like a horse that had fallen down on a slippery street.

The home-made furniture survived the Pounds' various moves, or was
replaced by Ezra with similar constructions – he was making a table as late
as 1958.

He performed similar feats for Sylvia Beach at her bookshop, mending a
cigarette box and a chair. She noted that everybody was impressed except
Joyce, who 'wondered why Ezra wasted his time on labors that any
competent workman could perform for him'.

Sylvia Beach was already an admirer of Ezra's work, and stocked it in
her shop; she claimed that the first book by an American sold to a paying
customer had been *Cathay*. Now that the serialization of *Ulysses* had come
to an end in the *Little Review* for legal reasons, she proposed to Joyce that
Shakespeare and Company should publish and sell the book. Notices were
sent out soliciting subscriptions, Ezra supplying many names for the
bookshop to approach. Yeats agreed to subscribe, but George Bernard
Shaw refused, writing that while he was impressed by the book's 'hideously real' account of Dublin, this was something he had run away from
as a young man, and as an 'elderly Irish gentleman' he would not pay 150
francs for the dubious privilege of revisiting it. Ezra sent him a stern
rebuke, and a lively argument ensued, during which Ezra branded Shaw, in
the *Dial*, 'a ninth rate coward'.

However as the *Ulysses* publication day approached – it was to be
2 February 1922, Joyce's fortieth birthday – Ezra began to show signs of
resentment. Shakespeare and Company announced a public 'séance' at the
bookshop to promote it, with the leading Parisian writer Valéry Larbaud as
speaker, but, perhaps because he himself was not being asked to hold forth
about his 'discovery', Ezra declined Sylvia Beach's invitation to attend. He
was beginning to turn perceptibly against Joyce, his irritation springing
largely from jealousy of what he called the 'great hullabaloo' of enthusiasm
surrounding the book.

4

Caro Lapino

Eliot, on his way to a rest-cure at Lausanne, stopped briefly in Paris in mid-November 1921 and showed Ezra a long poem on which he had been working for much of the year. Originally entitled 'He Do the Police in Different Voices' (a quotation from *Our Mutual Friend*), it was known by December 1921 as *The Waste Land*. Eliot had mentioned it to Dorothy in a letter of 22 May 1921: 'In October I shall be ready for a little mountain air, after I have finished a little poem which I am at present engaged upon.'

Eliot may have considered the poem finished when he set off for Lausanne, but Ezra did not. On being shown it in Paris he evidently made some harsh comments, for when Eliot reached Switzerland he redrafted it substantially, and added the section 'What the Thunder Said'. Afterwards he told John Quinn that the entire *Waste Land* was written 'mostly when I was at Lausanne', so unimportant did his earlier work on it now seem to him.

Ezra greatly approved of what Eliot had done in Switzerland, telling Quinn: 'Eliot came back from his Lausanne specialist looking OK; and with a damn good poem (19 pages) in his suitcase; same finished up here; and shd be out in *Dial* soon, if Thayer isn't utterly nutty.' He introduced Eliot to Horace Liveright of the New York publishers Boni & Liveright, who was then in Paris, with the consequence that Liveright gave Eliot a contract for *The Waste Land* in book form. Eliot then returned to London, leaving Ezra a typescript, and Ezra began to read the poem again with close attention.

On 24 January 1922 he wrote to Eliot: 'Caro mio: MUCH improved . . . Complimenti, you bitch. I am wracked by the seven jealousies.' He also suggested a number of further alterations; the typescript became scrawled over with his comments. Eliot afterwards recalled how 'I placed before him in Paris the manuscript of a sprawling chaotic poem called *The Waste Land* which left his hands, reduced to about half its size, in the form in which it appears in print.'

In its post-Lausanne stage the manuscript still included, as well as the main *Waste Land* sequence, a number of short poems placed to follow 'What the Thunder Said' at the end. In his January 1922 letter Ezra recommended the total exclusion of these 'superfluities', saying: 'If you MUST keep 'em, put 'em at the beginning before the "April cruelest month".' He insisted that the work must end with the 'Shantih shantih shantih' which terminates 'What the Thunder Said'.

Either at this stage, or possibly when he was first shown the poem in November, he wrote 'Bad' alongside the 'Death by Water' section, which at that stage included a lengthy narrative of a shipwreck in the Arctic. Eliot was prompted by this criticism to abandon all of this section, apart from the brief lines beginning 'Phlebas, the Phoenician' – and these he retained only after persuasion from Ezra. Presumably Ezra disliked the matter-of-fact, at times banal tone of the shipwreck story. It may also have been his criticism that made Eliot discard the original opening passage of 'The Fire Sermon', a pastiche of *The Rape of the Lock* in heroic couplets. Alongside it Ezra wrote: '?Too loose = rhyme drags it out to diffuseness'. On the other hand one of the most radical changes, the exclusion of the opening section of 'The Burial of the Dead', which described a seedy night on the town ('First we had a couple of feelers down at Tom's place'), was apparently made by Eliot alone, since there are no comments by Ezra on the typescript, nor is it mentioned in their letters.

In the section of 'The Fire Sermon' describing the seduction of the typist by the 'small house agent's clerk', Ezra hacked up Eliot's regular Gautier-style quatrains, criticizing or rejecting virtually every other word. Eliot followed most of the suggestions, remodelling the passage into a far more terse and chilling narrative. Ezra tended to push Eliot into pruning the over-abundance of statements and images, which the poem contained in early drafts. He drastically reduced the element of pastiche and impersonation (the 'Different Voices' of the original title) and nudged Eliot in the direction of something far more gnomic and oblique than the sprawling collection of narratives that had made up the original text. He drew out the best lines and phrases, encouraging Eliot to isolate them, according to the Ideogramic Method, so that the poem came to resemble an archipelago of 'obstinate isles' - to quote *Hugh Selwyn Mauberley* - reluctant to yield their whole meaning even to the most attentive reader; but isles full of noises that allure and amaze. After Ezra's surgery *The Waste Land* emerged as the supreme piece of modernist verse, terse and allusive where it had originally been much less opaque – yet retaining enough of its original matter to suggest (in a way that a work composed on modernist principles from the outset is less likely to) an underlying coherence and clarity of meaning.

Ezra knew that his surgery on the poem had been crucial to its survival. Accompanying his January 1922 letter to Eliot was a squib headed 'Sage Homme':

> These are the poems of Eliot
> By the Uranian Muse begot;
> A Man their Mother was,
> A Muse their Sire.
>
> How did the printed Infancies result
> From Nuptials thus doubly difficult?
>
> If you must needs enquire
> Know diligent Reader
> That on each Occasion
> Ezra performed the Caesarean Operation . . .

This delighted Eliot, who said he wanted to print it at the front of *The Waste Land*, but he never did.

*

Although publication in book form had been arranged with Boni & Liveright, Eliot also offered the poem to Scofield Thayer for the *Dial*. After some haggling, it was agreed that he would receive the annual *Dial* award of $2,000 for the best contribution, in return for its appearance in the magazine. Eliot wrote to Ezra: 'Dam but why dont they give the prize to you?' And to John Quinn:

> My only regret . . . is that this award should come to me before it has been given to Pound. I feel that he deserves the recognition much more than I do, certainly 'for his services to Letters', and I feel that I ought to wait until after he had received this public testimony. In the manuscript of *The Waste Land* you will see the evidences of his work, and I think that this manuscript is worth preserving in its present form solely for the reason that it is the only evidence of the difference which his criticism has made to this poem.

Scofield Thayer resented having to pay $2,000 for the poem. He grumbled about 'the very disappointing *Waste Land*' and 'the silly cantos of Ezra Pound', and said he would much prefer to publish 'the work of such recognized American authors as Edith Wharton'.

On 12 March 1922, Eliot wrote to Ezra and, after telling him the latest news of negotiations with the *Dial*, said that Lady Rothermere was prepared to back 'the quarterly review' he was hoping to start, adding that she 'is a particular admirer of yours and especially anxious for your collaboration'. Eliot, agreeing that such collaboration would be 'an essential condition' of the venture, asked Ezra whether he would consider

1. A Paris letter every quarter as per Dial, say 1500 words.
2. Of course cantos etc. except that I suppose you would get more by putting them in the Dial, but I shall hope to arrange much higher rates for verse.
3. Sending over contributions by the best people. I am particularly anxious to obtain Picabia, for whom I have much respect. None of these people can get printed in England otherwise. When you translate, translator's fee also.

It is of course clear that the selection of contributions is entirely in your hands . . . I want the paper to be good while it lasts, and if at any time I could not have my own way with it I should drop out and publish the fact . . . Please consider that this venture is impossible without your collaboration.

The terms could scarcely have been more attractive to Ezra, whose likely objections Eliot had cunningly anticipated.

Yet his reply on 14 March was strikingly unenthusiastic:

Cher T,
Willing to do anything I can for you personally, but do consider the following points: I have not the slightest interest in England . . . I am not the least interested in the fortunes of any writer in England save yourself . . . I absolutely refused to have anything to do with another projected English review (only last week) unless they wd. guarantee to get you out of your bank. I am not the least interested in any scheme concerning you which has not that for its aim . . . I cant see that England deserves a good review.

Of course if Lady R. is willing to cooperate with me in a larger scheme which wd. mean getting you out of your bank, and allowing you to give up your whole time to writing, I might reconsider these points . . . I cant see that editing a quarterly will give you any more leisure to write poetry.

This response was doubtless a little motivated by jealousy. Eliot had suddenly succeeded in achieving what Ezra had always wanted: had set up a literary magazine on a firm financial footing. Despite Ezra's refusal to co-operate with the new magazine – the *Criterion* – Eliot went ahead with the plans. Ezra's collaboration was, after all, not essential, and Eliot might not have pressed him for it quite so warmly had he not been so immensely grateful for the recent surgery on *The Waste Land*.

Ezra, meanwhile, had his own plans for Eliot, which he now rushed into action lest the *Criterion* steal all the thunder. 'It is rather odd your writing just at this time,' his letter to Eliot of 14 March 1922 continued. 'I had not intended to say anything to you about the scheme until I had got it into writing. However –' And he enclosed a copy of a document which demanded that

> T. S. Eliot be endowed for life . . . and give his entire time to literature . . . The greatest waste in ang-sax letters at the moment is the waste of Eliot's talent; this wd. not be remedied if he left Lloyds and were compelled to spend his time doing journalism, or to review books etc. He must have *complete* liberty.

It was, in other words, a scheme to get Eliot out of the bank, though to increase its appeal Ezra formulated it as a project to raise money for any suitable 'prisoner' who needed to be released from a job and given liberty to work at his art. He wrote to Agnes Bedford: 'We are saving civilization.'

The idea was that thirty people would pledge themselves to donate £10 a year as long as Eliot – or any other 'prisoners' – needed it. It was 'not charity' but 'release of energy for invention and design . . . It is a new order, called Bel Esprit.' It sounded like some mock medieval order of chivalry. The name was chosen by Natalie Clifford Barney, whose Temple à l'Amitié became the 'trademark' of the venture.

Ezra was the first to subscribe. He persuaded Richard Aldington to contribute, and May Sinclair also agreed. 'Various people including Aldington and myself are IN,' Ezra told Agnes Bedford, with studied vagueness as to numbers.

> Others ought to be. It doesnt stop with Eliot. he is merely the first. Got to be one star case . . . IT is the restart of civilization . . . ANYone who disapproves the choice of the Paris group is at liberty to start group of their own for upkeep of . . . whom they DO like.

He further explained to William Carlos Williams that 'AFTER Eliot is freed it will be much easier to get out the second, third, and tenth prisoners. I wd. back you for the second, if you wished.' (Williams, working contentedly as a doctor in Rutherford, New Jersey, had no such desire.) Ezra even envisaged running 'a yearly trip from America', shipping over the freed captives to Europe like some slave-trader in reverse. 'Or at least you one summer,' he told Williams, 'Marianne another, etc. when there was someone worth it.'

Eliot became very uneasy. At first he sat by in silence, then on 28 July

1922, when he saw a typed circular advertising for subscriptions, he wrote
to Ezra:

> If this circular has not gone out, will you please delete <u>Lloyds
> Bank</u>, to the mention of which I <u>strongly object.</u> If it is stated so
> positively that Lloyds Bank interferes with literature, Lloyds
> Bank would have a perfect right to infer that literature inter-
> fered with Lloyds Bank. <u>Please see my position</u> – I <u>cannot</u>
> jeopardize my position at the Bank before I know what is
> best . . . If this business has any more publicity I shall be forced
> to make a public repudiation of it and refuse to have anything
> more to do with it.

The circular was a breathless, rather hysterical document, full of such
exclamations as 'Must restart civilization; people who say they care,
DON'T care unless they care to the extent of £5 in the spring and £5 in
autumn, ridiculous to say they do, if they won't run to that, can't expect a
civilization or grumble if they don't.' A rather more sober printed missive
was eventually produced by John Rodker, and Ezra wrote about Bel Esprit
in the *Dial* of September 1922 without mentioning Eliot's name. Nevertheless Eliot reported gloomily that Aldington 'evidently regards Bel Esprit as
entirely a personal favour to me'. He had not yet determined to pull out,
admitting that the scheme might help him with 'the production of verse, a
very small, but still a public utility work', but he doubted whether it could
raise enough money to support him. 'I dont think 300 a year . . . is a living
income for me,' he wrote to Ezra on 19 July 1922,

> especially with vagueish guarantees, unless some very definite
> way is shown me of getting another 300 by not too close or
> bestial labour. I shall not stand in the way of your finding out
> just how much money can be got and how many people will
> give it for the arts in any form, *only* I do not at present find 600
> a penny too much and cannot accept one bed room as being
> liberty in comparison with my present life.

Meanwhile, Wyndham Lewis fancied benefiting from Bel Esprit himself.
Ezra wrote crossly to him: 'Certainly can't start on you as you have to the
public eye had nothing but leisure for years. Nothing to prevent or to have
prevented you doing any damn thing you liked, save yr habit of fuss and of
having a private life and allowing it to intrude on yr. attention' – a reference
to Lewis's illegitimate offspring.

Bel Esprit spluttered on for a while, Eliot worrying about what the bank
and his very correct family in America would think, and finding most of
Ezra's communications 'extremely obscure'. By midsummer 1922 Ezra
said he had received twenty-one of the thirty subscriptions required to

'release' Eliot. Yeats wrote that he had meant to contribute, but family troubles made it impossible. Almost the only person to refuse point blank was Amy Lowell. Ezra wrote to her: 'Auw shucks! dearie, aint you the hell-roarer, aint you the kuss.'

Eliot genuinely wanted to leave the bank – 'the prospect of staying there for the rest of my life is abominable to me' – but said he would not help Ezra obtain money for Bel Esprit from Lady Rothermere, backer of the *Criterion*: 'I can't go about passing the hat for myself . . . If you call her answer an insult, I don't think you know what insults are: I should like you to see a few of her notes to me.' He now gave the state of his wife Vivien's health as the reason for tolerating Bel Esprit, and pointed out that while Ezra could live on Dorothy's funds, Vivien had no private means and 'will *never* be strong enough to earn her own living. If I had only myself to consider,' he went on,

> I should not bother about guarantees for a moment: I could always earn my own living. But I am responsible toward her in more than the ordinary way. I have made a great many mistakes, which are largely the cause of her present catastrophic state of health, and also it must be remembered that she kept me from returning to America where I should have become a professor and probably never written another line of poetry, so in that respect she should be endowed . . . I will leave the Bank as soon as I have such guarantees – for my life <u>or</u> <u>for Vivien's life</u> – as would satisfy a solicitor.

In September 1922 Eliot told Ezra that Aldington, who had not exactly been 'sympathetic', was stirring up trouble over Bel Esprit, though he did not say what. Two months later Vivien wrote Ezra a frantic letter reporting that Eliot was 'running down again', and that Lady Rothermere was being 'offensive' about the *Criterion*: 'She is unhinged – one of those beastly raving women who are the most dangerous. She is now in that asylum for the insane . . . where she does religious dances naked with Katherine Mansfield . . . [who] hates T. more than anyone. Can you get for T. this money (Bel Esp.) which you speak of in yr. letter, without the condition that he leaves the Bank *immediately*? . . . Write at once. V.'

Eliot himself followed up Vivien's letter the next day and confirmed everything she had said: Lady Rothermere was becoming 'increasingly offensive', especially since she 'entered her retreat for maniacs'. Would Ezra please see her in Paris and 'tell her bluntly that the *Criterion* is a SUCCESS' (the first number had now appeared). Eliot suggested that the Bel Esprit money might be used to finance the magazine: 'If you and I could get the *Criterion* into our own hands and could only find the money to run it for a couple of years, it would be the thing of our lives.'

Ezra ignored this suggestion, and now Bel Esprit finally foundered. Lady Ottoline Morrell (with whom Ezra had no contact) had decided to establish a rival scheme, the Eliot Fellowship Fund, and in November 1922 the *Liverpool Daily Post* alleged that Eliot had received £800 from sympathizers but was refusing to give up his bank job. Eliot told Ezra he was treating this as libel and had put it in the hands of his solicitor. He added: 'You ought to know as well as I from what sources it is likely to emanate' (meaning Aldington).

The newspaper published a retraction, but Eliot said it had all given him 'a devil of a lot of trouble', and he had suffered such nuisances as 'an anonymous letter from a "Wellwisher" offering me 6d in stamps' (probably Aldington again). But he told Ezra he did not want to seem ungrateful: he really felt the efforts on his behalf to have been 'wonderful'. The following year Ezra sent him such funds as Bel Esprit had actually accumulated (apparently about £120), which Eliot received, in two instalments, with gratitude: 'As I have no immediate crying need to spend the money and havnt time for a 3 days debooch, I shall bank it or invest it temporarily.' Ezra's final word on Bel Esprit was that it had been 'a dismal nerve-wracking failure for everyone concerned', though he said it had inspired a group of Frenchmen to subsidize Paul Valéry. Eliot remained in the bank for a little over two years, after which he became a publisher, joining the staff of the newly formed Faber and Gwyer, soon renamed Faber and Faber.

*

In the early days of the *Criterion*, Eliot continued to try to involve Ezra editorially. The magazine's name was originally suggested by Vivien Eliot, who thought Eliot's own idea, 'The London Review', was dismal. Almost simultaneously Ezra sent a letter suggesting the same name – he had thought of using 'Criterion' some time before for one of his own projects. Eliot was delighted at this 'most auspicious confirmation . . . I told Lady R that you had suggested the same title as had been agreed upon 2 days before, and she was mightily pleased.'

Ezra's own first offer for the *Criterion* was a piece that Eliot described as 'notes on the slave trade'; he turned it down as 'not quite the thing to make an impression in an early number', and asked instead for an article on Impressionism that Ezra had promised. He continued: 'I don't ask for Cantos simply because I know you can get more money from the Dial.' And a few days later: 'I hear good report of the progress of Cantose. If the Dial refuses please let me inspect, but probably unwise to make the paper too conspicuous at first, if the rape of the bishop is an integral part.' (No bishop is raped in the Cantos, though there are derogatory references to one in the second of the Hell Cantos.) In the event the first number of the

Criterion contained nothing by Ezra, his name not appearing until the second (January 1923) where he wrote on 'Criticism in General'.

Eliot himself was the first to point out the shortcomings of the new magazine. 'You will possibly observe,' he wrote to Ezra of the opening number, 'a few passengers who will have to walk the plank as soon as the ship gets out of sight of land.' And a year later: 'Of course I don't think ¾ of the stuff worth printing, but ¼ is a larger proportion than any other paper can show.' Ezra's own first reaction was wary. 'Eliot's new Quarterly very good, in octogenarian way,' he told his father. 'Will be more intelligent than Dial, but possibly no more lively.' Two issues later he described the magazine as 'so heavily camouflaged as Westminster Abbey, that the living visitor is not very visible'. By 1930 he was using the word 'Criterionism' to mean a preference for 'dead and moribund writing', and alleging that 'Criterion has printed in seven years about enough live stuff for one; if that'. To Eliot in 1935 he wrote:

> KIRYypes!! I keep on reading at this Morterarium. Waal, I suppose it is a just estimate of the mortician's parlour which is England . . . It wd. be nice if you wd. reserve say 4 pages per issue to tell the reader honestly what is fit to read.

Eliot's reaction to letters like this was 'Lawd how you cuss and rave.'

Ezra had no higher opinion of the value of Eliot's work as a publisher. In *Guide to Kulchur*, itself published by Faber and Faber, he wondered which of Eliot or himself had 'wasted the greater number of hours', Eliot by 'attending to fools', himself by 'alienating imbeciles'. He also thought little of Eliot's published criticism. 'Not that his crit. is *bad* but that he hasn't seen *where* it leads.' Eliot, he alleged, wasted his time attending to 'lesser rather than greater'. In 1930 he suggested that Eliot had 'arrived at the supreme Eminence among English critics largely through disguising himself as a corpse'; and by 1933, looking back at modernism, he felt that if he himself had been 'in any sense the revolution', then Eliot had become 'the counter-revolution' (again this insult was printed in a Faber book). But he admitted that the *Criterion* had tried – and partially succeeded – to establish 'a medium for careful criticism as distinguished from the slop that preceded it'.

Despite this frequent sniping, Eliot continued to commission pieces from Ezra for the *Criterion*, occasionally disciplining him into sober prose, but often allowing him to ramble about his current obsessions. In 1923 he published the Malatesta Cantos in the magazine, and later excerpts from the Cantos occasionally appeared in its pages. 'What I really want is a canto or two,' Eliot wrote to Ezra in December 1924. 'Can you inform me as to present condition and prospects?' And ten years later:

what about a cantoo for December . . . we might have a canto canto canto three cheers for the Headmaster three cheers for the governors three cheers for the Dean hip hip canto cantoo cantooo.

He continued to consult Ezra about his own work. In October 1925 he sent him *The Hollow Men*, asking 'Is it too bad to print? If not, can anything be done to it? Can it be cleaned up in any way? I feel I want something of about this length (I-V) to end the volume [*Poems 1909–1925*] as post-Waste, but if you think it is . . . [the rest is missing].' But despite this appeal, Ezra does not seem to have offered any suggestions for improvement.

At some time during the 1920s Ezra took to calling Eliot 'Possum'. A letter from him to E. E. Cummings refers to 'Possum's rep[utation] for decorum and subtlety'. In 1946 Ezra asked Charles Olson: 'Why do you think I baptised him? . . . The possum: ability to appear dead while it is still alive.'

It was part of a whole game with names from *Uncle Remus*. A 1926 postcard from Eliot to Ezra is signed 'Tar Baby', but 'Possum' stuck, and appealed to Eliot who sometimes signed letters to other friends 'T.P.' for 'Tom Possum'. In 1934 he made unsuccessful efforts to get hold of a framed picture of a real possum to send to Ezra.

In the game, Ezra himself was Brer Rabbit – Joel Chandler Harris's canny and resourceful hero. Eliot's letters to Ezra often begin 'Dear Rabbit', 'Rabbit My Rabbit', or 'caro lapino'. In response, Ezra: 'Waaal Possum, my fine ole Marse Supial . . .' Others were drawn into the game: Frank Morley, an American-born director of Faber and Faber, was 'the Whale'; Laurence Pollinger, who had the (far from enviable) task of acting as Ezra's literary agent for some of his projects, was 'the Hipol' (presumably a variant of 'Hippo'); Geoffrey Faber, founder of the publishing house, became 'the Coot'; and Eliot's friend John Hayward was named 'the Tarantula' because of his often poisonous wit. Ezra eventually dropped out of the game, but he continued to use the 'Possum' joke, claiming that Eliot's 'low saurian vitality' would sustain him almost indefinitely: 'When Joyce and Wyndham L. have long since gag'd or exploded, ole Possum will be totin round deh golf links and giving bright nickels to the lads of 1987.'

*

Ezra and Dorothy were drawn into some of the turmoils of Eliot's first marriage. The work of a Dr Louis Berman, who believed that 'glands' lay at the back of most illnesses, interested Ezra for a time – he wrote about it in *New Age* in March 1922 – and he suggested to Eliot that Berman might be able to help Vivien, who was (or claimed to be) constantly ill. Vivien herself wrote to Ezra in June 1922 to tell him she would have 'great faith' in anything he might suggest. She listed her symptoms: colitis, a high temperature ('I very often have a temperature of 99.4 for two or three weeks at a time for no obvious reason'), migraines, insomnia, and 'Increasing mental incapacity. I have a horror of using my mind and spend most of my time in trying to avoid contact with people or anything that will force me to use my mind.'

Eliot himself added at the bottom: 'Vivien has shown me this letter and I think it is *quite inadequate* as a description of her case, but she is *very* ill and exhausted and I do not think she can do any better now.' He told Ezra he would 'like to put her into your hands', except that she seemed too unwell to go to Paris. However, at some point she did make the journey: Olga Rudge remembers seeing her there with Ezra and Dorothy, and describes her as 'very charming, perfectly normal'. By May 1923 Eliot was reporting having 'a hell of a time' with Vivien, and told Ezra she had been contemplating suicide and 'was going to leave you a letter'.

Eliot was clearly very fond of Dorothy, given the number of letters from him to her trying to arrange a meeting when she was visiting London from the Continent. For example: '*Could* you meet me tomorrow (Wed.) night at 8^{30} at the Café Royal for a ¾ of an hour? . . . I sh^d be very sorry to miss you.' And on another occasion: 'My dear Dorothy . . . Will you have tea with me on Wednesday at the Carlton at 5^{30}? That is the easiest place to get to from the bank. I hope you can.' Once when they failed to meet he was 'indeed very disappointed'. It was difficult to pin her down; Eliot refers in one note to her 'mysterious movements', and he observed that unlike him she hated using the telephone to make arrangements. (So did Ezra, who regarded the 'gorbloody tHellerfone' as a trap rather than a convenience.)

Dorothy and Eliot continued to meet whenever she was in London during the 1920s and 1930s, and his letters to her were always playfully affectionate. A 1934 postcard, thanking her for the gift of a Simenon novel (always his favourite light reading), is signed 'Yr dear   Eliot'.

*

The Waste Land made its first appearance in print in the first issue of the *Criterion* in October 1922, and in the November 1922 *Dial*. The Boni & Liveright edition, with Eliot's notes to the poem, came out in mid-December, and the Hogarth Press edition in September 1923. When Eliot received his first Boni & Liveright copies he sent one to Ezra in Paris with the inscription 'for E.P. / miglior fabbro / from T.S.E. / Jan. 1923.'

Eliot's inscription alludes to Dante's words of praise for Arnaut Daniel, in Canto 26 of the *Purgatorio*: 'Fu miglior fabbro del parlar materno' ('He was the better craftsman in his mother-tongue'). Ezra had used 'Il Miglior

Fabbro' as the title of his chapter on Daniel in *The Spirit of Romance*. The dedication was put into print by Eliot when *The Waste Land* was reprinted in his *Poems 1909–1925*, where it is preceded by the words 'For Ezra Pound / il miglior fabbro'. Eliot explained in 1938 that he had 'wished at that moment to honour the technical mastery and critical ability manifest in his [Ezra's] own work, which had also done so much to turn *The Waste Land* from a jumble of good and bad passages into a poem.'

Ezra's own judgement of himself and Eliot, in 1942, was that in the matter of logopoeia 'Eliot surpasses me'; in melopoeia 'I surpass him', but 'part of his logopoeia is incompatible with my main purpose'. He did not mention phanopoeia, but perhaps thought that they were equal masters of it – which they were.

Whatever his view of his own abilities, Ezra was well aware that *The Waste Land* achieved far more than he had yet managed. In July 1922 he wrote to Felix Schelling: 'Eliot's *Waste Land* is I think the justification of the "movement", of our modern experiment, since 1900.' And to John Quinn in February 1922: 'About enough, Eliot's poem, to make the rest of us shut shop.' William Carlos Williams felt much the same: 'It wiped out our world as if an atom bomb had been dropped upon it and our brave sallies into the unknown were turned to dust . . . I felt at once that it had set me back twenty years.'

Wise Guy

But Ezra did not shut shop. As soon as he had finished helping Eliot with *The Waste Land* he returned to the Cantos, which he had not touched for more than two years. 'There is a new canto done,' he told Agnes Bedford on 17 February 1922. During March he revised it: 'a decent VIIIth,' he called it, 'which the Dial will print in due course'. He liked to publish cantos as soon as they were finished, preferring to 'get 'em out of the shop'.

The 1922 eighth Canto – eventually renumbered Canto 2 – describes the young god Dionysus being kidnapped by Pentheus and taken on a ship to Naxos, and the strange metamorphosis undergone by ship, sailors, and sea. The story, taken from Ovid, is told by the sea captain Acoetes, and for a time Ezra considered making him the narrator of the Cantos from now on. He wrote to Ford: 'I dare say it wd. be easier to . . . let Acoetes continue – only I dont see how I cd. get *him* to Bayswater' (make him an observer of modern events).

Up to now, the Cantos had been a rather humourless enterprise, but the new one contained suggestions of comedy:

> 'To Naxos? Yes, we'll take you to Naxos,
> Cum' along lad.' 'Not that way!'
> 'Aye, that way is Naxos.'
> And I said: 'It's a straight ship.'
> And an ex-convict out of Italy
> knocked me into the fore-stays . . .

Ezra wrote it while reading *Ulysses* right through in book form – he completed the first draft just as he had 'finished the 732 pages' of Joyce's book. Judging by the turn the Cantos now began to take, Joyce's huge range of humour had suggested to Ezra that he need not be quite so solemn. *The Waste Land* probably nudged him in that direction too.

Nevertheless he was still fumbling in the dark. 'Having the crust to attempt a poem in 100 or 120 cantos long after all mankind has been commanded never again to attempt a poem of any length, I have to stagger as I can,' he wrote in the summer of 1922 to Felix Schelling. He said that everything he had written so far had been mere 'preparation of the palette. I *have* to get down all the colours or elements I want for the poem. Some perhaps too enigmatically and abbreviatedly. I hope, heaven help me, to bring them into some sort of design and architecture later.'

His next piece of subject matter suggested itself to him during a visit to Italy in the spring and summer of 1922. He was away from Paris for about three months; he stayed in Siena, went north again to Venice and Sirmione, and also visited Rimini, Ravenna, and Verona. In Rimini he visited the Tempio Malatestiano, one of the most striking buildings of the Italian Renaissance. Originally a Franciscan church, it was reconstructed in the fifteenth century by direction of Sigismundo Pandolfo Malatesta, ruler of Rimini, virtually as a monument to himself and his mistress Isotta (later his wife). Ezra decided to make Sigismundo the subject of a canto.

Back in Paris in August, he told his mother he had 'various materials for my Malatesta canto lying about'. A couple of weeks later he was 'plugging away' at it, and thought it might stretch to two cantos. By December there were three, 'in some sort of shape'; by the summer of 1923, after he had paid a return visit to some of the Malatesta sites, four. They were published in the July 1923 *Criterion* as 'Cantos IX to XII of a Long Poem'. (They are now numbered 8 to 11.)

Sigismundo Malatesta was cultivated but also brutal and treacherous, a challenge to historians and biographers. Ezra read a nineteenth-century French life of him by C. E. Yriarte, which (in Ezra's words) presents him as 'a failure worth all the successes of his age', 'an entire man', an example of 'the factive personality'. In the Malatesta Cantos he calls Sigismundo 'POLUMETIS', 'many-minded', a Homeric adjective for the versatility of Odysseus. Elsewhere, Ezra described this Odyssean character as '"the wise guy"', the downy, the hard-boiled . . . His companions have most of them something that must have been the Greek equivalent of shell-shock.' The Malatesta Cantos are an idealization of this personality, the kind of tough guy to whom Ezra was always attracted, and on whom he liked to model himself.

'No one has claimed that the Malatesta cantos are obscure,' he wrote with some pride, and certainly the dense narrative style of earlier cantos is replaced by a disarmingly open and colloquial manner:

> These fragments you have shelved (shored).
> 'Slut!' 'Bitch!' Truth and Calliope
> Slanging each other sous les lauriers . . .

The first line is a nudge at Eliot's 'These fragments I have shored against my ruin' in *The Waste Land*. Eliot was rather nervous about it when Ezra sent him the typescript for printing in the *Criterion*: 'I object strongly on tactical grounds to y^r 1st line. People are inclined to think that we write our verses in collaboration as it is, or else that you write mine & I write yours. With your permission we will begin with line 2.' Ezra also seems to be glancing at Eliot and Bel Esprit when he makes Sigismundo say, of an artist he is patronizing: 'I want to arrange with him to give him so much per year / . . . So that he can work as he likes / Or waste his time as he likes.'

The artist – probably Piero della Francesca – was engaged in decorating the walls of the Tempio in Rimini. The building was not completed in Sigismundo's lifetime; Ezra judged it both 'a monumental failure' and 'perhaps the apex of what man has embodied in the last 1000 years . . . A cultural "high" . . .' The Tempio attracted him because it was nominally a Christian building with strong pagan connections. In a niche in the outside wall, Sigismundo interred the ashes of a Neoplatonist philosopher, Gemisthus Plethon, who had helped to revive Greek learning in the medieval Western world, and had tried to synthesize Plato and Christianity. Ezra chose to regard him as one of the links between the Greek Mysteries (origin of his troubadour love cult) and Europe. The Tempio thus suggested that 'there could be clean and beneficent Christianity restarted'.

As the Malatesta Cantos continue, Sigismundo writes a letter agreeing to give his services as a commander of mercenaries, sings a song he has written to Isotta, reports awful weather as he prepares to fight, and recalls how he met Gemisthus the philosopher. Sometimes Sigismundo himself narrates, and sometimes the voice – as in this passage about Federigo, Lord of Urbino – is that of one of his men:

> And he said. 'This time Mister Feddy has done it.'
> He said: 'Broglio, I'm the goat. This time
> Mr Feddy has done it (*m'l'ha calata*).'
> And he'd lost his job with the Venetians,
> And the stone didn't come in from Istria;
> And we sent men to the silk war;
> And Wattle never paid up on the nail . . .
> And the jobs getting smaller and smaller,
> Until he signed on with Siena;
> And that time they grabbed his post-bag.

Sigismundo, short of work as a *condottiere* or leader of mercenaries, signed on with such minor powers as the Sienese, who after a disagreement captured his mail bag with five months' letters in it. Ezra may have seen these in the municipal archives in Siena; he goes on to quote from one of them. Here for the first time the Cantos drop into prose, and the Italian names are translated into equivalent English ones – Luigi Alvise, overseer of the Tempio workmen, becomes 'master Alwidge', and a stonemason, Giorgio Ranbutino, is transformed into 'George Rambottom'.

The Malatesta Cantos nearly succeed, as Eliot observed, in extracting the 'essentially living' from fifteenth-century Italy. But the sheer weight of detail becomes burdensome, and the style declines into catalogue:

> And the Angevins were gunning after Naples
> And we dragged in the Angevins,
> And we dragged in Louis Eleventh,
> And the *tiers Calixte* was dead, and Alfonso;
> And against us we had 'this Aeneas' and young Ferdinando . . .

The conception of the Malatesta Cantos is close to that of *Homage to Sextus Propertius*, with its scheme of bringing a historical figure alive from the inside. But the sequence is more raggedly written, less deft, and for elucidation requires constant reference to fifteenth-century Italian political history. Sigismundo never comes alive as does Propertius.

Ezra, pleased enough with the Malatesta Cantos, decided to look for some other 'bhloomin historic character' on whom a further section could be built, somebody else who could illustrate 'intelligent constructivity' and who also had a 'private life'; but most historical figures seemed 'fatally deficient' in one or other of these categories. The next canto, half done by the summer of 1923 and numbered 12 in the finished work, was the first to introduce a modern character: 'Baldy' Bacon, the New York entrepreneur with whom Ezra had hoped to go into business in 1910. The canto presents him as an example of a creative user of wealth, however shady.

Canto 13, written immediately after, was described by Ezra as announcing the 'backbone moral' of the Cantos. Its subject is Confucius ('Kung'). On 21 June 1923 Ezra told his father: 'I'm doing a canto on Kung; don't know about english translations of him. I have Pauthier's french translation of the Four Books; and a latin translation of the Odes.' He said he found the teachings 'very refreshing' after 'Christianchurchism', which taught 'thou shalt attend to thy neighbour's business before thou attendest to thine own'; whereas Confucius recommended beginning with oneself. He might have added that the Confucian method of organizing one's personality – assuming a mask of correctness, and repressing all immoderate tendencies – was the opposite of Freudianism and other forms of psychoanalysis, which begin by uncovering weaknesses. 'Anyone can run to excesses,' says Kung in Canto 13. 'It is easy to shoot past the mark, / It is hard to stand firm in the middle.'

Next in numerical order come the two Hell Cantos, 14 and 15. In June

1922 Ezra told Agnes Bedford they were 'unprintable – dealing with modern life'. Intended to be 'a portrait of contemporary England', of 'LONDON . . . in 1919 and 1920', and superficially modelled on Dante, they picture their victims as condemned not to any Christian hell but to a mire of human excrement. There are some richly comic images: the public leader with 'a scrupulously clean table-napkin / Tucked under his penis', and a bishop 'waving a condom full of black-beetles'. But even these seem rather randomly conceived, while the portrayal of pompous personages squelching through a world of faeces soon palls. The images are so extreme from the outset ('Profiteers drinking blood sweetened with shit') that there is no build-up of revulsion or amusement as the cantos proceed. Names are left blank, partly no doubt for fear of libel, though Ezra said he meant it to seem that they had decayed through corruption. In the few instances where individuals can be identified, the insults do not seem particularly appropriate; for example, Lloyd George and Woodrow Wilson 'Addressing crowds through their arse-holes', and Churchill (in those days Secretary for War) looking like 'a swollen foetus'.

The Hell Cantos were not meant to be funny; Ezra said he objected to *Punch* treating the iniquities of England as a laughing matter. Yet he can scarcely have meant them to communicate – as they do – an obsession with defecation and its physiology, which he regards with horrified fascination:

> Above the hell-rot
> the great arse-hole,
>   broken with piles . . .
> endless rain from the arse-hairs . . .
> a continuous bum-belch
>   distributing its productions.

Eliot, disconcerted by the Hell Cantos, pointed out that Ezra's hell consists entirely of '*other people*, the people we read about in the newspapers'; there is no suggestion of self-accusation – an attitude that runs throughout the Cantos; except for a celebrated moment in Canto 81, the blame is always attributed to others. Eliot wrote to Ezra in 1933:

> The Cantoes is all right but here & there a little humanitarian pus might have been squeezed out you need a canto or two with a REAL hell in it somebody feeling something but I know I know 300 years of Calvinism from Calvin to Coolidge makes it come hard.

And in another letter the same year:

> I dont see what you can do with Hell without Sin & sinners This is not a theological argument its just the way it seems to me

things hang together or dont It may be allright just as an
interlude in Limbo but it wants to be supported by a real Hell
underneath with real people in it Put me in if you Like Anyway
without that it just Oh well

Ezra paid no attention.

Canto 16, which concludes the first section of the Cantos to be printed
as a book, begins in the manner of a *Purgatorio*, with a description of hell
mouth. Ezra wrote in 1927: 'You have had a hell in Cantos XIV, XV,
purgatorio in XVI etc'. In the canto, purgatory chiefly takes the form of
certain individuals' war experiences, especially of the First World War – a
montage of anecdotes that Ezra had heard recounted by such diverse
people as Victor Plarr, Aldington, Wyndham Lewis and the American
journalist Lincoln Steffens, who gave a talk in Paris in October 1922 about
his eye-witness memories of the Russian Revolution.

Having written the sixteenth canto in the summer of 1923, Ezra then
reorganized the opening. In mid-August he told his father that he had
'revised earlier part of the poem'. He scrapped the first of the original
'Three Cantos' (the Browningesque apology for the whole project),
retaining only its very opening ('Hang it all, Robert Browning, / there can
be but the one "Sordello"') for the beginning of what now became Canto 2
(formerly Canto 8), while part of the second of 'Three Cantos' was used to
make up a new, very short Canto 3. What had been the third of the 'Three
Cantos', the 'Nekyia' describing Odysseus' visit to Hades, now became
Canto 1.

Though these changes were elaborate, they failed to bring to light any
structure, plan, or purpose within the complete work. Indeed the *Dial*
reviewer of the first sixteen cantos observed that they were harder to read
en bloc than piecemeal; they gave each other 'little aid'. The purpose of the
revisions was not to clarify, rather the reverse – to remove what Ezra now
evidently regarded as the damaging admission, made by the narrator of
'Three Cantos', that the 'endless poem' was simply 'a rag bag' in which he
could 'stuff' all his ideas. It would have been more honest to allow the
admission to stand, and not necessarily damaging. The same *Dial* critic
perceived that the poem was really 'a rag-bag like *Sordello*', but said this
scarcely mattered, for 'the rhythm is breathless and breath-takingly
beautiful'. (The reviewer, the novelist Glenway Westcott, had been office
boy on *Poetry* and was a longstanding admirer of Ezra.) May Sinclair had
pointed out in her review of 'Three Cantos' that the very formlessness of
the work was perfectly suited to the mind of its author: 'The form gives
scope to his worst qualities and his best.'

His 1923 revision was the last major change Ezra made in any part of the
Cantos after initial publication. He reserved, at least for a time, the right to

revise: the first two sections included the word 'Draft' in their titles, Ezra explaining that they were a 'half-time report' rather than necessarily the finished text. But it became apparent that he intended to try to clarify the structure and meaning by adding further sections rather than by revising, re-working, or adding notes. This set a considerable challenge.

*

A Draft of XVI Cantos, as the first section was called, was ready for press by the autumn of 1923, but did not appear until January 1925, owing to the leisurely pace of its printer, William Bird, an affluent American journalist living in Paris who produced hand-made books as a hobby under the name Three Mountains Press. Ezra described Bird's printing of the sixteen cantos as 'a dee looks edtn . . . of UNRIVALLED magnificence . . . one of the real bits of printing; modern book to be jacked up to somewhere near level of mediaeval mss.' With its hand-made paper, elegant typography, and extravagant bindings, it was certainly a luxury product, while the price – 400 francs for ordinary copies, 1,600 francs for those on Imperial Japan paper, bound in blue morocco – put it exclusively in the collectors' market.

Because the Cantos were such a hold-all, Ezra now ceased to write any other serious poetry. Apart from translations and occasional excursions into light verse, from his Paris years onwards he turned out cantos and nothing else. 'Am plugging on my next batch of cantos,' he told his father. 'Don't know what else is to be expected of me during the oncoming years.' And to an enquirer: 'There is no other verse available, and will be none.'

6

Fiddle Music

Among those whose war experiences were mentioned in Canto 16 was Ernest Hemingway. He and his wife Hadley had come to Paris late in 1921 in the hope that he could make his mark as a writer. He accepted an invitation to tea at 70 *bis* rue Notre Dame des Champs and listened, mostly in silence, while Ezra held forth.

Afterwards, he wrote a satire on Ezra's Whistler pose and his self-conscious bohemianism, intending to offer it to the *Little Review*. But before he could do so he discovered that Ezra might be of use to him – Ezra praised some poems Hemingway let him see, and passed on a short story of his to the *Little Review*. Though neither poems nor story were printed, Hemingway began to realize that Ezra had a considerable fund of kindness, was indeed 'kinder . . . than I was'. Certainly he could be silly, but he was, Hemingway decided, 'sincere in his mistakes'. From despising Ezra's pretensions, Hemingway swiftly moved to a position of almost doglike devotion, saying that he thought of Ezra as 'a sort of saint. He was also irascible but so perhaps have been many saints.' He paid great attention to Ezra's criticisms of his writing.

Ezra discovered that 'Hem' was (or claimed to be) an experienced boxer, and asked for lessons. The report went out: 'He's teaching me to write . . . and I'm teaching him to box.' Wyndham Lewis called at 70 *bis* and found the pair in action:

> A splendidly built young man, stript to the waist, and with a torso of dazzling white, was standing not far from me. He was tall, handsome, and serene, and was repelling with his boxing gloves – I thought without undue exertion – a hectic assault of Ezra's. After a final swing at the dazzling solar plexus (parried

effortlessly by the trousered statue) Pound fell back upon his settee.

Hemingway was uncomfortable at their being observed by a third party: 'Ezra had not been boxing very long and I was embarrassed at having him work in front of anyone he knew, and I tried to make him look as good as possible.' He said Ezra boxed like a fencer. (William Carlos Williams thought he fenced like a boxer.) Hemingway was 'never able to teach him to throw a left hook', which was probably just as well.

In March 1922 Hemingway reported to the friend who had arranged the introduction to Ezra:

> I've been teaching Pound to box wit [*sic*] little success. He habitually leads wit his chin and has the general grace of the crayfish or crawfish. He's willing but short winded . . . It's pretty sporting of him to risk his dignity and his critical reputation at something that he don't know nothing about. He's a really good guy, Pound, wit a fine bitter tongue onto him.

But progress was evident after a week or two:

> Pound . . . has developed a terrific wallop. I can usually cross myself though before he lands them and when he gets too tough I dump him on the floor . . . Some day I will get careless and he will knock me for a row of latrines.

Ezra invented a showcase for Hemingway's writing: a series of small books to be printed by Bill Bird at Three Mountains Press under the overall title 'The Inquest' – it was supposedly an enquiry into 'the state of prose after *Ulysses*, or the possibility of a return to normal writing'. Ford Madox Ford and William Carlos Williams agreed to contribute, and the star item was to be a collection of very short prose vignettes by Hemingway entitled *in our time*. Ezra had high expectations of the series, but Bird took so long to print each book that they appeared too far apart to attract any collective attention. However, *in our time* did the trick for Hemingway: it was noticed and reviewed in America, and played a large part in getting him a contract for his first novel. (A much expanded version, entitled *In Our Time* and including a number of short stories, was issued in New York a year after the Paris publication.)

Ezra was soon speaking of 'the sensitivity of real writing like Hem's', saying it showed the 'touch of the chisel'; but Hemingway's reputation grew too swiftly to need a further boost from Ezra: *The Sun Also Rises* appeared in 1926 and *A Farewell to Arms* three years later. Hemingway was lavish, however, in acknowledgement of what he claimed Ezra had taught him: in 1933 he told Ezra he had learnt more about 'how to write and how not to write' from him than from anyone else, and had always said so. There was a degree of hero worship on each side, Ezra being attracted by Hemingway's tough physique and his ability to combine literature with pugilism. James Laughlin suggests that the literary influence went both ways: that the furiously aggressive, jabbing style that characterizes Ezra's prose from the late 1920s grew from those attempts, under Hemingway's tuition, to throw a left hook to the jaw.

*

'My income is still extremely unsteady & has no settled elements,' Ezra wrote to his mother in January 1923. But during this year Dorothy's father died, and her mother gave up the Kensington house, thereby releasing more family funds. Almost simultaneously an aunt of Dorothy's left her a substantial legacy; so by August, Ezra could tell his parents that 'our combined intake is now probably more than yours'. It was scarcely 'combined', for he was still earning virtually nothing. But Dorothy continued to support him, and they spent much of 1923 travelling in Italy.

Paris had not lived up to its promise; Ezra now felt the place to be typified by the 'enervation' of Proust. In his 'Paris Letter' for the November 1922 *Dial* he made unflattering comparisons between Proust and *Notturno*, a newly published autobiographical novel by Gabriele d'Annunzio, written while he was temporarily blinded on active service in the war. 'Gabriele is male, civilized,' he alleged. As opposed to Proust's 'meticulous record of minor annoyance', d'Annunzio was a typical example of 'Italian vitality'.

In fact he now thought as poorly of Paris as of London. 'Is it possible,' he asked in the same *Dial* article, 'to establish some spot of civilization, or some geographically scattered association of civilized creatures? One is up against this problem in a decadent wallow like London, in an enervated centre like Paris.' In contrast, Italy was clearly 'reawakening'. Soon he extended his strictures to the whole of France, which he said was 'in her dotage'.

He had paid no serious attention to French intellectual life since settling in Paris. His initial enthusiasms for Cocteau, Picabia, and Brancusi had led nowhere, and in 1923 in the *Dial* he was alleging that such nineteenth-century stars as Flaubert, Laforgue, and Rimbaud were still 'the latest real news' in France, the rest being merely passing fashion. Though he had met and read Valéry, he thought him 'of less interest than Eliot'; and Valéry was certainly 'the best they've got at the moment'.

At the beginning of 1923 he and Dorothy spent some weeks in Rapallo, on the Riviera di Levante, a few miles east of Genoa. Ezra had visited it briefly the previous summer, and thought it 'hard to beat', the sort of place for which he and Dorothy had been searching. Now in 1923 they both gave it an extended test.

The Italian Riviera had begun to be favoured by English and other northern European travellers making the Grand Tour in the eighteenth and early nineteenth centuries. The English Romantic poets were among those who passed through; somebody told Ezra that Keats had stayed in Rapallo, and he was inclined to believe it. 'The magic casements are here,' he wrote, 'though I have always suspected a different and less perfect edifice suggested 'em.' After the arrival of the railway, Rapallo became, for a time, a haven of the élite, but by the 1920s other resorts had grown more fashionable, and the steep rise of hills behind the town made more than a modest expansion impossible. When Adrian Stokes visited Rapallo at the impressionable age of nineteen, he was enchanted: 'The air held scents of flowering trees and of eucalyptus enclosing and disclosing the villas mounting on their gardens. I drove in a carriage through the town to the pension . . . The scents intensified: there was the sound of waters falling to the sea.' Yeats came there a few years later, in Ezra's wake, and was equally moved, describing

> Houses mirrored in an almost motionless sea, mountains that shelter the bay from all but the south wind, bare brown branches of low vines and of tall trees blurring their outline as though with a soft mist; a verandahed gable a couple of miles away bringing to mind some Chinese painting, and Rapallo's thin line of broken mother of pearl along the water's edge.

Ezra's own delight in Rapallo and the sense of liberation he felt there after London and Paris seems to be expressed in Canto 17, written during 1924, which describes an earthly paradise that has recognizable touches of the place:

> So that the vines burst from my fingers
> And the bees weighted with pollen
> Move heavily in the vine-shoots:
>   chirr – chirr – chir-rill – a purring sound,
> And the birds sleepily in the branches . . .
> The light now, not of the sun.
>   Chrysophrase,
> And the water green clear, and blue clear;
> On, to the great cliffs of amber . . .
> Beyond, sea, crests seen over dune
> Night sea churning shingle . . .

Rapallo was a favourite retreat for other writers and artists. On the terrace of the Albergo Rapallo one might occasionally see Thomas Mann or

Oskar Kokoschka, or more often the Nobel Prize winner Gerhart Hauptmann, or Max Beerbohm who had a villa just outside the town. The other
fashionable café, the Chuflay, was frequented by the American 'smart set',
who played bridge and backgammon and escaped Prohibition. Both
groups met amicably at the town's tennis club. Yeats describes the mixed
society with some relish:

> On the broad pavement by the sea pass Italian peasants or
> working people, people out of the little shops, a famous
> German dramatist, the barber's brother looking like an Oxford
> Don, a British retired skipper, an Italian prince descended from
> Charlemagne and no richer than the rest of us, and a few
> tourists seeking tranquillity. As there is no great harbour full of
> yachts, no great yellow strand, no great ballroom, no great
> casino, the rich carry elsewhere their strenuous lives.

Ezra had no objection to the literary company. He made friends with
Gerhart Hauptmann, persuading him to read Joyce and Yeats, and would
have liked to cultivate Beerbohm; but the latter felt disinclined to extend
the acquaintance, observing that Ezra 'seems out of place here. I should
prefer to watch him in the primeval forests of his native land, wielding an
axe against some giant tree. Could you not,' he asked Ezra's friend Phyllis
Bottome, 'persuade him to return to a country in which there is so much
more room?'

*

Almost as soon as he and Dorothy had arrived in Rapallo, Ezra urged
Hemingway to come there with his wife Hadley, so that they could all set
out on a walking tour in search of places associated with Sigismundo
Malatesta. 'As I was very vague as to who Sigismundo was,' writes
Hemingway, 'and had no wish to eat bad food and sleep in poor inns in
Italy in February following the trail of a historic personage . . . I put off
going as long as possible.' Hemingway was at Lausanne, where he had been
observing Mussolini at the Peace Conference, and consequently sensed the
political implication of Ezra's new love of Italy even before Ezra had
realized it himself. 'Can I,' he wrote to Ezra, 'preserve my incognito
among your fascist pals?' Ezra did not yet read newspapers, but he soon
began to gather that 'the governing class of germany does not wish the
place to be a republic', and rather hoped that 'the argument wont extend to
Rapallo'. If it did, he said he would go to Spain instead.

Despite their doubts, the Hemingways joined the Pounds in Rapallo in
early February 1923. Hemingway was at first disappointed. 'The sea is
weak and dull here, and doesn't look as though there was much salt in the
water. The tide rises and falls about an inch . . . The place aint much.' But

the walking tour went splendidly. They explored Orbetello and much of the coast between Pisa and Rome, Hemingway gratifying Ezra by explaining, on the basis of his own supposed military experiences, 'how and why Sigismundo Malatesta would have fought where and for what reasons'. He imagined he had misled Ezra badly.

After the walking tour the Hemingways went on to the Dolomites while Ezra and Dorothy briefly visited Rome and then Florence, which Ezra hated. 'Firenze the most damned of Italian cities,' he calls it in *Guide to Kulchur*, 'wherein is place neither to sit, stand nor walk'; there seemed to be 'a curse of discomfort' on it for casting out Dante. Ezra then went on to Rimini and Cesena for more Malatesta material, and at the Malatestine Library in Cesena was much struck by the personality of the librarian, Manlio Dazzi, a man of 'proper Dantescan education' who organized concerts by local musicians. By late April 1923 Ezra was back in Paris, telling the *Dial* that 'three months sweat in Italy' had brought to life the 'skeleton' of the Malatesta Cantos.

Though the *Dial* published them in July, Scofield Thayer had lost patience with Ezra's writings, being particularly irritated by a 'Paris Letter' in which, absorbed in Sigismundo and Bel Esprit, Ezra had alleged that patronage was now extinct. Thayer thought this no way to treat the backers of the *Dial*, who produced $84,000 a year, not to mention the annual $2,000 award (which, to Thayer's disgust, had gone to Eliot). 'The *Dial* has sacked me,' Ezra reported just after his return from Italy, 'so there will be no more Paris letters.' He claimed the loss was 'serious financially', but thanks to Dorothy's income it was not a major problem. On the other hand it was 'the last link severed' as far as American magazines were concerned, and 'I don't know where to go next'.

*

The problem seemed to resolve itself almost at once when Ford Madox Ford, who was wandering about France with Stella Bowen, announced his intention to start a magazine. Ezra knew nobody would make a fortune from the project – 'Dont for Gawds sake put any money into the Transatlantic Review,' he warned his father – but he did his best to persuade John Quinn to contribute cash. Quinn visited Paris and came to 70 *bis* in October 1923; he was photographed there in the company of Ezra, Ford, and Joyce.

The photograph is very comic. Ford, trapped in one of Ezra's home-made armchairs, his mouth hanging open as usual, is engaged in pretending to examine a large piece of stone, presumably one of Ezra's 'sculptures', while Joyce looks on with understandable curiosity. Ezra stares broodingly away from the camera as if he now regretted having organized the gathering, while Quinn eyes the lens warily. Ford has explained that

I was engaged in avoiding Mr Quinn, whom I disliked because he had pretended to mistake me for George Moore. I was also engaged in trying not to be near Mr Joyce . . . To be anywhere near Mr Joyce, at any sort of reception or public event, was embarrassing. I should be at once . . . surrounded by a ring of Mr Joyce's faithful, we should be expected to talk . . .

Despite the evidently strained nature of the meeting, Quinn agreed to back the magazine to about $2,000. It was one of his last pieces of patronage: he died in the summer of 1924, aged fifty-four, of cancer of the liver. Ezra showed remarkably little concern at the break-up of Quinn's art collection after his death, saying there was almost nothing in it 'to which I am personally attached'.

Ford and Stella Bowen somehow found the rest of the money for the magazine, and the first issue of the *transatlantic review* (the use of lower case was purely for reasons of typographical design) appeared in December 1923. The name was chosen to reflect the considerable literary traffic between America and Paris.

The magazine was produced at Bill Bird's Three Mountains Press, in conditions (said Stella) of 'the utmost confusion'. Ford was provided with a tiny balcony above the printing machine as 'office'; when he stood up, his head touched the roof and the whole antique structure was felt to tremble. The first sub-editor was allegedly a White Russian prince who spoke no English, but claimed to be able to persuade booksellers to stock the magazine. He was soon replaced by Basil Bunting.

Bunting was a doctor's son from the north-east of England; Ford labelled him Ezra's Conscientious Objector because at the age of eighteen, although the First World War had just ended, he had accepted imprisonment on the principle that 'if there was a war he wouldn't go'. He had studied briefly at the London School of Economics before 'clearing off to France with no money at all. I landed in Paris and, well, had the usual sort of adventures that young men had.'

Ford describes Bunting at this time as 'a dark youth with round spectacles, in a large Trilby hat and a blue trench coat with belt'. Bunting believed that Ezra's *Propertius* was 'the finest of modern poems' – it 'gave me the notion that poetry wasn't altogether impossible in the XX century'. He first came across Ezra at the Dôme café, playing 'a swashbuckling kind of chess' with Ford. Bunting was earning a few francs as a roadmender outside Paris, and soon after having met Ezra was 'locked up for a colossal drunk'. Ezra found him in prison, 'and perjured himself in the courts to try to get me off'. (Pressed for further details, Bunting explains that after a drunken binge he had absentmindedly forced his way into the wrong hotel, had made advances to the concierge's wife, had given the police 'a good swift kick in the pants' when they tried to arrest him, and had found himself in jail 'with a copy of Villon in my pocket'.)

Bunting was taken on at the *transatlantic review* as 'sub ed. and sec.', with duties that included bathing Ford and Stella's baby daughter. He only stayed with the magazine a few months, then followed Ezra to Rapallo and made a living for a while on the coastal cargo boats. He was labelled by Yeats as 'one of Ezra's more savage disciples'.

The *transatlantic review* acquired some respectable contributions. It serialized the first part of Ford's own *Parade's End*, and printed excerpts from Joyce's 'Work in Progress' (the future *Finnegans Wake*) and Gertrude Stein's *The Making of Americans*. But it was shabbily produced and rather muddled in its aims, and after a year it ran out of money and closed. Ezra found it of use in only one respect: it gave him a platform on which he could present his latest 'discovery'. In mid-August 1923 he wrote to Agnes Bedford: 'The young Antheil is here in Paris, possibly the salvation of music. Has been causing riots in Budapesth; I think by playing Strawinsky . . . I think he has something to him.'

George Antheil was a twenty-three-year-old American, born in Trenton, New Jersey, the son of a shoe-store owner of German descent (he liked to claim Polish blood). He was expelled from school but studied the piano with a pupil of Liszt in Philadelphia, and at the age of twenty wrote his first symphonic work, a musical portrait of industrial Trenton. Supported by a wealthy Philadelphian, Mrs Edward Bok, he left for Europe in May 1922 and managed to have his First Symphony performed by the Berlin Philharmonic. He also gave a Wigmore Hall piano recital and played in several European capitals.

He looked much younger than his twenty-three years. With his 'smashed nose, interesting but wicked-looking eyes, a big mouth and a big grin,' said Sylvia Beach, he seemed 'like an American high-school boy'. He also behaved like one. His avowed aim was to produce a counterblast to 'the mountainous sentiment of Richard Strauss' and 'the fluid diaphanous lechery of the recent French impressionists', but his music was no more than pastiche of Stravinsky (whom he had met in Berlin) with the addition of 'machine' and jazz gimmicks. He wrote piano pieces with such titles as 'Mechanisms', 'Jazz Sonata' and 'Airplane Sonata', avant-garde enough to cause an audience to riot in Budapest. Antheil claimed that he bought 'a small thirty-two automatic' and placed it ostentatiously on the piano at his next recital, thereby ensuring silence. Actually he commanded attention through sheer noise. Ford called him 'the heaviest living piano player'.

In Paris, Antheil and his girlfriend Boski Markus rented a room above Shakespeare and Company and soon met Ezra, whom Antheil perceived as 'a Mephistophelian red-bearded goat'. Margaret Anderson had already told Ezra that Antheil was a genius, so he handed Antheil some money he had just been given, realizing that he was short of cash. Antheil thought him 'unusually kind'. There was no piano at Shakespeare and Company, so Ezra took him to Natalie Barney's in the rue Jacob where Antheil 'played for hours, and Ezra seemed very pleased with it all'.

Ezra asked if Antheil had written anything about music, and Antheil told him he had

> occasionally amused myself with typing out pronouncements on art and music which would have blown the wig off any conventional musician; among other things I said that melody did not exist, that rhythm was the next most important thing to develop in music and that harmony after all was a matter of what preceded and what followed.

This fitted strikingly with what Ezra himself believed, so he immediately borrowed Antheil's jottings on music. After a while, Antheil heard that 'Ezra was planning to write a book about me, and that . . . Bill Bird . . . would publish it. This scared me. Two months later Ezra was to bring me proof sheets with big black letters on the front page: ANTHEIL AND THE THEORY ON HARMONY.'

Antheil exaggerates the speed of this operation. The book, actually entitled *Antheil and the Treatise on Harmony*, did not appear until over a year after their first meeting, though by that time substantial portions of it had already been printed in the *transatlantic review* and the *Criterion*. Despite its title, it contained remarkably little information about Antheil or his music. Ezra described him as a late-arriving Vorticist who compensated for the absence of music from the original Vortex of 1914, and said that like Picasso, Wyndham Lewis, and Brancusi he was concerned to make his audience 'increasingly aware of form'. But there was no analysis of his music or even examples of it. A large proportion of the volume was made up of reprints of Ezra's 'William Atheling' music reviews from the *New Age*. There were also some comments by Antheil on Ezra's observations in these reviews. The only striking part of the book was 'The Treatise on Harmony'.

This was Ezra's attempt to expound his theory that pitch is unimportant and only rhythm, or the correct duration of each sound, really matters. The theory was mostly set out in capital letters: 'A SOUND OF ANY PITCH, or ANY COMBINATION OF SUCH SOUNDS, MAY BE FOLLOWED BY A SOUND OF ANY OTHER PITCH, OR ANY COMBINATION OF SUCH SOUNDS, providing the time interval between them is properly gauged; and this is true for ANY SERIES OF SOUNDS, CHORDS OR ARPEGGIOS.' (Ezra later developed this eccentric idea in *Guide to Kulchur*, where he asserted that the sound frequency of a note (beats per second) governs 'the whole question of tempo'. He called this the theory of 'Great Bass' because he believed the governing frequencies to be those of the very lowest, inaudible notes.)

Antheil found the book about him embarrassing and its theories eccentric. 'From the first day I met him Ezra was never to have even the slightest idea of what I was really after in music. I honestly don't think he wanted to have. I think he merely wanted to use me as a whip with which to lash out at all those who disagreed with him . . . I still do not know why I permitted Ezra to issue his book . . . My error and lack of judgement were to cause me a lot of future grief . . . It sowed the most active distaste for the name "Antheil".' He never became a serious composer, but took to writing background music for Hollywood.

*

Soon after Antheil had arrived in Paris, Ezra told him he needed '*several* violin sonatas' for 'a friend of his, Olga Rudge, the concert violinist'. Ezra said Antheil was to accompany her, and 'all of important Paris' would be present. He introduced Antheil to Miss Rudge, 'a dark, pretty, Irish-looking girl,' recalls Antheil, 'and, as I discovered when we commenced playing a Mozart sonata together, a consummate violinist. I have heard many violinists, but none with the superb lower register of the D and G strings that was Olga's exclusively.'

Ezra had heard her play just before he left London at the end of 1920, but did not speak to her at that concert. She first became aware of him when giving a recital in Paris in 1923 with her accompanist Renata Borgatti: 'I saw Ezra first in a concert hall, and noticed him. The hall was emptying. We said: "Who is that? Must be a painter." He had on a brown velvet jacket. I didn't know anything about Ezra Pound, had never heard of him. I went to Natalie Barney's, and he was there.'

One of their first subjects of conversation was Gautier's daughter Judith, whose Paris salon Olga Rudge had attended as a child. She told Ezra how the house had been left just as it was in Gautier's time, with 'the very chair of the great Théophile himself in a small detached sitting room'. (Ezra later put this into Canto 80: 'Judith's junk shop / with Théophile's arm chair.') The talk then turned to music. Ezra mentioned George Antheil, and Olga asked if he had written anything for the violin. Ezra said: 'Don't know, I'll ask.' And Antheil, when approached, answered: 'No, but I will.' Shortly afterwards, Olga found herself due to give the world première of two sonatas for violin in the concert hall of the Paris Conservatoire. It was a brisk demonstration of Ezra's ability to make things happen. Olga observes: 'He didn't talk about things – He wanted something *done*.'

She herself was equally determined. A professional studio photograph taken in the 1920s emphasizes only one side of her personality: she poses aloofly, eyes cast away from the camera, eyebrows and lips sharply made up in the mask-like, almost harlequin fashion of the day. But in the flesh she was vigorous and fiercely energetic. Antheil was struck by what he called her 'Irish adrenal personality'. The contrast with the silence and remoteness of Dorothy Pound could not have been more marked.

She was not Irish but American, though by 1923 it was impossible to detect it in her accent or manner. Born in Youngstown, Ohio, ten years after Ezra's birth, she was the granddaughter of an English settler and the daughter of a real-estate businessman. At the age of nine months she was brought to London by her mother, an ex-professional singer who cared little for Youngstown and soon settled in Europe without her husband, supporting her daughter and Olga's two brothers by giving singing lessons. The children were educated in Catholic schools in Paris and London. Ford Madox Ford, meeting Olga in Paris, expressed astonishment when he learned where she had been born: 'I did not know such beautiful flowers blossomed in that desert.'

Her brothers settled in England; one was killed in the First World War, the other became a doctor. Olga, supported to some extent by family money, began to pursue a cosmopolitan career as a solo violinist, giving recitals in several European capitals. She performed in London for the first time when she was twenty-one, and *The Times* spoke of her 'excellent technique and fine taste'. Her repertoire was adventurous in including some modern works. She was beginning to make a reputation; Antheil says that her name was already 'well known' to him when they first met.

Armed with an unceasing flow of high-speed conversation, the small, slightly built young violinist could, as she herself put it, usually 'fall on my feet'. She feels that when she met Ezra he was the more determined of the two, and she allowed him to boss her: 'I hadn't got the sense in those days to say no. If I was told to do a thing, I did it.' But all the evidence suggests the opposite: that for the first time in his life Ezra had come into the hands of somebody more obstinate and resourceful than himself. One of Olga's relatives has observed: 'I shouldn't think he stood a chance.'

*

Antheil's Violin Sonatas seemed to Ezra to give birth to 'a new violin technique' with their 'violent' and 'demoniac' character, though to Antheil himself twenty years later the effect seemed merely 'great empty chic'. By the end of September 1923 he and Olga were practising hard, their work only being interrupted by his first Paris piano recital, arranged by Margaret Anderson. 'Ezra seemed concerned that I would first appear in Paris without his personal sponsorship,' says Antheil, but he 'soon became reconciled to the idea, even enthusiastic'. The concert provoked the expected rage from much of the audience, but Antheil's music won the approval of Erik Satie, and he became a Paris celebrity overnight.

Ezra made two contributions to the Antheil–Rudge concert, which took place on 11 December 1923. It opened with his own transcription for unaccompanied violin of the twelfth-century 'Plainte pour la Mort du Richard Cœur de Lion', one of the works he had found in the Ambrosian Library in Milan in 1911. Olga also played one of his original pieces, 'Sujet pour Violon (Résineux)' which drew limited praise from the Paris edition of the *Chicago Tribune* – whose critic recorded that the Antheil sonatas 'caused the audience to disagree', and said that many people found them 'degenerate noise and crash'.

Antheil and Olga gave further concerts together in succeeding months. In London in May 1924 their recital at the Aeolian Hall included Ezra's 'Fiddle Music, First Suite'. In Paris two months later Olga played what Ezra described as a fifteenth-century piece he had 'dug up in Perugia'. There was also a 'fanfare, violin and tambourin, by E.P. to celebrate George's entrance', Ezra himself probably playing the 'tambourin'. Some of the songs from his opera were sung at this concert by Yves Tinayre. Ezra reported to Agnes Bedford that, being French, Tinayre had the advantage of understanding the words, and had done very well in the circumstances. 'After all I only found him in Paris on Thursday ten days ago, and didn't get my violin accomp. into final shape until a few hours before the show.'

One evening in a small hall in Montparnasse, Antheil performed a Sonata for Drum and Piano, with Ezra on percussion. A member of the audience suspected Antheil of improvising the piano part, while Ezra 'was obviously trying to communicate some sort of narrative with his drumming'. This listener rather hoped for the usual Antheil riot, but 'Pound's seriousness of mien in beating his big bass drum won the day', and the performance was heard out respectfully.

Ezra reported to his father that he had been pounding the percussion, and received this reply:

> Dear Son – Certainly glad to receive the clippings in re concert – Wish we had been there – I could hold the drums – Why not have a Victrola record made of your 'fiddle music' then we could hear it over here . . . Hope that the concert did not injure your state of health – Guess Antheil – does not feel as good as you do over the result of the grand slam bang music – Lovingly Dad.

*

Ezra decided that a performance of the opera would be more practicable if Antheil put proper instructions into the score for singers and instrumentalists, correcting the music where he thought necessary. He reported to Agnes Bedford in February 1924:

> Re opera. Antheil has re-rited it all with highly fractional
> notation = bars all sorts of lengths from ⅛ to ¹⁷/₃₂ etc = I am
> assured it is now correct & that McKee [?] can conduct from
> these fractions.

He added that 'a new art theatre in Paris' had shown an interest in the
possibility of a production.

A manuscript score of the opera describes the work as 'edited 1923 by
George Antheil'. It appears to be chiefly in Ezra's hand, but contains time
signatures in the hand of Antheil, which are indeed as Ezra describes them.
Besides those he mentions there are such eccentric markings as $\frac{13}{16}$, $\frac{10}{16}$, and $\frac{22}{16}$,
which seem designed to terrify performers. Far from 'editing' the music
into a more accessible state Antheil had made the work virtually unperfor-
mable.

He seems to have decided that the very unorthodox rhythms and implied
bar lengths of Ezra's vocal and instrumental writing could not be left
without time signatures (as would have been the practice in medieval
music) but must be provided with a modern system of barring and
indications to time. Since the music was not meant to fit into any regular
scheme, the result was a ludicrously complicated set of markings. Ezra
himself proposed a far better solution to the problem in a note on the
score: 'I doubt if the instrumentalist will get much help from "counting
measures". Let him learn the *words* & make his noises when singer reaches
the *syllable* the instrumentalist is to emphasize.' But Antheil was opposed
to this, and declared that he had arranged things 'so that nothing at all is left
to the singer'. Moreover, 'the editor would be obliged if the singer would
not let the least bit of temperament affect in the least the correct singing'.

Ezra asked Yeats if the Abbey Theatre in Dublin might be interested in
the opera, adding: 'I DO NOT want operatic voices, I want a few singers
who can understand the text.' Meanwhile in December 1923 a dispute
broke out in his studio at 70 *bis*. He was already on bad terms with some
Swedes on the floor above, who had 'propensities to dance . . . at three
a.m.', so he installed a piano in his room and encouraged Antheil to
practise on it. The ensuing altercation involved the police. Ford Madox
Ford recalls how Ezra

> persuaded Mr George Antheil . . . to practise his latest sym-
> phony for piano and orchestra in Mr Pound's studio. This
> lasted all day for several weeks. When Mr Antheil was fatigued,
> his orchestra played unceasingly Mr Antheil's own arrangement
> of the 'Wacht am Rhein'. In the meanwhile, turning sculptor,
> Mr Pound fiercely struck blocks of granite with sledge
> hammers.

Unlike some of Ford's stories, it is essentially true.

7

Ez He Lives On The Roof

Ezra had a tendency towards hypochondria, but was usually perfectly well. Around 1924, however, he had some genuine trouble with his health: first a grumbling appendix, which 'cooled down' after bed rest at the American Hospital in Paris, then a recurrent anal fistula, which over the next few years was operated on three times, but was still giving trouble in January 1928, when he called it 'a demnition bore'. Partly so that he could convalesce after the appendix, he and Dorothy went down to Rapallo again in February 1924, staying at the Hotel Mignon with the vague idea of finding something more permanent there.

'At present our only plans are to have as few plans as possible,' Ezra told his mother, 'not to feel that we *have* to do anything in particular . . . We hope to look for some sort of villa – or at least possible situation for one – sometime – neither too remote – too hot nor too cold etc.'

From Rapallo they moved further south to Assisi and Perugia. At Perugia, Ezra began to consider 'American Presidents' as possible material for future cantos, and asked his father what he knew about any of them. 'I dont care a damn about their public eyewash,' he wrote to Homer. 'I want facts indicative of personality . . . Jefferson's letters I have read. He was probably the only civilized man who ever held down the job . . . I can't remember the names of a lot of them. There was a Johnny named Polk & two bums called Adams/ . . .' He also asked Homer for details of grandfather Thaddeus's life and character. 'Do *you* know definitely what he did in way of originating & putting thru legislation . . . Sorry he burnt his papers. – they might have had educational value for yrs. truly.' By mid-May he had 'blocked out course of a few more cantos'.

He was back in Paris in May. During the summer and early autumn, Dorothy was in England with her mother. Ezra was seeing a lot of Olga.

When writing to her he would often use the third person. They were trying to find singers for the opera; he told her: 'She fish a basso and a contralto out of the lake for him. Ought to be bass in lake.' It was a private language, used also when they talked: 'He liked it there, didn't he?' 'Yes, ma'am.'

Dorothy returned from England in October 1924, and immediately set off for Rapallo with Ezra. But if her aim was to extract him from an involvement with Olga, it was too late. At some time during the autumn Olga conceived a child by him.

She has said of this: 'I wanted a child. There was no question about that. But Ezra didn't, and it took a year to persuade him. Even then, he said it was *my* decision, not his.'

*

The Pounds settled as usual into the Hotel Mignon at Rapallo. 'D. just back from dip in the gulph of Tigullio – summer at last,' Ezra told his mother on 14 October 1924. 'Will write of last weeks in Paris sometime soon.' It appeared, suddenly, that they had left Paris for good. 'We have taken an extra room here . . . D's trunk and various suitcases seem to contain most of the necessaries, racquet, typewriter, bassoon, in fact about everything save the clavichord and a few woiks of Aht.'

Ezra now thought that living anywhere on 'the north side of the alps' had been 'an error, useful only to make one glad to get to this side. An error I hope not to repeat.' He and Dorothy considered renting a house or an apartment, but there was 'no pressing hurry'. His thirty-ninth birthday found him in a 'state of tranquillity'. He said he had added ten years to his life by getting out of Paris; it was very pleasant to be away from the 'maelstrom' of a capital city 'with leisure to do my own job'. Yet he did not have much of a job to do at present, other than turn out more cantos when he felt so inclined. One day he leafed through an old copy of *BLAST*, and wrote to Wyndham Lewis with uncharacteristic nostalgia: 'We were hefty guys in them days . . . Can we kick up any more or any new devilment?'

In December 1924 he and Dorothy went to Sicily, wondering whether they might settle there instead of in Rapallo. Ezra wrote to his father from Palermo at the end of January 1925: 'I reckon it'll be Rapallo . . . This country is interesting, but not exactly habitable.'

They were back in Rapallo at the end of February 1925, and chose an apartment for themselves on the seafront, moving in during the second week in March. 'Vast surprise yesterday when the elevator suddenly began to function,' Ezra told his father, 'having signed special clause in lease that we wouldn't go to law if it didn't. And it having been out of whack when we inspected the building.' The elevator was a not unimportant detail, the apartment being on the top floor of a six-storey building, with more than 100 steps to climb. After this brief resurrection, it never worked again in twenty years. Ezra did not mind; it kept away unwanted visitors.

By the end of April he had had a letter-head printed:

EZRA POUND   RAPALLO
VIA MARSALA, 12 INT. 5

'Yes, ciao,' he wrote to Olga on a sheet of it, 'his new paper or "stationery" perhaps they call it in more conservative countries.'

The address was slightly misleading, for though the entrance to the apartment building was in Via Marsala (a narrow alley at the back) the flat itself overlooked the promenade, and the Pounds had an almost unrivalled view of sea and harbour. 'We front on the bay,' Ezra told his father. 'I think it is about the best position in Rapallo; and very convenient, as we still feed at the Mignon.' They soon changed their habits and began to take their midday and evening meals at the café of the Albergo Rapallo, which occupied the ground floor of their building, with a terrace on the seafront. This was after all Rapallo's 'literary' café, and Ezra sent a picture postcard of its *terrazza* to a friend, explaining that 'the eel/light life of the village is centred HERE . . . Ez he lives on the ROOF to the left (invisibl above this tea-razzer).'

A visitor, meeting Ezra on the café terrace and finding himself invited upstairs to the apartment, would be astonished at the speed with which he went bounding up the stone staircase to the top floor. 'By the time I had reached the landing, rather winded,' writes Daniel Cory, 'Ezra was already seated at his broad desk.' Although the flat was strictly speaking a penthouse, it had none of the opulence that this might suggest: the rooms were very small and narrow. However, most of them looked out to sea, across the apartment's own terrace, which seemed vast by comparison with the indoor accommodation and was dignified by a large flagpole.

'Ezra Pound strode up and down the broad terrace of his own roof-tree at Rapallo,' wrote a reporter. 'A turbulent wind stirred up the blue waters of the gulf below . . . The sun was fast disappearing over the cypress hills, but it was still a magic flame upon the entire landscape; still burned upon Pound's alert head, fusing it in bronze.' Dorothy said that on 25 March each year they would see the swallows flying overhead on their way north. Ezra enjoyed ship-spotting more than bird-watching. 'The, or *a* fleet has been in here, oiling the front yard,' he reported to Agnes Bedford a few weeks after moving in. He said the 'net profit' to him from this naval presence had been 'one excellent dinner and an augmentation in the quality of tennis. The two light cruisers that have just replaced 'em (carsting hankor with large rattle at 7.05 this a.m.) are said to contain two good players.' And on another occasion: 'Marconi's yacht is visible from breakfast table.'

One room looked out over the slanting roof of a lower storey, corrugated with red Mediterranean rounded tiles. At mealtimes, says Brigit Patmore, about twenty cats would collect on this, waiting for Ezra to feed them.

> I had never realized how much Ezra cared for cats, but *they* knew – those multi-coloured ravenous Italian cats, tortoiseshell, white, tabby, black and in-between mixtures . . . Each seemed to have its own position and there was no quarrelling. But this palpitating crowd quivered like the outspread tail of a strange peacock. Ezra must have trained them well.

When Yeats came to Rapallo in 1928 he, too, observed this close relationship between Ezra and the local feline community, but he guessed that it was not simply a case of Ezra 'caring for cats':

> Sometimes about ten o'clock at night I accompany him to a street where there are hotels upon one side, upon the other palm trees and the sea, and there taking out of his pocket bones and pieces of meat he begins to call the cats. He knows all their histories – the brindled cat looked like a skeleton until he began to feed it; that fat grey cat is an hotel proprietor's favourite, it never begs from the guests' tables and it turns cats that do not belong to the hotel out of the garden; this black cat and that grey cat over there fought on the roof of a four-storeyed house some weeks ago, fell off, a whirling ball of claws and fur, and now avoid each other. Yet now that I recall the scene I think that he has no affection for cats – 'some of them so ungrateful' a friend says – he never nurses the café cat, I cannot imagine him with a cat of his own. Cats are oppressed, dogs terrify them, landladies starve them, boys stone them, everybody speaks of them with contempt. If they were human beings we could talk of their oppressors with a studied violence, add our strength to theirs, even organize the oppressed and like good politicians sell our charity for power. I examine his criticism in this new light, his praise of writers pursued by ill-luck . . .

Ezra had his own study in the apartment, looking out over the terrace, next to the french window. Nearby stood the Dolmetsch clavichord, brought over from London. Over the desk hung what Ezra called his 'active filing system': a network of string from which dangled envelopes, sheaves of manuscript, a pair of pince-nez, pens, scissors. Dorothy had her own 'studio', decorated with a few Wyndham Lewises and other pictures of her choice. The whole apartment was, as Ezra put it, 'more or less veiled in various devices of me-yown conskruktion' – his usual home-made furniture.

There was a kitchen, but they usually ate out 'because we are too lazy to use the three kinds of range'. They could easily afford restaurant meals downstairs, thanks as always to Dorothy's income. 'I can't get interested in being paid,' Ezra wrote. 'I know it is my duty to my dependents – etc – but –' If money happened to run short, they could still dine at the Albergo Rapallo for months at a time 'without either paying a bill or causing the proprietor any anxiety'.

*

But he was still concerned with the financial well-being of his friends. He had recently helped a third-rate neo-Victorian poet named Cheever Dunning, who had been a neighbour in Paris, looking after him when he was ill, giving him money, and even convincing himself that Dunning's poetry was publishable, getting it printed with enthusiastic introductions by himself. Archibald MacLeish, who knew nothing of Dunning's personal circumstance, thought this enthusiasm for his verse proved that Ezra was now just 'cucku' and 'an ass'. Ezra also supported the ailing Italian poet Emmanuele Carnevali (who wrote in English), sending books and magazines to his hospital bed in Bologna and raising money to pay his medical expenses.

Knowing his generosity, old friends would turn to him in emergency. In 1931 Ford Madox Ford asked if Ezra could possibly lend him some money, since he and Stella had now been 'without enough to eat for many weeks'. Ezra immediately sent $100, though he had to borrow much of it himself. Raymonde Collignon wrote from London to thank him for a cheque he had sent to help her in a difficult time; and when he received the annual $2,000 *Dial* award in January 1928 – Marianne Moore had taken over the editorship from Thayer – he immediately invested it and began to give away the interest to various needy friends.

Yet his capacity for prickliness still knew no bounds. He had accepted the award, offered for 'services to literature', only on condition that it was given specifically for the Cantos or 'my verse as a whole'. Marianne Moore thought this unnecessarily rude, though she complied. He also behaved obtusely over the matter of the piracy of *Ulysses*.

In 1926 a New York publisher, Samuel Roth, began to serialize the book in his magazine *Two Worlds Monthly* without authorization or any payment to Joyce. Ezra received a letter from Joyce asking for help and advice, but would only answer: 'Sorry, I dunno no lawyer.' Eventually a letter of protest was organized for the eminent to sign, and more than 150 put their names to it, including Eliot, Yeats, and Wyndham Lewis. But Ezra refused, claiming that Joyce was making far too much fuss about a particular case, and the really important thing was to change the whole copyright law so as to make such piracies impossible. He himself had not organized the petition, and he still resented the fanfare that had accompanied the publication of *Ulysses*.

Joyce did not realize that his old champion had retired from the lists, indeed had virtually defected. He sent to Rapallo a typescript of some 'Work in Progress' chapters that the *Dial* had turned down, but Ezra was very discouraging: 'Nothing short of divine vision or a new cure for the clapp could possibly be worth all the circumambient peripherization.' Joyce was upset, not least because most of his friends were responding in the same way to the new book, and he wrote to Ezra arguing his case. But Ezra stuck to his ground.

Eleven years later he dismissed 'Work in Progress' (the still unfinished *Finnegans Wake*), of which he had seen nothing more in the interim, as 'that diarrhoea of consciousness'. He never repented of this opinion, nor could he find anything enthusiastic to say about a small collection of Joyce's poems that Sylvia Beach published in 1927 as *Pomes Penyeach*. Joyce showed Ezra a couple of them during one of Ezra's visits to Paris, and was told bluntly: 'They belong in the bible or the family album with the portraits.' Joyce asked if he didn't think it might be worth printing them some time, and Ezra answered: 'No, I don't.' To make the insult worse, he told Joyce that Cheever Dunning's poetry was as good as Verlaine.

This marked the end of the association between the two; Joyce summed up his feelings by observing to Harriet Shaw Weaver that Ezra 'makes brilliant discoveries and howling blunders'. Ezra, meanwhile, developed a vitriolic attitude to Joyce's Paris entourage, which included the young Samuel Beckett. Beckett describes how he met Ezra 'one evening at dinner with the Joyces in the Trianons, Place de Rennes. He was having great trouble with a fond d'artichaut and was very aggressive and disdainful.' He turned to Beckett and asked in withering tones whether he were writing the next *Iliad*, or was it a new *Divine Comedy*? In those days Beckett felt equally scornful towards Ezra's poetry, describing his and Eliot's work as wholesale borrowing from others.

By 1931 Ezra was openly attacking Joyce in print, saying that he respected his integrity as an author 'in that he has not taken the easy path', but that he had 'never had any respect for his common sense or for his intelligence, apart from his gifts as a writer'. He was now only residually loyal to *Ulysses*, merely allowing it to be in 'the line of great unwieldy books, *Gargantua*, and *Don Quixote*'; and in 1935 he welcomed Henry Miller's *Tropic of Cancer* as 'a bawdy' which would put Joyce into his 'proper cubby-hole', since Miller was sexually 'sane and without kinks'.

After he had begun to evangelize Social Credit he liked to accuse Joyce of failing to concern himself with economics, and paired him contemptuously with Gertrude Stein as two writers who had nothing of interest to say. By 1942 Joyce had become, in his judgement, a writer with 'a VERY conventional outlook' with whom he, Ezra, had 'nacherly never agreed about much of anything'. Later still, in the St Elizabeths days, he was bitterly scornful of the 'Joyce inflation' (his term for the burgeoning Joyce scholarship industry), and complained that while his own writings on economics had been ignored or suppressed by the publishing powers, they had left unpublished 'no cigarette butts of the late J.J.' He said that the 'weakness of the Joyce cult and quality of his parasites' was that 'his rustlers never read ANY good authors except Jim himself, IF they read him' – a criticism that could have been directed with equal justice at many of his own followers.

Joyce, in the remaining years of his life (he died in 1941), viewed Ezra's disloyalty without surprise, observing: 'The more I hear of the political, philosophical, ethical zeal and labours of the brilliant members of Pound's big brass band the more I wonder why I was ever let into it "with my magic flute".' In fact Ezra had chiefly valued him for his least Joycean, least modernist qualities. Surveying Joyce's achievements, he praised the clarity of his early writings, his refinement of the craft of fiction, rather than any revolutionary qualities: 'In *Dubliners*, English prose catches up with Flaubert.' And he hinted that his own intellect was some distance away from the mainstream of modernism. He said that his 'editorial function' – his part in getting modernist work into print – had been 'something very different' from his own inclinations as a poet. The fact that he had promoted 'Joyce, Lewis, Eliot, D. H. Lawrence etc.' had made his life much more 'interesting' than if he had merely followed 'what my taste was in 1908'. He implied that his own literary preferences had changed little since that date.

This was borne out by his attitude to his own early poetry. Soon after settling in Rapallo, towards the end of 1925, he prepared what was intended as his Collected Poems (excluding the Cantos) for Boni & Liveright in New York, but which became a selection. He discarded what he now regarded as mere 'soft stuff' and 'metrical exercises', things which 'no longer convince me that I had anything to say when I wrote 'em'; but retained, without any apology or revision of the text, a considerable amount of his work from his earliest volumes, and called the book *Personae*, which title he had first used in 1909. Published in December 1926, it was the first of his books to remain in print in various forms for the rest of his life.

Eliot made a slightly different selection for a Faber edition, entitled *Selected Poems* and published in 1928 – Ezra called this 'Eliot's castrated edition' (actually it is a better selection than his own). Afterwards Eliot judged his own very formal introduction to the book 'pretentious', though he said it had been 'appropriate to talk that way' at the time.

*

'Wot ells. Have typed out most of seven cantos, taking it up to XXIII,' Ezra told his father at the end of March 1925. Canto XVII deals with a sort of paradiso terrestre. XVIII and XIX . . . Geryon, fraude. You can look it up in yr. Dante. the minor hell of rascality. XX lotophagi; further sort of paradise. or something in that direction. then some narrative. Medici and Este.'

The new cantos were as varied as this suggests. Canto 17 conveys a sense of an earthly paradise by presenting a scene that is sometimes Sirmione or Rapallo, sometimes Venice. A fine passage describes gondolas in the evening torchlight:

> There, in the forest of marble,
> the stone trees – out of water –
> the arbours of stone –
> marble leaf, over leaf,
> silver, steel over steel,
> silver beaks rising and crossing,
> prow set against prow,
> stone, ply over ply,
> the gilt beams flare of an evening.

Yet there are disconcertingly inexplicable details. Nerea, a goddess whose name comes from Homer's Nereids (sea sprites), is described like Botticelli's Venus: 'she like a great shell curved / In the suavity of the rock'. But she is an invention, and the context does not make it clear what she is meant to represent. Nor is it obvious why 'a sort of paradiso terrestre' should be described at all at this stage, unless it is simply meant as a contrast with the squalor of the Hell Cantos and the 'purgatorial' accounts of war in Canto 16.

Nevertheless, Canto 17 reaches a peak of expressive power not achieved before in the Cantos. The description of the Venetian scene – which includes a memory of the gondola repair yard opposite Ezra's room in San Trovaso in 1908 – has a luminosity of detail that truly demonstrates his power of phanopoeia and melopoeia:

> And the waters richer than glass,
> Bronze gold, the blaze over the silver,
> Dye-pots in the torch-light,
> The flash of wave under prows,
> And the silver beaks rising and crossing . . .

Yeats selected this canto for his *Oxford Book of Modern Verse* (1936); it was an inspiration to a young Englishman, Adrian Stokes, to begin his own work as a latter-day Ruskin. Stokes first met Ezra at the Rapallo tennis club in 1926, and eight years later there appeared his study of the aesthetics of the Renaissance, *The Stones of Rimini*. Yet though the book was grounded in a passion for the Tempio Malatestiano that equalled his own, it only drew reserved and condescending praise from Ezra when he reviewed it in the *Criterion*. The most he was prepared to call Stokes was 'not merely another follower of Walter Pater'.

Canto 18 turns abruptly from the stones of Venice and their watery setting to economics, and presents examples of financial activity ranging from Kubla Khan's issue of paper money (which is deplored) to the doings of 'Metevsky', a crooked armaments manufacturer. The economic theme is continued in Canto 19, which has an exclusively modern setting and describes big companies' fear of the enterprise of individuals. In Canto 20 there is another sudden switch, this time to the lotus-eaters of the *Odyssey*, seen, for reasons which are not clear, through the agonized vision of the fifteenth-century Italian ruler Niccolò d'Este, after he has ordered the beheading of his wife and natural son because of their adultery together. Ezra explained to his father that he was portraying d'Este in 'a sort of delirium', and that the details of Canto 20 were 'jumbled or "candied"' in Este's delirious mind. 'Take that as a sort of bounding surface from which one gives the main subject of the Canto, the lotophagoi: lotus eaters, or respectable dope smokers; and general paradiso.' But the canto itself fails to make it clear that Este is the observer, and one searches in vain for any definite reason for the lotus-eaters to be there.

Canto 21 introduces the Medicis, describing the beginnings of their financial empire, in a manner familiar from the Malatesta Cantos; into the middle of this is thrust a letter from Thomas Jefferson, in which he expresses the hope of acquiring servants who are also competent musicians. This is supposed to suggest the possibility of Renaissance Man existing in America, but it seems to have nothing to do with the emphasis in the rest of the canto on the purely financial activities of the Medicis.

Canto 22 seems refreshingly straightforward by comparison, describing, with some real comedy, Thaddeus Pound's railroad building enterprises, and Ezra's own experiences in Gibraltar in 1908. Canto 23 contains an array of experiences and remarks that seem arbitrarily selected and organized: a glimpse of the Neoplatonist philosopher Gemisthus Plethon (whose ashes Sigismundo interred in the Tempio); Pierre Curie testing radium; the sack of the castle of Montségur during the Albigensian Crusade. These and other items from Ezra's personal store flicker on the poem's screen with no sense of luminosity, 'No light reaching through them,' as the last line of the canto says. Homer Pound, trying to puzzle out what his son had sent him, appealed for help and was told: 'there ain't no key. Simplest parallel I can give is radio where you tell who is talking by the noise they make.'

*

The Gaudier head of Ezra arrived in Rapallo from Violet Hunt's front garden on Campden Hill, and, since getting it upstairs seemed impracticable, the proprietor of the Albergo Rapallo was persuaded to place it in his café, in the corner near the door. Later Ezra (or the proprietor) persuaded somebody to manhandle it up to the top floor, and had it positioned on the terrace outside his study window, where its slit eyes gazed impassively seaward, alongside the dog kennel and the flagpole.

Ezra was now known in Rapallo as 'Il Signor Poeta', and he played up to the role. Several times a day he would be seen striding along the promenade in a swirling cape and the wide-brimmed sombrero which had replaced the Latin Quarter beret, a great yellow scarf flapping round his neck as protection against the Mediterranean breeze, as he brandished his malacca cane. He was also to be found regularly at the tennis club, where he shocked the ladies with his language as he leapt explosively about after the ball. Sometimes he was partnered in a game of doubles by Giuseppe Bacigalupo, son of the local woman doctor who attended most of the expatriates. Ezra would tell Giuseppe to hit anything that he himself missed, but otherwise to keep out of the way and leave it all to him. He would plunge wildly around the court, somehow managing to be in several places at once, so that very few volleys escaped him. Another young man who played with him describes 'the Poundian brand of tennis' as 'eccentric, surprising, and scattershot, filled with bounding rushes, wheezes, shouts and many cries of "Egad!"'

After lunch he would take a siesta. James Laughlin remembers him (in an autobiographical poem) 'on your bed with your cowboy hat shielding the sea light from the window / with the big Chinese dictionary on your stomach / and you stared at the characters, searching for the true glyph of meaning in the calligraphy'. Later in the afternoon, if there was a visitor, a tea party might be held. Ezra would eat little Italian pastries with animal vigour while Dorothy silently poured China tea from a silver pot. Then she would withdraw to her own room and read Henry James, while Ezra banged about with books and papers he wanted to show his guest. There might also be an expedition to the cinema (Dorothy never went). He liked the front row of the gallery, because he could put his legs up on the balustrade, and he expressed noisy enjoyment – the trashier the film the better. Sometimes he would pass the evening with a thriller, perhaps an Edgar Wallace or a Dorothy Sayers. In one letter Dorothy mentions that 'Ezra is deep at the moment in a v. bad Agatha Christie.'

Dorothy liked to sign her letters 'Cordiali Saluti', or with some other Italian tag, but she never became fluent in the language, learning only enough for shopping and other necessities. Laughlin says, however, that Ezra 'was very fast in it, and it sounded all right to me, except for his cracker-barrel accent!' Similarly, while Ezra mingled with the upper levels of Rapallo society – the Italian princes who were, as Yeats said, 'no richer than the rest of us' (though some had wealthy American wives) – Dorothy held herself aloof, regarding them with a very English suspicion of possibly fake European titles.

Ezra was inclined to take Rapallo life for granted, rarely commenting on it in letters or in print, though he liked to assert that the cultural level was high. He would cite the local chemist's remark that a brand of imported lavatory paper cost more than a copy of the *Divine Comedy*, and said that at the lunch table at the 'Albuggaro Rapallo' one might get plunged into 'a good three-cornered discussion of the respective merits of Horace and Catullus'. He was also favourably impressed by the priests, much of his anti-clericalism petering out in the face of amiable, tolerant, cassocked Italians. When he told a nun he believed in Zeus and Apollo rather than Christ, she remarked cheerfully: 'Well, it's all the same religion.'

Perhaps the inclusion of the lotus-eaters in the new Cantos simply reflected his own life in Rapallo. Giuseppe Bacigalupo, recalling the late 1920s in his home town, says its remoteness from the rest of the world and the Arcadian character of daily existence cannot be over-emphasized. 'It was an unproblematic world, not yet bombarded by daily news of catastrophes. The radio had only just started; newspapers were read absent-mindedly because they always promised fair weather. And they were usually right.'

8

Human Complications

At midsummer 1925, less than four months after he and Dorothy had moved into the Rapallo apartment, Ezra slipped quietly away and joined Olga Rudge in the Italian Tyrol, where on 9 July at a hospital in Bressanone she gave birth to a daughter. The child was given the name Maria. The birth certificate stated that the father's name was Rudge.

The baby was premature, and spent the first nine days of its life in an oxygen tent. When its survival seemed likely, Olga and Ezra arranged that it should be handed over to a peasant woman, Johanna Marcher, who was at the hospital, having just lost her own baby at birth. Frau Marcher was used to fostering; a child had already been dumped on her by a wandering basket-maker. She and her farmer husband Jakob agreed to take care of the baby for 200 lire a month.

She began to breastfeed the baby herself while still at the hospital, and Olga, anxious to make sure the child was getting enough milk, had it weighed before and after each feed. Then, when the time came to leave Bressanone, she and Ezra travelled in a taxi up to Gais, the mountain village where the Marchers lived, in order to inspect their house.

The Italian Tyrol had been part of Austria until the Armistice, and the people spoke a dialect German rather than Italian. Jakob Marcher had a crippled back and wounded leg from war service, and was proud of a medal awarded by Austria for his part in fighting Italians on behalf of the Kaiser. In Canto 35 Ezra amuses himself with the 'century-old joke' of the Tyrol being wedged awkwardly between Italy and the German-speaking powers, but to its inhabitants in 1925 their recent enforced change of nationality was no laughing matter.

Ezra thought the mountain air and simple farm life would ensure a good start for the child, whatever might happen to her later. He and Olga left a

500 lire note, as two months' payment with an extra hundred as gift, then departed in the taxi.

In her autobiography, *Discretions* (1971), Maria Rudge (now Mary de Rachewiltz) gives a rose-tinted account of her foster parents and her upbringing on the farm, reserving such harsh feelings as the book expresses for her mother. Elsewhere she has spoken much less warmly of the Marchers, describing her foster mother merely as her 'nurse', hinting that she was not treated altogether kindly, and making it clear that she was reared casually 'among a crowd of children'. Even in *Discretions* she admits that over the years Frau Marcher had no less than sixteen other foster children passing through her hands. Her overall feeling (in the later interview) was: 'I really don't like to dwell on my past at all.' Her account in *Discretions* emphasizes that at the time of her conception and birth 'I, the child, was wanted.' But Ezra once told her that Olga had hoped for a son.

*

No faint allusion to these events appeared in Ezra's letters to his parents, or to other intimates. He had always despised the way Wyndham Lewis wasted energy on coping with the existence of his own illegitimates. It was not remotely in Ezra's nature to boast about such a thing. Quite the opposite: as late as 1946, when Maria's existence was known to several of his close friends, he showed considerable reluctance to talk about her to the doctors at St Elizabeths. It was partly his old inclination to compartmentalize his life, but he also had a prudish streak, inherited from his mother; perhaps the child's existence disturbed him at the deepest level.

Certainly he knew his life could no longer be entirely under his own control. He wrote to Olga: '*Her* affairs don't bear looking at. *His* affairs don't bear looking at. The past is forgotten, the future is ominous, the present is beyond words . . . Need I go into details. I need not.'

*

He spent part of the autumn after Maria's birth in Venice, probably with Olga. Dorothy was in Siena with her mother. Richard Aldington writes of her response to what had happened: 'The impression she gave was not of a woman who is hurt and offended by infidelity, but simply a pathetic *quelle morne soirée* feeling. Why should she object, merely because her husband had found the only trained musician in the world who would take his ridiculous vapourings and caperings seriously?'

The Pounds were together again in Rapallo by the end of October, when Ezra's fortieth birthday fell, but shortly before Christmas, Dorothy left again, for a holiday in Egypt alone. Her place was taken by Olga, who was there when Eliot came for a short visit.

'Me & my lil ole saxophone will be with you some day next week,' Eliot wrote from the Alpes Maritimes. 'Must get new passport & hire a newt to tote my traps down the mountain . . . It *cant* be colder than here – they have to break the ice in the horsetrough to wash mah pants.' He told Ezra: 'dont give my address to *anyone*' – then added, on the postcard, the bold signature 'T. S. Eliot' and a clearly written address. Olga remembers that when he arrived in Rapallo he was very worried about Vivien and the future. 'Ezra said to me: "Poor Possum, you ought to play for him." So I played him the Bach Chaconne before breakfast, in cold blood.'

Ezra told his parents on Christmas Eve: 'Took Possum Eliot to tea with Beerbohm yesterday . . . [Eliot] has just been here for four days. has at last escaped from Lloyds' Bank and is more alive than might have been expected.' He added: 'D. is in Cairo, when last heard from she had been there "24 hours without a flea" but didn't expect it to last.'

On 19 January 1926 he reported: 'D. seems to be enjoying Cairo and pyramids, she has chosen a good winter for the south.' Dorothy was away until 1 March. On her return Ezra wrote to his parents that she 'has had about enough of Egypt, interesting place, but not very habitable'. She seemed 'somewhat worn by trip; or at least desiccated with Egypt, and disliking sea travel'. And on 24 March: 'D. has been under the weather, but up again yesterday.'

*

Ezra spent the spring and early summer in arranging for his opera to be performed at last. He now realized that he would have to organize the whole thing himself, and decided on a modest concert performance of a shortened version in Paris, with only two singers – Yves Tinayre, and a bass for Bozo the brothel keeper. There would be the minimum of instrumental accompaniment: harpsichord (to be played by Agnes Bedford), violin (Olga, of course, who had a great deal to play), and two hired trombonists for Bozo's song. Ezra also thought he might add 'a drrrumm' to the score and play it himself. 'I *seem* able to beat the time . . . at any rate to hit the front of the bar,' he told Bedford, adding: 'dont mention this, can be abandoned in rehearsal.'

By the beginning of June 1926 he and Dorothy were in Paris, installed in the Hôtel Foyot in rue du Tournon. Agnes Bedford said she could not manage to come over after all, so Ezra got 'Tinayre's kid brother' to take her place at the keyboard, though he soon proved to be an 'idiot' who 'has to be kept in shape by others'. Meanwhile Ezra was having difficulties as a percussionist. 'Touch and go wot I do at kettles – I hit it once & then miss.' They had found a bass singer named Maitland, 'magnifique but hardly bowsy enough', and the trombones did not make enough noise. There were other problems, too, not musical ones. 'Awfully surrounded by human complications,' Ezra wrote to Agnes Bedford on 3 June. He now realized that Dorothy, at the age of thirty-nine, had returned from Egypt pregnant.

*

Shortly before the opera was due to be performed, George Antheil's new piece *Ballet Mécanique* received its première in Paris, the audience eagerly anticipating a musical outrage to beat even previous offerings by the man Ezra now called 'Anthill'. The work was scored for eight grand pianos, a battery of percussion, and two large aeroplane propellers. A riot resulted. Sylvia Beach describes Ezra's voice rising above the others in support of Antheil, and says he was seen 'hanging head downward from the top gallery'. Ford Madox Ford tells of him rising from his place and yelling 'Dogs! *Canaille*! Unspeakable filth of the gutter!' Then, goes the story, the aeroplane propellers began to turn, beating down the catcalls and yells with their hurricane.

At least part of this is true; Ezra afterwards advertised his Antheil book as 'Ezra Pound answers the jeers and laughter of the mob . . . as he did at the premier of the Ballet Mécanique in Paris'. But he wrote in rather restrained terms when reviewing the performance in the *Criterion*, saying only that the music demonstrated the 'possibilities' of making a work of art out of factory sounds.

Ten days after this event, on the evening of Thursday 29 June 1926, *Le Testament de Villon* was given its own première at the Salle Pleyel, rue Rochechouart, in front of an audience invited by 'M. et Mme. Ezra Pound'. Ezra said he wanted to keep the 'opry' a semi-private matter until it could be staged in full. Yves Tinayre sang the part of the old prostitute La Hëaulmière in falsetto with a shawl over his head; Ezra played the percussion (though he modestly omitted his name from the programme); and at the last minute Paul Tinayre, the 'kid brother' was provided with a five-foot alphorn from which he managed to produce two deep notes. 'Anthill' had taken over the harpsichord part, disrupting rehearsals by playing noisy jazz. The audience included Joyce, Eliot, Hemingway, and other members of the American community, including Robert McAlmon, Djuna Barnes, and the composer Virgil Thomson.

'Dare say it went fairly well,' wrote Ezra to Agnes Bedford next day. 'Various people seemed to take it – no riots or departures.' Tinayre had given rather a 'sloppy' performance and botched several songs, but no one seemed to notice. Maitland, the bass, was a real musician; the two trombones had been 'vurry vurry delightful', though Ezra said he would use four of them next time. And the 'faked up' two-voice version of the final motet was 'magnifique – even with me at les timballes'.

Members of the audience reacted variously. Brancusi was said to think it 'a scandal'; Virgil Thomson judged it 'not quite a musician's music, though it may well be the finest poet's music since Thomas Campion . . . and its sound has remained in my memory'. Yves Tinayre was inclined to laugh about the whole thing (though Ezra said he had never really been in sympathy with it). The performance certainly raised interest in the work, and the BBC eventually decided to mount their own radio broadcast of the full opera, although this did not happen until 1931.

Ezra took no part in the radio production – 'It wd. cost 50 quid to get me to London, and the hopera only pays me that MINUS the bloody inkum tax' – but Agnes Bedford represented him at rehearsals. Maitland again sang Bozo, and Tinayre was replaced by a baritone named Ferrari. The songs were interspersed with what the *Radio Times* called 'brief snatches of dialogue in "hobo" language'. The broadcast was on the National Programme on 26 October 1931, and was repeated the next night on the London Regional service. The *Manchester Guardian* called it 'one of the best plays [sic] the BBC has given' but the *Sunday Referee* judged it an hour of 'clotted nonsense'. Ezra himself heard it on a wireless set 'in the electrician's kitchen in Rapallo'.

The broadcast spurred him into a new burst of musical activity. During 1932 he composed a second opera, entitled *Cavalcanti*, with words taken from that poet and from the works of Sordello. The score was even less conventional than *Le Testament de Villon*, with one voice taking over from another in the middle of a word – another technique that later became popular with the professional avant-garde. 'Gheez I had orter have learned something since 1920!!!' Ezra wrote of it to Agnes Bedford, but he did not complete the work, because it lacked 'the variety of theme and drive of the Villon text, and contrast in melodic shape had to be imported from poems of Sordello's'.

Ezra took to describing himself in the British *Who's Who* as 'poet and composer', but *Le Testament de Villon* received no further performances for thirty years, and Ezra never saw it staged in quite the harsh style he wanted. He suggested that the ideal singer for La Hëaulmière might be Ethel Merman.

*

Ezra and Dorothy stayed on in Paris after the performance of the opera, remaining at the Hôtel Foyot. Dorothy wanted her child to be born at the American Hospital in Paris, where she had once been a patient for some minor ailment.

Ezra made no mention of the pregnancy in letters to his parents. Indeed he scarcely wrote to them at all, or to anyone else, during the weeks before the birth. Olivia Shakespear must have been told, though, because Yeats wrote to her on 5 September: 'I hear that you are to be a grandmother and that the event is taking place in the usual secrecy . . . I congratulate you upon it. Dorothy . . . will make an excellent mother.'

When the time came, Ernest Hemingway accompanied Dorothy to the hospital. Ezra was apparently not with them. In 1951 Hemingway wrote to Dorothy recalling 'the taxi ride out to the hospital in Neuilly and how you finally told me it was time to go . . .'

The child, a boy, was born during the afternoon of 10 September 1926. He was named Omar. The next day Ezra went to the Mairie at Neuilly and signed the birth certificate:

> . . . Omar, du sexe masculin, de Ezra Pound . . . homme de lettres, et de Dorothy Shakespear . . . Dressé le onze Septembre mil neuf cent vingt six, seize heures quinze, sur déclaration du père . . .
>
> Ezra Pound

The same day he wrote his first letter to his parents for six weeks:

> Dear Dad
>   next generation (male) arrived. Both D & it appear to be doing well.
> _____
> Ford going to U.S. – to lecture in October. Have told him you wd. probably be glad to put him up.
>   more anon.
>   Yrs
>   E

Before he had a reply from Homer and Isabel, Ezra left Paris and went back to Rapallo. His next letter to them was written there 'sometime in October':

> Damn glad to be back here. Had week in hospital before leaving Paris, and then a bit of rest. Now supposed to be o.k.; had all the possible taps, tests, analyses etc. am supposed to be suffering from health [sic] , but completely exhausted . . . Bhloody glad to be back here. Wore aht completely . . .

He made no mention of Dorothy or the baby.

*

He continued to write to his parents, sending off four more letters, none of which made any reference to the birth, containing merely the usual chat about his own concerns. Then he heard back from his parents for the first time since he had broken the news to them, and on 18 November he replied to Homer:

Re/ your enervé epistle of 3d. inst. Omar born 10 Sept. My illness nothing whatever to do with it. Source of supplies presumably sound. Dutch East India 6%, some of it. I spose that is O.K. or as solid as anything in world of crazy finance.

His parents had apparently asked why the child was not born in Rapallo. He wrote:

Much more sensible that infant shd. be reared near some sort of proper medical attendance, i,e, American hospital, than here. Where I have vivid recollection of Berman [Dr Louis Berman, expert on glands] looking for sterilized food, and finding fly down neck of Strater's infant's bottle . . .
Yes, D. in perfect health.

Naturally the absence of any mention of Dorothy or Omar in his letters following the birth had upset and alarmed Homer and Isabel. When Ezra eventually learnt of their anxiety, he wrote, on '19 or 20 Nov.':

Sorry you seem to have been worrying; not like you to worry.
In any case no expected calamity ever arrives. Them that arrives is onexpected [*sic*]; and usually a blessing in disguise. Them that etc – in short anything that falls on ones head is not what one expects to have fall, so foreboding is at a discount.
In any case, DONT. you have enough bothers of your own.

//////

re/ package. A package for D. or rather O. arrove that's all right . . . Understand O. doing O.K. so thass that.

Homer's and Isabel's concern was only increased by Ezra's current letters, which were enigmatic even by his standards. They could not make out what he was trying to tell them, though they did perceive that he had no interest in the child. After receiving a letter from them,* he wrote to his mother on 23 November:

Omar is not up for adoption by the local worthies, if that is what you mean to suggest.
If on the other hand your information is meant to indicate that the ancient neosaurian race that used to inhabit Wyncote about the years 1895 to 1900 is in the act of dying out, I can but regard you as over optimistic; much as I might like to accept the idea, I must insist on a wider survey.

---

*Their side of the correspondence does not survive.

He could hardly expect them to make anything of this oblique reference to his own illegitimate child – of whose existence, of course, they did not know. Hereafter Homer and Isabel gave up trying to puzzle out what had been going on, and merely sent regular fond enquiries as to Omar's progress.

Others, however, wished to know more. Eliot wrote to Ezra demanding 'the main facts regarding D. the child and yourself'; a previous letter to him from Ezra had been clouded with 'mysterious allusions'. William Carlos Williams facetiously alleged that Dorothy had not had a baby at all, but had merely stuffed a pillow under her clothes for a while, and 'gone away letting Ezra announce the birth of a son'. There was also a certain amount of joking about the child's name, Basil Bunting referring to him as 'Omar-i-bin-Ezra'. Probably Ezra had concurred in the selection of it, since four years before Omar's birth he wrote: 'Fitzgerald's trans. of Omar is the only good poem of Vict. era that has got beyond a fame de cénacle.' The name was usually given in full as Omar Shakespear Pound. Olivia Shakespear told John Cournos that Ezra was supposed to have remarked of this: 'Just note the crescendo.'

The most elaborate commentary on the business came in Richard Aldington's 1932 short story 'Nobody's Baby', in which a great mystery surrounds the birth of a daughter, Juliette Isolde, to the Ezra-like Charlemagne Cox. There is much speculation not only as to whether Cox is the father but even whether Ophelia his wife is the mother, the situation being complicated by the presence of 'Maggie' (Olga). 'Was it possible, writes Aldington, 'that the child was really Ophelia's but not Charlemagne's, and that all the curious hanky-panky in Paris which had perplexed us so much was simply a clumsy but generous plot on the part of Charlemagne and Maggie to shield the erring but repentant wife?'

*

Yeats wrote to Olivia Shakespear on 24 September 1926, two weeks after Omar's birth: 'I divine that you have already adopted the grandchild.' Dorothy took the baby to England and remained there for a year. During this time it was arranged that Omar would be sent to live in the country with the retired superintendent of a Norland 'nanny' training institution who lived in the Sussex village of Felpham, by the sea just east of Bognor Regis. Dorothy went there to see him settled in, and wrote to Ezra's parents: 'Am just going over the hill to pay my respects to Omar . . . P.S. Omar appeared flourishing this morning. I saw him have his bottle, and he is then put to sleep out in the garden for a while . . . He smiled broadly and indiscriminately.'

During these months Ezra would occasionally mention the child in letters to his mother ('Omar cutting back teeth'), but he never explained that Omar was not in Rapallo. He passed on news as if Dorothy and the baby were there with him.

Omar continued to live at Felpham until adolescence. At about the age of seven he began to attend a preparatory school in Bognor Regis, cycling there daily. Each Christmas he went to London to see the pantomime and visit his grandmother. In the summer his mother came over from Italy and took him to Hindhead or Malvern to stay in a hotel. He does not remember seeing Ezra until he was twelve.

When Mary Moore of Trenton visited Rapallo in 1932 she asked Dorothy whether Omar liked living in England. Dorothy answered: 'He jolly well better.' Omar himself has said that he feels 'totally indifferent' about his childhood and the manner of his upbringing.

*

Dorothy returned to Rapallo in September 1927, a year after Omar's birth. Ezra came back from Venice, where he had spent part of the summer. Life carried on as before.

Only a few people were allowed to know something of the real state of affairs. When Ronald Duncan was in Rapallo in 1938 he was given the usual formal tea party in the apartment; afterwards Dorothy went into the kitchen and Ezra 'furtively took a small snapshot from a wallet in his desk and passed it to me, his face beaming with pleasure. "That's Mary," he said proudly. "My daughter; Olga's daughter." There was a noise off. Ezra hastily stuffed the photograph into his desk, locked it and began talking in a loud voice about Baudelaire as Dorothy entered. Perhaps she had been listening. At any rate she immediately began talking about Omar.'

9

Giving 'Em The Medicine

On 19 February 1927, Olga Rudge had an audience with Mussolini in Rome. She and George Antheil had been taking part in a concert there along with another pianist, Daniel Amfitheatrow (whom Ezra described as having 'a name like Circus Maximus'). Ezra reported what had happened to William Carlos Williams. Olga, he said, had managed to arrange the audience without the help of the American Embassy or any other institution. Amfitheatrow had gone with her but not Antheil. 'Muss prefers classics, but O. did what she cd. to pave her way for Antheil audition later, bringing talk round to modern music and machines. The lowdown Greek Rhosshian Amphitheatre tried to crab Gawge and spake contempshus of people who take piano for "percussion instrument". "So it *is*," sez Muss, taking the wind out of Mons. Circus Minimus.'

Recalling the occasion half a century later, Olga explained that the meeting had been arranged for her by a friend who was giving Mussolini some English lessons. She said that Mussolini was himself a violinist, who 'played well for an amateur', and 'had the manners of an archbishop'.

Mussolini was two years older than Ezra. He had been in power since the so-called March on Rome in 1922, and had formed a dictatorship in 1925. Stella Bowen, visiting Rapallo and the Pounds, was upset to find his 'heavy features' stencilled all over the town walls, 'glowering at me from every corner', but at this time the rest of the world generally regarded his régime with benevolent curiosity. No small number of politicians and intellectuals took an interest in what John Buchan called 'the bold experiment of Fascism'. Even after parliamentary government was abandoned in Italy in 1929 there seemed, as H. G. Wells put it, to be something 'of a more enduring type' in the Mussolini régime than in most dictatorships. British support came largely from such predictable quarters as

Belloc and Chesterton, while Shaw praised Mussolini chiefly to annoy his fellow Fabians; but Yeats was interested too, wondering if 'Fascism modified by religion' might be the right weapon against Communism – though he was only seriously concerned about Irish politics.

'Il Duce' was willing to talk to Olga about Antheil's music because at the time he was trying to take a conspicuous interest in the contemporary arts, in the hope of getting support from their practitioners (Marinetti, Pirandello and d'Annunzio were in sympathy with him at this period). Olga thought that in this climate she might manage to 'pave the way' for some official patronage of 'Gawge'. Ezra could see nothing wrong with this: after spending a couple of years in Italy he liked the régime, or what he could see of it, chiefly because it had not interfered with his own life. 'I personally think extremely well of Mussolini,' he wrote to Harriet Monroe at the end of 1926. 'If one compares him to American presidents (the last three) or British premiers, etc., in fact one can NOT without insulting him. If the intelligentsia don't think well of him, it is because they know nothing about "the state", and government, and have no particularly large sense of values. Anyway, WHAT intelligentsia?'

He was inclined to think just as highly of Lenin, who had died in 1924. When the New York left-wing journal *New Masses* sent him some recent issues, he read them 'with a good deal of care' and said he thought 'Fascio and the Russian revolution' were equally 'interesting phenomena', though he did not expect much of Russia because it had just lost its great revolutionary leader: 'No country produces two Napoleons or two Lenins in succession; so we may expect Russia to be reasonably slow in producing Utopia.' The only political doctrine that really annoyed him was liberalism, 'a mess of mush'.

Many of these observations on the contemporary political scene were printed by him in *Exile*, a magazine which ran for four issues during 1927–8. He himself was its editor, publisher, and chief backer. At last he had achieved his long-cherished plan of running his own journal; but the results were lamentable. He said that '*Exile* was undertaken to print what no other mag. wd. print', but no sensible editor of any persuasion would have given page room to most of its contents. There was an appallingly written novella by John Rodker, turgid verse by poor Cheever Dunning, and a 'True Confessions' narrative supposedly by a woman with five husbands, actually the work of a male literary hack in Chicago. Many of the worst contributions were probably written by Ezra himself – one of them is signed 'Payson Loomis' – and possibly the whole thing was meant as an off-beat joke. The only serious discovery was the young New York Russian Jewish poet Louis Zukofsky, whose eccentric 'Poem Beginning "The"', rather Pound-influenced but thoroughly independent-spirited, appeared in the third issue. Apart from that, *Exile* is only worth looking through because it shows how Ezra was beginning to be drawn, moth-to-candle fashion, into making brash statements on public issues that had little or nothing to do with literature.

In the second number, right in the middle of the poetry section, he breaks into an editorial snarl against the 'drear horror' of American public life. And the third issue concludes with a series of violent assertions. Both Democrats and Republicans, he says, deserve to be 'forever excluded' from American politics for having provided 'the last three presidents' (Wilson, Harding, and Coolidge). All officials in the State Department 'ought to be vacuum cleaned'. Anything is preferable to having another Democrat as President, 'but there is nothing in sight which can be preferred very much'.

Given the state of American politics at this period, these protests were in themselves comparatively mild. What is surprising is that an exiled poet who had shown no interest in the affairs of his homeland for two decades should be suddenly moved to voice them. Ezra admitted in a 1928 letter to H.L. Mencken that 'the State of Pound' had severed itself from the Union '20 years ago', so why the change of attitude?

An immediate cause of his anger with the USA seems simply to have been the difficulty of importing *Exile* into America without threat of censorship (not that there was anything in it worth censoring) or loss of copyright. Once he had become angry about America on these specific issues, other grudges rose to the surface. There was the old one about 'faddle of passports and *cartes d'identité*', and he continued to be outraged by Prohibition. He grumbled about these in *Exile*. But they were not the cause. He was looking for a new persona, a new subject matter, and public affairs seemed promising ground in which to search – more promising now than literature.

He half hinted that he was short on ideas for his own writing in a letter to Archibald MacLeish, who had offered to help finance *Exile* because of his admiration for Ezra's poetry, and had submitted some of his own work – a section of his long poem *The Hamlet of A. MacLeish*. Ezra turned it down. He said it was little more than a parroting of himself, mixed up with bits of Eliot, Joyce, and Gertrude Stein. And in a long letter of December 1926 he emphasized that the important thing for a poet was, in the end, not style or rhythm but subject matter, 'the lasting vitality of SUBJECT, and yet again subject . . . Hell yes, the rhythm has to be, but it must be the content; it must be so much the content.' A poet needed 'alternative elements' all the time to stop him merely regurgitating his own notions again and again. He admitted that he himself was 'a little short' of such elements at the moment, 'but they must exist'.

At cooler moments he seemed to think the idea of becoming involved in public affairs rather absurd. He observed in *Poetry* in December 1928 that neither he nor any other writer was likely to 'invade the halls of Congress or lead anyone over the barricades'. But it was not in character for him just to sit and complain. 'Wot's use telling 'em they are damn sick?' he wrote to an American correspondent. 'I prefer trying giving 'em the medicine.'

*

Ezra's first determined attempt to administer 'medicine' directly to an ailing society was also his most ludicrous. The newly established Carnegie Endowment for Peace had appointed as its chairman Professor Nicholas Murray Butler, President of Columbia University. Ezra wrote to Butler, making C. H. Douglas's point that one of the causes of war is over-production, particularly of armaments, and asking if Carnegie money would be spent investigating this. Butler sent him a rather bland reply, which infuriated Ezra, and thereafter Butler became a target for personal abuse by him.

In print, Ezra was soon calling him 'a vain and pretentious seeker after glory' who, apart from 'all his obvious grossness', had 'sabotaged the Carnegie fund' and was 'a particularly good example of the murderer's accomplice', 'a toady to rich men'. By 1938 and *Guide to Kulchur* Ezra had invented a disease of civilization which he called 'Butlerism, the little Nicky Flunkies hiding their heads in their plush britches'. He continued to write to Butler, pouring out such abuse as: 'You will go down to whatever history takes note of you as one of the most loathsome figures of a time that has not been particularly creditable even to humanity . . . Coward is the softest name one cd. call you.'

He was not yet certain that the 'medicine' should consist of direct pronouncements about public issues, and he turned to Confucius to see if an ethical solution might not be propagated to the evils of modern life. In *Exile* he alleged that not merely moral but even 'economic' problems could usually be solved 'by ref. to the *Ta Hio*', and in the autumn of 1927 he spent a couple of weeks translating it.

The immediate reason for this was a request from Professor Glenn Hughes of the University of Washington, Seattle, that he should write his 'literary autobiography' for a series of 'Chapbooks' which Hughes was editing. Ezra said this 'wd. not interest me in the least', though Hughes might profitably put one of his own students on to it – it 'wd. probably educate *him* a good deal'. Instead he offered to make Hughes a translation of the *Ta Hio*, one of the classic Confucian texts. It was published in the Chapbook series a few months later.

He translated not from the Chinese, but from J. P. G. Pauthier's 1858 French version, which is more in the spirit of the Enlightenment than of the original Confucian text. Ezra's *Ta Hio* is an almost absurdly literal rendering of Pauthier:

The law of the Great Learning . . . lies in developing and

making visible that luminous principle of reason which we have received from the sky [in Pauthier '*le principe lumineux de la raison que nous avons reçu du ciel*'], to renew mankind and place its ultimate destination in perfection, the sovereign good.

One should first know the target toward which to aim . . . and then make up one's mind . . . one can then have the spirit calm and tranquil ['*l'esprit tranquille et calme*']; and . . . one can then enjoy that unalterable repose which nothing can trouble . . . [and] attain that desired state of perfection ['*l'etat de perfectionnement désiré*'].

Only once does Ezra's own character break through this phoney Gallicism, when he cites the words that were displayed on the bathtub of an ancient Chinese ruler. Pauthier gives them elegantly as '*Renouvelle-toi complètement chaque jour; fais-le de nouveau*'; Ezra has 'Renovate, dod gast you, renovate.'

It seems very odd at first sight that Ezra of all people should be attracted to Confucianism, which teaches that a man can only master others when has mastered himself, and that he must aim for moderation in all things, learning to consider his motives before taking action. Ezra himself never seems to have understood why Confucius appealed to him. Once, he said he regarded his teaching as 'a reaction against Christianity'; but this is nonsense as a historical description of Confucianism, which antedates Christianity by more than 500 years and contains nothing that conflicts with its ethics. It can only mean that he hoped to shock people by preferring Confucius to Christ.

Rather more revealingly, he remarked in 1942: 'You read a sentence by Confucius and it seems nothing. Twenty years later you come back to it to meditate on its significance.' He seems to have felt that the very blankness of the surface of most Confucian writing – which to Western eyes often seems to have little worth saying – would yield some depth of meaning if he contemplated it for long enough; it was thus the philosophical equivalent of the Chinese ideograms.

Confucianism also attracted him because it shies away from any interest in personality, private characteristics, psychology, traits, or weaknesses and speaks persuasively in favour of the assumption of a mask of correctness. As Ezra's *Ta Hio* translation has it, the Confucian disciple is 'corrected and ameliorated' by his contemplation of his own motives, his 'manners' are governed by 'probity and rightness', he and his family are 'well governed' by what he has learnt. There is no question of untangling private confusions, but rather of keeping them beneath the surface. It was a method that Ezra himself had practised since his undergraduate days at Hamilton.

*

Yeats was amused by Ezra's obsession with Confucius, whom he said 'should have worn an eighteenth-century wig and preached in St Paul's'. Similarly, Wyndham Lewis's remark in his *Time and Western Man* (1927) that Ezra was 'a sort of revolutionary simpleton . . . a genuine *naïf*' might well have been applied to his enthusiasm for Confucius, though at the time Lewis was not aware of this latest passion. Ezra took the remark as a compliment, saying that a revolutionary simpleton seemed to him a 'serviceable figure'. He was never very good at hearing warnings.

In 1929 Yeats, becoming aware of Ezra's increasing tendency to pontificate on political matters, admonished him in print:

> My dear Ezra, Do not be elected to the Senate of your country.
> I think myself, after six years, well out of that of mine. Neither
> you nor I, nor any other of our excitable profession, can match
> those old lawyers, old bankers, old business men, who, because
> all habit and memory, have begun to govern the world.

Ezra, curiously, did not understand what Yeats was driving at. 'That remark always seems funny to me,' he told Charles Olson in 1946.

Lewis's *Time and Western Man* contained two entire chapters attacking Ezra, asserting that there was a discrepancy between his real interests (ancient poetry) and his fire-eating support of modernism; that he was essentially parasitical in his enthusiasm for such people as Antheil, finding it easier to bask in their reflected energy than to create his own; and that he had no poetic personality of his own, and was at his best when mimicking 'a Propertius or an Arnaut Daniel'. But these well-aimed shafts were sent on their way with an air of affectionate banter rather than serious criticism, and Ezra told Agnes Bedford he preferred 'dear Wyndham's' assaults to praise from imbecile critics; he hoped the book had made plenty of money for Lewis. Four years later he was praising Lewis's *The Apes of God* as 'the only major manifestation' of literature that had come out of England 'for now nearly a decade'.

Yeats wrote some observations on Lewis's attack on Ezra, but then tore them up because he wanted to keep on good terms with Ezra, as they had become neighbours. A brief visit to Rapallo in February 1928 had so pleased Yeats – Canto 77 shows him looking out at the sea mist descending on the bay and murmuring 'Sligo in heaven' – that he and his wife decided to return in the autumn and take a flat there. In their apartment at 12 Via Americhe, Yeats finished *A Packet for Ezra Pound* (1929), an engaging little bundle of a book which contains the exhortation to Ezra not to become a senator, the description of him feeding the Rapallo cats, and other such trifles, though much of it is concerned with Mrs Yeats's automatic writing and other supernatural experiences. Ezra thought such stuff 'very very very bughouse', and described Yeats's beloved tower near

Coole Park, Thoor Ballylee, acquired in 1918, as 'his phallic symbol on the Bogs. Ballyphallus or whatever he calls it with the river on the first floor.'

Richard Aldington says Ezra liked to give the impression that Yeats being drawn to Rapallo was a case of the lesser poet being pulled irresistibly into the orbit of the greater, for he now regarded himself as Yeats's equal. Yet he constantly sought out the older man's company. 'I see Ezra daily,' Yeats told Lady Gregory. 'We disagree about everything, but if we have not met for 24 hours he calls full of gloomy and almost dumb oppression.' Ezra said that Yeats would often 'pester' him to be 'a 4th at table-rapping', and he helped Yeats to punctuate new poems, as in the old *Poetry* days. Another motif from the pre-1914 period seemed to be recurring. 'Ezra . . . constantly comes round to talk of Guido who absorbs his attention,' wrote Yeats to Olivia Shakespear in November 1928.

Lewis's assertion that Ezra was still only interested in old poetry seemed to be true. He was working on Cavalcanti again, and he proposed to Eliot that Faber and Faber bring out a revised edition of his translation of Cavalcanti poems, to which he would add a commentary and facsimiles of manuscripts. Eliot and his co-directors agreed. A chunk of the introductory material was printed in the *Dial* in March 1928, and in the following months Ezra did 'a great deal of work of plodding kerakter', enlisting Manlio Dazzi of the Malatestine Library in Cesena to help him on scholarly points, and looking forward to producing a 'standard woik'.

But his requirements soon became too expensive for Faber and Faber and by the spring of 1929 Aquila Press, a small London publisher, had taken over what was now announced as 'a monumental and definitive edition' with 'a full critical text . . . an extensive commentary and variant readings'. Then Aquila went bankrupt, so Ezra had the Italian texts and the scholarly apparatus printed in Genoa, and the facsimile plates made in Germany, all at his own expense. He also rescued sheets of that part of the Aquila edition that had already been printed, including his commentary on the celebrated 'Donna mi prega' poem, and had them bound up with the other material. The resulting volume was utterly chaotic in character, several texts appearing twice and the English translations breaking off incomplete. It was published in an edition of 500 copies in January 1932; Ezra told Louis Zukofsky some time later that he had been 'short of cash for three years: due to bein such a godd damn fool as to try to do a decent job over the Cavalcanti'. During this period of comparative penury, he asked Hemingway if he thought it might be possible to make money writing songs for American election campaigns.

Despite the botched appearance of the book, he was immensely proud of the Cavalcanti as a work of scholarship, something he usually claimed to despise. One reviewer, Étienne Gilson in the *Criterion*, gave support to this confidence in the book, praising the 'care and accuracy' with which the

Italian text had been transcribed, and saying it was 'on a higher level than the ordinary reprint of an old text' – though he strongly disagreed with Ezra's interpretation of Cavalcanti's philosophy of love, which he thought was altogether simpler than Ezra suggested in his commentary on 'Donna mi prega'. Mario Praz, however, could find nothing at all to praise, branding the book as 'that unbelievable olla podrida', and saying it seemed to have been put together by the proverbial monkeys who, given type-writers, might eventually produce a Shakespeare sonnet. 'In the case of Pound's *Cavalcanti* this seems to have been the method followed, though the result is not as satisfactory.'

Ezra responded by calling Praz 'a Bloomsbury snob', and, undeterred by the book's mixed reception, tried to submit it for his long-deferred doctorate at the University of Pennsylvania. He wondered if there was anything that 'rules out work done in absence after so great an interval'. The University invited him to submit a copy, but told him he would have to return to Philadelphia and take various courses before he could be examined for the doctorate. Ezra had justified an attempt in 1920 to be awarded the doctorate as 'an enquiry into the psychology of the University . . . a record of The Spirit of the Age', rather than a serious 'desire on my part to possess a futile decoration'; but it was clear that his rejection by Penn twenty-five years earlier still rankled.

10

How To Read

A community seemed to be forming around him in Rapallo. During 1928 Richard Aldington and Brigit Patmore, then living together, set up temporary home there in hotel rooms found for them by Ezra. Yeats would take Aldington for walks and ask him: 'How do you account for Ezra?' Aldington knew no simple answer, but 'with Yeats that never mattered. He proceeded in his pontifical style: "Here is a man who produces the most distinguished work and yet in his behaviour is the least distinguished of men. It is the antithetical self . . ."' And in the summer of 1928 Homer and Isabel Pound arrived to see their son for the first time since 1914.

Homer had now retired from the Mint. They had booked their passage back to the USA, but wondered whether they might not stay in Italy. By September they had decided to make Rapallo their retirement home. 'It is surely a loss to Wyncote to lose such charming people,' reported the *Jenkintown Times–Chronicle*. At first they lived in a hotel, then borrowed Yeats's flat, finally taking their own house, the Villa Raggio, on a hill overlooking the town. 'Wyncote is lovely, but does not equal Rapallo (Italy),' Isabel wrote to the *Times–Chronicle*. 'We now have a blue cottage amid the grey green olive trees where the birds sing, the sea chants, waves roam . . . We have lots of fruit, walnuts and almonds, and life goes very pleasantly.'

The Rapallo locals took quickly to Homer, whom they dubbed *simpatico, una past' d'uomo*, a wholesome man. Isabel held herself more apart. The original Blakes, Burne-Joneses and Gordon Craigs that covered the walls of the Yeats apartment were soon joined, during their tenancy, by a gallery of snapshots of Ezra from childhood.

Ezra would often billet friends on his parents. Louis Zukofsky stayed with Homer and Isabel when he visited Rapallo in 1935, and was overwhelmed by their hospitality. He was supposed to take his meals at Basil Bunting's lodgings (Ezra was paying for them), but when he tried to slip out, Homer would bar his way benevolently and escort him to the dinner table. Guests would have to listen to Isabel reciting Ezra's juvenilia. 'Any attempt to put in a word for the greater importance of Ezra's maturer work,' writes one of them, 'would be quenched by a glance, while the early verses swept on to their ninetyish close.'

As Homer received his pension from the USA the 1929 Wall Street crash affected him a little, but not seriously. Ezra referred casually to his father's reduced income in a few letters, saying the situation was not grave. In general Rapallo was untouched by the Depression, which, writes Giuseppe Bacigalupo, 'hardly affected our economy, predominantly agricultural, compared with the disasters in Germany and the States'. Ezra saw nothing of the widespread poverty of the period, and admitted this in a 1941 broadcast: 'I can't wring anyone's heart.'

It was during the Depression that C. H. Douglas's Social Credit, which up to then had commanded little general attention, began to acquire cautious support from a number of intellectuals and writers, among them William Carlos Williams and Archibald MacLeish, and, in England, Herbert Read, Storm Jameson and Bonamy Dobrée (not to mention Hilaire Belloc, who liked it because it was potentially anti-Semitic). But Ezra's resurgence of enthusiasm for Social Credit in 1933 had nothing to do with the Depression.

Homer Pound's arrival in Rapallo affected Ezra's writing in one small but not unimportant detail. Homer brought with him from Wyncote the family scrapbooks, with old newspaper cuttings about grandfather Thaddeus Coleman Pound. Ezra began to study them with interest, and came to the conclusion 'that T.C.P. had already in 1878 been writing about, or urging among his fellow Congressmen, the same essentials of money and statal economics that I am writing about today'. There were few points of real similarity between Ezra's economic theories and his grandfather's activities in Congress or as a business entrepreneur, but Thaddeus's irrepressible energy, his loud-mouthed approach to matters of public concern, clearly seemed to offer a model.

*

Soon after his parents had arrived in Rapallo, Ezra told his father, in the strictest confidence, of the existence of Maria Rudge, now aged three and still living at Gais in the Tyrol. He did not tell his mother or if he did, she shut her ears; it was something not to be contemplated. Ezra remarked succinctly that 'two emotions at once' – the discovery that she had an illegitimate granddaughter, and learning the truth about Omar – would be too much for her. Isabel eventually recognized Maria's existence, but she made no attempt to see her grandchild for seventeen years. However, she added photographs of Omar, taken in England, to the family gallery of snapshots.

Homer took the news calmly, and agreed to accompany Ezra to Gais to see the child and consider whether she should be brought out of her retreat into 'civilization'. When they reached the Tyrol, Homer was captivated by his granddaughter, and the three generations of Pounds posed for the photographer in Bruneck. Maria, blue-eyed with golden hair and high cheekbones, sits seriously on a high stool, not altogether certain of what is going on. Ezra, on a lower chair, characteristically ignores the camera, and gazes at her adoringly, a hand resting gently on her shoulder. Homer stands benevolently over them both, in one of Ezra's wide-collared shirts and floppy ties, managing to look at once patriarchal and childlike.

Homer and Maria could not understand a word of each other's language – she could speak only Tyrolean German – but it was clear that she was being brought up strong and healthy, and Homer's verdict was that it would 'kill her' to tear her away from the place. Short trips might soon be tried, but at no cost must she yet be separated from the foster mother. Everyone was happy with the decision.

Afterwards Maria thought that Homer's visit to Gais had helped her find a sense of stability in a very confusing world. Her foster parents, 'Mamme' and 'Tatte' in her vocabulary, would speak mysteriously of her real father and mother, 'the Herr' and 'the Frau', whom she rarely saw and could not yet take in. But Homer was different. 'A *Grossvater* you do not conjure up out of nowhere,' she writes. 'His first visit left a landmark . . . It seems to me we were always hand in hand . . . He drew funny faces on our breakfast eggs and produced the most vivid animal shadow plays with his hands on white walls . . . He gave me a beautiful doll, and I called it Rosile.'

*

Ezra continued to give America the medicine for its shortcomings in 'How to Read', a series of three articles that he managed to place with the 'Books' section of the *New York Herald Tribune* in January 1929. The articles castigated the usual system of teaching literature in American universities, by which, he said, students were not simply given great books to read, but were expected to endure a 'dead and uncorrelated' syllabus in which 'one was asked to remember what some critic (deceased) had said'.

He proposed that instead, instructors should present their pupils only with literature that contained real 'discoveries'. They should be made to read only the work of 'the inventors', such as Arnaut Daniel who 'introduced certain methods of rhyming' and Cavalcanti who developed a new 'fineness of perception', and 'the masters', the great writers who had not only invented but assimilated and synthesized the work of others. They should pay little heed to 'the diluters' or to the great mass of writers who can only offer 'some slight personal flavour'. He then went on to outline a specific curriculum.

This was chiefly remarkable for what it omitted. From 'the Greeks' he recommended only Homer and Sappho, dismissing the dramatists as 'diluters'. From Latin poetry, merely Catullus, Ovid and Propertius – 'I am chucking out . . . Virgil without the slightest compunction,' he said; indeed one could really 'throw out at least one-third of Ovid'. From the Middle Ages, it only seemed worth looking at the *Seafarer* and taking 'some cursory notice of some medieval narrative, it does not greatly matter what', perhaps *Beowulf* or *El Cid*. The troubadours, as might be expected, featured on his list. Villon must be read because he was 'a pivot' for understanding poetry both before and after his time. Dante was allowed a brief mention.

Shakespeare was comparatively unimportant, rather spoilt by 'embroidery of language'. Stendhal and Flaubert deserved close inspection by anyone who wanted to write good verse, since they understood 'the art of charging words'. Henry James was the only author who added 'anything to the art of the nineteenth-century novel not known to the French'. Gautier and Browning were worth a look. Confucius was added rather as an afterthought. 'How to Read' concluded with the comforting assurance that the curriculum 'would not overburden the three- or four-year student' who, after this 'innoculation', could be safely exposed 'to modernity or anything else in literature'.

Archibald MacLeish received 'How to Read' with some astonishment. He thought it 'a little masterpiece . . . It is about great poets. There are practically no first rate poets in Pound's list but still that would seem to be a minor weakness. I expect his next will be How To Dance or How To Vote Republican. The man has sheep herder's madness. I wish he would stick to Cantos.'

As a piece of intellectual autobiography, 'How to Read' has its value; taken literally as a curriculum it is very nearly as ludicrous as MacLeish suggested. But it needs to be seen as part of Ezra's efforts to set things right in the USA. The idea of reducing all literature to a small collection of 'essential' books, in itself quintessentially American, was inspired by 'Doctor Eliot's Five-Foot Shelf of Books', the popular name for the fifty-volume Harvard Classics series of world literature selected by Charles W. Eliot, President of Harvard, published just before the First World War. MacLeish observed that Ezra's enterprise was 'Eliot's Five Foot Shelf cut down to Five Inches. Showing how much smarter Pound is.' Shortly before writing the articles, Ezra had asked his father (then still in Wyncote) for a 'full list of woiks included in Doc. Eliot's "bookshelf"'.

He was thoroughly pleased with 'How to Read', calling it 'my conclusions after 25 years of examination of comparative poesy', and saying it proved that all his writings and literary studies had not been 'hap hazard dilletantism' but were according to 'plan and coherent design'. He meant it to be used in colleges, telling his old teacher Professor Ibbotson at Hamilton that students should be issued with 'an encyclopaedia or a few vols/' incorporating in it the literature he recommended; and for some people 'How to Read' really was a valuable eye-opener. The English writer C. H. Sisson picked up a copy in booklet form – it was published in London in 1931 – while still an undergraduate, and found it an exciting encouragement to rebel against the system. 'I cannot say that . . . I got very far with Pound's dramatic short reading list, but I did dip into Villon and Dante . . . I even read Pauthier's version of Confucius. In each of the books recommended by Pound I found something new, interesting, and . . . blazingly illuminating.'

F. R. Leavis picked up the pamphlet too, and in 1932 published a riposte, *How to Teach Reading: a Primer for Ezra Pound*. He allowed that Ezra had delivered a much-needed kick to the shins of literary studies. 'One may quarrel with it, but that is its value: it is a thing to quarrel with. Some such challenge was badly needed. It is a challenge to a stock-taking that has long been overdue, to a radical inquiry into the state of literary culture . . . Why do we read, and what should it be?' Leavis found Ezra's proposals for jettisoning so many 'great' writers 'exhilaratingly drastic'. But he accused him of 'perversity' in his choices – for example, his exclusion of Shakespeare, and of Donne, whom Ezra put in the class of writers who only offer 'personal flavour'. Leavis went on to propose his own programme of study, with a 'focus of interest in the present', saying he wished to consider 'the whole question of the relation of reading to education and culture' – a matter that Ezra had not discussed at all, offering no definition of who his hypothetical reader might be.

'What is Leavis? He recently sent me his "Primer"?' Ezra asked in February 1932. But he did not read the book. Some years later he told Huntington Cairns he had 'looked at it once' but 'one did not have to eat the whole of a rotten egg to know that it was bad'. He paid no attention to Leavis's *New Bearings in English Poetry* (1932) with its sustained panegyric of *Hugh Selwyn Mauberley* and also an attack on the Cantos, though he once glanced at an issue of his journal *Scrutiny* and judged it 'quite awake'.

'How to Read' played a part in setting Leavis on his own course as a castigator of received ideas about culture, and so may be said to have influenced the teaching of literature in England. In America it made no such mark. The original series of *New York Herald Tribune* articles attracted little attention, and there was no reprint in pamphlet form.

Harcourt Brace offered Ezra a contract to expand the articles into a book, but he decided that the small print was designed to let them 'swindle' him, and refused to sign. Eventually he enlarged 'How to Read' into his *ABC of Reading* (1934), which was published on both sides of the Atlantic. This attracted a wide readership in the years that followed; but while it is full of well-aimed jabs at received opinions, and makes a fizzy introduction to Ezra and his works, it is a more rambling affair than the original articles, less likely to create cónverts or provoke spirited responses.

*

In April 1929 Yeats sent out one of his occasional conduct reports on Ezra, this time to Sturge Moore: 'He is sunk in Frobenius, Spengler's German source, and finds him a most interesting person.'

Leo Frobenius was a German anthropologist, six years older than Ezra, who from the early 1900s conducted expeditions in Africa. Inspired by the newly discovered palaeolithic cave-paintings in Europe, he wished to examine the theory that European culture originated in Africa and swept northwards in what he called a continuous *Kulturmorphologie*. He investigated African folk tales, and certain of his discoveries were taken up in Spengler's *Decline of the West* (1918), which Ezra disliked, saying that Spengler was merely a German equivalent of H. G. Wells.

Ezra gave this example of the material collected by Frobenius and printed in the seven volumes of his encyclopaedic study of mythology, *Erlebte Erdteile*:

> It began . . . with his hearing that certain railway contractors were in conflict with some local tradition. A king and a girl had driven into the ground where there was a certain hillock: they ought not to make a cutting through the sacred place. The materialist contractors took no notice and went ahead – and unearthed a bronze car with effigies of Dis and Persephone.

In *Guide to Kulchur* Ezra describes Frobenius's book as a tool 'without which a man cannot place any book or work of art in relation to the rest', but it seems unlikely that he studied very much of it. In 1941 he described his command of spoken German as 'broken', and it is doubtful that he could have waded through seven volumes of abstruse German prose.

One thing he did take from Frobenius's writings was the word 'paideuma'. Frobenius had used this as the title of a section of the book, and it caught Ezra's fancy. He was soon using it with rapidly increasing frequency. Writing of Ford Madox Ford's memoirs, for example, he spoke of 'assessing Ford's position in the "paideuma", in the mainstream of English culture'. According to Frobenius's protégé and assistant, a young American named Douglas Fox, the anthropologist had used 'paideuma' to mean 'the tutorial essence of culture *per se* . . . culture [as] the tutor of mankind'. Ezra decided, however, that it referred to 'the tangle or complex of the inrooted ideas of any period', 'the gristly roots of ideas that are in action'. Where he got this 'root' notion from is a mystery: he seems to have ignored the fact that the classical Greek word παίδευμα (*paideuma*) is derived from παῖς (*pais*), 'a child', and according to Liddell and Scott's dictionary means: 'that which is reared up or educated, i.e. nursling, scholar . . . [hence] thing taught, subject of instruction . . . [or] 'means of instruction . . . [or] process or system of education, culture, learning'. Thus it is a term solely concerned with education, and has nothing to do with 'ideas in action'.

Ezra made personal contact with Frobenius, meeting him when he went to Frankfurt to attend the première of Antheil's opera *Transatlantic*. He even persuaded him to go to the performance with him, but the anthropologist disliked it intensely (as did Albert Einstein, who wrote in the *New York Times* that 'its creator is quite unable to compose opera . . . he is quite unable to compose anything whatever'). Yet Frobenius seemed glad of Ezra's attention, while Ezra was struck by his own physical resemblance to the anthropologist. At St Elizabeths in 1946 Charles Olson asked him 'what Frobenius looked like', and immediately

> stumbled on the fact that Pound sees himself as a cat man . . .
> Said he, 'There were three men' – it was almost as though he
> said, 'Once upon a time, there were three men who might have
> come from the same genes . . .' [Dorothy] went on making with
> her hands, seeking further to show the differences – F not so
> wide at the temples, a V for F's beard, when all of a sudden old
> Ez lets it out . . . 'cat family, cat family'!

(The third man was a Russian diplomat named Barkov.)*

During the 1930s Ezra constantly wrote to Frobenius at his 'Forschungsinstitut für Kulturmorphologie' in Frankfurt asking for information. Frobenius was not fluent in English, and would pass on the letters to Douglas Fox, who observes that 'no one with only a conventional knowledge of English and practically no knowledge of Pound' could have made head or tail of most of them. Often he 'did not get what E.P. was driving at either'. But 'we communicated, and Pound apparently got the feeling that here was someone who understood. I was not so certain.'

Ezra used the Frobenius institute as a source of 'lowdown' on all kinds of topics. 'If I wish to know, for example, if J. S. Mill is right in saying that certain African tribes have a money of account . . . a means of exchange . . .

---

*Another look-alike was Silvio Gesell, an economist whose theories later attracted Ezra's passionate support.

I write to Frankfurt . . . When I wanted to know how the primitive telegraph, tapped out on wooden drums, worked, I write to Frankfurt . . . One cannot fully understand modern thought without some awareness of Frobenius's work.'

11

ABCD And Then JKLM

By the end of the 1920s Olga Rudge had a small house of her own in Venice, paid for by her American father shortly before he lost much of his money in the Wall Street crash. It became customary for Ezra to spend the late summer and early autumn there with her each year, while Dorothy was in England with her mother and Omar.

The Venice house, 252 Dorsoduro, was a three-storey terraced artisan dwelling in a narrow blind alley, the Calle Querini, leading off a quiet side canal near the great church of Santa Maria della Salute. It was not far from the district where Ezra had lived in 1908, in one of the most secluded spots in Venice, yet only a few minutes' walk and boat journey from the most fashionable part of the city. Ezra and Olga named it 'the hidden nest'.

To this house, their child Maria was first brought at about the age of four, according to Homer's advice of gradual weaning from her Tyrolean home. Frau Marcher accompanied her from Gais by train, afterwards describing this great adventure as if it had taken three days and three nights instead of a mere ten hours.

The house was tiny – one visitor described it as three matchboxes on top of each other – but Maria, led in through the narrow front doorway from canal and alley, found it a new world of colours, objects, and figures. The front door opened straight into a living room, decorated with painted yellow columns on the walls. A lamp in the form of a glass star hung from the ceiling. 'The Herr', whom Maria had probably not seen since he came to Gais with the *Grossvater*, sat waiting on a low bench or divan (which he had made himself), covered with dark blue cotton, against the opposite wall. Maria was lifted on to a high armchair that had been bolstered with cushions. Watching her across the dining table sat 'the Frau' – Olga, her mother – 'a queen towards me,' wrote Maria long afterwards, but 'soft and willowy, smiling like a fairy' towards the Herr.

The foster mother remained at the house for the few days of this first visit, supposedly to ease the child's passage into civilization, but was greatly disconcerted by Venetian life. The tap water smelled foul to her after the mountain springs of Gais, and Olga's clothes surely indicated that she was a loose lady. The Herr consoled Frau Marcher for her homesickness, buying her knick-knack souvenirs, putting an arm around her shoulder when she looked unhappy – '*Gut, alles gut.*' Nor did he show any reserve towards the child. 'He never had any whims and looked at me approvingly and hugged me . . .'

Olga was strict. Maria must wear gloves. She must behave like a lady, and call her parents Mamile and Tattile – though her foster mother could still be Mamme. It was confusing, yet gradually the child began to feel curiosity about her surroundings. 'I liked Mamile's room upstairs the best; it had no open fire and the most beautiful dress hung on the door. The door was a looking glass, facing the king-size, pearl-grey velvet couch. On the long, low bookcase stood two pairs of strange shoes . . . and the jewel-studded silver bird . . .'

Gradually she put together her personal map of the house. Later she learnt that the dress and shoes were Japanese; the bird a gift from d'Annunzio; the grey opaque canvas on the stairs a painting by Tami Koumé; the huge book with a wooden binding in the top-floor studio the works of Ovid; the marble face set into the wall by the desk in that top room a bas-relief of Isotta da Rimini. But at first they were just hard, unyielding symbols which she would scan each summer, on her yearly visit to the hidden nest.

She was told neither of the existence of Dorothy, nor of Omar. She was an inhabitant of one of the sealed compartments of her father's life.

*

Those who saw Ezra and Dorothy together were not shown so much as a hair-crack in the façade. The wife of an American who was working as secretary to Ford Madox Ford watched them both at a Paris dinner party in 1930. Sitting side by side on a sofa, they looked 'devoted'. In certain respects they were. When *A Draft of XXX Cantos* went to press in 1930 Dorothy undertook to draw initial letters for the volume, and did so with no little skill and sympathy.

Bill Bird's Three Mountains Press had been bought by Nancy Cunard, whom Ezra had known since London days when he had solicited patronage for Joyce from her. She was now publishing in Paris on the same small scale as Bird, under the name Hours Press. She usually did the printing herself, but the length of the thirty Cantos that Ezra had given her made this too daunting, and Ezra found a Paris master printer to take on the job for her. He derived amusement from Nancy's black American lover

Henry Crowder. 'Nancy Cunard's "coon", he and I the only civilized creatures,' Ezra told Charles Olson. 'Says Henry: "Ah been readin' Mr Pound's Cantos. And Ah don' know why I read 'em, 'cause I don' understand 'em. Snobbism, I guess."'

F. R. Leavis would have applauded this judgement. His attack on the Cantos in *New Bearings in English Poetry* was chiefly directed at Ezra's obscurity. Leavis compared his use of allusion to Eliot's in *The Waste Land*. He judged that in the Eliot poem 'the intrinsic power of his verse' could force meaning through, even to a reader 'who does not recognize what is being alluded to'. But in the Cantos 'even when one is fully informed about Mr Pound's allusions, one's recognition has no significant effect: the value remains private to the author . . . The Cantos appear to be little more than a game – a game with the seriousness of pedantry.'

Ezra's response to such accusations was usually to say that everything would become clear when the entire Cantos were finished. He would, he said, eventually 'get all the necessary notes into the text itself'. Yet he never attempted to build 'notes' on earlier cantos into later ones (it seems an impossible scheme), and the most he ever undertook was occasionally to echo earlier passages, a device that gave some appearance of structure, but did little to clarify meaning. Certainly, the last seven cantos in the 1930 *Draft of XXX Cantos* did nothing to enlighten readers about the earlier parts of the poem.

Cantos 24 to 26 form a group which is sometimes called 'Historical Venice', and which attempts to repeat the method of the Malatesta Cantos. The group lacks the binding presence of a Sigismundo. Niccolò d'Este comes near to occupying his place: Canto 24, as Canto 20, alludes to the execution of d'Este's adulterous wife and natural son – a theme that understandably seems to have fascinated Ezra at this period – and describes his pilgrimage to the Holy Land, in an account taken from a book in the Vatican Library. It seems, however, a curiously dispirited enterprise, as if Ezra were merely parroting his own manner from earlier cantos. Next, Cantos 25 and 26 present a collection of decrees by the Doge of Venice, and other fragments from the city's past, sometimes lapsing into prose. Cantos 27, 28 and 29 defy any connected interpretation, consisting of a collage of such private memories as 'that music publisher, / The fellow that brought back the shrunken Indian head'; Professor Rennert teaching at Penn ('And old Rennert wd. sigh heavily / And look over the top of his lenses'); and Eliot in France in 1919 saying he was 'afraid of the life after death'. Canto 30 returns to apparent clarity, beginning with a pastiche of Chaucer, touching on Lucrezia Borgia, and ending with the death of Pope Alessandro Borgia. William Carlos Williams claimed it represented 'Pound's main philosophic tenet' this being (said Williams) 'Keep what is "good", keep what is lovely. Let all that is ugly be clean slain . . . To Ezra much of everything in the world today is sloppy and mushy . . . There is no order in the world. It should be clean slain, slain.' But Canto 30 scarcely seems to exemplify this, or anything else. It concludes this part of the Cantos with a montage that has moments of beauty, but which seems quite insufficient as a major punctuation mark in an enterprise of this scale.

However, in essence Williams was right, for by 1930 Ezra wanted the Cantos to express what he believed to have been the 'radiant' nature of the medieval world, as contrasted with the 'fog' of the present age. Ezra wrote in the *Dial* in March 1928 on medievalism and Cavalcanti:

> We appear to have lost the radiant world where one thought cuts through another with a clean edge, a world of moving energies . . . A mediaeval 'natural philosopher' would find this modern world full of enchantments, not only the light in the electric bulb, but the thought of the current hidden in air and in wire would give him a mind full of forms . . . Or possibly this will fall under the eye of . . . a painter who will answer: confound you, you *ought* to find just that in my painting.

He clearly thought it could be found in the Cantos, and at their finest moments, such as Canto 18 with its evocation of an earthly paradise, there is indeed a representation of such a 'radiant' world. But too often Ezra now took that effect for granted.

*

He showed no urgent desire to secure a wide readership for *A Draft of XXX Cantos*: Nancy Cunard had only 200 copies printed, and they were soon sold. Ford Madox Ford tried to interest British and American publishers, but Ezra gave him small encouragement, and when Archibald MacLeish recommended the book to Farrar & Rinehart of New York Ezra snarled at him for his pains. 'For Christ's sake lay off the abuse,' MacLeish wrote in response. 'I have no intention whatever of holding onto the shitty end of one of your famous correspondences. I know what you think of me and frankly I don't give a good goddam. You have praised too many really rotten writers for your condemnations to go very deep. What I am interested in is your poetry and fixing things up so that you can go on writing it.'

Ezra answered: 'I wasn't abusin *you*. I wuz seekin' light.' But he remained ungrateful, only letting Farrar publish *A Draft of XXX Cantos* in 1933 because by then he wanted a big readership for the next section of the Cantos, which propagated Social Credit. In London, Eliot decided that Faber and Faber should print their own edition, but the firm took its time over it. Ezra did not mind: 'Faber flowing slow & majestic,' he reported contentedly to MacLeish. Eliot, meanwhile, assured Ezra that henceforth he must regard Faber and Faber as having a standing order for future Cantos: 'I mean release them in chunks according to your own sense of time and consuitability.'

With thirty Cantos available in print, critics felt inclined to look for some evidence of structure and overall purpose in the work. Yeats had raised this matter with Ezra in Rapallo, saying that he had often found 'some scene of distinguished beauty' in a particular passage, but could not make out 'why all the suits could not be dealt out in some quite different order'. Ezra told him what he always told people who asked this question. 'He explains,' said Yeats, 'that it will, when the hundredth Canto is finished, display a structure.' But this time Ezra went further. He told Yeats it would be 'a structure like that of a Bach Fugue. There will be no plot, no chronicle of events, no logic of discourse, but two themes, the descent into Hades from Homer, a metamorphosis from Ovid, and mixed with these medieval or modern characters.'

This conversation was in February 1928. Yeats wrote to his wife that Ezra said 'there is a structure & that it is founded on that of a fugue – that word looks wrong.' Ezra was not sure how to spell 'fugue' either. After Yeats had printed his account of the conversation he wrote: 'CON-FOUND uncle Bill YEATS' paragraph on fuge/ blighter never knew WHAT a fugue was anyhow. more wasted ink due his "explanation", than you cd. mop up with a moose hide.'

During their Rapallo talk he offered Yeats another 'explanation', which Yeats recorded:

> He has scribbled on the back of an envelope certain sets of letters that represent emotions or archetypal events . . . ABCD and then JKLM, and then each set of letters repeated, and then ABCD inverted and this repeated, and then a new element XYZ, then certain letters that never recur and then all sorts of combinations . . .

Yeats concluded bemusedly: 'It is almost impossible to understand the art of a generation younger than one's own.' And he wrote to Ezra in September 1928: 'Your "Cantos" are a fine book to look at & full of beautiful things . . . I doubt however that I shall ever see the picture that all these bits of mosaic compose into.'

Writing to his father, Ezra used both the 'fugue' and the alphabetical explanations of the structure of the Cantos, saying that the 'main scheme' was rather like 'subject and response and counter subject in fugue' (he actually seemed to be thinking of sonata form), and identifying the poem's themes as

A. A. Live man goes down into world of Dead
C. B. The 'repeat in history'
B. C. The 'magic moment' or moment of metamorphosis, bust thru from quotidien into 'divine or permanent world'. Gods, etc.

These three elements recur throughout the first thirty Cantos, but haphazardly and with little evidence of a plan. The truth was, as Ezra admitted in a candid moment to James T. Farrell in 1932, that the 'first 2/7ths' of the poem had been filled with 'ANY bloody thing to xcite curiosity'.

*

One or two sympathetic reviewers of *A Draft of XXX Cantos*, hoping and expecting to find a structure revealing itself, convinced themselves that they had. Dudley Fitts wrote in *Hound & Horn* that he had not only perceived a 'rhythmic balance' within each canto, but believed that 'as the individual verse is to the complete cadence, so is the single Canto to the poem as a whole'. Fitts judged the Cantos 'the most ambitious poetic conception of our day . . . so nearly successful in execution that fault-finding seems invidious'. Ezra, however, did not want flattery. 'Fitts is from my point of view, very nearly hopeless,' he wrote of this review, though he did not say why.

Eda Lou Walton in the *New York Times* perceived that the only 'structure' was autobiographical: the poem was 'a kind of odyssey of the literary mind'. She thought it was all intellect and no feeling, and even the sympathetic Fitts felt Ezra had 'substituted book-learning for actual life'. In England, Geoffrey Grigson, in his own journal *New Verse*, accepted that the Cantos had some homogeneity of material and style, but thought they lacked the 'discipline' needed to bind them together, and, like Walton and Fitts, he was disturbed by the 'second-hand', predominantly book-acquired nature of most of the narrative. He missed the 'extreme physical shock' he said, which even a cursory reading of Dante, or of Eliot, could bring. In her *Aspects of Modern Poetry* (1934), Edith Sitwell compared the absence of structure in the Cantos to 'the lost luggage office at a railway station' where the individual trunks might be carefully labelled but were 'strewn about'. And D. G. Bridson, a young BBC radio producer much attracted by Ezra's work, while arguing that it was absurd to talk about a lack of 'real' life in the Cantos when so many passages described Ezra's own experiences, felt he would have been better advised to make it all less obscure, to 'compromise by meeting his audience half way'.

Ezra, always glad to stamp on the toes of a potential disciple, growled back at Bridson: 'WHAT audience . . . London is, as you know, full of pimps who do not want to look either facts or ideas in the face . . . Are these the vermin for whom one should write footnotes?' But it was not just that. The whole notion of explanation, of unravelling the obscurities, annoyed him deeply. Later, when his daughter asked him about some name or allusion in the Cantos that meant nothing to her, he would reply 'It doesn't matter.' And when Nancy Cunard asked him if he thought any single person would be capable of recognizing all the references and allusions, he laughed and shook his head and said 'Waal, perhaps some learned old *Turkish* scholar, someone like that.'

12

The Ink Is Mostly Green

In 1927 a contributor to *Poetry* was asked to report on 'what the younger poets now think of Mr Pound'. He answered: 'So far as I can tell they do not think of him. I find no curiosity about him among young people who read or write poetry. Only here and there one runs across some vague knowledge of him. But he is spoken of without enthusiasm.' Archibald MacLeish had much the same impression, remarking in 1930 that if Ezra returned to the USA, far from being 'lynched' as he (Ezra) had suggested, 'Poor devil, not more than ten people would know who he was.'

His early poetry had been regarded as mildly revolutionary. The Cantos, coming much later and not reaching a wide audience until more than ten years after the publication of *The Waste Land*, were received by that audience as a little *passé*. He had helped to set the fashion, but he was late in catching up with it himself.

By the 1930s, Ezra was looking back to the early modernist period as something definitely over, as the 'decade or so' in which 'we tried to get the arts sorted out'. He was now settling into what he liked to think of as a complacent middle age – he was forty-five in October 1930. 'One of the pleasures of middle age,' he wrote in 1934, 'is to *find out* that one WAS right.' This was not a convincing pose. His letters still had all the energy, naïvety, and enthusiasm of a young man. By comparison Eliot, in his public utterances, seemed, as Ezra loved to point out, prematurely ancient. And, thanks largely to his unimpaired effervescence, Ezra began at last to attract disciples.

Several people around 1930 observed that, mercifully, there was no 'Pound school' of poetry. Geoffrey Grigson said he was the kind of poet who would not be a healthy influence on others, because he mostly derived his own poetry from imitating other works of art rather than from personal experience, and if this was imitated in turn the result would be a very unnourishing potation. 'Mr Pound should be allowed to drive his rich, royal coloured coach down his blind boulevard without rearguard or procession,' said Grigson. But the procession was already starting to form. Grigson's own generation, which had grown up reading Eliot and, to a lesser extent, Ezra, was beginning to produce its own work, and imitation was inevitable. Eliot had remarked in the *Dial* in January 1928 that 'Pound has had . . . no disciples'. Four years later this was no longer true.

He had already enjoyed one period of authority as a teacher-cum-leader of 'les jeunes', when he had founded the Imagist movement in 1912. This was one of the roles in which he was happiest, but since then he had had little chance to assume it again. Now, when a new generation discovered him for themselves, it could all begin once more.

He started to pose as Old Ez, the experienced old hand warning the youngsters. He wrote to John Drummond, an enthusiast of his work, in 1932: 'You young, and more especially the chaps who were young ten years ago, don't yet realize how much little pimps and edtrs. have done yew wrrrong.' Some certainly thought of him as a patriarch. John Crowe Ransom, writing in 1935, labelled him 'the father of modernism'. Quick to respond to this, Ezra began to start a new 'movement', herding all his potential disciples into a group.

His chief – and ingenious – technique was to encourage them to communicate with each other as much as with him. He sent a young Italian poet in New York, Lauro de Bosis, to look up Louis Zukofsky, telling him that 'Zuk' was 'the only intelligent man in America'. Similarly, Zukofsky was instructed to make contact with Basil Bunting. Ezra did not, however, simply want to set up a school of imitators. He reproved Archibald MacLeish for borrowing wholesale from the Cantos: 'DON'T work on some damn thing that I have already chewed over . . . Get some gorbloody thing that I have NOT chewed.' Quite what he did want from admirers was not yet clear, least of all to him.

The best of the followers was undoubtedly Bunting, though no publisher in England would touch his work. Eliot rejected a manuscript in 1932 as merely 'a rather fuzzy imitation of the cantos'. Ezra's response was to defend Bunting's work as 'not simple steal from my language and metric/ at least a subject matter is dealt with'. Bunting had learnt a lot of his technique from Ezra's poetry without submerging his own very strong personality beneath it. Also, unlike most of Ezra's disciples over the years, he retained his own style in letters to Ezra, and did not adopt the 'Ez' mannerisms – the peculiar spellings, abbreviations, and punctuation – which were usually mimicked by the weaker brethren. (Later, Bunting also studiously rejected anti-Semitism. In a letter to Dorothy he calls it 'this obsessing redherring', and there follows a wonderfully articulate defence of

Judaism.) Nor, despite Ezra's attempt to make Bunting and Zukofsky into the twin moons of his planet, did Bunting care for Zukofsky's work. In a letter to Dorothy in 1946 he described Zukofsky as being quite sincere and un-sham, but said his poetry was the extreme of subjectivity, which 'nobody *can* read'. However, in his *Collected Poems* (1968) Bunting acknowledges a debt to Zukofsky's 'sterner, stonier' poetry.

Zukofsky's early poems loudly proclaimed his admiration for Ezra. His 'Poem Beginning "The"', printed in *Exile*, might in places have been entitled 'Homage to *Hugh Selwyn Mauberley*':

> The broken Earth-face, the age demands
> an image of its life and contacts . . .
> And why, Lord, this time, is it Mauberley's
> Luini in porcelain . . .?

But he too was no mere Pound-imitator, 'sterner, stonier' indeed than the master, often incomprehensible, but never slavish.

Eliot had no more patience with 'Zuk' than with Bunting. 'His verse is highly intelligent and honourably jewish,' he told Ezra. 'But what the hell can I do with it in London.' And when James Laughlin made a similar comment about Zukofsky's obscurity and subjectivity: 'As to Z// yaaas, I dun told him THAT. Bunting and I both went on telling him JUST THAT.' But 'with so many damnd idiots, I spose when a man thinks at all, one has to put up with the rest of his limitations – but no need to pretend that they ain't there.' And to another correspondent: 'Zuk. understands a great deal/ and his expression gets worse and worse.'

Though he rather despaired of Zukofsky the poet, he encouraged him to write a critical study of the Cantos, telling him he was the first person to credit the work with 'an occasional gleam of intelligence' or the 'possibility of an underlying coherence'. This study was published in the *Criterion* in April 1931. In it, Zukofsky alleged, in prose scarcely more comprehensible than his verse, that the Cantos were 'an ideation directed towards inclusiveness, which sets down one's extant world and all other worlds existing within one', and that its 'general scheme' was 'closely related' to the 'kind of ideation' found in the *Divine Comedy*. Pound, he said, could not be understood by his contemporaries 'not because he is difficult, but because they find it difficult to assimilate the classic matter of the epic as new poetic creation'.

Not all the admirers were prepared to oblige like this. The young American poet and translator Robert Fitzgerald, visiting Ezra in Rapallo in 1932, became worried 'when it appeared that one thing I should do at his bidding was to write a review of his *Cavalcanti*, to be printed by Eliot or Orage'. Fitzgerald was flattered to be asked, but felt that this was not playing the game.

Ezra was soon writing to Zukofsky as 'Filius delectus mihi'. In turn, 'Zuk' described his mentor as 'the master of American poetry and in a sense its father'; and he established a group of poets calling themselves the Objectivists, who, like himself, admired Dante and Ezra and almost nobody else. Zukofsky defined Objectivism as 'Desire for what is objectively perfect, inextricably the direction of historic and contemporary particulars' [sic]. Sheltering under this odd umbrella could be found such diverse figures as Bunting, Robert McAlmon, and William Carlos Williams, who joined because Zukofsky promised that an Objectivist Press, financed by a wealthy young Objectivist, George Oppen, would publish Williams's *Collected Poems* (which it did). Ezra, not to be outdone, told them they should also print his own Collected Prose in twenty volumes. But the Press expired, and the nearest this project came to reality was the publication of *Prolegomena 1–2*, a volume containing 'How to Read' and five chapters of *The Spirit of Romance*, issued by a small publishing house in southern France which then went out of business.

Ezra schemed to get Zukofsky to 'Yourup' on a visit, and sent him his boat fare. Zuk refused to cash the cheque but wrote a poem celebrating the gesture, which Ezra published in the Rapallo newspaper, accompanied by a Latin translation by Bunting. Like all Zukofsky's work, it defied comprehension; Ezra said the Latin was much clearer than the original. Zuk made the trip at his own expense in 1933, being met on arrival at Genoa by Bunting. He proved to be as thin as a pencil, with a cadaverous face, unusually thick black eyebrows, and a voice faint as a whisper, a richly comic contrast with the fierce, bearded, and thoroughly corporeal Bunting. He was given a room in Homer and Isabel Pound's apartment. Homer would take him down to the beach and point at a distant figure swimming on its back, half a mile out: 'See that over there floating? That's my boy!'

Meanwhile, Ezra observed of a rising English enthusiasm: 'I personally do *not* share the Auden craze.' And in 1933: 'This Spender Auden/ particularly Spender bizniz or boo/um beats me. I spose Eng/z being so god damn dead for 12 years that ANY yawp is welcome. But ov all the post Abercrombie / Post Drinkwater trype!!!!' Yeats grouped the newcomers with Eliot and Ezra himself, regarding the whole thing as the incomprehensible younger generation, 'the Ezra, Eliot, Auden school'. He believed Ezra to be a definite influence on the Auden group, saying he was 'probably the source of that lack of form and consequent obscurity' that to him was their chief hallmark. Auden himself allowed that there were 'very few living poets' who could say their work would have been 'exactly the same if Mr Pound had never lived', though that was as far as he would go. He had scarcely looked at Ezra's work, and he owed – as Ezra perceived – almost as much to the Georgians as to modernism.

✳

Ezra continued to weigh up the relative possibilities of Fascism and Communism. In the autumn of 1931 he suggested that 'both the communist party in Russia and the fascist party in Italy are examples of aristocracy, active. They are the best, the pragmatical, the aware, the most thoughtful, the most wilful elements in their nations.' But he thought a Communist revolution would have little to offer the USA. It was not a case of needing to improve the living standard of the common people, as it had been in Russia, but of the Americans being 'too hog lazy and too unfathomly ignorant' to profit from their existing assets.

This inclination to write off Communism was reinforced when he read E. E. Cummings's *Eimi* (1933), a diary of a visit to the USSR, which attacked the regimentation of Soviet life. Ezra called the book 'more alive' and better than 'later Joyce or Gertie', and it finally dissuaded him from giving any support to an ideology that clearly set the needs of the masses above the talents of the individual, and which was never likely to give any special place to artists.

By the end of 1931 he had begun, provocatively, to date his own letters according to the Italian Fascist calendar, which numbered the years from 1922 and the March on Rome. He also designed a letterhead with a drawing of himself by Gaudier-Brzeska at the top. This was printed in red, then a year or so later in green, then blood-red, then dark blue, then black on yellow paper. By 1935 the Fascist date was printed too, so that it read:

ANNO XIII   E. POUND
1935   RAPALLO

Eliot commented:

I will arise & go NOW, & go to Rappaloo,
Where the ink is mostly Green, & the pencils mostly Blue.

Some of Ezra's dialogue with himself about the respective merits of Communism and Fascism took place in the *New Review*, edited by Samuel Putnam. Ezra was named as 'associate editor', and attended a Paris dinner to celebrate the opening number, where he was attacked by a drug-taking Surrealist, who had turned up hoping to stab Jean Cocteau but in his absence settled for Ezra instead. The man, said Putnam, was about to plunge 'a long, wicked-looking knife' into Ezra's back, but 'luckily Bob McAlmon . . . [seized] the assailant's arm'. Putnam adds that Ezra was 'not in the least ruffled'.

Putnam had hoped Ezra would keep the magazine in touch with the work of young writers in Italy, but soon discovered that 'he had quite as vague an idea of what "i giovanni" were doing in the peninsula as he had of the activities of "les jeunes" in France; his interests were wholly limited to the little hand-picked group about him in Rapallo'. The *New Review* soon packed up, and Ezra had similarly fruitless relations with *Hound & Horn*, a literary magazine founded in 1927 by Lincoln Kirstein and Varian Fry, both Harvard undergraduates, which took its title from a line in Ezra's early poem 'The White Stag' ('Bid the world's hounds come to horn!'). Ezra agreed to be an editorial adviser, and sent a group of new cantos for publication, but began also to bombard the magazine with unsolicited abuse about its contents. For example: 'I don't see any use in H & H printing Ed. Wilson, cheapens the periodical.' He and the editors soon wearied of each other, Ezra referring to Lincoln Kirstein by such names as 'Stinkum Cherrystein'. He concluded the affair by branding the magazine 'Bitch & Bugle', and saying it had the worst features of the *Criterion* without the redeeming presence of Eliot. To Kirstein in retrospect, the relationship seemed to have gone sour because 'in spite of his lovely poems and his marvelous letters, we couldn't face the attendant coterie of lame duck discoveries he was always harbouring'. Like Putnam, Kirstein found that the man who had discovered Joyce and Eliot now only wanted to publicize the small fry who happened to be swimming around him.

The only editor still prepared to put up with him *ad infinitum* was A. R. Orage. Not long after Ezra had left London, Orage gave up the *New Age* and, ever susceptible to an unorthodox enthusiasm, went off to America as a disciple of the occultist Gurdjieff. A little later, he came back to England and founded the *New English Weekly*, chiefly as an organ of Social Credit, to which he still adhered. Ezra once again became an Orage contributor, and in 1934 supplied the magazine with a set of extremely unfunny light verses on 'Social Credit Themes', supposedly the work of 'Alfred Venison'. The first of them, 'The Charge of the Bread Brigade', deals with the hunger marches on London (which Ezra had never witnessed). The speaker is supposedly an opponent of the marchers, a contemptible rich industrialist such as Social Creditors deplored. But his attitude to the mob seems to be half shared by Ezra:

> Half a loaf, half a loaf,
> Half a loaf? Um-hum?
> Down through the vale of gloom
> Slouched the ten million,
>   Onward th' ungry blokes,
>   Crackin' their smutty jokes!
> We'll send 'em mouchin 'ome,
> Damn the ten million!

Nearer at hand, Ezra was granted some regular space in the Rapallo newspaper *Il Mare*, to which he contributed a literary column once a fortnight. At first, his pieces were translated for him into Italian, but he was soon writing directly in the language. In September 1932 he told Ford Madox Ford he had been 'saluted as a master of Italian prose', but really his written Italian was idiosyncratic and unidiomatic. He took no trouble to pick up a style from contemporary Italian writers, holding that the country's literature had gone steadily downhill since Cavalcanti and Dante, and grumbling that modern Italians seemed to prefer 'a language of shopkeepers and hairdressers'.

Quite apart from style, readers of *Il Mare* must have been surprised by the content of his articles, which are fully comprehensible only to someone with an extensive knowledge of Ezra's personal history. For example, a 1933 piece, chiefly on women writers, is a series of unexplained staccato reflections on such figures as Harriet Shaw Weaver and Harriet Monroe, and ends – somewhat impertinently in the circumstances – with a gibe at the awfulness of modern Italian prose:

> Dear friends and colleagues 99% of the printed matter in Italy is completely unreadable because it's all written in a dead cadence, but DEEAAAD, dead in the tradition. Even brave and clever futurists fall back into this grey mud from time to time.*

On another occasion he persuaded *Il Mare* to print a conversation between himself and Ford Madox Ford, who was visiting Rapallo. It is hard to imagine what native Rapallesi can have made of several columns comically describing Ford's resolute refusal to give advice about novel-writing.

On his own initiative, Ford organized an elaborate testimonial in support of the Cantos, which was eventually issued as a pamphlet by Farrar & Rinehart, when they published their edition of *A Draft of XXX Cantos* in New York in March 1933. Entitled *The Cantos of Ezra Pound: Some Testimonies*, it included contributions by Ford himself, Hemingway, Eliot, Hugh Walpole (who, said Ford, 'claims to represent English Cathedral closes'), MacLeish, Joyce, Edmund Wilson, William Carlos Williams, Allen Tate, 'H.D.' and Bunting. Ford told Farrar he had done it 'because Ezra is not half as much recognized as he ought to be in his own country', but it was a somewhat backhanded compliment.

It opened with a facetious piece by Ford himself, declaring that 'The periodicals that have supported Ezra Pound have usually lacked readers', and listing him among those artists who have gone 'without recognition' in their entire lifetime. He said almost nothing about the Cantos themselves, being more content to harp on Ezra's personal oddities. Hemingway's tribute was rather vaguely worded ('The best of Pound's writing – and it is in the Cantos - will last as long as there is any literature'), while Joyce, true to form, did not even mention the Cantos, but merely submitted his usual

*English translation by Tim Redman.

thanks for Ezra's efforts on his own behalf. Ezra wrote a note of muted gratitude to Ford: 'Thanks for the abundant wreaths.'

*

He continued to produce more cantos at what he termed a steady 'canter', and published Cantos 31 to 33 in a Massachusetts literary magazine in the summer of 1931. Canto 31 begins with Sigismundo Malatesta's motto, adapted from Ecclesiastes 3: 7, '*Tempus loquendi, Tempus tacendi*' ('A time to speak, a time to be silent'). It consists of prose fragments from the letters of Thomas Jefferson and John Adams.

To Ezra, these men's correspondence seemed 'a still workable dynamo' left from a period when 'CIVILISATION WAS in America', and Canto 31 was meant to show their wide variety of interests, their precision of language, and their clear-headedness in economics. Ezra composed it from a 1905 edition of the works of Jefferson which Eliot had given him, but Eliot did not care for the result, and wrote to Ezra turning down Canto 31 for the *Criterion*:

> Right Honourable Rabbit,
> . . . I enjoyed your Canto, featuring Mr Jefferson, Dr Franklin, and my uncle John, but I am not sure that it is the most suitable to impose upon the illiterate public of Britain. Would you permit me to select one out of Nancy's book . . .?

Elsewhere, Eliot described Ezra's '*longueurs* . . . about mysteries of American history . . . in which I, like most readers, am not adept'.

MacLeish thought that even Ezra himself was not adept in them. He wrote to Hemingway of Ezra's 'conviction that he has read American history – which the facts don't seem to support'. Certainly, Canto 31 treats its sources very oddly. Ezra praised the Jefferson–Adams correspondence for its 'excellent prose', but in the canto he quotes fragments from it (in prose, broken up arbitrarily into verse lines) with a curious disregard for its original cadences, making Jefferson seem more like a modernist poet than an early American president.

Canto 32 applies the same technique to John Adams's letters, while Canto 33 presents a set of prose snippets from various books on government and society. Canto 34, which concludes the group but was published on its own in *Poetry* in April 1933, delves into the diary of John Quincy Adams, Ezra again selecting arbitrarily and abridging with insensitivity to the character of his source. This canto omits its subject's first two names and refers to him simply as 'J. Q. Adams', which is probably just as well in view of a postcard from Eliot to Ezra in October 1934:

> this is to try to stop you from spelling Quincy Quincey where

did you get that Quincey from old John was no Opium Eater though they do say Mrs John was a Great Trial to him you aint got that bit of gossip in yet but you can take it from me Come on we mustnt let you show your ignurance of American literature.

13

Me And Muss/

'Don't knock Mussolini,' Ezra wrote to a young admirer of his poetry in February 1932, 'at least not until you have weighed up the obstacles and necessities of the time. He will end with Sigismundo and the men of order, not with the pus-sacs and destroyers . . . Don't be blinded by theorists and a lying press.' But he was not yet ready to say such things openly, and he prefaced this section of the letter 'private', not among the part that 'you can cite publicly'.

The Futurist leader Marinetti played some part in pushing him over the brink into active support of Mussolini. During the spring of 1932 Ezra was in Rome, where he 'had amiable jaw with Marinetti' and came back 'loaded with futurist and fascist licherchoor'. Most of the Futurist writing was old hat to him – it chiefly 'dated from before 1924' – but the Fascist pamphlets stirred him into a new wave of interest in what the régime was doing. He was on the look-out for a new Sigismundo Malatesta among modern leaders, and he began to think he had found one in Mussolini.

What such a man *did* mattered rather less than what he was *like*. Ezra wrote of Sigismundo that he had 'got things done *Because* never knew what next. – didn't *wait* to do it'. This was usually his own principle, action before reflection. That the Fascists had 'got things done' in Italy, had reformed the transport system, drained the marshes, and carried out other visible public works, seemed an adequate indication that a Malatesta-style ruler was once again in power. And if this were true, then such a ruler would, of course, find room in his new order for great artists and writers.

In April 1932 Ezra began to try to make personal contact with Mussolini. He wrote in Italian to Il Duce's private secretary, Alessandro Chiavolini, stating his desire to communicate to the leader his *proprie impressioni* (personal impressions) of Italy. He received the reply that

Mussolini could not give him an audience, but he was invited to communicate what he had to say in writing. Ezra duly sent back a letter, saying he wanted to talk to Mussolini about:

> I. Some details observed by me while travelling in various parts of Italy in the last ten years, which allow me to appreciate the obstacles overcome by the Fascist effort (marsh-draining, restorations, etc.)
> II. Two areas of anxiety: A. The working conditions in the sulphur mines of Sicily, except in the modernized ones visited [by Mussolini] seven years ago. B. The productivity of the cork industry as compared to that of Portugal, Spain or France.

Not surprisingly, this elicited no reply, for Ezra seems simply to have sought an excuse to meet the man.

His next contact with Mussolini's office was in December 1932, when he sent the script of a film on the birth of Fascism, on which he had been working. This abortive project appears to have been initiated by an Italian named F. Ferruccio Cerio, and Ezra's contribution was to adapt it for a foreign audience. (The film was never made.) In the letter enclosing the script, he asked again to see Mussolini, specifying that he had certain information that could be used in answer to criticisms of Il Duce in the American press. This time he received a reply granting him an audience.

*

They met at 5.30 p.m. on Monday 30 January 1933, in the Palazzo Venezia in Rome. Mussolini received him in the Mappamondo chamber, sitting behind a desk at the far end of the room.

Ezra never gave an account of exactly what took place – as with any other crucial event in his life. He only spoke eulogistically of the impression that Mussolini made on him, describing 'the swiftness of his mind . . . the speed with which his real emotion is shown in his face, so that only a crooked man cd. misinterpret his meaning and his basic intention'.

He had either sent in advance, or brought with him, a copy of *A Draft of XXX Cantos*. Glancing at it while Ezra was speaking, perhaps giving the impression that he had already read it, the dictator remarked that he thought it '*divertente*' (amusing). It can scarcely have been the reaction Ezra had expected, but he chose to take it as a great compliment – indeed, as a brilliantly perceptive judgement of the whole Cantos. In Canto 41, recounting the incident, he says that Mussolini was 'catching the point before the aesthetes had got there'. If Il Duce had really had time, inclination, and enough knowledge of English to look thoroughly at *A Draft of XXX Cantos*, he would probably have been contemptuous. Despite superficially good relations with practitioners of the contemporary arts, the Fascists tended to label anything even remotely avant-garde as 'degenerate'.

After the initial pleasantries were over, Ezra ignored the pretext on which he had gained the interview (Mussolini's portrayal in the American press), and swept on to the matter that most concerned him at present. He handed Mussolini a document that summed up what he believed to be the essentials of Social Credit in eighteen paragraphs. Perhaps Il Duce, not expecting anything like this, frowned as he studied it, for Ezra seems to have made some apology for his inability to present C. H. Douglas's economic theory more clearly, saying that he needed to organize his ideas. In *Guide to Kulchur*, he describes Mussolini asking him: '*Perchè vuol mettere le sue idee in ordine?*' ('*Why* do you want to put your ideas in order?')

It was not totally unreasonable for Ezra to hope that the Fascist Government might listen to Douglas's economic views. Fascism had no economic policy of its own, and the Mussolini régime was not committed to an economic dogma. Its only influence on the economy so far had been to oppress industry with a hierarchy of civil servants, who were intended to police the so-called 'Corporative State', in which management and workers theoretically shared power but which was really run by the bureaucrats.

After half an hour or so, Mussolini indicated that the interview was at an end, and Ezra was shown out. He gathered that he should remain in Rome the next day, in case the dictator wanted to see him again, but no further summons came.

The interview had no effect whatever on Mussolini's economic policy, but Ezra felt that the dictator was thoroughly sympathetic to the objectives if not the methods of Social Credit. He claimed that while Italy was clearly not about to adopt 'the political ideas of Major Douglas', it was nevertheless 'driving towards the result desired . . . by Social Creditors in the economic domain'. In fact, Ezra had little idea of Italian Government policy, and even less of what Fascism meant. But a Sigismundo could do no wrong.

*

Giuseppe Bacigalupo has recalled that when Ezra returned to Rapallo from the interview with Mussolini, 'the town band greeted him'. The residents, Bacigalupo's family among them, were generally sympathetic towards the Government at this period. 'Fascism,' he writes, 'seemed the least of evils compared with the cruel extremes of Stalin's Russia, Hitler's Germany, and unstable and impotent democracies . . . Fascism had repainted the façade even if, behind, the eternal problems were still unresolved. But people were happy with the façade.'

On his return home from Rome, it might have seemed a natural step for Ezra to join the local Fascist Party organization, but he did not. 'I never was a member of the Fascist Party,' he told his captors in 1945, and in 1948 the mayor and some sixty citizens of Rapallo signed a declaration in his support that 'he did not take part in fascist activities in this town. He was not present at local meetings, nor was he a member of fascist organizations'. Ezra himself claimed that he had only entered Fascist headquarters in Rapallo 'once before the war', when 'a Genovese sculptor' had invited him there, 'to see how things were done'.

With hindsight, he stated twenty years later that he had held back from membership or participation because he was 'not dazzled by Mus/' and 'never ceded an inch' of his principles. He even said he had been a 'critic of fascism' rather than a supporter. The only thing he had approved were Mussolini's 'emergency measures IN time and place', certainly 'not a dogma'. But this misrepresented his view in 1933.

He did not join the Fascist Party chiefly because he rarely enrolled in other people's organizations; he preferred to set up his own. And now, after the meeting with Mussolini, he swiftly developed a world view in which the Fascist leader played a central part, and was portrayed as the ideal ruler, but where Social Credit rather than Italian Fascism was the political dogma.

Mussolini was at the centre of his world view because Ezra now hero-worshipped him as a man. 'As a PERSON,' he wrote sixteen months after the audience in Rome, 'M. is more *alive* than anyone except Gaudier, or Picabia WHEN Picabia was himself, whom I have met. Hem. may shoot lions; but he don't play with 'em, in the domestic cage. I like my photo of M. with a live one, better than Hem's with a dead one. And allus regret they disagree. Put it this way: AS A MIND, who the hell else is there left for me to take an interest IN??'

Mussolini had been photographed playing with a young lion, and Ezra told an acquaintance that he had said to Mussolini that 'the only thing he envied him was his lion-cubs'. The comparison with Hemingway is striking; as with 'Hem', Ezra seems to have been attracted to Mussolini largely as an image of tough masculinity. After their meeting he took to referring to the dictator as 'the Boss' or even 'Bull'. In 1934 he wrote to James T. Farrell: 'There is no use . . . blahing about fascist tyranny. Bull Muss has DONE more, and distributed More to the PEEPUL than any yourpeeing govt. and is still going.' And to James Laughlin a year later: 'The Boss here is breaking it gently that the population might conceivably be HOUSED.'

Ezra hung the official summons to meet Mussolini on the wall of his study, and began to keep a scrapbook of the 'Bull's' life and activities. But there was more to this new passion than the hero worship of a masculine image. 'AS A MIND, who the hell else is there left for me to take an interest IN??' That was the candid truth. All Ezra's serious literary interests, apart from the encouragement of a few *jeunes*, had burnt out. He badly needed something else to fuel the fire; had needed it, indeed, for at least the past ten years.

Now that he had finally found the fuel, there was an immediate blaze. Immediately after his meeting with Mussolini he began a period of frenetic activity, in which he set himself up as a prophet of salvation through right economics, an interpreter of history who could save the world from its errors, a scourge of government who could unmask international conspiracies. It seemed as if he felt that his audience with the dictator, however slight its practical outcome, had been almost a divine blessing or laying-on of hands. Filled with apostolic fervour, he began a full-time evangelism of his world view, relegating literature overnight to a status of secondary importance.

It might be supposed from this that he had lost his sense of proportion; yet he was only behaving in character. The fervour he now devoted to questions of economics and government was the same with which he had pushed himself into the London literary world in 1909, had set up Imagism, promoted Vorticism, and championed Gaudier Brzeska, Joyce, and Eliot. If he devoted extra vigour to the job in 1933, it was because he had spent years in search of a new cause, and he was euphoric at having found one. It was like the bursting of a dam. 'Having been a suppressed author for 25 years the stuff DEW mount up,' he told MacLeish, soon after the frenetic activity had begun.

The new field of operation was familiar; the giving of 'medicine' to the USA; trying to set its internal house in order; 'getting ideas into the heads of a few men near the centre of power in the U.S.' After meeting Mussolini, he felt doubly certain of the importance of this, and, during the month following the meeting, he wrote two entire books about it.

*

The first, *ABC of Economics*, was completed in about ten days. It was really a long pamphlet (12,000 words), though Faber and Faber published it as a hardcover book of over 100 pages. The book describes itself at the outset as wishing 'to express the fundamentals of economics so simply and clearly that even people of different economic schools and factions will be able to understand each other when they discuss them'. But this is highly misleading; simplicity and clarity eluded Ezra from the start. He admitted that *ABC of Economics* 'isn't as good as my ABC of Reading'; he promised it would be 'by the time I get to the final revision of it', but there was no revision.

Its chief fault – if one chooses to regard it as a serious textbook – is

Ezra's assumption that the reader already knows and understands C. H. Douglas's Social Credit theory, which the book is supposed to expound. Consequently it becomes a series of Poundian 'divagations' from Douglas, a set of off-beat thoughts on economic or social matters, presented in the form of aphorisms or *pensées* rather than as a connected argument.

William Carlos Williams observed this tendency of mind growing in Ezra during the 1930s: 'He has taken the attitude of being little interested in the intermediary steps [of an argument], his attack and thoughts being occupied with nothing but the peaks of interest. I hope he wears the right glasses or he may in the near future trip over the hem of his skirt.' Eliot, too, noticed this increasing mental habit. After commissioning Ezra to write on one aspect of his economic programme for the *Criterion*, Eliot complained: 'I asked you to write an article which would explain this subject to people who had never heard of it; yet you write as if your readers knew about it already, but had failed to understand it.' Eliot felt that the same defect was present in many of the Cantos, where passages about historical figures read 'as if the author was so irritated with his readers for not knowing all about anybody so important . . . that he refused to enlighten them'.

Ezra was well aware of the unconventional style of argument in *ABC of Economics*, but defended it on familiar grounds. 'Very well,' he writes near the beginning of the book, 'I am not proceeding according to Aristotelian logic, but according to the ideogramic method of first heaping together the necessary components of thought.' But while the Ideogramic Method was sometimes a good tool for poetry, it was ill-shaped for clarifying Social Credit.

ABC of Economics is therefore thoroughly disconcerting if one comes to it hoping to understand what Ezra had picked up from C. H. Douglas. On the other hand, if treated as a set of extra cantos, a collection of Luminous Details from Ezra's imagination, it can at times be rewarding; and, if only for its eccentricity, it is often *divertente*.

Inasmuch as one can distinguish 'steps' in the book's 'argument', they are as follows:

1. With everyone working an eight-hour day, and with increasing mechanical efficiency, there will be over-production. Already, more than enough is being produced for the general need.
2. Nevertheless, many people at the moment who work, or are able-bodied enough to work, do not earn enough money. Meanwhile, someone else has become rich without justification.
3. One source of redress would be to shorten the working day, resulting in a fairer distribution of labour and hence of earnings, but this is not a complete solution.
4. An increasingly large proportion of goods produced never earn proper

wages for the workers. This is because 'some fool or skunk plays mean' with money. So there must be a fairer distribution of 'certificates of work done' (an idealized form of currency).

5. There can be no objection to inflation (the creation of more paper money when more goods are produced), providing it is not merely for the benefit of a few back-room financiers.

6. On the other hand, over-production should not be rewarded. Prices should drop if too many goods are produced.

7. Lower wages but more spare time is an attractive proposition: 'A man with a lot of spare time', Ezra writes, 'can get a great deal more out of life with very little money, than an overworked man with a great deal.' There should also be birth control to limit the size of families and the drain on their resources.

8. In other words, the solutions cannot be achieved only by tampering with the economic system. It may be that there are several possible economic solutions to one particular problem.

9. Nevertheless, the overwhelming question seems to be economic: the problem of how to achieve 'a fair and/or adequate distribution' of 'credit slips' (wages for work done). Ezra has no answer to this, other than to 'keep the work distributed among a sufficient proportion of the people'. To achieve this 'there is probably no equation other than the greatest watchfulness of the greatest number of the most competent'.

10. He now joins with C. H. Douglas in saying that at present 'the manufacturers, owners, traders, etc.' demand from the public more credit slips than the work is worth (that is, charge too high a price), 'or at any rate more credit slips than the government and banks will permit to be available against that work'. So 'there are constantly more goods and constantly fewer and fewer valid certificates' (that is, there is over-production and not enough spending power among consumers). He quotes Douglas's solution: either to 'print more slips' – inflate – or to 'compute the cost in some other way, i.e., to distinguish between real costs and costs according to the traditional book-keeping' – to lower prices artificially in order to bring goods within the spending power of the public.

11. Ezra seems inclined to leave this technical problem to one side, and concludes by reasserting his formula: 'a small amount of work for everyone, with a certificate of work done as the consequence'.

12. He emphasizes finally that the function of bankers and economists is to consider 'the *bonum publicum*, the commonweal and not the shifting and shaking the sieve for the benefit of a few highly placed crooks, scoundrels and exploiters'.

The book's thread of argument is entirely reasonable, even liberal – though Ezra would have disdained that word – in its attitudes to society. But to extract the thread like this is to misrepresent the nature of *ABC of*

Economics, for the argument is buried in a mass of inchoate material which makes it almost impossible to know where – if anywhere – Ezra wants to lead the reader – though much of this material is in itself very amusing, even wise:

> The minute I cook my own dinner or nail four boards together into a chair, I escape from the whole cycle of Marxian economics.
>
> I know, not from theory but from practice, that you can live infinitely better with a very little money and a lot of spare time, than with more money and less time. Time is not money, but it is almost everything else.*
>
> Leisure is spare time *free from anxiety*.
>
> I am an expert [on unemployment]. I have lived nearly all my life, at any rate all my adult life, among the unemployed. All the arts have been unemployed in my time.
>
> One man asleep at a switch can very greatly discommode quite a good railway.

Some of Ezra's arguments have proved prophetic – his call for a shorter working day to decrease over-production and create leisure, and his recommendation of state lotteries as a way of raising money – but on the other hand there are moments when his grasp on the material seems to slip, and he rushes at the task without giving himself a moment to think, let alone research the subject properly:

> What the Major [C. H. Douglas] said fifteen years ago matters less than getting a valid and clear statement . . . If I remember rightly, Major Douglas explained how the wangle was wangled. According to him, if I translate correctly, a certain part of the credit-slips received by the entrepreneurs was wormed down a sort of tube . . . THE BASES OF ECONOMICS are so simple as to render the subject almost wholly uninteresting . . .

A few months after writing *ABC of Economics*, Ezra claimed, in the *New English Weekly*, to be 'an orthodox Douglasite'. But this was in response to an assertion by Orage that he had lost touch with what Douglas believed, and *ABC of Economics* bears Orage out. He had started with only a shaky grasp of the intricacies of Social Credit, and, as he went on, this reduced

*It may be objected that this panegyric of shorter working hours, lower wages, and greater leisure merely reflected his own enjoyment of what he chose to call 'poverty' in the Riviera lifestyle of Rapallo, and is nonsense if applied to the lives of most working people in industrial societies in the 1930s.

further to a set of crude outlines. To these, he attached ornaments of his own, supposing that he was illustrating Douglas's ideas, but in truth constructing his own Gothic cathedral of neo-economics.

ABC of Economics is dated, on its final page, 'Feb. 12 anno XI dell' era Fascista', and contains Ezra's first public statement in support of Mussolini. In the fourth part of the treatise, he asserts that it does not make any difference to the working of an economy whether the orders are issued by 'an intelligent democracy' or by 'an omniscient despot'. Later, he repeats this, and adds that it is of no importance whether the power is in the hands of 'republic, monarchy, or soviet or dictatorship', providing the orders are the right ones. A dictator is defined, in a phrase perhaps deliberately reminiscent of Anglo-Saxon verse, as a 'man of the hour, force of will, favoured of fortune'. Finally, there is a discussion of Mussolini in person.

'Mussolini,' Ezra writes, 'as intelligent man is more interesting than Mussolini as the Big Stick. The Duce's aphorisms and perceptions can be studied apart from his means of getting them into action.' He quotes two of the aphorisms:

> We are tired of a government in which there is no responsible person having a hind name, a front name and an address.

> Production is done by machines but consumption is still performed by human beings.

Ezra asserts that such observations indicate that Mussolini is one of those rulers who perceive the 'dimension QUALITY' as an economic factor as well as quantity.

*

Ironically, in view of Ezra's desire to drive 'facts' chiefly into the heads of leaders and men of intelligence in the USA, *ABC of Economics* was at first only published in London, where a few hundred copies of the Faber and Faber edition reached bookshops in the spring of 1933. Nevertheless Ezra claimed in a letter to Archibald MacLeish a year after writing it, that 'The ABC has brought many souls to the Lord/// They can understand it a damn sight easier than they can Doug// after all it wuz Doug/ told Faber it ought to be printed.' MacLeish commented of the book: 'Pound is really such a bleeding fool when he is doing anything except writing verse.'

Hemingway seems to have seen a copy, or at least was aware that Ezra was now enamoured of Mussolini, since in the spring of 1933 he wrote to him reminding him how little he himself thought of the dictator. Ezra replied that Hem was 'all wet' on the subject. He said that Mussolini had told him the Fascist Government did not 'step in' until people had been given a chance to handle things themselves. Other countries were talking, but Italy was acting. There were new houses, grain was growing where there had been marshes, the trains were smokeless. Hem should get all his money 'out of America' and invest in Italy. Ezra did not wish to 'advocate boy scouts' – the wearing of Fascist uniform – for America, but the USA could profit from the essence of the Italian experiment. He added that Hem would probably disapprove of his new book about it, *Jefferson and/or Mussolini*.

This book, too, was written during February 1933, immediately after the *ABC of Economics* had been rushed through the typewriter. A typescript went at once to his agent Laurence Pollinger in London, but after six months Pollinger had not found a publisher to take it. Oddly, Eliot claimed he had not been shown it, and he wrote to Ezra in November 1933:

> Respected Remus & Limb of Satan,
>   Re Jeff & Mutt what the ell can i do about It when I avnt yet seen that corpussle? why dont you get Round to tellin somebody to show it to me.

Ezra offered it to him, but Eliot replied in January 1934:

> Britons . . . dont know who Jefferson was and never heard of John Quincy etc. You might as well talk to Tammany Hall about the foreign policy of Castlereagh . . . Ought . . . to be published in New York.

Ezra had told Ford he believed that, thanks to the widespread interest in Mussolini, the book would be a real 'seller' and might also 'open up publ/ for the Cantos'; but even the British Union of Fascists (BUF), to whom he offered it in the summer of 1933, turned it down. Consequently, in the *New English Weekly* during the spring of 1934, Ezra described himself as now being 'without the full rights of debate in England, such as are granted to 400 sub-human imbeciles, paid pimps and immature perverters of reason'. Finally, in 1935 Stanley Nott, a London publisher sympathetic to Social Credit, took on the book and issued it in the summer; Boni & Liveright published it in New York the next year. Ezra wrote in the foreword that '40 publishers have refused it . . . It is here printed verbatim . . . as record of what I saw in February 1933.'

Jefferson and/or Mussolini begins by asserting of its two subjects that 'the fundamental likenesses between these two men are probably greater than their differences . . . The heritage of Jefferson, Quincy Adams, old John Adams, Jackson, Van Buren, is HERE, NOW *in the Italian peninsula* at the beginning of fascist second decennio, not in Massachusetts or Delaware.' American liberals are 'completely, absolutely, utterly, and possibly incurably, ignorant of Jefferson'.

Ezra then begins to argue his case, asserting that Jefferson, like Mussolini, 'governed with a limited suffrage' and ran the country chiefly 'by means of conversation with his friends', but he quickly abandons this comparatively logical procedure, observing: 'I am not putting in *all* the steps of my argument but that don't mean to say they aren't there.' He then digresses into such matters as the meaning of the *Divine Comedy*, a definition of '*real* intelligence', and the reader's own supposed reaction: 'I really do not give an underdone damn about your terminology so long as you understand it and don't mess up the meaning of your own words.' And an old friend reappears: 'If the gentle reader wants to think, he can learn how to start from Fenollosa's essay on the Chinese Written Character.'

Eventually, we are brought back to the true subject of the book, which is now dealt with by assertion rather than argument. For example: 'The fascist revolution is infinitely more INTERESTING than the Russian revolution because it is not a revolution according to preconceived type.' He claims to find in Fascism a clear echo of Jeffersonian oratory, describing its proclamations as 'almost a refrain out of Jefferson'. Occasionally, a shaft of uncertainty penetrates his conviction: 'Any thorough judgement of MUSSOLINI will be in measure an act of faith, it will depend on what you *believe* the man means.' He admits that the 'details' of Mussolini's 'surfaces' are 'un-Jeffersonian', but alleges that if one treats Mussolini as '*artifex*' or 'artist', as 'driven by a vast and deep "concern" or will for the welfare of . . . Italy organic', then 'all the details fall into place'.

He would use the term 'artist' of Mussolini often over the years, claiming that Il Duce had the artist's self-confident, inspired, intuitive approach to the business of government. By looking at the dictator in this fashion, he had found a way of coping with the fact that the man *was* a dictator. If he was an artist, then obviously he had the right to do as he saw fit. Art is not a product of the democratic process.

Of Mussolini's specific actions and policies we learn almost nothing from the book. It appears (yet again) that he has drained marshes; he has 'persuaded the Italians to grow better wheat, and to produce Italian colonial bananas'; but few other facts are supplied. Ezra denies that the Fascist censorship of the press amounts to more than the gentle reprimanding of editors who disagree with the Government, and says he prefers this to the self-censoring attitude of the English press, which simply dares not publish reports on the true state of the nation: 'A great deal of yawp about free Press proves on examination to be a mere howl for irresponsibility.' As for personal liberty, the 'freedom' valued by present-day liberals is merely a shunning of responsibility, and 'NOT the ideal liberty of the eighteenth-century preachers'. Certainly one should demand justice, 'but

Mussolini has been presumably right in putting the first emphasis on having a government strong enough to get the said justice'.

After this, it seems odd to find Ezra winding up the book in moderate terms:

> This is not to say that I 'advocate' fascism in and for America, or that I think fascism is possible in America without Mussolini, any more than I or any enlightened bolshevik think communism is possible in America without Lenin.
>
> I think the American system *de jure* is probably quite good enough, if there were only 500 men with guts and the sense to USE it, or even with the capacity for answering letters, or printing a paper.

He asserts that Mussolini has simply shown America that, by comparison with Italy, the country is not managing any longer to execute 'the driving ideas of Jefferson'. Those ideas do not 'FUNCTION actually in the America of this decade', and a 'vigorous realignment' will be necessary in the USA before they can. This does not mean a revolution, Italian or Russian style, but it definitely requires 'an orientation of will'. On the last page, he affirms that 'the Duce will not stand with despots and the lovers of power but with the lovers of ORDER, τὸ καλόν'.

The conclusion, then, is a disappointing splutter. Mussolini is returned to his pedestal; there is no call for any radical external change in the American system of government; and Ezra tells the reader that the ultimate responsibility for the future lies not in any political ideology, but in the good sense of the individual. Again, the word 'liberal' seems the only appropriate term, although he hated even the faintest suggestion that the label might be appropriate to him. 'Call me a liberal and I'll knock yr/ constipated block off,' he wrote to Louis Zukofsky around 1935. Yet he declared in print: 'A good state is one which impinges least upon the peripheries of its citizens. The function of the state is . . . to prevent the citizens from impinging on each other.'

As soon as *Jefferson and/or Mussolini* was finished, Ezra sent a typescript to Mussolini with a brief summary of the book, together with a printed copy of *ABC of Economics*. They reached Il Duce from the Press Office of the Ministry of Foreign Affairs, who passed them to him with the comment that they 'clearly demonstrate a friendly feeling for Fascism'.

In December 1934 when someone asked him to write another piece on Joyce, Ezra replied: 'I will not LOT'S WIFE. There is too much future, and nobody but me and Muss/ and half a dozen others to attend to it.'

14

Rabbit So Bad

Wyndham Lewis had meanwhile become an admirer of Hitler. After visiting Germany he called the Führer 'the expression of current german manhood', and praised the people's determination 'not to take their politics at second-hand'. He had not bothered to read *Mein Kampf,* and simply thought he had found a kindred spirit. He persuaded himself that Hitler was essentially peaceful, and would moderate his anti-Semitism once he had fully grasped power. Lewis tried to convince the British public of this in his hastily written *Hitler* (1931), a book of which Ezra approved.

Eliot, too, had flirted a little with Fascism, writing in the *Criterion* in 1929 that 'it is conceivable that in particular circumstances fascism might make for peace, and communism for war . . . I believe that the fascist form of unreason is less remote from my own than is that of the communists'. But his 1931 poem 'Coriolan' was intended to show the futility of political power, and in *After Strange Gods* (1933) he preached a society founded on religious rather than political stability. Three years later he defined 'the movement towards the Right' as 'a symptom of the desolation of secularism'.

Eliot's return to religious belief did not surprise Ezra; he said Eliot had always seemed Christian to him. But he got endless delight out of caricaturing Eliot as a desiccated clergyman, 'the Reverend Eliot' – an image that Eliot liked to live up to. 'In virtue of the authority given to me as a Director of this firm,' he wrote to Ezra from Faber and Faber, 'I give you my blessing for 1934, expiring on Dec. 31st.' And, referring to his official duties at St Stephen's Church, Gloucester Road, he signed one letter 'Vicar's Warden'.

Throughout the 1930s Eliot continued to find Ezra an endless source of amusement, often writing to him in a parody of Ezra's own irascible style.

Ezra was not sure how to respond; increasingly trapped in his own performance, he now lacked the agility to cope with the variety of poses Eliot was still able to adopt. Yet he admitted that Eliot was 'constantly ALIVE in private letters, at least to me', and regretted that prudence prevented him from writing publicly in the same style.

He discussed – or rather ranted about – Eliot's choice of a religious rather than an economic dogma, in a review of *After Strange Gods* in the *New English Weekly*, dismissing the modern church as 'an irrelevance' because it did not concern itself with 'vital phenomena in ECONOMICS'. He said nothing whatever about Eliot's book, except that it was 'full of lacunae'. In fact, Eliot did take an interest in economic solutions: in the spring of 1934 he was one of those who helped circulate a letter urging some 'scheme of national credit' to ease the Depression. Replying to Ezra's review, he said he was 'in sympathy' with Social Credit, but complained of the 'fanaticism' of Ezra's writings about it, saying they 'seem to degrade it', to which Ezra observed: 'It is amusing, after so many years, to find that my disagreement with Eliot is a religious disagreement, each of us accusing the other of Protestantism.'

He still admired some of Eliot's new work; he wrote of *Sweeney Agonistes*: 'His fragments of an Agon are worth all his stage successes.' Eliot as popular playwright did not appeal to him. 'Waal, I heerd the MURDER in the Cafedrawl on th radio/ lass' night,' he wrote to a friend in January 1936. 'Oh them Cowkney voices, My Krissze them cawkney woices! Mzzr Shakzpeer STILL retains his po/sishun.' And he had nothing better to say about *Old Possum's Book of Practical Cats* (1939). 'Waaal I dont think much of pollical CATS/' he told Agnes Bedford, and continued

> sez the maltese dawg to the Siam kat
> Whaaar's old parson Possum at?
>   etc//

He could be scathing about all that Eliot had done since *The Waste Land*, telling Charles Olson: 'We mowed the grass for him, so he could set up his doll house.' Yet his attacks on Eliot were largely sham. He admitted to Olson that he had never read *After Strange Gods* properly, and when James Laughlin criticized Eliot Ezra replied: 'Possum . . . is carryin' on. He maintains a bulletin board / almost only one in Eng/ where honest news CAN be placarded . . . also he and F.V.M. [Frank Morley of Faber] are getting me slowly into print.'

There was nothing personal in the attacks. He now treated all living writers (and many dead ones) as 'irrelevant' if they did not deal with economics. The 'limitation' of all modern American fiction, he said, was that its authors did not 'place their characters in an economic setting'. Joyce was useless because he was uninterested in Social Credit and the machinations of international bankers. 'People too lazy to examine the facts are not intelligent enough to write interesting books,' he told Robert McAlmon, attacking McAlmon and Hemingway. 'And thass that.'

His last meeting with Joyce was in Paris in 1934. The two of them had dinner with Hemingway, who nine years later described the occasion: 'Joyce was convinced that he [Ezra] was crazy then and asked me to come around when Pound was present because he was afraid he might do something mad. He certainly made no sense then and talked utter rot, nonsense and balls as he had made good sense in 1923.' But this was written after Hemingway had seen a transcript of one of Ezra's wartime broadcasts, when the question of his sanity had begun to be raised, and Hemingway's recollections were probably influenced by this.

Nevertheless by the mid-1930s some of Ezra's old friends were becoming wary of him. Yeats kept his distance after 1933, a year in which he received a rebuff. Now sixty-eight and feeling that he was too 'barren' to write poetry, Yeats had nevertheless forced himself to complete a new play, *The King of the Great Clock Tower*, and he went down to Rapallo to ask Ezra what he thought of its lyrics. Yeats continues:

> I asked him to dine, tried to get his attention . . . but he would not speak of art, or of literature, or of anything related to them . . . He said, apropos of nothing, 'Arthur Balfour was a scoundrel', and from that on would talk of nothing but politics. All the other modern statesmen were more or less scoundrels except 'Mussolini and that hysterical imitator of his Hitler' . . . He urged me to read Captain [*sic*] Douglas who alone knew what caused our suffering. He took my manuscript and went away denouncing Dublin as a 'reactionary hole' because I had said that I was re-reading Shakespeare, would go on to Chaucer, and found all that I wanted of modern life in 'detection and the wild west'. Next day his judgement came and that in a single word 'Putrid'.

In a private journal, Yeats gives a more detailed account of the episode. Ezra said the lyrics had been written in 'Nobody language' and would not do for drama. Yeats at first took this as confirmation of his worst fear – that he was too old for poetry. But then he decided that 'nobody language' was something he could remedy, and he apparently worked at the play again before it was published and performed. In 1934 he asked Olivia Shakespear to send Ezra a newspaper cutting describing its successful stage presentation, 'that I may confound him. He may have been right to condemn it as poetry but he condemned it as drama. It has turned out the most popular of my dance plays.'

Ezra showed no remorse. 'So difficult to kick old friends in the fyce when they get sloppy,' he wrote. 'I have, but very few do.' Many years later he recalled how 'I tried for God's sake to prevent [Yeats] from printing a thing. I told him it was rubbish. All he did was print it with a preface saying that I *said* it was rubbish.' He told Basil Bunting in 1936 that Yeats was now 'dead', was 'clinging to the habit of being a writer', that his recent poetry was 'slop', and that he himself found 'increasing difficulty' in 'reading the buzzard'.

Yeats got his own back when he discussed Ezra's poetry in his *Oxford Book of Modern Verse* in 1936. 'When I consider his work as a whole,' he wrote,

> I find more style than form; at moments more style, more deliberate nobility and the means to convey it than in any contemporary poet known to me, but it is constantly interrupted, broken, twisted into nothing by its proper opposite, nervous obsession, nightmare, stammering confusion; he is an economist, poet, politician, raging at malignants with inexplicable characters and motives, grotesque figures out of a child's book of beasts. This loss of self-control, common among uneducated revolutionists, is rare – Shelley had it in some degree – among men of Ezra Pound's culture and erudition.

Yeats said privately that he had exhausted himself reading through Ezra's work for the *Oxford Book* – he had constantly found 'a single strained attitude instead of passion, the sexless American professor for all his violence'. Nevertheless he asked Ezra for permission to use a large number of his poems: three from *Cathay*, three from *Homage to Sextus Propertius*, three from *Hugh Selwyn Mauberley*, 'The Lake Isle' (Ezra's parody of Yeats), 'The Return', 'Ité' (a short piece from 'Lustra'), and Canto 17 (the earthly paradise). Ezra replied to him: 'Dear W.B.Y./ My regular fee is five guineas per poem to all anthologists . . . This does NOT cover America, where there is an equivalent fee of 25 dollars per poem.' (This was at a time when Americans could eat for a dollar a day in Europe.) To which Yeats answered:

> There is only one man in the English language as expensive as you and I am going to reduce him to one poem . . . I can spend twenty pounds on poems from you . . . I should like to use Canto XVII and anything else from my selection you can throw in. I have personally never got more than two guineas for a poem on either side of the water. It is clear that I shall have to raise my charge.

Ezra agreed to let him have 'The River-Merchant's Wife' and one of the *Propertius* poems 'thrown in' with Canto 17.

The two men met again when Yeats paid a last visit to Rapallo in the winter of 1934. Ezra afterwards said he wanted friends 'to chloriform me before I get to THAT state'. Their final encounter was during a visit by Ezra to London in the autumn of 1938. Yeats's *New Poems* had just appeared, and Ezra remarked that some of them were 'quite good' – which, said Yeats, was 'very high praise from Ezra'.

Yeats died in January 1939; Ezra afterwards provided his own version of the celebrated epitaph:

> 'Neath Ben Bulben's buttocks lies
> Bill Yeats, a poet twoice the soize
> Of William Shakespear, as they say
>
> Down Ballykillywuchlin way.
>
> Let saxon roiders break their bones
> Huntin' the fox
>   thru dese gravestones.

*

He had indeed, as Yeats observed, reduced literature to a branch of politics. In September 1933 he defined literature as 'journalism that *stays* news'. The only literary activity that really interested him at present was translation; he wrote to encourage Laurence Binyon with his English version of Dante, and similarly egged on W. H. D. Rouse with a prose translation of Homer. But even this had an economic tinge: he told Rouse that the present economic 'sabotage and obstruction' had put the modern world out of contact with the classics, and a new translation was therefore a blow against the usurers.

He took a little interest in the Basic English movement (a proposed simplification of the language for international use), telling its inventor C. K. Ogden that with fifty more words than Basic at present allowed, he could make it 'into a real licherary and mule-drivin' language . . . You watch ole Ez do a basic Canto.' But his own vocabulary was becoming anything but basic. In 1936 he drew up a manifesto demanding clearer terminology in the public discussion of economic issues; yet it was couched in such obfuscating and idiosyncratic language as to be scarcely comprehensible. He now used his personal collection of favourite words to the point of self-parody: '. . . the putrid habits of the bureaucracy . . . you cannot get the whole cargo of a sinking paideuma into the life-boat . . . You can divagate into marginalia . . .'

His published writings now assumed that the reader shared his know-ledge of such people as 'Steff' (Lincoln Steffens) or Frobenius and Fenollosa, who were referred to as if they were as well known as Dante and

Cavalcanti. As Eliot wrote to Ezra in 1934: 'I dont mind printing things I disagree with . . . But I do worry about printing what I dont Understand.'

Ezra's frequent insistence on accuracy of expression now seemed to count for nothing, at least in his own writing. *ABC of Economics* and *Jefferson and/or Mussolini* are full of vague allusions and loose terminology, and he was less inclined than ever to check facts. He wrote in the latter book, of the Fascist revolution in Italy:

> I can't remember which year contained what, possibly in '21 the cavalieri della morte passed through the Piazza San Marco, and when I got to Milan that year I asked my friend what about it . . . Or perhaps that was the year when one was lucky to get there at all. I did go out via Chiasso by tramway but I suspect that was 1920 and that in '21 or '22 or whatever spring it was, I hadn't any excuse save an interest in other matters . . .

Yet at this period he could still say to Basil Bunting: 'The poet's job is to *define* and yet again define . . . LUCIDITY.' And in a 'digest' of the *Analects* of Confucius, made by him in 1937: 'If the terminology be not exact . . . you cannot conduct business properly . . . An intelligent man cares for his terminology.'

Robert Fitzgerald admitted that Ezra's letters and other missives to the outside world from Rapallo had 'the tone of a man no longer in touch . . . What had seemed high-hearted and really Olympian fun began to seem childish and beside the point . . . Only a man working in isolation, without criticism or ignoring it, could have failed to see the fretfulness and poverty of argument.'

Part of the trouble was simply that he wrote too much, too fast. Now that he was into what he called one of his 'fits of work (bordering on insanity)' he simply did not stop to think, to re-read or consider what he was turning out. 'God I beat this eight hours,' he wrote on his typewriter to James Laughlin in December 1935, 'and forgot what I meant to start the day with.' And to Agnes Bedford: 'I seem to beat this damn machine progressively more hours per day as the working day gets shorter.' Giuseppe Bacigalupo, by then in his mid-twenties and training in medicine, saw little of Ezra in Rapallo during this period, but at their occasional meetings was struck by his changed manner: 'It was not possible to hold a normal conversation . . . He had come increasingly to adopt the attitude of someone who assumes that the person he is talking to shares his own interests and knowledge, so that some cryptic allusion seemed to him to be enough to explain what he was thinking – a hypothesis which was far from well-founded.'

Though the haste with which he conducted his work was principally motivated by an urgent desire to set the world right, Charles Olson, talking to him a decade later, perceived that it was also haste for its own sake, a sheer love of headlong speed. 'There is haste in Pound,' Olson wrote, 'but it does not seem to be rushing to any future or away from any past. It is mere impatience (it is how he got his work done) and, more important, an intolerance of the mind's speed (fast as his goes), an intolerance even of himself.'

If this impatience was intended to lead to the achievement of his economic and political objectives, it was utterly counter-productive. Many of his articles written during this period make the confused and over-hasty *ABC of Economics* seem, by comparison, a model of clarity. A typical piece, printed in *Hound & Horn* under the title 'Criterionism', begins by giving some mild praise to the *Criterion* for raising British standards of criticism, goes on to allude in vague terms to an essay in an earlier issue, asserts that *Ulysses* is 'a diagnosis of the *Daily Mail*', wonders how Christendom lost its 'unity', compares this to the present situation in Russia, and says it is pointless 'stopping to argue about free will and the immortality of the soul' with 'European civilization going to Hell and America not getting on with the work fast enough'.

This piece was unsolicited, and he bombarded other journals with similar verbose contributions. (Favourite targets were the Paris editions of American newspapers, which received a ceaseless flow of letters from him on his political and economic obsessions.) Bernard Bandler of *Hound & Horn* eventually tired of this bombardment, and rejected an article by Ezra on the grounds that it was merely 'a vast assortment of information and ideas which you have dashed off on a typewriter'. He asked, 'What exactly is the relation of all these [ideas]?' To which Ezra answered: 'Damn it all the reader must do something, can't have it all predigested and chewed and peptomized.'

In a later *Hound & Horn*, Dudley Fitts echoed Bandler: 'Mr Pound's prose sounds as though its author were trotting in his nightshirt through a cobbly street, prodding an ancient typewriter suspended upon his bosom.' Ezra defended himself against such attacks on the grounds that 'There are more questions in my head than I can set down with apparent coherence.'

By the mid-1930s Robert Fitzgerald that that 'in that beautiful intelligence all was not going well'. Yet Fitzgerald had to admit that, when one met him face to face in Rapallo, he was 'quieter in talk and less positive than his writing; he did not impose himself, as the writing rather did'. Certainly, as Bacigalupo observed, his conversation was often incomprehensible, but the sheer fury was mostly restricted to the typewriter, and usually came to an end when the machine was pushed aside. He still loved the leisured Riviera life, was still prepared to observe his own precept in the *ABC of Economics* about the value of free time. 'Don't work more than the legal hours as envisaged by Forward Lookin' economists,' he told

MacLeish. And as for reports that he had become embittered and abrasive: 'It won't wash, everybody who comes near me, marvels at my good nature.'

Eliot continued to derive amusement from the spectacle of Ezra Furioso, remarking of it (in a letter to Ezra) that 'the rattle of musketry is reported from the Ligurian Coast and it is Said that an allgemeine Mobilmachung of the Swizz Army has been ordered'. As in London days, the language of Ezra's letters and published writings was less like genuine anger than a man pretending to be angry. 'God damn it . . . damn it . . . god damn blithering idiots,' run the expletives in a letter typical of the mid-1930s (to MacLeish), 'God damn 'em . . . why the hell . . . the bastards . . . shotten shitten and pewky potbellied bastard . . . arserag . . .' Eliot knew how to treat such missives when they arrived at Faber and Faber: he wrote back after one such:

> Your undated communication to our accountant has been passed to me. Without animadverting on the tone which you thought fit to adopt toward an accountant who is young and unmarried and has never heard such words as you have introduced into your invective . . .

In another note to Ezra, signed 'F. X. Sweeney', Eliot writes that 'Owing to the Obsxurity of yr. episstlary style I had done nothing about anything . . . me ead was dizzy & when I got yr. Letters I come over all of a Hoo Ha. & I aint done nothink . . .' In a 1934 note to Dorothy, Eliot speculated: 'I wonder what makes the Rabbit so Bad I think he must have been a Choir Boy when he was young thats an Idea . . .'

Ford Madox Ford expressed no opinion, but might have cited words he had used in his novel *A Call*: 'Don't you think that, since his mania, if it is a mania, is so much along the lines of his ordinary character, that it is an indication that his particular state is not so very serious?'

Ezra admitted in private that he was enjoying himself in this new role. In 1934 he told MacLeish: 'The Economic scrap is more important/ immediate/ in general, more fun.' And to James Laughlin he reported contentedly: 'Am running top speed and likely to emit folly.'

15

Casa 60

All this manic activity was reflected in the Cantos. Though it had taken him fifteen years to write the first thirty, in the seven years from 1934 to 1940 he produced forty-one more, most of them intended to be taken as instruction in economics or government. *Eleven New Cantos: XXXI–XLI* was published by Farrar & Rinehart in New York in October 1934, and by Faber and Faber (as *A Draft of Cantos XXXI–XLI*) the following spring. This time Ezra was willing to put them at once 'into cheap edtn. (sacrificing the folio profits) pro bono pubco'.

The new set opened with the four American cantos (Jefferson and John Quincy Adams). Then came Canto 35, which begins 'So this is (may we take it) Mitteleuropa', and is an attempt to convey the character of mid-European culture following the First World War. After dismissing the Emperor Franz Josef as 'that lousy old bewhiskered sonvabitch of whom nothing / good is recorded', it proceeds to narrate, in their own voices, some of the memories of the aristocratic and bourgeois relics of the Austro-Hungarian Empire. There are some good moments, good phrases – particularly the term 'general indefinite wobble' to express the cultural and racial uncertainty of the era. The canto's sole purpose, apparently, is to portray this 'wobble', to demonstrate what Ezra elsewhere called 'the difference of races inside the Austrian conglomerate ... stuck together, glued together, tied together with stray string dynastic contraptions'. (He drew his material mainly from what he was told during a visit to Vienna with Olga in 1928.) But the canto itself suffers from 'indefinite wobble', has too many unidentifiable names and half-explained anecdotes to convey even this simple message satisfactorily.

Canto 37 deals with the public activities of Martin Van Buren, another early American president whom Ezra regarded as heroic, this time because of his fight against the banks. Canto 38 is another montage of Mittel-europa, but also contains one of Ezra's rare lucid explanations of the problem that Social Credit claimed to cure:

> A factory
> has also another aspect, which we call the financial aspect
> It gives people the power to buy (wages, dividends
> which are power to buy) but it is also the cause of prices
> or values, financial, I mean financial values
> It pays workers, and pays *for* material.
> What it pays in wages and dividends
> stays fluid, as power to buy, and this power is less,
> per forza, damn blast your intellex, is less
> than the total payments made by the factory . . .
> and the power to purchase can never
> (under the present system) catch up with
> prices at large . . .

Canto 40 concludes with a summary of the *Periplus of Hanno*, an account of an Odyssey-like voyage to Morocco by a fifth-century BC Carthaginian. Its significance to Ezra is not made clear by the canto, but the word *periplus*, usually (though incorrectly) in the accusative form *periplum*, was hereafter added to his store of favourite code words. Strictly speaking, the word, which came into Latin from the Greek language, means 'circumnavigation', but Ezra used it idiosyncratically to describe the limited but supposedly truthful view one may obtain through the use of the Ideogramic Method. Canto 41, which concludes this batch, begins with a thumbnail sketch of Mussolini and his achievements, echoed from *Jefferson and/or Mussolini*: 'Having drained off the muck . . . / From the marshes . . . / Water supply for ten million . . .'

Even Ezra was not sure how to treat many of these cantos. Writing to Harriet Monroe, who disliked Canto 37, he admitted that 'economics are *in themselves* uninteresting, but . . . Van Buren was a national hero, and the young ought to know it'. He told a reader in 1934: 'Skip anything you don't understand and go on till you pick it up again.'

Among reviewers of the new sequence, John Crowe Ransom in the *Saturday Review of Literature* felt that the 'solid material ingredients' which had gone into most of the cantos 'involve the reader in a gigantic feat'. The greater part of the sequence certainly offends against Ezra's own maxim in 'How to Read': 'Great literature is simply language charged with meaning to the utmost possible degree.' Similarly in *ABC of Reading* he declared: 'Incompetence will show in the use of too many words.' And he cited with delight Bunting's discovery that a German–Italian dictionary rendered *dichten* (to write poetry) as *condensare*, to condense. Yet the greater part of his poetry was now written on the principle of accumulation rather than condensation. The more 'facts' he could cram into it, the happier he was.

Eliot teased Ezra about this at Christmas 1934 when he sent him a copy of a new book entitled *The Money Supply of the American Colonies before 1720*, inscribed

> Rabbit from Possum
> for Canto XCI
> Noel Noel!

Ronald Duncan asked Ezra why he no longer wrote in the manner he had perfected in *Hugh Selwyn Mauberley*. He received the curt answer: 'You write it.'

However, two cantos in the new sequence were very different both in subject matter and voice. They show him still thoroughly capable of fine poetry, and belong to quite another area of his experience and outlook. Canto 36 is for the most part a translation of Cavalcanti's canzone 'Donna mi prega'. Ezra had already translated it in his 1932 Cavalcanti book; that rendering of the poem was criticized by Étienne Gilson in the *Criterion* (October 1932), which may have encouraged him to make a new one for the Cantos. More probably, he was not yet satisfied with his attempt to transpose into English something of personal importance to him, and he wanted to try again.

The language of the canto is archaic: an attempt to translate Cavalcanti's medieval Italian terminology, of which Ezra did not claim to have a complete understanding, so it is particularly difficult to comprehend at first reading; but in it Ezra is undoubtedly trying to explain his own beliefs about love and sexuality. 'A lady asks me . . .' begins the canto; her question is, how does love operate? Ezra/Cavalcanti delivers this answer:

> Where memory liveth,
>   it takes its state
> Formed like a diafan from light on shade . . .
> Cometh from a seen form which being understood
> Taketh locus and remaining in the intellect possible
> Wherein hath he neither weight nor still-standing,
> Descendeth not by quality but shineth out . . .
> He is not vertu but cometh of that perfection
> Which is so postulate not by the reason,
> But 'tis felt, I say . . .

It is almost impossible to translate this into comprehensible prose, but the gist appears to be that love is not a rational process, but the passive experience of pure form. This is felt in the same part of the mind that experiences memory ('dove sta memoria' is Cavalcanti's phrase, 'where stands memory'). The general idea, as Ezra himself said, 'is Platonism' – the perception of perfect forms. He also observed: 'It is a truth for elect recipients.'

He may have completely misunderstood the Cavalcanti canzone, which could be simply a poetic description of ordinary mental processes, rather than an attempt to say anything erudite. But Ezra had convinced himself that Cavalcanti was some sort of religious–philosophical heretic, who had a message of special value about the nature and function of love.

Eliot realized this. In *After Strange Gods* he remarks that Ezra 'finds Guido [Cavalcanti] more sympathetic than Dante . . . on grounds which have very little to do with their respective merits as poets: namely, that Guido was very likely a heretic, if not a sceptic – as evidenced partly by his possibly having held some pneumatic philosophy and theory of corpuscular action which I am unable to understand.' Yeats was also unable to understand it. After puzzling over Ezra's earlier attempt to translate 'Donna mi prega', he wrote to him saying he realized it was obviously 'your religion, your philosophy, your creed, your collect', but the poem was 'far from explaining itself'.

This was fair comment, and perhaps because of it, Ezra provided Canto 36 with one line of thoroughly clear explanation – in Latin of apparently his own composition: 'Sacrum, sacrum, inluminatio coitu'. ('Sacred, sacred, the illumination in intercourse.') This is a recapitulation of his assertion, in his 1921 postscript to the Remy de Gourmont book, that sex leads to mental enlightenment.

The theme of sexual love as an experience of 'sacred' intellectual illumination is taken up again in Canto 39, which begins with a description of Odysseus' men at the house of Circe – differing from Homer in that, alongside men transformed into beasts, there are girls sated with sex: 'Girls talked there of fucking, beasts talked there of eating, / All heavy with sleep, fucked girls and fat leopards.'* Circe is described in sexual terms: 'Venter venustus, cunni cultrix' ('Beautiful belly, cultivator of the cunt') and 'Song sharp at the edge, her crotch like a young sapling'. Sexual pleasure is portrayed in lines taken from the *Paradiso*: 'Che mai da me non si parte il diletto' ('So that never will the delight leave me'), 'Fulvida di folgore' ('luminescent in its splendour') – the latter being Dante's description of the heavenly light. Canto 39 concludes with a description of a fertility rite, which leads to the conception of a god:

*The 1934 Farrar & Rinehart and 1935 Faber and Faber editions of these Cantos printed all the text uncensored. The 1933 *Draft of XXX Cantos* issued by these publishers had left the text of the Hell Cantos unaltered, except that Farrar & Rinehart printed 'sh-t' instead of 'shit'.

Beaten from flesh into light
Hath swallowed the fire-ball . . .
His rod hath made god in my belly . . .
I have eaten the flame.

Ezra still held to his old obsessive interest in the love cult of the troubadours and its supposed descent from the Eleusinian Mysteries. Indeed, Canto 39 is his first full statement of this sexual–religious credo.

In *ABC of Reading*, published the same year as Canto 39, he speaks cryptically of 'a whole body of knowledge, fine, subtle' which he alleges had 'lain in the secret mind of Europe' in the medieval period, and which is 'far too complicated to deal with in a primer of reading'. Elsewhere in the book he speaks, again mysteriously, of 'certain problems' which are not susceptible to 'laboratory proof and experiment' and can only be examined through 'the introspective analysis of highly sensitized persons'. In *Guide to Kulchur* he writes rather more explicitly on the subject. The Platonic tradition, he says, has caused 'man after man to be suddenly conscious of the reality of the *nous*, of mind, apart from any man's individual mind, of the sea crystalline and enduring, of the bright as it were molten glass that envelops us, full of light'. (He derived the association of sexual love with light from such Neoplatonist philosophers as Erigena, mentioned in Canto 36, who believed that all created matter is filled with divine light.) But such an experience is only for the elect. These are 'the mysteries, Eleusis. Things not to be spoken save in secret,' he continues in *Guide to Kulchur*. 'Fools can only profane them. The dull can neither penetrate the secretum nor divulge it to others.'

He had no intention of discussing his Mysteries in more explicit terms. He wrote to a correspondent in 1939: 'The mysteries are *not* revealed, and no guide book to them has or will be written.' And to another correspondent the same year: 'The minute you proclaim that the mysteries exist *at all* you've got to recognize that 95% of yr. contemporaries will not and can not understand *one* word of what you are driving at.'

His irrational attitude to sexuality affected the general drift of his life in the 1930s – not domestically, for the Ezra–Dorothy–Olga triangle persisted without variation during these years, but intellectually. If enlightenment could, as he believed, come to the intellect in this mysterious fashion, through coitus, it should not, he felt, be sought in more cold-blooded ways. In *Guide to Kulchur* he complains that the Mysteries are banished by rational thought, by logical argument: 'Some sort of vital instinct . . . [feels] the menace of logic-chopping, of all this cutting up, rationalizing and dissecting of reality.' His obsession with the Mysteries was therefore an oblique contribution to his growing irrationality and loss of judgement as the 1930s advanced.

*

Circe's 'ingle' in Canto 39, with its sex-sated girls, is introduced by a description of a hill path: '"thkk, thgk" / of the loom / "Thgk, thkk" and the sharp sound of a song / under olives'. This is a depiction of the track leading up from Rapallo to the hilltop hamlet of Sant'Ambrogio, where from 1929 Olga rented a small apartment in the upper storey of a peasant house. This was to be her home for part of the year; she could live there more cheaply than in Venice, and could sublet her Venetian house profitably during the tourist season.

Ezra found the apartment for her, at Casa 60, Sant'Ambrogio, a mile or two above the town. 'I never actually cared very much for Rapallo myself,' Olga has said. 'If you once get *outside* Rapallo it's all right, but Rapallo itself as a place –!' More sophisticated in her social tastes than Dorothy and Ezra, she preferred village life to the rather tawdry resort.

Maria Rudge first came to her mother's apartment in Sant'Ambrogio in 1939. She describes the approach from Rapallo:

> We climbed for almost an hour on a broad cobbled path, on narrow stone steps flanked by gray holding walls, upwards under olives, past eucalyptus and lemon trees. The sea so different from the Venice sea, colors sharp and clear . . . Casa 60 was orange-coloured, with Ionic columns painted on the outside walls, a flight of smooth black lavagna steps leading up to the green front door half hidden by Virginia creepers and honeysuckle. *Thk thk thk* GRR: the sound of the olive press on the ground floor. *Ploff, chuu*: the bucket hitting the water in the well.

Stella Bowen, now separated from Ford Madox Ford, visited Rapallo and was invited by Olga to spend the night at Casa 60:

> She warned me to wear stout shoes and to bring the smallest possible luggage. We left the lights of Rapallo at midnight [after a concert], and as soon as we were outside the town, Olga changed her evening slippers, hitched up the skirts of her evening dress, and slung her violin-case on a strap over her shoulder. Then we began the slow, steep ascent of a cobbled, zig-zag mule track through the pitch-black olive terraces, losing our way, stumbling on invisible steps, and bumping into someone's silent cottage. It was a long way up . . .

Ezra was amused by the pronounced differences between Sant'Ambrogio and Rapallo – differences seen, at least, in the eyes of the two communities. 'Mrs B's cook is taken to the "mountains",' he writes in

Jefferson and/or Mussolini, 'that is to say she is taken uphill about a mile and a quarter, and she weeps with nostalgia for the sea, said sea being clearly visible from the kitchen window.' Indeed it was: walking on the old Roman road on the hilltop, or standing by the church wall, gazing over the Zoagli cliffs, one could see across the bay and almost pick out individual figures on the promenade outside the Pounds' flat in the town below.

'In twenty minutes,' wrote Ezra, 'I can walk into a community with a different language, the uphills speaking something nearer Tuscan and the downhills talking Genovese.' Even the weather was different. Canto 46 portrays a typical hilltop day in Sant'Ambrogio:

> That day there was cloud over Zoagli
> And for three days snow cloud over the sea
> Banked like a line of mountains.
> Snow fell. Or rain fell stolid, a wall of lines
> So that you could see where the air stopped open
> and where the rain fell beside it.

Ezra did not sentimentalize the life of the Sant'Ambrogio peasants. Olga says that the olive press produced 'awfully good olive oil', but Ezra was more interested in persuading the locals to grow peanuts. They in turn paid little attention to him; the husband of the family on the ground floor of Casa 60 described him as 'always working'.

Maria found Casa 60 as striking as her parents' hidden nest in Venice:

> The house inside: light. White and empty. Polished red brick-tile floors. A square entrance, and four doors open on rooms with a view to the sea, olives and a blossoming cherry tree. Pale blue and pink vaulted ceilings with painted morning glory convoluting into bouquets and wreaths.

Stella Bowen provides practical details:

> Her home was the upper floor of a peasant's house, every room of which seemed to be surrounded by windows . . . The house had no water-tap and no electricity, and the cooking was on charcoal. Olga preferred pine-cones, and used them with as much success and precision as most people achieve with a gas-tap. She had almost no material possessions, but her well-proportioned rooms furnished with big rectangles of sunshine had a monastic air which was highly conducive to the making of music. Her rent was seventy-five lire a month and she supported herself by the sporadic letting of a charming little gondolier's house which she still owned in Venice.

As usual, Ezra provided home-made furniture, all of it unpainted this time, and very plain: a long bookcase and a mirror in the entrance hall, a dining table and four straw-bottomed chairs, a desk, a shelf for music and the violin, a bookcase under the window in Olga's bedroom. These were augmented with a few pieces known as 'the Yeats furniture' because they had come from the flat Homer and Isabel had taken over from the Yeatses.

Maria has described her father arriving at Casa 60 after the long climb up from Rapallo:

> 'MIA' – and the rattle of Babbo's stick on the front door. He was laden with parcels, papers and envelopes sticking out of his pocket. We relieved him of the encumbrances while being kissed and gently buffeted on the cheeks. He went into his room to change and then threw himself on the orange couch. There was nothing in 'his' room except two of his stools, a change of clothes and a packing-case dresser ingeniously disguised by chintz. Mamile in the meantime prepared the tea . . . Her room was the centre of the house. After the tea ritual and some chitchat, Babbo: 'She feel up to the Chaconne?' And I heard Bach's Chaconne, probably for the first time.

Maria was the only person to be admitted, in those days, into the private world of Ezra and Olga. She notes that they spoke to each other in 'their third-person language': '"He take the child for a walk and show her." "Yes, ma'am."'

On that first visit, when her mother played the Chaconne, she had some understanding of what they felt for each other: 'In Venice I had heard her practice for hours and had been oppressed by the sound . . . Now a new person stood in front of me . . . I had a glimpse of their true world.' Only a glimpse; and she does not speculate about their life together, their feelings for each other. Olga's house, in Canto 39, appears by implication as Circe's bower, but it is hard to believe that Ezra saw her as Circe, though she had persuaded him to beget their only child.

Meanwhile, others, not in this innermost circle, began to gossip about Ezra dividing his life between Dorothy in Rapallo and Olga up the hill. Ronald Duncan alleges that he 'used to spend his evenings with Olga, his days with Dorothy'; another version has it that five nights were allocated to Dorothy and two to Olga. 'It was apparent,' says Duncan,

> that he had a deep affection for both, but neither ever referred to the existence of the other. This omission gave the situation an appearance of Jamesian unreality: but it appeared sophisticated and civilised on the surface. Rose Marie [Duncan's mistress]

and I tried to remain that on the surface, though we lunched
with Dorothy and dined with Olga.

Daniel Cory, who lived in Rapallo at this period, had always thought
Ezra and Dorothy 'happy enough together', so he and his wife were now
amazed to hear 'from the gossip of the small English colony' the
complications of Ezra's life. 'Perhaps something I said to Ezra one evening
betrayed the fact that I had got wind of this arrangement: he suddenly
started to rave against "the middle-class mentality of this bloody English
bunch".'

16

Ezuversity

The presence of Olga spurred Ezra into organizing concerts in Rapallo, following the example of Manlio Dazzi, the librarian at Cesena whom he had met ten years earlier. The first Rapallo performances were in June 1933, when Olga and a pianist, Gerhart Münch, gave a Mozart Week of a dozen sonatas in the local cinema, 'under the auspices of the Fascist Institute of Culture'. Ezra wrote a programme note in Italian, describing the sonatas as the musical equivalent of the *Paradiso*, and Basil Bunting, who, like Ezra, had once written music criticism, contributed a front-page article boosting the concerts to *Il Mare*.

The success of this first series led to the inauguration of a grander project, which Ezra entitled 'Concerti Tigulliani' after the Bay of Tigullio on which Rapallo is situated. He was allowed free use of the town hall, and he acquired financial support from Homer, Dorothy, and Father Desmond Chute, a languid Anglo-Catholic who had exiled himself to Rapallo. The charge for admission, wrote Ezra,

> is ten lire *to those who can afford it*, five lire to anyone claiming student privileges . . . two lire to members of the Circolo de Cultura and to members of the town bands of Rapallo and Santa Margherita; and I might add free admission to a few people who deserve it.

All the proceeds went to the performers, save a 10-lire tip to the town hall caretaker and payment of printing expenses.

The first of the Concerti Tigulliani was in October 1933. Olga and Münch were again among the performers, but other professional musicians took part too, and the season included music by Debussy and Ravel as well as items from the baroque repertoire. Homer and Isabel 'came to the concerts loyally', Olga remembers, and Ezra proudly reported an appearance by the Princess de Polignac, née Singer, daughter of the sewing-machine millionaire and former patron of Stravinsky, who 'sat thru the second show after 9 hours train trip from Rome and no dinner . . . She is now among the "sostenitori" [patrons]. We have also bought a Steinway pyanny and will give it to the town, after which we will possibly procede towards the amortization of the third foot of the instrument, now aerially suspended over my credit.' Naturally, Ezra reviewed the concerts himself. His first report in *Il Mare* described how

> the Town Hall was crowded with the most distinguished clientele, mainly from the tourist colony . . . [It is] one of the finest and most successful attractions that Rapallo has succeeded in organising . . . It is my belief that the taste, at least the official taste in Rapallo, is for the moment pure (100%). We prefer Bach unadulterated, we do not ask for concessions from the ideas of the pre-fascist era.

Sometimes in these reviews he would lavish praise on Olga: 'Olga Rudge's sound, her tidy technique . . . the truly aulic rhetoric of her music . . .' and in *Guide to Kulchur* he writes: 'We have not had an unlimited number of executants having sensibility such as that possessed by Olga Rudge and by Münch.' Privately he was not always uncritical. 'Münch plays in time / Olga can now play in time/,' he told Ronald Duncan in 1938, five years after the start of the concerts. Münch, said Ezra, was a prickly character whose lack of 'social suppleness' had stopped him having a 'career'. Ezra thought poorly of his attempts at composition, but when Münch made a version for violin of a Jannequin piece imitating birdsong, Ezra eventually printed the music as Canto 75.

Later Concerti Tigulliani included performances of music by a newly rediscovered seventeenth-century composer, William Young, and, in a private house, Münch playing the complete 'Well-Tempered Clavier'. Ezra was quick to make use of any professional musicians who happened to be within reach; Father Chute recalls how 'rare and unforgettable little concerts' would spring up at short notice. Needless to say, Ezra had his own principles on which he believed that a concert programme should be constructed. '*Block* in this context was a great word with Ezra,' writes Father Chute; 'not only did he insist at rehearsals on "blocks" of light and shade in the performance of old music, he also demanded integrated and consecutive programmes.' In *ABC of Reading* he asserts that the juxtaposition of Bach and Debussy, and of Bach and Ravel, in two consecutive concerts, taught the audience 'a great deal more about the relations, the relative weight, etc., of Debussy and Ravel than they could possibly have found out by reading ALL the criticisms that have ever been written of both' – the Ideogramic Method applied to the concert hall.

Although the concerts were very much an Ezra–Olga enterprise, Dorothy supported them uncomplainingly, and wrote enthusiastically about one of them to one of Ezra's correspondents in America: 'I am sorry you missed our Nuovo Quartetto Ungarese – as they are the most extraordinary performance . . . The Bartok V quartet took me to Genghis Khan and the Golden Horde! and a whole series of fantastic Paolo Uccello's.' But the real discovery of the concerts was Vivaldi.

Vivaldi's music had been neglected since immediately after his death in 1741, and was generally judged 'only a fit amusement for children' – a reference to the fact that the composer had taught at a girls' school in Venice. Part of the trouble was sheer over-production: among his surviving compositions are nearly 500 concerti. By the 1930s there was beginning to be some scholarly interest in him, but very little.

He was brought to Olga's attention by Manlio Dazzi, who had moved from Cesena to be curator of the Querini Stampalia collection in Venice; he showed her some Vivaldi letters, and explained that the principal collection of manuscript scores was in Turin, where they were being guarded by a jealous professor. Reluctantly, this scholar allowed Olga to examine them, and it immediately became clear to her, as Ezra put it, that 'the enormous "continent" of Vivaldi's work has not yet been explored, let alone catalogued with precision'. He wrote a note to Olga urging the fullest investigation: 'I want all the facts . . . Find out just what you are allowed to study/ and what notes are permitted . . . Dont waste any time feeling indignant.'

The result, according to Ezra, was that Olga turned up 'three hundred and nine inedited concerti', and began to make a 'thematic catalogue', which Ezra hoped to have published. He was as much delighted by the technical challenge of the operation as by the actual music. Having stumbled across the use of microfilm when working on Cavalcanti manuscripts, he saw the immense possibilities it offered for Vivaldi, and immediately sent for a film of items from the second largest holding of the composer's manuscripts, at the Sächsische Landesbibliothek in Dresden. He began to make transcripts from the film, and admitted that he was more excited 'copying out the Dresden concerti . . . note by note, and being pleased by the quality of Vivaldi's mind therein apparent' than by hearing the same music played by 'a heavy and heavily led orchestra'.

This operation went on during 1938, when he reported having to use a 'desk magnifying glass' to study the film because a microfilm reader was not available (he had spent '15 months' trying to get 'ANY precise answers' as to what they cost and where they could be bought). However, he had enlargements printed from the film, and with the aid of these he embarked on adding a keyboard continuo part to some of the concerti, with a view to performance. 'Shd/ like yr/ opinYun as to whether I have done enough or not enough filling of pyanny part//,' he wrote to Agnes Bedford. 'The syncopation etc/ will give PYANNER enough to occupy attention.' And in another letter: 'Have just done 3 photopages of a nother/ not much fun as Viv. has written in parts so fully that there is vurry little one can add on the PY/a/no.'

In Rapallo, he and Olga announced a 'study-workshop' which would begin by 'reading all Vivaldi's works for two violins and piano'. Ezra was exultant about their discoveries. Bach's music seemed to him materialist by comparison: 'Vivaldi moves, in his adagios, in the sphere of the Paradiso.' And 'Viv's' oratorios made 'ole pop Handel look like a cold poached egg what somebody dropped on the pavement'. He felt he and Olga were especially suited to the task of discovery and transcription; there had been 'too much musical scholarship by non-performers'. He contemplated instigating 'a decent LIBRARY of the chief composers/ beginning with the greater *inedits*'.

The culmination of the enterprise came in September 1939, when the Accademia Musicale Chigiana in Siena held a Vivaldi week, with prominent Italian musicians taking part and performances of works that Olga and Ezra had discovered. The Accademia was the creation of Count Chigi, a Renaissance-style patron who gave over his Sienese *palazzo* to an annual musical festival; Olga worked as his 'public relations secretary' for part of the year. She and Ezra also staged some Vivaldi concerts in Venice. The Second World War interrupted the project, and when the widespread Vivaldi revival began in the post-war years the Olga–Ezra work played no significant part in it. It has been said that Ezra and Olga preserved a number of Vivaldi works from being utterly destroyed, by obtaining a microfilm of the Dresden collection and placing it in the hands of the Sienese academy, but though the Dresden library suffered in the bombing of that city, only one manuscript that had been microfilmed for Ezra was damaged, and none destroyed.

The Rapallo concerts were never a success with the public; in his *Il Mare* notices, Ezra complained that they were ignored by 'the bourgeoisie, the inhabitants of the great villas and backward, short-sighted hotels . . . We expected a reasonably large public. It was bitterly disappointing. It was almost as if the idea of a better and nobler culture was hateful. But I console myself by remembering the gratitude and warm response of the small handful of people.'

*

He was now writing dozens of letters each week to monetary reformers, politicians, and public figures of every kind. He claimed that postage stamps were now the biggest item in his budget, while the return mail was so great that 'Pound, Rapallo' was sufficient for the postman to find him. Some of his correspondents began to show strain. Eliot alleged that he was now being retained by Faber and Faber 'at a salary named in five or six figgers' solely 'to superintend the department devoted to correspondence with Mr Ezra Pound'; and Major C. H. Douglas himself, whom Ezra consulted on the finer points of Social Credit, said he would soon have to engage 'a whole-time secretary to correspond with you'.

Ezra now regarded the world beyond Rapallo largely as a source of 'snippets' of news, of 'factual atoms' which, if laid side by side Ideogrami-cally, would prove his hypotheses about an international financial con-spiracy. To an American senator he wrote pointing out that Anthony Eden, a newly appointed British cabinet minister, 'is the son-in-law of the Westminster Bank, so THAT mystery is largely explained' (that is, the bankers and the politicians were clearly in cahoots against the real needs of society). He said he often 'howled in vain' for 'odd bits of supplementary knowledge' of this kind, which would (he believed) prove the Ezra–Douglas theories right. To one correspondent he wrote asking for 'a list of serious characters in England, if any known to you. My own, outside the field of economics, is very short.'

New catchphrases began to appear in his vocabulary. He wrote to a professor at Penn that there was a 'Time Lag, between real culture and that TAUGHT'; he became obsessed with the notion that it took ideas an appallingly long time to filter through to the population. Another favourite phrase was 'Volitionist Economics', the title he gave for a while to his own brand of Social Credit. He distributed a questionnaire under this heading to public figures around the world, asking them what side they were prepared to take in the economic struggle.

In April 1934 Frank Morley played a practical joke on him. He sent Ezra a copy of a new book by Franklin D. Roosevelt, *On Our Way*, with a fake autograph and supposed personal inscription to Ezra from the President. Ezra spotted that the inscription was a fake, but took the autograph as genuine. Since he had found a small misprint in the book ('willing' for 'unwilling') he wrote to the President to point this out. He signed the letter – which was dated according to the Fascist calendar – 'With best wishes and . . . convictions that you have not yet publicly shared.' (The President apparently read the letter, for his copy of the book contains a correction of the error initialled by him, and the mistake was rectified before Faber and Faber produced their edition.) Morley's joke had unwittingly turned Ezra's sights on Roosevelt.

Roosevelt had come to office in 1933, promising vigorous action against the Depression, and had instituted his first New Deal programme in the following year, providing public-funded work for the unemployed and trying to mend the shattered economy. At first Ezra judged him 'still a more or less nebulous figure' to whom was attached merely 'a little discreet hope and family rumour that F.D. understands this and that'. By contrast, Mussolini seemed 'a male of the species'.

Ezra hoped vaguely that he himself might have some part to play in the New Deal. In August 1934 he asked Hemingway if he could 'push me over on Washington'. He thought Roosevelt should be criticized for not calling home 'the best brains from abroad'. Around this time he wrote to MacLeish: 'If Frankie DON'T see C. H. Douglas he is just a plain god shatten fool . . . My feeling re/ F/D is that he either *WANTS* or NEEDS to be pushed along.'

He sent a picture postcard to Roosevelt. He had had it printed himself; it bore a photograph of a 'banknote' his grandfather Thaddeus had issued to his employees at the Union Lumbering Company in Chippewa Falls. On the back of the card Ezra wrote:

> Lest you forget the nature of money/ i;e; that it is a ticket. For the govt. To issue it against any particular merchandise or metal, is merely to favour the owners of that metal and by just that much to betray the rest of the public. You can see that the bill here photod. has SERVED (I mean by the worn state of the note).
>
> Certificates of work done. That is what these notes were in fact/ before the bank swine got the monopoly.
>
> Thus was the wilderness conquered for the sake of pork-barrelers who followed?

He signed himself: 'Cordiali saluti.'

He had similar hopes of teaching Social Credit to the USSR; he wrote to John Cournos: 'Are you in touch with any of these Rhooshun blokes you write about in *Criterion*? Would there be any way of inducing any Rhooshian intelligentsia to consider Douglas and Gesell?'

*

'Gesell' was Silvio Gesell (1852–1930), who now began to replace C. H. Douglas in Ezra's mind as the economic Messiah. Born in Germany, Gesell made a fortune in business in South America, then briefly served as Minister of Finance in the short-lived Lindhauer Government in Bavaria in 1919. He was later imprisoned, his ideas having been rejected by the Nazis. Though he shared Douglas's hatred of the existing capitalist system, Gesell believed its injustices should be remedied not by Government intervention in the form of subsidies or dividends, but by changing the nature of money itself, so that the rich were actually penalized rather than rewarded for hoarding capital. He expounded his theory in *The Natural Economic*

Order, first published in 1906 and subsequently enlarged. The frontispiece of the 1929 English translation shows him to have been virtually a *doppelgänger* of Ezra, fierce-eyed, bearded, restless-looking.

Gesell proposed that the existing currency system, in which coins and banknotes are themselves regarded as having an intrinsic value, should be entirely abandoned. Instead, he argued for the establishment of 'Free-Money', a currency which, if it is not used quickly to buy something, 'goes out of date like a newspaper, rots like potatoes, rusts like iron', and is therefore valueless for hoarding. Spending and keeping money in circulation becomes the only logical thing to do. The system by which the rich accumulate money and lent it at interest disappears overnight.

This is to be achieved by a simple process. 'Free-Money' takes the form of pieces of paper resembling ordinary banknotes in that they bear a printed statement as to their value, but they also contain blank spaces on which small stamps must be stuck at regular intervals to keep the Free-Money at its face value. These stamps have to be bought from the Government. The purchase of them is therefore a tax on money, and produces revenue for the public benefit. If no stamps are purchased, the note becomes valueless and cannot be exchanged for anything. Because of the stamping system the Free-Money has often been referred to as 'stamp-scrip'.

Gesell intended to put the system into operation in Bavaria, but the Government in which he held office fell from power. However, his theory caused some interest among economists. J. M. Keynes described it as essentially 'an anti-Marxian socialism' and said that the idea was certainly 'sound', though he believed that in practice a series of substitutes for currency would be found which could be hoarded with impunity – jewels, precious metals – so that the problem would remain unsolved. He allowed, however, that Gesell had 'flashes of deep insight and only just failed to reach down to the essence of the matter'. In the USA Irving Fisher wrote a book on Gesell, and Ezra first heard of stamp-scrip when he read and reviewed it for the *New English Weekly* (October 1933).

He was immediately impressed by the simplicity and clarity of Gesell's system, which harmonized with Douglas and Social Credit in that it regarded money as simply 'certificates of work done', but claimed to abolish the evils of usury at a blow without any of the dubious complexities of Douglas's dividends and subsidies. Unlike Social Credit, there was no evidence that it would create inflation. It was also, Ezra observed, 'a sane mode of taxation . . . a tax on . . . stagnant money, which is obviously money for which its owner has no immediate need, or is too stupid or torpid to make use of'.

From now on, his own economic writings gave much more emphasis to Gesell and stamp-scrip than to Douglas and Social Credit. He wrote: 'If

Douglas really does not understand Gesell, then Douglas is done for. If his clique is afraid to discuss Social MONEY, then we must dismiss them as impotent sectaries.' He later recorded that he had 'dropped soc/ credit schemes for Gesell/ precisely because Gesell needs LESS bugogracy', whereas Douglas would have increased the bureaucrats. (It was not precisely true to say he 'dropped' Social Credit; as with all his fanaticisms, he retained it in his writings, even though he had moved on to something else. He never rejected old ideas, merely assimilated them into new ones.) He was also bored with the sectarianism of the Social Credit movement, which had split up into various warring factions, and he hated 'the sort of paralysis' which he said always seemed to creep over Social Creditors as soon as they got 'near action'. In response John Hargrave, a prominent member of the Social Credit movement in Britain in the 1930s, called Ezra's contributions 'worthless . . . a series of explosions in a rock quarry'.

*

His visitors in Rapallo were lectured on Gesell and stamp-scrip. They were becoming more numerous; Ezra might have lost interest in most purely literary projects, but an increasing number of young writers and poets wanted to sit at his feet. Among them was Ronald Duncan, who had first corresponded with Ezra because he wanted to interest him in a pacifist pamphlet he had written. Ezra told Duncan that he had failed to give a proper emphasis to economics; Duncan replied with 'a rude postcard in verse, mourning the black-shirted poet and pointing out that the black shirt was probably because he was mourning for the talent he had lost since writing "Mauberley". This . . . only produced more letters from Pound, who approved my rude verses and urged me to start a poetry magazine.'

Duncan's first visit to Rapallo was in 1937; Ezra reported that he 'had the sense to come down here from Marseilles for 12 hours in order to consult the high and final EZthority, you can see he knows eggs'. He bombarded Duncan with instructions about the magazine, which was to be called *Townsman*, and suggested its motto should be 'Duncan hath banished sleep'. Duncan afterwards recorded of this first encounter that 'Ezra taught me more in one day than I had learned in a year at Cambridge . . . And, like many other students at Rapallo, I continued to have, as it were, a post-graduate course by postcard from the Chancellor.'

Duncan was lucky in that this first tutorial concentrated chiefly on literature (particularly Cavalcanti). Others hoping for literary instruction would get Gesell and stamp-scrip instead. Carlo Izzo, Professor of English and American literature in Venice, sometimes brought 'some shy young man interested in poetry', whereupon all too often Ezra would

challenge the newcomer by pulling out a ten-lire note and

telling him to look at it carefully, to read the fine print. What did it mean, what did it say, what did he know about the nature of money? Nothing. Unless he understood the nature of money he could not understand or write good poetry. Then followed a list of assignments. The young man seldom came a second time.

Even Homer Pound was called into this battle. Ezra had already told Louis Zukofsky that unless his poetry became 'econ/ conscious' he would be excluded from Ezra's next anthology. (There was no such anthology.) Homer backed this up a month later when he wrote to Zuk: 'Ezra had me read your book of poems and I must confess that it seems to me you could spend your time and talents on a much more needed Message to the world. Put your book aside, take up Social Credit.'

Homer (who evidently had not yet caught on to Gesell) wrote on a letterhead printed with the Ezraic motto 'LEISURE SPARE TIME FREE FROM ANXIETY'. Zukofsky responded to this by writing angrily back to Ezra, complaining that Ezra himself no longer bothered to 'weigh each word' in his own writings, and wishing he would go back to producing poetry in the vein of the best Cantos.

Ezra was only willing to let Faber and Faber publish a collection of his purely literary essays, without any economic content, after persuasion by Frank Morley. He decided to call it *Make It New*, this being his current translation of the inscription on the Chinese bath tub which is cited in the *Ta Hio*. In Canto 53 he writes:

> Tching . . .
>   . . . wrote MAKE IT NEW
> on his bath tub
>   Day by day make it new
> cut underbrush,
> pile the logs
> keep it growing.

Eliot told him that he and Morley did not feel 'altogether happy about your new title MAKE IT NOO we may have missed subtle literary allusion but if we do I reckon genl public will also'. Ezra, unrepentant, kept the title; in *Make It New* he chose to print various essays on the troubadours, Arnaut Daniel and Elizabethan classicists, making it another 'course' on comparative literature, like his earlier prose collections. The book, published late in 1934, was reviewed appreciatively in the *Bookman* by Samuel Beckett, who called it 'education by provocation'. (A second similar volume was published by Faber and Faber in 1937, this time consisting of what Eliot and Morley had wanted all along – fairly recent and largely abusive pieces by Ezra about contemporary authors, selected by Eliot, who gave it the ironic title *Polite Essays*.)

One visitor came to Italy in 1936 to meet Ezra the economist rather than Ezra the poet. This was the only American politician willing to pay serious attention to Ezra's letters: George Holden Tinkham, a rich Republican congressman from Boston, who had once fought a campaign to keep the United States out of the League of Nations. Ezra had been alarmed by a photograph of Tinkham which suggested that he might be Jewish, but this proved misleading – 'Waal, I been took fer one me self,' said Ezra.

Tinkham was taken to meet Maria Rudge, who was told to call him Uncle George. But she did not warm to him. 'How his dirty fingernails and his smacking the waitress's young fanny were compatible with being a great man and a friend of Babbo's I could not quite figure out.'

'Uncle George' was an adventurer who claimed to have been round the world twelve times. He took Ezra and Maria to places he said he remembered from military service in the First World War, and told tall stories about big game hunting, fragments of which are to be found in *The Pisan Cantos*. In 1939 Ezra wrote to the *Boston Herald* proposing 'Uncle George' for President: 'It is time we had something AUTHENTIC in the White House.' To Wyndham Lewis he described him as 'male 100%'.

Another visitor pleased Maria much more: 'The tallest young man . . . anyone had ever seen . . . he . . . tried to talk to me in German and in Italian.' Afterwards he sent her two books from America, Celtic legends and the *Arabian Nights*, inscribed 'Love from Jas.'

James Laughlin IV, aged eighteen, wrote his first letter to Ezra from the Alps in August 1933: 'Dear Ezra Pound – Could you and would you care to see me in Rapallo between August 27–31?' Back came the reply by telegram: 'VISIBILITY HIGH.'

Laughlin's letter explained that 'I am American, now at Harvard, said to be clever . . . I presume to disturb you, because I am in a position (editor *Harvard Advocate* and *Harkness Hoot* (Yale)) to reach the few men in the two universities who are worth bothering about, and could do a better job of it with your help.' Specifically, Laughlin wanted 'advice about bombarding shits like Canby & Co' (Henry S. Canby, editor of the *Saturday Review of Literature*), and 'sufficient elucidation of certain basic phases of the Cantos to be able to preach them intelligently'.

It was the sort of letter Ezra himself might have written at eighteen, and there were a number of resemblances between him and his correspondent. Born in 1914 in Pittsburgh on the same date as Ezra, 30 October, into a family with a large share in the huge Jones & Laughlin steel company, James Laughlin 'simply could not get on' in the 'country-club existence' offered by his parents' social milieu, particularly after Dudley Fitts, who taught him at Choate School, Connecticut, had opened his eyes to modern literature, including Pound and Eliot. He went on to Harvard, but was a loner there: 'I was . . . not good at getting on with people. Harvard was very cliquish and socially conscious. Coming from Pittsburgh, I didn't rate with the boys who had been to Groton or Milton.'

His chief desire after a 'boring Freshman year' was to take off for Europe, and he was granted leave of absence for the trip on the grounds of strained eyesight. Armed with an introduction to Gertrude Stein, he spent a month in her company in Haute-Savoie, during which she made him write press handouts for her forthcoming American lecture tour, mend punctures on her little car, and look after her dogs. Worn out by this, he decided to take advantage of the epistolary friendship that existed between his old teacher Dudley Fitts and Ezra.

'Expect, please, no fireworks,' Laughlin told Ezra by letter. 'I am bourgeois-born . . . But FULL of "Noble Caring" for something as inconceivable as the future of decent letters in the US.' When he arrived he proved to be six feet five inches tall, with a genial, steady manner, ready to be instructed by Ezra, but stubborn too. 'So I came to Rapallo, I was eighteen then,' Laughlin writes in an autobiographical poem,

> And you accepted me into your 'Ezuversity',
> Where there was no tuition, the best beanery since Bologna,
> And the classes were held at meals in the dining room of what
>   you called the Albuggero Rapallo,
> Where Gaudier's head of you sat in the corner, an astonishment
>   to the tourists.
> Because it was too heavy to tote up to the fifth floor of Via
>   Marsala 12/V
> And might have bust through the floor.
> And you showed me with some relish that if one looked at the
>   back of the cranium it was quite clearly a scrotum.
> Literature (pronounced literchoor), you said, is news that stays
>   news . . .
> Your conversation was the wittiest show in town,
> Whatever you'd heard or read was in your head as fresh
>   as when it first came there.
> The books you loaned me were filled with caustic
>   marginalia . . .
> And in de Maille's *Histoire de la Chine* (Paris, 1777) you'd
>   put a big star
> Beside the part where he tells how Emperor Tching had MAKE
>   IT NEW painted on his bathtub . . .

When the Ezuversity was not in session, Laughlin would accompany Ezra for a swim or a game of tennis, or would go to the cinema with him:

'The movies were simply awful, but Ezra loved them. He'd sit up in the gallery with a cowboy hat on and his feet up on the rail, eating peanuts, roaring with laughter.' Sometimes Dorothy would take Laughlin into her own sitting room and, solicitous towards his eye trouble, would read to him from Henry James.

Laughlin did not immediately take in the complexities of Ezra's life. Olga would often turn up at the Albergo to eat with him and Ezra, but there was no indication of anything other than friendship between them. Laughlin, though nearly twenty years her junior, made a mild pass at her; Gerhart Münch had to explain the situation to him in private.

Laughlin showed Ezra some of his own poetry, wry and self-deprecating, lucid and amusing, displaying not the faintest trace of any Pound influence. Possibly for this reason Ezra was unjustly dismissive of it, telling him: 'No, Jas, it's hopeless. You're never gonna make a writer . . . I want you to go back to Amurrica and do something useful.' Laughlin 'said "Waal Boss," (I used to call him "Boss"), "Waal Boss, what's useful?" He thought a moment and suggested . . . "Go back and be a publisher."'

But first, said Ezra, Laughlin must return to Harvard and finish his studies, so that his family would agree to finance his publishing activities. This Laughlin did, majoring in Italian and Latin. On his return he determined to make over the *Harvard Advocate* to Ezra – to print new Cantos in it, then 'publish them in good type and format' via someone else's small press. Meanwhile, his letters to Ezra from Harvard began to parrot the 'E.P.' manner. In October 1933 he wrote: 'I should be orgasmikally content to see Cantos invade Cambridge . . . the lady publisher [with whom he intended to collaborate] . . . knows shit & non-shit . . . goddamitall Harvard is the best over here . . .'

Laughlin has said he was 'raised with 100% anti-semitism' in Pittsburgh. Ezra now found that this 'diffident' but also 'savage' young man (as he described him in a letter to Laurence Binyon) was a ready audience for his own attitudes. Indeed Ezra himself was a little perturbed by Laughlin's fierce determination to publicize and publish every facet of his work. 'DON'T for gards zake print anything of mine, merely because it is me,' he counselled him in December 1933.

Laughlin printed Canto 38 (the second *Mitteleuropa* canto) in the *Advocate* in February 1934, and began to look for a second-hand printing press. 'May be able to get Jeff & Muss printed yet,' he told Ezra, whom he was now addressing as 'Granfer', signing his own letters, 'Laughlin'. Ezra in return began one letter 'Dilectus Filius (or wotever the god damn vocative may be).'

Laughlin was back in Rapallo in the summer of 1934, and Ezra took him, Olga, and Laughlin's Harvard classmate John Slocum up to Salzburg in a hired car. Toscanini was conducting *Fidelio*. 'Ezra didn't think much of

Beethoven. After about twenty minutes into the opera, Ezra rose up and said in a very clear voice, "No wonder! The man had syphilis!" He started out, and we all, of course, felt we had to file out with him.' Laughlin adds that the audience thought Ezra was referring to Toscanini.

At Salzburg they met Douglas Fox, assistant to Frobenius, and Laughlin was indoctrinated in this part of the Pound canon. They also made an expedition to the small Tyrolean town of Wörgl, which had carried out the experiment of issuing 'stamp-scrip' according to Gesell. 'The town had been bankrupt,' writes Ezra; 'the citizens had not been able to pay their rates, the municipality had not been able to pay the schoolteachers, etc.' But in less than two years after the introduction of stamp-scrip, with its automatic tax on money, 'everything had been put right, and the townspeople had built a new stone bridge for themselves etc.' Their rate of taxation was in fact higher than Gesell had contemplated. In his book he suggests 5 per cent per annum on the face value of each note, but Wörgl required its citizens to purchase a stamp each month equal to 1 per cent. 'All went well,' continues Ezra's account, 'until an ill-starred Wörgl note was presented at the counter of an Innsbruck bank.' (The notes were only valid within the municipality.) 'Threats, fulminations, anathema! The burgomaster was deprived of his office . . .'

So by the time that Ezra and Laughlin arrived the experiment was over; but Ezra was convinced that 'the ideological war had been won'. They all went to call on Herr Unterguggenberger, the Burgomaster. He was out chopping wood, but his wife showed them some of the abandoned stamp-scrip notes, and Laughlin was allowed to take away one of them worth 10 schillings, with a single tax stamp stuck on it. Ezra afterwards wrote in print of 'Unterguggenberger, the Austrian monetary reformer' as if he were someone as well known as Keynes. He extracted plenty of 'copy' from the visit, telling MacLeish: 'Woergl IS history – it also makes a damn good "story".'

*

Ezra settled down into addressing Laughlin as 'Jas', pronounced 'Jazz', as if that had always been his nickname, though up to then Laughlin's friends had always called him 'J'. He decided to arrange an outlet for Laughlin in an American Social Credit journal called *New Democracy*, published in New York by the literary critic Gorham Munson. Laughlin went to see Munson in September 1935, and described him to Ezra as 'a very nice chewish chennlmn inteet', remarking that he would not trust him 'with a nickel'. Ezra replied: 'I thought he was [Jewish] till I saw his pixchoor/ but that *dont* look as if they once spelled it Mendlesohn.' Munson had already rejected a Social Credit poem by Ezra because 'Your last lines about the Jew, we would not like to print . . . we have to consider some non-poetic

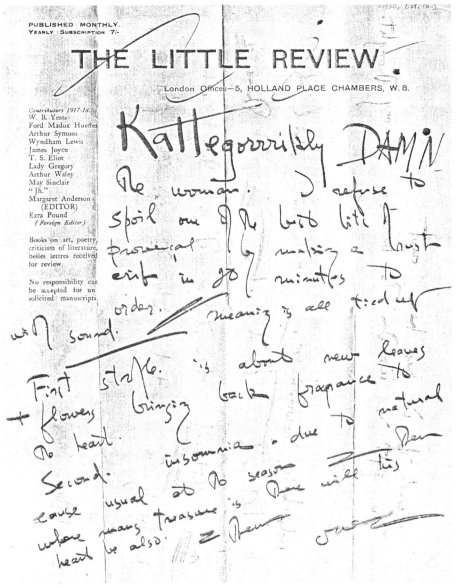

PUBLISHED MONTHLY.
YEARLY SUBSCRIPTION 7/-

THE LITTLE REVIEW

London Office:—5, HOLLAND PLACE CHAMBERS, W.8.

Contributors 1917-18.
W. B. Yeats
Ford Madox Hueffer
Arthur Symons
Wyndham Lewis
James Joyce
T. S. Eliot
Lady Gregory
Arthur Waley
May Sinclair
"Jh."
Margaret Anderson
(EDITOR)
Ezra Pound
(Foreign Editor)

Books on art, poetry,
criticism of literature,
belles lettres received
for review.

No responsibility can
be accepted for un
solicited manuscripts.

Kattegorrribly DAMN

Re woman. I refuse to spoil one of the best little provencal tale by making a burst exist in 90 minutes to order. meaning is all tied up with sound.

First strophe is about new leaves + flowers bringing back fragrance to the heart.

Second. insomnia — due to natural cause usual at the season where mans treasure is there will his heart be also. E Pound

This page and overleaf: A typically explosive letter from Ezra, written on his *Little Review* paper in October 1920, to Agnes Bedford. *(Lilly Library, Indiana University)*

And — I see here not
the sight is ... word the beauty

my thought

which is the knowable.

detached read the

literal translation ... a thing where
the beauty is mattled in ... original phrase
of ... take a literal

To tell the truth to
history. The meaning of Plato

Ezra soon after he had settled in Paris, in 1921, photographed by Sylvia Beach in her bookshop, Shakespeare and Company. *(Princeton University)*

Ezra in the courtyard outside his Paris studio, at 70 *bis*, rue Notre Dame des Champs. *(Culver Pictures)*

A group of Dadaists and their friends, taken at the opening of the Jockey Club in Montparnasse, 1923. Man Ray stands on the left, with camera; Hilaire Hiler, the club's proprietor, is next to him, wearing a bowler hat and carrying a coat; Ezra, in the middle, is wearing his Whistler outfit; on the ground squat Tristan Tzara (with monocle and cigarette) and Jean Cocteau. *(Mary de Rachewiltz)*

Left to right: James Joyce, Ezra, Ford Madox Ford, John Quinn: a summit conference to mark the founding of the *Transatlantic review*, taken in Ezra's Paris studio in 1923. Note that two out of the three chairs have been made by Ezra. As usual, Ford seems to be doing all the talking. *(Mary de Rachewiltz)*

Olga Rudge around the time Ezra met her, in 1923. *(Mary de Rachewiltz)*

George Antheil at the piano, Olga with violin. *(Mary de Rachewiltz)*

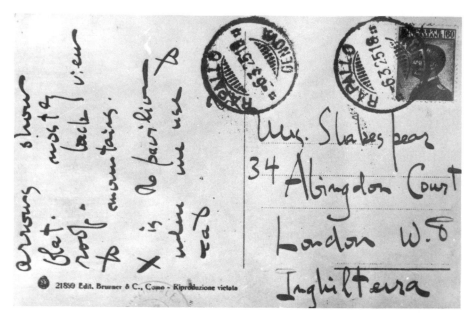

A postcard sent by Ezra to his mother-in-law from Rapallo in March 1925, indicating the position of the flat he and Dorothy had just taken on top of a building overlooking the sea. (*Omar S. Pound*)

The entrance to the Pounds' apartment building at 12 via Marsala, Rapallo. *(Photo by Antonio Carta, lent by Massimo Bacigalupo)*

Ezra playing tennis at Rapallo; Ford Madox Ford said he played like 'an inebriated kangaroo'. *(Mary de Rachewiltz)*

Maria Rudge, her grandfather Homer Pound, and her father Ezra, in 1929, when she was four. *(Mary de Rachewiltz)*

Maria and Ezra. *(Mary de Rachewiltz)*

Maria and Olga, her mother.
(Mary de Rachewiltz)

Calle Querini, the Venice alleyway that concealed Olga's house, 'the hidden nest'.
(Photo by Humphrey Carpenter)

Olga in the 1930s. *(Yale University)*　　　Dorothy c. 1930. *(Mary de Rachewiltz)*

Homer and Ezra on the steamer at Sirmione, on Lake Garda, opposite the Hotel Eden where Ezra always stayed. *(Mary de Rachewiltz)*

Above: Isabel, Ezra's mother, during her years of retirement in Italy. *(Mary de Rachewiltz)*

Above right: Basil Bunting. *(Paideuma)*

Right: Louis Zukofsky. *(Paideuma)*

T. S. Eliot in middle age. *(BBC Hulton Picture Library)*

W. B. Yeats in the 1930s. *(Photo by Howard Coster, National Portrait Gallery)*

Two of Ezra's heroes in the 1930s bore a striking facial resemblance to him: Leo Frobenius, anthropologist, *(Interfoto, Munich)* . . .

. . . and Sylvio Gesell, inventor of 'Stamp Scrip' money. *(Julius Gross, Berlin)*

Ezra around 1933: 'Am running top speed and likely to emit folly.' *(Mary de Rachewiltz)*

James Laughlin in his early years as Ezra's publisher. *(Photo by Polly Forbes-Johnson, from the Paris Review)*

Dorothy in Italy *c.* 1938.
(Mary de Rachewiltz)

Wyndham Lewis's portrait of Ezra, begun late in 1938 and exhibited the next year. *(Tate Gallery)*

points.' These differences were smoothed over, and in November 1935 Laughlin began to edit a literary section of the paper under the heading 'New Directions'. Munson, who had devised this title, observed that Ezra 'exerted a strong influence' over young Laughlin. After less than a month Ezra was punning about 'Nude Directions' and 'Nood Damnocracy'. But he left Laughlin to make his own decisions about what to print, offering suggestions rather than instructions. He was also concerned that 'Jas' shouldn't 'over balance yr/ pages with EZ'.

Laughlin soon began to part from the strict Ezra line. After a few months of 'hard experience' trying to propagate Social Credit, he decided it was 'the poet' rather than 'the economist' who must lead the world. In 1936 he followed his plan of starting a publishing house, fortified by family funds donated by a benevolent aunt in Connecticut with whom he was living. Ezra was all in favour of this. 'The foetor of the pub/ing system,' he wrote in 1936,

> makes it quicker to start a new publishing house than to get an extabd. one to print anything containing an invention or a disturbing element . . . Faber's want what I did 20 years ago . . . Eliot and ole whale Morley seriously concerned to get something that wont disturb British SUET.

Laughlin's operation began with the first number of what was to be an annual anthology, *New Directions in Prose and Poetry*. The next year, 1937, he brought out William Carlos Williams's *Life Along the Passaic River*, and in 1938 his *White Mule*. Williams also appeared in the first volume of the anthology, as did Gertrude Stein, Marianne Moore, E. E. Cummings, Elizabeth Bishop, Dudley Fitts, Henry Miller, Laughlin himself, and Ezra's Canto 44. The operation was conducted from the stable of Laughlin's aunt's house in Norfolk, Connecticut, with young writers providing such staff as were required. The first of Ezra's books to come out under the New Directions imprint was the American edition of *Guide to Kulchur*, though Laughlin felt the title to be too strong for the American market, and issued it as *Culture*.

Ezra had not warned Laughlin 'how difficult it was to *market* books', and the early New Directions titles 'were greeted with a sublime indifference by critics and booksellers alike'. But Laughlin was 'full of youthful bash and was not daunted'. He kept complete editorial independence from Ezra, despite instructions from Rapallo to print Martin Van Buren 'or some economist who lived in God-knows where'.

By 1940 Laughlin had so much abandoned his own anti-Semitism as to ask Ezra that there should be no anti-Semitic material in the Cantos. Ezra wrote back snorting that 'The pubr/ can NOT expect to control the religion and philosophy of his authors,' but admitted that 'certain evil habits of language etc/ must be weighed/ and probably will be found wanting'.

By his own description, Laughlin was a very dilatory publisher in the early days – 'I used to go skiing about half the year' – and Ezra often fumed about this: 'Of course if you spend ¾s of your time slidin' down ice cream cones on a tin tea tray . . .' He could be disloyal to Laughlin, telling Charles Olson in 1946 that he had 'no flair as a publisher' – which was quite untrue, for New Directions quickly became an outstanding, if usually non-profit-making, literary imprint, while such delays as Ezra's books encountered were more often at Faber and Faber than at New Directions. Immediately after this attack, said Olson, Ezra went on to give 'the sense of Laughlin as the last hope here of publishing surviving the deluge'. He spoke of the enterprise with unvarying flippancy, giving its address in such fashion as 'Nude Erections/ Norfuck, Conn'; but he was profoundly glad of the outlet Laughlin had given him, while Laughlin writes of him as 'a second papa to me. With all his warts, I loved him.'

17

Fighting A Wasp Nest

In the summer of 1934 Maria Rudge, now aged nine, began to become aware of her father's politics. Ezra came to Gais to visit her, before taking her for her annual stay in Venice. Once, he contemplated buying a field at Gais himself as an economic experiment, but single fields were not to be had. Another time he sent money to Maria's foster parents to buy one of their sheep on the child's behalf; she was to keep a detailed account of how much it cost to feed, house, and pasture. Her own hope was that he would purchase her a beehive, 'and when I come to Venice I will bring you the honey and there will be enough for grandfather too'. He sent the money, and she bought the hive.

At the farm he was treated as an honoured guest. Arriving with Olga, he was amused to see that Frau Marcher had sewn yellow ruffles for the bedroom window with an O.R. monogram. A sumptuous dinner was served for the visitors, Frau Marcher waiting on them while her husband watched from a bench near the stove. Ezra, having failed to get the rest of the family to sit with him, told Maria she must get up and clear the table; that was her job. 'No one must expect to be served. Everyone must work, either with his head or with his hands. He worked with his head. Hard work. Much thinking.' All this in rather broken German.

He lectured the Marchers in economics, telling them about the Depression and its real causes. Maria only caught stray words, but afterwards heard her foster father explain it to neighbours: '*Arbeit, Kredit, Gold, Schuld, Jude, Bank* . . . Perfect agreement on that score.' But Ezra and the Marchers disagreed over Mussolini, the husband declaring that neither Il Duce nor Hitler had manners or religion; he said he had been beaten up by blackshirts for not taking off his hat to the Italian flag – 'It had not occurred to him, it wasn't his flag.' The Fascists forbade the speaking of

German in Tyrolean schools inside the Italian border, and the use of the Italian language by the police and bureaucrats gave the peasants no chance to defend their rights. Franz Josef may have been a lousy old bewhiskered sonvabitch, as Ezra had called him in Canto 35, but, said Maria's foster father, he had bothered to inspect his troops at the front, and had good manners, and the taxes were lower before the war. The argument went on into the night, and Maria was sent to bed.

After this conversation at Gais, Ezra began to show faint doubts for a while about the Mussolini regime. In January 1935 he remarked to E. E. Cummings that 'this bootshaped pennyinsula' was 'sufferin from premature bureaucracy'. The older inhabitants like Herr Marcher were cynical about the 'new boys' in '40 lire necties and a forrinoffice manner'. In Canto 77 he admits that 'the dog-damn wop is not, save by exception, / honest in administration any more than the briton is truthful'. But the shortcomings of the underlings did not reflect discredit upon the supremo; the important thing was that 'the boss can git on WIFF it', however second-rate his minions. When Mussolini ordered the invasion of Ethiopia in October 1935, Ezra was right behind him, attacking the League of Nations, which was debating Italy's conduct, as 'an assembly of bank pimps . . . a packed jury'.

Ezra went to Rome during the Ethiopian crisis, apparently feeling that he should be near the seat of government at this crucial moment. 'I was in Rome during the two months of greatest tension and did not leave the Capital until, to my mind, the time of that particular danger was past.' He apparently had some contact with the propaganda authorities, since soon after the invasion he became a regular contributor to the *British–Italian Bulletin*, an English language propaganda newspaper that began to be produced by the Mussolini Government for distribution in Britain. The *Bulletin* supported the invasion in such terms as 'A strong Italy is the keystone of Europe for peace, for the good life, for civilisation. No man living has preserved the Peace of Europe so often as has Benito Mussolini.'

Ezra's articles in the *Bulletin* praised the intellectual climate of Fascist Italy ('The Corporate State is not composed of tame robots'), observed that cheese at the Albergo Rapallo had actually been better since sanctions had been imposed on Italy, and harped on his old theme of the improvement of life under the Fascists: 'You cannot open the cheapest bit of newsprint in Italy without finding notice of war on tuberculosis, war for better wheat, better houses for agricultural workers, an end of exploitation.' To allegations that true opinion in Italy was being held down by the censorship of newspapers, he answered that in fourteen years he had never heard of an idea being suppressed 'when it could be shown to be of public utility'.

At first, he avoided discussing the invasion of Ethiopia, but he finally turned to it twelve weeks after beginning to write for the paper. 'Italy

needs Abyssinia,' he told his readers, 'to achieve ECONOMIC INDE-
PENDENCE . . . the MATERIAL WEALTH, the raw materials necessary to feed and clothe the people of Italy. And I hope Italy gets every inch
of it.' It was not necessary that Italy should have sought 'written
permission from the enemies of mankind before taking this step'. He
added: 'I am, if you like, writing European propaganda for the sake of a
decent Europe wherein the best people will not be murdered for the
monetary profit of the lowest and rottenest.' That he felt obliged to defend
himself from a charge of propaganda shows he was not altogether easy
about this new role. He wrote to an American acquaintance that his articles
for the *Bulletin* had possibly been 'too jabby/ but that has been emergency
work, pro Ethiopia'.

In private, he took the line that 'Abyssinian habits are unprintable', and
that the invasion was saving Ethiopia from atrocities. To James Laughlin he
reported having been told by a 'Colonel Rocke' the story of a 'slave of
Coptic priest whom he had met. suspected of infidelity to owner, they
"destroyed her clytoris by injectin boilin' oil".' The story seemed to excite
him. Laughlin also noticed how at the Albergo Rapallo he would hand
round photographs of the bodies of Italian farmers in Ethiopia, dismem-
bered by the natives. Laughlin thought this 'a bit off, a bit peculiar'.

*

With the compulsory Italianizing of her part of the Tyrol, Maria was now
only able to study German twice a week in an 'underground' school, in
conditions of complete secrecy. When she arrived in Venice with Ezra, she
was told by Olga that 'I must speak Italian all the time' and must call her
father 'Babbo'. If he addressed the child in German, Olga would knit her
brows and say reprovingly: '*Caro!*' Frightened and confused, Maria, for
fear of lapsing into German or saying the wrong thing, 'turned poker face'
and would hardly talk. She was further muddled by her parents, between
themselves, continuing to speak English, of which she knew scarcely a
word.

Olga rejected the clothes Maria had brought with her from Gais – 'all too
long . . . Frau Marcher had bad taste'. Instead, she was given two dresses
'that made me feel like a doll, and an indecent one at that: too short'. Olga
seemed 'an incomprehensible entity with a grudge, a dark resentment as
though I were permanently doing her wrong'.

She sometimes demonstrated the same fierceness to Ezra. One afternoon
at the Lido, Maria cut her toe and limped up to her parents, who were
sitting on a restaurant terrace waiting for lunch. Seeing Ezra glowering
darkly, Maria took it for a reproof ('I should not have cut myself, should
not have held up the bleeding toe, a breach in manners'), even though he

rushed her solicitously down to the sea, bathed the toe, bound it with his handkerchief, and carried her back. His silence continued throughout lunch: 'he sat furious and ate almost nothing'. Later, Maria discovered that it had nothing to do with her: Olga had scolded him for being extremely rude. 'A group of friends led by Giorgio and Alice Levi had turned up, and one of the ladies asked for an autograph. She got an *E.P.* signature. She insisted on a few lines from the poet, and received: "a lesson that no school book teaches: some women's b——s are too big for their breeches".'

Maria was a little shaken, even when she had discovered it was not her fault, to see him in such a fury after the talking-to from Olga. 'It was the first time I had seen him angry . . . Quite different from when he was merely pensive. That occurred often, and I knew immediately that he wanted me to refrain from talking.' But this time 'it seemed as though he were visibly fighting a wasp nest in his brain'.

Maria's life in Venice during these summer visits began to assume a familiar pattern. After breakfast, 'Babbo' would leave the tiny house, walk down Calle Querini, and cross the canal on a footbridge to 310 San Gregorio, where he rented a room from a Signora Scarpa to do his typing. It was also his postal address in Venice, a device to protect this compartment of his life from intruders. At the end of the morning Maria would listen hopefully for his return. 'The tapping of his black malacca cane up the cul-de-sac Calle Querini. A rattle downstairs and a long, prolonged *Miao*. From the first floor, *Miao* – Mamile answered, and my tedium was over.' She would rush down the two flights of stairs, eager to go out.

'Shopping, a blissful ritual.' Sometimes they stopped at the Banca d'America e d'Italia to cash a dollar cheque, and if there were some small coins in the exchange Maria would be allowed to pocket them, while the bank clerk smilingly complimented her father, in the Venetian dialect, on her hair: 'Che bei capei, che bei capei.' There were compliments in the street too – blonde hair like Maria's was unusual among Italian children – and in reply Ezra would take off his hat 'and bow and chuckle with pleasure in his characteristic hissing fashion'.

They would take the cheap *traghetto*, the public ferry-gondola, across the Grand Canal to San Marco, and make a ritual first stop 'at the American Bar under the Clock for a small sandwich and an orangeade. Nowhere else in the world have sandwiches tasted so good . . . We would proceed up the Mercerie to a small coffee shop where he would select a mixture of grains and have them ground . . . Here he also bought blocks of dark bitter chocolate, and the dainty parcel was handed to me.

'Thence to Moriondo, the pastry shop with fragrant *apfelstrudel*, cream chocolate and mints. The white-haired man in a brown duster who owned the shop was a special friend and there were long conversations, mostly about politics and prices.' Ice cream was still Ezra's favourite food, and sometimes in the evening he would take Maria to Piazza Santo Stefano to buy ices, 'the best in all Venice, Babbo declared. Mamile soon gave up trying to convince him that the only place fit to be seen was a caffè in Piazza San Marco – so and so would be there in such and such a dress. No, the ice cream was bad and expensive and so and so a chicken head without historical interests.'

The morning shopping done, they returned home triumphantly. 'Inevitably the sound of the violin met us at the door . . . We deposited the parcels in the kitchen with a hush, but the playing stopped. *Miao.* Babbo went upstairs with the sweets and the papers and I could start unwrapping the fruit and the bread and put things in their place until Mamile descended and together we prepared lunch.'

Ezra put all his care into the choice of food; Olga's concern was its presentation at the table. The little house had no garden, but a passion-flower trailed over from next door, and they had permission to pick any blooms they could reach from the back windows. 'Mamile told me I must always try and find a flower for the fingerbowls and invariably Babbo was told not to eat it.' Olga had no more flair for cooking than Dorothy. 'If they wanted something that tasted really good, Babbo had to cook it. A variety of omelets (and the secret lay in adding half a shell of water to each egg, salt and pepper and beat it very briskly) lavishly filled with ham, cheese, or apricot jam.' If there were guests, a hired cook would come in a black dress with a white apron. 'He didn't like to see me working in the kitchen, doing dishes,' says Olga. If he thought she was immersing herself in chores he would call out impatiently: 'What are you doing in there?'

Apart from the food, Maria did not enjoy meals. There was the tedium of 'long conversations I could not follow, a painstaking imitation of their ways of eating – *drink* the soup from the spoon – *never* stick the spoon into your mouth, hold it to the lips sideways – *always* tip the plate away from you – never touch a peach with your fingers when you peel it . . .' And then after lunch 'the dreaded siesta'. She was supposed to go to sleep, but she could not. Up in the top-floor studio, Olga's practice-room and the child's bedroom during her visits, 'I lay listening to the voices downstairs, then to the turning of the newspaper pages and finally deep silence.'

Waiting for what seemed hours, the studio felt to her like 'a desert'. Pushing aside the voluminous mosquito net which covered her bed, she would cross the room stealthily – the floorboards creaked – and sit in front of the long bookcase that fenced off the stairs down to Olga's bedroom. 'I pulled out one book after another in search of illustrations, or some German or Italian I could read, but everything was in languages I did not understand, and no pictures.' One afternoon, in the usual boredom, she took a pencil and painstakingly worked the face of Isotta da Rimini, on the bas-relief by the desk, into a shiny black. 'I was rather pleased with the effect.' Later, nursing smacked hands, 'studiously, tearfully', she restored it to something like its original whiteness.

When the ordeal of the siesta was finally over, they might take her by *vaporetto* to the Lido. Her visit to Venice was usually late in the summer or in early autumn, and the beach was deserted. 'Babbo loved to row. He and Mamile would get into the water when we were way out and I was left in charge of the oars. I was a coward and never learned to swim properly . . . No loafing around on the beach; we were there to swim and row and it was done with zest and speed. One could idle on the *vaporetto* on the way back.'

If it was not an afternoon for bathing, her father would go back to his typing across the canal, 'and Mamile would tell me to stretch out beside her on the big velvet couch and would read to me in English . . . Then she summarized it into Italian and at the end of the story showed me the pictures: the ogre, Puss-in-boots, etc. Sometimes some frightening ones in *The Ingoldsby Legends* . . . Those were enjoyable afternoons, up to a point: I never felt safe. All of a sudden Mamile might ask me to repeat a word in English, or make me retell the story I had just heard in Italian. My mind stopped . . . The more I liked the story the more I would assimilate it into my dialect and only German words would come.'

They wondered if Maria might be profitably occupied in learning music. A violin was brought, but 'Mamile never got around to teaching me'; the child must learn sol-fa first. 'That was another failure.' One time she was told to go skipping on the Zattere, a couple of hundred yards away. 'I was too heavy and clumsy and must practise being light and graceful . . . I was growing into a problem: a clumsy pig-headed peasant instead of a graceful bright sprig.' Feelings between mother and daughter were not eased by Maria's having inherited all Olga's wilful determination; they were 'very much alike'.

Once, her misery was discovered. She was swimming at the Lido with her father; Olga was not there. 'He smiled and blinked, and I was happy and off guard . . . He must have inspired me to prate about Gais, for suddenly he asked: And when do you want to go home? He said *a casa*. I was not sure whether he meant Calle Querini or Gais, I did not think I had a say in such matters. I replied: *Presto*. So he knew I meant Gais . . .

'When we got back, Babbo and Mamile talked for what seemed an interminable time. Finally she turned to me: So you want to go back soon? *Sì*. And that was all I managed to say. The room filled with repulsion and hostility. A solid blackness. She started to cry. Babbo took her on his knees and tried to soothe her . . . I sat on the floor . . . and began crying too, like a grown-up at first, silently. Then, loud sobs, clamouring for attention. Babbo told me to come over to them, and sat me on his other knee and patted us both until the sobbing ended.

'Then he handed me his big handkerchief and dashed out of the house; he found out about trains, bought me a ticket and sent a telegram to Mamme asking her to meet me in Bruneck next evening.' Afterwards, Maria wondered who (if anyone) had really decided that she should go at once. 'Why did not Babbo smooth out my blunder and prevent futile suffering?' She had an uneasy feeling that he had betrayed her trust, that she had been exposed to Mamile yet again as a failure. But it was just his habitual running away from an awkward situation.

He was full of admiration for his daughter. 'That amazin kid,' he told Laughlin soon after Maria had passed her tenth birthday, 'has just sent me a communique which went straight on the PAGE of the noo econ.book at the exact place i was typing.' He quoted it in Italian. 'At this rate papa wont have to do no woik not any more . . . Maria di Ez P achieved several swimmin strokes includin' a roll over and to dormire sul acqua, alias float, before leavin the adriatic front.' (So her swimming was not so bad after all.) 'How much of this fond parent stuff you can stand, dunno.'

About this time he wrote for her 'Laws for Maria':

1. That she is not to lie, cheat or steal.
2. If she asks inconvenient questions, to be told
      All countries do not have the same customs . . .
3. That if she suffers, it is her own fault for not understanding the universe.
      That so far as her father knows suffering exists in order to make people think. That they do not usually think until they suffer.
4. That she is not to judge other people's actions save from two points of view: (A) objectively as elements in a causal sequence . . . (B) as to whether such action . . . is one she wd. LIKE for herself. A preference which has NOTHING whatever to do with its being suitable or likeable for someone else.
5. In case of disliking things, to blame 'em on the universe or on herself. The former course is in some religions considered presumptuous.

There was more in this vein: she was to learn 'NOT to be a nuisance (I think you have learned this)'; to be able to cook, sew, and keep house ('otherwise unfit to marry'); to be economically independent. She should learn typewriting, Italian, how to translate, possibly inventive writing too: 'first simple articles, then the novel. That is to say, I can only teach you the profession I know.' Maria was not shown or given this document, nor could she have read it, since she knew virtually no English. 'But the gist I knew.'

At Gais, she was sent home from school one day with a circular requesting that children whose parents had sufficient means be provided with Fascist uniforms. Her foster mother called it all nonsense, but told Maria she had better write to Venice to see what the Frau thought. In due course a parcel arrived with the complete uniform. Maria was on the whole pleased; 'after all, it was a new dress . . . We had to stay on after class on Saturday to learn the *giuramento fascisto* and songs . . . the oath and the anthems.' But in the oath 'we slipped in a *non* as a private reservation . . . In the name of God and Italy I swear *not* to serve faithfully my country.'

*

The publication of *Jefferson and/or Mussolini* in 1935 encouraged Ezra to try to get once more directly in touch with Mussolini. Sending the book to Il Duce, he said he now wanted to write an account of the more recent years of Fascism, and asked if he could interview him. The request was refused. Next, he sent Mussolini's office a proposal for an organization to replace the League of Nations. This time an internal memorandum by one of Mussolini's staff described his letter as 'a botched plan conceived by a nebulous mind devoid of any sense of reality'.

Over the years Ezra sent more than fifty communications to Mussolini, to his foreign minister Ciano, and to other top officials. One of the staff who had to deal with this flow of paper grumbled that his Italian was 'incomprehensible' and said it was 'clear . . . that the author is mentally unbalanced'. But on the whole he was dealt with patiently.

Certainly he was not discouraged. He sent a copy of his translation of the *Ta Hio* to the Palazzo Venezia in October 1935, and once again asked for an audience with Mussolini: 'It is in the nature of things and in my own nature that I desire the honour of a second audience with the head of government; whom I have only seen on 30 January of Year XI.' This time the proposed subject of conversation with Mussolini was to be 'the New Economy' and 'affairs in Spain'.

An audience was again refused, and Ezra became convinced that Alessandro Chiavolini, Mussolini's private secretary, was blocking him (which, of course, for understandable reasons, Chiavolini was), so he sent a letter (in Italian) personally to Mussolini:

DUCE! DUCE!
    Many enemies, much honour.
    I want to see all USURERS identified as the enemies of Italy.
    But, Duce! the system is a pernicious superstition, a corpse, which should be burned with Re Bomba and Francesco Giuseppe. From the moment the STATE supplies a MEASURE of exchange, the state works. The State has a right to reward for

this work. And this reward is fundamentally different from a tax.

From the moment a STATE bank-note exists, the state works and supplies the MEASURE and has the right to a reward (tokens, stamps, invented by Avigliano, and by Gesell) 1% interest per month maximum. The savage uses one instrument, where the civilised man uses a hundred.

One means for EXCHANGE.

Another for saving.

All the expenses of the State must be paid for with prescriptable money.

All the services, everything that goes with each day is and renewed each day must be paid for with a money which is not permanent.

I GET ANGRY EVERY TIME THEY TELL ME WORK IS A COMMODITY . . .

. . . LONG LIVE ITALY.

> Ezra Pound
> jure italico.

The letter was an attempt to explain Gesell's stamp-scrip system. Or rather, as Eliot might have said, it was not an explanation so much as an explosion of rage that his reader did not know all about stamp-scrip already. It was remarkable that he could adopt this tone towards Mussolini, with whom he had never previously raised the subject of stamp-scrip, treating him as if he were a benighted reader of the *Criterion* wallowing in shameful ignorance.

Neither Mussolini nor his staff sent any reply, and Ezra's next communication with the Palazzo Venezia was in May 1937, when he posted the dictator an article entitled 'Europe MCMXXXVI' which he had written for an obscure American periodical, together with a letter asking if he could become a regular contributor to *La Stampa*. Again, this produced no response, and he made no further attempts to communicate with Il Duce's office until 1940.

Although some of the officials who handled his letters were inclined to treat him as mentally incompetent, he was invited by a department of the Foreign Ministry to take part in an 'American Hour' which was being broadcast regularly on short-wave radio to the USA from Rome, and on 11 January 1935 he gave a talk on the programme. His intended title was 'Italy As I Have Seen It', but he was apparently persuaded to change his subject matter to something more propagandist, since the published radio bulletin announced his talk as describing 'come Il Duce resolve il problema della distribuzione' (which sounds as if he may have been asked to read from a prepared script). A few years later he recalled how 'shortly after they started short wave Rome to America . . . I . . . said a few words . . . BUT the boys here didn't tell my friends I was going to speak, so I think my audience consisted of one young lady on Broadway.' A few days after the broadcast he wrote to Agnes Bedford: 'Broadcast from Rome on the 11th short wave for the U.S. not much heard in Your/up.'

*

His long failure to get *Jefferson and/or Mussolini* into print persuaded him he was being deliberately excluded. 'Hell, Eliot won't print me . . . except when I am harmless.' Actually, Eliot was always on the lookout for some typically 'jabbing' stuff from Ezra, provided it was entertaining and reasonably comprehensible. Faber and Faber noticed that *ABC of Reading* was selling well, so Frank Morley wrote to Ezra asking if he would produce something else for them along the same lines. This time he might like to give a 'more comprehensive' survey of the world. Ezra wrote back enthusiastically. 'Do I gitt you? . . . Wot Ez knows, all of it, fer 7 an sax pence. O'Kay by me.' He wanted to call it *Paideuma*, but he could see that this was 'too long a word for the public', so how about 'The New Learning'? Morley (with a touch of irony) suggested that 'Guide to Culture' might be better. Ezra thought that was fine, and 'if your public is rough you can call it the *Guide to Kulchur*'.

He wrote *Guide to Kulchur* at his usual speed, nearly 100,000 words in about six weeks. It was not a guide to anything except the labyrinths of his own preoccupations, nor a book about culture, a concept that did not greatly interest him. Regardless of the new title, he stuck to his original notion, and itemized those elements of the arts he believed could contribute to the 'New Learning'.

He never defined the New Learning, which he also called the New Paideuma. In a prefatory note, he explained that the book and its concepts were not 'for the over-fed' but for 'men who have not been able to afford a university education or for young men . . . who want to know more at the age of fifty than I know today'. (He was now fifty-one.)

In fact a poorly educated person looking for information would learn little from *Guide to Kulchur*. From the beginning, it seems to demand an enormous range of existing knowledge in the reader – though in truth the only 'learning' required is an acquaintance with Ezra's favourite authors. The book is peppered with casual and unexplained references to figures who happened to interest him at this moment, such as 'the good father Cairoli' (an obscure Italian writer on medieval economics), 'Prof. Rostovtzeff at Yale' (a specialist in Russian history), and 'Dr Soddy' (a contributor to a recent book on economics, though we are not told what he said in it). At times this assumes a dimension of self-parody: 'Are we to assume that

Radloff buried a few lively poems in a mass of dullness? . . . Did Père Lacharme's latin arouse NO curiosity whatever? . . . Who saw it before Mohl?' None of these persons is identified.

There is a strong air of opportunities wasted. Subjects are skimmed over at enormous speed, as if everyone already knew them intimately. 'May we not suppose that XII, 9 of the Analects teaches the folly of taxation?' he asks breathlessly of Confucius, but he does not bother to tell us what 'XII, 9' actually says.

Dudley Fitts wrote in the *Saturday Review* when *Guide to Kulchur* was published: 'If only Mr Pound could forget that it is not necessary to sustain the proud scolding pitch for ever!' To Fitts, far too much of it was 'the bad boy strutting and shocking'. This is Ezra on French history: 'The Bourbons were garbage. The French court was punk.' Back to England: 'The WHOLE of 18th century literature was a cliché.' Samuel Johnson's *The Vanity of Human Wishes* is a silly poem because 'human wishes are not vain in the least'. The nineteenth century was 'mainly MESS'.

One of the most sustained demolitions is of Greek philosophy: 'You may with almost complete justice assert that greek philosophic thought is utterly irresponsible. It is at no point impregnated with a feeling for the whole people. It was mainly highbrow discussion of ideas among small groups of consciously superior persons.' This seems rather a curious accusation from someone who invariably disdained the herd, and kept calling for the world to be steered by a nucleus of intelligent men.

But in this mood any mud is worth slinging. Facts do not matter: 'Any sophomore fresh from a first reading of Plato cd. argue against me. I cd. by opening volumes I haven't seen for 25 years or more find data that run counter to what I am saying or what I shall say in the next ten pages.' But to do that sort of research would be using 'an inch rule' where 'a balance' is the right tool. He wants 'to write this new Vade Mecum without opening other volumes', to put in only 'what has resisted the erosion of time' in his own memory. He does not care if the uneroded bits are simply wrong.

He admires Socrates for trying to make his listeners 'distinguish knowledge from not-knowledge', but himself does not even bother to look up a name: 'There are passages in what's-his-name's *Glaucus* and in his *Ixion*.' The only definition of 'culture' he gives in the book is 'what is left after a man has forgotten all he set out to learn'.

He takes the trouble to support his attack on Aristotle with many pages of detailed grumbles about the *Nicomachean Ethics*, but rarely cites what 'Arry' actually said (and when he does, usually leaves it untranslated). Robert Fitzgerald was particularly disturbed by this section of *Guide to Kulchur*, calling it 'fairly alarming'.

There is also the question of prose style. In *ABC of Reading* Ezra declares that 'good writers are those who keep the language efficient . . .

keep it accurate, keep it clear'. But in *Guide to Kulchur* he oscillates between his Old Ez cracker-barrel manner ('I wd.nt condemn a mad dog on the strength of Gbt [Gilbert] Murray's evidence') and a terrible convolution of sentences which anticipates the modern academic style at its worst: 'It failed perhaps from disrespect of perceptions which are in excess considered, perhaps wrongly, a danger to communal life.' Even short sentences are sometimes dreadful: 'That is the statal adjunct.'

Guide to Kulchur is extraordinarily diffuse, hopping from one subject to another in a manner that indicates a lack of any detailed plan. Some subjects, such as the 'Vou' group of Japanese poets, are included simply because they happened to have cropped up in Ezra's postbag literally on that day. The chapter on the 'Vou' is entitled 'March 12th' because that is when it was written. The order of themes completely defies expectation: at one moment Ezra is disembowelling 'Arry Sttol', the next, expounding his theory of Great Bass in music, then Neoplatonic writers on Light. Occasionally he inserts a half-apology for this: 'These disjunct paragraphs belong together, Gaudier, Great Bass, Leibniz, Erigena, are parts of one ideogram, they are not merely separate subjects.' At a more candid moment he calls *Guide to Kulchur* 'a book of yatter'. And at times he becomes furious with himself: 'I am, in these paragraphs, doing no better than any other DAMNED writer of general statements. I am too far from concrete and particular objects to write any better than Bertie Russell or any other flat-chested highbrow.'

The book demonstrates his increasing obsession with 'usury' as the cause of failure in human endeavour of any kind: 'I suggest that finer and future critics of art will be able to tell from the quality of a painting the degree of tolerance or intolerance of usury extant in the age and milieu that provided it.' This leads him to the Jewish question. At one moment he asserts: 'Race prejudice is red herring. The tool of the man defeated intellectually and of the cheap politician.' But the very next sentence is: 'No one will deny that the jews have racial characteristics, better and worse ones.'

*

He discussed Jews and usury in a letter to the *New English Weekly*, saying that his hatred of usury made him 'equally ready to shoot quakers and calvinists', but arguing that 'a general loathing of a gang or sect usually has some sound basis in instinct'. He was in agreement with the general tone of other letters to this journal, whose support of Social Credit attracted anti-Semites. Another correspondent in the same issue stated: 'The Jew is not disliked on account of his breed or creed, but for the financial persecution of the Gentile.' And though a writer of one article tried to draw attention to 'what has happened, and is happening, in Germany', which he called 'vile', many readers seem to have shared Ezra's view.

It would be wrong to regard his increasingly anti-Semitic opinions as simply a concomitant of his enthusiasm for Mussolini. There was very little popular anti-Semitism in Fascist Italy, and at this period the Government took no anti-Jewish measures. In England, however, C. H. Douglas was becoming more overtly anti-Semitic. In his *Social Credit* (1935) he discussed *The Protocols of the Elders of Zion*, a supposed account of a Jewish plot for world domination, and wrote that its authenticity 'is a matter of little importance; what is interesting about it is the fidelity with which the methods by which such enslavement [of the world by Jews] might be brought about can be seen reflected in the facts of everyday experience'.

*

Faber and Faber made no attempt to tidy up *Guide to Kulchur* for publication. Probably nobody there gave the manuscript more than a glance before sending it to the printer, for the book is scattered with small errors - missing punctuation, parts of speech absent – quite apart from preserving all Ezra's eccentricities of style. Not until copies were already bound and waiting for distribution did someone notice that certain passages looked libellous. Publication was consequently delayed from June to July 1938, while about fifteen pages were reprinted and pasted in by hand.

Gilbert Murray, described by Ezra as 'unspeakable' on account of his bad translations from the Greek, now became 'the Genevan pacifist'. 'One of Roosevelt's gang' (though not named), originally described as 'a shark', now became 'a dogfish'. A description of Cosmo Lang, the Archbishop of Canterbury, supposedly by an unnamed colonial parson (no doubt Ezra himself), as 'probably the wickedest man who ever sat in the seat of St Augustine', was removed and replaced by '. . . I can't print what he says without danger of libel'. The remark that England was now ruled by a 'gang of punks, pimps and cheap dudes' was to change to 'the gang now ruling England', as if Faber and Faber feared that the entire Cabinet would sue.

Guide to Kulchur contained a defence of the Cantos: 'There is no mystery about the Cantos, they are the tale of the tribe – give Rudyard the credit for his use of the phrase.' (Ezra did not say where in Kipling's works he found this expression, which resembles Eliot's 'purify the dialect of the tribe' in *Little Gidding*, though that was a rough translation from Mallarmé.) Just before beginning work on *Guide to Kulchur*, Ezra had completed the next ten Cantos. '42–51 are in page proof,' he wrote in April 1937. 'Should be out any day. I believe they are clearer than the preceding ones.' They were published in June 1937 by Faber and Faber and in

November by Farrar & Rinehart in New York, as *The Fifth Decad of Cantos*.

This section of the Cantos consists mainly, as Stephen Spender wrote in *Left Review* when they were first published, of 'great tracts of the Social Creditor looking at history and life'. The first three, Cantos 42, 43 and 44, give a discursive account of the creation of what Ezra regards as the ideal bank, the Monte dei Paschi ('Mount of the Pastures') – established in Siena in the seventeenth century and still flourishing today. Its perfection in his eyes lay in its original funding having come from the pasturelands south of Siena. According to him, it would only lend money 'to whomso can best USE it'; it distributed its profits to the workers; it would not allow long-term debts – all according to Social Credit principles. Now and then these cantos are quite attractive – there is an amusing account of a parade to celebrate the foundation of the bank, with such details as 'four fat oxen / having their arses wiped' – but in general they are, as Edwin Muir said in the *Criterion*, 'rough notes and excerpts' rather than poetry. Ezra wrote to Ford Madox Ford: 'Waaal I have just knocked off three more Cantos on a patch of history wot the woild needz to be told and have a fourth nearly set up. and this time it is Siena.'

The desultory tone of Cantos 42 to 44 gives way abruptly in Canto 45 to one of the most passionate moods in the whole work. This canto is a litany against 'Usura':

> With usura hath no man a house of good stone
> each block cut smooth and well fitting
> that design might cover their face,
> with usura
> hath no man a painted paradise on his church wall
> *harpes et luz*
> or where virgin receiveth message
> and halo projects from incision,
> with usura
> seeth no man Gonzaga his heirs and his concubines
> no picture is made to endure nor to live with
> but is made to sell and sell quickly
> with usura, sin against nature,
> is thy bread ever more of stale rags
> is thy bread dry as paper,
> with no mountain wheat, no strong flour
> with usura the line grows thick
> with usura is no clear demarcation
> and no man can find site for his dwelling.
> Stonecutter is kept from his stone

weaver is kept from his loom
WITH USURA
wool comes not to market
sheep bringeth no gain with usura
Usura is a murrain, usura
blunteth the needle in the maid's hand
and stoppeth the spinner's cunning . . .
They have brought whores for Eleusis
Corpses are set to banquet
at behest of usura.

Canto 45 deservedly attracted a lot of praise when it was published. Delmore Schwarz, writing in *Poetry*, said there was 'nothing like it in English'. It would be a magnificent, perhaps unflawed piece of work, were it not for the uncomfortable fact that it is a hymn to an obsession.

Economics are treated in the familiarly diffuse way in Cantos 46, 48 and 50, which contain such assertions as 'the arts gone to hell by 1750', 'Wellington was a jew's pimp', and so on. Canto 51, which concludes *The Fifth Decad of Cantos*, consists principally of a reprise of the anti-usury litany, on which is superimposed instructions on fly-fishing from a nineteenth-century anglers' manual. This canto also quotes Rudolf Hess's dictum 'Between peoples a way of life will be achieved', which suggests that Ezra was now seeking European Fascist unity.

The volume ends with two Chinese ideograms quoted from Confucius, meaning literally 'right name' or, as Ezra puts it, 'precise definition'. Yet imprecision and inaccuracy haunt *The Fifth Decad of Cantos*. For example, in Canto 46: 'Said Mr RothSchild, hell knows which Roth-schild / 1861, '64 or there sometime . . .' The remark in question was, as Ezra admitted elsewhere, really made by one John Sherman in 1863, and was only quoted by Rothschild Bros in a letter. Similarly in Canto 48: 'Bismarck / blamed american civil war on the jews.' He did not; Ezra took the remark from the *Liberator*, an anti-Semitic periodical published in North Carolina, and admitted that he had not verified the truth of it. (Bismarck was, in fact, pointedly pro-Jewish.) And it is hard to see what 'accuracy' resides in a long passage in Canto 48, in which four lines taken from a letter from Olga describing a shopping expedition in Paris are juxtaposed with one from Maria at Gais, giving an account of festivities when a priest said his first mass – all within the same set of quotation marks, as if one speaker were meant to be indicated.

Apart from the resounding Canto 45, two cantos stand out from the main body of the sequence as entirely different in tone and subject matter. Canto 49, like others before it, presents a brief glimpse of an earthly paradise, this time in a Utopian China of the distant past, by means of translation from poems in a manuscript book of Chinese and Japanese verse belonging to Homer and Isabel Pound. (Literal English versions were provided by a Chinese lady teacher who was passing through Rapallo.) This canto shows that when Ezra wanted to, he could still achieve, in the words of the canto itself, the 'dimension of stillness', which had superbly distinguished *Cathay*:

> Wild geese swoop to the sand-bar,
> Clouds gather about the hole of the window
> Broad water; geese line out with the autumn
> Rooks clatter over the fishermen's lanthorns,
> A light moves on the north sky line
> where the young boys prod stones for shrimps . . .
>
> Sun up; work
> sundown; to rest
> dig well and drink of the water
> dig field; eat of the grain
> Imperial power is? and to us what is it?

More puzzling is Canto 47, which returns to the theme of Odysseus' descent into the underworld. But now Odysseus seems not so much the protagonist, *polumetis*, as the victim of two women, Circe and Penelope. He has been 'freed from the one bed' (Circe's) that he may 'return to another'. This is surely autobiographical, though it is impossible to determine exactly what it means. There is also a curious passage which seems to depict Woman as a predatory beast intent only on sexual satisfaction:

> Two span, two span to a woman,
> Beyond that she believes not. Nothing is of any importance.
> To that she is bent, her intention
> To that art thou called ever turning intention,
> Whether by night the owl-call, whether by sap in shoot,
> Never idle, by no means wiles intermittent
> Moth is called over mountain
> The bull runs blind on the sword, *naturans*
> To the cave art thou called, Odysseus.

Canto 47 contains an assertion of virility – 'By prong have I entered these hills' – but has, as doleful refrain, words from Bion's lament for Adonis, whose fate was not only to be the lover of Aphrodite on earth, but, after his death by goring, to spend half the year in Hades with Persephone. There is clearly some reference to Ezra's own situation here, suggesting a deep weariness and sense of doom.

*

Sometimes Ezra's Venetian literary friends gathered at Calle Querini, after dinner, to hear him read aloud from the Cantos. Maria was occasionally present at these sessions. The guests were usually Manlio Dazzi, who would look dreamily at Ezra and tell the child 'Il tuo Babbo è un fenomeno'; Aldo Camerino from the Venice newspaper *Il Gazzettino*, 'tall with a prominent nose and shiny black eyes'; and Professor Carlo Izzo, 'roundish, reddish, with spitting protruding lips'. Izzo translated some of Ezra's work into Italian; during 1938 he was working on Canto 45.

Maria afterwards recalled these evenings, with 'the audience grouped in a semicircle around Babbo in his big, straw-bottomed, wood-framed arm-chair by the green reading lamp . . . constantly changing his three sets of rimless pince-nez . . . Dazzi in a similar chair, except for size – man and chair were half the size – facing him; Izzo and Camerino on two stiff plain *careghe* or Chiavari chairs painted dark blue, facing the big velvet pearl-grey couch, upon which lay Mamile, dressed in a Duchess of Alba pose with me beside her, equally dressed up, my hair loose and shiny after the obligatory hundred *coups de brosse*.'

Maria liked the preparations and the careful dressing-up. 'It was my job to squeeze lots of oranges, enough to fill a big green glass jug. The guests were never offered anything alcoholic.' While Ezra read aloud from the Cantos, 'no one stirred. A sort of tinkle hung in the air . . . Since Dazzi understood no English, at the end of each Canto, Babbo would translate for him; then followed questions and long arguments. This bored me, so I would retire to the bathroom and there try out Mamile's rouge and powder and creams, scrubbing my face violently and resuming my place on the couch as soon as I heard Babbo's pince-nez case click; I knew he was on the point of resuming his reading. Silence.'

In the autumn of 1937, just as *The Fifth Decad of Cantos* was reaching the bookshops, Maria, now aged twelve, was finally taken away from Gais in preparation for boarding school. 'I don't remember any special anguish at leaving Gais for good or whether it was clear it was for good. Babbo met me at the station and filled the day . . . In the shoe shop he sat back and told them to bring something beautiful for the signorina. And when I picked a pair of brown suede with a bit of a heel, he gave me an approving look . . . On arriving at Calle Querini, Mamile said those shoes were not suitable, too grown-up. She would keep them for herself and get me another pair.'

After a few weeks in Venice, Maria went to a convent school in a villa above Florence, where she ceased to be addressed as Maria, and became Mary Rudge. 'I spent the first three months huddled up behind the grand piano, crying.'

18

First Clawss To Amurika

'Rabbit I don't much mind what you do as long as you don't go involve yourself with that Mosley that is only a place fit for Bad rabbits,' Eliot wrote to Ezra in March 1934. It was already too late. During 1933, Ezra had offered Oswald Mosley's British Union of Fascists (formed the previous year) the chance of publishing *Jefferson and/or Mussolini*. At first he had a quarrelsome relationship with them. Annoyed by their lack of interest in his work, he wrote them a rude letter calling them reactionary and unconstructive. This elicited a brusque response from one of their officials, G. A. Fisher ('M.A., D.Litt., Dr. Phil.'), who told him that Mussolini greatly admired the BUF. Back came the reply from Ezra:

> Dear Mr Fletcher [sic]
> GOr-DDDAMMM mit!!! You can't regenerate ANY-THING so long as you are AFRAID to look facts and ideas in the face . . . On the most enjoyable occasion when I met the boss he didn't get under the table and ask me not to have such active ideas.

Mosley had himself originally preached an economic doctrine that strongly resembled Social Credit. In 1930 while still a Labour MP he had proposed a 'credit policy' that would expand purchasing power, take public control of banks and industry, and alleviate unemployment by a large-scale plan of public works. Only when Labour refused to countenance this did he set up his New Party, initially intended to bridge the gap between Left and Right. Far from seeming Fascist at this stage, its character was 'vague and feeble' – Eliot's term for it in the *Criterion* in April 1931. Only after its complete failure to make any impact on Ramsay Mac-Donald's Coalition Government did it reform in the spring of 1932 and declare itself Fascist.

Mosley then began to call for a one-party state in which Parliament would play virtually no part. Public works, bank control, and a planned increase in the purchasing power of the people still featured as elements of its programme, but after the rally at Olympia in West London in 1934, when Mosley's blackshirt stewards attacked hecklers, it lost almost all support from intellectuals. (An exception was Henry Williamson, author of *Tarka the Otter*, who backed Mosley as someone who could shake England out of inertia, and who in 1939 wanted to fly to Berlin to persuade Hitler not to wage war. Williamson regarded the Führer as 'the only true pacifist in Europe'.)

Ezra met Mosley when he made a visit to London at the end of 1938; Mosley writes that he found Ezra 'exactly the opposite of what I expected from the abstruse genius of his poetry . . . He appeared as a vivacious, bustling and practical person, making the shrewd observation that Englishmen of my class never grew up until they were forty.'

Ezra had earlier been critical (writing in the *New English Weekly* in December 1935) of 'the antics of Sir O. Mosley', calling it one of those 'travesties of Fascism' that he did not advocate. The BUF costume struck him as ridiculous; in a 1935 pamphlet on Social Credit he wrote that 'the British Black Shirt is an annex to the Gaiety Chorus'; but by 1937 he was changing his mind. 'I dont make out Mosley/ appearances are against him, and yet several good guys are for him.' (He did not mention who they were.) And he judged the *Fascist Quarterly*, organ of the BUF, to be 'much better edited than the soc/ credit papers'. A year later he told Agnes Bedford: 'Watch Marse Mosley, I think the mind of that orgumization iz rizin.'

He did not join the BUF himself, just as he had held back from joining the actual party organization in Italy. Nevertheless, the first issue of the renamed *British Union Quarterly*, published in January 1937, proclaimed:

Contributors include:

WYNDHAM LEWIS   EZRA POUND   ROY CAMPBELL   VIDKUN QUISLING

Lewis contributed a facetious and somewhat guarded piece about 'the extreme bogusness of the non-fascist or the anti-fascist "fronts"', without giving his explicit support to the BUF; Campbell sent the magazine three poems from the Nationalist front in Spain; and Quisling (leader of the Norwegian National Socialists) wrote on an 'international Nordic movement' to combat 'the Jewish international Marxist conspiracy'. Ezra's piece, headed 'Demarcations', was simply a collection of explosions on Social Credit. For example: 'You would think that this would be clear even to amoebic minds like Stan Baldwin and Neville [Chamberlain] the damned.' He gave no explicit support to Fascism – not even to Mussolini – and his only anti-Semitic remark was a reference to the 'schnorrer press'.

In a later issue, he described the *British Union Quarterly* as 'the only English review in which I have been able to read the writings of the other contributors', comparing it favourably with the 'pallid . . . English suburban temperament' of the *New English Weekly*. The paper reciprocated by invariably putting his name on the front cover whenever he appeared in it. Evidently the BUF now valued his support, even if his ideas were at a tangent to theirs.

In the issue of January–March 1938 he was more eloquently anti-Semitic than he had yet been in print. Discussing the betrayal of the original American spirit, he attacked not Jews but 'the pinch-penny aryio-kikes', non-Jewish financiers who were 'able to take a dirty line and stick to it without deviation or shadow of turning, with none of the Jews' moments of pity, excitement, or need of opulent display'. On the other hand he suggested that

> A race may possibly be held responsible for its worst individuals . . . If you believe that a whole race should be punished for the sin of some of its members, I admit that the expulsion of the two million Jews in New York would not be an excessive punishment for the harm done by Jewish finance to the English race in America.

Though there is a pretence of caution here, he now accepted the attitudes of hard-liners in the Fascist movement on the Jews. He corresponded with Arnold Leese (not an orthodox Mosleyite, but the self-styled Director General of the Imperial Fascist League) who took precautions to exclude Jewish infiltrators by examining the shape of members' heads, which he believed to be a certain test of race. When Leese asked Ezra whether he might have Jewish blood, Ezra replied with a lengthy genealogy to prove that this was impossible.

He continued to be obsessed by the idea that the Jewish character was influenced by circumcision. He wrote to William Carlos Williams in 1936 arguing that 'history is written and character is made by whether and HOW the male foreskin produces an effect of glorious sunrise or of annoyance in slippin backward . . . the whole of puritan idiocy is produced by badly built [i.e. tight] foreskins.' His attitude was that circumcision diminished sensitivity and thus decreased interest in sex, encouraging Jews to find satisfaction from usury instead.

At times his failure to discuss Fascism itself, in the *British Union Quarterly*, seemed deliberate. He often came close to the subject, as in an article where he chided Eliot for declaring that there was no 'intellectual interest' in British Fascism, and when he claimed that 'Mr Bunting considers himself anti-fascist, nevertheless he and Mr Jorian Jenks [a regular contributor to the paper] are ineluctably OF the same party, when you get down to any real bedrock, to any real honesty.' But that was as far as he would go politically. He also contributed to *Action*, a weekly paper of the Mosley movement, from November 1937 onwards. As in the *British Union Quarterly* his articles were, to say the least, tangential to the main issues of Fascism: he wrote on the poor intellectual powers of the British Parliament, and suggested this body would be improved if, as in Italy, the proceedings were broadcast on the radio. In *Action* he took an ambiguous line towards anti-Semitism: 'As to the investors I do not care a twopenny damn whether they be Jews, semites, quakers, or anglican frogs or Britons. A usurer is a usurer.'

His private letters, however, were unrestrained. His correspondence with James Laughlin from 1933 onwards was peppered with such remarks as 'the little kike snot'; and when Laughlin had a Jewish girlfriend in 1936: 'NO/ no/ jews IZ temptin when 18, but about 26 they begins to THICKEN, and the older they gets the MORE RACE shows, more it oozes thru every pore.'

By December 1936 he was at least partly aware of, and did not censure, events in Germany. He wrote to Laughlin of an unfavourable American review of *Jefferson and/or Mussolini*:

> This is typical communist mentality in the U.S.A. it is also the
> kind of jew impertinence that creates antisemites nazism and
> pogroms with the nazi desire of independence from usury, and
> the nazi 'idealism' such as it is.

But he warned Laughlin against public expressions of unmitigated anti-Semitism, telling him: 'The line to take is as in my "USURERS have no RACE".' Meanwhile; he remained extraordinarily ignorant of the real nature of Fascism itself, judging from a 1941 letter to a pro-Fascist economist in Italy, Odon Por, in which he defines it as: 'Fascio, fasci, informal group or groups who agreed to meet for the good of the country BEFORE having decided on a programme or any details of the same.'

He and the Mosley supporters never came to a close understanding. In June 1938 a puzzled member of the BUF wrote to him: 'What do you mean by "Ta Hio"? Is it a tax on money? If so, I think it need only be adopted in an emergency.'

*

In the autumn of 1937, Nancy Cunard compiled and published the questionnaire *Authors Take Sides on the Spanish War*. Ezra's comment was printed in the section headed 'Neutral?' It reads:

Questionnaire an escape mechanism for young fools who are too cowardly to think; too lazy to investigate the nature of money . . . Spain is an emotional luxury to a gang of sap-headed dilettantes.

His place in the neutral section was shared by (among others) Eliot, who wrote that 'at least a few men of letters should remain isolated'. There was also a pro-Franco section, which included statements by Edmund Blunden and Evelyn Waugh.

A few months after sending Nancy Cunard her answer, Ezra was approached by a pro-Franco organization, the Friends of National Spain, who hoped for his support. Once again he refused to take sides, telling them that their letter did not touch upon the all-important question of economics. And in a scribbled note some years later he wrote of Nancy Cunard's attitude to Spain: 'N. incapable of understanding that ONLY reason anyone has been allowed to hv. war in Spain is because $1 of petrol can be sold for $5 during civil war.' He added that at the time he had been 'too weak to write necessary 600 pages' on this subject, though Nancy's 'serious letters' to him had deserved a proper answer.

Temperamentally, the Spanish war interested him not in the slightest. In 1936 he observed in the *New English Weekly* that 'Europe ENDS with the Pyrenees. Neither Spain nor Russia has ever contained more than a handful of civilized individuals.' And to an American correspondent the same year: 'Spain is a damn'd nest of savages/ and Russia shall not haa/a/AV Bar/Bar/Bar Barcelonah!!!'

*

At the beginning of October 1938 Olivia Shakespear, then aged seventy-four, was taken seriously ill in London. Dorothy was herself unwell at the time, so Ezra went to England on her behalf. By the time he arrived Olivia had died, so he remained there to settle her affairs, close up her Kensington flat, and see Omar, then aged twelve and soon to leave his preparatory school for Charterhouse.

Ezra had been summoned to London from Venice, where, as usual, he was spending the early autumn with Olga and Mary, who remembers how 'the holiday got disrupted by a telegram. Although I was now making real efforts to learn English, I still caught little of the conversations going on between my parents. Babbo must leave for England: an old friend of his had died. When I told him I was sorry he had lost a friend, he realized I thought it was a male friend, but he did not correct me. Mamile was very animated and indignant. Babbo struck his characteristic pose: hands deep in trouser pockets, balancing on toes and heels, looking straight ahead of him toward the window, lips tightly closed.'

In London he visited Violet Hunt, and with her help made contact with some of his former girlfriends from the Bohemian days in 1917, most of whom were now respectable married women. Ronald Duncan had heard that he was coming to London, and he and his mistress Rose Marie were suddenly summoned by Ezra to 'some Italian restaurant which he named in Dean Street. Rose Marie and I went along, but found that Pound's restaurant was long bankrupt and had closed eight years ago . . . We had arrived a little late and there was no knowing whether Pound had already been there. We hung around for ten minutes and then I noticed a bit of paper stuck to the wall giving an odd clue to Pound's whereabouts. "Where it says: *no dogs or Japs admitted*," we read. This baffled me. It was Rose Marie who solved the message and led off for the nearest Chinese restaurant. The notice was in the window: Pound was inside, ordering a meal sufficient for sixteen.'

After the dinner they all went in a taxi to Olivia Shakespear's flat. 'The rooms,' writes Duncan, 'were stuffed with the ivory and brass trophies of colonialism, silver photograph-frames, ornaments à la Harrods, and all the bric-à-brac of a predatory dowager with an assured income. Ezra looked cornered in these surroundings . . . For some inexplicable reason Ezra's wife, Dorothy, had been foolish enough to ask Ezra to dispose of the furniture and effects . . . [His] method of doing business was simple but hardly profitable. He merely asked his friends to help themselves. Rose Marie and I staggered off, our pockets bulging with Chinese ivory and jade, fish knives and forks, an inscribed copy of Yeats's poems, several cushions, and a stool ornamented with quotations from Virgil.'

Ezra set himself various political tasks before he went back to Rapallo. It was now that he met Mosley (nothing of consequence came of the meeting); also he had 'the wild idea that I ought to TELL Chamberlain what he was headed for' - that is, war, though the Munich agreement had been signed at the end of September. Ezra managed to contact Downing Street by telephone, but then 'missed a phone call' back from the Prime Minister's office which he believed might have led to a meeting. (He had remarked of Chamberlain in 1936 that he 'wd. trust [him] with one half of a bad potato'.) Typically, during this London visit he managed to get some 'lowdown'. He ran across a 'bloke who had been in their [the British] secret service' who 'said he could buy any of the big politicians, except Chamberlain', and who 'had the dope on all the communist leaders'. Eight years later Ezra told Charles Olson that he regretted not having got the Communists and the Fascists together in London during this visit; something might have come of it.

He went to Wyndham Lewis's studio in Notting Hill to sit for his portrait. A 1920 Lewis drawing of him had emphasized his strength, portraying him like an upright mountain, recognizably the man who had sat for the 1914 Gaudier-Brzeska head. But the 1938 oil shows him sloping back in an armchair, exhausted and brooding, with half-closed eyes that suggest both great tiredness and a smouldering anger.

Lewis had recently painted Eliot, at a sitting that produced a great deal of talk and laughter. But with Ezra it was a different matter. Lewis has described how he

> swaggered in, coat-tails flying, a malacca cane out of the 'nineties aslant beneath his arm, the lion's head from the Scandinavian North-West thrown back . . . He flung himself full length into my best chair for that pose, closed his eyes, and was motionless . . . He did not sleep, but he did not move for two hours by the clock. 'Go to it, Wyndham!' he gruffled without opening his eyes, as soon as the mane of as yet entirely ungrizzled hair had adjusted itself to the cushioned chair-top.

The pose was becoming characteristic. In 1939 somebody wanted to take his photograph, but he told them he did not want them to, then slumped down in a chair, and closed his eyes – in which position the picture was taken. He would say that one of his concerns was to rest his neck, which he regarded as an especially sensitive part of the body, the vital connection between brain and physique.

Lewis was now recanting his support of the Nazis: in 1939 he published *The Hitler Cult*, in which he firmly denounced his former hero – though the book came too late and was too superficial to change many people's belief that he was a Fascist. (He spent the Second World War in Canada and America.) Ezra was distinctly unimpressed by this change of heart. He wrote to Lewis in February 1940 suggesting that the book had been undertaken to earn a boat fare across the Atlantic. 'Why all this slap stick about Adolf – ? wot you need is a bit of economic background.' He and Dorothy provided some much-needed financial help for Lewis. Ezra bought drawings and Dorothy advanced £30 against future work. Lewis told her: 'A beautiful portrait of you will result,' though it never did.

*

After her mother's death, Dorothy's solicitor described her as having 'substantial means'. The Pounds' lifestyle at Rapallo did not change, but Ezra admitted: 'We had money from then on.' Early in 1939, soon after returning from London, and doubtless partly because of this increase in financial resources, he planned a trip to the United States.

Since 1937 Ford Madox Ford, who was now spending much of his time in America, had been making intermittent attempts to persuade Ezra to come over and earn some money by lecturing. Ford held a specially created chair of comparative literature at Olivet College, Michigan, and during 1938 persuaded the authorities there to invite Ezra. Back came the response to Ford: 'I do NOT propose to go into any sort of YOKE, whether devised by the Prex of Olivet or by you.' In his reply Ford expressed his infuriation with Ezra's epistolary style: 'Your incomprehensible scrawls are a torture to me . . . Get the waiter at your hotel to write your letters for you.' (Yeats had been moved, towards the end of their friendship, to complain in similar terms: 'Your letter . . . followed me to America . . . I have read it without much understanding, I wonder if you could bring yourself to tell me what you want in old-fashioned English.')

William Carlos Williams wanted Ezra to come to the USA for his own good, to shake him out of his obsessions. 'You belong in this country,' he wrote in April 1938. 'I think that if anyone needs a change, a new viewpoint, it's you. You can't even smell the stink you're in any more.' But when Ezra finally decided to go, it was not for his own good, nor because any college had invited him, but because he felt that the USA needed his presence.

He still felt 100 per cent American. 'I don't have to *try* to be American,' he wrote in February 1939. 'Am I American? Yes, and buggar the present state of the country, the utter betrayal of the American Constitution, the filth of the Universities.' He had recently been elected to membership of the American Institute and Academy of Arts and Letters, and he wrote wrathfully to Van Wyck Brooks and other senior academicians about possible improvements in the organization, suggesting that it 'COULD with a little gumption at least stimulate the reprint of American classics . . . the letters of Adams and Jefferson'. He compiled a three-page pamphlet entitled 'Introductory Text Book', which he circulated to correspondents; it consisted of quotations from John Adams, Jefferson, Lincoln, and Washington, all intended to prove that in the early days of the Union these men had perceived the real nature of money and credit.

He had never entirely abandoned his hope for a Renaissance in America, though he now regarded it as an economic rather than a literary rebirth. 'Are you now ready for a revival of American culture considering it as something specifically grown from the nucleus of the American Founders, present in the Adams, Jefferson correspondence?' he asked John Crowe Ransom in 1938. He complained that 'Marx and Lenin are reprinted at 10 cents and 15 cents in editions of 100,000 and Adams' and Jefferson's thought is kept out of the plain man's reach, and out of my reach considering that for three years I have tried in vain to buy John Adams's letters.'

It was not clear to what extent, if at all, he wanted to impose Fascism on the USA. In a 'manifesto' that he published during 1938, entitled *National Culture*, he wrote that the idea of 'total democracy' was 'bilge . . . clichés . . . cant', a 'perversion of ideas by means and misuse of words . . . There is no more equality between men than between animals. Jefferson never thought there was.' The only equality he demanded was 'equality before the law courts', and liberty was defined as 'to do that which harms not another'. But it was not clear as to what all this added up to, and he made no recommendations for any changes in the Constitution.

He kept very quiet about his plan to go to the USA in advance of the trip, scarcely mentioning it in letters, as if he himself were unsure about the wisdom of it, let alone the outcome. But by the end of March 1939 he had his passage booked, and Mary travelled from her boarding school at Florence to Rapallo so that she could say goodbye to her father. Ezra did not know how long he would be gone.

*

'In April 1939 I saw Rapallo for the first time,' writes Mary. Ezra talked to her confusedly about his plans, 'as though placing the needle on a record at random – well knowing the beginning and the end'. He told her that if he could get anyone over there to listen to him, 'if I can talk some sense into the President, to stop him from allowing the country to be run by crooks, help prevent the ruin of Europe, perhaps in the future America will become a fit place to live in, for all of us. They take me to the boat tomorrow. There is not room for everybody in the car . . .'

It took some time for her to realize that this meant she and her mother would not be allowed to see him off. She did not know why, having no inkling of another life than that which he led with Olga.

He sailed on 13 April 1939, on the Italian liner *Rex*, occupying a first-class cabin. This afterwards gave rise to speculation that his ticket had been paid for by the Italian Government, who might have been sending him across the Atlantic as their unofficial envoy; but, apart from the improbability of their doing any such thing, it is clear that he himself had decided to travel in style, at his own cost, since with Dorothy's new wealth he could afford to. A month before sailing he wrote to Wyndham Lewis:

> I have bin TOLD that it is 'necessary' to go FIRST CLAWSS to Amurika, if anything is to be accomplished . . . Do you advise it. I shall go on Rex or something large / prefer 2nd. on colussus to capn's kaBIN on a small tub. Purrvided they dont stik one 80 quid for a foist.

The letter was signed 'EZ' with the E in the shape of a swastika, to which was added: 'sig. chur for use in Murka? or not.'

Gorham Munson went to the expense of dispatching a wireless message to Ezra on board the *Rex* advising: 'GIVE ECONOMIC BUT NOT POLITICAL VIEWS TO THE PRESS WHEN INTERVIEWED.' He also went to meet the ship as it docked in New York on 21 April. But he was too late: Ezra had already held an impromptu press conference. Hunched in a chair in the ship's lounge, clasping his pince-nez, he took each question as a starting point for a homily.

One journalist asked, would there be a war? Ezra answered: 'The bankers and the munitions interests, whoever and wherever they may be, are more responsible for the present talk of war than are the intentions of Mussolini or anyone else.' He had met Mussolini, hadn't he, so what did he think of the Italian dictator? 'He has a mind with the quickest uptake of any man I know except Picabia.' Who is Picabia, Mr Pound? 'Picabia is the man who ties the knots in Picasso's tail.' Mr Pound, who are your favourite poets in America today? 'I can name one poet writing today. I mean Cummings.'

He did not especially care for Cummings's verse – he admired him much more for *Eimi*, his prose book on Russia – but Cummings had offered to be his host in New York and put him up at his apartment on Patchin Place. Cummings describes how, fresh from the boat and the press conference, Ezra 'zoomed into Patchin, all of a gloat and gasping against . . . the heat and juggling all his mythical realities like "Possum" and "Brancoosh" [Brancusi] and "Uncle Jarg" [Ezra's pet Congressman, 'Uncle' George Tinkham]'.

Cummings declared: 'I'm very fond of Ezra', but he and his wife Marion quickly found they had an impossible guest, who was 'gargling anti-semitism from morning till morning . . . He continually tackles dummies, while uttering ferocious poopyawps & screechburps . . . [saying] if you don't know money you don't know nothing.' In this letter, written to a friend while Ezra was still staying with them, Cummings continued: 'We don't know if he's a spy or merely schizo, but we do feel he's incredibly lonesome.'

After a few days, the Cummingses fled to New Hampshire, and Ezra moved on to Washington. He hoped to see the President, though over the past few years he had developed a strong antipathy to Roosevelt, and now had nothing but contempt for the New Deal. 'FIVE million youths without jobs,' he had written in Canto 46,

> FOUR million adult illiterates
> 11 million 'vocational misfits', that is with small chance for jobs
> NINE million persons annual, injured in preventable industrial
> accidents
> One hundred thousand violent crimes. The Eunited States ov
> America
> 3rd year of the reign of F. Roosevelt

In Washington, he stayed in the Georgetown home of the Misses Ida and Adah Lee Mapel, whom he had not seen since 1919 when he and Dorothy had met them in Paris. He described them to Wyndham Lewis by saying that 'gawd and the angels wd/ NOT impress Miss Ida and Adah Lee is perfectly cable of continuin' to sip her tea quietly in the midst of an earth quake'.

He attended a session of Congress, acquiring a seat in the section of the public gallery reserved for Congressmen's relatives, on the strength of being the grandson of Thaddeus Coleman Pound; found it a stupid, boring spectacle; and began to lobby members of the Government. He called on Henry A. Wallace, then the Secretary of Agriculture, who agreed to see him for a few minutes and had to listen to a lecture on Social Credit. Ezra also made himself known to half a dozen senators, thanks to a batch of introductions provided by 'Uncle Jarg', though he seems to have knocked on doors *ad lib*, since William Carlos Williams said that a friend of Skipwith Cannell's had run across him 'wandering around more or less blindly' in the labyrinth of administrative buildings on Capitol Hill. In this process he picked up some 'lowdown'. Senator Burton Wheeler, later a leader of the movement to keep America out of the war, told him that Roosevelt had 'packed the Supreme Court' so that 'they will declare anything he does constitutional' (a charge often levelled against FDR). Senator J. H. Bankhead remarked to him that the President 'chop an/ change all the time' and was 'stubborn az a mule, sah, stubborn as a MULE' (Canto 84). And Senator William E. Borah, from what was technically Ezra's native state, Idaho, had to listen to Ezra asking if he might not be able to serve the Government himself in some official capacity. Ezra afterwards wrote that he could still feel Borah's hand on his shoulder 'just before he was getting into an elevator in the Senate building ... sayin': "Well, I'm sure I don't know what a man like you would find to DO here."'

He applied to the White House to see the President, but was told that this was impossible, and never referred again to this failure of his central hope for the trip. Instead, he occupied himself with the collecting of further 'lowdown' – and its dissemination. He had lunch with the Polish ambassador, Count Patocki, whom he warned against Winston Churchill: 'God help you if you trust England.' He visited the Library of Congress, where 'Arch MacLeish' was now Librarian (though they did not meet), and inveigled the chief of the library's Japanese section ('a japanese female Dr Sakanishi ... VERY much on the spot') into allowing him to see a film of a Noh play as actually performed in Japan. She caused him some unease by casting doubt on Fenollosa's accuracy as a translator. The existence of Noh films excited him, and at several points during the next few years he suggested, in all seriousness, that the USA should hand over the disputed Pacific island of Guam to the Japanese in exchange for '300 sound films of Noh plays'.

After a couple of weeks he left Washington, confirmed in his belief that

'Uncle Jarg' was the only fit man to be President. He told a reporter: 'If God loved the American people, the Republican party would nominate for President George Holden Tinkham, the representative from Massachusetts.'

Back in New York during mid-May, he began to examine the Museum of Modern Art in some detail, and was critical of its collection. Lewis and Gaudier were not represented and what was there seemed merely the leftovers after Europe had taken the best. Meanwhile he was not thinking much about going back to Rapallo.

Observing that Gorham Munson's apartment on Fifth Avenue included a large studio, he considered holding regular evenings there devoted to the arts. He also contacted a Hungarian-born composer, Tibor Serly, who had been a member of the Rapallo musical set, and, considerably to Serly's irritation, began to bring a 'crowd' to his apartment, mostly from the Museum of Modern Art.

At Serly's he met Louis Zukofsky, whom he had not seen for six years. Zukofsky told him he did not doubt the integrity behind all his political–economic activity, 'but I pointed to his head, indicating something had gone wrong'. Zukofsky was particularly alarmed by Ezra's enthusiasm for the American popular orator Father Charles Coughlin, whose paper *Social Justice* printed anti-Semitic propaganda received from Germany, and who made regular broadcasts which were virtually Nazi in character and content. 'Whatever you don't know, Ezra,' said Zukofsky, 'you ought to know *voices*.' But Ezra paid no attention. 'Father Coughlin speaks regularly to millions of Americans,' he had written in the *British–Italian Bulletin*,

> and that means that he speaks also *for* them: I mean the fact that they listen regularly means that they share to a great extent the hopes of the speaker : . . . Coughlin has the great gift of simplifying vital issues to a point where the populace can understand their main factor if not the technical details.

Undoubtedly Ezra took Coughlin as a model when he began to broadcast regularly in 1941.

It was afterwards alleged that during his time in New York he had refused to enter the Gotham Book Mart because its proprietor Frances Steloff was Jewish, but this story was denied by Miss Steloff, who called it 'an absolute falsehood'. Louis Zukofsky, himself a Jew, 'never felt the least trace of anti-semitism in his presence. Nothing he ever said to me made me feel the embarrassment I always have for the "Goy" in whom a residue of antagonism to "Jews" remains. If we had occasion to use the words "Jew" and "Goy" they were no more or less ethnological in their sense than "Chinese" and "Italian".'

William Carlos Williams met him in Washington and took him to stay briefly in Rutherford on his way back to New York. Writing to Laughlin on 7 June 1939, a few weeks later, Williams comically describes Ezra's appearance when he first saw him: 'wrapped in sweaters and shirts and coats until I thought him a man mountain . . . I think he was afraid of our damp spring weather!' (His daughter Mary has observed that whenever he had a cold 'the fuss and the precautions seemed to me excessive'.)

Williams was worried about him. 'I found, unfortunately,' he told Laughlin, 'that he has acquired a habit of avoiding the question at issue when he is pressed for a direct answer . . . The man is sunk, in my opinion, unless he can shake the fog of fascism out of his brain.' If the subject of Fascism were raised with him, he was defensive rather than aggressive, telling one of the people he met in New York: 'Fascism only regiments those who can't do anything without it. If a man knows how to do something, it's the essence of Fascism to let him alone.' One of his hosts asked him if he thought Fascism would work in America, and he replied: 'No, I don't think so.'

Old friends constantly surfaced and pressed him to come and stay. He afterwards said he only needed to spend one night in an hotel the entire trip. Among those he visited was Viola Baxter, now married to a man named Jordan and living in Connecticut with two children. He also saw Kitty Heyman, met Marianne Moore for the first time, and had lunch with H. L. Mencken. However, he was rather dilatory about looking up Ford Madox Ford, even though Ford was currently in New York.

On 3 May, Ford wrote to Allen Tate: 'He has made no sign to me.' They met in the end, but it was not a happy occasion. Janice Biala, with whom Ford was now living, recalls: 'He seemed irritated at the thought that Ford might think he was in Mussolini's pay because he came over in the royal suite on an Italian boat. (I don't think Ford thought it.)' On 25 May he was expected at Ford's again to say goodbye – Ford and Janice were about to depart for France – but he failed to appear. They never met again, for on 24 June, Ford died in Normandy from heart failure.

Ezra wrote an obituary of Ford in the August issue of the magazine *Nineteenth Century and After* – 'only hole left', he explained of this rather *outré* burial ground. He termed it 'an inadequate oration', but it was actually one of his most eloquent tributes:

> There passed from us this June a very gallant combatant for those things of the mind and of letters which have been in our time too little prized. There passed a man who took in his time more punishment of one sort and another than I have seen meted to anyone else . . . The elder generation loathed him . . . He disturbed 'em . . . And he got all the first-rate and high

second-raters of my decade [in the *English Review*] ... His own best prose was probably lost, as isolated chapters in unachieved and too-quickly-issued novels ... He took up the fight for free letters in Paris, he took it up again in New York, where I saw him a fortnight before his death, still talking of meritorious novels, still pitching the tale of unknown men who had written the *histoire morale contemporaine* truthfully and without trumpets ...

*

Having dealt with Washington, Ezra now turned his attention to the universities. He hawked his three-page 'Introductory Text Book' and a tract, 'What Is Money For?' around several campuses. The 'Introductory Text Book' was printed in a student magazine at Yale. He met a Jesuit, who was teaching at a college in the Bronx, and persuaded him to study the money pamphlet, afterwards describing this priest (Father Moorhouse Millar) as 'one of the serious characters I saw in U.S.' From New York he went on to Harvard, where he stayed with the poet Theodore Spencer, who taught in the English department, but said that he did not wish to see any other English department professors, only the people who taught economics. However, he did agree to give a poetry reading.

Remarkably, this seems to have been his first public reading since the days of the *BLAST* group, twenty-five years earlier. A student who was present when he read at Harvard recalls how he 'seemed to read an extraordinarily long time on one breath, and then take a deep one, and go on again ... He read sitting down ... The voice was too soft to be heard, unless, as he did unexpectedly, he yelled.'

He agreed to make some gramophone records of his poetry for a series being compiled by the Department of Speech. He asked to play a set of kettle drums while recording 'The Seafarer'. This was arranged, and the general opinion was that his performance would have been 'magnificent with a rehearsal'. As it was, he merely gave 'a few reverberating strokes', then waved his sticks in the air, with only an occasional thump on the drums, being too engrossed in the words.

He also read for the recording Canto 17 (the earthly paradise), and what he called the 'Bloody Sestina' ('Altaforte'). The drums were used again for this, and Donald Hall, who heard the recording many years later, describes how it made him jump in his chair – it begins with a shout, and during it there is a thumping which 'sounded as if he were kicking a filing cabinet'.

*

Before leaving Rapallo he had been in correspondence with the President of Hamilton College about the methods used there to teach history and economics. Learning that Ezra was about to come to the USA, the President invited him to visit Hamilton and receive an honorary doctorate – this in spite of the characteristically abusive tone Ezra had used in his letters.

The invitation from his old college did not reach Rapallo before he sailed, and finally caught up with him in Washington. When he received it he was delighted. After all, he had always wanted his doctorate from Penn, which he believed he had earned. Having written to Hamilton to ensure that he would not be required to pay a fee, he accepted, and in New York he rushed round to Tibor Serly's apartment to raid it for black shoes, which he lacked. 'My feet were too small,' writes Serly, 'but I think I finally found a pair to fit him.'

Ezra's idiosyncratic clothes had been causing comment throughout the trip. One evening (says John Slocum, another of his New York hosts) 'we were refused admission to the Stork Club because of Pound's costume – tieless, in a shirt open at the throat, with broad purple stripes'. At Hamilton he struggled into a tie, but a photograph shows it to have come adrift as usual, and his academic robe sits very oddly on him.

The degree was to be conferred along with others at Commencement on 12 July. At Hamilton he stayed with Edward Root, who taught art appreciation and was related to a professor from Ezra's own college days there. He hoped to have a chance to talk to the students about economics and American history, but said he was carefully sheltered from them '& they from me'. However, it took more than these precautions to damp him down.

The degree ceremony itself went smoothly enough, and the citation addressed to him was witty and tactful. 'Your Alma Mater,' it read,

> is an old lady who has not always understood where you have
> been going, but she has watched you with interest and pride if
> not always with understanding.

But then came the official lunch, at which the principal speaker, another honorand, was a veteran political journalist and commentator, H. V. Kaltenborn, who launched into a speech which was anti-Fascist and therefore implicitly critical of his fellow guest. 'It is written in history,' he said, 'that dictatorships shall die, but democracies shall live.' He also referred to the 'doubtful' alliance between Italy and Germany. This was too much for Ezra.

He interrupted in a loud voice, asking what Kaltenborn meant by 'doubtful'. Kaltenborn attempted to explain, but was not happy at departing from his written speech, and began to stumble. Ezra leapt in and apparently began a panegyric of Mussolini, whereupon Kaltenborn tried to soothe things by declaring blandly: 'Praise God that in America people of varying points of view can still speak out.' Ezra continued his monologue, whereupon Kaltenborn, in contradiction of what he had just said, began to complain that anti-democratic doctrines ought not to be preached within the confines of an American college.

Reports of the dogfight are sketchy, but the daughter of one of the professors says that 'the situation almost got out of hand'. Another onlooker describes it as 'a hot dispute', and says 'the President intervened and stopped the uproar'. Ezra's neighbour on one side at the lunch, Wallace B. Johnson the college secretary, is emphatic that Ezra 'displayed bad manners'. Seated on the other side was Professor 'Stink' Saunders, an old friend of Ezra's from Hamilton days; he said he 'sought to calm Pound down'.

Following this Marx Brothers-style fracas, which the students doubtless enjoyed immensely, Ezra was allowed to give his own speech. He repeated his usual remark about it being possible to buy cheap reprints of Marx and Lenin in the USA but 'I spent seven years trying to get hold of a copy of John Adams's writings'; and he told them they should read his 'Introductory Text Book'. The luncheon then lurched to an end.

Writing to Wyndham Lewis some years later, Ezra looked back with pleasure on the occasion: 'That was a music hall day. with a stage set/ only at a Kawledg Komencement wd/ one git in mouth-shot at that sort of wind-bag/ that fahrt Kaltenbourne.' At the time, he referred to Kaltenborn as 'Kaltenstein'.

He left Hamilton, according to one report, 'disgruntled'; more probably he was in high spirits. Certainly on his journey back to New York he wore out a fellow alumnus with a ceaseless monologue on economics. The only use he afterwards made of the title 'Dr Pound' was in the introduction to his broadcasts on the Fascist radio in Rome.

19

Get Hold Of Their Microphone

He sailed back to Genoa from New York a few days after returning from Hamilton, on another Italian liner, the *Conte di Savoia*. Far from being disconcerted by the failure of his American visit, he seemed to believe that it had achieved something, since a few months later he was talking about his economic work as being 'done (in the main)'. He said too that he was 'inclined to come to the U.S. again next spring', perhaps even to 'make a li'l nest for ole Ez/ in N.Y.' Despite his behaviour at Hamilton he believed he might be invited back to lecture, and suggested that such an event might have 'publicity value' for the college.

Two and a half months after he returned to Rapallo, Britain and France declared war on Germany. Although the Rome–Berlin Axis had been formed in 1936 and there had been a full military and political alliance between Mussolini and Hitler since May 1939, Italy remained out of the conflict for the time being. Ezra's circle of acquaintances in Rapallo and Venice, mostly elderly expatriates, took refuge in the belief that the country did not want war at all. They pointed out that recent fortification operations along the Brenner Pass between Italy and Austria indicated that 'Mussolini's heart was in the right place'.

Ezra carried on as if nothing out of the ordinary were happening. A letter to a Social Credit supporter in England on 2 September, the day after the German invasion of Poland, asked him to check the proofs of the next section of Cantos 'if for any reason postal communications are interrupted'; but another letter written the same day, to an American who wanted to start a new magazine, entirely ignored the European situation, and said there was a 'crying need' for something like the *Little Review* which would 'fight and will include *all* the mental life of its time'. In the same letter he asserted that 'the *only* American book that *needs* reading' was Willis A. Overholser's *History of Money in the United States* (1936).

'Uncle' George Tinkham told him in an August letter that if there was a war, Roosevelt would want to propel America into it because it was the only thing that would save him politically. Ezra, all too ready to believe this, began a letter-writing campaign to keep America neutral, on the grounds that the conflict was caused by 'international usury' and by England's unjustifiable attempt to embezzle mandated territories that had formerly belonged to Germany. He told one correspondent: 'This war is no place for boys, especially American boys.' And in Canto 65, written during this period, he cited John Adams's observation that America had been for too long the puppet of Europe where wars were concerned. In the printed text he put a black line alongside this passage, to indicate its relevance to the contemporary situation:

> . . . easy to see that
> France and England wd/ try to embroil us OBvious
> that all powers of Europe will be continually at manoeuvre
> to work us into their real or imaginary balances
> of power; J. A. 1782

He had begun to contribute to the Fascist-dominated periodical *Meridiano di Roma*, and in November 1939 wrote to its editor Cornelio di Marzio, suggesting that the Italian Government should establish, presumably under his own supervision or at least with his participation, a series of publications in English that would make American readers understand and sympathize with Fascism as it actually existed in Italy. There should, he said, be studies of great American politicians of the past, whose ideas could be compared with Fascism; also a periodical devoted partly to Italian and partly to American ideas and culture, and a weekly summary of articles that had been published in Italian daily papers. Di Marzio recommended Ezra to contact the Institute for Overseas Cultural Relations. In December 1939 a note from Ezra reached Luigi Villari, in charge of relations with the USA, who rejected the plan on the grounds that it would be a tactless intervention in American domestic affairs at a time when there were no hostilities between the two countries. Villari had a shrewd idea of whom he was dealing with. In an internal memorandum he wrote:

> Mr Pound . . . is a gifted and cultured man with excellent impulses towards us, but is a dreamer who also wants to be involved in economic and financial matters about which he has some pretty fantastic notions. In the United States, Pound is appreciated as a poet, but as a political and economic writer he is not taken seriously, so that an initiative originating from him would not carry much weight.

Ezra now thought of using the radio as an alternative means of communication between Italy and America. He visited Rome and suggested to the propaganda authorities – apparently to the Minister of Popular Culture himself, Alessandro Pavolini, the supremo of all propaganda activities – a wireless programme on the lines of the printed matter he had proposed to Villari:

> I . . . suggested that as it cost 30 cents per letter [to write to America], it would convenience me to use the air in communicating with several etc. Well the Ministro looked at me careful and said in perlite words to the effect that: Ez, or probably he said 'Mio Caro Signore', if you think you can use OUR air to monkey in America's INTERNAL politics you got another one comin'.

Later, Ezra would say: 'It took me, I think it was, TWO years, insistence and wangling etc to GET HOLD of their microphone.'

He had declared for years that wars are created by the greed of usurers and armaments manufacturers, so of course he took that line now, writing to one correspondent during 1940: 'The war is mainly for money lending and three or four metal monopolies'. Roosevelt was merely the tool of 'Jewry, all Jewry, and nothing but Jewry'. He began to speak of Roosevelt as 'Jewsfeldt' and 'Stinkie Roosenstein'.

Not all his prognostications were entirely foolish: in October 1939 he wrote to a correspondent that the war would undoubtedly profit Russia, which had already received 'an enormous slice' and would doubtless get more. Also he showed sympathy with certain aspects of the British war effort, writing to British correspondents about the advisability of getting as much land as possible back into cultivation, and emphasizing the importance of self-sufficiency in farm products during wartime. 'The place to defend England is on the *land*,' he wrote to Ronald Duncan, who was himself taking up small-scale farming in the West Country.

He liked to think that the British did not really want the war: they had not been allowed to vote on it, and he alleged that 'every English friend I got in the world' had tried to 'keep England from makin' such a thunderin' and abysmal ass of herself'. But since Britain was in it now, and probably could not defeat Germany, the result would be 'infinite harm', and he hoped this could somehow be alleviated.

*

By March 1939 a new section of the Cantos, numbered 52 to 71, had reached Faber and Faber. It was published in January 1940; New Directions issued an American edition in the following September. In each case only 1,000 copies were printed; the Cantos could not yet be judged a popular success.

Ezra told Agnes Bedford he believed that *Cantos LII–LXXI* showed 'a progruss on the earlier ones/ tenny rate somfink different'. Although this latest section occupies almost 200 pages, it had been written in no more than six months, beginning no earlier than the summer of 1938. This high speed was the consequence of what Ezra described to Frank Morley as 'two advances in mode'. By this, he meant that he was now lifting material wholesale from prose sources, and was making almost no attempt to relate the new cantos to earlier parts of the work.

It is true that, for the first time, he made some effort to explain the new cantos to the reader. The section begins with a summary of their contents (though a very bare one) and an assurance that foreign words and Chinese ideograms, both here and in earlier cantos, 'seldom if ever add anything not stated in the english'. (This is untrue of a number of passages earlier in the Cantos.) James Laughlin requested more explanation in a preface, but Ezra told him to provide one himself if he really thought it necessary, and in any case the new cantos consisted simply of 'plain narrative with chronological sequence'.

Canto 52 opens the new section attractively enough. Drawn from the *Li Ki*, a Chinese classic setting out the correct rituals for each season of the year, it is another return to the cool beauty of *Cathay*:

> This month are trees in full sap
> Rain has now drenched all the earth
> > dead weeds enrich it, as if boil'd in a bouillon.
> Sweet savour, the heart of the victim
> yellow flag over Emperor's chariot
> > yellow stones in his girdle.
> Sagittarius in mid-course at sunset
> > cold wind is beginning. Dew whitens.
> Now is cicada's time,
> > the sparrow hawk offers birds to the spirits.
> Emperor goes out in war car, he is drawn by white horses,
> white banner, white stones in his girdle
> eats dog and the dish is deep.
> > This month is the reign of Autumn . . .

This canto also states the pivot on which the whole work was currently resting in Ezra's mind: 'Between KUNG and ELEUSIS' – that is, between Confucian ethics and Eleusinian sexual mystery. (In the next canto he emphasizes that these truths are accessible only to initiates: 'Kung and Eleusis / to catechumen alone.')*

---

*He fails to point out that Confucius would have disapproved deeply of 'Eleusis'. In his own translation of one of the Confucian texts (*The Unwobbling Pivot*) in 1945, he quotes the master as saying: 'To seek mysteries in the obscure, poking into magic and committing eccentricities in order to be talked about later, this I do not.'

But even the limpid Canto 52 is marred by its muddled, aggressive opening, which is spattered with anti-Semitism – such as Benjamin Franklin's supposed remark (in fact taken from a forged document) that Americans had 'better keep out the jews/ or yr/ grand children will curse you'. There are several blacked-out lines,* which mark the omission of a passage hurling abuse at the Rothschilds: 'Spécialité of the Stinkschuld / bomb-proof under their house in Paris / where they cd/ store aht voiks, / fat slug with three body-guards / soiling our sea front with a pot-bellied yacht in the offing' (a reference to the Rothschild yacht visiting Rapallo harbour). Ezra blamed Laughlin for the censorship, but Faber and Faber, who published first, cut the lines out too. Laughlin recalls that his chief problem in these cantos was not censorship, but 'getting the Chinese characters upside down . . . I would blame it on the printer. The printer would deny it . . . Finally . . . for every character, Ezra wrote "top" and "bottom" on the back of the page.'

After Canto 52 come the nine Chinese History Cantos (53 to 61), in which Ezra presents his historical raw material in a more undigested form than ever before in the Cantos. Chiefly based on a thirteen-volume history of China by a late eighteenth-century French missionary named de Mailla, they cover about 5,000 years of Chinese history, from 3000 BC to the eighteenth century AD. The purpose is to present an account of an ideal civilization, founded upon Confucian rather than Aristotelian ethics, whose efficacy can be demonstrated from history. But, as usual, Ezra assumes that the reader already understands the main outlines of what he is trying to convey, and gives only surface details without explanation of their significance. Take Canto 53:

> Then an Empress fled with Chao Kang in her belly.
> Fou-hi by virtue of wood;
> Chin-nong, of fire; Hoang Ti ruled by the earth,
> Chan by metal.
> Tchuen was lord, as is water.
> CHUN, govern
> YU, cultivate,
> The surface is not enough,
> > from Chang Ti nothing is hidden.

The surface is indeed not enough for comprehension, but it is all that is given, and almost everything else *is* hidden.

Ezra's technique was to read through de Mailla, copy extracts into his notebook and type them out in paraphrase, broken up into lines of free verse. One evening while engaged in this, he went to the cinema and

---

*The blacking-out has now been removed (1987).

watched a newsreel about Hitler visiting Italy. The film showed a group of submarines diving and surfacing in formation in honour of the Führer. Ezra was told by a retired admiral, Ubaldo degli Uberti, who had translated some of his journal into Italian, that this was an extremely dangerous manoeuvre. Ezra happened to be taking notes from de Mailla on the visit of a Tartar ruler to a Chinese emperor; believing that there was a parallel, he made use of this incident in Canto 54:

> And the Tartar ran from his car to HAN SIEUN
>> held out his hand in friendship
>> and then remounted his war horse . . .
> to the joy of HAN SIEUN TI
>> (Pretty manoeuvre but the technicians
>> watched with their hair standing on end
>>> anno sixteen, Bay of Naples)

The passage makes absolutely no reference to submarines, and would have remained incomprehensible had not Hugh Kenner examined the notebook about twenty-five years later.

At moments, Ezra's working method in these cantos has its virtues. A Chinese critic (Woon-Ping Chin Holaday) has remarked that for example some lines in Canto 53

> Wars,
>> wars without interest,
> boredom of an hundred years' war

are a perfectly acceptable summary of a period of petty strife, while the preceding lines

> Sky dark, cloudless and starless
>> at midnight a rain of stars

refer elliptically but perfectly correctly to the physical phenomena recorded during this period. But Holaday admits that Ezra's fragmentary approach to the material deprives the reader of any sense of historical cause and effect, or even of the true character of particular periods of history. Such facts as he gives seem meaningless because they are isolated. Holaday concludes that these cantos 'contain more of Pound than they do of Chinese history' – and an infuriatingly incomprehensible Pound at that.

There are occasional hints that he may be wishing to draw parallels between ancient Chinese civilization and the achievements of Mussolini's rule: there are the submarines, the reference in Canto 53 to *Ammassi* (grain-stores erected under Fascist rule in Italy), and the lines describing navigational works and the construction of the Great Wall of China: 'great works by oppression / by splendid oppression'. But most passages lack even this faint suggestion of purpose; they have no 'luminous details', and consist only of the most dry and public facts about the reigns of emperors and their families:

> OUEN kept up mulberry trees
>   and failed with his family
> YANG (kouang) TI ordered more buildings
>   jobs for two millyum men
>   and filled his zoological gardens
> 1600 leagues of canals 40 ft wide for the
>   honour of YANG TI of SOUI
> the stream Kou-choui was linked to Hoang Ho the river . . .

The impression prevails that Ezra did little more than rush through his source-material, picking out randomly such economic or political facts as appealed to him. At times, he even admits to being bored himself:

> Han, Khitan, tartar wars, boredom of.
> Money and all that, stabilization,
>   probably racket . . .

*

At least in the Chinese History Cantos the reader has a vague idea of what is going on. By comparison, the John Adams Cantos which follow (numbered 62 to 71) are three-quarters opaque.

John Adams was the second President of the United States. Ezra here singles him out for the most extended treatment of the Odyssean personality in the entire Cantos – he has ten cantos as opposed to Sigismundo Malatesta's four, the three devoted to the Jefferson–Adams correspondence, and the single one from the diary of John Quincy Adams. Oddly enough, up to now Ezra had shown no particular interest in John Adams himself. He often mentioned him in connection with Jefferson, and in *Guide to Kulchur* had observed that 'John Adams had the corrective for Jefferson', but he did not say what he meant by this. His interest in the Adams family came late; in the spring of 1924, while reading Jefferson's letters, he admitted that he could not 'remember the names' of most of the early presidents, and referred vaguely to 'two bums named Adams'. Indeed, the chief motive for the John Adams Cantos was simply his belief that Adams's writings were not available in print in the 1930s and needed to be disseminated. This was not true: the ten-volume edition of the *Works*, edited by Adams's grandson, was widely available in American libraries, while the five pages of entries for John Adams in the *National Union Catalog*, many of them dating from the 1930s, suggest that Adams was scarcely an obscure figure at that time, if not popular bedside reading. No good selected edition was available, but the man's total range could be quickly perceived by anyone seriously interested.

It is striking that the most obvious characteristic of the major historical figures in the Cantos is their comparative obscurity; this seems to have been a large part of their attraction for Ezra, who infinitely preferred cultivating his own 'discoveries' to celebrating the achievements of, say, a Cosimo di Medici or a George Washington. John Adams was intended by him, as Sigismundo had been, to exemplify 'intelligent constructivity' combined with an adequately interesting 'private life'. The very neglect from which he supposed Adams to be suffering gave the man a luminous importance. What actually went into the John Adams Cantos was of little significance.

Ezra rushed through the ten-volume Charles Francis Adams edition of the John Adams *Works* (1850–56) – as he had done with de Mailla – picking out incidents from Adams's life and activities that caught his eye, and transposing them into the Cantos. However, whereas de Mailla presented his Chinese information chronologically, the Adams *Works* were organized differently, with the material divided according to sources. Hard as it is to believe, Ezra simply ignored this, and put his chosen quotations into the Cantos in the order in which they happened to appear in print in the *Works*. In consequence he made complete nonsense of Adams's life.

For the most part he trawled wildly through the *Works*, picking up some phrase or event every page or so that took his fancy, rather than looking for any special catch. This means that no reader can make more than the most fragmentary sense of John Adams and his activities without the *Works* at hand (or at least an exegesis based on them), and even that does not facilitate interpretation, since Ezra is quite capable of taking a line or phrase from one passage in the *Works* and grafting it on to something lifted from somewhere else. On top of this, there are frequent inaccuracies in transcription.

The Chinese History Cantos are often, indeed usually, turgid, but it is possible to determine something of what is going on in each incident described. In the John Adams Cantos we encounter a mind in chaos. Ezra purports to give Adams to us as an example of pragmatic wisdom, an embodiment of Confucian ethics. But he actually presents a frighteningly candid picture of his own intellect – a mind scarcely willing to fit anything together, to distinguish between the significant and the trivial, or to convey anything of its own interior pattern to the world outside; 'a broken bundle of mirrors' indeed.

This is a typical passage (from Canto 62):

> BE IT ENACTED / guv-nor council an' house of assembly
>   (Blaydon [sic] objectin' to form ov these doggymints)

Encourage arts commerce an' farmin'
not suggest anything on my own
            if ever abandoned by administration of England
            and outrage of the soldiery
the bonds of affection be broken
till then let us try cases by law IF by
            snowballs oystershells cinders
            was provocation
            reply was then manslaughter only
in consideration of endocrine human emotions
unprootable, that is, human emotions –
                        merely manslaughter
                        brand 'em in hand
but not hang 'em being mere human blighters
                        common men like the rest of us
                        subjekk to
                                    passions . . .

These lines mostly concern Adams's defence of Captain Thomas Preston and the British troops who had been involved in the 1770 Boston Massacre, during which five American rioters were shot and six wounded. Snowballs, oyster-shells and cinders were among the missiles thrown by the crowd; Adams's argument was that if attacked the troops were entitled to retaliate. Two of them were punished by branding, having been found guilty of manslaughter. But the opening lines of this passage concern quite different matters: the objection by a Colonel Bladen, a member of the British Board of Trade and Plantations, to the words 'be it enacted' in colonial laws, which he said usurped the authority of the King; and the establishment of a committee, with Adams as member, to 'mature a plan for the encouragement of arts, agriculture, manufacturers and commerce' (this is referred to obliquely in the third line).

Even Donald Davie, whose book *Poet as Sculptor* (1965) makes heroic efforts to see some good in every page of the Cantos, has to allow that the handling of the John Adams material reduces Adams's 'admirably purposeful' life to 'a non-sensical hurly-burly'. And yet, just as Ezra seems to be touching bottom in the whole enterprise, it is possible to see some sort of perverse achievement, to have some sense that he is on his way up again, towards better things. William Carlos Williams was amused and delighted by Ezra's latest outrage, perceiving that something enjoyable had come of it. 'He thinks he's being terribly profound, frowningly serious,' he wrote to Laughlin, 'and all he's doing is building blocks, and it's lovely.'

*

Ezra sent the new cantos to Mussolini, together with a translation of one of his articles in the *British Union Quarterly*, saying in his accompanying letter:

> DUCE
>   I hope I have done some useful work, especially in conden-
> sing some historical facts in my CANTOS 52/71.
>   The book is accordingly hardly neutral and my editors have
> cancelled the name Rothschild from the first page . . .
>   very truly yours
>   Ezra Pound

He felt that the Cantos should now change direction; he said that he did not propose to go on dealing with 'dead matter and negations'; it was time for 'positive statements'. He reiterated that his economic work was mainly done (though there was still a need to compress, restate, and distribute it), and he was 'now definitely onto questions of BELIEF'. He was envisaging only one more volume of cantos; in 1940 he wrote that 'there's a final volume to be done'. And he told Agnes Bedford he would shortly be 'plungin' into philosophy'. This propelled him in the direction of George Santayana.

Half-Spanish and half-American, Santayana had been for many years an instructor in philosophy at Harvard. Politically conservative, since 1924 he had lived in Rome. Now in his late seventies, he was pro-Christian and opposed to Hegelian idealism, but disliked the credulous and superstitious aspects of religion. Daniel Cory, who was often in Rapallo, acted as his secretary and assistant for much of the time; hence Ezra's knowledge of him. Ezra had tried to meet him in September 1937, but Santayana fended him off – 'For heaven's sake, dear Cory, do stop Ezra Pound from sending me his book.'

In January 1939, while briefly in Rome, Ezra called on Santayana at the Hotel Bristol. Santayana afterwards wrote to Cory that Ezra 'reminded me of several old friends . . . who were spasmodic rebels, but decent by tradition, emulators of Thoreau, full of scraps of culture, but lost, lost in the intellectual world . . . On the whole we got on very well, but nothing was said except commonplace.' The meeting entertained Santayana enough to make the idea of another encounter not unpalatable, and when in the autumn of 1939 he finished writing *The Realm of Spirit* he felt himself briefly 'free to amuse myself with other things', he decided to look up Ezra again, as a recreation, and wrote to him proposing that they might meet in Rapallo or Venice, where he was going to winter in the Danieli. This fitted perfectly into Ezra's plans, since he was to spend Christmas in Venice with Olga and Mary.

He told Santayana in a letter at the beginning of December:

> I have . . . got to the end of a job or part of a job (money in
> history) and for personal ends have got to tackle philosophy for
> my 'paradise' and do badly want to talk with some one who has
> thought a little about it. There is one bloke in England, whose
> name escapes me, who has dropped an intelligent aside in a
> small book on Manes [founder of the Manicheans]. Otherwise
> you are the only perceivable victim . . . There are one or two
> gropings in my notes to Cavalcanti and one or two Chinese
> texts whereupon sidelight wd. be welcome.

This indicates all too clearly the kind of 'philosophy' he really wanted to
discuss: he had simply plunged himself back into the Mysteries. Having
acquired at last a copy of the works of the Neoplatonist philosopher Scotus
Erigena, he was now making such observations in his correspondence as:
'Re Cavalcanti: Erigena certainly throws doubt on various readings . . . I at
any rate have got to digest Erigena and then review the whole "Donna Mi
Prega".'

Santayana perceived something of what was in store for him. He wrote
back agreeing to meet in Venice just after Christmas, but added: 'You must
not count on my philosophy to answer your questions, because questions
are apt to imply a philosophy and don't admit of answers in terms of any
other' (which was certainly true of Ezra's Mysteries). Ezra had better 'find
your answers for yourself. But you might show me some of the beauties of
Venice, which I have very likely missed all my life.'

Ezra, Olga and Mary spent Christmas not at the hidden nest, but in a
borrowed flat in a *palazzo* overlooking the Grand Canal – Olga's house
had been let as was usual at that time of year. She insisted 'how elegant and
right' things were in the *palazzo*, but Ezra found it appallingly cold, and
after two nights persuaded her to move to a *pensione* on the Zattere. 'There
was some talk about a friend of Babbo's joining us,' writes Mary. 'He was
referred to as the Possum . . . The Possum never showed up.' Ezra wrote
to Eliot on 18 January: 'I am sorry yew missed the outlook from the
Palazzo, but it got so goddam cold we emigrated to a steam-hot and damn
good eatin pension.' One evening they all went to see a Fred Astaire–
Ginger Rogers movie, and came home late. 'All the way home from the
cinema,' writes Mary

> Babbo tapped and leapt and encouraged me to do likewise and
> 'get nimble', Mamile laughed and we were very gay. As we
> started to undress we heard a loud fracas in Babbo's room –
> now that he had thrown off his coat and jacket he leapt and
> tap-danced more freely. Mamile had quite a bit of difficulty in

putting an end to it: '*Caro*! I refrain from practising for fear of disturbing the other guests and you bring the house down in the middle of the night.' Babbo was mortified and sorry; it was hard for him to keep still before having fully danced out the rhythm he had absorbed.

Ezra's letter to Eliot continued: 'Had a lot of jaw with Geo. Santayana.' They met at the Hotel Danieli, Mary being allowed to accompany her father only to the door: 'No philosophy until you are forty.' Afterwards, she had 'seldom seen Babbo so eager and yet so contented. "A relief to talk philosophy with someone completely honest – a nice mind."' From odd remarks dropped by Ezra, Mary gathered that they had strayed into politics now and then, 'and saw eye to eye on most things. They believed in Mussolini's basic humaneness and peaceful intentions; certain foibles in his character did not diminish the fact that the country had improved greatly under his regime.'

Ezra's opinion of Santayana (expressed to Eliot) was 'Never met anyone who seems to me to fake less. In fact, I gave him a clean bill . . . Wot wiff ideograms and all, George *is* trying to see the connection. I have fed him the Cavalcanti . . .' He also lent Santayana Fenollosa's essay on the Chinese Written Character. Santayana returned it by post, saying he wished there had been more in it about the actual composition of the ideograms and 'less romantic metaphysics'. He ended: 'You see I am floundering in your philosophy, badly but not unpleasantly.' The tone of the letter indicated that he had had quite enough of the whole business.

Ezra did not read it like that, and wrote back addressing Santayana as if he were now a potential convert to all his ways of thinking, including monetary reform. He talked about his belief in that method of thought which involved mental jumps between 'ideograms' as opposed to logical abstract argument. Santayana replied asking if he really meant that he could jump legitimately from one idea to another, just as he chose. He remarked that certainly 'your tendency to jump is so irresistible [to you] that the bond between particulars jumped to is not always apparent . . . It is a mental grab-bag. A *latent* classification or a *latent* genetic connection would seem to be required, if utter miscellaneousness is to be avoided.'

Ezra ignored this slight on his Method, and pressed on with his plan to enrol Santayana in his team. He proposed to Eliot that they should all three collaborate on a book, the subject to be 'The Ideal University, or the Proper Curriculum'. Eliot, either teasing Ezra or genuinely misled as to Santayana's supposed willingness, wrote back that Santayana 'adds just the spot of respectability that makes the book queer whereas if you and me didn't have him I don't say we couldn't make the book just as queer, but the public wouldn't be so surprised'. But Santayana had now had enough of Ezra, and said he could not possibly collaborate on a subject 'about which I have no ideas . . . And it would always be impossible morally because you and T.S.E. are reformers, fully of prophetic zeal and faith in the Advent of the Lord; whereas I am cynically content to let people educate or neglect themselves as they may prefer.'

Ezra, brought up short by this, made no further attempt to involve Santayana in his plans to turn philosopher, but for a time simply continued on that course alone. He contemplated writing 'quite a chunk' about Erigena, and suggested to Eliot that this might form part of a prose trilogy of which the other two sections would be the *Ta Hio* and his article on 'The Ethics of Mencius' published in the *Criterion* in 1938 – though he added modestly: 'I don't feel ready to knock off "The *whole* of Philosophy" in six months".'

He also contemplated writing new cantos which would follow Frobenius's belief about the spread of culture from Africa into Europe, but would apply it to religion – 'an analysis of Christianity into its various racial components . . . I shd. claim to get on from where Frobenius left off, in that his Morphology was applied to savages and my interest is in civilizations at their *most*'. One may guess at the sort of cantos that would have emerged, if this idea had been pursued, from a passage in a letter of March 1940 to the Reverend Henry Swabey, an Anglican clergyman who was an enthusiastic Social Creditor:

> Re European belief: Neither mass nor communion are of Jew origin. Nowt to do with that narsty old maniac JHV [Jehovah] and are basis of Xtn relig. Mass ought to be in Latin, unless you cd. do it in Greek or Chinese. In fact, *any* abracadabra that no bloody member of the public or half-educated ape of a clargimint cd. think he understood.

However, in the same month, in an uncharacteristic mood of self-doubt, he wrote to Ronald Duncan: 'Mass and communion not Jewish in origin – What's use my saying *that* especially as I have *not* studied the Mass and am not absolutely sure what mightn't be tucked into it . . . Christianity is (or was when real) anti-Semitism, etc. What is the use of arguing (my arguing) with undefined terms.' This was itself thoroughly un-Ezraic, and went on: 'I am getting to age where at bloody last I occasionally wonder whether I don't talk too much – or at any rate stop and ask myself: *is it useful* to say this or that – at a particular time . . . And at the end of the same letter: 'Damn it all, I am a poek [*sic*], partly a musician, i.e. in one corner up to a point, and an economist. I can't become an authority on another dept. in six weeks or even six months . . . Speculation is one thing; dogma another. And I don't think it opportune to print speculation at the moment . . . Tempus tacendi. I don't know how long it will last.' The answer was, not long.

*

In any case it was only *tempus tacendi*, time to be silent, in the matter of the origin of Christianity. He had no intention of keeping quiet in his attempts to encourage the USA to become sympathetic to Mussolini. Though his earlier approaches to the authorities had met with a rebuff, he tried again.

On 25 April 1940, while in Rome, he went to the Ministry of Popular Culture, this time hoping to see the Director General of the Propaganda Service, Armando Koch, and to convince him that 'the absolute domination of the Jews in the North American press and publishing' made it quite impossible to have the Italian viewpoint aired there. His argument was that 'at least those few Americans who see the truth' should 'illuminate their own fellow-citizens'.

The Ministry of Popular Culture, 'Minculpop' in common parlance, was intended to control all areas of Italian cultural life as well as administer press censorship and propaganda. In practice it was far less effective than Goebbels' similar enterprise in Berlin, not least because of shortage of cash. The official who saw Ezra on this visit said his proposals were impossible because it 'would need a lot of money' to launch effective propaganda at America; to which Ezra replied: 'It doesn't need a lot of money but a lot of intelligence.'

He now began again to consider whether broadcasting might be more effective than writing. On 31 March 1940 he wrote to Ronald Duncan from Rapallo:

> Blasted friends left a goddam radio here yester. Gift. God damn
> destructive and dispersive devil of an invention . . . Only stuff
> fit to hear was Tripoli, Sofia and Tunis. Howling music in two
> of 'em and a cembalo in Bulgarea. And a double sense of the
> blessedness of silence when the damn thing is turned off.

But the radio set, left by Natalie Barney and a companion, made him think seriously about the medium, or at least about its potential.

'What drammer or teeyater *wuz*, radio is,' he told Duncan dogmatically. He suggested that, if properly used, radio might 'stop diffuse writing' by imposing more concision and clarity than print demanded. There were also 'the histrionic developments in announcing' – the actual techniques of performance at the microphone, which would present a new challenge to someone who had previously only used pen and typewriter.

He started listening regularly to the radio. It occurred to him that he had really anticipated the radio effect 'in first third of Cantos' (the montage of different voices), and had been able to write the John Adams Cantos, a monologue by a single voice, 'because I was the last survivin' monolith who did not have a bloody radio in the 'ome', but now it was impractical to ignore the medium. 'As Mr Cohen said: "Vot I say iss, we got to svallow 'em, vot I say iss, ve got to svallow 'em." Or be boa-constricted.'

He had, of course, no shortage of potential subject matter for broadcasts, were he given a chance to address the world. His observation that he had finished his economic work now seemed only to have referred to the Cantos, for during 1940 he poured out as many letters as ever dealing with economic and political problems as he saw them. He added two books to his list of approved authors on these subjects: D. R. Dewey's *Financial History of the United States* (1905) and Brooks Adams's *Law of Civilization and Decay* (1895). Adams, a great-grandson of John Adams, had anticipated Ezra's view not merely of usury but of the decline of art since the rise of money-lending, claiming that there had been a perceptible decay in the imagination; Dewey's book seemed proof to Ezra that Social Credit worked, since it described how something resembling a Douglas-style National Dividend was paid in America in 1837. Another talisman for him during this period was *The Two Nations* (1935) by the British writer Christopher Hollis, which followed in the steps of Hollis's fellow Roman Catholic, G. K. Chesterton, by attacking monetarism, international banking, and the division into rich and poor which this created. Hollis was later deeply embarrassed to hear that Ezra had cited him approvingly in a broadcast from Rome, since he was at the time a monitor of enemy broadcasts at the Air Ministry.

*

France surrendered in June 1940, and Ezra referred affectionately to 'ole Pete Pétain', who now had Berlin's mandate to govern the unoccupied part of the country from Vichy. In September, Ezra tried to arrange another visit to America, in the hope of carrying out the propaganda programme he had proposed to Minculpop, and of persuading the USA to keep out of the war (as he put it in a letter to a friend in Japan, he 'thought of going to U.S. to annoy them'), but he was told that no passage was available until December. 'Thank God I didn't get as far as Portugal and get stuck there.'

America continued to remain out of the conflict, but Italy invaded Greece in October, and Ezra found himself abruptly cut off from his London friends. 'Gornoze what's become of Possum and Duncan . . . or the pacific Bunting.' He was soon reduced to asking his contact in still-neutral Japan (the poet Katue Kitasono) if *he* was in touch with Duncan or Eliot and could pass on any news of them. Mail could still be exchanged with America, but H. L. Mencken wrote to say that he could not think of any periodical likely to print contributions by Ezra supporting Italian Fascism. It seemed absurd, said Ezra, for a man 'at my time of life' to find himself 'with no means of communicatin' wiff his com/damn/ patriots save by private letter'. He told William Carlos Williams dolefully that enormous harm had been done to England during the Napoleonic Wars 'by simply being cut off from ALL contemporary thought', adding: 'Same goes for U.S. now . . . gross ignorance [in America] of thought on the Axis side of the line . . . gross ignorance . . . of English thought.' This was nonsense as a summary of America's current situation, but it exactly described his own.

He was isolated in Rapallo, with little coming in from the outside world, dependent on what was in his own head, his small library, and the heavily censored propaganda-laden Italian and German newspapers. Only the radio kept him in touch with the world as it seemed outside Italy and his own mind. He listened to the BBC, but did not care for it, remarking that it sounded like 'the cold, evil voice of mendacity, and needless excitement'. He was reduced to reading anti-Semitic material that the Mosley organization had sent him in the mid-1930s, which at the time he had tossed aside. In one of their books he found the allegation that the Jews were controlled by a central authority, the Kahal, which wanted to stir up war because it would benefit nickel production. He wrote about this in *Meridiano di Roma* in March 1940, where his article was found and reprinted by the Nazi *News from Germany*, which Ezra took throughout the war.

At the beginning of June 1940, shortly before communication with London was broken off, he told Eliot that he was continuing with the Cantos, and had some material about silver mines which would fit with Erigena's '*Omnia quae sunt, lumina sunt*'. A few months later he sent Katue Kitasono in Japan some lines 'to go into Canto 72 or somewhere' beginning 'Now sun rises in Ram sign'. These suggested that he was returning to the style of those earlier cantos which had described lotus-eaters and an earthly paradise. And for the moment that was all, as if he sensed that neither of these starts was in the right direction. Gradually, under the pressure of other concerns in the following months, work on the Cantos, for the first time in nearly twenty years, came to a halt.

٭

English and American periodicals might be beyond Ezra's reach now, but the Italian papers often welcomed him into print. He contributed to the daily *Giornale di Genova*, to a Milan journal of Fascist groups in universities, and frequently to *Meridiano di Roma*, where he usually wrote on economics, and where his articles were almost always placed on the front page alongside speeches by major Fascists. However, the editor, Cornelio di Marzio, took pains to dissociate the paper from necessary concurrence with Ezra's views, and deliberately left his many errors of grammar and spelling uncorrected, to underline the impression that he and his staff regarded the American poet as an oddity, an amusement rather than a serious commentator.

He spent part of the late summer of 1940 in Siena, where Olga was still helping to run Count Chigi's annual Accademia Musicale. Mary joined them, and he 'showed me Siena stone by stone, as he had done in Venice . . . As usual, he would make me describe in writing what we had seen.' But she noticed that when they spent a few days together in Rome he 'seemed harassed, as though something was out of control'. In her company he kept saying to an American journalist, Reynolds Packard: 'Tell the American people, tell the American people . . .'

During this Rome visit, he probably paid another call on Minculpop. Certainly in November 1940 he wrote asking for an audience with Pavolini, and was told that this was out of the question and referred back to Propaganda Services. To them, he wrote from Rapallo offering to 'come down to Rome at once if you telegraph and carry on for at least six brief talks of this sort', and enclosing a sample script. He suggested he might 'register 'em on discs' so they could be repeated. 'Might even make my talks SHORTER, as NO ONE can take in more than one economic or monetary idea or point at one time.'

Still the answer was no: the Radio Department of Minculpop answered that they could not at present make use of his scripts in broadcasts to America. Yet now that Italy was involved in the war, propaganda broadcasts were going on, and Ezra could no longer be fobbed off with the excuse that it would be an impertinent interference in the domestic affairs of the United States. Behind the scenes, the Radio Department began to undertake a confidential vetting of his history and character, with a view to enlisting him to speak over the air.

20

Europe Calling! Pound Speaking!

While the vetting was going on, Mary was in Venice with her parents for a few days before returning to school. It was October 1940, their last holiday there together. 'It was too cold to do much swimming. . . There were no concerts. The sparkle had gone out of Venice. . . Mamile's main concern was finding new tenants for the house. She had always leased to foreigners; now they had all gone. A plump elderly lady came to look at the house. . . In the end she sighed and gave up: no, too small, too expensive. When she left, Mamile said: "Poor thing, all these Jews not knowing where to go and with so little money left. But we are no better off either." I sensed the great shortage of money and that my school fees were a burden.'

Mary went back to Florence and her convent school. She was showing signs of her father's independence of mind: in an unprecedentedly short time she rose to the envied position of President of the Daughters of Mary, but soon afterwards declared herself a heretic and began to read Confucius, encouraged by letters from Rapallo. Her father's opinion on any subject 'became dogma to me and no one was to question it'.

*

Nobody in authority in Rome objected to Ezra's enrolment as a broadcaster. The security services questioned whether his offer to collaborate might have 'ulterior motives', but did not suggest what these might be. Ezra afterwards said the final decision to employ him was made by Adriano Ungaro of Minculpop, 'an Italian liberal who had the guts to initial my broadcasts'.

At first, during the closing weeks of 1940, he was only invited to send in scripts to Rome for others to read on the air, but on 21 January 1941 he had his first appointment to go in person to the studios that Ente Italiano

Audizione Radio, the Italian broadcasting service, had established for short-wave overseas transmissions. These were on the top floor of Minculpop, in Via Veneto. That day, Ezra made his first recording for the 'American Hour', a programme of news, comment and music, which had been transmitted for the previous three and a half months and was audible in Britain and much of Europe as well as the USA and the Pacific.

'The United States,' he began his talk,

> should try to understand the last twenty years of European history, before going too far in finding themselves involved in the war. Democracy was created in America and this is the place where it must be saved. The peace of the world is set forth through the good government from the interior.

It was mild stuff. After all, America was not yet participating in the war and a strong lobby existed in Washington that wished to leave Europe to sort out its own mess. No one in Rome could object to beaming comment such as this across the Atlantic, and on the strength of his first recordings Ezra was engaged to supply the American Hour with regular broadcast talks, and to come to Rome to record them in batches.

After a few further sessions in the studio, it became apparent that he was not a run-of-the-mill political commentator. First, there was the matter of his opening words. He was asked to begin each talk by identifying himself in some such form as 'Ezra Pound speaking'. In practice, after the scripts had been vetted by a Minculpop official, and he was left in the studio with only a recording engineer who did not understand English, he would depart from the typed text and provide himself with a real P. T. Barnum send-off:

> 'Europe calling! Pound speaking! Ezra Pound speaking!'
> 'Old Ezra speaking! Pound speaking!'
> 'Ezra Pound speakin' from Europe for the American heritage!'
> 'Dearly beeloved brevrem, this is ole Ezra speaking'.'

The medium of radio was absolutely irresistible to him. 'I don't so much write as I roar,' he remarked in a letter to James Laughlin. 'A New technique/ vurry funny after WRITING.'

He approached the microphone just as he had tackled any art or subject that was unfamiliar to him: as something that he could master overnight, providing he were sufficiently critical of his own work. There was no need to refer to the so-called professionals. When the studio engineers, struggling to balance his unpredictable decibels, which ranged from whisper to shout, asked him to keep a more 'even tone of voice', he told them that if he was too quiet they could 'turn on more current'. He would not be overawed by technicalities.

The Italian Government officials whose duty it was to monitor overseas broadcasting began to wonder what the American Hour had let itself in for. Two months after Ezra had recorded his first talk, the Military Intelligence department contacted the radio staff to say that one of their colonels had had a talk with the American ambassador, and neither of them felt Ezra should continue to be let anywhere near a microphone. Similarly, Luigi Villari of the Institute of Overseas Cultural Relations tried to warn the radio people:

> There is no doubt in my mind that Ezra Pound is insane! He is a pleasant enough madman and he is certainly a friend of Italy, but in the course of two interviews I recently had with him, I heard criticism, circumspection, accusations, etc. that have rather alarmed me. . . It is advisable that such things be stopped from the start.

Ezra had apparently been grumbling about the behaviour of those officials who had tried to block him. When he heard criticisms such as Villari's he dismissed them, in rather curious terminology, as a plot by 'capitalist reactionaries'. Now he had arrived in the studio, he was not going to be pushed out again.

He acquired a journalist's rail pass, which made travel from Rapallo much cheaper, and would go to Rome for a couple of weeks at a time, to record two dozen or so scripts that he had written at home. He always stayed at the Albergo d'Italia in the Via Quattro Fontane; he would arrive there with his portable typewriter and a pile of books, so that he could look up quotations and make last-minute changes in the scripts.

On his recording days, he would hurry off to the Via Veneto in his big hat and thick tweed overcoat, a garment ridiculously heavy for the Rome weather, and would arrive at the studios in the rushed manner that had become habitual. 'Time, damn it/ never enough TIME,' he wrote in a 1936 letter. Charles Olson noted that he would enter a room

> with a movement peculiar to himself, both like a loaded gun and with the sort of blind swing of a battering ram. . . Part of it's restlessness to get things going, which accounts for a motion to the right and ahead, as though to hurry past one. And some feeling of anxiety that if he doesn't unload, he may lose what's on his mind. . . But it is the blindness which is the remaining sense, over concentrated, obsessional, rushing ahead of the reality. . . impatience, impatience, impatience.

When he had finished at the studio, there were friends to see. Mary, visiting Rome with her father, was struck by the number of acquaintances he had made there, all of whom seemed eager to entertain and feed him.

There was Princess Troubetzkoi, a novelist and playwright in her late seventies who spoke on the American Hour, giving cosy talks about how pleasant life was in Italy. She told Mary that 'young people in Italy were wonderful, intelligent, serious, that all this talk about Fascist education being bad was nonsense'. Russian by marriage, she had been born Amélie Rives in Richmond, Virginia. Her death in June 1945 is commemorated in Canto 74, where Ezra calls it 'the end of that chapter'.

Mary was also introduced to Luigi Villari, the only person she met who made even mildly anti-Semitic remarks – and he was immediately silenced by another of Ezra's friends and fellow-broadcasters, Olivia Rossetti Agresti, daughter of William Michael Rossetti and niece of Dante Gabriel and Christina. Married to an Italian, she told Mary that she believed in 'cultural rather than racial values'; she had a boundless admiration for Mussolini. Other speakers wandered in and out of the radio station, exotic figures from India or Afghanistan, deposed monarchs, princes in exile; 'all eccentrics', says a former employee, 'so that Pound did not stand out'.

The editor of the American Hour was George ('Giorgio') Nelson Page, whose family came from Virginia but who had spent most of his life in Italy. During the war he renounced American citizenship and became legally an Italian. There was also an Englishman, James ('Giacomo') Strachey Barnes, an avid supporter of Mussolini since the 1920s, who described himself as 'chronicler and prophet of the Fascist Revolution', and had written several books in English in support of his political beliefs. After the war he vanished.

Now that Ezra had become a regular contributor to the programme, he was sometimes asked to take part in unscripted round-table discussions of the news, but he was never comfortable in these, and would ask the producer to map out topics in advance so that he could prepare what he was going to say. In the event the plan was not usually adhered to, and this disconcerted him. Once or twice he tried his hand at writing slogans for use in other parts of the programme; the art of propaganda fascinated him, and he suggested that a chair in such a discipline should be established in some university. Occasionally his proposals for music broadcasts were followed – 'I had them play Vivaldi until the disks wore out,' he told Charles Olson. Mostly 'Giorgio' Page restricted him to writing and recording his own talks, which were used at the rate of two or three a week, each being broadcast three times (the programme was repeated so that it could be beamed at different parts of the world).

Ezra always emphasized that he was 'an independent speaker', an outside contributor as opposed to 'the REGULAR staff speakers', and that he had only 'obtained the concession' to speak on the radio after battering on the doors of authority, rather than accepting any offer of a job. Moreover 'no one ever suggested to me what I should say over the radio. . . All talks were my own idea and I was at no time ever coerced by anyone in any way either directly or indirectly.' (He said this during a 1945 interrogation, when it would have been in his interest to claim the opposite – to say that he had only broadcast as the result of coercion, and was not expressing his own opinions at all.) Nevertheless, though not a staff member, he was paid for his broadcasts from the outset.

For the first time since his marriage in 1914 he found himself obliged to try to earn a living. Since Italy had entered the war, Dorothy's income from England had stopped coming through, and her assets there were sequestered by the authorities for the duration of hostilities, under Enemy Property regulations. Such royalties as Ezra was owed by Faber and Faber or any other publisher could not be sent, and Homer's pension from the USA was only arriving erratically. Italian banks now generally refused to cash American cheques, on the grounds that mail boats were being intercepted by British warships. Ezra said he had applied to become a regular broadcaster largely because a German officer at the Rapallo tennis club 'told me they were paying good money'.

He was indeed paid 'quite a good sum', as one Minculpop official put it – a little over 350 lire per talk, which (thanks to inflation) had become the equivalent of $17, the price of half a dozen new books. If he had recorded only one broadcast at a time, the money would scarcely have covered his travel and accommodation in Rome, but in batches of two dozen for each journey from Rapallo it produced a modest but steady and valuable income for himself and his dependants. His need of it is indicated by the frequency with which he complained to Minculpop's finance department about the tardiness of payments.

*

His talks were supposed to last about ten minutes, though since they were not broadcast live, he could vary the length a little as he chose. When preparing them, he would look through the Italian papers and listen to any foreign radio station he could tolerate. 'I definitely tried to listen to London,' he said in one of his talks, 'but with the passage of time I listen to London less.' Off the air he spoke of 'the shit of BBC'.

His main purpose in writing the scripts, he said, was to induce his audience to 'listen to historic information in order to understand fascism and how to beat the financiers'. He claimed that this could not be called propaganda, at least not official propaganda: 'I was not sending axis propaganda but my own.' Certainly neither Minculpop nor the radio staff gave him more than minimal guidance on subject matter. Consequently he produced the usual Poundian *mélange* on current affairs, 'broken mirrors' from his reading and reflection, clusters of favourite codewords, familiar names, and stock ideas.

He claimed not only that each talk fitted together into a perceptible shape, but that there was also a sequence of ideas running right through the series, so that 'the conversation of February coheres with that of April'. In fact, though certain themes rose to the surface and recurred for several weeks, they usually vanished and gave way to other preoccupations. Shrewdly, he perceived that too smooth a presentation at the microphone would be deadening: 'Nothing solemn or formal will hold the American auditor. If I don't sound a bit cracked and disjointed, they will merely twirl the button and listen to the next comic song, dance or ballyhoolah "Soapopry". Hence the. . . American dialects etc.' So at last he was able to do with his voice what he had done on paper for years; and he gave a truly spectacular performance.

*

A typical broadcast – many have been preserved on record in Washington – begins with 'filler' music, after which a female announcer with a flat, formal voice reads a station identification, first in Italian, then in English: 'Good evening. This is the Italian Broadcasting System, transmitting a special programme for the Western United States and Canada, the Pacific area, New Zealand and Australia. We open our programme this evening with a talk by Ezra Pound, entitled "To Be Late".'

There is a brief pause as the disc of Ezra's talk is started; then a powerful shout: 'EUROPE CALLING! EZRA POUND SPEAKING!'

The voice drops into a cosy, folksy drawl for the opening remarks: 'Ah hear one of mah ex-editors has bin' sayin', oh yeah, Pound talks are all right, but they *arrrrre* –' (he rolls his r's with ridiculous exaggeration) – what was it? "belated"? No, he said, uh, they're "retarded" was it? *Out of date*, um, *out of date*, that was it.

'Well, dammit, two things. If yew hadn't bin such *mutts*, you woulda *heerd* me, and Céline for that matter, long before now! Some of yew woulda thought about what that good man, L.-F. Céline, an' the present speaker, started sayin' a long *taime* ago' (an almost Texan drawl on *taime*).

'Ah started long befoh' Céline, 's far 's Ah can make aht, Ah spose he's fifteen or twenty years younger 'n Ah am, unless o' coss he took up his young days doctorin' in the Paris suburbs, an' only got roun' t' writing' as he had got through with his patients.

'He says in one place, folks don' unnerstan' him, or they unnerstan' him all wrong. . . Ah'll translate it from the original . . .' And off he goes into a long quotation from Céline about his patients' perpetual inability to follow the precise instructions on a prescription – having given his audience no information about who Céline might be.*

---

*Louis-Ferdinand Céline (1894–1961), French doctor and novelist, anti-Semite and wartime contributor to the French collaborationist press.

'The Yew-nited States,' he eventually continues, 'may take twenty years or more t' get t' where Céline was ten years ago. Ah be late? Ah am belated? Ah am not an *alarrrm clock*, expected t' tell unhearing America about every fust book by a noo European author, especially if Ah've said things analogous before the said author had broken into print.

'Céline writes with the clarity of Remy de Gourmont. He is a *grrrreat wrrrriter*. The search for *rrrreality* leads men of differrrrent races t' similar private discoveries. In fact that is the basis of science, which *rrrrelativity* tries to destroy.

'Céline denies that there is any fundamental and *irrrrremediable* hate between the Frrrrench and the Gerrrrmans, That was mah own conclusion after four years in Paris. Hence of course Mister Rooo-se-velt's dee-term-in-ation to starve the French in unoccupied France . . .'

And so he continues for another five or six minutes, oscillating between Roosevelt's supposed desire to embroil the USA in the war for his own unscrupulous ends, and the wisdom of Céline, whose remarks on 'Yew-genics' and the Jews are quoted with relish. Then comes the pay-off:

'Mebbe in time the Amurrican cawledge boys will git roun' t' readin' me, or Céline, or some of the livin' authors. . . Time t' read Céline for the simple truths. . . You may be a bit late in startin'. . . Ezra Pound speakin'."

The announcer returns to the microphone with her flat, rather bored tones: 'You have just heard a talk by Ezra Pound entitled "To Be Late". This is the Italian Broadcasting System. Our musical presentation this evening consists of a concert of light music . . .'

*

Occasionally in the talk he makes a slight slip and corrects himself; often it is hard to distinguish the names he is citing; but in general it is a masterly performance. The voice is clearly pitched – the absurdly rolled r's help to throw the words across the poor-quality short-wave transmission, so that he comes over far better than the professional announcer – and the folksy manner is perfectly attuned to the style of the 'fireside chat'. Some of his listeners in the USA were astonished by the whole act, observing that the accents adopted were simply stage-American: 'if Yankee,' writes Charles Norman, 'more nasal than anything ever heard north of Boston, if western, more "folksy" and drawling than anything ever heard west of the Mississippi.' But the very absurdity was itself a draw to listeners.

*

In the early days he would rehearse his broadcasts at home. Mary found his radio voice unnerving, 'angry, sardonic, sometimes shrill and violent', but apparently never funny, which was what, for much of the time, he meant it to be. Olga sometimes made suggestions for the broadcasts, of which she thoroughly approved, but Dorothy cared less for them and commented unfavourably on the frequent jumps in sense, saying the scripts were hard to follow; possibly the Kensington streak in her found the performance vulgar.

But she did not dissent from the political content. Indeed, she had a simpler and more hard-line feeling of support for the Axis than Ezra. In 1949 she wrote that the Allies had disseminated 'very little but destruction' and that 'Hitler & Mussolini, especially the latter, were certainly trying against awful odds, to further civilization'. Charles Olson judged: 'Hers is just anglo-saxon fear and hate, the weak of the world.'

The Céline script is typical of what Ezra wrote for the microphone. His talks usually began with the bold statement of a theme, such as: 'Brooks Adams observed that after Waterloo no power had withstood the power of the usurers.' The exposition of the theme (if it could be called that) would include citation of personal experience, recollections of remarks made to him, and snippets from his own reading and published writings, with allusions rarely explained. Such names as 'the *Little Review*', 'Major Douglas', and 'Doctor William C. Williams' would be dropped in throughout with no concession to the listener. He often made play with puns, such as 'Chiang Kike Shek', or 'the nude eel' and 'new steal'. The broadcast would sometimes end with an injunction to the listener to 'look into that', or a rhetorical question such as 'Why did you get into this war?'

Just now and then, doubts crept into the talks about who, if anyone, might be listening: 'I was wonderin' if anybody listened to what I said on Rome Radio and an experienced well-broken journalist said: don't worry, there'll always be some fellow in a newspaper office sitten there, trying to get something for his column or something.' As late as 1945, he was still wondering about this: 'What I am in absolute ignorance of is: whether anyone actually heard my broadcasts . . . The only auditors I know of were foreigners in Florence.'

*

But he thought highly of the broadcasts, and hoped to print them in book form, available in England and America (though even he could not imagine when this would be possible). Indeed, he regarded the scripts as essential instruction for the rising generation; he said that he honestly did not know where else 'the young men of England and America' could get material 'to build their souls, or at least their minds for tomorrow . . . except from my broadcasts'.

After a few months, he was officially warned to stick to literary matters and not to pontificate about current affairs. 'I gather that if I am to go on with these talks,' he told his listeners during 1941, 'I shall have gradually more to say about letters and less about international politics.' He was asked if he could not discuss contemporary American writing – that was the sort of thing a poet should talk about – but he discovered a Minculpop official who backed him, and who was 'furious at the idea that ANYbody in the office would have thought they knew enough to amend my Ezment'. Eventually his critics gave up, and left him entirely alone to pursue his idiosyncratic course; he said he had refused to let them 'change a comma' in his texts.

Nothing could rein him in. In the same broadcast in which he mentioned the attempt to restrict him to literature, he revived his 1939 idea that America should

> give Guam to the Japanese in return for one set of colour and
> sound films of the 300 best Noh dramas. The films could not be
> delivered at once, so we would not need to give up Guam all at
> once . . . I ask the impartial auditor whether the individual
> American citizen wouldn't get a great deal MORE out of a set
> of such films as I saw, the one I saw in Washington two years
> ago, than the world out of a few tons of tungsten, with possibly
> a few family coffins thrown in.

The Rome Radio staff, if they listened closely to the broadcasts (which seems doubtful), must have been astonished at the subjects he would turn to: a Vivaldi oratorio he had just heard in Siena, poor Nicholas Murray Butler, who as head of the Carnegie Fund had annoyed him in the 1920s ('Ole Nick . . . oleaginous . . . the old scamp'), A. R. Orage of the *New Age,* and a host of other characters from Ezra's past. At the microphone on 12 February 1942 he read his audience Canto 46, full of references to 'the Reverend Eliot', 'Max's drawings', 'G.B.S.', and 'Mr Wells'. Even his more comprehensible paragraphs were laced with such allusions as 'Ole Frida started the cave of the calf' (Madame Strindberg, whose Golden Calf night-club had been a Vorticist haunt), 'Kumrad Kumminkz' (E. E. Cummings, who had written about the USSR), and 'ole Doc Williams'.

One day in New Jersey, William Carlos Williams's wife Florence was told by a bank clerk that he had heard a curious voice on the radio the other night. It was coming from Italy, and it was muttering about 'ol' Doc Williams of Rutherford, New Jersey'. Williams snapped to his wife: 'What the hell right has he to drag me into his dirty messes?'

*

If Ezra had known about Williams's reaction he would have been puzzled. In the broadcasts during 1941, he unvaryingly spoke of 'We Americans', never 'you'. On one occasion he described his work at the microphone as 'exercising my native right as an American to speak to my own compatriots'. And during these months before the USA entered the war it would have been hard to prove, in a court of law, that he was doing anything else.

He soon began to regard himself as an expert on radio technique, and he offered the Rome Radio staff some hints for a more 'snappy' style of presentation, which the programme certainly needed. The American Hour, he said, might begin with a crisp slogan, something on the lines of '*What about freedom from debt?*' The news bulletin should be 'so condensed as though for every useless word there were a fine'. Then might come a 'Fanfare', followed by the announcement: 'Dr Pound is approaching the microphone!' The only one of these suggestions to be followed was the use of 'Doctor' to introduce him. He also sent in technical reports on the quality of his own transmissions. On 28 July 1941: 'Excellent delivery last night. Voice absolutely clear and every word "visible", except for a few ORful KRRumpzzz! of static or atmospheric or whatever that BLITZED out a few phrases – afraid "scum at the top" was lost in the thunder.'

In this mood of professionalism, he began to correspond with a fellow broadcaster in Berlin. An émigré from the British Union of Fascists, William Joyce had originally been employed by the Reichsrundfunk as a newsreader in English. Like Ezra, he thought that the bulletins were poorly written – as indeed they were; once, Joyce had to read a report in which a torpedo was described as having struck 'the machines and kettles of the boat'. So he began to write his own topical talks, which he was allowed to broadcast. Just as Ezra caricatured his own imagined listeners by adopting a folksy mid-American drawl, so Joyce, an Irishman, aped the 'typical' Englishman by assuming an absurd upper-crust manner, which quickly earned him the nickname 'Lord Haw-Haw'. Unlike Ezra he broadcast anonymously, but Ezra discovered his identity when, in May 1941, four months after he had started his own broadcasts, he wrote a fan letter to him.

'Lord Haw-Haw' replied on 3 June, saying he had been 'delighted' by Ezra's praise, telling him that the time of the broadcast had been altered, and warning him amicably that 'in the very near future I propose to inflict a real letter on you. Meanwhile all the best. Heil Hitler. William Joyce.'

Unlike Ezra, Joyce had swiftly created an enormous popular audience, thanks to the eerily knowing manner in which he referred to events in Britain, as if he were being supplied with intimate inside knowledge by a network of spies. In fact, like Ezra, he simply picked up material for his talks from the news bulletins. Like Ezra, too, he believed that what he was doing was for the good of his own country: he wanted to save Britain from the domination of Jewish financiers. His last message before his execution in 1946 was: 'May Britain be great once again . . . I am proud to die for my ideals.'

Ezra wrote back to him during June 1941:

> Dear Joyce,
>   Do write at length, if ever you get time . . . Present schedule I
> am supposed to be shot over the air at 4.10 a.m. twice a week
> Tuesday and Thursday which I don't hear as I have only
> medium wave receiver . . . I don't suppose you have time to
> listen, but shd be glad to profit by experienced criticism. God
> knows HOW one gets an idea into a lunatic asylum. And the
> idea that Brits/ are subject to REASON is probably an error if
> not downright lunacy. Can't remember when I first heard of
> yr/ transmissions, but have been hearing 'em daily ever
> since . . . I suffer from lack of NEW information. Stuff I wrote
> three years ago can not be regarded as war propaganda. But I
> lack new data . . . I dont know whether anyone in Berlin reads
> what I write in Italian??

Joyce replied to this on 30 June:

> . . . my work is heavier than ever just at present . . . I agree with
> you that it is not easy to make an impression of an obvious
> nature on the thing called the British public, but I nevertheless
> think that we are succeeding and that the results will be
> cummulative [*sic*] when they emerge. I shall certainly make a
> point of listening to your transmissions, though I shall not
> presume to criticise. Your methods are unique and they belong
> to you alone. I am quite sure that nobody could imitate them
> successfully. With kindest regards . . .

Ezra did not hesitate to bother a busy man if he thought the cause required
it. He wrote to Joyce on 18 July:

> You needn't worry about the word 'criticize'/ call it guidance if
> you like. You have been at the job longer than I have. New
> technique for Uncle Ez . . . I think I have got my voice right at
> last. I . . . got back in time to hear . . . the eleven P.M. medium
> wave transmission for England/ . . . I think I was right to
> transmit from Rome/ I know this country and do not know
> Germany: and can not speak German well enough to make my
> ideas clear. Also I cd/ never stand a winter in Berlin . . . I shd/
> like a few German contacts . . . I couldn't get to Berlin except
> by official invite with paid expenses . . . HEUL [*sic*] HITLER
> and nach Vladivostock.

He wrote to Joyce again on 29 July asking him to draw his department's
attention to 'A talk by Princess Troubetzkoi' on the Bolsheviks. Joyce

acknowledged this briefly. Ezra wrote again on 16 September:

> Am still feeling lack of coordination . . . I mean IF we can hold out a few months longer, the American electorate will I think squash that unspeakable louse, that cunt of all infamy Roosevelt at the autumn elections next year . . . I am not convinced the kikes meant England to WIN/ or that the drive to war is the same as a drive to WIN a war . . . I hear you three times an evening when I am here in Rap/ . . . but I go it blind/ I have no idea if anyone listens . . . I want more printed matter from Germany . . . Is there anybody in the Rundfunk that can send 'em to me . . . Isn't it time to be more specific about JEW interests in Finland . . . Also a little more information about Hambro might be got from Quisling or someone . . . yrz. E.P.

This letter was four pages long. Joyce did not reply, and there was no further correspondence.

*

Anti-Semitism was the chief motif of one of Ezra's 1941 broadcasts. His theme was that those who wanted to 'destroy every last vestige of the AMERICAN heritage' were influenced by 'hearin' kike radio, and I propose to use the word KIKE regardless of race. Use it to cover honorary Jews, AND TO EXCEPT honest Jews where we find 'em.'

There were, he said, 'clever Kikes runnin' ALL our communication system'. And he concluded: 'You can't go to war without small meanness to SOME of the neighbours. You get het up over the sorrows of Mrs Ikestein, the tailor's wife; you can't DO anything about it without doin' dirt to Giovanni the grocer, and the Hungarian livin' next door.' In the same talk he seemed also to attack anti-Semitism. He said it was nonsense to regard the USA as racially pure – 'We are all intermixed' – and remarked that racism begins when 'things are scarce' and consequently 'there is a conspiracy, to shut out someone or other'. But such disclaimers were becoming rarer now, and a hatred of Jewish usury was a fundamental assumption of his broadcasts from the start. The scripts are spattered with such phrases as 'kikery', 'Anglo-Judaea', 'Kike propaganda', 'shyster', 'judaeocracy'.

As the war and the broadcasts went on, he seemed to feel less and less need to mince matters about the Jews. He was not ordered to take an anti-Semitic line by the propaganda staff in Rome – the Mussolini Government was not yet concerned with the Jewish question – but he could hear Lord Haw-Haw and other Berlin broadcasters ranting about the Jews, and in such a climate he was unlikely to play the liberal.

Alongside the increasing expressions of anti-Semitism and the almost incomprehensible allusions to old friends and enemies which made up much of the broadcasts there were, now and then, some shafts of perception. During 1941 he observed that 'a peace with American war bases all over the whole of the planet would be no more a real peace than Versailles was'; and of twentieth-century American presidents: 'You can't tell me that . . . any of 'em were chosen, nominated because anybody really felt: well now, that is what we need in the White House.'

He regarded his audience for the earliest talks as exclusively American, but later turned his attention to Britain, telling his listeners some time around mid-1941: 'I have not considered it suitable to meddle in the internal affairs of another country.' He still believed the majority in Britain did not want war, yet there were moments when he seemed almost to understand how the conflict appeared to them:

> Yes, I know what the decent English are resistin' and what they were even ready to fight to resist. And if they had any clear headedness, that would be dandy. They want their cultural heritage, they think the English once had nice manners.

But he went on to say that the Nazis had 'wiped out bad manners in Germany'; whatever this was supposed to mean, he no longer felt the need to consider the British view further.

If the British Government had their way, he felt, 'England is to be a Jew-owned deer park with tearooms'. And in another script, entitled simply 'England', he branded the entire nation as Jew-ridden:

> Nothing can save you, save an affirmation that you are English. Whore Belisha is not. Isaacs is not. No Sassoon is an English-man, racially. No Rothschild is English . . . no Baruch, Morgenthau, Cohen, Lehman, Warbugh, Kuhn, Khan, Schiff, Sieff, or Solomon was ever yet born Anglo-Saxon. And it is for this filth that you fight.

He took the anti-Semitic line towards Russia too: Churchill, Roosevelt and Stalin presented a 'triangual Darby and Joan of the three hebraicized governments.' Stalin he dismissed as a criminal, a 'Georgian assassin', 'the old Georgian train-robber'. The 'Bolshevik anti-morale' came, he said, 'out of the Talmud, which is the dirtiest teaching that any race ever codified'. And he began to preach racial purity. In the Céline talk he spoke of the desirability of breeding 'thoroughbreds', while in another script he recom-mended 'two children MINIMUM' for 'real Americans', ''cause if two people don't reproduce two people, the race DIMINISHES and you get invaded: as the United States has been invaded by VERMIN'.

He had begun to sign other letters besides those to William Joyce with 'Heil Hitler'. He concluded a letter to old Professor Ibbotson with a swastika. Yet, just as before the war, he seemed studiously to be avoiding any discussion of Hitler's character and objectives. He suggested to his British listeners that, in return for the German attack on Russia, Britain should have said to Hitler: 'If you can stop the Moscovite horror, we will let bygones be bygones. We will try to see at least HALF of your argument.'

At times he seemed to have devised his own version of Nazi doctrine. 'HITLER stands for putting men over machines,' he told his audience. 'If you don't know that, you know NOTHING.' He gave no explanation of what he meant.

His daughter Mary noticed that

> emotionally he had no leanings towards Germany. The same Boches who had killed some of his best friends . . . were lurking in the background . . . Culturally . . . the *Götterdämmerung* and a Valhalla at the end of it was far removed from his aesthetic imagery. But there was a certain kind of discipline and honesty that seemed to appeal to him . . . And there had been that attempt in Wörgl to introduce money based on work.

He might have committed himself further to the Nazi cause if he had not found Germans so comic. Rapallo became a favourite resort for off-duty German officers, and when out walking with Mary, Ezra would shake his head as they passed: 'They walk as though they had swallowed a broomstick. You should see their necks at table, stiff, stiff, stiff.' He wrote to Wyndham Lewis that while most 'teutons' were certainly 'as good as frawgs', one had to admit that 'the hun comic, is comic, vurry visibly so'. He wished that all Germany could be 'peasants like the Tirol', and after the war he emphasized: 'I did NOT want a Kaisertum uberalles. Or an ADOLF uberalles'; but while broadcasting from Rome he simply kept silent on this issue.

*

At no time, either before or after America entered the war, did he specifically address Allied troops and suggest they should mutiny or revolt. He emphasized this in his own defence in 1943. His claim all along was that he was supporting the 'United States heritage', and he challenged his listeners to 'find anything hostile to the Constitution of the USA in these speeches'. He was, he often said, 'speaking as an American citizen'. And in his book on Ezra, the man who conducted his legal defence in 1945 argues that he was doing nothing in the broadcasts but 'exercising the good old American prerogative of criticizing his government . . . The criticism . . . reminded me of the way Wall Street bankers and lawyers used to talk.'

Certainly there were Americans who, in 1941, would have agreed with virtually every word Ezra said at the microphone about the United States Government, the European conflict, and the power of the Jews. Joseph Kennedy, father of the future president, had told Roosevelt that England would not fight, and tipped off the German ambassador in Washington that many Americans, like himself, were sympathetic to Hitler and his ideals. The ambassador reported to Berlin that Kennedy had told him:

> It was not so much the fact that we wanted to get rid of the Jews that was harmful to us, but rather the loud clamour with which we accompanied this purpose. He himself understood our Jewish policy completely; he was from Boston and there, in one golf club and in other clubs, no Jews had been admitted for the past 50 years.

During the Battle of Britain, when Kennedy was ambassador to London, he kept out of the capital for fear of the bombing, and declared that 'the British have had it. They can't stop the Germans and the best thing is for them to learn to live with them.' His remarks became so embarrassing to Washington that he was withdrawn from his embassy. This, like later disgraces, he blamed on the influence of the Jews.

American anti-Semitism, temporarily diminished in some quarters when news of the German treatment of Jews began to filter through during the early 1930s, had been fuelled again by the continuing Depression, the unthinking choosing to blame Jewish financiers. During 1933 to 1940 well over 100 anti-Semitic organisations sprang up in the USA. Polls taken during the 1930s and 1940s showed that about a third of the American public was inclined to be suspicious of Jewish influence. In 1938 a national sample was asked: 'Do you think the persecution of Jews in Europe has been their own fault?' Ten per cent said 'entirely', 48 per cent 'partly'.

*

Mussolini knew nothing of Ezra's broadcasts. When a secretary passed one of Ezra's letters to him in 1943, he had to explain – since Il Duce had evidently forgotten – that its author was 'an American'. Camillo Pellizzi of the Fascist Institute of Culture observed Ezra at work at Rome Radio, and says that anyone in the régime who knew about the broadcasts was thoroughly puzzled by Ezra's motives: 'Those in authority more than once asked me: "But what does the fellow want? Can we be really sure that there isn't a code of some sort in what he says? Can you guarantee that he is not a spy?"' To which Pellizzi would reply that it required 'an entire university course' to explain what was going on in the head of Ezra Pound.

21

Recoming To U/S/

His Italian acquaintances were equally puzzled as to why he was undertaking the broadcasts. Mary describes him in Siena in 1941: 'groping for facts. But few Italians were eager to enlighten him. In Siena they were mostly artists not interested in politics, or aristocrats interested mainly in keeping old privileges. They could not understand why an American should feel so strongly about saving Europe. Or why a poet should bother about economics.'

Mussolini's increasing toadying towards Hitler had by now undermined much of his popular support in Italy. The country had on the whole been reluctant to enter the war, and many intellectuals who had pledged themselves to Fascism in the 1920s and 1930s now privately withdrew their support, not least because they objected to the anti-Semitism Berlin was trying to foist on them. Ezra's broadcasts could in no sense be said to represent Italian feeling – not that anyone who listened to them could have imagined them to be anything except the product of a highly eccentric mind.

*

On his journeys between Rapallo and Rome he sometimes stopped off in Viareggio to see the novelist Enrico Pea, whose *Romanzo di Moscardino* Ezra had decided to translate into English. Pea had worked as a marble cutter, sailor, mechanic and pedlar before turning writer. *Moscardino* is an intense tale of a household whose chief occupants are three mad brothers. There is violent death, the impregnation of a servant girl, and an atmosphere somewhere between Poe and Hardy. Ezra had been recommended the book by a Rome journalist friend, and said it was 'the only time in my life I have ever wanted to translate a novel'. He felt it was the sort of thing 'Tom Hardy' might have written if he had lived in rural Italy.

Pea gives a vivid description of Ezra at work with him in a café in Viareggio, with his typewriter on the table, typing English equivalents to the dialect words in the original. Afterwards he would rush off to catch his train, clutching the typewriter in one hand and, if he had cut it fine, taking 'a flying leap over the barrier' and jumping on to the moving train 'with all the ability of an American cowboy who vaults on to the back of a fleeing horse'.

Ezra wanted *Moscardino* to be published in America, but because of the war and events in his own life the project was never completed. However, his English version of the first of the novel's four volumes appeared in the 1955 *New Directions in Prose and Poetry*. The book begins with Signora Pellegrina going into mourning at the death of her husband. She shows no grief, but after dividing the family property 'she forgot to talk, as if turned mute . . . trembled and stared into nothingness, rolled her eyes from the depth of her armchair – and didn't answer'.

*

Other than writing the broadcasts, translation was his chief literary activity in 1941 and 1942. He began to render the *Ta Hio* into Italian (it was published in Rapallo in 1942), and he made an English version of a book on Italian economic policy by Odon Por, a Hungarian exile who supported Mussolini, which was published in Milan in 1941. He spent part of the summer of 1941 in Siena, where Olga and Mary were again attending Count Chigi's music festival. 'Babbo banged the typewriter most of the day . . . I felt sure he was enunciating eternal truth . . . "Trying to save the world" . . . the seriousness of purpose and dedication were such as to turn the hyperbole into an understatement.' But with hindsight, she felt that there had also been 'an inner, metaphysical war' going on in him, that he was 'losing grip over what most specifically he should have been able to control, his own *words*'.

Suddenly he hurried off from Siena to Rome, then came back abruptly to say he would shortly be leaving for America. Precisely what was going on is not clear. According to an Italian journalist friend, he had decided to return to the USA because the American Government had notified its citizens around the world that they should come home for their own safety. But no such announcement was made until Pearl Harbor and America's entry into the war. More probably Ezra was planning to go to America again on his own initiative, partly so that, as in 1939, he could attempt to divert Roosevelt's Government from entering the war; but it seems that this time he intended to stay there, if not for good then at least for the duration of European hostilities. He wrote to his friend, the retired admiral Ubaldo degli Uberti, who lived in Rome, asking him to look after his Gaudier-Brzeska sculptures and drawings, the Dolmetsch clavichord, and certain books. This indicates that Dorothy was to go with him – she was an American citizen by marriage – and perhaps Homer and Isabel too, but there is no evidence that Olga and Mary featured in the arrangements. Certainly Mary remembers that in Siena he said goodbye to them both. Possibly he intended to leave them to fend for themselves – after all, Mary's surname was Rudge, and neither of them was legally tied to him.

In Rome, he had visited the US Consulate General to ask for the renewal of his passport, which had almost expired. (Dorothy had her own passport.) He was dealt with at the top level, by the US Chargé d'Affaires, George Wadsworth, whose surname must have aroused Ezra's interest and hope. But Wadsworth knew about the broadcasts, and instead of renewing the passport he confiscated it on the spot. Ezra was told that the question of renewal would have to be referred to Washington. He lost his temper with Wadsworth; it was reported that he made 'undignified remarks concerning the United States Government', and that on leaving the office he 'gave the Fascist salute'. (After the war he admitted to having given that salute 'occasionally'.) At this stage, however, he still expected the passport to be renewed, for it was now that he returned to Siena and announced his imminent departure for America.

However, the Washington authorities decided to take advantage of his plans. Certainly they were prepared to allow him to return home, but only on condition that he did not leave for Italy again until after the war was over. They told Wadsworth that the passport could be renewed for just long enough to get him across the Atlantic, but no longer. Although the USA was still not officially in the war, hostilities seemed near; in mid-July 1941, in reprisal for the closure of German consulates in the USA, the Italians ordered American consular staff out of the country, and towards the end of that month a diplomatic train was scheduled to leave Rome.

Olga did not know what was happening; she left Mary in Siena and hurried to Venice to 'see about things', and 'make arrangements about the house in case we too should be leaving Italy'. Mary found herself abandoned in a student boarding-house; her mother had told her to get on with her studies alone. She was now sixteen. 'I had fears that my parents might be going to America without me, and instead of studying fretted away my time.'

*

At this point, Ezra made another visit to the US Consulate in Rome, and was told the condition on which he could have his passport renewed. He refused to accept it. The authorities had proposed no more than he evidently intended himself – that he should go back to the USA and stop broadcasting – but he was not going to be dictated to by bureaucrats. His behaviour on this second occasion further enraged Wadsworth and his staff (who were now packing up to go); in a report they described him contemptuously as a 'pseudo American'.

Despite the impasse about the passport, he spent much of the late summer and autumn of 1941 trying to get a passage for himself (and presumably for Dorothy) on the Clipper flying boat from Rome to the USA. A note sent to Homer from Rome refers to this:

> Friday
> Dear Dad
>   all vurry interestin' – but also wearing to nerves.
>   nothing very clear yet & several people wanting clipper
> passages.
>   love to mother
>   EP

But during the latter part of 1941, Homer, now aged eighty-three, fell out of bed and broke his hip; while he was convalescing he contracted a chest infection. Travel became out of the question for him at present – another factor to make Ezra's plan difficult.

Mary was told, around the beginning of August, that the original plan had been abandoned. Olga wrote to her telling her to come to Rapallo. 'Were we not going to America? Not even Babbo? Not for the moment. Impossible. The officials at the American Consulate had been very nasty.'

She took up residence with her mother in the Sant'Ambrogio apartment, at Casa 60, overlooking Rapallo. Olga decided to pass her off as her cousin, using an Italian identity card, rather than admit she was a foreigner. 'One never knows what might happen to foreigners. Permits, reports to the police. We might be deprived of our ration cards.' Mary was uncomfortable about this – 'I was young and objected to scheming and pretending' – and she winced when the peasants and shopkeepers asked her arch questions about the *signorina*, her 'cousin', sensing the malice in their tone. 'However, I never put questions to Mamile.' Unlike the locals, to whom rumour had inevitably spread from Rapallo, she still had no notion of the existence of Dorothy.

Olga worked out a strict schedule for herself and Mary. The alarm clock was set for six in the morning. 'Exercises . . . the ten genuflections, palms to the ground, stiff knees, prescribed by *Vogue*.' Washing in a basin of cold water, getting dressed with her mother snapping '*Quick*!' at her, Mary rebelled for a while; then she began to discover 'the logic and the beauty of her new life: strict discipline and routine left more freedom for one's thoughts'. But she was homesick for Gais and the Tyrol. And, apart from her mother and 'Babbo', the only person she could talk to was Father Desmond Chute, to whom she went twice a week for lessons in French and Latin.

'Mamile practised the violin all morning. I worked by the little iron stove which was installed in her room to take the chill off the house. We burnt pine cones and boiled dried chestnuts and potatoes on it. In a sense our life had become a work of art: nothing wasted, nothing sloppy.'

Ezra spent every other afternoon with them; occasionally he came to lunch or stayed for the evening meal. When he arrived up the hill from Rapallo, he would bring a few chestnuts or peanuts, or a slice of pancake, 'and in an old envelope the cat's food, scraps from his lunch'. One Christmas, an old woman sidled up to Mary on the *salita*, the hill path down to the town, and offered her three eggs, 'a splendid addition to our Christmas dinner'. But when he saw them, her father disapproved strongly: 'Italy was fighting a war and no one must indulge in black market.' Similarly, in Rome during 1943 at the dinner table of a journalist friend and his wife, when a bottle of champagne was brought in his honour he refused to drink it, and took Mary home abruptly as soon as the meal was ended, though the hosts were distressed and perplexed. 'Non è tempo per frivolezze,' he told Mary as they hurried out of the dinner party, 'this is no time for frivolities.'

*

Mary was now old enough to be enrolled in the Ezuversity. Her father brought her Hardy's *Under the Greenwood Tree* to translate into Italian. She found the job tough, but 'listened more and more eagerly for his cane on the cobblestones of the *salita* and then the rattle on the door, for he brought with him a dimension of – no, not stillness, but magnitude, momentum. He made me feel that work, learning, was worthwhile, exciting.'

After rehearsing aloud his latest broadcast script, he would ask her to recite five lines she had learnt from the *Odyssey*, and then translate. He would himself read out the next five she was to learn. 'And it seemed as though he possessed two voices: one angry, sardonic, sometimes shrill and violent for the radio speeches; one calm, harmonious, heroic for Homer . . .'

From Hardy she moved to the Cantos, beginning to translate them into Italian. 'I think he made me do over the first line of Canto 10 at least twenty times – we spent two years over twelve cantos.' The task was 'really beyond my capacity', but her father never lost patience, 'just corrected and recorrected'. After the day's task was finished came tea (camomile or mint, all that could be obtained), then Olga's violin. 'Mozart, Bach, Vivaldi, Beethoven . . . For me nothing, stillness – stillness outlasting all wars – Mamile playing. Babbo and I walking down the path to Rapallo. A crystallized image set amongst grey-green olives by the changing sea.'

*

His broadcasts continued throughout the autumn and early winter of 1941. One of them was transmitted on the evening of 7 December, the day on which Japan bombed Pearl Harbor. Ezra was in Rome when the news came through; he hurried back to Rapallo.

The Japanese attack astonished him. A few weeks later, in a broadcast, he described how 'the last American journalist I saw, and that was the night before Arbour [sic] Day, told me the Japs would never etc. etc.' He could not properly take in what had happened, or readjust his mental picture to fit it, for a full two months after the event. It was not a question of the USA voluntarily entering the war for dubious reasons (which he had expected), but of being dragged into it by the aggression of Japan, a nation for which, since his early Fenollosa days, he had felt deep admiration. On top of this was the blunt fact that, with America in the war, he would be apparently siding with the enemies of the USA if he continued to broadcast from Rome. A few weeks later he described his state of mind during the crisis:

> On Arbour Day, Pearl Arbour Day, at 12 o'clock noon I retired from the capital of the old Roman Empire to Rapallo to seek wisdom from the ancients. I wanted to figure things out. I had a perfectly good alibi, if I wanted to play things safe. I was and am officially occupied with a new [Italian] translation of the Ta S'eu [*Ta Hio*] of Confucius . . . That is, I have WORK thaaar for some years, if I don't die before I git to the middle. . . . There was to face this, the SITUATION. That is to say the United States had been for months ILLEGALLY at war, through what I considered to be the criminal acts of a President whose mental condition was NOT, as far as I could see, all that could or should be desired . . . It was obviously a mere question of hours . . . [before] the United States of America would be legally at war with the Axis.
>
> I spent a month tryin' to figure things out, well did I? Perhaps I concluded sooner. At any rate I had a month clear to make up my mind about some things . . . There was my old dad in bed with a broken hip; Lord knows who is going to mend it or whether it will mend. So – I read him a few pages of Aristotle in the Loeb Classical Library, English version, to take his mind off it. Also to keep my own work in progress. Because for some time I have had in mind the need of comparing the terminology of Chinese and Greek philosophy, and also comparing that with the terminology of mediaevil [sic] Catholic theology.
>
> No. For a man cut off from all his NORMAL contacts with the non-European world, I can't say I was destitute – mentally – there was plenty lyin' there for me to be busy about.

He breaks off this account of his self-questionings inconclusively.

His remark that he 'had a month clear to make up my mind' suggests that Rome Radio had told him to take the month off to consider his position. (He was away from the microphone for nearly two months.) Elsewhere in the same broadcast, he observes that the study of Confucius and Mencius was appropriate for his dilemma, since both men had been 'up against similar problems . . . and seen empires fallin''. But he was in more difficulties than could be solved by the contemplation of ancient Chinese ethics.

As Mary recalls, it was now that 'impressive envelopes arrived summoning all American citizens to return to the States, to get in touch with the Swiss legations. Mamile seemed at a loss. And what about me? What, who, was I?'

According to her recollection, her father came back from Rome, just after the news of Pearl Harbor, 'indignant and discouraged. They would not allow him on the last clipper out of Rome. It was reserved for American diplomats and press envoys. If he and his family wanted to leave Europe it would have to be by slow boat. Months on a route full of mines and torpedoes. "Is that the way they want to get rid of me?". I think a way out was suggested by train to Portugal. I do not remember details. The words that stick in my mind are: clipper, the last clipper, frozen assets, frozen bank account. Grandfather's US Government pension withheld, the old man in hospital with a broken hip. Mamile's house in Venice sequestered as alien property.'

Ezra himself, a few weeks after the event, said he had 'tried at the last moment in the flurry' to 'get "home" by Clipper', but had found the plane 'entirely full of escaping diamond merchants, secret (more or less) agents, delayed mail etc. to such degree that no simple and private Americans could find place'. The question arises, once again, as to how many places he was seeking.

Olga is convinced that Homer's illness was 'the principal reason why Ezra didn't go back'. Yet by his own admission he had tried to book a passage after Homer had already gone to hospital. On the other hand there were a number of motives, quite independent of his family, why he should not wish to return to the USA.

In September 1941, three months before Pearl Harbor, he discussed the possibility of such a return in a letter to Laughlin, who had evidently urged him to go back:

> Wot do you suggest I come home ON? and then: WHY? If you can't find anything up to yr mental level; how shd/ I find anything up to mine? At any rate I can see here one first rate writer, namely Pea/ and the kid is translatin' Hardy, and Pea

> sez it is better'n' etc/ and he will look thru the finished
> product . . . No use yr/ saying I am disliked/ I wanna know
> HOW, and by whom details welcome. Wot you need is a lil'l
> trip to Yourup as a refresher/ yrz. EZ

The letter made no reference to the broadcasts. He had aired the same
problem nine months earlier in another letter to Laughlin:

> Waaal, as to my recoming to U/S/ what do I DO when I get
> there/ go on board of Chase Bank or teach tennis in Noo putt?
> Or clean latrines in the MacLeishery?

A report in the *Philadelphia Evening Bulletin* of 5 June 1942 quoted
'Nancy Horton, American woman who returned Monday from Italy' as
saying 'Ezra Pound . . . was refused permission to leave Italy aboard a
diplomatic train carrying other Americans', but this may have been
rumour, or perhaps it was the defence that Ezra was using by that time to
any Americans he met. The last 'diplomatic train' as such had departed five
months before Pearl Harbor, in mid-July 1941, after the American
consulates in Italy had been closed down.

Yet another account of Ezra's movements and intentions, at variance
with all these, is provided by an American journalist, Reynolds Packard,
Director of the United Press bureau in Rome, who had known Ezra since
Paris days and writes in his autobiography (1943):

> The day of Pearl Harbor, Pound unexpectedly came to our
> house and told us that war between the United States and Italy
> was inevitable but that he intended to stay on. [I] told him that
> he would be a traitor if he did so, and that now was the time for
> him to pipe down about the alleged glories of Fascism. 'But I
> believe in Fascism,' Pound said, giving the Fascist salute, 'and I
> want to defend it . . . I tell you I want to save the American
> people.' There was no way to reason with him.

Following Pearl Harbor, those American journalists who had not left
Italy were interned in Siena, then repatriated in May 1942. Ezra would
have had to make strenuous efforts to get to the USA by this time, and in
trying to do so might well, together with his family, have been interned for
the duration of the war. This was how Laughlin read the situation when he
wrote in the 1941 *New Directions* anthology, with covert reference to
Mary:

> People who hear him broadcasting for the Italian Government
> do not realize that possibly he has no choice in the matter. If
> they knew, for example, that he cannot leave Italy because he
> has close dependants who are not American citizens, they

would perhaps be more charitable in their judgements. Those are the facts in the case.

Ezra himself, interviewed for the *Paris Review* in 1960, said he could not reconstruct the details of his attempt to leave Italy: 'I am a bit hazy in my head about a considerable period, and I think that – I know that I had a chance to get as far as Lisbon, and be cooped up there for the rest of the war.' But it was not like him, even in old age, to be 'hazy' about facts from his past.

Olga remained puzzled by the episode, and was never taken fully into his confidence. 'I wish I knew all the ins and outs,' she has said, 'because honestly I don't. It's still a mystère, that whole thing.'

22

8 From US Indicted

The possibility of flight from Italy soon faded from his mind, and he decided to carry on as before. As early as 9 December 1941, two days after Pearl Harbor and just before news reached Italy that America had come into the war, he wrote to Adriano Ungaro at Minculpop that

> even if America declares war on the Axis, I see no reason (from my point of view) why I should not continue to speak in my own name, so long as I say nothing that can in any way prejudice the results of American military or naval (or navel) action, the armed forces of the U.S.A. or the welfare of my native country.

And three days later he told Ungaro: 'Damn it all, nothing but propaganda can prevent it degenerating into a ten year war of inexhaustible exhaustion.' Ungaro and his colleagues suggested that he might broadcast anonymously, but he refused: 'It seems to me that my speeches on the radio must continue IN MY OWN NAME and with *my* voice, and NOT anonymously . . . Either one fights, or one does not fight.'

He applied for official Italian permission for himself and Dorothy to remain in the country; it was granted in the last week of January 1942. His bank account had been frozen by the Government since Pearl Harbor, but he managed to gain the use of it again, through influence at Minculpop, and by pointing out to the authorities that his and Dorothy's capital (such as they had access to at present) was mostly in Italian Government bonds and loans. He had bought these shortly before the outbreak of war, transferring money from the USA.

On 26 January 1942, *Time* magazine printed a story that he had 'retired to Rapallo to continue his study of Chinese philosophy.' The article, which probably emanated from Reynolds Packard, was captioned 'No Haw-Haw He'. Quite apart from ideological considerations, he had to resume broadcasting now that he had decided to stay to survive financially and help maintain several households. The scripts, and such journalism as he could place with Italian papers, 'had to be written regularly,' says Mary, 'we now all depended on them for our subsistence.'

He was next heard on the air on 29 January 1942, three days after the *Time* story was printed. (In 1946 he said: 'My mistake was to go on after Pearl Harbor.') He took one step that he thought would offer him some protection. For a while his broadcasts were preceded by an announcement (drafted by him) intended to emphasize that he was broadcasting of his own free will and not acting as an enemy agent:

> Rome Radio, acting in accordance with the Fascist policy of intellectual freedom and free expression of opinion by those who are qualified to hold it, following the tradition of Italian hospitality, has offered Dr Ezra Pound the use of the microphone twice a week. It is understood that he will not be asked to say anything whatsoever that goes against his conscience, or anything incompatible with his duties as a citizen of the United States of America.

Yet by emphasizing that the broadcasts were entirely his own work and not the result of coercion, he was publicly taking full blame for the decision to carry on; and by informing listeners that he was still 'a citizen of the United States' he was making himself even more vulnerable.

It would have been comparatively easy at this juncture to have taken Italian citizenship – several of his fellow broadcasters did so – and as a citizen of Italy he would have been entirely beyond the jurisdiction of the US Government and law courts; but there is no indication that he considered this step at any time. Apparently he had never entertained the possibility that legal charges might be brought against him, and even if he had, it is highly unlikely that this would have driven him to renounce American citizenship. The theme of his broadcasts was that the USA should set its house in order, and he only claimed that he had the right to make such demands because he was a member of the American nation.

The pre-broadcast announcement was only used a few times. Ezra did not care for its 'rather forced definition of Fascism', and after a few weeks he and the radio authorities regarded it as unnecessary. However he continued to take the line, for the rest of his life, that his broadcasts had simply been a manifestation of 'free expression of opinion' – in 1946 he told a doctor in St Elizabeths that he had been practising 'a form of freedom of speech in a radio age', and the same idea is stated in Canto 74: 'free speech without radio free speech is as zero'.

*

In his first broadcast after Pearl Harbor, he spent much of the time ruminating about his two-month 'retirement' from the microphone, though without explaining why he had decided to return to it. He went on: 'It [is] my private belief that I could have avoided a war with Japan, if anybody had had the unlikely idea of sending me out there with any sort of official powers.'

His chief theme during the next few weeks was deep regret that America had come into the conflict:

> America COULD have stayed out of the war . . . IF America had stayed neutral the war would now be over . . . For the United States to be makin' war on Italy AND on Europe is just plain damn nonsense . . . And for this state of things Franklin Roosevelt is more than any other one man responsible.

He feared that America would be in the war for thirty years, and told his listeners on 3 February 1942: 'You are in it, and Lord knows who is goin' to git you out . . . You are at war for the duration of the Tenno's pleasure.' ('Tenno' is the Japanese Emperor.) Note the use now of 'you' instead of 'we Americans', which he had always said before Pearl Harbor. He continued: 'Nothin' in the Western World, nothin' in the whole of our Occident can help you to dodge that. Nothing can help you dodge it.'

His broadcasts were now monitored and transcribed in Washington, where the official transcript of this talk (supposedly as broadcast) reads: 'You are at war for the duration of the General's pleasure. You are at war for the duration of Japan's pleasure. Nothing in the Western World . . . (etc.)' Charles Norman's *The Case of Ezra Pound* (1948) quotes it with yet another variation: 'You are at war for the duration of the Germans' pleasure. You are at war for the duration of Japan's pleasure. Nothing in the Western World . . . (etc.)' The Norman version has been taken up by other writers. The distortion of what he actually said is not perhaps so very great – in many people's eyes the Japanese Emperor was almost as heinous as Hitler – but in a court of law his fate could have hung on such quotations and misquotations.

His attitude after Pearl Harbor was that the Allies had fallen into an even worse mess than before. 'You do not know what has HAPPENED,' he told his listeners on 28 May 1942.

> And the first thing to DO about it is to pull OUT of this war – a war that you never ought to have flopped into. Every hour that you go on with it is an hour lost to you and your children. And every sane act you commit is committed in HOMAGE to

Mussolini and Hitler. Every reform, every lurch towards the just price, toward the control of the market is an act of HOMAGE to Mussolini and Hitler. THEY are your leaders however much you are conducted by Roosevelt or sold up by Churchill . . . You follow Hitler and Mussolini in EVERY CONSTRUCTIVE act of your Government. Damn you, you follow Mosley, go back and read over his programmes.

No doubt a prosecuting lawyer would have quoted this as evidence that Ezra was inciting mutiny or desertion among Allied troops. In fact he was discussing the conflict solely in terms of economics – of the 'just price', 'control of the market', terms from Douglas and Gesell. The Mosley 'programmes' he had in mind were the BUF leader's early attempts to preach something like Social Credit. Ezra's view of the war was as unrealistic as ever.

Though he was not addressing the troops specifically, he was heard by them. George Dillon, Harriet Monroe's successor as editor of *Poetry*, wrote in that magazine describing how during military service in Europe 'when we dialed the short-wave programs during rest periods, Pound was sometimes good for five minutes of modest entertainment. That is all it was, and I doubt whether any of us who listened to him felt anything but amusement, though we were not in a kindly mood . . . Pound . . . went on and on. But it was impossible to have any serious reaction.'

The broadcasts were not treated as entertainment in Washington, where monitors did their best to make transcripts of Ezra's tirades of obscure names, heard through bad short-wave reception. One monitor transcribed 'Confucius' (frequently cited by Ezra) as 'confusions', while 'Mencius' became 'Mencken'. Despite such errors, there was no doubt in official circles as to the nature of the broadcasts.

In April 1942 the monitoring service notified the Department of Justice that Pound, behind enemy lines, was producing 'a vicious tirade of anti-Administration and anti-American conversation', and in due course the FBI was requested to discover what it could about the poet and his activities before the war. Investigations began in December, and one of J. Edgar Hoover's agents visited William Carlos Williams to ask if he had heard the broadcasts. 'I told him, no,' says Williams, 'though I had heard about them. Would I be able to identify the voice if I did hear it? No. I didn't think that would be possible though I might be fairly certain that it was he who was talking.' Williams was told that the FBI would bring him records of the broadcasts (they were never in fact brought), and was asked if he himself were a loyal American citizen.

Williams had recently attacked Ezra in the American literary magazine, *Decision*, where, in view of what he had heard about the broadcasts, he called him 'Lord Ga-Ga' and said he was a 'pitiable spectacle', a 'fool', a 'case for the psychiatrists', who was bitter over his 'failure to be recognized as a great man', a 'spoiled brat' who had always longed to be the centre of attention. He asserted that Ezra was rooted in the past, could not understand the present, and 'I think he hates humanity'.

Ronald Duncan's West of England cottage was raided by plain-clothes police who observed accusingly: 'You've printed Ezra Pound in your magazine.' They searched the place for a radio transmitter. After they had gone, Duncan took all his letters from Ezra to be locked away in the Faber and Faber safe.

The April 1942 issue of *Poetry* had carried an article by an American poet, Eunice Tietjens, headed 'The End of Ezra Pound'. It began:

> The time has come to put a formal end to the countenancing of Ezra Pound. For a number of years . . . he was associated with *Poetry*, and the association was valuable to both sides. Then he quarreled with us, as he has quarreled with everyone, yet continued to use the magazine as an outlet . . . Now, so far as he and the rest of the English-speaking world of letters are concerned, he has effectively written *finis* to his long career as inspired *enfant terrible*.

Miss Tietjens – Ezra would surely have found amusement in that she bore the same surname as Ford Madox Ford's perfect gentleman in *Parade's End* – judged him to have been 'of . . . great service to the art of poetry' but 'never a major poet himself', and went on to various kinds of abuse before turning only at the end directly to the matter of the broadcasts. These she described as a

> deliberate attempt to undermine the country of his birth through enemy propaganda. Whether he is committing treason or not depends, technically, on whether he has become an Italian citizen or still retains his American passport . . . That it should be one of the poets who is thus playing Lord Haw-Haw, no matter how ineffectually, seems to cast a slur on the whole craft. In the name of American poetry, and of all who practise the art, let us hope that this is the end of Ezra Pound.

This was the first suggestion in public that he might be committing treason.

Miss Tietjens gave no practical hint as to how Ezra should expedite his own end, but eighteen months later Hemingway had a specific suggestion. 'If Ezra has any sense,' he wrote to Archibald MacLeish, 'he should shoot himself. Personally I think he should have shot himself somewhere along after the twelfth canto although maybe earlier.'

*

Ezra did not see the *Poetry* article, but he did hear that the London papers were reporting his broadcasts, and he quoted the *Sunday Times* calling his support of Fascism 'an aberration'. He answered this in a broadcast on 20 April 1942: 'Has a fascist government itself ABerrated, or has it aberred?' And he went on to cite the Mussolini régime's economic and industrial achievements: 'Do I aber in admiring it? I think I do not . . . And I reckon even the *Sunday Times* is about ready to wish some of the stuffed British shirts had aberrated more in my fashion.'

He was now becoming more explicit about the treatment he envisaged for the Jews. 'Don't start a pogrom,' he said on 30 April 1942,

> that is, not an old style killing of small Jews. That system is no good whatsoever. Of course if some man had a stroke of genius and could start a pogrom UP AT THE TOP, there might be something to say for it. But on the whole, legal measures are preferable. The sixty Kikes who started this war might be sent to St Helena as a measure of world prophylaxis. And some hyper-kikes, or non-Jewish kikes along with them.

The next month he described Jewry as 'these dirty swine, out to destroy Bach's music. Bach? OUT. Shakespeare? OUT . . . Damn civilization. The Kike is all out for power.'

He was perhaps thinking of Zukofsky and other Jewish friends when he said on 1 June 1942: 'The lone Jew is a subject of study. He seems a good fellow, but is he in some way cut off from the organization? Has he declined to kiss the magic rod – is he in exile – is that why he apparently has no more luck than the goyim?'

Olga has always maintained that 'none of Ezra's Jewish friends ever ratted on him' – that is tried to harm him as a result of what he said in the broadcasts. His daughter Mary, when faced with this issue, is equally keen to defend him, but, like her mother, cites no particular argument. In a filmed interview she has said: 'I shall make myself completely unpopular if I say that I think certain things have been distorted and blown up out of all proportion . . . It's just one of those points where everyone becomes hysterical.'

After the war, Ezra justified what he had said largely on the ground that it was spoken in ignorance of the Final Solution being implemented in Germany by the Nazis. 'There were no gas ovens in Italy,' he wrote to MacLeish in 1956. It is true that no internment, deportation, or slaughter of Jews took place in Italy until after Mussolini's downfall in 1943, but thereafter the situation changed drastically. Ezra's defence of himself to MacLeish continues: 'E.P. did NOT, as you may, or possibly do NOT know, advocate violence.' But the suggestion of starting a pogrom 'UP AT THE TOP', whether or not he meant it to be taken seriously, is nothing if not an incitement to violence.

He told Donald Hall in 1960 that the first he had learnt of the death camps was from the doctors in St Elizabeths. But it appears that he had gained a fairly detailed idea of the Nazi treatment of Jews during the war, by listening to Romano Bilenchi, a left-wing sympathizer, who had talked to him in Rapallo during 1941 and told him about his meeting with a young German Jew who had escaped to Italy after the SS had massacred his family. Bilenchi records that this story 'shook' Ezra, who

> said I was probably right . . . that the Jews taken individually, especially if they were poor, were human beings like ourselves. However, collectively, and controlled by the capitalists as they were, they had organized a relentless conspiracy against mankind. The conspiracy should be denounced, combated, and destroyed by political action and not, surely, by murders and massacres. Our discussion became rather heated . . . I told Pound that it was Hitler and Himmler who had organized a conspiracy.

But Ezra remained 'stubborn'.

He was certainly prepared to let individual Jews undergo personal suffering for what he believed to be the public good: when in 1938 the Italian Government banned Jews from public office, from working in major industries or on large farms, and from marrying non-Jews (regulations that were only half-heartedly observed), he told a Jewish friend, Aldo Camerino: 'I'm sorry for you, but they have done the right thing.'

*

'I ask you WHY WAS CHRIST CRUCIFIED?' he asked listeners to the American Hour. 'He was crucified for trying to bust a racket.' The whole war seemed to him, in July 1942, to be Europe's 'rebellion against the pervasive, the ubiquitous Yidd.' He now completely accepted the 'truth' of the *Protocols of the Elders of Zion* (the document that was supposed to prove the existence of a Jewish conspiracy). 'For God's sake, read the Protocols,' he exhorted listeners in June 1942, 'if the last copy hasn't been taken out of the bookstores. They were printed twenty years ago. I never bothered to read 'em till I had learned all that is in them from other sources, thereby convalidatin' the evidence.' He was prepared to admit that 'certainly they are a forgery', but that was 'the one proof we have of their authenticity. The Jews have worked with forged documents for the past 24 hundred years.'

He now mocked people who, like himself before the war, admitted to having a few likeable Jews among their friends, suggesting that anyone his listeners happened to dislike was probably Jewish. 'What chance the Frenchman you dislike ISN'T a Frenchman AT ALL? . . . They are everywhere.' He returned to his call for a pogrom at the top: 'Kill 'em off at the top, pogroms start at the bottom and are NEVER so very effective.' Another suggestion was 'Don't start a pogrom; SELL 'em Australia . . . if they'll buy it.'

He saw himself as participating in the same struggle as his grandfather Thaddeus, 'fighting the same kikified usurers . . . trying to have the Government money run honest'. Indirectly but definitely, he predicted an Axis victory: 'The next peace will not be based on international lending . . . And England will certainly have nothing what bloody ever to say about what its terms are.'

More specifically, on 28 June 1942 he told English listeners: 'You are NOT going to win this war. None of your best minds ever thought you could win it.' England had made such mistakes as choosing 'birth control INSTEAD of eugenics.' And on 'thoroughbreds':

> Seems fairly clear that you fix a breed by LIMITING the amount of alien infiltration. You make a race by homogeneity and by avoiding INbreeding . . . Means no hardship to anyone . . . No argument has ever been sprouted against it. You like it in dogs and horses.

He admitted that 'halfbreeds' might have 'cleverness' sometimes, but they 'don't come quite solid, sometimes from a peculiar sort of stoppage INSIDE the head, leadin' to a kind of sense of frustration'.

On 18 May 1942, he began to talk directly about Hitler and Germany. He called Hitler 'that opponent of your infamies' and argued that

> the Anglo-Jew world is fighting . . . the German PHANTOM, NOT the reality. And that phantom has been built out of lies . . . Now I almost never talk of Germany because I have seen very little of Germany . . . Ole Ford toted me about Hessen Darmstadt in 1911 . . . Since then I have been to Vienna and to Frankfurt for Antheil's opry, and passed thru Munich and from Wien I went up to Wörgl.

But in youth he had so soaked himself in the Mediterranean that

> I didn't cotton to German literature. And then philology, ERROR of old German university system got my goat . . . Also being in England 12 years, I certainly saw the last war from the London angle . . . BUT JUSTICE IS JUSTICE. And as to LYING I reckon Hitler has been lied about more than any man livin' except Mussolini.

In this broadcast he examined *Mein Kampf*, which he said he knew from the Italian translation. He described its ideology as follows:

> First, HEALTH, health of the race . . . Breed GOOD and preserve the race . . . SECONDLY . . . a political system in which you can't pass the buck . . . Hitler, having seen the Jew puke in the German democracy, was out for responsibility . . . And the THIRD point was a study of history. To look at the history.
>
> Waaal, now WHAT program does this CONTRADICT? . . . You may see why the stick screen was erected, and people began to speak evil of Hitler.

He was now prepared to describe Nazi Germany and Fascist Italy as 'those two great movements'.

*

No scripts, transcripts or recordings exist for any broadcasts made by Ezra between 16 July 1942 and 18 February 1943 (with the exception of a talk broadcast on 19 September and another on 9 December, but very likely these had been recorded earlier in the year). Payments to him from Minculpop stopped too, though for a shorter period, from 12 August to 19 October 1942. Clearly, he ceased broadcasting for a time, but there is no indication as to why.

A story circulated in the late 1940s that at some time during the war Ezra went to Berlin and met Hitler. Isaiah Berlin, who was in America during this period, says he heard that such a meeting took place and that Ezra 'did not like [Hitler] at all'; but Berlin is inclined to dismiss the story as 'pure fantasy', and there is indeed no evidence to support it. If it had actually happened, Ezra would have been unable to keep quiet about it, while Dorothy, an admirer of Hitler who would have seen little reason to cover up such a visit, categorically denied that it had ever taken place. (The story of the Berlin trip has been given some credence by E. Fuller Torrey in his study of Ezra, *The Roots of Treason* (1984), but this is entirely due to a misunderstanding. Torrey cites as evidence a note in the Huntington Cairns papers in the Library of Congress, which he alleges records that Ezra was 'invited by the German Press Association to give a lecture on "the principles of Italian Fascism" . . . [in] Berlin in April 1942'. In fact the note in question is a transcript, made by Ezra for Cairns, of an account by Camillo Pellizzi, describing a lecture Pellizzi gave under that title in Berlin during that month. Ezra took it from Pellizzi's book *Una Rivoluzione Mancata*.)

*

'End of February 1942,' writes Mary, 'Babbo stood at the door with red eyes. He hugged me and said: "Il tuo nonno è morto." – Grandfather was dead. Mamile led Babbo into her room. I knew they needed to be alone. He left early and I walked down the *salita* with him. He was silent and I did not dare break the silence.'

After the funeral, Ezra followed 'certain Confucian rites' and placed some jade on his father's body. For a few visits to Olga and Mary, he 'just threw himself on the couch and wanted to be left in peace and listen to music. Then he went to Rome again.'

In April 1942, Eliot managed to contact the Pounds by letter, posted by a friend in Portugal, to tell Dorothy that Omar was in good health at school at Charterhouse. 'I hope to continue to see him from time to time, and he can always get in touch with me,' Eliot wrote. Dorothy had reported to Agnes Bedford two years earlier:

> Omar goes to Charterhouse now. Mrs Dickie is arranging to look after him during holidays as long as this filthy mess continues – Did I tell you he has been *Baptized*! What unscrupulous morals Christians have! I was, am, very angry with her – not with him, poor child! I believe, & hope, that it is partly because he wishes to be like everybody else at Ch: *Is* everybody baptized? Olivia would have agreed for this reason: we didn't see alike on the point.

Eliot sent further news of Omar in October 1943, saying he had 'recently left Charterhouse, and is starting to learn the business of hotel management in London.' Omar's legal guardian during the war was the Pounds' solicitor, Arthur Moore, a partner in Dorothy's father's old firm, Shakespear & Parkyn; but Eliot took an avuncular interest. In 1945 when he was able to resume direct correspondence with Dorothy, he told her that he had 'not been very happy about Omar working in the hotel'; but by then Omar, aged twenty, had gone into the army, and seemed to be taking well to military life.

During 1942, Mary continued with her task of translating the Cantos into Italian. Now, 'unless I had reached some insurmountable impasse, I was not to show him my translation before having a full typed page. Inevitably he set to tear it to pieces. Gradually I realized that this was a way for him to reconstruct his own Cantos in Italian, a trying-out of his principles on translation with his own poetry.' She became absorbed in the background material. 'Three volumes on the life and work of the troubadours became light reading.'

*

Ezra resumed regular broadcasting in February 1943 with a talk on 'Franklin D. Frankfurter Jewsfeld'. In April he suggested: 'I think it might be a good thing to hang Roosevelt and a few hundred yids IF you can do it by due legal process, NOT otherwise', though 'sometimes one feels that it would be better to get the job done somehow, ANY how, than to delay execution.'

Though to Mary, 'it looked as though the war would go on forever', the Germans were beginning to retreat in Africa and Russia, and there was an air of desperate optimism in the Axis news bulletins rather than real confidence. Ezra's broadcasts, however, made no reference to Allied advances – indeed, he scarcely ever spoke of actual events of the war, for the conflict seemed to exist for him on a purely intellectual plane. If ever he alluded even faintly to Allied victories, he would immediately assert that the Allies were losing the *real* war: 'Quite apart from military operations, from the results of military operations, from the possible results of any military operations that may occur, the American people appear to have suffered crashing defeat, at the hands of the financiers.' Similarly of Britain: 'Some people fear NOT the outcome of the war, but the END of the war. Churchill, for example . . . sees the end of monopoly and privilege when the war ends, no matter HOW.'

And of American advances in North Africa in the spring of 1943: 'I think quite simply and definitely that the American troops in N. Africa, all of 'em ought to go back to America: IF they can get there.' (It was the nearest he came to inciting mutiny.) In May 1943 he criticized the USA for 'the bombing of civilians, the sinking of hospital ships', and 'vandalism' towards monuments and works of art.

The first report of wartime atrocities to reach him was the news, in April 1943, that mass graves of Polish officers had been discovered by the Germans in the Katyn forest near Smolensk; Berlin accused the Soviet authorities of having executed them two years earlier, and the Polish Government in exile requested that the International Red Cross should be allowed to examine the graves. Ezra reacted energetically to the news, telling his listeners that the mass graves 'surprised NO one', and he tried to join the Red Cross commission himself. Mary gathered that if he failed, he hoped to be able to make the journey at his own expense to collect with his own eyes evidence of Russian guilt. All his requests were turned down. 'I think Babbo had the vague suspicion that Italy did not trust him out of the country.'

In February 1943 he made another approach to Mussolini, sending him *Carta di Visita*, in effect a new version of *Guide to Kulchur* written in Italian and published in Rome, a copy of his Italian translation of the *Ta Hio*, and a note to Il Duce asking him to accept these 'two testimonies to fascist faith'. Two months later he wrote to Mussolini again, this time asking that Il Duce study the idea of 'prescriptible (or redeemable) money' – the Gesell stamp-scrip system. This letter, signed 'with fascist devotion', was no more comprehensible than his previous missives to the Palazzo Venezia, but this time it was noticed and passed to Mussolini himself, with a brief explanatory note by his personal secretary Chiavolini:

> – It is an American who is setting forth his ideas to the DUCE.
> – He refers to a project of monetary reform . . .
> – He . . . maintains he is proposing an 'invention' to defend the lira and the country . . .
> – The project would bring the nation a profit of 17% compared to the 1% loss suffered by the well-off, industrialists, etc.

Mussolini read the letter, and asked that Ezra should be summoned to explain 'this prescriptible money of his'. On 15 May, Chiavolini wrote asking him to come for a meeting with Il Duce. But Ezra had sent his letter from a Rome address, and had now gone back to Rapallo. The communication from Mussolini's office was not forwarded to him, and he never knew anything about it.

*

For Christmas 1942 he gave Mary 1,000 lire, encouraging her to use it: 'Money must be spent, money must circulate.' This gave her the courage to say she wanted to visit Rome with him. Olga made difficulties: 'The child has nothing to wear . . . too plump according to measures set by *Vogue* . . . did not know how to smile', so a period of 'fencing and face-exercise' started, with Ezra as tutor. As soon as he arrived up the hill at Casa 60 it was 'hop, with a broomstick, one two, keep your back straight . . . He pranced around and I was supposed to do likewise . . . The worst of all was moving the face muscles: I felt embarrassed, but Babbo seemed ready to push his face into the most extraordinary grimaces to show me how the muscles worked.' When on top of this she was made to learn Eliot's 'The Hippopotamus' by heart, she was almost ready to forget about Rome. But by April 1943 she was judged to have reached the *Vogue* standard, and off they went, Mary staying with Olga's Rome friend Nora Naldi.

She was taken to meet some of her father's Rome Radio acquaintances, and, somewhat to her surprise, also found herself in the middle of an anti-Mussolini group – or at least among individuals who believed there were serious flaws in the regime. This was in

> the house of Felice Chilanti in Via Frattina . . . We met a group of young people, enraged, tense, opposed not so much to Mussolini and to Fascist ideology as to . . . 'the assassins surrounding Mussolini' . . . They had a paper, *Origini*, on which they invited Babbo to collaborate. He was tempted, for they

advocated freedom of speech, frank exchange of ideas between Fascists, anti-fascists and Marxists. But the situation was tricky. There was an air of conspiracy. I heard the word *Resistenza* for the first time . . . '*Sono svegli*,' Babbo said as we left – Wide-awake, those boys. But too violent for his taste. Chilanti's twelve-year-old daughter had suggested Ciano should be poisoned. But crime is stupid, not the right way out.

The remark appears in Canto 77: ' "I would do it" (finish off Ciano) "with a pinch of insecticide," / said Chilanti's 12 year old daughter.'

Galeazzo Ciano, Mussolini's son-in-law and foreign minister, was widely regarded as unsuitable for office, and early in 1943 was sacked by Il Duce, who took over the post himself. Even after this, Mussolini chose to surround himself with second-raters to make himself seem the more brilliant. Ezra's loyally Fascist friend Admiral Ubaldo degli Uberti grumbled about the quality of Il Duce's subordinates ('If he wd/ *only* get rid of Ciano,' Uberti says in Canto 77), and in Canto 80 Ezra himself reflects on their absurdities:

> and as to poor old Benito
>   one had a safety-pin
> one had a bit of string, one had a button
>   all of them so far beneath him
> half-baked and amateur
>   or mere scoundrels.

While Mary was in Rome, Allied planes flew overhead dropping propaganda leaflets. Africa was now in Allied hands, and they called on Italy to surrender. Allied air raids had started over Genoa, while in Rapallo there were now Axis soldiers stationed along the railway line, and the beach was guarded against coastal invasion by high cement walls. By midsummer, Olga felt that Mary should go back to the Tyrol 'for a month or so'. The 'change of air' would do her good, and at the same time I could leave my ration card behind and it would mean a little extra for Babbo. He was not getting enough to eat and he was overworking.' In July 1943 she went.

Mussolini's downfall came when the Allied bombing of Rome began on 19 July 1943. For some time those around him had begun to despair of his mental condition. He was still talking about victory being round the corner, but was unable to explain how he thought it would be achieved. On 24 and 25 July the Grand Council met and voted to disband the existing structure of government; Victor Emmanuel III, still King in name, informed Il Duce that Marshal Badoglio would take over as Prime Minister, and Mussolini was arrested. The new Government immediately tried to begin peace negotiations with the Allies.

On the day after Mussolini's deposition, Ezra was indicted for treason in Washington.

*

Since the USA had entered the war, there had been a number of newspaper and magazine articles about 'broadcasting traitors', Americans speaking on Axis propaganda radio. Eight had been identified: Robert Henry Best, Douglas Chandler, Edward L. Delaney, Constance Drexel, Max O. Koischwitz, Jane Anderson, Frederick W. Kaltenbach, and Ezra Pound. All except Ezra were broadcasting from Berlin. In each case they were US citizens who had been in Europe when war broke out. Several were journalists; Anderson was an art and music critic. Ezra discussed two of them many years later in a letter to his London lawyer: 'Believe both Chandler and Best were honest and trying to save Europe from Moscow/.' He suggested they had been coerced in Berlin in a way that he had not in Rome.

Demands for the broadcasters' indictment soon began. In August 1942 Oscar R. Ewing, Special Prosecutor in New York, called for them to be charged with treason, and in January 1943 Representative Celler of New York was reported to be seeking to 'amend the Articles of War to permit the trial "in absentia" of these people'. Though Celler's demand was a travesty of the principles of justice, it brought the matter to the official attention of the Secretary of War, Henry L. Stimson, and the Attorney General, Francis Biddle.

The former wrote to the latter in February 1943 proposing 'their indictment "in absentia", leaving their trial and conviction until the successful conclusion of the war'. The main aim for the moment (continued Stimson) was 'that the public, at home and abroad, will be convinced of our determination to punish these traitors'. Thus, the eight would be 'indicted simultaneously', and a news story 'which thoroughly discredits them' would be released for publication by the Attorney General's office.

There was some delay, presumably because of the necessity of collecting evidence, but on 26 July 1943 a Federal Grand Jury in Washington DC returned indictments on all eight. That in Ezra's name stated

> that Ezra Pound, the defendant herein, at Rome, Italy, and other places within the territory of the Kingdom of Italy . . . being a citizen of the United States, and a person owing allegiance to the United States, in violation of his said duty of allegiance, knowingly, intentionally, wilfully, unlawfully, feloniously, traitorously, and treasonably did adhere to the enemies of the United States, to wit, the Kingdom of Italy, its counsellors, armies, navies, secret agents, represen-

tatives, and subjects . . . with which the United States at all
times since December 11, 1941, have been at war.

There was no mention in the indictment of the broadcasts, though a later
passage alleged that Ezra had 'asserted that citizens of the United States
should not support the United States in the conduct of the said war'.

In 1945 it was pointed out to the court that 'the crime of treason is the
only crime which, because of its importance in Colonial times, was defined
in the Constitution of the United States'. The actual definition in the
Constitution (Article 3, Section 3) reads as follows:

> Treason against the United States, shall consist only in levying
> War against them, or in adhering to their Enemies, giving them
> Aid and Comfort. No Person shall be convicted of Treason
> unless on the Testimony of Two Witnesses to the same overt
> Act, or in Confession in open Court.

This last provision (which was interpreted as meaning eyewitnesses) would
cause the prosecution some problems after the war was over, and not just
in the Ezra Pound case.

On the morning after the Grand Jury hearing, 27 July 1943, the *New
York Times* carried this front-page headline:

8 FROM U.S. INDICTED
AS AIDING THE AXIS

Ezra Pound, Jane Anderson
and Other Expatriates Face
Trials for Treason

The report stated that 'on conviction [they] can be punished by penalties
ranging from death down to five years and a $10,000 fine.' It was also
stated that 'Pound broadcasts from Rome, whence he spoke last night.'

The punishment for treason was specified in Section 2 of the US
Criminal Code:

> Whoever is convicted of treason shall suffer death; or, at the
> discretion of the court, shall be imprisoned not less than five
> years and fined not less than $10,000 to be levied . . . out of any
> or all of his property . . . and every person so convicted shall,
> moreover, be incapable of holding any office under the United
> States.

The *New York Times* quoted Attorney General Biddle as saying: 'It is
our intention when we can to apprehend these defendants and to bring

them to trial before a jury of their fellow-citizens, whom they are accused of betraying . . . These indictments are based not only on the content of the propaganda statements, the lies and falsifications which were uttered, but also on the simple fact that these people have freely elected, at a time when their country is at war, to devote their services to the cause of the enemies of the United States. They have betrayed the first and most sacred obligation of American citizenship.'

Ezra said that he heard the news of the indictment 'via the BBC'.

23

Out Fer The Mountains

In 1960 Ezra told Donald Hall he was 'completely surprised' to find himself charged with treason: 'You see I had that promise . . . "He will not be asked to say anything contrary to his conscience or contrary to his duty as an American citizen." I thought that covered it . . . I thought I was fighting for a Constitutional point. I mean to say, I may have been completely nuts, but I certainly *felt* that it wasn't committing treason.' In the same interview, he compared his case to that of P. G. Wodehouse, whose broadcasts from Berlin in 1941 had aroused British and American outrage: 'Wodehouse went on the air and the British asked him not to. Nobody asked me not to. There was no announcement until the collapse [of the Mussolini régime] that the people who had spoken on the radio would be prosecuted.' And of the justice of the indictment: 'I don't know whether I was doing any good or not [in the broadcasts], whether I was doing any harm. Oh, I was probably offside. But the ruling . . . was that there is no treason without treasonable intention.'

*

He was in Rapallo when he heard the news of the indictment. Two days earlier he had learnt of the 'resignation' of Mussolini. Mary, who had left Rapallo for Gais, wondered 'how the news of Mussolini's fall . . . affected Babbo'. She knew nothing of the other development.

On about 1 August, four days or so after he had heard of the treason indictment and a week after Mussolini's downfall, he went to Rome 'to see what was going on'. Rome Radio had broadcast one of his talks on 26 July, the day after the coup, but no more of his scripts had been transmitted since then, though the short-wave transmissions were continuing. Perhaps the radio staff had heard of the treason indictment, and wished to protect him, or possibly his talks seemed unsuited to the unpredictable political climate now that Il Duce had gone.

In Rome, Ezra went to the American Embassy, which was being managed by the Swiss, in the hope of acquiring official notification of the charges against him and what they meant, but he could learn nothing there, for the Embassy was only nominally open and had no contact with Washington. He returned to Rapallo to think things out, just as he had after Pearl Harbor.

On 4 August he wrote to US Attorney General Francis Biddle:

> I understand that I am under indictment for treason. I have done my best to get an authentic report of your statement to this effect. And I wish to place the following facts before you.
>
> I do not believe that the simple fact of speaking over the radio, wherever placed, can in itself constitute treason. I think that must depend on what is said, and on the motives for speaking.
>
> I obtained the concession to speak over Rome radio with the following proviso. Namely that nothing should be asked of me contrary to my conscience or contrary to my duties as an American citizen. I obtained a declaration on their part of a belief in 'the free expression of opinion by those qualified to have an opinion'.
>
> The legal mind of the Attorney General will understand the interest inherent in this distinction, as from unqualified right of expression.
>
> This declaration was made several times in the announcement of my speeches; with the declaration 'He will not be asked to say anything contrary to his conscience, or contrary to his duties as an American citizen' (Citizen of the U.S.).
>
> These conditions have been adhered to. The only time I had an opinion as to what might be interesting as subject matter, I was asked whether I would speak of religion. This seemed to me hardly my subject, though I did transmit on one occasion some passages from Confucius, under the title 'The Organum of Confucius'.
>
> I have not spoken with regard to *this* war, but in protest against a system which creates one war after another, in series and system. I have not spoken to the troops, and have not suggested that the troops should mutiny or revolt.
>
> The whole basis of democratic or majority government assumes that the citizen shall be informed of the facts. I have not claimed to know all the facts, but I have claimed to know

some of the facts which are an essential part of the total which should be known to the people.

I have for years believed that the American people should be better informed as to Europe, and informed by men who are not tied to a special interest or under definite control.

The freedom of the press has become a farce, as everyone knows that the press is controlled, if not by its titular owners, at least by the advertisers.

Free speech under modern conditions becomes a mockery if it do [*sic*] not include the right to free speech over the radio . . .

The letter continued in this fashion for a further six paragraphs, citing Brooks Adams, 'the course of events following the foundation of the Bank of England', Ezra's membership of the American Academy of Social and Political Science (which he had been invited to join just before the war), and a variety of other topics. It concluded:

At any rate a man's duties increase with his knowledge. A war between the U.S. and Italy is monstrous and should not have occurred. And a peace without justice is no peace but merely a prelude to future wars. Someone must take count of these things. And having taken count must act on his knowledge; admitting that his knowledge is partial and his judgement subject to error.

The letter also contained 'an application for the renewal of the passport which you took from me when I called at your office'.

*

Francis Biddle was married to a poet, Katherine Garrison Chapin, so perhaps he had a little private understanding of, or sympathy for, Ezra Pound. He was also a descendant of Nicholas Biddle, an early nineteenth-century American economist whom Ezra had criticized for his belief that the circulation of money should be put into private hands. He was the brother of George Biddle, a painter and sculptor who had met Ezra in Rapallo and corresponded with him.

But the machinery of justice was now in motion. No reply was sent from Biddle to Ezra (though his letter was eventually received in Washington), and on 24 January 1944 Biddle sent a request to Stimson that

in the event that Dr Pound is taken into custody by the military authorities, it is requested that he be thoroughly interrogated concerning his radio broadcasting and other activities on behalf of the Italian Government. It is also desired that an effort be made to locate and interview persons, particularly American citizens, having information regarding his acts of treason who might be utilized as witnesses in the event of prosecution.

The letter also mentioned the possibility of 'effecting Dr Pound's return to the United States'.

Among Ezra's American acquaintances who now began to consider his likely fate was Archibald MacLeish, Librarian of Congress and influential in Government circles (he had been appointed personally by Roosevelt). In September 1943 MacLeish wrote to the Assistant Secretary for War, Harvey H. Bundy, accepting that the indictment itself was 'understandable enough' in the circumstances, but wondering whether the consequence might not be 'to confer the paraphernalia of martyrdom upon a half-cracked and extremely foolish individual'. MacLeish was worried that 'summary action' (the execution of Ezra) might be taken 'by Allied military quarters in Italy as we occupy the country'. He was anxious that Ezra should be 'brought to civil trial' without fuss, whereupon (MacLeish was sure) the 'punishment will very precisely fit his crime'.

*

Ezra remained in Rapallo for the rest of August, waiting to see what would happen. The new Badoglio Government was trying to negotiate a peace with the Allies – Ezra afterwards coined the word *badogliare*, which he said meant 'to be a traitor' – but in the meantime the short-wave overseas broadcasts were continuing as usual from Rome Radio, and he had no wish to remain off the air. During August he sent them four or five more scripts, and these were read on the American Hour, though they were announced as being the work of 'Piero Mazda'.

On 6 September he went to Rome again, and he seems to have convinced Minculpop that he should be allowed on the air again in person, since the next day they announced that his broadcasts would resume. But on 8 September came the notification of Italy's official capitulation to the Allies.

It was expected that in consequence of the Badoglio surrender, American and British troops would shortly enter Rome. Allied forces were indeed landing from Sicily on the 'toe' of the peninsula, and at Salerno, south of Naples, but they only advanced with difficulty, thanks to resistance by German troops who had poured into the country in expectation of such an offensive. For the time being the Allies never came within less than eighty miles of the capital. Instead, from 10 September, Rome was occupied by German forces.

Ezra afterwards talked of 'the confusion at the Radio offices as soon as it was known that the Allies had landed. All the high officials moving out of Rome, some to the south, some to the north.' He himself lingered for about two days, and was seen in the Minculpop building, wandering around the offices. One employee had the impression he was trying to collect the scripts of his broadcasts, which she supposed he wished to destroy as compromising documents. He told her that the Americans would probably shoot him when they found him. But if he was collecting the scripts, it was probably in the hope of using them in his defence, as proof of his innocence of treachery.

On the morning of 10 September, before the Germans had occupied the city, he paid his bill at the Albergo d'Italia, and asked the clerk to look after his malacca cane, his wide-brimmed hat, and his small leather case: he wished to disburden himself of certain distinguishing marks. Then he went to call on Admiral Ubaldo degli Uberti and his wife. He asked if they could lend him a walking stick and a pair of stout boots. They agreed readily, and also provided a narrow-brimmed hat and a rucksack. They offered him shelter in their apartment from the Allied troops, who were still expected hourly; but he refused, and said goodbye.

At midday he rang the doorbell of Olga's friend Nora Naldi and her husband. He said he hoped to get up to the Tyrol, to see Mary in Gais. They were astonished – a 450-mile journey would be impossible with the country in such chaos. Why did he not stay with them? The war might be over in a few days. No, he said.

Nora Naldi cooked him two eggs, which he ate, even though they were black-market, along with a cup of tea and some bread. She put a hard-boiled egg, some fruit, and more bread in his rucksack. He asked the best way to leave the city on foot, unostentatiously, and they marked his map for him. Signor Naldi accompanied him along the street for a short distance. 'At the corner, I showed him the right way to go. He shook my hand, without speaking . . . I watched him go off, his stick striking the footpath regularly.'

*

'. . . an' Brer Rabbit he litt out fer the mountains! Right into the Homeric world . . .' So Ezra wrote in an unpublished broadcast script, remembering that journey. It was partly a flight – his old habit of simply disappearing from view in a crisis – but not a fearful one. It was euphoria, a sense of freedom such as he had not known since he walked the roads of the Dordogne and Provence in 1912.

He describes his journey in lines written for Canto 84 but never published:

> INCIPIT VITA NUOVA:
> 　　　　Tea at Norah's
> and then @ the air-port:
> 　　　　'what shall we do? we have no officers.'

And @ Sette Bagni nothing to pay for good bread –
   that after Roma –
nothing to pay for that egg
or those grapes
    or that double minestra
'Cosa fanno a Roma?'
    Wd/ I stay for the night,
and the first day they kept their packs
    and the second got rid of
    all military impedimenta
in fact of *all* impedimenta
    ready to escape in their underwear,
One night under the stars
    one on a bench at Rieti
one on Bologna platform
    after food at the cab-driver's friend's trattoria
Lo sfacelo, understood why Hem had written,
that is, his values.

  The journey was indeed like something from Hemingway. Ezra afterwards alluded to it in prose in one of his economic pamphlets, but even there he could not keep euphoria out of the account: 'On the 10 of September last, I walked down the Via Salaria and into the Republic of Utopia, a quiet country lying eighty years east of Fara Sabina . . .'

  He walked from Rome to Rieti, about fifty miles north-west of the capital, taking this route because it was 'the only road going north not infested by troops'. Only afterwards did it occur to him that his map, provided by the old admiral, was a military one, 'and if they caught me with it they might have taken me for a spy'. From Rieti he took a train, going on north 'with a herd of the dismantled Italian army'. At some point during the journey he ran into trouble with the German military authorities, and had to continue on foot. He found another train at Bologna which took him to Verona, where he spent a day deciding whether he should continue north, or give up and go to Rapallo. The situation on the railways was better – in this area they were under efficient German control – so, says Mary, 'he decided he would stick to his original plan and come and see me first; he had something important to tell me'.

*

One afternoon – 'a carefree and lovely September day' – Mary was returning on her bicycle to the Gais farmhouse. 'I saw Mamme standing at the corner of the house as though on the lookout for me, her hands curiously wrapped up in her apron, which I knew to mean she was upset and trembling ... As I halted my bicycle: "Iz isch's Tattile kemm!" She saw I did not grasp ... "Do Hearr!" The Herr had come.'

He had walked into the kitchen, and Frau Marcher did not recognize him. 'I said to myself: what new beggar is this? Then he said: Grüss Gott, and I recognized his voice: Der Herr! ... I gave him water to wash with; he was all covered with dust, like a beggar. Like a beggar, but he wouldn't eat anything. He said: Müde [weary]. He is lying down on your bed.'

Mary 'ran upstairs. A long silent embrace. Finally I managed to speak: How did you get here, where from? And he pointed to his feet, red, full of blisters, his ankles swollen. "I walked out of Rome ... "'

She brought him his supper, and the Marchers, unable to hide their perplexity and curiosity, crept up to wish him goodnight. Then at last he started to talk to Mary.

*

'"I don't know how much of this you already suspect, the doors at Sant' Ambrogio are not exactly soundproof." No, those doors did not close very well, but I had never overheard any conversation between him and Mamile. I felt he almost wished I had, it might have made things simpler for him. Not only did I show no curiosity, but I was completely unsuspecting about what was on his mind. He tossed about for a beginning. Where? When? And it was almost three o'clock in the morning when he finally thought he had said everything ...

'Now I learned that in Rapallo there was also a wife. His wife, with a son back in England. The news was not imparted as a secret, simply as facts that I was now old enough to understand. Things would be set right – "if this war ever ends ..." All plain and simple. I felt no resentment, only a vague sense of pity ...

'All plain and simple. But that was not the way it worked out.'

24

Civilized

What Ezra told Mary at Gais that night only intensified her desire to be her father's child, his true inheritor. She now plunged herself even deeper into his poetry, his ideas. To 'participate in Babbo's work' now 'meant more to me than being legitimate or illegitimate . . . What carried weight in my life then was Babbo's inner order; everything would forever depend on that.'

Word quickly got around Gais that there was a foreigner at the Marchers'. 'The commissioner from Bruneck, Herr Bernardi the butcher, and Herr Bacher came to the house. They were old friends, but Mamme and Tatte looked frightened when they entered with rifles over their shoulders . . . "Who is this man out of Italy who says he is an American? What business can anyone like that have in Gais?"' But Herr Bacher had a brother in America, and the investigation soon dissolved into a good-humoured discussion of politics, thence into economics, with Ezra holding forth about the experiment in Wörgl. Naturally, he did not mention his indictment for treason; he had not told Mary about that.

Herr Bacher was a wood carver by profession, and began to study Ezra's head. Would the Herr care to come to his studio? Mary accompanied him there the next afternoon. In Canto 74 it is told that 'Herr Bacher's father made madonnas still in the tradition / carved wood as you might have found in any cathedral'. And Ezra wondered: would Herr Bacher take him on as an apprentice? 'It might be interesting to see what he could do with his own hands, he had tried marble once . . . Or perhaps, under the circumstances, he might be suited to the sawmill, physical labour might be better. And so we walked to the sawmill . . .'

He wanted to stay, to escape from his obligations, to manage, as he had so often managed before, to start completely afresh. This time it was not so easy. 'I could not visualize Babbo lifting tree trunks and boards in the roaring noise and velocity of the mill and said so, venturing advice. He told me of his grandfather's lumber business . . . Had he ever tried handling trunks? No. To the owner of the mill he looked strong enough; they were in need of help, the sons were in the war . . . We would call again.'

But he had already lost the chance of escape. The morning after his arrival, he told Mary to send a telegram to Olga. Receiving it, she went down the hill to Dorothy and gave her the news. They gathered that he was safe, that he had slept in the open, that he had sore feet. They acted in harmony: Olga sent Ezra some Papier Fayard onionskin bandage that he had used ever since his walking tours in France in the old days. With it was a note saying that everything was calm in Rapallo. 'Babbo's vague plans to settle down in Gais to manual labour were dismissed.'

*

The Gais people treated him with an affectionate concern. Herr Bernardi's brother, the Nazi commandant in Bruneck, said he should go to Berlin and broadcast on the Rundfunk – 'That was the place for such a brain!' Frau Marcher's brother thought he ought to try Switzerland, said he would show him a safe way across. But Ezra had decided: 'No, he would return to Rapallo.'

To return might, however, not be so easy. He and Mary went down to Bruneck for a permit, but the authorities were doubtful, could not allow him outside their district. So father and daughter went on to Bolzano, now under its German name of Bozen. Ezra was depressed and bewildered by the town's desolate, militaristic appearance, and Mary, now eighteen, did all the talking: 'Look here – this man has to catch a train!' Catching a train, she sensed, would carry some prestige. 'By early afternoon Babbo had his permit.' She was certain that, had he been less law-abiding, he could have left without one.

The train was of sinister appearance: there was a single carriage with wooden benches for passengers, the remainder a long row of open freight trucks laden with heavy guns. As he said goodbye to Mary, Ezra looked at them wryly: 'I moved out of Idaho in 1887 behind the first rotary snowplough.'

*

There were, of course, adventures on the way back; Dorothy half remembered some story he told about two Japanese with a volume of Confucius in a restaurant in Milan. In any case he did not hurry; it seems to have been on this journey that he made contact with the new Fascist 'republic' that was being hastily set up in the north of Italy.

Mussolini, under house arrest at a hotel in the Apennines, had been snatched by a German airborne commando operation and taken to

Gargnano on the western shore of Lake Garda, to be used as figurehead in a puppet Government operating from the nearby town of Salò. By the end of September 1943 this Repubblica Sociale Italiana, or Repubblica di Salò, had pledged its loyalty to Berlin and drawn up a new and strictly Fascist 'programme'. Italy north of (and including) Rome was now nominally under its control, though real power and policy-making were in the hands of Berlin. Il Duce had very little influence on the Republic's decrees.

The Salò Republic immediately began to carry out Berlin's anti-Semitic policies, which up till now Italy had fended off. On 16 September, the day after the Republic was proclaimed, twenty-five Jews were arrested in Merano. Ten days later the methodical deportation of Jews started. There were raids in Trieste, and in Rome, where just over 1,000 were rounded up by the authorities, of whom only twelve survived the war. Similar raids took place in Genoa and Milan in November, deportation camps were set up near Modena and Bolzano, and near Trieste an extermination camp and crematorium were built; Ezra was therefore incorrect in saying that there were 'no gas ovens' in Italy during the war. By Christmas 1943 almost 10,000 Jews had been arrested; most of them were deported, the greater number to be murdered at Auschwitz.

Ezra, who, like most people in Italy, was unaware of this, contacted officials of the new Republic as soon as it was set up, and was invited to visit its headquarters at Salò, 'if I could get there'. He managed the journey during the autumn of 1943 – possibly on his way back from Gais – and met various officials, proposing to them that they should adopt stamp-scrip money and other Utopian economic measures. He was given an interview with Fernando Mezzasoma, the new Minister of Popular Culture, a hardliner who remained fanatically loyal to Mussolini and wanted to wipe out all 'traitors' and anti-Fascists. He approved of Ezra, describing him in December 1943 as 'the collaborator Ezra Pound, American writer, old and proven friend of Italy, in the service of which he has placed his intellectual bearing'. Certain of the Salò ministers were less enthusiastic. There is a report of the Foreign Minister speaking critically to Ezra about his Rome broadcasts; to which Ezra replied that he had been 'guided by an interior light'.

*

He hoped to broadcast again, for the Salò people were making efforts to beam propaganda at the outside world, this time from Milan. Mezzasoma told him he could certainly go there and offer his services. Ezra went, 'on a cattle truck', at the end of November 1943, and 'found the Republican Fascist Radio in disorder, with a few honest men wanting a radio station and the "wise guys" sabotaging and none of them being free from German control. The Germans censored all the programmes.'

. The station manager said there was no job for him; he would serve the cause better by broadcasting from Berlin or Paris. Ezra strongly resisted the idea. 'Give me a bed, a bowl of soup and a microphone,' he announced dramatically. But none of these was offered. It was suggested that he might read official propaganda over the air to American troops, but this he refused to do. There is a note among his papers, dated November 1943, which reads: 'Nein, ich spreche nicht gegen mein Vaterland.'

He wrote to one of the Ministry of Popular Culture staff during December: 'I see you refuse to pay my hotel bill.' Another note complains: 'I've slept two nights in a kind of corridor.' But then, on this visit to Milan, he came across Carl Goedel, a Philadelphia-educated German who had worked alongside him at Rome Radio. Goedel had an influential position in the Salò Minculpop, and arranged for one of its officials to give Ezra 3,000 lire 'towards expenses'. There is an acknowledgement in Canto 78 – 'Goedel's sleek head in the midst of it'.

On 10 December, thanks to his persistence, Ezra was finally allowed on the air. On the 'Tunis' transmission, beamed at American troops in North Africa, he gave a talk about Badoglio and the other 'defectors' who had betrayed the Fascist cause in Italy, calling for their summary execution. He was delighted to be back at the microphone, and proposed that he should adopt the same sort of timetable as in his Rome Radio days – 'go to Milan occasionally . . . for two or three weeks at a time. In other words, I want to use the same system which worked for me so well before.'

The radio staff were not prepared to agree to this, but he was told he could send in scripts, which others could broadcast at the rate of two or three a week, and he would be paid for them. This arrangement began in the spring of 1944, and Ezra afterwards described the material he wrote as being 'along the same lines' as his Rome scripts. For it he received 'about eight thousand lire per month'. The director of the radio station later described how, presumably because he could not perform the scripts in his own cracker-barrel voice, Ezra 'created a character known as "Mr Dooley"' for whom he would 'think up humorous remarks' to make in the broadcasts. Mr Dooley was not his own invention, but that of the American comic writer F. P. Dunne – and had probably been one of his models for the 'Ole Ez' performance all along.

Ezra never heard these broadcasts; the Salò radio 'was not on any wave length I ever heard in Rapallo'. As before, he was concerned to emphasize that he was not on the staff payroll. When they sent him an employment application form, 'I declined to return it', and on his payslips he would cross out the word 'salary' and insert 'for services rendered'.

After a while the radio station moved to Lake Como, and Ezra, for some reason, began to send his scripts via Carl Goedel at the German Consulate in Milan. Again, he wished to emphasize that this was purely because he happened to know Goedel, and that he was not himself working for the Germans. (Possibly the scripts were not being used at all, and Goedel was benevolently conjuring up regular payments to keep Ezra going.) However, Ezra pledged his loyalty to the Salò Republic in an eccentric manifesto which he drew up in February 1944, and persuaded some other writers in the Rapallo area to sign. It began with the assertion that 'The live thought of the epoch is permeated by the Fascist spirit', then turned to such matters as Frobenius, Confucius, and the liberation of Christianity from Judaism.

He began to bombard Mezzasoma almost daily with letters containing such observations as

> I am anxious to help . . . Anyone involved in Italy's propaganda broadcasts should at least be acquainted with the cast of mind of those who live in England and the United States . . . We are wasting time . . . Nothing will be done until I or someone who understands the meaning of this war has been granted the use of a printing press . . . The Fascist regime is only as good as its propaganda . . . My own voice should probably be used . . .

Besides proposing his familiar economic measures to the Salò people, he called for the introduction of a through bus service from La Spezia to Salò via Genoa (thereby handy for Rapallo), saying it would 'give the Republic a new backbone'. He wrote on every kind of subject to the Minister of Finance, to the Army Chief of Staff, to the Mayor of Milan; to anyone he could think of, even to a discarded mistress of Mussolini. As late as 20 April 1945 he could still be found making suggestions to the Salò authorities; by this time they themselves were desperately packing up and fleeing for their lives before the advancing Allies.

*

Though he could not return to his old position as a broadcaster, he managed to find a newspaper that would print him regularly, the *Popolo di Alessandria*, a bi-weekly Fascist journal. It had only a small circulation, but Ezra, typically oblivious to this, wrote with as much passion as ever, calling on his handful of readers to attend to such sacred names as Frobenius and Gesell. Now and then his articles were printed in other papers, and he managed to persuade the Salò Minculpop to publish some of his writings in Italian in book form, under the imprint of Edizioni Popolari in Venice. In the spring of 1944 they issued a thirty-two-page pamphlet by him on Roosevelt and 'le Cause della Guerra'; in June, another on the 'nature of economics in the U.S.A.'; in July, the *Ta Hio* in Italian; in September, *Jefferson and/or Mussolini*, which he updated while translating it; in February 1945 the Confucian text he later rendered in English as *The*

Unwobbling Pivot. He referred to all this as his 'main work' during 1944 and early 1945. *Orientamenti*, a collection of his articles written for the *Meridiano di Roma* between 1939 and 1942, together with selections from the Cantos translated into Italian by Olga, was ready for publication by Edizioni Popolari in September 1944 when it was decided to scrap the entire book. Either the Salò authorities disapproved of it, or somebody considerately felt that, with an Allied victory now almost inevitable, its distribution would do Ezra no good at all. (Indeed, during their 1945 investigation into his activities in Italy the FBI translated the book in full.) Similarly the new edition of *Jefferson and/or Mussolini* was scrapped before distribution – though Ezra afterwards claimed the book had been 'quoted on fascist posters'.

These, however, were probably posters that he himself composed and had printed in Rapallo. Some were full size, others mere strips a couple of inches wide. On the strips, in Italian, were such Confucian maxims as 'The archer who misses the mark turns and seeks the cause of his failure in himself.' The larger posters bore economic slogans: 'A Nation that will not get itself into debt drives the usurers to fury.' It seems unlikely that they were ever stuck on walls; the authorities would probably have removed them. Even Confucius began to seem dangerous: the Venetian printer of Ezra's work decided, at the Liberation in 1945, that the remaining copies of *The Unwobbling Pivot* had better be burnt because the last word in the title was rendered in Italian as *Asse*, and this might be misunderstood to mean Axis.

*

The Germans strengthened the coastal defences at Rapallo, and in May 1944, eight months after Ezra's journey from Rome to Gais, he and Dorothy were ordered out of their apartment at 12 Via Marsala, as 'aliens in a prohibited area'. They moved in with Olga at Sant'Ambrogio.

Dorothy's only reference to this episode in their lives is a simple statement in a letter to James Laughlin in 1945: 'We spent a year up at Olga's house.' Mary, who was still in Gais and heard about it from her mother, describes how 'the accumulation of twenty years of books and papers, letters, manuscripts, drawings, was all slowly carried up hill. Old Baccin gave a hand now and again, but most of it was carried by Babbo and Mamile in briefcases and knapsacks' (and by Dorothy, to whom Mary simply refers in this passage as 'his wife'). Dorothy describes how they 'found a cart with two horses to haul the books and heavy things up the hill'. Some of the furniture remained in the flat; they hoped to move back soon. A nearby family stored other pieces. The Gaudier-Brzeska head kept guard over the empty apartment.

With the books and papers crammed into it, Casa 60 at Sant'Ambrogio ceased to be a place of light and empty space, and became cluttered with furniture, trunks and boxes. Dorothy was given Mary's room in which to sleep. Ezra kept his own.

Had Dorothy not wished to come to Sant'Ambrogio she need not have done so. She could have moved in with Isabel Pound, who was still living in her own house, on another hill overlooking the town. But Dorothy and her mother-in-law never got on very well, and since Ezra was now clearly going to live with Olga whatever Dorothy did, she chose to accompany him.

*

The two women concentrated most of their effort on survival. 'Dorothy had nothing,' says Olga of their financial situation, 'I had nothing, and it was extremely tight.' Ezra was earning something from Salò, but after several months his payments were reduced because of a general salary cut. The Italian Government bonds he had bought shortly before the war had become worthless with the fall of Mussolini in July 1943; so Olga earned what she could by teaching. 'The Italians were anxious to learn German . . . This suited me, right? So I took them.'

The household had to do without most foods. 'Ezra lost 25 kilos,' says Olga. 'I used to get dried fruits from the peasants.' She herself did most of what shopping they could afford, since of the two women she spoke better Italian. For the first time in her life, Dorothy shared the cooking.

In Rapallo there were now occasional Allied bombing raids, on the railway line to Genoa. 'Bombs fell, but not quite on Sant'Ambrogio,' says Canto 87. One of the Allied officers involved in the operation was Squadron Leader Basil Bunting – a pacifist in 1918. 'It was a flight of Mitchells that first bombed Rapallo,' Bunting wrote to Dorothy after the war.

> They were sent to get the Zoagli viaduct but couldn't get in to it because of weather conditions. One of them landed at Catania where I was, for the moment, in charge. I had to de-brief the pilot. It was part of the preparation for Anzio.

*

Mary afterwards wrote of 'the stress' of these months when her father was 'pent up with two women who loved him, whom he loved, and who coldly hated each other'. But Mary was not there, and Olga strongly rejects this picture of the household, saying: 'We were all civilized people.' According to her, there were only the usual minor domestic irritations, misunderstandings over cooking or shopping. The word 'civilized' recurs again and again in her remarks (such as they are) about these months. To which Mary rejoins: 'Whatever the civilized appearances, the polite behaviour and façade in front of the world, their hatred and tension had permeated the house.'

Mary further suggests that the moments of self-reproach and regret in the Pisan Cantos, written a few months after the household had broken up, resulted not from her father's imprisonment but from the misery of that time at Sant'Ambrogio. She indicates a cry of 'AOI!' in Canto 81, calling it 'an outburst more personal than any other in the Cantos'. Similarly the lines in Canto 80:

> Les larmes que j'ai creées m'inondent
> Tard, très tard je t'ai connue, la Tristesse,
> I have been hard as youth sixty years.

'Until then,' observes Mary, 'the attitude toward personal feelings had been somewhat Henry Jamesian: feelings are things other people have. One never spoke of them or showed them.'

Yet Mary admits that during the Sant'Ambrogio months 'the letters I had received from Babbo . . . had been calm and enthusiastically concerned about his work'. That Jamesian distancing from emotion could not, perhaps, be broken down so easily; it seems to have made life in the triangular ménage, if not pleasant, then at least endurable. After all, Dorothy and Olga were practised at it too: each of them was a thoroughly 'civilized' character.

An unpublished passage from the Pisan Cantos suggests that Ezra had a certain pride in making such an unlikely ménage work:

> So the old Emperor said to Shun . . .
> 'If you can keep the peace between those two hell-cats
> you will have no trouble in running the Empire.'

*

He began work on the Cantos again, but this time in Italian. Cantos 72 and 73, written during 1944, were printed in a Salò journal, *Marina Repubblicana*, edited by Ezra's old friend Admiral Ubaldo degli Uberti, in January and February 1945. They have never been included in the collected editions of the Cantos; Ezra's family has preferred to keep them out of sight.*

Canto 72 begins:

> Purchè si cominci a ricordare la guerra di merda
> Certi fatti risorgeranno. Nel principio, Dio
> Il grande esteta, dopo aver creato cielo e mondo,
> Dopo il tramonto vulcanico, dopo aver dipinto
> La roccia con lichei a modo nipponico,
> Cacò il gran' usuraio Satana-Gerione, prototipo
> Dei padroni di Churchill.

---

*Since this was written, they have been added to a new edition (1987) of the *Cantos*, in their original Italian, without translation.

'As soon as one begins to remember the shit war, / certain facts will rise to the surface again. In the beginning, God / the great aesthete, after creating heaven and earth, / after [making] the fiery sunset, after having painted / the rocks with lichen like a Japanese print, / Shat the great usurer Satan-Geryon, prototype / of the masters of Churchill.'*

We are back in the Hell Cantos, but now it seems a Dantean hell, for Ezra himself, narrating directly for the first time in the Cantos, describes how he is visited by a series of spirits of the dead. First comes the Futurist leader and Fascist supporter F. T. Marinetti, who died during 1944. He tells Ezra: 'Well, I'm dead. / but I don't want to go to Paradise, I want to go on fighting.' He asks to borrow Ezra's body, but Ezra answers that it is too old to lend (he was fifty-nine in October 1944). He advises Marinetti to find some youngster's instead, by which he may escape the Purgatory in which he has lingered since the 'September treason' – the signing of the armistice with the Allies by the Badoglio Government in September 1943.

The next ghost is Manlio Dazzi – still very much alive when Canto 72 was written – whom Ezra accuses of immersing himself too much in the culture of the past (an odd accusation, coming from him), just as he believes Marinetti to have wasted his time in Futurism. But suddenly Marinetti's voice is heard, telling Ezra: 'Go! Go! / From Makkalè, on the edge of / the Gobi Desert, a white skull in the sand SINGS / without tiring, it sings, and sings: / "Alamein! Alamein! / We will return!"' (Makkalè was an outpost surrendered in 1941 when Italy lost Ethiopia to the Allies, while the Axis defeat at Alamein in 1942 was generally regarded as the turning point of the war.) Ezra is declaring that Italy and Germany will yet arise and be victorious.

Now a third voice cuts in, and begins to curse the 'shit' of multi-racial Allied forces, which are penetrating northern Italy, 'raping and setting fire'; there are 'moroccans and other filth / too foul to name'. It also curses 'that demi-foetus' Victor Emmanuel for having 'sold all Italy and the Empire'. The voice declares that 'Rimini is burnt down / Who now will see the tomb of Gemisthus / . . . The arches have fallen, the walls are burned / of the resting-place of the divine Isotta.' Ezra had been reading a newspaper report of severe damage to Sigismundo's Tempio at Rimini during the Allied advances, though in fact the building was not irreparably destroyed, and was completely restored after the war.

Ezra asks if it is Sigismundo himself speaking, but learns that the voice actually belongs to 'Ezzelino who did not believe / that the world was created by a Jew' – Ezzelino da Romano, known in his day as a tyrant, 'son

*I have translated these two Italian cantos with the aid of a literal prose English version by Mary de Rachewiltz.

of the devil'. He seems to stand for Ezra himself, or some aspects of him, since he defends having 'made fun of reason', and says that 'one single falsification' does more harm to the world than 'all my outbursts'. He asserts as Canto 72 ends that 'where the skull sings / the soldiers will return, the banners will return'.

There is nothing even faintly ambiguous about the political stance of this canto, but its support of Fascism and the Axis seems mild by comparison with Canto 73, the second of this Italian pair. This begins with the spirit of Cavalcanti introducing himself to Ezra as 'that Guido whom you loved / for my lofty spirit / and the clarity of my intellect'. The imitation *terza rima* of parts of Canto 72 now gives way to a looser metrical form as the Italian poet tells the story of a recent event.

Passing through Rimini, he met a 'gallant spirit', the ghost of a peasant girl only just killed, 'a bit stocky but a beauty / who had a German on each arm'. She was singing because of the way in which she had met her death. Cavalcanti explains that some Canadian troops had been on their way to rout the German occupying forces in Rimini, and to destroy what still stood of the town. Some of them raped the girl. Four or five of them, guarding German prisoners, then told her to direct them to the Via Emilia. The girl answered that she would lead them there herself, and she set off, deliberately taking them through a field which she knew her brother had laid with mines. 'What a brave girl!' declares Cavalcanti.

> What splendour!
> To hell with the enemy,
>   twenty of them were killed,
> the maid herself dead
>   among that rabble,
> the [German] prisoners were rescued.
>   The bold spirit
>   of that girl
> sings, sings
>   a song of joy,
> at this very moment on the road
>   that goes down to the sea.
>   *Gloria della patria'*
>   *Gloria! Gloria!*
> To die for *la patria*
>   in Romagna!
> The dead are not dead,
> I have come back
>   from the third heaven
>   to see Romagna,

> to see the mountains
> during the uprising,
> what a beautiful winter!
> In the north the fatherland is reborn.
> What a wench!
> what fine girls
> what fine lads
> wear the black!

*

By the end of April 1945, the reality of Italy was somewhat different from the picture of the country in these two cantos. A resistance movement against Fascism had begun in the German-occupied north after Mussolini's downfall in 1943, and from June 1944 partisan groups, organized by the Corps of Volunteers for Liberty, harassed Nazi and Salò troops at great loss of life to themselves. There were also anti-Government strikes. The extreme left wing was involved from an early stage, but the resistance movement was not exclusively or even predominantly Communist.

Ezra had his own explanation for the Allied victory. In January 1946 he told Charles Olson that 'radar had won the war, American production second, and the military strategy third'. Olson gathered that he had 'thought the war was lost [to the Allies] until radar began to sink the submarines'. And he wrote to Wyndham Lewis in 1951: 'without radar yr/ bottle [*sic*] fleet wd/ have been sunk/ exercise in bay of Naples, seen on film, and also discussed with technician, ole admiral had submarined'. Dorothy wrote to Ronald Duncan in 1947:

> Ez sez: 'England better off had she got out of war after having been defeated by Germany at Dunkirk, than to stay on for triple defeat by Germany, Russia & the U.S.A.

Dorothy added: 'Does she know she was defeated at Dunkirk? or has it been hidden from her?'

On 25 April 1945 there was an uprising of Italian partisans against the Germans. Three days later Mussolini and his mistress Claretta Petacci tried to escape from the overrunning Allied forces, but were caught and killed by a band of partisans near Lake Como. Orders went out to German commanders in Italy not to resist the partisan takeover, and at noon on 2 May, six days before the final surrender in Europe, German envoys signed a document pledging the unconditional surrender of Italy, to prevent further loss of life.

*

Ezra continued on his course quite unabashed. Though the Salò radio station was abandoned a couple of weeks before the surrender, he continued to write articles on economics for the newspapers. One was published the day before the partisan uprising. Allied troops began to appear in Rapallo at the end of April, and Olga went down to the town every day to see what was happening; she told Ezra that the Americans were setting up headquarters in one of the waterfront hotels. He decided to go and identify himself to them, not in any spirit of guilt or surrender, but simply so that, as Mary puts it, he could 'explain his ideas and actions'. In fact, he wanted to do more than explain: he wanted to be recognized as an expert. In Dorothy's words, he had 'lots of information about Italy which could be of use' to them. Ezra himself told Donald Hall in 1960 that he 'expected to turn myself in and to be asked about what I had learned'.

On the morning of Wednesday 2 May he dressed himself rather more smartly than usual, and set off calmly down the hill. A few hours later he came back again. He had talked to some Americans, and had told any of them who would listen that he should be taken to the USA 'to give information to the State Department'. But there was no one in authority, no one who understood what he wanted or who he was. (He had omitted to mention that he was under indictment for treason.) So he simply went back to his desk at Sant'Ambrogio and got on with his work, which happened to be an English translation of a Confucian text.

The next day, Thursday 3 May, Olga went off on her usual morning shopping-and-newspaper-buying expedition, and Dorothy set off for the other side of town, on her weekly visit to Ezra's mother. Ezra stayed at home, at the typewriter, working on at the Confucius. 'The man of breed,' he wrote,

> stands firm in the middle of what whirls without leaning on anything either to one side or the other, his energy is admirably rectificative . . . He comes into harmony with the process and continues his way . . . He pivots himself on the unchanging and has faith.

He was engrossed in this when, as he afterwards described it, two partisans 'came to the front door with a tommy-gun'.

Mary says they were 'two common ex-Fascist convicts'; Olga calls them 'common thieves! simply thieves!' According to Mary, they had heard there was 'a ransom of half a million lire on the head of the Poeta Americano'; they were men whom the peasants of Sant'Ambrogio knew well and 'despised'; one of them, she says, was later accused of man-slaughter 'and got killed', the other 'was imprisoned for theft'. Dorothy describes them as 'a couple of vicious Italian Communists'.

The men knocked on the door, Mary says, 'with their gun butts', though Ezra states that they carried only one weapon between them. According to

Mary they said to him: 'Seguici, traditore!' ('Come with us, traitor!'). Ezra put the Confucius into his pocket ('Slipped into pocket when partigianni came to door with tommy-gun,' he writes), and he also picked up his Chinese dictionary, to take some work with him because, he told Charles Olson, 'he didn't know what kind of floors of what Italian jails he'd be lying on', nor for how long.

The partisans allowed him to lock up and take the key down to Anita, the woman who lived on the ground floor of Casa 60. She asked where they were taking him. 'To the commando in Zoagli,' they answered. She told them: 'Il Signore è un galantuomo, non stategli a far male' ('He is a gentleman, don't do him any harm'). Ezra's only comment was to put a hand to his neck, and mime the action of a noose.

The men led him off down the *salita*. On the way, he stooped to pick up a single eucalyptus pip, 'one eucalyptus pip', he writes in Canto 80, 'from the salita that goes up from Rapallo'. Olga came home a few hours later, heard from Anita what had happened, and rushed off immediately in search of him. Dorothy writes: 'I came home about 6 p.m. – E. and O. both gone.'

Part Four

1945–58
'Grampaw'

1

Definitely Not Senile

Olga ran down the hill to Zoagli. She found Ezra under guard in the makeshift partisan headquarters there. They told her they were going to take him to Lavagna, to a more important command post. She asked, why not to Rapallo? They said: 'He has too many friends in Rapallo.'

Lavagna was about ten miles along the coast. Olga asked if she could come too. They agreed, but she and Ezra had to wait what seemed like hours for transport.

At Lavagna they were driven into a courtyard. Olga saw that 'the walls were all bloody, they had been shooting people'. Ezra, too, spotted the evidence of summary executions, 'and I thought I was finished there and then'. But to their surprise a partisan officer informed him: 'There is no warrant to arrest you. As far as I'm concerned, you're free.'

Ezra, however, did not want liberty as offered by this 'Communist mob', as he afterwards called them. There was no guarantee that another partisan band, less cool-headed, might not snatch him, and if that happened, the state of the walls indicated his likely fate. He decided to make another attempt to contact the American authorities.

But this was not easy. Ezra describes how, at this point, he 'tried to report . . . to the military . . . and didn't find a military save one negro who offered to sell me a bicycle and who was equally "lookin' fo' his comman"'.

The nearest American military post eventually proved to be in Lavagna, almost next door to the partisan headquarters. 'They were a negro troop,' says Olga (the US Army in 1945 was still segregated). 'They were all extremely nice (the officers were white), and they offered us refreshment.'

When the Americans understood – at least to some extent – who and what Ezra was, they decided that he should be taken to Army Intelligence, who would know what to do with him. The Counter Intelligence Center in Genoa was contacted and told to expect him. Once again there was a wait for transport; once again Olga was told she could come too.

*

Dorothy, coming back to an empty house at Sant'Ambrogio, made no attempt to go in pursuit of Ezra and Olga. When more than a day had passed and neither of them had reappeared, she decided she would move out. Leaving a note, she went down to the town, and found a room for herself.

After a while she was able to get back into the flat at 12 Via Marsala. The ceiling was down in several places, thanks to the bombing, and the water and electricity had been cut off, but she persuaded some South African troops to help her make the place habitable.

*

Ezra and Olga were taken to Genoa by jeep. The Counter Intelligence Center (CIC) was on the top floor of a modern office building in the middle of the city. 'There was a big hall,' says Olga, 'with two *carabinieri* guarding the door, and those American office chairs, shiny and hard and very stiff. And we sat down to wait.

'Nothing happened. And there were people coming in and out of the offices; and then there were fewer and fewer people, and it was getting cold. I was cold! Ezra always covered up a great deal. I said to one of the young men, "It's cold, can I borrow your coat or something?" So he lent me a coat. But we sat there, and it got to nine o'clock, ten, eleven.

'I said to the *carabiniere*, "When do they close?" He said, "Oh well, when they are all gone." One could hear, in the distance, in another room, people crying, as though they were being – Lord knows what.

'We were left there to sit from about seven o'clock, all night, until in the morning they started to come in. I said, "This is ridiculous, we haven't had anything to eat." And the *carabiniere* said, "The soldiers in the trenches haven't had breakfast." Blah! There was no point in going hungry in a place like Genoa, when all the cafés were open. But I kept quiet until after lunch.

'Just sitting there, on those hard chairs! If you went to the bathroom you had the *carabiniere* following you – and when you got there, there weren't any towels.'

*

Ever since the treason indictment of July 1943, Ezra had been the subject of a series of cables, letters, and memoranda between Washington and the Allied armies in Europe. A photograph of him and a written description was on file at HQ, Commanding General, US Forces. But this information had not percolated through to local Intelligence officers, and when he was first brought in from Lavagna, CIC Genoa did not know who he was or what to do with him. During the apparently pointless delay endured by Ezra and Olga, hasty efforts were being made to discover what action was required.

Ezra himself was expecting to be taken swiftly to Washington. He had contacted the American authorities voluntarily, twice, and he still wanted to impart to them his own detailed knowledge of the Italian situation. He emphasized, a little later, of his behaviour during these days: 'I was not fleeing from justice.'

Naturally he had not forgotten the treason indictment, but that had happened almost two years earlier, and he had never had any official notification of the charge, nor a reply to his letter to the Attorney General. It was not unreasonable to hope that in the interim the situation had changed, and that, even if the indictment still stood on record, it should be possible to explain to the authorities the real nature and purpose of his broadcasts – that they were not treasonable, but were merely the free expression of his own opinions – and to have the charge dropped.

He was also as anxious as ever to explain to Washington the true nature of the international situation, the 'real' war of usurers against humanity. As in 1939 he wished, if possible, to see the President himself – especially as Roosevelt had just died and been replaced by Vice-President Harry Truman. Ezra was rather disconcerted by this abrupt vanishing of his old enemy – in January 1946 he was still saying: 'Who is this Truman?'

*

At last, in the early afternoon, an official arrived at CIC Genoa from Rome. He knew all about the Pound case. 'And so,' says Olga, 'Ezra went in; and after a while, somebody brought me some coffee. So Ezra had his first examination certainly not under the proper conditions! It's not the way you should treat political prisoners, is it?'

Frank L. Amprim was not an army officer, but an FBI agent stationed in Rome, dealing with war crimes; to help him carry out his duties he had an army uniform and the acting rank of Major. He was young, and had a patient, rather friendly manner.

It was now his task to carry out the Attorney General's request, made in January 1944, that 'in the event that Dr Pound is taken into custody . . . it is requested that he be thoroughly interrogated concerning his radio broadcasting and other activities on behalf of the Italian Government'. Amprim started to question Ezra, thoroughly but unaggressively. Ezra liked his manner, and began to talk freely. Here, at last, was the chance to explain everything to an American in authority. Amprim listened, and took careful notes.

Ezra began to explain what he had been doing since the early months of 1941, when he had started to broadcast. He jumped about from subject to subject in his usual manner, but at all times he kept his head. Nevertheless, some of the observations recorded by Amprim in the report of the 'interrogation' looked damning. No doubt they were given in answer to leading questions. For example.

> I believe [said Ezra] that I was justified in continuing to criticize President Roosevelt after the United States entered the war . . .
> I was told that my radio talks were giving comfort and aid to the enemies of the United States.

By having manipulated Ezra into saying this, Amprim had virtually made him admit to treason, since the Constitution defined that crime as 'adhering to . . . Enemies, giving them Aid and Comfort'. On the other hand, Ezra seems to have spotted this, since on looking through Amprim's transcript of his answers, he was allowed to add in his own hand in the margin: 'I think my talks were giving pain to the *worst* enemies of the U.S.A.'

He told Amprim again and again that the decision to broadcast, and the content of his scripts, was entirely his own. There had never, he said, been the slightest pressure on him from anyone in authority. It would have been easy for him to claim that he was coerced, and difficult for the investigators to obtain evidence to the contrary, but clearly he never entertained the idea for a moment.

He was not content to leave Amprim to handle the presentation of his opinions to the authorities. He dictated this sentence:

> This statement should not be considered separate from a statement which I will write out myself as to the main foundations of my beliefs and the object of my thirty years' writing.

The transcript of his answers concluded:

> I am willing to return to the United States to stand trial on the charge of treason against the United States. I will admit the contents of this statement in open court since this statement is the truth.

*

It was now clear to him that the treason charge was still pending, and that what he had undergone was an interrogation relating to a supposed criminal offence, rather than the high-level discussion about economics and the Italian situation for which he had hoped. But Amprim seemed sympathetic and sensible, so Ezra had some hope that he would make the authorities understand the true situation.

Olga had remained in the waiting room. She was allowed to talk to Ezra between his sessions with Amprim, and, as nobody seemed to object, she stayed on for a day or two more, camping on the hard chairs, while Ezra and Amprim talked and talked in the interrogation room. She managed to buy rolls and coffee from a café in the square.

Eventually Amprim realized that something would have to be done about her. He told her she had better go home to Sant'Ambrogio, but must keep herself at the disposal of the American authorities, must be 'ready to testify in case there was going to be a trial'. She asked when and where that might be. Amprim did not know. Ezra Pound, he said, was now officially in custody (a report of his 'arrest' had just been sent out to the American papers), and 'no one was to see him or communicate with him till further notice'. He arranged for her to be driven back to Sant' Ambrogio in a jeep, and when he came out there himself a day or two later to look through Ezra's papers and confiscate anything that seemed relevant, he was unfailingly courteous.

A week later he returned, and took more papers and the typewriter, to prove that Ezra had typed the broadcast scripts (the letter 't' was out of alignment). He was still very polite and considerate, but he said he could give no information as to what was happening to Ezra, and what would happen next.

*

In Rome and at Salò, other FBI agents received instructions to look for any correspondence with Ezra that might be in the Fascist Government files. They started a search, and found a great deal. Some of the material was sent to Genoa, where Ezra agreed to sign acknowledgements that it was his own work.

Inventories were made:

> Two pencils and a black (Swan) fountain pen and ten sheets of paper bearing the known handwriting and handprinting in ink of Ezra Pound.

> Everest portable typewriter, Model 90, serial no. 27780, in blue and black ink, two sheets of carbon paper, one sheet of thin white paper and two sheets of paper containing handwriting in a foreign language . . .

Ezra was impressed by all this thoroughness. He later told his lawyers that Amprim and his colleagues had 'with great care collected far more proof . . . than I or any private lawyer could have got at'. It was proof, in his eyes, not of any guilt, but that everything he had told Amprim was 'the absolute truth'.

*

At the CIC they made him reasonably comfortable, with adequate food and makeshift bedding. He did not worry about his situation. 'My instinct all along,' he said a few weeks later, 'has been to leave the whole matter to the U.S. Dept. of Justice, the good faith of whose agent I have no reason to doubt.'

Possibly his predicament was not a wholly unwelcome relief from life in recent months, from the *ménage à trois* at Sant'Ambrogio. Certainly it delayed the difficulties he might have faced with the war ending and life expected to return to 'normal'. Like Richard Aldington's George Winterbourne in *Death of a Hero*, not dissimilarly faced with both wife and mistress, his situation was not impossible, 'but it would have needed a certain amount of patience and energy and determination and common sense to put right'. And even if he were to be taken to the USA not as presidential adviser but as prisoner, the prospect of conducting his own defence in court – and to whom else would he dream of entrusting it? – was not unattractive. It might indeed be the triumph of his life.

*

The interrogation was finished; the material was gathered from Sant' Ambrogio, from Rome, from Salò; and Amprim and his colleagues wondered what they should do next. The 1944 memorandum from the Attorney General said that 'consideration will be given . . . in the event that Dr Pound is taken into custody . . . to the advisability of effecting Dr Pound's return to the United States', but this did not amount to a clear order. Amprim wired for further instructions.

Meanwhile, though he had told Olga that neither she or anyone else could see Ezra at present, he allowed a journalist to meet and interview Ezra for the American newspapers. It seems a curious decision, but apparently there was nothing in the rule-book that forbade it.

The journalist, Edd Johnson, represented the *Philadelphia Record* and the *Chicago Sun*. Both papers printed his interview with Ezra on the morning of Wednesday 9 May, after Ezra had been at the CIC nearly a week:

Confucius and Kindred Subjects
**Pound, Accused of Treason,
Calls Hitler Saint, Martyr**
By Edd Johnson
Chicago Sun Foreign Service.

GENOA, May 8.

With millions of Italians and United Nations troops in Italy celebrating the announcement of Germany's surrender, Ezra Pound, an erudite poet and scholar, talked today about Confucius and kindred subjects.

I talked with Pound, now 59 years old and with a grayish pink beard, on the sixth floor of an office building overlooking the main square of war-battered Genoa.

Pound, a native of the United States, has been a self-styled expatriate in Italy since 1908 [*sic*]. He was taken into custody Saturday* near Genoa by American authorities on charges of treason. He was indicted on July 26, 1943, because he was broadcasting anti-United States and pro-Fascist propaganda in an English-language program beamed to America over Benito Mussolini's shortwave radio station in Rome.

Among the many things he said today were these:

'Adolf Hitler was a Jeanne d'Arc, a saint. He was a martyr. Like many martyrs, he held extreme views.

'There is no doubt which I preferred between Mussolini and Roosevelt. In my radio broadcasts I spoke in favor of the economic construction of Fascism. Mussolini was a very human, imperfect character who lost his head.

'Winston (Churchill) believes in the maximum of injustice enforced with the maximum of brutality.

'Stalin is the best brain in politics today. But that does not mean that I have become a Bolshevik.

'I do not believe that I will be shot for treason. I rely on the American sense of justice.'

*　*　*　*

Now all this might sound like gibberish, and it would be easy to write off Pound as a senile old sinner who has gone off his rocker. But Pound is definitely not senile. And if he is off his rocker, it does not show in any of the usual manifestations of nuttiness.

Pound told me that he received 300 lire each for the scripts that he wrote for other broadcasters, and 350 lire for those he wrote and voiced himself. He made much of the point that while he said the United States should not be in the war, he never urged American soldiers to lie down on their job once they got in battle.

Pound said that the last money he received for any writing

*The day on which he was officially charged, though by then he had been at the CIC about 48 hours.

other than his radio scripts was a check that he received for articles published in the Japan Times, a Tokyo newspaper.

The idea of making pro-Fascist broadcasts came to him from a German officer with whom he was playing tennis. He talked about his economic theories to the officer, and then asked him what they were saying up in Berlin.

'He said: "They are saying just what you are saying," and he told me these things paid well. But I knew that if they paid well they would want to control me, so I went to see Alessandro Pavolini (the Fascist propaganda minister) instead.'

I asked Pound if he really believed either President Truman or Premier Stalin would be interested in seeing him. He replied:

'One might say that I am in an unfavorable position at the present time to be received at the White House. If I am not shot for treason, I think my chances of seeing Truman are good.'

Pound's interest in Confucius is profound. He is probably the only man ever to be interviewed while awaiting trial for treason who talked more of various interpretations of Oriental ideographs than he talked of his own impending trial.

Pound believes that Hitler and Mussolini were successful in so far as they followed Confucius, and that they failed because they did not follow him more closely.

When I had to terminate the interview, Pound was just beginning to discuss the astrological era of dictatorship.

But I still say that the old sinner is not crazy.

Ezra may have struck Johnson as amazingly pro-Axis, but his remarks about Hitler and Mussolini show that he was beginning to shift his ground. The essential doctrine was, after all, the attack on usury; it might be wise now not to cloud the issue by supporting the defeated Axis leaders too vehemently. So he allowed that they had 'failed', and called Mussolini 'a very human, imperfect character' – a change from naming him 'the Boss' and describing him as a flawless artist.

Later he would become more critical still, censuring Mussolini, in a 1949 letter, for not 'working in centre' – for failing to observe the Confucian principle of balancing at the still centre or pivot – and criticizing Il Duce's policies for 'plunging into the swamp instead of improving FROM the centre'. In 1946, talking to Charles Olson, he even indulged in personal abuse, alleging that Pavolini had told him that 'he couldn't walk on the side of the street under M's Palazzo because of the stink of the boss!'

*

Twelve days after the publication of the Edd Johnson interview, Ezra was still at the CIC. Washington had sent no orders as to what should be done with him.

Dispatches went out with increasing urgency from the CIC, requesting instructions about the prisoner, who was referred to variously as 'the American Doctor', 'American expatriate', 'War Criminal'. In the end the matter reached the level of Supreme Commander, Mediterranean – Field Marshal Sir Harold Alexander of the British forces – who on 21 May told the War Department in Washington that he must have an immediate decision about Ezra Pound.

A response came the next day, and was sent on to Genoa and the other relevant command post in code:

> May 22, 1945
> TO FOR ACTION: CG FIFTH ARMY
>   CG REPLACEMENT AND TRAINING COMMAND
> SIGNED: CG MTOUSA
>   American Civilian Doctor EZRA LOOMIS POUND reference Fifth Army cable 2006 under Federal grand jury indictment for treason.
>   Transfer without delay under guard to MTOUSA Disciplinary Training Center for confinement pending disposition instructions. *Exercise utmost security measures to prevent escape or suicide*. No press interviews authorized. *Accord no preferential treatment*.

The initials CG MTOUSA stood for Commanding General, Mediterranean Theatre of Operations, USA, but the cable had been composed by an anonymous official, probably in Washington.

There can be little doubt that the Edd Johnson newspaper interview was responsible for the concluding instructions. Obviously up to now Ezra had been accorded some preferential treatment. He was only under what amounted to house arrest, and he was being allowed to talk to journalists. The Department of Justice wanted the case to be treated with the gravity demanded by a charge of treason.

As to the observations about 'escape or suicide', someone had, perhaps understandably, considered these possibilities, though CIC Genoa could see that he showed no signs of contemplating either course of action. But the cable had been sent, and its instructions were now followed to the letter.

2

Gorilla Cage

The cable reached CIC Genoa, and on the morning of 24 May 1945, Ezra was handcuffed and taken downstairs to a waiting jeep, manned by military policemen. He was driven off, believing (as he later said) that he was 'bound for an airport and a plane to the United States'.

*

Mary had now left Gais. For the past year she had been working as secretary to a German military hospital at Cortina in the Dolomites. After the surrender, 'nothing gave me a clue as to what might have happened to my parents. The gory pictures of Mussolini and Claretta Petacci with their entourage, hanging by the heels . . . filled me with horror and forebodings . . . I felt the humiliation and the defeat.'

She decided she must go to Rapallo. She travelled part of the way in a jeep, but the journey was almost as difficult as her father's to Gais in 1943. 'Mamile opened the door, very pale and tense. "And Babbo?" "My dear, I don't know." We embraced and cried for a while.'

Olga told her what had happened, and said: 'We must be prepared. There will be a trial. His life is in danger.' Mary's having worked in a German war hospital might count against him, and the American gutter press could make a nasty story out of an illegitimate daughter. It would be wise, said Olga, for Mary to try to get a job with the Americans. 'The thought revolted me,' writes Mary.

Olga decided that Mary must go to CIC Genoa. 'Perhaps a young girl could more easily touch the officer's heart and he might tell me where Babbo was; perhaps even give me permission to see him.' She gave Mary Ezra's seal ring: 'It was as though I had been entrusted with the Holy Grail.'

She had no luck at Genoa. 'An impassable officer – Major Amprim was not there – who seemed neither to believe me nor to care whose daughter I was, said: "Sorry, I can tell you nothing."' She did not return to her mother, but went back to Cortina with the ring in a little bag around her neck. 'Somehow it gave me a glimpse of how tenuous a thread tied me to Babbo . . . I began from then on to idolize him. Now that I did not even know his whereabouts, he was no longer merely the Herr, il Signore, the Teacher, Tattile or il Babbo, but the hero, the victim, the righteous man who had tried to save the world and had fallen prey to evil powers. The Infallible.'

Her hospital work at Cortina soon came to an end, and she went to Gais. There, she received a letter from Olga telling her to come to Rapallo with her things as soon as possible. 'She still did not know where Babbo was, but she gathered he had been taken to the States and felt that we must try to join him there.'

Transport was again a problem. Eventually Mary managed to get a lift on a truck going to Genoa. She put all her belongings into one big trunk, so heavy that no one could possibly steal it. 'Inside it I placed my locked treasure box: Babbo's ring, my emerald ring and gold brooch that Grandfather Homer had given to Mamme and she had given to me . . . as well as all the money I had saved from my salaries.' By the time she arrived, the trunk had vanished. 'At the beginning Mamile was full of sympathy . . . Then suddenly: "But you have Babbo's ring?" "No." I had not had the courage to say it . . . She pushed me away: "Naughty child, I knew you couldn't be trusted! This is a sign, this is a sign." And she started to weep.'

A strained, painful four months followed at Sant'Ambrogio. Finally, late in September, 'a letter from Babbo arrived. A short note in pencil. The address was typed on a brown envelope that had BASE CENSOR over it . . . He was – had been all the time – barely two hundred miles from Rapallo.'

*

During the Liberation, the US Army had hastily set up a prison and rehabilitation camp for its own malefactors in a big field just north of Pisa. The camp had the euphemistic name Disciplinary Training Centre (DTC). Situated just off the Viareggio road, it was intended to provide summary punishment – imprisonment and intensive drill – for malingerers, brawlers, cowards, deserters, and other recalcitrant military. It also served as a temporary jail for more serious offenders – particularly rapists and murderers – who were awaiting transfer to the USA for federal trial. Around the perimeter, ragged barbed wire supported by concrete 'gibbets' was topped by an electric fence. At intervals stood guard towers, their sub-machine-guns and Browning automatic rifles trained on the wire.

The prisoners were divided into companies, each being separated from the others by its own barbed wire. Ordinary detainees – those who would eventually be returned to their units – were given one-man 'pup' tents to sleep in. They underwent an exhaustive 'retraining' programme of fourteen hours daily, starting at dawn. The US Army's magazine for the troops, *Yank*, described it as 'the toughest training detail in the Army . . . tougher even than front-line combat'.

The more serious offenders were confined in a maximum security compound. Some of these – particularly prisoners suspected of being 'escape-artists' – were put in cages, with stout wooden frames and strong steel mesh, where they could be kept under continuous observation, though they were usually allowed to pitch a 'pup' inside for sleeping and protection from the weather. They tended to be prisoners due for trial in the US, though occasionally hangings or execution by firing squad took place at the DTC itself (a local priest has described attending the execution of an officer). In this case the cages were used as death cells. Equally unpleasant for the prisoners were the 'boxes', three rows of concrete cells with no windows, merely a small observation flap in the door. These were used for solitary confinement, which usually meant two weeks on bread and water. Escape attempts were treated with the utmost severity. One day, eight men from Special Company, the section consisting of mental defectives, tried to get out across the drill field, and were shot down from the guard towers. One of the medical staff, Robert L. Allen, describes how he 'rode to the hospital with two of them while they bled to death'.

The intention of the Department of Justice in Washington was to house Ezra here until arrangements had been completed for his trial. The commanding officer of the DTC, Lieutenant Colonel John L. Steele, assumes that he was sent there simply 'because there wasn't any place else. We were primarily a retraining center, but we were also a holding camp for prisoners to be sent back to the States, and the Army was of course the government in the area at the time'.

Lieutenant Colonel Steele was away from the DTC attending a family funeral in the USA when Ezra arrived, and was not due to return for a month. He said afterwards that he was one of the few officers there who had heard of Ezra Pound and would have realized who and what he was. Most of his subordinates (who, he says, were young and relatively inexperienced) only understood that the new prisoner was a civilian charged with some war crime or other. They noted the cable's instructions, which came from the highest level, that they must exercise 'utmost security measures', and the warning about 'escapes or suicide', combined with the caution against 'preferential treatment'.

So it was that, as Lieutenant Colonel Steele put it, 'somebody over-eager to obey explicitly the order from central command' decided not only to use one of the 'death cell' cages for Ezra Pound, but to give orders for the regular steel mesh on this cage to be replaced by a tougher grille. On the night before Ezra was due to arrive from Genoa, military engineers cut away the existing mesh with oxy-acetylene torches, and replaced it with sections of heavy 'airstrip' steel, so-called because it was used to make temporary runways for aircraft. A report to Washington later explained that 'extreme precautions were used to prevent suicide or escape', and that it had been decided to place the prisoner 'in a small open cell with walls of steel grating in order that he might be under constant observation'.

Orders also went out that all DTC personnel, both prisoners and guards, should keep away from Ezra Pound's cell, and that no one was to speak to him. This, combined with the glimpse that some prisoners had had of the flashing blue oxy-acetylene, understandably caused interest to be taken in the new arrival. Rumours circulated that in his last prison he had not merely been fettered, but shackled to a huge iron ball. Somebody said he had heard that the list of charges against the fellow occupied twelve sheets. All this amounted to 'really big-time stuff'.

*

The jeep carrying him arrived at the main gates of the DTC around 1500 hours on 24 May 1945. Robert Allen of the medical staff 'recognized him easily by the beard and the glasses'.

Ezra's lawyer later claimed that, on arriving at the DTC and discovering what it was, Ezra 'was at once beset with fears – that he would be thrown with murderers and felons who would kill him; that nobody knew where he was and nobody would ever know what had happened to him'. A very different account is provided by a British officer in charge of another Allied prison camp in Italy, who was visiting the DTC in order to learn how things were run there. This Englishman, Peter Brown, alleges that Ezra 'behaved like a visiting lecturer, expecting a reception of dons and pressmen as a matter of course, before being escorted to his podium. He waved cheerfully at some of the inmates. It was said that his first words, on looking around, were "Dis is a crummy stir."' More plausible than either of these is Robert Allen's impression, gained from later conversations with Ezra, that, 'even when the vehicle carrying him stopped at the DTC, he thought that his visit [there] would end as soon as a plane was readied at Pisa airfield'. In other words he expected to be there only for a matter of hours, or at the most days, before being flown to Washington.

He dismounted from the jeep, his handcuffs were removed (he after-wards complained that it was illegal to handcuff a man in a moving vehicle), and he was stripped of his own top clothing and given an Army 'fatigue' uniform – a pair of loose trousers and a battledress blouse. It was hot, and he was allowed to leave the blouse hanging wide open at the neck.

He was not permitted belt or shoelaces, for fear that he would use them to hang himself – a standard precaution for high-risk prisoners – but he asked if he could keep the Confucius and the small Chinese dictionary he had brought from Sant'Ambrogio, and this was allowed. He was also given the Bible, Authorized Version, US Army issue. The door of the specially reinforced cage was then opened, and he was put inside and locked in.

*

The cage chosen for him – rather surprisingly in view of the caution against escape – was at the end of the row, next to the perimeter fence, with a view across the drill field to the Pisa–Viareggio road. Behind it stood the concrete boxes for solitary confinees. To the left were the rest of the cages, while in front lay a cramped wire compound into which prisoners were herded in the daytime. He was easily within earshot of them, and of the occupants of the other cages, but he was told not to talk to anybody.

'Not allowed to talk to other prisoners,' he afterwards noted. He also made these jottings about the conditions in which he was kept:

> Barbed wire cage/ special cage made out air strip/
> cages werent barbed wire they were inside several fences
> of same
> the line of cages inside the punishment area, labelled
> 'DEATH CELLS'

This information was provided for a friend in 1953. It was followed – in the same letter – by the request: 'Dont' putt in inexact sobb stuff. svp.'

Far from trying to stir up sympathy for the way he was treated at the DTC, he would afterwards speak of his confinement with scarcely suppressed pride. To Charles Olson in 1946 he 'always referred to it as Gorilla Cage' and observed that to have been shut in it was really 'something' at first. And an article in *New Republic* in 1957 records him as saying:

> Ha, I was a dangerous criminal . . . They thought I was a dangerous wild man and were scared of me. I had a guard night and day and when they built a cage out of iron mats from airplane runways and put me in the cage for the merriment of all, they posted a guard outside. Soldiers used to come up to the cage and look at me. Some of them brought me food. Old Ez was a prize exhibit.

*

During the first afternoon and early evening he was not particularly uncomfortable. Robert Allen remembers how he 'walked back and forth on the concrete floor'. When night came it rained. The cage had a slanting wooden roof, but there was no other protection against the weather, and the rain could come in through the mesh on all four sides. Ezra now learnt that, unlike other caged prisoners, he was not going to be supplied with a 'pup' tent for shelter – the orders were that he must remain under observation throughout the twenty-four hours – and the guards would only give him a pile of blankets, which he must put on the damp cement floor. This was no joke to a man who had always wrapped up well at any hint of bad weather, and would retire to bed at the slightest sign of a sore throat. He could not even take shelter by going to the latrines; there was a can in the corner of the cage, which they would not remove until it was completely full and stinking. A guard stood outside the cage, watching him all through the night, and bright lights shone continuously on him. Naturally he could not sleep.

In the morning, when the guards let most of the other caged prisoners out for exercise, he gathered that this too had been forbidden in his case: he must remain penned inside continuously. It was also made clear to him that none of his relatives, no one in Rapallo or Sant'Ambrogio, was being told what had happened to him. This disturbed him. It also began to become apparent that no plane was waiting to take him to Washington.

*

The next night came. Once again the powerful floodlights glared into the cage, and his eyes felt sore. In the day, worn by lack of sleep, he took relief in Confucius and the Chinese dictionary. At other times he simply stared out at the road and the countryside. One of the guards, David Park Williams, writes: 'Pound's volume of Confucius was by his side continually, and the prisoner read for hours, or simply sat and combed his ragged beard, watching the Pisa road where passers by and an occasional white ox were visible.' Later, in the Pisan Cantos, Ezra ironically compared his situation with Basil Bunting's imprisonment in 1918 as a conscientious objector: 'Bunting / doing six months after that war was over.'

Food was brought to him once a day by a black soldier named Whiteside. 'Spoke only to Negro attendant who brought food,' Ezra noted. One of the guards describes Whiteside as 'Stocky and grave, a person beautiful in his simplicity . . . the bearer of news and refreshment to Pound and the other caged men.'

Rain alternated with hours of hot sun and dust; it was late May, approaching June. The other caged men could crawl into their pup tents at midday, but Ezra was left in the open. 'And the wind came as hamadryas under the sub-beat,' he writes in Canto 74. Yet he goes on:

> The wind is part of the process
> The rain is part of the process.

– an allusion to words in the *Chung Yung* of Confucius:

> What heaven has disposed and sealed is called the inborn nature. The realization of this nature is called the process. The clarification of this process . . . is called education. You do not depart from the process even for an instant; what you depart from is not the process.

That is, all experience is a valid part of the search for truth.

Perhaps, too, he remembered Confucius's praise, in the *Analects*, for one of his disciples:

> How admirable Hui is! Living in a mean dwelling on a bowlful of rice and a ladleful of water is a hardship most men would find intolerable, but Hui does not allow this to affect his joy.

Certainly he was supported by his belief that, despite present delays, he would eventually get to Washington, where he still expected to be able to exonerate himself completely. Admittedly something had gone wrong: as he said, a few months afterwards, he suspected that someone from the real enemy, the usurers, had deliberately 'maltreated and double-crossed' him. But even so, he was certain that there would be 'some way out', so that he could divulge what he knew to 'the proper people'.

*

He found it hard to sleep. There is a repeated motif in Canto 74:

> of sapphire, for this stone giveth sleep . . .

> Kuanon, this stone bringeth sleep . . .

> for this stone giveth sleep . . .

The days were often so scorching and the nights so cold that at last he was allowed to have a pup tent for shelter inside the cage. Robert Allen noticed how ingeniously he would organize its two halves, which buttoned together, so as to make the best of the tiny space (6 ft by 6½ ft).

Often, he occupied his mind by examining his surroundings. To the north and east lay the Carrara hills; one cone-shaped peak he named Mount Taishan after a sacred Chinese mountain, not far from the birthplace of Confucius. Looking the other way, through the tangles of steel mesh and barbed wire, he could just make out the roofs of Pisa and the Tower. Two other hills he named the Breasts of Helen. There are glimpses of all this in the Pisan Cantos:

from the death cells in sight of Mt Taishan @ Pisa . . .

> from Mt Taishan to the sunset
> From Carrara stone to the tower . . .

Mist covers the breasts of Tellus–Helena and drifts up the
> > > > Arno . . .

> 10,000 gibbet-iform posts supporting barbed wire . . .

Occasionally there was an animal or bird to glimpse or examine:

> > came a lion-coloured pup bring fleas
> > and a bird with white markings, a
> > > stepper . . .

and a white ox on the road toward Pisa as if facing the tower,
dark sheep in the drill field and on wet days were clouds
in the mountain as if under the guard roosts.
> > A lizard upheld me
> > the wild birds wd not eat the white
> > > bread . . .

Be welcome, O cricket my grillo, but you must not sing after
> > > taps . . .

> squawky as larks over the death cells . . .

> and Brother Wasp is building a very neat house
> of four rooms, one shaped like a squat indian bottle . . .

Ezra told Robert Allen that he had spent 'hours watching wasps construct a nest', and had been fascinated by an ant colony. He also looked at the life of the ground itself:

> > dry friable earth going from dust to more dust
> > grass worn from its root-hold . . .

> niggers scaling the obstacle fence in the middle distance . . .

Occasionally he described himself:

> > the leopard sat by his water dish . . .

> But in the caged panther's eyes:
> > 'Nothing. Nothing that you can do . . .'

This was a rare moment of self-pity. Usually he was more detached:

> Nor can who has passed a month in the death cells
>   believe in capital punishment
> No man who has passed a month in the death cells
>   believes in cages for beasts.

*

He made constant efforts to stay healthy. He was observed by the other inmates as he boxed, fenced, and played imaginary tennis with himself to keep fit. Robert Allen describes him 'making graceful leaping forehands and backhands. He assumed fencing stances and danced nimbly about the cage, shadow boxing.' But he did not feel very safe; when hastily fitting the airstrip steel, the workmen had left the jagged edges of the old mesh protruding where they had cut it away about ten inches above the ground, and it formed a hedge of murderous spikes. Ezra regarded it as a half-invitation to suicide, an easy way to slash the wrists. Afterwards Mary gathered that 'during certain hours of despair the temptation had been very great'.

> the loneliness of death came upon me
>   (at 3 P.M., for an instant) . . .
> There is fatigue deep as the grave . . .

Meanwhile the sun and dust, and the glare of the lights at night, made his eyes more and more inflamed –

> the dust and glare evil

– so that the cage became quite simply

> hell, the pit.

*

After two weeks, he began to experience giddiness and claustrophobia:

> hast 'ou swum in a sea of air strip
>   through an aeon of nothingness,
> when the raft broke and the waters went over me . . .

He reported his condition to the guards. Robert Allen also noticed the increasing inflammation of his eyes, and another guard observed that he was losing weight very fast.

It was decided that he should be given a medical examination, and this took place on two consecutive days, 14 and 15 June, by which time he had been in the cage exactly three weeks. Since his complaints were of claustrophobia and mental confusion rather than of physical symptoms, the Acting Camp Commander detailed two psychiatrists, Captain Richard W. Fenner and Captain Walter H. Baer, to discover what was wrong with him. The first report, by Fenner on 14 June, reads:

> Placed in confinement here at the DTC he had a 'spell' about a week ago. This occurred while he was sitting in the sun, and the patient describes it as a period of several minutes during which he had great difficulty in collecting his thoughts.
>
> There has recently been some difficulty in concentration. Easy fatiguability has also recently been noticed by the patient . . .
>
> Patient talks a great deal. He wanders from the subject easily, and needs to be constantly reminded of a particular question to which a complete answer is sought . . .
>
> Patient states that he has been confined in a rather small space, he has become afraid of the door and the lock of his enclosure. Also states he worries a great deal that he'll forget some messages which he wishes eventually to tell others.
>
> No paranoia, delusions nor hallucinations . . .
>
> Patient is oriented as to place and person; knows that it is June, but does not know the day of the week nor the date of the month.
>
> Memory for remote events is good.
>
> Memory is also good for recent events, and is likewise good on testing. Patient states he is having great difficulty keeping in mind some facts which he wants to deliver at some time . . .
>
> No evidence of emotional instability.
>
> Insight – good.
>
> His fund of general information on geographical, historical, political, economic and artistic subjects, as well as others is apparently very superior . . .
>
> Apparently very superior intelligence. No evidence of disease of the central nervous system, and no notable personality defect.

This was Baer's report the next day:

> His present complaints are temporary periods of confusion, anxiety, feelings of frustration, and excessive fatiguability. There is no evidence of psychosis, neurosis or psychopathy. He is of superior intelligence, is friendly, affable, and cooperative. He does, however, lack personality resilience, shows some

anxiety, restlessness, tremulousness and has had an attack of confusion.

Due to his age and loss of personality resilience, prolonged exposure in present environment may precipitate a mental breakdown, of which premonitory symptoms are discernible. Early transfer to the United States or to an institution in this theatre with more adequate facilities for care is recommended.

In consequence of these reports, particularly the second, Ezra was taken out of the cage and moved to the medical compound, where he was given an officer's tent of his own in which to live.

3

It Exists Only In Fragments

He 'kissed the earth after sleeping on concrete'. In the tent he slept well, had a good appetite, and no longer felt confusion or claustrophobia. It was now mid-June and very hot; he abandoned his army fatigue dress, spending many days lounging in his tent clad only in army drab olive underwear, a fatigue cap, and GI shoes and socks.

Every evening he would report on sick call to one of the medical huts, after the other 'trainees' had been seen, so that he could be checked over and given any necessary treatment. They prescribed him medication for a urinary discomfort ('methenamine eases the urine', he says in Canto 74), and gave him drops for his inflamed eyes.

The DTC commanding officer, Lieutenant Colonel Steele, returned to the camp a week after Ezra had been taken out of the cage, and decided to inspect him. Ezra had put in a request for more blankets (which, says Robert Allen, was delayed while an officious corporal pondered the matter), and Steele used this as the excuse to go and speak to him.

> We talked for over an hour [says Steele], but he did most of the talking, and for two reasons: he talked very fast and had a lot of things to say, and it took me a long time to think of anything worth saying . . . One of the first things I spoke to him about was whether he was warm enough and had enough blankets – although it seemed to take two or three hours to find this out, because of the way he talked.

Ezra was amused by the Commandant's name; in Canto 78 he quotes Guard Whiteside: – '"Steele that is one awful name," sd/ the cheerful reflective nigger'– and adds that Steele's junior officers included two men named Blood and Slaughter (actually these were prisoners' names). Steele himself saw the joke: 'Steele is the sort of name somebody might dream up if he wanted a prison warden in a story.' Ezra went further in the Pisan Cantos and implied that Steele's bearing suggested he was a cruel man, alluding to 'The touch of sadism in the back of his neck'. Steele refutes this charge, saying that if he did 'hold back' in his dealings with Ezra, it was 'because of the distance that you ordinarily keep between yourself and the prisoners . . . Here was a citizen charged with treason.' He adds: '"Pound" is not such a pretty name itself.'

During their first conversation, Ezra, says Steele, 'wanted to talk only about economics, and the fact that he needed to go straighten out Truman. He thought that this could be done if he could get to Washington.' Steele had some sympathy for this passionate concern with economics, since he himself had taught the subject at Boston University before the war. But 'it seemed a little bit strange to me that he thought . . . he could go and see Truman.' Steele was also struck by the force with which Ezra spoke: 'He was very animated, and the piercing eyes were just fascinating.'

Steele has said he feels that after the initial mistake of putting Ezra in the cage 'it worked out pretty well . . . We did what we could [though] he would still be confined.'

*

Ezra spent most of his first couple of weeks in the tent resting and letting his sore eyes ease themselves. The dim cool under the canvas was a blessed relief after the glare of sun and floodlights:

> Only shadows enter my tent
>> as men pass between me and the sunset . . .
>
> in the drenched tent there is quiet
>> sered eyes are at rest . . .

He took exercise or walked in the grass compound for about two hours each day; the remainder of the time he passed lying down.

He still derived pleasure from looking at small details of the scene around him:

> a black delicate hand
> a white's hand like a ham
>> pass by, seen under the tent-flap
>> on sick call . . .
>
> and this grass or whatever here under the tentflaps
>> is, indubitably, bambooiform
> representative brush strokes wd/ be similar . . .

Other DTC personnel were still supposed not to talk to him, but there were loopholes:

> . . . Mr Edwards superb green and brown
>   in ward No 4 a jacent benignity,
> of the Baluba mask: 'doan you tell no one
>   I made you that table.'

The 'table' was just a packing case, but Ezra saw it as a step towards the resumption of normal life:

>   . . . this table ex packing box
> 'doan yu tell no one I made it'
>   from a mask as fine as any in Frankfurt *
> 'It'll get you offn th' groun' . . .

Ezra was able to add to his reading matter. He was now allowed to use the communal latrines, and one day 'on the jo-house seat' he found a copy of *The Pocket Book of Verse*, an American anthology edited by Morris Speare. He pocketed it, and began to pore over it eagerly.

He found a pencil and some cheap lined writing paper, army issue, and was given hard ration biscuits to stave off hunger outside meal times:

> Prowling night-puss leave my hard squares alone
>   they are in no case cat food
>   if you had sense
> you wd/ come here at meal times
>   when meat is superabundant
> you can neither eat manuscript nor Confucius
>   nor even the hebrew scriptures
>   get out of that bacon box
>   contract W, 11 oh oh 9 oh
> now used as a wardrobe . . .

He was good at finding alternatives for the necessities of life. He acquired an old broom handle, which became a substitute for his usual malacca; wielding it on his endless circular perambulations around the perimeter of the medical compound, he walked with the same flourish that he had shown in the streets of Paris and Rapallo. It was soon noticed that he had worn a path in the grass. Lieutenant Colonel Steele remembers how 'he had a spring in his step which was quite remarkable', and says how, whenever he himself paid a visit to the medical compound, 'Ezra could be seen either walking or sort of dog-trotting; he had a lot of push'. One of the other prisoners asked: 'What's he training for?' Robert Allen observed that the

---

*That is, from Frobenius's collection of African masks at his Institute in Frankfurt.

bounce had returned to his manner: after his evening sick-call, 'he would stride to the door of our prefab, put his crumpled Army fatigue hat onto the back of his head, tuck his stick under his arm, and wave an appreciative and smiling good night'.

*

July came, and the DTC received no further instructions as to what was to be done with him. This did not much surprise Steele or his staff, since most detainees remained in the camp for several months, and they did not press HQ MTOUSA or Washington for orders about Ezra.

The delay was being caused by further painstaking collection of evidence, both in Italy and America. Meanwhile the Department of Justice in Washington kept a sporadic watch on his condition. When word reached them from the FBI at the beginning of July (incorrectly, as it happened) that the DTC psychiatrists had found 'strong indications of a mental breakdown' in him (this was a garbling of Captain Baer's report that a breakdown might occur if he were not better treated), they sent a request to the army that a further psychiatric examination should be conducted and a report sent to them.

This was performed at the DTC on 17 July, the examining psychiatrist this time being Major William Weisdorf, a rank higher than the two doctors who had talked to Ezra in June. His report began: 'The prisoner is an elderly appearing white mail [*sic*] . . . Appearance is somewhat bizarre due to the affectation of a small irregular beard.' He found no instability or mental abnormality:

> His facial expressions are animated and alert. Speech is voluble, highly productive with a prodigious flow of thought largely centered about his economic theories, and illustrated by quotations from classical and modern sources. There is some circumlocution and repetitiousness, but speech is on the whole relevant and coherent . . . He defends his radio broadcasts . . . as the right of free speech and contends he was not treasonable. There is no evidence of hallucinations or delusions. Emotionally he exhibits mild tension, but there is no evidence of depression . . . Intellectual powers . . . are superior . . .
>
> The prisoner apparently developed transitory anxiety state, as the culmination of several weeks in close confinement . . . These manifestations cleared up rapidly as the prisoner was made more comfortable physically. He shows no evidence of psychosis, or neurosis at the present time.

To this report, Lieutenant Colonel Steele added his own observation that Ezra had 'made a satisfactory mental adjustment to his present situation and is mentally competent'. Meanwhile, Robert Allen relates that the story flew round the DTC that 'Uncle Ez', as they were now calling him, had 'made a dummy of the psychiatrist', that he had 'turned questions around so that even the psychiatrist became confused'. Allen adds that the camp accepted the verdict that he was 'sane', but felt him to be 'a little exotic'.

The Weisdorf psychiatric report concluded with a recommendation that he be allowed more reading matter, to promote 'mental hygiene', but Ezra was now more concerned to write than to read. He had his packing-case table and his writing pad and pencil, and soon he was granted another unofficial concession: to use the dispensary typewriter in one of the medical huts. Steele says a blind eye was turned to this because 'it was felt that Ezra, as a professional author, needed his work to keep him healthy'.

In return for this favour, Ezra expressed himself willing to help illiterate and semi-literate prisoners with their correspondence. Robert Allen says 'it was not unusual to see him typing a letter to some trainee's girl or mother with the trainee dictating at his shoulder and Pound interpreting for him'. His skill with words and his privileged use of the typewriter gained him the reputation at the DTC of being enormously influential with the authorities. Peter Brown says the two chief 'barons' (criminal bosses) among the prisoners 'had to look to their prestige', and one of them remarked: 'Maybe Ezra could fix it so I get a pardon.'

*

Dorothy was trying to extract news of him from the authorities. The American Consulate at Rome would not help other than to refer her to the army. However, she was able to turn to John Drummond, a young English friend of Ezra's who had lived in Rapallo before the war, and was at present a lance-corporal at HQ Allied Commission in Rome. Drummond wrote to Dorothy on 11 July that he had talked to the authorities, but had been told there could be 'no communication whatever' between Ezra and his family. Frank L. Amprim was still in charge of the Italian end of the investigation, but the US Army was now responsible 'for the custody of his person'.

Drummond saw Amprim at his Rome office. Amprim said he was glad to meet a friend of Ezra Pound's, and asked if Drummond would be prepared to go to Washington as a witness for the defence, which Drummond readily agreed to do. Drummond said that Amprim, who struck him as 'a very decent and fair-minded fellow', had explained that it was his job to 'collect what material there was over here, to get in touch with possible witnesses etc., purely in the interests of justice, irrespective of whether the material, or witnesses, would be more useful to the prosecution or the defence. He seemed optimistic on the whole and said that reading through the MSS [of the broadcasts] there was a great deal less in them on which accusations might be based than one would have imagined from journalistic accounts of the case. He quite appreciated Ezra's integrity and sincerity.'

Amprim was not allowed to tell Drummond where Ezra was being held, but he did report that he was 'eating well, but . . . impatient to get to the States and have the matter "cleared up"'. Ezra had told Olga at the time of his arrest that he wanted to find a lawyer to advise him on how to conduct his defence in the USA, and would like 'to have his old friend Elihu Root' – a member of the Root family of Hamilton College – who was now a top New York lawyer. Drummond passed on this request to Root himself, and heard back from him on 13 July. Root said he scarcely knew Ezra and was not 'very sympathetic'; he was also 'not a barrister, I do not try cases'. He recommended 'Lloyd Stryker, of the Class of '06 Hamilton', an experienced criminal lawyer who 'warms up to the battle when he thinks that someone is being oppressed. Pound will know all about him.'

Indeed Ezra did, for Stryker was the son of that 'Prex' Stryker whose sermons had so enlivened the college chapel in 1903. It was quite an appealing idea to be defended by someone who had oratory in the blood.

*

Each evening after 'taps', in the corner of the dispensary, Ezra could now be found hammering away at the big office Remington. Robert Allen describes how 'the constant clanging and banging of the typewriter, which he punched angrily with his index fingers, was always accompanied by a high-pitched humming sound'. The humming meant that he was composing poetry.

The Pisan Cantos, Ezra told Agnes Bedford, were all written at the DTC: 'All Pisans @ Pisa.' He added that 'not more than 3 lines' were emended after he had left, 'and I can only recall one'. (He did not say which.)

He probably began work on them shortly after his release from the cage, possibly while still in it, since at least one person saw him writing when caged, and he later told Louis Dudek (a disciple) that he had been given pencil and paper while still shut in there. Dudek asked him 'what moved him to begin writing them at the time he did and how could he have written all that poetry in a prison camp. He said: "What else was there to do?"'

The opening lines of Canto 74, the first of the new sequence, have been found in his handwriting on two sheets of toilet paper, and this may have been the start. The greater part of the sequence was roughed out in pencil on his packing-case table in the tent, much of it on his grainy blue-lined army writing pad (he used it sideways, so that the ruled lines ran vertically through his handwriting). He also used airmail sheets or anything else he could lay his hands on. Some pages are filled with Chinese characters, others with incomprehensible jottings such as

R.D. June – foetid ig. of [   ] 300 yrs ago Electra

On other sheets the text is worked out in considerable detail, ready for the evening sessions at the typewriter, when the cantos were steadily pounded out in their finished form, with little or no hesitation.

To the Base Censor, when passing on the typescript of *The Pisan Cantos* for examination, Ezra alleged: 'The proper names given are mostly those of men on sick call seen passing my tent.' In fact, the eleven new cantos, which occupy 115 pages of print (the same space as Cantos 1 to 24), are crammed with mythological and literary allusions, including many Greek tags (rarely remembered correctly) and fragments of Latin and French, not to mention a plethora of personal memories and glimpses of Ezra's own life before 1945. One thing they demonstrate is how richly stocked was his memory; he had no need of a library.

He took some trouble to tie the Pisan Cantos thematically to the rest of the Cantos. They contain allusions to the Mysteries, to the dream of the earthly paradise, to Sigismundo, to Erigena, to John Adams and the Chinese emperors. In his determination to pick up the threads already lying in the Cantos, he echoed not merely such phrases as 'in coitu inluminatio', 'Tempus tacendi, Tempus loquendi', and 'Sunt lumina', but even recalled a line from the first of the rejected 'Three Cantos': 'ghosts move about me patched with histories'.

Given their position in his life story, and their distinct and pervading tone of regret, it is not surprising that since their first publication the Pisan Cantos have been widely regarded as an act of contrition, renunciation and expiation, a confession of failure and error – particularly, of course, the errors of Fascism and anti-Semitism. James Laughlin seemed to be hinting at this in his dust-jacket blurb to the New Directions edition, when he wrote of them as a 'revelation of the poet's personal tragedy'.

Yet the Pisan Cantos begin not with any abandoning of hopes, but with a clear statement of profound regret at the downfall of Mussolini:

> The enormous tragedy of the dream in the peasant's bent
> > shoulders
>
> Manes! Manes was tanned and stuffed,
> Thus Ben and la Clara *a Milano*
> > by the heels at Milano . . .

A phoenix rises from these ashes. 'Yet say this to the Possum,' Canto 74 continues: 'a bang, not a whimper, / with a bang not a whimper.' By this allusion to the concluding lines of Eliot's *The Hollow Men*, Ezra asserts that Fascism at least died a noble death.

He himself now steps explicitly into the poem. He is perhaps Odysseus, but also the 'No-man' that Odysseus becomes:

ΟΫΤΙΣ [Outis], ΟΫΤΙΣ ? Odysseus
    the name of my family.

This is an allusion to Book 9 of the *Odyssey*, where Odysseus answers the Cyclops' demand for his name by saying punningly: 'My name is Nobody (*outis*). That is what I am called by my mother and father and by all my friends.' The same cry is reiterated later in Canto 74:

ΟΫΤΙΣ
ΟΫΤΙΣ
'I am noman, my name is noman' . . .

ΟΫΤΙΣ
a man on whom the sun has gone down . . .

This is as far as he will go towards regret in Canto 74: he is one no longer in favour with the gods, one whose time of fortune is ended.

This does not amount to any admission of failure or abandonment of old ideals: a few lines later he asserts that 'free speech without free radio speech is as zero', and says he hopes to talk to Stalin and tell him that money is simply a device 'to signify work done'. The remainder of Canto 74 is scattered with assertions of familiar beliefs: there are allusions to the sinister influence of Meyer Anselm, founder of the house of Rothschild – 'more fool if you fall for it two centuries later' – along with such statements as 'the yidd is a stimulant, and the goyim are cattle' and remarks about the 'racket' of usury. Certainly the tone may be regretful, but there is not the slightest ideological shift; and as usual the reproaches are all directed at others.

He took a similar line when talking to the medical staff who were with him in the dispensary at the DTC, while he was typing these cantos.

> During the late evenings [writes Robert Allen] the only person with him was the Charge of Quarters and often, after typing, Pound would let down completely to rant and rave about the 'dunghill usurers' and 'usuring cutthroats' . . . His green eyes snapped as he tapped his glasses on the desk and shouted.

Such degree of resignation as the Pisan Cantos do seem to express arises chiefly from his admission that the actual 'resurrection' of Fascist Italy, the building of his political and economic dream in any worldly form, is now an impossibility.

For this worldly dream, Ezra begins now to substitute his own ideal city or community of the mind, chiefly expressed in mythological terms. At the beginning of Canto 74, he resolves 'To build the city of Dioce whose terraces are the colour of stars'. This is another name for the Ecbatan of Cantos 4 and 5, the city of the *paradiso terrestre*. A little later in the same

canto: '4 times was the city rebuilded, Hooo Fasa / Gassir, Hooo Fasa dell'
Italia tradita [of the betrayed Italy] / now in the mind indestructible, Gassir
Hoooo Fasa'. This alludes to the story 'Gassire's Lute', collected in
Frobenius's and Douglas Fox's *African Genesis* (a book for popular
readership explaining Frobenius's work), though in that story the name of
the perfect city is actually 'Wagadu'. This mythological city is, write
Frobenius and Fox, a symbol of 'the strength which lives in the hearts of
men and is sometimes visible because eyes see her and ears hear the clash of
swords and ring of shields, and is sometimes invisible because the
indomitability of men has overtired her, so that she sleeps.'

So, in Canto 74, the city is described as 'now in the mind indestructible'.
It has become internalized, subjectivized, a place of the mind. In the face of
adversity, Ezra is withdrawing his ideals into his private mental world.
This is the principal message of Canto 74, and really of the entire Pisan
Cantos, which exemplify it by exploring the crannies of Ezra's own mind
and memory, in search of the perfect city he believes to lie there.

Hence the plethora of personal memories and references which make up
the greater part of the Pisan Cantos. They are not, as some critics suggested
when the sequence was first published, just random jottings from a poet's
notebook, but are supposed to indicate a purposeful search through the
memory in the hope of finding the perfect city, or at least the materials
with which it may be built. Certainly Ezra dredges up only fragments, but
he now believes (as he says half-way through Canto 74) that 'Le Paradis' is
only to be found in, or built from, splinters like this. Perfection is of
necessity 'spezzato' (broken, fragmented); 'apparently / it exists only in
fragments'.

There are other moments when he seems to have found the Perfect City
in, of all places, the DTC itself. For the first time in his life he has come,
through his confinement, to contemplate the virtues of ordinary, unedu-
cated people. He is interested in the conversation of the black prisoners:

> 'Hey, Snag, wot are the books ov' the bibl''
> 'name 'em, etc.
> 'Latin? I studied latin.'
>   said the nigger murderer to his cage-mate.

The rhythm of black speech particularly delights him:

> young nigger at rest in his wheelbarrow
> in the shade back of the jo-house
> addresses me: Got it *made*, kid, you got it made.

'We had a large percentage of Negro soldiers,' says Lieutenant Colonel
Steele. 'We were, by the way, the only integrated command until the whole
army was integrated.'

'c'mon small fry' sd/ the little coon to the big black . . .

present Mr G. Scott whistling Lilli Marlene
          with positively less musical talent
          than that of any other man of colour
                    whom I have ever encountered
but with bonhomie and good humour . . .

or Whiteside:
          'ah certainly dew lak dawgs,
          ah goin tuh wash you'
(no, not to the author, to the canine unwilling in question) . . .

Ezra was fascinated to discover that several of the blacks bore names of
former American presidents, concluding that these must be descendants of
slaves who had taken the names of their masters. By contrast, there were
few Jewish or other recent immigrant names. His attitude to the blacks was
patronizing but affectionate, and any tendency towards expressions of
superiority was swept aside by sheer anthropological curiosity:

          I like a certain number of shades in my landscape . . .
whereas the sight of a good nigger is cheering
          the bad 'uns wont look you straight . . .

He was fascinated by the toughest criminals, their exploits, and their
fates:

and Till was hung yesterday
for murder and rape with trimmings . . .
                    thought he was Zeus ram or another one . . .

'the pride of all our D.T.C. was pistol-packin' Burnes'

As Arcturus passes over my smoke-hole
          the excess electric illumination
          is now focussed
on the bloke who stole a safe he cdn't open
(interlude entitled: periplum by camion) . . .

He suggests that in a society founded on usury, criminals may be within
the bounds of morality: 'not of course that we advocate – / and yet petty
larceny / in a regime based on grand larceny / might rank as conformity'.
    There are moments in the Pisan Cantos when he suffers doubts and fears
about his situation and the future. After recalling his walking tours in
France in 1912 and 1919 he remarks: 'we will see those old roads again,

question, / possibly / but nothing appears much less likely'. At one moment he even appears to half contemplate suicide: 'nor shall diamond die in the avalanche / be it torn from its setting / fire must destroy himself ere others destroy him'. At another he asks: 'in sort shall we look for a deeper or is this the bottom?'

Canto 74 ends however, with the impression that the Inferno has been endured and escaped from. He is one of those who has 'seen the rose in the steel dust' (an alluring reassurance of the pattern of life, remembered from Allen Upward's *The New Word*); * and the last line of Canto 74 is 'we who have passed over Lethe'.

'As to POETRY//' Ezra had written prophetically in 1936, nine years before composing the Pisan Cantos, 'it just ain't till it is lived / Best of it has to be knocked out of man; at the end of his tether/ no matter what tether// The real thing is the LAST resource/'

*

Canto 75 is a shock to the eye; it consists almost entirely of a musical score – the violin part of an arrangement by Gerhart Münch of a Janequin tune imitating birdsong. Ezra, in a note in the typescript of *The Pisan Cantos*, refers to it as the 'Canzone de li Ucelli' (Birds' Canzon). It was first printed by Ronald Duncan in *Townsman*. The idea is to offer the reader pure melody after the troubled logopoeia and phanopoeia of Canto 74.

Canto 76 repeats some of the questions of Canto 74 in more subdued fashion, and some positive answers (if only very limited ones) are found. Two frequently quoted lines from Canto 76 –

<blockquote>
As a lone ant from a broken ant-hill
from the wreckage of Europe, ego scriptor
</blockquote>

might be taken to imply defeat. But though the ant-hill is broken, the ant is not, and he can announce himself with the confidence not merely of a survivor but of one set apart from the tribe: 'ego scriptor', 'I the writer'.

Canto 77 is little more than a quiet reiteration of statements already made. Canto 78 begins with nostalgia for recent events – 'Salò, Gardone / to dream the Republic' – and alludes to Ezra's 1943 walk out of Rome. But there is now almost more repetition than advance, and little comprehensible fresh material. The reader is reminded of a passage in Ezra's 1912 poem 'Portrait d'une Femme', which now seems like a prophecy of the method of the Pisan Cantos:

---

*Upward writes: 'He who has watched the iron crumbs drawn into patterns by the magnet; or who in the frostwork on the window pane has apprehended the unknown beauty of the crystal's law, seems to me to have an idea more wholesome to our frail imaginings of the Mystery of Life.' (*The New Word*, A. C. Fifield, 1908, p. 218.)

> Trophies fished up; some curious suggestion;
> Facts that lead nowhere; and a tale or two,
> Pregnant with mandrakes, or with something else
> That might prove useful and yet never proves ...

Even in the more intense passages there are scatterings of obscure Greek tags, classical Latin and Italian dialect references. The suspicion begins to arise that at such moments Ezra is posing, is uncomfortably aware that he has still not really 'modernized' himself, and is belatedly hurrying to catch up with some of the devices of *The Waste Land*.

By Canto 79 the narrative of the Pisan Cantos has deteriorated into tiny fragments, few of which have much discernible meaning (though some are attractive enough in themselves). The only certainty is the DTC, with Ezra as the central figure in the landscape:

> and when the morning sun lit up the shelves and battalions
> of the West, cloud over cloud
>   Old Ez folded his blankets ...
>   O Lynx, wake Silenus and Casey ...
> Salazar, Scott, Dawley on sick call ...

One notes the 'Old Ez'. He was only turning sixty, but that was how the young men of the DTC thought of him, and he was glad to adopt the role.

The memories that tumble out in Canto 80 are more those of an old man recalling his youth than of a seer or man of action looking at the past in order to find the way forward. He seems to have given up the struggle; the future holds nothing. He reminds himself that he is *outis*, no one; he is even *achronos*, no time. He is not at all sure that he will be taken to the USA:

> so that leaving America I brought with me $80
>   and England a letter of Thomas Hardy's
>   and Italy one eucalyptus pip
> from the salita that goes up from Rapallo
>   (if I go) ...

*

Having reached a state of profound loss and regret that his active life seems to have come to an end, he now finds comfort, in Canto 81, in what is apparently meant to be regarded as an imaginary scene. Alongside its opening lines is the marginal heading '*libretto*' – that, is, words intended for music, probably an opera. To the refrain 'Lawes and Jenkyns [*sic*] guard thy rest / Dolmetsch ever be thy guest', he describes how 'Borne upon a zephyr's shoulder / I rose through the aureate sky'. The reader is suddenly in a masque, for which Lawes or his fellow seventeenth-century composer John Jenkins might have provided music. The canto goes on: 'Ed ascoltando al leggier mormorio [and listening to the light murmur] / there came new subtlety of eyes into my tent . . . ' In the passage that follows, Ezra describes those eyes, from which there shines 'sky's clear / night's sea / green of the mountain pool'. The eyes seem to belong to a god, possibly Aphrodite, since she is frequently described in the Cantos in terms of her eyes.

It is the possessor (or possessors, since there seem to be more than one pair) of the eyes, and emphatically *not* Ezra himself, who is (or are) the speaker or speakers of the words that follow, the passionate, enigmatic and famous 'Pull down' stanzas:

What thou lovest well remains,
>   the rest is dross
What thou lov'st well shall not be reft from thee
What thou lov'st well is thy true heritage
Whose world, or mine or theirs
>   or is it of none?
First came the seen, then thus the palpable
>   Elysium, though it were in the halls of hell,
What thou lovest well is thy true heritage
What thou lov'st well shall not be reft from thee

The ant's a centaur in his dragon world.
Pull down thy vanity, it is not man
Made courage, or made order, or made grace,
>   Pull down thy vanity, I say pull down.
Learn of the green world what can be thy place
In scaled invention or true artistry,
Pull down thy vanity,
>   Paquin pull down!
The green casque has outdone your elegance.

'Master thyself, then others shall thee beare'
>   Pull down thy vanity
Thou art a beaten dog beneath the hail,
A swollen magpie in a fitful sun,
Half black half white
Nor knowst'ou wing from tail
Pull down thy vanity
>   How mean thy hates
Fostered in falsity,
>   Pull down thy vanity,

Rathe to destroy, niggard in charity,
Pull down thy vanity,
            I say pull down.

But to have done instead of not doing
                this is not vanity
To have, with decency, knocked
That a Blunt should open
                To have gathered from the air a live tradition
or from a fine old eye the unconquered flame
this is not vanity.
                Here error is all in the not done,
all in the diffidence that faltered . . .

And with this ellipsis, Canto 81 ends.

The lines offer chiefly comfort and reassurance. Firstly they tell Ezra that 'What thou lovest well remains'. This is the answer to the question he has asked himself again and again in the preceding Pisan Cantos: does anything at all that he loves survive in the chaos of a ruined Europe? Yes, say the eyes in Canto 81, it does, precisely because he loves it. His love has fixed it in memory and therefore it 'remains' it 'shall not be reft from thee', it 'is thy true heritage'.

In reply, he questions the eyes: 'Whose world, or mine or theirs / or is it of none?' – who may rightly lay claim to the possession of what he (Ezra) loves? Only himself, or those he implacably opposes? He wonders whether the apparition of the eyes and what they tell him is not merely a deceiving vision. Is he merely reassuring himself falsely?

In response, the eyes repeat their assurance, this time as a refrain: 'What thou lovest well is thy true heritage / What thou lov'st well shall not be reft from thee.' Now and only now, in the comfort of this reiterated assurance of the survival of all his ideals, does Ezra allow the vision to reproach him with any shortcomings.

'The ant's a centaur in his dragon world,' the vision tells him, recalling his description of himself as 'a lone ant from a broken ant-hill / from the wreckage of Europe'. He has had an inflated view of himself, is indeed an ant and not a centaur, has suffered from the sin of vanity. He is to learn his true place from that which he has been observing in minute detail (for the first time in his life) while in the DTC: the 'green world' of nature that has 'outdone your elegance'.

Paquin, the epithet he applies to himself here, seems an odd choice. Madame Paquin was the first successful woman in Parisian *haute couture* (she opened her premises in 1891), so she might be a symbol for vanity. Yet when speaking briefly of Olga in Canto 74, Ezra seems to approve of her

Paris dresses ('the dress she wore Drecol or Lanvin'). Possibly he is thinking of 'Pasquin', an English word for 'lampoon', derived from the Italian Pasquino, the name of a statue in Rome which from the sixteenth century was annually dressed up in the guise of some historic personage and addressed in mock verses. This seems a more suitable image for vanity than a skilled Parisian dressmaker.* At all events the speaker of these lines is mocking Ezra for a vanity which seems absurd rather than seriously culpable. Whether it be Paquin the dressmaker or Pasquin the lampooned statue, the image is clearly meant to be comic, and the 'elegance' is ascribed to Ezra /Pa[s]quin as a sneer, not in a tone of stern rebuke.

The speech continues with an allusion to Chaucer's 'Reule wel thyself, that other folk canst rede', from the 'Ballade of Good Counsel', which was printed in a modern English version in *The Pocket Book of Verse* as 'Subdue thyself and others shall thee hear'. In Ezra's text, 'beare' is probably a typing error for 'heare', since it is clear that Chaucer's advice (especially in the modern version Ezra had) is intended to lead to being *heard* and *attended to*, not to improving oneself for the sake of being *bearable*. Ezra apparently wants people to listen to him again, and feels that a more subdued approach might succeed.

The lines that follow, which speak of 'a beaten dog beneath the hail', a 'swollen magpie . . . Half black half white', have sometimes been thought to refer to Ezra's captors, the US Army, with its mixed races, but all the evidence of the Pisan Cantos is that he liked and was amused by the black inmates of the DTC. The magpie line, together with the charge of being 'a beaten dog beneath the hail', is more likely an accusation against himself – not of wrongness or mistaken ideals, but of wavering, of accepting apparent defeat when, as Chaucer counsels, he should be ready to 'master himself' and carry on the fight.

Yet now follow three lines which seem to accuse him of wrong doctrines – maybe even of anti-Semitism: 'How mean thy hates / Fostered in falsity . . . / Rathe to destroy, niggard in charity'. The meaning of 'rathe' is hasty, too hasty. But what 'hates' is he thinking of? A clue seems to lie earlier in the Pisan Cantos, in Canto 76:

> . . . gli onesti
> J'ai eu pitié des autres
> Probablement pas assez, and at moments that suited my own
> convenience.

If 'des autres' were taken to mean those who were *not* 'gli onesti' ('the honest ones') – that is, the rest of humanity – he would be accusing himself simply of a failure of charity towards the great mass of flawed and

---

*I owe this suggestion to Mari Prichard.

somewhat *dis*honest humanity. In other words, here and in the lines beginning 'How mean thy hates', he may be simply chastising himself for impatience with what (long ago in 'To Whistler, American') he had called 'that mass of dolts'.

It does not seem, then, that the self-accusations are so very great. He has admonished himself for a failure of charity towards *hoi polloi*, and for losing his nerve in a time of trouble; and he exhorts himself to learn modesty from the world of nature. There is no question of reproaching himself for his *intentions*, his choice of ideology. And from these mild self-chastisements he moves on briskly to a final affirmation of the rightness of his cause.

He has, he claims, 'done instead of not doing', and 'this is not vanity'. He has 'with decency knocked / That a Blunt should open'. (How typical of him to choose someone so *outré* as Wilfred Scawen Blunt, whom he and Yeats had fêted in 1914, in such a context.*) He has 'gathered from the air a live tradition' and 'from a fine old eye the unconquered flame' – a claim that his interest as a young man in such surviving Victorians as Blunt has led him to inherit the best of their values. All this 'is not vanity'. The only real failing has been inadequate resolve: 'here error is all in the not done, / all in the diffidence that faltered . . . ' And so, breaking off like this, Canto 81 ends in a mood that can hardly be construed as repentance.

After this climax at the end of Canto 81, the remaining Pisan Cantos seem slightly bored. There are further fragments of memory, but towards the end of the sequence, in Canto 83, an uncharacteristic note of weariness creeps in: 'and that day I wrote no further' (an echo of Francesca da Rimini's 'And that day we read no further' at the end of the fifth canto of the *Inferno*), and – shades of Edward Lear this time – 'Down, Derry-down / Oh let an old man rest'. The final canto – 84 – is headed '8th October' and is almost careless. It concludes with disarming simplicity and abruptness.

> If the hoar frost grip thy tent
> Thou wilt give thanks when night is spent.

*

One of the most balanced comments on the Pisan Cantos came from Robert Lowell, who wrote to Ezra about them in 1952: '. . . long stretches . . . have a loveliness and humor that's hard to find anywhere else. But damn it – I wish you'd read them over, they're too long, the drift must be *cut* somewhere. I think I get, or can suppose, most of the connections; yet there's something that blankets me . . . '

---

*He was reminded of Blunt by finding one of his poems in *The Pocket Book of Verse*.

4

Talk When He Wants You To Talk

In late August, Dorothy was at last given official notification of Ezra's whereabouts, and was told she could visit him. Passing on this news to John Drummond who had been helping her in Rome, she asked him not to give Ezra's address to Olga 'anyway yet awhile – as she'll go rushing round & minimizing my chance of success!' Drummond replied to Dorothy eloquently arguing that both women had 'a claim to see him', and that they should present 'a united front'.

Dorothy heard directly from Ezra at the end of September, and wrote at once to Laughlin: 'He says health O.K., putting on weight on U.S. Army food – he was a skeleton before.' She added: 'I can't get money out of England: all v. tiresome.'

It took her many days to get a lift down the coast from Rapallo to Pisa, but at last she managed it. Afterwards she described

> the saga of my two trips to the camp, one in a strange car, the other in a camion with a New Zealand football team . . . with sandwiches, my first meat for weeks – and how I walked several miles to get home after seeing E.P., with an unknown doctor who took me to his house at Massa Carrara for the night – his antique house devastated by troops – his wife and son so kind – cold soup and hot milk was all the food they had . . . Why and how one survives!

Dorothy's first visit to the DTC was on 3 October 1945. Wearing an old mackintosh of Homer's, she gave the gate sentry her name, and he rang through on the telephone: 'Tell Uncle Ez his wife is here.' She was allowed half an hour with him in an office, with a guard looking on. He had asked her to copy out and bring some ideograms from a Confucius text that he did not have with him. The DTC gave her a meal before she set off for home.

Two days after her visit, Ezra wrote to his and Dorothy's lawyer in London, Arthur Moore of Shakespear & Parkyn. Ezra had received a letter from Moore advising him to 'obtain the best possible lawyer' and not to 'attempt to address the Court' himself; Moore mentioned the names of Lloyd Stryker (the Hamilton alumnus also recommended by Elihu Root) and Archibald MacLeish (a lawyer by training) as possibilities. Ezra replied:

> I am not sure that your advice is given in full knowledge of certain essential facts in my case.
>
> For example I was not sending axis propaganda but my own . . .
>
> I had hoped to see Mr MacLeish in Washington in May while he was still in the State Dept . . . I have very cordial recollections of Lloyd Stryker, he is now I believe one of the best known big lawyers in the U.S. whose fees are probably far beyond anything I could pay . . . BUT I should much prefer to see Mr MacLeish before deciding on so important a step as NOT speaking on my own behalf . . .
>
> The agent of the Dept. of Justice started by saying that they proposed to consider my past 30 years work. I do not know whether Mr Stryker would be prepared for such labour, and without it, I do not know how he could tell the Court what the case is about . . . I do not think it is an occasion for great skill in presenting a case so much as for great patience in making clear the bearing of known and knowable facts . . . I want very much to know the source or reason for your opinion that I should not address the Court. Is it due to your not knowing what I actually said on the air? . . .
>
> Mr MacLeish . . . might . . . communicate with Roger Baldwin of the Civil Liberties Union as the question of Freedom of speech on the air . . . should interest them . . .
>
> Have I a balance at Faber and Fabers that could be sent to Dorothy pending the release of her own funds?
>
> Also can you ask Mr Eliot whether Faber will be ready to print another volume of Cantos . . . ?
>
> I dont want to extend the present letter indefinitely.
>
> > Sincerely yours,
> > Ezra Pound.

The letter was in any case very long. It contained the assertion that Social Credit and other points from his 'program' were now being 'tacitly accepted' as valid, and wandered into other such matters. There were repeated expressions of determination to contact MacLeish, who had ended the war as Assistant Secretary of State for Public and Cultural Relations, but since its conclusion had returned to private life. (Eliot had already contacted MacLeish about Ezra's case; MacLeish observed to him that some sort of 'mitigating circumstance' would have to be presented in defence.) Ezra's own determination to defend himself in court was perhaps influenced by the way in which the Vichy leader Pierre Laval was currently dominating his own treason trial with considerable eloquence.

A few days before Ezra's letter to Shakespear & Parkyn was written, James Laughlin contacted Arthur Moore to make another suggestion about a defence lawyer:

> I do not believe that . . . Stryker . . . is at all suitable . . . He is a man noted for his work in defending murderers and the like. I would much prefer . . . a more intellectual approach . . . I suggest Julien Cornell, whose address is 15 William Street, New York City . . . Cornell has defended many conscientious objectors and has made himself a good reputation in cases involving civil liberties. He has written a book on this subject which is widely quoted . . . Cornell is a Quaker and a man of the highest refinement and character. I have known him for some three years . . . Mr Cornell has read the indictment and expressed the opinion that it would be extremely difficult to convict on the basis thereof as it is now worded. Public sentiment, however, is very strong in favour of conviction, and that, I think, is the force which we have to fear.
>
> I should like, of course, to make it clear to you that I do not share the incorrect political opinions that are involved in this affair, and I am acting only out of a sense of deep personal loyalty for someone whose friendship and kindness has meant much to me.

*

Julien Cornell was then thirty-five, a graduate of Swarthmore and Yale Law School. He readily agreed to look into Ezra's case,

> as I had always enjoyed fighting for an underdog. Much of my time in those days was spent defending the civil liberties of persons who had become entangled with the law in one way or another, such as aliens, ministers [of religion] and conscientious objectors who were having difficulties with the Selective Service law. *

*In a letter to the author (3 July 1986), Julien Cornell adds: 'From 1933 to 1940 I was associated with my father's law firm in New York City, Davies, Auerbach & Cornell. My

Although Cornell's Quaker and pacifist leanings might seem a far cry from Ezra, it is possible to detect a certain similarity of outlook in Cornell's book *New World Primer* (1947), which argues that in an atomic age the United Nations is inadequate, and proposes instead a 'world federal government' that would have more effective powers in maintaining peace. The book is idealistic to the point of naïvety, and recalls Ezra's equally simplistic arguments on politics and economics. It is tempting to speculate as to what the adept criminal lawyer Lloyd Stryker might have made of Ezra's case; Cornell treated it from the outset as if it were another civil liberties affair.

Cornell's first action, before anyone had confirmed that he was to be engaged to defend Ezra, was to try to obtain the radio speeches. Although Amprim had assured John Drummond that the material he had collected could be used for the defence as well as for the prosecution, the Department of Justice turned down Cornell's request to see the official transcripts of the broadcasts or to hear the monitors' recordings – though of course the Department planned to make use of them in the trial. However, the British Information Service (BIS) in New York had some recordings of its own and allowed Cornell to listen to them. He found them 'dreary', but

> they did not sound treasonable to me . . . There was no criti-
> cism of the allied war effort . . . nothing was said to discourage
> or disturb American soldiers or their families . . . The broad-
> casts were in essence lectures in history and political and
> economic theory.

Arthur Moore of Shakespear & Parkyn wrote back to Laughlin thanking him for suggesting Cornell as 'Counsel for defence of our friend' – somewhat conspiratorially he refrained from using Ezra's name in corres-pondence – and told Laughlin that while he agreed in principle that Cornell's services should be retained, he was not yet able to give definite instructions until he had heard from 'our friend' that *he* was in agreement.

However, Cornell now seemed to assume that he would be appointed as lawyer for the defence, and wrote to Moore explaining that it would not be necessary to employ a firm of American lawyers as well ('in this country the functions of solicitor and barrister are combined'). He observed that when the case came to court it might be necessary to engage 'some other trial counsel', but emphasized that he himself was 'quite willing' to

---

work there had to do principally with estates and trusts, real estate, corporation practice and taxation. When the war came along, I became counsel to the American Civil Liberties Union and for two or three years I spent a considerable amount of time in civil liberties work but, at the same time, I continued to be in general practice associated with a small law firm. My civil liberties cases involved a substantial number of criminal trials.'

represent Ezra for the time being. The question of which lawyer Ezra wanted began to fade from the picture.

*

Arthur Moore sent on to Faber and Faber the letter from Ezra asking if Eliot would consider more cantos. Eliot replied directly to Ezra at the DTC:

> Dear Ez,
>   ... As for Cantos. We see no reason for not continuing the Opus. Will you get the Cantos sent to Faber & Faber when you can, and at the same time make clear whether this completes the work; or, if not, how much more of it you project ... Royalties have been paid over as they accrued ... so we have no funds at your disposal ... Now the great thing is that you should get the best possible counsel in America, and on this point Laughlin has sensible views. I hope that you will see Archie MacLeish and Laughlin if possible as soon as you get there. The other thing is that you do exactly what your lawyer tells you to, and only talk when he wants you to talk. It must be a laywer who is prepared to read all your works and try to understand them ...
>   Fraternal greetings, and on this occasion I shall subscribe, probably for the first time in our correspondence of many years, my public signature,
>   T. S. Eliot

In October 1943, three months after Ezra's indictment for treason, Eliot had written of him to a correspondent: '[He] is an honest but silly man; I owe him much gratitude for kindness in the past: I remain as much admiring his poetry and literary criticism, as exasperated by his political opinions.'

*

Mary was still with her mother at Sant'Ambrogio, knowing now where her father was and hoping to be able to see him before he was taken to America. One day she and Olga were talking to John Drummond, in the Rapallo café they used as meeting place and unofficial post office for the exchange of such letters as had to be sent to Dorothy, when, 'whether by design or by chance, a very young American soldier came into the bar. Dark, spectacled, he looked frail and shy. Drummond knew him; confusedly he muttered introductions. So this was Omar!'

Now nineteen, Omar had been called up for the US Army, as he had been registered as American at birth. He underwent basic training in France, then served in the Army of Occupation in Germany and Italy. He had come to Rapallo to spend some leave with his mother.

Mary wondered: 'Does he realize who I am, shouldn't we embrace?' But 'No ice was broken. We evidently had nothing in common.' (Actually Omar had no idea who she was – no idea, even, of the existence of Ezra's daughter.)

Olga told her afterwards: 'it is a very good thing he has joined the American army. It will be of great use to Babbo.' Whereas (added Mary to herself) 'my having worked in a war hospital with the losing side would harm him. It hurt. It did not tally.'

*

'Visit from daughter Oct. 17', reads Julien Cornell's note on preliminaries in the Pound case. In fact, this visit to the DTC was from Olga and Mary.

Mary had applied for permission to see her father, simply stating that she was his daughter. The authorities asked no questions, and sent a permit for his 'minor child' to come to the camp. She and her mother 'were elated, and apprehensive as to how we would find him, turning over in our heads what to say during a precious half-hour. The permit said thirty minutes once a month, in the presence of two guards.'

They managed to get a lift to Pisa in a jeep. 'We arrived at the camp when it was already dark . . . Mamile handed the permit to the sentinel who shouted into a telephone: "Two young ladies." . . . We had feared Mamile might not be let in since the permit was only for me, but either because it was assumed that a minor must be chaperoned, or, more likely, because under dramatic circumstances she automatically turned into an irresistible force, we were both led into a big tent.'

There was a desk and some iron chairs. Ezra walked in. 'I had last seen him in Gais weary and full of dust, with crumpled clothes, so his appearance was not too surprising. He had aged a lot and his eyes were inflamed. It was the dust and light, he said, but now he was getting treatment. He sounded grateful, he had kept his trait of being most appreciative of small kindnesses and he made the medical care and the tent that he was allowed to sleep in sound like great blessings. In the *gabbia* he had collapsed. A severe sunstroke, he thought. He used the Italian for cage, and since we had not seen the cages we did not have a clear idea of what he meant.'

Olga noticed how 'he had grown stouter, because he had lost a lot of weight during the war. A change of diet.'

After half an hour the guard announced: 'Time to go, Mr Pound,' then left the three alone for a moment to say goodbye. 'One embraced each other and wept,' says Mary, 'and that was it . . . The image of Babbo . . . with this old twinkle and bear-hug, stands as on a huge screen in the foreground.'

*

Dorothy wrote to Laughlin on 31 October that she had 'heard today from my good man'; he had a message for Laughlin:

> Say I want the Chinese and Adams Cantos . . . sent to a few adults . . . Get him off the subject of me personally, and on to larger issues.

Business was beginning to get back to normal in Ezra's mind – if indeed it had ever been anything else.

During October he finished typing the Pisan Cantos. Shortly after Mary and Olga had paid their visit, a batch of typescript reached Mary. 'He wanted me to type them up and make several copies. For the Base Censor to allow them out he had written a note to the effect that they contained nothing seditious, no private code or personal message.' The typescripts went first to Dorothy, who sent them on to Mary up the hill (though they had never yet met). 'I have had another canto today – about lynxes and pumas!' Dorothy wrote to Laughlin on 31 October. In early December she received a 'thick batch' and said she was 'doing the characters out for Porteus or somebody to deal with' – Ezra wanted the sinologist Hugh Gordon Porteus to check the ideograms after Dorothy had painted them. But he took no such trouble with his Greek and Latin quotations, and when the Pisan Cantos were published Robert Fitzgerald – an expert classicist – found them full of errors. (In later printings of the Cantos, Laughlin got Dudley Fitts to check and correct the classical allusions.)*

Lieutenant Colonel Steele of the DTC felt that to have prevented Ezra from sending out the new cantos after they were completed 'would have had the same effect as forbidding him to write altogether'. Yet it is curious that the Base Censor raised no objection to the very thing which Ezra carefully pointed out to him: the Pisan Cantos are peppered with the names of actual prisoners. Steele records that 'the prisoners themselves were usually vague about their exact whereabouts in their own letters home, and all the photographs [of the DTC] have careful deletions where the soldiers' names appeared in large letters on their uniform shirts'. Steele had a transcript made of five pages of the Pisan Cantos to show his superiors if any questions were raised, but no query ever reached him, 'so I assumed it was all right'.

Mary, faced with the task of retyping the new cantos, was 'overwhelmed . . . What if I misspelled? I remember pondering for hours over

---

*Laughlin estimates that over the years about 600 corrections have been made to classical and other quotations in the Cantos. 'Then at a certain point, Hugh Kenner said, "Look, fellows, we'd better stop correcting, because we may be spoiling some of his best puns.'"

Vai soli, not knowing the origin of the quotation, I felt sure it must be *Mai soli*, but dared not alter it. And fountain pan? – "dust to the fountain pan". It was only after I had detached myself from the chore and responsibility of the typing that slowly the entire passage crystallized and I could see the rose in the steel dust.'

*

In his letter of 5 October 1945 to Shakespear & Parkyn, Ezra also mentioned the Confucius translation at which he was now working in the DTC. Eliot was unenthusiastic; he wrote back to Ezra: 'The demand for Chinese wisdom is not so great; and I find no enthusiasm for it amongst my colleagues. Yet it seems to me sensible to ask you to get this stuff to us as well.'

The Confucius work was done after the greater part of the Pisan Cantos had been finished; it is dated 'D.T.C., Pisa; 5 October – 5 November, 1945.' Ezra described it as 'a new translation of the Ta S'eu [Ta Hio]; and the first proper translation of the Chung Yung, plus an abridgement of the analects and of Mencius.' He felt his personal situation had helped the work: 'I do not know that I would have arrived at the centre of [Confucius's] meaning if I had not been down under the collapse of a regime . . . The Chinese Empire during its great periods offer[s] the ONLY working model . . . that can possibly serve in the present situation.' He was referring to Confucius having promulgated his teachings in an attempt to revive old values at a period of considerable public turmoil. Ezra told Charles Olson in January 1946: 'If I had only read Confucius earlier I would not be in this mess.'

The *Chung Yung* ('Doctrine of the Mean'), the second of the so-called Four Books of Confucius, is really an extraction by a twelfth-century Confucian disciple from the ancient *Li Chi* or book of ritual. Ezra's name for it, *The Unwobbling Pivot*, was suggested by one of the two ideograms in the original title, which shows a rectangle balancing on an upright, an image for the unmoving centre of the universe. Though Eliot alludes to the same concept in '*Burnt Norton*' ('At the still point of the turning world . . . / Neither movement from nor towards, / Neither ascent nor decline'), Ezra had not seen that poem – first published during 1941 – when he worked at *The Unwobbling Pivot*.

His 1928 translation of the *Ta Hio* had been taken from a French rendering. This time he used an English text – the standard Victorian version, by James Legge, Professor of Chinese at Oxford. Or rather, he worked from his own Italian translation of Legge, made in 1942 and published in Rapallo. The result was vastly more enjoyable than his 1928 version, and much more vigorous than Legge's. This is how Legge renders one passage:

I know how it is that the path *of the Mean* is not walked in: –
The knowing go beyond it, and the stupid do not come up to it.

And Ezra:

Those who know how, exceed. (The intelligentzia go to
extremes.) The monkey-minded don't get started.

Yet, as with Ezra's version of the *Ta Hio*, one ends *The Unwobbling Pivot*
without the conviction that the Mean or Pivot on which we should balance
our lives has been properly identified either by Confucius or his translator
– and with the realization that this 'metaphysic' can just as rationally lead
to Fascism as to enlightenment.

*

Ezra's sixtieth birthday, on 30 October 1945, came and went. Robert Allen
noticed that he now 'read voraciously – novels, magazines, everything that
was given to him. The Mediterranean edition of *The Stars and Stripes* and
the overseas edition of *Time* and *Newsweek* were his sources of news.'

Now that he had finished *The Pisan Cantos* and *The Unwobbling Pivot*
he gradually became depressed. 'His tone of conversation changed,' says
Allen, 'and occasionally he spoke of himself in the past tense.' In *The Stars
and Stripes* he read of the trial of Pétain, head of the Vichy Government,
which ended with a death sentence, commuted to life imprisonment.
Vidkun Quisling in Norway went to execution, while in London during
September the trial of Lord Haw-Haw (William Joyce) also terminated in a
death sentence. And though Pétain's second-in-command Laval had
defended himself eloquently, just as Ezra hoped to do, he was executed by
firing squad on 16 October. It was with these in mind that Ezra said several
times to Robert Allen: 'If I go down, someone must carry on.'

The weather became cold and wet; there was no communication from
the authorities about his own trial; and Allen realized that he 'almost
despaired of ever leaving Pisa'.

*

The Department of Justice wished to leave him where he was until Amprim
had finished his investigation in Italy, and everything was ready for the
trial. But the US Army was becoming anxious to get him off their hands.
On 4 August HQ MTOUSA sent a cable to the War Crimes Office in
Washington saying that

THE F.B.I. AGENT, FRANK AMPRIM . . . NOW IN ROME, WAS
REACHED ON THE TELEPHONE AND HAS AUTHORIZED HIMSELF
TO BE QUOTED AS SAYING THAT THE IMMEDIATE RETURN
OF POUND TO THE U.S. WILL IN NO WAY PREJUDICE THE

INVESTIGATION HE IS MAKING OF THE CHARGES . . . IN VIEW [OF
THIS], IT IS URGENTLY RECOMMENDED THAT THE DEPARTMENT
OF JUSTICE . . . AUTHORIZE HIS RETURN.

But two and a half months later, in mid-October, there was still no sign of
the Department of Justice moving; the US Army sent a message to their
own headquarters in Washington that unless Ezra were taken off their
hands very swiftly the DTC would simply release him.

It now transpired that the trial had been delayed so long because the
Constitution (upheld by a 1944 Supreme Court ruling) laid down that a
treason prosecution had to be supported by the testimony of two
independent witnesses to each 'overt act' – a clause designed to avoid
conviction merely on malicious testimony. The Department of Justice was
finding it singularly difficult to locate the necessary witnesses for the case,
as was admitted in a letter from Brigadier General John M. Weir of the War
Crimes Office to Brigadier General Adam Richmond, Theater Judge
Advocate, MTOUSA, on 3 July:

> Dear Adam,
>   . . . Mr Ely of the Department of Justice says the long delay
> in holding Dr Ezra Pound has been due to the necessity of
> securing two witnesses to the overt act of treason . . . Mr Ely
> feels that it would be unfortunate to bring Pound back to the
> United States and then find that he would be needed in Italy for
> the effective building up of the case . . .

Sufficient witnesses had still not been found by as late as 29 October, when
the *DC Times Herald* in Washington carried a report that

> Justice officials . . . have been unsuccessful in locating witnesses
> who actually saw Pound making the disputed broad-
> casts . . . Without such witnesses it is 'doubtful' conviction can
> be obtained, they admitted.*

On the same day, an internal FBI memo to J. Edgar Hoover admitted
that 'there are no two witnesses at present who can testify that they both
saw Pound broadcast at one time', though the FBI official said they had
located 'two witnesses to overt acts of treason other than the act of

---

*The same problem was encountered three years later when the FBI and Department of
Justice were trying to bring to trial the so-called 'Tokyo Rose', Iva d'Aquino, an American
citizen who had participated in Japanese broadcasts to American troops, and on whom most
of the blame for these broadcasts had (unjustifiably) been put. Again, it proved very difficult
to locate and obtain the co-operation of two independent witnesses to the act of broadcasting,
and when the case came to trial in 1949 it was widely expected that there would be an acquittal
for lack of evidence. In fact Mrs d'Aquino was found guilty on one charge of treason; she was
imprisoned for ten years and fined $10,000.

Ezra, arriving in New York on 21 April
1939, gives an impromptu press
conference on board ship: 'Mussolini . . .
has a mind with the quickest uptake of any
man I know . . .' *(Wide World Photos)*

The degree ceremony at Hamilton College, 12 July 1939. H. V. Kaltenborn, with whom
Ezra joined battle ('that fahrt . . . Kaltenstein') is in the centre, next to Ezra.
(Hamilton College)

Ezra outside the hotel where he stayed in Rome while making his broadcasts in 1941–3. *(Wide World Photos)*

Ezra, under arrest, answers questions from Frank L. Amprim of the FBI, Genoa, May 1945: 'I believe that I was justified in continuing to criticize President Roosevelt after the United States entered the war.' *(US Army)*

The punishment stockade at the DTC, Pisa. The row of cages is in the centre; Ezra's is the nearest to the gate. Note the prisoners crowded in the wire compound on the right. *(US Army)*

Close-up of the cages. Ezra's is on the extreme left of the picture, with its specially reinforced steel mesh, fitted because he was regarded as a high-security risk. *(US Army)*

Ezra at the typewriter in the medical office, DTC, typing his Confucius; a bilingual Chinese–English text lies on the table beside him. *(US Army)*

Ezra, arriving at Bolling airfield, Washington DC, on the night of 18 November 1945. He has been handcuffed to one of the Department of Justice marshals, but looks in good spirits: 'Does anyone have the faintest idea of what I actually said in Rome? Get over the idea that I betrayed anybody.' *(Wide World Photos)*

St Elizabeths Hospital, showing Center Building. Ezra's room was one floor above ground level on the other side of the building, facing the lawns. *(St Elizabeths Hospital)*

Mug-shot of Ezra taken on his admission to St Elizabeths, 21 December 1945. *(Wide World Photos)*

Dr Winfred Overholser, Ezra's 'keeper' for twelve and a half years. *(St Elizabeths Hospital)*

Above: Ezra in a folding chair on the lawn of St Elizabeths: 'One has to go nuts before you have the sense to buy proper chairs.' *(Eva Hesse)*

Above right: Sheri Martinelli: 'Grandpa loves me'. *(Eva Hesse)*

Right: Marcella Spann: 'The three of us.' *(Mary de Rachewiltz)*

Above left: Olga in the 1950s.
(Mary de Rachewiltz)

Above: Dorothy in 1958.
(Wide World photos)

Left: Ezra at the Gatters' house – his old home in Wyncote – on 18 June 1958: 'Grandpop's head needs support.'
(University of Texas)

Above: Dorothy at the Gatters' on 18 June 1958, looking as if she knows there is trouble ahead. *(University of Texas)*

Above right: Ezra, for the last time, taking charge of William Carlos Williams, on his flying visit to Rutherford, New Jersey, before sailing for Italy in June 1958. *(University of Pennsylvania)*

Right: Ezra gives the fascist salute on board ship at Naples, 9 July 1958: still 'the bad boy strutting and shocking'. *(Wide World Photos)*

Ezra arrives at Brunnenburg, 12 July 1958. *Left to right:* (at rear) Mary de Rachewiltz; Patrizia de Rachewiltz and her father Boris; *(at rear)* Dorothy; Ezra with his arm around Walter de Rachewiltz; *(at rear, with handbag and coat)* Marcella Spann. *(Wide World Photos)*

Brunnenburg. *(Photo by Humphrey Carpenter)*

Ezra at Brunnenburg: 'I can't live at this altitude.' *(Mary de Rachewiltz)*

Ezra and Dorothy touring Italy in May 1959. *(Mary de Rachewiltz)*

Ezra and his host Ugo Dadone sightseeing in Rome in January 1960: 'One day I talk like a parrot and the next I can find nothing to say.' *(Wide World Photos)*

Ezra convalescing at Villa Chiari nursing home, Rapallo, in the summer of 1962, with his grandson Walter de Rachewiltz. *(Giuseppe Bacigalupo)*

Dorothy at Rapallo towards the end of her life: 'She just sat in her room and looked out of the window.' *(Massimo Bacigalupo)*

Ezra at Casa 60, Sant'Ambrogio, in July 1963. *(Wide World Photos)*

Ezra on the *salita* up to Sant'Ambrogio, 1964. *(Massimo Bacigalupo)*

Ezra and Olga with the Misses Heacock *(far left and right)* during the visit to America in 1969. *(University of Pennsylvania)*

Ezra and Olga at a memorial service for Stravinsky, Venice, 15 April 1971. *(Yale University)*

Ezra in 1971. *(Wide World Photos)*

Ezra poses for the camera for the last time:
a photograph taken by Horst Tappe in
Venice, autumn 1971.

The gondola leaves the island of San Giorgio Maggiore after Ezra's funeral, on
3 November 1972, carrying his body across the Grand Canal on the start of its voyage to
San Michele cemetery. *(Wide World Photos)*

broadcasting' (no details were given). However, under increasing threats from the US Army to release its captive, the Department of Justice decided to make use of five technicians from Rome Radio whom the FBI had identified and located.

On 6 November, Attorney General Tom Clark (who had replaced Francis Biddle) gave a press conference saying that these men were being brought to the USA, and that Ezra Pound would shortly be repatriated. He added that the five technicians were 'ready to give testimony'; they were 'in the radio studio when Pound made his broadcasts, and thus could swear to the circumstance'. An internal Department of Justice memo dated 5 November named them as Giuseppe Bruni, Armando Giovagnoli, Walter Zanchetti, Fernando de Leonardis, and Fernando Luzzi.

Ezra himself read an account of the Attorney General's press conference in *The Stars and Stripes*. Robert Allen says he 'made light of the whole story and asserted that no one had ever seen him broadcast. He said that the technicians were obviously imposters "just making the flight to get some decent food".'

By 14 November the men had arrived in Washington, where they immediately claimed their usual monthly salaries of 15,000 lire each, demanding to be paid this as long as they remained in the USA. It transpired that none of them could speak English, so they could not testify to having heard Ezra make any particular remarks in the broadcasts. Moreover, there had usually only been one of them in the studio during the actual recordings. The 'witnesses' were, nevertheless, housed in first-class hotels in the Washington area, at the expense of the Government. They remained there as the weeks passed. Later, when the trial was further delayed, they were sent off to Hot Springs, Virginia, where as Julien Cornell observes, they enjoyed 'a luxurious vacation at the American taxpayers' expense', before being sent home as not needed after all.

A new indictment of Ezra being prepared by the Department of Justice during November 1945 had to be drawn up carefully to disguise the lack of effective witnesses and uncertainty about actual details. Five technicians and two Minculpop officials were named as being ready to give evidence, but there was some hazy wording about dates of recording and transmission – such phrases were used as 'On or about February 4, 1943', or 'Between June 29 and July 15, 1943'. The prosecution case was far from cast iron.

❊

On 3 November Dorothy reached the DTC for a second visit. Two days later the War Department sent out a cable to CG MTOUSA in Italy:

THE DEPARTMENT OF JUSTICE SHORTLY WILL ASK FOR RETURN TO THE UNITED STATES OF EZRA POUND, 14 NOVEMBER PROB-

ABLE TARGET DATE. WE WILL GIVE YOU ABOUT 3 DAYS NOTICE OF
DATE FOR POUNDS ARRIVAL HERE.

The time was drawing near for Mary's and Olga's next permitted visit to him. 'We went into town to make arrangements about transportation . . . But when we bought a paper we read that Ezra Pound had been flown to Washington to be tried for treason . . . There was no further need for transportation.'

Omar, curious to have another glimpse of the man he only remembered seeing once, in 1938, was able to get to the DTC, where he expected to be able to use his GI uniform to obtain permission for a visit; but he arrived the day after Ezra's departure. He went straight back to Rapallo to tell his mother the news.

*

Mary decided to go back to Gais, but Olga waited to follow Ezra to America. Together they made an inventory of Ezra's books and papers at Sant'Ambrogio, so that these could be packed up safely. One day in Rapallo, Mary saw Dorothy (whom she now knew by sight) on the opposite side of the street. Dorothy crossed over and said: 'I hear you are going back to Gais. I shall be leaving soon for America. If there is anything I can do for you, you must let me know, you must think of me as your stepmother.' But Mary 'felt no need of a stepmother'.

Ezra's mother, Isabel, now began to acknowledge Mary's existence. At Christmas she sent her a few pieces of old fur. Mary 'would have preferred an invitation to go to see her'. Mary gathered from Father Chute that the old lady wanted at all costs to get to America.

*

Ezra's departure was delayed by several days from the date envisaged, but on 16 November a cable went from Washington to CG MTOUSA:

SECRETARY OF WAR DIRECTS THAT ATC PICK UP POUND ON HIGHEST PRIORITY ON REGULAR FLIGHT LEAVING ROME 17 NOVEMBER AND ARRIVING U.S. 18 NOVEMBER.

POUND IS TO BE TRANSPORTED UNDER MILITARY GUARDS UNTIL RELINQUISHMENT TO FEDERAL AUTHORITIES IN U.S.

An earlier cable had warned of a special legal requirement:

LEGAL JURISDICTION REQUIRES THAT PLANE RETURNING PRISONER LAND AT BOLLING FIELD IN THE DISTRICT OF COLUMBIA AND NOT REPEAT NOT AT NATIONAL AIRPORT OR OTHER AIRPORTS IN THE UNITED STATES.

Bolling, a US Air Force field in Washington, lies within the boundary of the District of Columbia (DC), in which the Federal buildings are situated. If Ezra was to have a Federal trial, the plane carrying him must touch down in that District, and not at National Airport on the opposite bank of the Potomac, which lies in Arlington, Virginia. The reason for this was (as the Attorney General's office reminded the War Department) that

> jurisdiction over crimes committed outside the United States is in the District in which the defendant is first found or first brought ... Should a forced landing elsewhere be necessary, custody over Pound should be retained by military authorities until he can be released to officials of this Department in the District of Columbia.

Ezra seemed to anticipate his departure from the DTC in Canto 79:

> 'paak you djeep oveh there.' . . .
> 'Bless my buttons, a staff car . . .'
> 'Prepare to go on a journey.'
> 'I –'
>   'Prepare to go on a journey.'

5

Very Wobbly In His Mind

'One evening after taps in the middle of November,' writes Robert Allen, 'Pound was sitting in the dispensary reading Joseph E. Davies's *Mission to Moscow*. The Charge of Quarters sat at the desk next to him. From time to time Pound commented on the book. Suddenly the door opened and two young lieutenants entered. They told Pound that he would be flown to Washington in one hour and to get his personal effects together. They turned and left. Pound handed the book to the C.Q. He asked him to thank all of the medical personnel for their kindness. He then walked to the door of the prefab, and, with a half-smile, put both hands around his neck to form a noose and jerked up his chin.'

Ezra left the DTC escorted by military police at 2030 hours on 16 November 1945. He was driven by jeep to Ciampino airport, near Rome; the journey, on a cold raw night, took six hours. He was to be accompanied on the flight by Lieutenant Colonel P. V. Holder, together with a Lieutenant Colonel Donaghy and a Captain Manus. Holder afterwards wrote this account of their trip:

'Pound arrived at Ciampino airport at 0445 hours and was detained in the guard house with escort. At 0630 I went to the traffic office to check on the readiness of plane, priorities, tickets, etc. I was told that we were leaving at 0800 hours for Marseilles, Lisbon, Santa Maria (Azores), Bermuda and Washington. Col. Donaghy and Capt. Manus arrived at the airport at 0700 hours. We picked up Pound and all had breakfast, changed our money, weighed in and were on the plane at 0800. Traffic officers had arranged that we have the first three rows of seats in the front of the plane, i.e. twelve seats, so that no one would sit in the immediate vicinity of Pound but his escorting officers.

'We took off at 0830 hours and headed North. The pilot told me that at the last moment orders had been changed and we were routed through Prague, Brussels, Bovington (England), Greenland, Newfoundland. Arrived at Prague approximately 1330 hours. The plane had no lunch baskets on board and there were no facilities for feeding at Prague. After an hour's wait, to no purpose that I could see, we took off again for Brussels, arriving at approximately 1700 hours. The wait there, also, was to no purpose that I could discern. No petrol was taken on and we were not permitted to leave the vicinity of the aircraft to go to the lunch counter, which was some distance away. We took off in about forty-five minutes and arrived at Bovington approximately 1830 hours (GMT). There we had an ample dinner, the first food since 0600 hours (GMT). Mr Pound was suffering acutely from hunger and was extremely nervous.

'There was considerable uncertainty at this point as to our next move. One source stated that we were to wait four hours to see whether the weather cleared over Stephensville (Newfoundland); if it didn't we were to go to the Azores and see what the situation was from there. The uncertainty of the situation concerned me no little, so I went to operations and after some argument and flaunting of orders, copies of signals etc. induced them to order our immediate departure for the Azores.'

Though Ezra had been nervous during the first few hours of the flight – apart from everything else, it was his first time in a plane – he soon regained his usual composure, and, says Holder, 'conversed freely with all three of the escorting officers. Since he was not charged by Army authorities for any crime that we knew of, we were disinclined to interrogate him or to conduct any conversation which might have the appearance of interrogation. Pound . . . is an extremely well educated man . . . His hobbies are the translating of ancient documents such as Pluto [*sic*] and Confucius. The bulk of our conversation was carried on concerning these matters. He explained in detail the sources of his knowledge and the means by which his translations were accomplished. Also he is a keen economist, although in my opinion his arguments are not entirely sound. In so far as his attitude toward the United States is concerned I got the impression that he was anxious to impress upon us his loyalty and his desire to be considered as an American who was trying to help America rather than hinder her. He is distinctly anti-Jewish and anti-Communistic. He denies that he is pro-Fascist and pro-Nazi. He made statements that he considers Hitler a mountebank and thought that Mussolini was much the better man of the two. Among the heads of the American Government he considers Mr Morgenthau a dishonest man and stated that he knew approximately forty instances where the finances of the United States were used to improve the position of Jews in Europe or America . . . Pound endeavored to interest me in securing for him interviews with G-2 Section of the War Department on the grounds that through his contacts in Japan and China he is in possession of information which is of much more importance to the United States than his trial as a traitor.

'He discussed his visit to the United States in 1939 and stated that there were many Americans with whom he talked at that time who understood his views and who would be willing to testify that at the time there was nothing traitorous in his ideas and he wanted me to contact one or two of them and ask that they visit him. I did not make a record of their names since I did not want to become involved in his case. I suggested to him that he employ an attorney whose duty it would be to make such contacts for him. He stated that there was no attorney in the United States that he knew of who had sufficient information or knowledge of his works and studies. He stated that his whole defense was based upon the fact that his mental capacities and studies placed him in a sphere above that of ordinary mortals and that it would require a "superman" to conduct his defense. He stated that he proposes to conduct his own defense. My impressions of Mr Pound were that he is an intellectual "crack pot" . . . '

The plane arrived at Santa Maria airport in the Azores at three o'clock on the morning on 18 November. 'First we were told,' continues Holder, 'that No. 4 engine had to be checked and our departure would be delayed until 0600 hours. Then we were told that Stephensville (Newfoundland) was closed in and we would not leave before 1000 hours, if then. Having some knowledge of North Atlantic weather conditions my concern grew to the extent that I took issue with traffic officers. Finally I flatly refused to go to Stephensville at any time and requested that the first ship enroute to U.S. by way of Bermuda be off loaded sufficiently to accommodate our party. In the meantime Pound under the escort of Col. Donaghy and Capt. Manus had retired to the Stockade to shower and rest.

'A plane arrived from Paris at 0700 and two passengers were disembarked. I requested that Air Traffic Control make the same arrangements as previously, that is, that we occupy the first twelve seats in the aircraft. I learned later that the French Ambassador, his wife and two Colonels had been obliged to move their seats.' Ezra was delighted that he had 'kicked out' the Ambassador, whose wife (he said) was astonished by the 'AMOUNT of armed force' required to transport him to Washington.

They took off at 0830 hours (GMT). Ezra had now run out of conversation, and a French official noticed how, 'in dirty shirt and soiled prison clothes', he 'sat silent and bored for hours'. Then around late morning, when they were in mid-Atlantic, the thick cloud cover broke for the first time, and the sun began to shine. 'Suddenly,' writes the Frenchman, 'Pound sprang up and, looking down at the tremendous sunlit sea, became, on his first ocean crossing by air, ecstatic, like a bird let out of a cage, like a man pulled out of a deep, dark hole. He paced the aisles declaiming in poetic rhapsody.'

*

They arrived at Bermuda at 2100 GMT, five o'clock in the afternoon local time. 'Here we found, for the first time,' writes Holder, 'that the Commanding Officer of the airport was on hand. A special building was reserved for us and we were fed an excellent dinner there. Here, also, there seemed to be some appreciation of the importance and emergency of our mission and everything was done to expedite matters. We were airborne at 1830 Atlantic time and arrived without further mishap at Bolling Field approximately 2230 hours Eastern time, 18 November.'

*

Afterwards Ezra questioned the legality of his repatriation. He observed in 1946: 'Treason is not an extraditable offence.' He also claimed that he had been brought back to the USA under false pretences, alleging that he had been told he would be able to talk to Government officials about his special knowledge of Italy and the Far East. It had, he said, been a complete surprise to find himself a prisoner on a treason charge, and he supposed that he must have been 'double-crossed' by someone, possibly 'the British Intelligence Service or Commandos'.

This was all bluff. His letter from the DTC to his London lawyer Arthur Moore shows that he knew perfectly well what was in store for him in Washington. However, it is clear that on his arrival in the USA he still hoped to find some way out of his situation, and to be able to 'divulge what he knew to the proper people'. Meanwhile he had no idea of the degree of hostile feeling towards him in America. As Laughlin had written to Moore, 'Public sentiment . . . is very strong in favour of conviction.'

As long ago as August 1943, a month after the original indictment against him, an article in the New York newspaper *PM* had suggested that he might – perhaps should – be given the death sentence. The next year a pamphlet was published in Washington under the title *The Black Badge of Treason*; fifteen pages of attack on him ended: 'Will he inflict the penalty upon himself, or will he allow the country of his birth to give him his death?' Now, in November 1945, just as he was being transported across the Atlantic, a journalist and author named Charles Norman was putting together a lengthy article about him for *PM*, a symposium in which Ezra's literary friends were asked to express their opinion on what he had done and what punishment, if any, he deserved. The symposium was printed on 25 November, a week after Ezra arrived in Washington.

Among those solicited for an opinion was William Carlos Williams. He replied:

I can't write about Ezra Pound with any sort of composure. When I think of the callousness of some of his letters during the last six or seven years, blithe comments touching 'fresh meat on the Russian steppes' or the war in Spain as being of 'no more importance than the draining of some mosquito swamp in deepest Africa', 'Hitler the martyr' and all that – I want to forget that I ever knew him. His vicious anti-Semitism and much else have lowered him in my mind further than I ever thought it possible . . . But that isn't the whole story . . . Ezra Pound is one of the most competent poets in our language . . . He is also, it must be confessed, the biggest damn fool and faker in the business. You can't allow yourself to be too serious about a person like that – and yet he is important . . . His stupidities coupled with his overweening self esteem have brought him down – but to try to make a criminal of him because of that is to lay ourselves open to the accusation of being moved by an even greater stupidity than that which we are facing . . . Ezra Pound . . . taken as any sort of menace to America when compared with some of the vicious minds at large among us in, say for instance the newspaper game . . . is sheer childishness. He just isn't dangerous, they are . . . I don't think we should be too hard on him . . . As a poet Ezra has some sort of right to speak his mind, such as it had become, and he did . . . When they lock the man up, I hope they will give him access to books, with paper enough . . . It would be the greatest miscarriage of justice, human justice, to shoot him.

Louis Zukofsky agreed to contribute to the *PM* article; his piece arrived too late for inclusion, but it eventually appeared in Charles Norman's *The Case of Ezra Pound*:

> I should prefer to say nothing now. But a preference for silence might be misinterpreted . . . His profound and intimate knowledge and practice [of literature and music] still leave that part of his mind entire . . . He may be condemned or forgiven. Biographers of the future may find his character as charming as that of Aaron Burr.* It will matter very little against his finest work overshadowed in his lifetime by the hell of Belsen which he overlooked.

Another contributor to the *PM* article, Professor F. O. Matthiessen of Harvard, called Ezra's economic tracts 'crackpot' and said that the broadcasts, 'vicious as they were in their anti-semitism', could not have had 'any ponderable force as propaganda'. He summed up Ezra as 'a tragic

*Burr (1756–1836), Jefferson's Vice-President, was tried for treason. Though acquitted, he was notorious for political double-dealing.

instance of the consequence resulting from the gulf between poet and audience'. Conrad Aiken, also quoted in the symposium, judged Ezra 'less traitor than fool', but said that whatever judicial sentence was passed on him 'we must all see to it that justice should be done to him also as a poet'.

Norman received complaints from a number of *PM* readers who accused him of defending Ezra. The Communist journal *New Masses* followed the *PM* piece with a symposium of its own in which, said Norman, 'all the contributors declared he should be executed forthwith – this was before any kind of trial had begun'.

Ernest Hemingway was not quoted in the *PM* piece, but he felt much the same as Williams. He had seen one of the broadcast transcripts back in August 1943, and wrote to MacLeish, who had sent it to him:

> He is obviously crazy. I think you might prove he was crazy as far back as the latter Cantos. He deserves punishment and disgrace but what he really deserves most is ridicule. He should not be hanged and he should not be made a martyr of.

On another occasion, while grumbling that Ezra really ought to shoot himself, Hemingway observed that his friends must try to keep him from a traitor's execution, 'even though we all should have to get up on the scaffold with a rope on our own necks'. Hemingway's more practical suggestion, to Allen Tate, was: 'He ought to go to the loony bin, which he rates and you can pick out the parts in his cantos at which he starts to rate it.'

MacLeish gave his own opinion of the broadcasts in his letter enclosing some of them for Hemingway to see: 'It is pretty clear that poor old Ezra is quite, quite balmy.' He continued:

> What will save him, if anything does, is the fact that no jury on earth could think this kind of drivel would influence anybody to do anything, anywhere, at any time . . . Poor old Ezra! Treason is a little too serious and a little too dignified a crime for a man who has made such an incredible ass of himself, and accomplished so little in the process.

While Ezra was still being held at CIC Genoa, MacLeish received a cable from Eliot in London: 'ANXIOUS DO EVERYTHING POSSIBLE MITIGATE TREATMENT OF EZRA POUND STOP PLEASE ADVISE ME.' Eliot also wrote, in a letter to MacLeish, that he had 'not heard a single voice express any desire except that Pound should be let off as lightly as possible and that the whole affair might be forgotten as quickly as possible'. But Ezra was brought to Washington just as the Nuremberg war trials were about to begin in Germany, and certain of those responsible for Nazi atrocities had already been executed or sentenced. On the very day of his arrival at Bolling Field, the *Washington Post* carried the headline: 'BELSEN BEAST, 10 OTHERS MUST HANG FOR DEEDS.' Reprisals were the mood of the moment, and whatever Eliot may have thought, it was not a climate in which Ezra's behaviour was likely to be regarded lightly.

*

His plane touched down at Bolling Field, as Holder records, late on the evening of Sunday 18 November 1945. He was led from it handcuffed to one of the escort, but wearing one of his own broad-brimmed black hats, and with his own overcoat, scarf, and even his walking cane. Though underneath his coat he was still dressed in US Army fatigue clothes, he looked more like a visiting lecturer than a prisoner.

At the airfield he was given into the custody of two plain-clothes law officers, who took him to the Marshal's office where, as the *New York Times* reported next morning, 'Government attorneys told him his rights before lodging him in the District prison. "Does anyone have the faintest idea of what I actually said in Rome?" he said to reporters. "Get over the idea that I betrayed anybody."'

He afterwards told Laughlin: 'I thought they were bringing me to Washington to forward me on to MacArthur in Tokyo to help him convert the Japs from Shintoism to Confucianism.' The MacArthur story was spoof, but perhaps he had not fully taken in that he would be treated just like any other criminal awaiting trial. Talking to him two months later, Charles Olson gathered he construed the Washington events as evidence of some kind of plot against him. He felt that 'somebody seemed to want these things to happen to him. "Who is this Truman? . . . What's behind it all, who wants this thing?"' Olson realized that this seemed like paranoia. He commented: 'This might sound like persecution, but in the light of the Army's Cage for him and a few other things, hasn't he a right to wonder?'

*

After one night in the prison – which was on 19th Street in the south-eastern sector of the city – he was brought before Chief Justice Bolitha J. Laws for a 'preliminary arraignment'. In court, he announced that he wished to act as his own counsel, and told the judge that 'he wanted Secretary of Commerce Wallace and Archibald MacLeish to testify for him at his trial' (he explained that he had met Wallace during his 1939 visit). The *New York Times* report continued: 'Pound . . . appeared tired and disheveled in court. He wore a dirty GI sweatshirt, a pair of baggy trousers and coat and GI shoes that were too large. Saying that he had only $23, Pound asked to act as his own counsel, but Judge Laws told him the charge was too serious for that. Pound then agreed to have the court appoint an attorney for him, and Judge Laws set Nov. 27 for a formal arraignment.'

The press were keen to get some colourful stuff out of him, and, of course, he obliged. 'Talking with reporters later,' said the *New York Times*, 'Pound said that he wanted to learn Georgian, Stalin's native tongue, so that he could confer with the Russian leader to "see what's in the back of his mind". Pound denied that he ever supported Benito Mussolini and called the Italian dictator "a puffed up bubble".'

He was taken back to prison. The next morning, Tuesday 20 November, he was visited by Miss Ida Mapel, one of the Washington spinster pair he had known since the early 1900s. She found him 'nervous' but otherwise well. The Miss Mapels were now both in their eighties; Ezra observed with some amusement that they were 'not used to having friends in gaol'. However, Miss Ida expressed no shock at his situation, and she and her sister began to call on him regularly, mending his clothes and performing other such useful tasks.

The same morning, Julien Cornell paid his first visit to Ezra. Having read a newspaper report on 7 November that Ezra would soon be repatriated and brought to trial, Cornell wrote to the Attorney General 'advising him that I had been retained to confer with Pound about his defense and asking to be informed when he arrived'. As yet, Ezra had not heard of Cornell, and was still expecting to discuss the matter of legal representation with MacLeish, and perhaps also with Laughlin, or at worst to accept the court's choice of lawyer.

Cornell, however, had Laughlin's strong backing, and as MacLeish did not appear at the prison (no one had asked him to), Ezra was faced with a *fait accompli*. On that Tuesday morning, 20 November, Cornell had come down early from his New York office, and had already had 'a talk with the Chief of the Criminal Division of the Department of Justice, Mr McInerney, and with his assistant who would have charge of the prosecution, Isaiah Matlack. They arranged for me to see Pound at the District of Columbia Jail. I also had a talk with the superintendent of the jail and with the Chief Judge of the District of Columbia District Court, Bolitha J. Laws. Judge Laws said he was very happy to know that I was going to appear for Pound because a Washington criminal lawyer of somewhat dubious reputation had been boasting that he was going to get Pound's case.'

Cornell then made a formal appearance before Judge Laws, 'after arranging for a Washington attorney of my acquaintance to introduce me formally to the court, as is the custom when a lawyer appears in a jurisdiction where he is not a member of the bar'. Cornell later explained to the court that he was appearing 'for the sole purpose of his [Ezra's] arraignment' – that is, not necessarily as counsel for the defence during an actual treason trial.

Afterwards he wrote to Laughlin describing his first talk with Ezra in the prison: 'I found the poor devil in a rather desperate condition. He is very wobbly in his mind and while his talk is entirely rational, he flits from one idea to another and is unable to concentrate even to the extent of answering a single question, without immediately wandering off the subject.'

Cornell spent two hours with Ezra. They passed 'most of the time', continues Cornell, 'talking about Confucius, Jefferson, and the economic and political implications of their ideas. I let him ramble on, even though I did not get much of the information which I wanted, as it seemed a shame to deprive him of the pleasure of talking, which has been almost entirely denied to him for a long while.' Cornell had no idea that he was simply encountering Ezra on typical form.

To Miss Ida Mapel Ezra had seemed 'nervous' but otherwise just as usual. Lieutenant Colonel Holder judged him 'crack pot', but never suggested that he was truly mad. The three psychiatrists who had interviewed him at the DTC, when he was under considerable stress, were unanimous in agreeing that he was not suffering from any form of mental disorder, either permanent or temporary. The journalist Edd Johnson, who had interviewed him at CIC Genoa back in May, had spontaneously emphasized that he was 'not crazy'. But Cornell's letter to Laughlin shows that Cornell had decided that he was not dealing with a person in a normal mental state, but with a man who must be humoured and soothed rather than treated as a responsible individual who could be encouraged and helped to formulate a coherent legal defence. Cornell was already forming the opinion, it seems, that the best tactic in court would be to claim that Ezra was insane.

6

Cornered

Ezra never felt that Cornell was the lawyer for whom he had been looking.
Dorothy told Cornell in 1946 that her husband 'does not feel, I rather
gather, that you are "on to" all his economic learning'. Cornell refuted this:
'I have a pretty good understanding of . . . his economic theories and the
motives underlying hs broadcasts. I have made it a point to study not only
his poetry but his economic tracts and I have read up on Social Credit in
general.'

Why did Cornell decide on a plea of insanity as a defence tactic? It is
understandable that a lawyer whose work up to now had largely involved
defending conscientious objectors, pacifists, and ministers of religion
might be inclined to doubt the sanity of a man who sat in a prison cell and
made such remarks to him as 'The greatest benefit which can come to a
poet is to be hung.' This was simply Ezra playing Villon, but Cornell was
not used to Poundian poses.

The idea that Ezra was crazy had already been suggested, of course, by
Hemingway and MacLeish, but there was a considerable difference
between calling him 'cracked' in private letters and publicly claiming, as a
legal defence, that he was clinically insane. It does not follow that
Hemingway or MacLeish would have repeated these remarks in court, and
there is no evidence that either of them suggested the insanity tactic to
Cornell. It is fairly clear that it was his own decision.*

---

* James Laughlin, when asked about Cornell's motives, said he was under the impression that
the insanity defence had originated with Arthur Moore, Ezra's solicitor in London. But
Moore made no such suggestion in any of his letters, and was content all along to accept the
advice of Ezra's friends in America and of Cornell. Laughlin himself feels that Ezra was
indeed of unsound mind during his first few months in Washington, just after he had been
brought back from Europe, and that the mental instability consisted of such delusions as
believing that he was to be sent by the US Government to the Far East.

His letter to Laughlin describing his first meeting with Ezra in the prison cell was at pains to emphasize the abnormality of Ezra's behaviour. Cornell reported that 'he kept talking about the possibility that government officials with whom he had no acquaintance whatever might interest themselves in his case if they could be persuaded of the soundness of his economic views'. Following this first conversation with Ezra, Cornell also made some notes which pointed out what he supposed to be the damaging effect on Ezra's mental health of his experiences at the DTC: '. . . he went out of his mind [in the cage] and suffered complete loss of memory, a state from which he said he did not fully recover until September.' Ezra did not mention to Cornell that the three DTC psychiatrists had judged him perfectly sane and in full possession of his memory in June and July. 'I would say,' wrote Cornell to Laughlin, 'that he is still under a considerable mental cloud.'

Cornell might perhaps have had grounds for regarding Ezra's mental health as unstable if he had reviewed his life over a long period of time – the years 1933 to 1943, during which Ezra had poured out economic and political dogma like a man possessed, and had seemingly lost the sense of proportion which he had had as a young man. It might have been possible to argue that those years saw the onset of some mental disorder (this is what Hemingway and MacLeish may have felt). But Cornell only considered his client as he found him at that moment. And the evidence is that in November 1945, in the DC Jail, Ezra was not 'mad' in any clinical sense; he was simply his usual highly eccentric self.

*

Cornell told Laughlin the procedure he had in mind. He planned to 'make an application for bail' on the grounds that Ezra's mental health had been 'seriously impaired by the brutal nature of his confinement and that his continued imprisonment may end both his life and his sanity'. This was not strictly a plea of insanity, merely an attempt to get Ezra out of prison for the time being. Cornell thought it would work; he said that the Government would 'probably oppose' the application for bail, 'but not strenuously, since they regard Pound's case as a rather mild one of its kind'.

This seems an extraordinary assumption, given the enormous official effort already expended on collecting evidence, detaining Ezra in custody for more than six months, and transporting him to the USA with a three-man guard, which included two colonels. The notion probably sprang from Cornell's private conversation with Judge Laws. Cornell reported that he had found Judge Laws 'most courteous and helpful'. Indeed, throughout the legal proceedings, Laws (a gentle-mannered Southerner) behaved with exemplary courtesy and benevolence towards all participants, including Ezra himself. But he was not the Government Prosecutor.

Even more strangely, Cornell reported (in this same letter written after his first meeting with him) that Ezra himself 'has no objection' to 'the possibility of pleading insane as a defense . . . In fact he told me that the idea had already occurred to him.'

This seems extraordinary. A matter of days earlier, on the plane journey from Italy, Ezra had been as determined as ever to conduct his own defence, claiming that no lawyer was clever enough to handle the case. He had also been characteristically garrulous in promulgating his economic views and in attacking the supposed international Jewish conspiracy. What could possibly have happened to make him abandon his wish to act as his own attorney, to reject the opportunity of demonstrating to the court and the American people that what he had said over the air was not treason but the truth, and to agree to be treated as a madman?

The only answer can be that he was led to believe that an application for bail, on the grounds of shaky mental health, would probably secure his immediate if temporary release from prison. Numb from six months of imprisonment and exhausted by a forty-eight-hour Atlantic crossing, completed only a day and a half earlier, Ezra can have been in no condition to judge the niceties of legal procedure, and he would very likely have found the prospect of release too tempting to refuse. It offered, too, the hoped-for chance to get in touch with Government officials and 'divulge' everything about Italy and the Far East which was on his mind. As a free man he could prepare his case at leisure, could get at the books he needed, and could work at an eloquent defence that would, in due course, hold the court spellbound.

He did not realize that a claim of insanity, once embarked on, would be very hard to retract. Perhaps Cornell had not considered this. Archibald MacLeish wrote to Eliot on 6 December that he had just met 'young Julien Cornell', who said he wanted to get Ezra out on bail. But 'beyond that', continued MacLeish, 'his plans for the case are not fully developed'.

*

Eliot began to sense that Cornell was making assumptions about Ezra's sanity. He had just heard from Dorothy about her visit to Ezra at the DTC, and had also been shown, by Arthur Moore, a copy of Cornell's letter to Laughlin describing Ezra's supposedly 'wobbly' mental condition. Eliot wrote to Moore on 3 December 1945:

> There is a curious similarity between Mrs Pound's and Mr Cornell's account of him in some respects and a complete difference of interpretation. One would suspect that Pound seems to his wife much more normal than he is, and to Mr Cornell, meeting him for the first time, he seems much more

unbalanced than he is. A good deal of what Cornell says about Pound's way of talking seems to me very much what I would expect of him at any time.

In the letter to Laughlin, which Eliot had seen, Cornell raised the possibility of using an insanity plea as defence when the trial finally began.

> I think there is a good chance that such a defense might succeed [Cornell wrote]. As you probably know, the trial of such an issue is almost always a farce, since learned medicos who testify for each side squarely contradict each other and completely befuddle the jury. It then largely becomes a question of the sympathy of the jury, assuming, of course, that there is no question of outright faking.

When discussing the matter with Ezra, Cornell even took the line that the insanity plea, if successful, would lead to his complete release and return to Italy – this at least was what Ezra afterwards claimed had been said to him. 'Cornell,' he wrote wryly eleven years later, 'thought I wd/ be back in Italy in six months a free man.' Evidently Cornell hoped he could convince the authorities that Ezra was mad enough to have made the broadcasts, but not mad enough to require locking up. If that was really in his mind, he was setting out to walk a legal tightrope.

Admittedly, the insanity tactic had one advantage: it was certain, if it succeeded in court, to save Ezra from execution. Cornell may have been working on this basis – that his ultimate responsibility was to save his client's life. Yet his assertion that the Government considered the case as 'rather a mild one of its kind' suggests that he had not seriously considered the death sentence as likely, and nowhere in his book on Ezra's trial does he mention the possibility of execution.

Cornell implied to Laughlin that he had now obtained Ezra's formal consent that he should act as his defence counsel: 'I told him that I want to postpone a decision as to who should represent him on the trial until I know more about the case, and he appeared to agree to all these suggestions.' No doubt Ezra still believed he could conduct the case himself when the trial actually opened. He had not been offered any other lawyer, and Cornell was a friend of Laughlin. Cornell effectively finalized the matter by sending a copy of his letter to Laughlin on to Arthur Moore at Shakespear & Parkyn. Thereafter all parties (except possibly Ezra) regarded him as the chosen defence counsel.

∗

A fresh indictment had been prepared by the Department of Justice to supersede that of July 1943. A much more lengthy document than the earlier one, it contained specific charges (though the dates of the broadcasts and other details were imprecise). While the 1943 indictment had merely accused Ezra in vague terms of having 'treasonably . . . adhere[d] to the enemies of the United States' and of having given them 'aid and comfort', it was now alleged that he was guilty of

> accepting employment from the Kingdom of Italy in the capacity of a radio propagandist and in the performance thereof which involved the composition of texts, speeches, talks and announcements and the recording thereof for subsequent broadcast over short-wave radio on wave lengths audible in the United States . . . counselling and aiding the Kingdom of Italy . . . and proposing and advocating to the officials . . . ideas and thoughts . . . which the said defendant . . . believed suitable and useful . . . for propaganda purposes.

His correspondence with Mussolini and other Government officials was being brought into the case too. The indictment alleged that all these activities were intended by him

> to persuade citizens and residents of the United States to decline to support the United States in the conduct of the said war, to weaken or destroy confidence in the Government of the United States and in the integrity and loyalty of the Allies of the United States, and to further bind together and increase the morale of the subjects of the Kingdom of Italy.

This was a fair summary of some of the aims of the broadcasts. If Ezra had been conducting his own defence, he would undoubtedly have retorted that it did not amount to treason, as defined in the Constitution and the US criminal code. Indeed, in April 1950, when the Department of Justice was reconsidering his case, a confidential internal memorandum within the Department – the work of a legal expert – expressed the opinion that only one of the nineteen specific accusations in the indictment (referring to a particular broadcast in February 1943) was likely to lead to conviction; the others either lacked the necessary two witnesses or 'could not properly be construed as giving aid and comfort to the enemy'.

In the new indictment, there were specific charges that 'on or about' certain dates, or 'between' certain other dates, Ezra Pound 'spoke into a microphone at a radio station in Rome, Italy, controlled by the Italian Government', and recorded 'for subsequent broadcast to the United States and its military allies' talks containing such material as:

> that the war is an economic war in which the United States and its allies are the aggressors . . . [statements likely] to create

racial prejudice in the United States . . . to cause dissension and distrust between the United States and England and Russia . . . [statements] that the true nature of the Axis regime has been misrepresented.

Again, this was a fair and accurate description of some of the material in the broadcasts; and again, the prosecution would have had to convince the court that it amounted to treason (for example, the charge of causing 'racial prejudice' scarcely constituted a treasonable action).

Besides giving this paraphrase of some of the broadcasts, the indictment also accused Ezra of receiving 'payment and remuneration', citing two particular dated payments to him from Minculpop (one of 350 lire, one of 700 lire). Other charges named seven witnesses – the five radio technicians who had been flown to Washington, and two Minculpop officials, Salvatore Aponte and Adriano Ungaro, with whom Ezra was alleged to have 'conferred and counselled . . . for the purpose of securing their approval of manuscripts'.

The indictment, signed by legal officials, was chiefly the work of Isaiah Matlack, Special Assistant to the Attorney General and Chief of the War Crimes Section of the Department of Justice, who was to be principal prosecutor in Ezra's case. The indictment was sent for hearing by a Federal Grand Jury on Friday 23 November 1945.* The day before that hearing, which he was to attend himself, Ezra wrote to his mother:

> District of Columbia Jail
>   Washington D.C.
>   cell CB 1.   22 Nov. 1945
> My dear Mother
>   Wonderful plane trip. includin Bermuda – escort most considerate. only blot was bein' tired by night djeep ride before start.
> –
> Note from Mencken. Mapel's have called – informal chess club amiable & play badly enough to stand my poor playing. fried chicken or rather poulade a la Virginia & chocolate ice cream today (thanksgiving) wish you cd/ have shared it – but the society is exclusive –
> Mr Peabody's anecdotes of Panama canal zone etc. in fact conversational level rather above that of the politer tea circles –

---

*A Grand Jury, which is used in the USA at both Federal and State level, hears evidence to decide whether there is a case to go to trial. The British equivalent would be a committal proceeding in a magistrate's court.

the papers seem to be expressin the views I held some years ago
with rather more ceremony that I ever did.
– Antheil publishin his autobiography. & Dali havin a picture
show. Poore ole F. Bacon is dead (2 or 3 years ago)*
–
Idea (i.e. mean idea in yr. last letter) perfectly sound. just have
patience.
                Love to you & D.
                        E.
            yr. obstreperous offspring

On the day of the Grand Jury hearing, he was, said Cornell, 'taken in the
police van to the "bull pen" at the courthouse and kept there all day shut in
with a group of prisoners, presumably because the Grand Jury was in the
process of indicting him'. Cornell claimed that this had 'aggravated' Ezra's
'poor physical condition'. Ezra was not called into court, and the Grand
Jury, after considering the evidence, formally approved the indictment.

It was now the weekend; on the Saturday (24 November) there was a
break out from the District Jail at lunchtime, five men escaping from a
recreation room. In consequence all prisoners were locked in their cells for
two days. Cornell afterwards alleged that this further period of confinement drove Ezra 'almost to the point of mental collapse'. Certainly he
found it a considerable hardship; he told Charles Olson a few weeks later:
'The jail at first was all right . . . and I wasn't bothered by claustrophobia.
But then that break, and they put us in the cells.' Nevertheless, on Sunday
he wrote a cheerful note from his cell to Ronald Duncan:

> Dear Ron,
>   Do send a copy of "Journal of a Husbandman" [Duncan's
> book about his wartime farming experiences] to Olga and Mary
> @ Casa 60 Sant Ambrogio (Rapallo).
>   All this is marvelous xperience if it dont break me and if the
> lesion of May cured (I thinks) in Sept. dont bust open under the
> renewed fatigues.
>   Love to Bunny
>   & Rose Marie
>   Yrs
>   Ez
>   Ezra Pound

The 'lesion of May' was his term for the mental confusion he had suffered
in the cage. He seemed to be hinting that the 'marvelous xperience' of being

*Frank 'Baldy' Bacon, the New York financial entrepreneur with whom Ezra had dealings in
1910, and who is mentioned in Canto 12.

in prison might lead to something else like the Pisan Cantos. By Sunday night, however, he had had enough of his cell, and he persuaded the authorities to transfer him to a bed in the prison hospital so that he could rest in more comfort. Cornell used this, too, as evidence that he was suffering a mental collapse.

*

On Monday morning, 26 November, the Grand Jury indictment was formally handed down to the District Court, and the beginning of the trial itself was scheduled for the next afternoon, Tuesday 27 November, before Judge Laws.

Cornell visited Ezra again on the Tuesday morning, and records that he 'spent about one hour with him reading over some of his poems, and at the end of the hour I mentioned for the first time the proceedings scheduled in court for that afternoon'. It seems that Cornell had now decided to treat him as a child, and felt that it was best to pass the time in amusing him rather than discussing the trial.

At the end of the hour, after he had sprung the announcement of the trial on Ezra, Cornell hurriedly suggested a tactic that would affect the whole case. He explained to Ezra.

> that he was to be arraigned [charged] and that he would have to plead to the indictment. I suggested that because of his condition it might be wise for him to remain mute rather than enter a plea of not guilty, and explained to him the implications of each course of proceeding. When I asked him whether he wanted to stand mute or would prefer to enter a plea, he was unable to answer me. His mouth opened once or twice as if to speak, but no words came out. He looked up at the ceiling and his face began to twitch. Finally he said he felt ill and asked if he could not go back to the infirmary.

This reaction was hardly surprising. Cornell said he had 'explained . . . the implications' of either pleading or standing mute, but he must have done so very briskly, since by his own admission the 'one hour' was almost up. Ezra had perhaps supposed Cornell had merely dropped by for a chat about the Cantos. Suddenly he was being expected to make a crucial decision, and understandably he felt unable to do so. Cornell took this as further evidence of insanity.

Cornell wrote to Arthur Moore, reporting Ezra's inability to answer the question about how he would plead in court. He observed:

> While he is able to converse extensively about literary and political matters, he appears to have great difficulty in concentrating upon his case and he appears to be unable to exercise any

judgement whatever regarding the impending trial. Because of his lack of ability to exercise any judgement and also because of his mental exhaustion, I considered him unable to plead to the indictment.

It was perfectly true that certainly Ezra did not like making decisions about the trial. His attitude was often to pretend that no trial would take place, as he had on previous occasions when faced with unattractive situations. Left to himself, however, he would undoubtedly have pleaded not guilty, and would have taken the opportunity to explain to the judge *why* he was not guilty. Cornell may have feared that he would interrupt the orderly proceedings of the trial, may have been appalled at the prospect of his client getting up and haranguing the court at the outset of the hearing, thereby seriously damaging his position with Judge Laws and the jury. But there may have been another reason why Cornell wished to take advantage of the fact that (as he explained to Arthur Moore) 'under our laws, when a defendant stands mute, a plea of not guilty must be entered by the court' – if Ezra refused to speak, it would help to suggest to the court that he was mentally incapable.

Ezra suddenly became alarmed at the prospect of being let out on bail. He had been in institutional care since May, and the prospect of the door opening began to frighten him. He told Cornell he had only $23 and asked how he was to manage. Cornell suggested that perhaps Dorothy's funds could be used as surety for the bail, and to cover his living expenses: but Ezra knew that her money was still in bond in Britain.

The trial started after lunch, and Ezra was brought from the prison. He was formally arraigned, whereupon Cornell got to his feet and told the court that his client was 'not sufficiently well to enter a plea'. Judge Laws said that Ezra might be permitted to remain mute, and could stay seated. A plea of not guilty was entered, which was reported next morning in the *New York Times*:

> A plea of innocent was entered . . . for Ezra Pound . . . after his attorney said his client was in no condition to make a plea for himself. 'Mr Pound is not sufficiently in possession of judgment and perhaps mentality to plead,' declared Julian [*sic*] Cornell, Pound's attorney. 'I ask that he be allowed to stand mute.' Mr Cornell said that he had asked Pound this morning [Tuesday] about his plea and Pound was unable to answer him.

*

Cornell claims, in his book on the case, that Ezra 'said not a word' during the proceedings, but simply 'sat with hands folded and eyes downcast'. However, Charles Olson, who was in the public seats at the hearing, describes his expression rather differently, as 'full of pain, and hostile, cornered'.

Olson gives a picture of the courtroom: 'The chief justice's chambers, made like some Episcopal chapel, with Negroes filling the pews for witnesses . . . Nothing disturbed the piety and quiet. It was a sleepy, do nothing world, waiting.' He watched Ezra examining the faces of everyone in court: 'He hunched forward, shot his head up and out like a beak, and squinting his eyes as though he missed glasses, though he had them on, moved along the jurors' faces, squaring at each direct and dwelling, as children and poets will and nobody else does because it is supposed to be rude.' Then he 'finished his examination and turned away to more immediate things, fingering one wrist with the other hand, removing his glasses and rubbing his eyes, slumping in his chair and then leaning on the table, twisting for comfort, always working his hands.'

The question of the plea having been dealt with, Cornell launched his insanity defence.

> I . . . handed up to Judge Laws my motion papers, at the same time giving copies to Isaiah Matlack, Assistant Attorney General in charge of the prosecution. I explained orally the general tenor of my motion, which was that Pound was suffering from mental illness, that he was physically fatigued and at the point of exhaustion from the rigors of his confinement at the concentration camp (there is no other word for it) of the United States Army at Pisa, that he was in urgent need of medical care, and that in my opinion he should never have been sent over here for trial. In view of the urgency of the situation, I asked the Judge to order Pound's immediate removal from the jail to a hospital.

Cornell's 'motion papers' were an affidavit stating what he believed to be Ezra's mental condition, and a brief, 'showing that there were precedents for his being admitted to bail despite the fact that treason is a capital offense'.

The affidavit alleged that since his arrest in May, Ezra had

> suffered a complete mental collapse and loss of memory. Although he has partially recovered his health, I believe that he is still insane and that if he remains in prison he may never recover, and not only will he be unable to stand trial on this indictment, but one of the greatest literary geniuses of these times will be permanently eclipsed. I urge this court to order his removal at once . . . to a civilian mental hospital or sanatorium under bail, or that if bail is not permitted, he be removed to a

civilian mental hospital or sanatorium operated by the United States and placed in custody of a civilian physician. I believe that such action is imperative, and that if it is not taken immediately, he will never recover his senses sufficiently to defend himself against the indictment.

Cornell was operating on two fronts: the humanitarian–literary (Ezra as the great writer who must not be caused further suffering) and the legal (if he were not given better treatment the court would not be able to put him on trial). There had been a subtle change from the plan he had put to Ezra that morning, and in his letter to Arthur Moore.

The original idea had been to free Ezra from prison for the immediate future, so that the matter of the defence could be considered at leisure. However, Cornell's application for bail stated that he was 'suffering from mental illness', while the accompanying affidavit made the further more serious claim that he had experienced 'a complete mental collapse' in May, from which he had not fully recovered, so that already he was completely incapable of standing a trial.

Although Cornell left open the possibility that a period in hospital might cure Ezra sufficiently for him to participate in his defence at a trial, he also made the suggestion – which he had not made to Ezra himself – that if the court found bail an unacceptable proposition, he might be put 'in custody' in a Federal-operated psychiatric hospital – a very different matter from being released on bail. Perhaps by now Cornell believed that this was where Ezra should be.

*

Though the affidavit submitted by Cornell to accompany his application for bail claimed to be 'confined to the facts of the case', it was a highly partisan summary of Ezra's life, character, and present position. Tracing his history, Cornell emphasized the respectability of his ancestry, his status in the field of letters (Cornell quoted from the Hamilton College honorary degree citation), his 1939 attempt to persuade US statesmen into 'paths which he thought were the paths to peace', his voluntary surrender to the Americans in May 1945, and the severity of the conditions in which he was kept at the start of his confinement in the DTC. The affidavit concluded:

> Only in a normal environment, free from the drastic restraints which are necessary in penal hospitals, can he possibly recover, in my opinion: only by such medical treatment does he stand a chance of regaining his sanity even to the point where he could stand trial on this indictment.
>
> I am confident that a disinterested psychiatric investigation of his condition would show that such measures are imperative.

It seems curious that at no stage in the proceedings did Cornell raise with Laughlin, Arthur Moore, or Ezra himself the possibility that it might prove technically impossible to convict him of treason on the charges contained in the indictment. Nor did he consider that, if the radio speeches were quoted in court, the jury might feel them too absurd, too irrelevant to the conduct of the war, in MacLeish's words, 'drivel', for them to be judged treasonable, or even able to 'influence anybody to do anything, any- where, at any time'. An experienced criminal lawyer would likely have concentrated on the technical loopholes in the indictment; but Cornell directed all his energies towards having Ezra judged insane, whatever the consequences.

*

Isaiah Matlack, the chief prosecutor, was, says Cornell, 'completely taken by surprise' by Cornell's move for Ezra to be judged insane – as well he might be, since it was not one that a defence counsel would be expected to make in the circumstances. Matlack asked for some time to read the affidavit and the 'brief concerning bail', and to consult with the Attorney General's office. There was, therefore, a brief recess. When the court reconvened, Matlack announced that 'the government had no objection to a medical examination'.

Matlack must have guessed that a likely outcome of an insanity plea by the defence would simply be the indefinite detention of Ezra in a psychiatric hospital; a not unsatisfactory result for the prosecution, especially since the case would not be easy to prove. But he was still astonished that Cornell had taken this course. The *New York Herald Tribune* quoted him as saying: 'It's a complete surprise.'

During the recess, Judge Laws had considered Cornell's application for bail, and when the court reconvened he gave the following decision:

> From the showing made before me by counsel for the defend-
> ant, it appears advisable to have an examination and observation
> of the defendant made by physicians and that pending such an
> examination and report of their findings and pending the
> granting of opportunity to counsel for the prosecution to reply
> to the motion for bail, no action should be taken on such
> motion.

In other words, bail was not yet granted. Certainly Ezra could be examined by psychiatrists, but this must be done in custody. The judge ruled 'that he be transferred to Gallinger Hospital or such other hospital as may be designated by authorized officials of the United States for examination and observation and for treatment, if found necessary'. He was to leave prison for the time being, and to enter a custodial psychiatric ward.

The motion for bail, continued Judge Laws, would be heard again on 14 December, in just over two weeks' time; by then, the court would have received the psychiatrists' reports, and a decision about bail could be given on the basis of them. In the meantime, the prosecution was invited to submit any 'showing' that they might wish to make in opposition to bail. The trial was then adjourned.

*

A reporter from *PM* watched Ezra talking to his attorney as they left the court: 'At the elevator . . . Cornell . . . said "maybe you'd like to read the paper while you're lying down", and handed him a folded newspaper. Pound looked at it and tossed it back to Cornell. "I don't read the *New York Times*," he snapped.'

7

He Is, In Other Words, Insane

It took several days for Ezra's transfer to hospital to be arranged. Meanwhile a journalist from *Time* managed to see him in prison. A report in that magazine on 10 December 1945 described him as

> lolling in the infirmary of the D.C. jail . . . last week . . . Most of the time . . . the ragbaggy old darling of the U.S. expatriate intelligentsia . . . just sat, wrapped in his grey flannel bath-robe . . . [He] did not seem to care very much [what was happening to him] . . . he denied that he ever talked treason: 'I was only trying to tell the people of Europe and America how they could avoid war by learning the facts about money.'

Julien Cornell reported the outcome of the court proceedings in a letter to Arthur Moore on 29 November, saying that he was planning to have an 'outstanding psychiatrist' examine Ezra, 'and his report together with the report of the government's physicians will be presented to the court'. Still hoping that bail would be granted when the court reconvened, Cornell also began to investigate the financing of a bail bond or surety. He said he hoped it would not be necessary 'to have Mrs Pound's funds put up as security' – he had, in any case, been told that it would be impossible to raise a bail bond in the USA with money that was in Britain, though perhaps Moore 'could find some way to do this through Lloyds'.

Cornell seems now to have decided that Ezra would not be given bail, but would be ordered to be confined to a private psychiatric hospital, at which he would be given treatment at his own expense. Cornell told Moore he had 'considerable doubt whether the case will ever get so far as to necessitate preparation for a trial', and said the defence would 'probably need a substantial sum to pay for medical treatment'. He hoped that 'some way can be found to release Mrs Pound's funds' for that purpose. He thought that hospital fees and the payment of the defence psychiatrist would necessitate the raising of about $5,000. He does not seem to have discussed this with Ezra; he simply continued with his own attempts at fund-raising from Ezra's friends.

In New York, he called on E. E. Cummings and asked if he would be prepared to offer funds should they be required. Cummings immediately handed Cornell a cheque for $1,000 that he had just received and said he did not need. (Later, Dorothy insisted on paying it back.) On top of this, Laughlin contributed $500, and the Boni & Liveright publishing company $300 that they owed Ezra in royalties.

Cornell therefore had $1,800 in hand. He had already run up an expenses bill of more than $1,000 for his work on the case, taking into account his trips from New York to Washington and two very expensive cables to Dorothy. However, he told Moore he would use all the cash he had raised for paying for the psychiatric report and 'hospital treatment', and would not submit any bill for expenses or fees until Dorothy's money had been released by the British Government, who were still holding it under Enemy Property regulations.

A letter from Cornell to Moore, dated 10 December 1945, suggests that he had no very clear idea of what might happen should a treason trial actually begin: 'I think he [Ezra] should be able to convince a jury of the sincerity of his motives although they will surely think that he was misguided and that his actions were subject to blame.' This seems to say: the jury will probably think that he believed in the rightness of what he was doing, but what he was doing was wrong, and he deserves to be punished for it.

There is no evidence that Cornell was devoting any serious attention to how he would conduct the defence. He told Moore that he had 'come to the conclusion that his [Ezra's] position would be very much better if he were defended by counsel assigned by the court'. He expected that 'in a case of this importance' they would 'assign eminent counsel'. He himself only wished to deal with 'the question of his mental and physical condition'.

*

On Monday 4 December 1945, Ezra was taken from the District Jail to Gallinger Municipal, a Washington general medical hospital with a psychiatric ward. He was installed in a private room and locked in. Cornell wrote to him promising to have him transferred to a more comfortable institution as soon as the psychiatric examination had been completed.

At Gallinger, he was given a thorough physical check-up, including X-rays, and at the request of one of the staff psychiatrists there was 'a special examination . . . of the genito-urinary system'. No explanation was given for this procedure, which Ezra cannot have regarded with enthusiasm. None of the tests showed any significant deviation from the norm. Indeed he was judged to be 'in at least as good, if not better, physical condition than the average sixty-year-old'.

The next step for Cornell was to send a psychiatrist of his own choosing to examine Ezra. A lawyer friend recommended Dr Winfred Overholser, Superintendent at St Elizabeths, the Federal psychiatric institution in Washington and a leading authority on legal aspects of psychiatry. Cornell sent a telegram asking Overholser if he could oblige, but Overholser said he must decline since he was a Government official. 'My next thought,' writes Cornell, 'was the famous Dr Adolf Meyer of Baltimore. Dr Meyer declined on the ground that he was an invalid and could not leave his home but he recommended several other doctors, including Dr Wendell Muncie, connected with Johns Hopkins University. Dr Muncie agreed to take the case.' Muncie, aged forty-eight, was an associate professor of psychiatry at Johns Hopkins, and in private practice. On 6 December 1945, Cornell wrote to him to confirm the arrangement for him to examine Ezra at Gallinger Hospital the following week and send a written report to the court. Muncie's fee was $250.

Cornell assumed that (as he had put it to Laughlin) the usual 'farce' would happen when the sanity issue was debated before the court. As he says in his book on Ezra's trial, in such cases 'the doctor for the prosecution testifies that the man is sufficiently sane to be tried while the doctor for the defense testifies to the contrary and the jury must choose between them'. Consequently, Cornell gave Muncie strong hints that he should declare Ezra insane.

Writing to Muncie, Cornell summarized Ezra's 'history'. He said it was 'conceded by the government that he became definitely insane during his imprisonment in Italy last summer' (the DTC psychiatrists had declared quite the opposite), and he stated firmly that at the DTC 'Pound's mind gave way'. Cornell added that he believed that 'even if he were sufficiently sane to understand the proceedings, the ordeal of a trial might bring on a relapse'. Cornell also enclosed a letter from Hemingway (who had not met Ezra for many years) saying that, in his opinion and that of James Joyce during the 1930s, Ezra was not sane. Finally in this package for Muncie, Cornell sent some lines from the Pisan Cantos which he said 'might afford some evidence of his mental condition' in the DTC – that is, proof of madness.

∗

Meanwhile the prosecution was choosing its own doctors to report on Ezra: Dr Marion King, medical director of the prison service, a fifty-six-year-old male general physician with no specialist training in psychiatry;

Dr Joseph L. Gilbert, one of the two resident psychiatrists at Gallinger, aged fifty-five and a run-of-the-mill hospital staff man; and Dr Winfred Overholser, aged fifty-one.

Winfred Overholser was tall, gentle, soft-spoken, and extremely obstinate. He had worked his way to the top of his profession thanks chiefly to a certain slow charm and a talent for making a good impression on Government officials. He had begun to specialize in psychiatry during the First World War, treating soldiers who had been sent home with trench neuroses. During the 1920s he had worked in Massachusetts psychiatric hospitals, rising to become Commissioner of Mental Diseases for that state in 1934. Three years later he went to St Elizabeths in Washington as Superintendent, remaining there until his retirement in 1962. He was also Professor of Psychiatry at George Washington University.

Overholser's attitude to psychiatric illness was liberal, in that he favoured out-patient treatment whenever possible, though this was principally a tactic to combat overcrowding in hospitals. He was always humane, believing in common-sense approaches to psychiatric disorder (for example, plenty of rest and exercise for depressives) rather than advocating the extensive use of drugs or electroconvulsive therapy. Nor was he committed to any school of psychoanalysis. But he had no flair as a therapist, as a theorist on psychiatric illness, or as an administrator, and during the years of his leadership at St Elizabeths there were no clear policies on how patients might be helped or cured.

One area that particularly interested him was the legal tennis match that (as Cornell had observed) tended to be staged in court when the question of a defendant's sanity came up. This seemed to Overholser to bring his profession into disrepute, and reputation always concerned him. In 1938 and 1939 he published articles urging that instead there should be a joint report to the court, made by doctors representing both sides, who would try to eliminate mere partisanship from their judgement and come to sincere agreement on the defendant's mental state. The Ezra Pound case seemed to offer him a well-publicized opportunity to put this scheme to the test.

Overholser was not necessarily disposed at the outset to assume that Ezra was insane. He himself had achieved a *cum laude* in economics at Harvard, and he had a number of literary friends, including the Boston poet–psychiatrist Merrill Moore. He was not, therefore, inclined to judge passionate intellectual activity to be *per se* a sign of mental instability. He had written in 1939 that geniuses are 'abnormal', but said this was quite different from calling them 'psychotic or mentally deranged'. Indeed, he did not accept that there was any clear division between sanity and insanity. 'Between the fully normal and the grossly abnormal,' he wrote in 1944, 'lies a vast no man's land of deviations from mental health, minor or major, slight or serious.' Three years later he dismissed in print the notion that any person could, beyond argument, be categorized as either ' "sane" and consequently fully responsible for all his acts, or else "insane" and wholly irresponsible'. But there was also his belief that psychiatrists involved in court cases should present a united front. This, rather than his good sense about sanity and insanity, was the dominating factor in Overholser's behaviour over the next few weeks.

*

Overholser and the other two prosecution-appointed doctors interviewed Ezra singly on various occasions between 4 and 13 December 1945. Dr King talked to him at least three times, Dr Gilbert (who was in charge of Ezra's psychiatric ward at Gallinger) saw him often in the course of duty, and Dr Overholser paid him one visit, possibly two. It is clear that, while the other two doctors developed no special interest in or sympathy for Ezra, and thought him merely a tiresome egocentric, Overholser was delighted to be involved in his case. Writing many years later, he described how he and Ezra 'discussed various persons and things of mutual interest', and said that his own 'literary interests' had fuelled these conversations.

Dr King, the head of the prison medical service, made an initial report to Overholser on 10 December in which he firmly judged Ezra to be sane. King had seen (or knew about) the reports of the DTC psychiatrists, and he pointed out that they had judged him not to be suffering from any 'mental or physical collapse'. It was his own impression that Ezra could not be classified as 'a psychotic or insane person' and therefore he 'should not be absolved from the necessity of standing trial'. Overholser's response was to send King back to take another look, with heavy hints that this was not to be just the usual game of defence versus prosecution. King then reported again, and this time allowed that during 'long periods' in Ezra's company, much of his talk had been 'definitely abnormal'.

Ezra took little interest in these proceedings. He had had enough of being pushed around; he complained that he was exhausted and wanted to rest. Dr Gilbert, in charge of the ward, recorded that he 'remained in bed practically all the time' and that he complained of being 'unable to get flat enough in bed', though Gilbert noticed that when he wanted to, he could 'move quickly about from the bed to a table nearby to get some paper, book or manuscript', and would then 'suddenly throw himself on the bed again and again assume the reclining position'.

Ezra knew that Cornell wanted him classified insane, so that (according to Cornell's hypothetical scheme) he could then be released on bail; possibly it was this that motivated him to tell King he was suffering from 'a queer sensation in the head as though the upper third of the brain were missing and a fluid level existed at the top of what remained'. More likely it was not a ruse, but an eccentric and rather hypochondriacal description of genuine feelings of exhaustion – influenced by his old notion that the brain was a 'great clot of genital fluid'.

Prompted by his instructions to declare Ezra mad, and encountering a man who talked non-stop and said the upper part of his brain was missing, Dr Wendell Muncie, for the defence, was naturally quite happy to state that Ezra was not sufficiently sane to stand trial. He only saw him once, on 13 December, the last day on which he could write his report before the court reconvened, so he was in a hurry. His hasty encounter with Ezra gave him the impression, he said, that he was dealing with 'a plain psychopath', someone who was 'not of sound mind and could not participate effectively in his own defense'. 'Psychopath' was scarcely a precise medical term, but little more than popular slang for almost any kind of madman. Overholser defines it in his *Handbook of Psychiatry* (1947) as meaning simply 'mentally diseased', and said it was applied to

> a large variety of maladjusted persons who are not definitely psychotic [mad] . . . They are lazy, eccentric, quarrelsome, fanatics, emotionally unstable . . . et cetera . . . people who have never grown up emotionally and cannot adjust themselves to the world.

Muncie had encountered Ezra in a characteristic mood. He complained that he had found it impossible to get him to talk straight, for 'if you touch on his case . . . Confucius and these other things seemed to get roped in'. Laughlin, who saw Ezra a few weeks later, reported that he was 'very much his old self'.

*

Overholser now assumed command of the proceedings. Immediately after Muncie had seen Ezra, Overholser arranged for him to meet with the three prosecution doctors and agree on a joint report which they could all sign. This move astonished Cornell when he heard about it, for he had not read Overholser's writings on psychiatry and court cases, and had expected the prosecution doctors to declare Ezra sane. Instead, however, he learnt from Muncie that all four doctors had judged him 'mentally unfit for trial'.

The doctors' report began by describing Ezra's career briefly, observing that his 'poetry and literary criticism' had won him 'considerable recognition', but remarking that in recent years his 'preoccupation with monetary theories and economics' had 'apparently obstructed his literary productivity'. They added that he had 'long been recognized as eccentric, querulous, and egocentric'. It was no more than a plain statement of the truth, as was the observation that 'at the present time he exhibits extremely poor judgement as to his situation, its seriousness and the manner in which the charges are to be met' – but then Cornell had scarcely given him a chance to form any proper judgement of these things, had encouraged him to believe that he would soon be let out on bail, had hinted (perhaps) that the Government really took the whole thing lightly.

The report – again accurately – went on to cite Ezra as insisting that 'his broadcasts were not treasonable', and that 'all of his radio activities have stemmed from his self-appointed mission to "save the Constitution"'. It was only now that Overholser – who clearly drafted the report himself – entered into specifically psychiatric territory:

> In our opinion, with advancing years his personality, for many years abnormal, has undergone further distortion to the extent that he is now suffering from a paranoid state which renders him mentally unfit to advise properly with counsel or to participate intelligently and reasonably in his own defense. He is, in other words, insane and mentally unfit for trial, and is in need of care in a mental hospital.

Overholser defines 'paranoid' in his *Handbook of Psychiatry* as a clinical term for someone who 'believes himself to be persecuted', somebody who thinks that 'various persons or organizations' are 'mixed up in plots against him'. This is a standard definition of a psychiatric condition usually associated with schizophrenia. But while it would have been possible for Overholser and his fellow doctors to argue that Ezra's ten-year preoccupation with the supposed international Jewish conspiracy was a symptom of a paranoid condition, Overholser was strikingly wary of pinning the 'paranoid' label on him too securely. Later, under cross-examination in court, he would only say that the condition of Ezra's mind 'resembles paranoia, if you wish to put it that way'.

He knew that to prove true paranoia, as it is normally understood in psychiatric circles, he would have had to show that Ezra suffered real and frequent delusions that people were trying to attack him personally – not just that humanity in general was threatened by a particular group of people. For example, in his definition of 'paranoia' in the *Handbook of Psychiatry*, Overholser cites the case of a man who thought, without any grounds whatever, that people were abusing him sexually. Overholser could see that Ezra showed no evidence of suffering actual delusions of persecution. Indeed, for all his ranting against the Jewish usurers, he had never claimed to have been singled out personally by them, or by any other of his supposed enemies.*

---

*A possible exception is Ezra's apparent belief that certain people or organizations had 'double crossed' him when he was brought to Washington, and had brought about his imprisonment; but Overholser was not aware that Ezra thought this.

Even Cornell admitted in private that Ezra was not exactly mad. He wrote to Dorothy on 25 January 1946 that she

> need not be alarmed about the report on your husband's mental condition . . . I feel quite sure that you will find, when you see him again, that he is his usual self, and that the mental aberrations which the doctors have found are not anything new or unusual, but are chronic and would pass entirely unnoticed by one like yourself who has lived close to him for a number of years. In fact I think it may be fairly said that any man of his genius would be regarded by a psychiatrist as abnormal.

*

The man of genius continued to send news to his mother in Rapallo:

> Gallinger Hospital
>   10 Dec.
> Dear Mother,
>   You might like this hospital better than Rapallo, @ least the steam heat & morning coffee.
>   One of my guardian angels is readin' Ron Duncan's 'Journal of a Husbandman' with great interest. –
>   Best wishes for as good a Xmas as possible.
>   By mistake some coffee was sent to me instead of to you. but hope you'll get some.
>   Love to D.
>   E.P.

*

The trial resumed on 14 December, but that day only saw a formal extension of Ezra's detention in hospital, so that the judge and prosecution could consider the unanimous report from the four doctors, which had just been submitted. The next hearing was fixed for 21 December.

*

When the court sat that day, the psychiatric report was read aloud by the judge. It would have been possible for him now to order the detention of the prisoner for an indefinite period in a Government psychiatric hospital, without further court proceedings, since all the doctors had judged him unfit to plead; but the prosecution indicated that this would be letting Ezra off too easily: Matlack told the court that he and his colleagues believed that Ezra Pound, 'like Rudolf Hess, might easily be feigning insanity to escape a trial that might cost his life'. (Hess, at Nuremberg, had claimed to be suffering from amnesia – which the court there did not accept.) Matlack asked that there should be a 'public insanity hearing' before a jury, at which the prosecution would be able to challenge the doctors' testimony, and the jury would deliver its verdict on the issue. Matlack further pointed out that the US Army psychiatrists had only thought the prisoner to be suffering from claustrophobia, and had suggested that 'in other respects, except for his usual eccentricity, the prisoner was sane and able to stand trial'.

Cornell said he had 'no objection' to a jury trial of the insanity issue, as well he might not, given the unanimity of the doctors and the likelihood that this would hold good in the face of cross-examination. Judge Laws therefore rejected the application for bail, and ordered Ezra's transfer from Gallinger to St Elizabeths Hospital, this being the statutory place of detention for all Federal prisoners regarded as insane. The judge then announced that the jury hearing on the sanity issue would be in 'late January'. The court adjourned for Christmas.

*

Late in the afternoon, after the court proceedings, Ezra was driven in a police van to St Elizabeths. Julien Cornell might have wondered, since four doctors had unanimously judged him insane, how he was ever going to get him out again; but the thought does not seem to have crossed his mind.

8

Hell-hole

St Elizabeths Hospital stands on part of the old St Elizabeth Tract, a high plateau in south-east Washington DC overlooking the Anacostia River, which joins the Potomac just below the hospital. The grounds, in the words of an early report, 'command a grand panorama of nature and art'. From a viewpoint opposite the hospital's Center Building there is certainly an impressive outlook across to the Capitol and other Federal monuments a few miles away, and the air is bracing. The hospital stands on land of more than 300 acres, and was opened in 1855 owing to the efforts of Dorothea Lynde Dix, celebrated campaigner for the better treatment of the mentally ill. Its original function was to care for the insane of the US Army and Navy, as well as for civilian patients from within the District of Columbia. The chief edifice (Center Building) was constructed of dull red brick in the Scottish baronial manner, suggesting a university campus rather than an asylum.

The wards spreading out from Center Building were given the names of trees that had been felled on the site to provide timber: Chestnut, Cedar, and so on. The main building also contained the Superintendent's apartment, where, at least in the early days of the hospital, that official lived in feudal style with a dozen rooms and a dining hall that could seat a banquet. His wife and children resided there too – all the doctors lived in – and they had not only a generous provision of maids, but the services of the hospital's own dairy and bakery. Other buildings soon appeared; in 1856 a 'lodge for colored insane' was set up, and in 1891 Howard Hall, a prison building with exercise compound for the detention of persons sent there by the courts, was erected in a rather remote corner of the grounds. Its high surrounding wall with dry moat behind were kept carefully out of the sight of distinguished visitors.

The first Superintendent, Charles H. Nichols, served as President of what is now the American Psychiatric Association, and all his successors up to and including Winfred Overholser followed suit. St Elizabeths liked to think of itself as 'the best known public mental hospital in the United States, and one of the few outstanding . . . in the entire world'. But during Overholser's régime it lost much of its prestige. There had been a distinguished Board of Visitors, but this was disbanded after the Second World War by the Truman Administration, and at the same time the army and navy connections with the hospital were severed. Overholser called these decisions 'an unpleasant shock', for both were erosions of his status. In December 1945 he may possibly have felt that the acquisition of a well-known poet as inmate would go some way towards restoring it.

By 1945 St Elizabeths was badly overcrowded. The bed capacity was supposedly 6,500, but 500 more patients were crammed in, and numbers continued to grow. The wards were choked with elderly institutionalized inmates incapable of facing life outside even though the mental condition of many no longer warranted confinement. The staff muddled along with a mixture of electroconvulsive therapy, insulin, and the experimental use of tranquillizers. Soon after the Second World War the Nurses' Training School had been closed, and many of the staff were under-educated in the care of the mentally ill. Even the classification of the patients' disorders was inadequately carried out: Overholser's predecessor, the widely admired Dr William A. White, had established the system of classification drawn up by Emil Kraepelin, a founding father of psychotic diagnosis; but Overholser had little interest in this, and let his staff use terminology virtually as they chose.

*

Ezra was taken straight to Howard Hall, the discreetly hidden penal building. He was escorted to an upper floor and locked up in a cell leading off a ward. Omar, who came to visit him there a few months later, describes the building as 'Faustian, with the sound of clanking chains and doors being bolted'. Charles Olson noted 'a black iron door with nine peep holes, cut in it in 3 horizontal rows'.

As soon as Ezra had arrived, an inventory was made of the personal property he had brought with him from Gallinger:

1 Bottle instant coffee	2 pr. slippers
1 Box Cookies	1 pr. checked pajamas
7 pr. shorts	6 pr. socks
7 Handkerchiefs	1 pr. shoes
4 towels	1 canvas knapsack
11 undershirts	1 bone handle cane

2 wash rags	1 brief case
2 shirts	1 wallet
1 pr. underdrawers	2 toilet articles
1 blue coat sweater	

He was given a physical check-up, and once again was found 'normal' in every respect.

In the evening he was subjected to a lengthy psychiatric examination, during which he launched into his habitual explanation of the Rome Radio broadcasts, attacking Roosevelt and the wartime Government, and quickly convincing the examining doctor of his 'egotism and belief in his infallibility'. However, the doctor recorded that he displayed 'no marked deviations from the normal . . . no outright deficiency in orientation'. It was also noticed that he seemed on the whole 'quite complacent if not actually pleased with his present status'. The only thing that seemed seriously to upset him was that his books and papers had been left behind at Gallinger.

He began to take a characteristically detached interest in his surroundings. He was impressed by the design of the strait-jackets: 'very neat and comfortable arrangement of leather cuffs and chain at waist to keep hands down and prevent wearers slugging others'. But he gathered that though most prisoners were allowed out every day for brief exercise in the walled compound of Howard Hall, no such arrangement would be made for him. He became upset about it; he complained to the doctors about 'the doors being locked', and said he was beginning to experience a return of the claustrophobia which had overcome him at the DTC. He was also annoyed by the clamour made by patients on the ward outside his cell, and was infuriated when a doctor offered him a radio to drown it – he angrily rejected this as 'just plain noise'.

Ezra had been put in a cell for his own protection. Though St Elizabeths was no longer the official asylum for the armed forces, there were still a number of military inmates among the criminal insane in Howard Hall, and a workman was heard to observe that 'if they put the son of a bitch down in Ward 1 the young fellows would give him the beating up he deserves'. The ward off which his cell led was full of dangerous men; Ezra told a visitor: 'Gallinger was better than this . . . There's an Indian in my ward who talks all the time about killing people. Last night he got the number up to 10,000 he wanted to bump off.' But while it was clearly best to have the safeguard of his own cell, he wished they 'wouldn't lock the door at night'. Later, in court, Julien Cornell cited this as yet further proof of his client's deteriorating mental condition: 'He found the confinement intolerable. The claustrophobia which had come over him in Pisa now returned.'

Sometimes he was quite amused by the other inmates. Charles Olson, who began to visit him soon after he arrived at Howard Hall, describes him half complaining, half laughing at the way the whole ward and its troubles seem to have to go through his room, by his door, illustrating 'the poor guy in the next cell' by suddenly going down on his heels, and squatting all bent over, his hands over his head, as agile and quick as you please, a Kollwitz pose of misery.

He told Olson: 'I guess the definition of a lunatic is a man surrounded by them.' Certainly he had moments of high spirits; some years later he said he remembered 'a moment of quite irrational happiness in the hell-hole'. But a hell-hole Howard Hall quickly became for him, and remained.

When the doctors came to inspect him he behaved just as usual. Dr Edgar Griffin, in charge of Howard Hall, turned up the day after he had been admitted, and Ezra snarled at him: 'If this is a hospital, you have got to cure me.' 'Cure you of what?' asked Griffin. 'Whatever the hell is the matter with me – you must decide whether I am to be cured or punished.' He insisted on getting things his own way whenever possible.

> He does no ward work [wrote one of the doctors in an internal report], eats regularly without complaint, and manages to sleep well. He has arranged to receive a newspaper daily, a pint of milk every other day, and ice cream at intervals. Provided with shower privileges, at his request, he insisted upon tub baths, which were provided. He has made the acquaintance of several patients, but engages only in brief conversation with them. At no time has he been assaultive or combative or involved in any altercations with other patients.

(Olga remarked to Noel Stock in 1966: 'Ezra will always eat ice-cream.')

Another psychiatrist noted that, since being confined in Howard Hall, Ezra had

> cooperated with hospital procedures and in no way obstructed normal routines except by his persistent demands for extra attention. He spends most of his time lying upon his bed in his room, reading a Chinese text and a few slim volumes of poetry, making a few notes on random slips of paper.

Some of his demands astonished the doctors.

> The patient [wrote one of them] does not appreciate his status as a patient in Howard Hall, and continually makes extraordinary requests, even so far as to ask permission to roam beyond the 'wall' surrounding Howard Hall. He is adamant to this request, and cannot see the 'logic' in his incarceration.

To Ezra there was no 'logic' in it at all. If they would give him ice cream, tub baths, and pints of milk, why should they not let him out for a walk?

*

Christmas 1945 came and went. Something of a curiosity now, Ezra was examined by those of the staff psychiatrists who cared to look at him. They noted his 'superior manner', 'traits of egotism', 'tendency toward the belief that he is infallible', and his feeling that 'there was no use to discuss his ideas about monetary and economic theories because most people, including the examiner, would not be able to understand and comprehend them'.

It was not immediately brought to Overholser's attention that all those who had taken a look at Ezra thought him, for all his eccentricities, fundamentally sane. One of them wrote: 'His language is often esoteric, but does not represent condensation in a schizophrenic sense . . . While he may be obscure he is never disconnected or irrelevant.' At a formal Admission Conference on his case, three days after Christmas, six staff psychiatrists agreed that he was not suffering from any insane delusions. For example he 'denied' the idea, put to him by one of them, 'that he was a world saviour'. One of the six, Dr Addison Duval, says that before seeing Ezra for himself

> I had assumed that he was psychotic because our boss had already made a diagnosis . . . But I couldn't elicit any symptoms of psychosis at all. There were no delusions, no thought disorder, and no disturbance of orientation. He definitely did not seem to be insane.

The difficulty, says Duval, was that Overholser, 'our boss', had already stated the opposite in his report to the court. The six doctors began to feel 'quite a bit of anxiety' as to what they should do.

Eventually it was agreed that Duval would call on the Superintendent and present their doubts as tactfully as possible. Meanwhile they refrained from recording any formal diagnosis in the case notes, so as not to put their dissenting views in writing. Duval went to the Superintendent's office, where Overholser was 'very cordial' to him. But he told Duval that it was not desirable 'to disturb the practicalities of the situation'.

Overholser did, however, feel he should take another look at Ezra, and make a further report. Shortly before the jury hearing on the sanity issue, he went over to Howard Hall and talked to him again. Afterwards, he recorded that Ezra was suffering from such 'delusions' as believing he had invaluable influences and connections 'in a half dozen countries', and that he should have been brought to the USA 'not as a prisoner but as an adviser to the State Department'. It was Overholser's sole recorded report on Ezra during his entire confinement at St Elizabeths.

Ezra himself began to feel that he had suffered a mental collapse since being brought to Washington. He had remarked, in his letter to Ronald Duncan from prison, that there was a possibility that the 'lesion' he believed he had suffered in the cage in May might 'bust open' again under the 'renewed fatigues'; and now he decided that this had actually happened, exacerbated by his being confined to the Howard Hall cell. On Christmas Eve 1945, Julien Cornell informed Arthur Moore:

> Contrary to your expectation, Ezra has made no objection to the plea of insanity, in fact he is inclined to agree that he is mentally abnormal, at least at the present time.

To the doctors at Howard Hall, Ezra began to repeat the assertion that something had happened to his mind – or at least to his energies: 'They won't believe me when I tell them the main spring is busted . . . Oh, you don't understand – no one seems to understand – fatigue – I told them in August that the main spring would bust . . . No, I don't think I am insane, but I am so shot to pieces that it would take me years to write a sensible piece of prose. I think I am of unsound mind, and I don't think I have been shown good treatment here. I am absolutely unfit to transact any business.'

James Laughlin suggests that, despite the remarks about hollowness in the top of the head, Ezra's complaint of the 'main spring' being 'bust' referred to his neck, which he regarded as the delicate point of junction between brain and body; perhaps, continues Laughlin, he believed that the supposed flow of sperm to the brain was being impeded by some sort of 'lesion' or fracture there. Perhaps fortunately, he did not mention this notion to the doctor. However, soon after arriving at Howard Hall, he did mention that he could not 'understand how incarcerated males can stand the strain of being sexually potent without a normal release', and said that he 'vividly remembers a "wet dream" while at Pisa' – though he now felt he was 'going through the "climacteric"' (menopause), which he said would be 'something to be thankful for'. (In fact a loss of sexual desire commonly accompanies fatigue and depression such as he was experiencing.)

Two of the four psychiatrists who reported on him to the court noticed that he was complaining of exhaustion. Dr Muncie noted that Ezra seemed to think exhaustion was the cause of 'the breakdown in his thinking processes', and Dr King observed that during psychiatric examinations he would talk himself to 'the point of exhaustion'. But Ezra realized that exhaustion did not amount to insanity, and that he was not experiencing the hallucinations of the truly mad. 'If I was a loony, as FDR's gang wanted me to be,' he wrote some years later, 'I wd/ be "seein' things".' Soon after being confined in Howard Hall he told Charles Olson calmly that 'he didn't think there was anything wrong with him', though he 'admitted his mind was distracted and said that if he had to stay there much longer he would go bust'.

For much of the time over Christmas 1945 he allowed fatigue to overwhelm him, and in this mood resigned himself to the insanity defence, since he did feel a loss of mental power. Quite apart from being worn out by the months of imprisonment and the continual uncertainty about his fate, he was suffering a natural reaction to the years of furious activity which had culminated with the Rome broadcasts. Yet at some moments he was still his usual energetic self, once more envisaging conducting his own defence when the trial finally began. Dr Muncie told the court:

> He has two minds . . . At times he believes he could persuade any jury who could understand him of the fact that he had not committed treason. At other times, he states categorically that he is not of sound mind and could not participate effectively in his own defence.

Meanwhile, it became the opinion of Dr Joseph Gilbert of the Gallinger that, because the physical examination of Ezra had shown him to be healthy and normal, his complaints of fatigue were 'out of all proportion of any physical defects', and were therefore themselves another demonstration of insanity; another example of the *Alice in Wonderland* logic which had taken over the case.

On 10 January 1946 he was examined yet again by a St Elizabeths psychiatrist, this time a Dr Kendig, whose report had absolutely no bearing on future events, but which deserves attention in itself for an astuteness not characteristic of the St Elizabeths doctors. Kendig described Ezra as 'a brilliant but pedantic individual with a marked personality disorder of long standing'. His report examined two areas of Ezra's character not previously discussed by the psychiatrists, and contained some very different observations from those previously recorded:

> He is profoundly introverted, narcissistic and egocentric and subject to outbursts of temper. His character structure is essentially anal-erotic, his attitude to women is contemptuous and he displays some homosexual trends. While many of these qualities are schizoid and some of his attitudes paranoid, there is no evidence of psychosis. What does appear, however, are certain constrictive changes which are the function of age, accompanied by depressive mood coloring.

In layman's terms, Dr Kendig was saying: this man is a self-regarding individual with a tendency to lose his temper, who is not really attracted to women. He is not mad (though he shows signs of certain mental abnormalities), but his eccentricities are becoming more exaggerated as he gets older, and he is also beginning to suffer bouts of depression.

Ezra's frequent and (in his early life) self-confessed use of different masks and personae as a way of making contact with the exterior world, and his fondness for private systems of esoteric knowledge, are both classic symptoms of the 'schizoid' or potentially schizophrenic personality, the type of withdrawn and 'split' character whose mental breakdown (if it happens) usually takes the form of paranoia. But Kendig was concerned to emphasize that Ezra showed no evidence of 'psychosis' of this sort – that is, he had not gone all the way to true paranoid schizophrenia. And Kendig observed that there was also 'depressive mood coloring', swings of mood which are not commonly shown by the 'schizoid' personality, but rather by individuals of the manic-depressive type. In other words, Kendig felt that Ezra showed what seemed a contrasting, even a conflicting, set of psychological symptoms and could not be classified as any one type. In any event he was not mad. Kendig also seemed to feel that as he grew older the depressions might increase.

Kendig's report went on to the file with all the others, and nobody read it.

*

When he was in one of his upswings of mood, and not overwhelmed by feelings of exhaustion, Ezra passed the time in his cell by drafting notes for use when defending himself in court. They covered familiar ground: his belief that he was absolved of the charge of treason by the assurance the Italian authorities had given him that they would not influence the content of his broadcasts, and his conviction that free speech in an age of broadcasting must mean the right to say anything over the air.

As to his anti-Semitism, he wrote to Cornell explaining that he wanted to see the peaceful resettlement of the Jews in Palestine: 'You might note that am Zionist @ least to xtent of having Zionist plan – (no longer much hope they wd ever use it -) at least worked out plan. to financing & a solution. not conscripting.'

Meanwhile he continued to concern himself with *The Pisan Cantos*. Cornell reported to Arthur Moore just before Christmas 1945 that Ezra wanted to go over the typescript again before it was printed; Cornell said he would send the MS to Faber and Faber when 'Mr Pound has made the final revisions'. In London, Ronald Duncan tried to find a publisher for *The Unwobbling Pivot* after Eliot had finally turned it down; he took it to Eyre & Spottiswoode, where it was read by Graham Greene, then a director. Greene wrote to Duncan: 'Much as I should like to have Ezra Pound's name on my list, I'm afraid I can't do his Confucius. It seems to me an example of the Master at his most wobbling.'

*

Ezra wrote to Cornell from Howard Hall soon after Christmas: 'Problem now is not to go stark screaming hysteric cent per cent 24 hours per day.' Cornell wrote back from his New York office:

> I have received your several letters, including one written last Wednesday, in which you complain of feeling hysterical and express the need for fifteen minutes of sane conversation daily.
>
> I am sorry that there is no way at present by which you can be removed to other surroundings. If you think you are not getting the treatment which you need, I should be glad to take the matter up with Dr Overholser, but for the present you will have to remain where you are . . . The hearing . . . is to take place February 13th . . . I will see you in court on that day.

(The jury hearing, for no known reason, had been postponed from the 'late January' date envisaged by Judge Laws.) Cornell also passed on some news from Dorothy, who, during the autumn, had written from Rapallo:

> Can you get a message through to EP? I have no address.
>
> I want him to know that Omar was here for ten days, and the greatest possible comfort to me and full of filial piety towards both of us.
>
> That I have now received some money.

Ezra, as Dr Kendig had surmised, was now suffering regular mood swings, ups and downs which had rarely been perceptible in him before 1945. He described these in one of his many undated notes to Cornell: '. . . relapse after comfort of Tuesday. – v. mute . . . velocity after stupour tremendous.' And in another: 'enormous work to be done. & no driving force & everyone's inexactitude very fatiguing'. Yet another, dated 'end of Jan' and written from 'Dungeon', reads:

> mental torture
> constitution a religion
> a world lost
> grey mist barrier impas[s]able
> 　　　　ignorance absolute
> 　　　　　　　　anonyme
> futility of might have been
> coherent areas
> 　　　　constantly
> 　　　　invaded
> 　　aiuto [Italian for 'help']
> 　　　　　Pound

It might have served as the next canto.

*

He soon began to get his 'fifteen minutes of sane conversation' at fairly frequent intervals. Early in January 1946 he wrote to Cornell: 'Olson saved my life.'

On 4 January, at the suggestion of James Laughlin, Charles Olson paid him a visit. Olson had sent Laughlin a poem entitled 'A Lustrum for You, E.P.', beginning 'So, Pound, you have found the gallows tree . . .' Laughlin told him:

> Go around and see him . . . He can't seem to concentrate on reading or writing but he does enjoy talking to people – it seems to release some of his woes – and he's just as amusing to listen to as ever. You won't get a word in edgewise but you'll like it, I think.

After his first visit to Howard Hall, Olson wrote to Overholser requesting permission to call on Ezra regularly:

> My motive is the simplest: I wish to proffer a helping hand to him, and a sympathetic ear. I do it out of respect for his published work and to do whatever chores one writer might do for another. I happen to live in Washington . . . I think that both you and Mr Pound will want assurance, because I am a writer, that there is no hidden motive of publication. There is none: I should not wish to abuse his confidence, in our conversations.

Olson made detailed notes of the conversations – he had a Boswellian ear and memory for detail – but they were not published until both men were dead.

Born in 1910 and educated at Harvard, Olson had held several public offices in the wartime Roosevelt administration – including a job in the Office of War Information – and was especially sensitive towards racial prejudice, writing in 1944 against Fascist anti-Semitism: 'Attack is the first and final weapon of the fascist.' He had not yet had any collections of poetry or other major work published – in 1946 his printed *œuvre* consisted only of two articles and four occasional poems – but he had written a good deal of Pound-influenced verse, which he described as 'dragging my ass after Ezra'. When he came to see Ezra he was at a loose end, having abandoned both academic and political life to write a book on Herman Melville, which he was just finishing without knowing what to do next. He turned to Ezra partly in search of an oracle for his own future.

They met on 4 January 1946 in one of the 'visiting cubicles' at Howard Hall, a grim room with barred windows and a guard always present. Olson had attended the first court hearing on 27 November, when he had his first glimpse of Ezra and thought him 'older and weaker' than he had expected; but now he was struck by his 'eagerness and vigor as he came swiftly forward into the waiting room'. Moreover 'his hand was as strong or more than my own. And his flesh was fresh and strong.' Olson was impressed too by his politeness: 'He was most gracious about his talking . . . Explained one gets egotistical in a place like this! Made an effort to allow me to also speak. Was neat about who I was. "Is it possible I have seen your name on something in print?"'

Olson told him he would like to do something to help, and Ezra 'mentioned the things at Gallinger, papers, clothes, money to get the boy to go for papers and candy bars for him. He kept coming back to it. He feels lost without them, naturally.' (The books and papers and other mislaid belongings eventually turned up; they included Ronald Duncan's *Journal of a Husbandman*, the Morris Speare *Pocket Book of Verse* that Ezra had carried off from the DTC, and – rather less predictably – *A Lawyer Examines the Bible*.) Ezra assumed vaguely that Olson was an emissary from New Directions, Laughlin's publishing company, and mentioned the proofs of *The Unwobbling Pivot*, which Laughlin was publishing. Olson noticed that he had a certain waywardness in his vocabulary (perhaps as a result of exhaustion); he 'kept using some word like souvenirs, or splinters, which conveyed to me the opposite sense of what he meant'. To Olson he also 'suggested I write cards to people asking them to write to him, and explain that he could not answer. He can't seem to put down more than one or two sentences. I made to do it, but he said, my addresses are at Gallinger. We will have to wait.'

He soon wandered into favourite topics, telling Olson he still contemplated 'going to Tiflis to learn Georgian so that he could be sent to talk to Stalin. Emphasized how little attention Stalin would pay to some fat from the State Department talking the old bankers' line. Said so far as he knew they had one man in the State Dept. who spoke Georgian.' He talked to Olson about his sources of ideas on American history and economics, especially Brooks Adams, who had been notorious for his anti-Semitism and other extreme opinions, and challenged Olson to say 'if Adams was a Fascist. Repeated it. From which I backed away. For I do not want to engage in politics with him . . . I don't wish to get into it . . . I only wish to offer him some personal comforts, do some chores for him.'

He asked Olson for help with sorting out his clothes, 'fingering back and forth the end of his shirt sleeves under his jacket, which appear to have had none, or lost their buttons'. Despite this somewhat disarrayed appearance, he seemed to Olson to display 'his normal fastidiousness about laundry etc. He mentioned how everything goes into service' (that is, was washed in the St Elizabeths laundry). 'Spoke of his pajamas at Gallinger. He is neatly shaved, and his chin beard trimmed. His hair . . . stays put.' Olson 'said I would bring my wife over one day, and said I imagined it would be pleasant for him to see a woman again. He agreed heartily, and said only the nurse at Gallinger, and somewhere, Pisa? some matrons whom he described in a spate of Italian, which I understood ? to indicate some big horsey creatures.'

Olson liked him, feeling 'the charm and attraction of his person . . . He is as handsome and quick and at work as ever. His jumps in conversation are no more than I or any active mind would make. Once in awhile he seems to speak with an obsession, but even this I do, and at his age, after the fullness of his life, I imagine I might be a hell of a lot worse.' Olson felt he was talking to a normal, sane, healthy man: 'Actually he looks as a writer might working at his desk.'

Other visitors began to appear. Caresse Crosby of the Black Sun Press (who had once published his and Wyndham Lewis's *Imaginary Letters* which they had written in 1917 for the *Little Review*) came to see him during early January 1946, between Olson's first and second visits. She made the trip, says Olson, 'at the request of the hospital staff, who wanted to hear the impressions of someone who had known him many years ago. To her Ezra seemed no different. She marked, as a sign of his continued coherence, the way he corrected her as to dates in the past . . . concerning people or events they had known in common.' He told her: 'It is a shame I am in here. It is a time when if I were out I could do so much good.'

Olson himself called again ten days later, and found Ezra clothed in a new suit provided by Mrs Crosby. But 'at one point he pulled up the top of his drawers and pointed out he had now to wear them all the time, night and day, because his things hadn't come from Gallinger . . . Asked me . . . to bring him . . . an old pair of mine. I said I didn't wear them.' During this second visit, he mentioned to Olson the name of Westbrook Pegler, a right-wing journalist who had won a Pulitzer for opposing corruption in labour unions. 'Does anyone know Westbrook Pegler?' Ezra asked. Olson indicated that he didn't, 'and must have froze more than I ever have with him. He then called him "the best man they've got". And with that, for the first time, the full shock of what a fascist s.o.b. Pound is caught up with me . . . For Pegler I have traveled through and understood. Pound's praise of him reveals his utter incomprehension of what is going on, and what has happened to himself. Just on a technical level, that such an ear as Pound's could permit itself to praise Pegler! What a collapse. I wondered then how long more I can hold out my hand to him as a poet and a man.'

'I suppose,' continues Olson in his notes on this second meeting, 'I shall tell him one day that I am the son of immigrants,' (a Swedish father and an Irish mother), 'this influx of second class citizens whom Pegler and Pound think has made impure their Yankee America of pioneers . . . That my father was killed fighting for the right of labor men to organize in unions.' (Olson's father died of a stroke in 1935 after campaigning against the US Post Office for the postal union.) 'Meanwhile I shall do what I can, as long as I can, for this fool of hate because once he was also a fool of love.' Ezra was not blind to Olson's racial status. 'I have as much or more of a quarrel with the Swedes and the Irish as with the Yids,' he told him at one of their meetings, 'so you better watch out.' Some years later he implied that Olson was Jewish: 'Mr Olson's (Chas) fambly is NOT of Schweeditsch origin.'

At the second meeting, Ezra asked Olson 'to write his daughter and tell her he was no maniac, and not "repulsive". I asked him if he had heard from them [Mary and Olga], and it seemed he had had a letter from them written in October.'

Although he still thought him sane, Olson decided that Ezra should definitely be kept in custody, 'or if released, he should be under the strictest of control . . . I should . . . put him in some less enclosed place, give him privacy and simple care, books and paper, and freedom to continue his literary work. This could be done within the framework of the Federal prison system . . . But he should under no circumstance be given any freedom which would allow him to do what he called to C[aresse] C[rosby] "good".'

This was in mid-January. Olson noticed that 'as things stand now he is not doing a bit of work. His mind flies off . . . He said that it had been hard going for him to get through Ayn Rand's *Fountainhead* [a 1943 American bestseller]. Apparently newspapers, and magazines, are about his limit.'

Olson asked him if Cornell or Laughlin had been down to see him. 'He said no, he had had a couple of postcards, they were off skiing somewhere. He then said I was his only anchor to windward.' However, the elderly Mapel sisters were still visiting him regularly, though he told Olson he 'couldn't expect much . . . they were too old'. Also, Laughlin had written to Overholser asking permission to visit: 'To see him now enmeshed in this terrible predicament is really heart-rending,' he wrote. 'I cannot endorse his anti-semitism – which I attribute to his disease, for certainly it is a fairly recent thing with him – but in spite of that I want to do anything I can to help him or to make him comfortable.'

Olson, still smarting from the remarks about Westbrook Pegler, ended their second meeting furiously angry at Ezra's evidence of Fascism: 'All he wants is the purring and tears of fellow fascists . . . Poor, poor Pound, the great gift, the true intellectual, rotting away, being confined and maltreated by the Administration. SHIT. And he is taken in by it! Here he's a punk like the rest of them.'

*

But when Olson called again, for twenty minutes on the afternoon of 24 January, everything 'was completely different in tone. It is strange, but the only word is gay. Right from the start it was wild and strong. I brought myself forward more, and Pound did too.'

They were in a different visiting cubicle, less forbidding. 'The guard was different too, less interesting than the regular one, so we sort of forgot him. Except when Pound as always so instantly gracious, was quick to suggest he have a cigarette as I was opening a package to give one to Pound.' (Ezra had not smoked regularly since his youth, but would occasionally do so if a cigarette were offered.) 'The guard declined, and with that Pound says, CHAW CUT PLUG. And repeated it, CHAW CUT PLUG. Explained to the guard he meant that's the only thing he guessed the guard did.' (He was no doubt remembering Ole Man Comley in Canto 28: 'Boys! / Never cherr terbakker.') 'The sudden explosion of Pound's voice in this phrase,' continues Olson, 'was quite total to me. It was the poet making sounds, trying them out to see if they warmed his ear. But it was the fascist, too, as a snob, classing the guard.'

Olson learnt that Ezra was being fatigued by the constant questions of one of the psychiatrists, a young doctor named Jerome Kavka. 'Poor Kavka does seem to be scared to death of this Pound business, and to be handling it in an absurd way because of his fear and uncertainty . . . Pound . . . says Kavka keeps pounding questions at him – and punched his fist against the wall of his other hand to illustrate the effect. He says he wakes up the following morning exhausted from trying to think back and work out the answers to his questions.'

Dr Kavka, apparently on his own initiative, was subjecting Ezra to sessions of intense questioning about his personal history, including sexual – which Ezra greatly resented, and about which he was thoroughly uncommunicative. Kavka afterwards wrote it up, with quotes from what Ezra had told him, in a fifteen-page document, unsophisticated to the point of naïvety, but full of nuggets of information that Kavka unearthed through sheer persistence. It is also refreshingly without the judgements, either psychiatric or political, which cloud most people's accounts of their conversations with Ezra in the hospital.

Kavka records that 'The formal interview was conducted over a period of several weeks. This was made necessary by the change in the patient's attitude from day to day. Occasionally becoming angry and irritated over his status, he would refuse to follow orthodox methods of questioning, and would ramble on in a devious fashion, skipping rapidly from one topic to another, with his own "trials and tribulations" always the center of discussion. On some days he would appear sullen and uncooperative, and the interview would have to be terminated after several minutes. Usually, however, the patient accepted the opportunuity to go to the examining room as a variation from what he called "boredom on the ward". Most interviews were relatively short, due to the early fatiguability of the patient. He . . . preferred to lie sprawled on a bed during the interview.'

Ezra exploded to Olson on the subject of Kavka: 'I never knew a doctor less scientific. If they want to examine me, why don't they give me some scientist, I wouldn't mind. He merely acts like a goddam bureaucrat. But this intolerable questioning. Good god, what the hell, what the hell difference does it make what I was reading in 1902!' At this point, Olson noticed, 'Pound just continued to swear, and wondering if there was any "lady" in the next cubicle, saying he wouldn't want to shock them, he jumps up and looks around the corner, and finding none, continues to let it rip.'

Olson told him not to worry about Kavka, reassuring him, from his own encounters with Kavka, that 'K is frightened to death, not of you so much, as of the fact that it is the Ezra Pound case . . . He's no more than a graduate student, trying to act professional.' The name Kavka does not seem to have struck any chord with Ezra, who if he had read *The Trial* and *The Castle* might have thought them not inapplicable to his own situation. He assumed Dr Kavka to be a Jew who hated him for his anti-Semitism. 'With ANTISEMITE spread all over the front page of *PM*,' he remarked to Olson, 'you can't expect much else.' In order to shock Kavka, he dug up from his memory a squib he had written in the 1920s.

'Pound,' records Olson, 'performed for K what he calls his YIDDISH CHARLESTON, composed originally for Louis Zukofsky.' The poem had been published by Zukofsky in his *Objectivists' Anthology* in 1932:

> Gentle Jheezus sleek and wild
> Found disciples tall an' hairy
> Flirting with his red hot Mary,
> > Now hot momma Magdalene
> > is doing front page fer the screen
> > > Mit der yittischer Charleston Pband
> > Mit
> > deryiddischercharles
> > > > tonband.

> ole king Bolo's big black qween
> Whose bum was big as a soup tureen
> Has lef' the congo
> > > and is now seen
> > Mit der *etc.*

> Calvin Coolidg dh' pvwezident
> He vudn't go but dh' family vwent,
> > > Vuddunt giff notding but his name vass lent
> > For deh yittischer *etc.*

> Red hot Mary of Magdala
> Had nine jews an a Roman fellow
> Nah she'z gotta
> > chob much swellah
> > Mit der yiddisher Charleston Band.
> > mit der YIDDISHER
> > > Charleston BAND.

Dr Kavka was amazed by this performance. 'K says it is something!' wrote Olson, 'and regrets he didn't get a recording.'

*

Olson hoped to get to know Kavka informally, and invited him to dinner; Kavka declined, 'for fear of compromising the case'. Olson surmised that 'probably K is also scared of that s.o.b. Griffin, who is his boss' (Dr Griffin, in charge of Howard Hall). However, at Olson's request, Kavka arranged to get Ezra some more pairs of long under-drawers, and 'at least had the curiosity to read his verse, and . . . in Chicago, when the book-stores said they wouldn't carry the books of a fascist, [Kavka] objected and damn well told them that was the same as burning books, and plain out and out fascist.'

Olson was struck that Ezra had taken Kavka's questioning with complete seriousness, however much it infuriated him; he did not, as some might have done, merely behave contemptuously towards Kavka or give frivolous answers. 'Pound will spend his night honestly seeking answers to K's questions, genuinely trying to give this Jew what he wants . . . He will mention his debt to the Jew in Rome who suggested to him to translate Confucius. He remains on the creative side of him, whole, and as charming and open and warm a human being as I know. Despite all the corruption of his body politic. It is this contradiction,' concluded Olson after his third visit to Ezra,' which keeps me from turning my back on him.'

Olson was now trying to show Ezra how much he disapproved of his politics. When Ezra mentioned another right-wing journalist, Mrs Austine Cassini of the Washington *Times–Herald*, who had shown a shallow sympathy towards him, Olson tried to lecture him about this and similar enthusiasms: 'Such people are not your friends, Mr Pound. They do you no good.' But he observed that Ezra paid not the slightest attention to this or any other attempts to make him consider himself. 'He made nothing of it, as he doesn't of any remark to him, actually. You can see him take such things into himself, and know he hears, but that's all.'

Olson had neither heard the broadcasts nor read any of the transcripts, and so had no idea what Ezra had actually said on the radio (Dr Kavka was similarly ignorant). Consequently he was deeply shocked when, during a visit to Ezra on 7 February 1946, Ezra described the second of the Italian Cantos (Canto 73), with its account of the girl leading the Canadian soldiers deliberately into a minefield, and spoke of her as 'one of the resistance'. Olson suddenly realized for the first time that he was listening to 'not only . . . a fascist, but the ENEMY'. His notes on the conversation continue:

> The strange thing was that there was no awareness on his part that we [Olson's wife was also present] might take this as what for the very first time I have seen: TREASON. There it was staring us in the face and speaking out bold. And yet let me record: merely there it was. A fact. I felt no surprise. Nor, I confess, did it shock and repel me as did his reference to Pegler or his antisemitism. I am bewildered.

Olson's visits continued at fairly frequent intervals. One day he would find Ezra feeling exaggeratedly sorry for himself – on 29 January 1946 he inscribed a copy of the Cantos to Olson as 'my onlye sustainer' – and a week later he was in the same mood: 'The whole effect today was of a demoralized man. He had nothing but the tatters of dignity left. It was all, cover my brother's nakedness . . . Even his parting remark: "Thank you for coming. You have saved my life more than once.". . . . At another point, he came up from his hands on his head, to sway out with, "I'm sorry to be so lachrymose."' Olson sensed more than a degree of theatricality behind all this, and found it 'very unpleasant'. On other days Ezra would be full of vigour and self-confidence. Olson even felt that his physical appearance was changing from day to day: one afternoon he would seem plump, healthy, fit; another time 'he looks bad, his skin scaly, his eyes ratty, his beard sparse . . . his hair mothy.'

His mood swings were perfectly genuine, but he was exaggerating them theatrically. And Olson had caught him while he was, so to speak, between personae. His pre-Pisa anger and volubility, the rage which had chiefly characterized him in the 1933 to 1943 period, could have no function at St Elizabeths, since he was among endless people who were just like that – such as the Indian who wanted to kill ten thousand. As Olson watched, he was beginning to develop a performance that would fit his new way of life and surroundings; but as yet it was scarcely formed in his mind; hence the frequent variations.

9

Unsound Mind

Cornell continued to be optimistic about the outcome of the legal proceedings. He wrote to Dorothy on 25 January 1946, three weeks before the postponed jury hearing:

> I have learned from questioning the doctors that they do not anticipate any substantial change in your husband's condition and also that they do not think he needs to remain very long in a hospital. I expect, therefore, that after a few months the case will be dropped and he will be set free.

It seems incredible that Cornell could really have believed this, or have been told it by Overholser or other doctors involved in the case. He was not even in Washington during this period, and there is no evidence that he was in touch with the doctors. It is almost impossible to understand how his mind was working.

He knew that the four doctors appointed by prosecution and defence would unanimously tell the court that Ezra was mad – he told Dorothy that the result of the jury hearing 'is a foregone conclusion since all the doctors are in agreement' – but he gave no explanation of how this could possibly lead to Ezra's release or the 'dropping' of the case. His letter to Dorothy concluded: 'You may rejoice that we have found a way to get round the difficulties presented by the indictment against him, and that these difficulties are all but surmounted.'

*

Quite apart from the sheer legal improbability that the court would unconditionally release, on grounds of insanity, a man found unfit to stand trial for a very serious crime, Cornell was taking no account of the continuing tide of anti-Pound public opinion. The *Saturday Review of Literature* said of him in its issue of 15 December 1945:

> There is no alibi for a charge of treason . . . He desires a world in which Mussolinis and Ezra Pounds could satisfy their egomanias . . . Such a man should not escape penalty for his misdeed.

Besides William Joyce (who was hanged on 3 January 1946), another English broadcaster from Berlin, John Amery, who had pleaded guilty to treason, had also now been executed. The *Washington Post* printed an editorial comparing Ezra's case to theirs, and doubting whether he 'was ever important or dangerous enough to exact the price of his treason in blood'; but other papers unquestioningly put him in the same category as Joyce, and a group of New York citizens signed a letter to President Truman claiming that he had 'assisted the perpetrators of the slaughter-chambers' and demanding that he 'suffer the same sentence meted out by the English people to traitors Amery and Lord Haw-Haw'. The 25 December 1945 issue of *New Masses* printed its symposium on Ezra's case, in which four writers all judged that his profession of poet should not automatically exempt him from the death sentence; among them was Arthur Miller, who declared that Ezra exceeded even Hitler in 'sheer obscenity . . . He knew all America's weaknesses and he played on them as expertly as Goebbels ever did'.

*

The prosecution did not initially intend to accept the four doctors' report without demur. Memoranda were passing within the Department of Justice and the FBI, emphasizing that the three army psychiatrists at Pisa had found the prisoner sane, and proposing that the contributors to Charles Norman's predominantly sympathetic symposium in *PM* (Williams, Cummings, and other of Ezra's friends) should be questioned as to their impressions of his mental health. The rumour had begun to emerge from St Elizabeths that the doctors there did not think he was mad, and that Overholser was suppressing the truth. On 7 January 1946 *Newsweek* published a report that 'so many curious psychiatrists' had been taking a look at Ezra's 'case reports' that the documents were now 'under lock and key' in case they be 'mislaid or lost'. The story concluded: 'Incidentally, some who have looked into the case believe the poet is sane enough to stand trial for treason.'

On 12 February, the day before the jury hearing, Overholser had a private talk with Cornell, who had just arrived from New York, and admitted to him that 'many of the young doctors' on his staff disagreed with the diagnosis that Ezra was mad. Overholser said he felt they were 'in

error'. He suggested that their judgement might be 'distorted by patriot-
ism', and said he himself was 'the responsible official, he had reviewed the
opinions of his juniors, and remained unshaken in his own opinion'.

Cornell was astonished at this confidential revelation from Overholser
that not everyone agreed with his diagnosis, especially as Overholser
followed it by saying he was not going to mention it to Isaiah Matlack, the
chief prosecutor. This was the prosecution's chief witness refusing to help
them, and imparting confidences to the defence. Cornell judged that
Overholser was 'a most unusual man'.

Actually, Overholser's behaviour was perfectly logical. He had no
intention of tolerating insurgence among his junior doctors, whose criticism of his diagnosis had made him all the more determined to push it
through in court. He was tipping Cornell off just in case the junior doctors'
opinion was brought to the notice of the court, whereupon Cornell would
be ready to attack it and help Overholser reassert his own view.

*

Olson found Ezra very edgy about the continued postponement of the jury
hearing. 'He said they had had him dressed and waiting to go all last
Tuesday, even after the hearing had been cancelled, but no one apparently
thought to let him or Howard Hall know. As he said: "I don't know what
goes on. Who to believe. Cornell writes that the hearing will be next week.
But what is going on?"' He fretted that 'Laughlin has not come, has not
sent him the proofs of the Confucius: "Which is the base of my defense."'

The hearing finally took place on Wednesday 13 February 1946. Cornell
was worried as to how Ezra might behave in court; he had not set eyes on
him since the previous hearing on 21 December, and Ezra's letters in the
interim had alarmed him. Fearing that Ezra might 'blow up', Cornell spoke
to him before the court convened, and 'told him that I would not put him
on the witness stand, and he did not need to do anything but listen to the
proceedings'. In other words, he wanted Ezra once again to play the
passive madman. Ezra's reply is not recorded. Perhaps it was one of his
'down' days, and he was prepared to let the chance of defending himself
finally slip past.

Cornell, arriving in court, observed that it was 'well attended. Laughlin
was there.' So was a large number of reporters, including Albert Deutsch,
who had persistently written anti-Pound pieces for *PM*.

Judge Laws opened the proceedings by announcing that he was 'going to
impanel a jury' to decide whether, as alleged, the defendant 'is not in
mental condition such that he is able to participate with counsel in the trial
of a criminal case, and is not in position to understand the full nature of the
charges against him'. The judge said that if 'the jury finds that his mental
state is as has been represented to me, then Mr Pound will not be brought

to trial because, under the law, it would not be proper to prosecute him'. A reporter from the *New York Herald Tribune* noticed that, during this, Ezra 'moved nervously in his seat, held his head in his hands or leaned back and stared at the ceiling'.

One juror was dismissed because he said he had known Ezra 'ever since he has been there in the hospital' (this was a man named John Wingfield, presumably on the staff of St Elizabeths). None of the others was challenged by prosecution or defence, but Cornell asked Judge Laws if the jury could seriously be expected to deliver an impartial verdict in view of the fact that the defendant had been critical of the US Government in his broadcasts, and had also made 'some statements which might be construed as anti-Semitic'. The clerk of the court put this question to the jury; no juror offered any reply, and Cornell and Matlack then declared themselves satisfied with the jury, which was sworn in.

Cornell called his first witness, Dr Wendell Muncie. Dr Muncie had seen Ezra again since he had been moved to St Elizabeths, and now told the court that he

> has a number of rather fixed ideas which are either clearly delusional or verging on the delusional. One I might speak of, for instance, he believes he has been designated to save the Constitution of the United States for the people of the United States . . . Secondly, he has a feeling that he has the key to the peace of the world through the writings of Confucius, which he translated into Italian and into English, and that if this book had been given proper circulation the Axis would not have been formed, we would be at peace now, and a great deal of trouble could have been avoided . . . Third, he believes that with himself as a leader, a group of intellectuals could have gotten together in different countries, like Japan, for instance, where he is well thought of, to work for world order . . . He feels he was being double-crossed in being brought back to this country, thinking that he was being brought back to aid the country.

He said that in general Ezra 'shows a remarkable grandiosity. He feels that he has no peer in the intellectual field, although conceding that one or two persons he has assisted might, on occasion, do as good work as he did.' Muncie observed that Ezra was unable to pursue his own ideas logically or methodically, but was lost in the vagueness of them: 'I would say he is unable to make a solution of his own fixed ideas, and he cannot explain the balance or significance.' He also suffered, said Muncie, from 'considerable distractibility . . . he moves from topic to topic'. He also alleged that there were moments when Ezra made 'a great push' mentally, but this only produced 'a condition which we refer to as stupor when nothing comes.

He just holds his head and nothing comes, and at those times he has complained of a feeling of emptiness in the forehead, or a feeling of pressure in the forehead.'

Muncie went on to cite what seemed to him definite evidence of mental unreliability, saying that the first time he examined Ezra he had mentioned to him that 'my brother had been a student at Wabash College . . . He obviously did not remember my brother and the matter was passed off lightly. When I saw him on January 7th I was reintroduced to him by the other doctors, and his immediate comment was, "Yes, you have a brother." and "he was my best student, he had just come back from Europe, and he came from a family of the highest culture in Indiana."' Muncie described this as 'pure confabulation . . . a confusion of facts in the face of real lack of memory about my brother'. (He did not say, however, whether Ezra's description of his brother was true or false, whether Ezra had in fact taught his brother or not, or whether there had been some other student by the name of Muncie in Ezra's class at Wabash in 1907 with whom Ezra might have confused him.) Questioned by Cornell, Muncie asserted that this 'confabulation' was caused by 'loss of memory', and 'usually appears in people with some kind of deteriorating process of the brain'. Muncie also alleged that, having 'read a great deal of his writings in connection with preparing this case . . . it is my idea that there has been for a number of years a deterioration of the mental processes'.

Cornell asked Muncie if he could supply any account or explanation of Ezra in 'medical diagnostic terminology . . . or doesn't that add anything to the picture?' Muncie answered:

> I don't think it does. Those are of a statistical nature. I would say in ordinary language he has been a peculiar individual for many, many years, and that on top of that in recent years, I don't know how long back, he has been engrossed with the things I have talked about as neurotic developments. For statistical purposes we could call this a paranoid condition.

Cornell asked Muncie if Ezra 'in his present condition would be able to stand up under the rigors of a cross-examination', to which Muncie replied: 'I think it would be rather dangerous to his welfare.'

Matlack now cross-examined Muncie, who conceded that 'a peculiar personality' did not necessarily 'denote insanity . . . in the strict sense of the term'. He also admitted that Ezra's particular 'delusions' – believing that he had a mission to save the Constitution, and that his translation of Confucius was a key to world peace – did not themselves prove that 'he was insane' and unable 'to consult with counsel and to understand the charge he is charged with'. Matlack cited Ezra's belief that he and other intellectuals could achieve world peace, asking Muncie: 'Does that indicate insanity?' Muncie answered: 'It indicates to my mind that he is getting farther and farther away from the reality of the situation. Whether that in itself constitutes insanity, I would say no, one is entitled to some queer ideas without being called insane.' Muncie also conceded that Ezra 'understands the nature of the charge' he was facing. Matlack asked whether his 'delusions' were 'any different than some of these other European leaders had in that they had an idea they were going to conquer the world?' To which Muncie replied: 'It might be, but I have never examined them.'

Without unduly exerting himself, Matlack had knocked a very large hole in Muncie's argument that Ezra was insane. If the members of the jury were attending properly they must have gone some considerable way towards being convinced that he was capable of standing trial for treason. But now, as later in the hearing, Matlack failed to press home the advantage, and seemed only to be going through the formalities of questioning the doctors' opinion. Albert Deutsch, writing in *PM* next day, drew attention to this, saying that Matlack and his colleague had shown 'an impressive unfamiliarity with the psychiatric issues at stake and a lacka-daisical interest in its political implications. They acted throughout as if they were going through the motions.'

It would seem that the Department of Justice now privately felt that the case would be best resolved by having Ezra Pound declared insane. Matlack doubtless realized that the prosecution would have a hard task proving that what he had said on the air from Rome really amounted to treason, not to mention the difficulties of producing two witnesses to each 'overt act'. For him to stand trial but then be acquitted would produce a howl of outrage from the American public, which might damage the Administration. Better in these circumstances to let him be swept under the insanity carpet, imprisoned without trial.

After Matlack had concluded his skimpy cross-questioning of Muncie, Cornell put some further questions to Muncie, who agreed that Ezra had 'a system of reasoning which is embedded in his mentality so that it is impossible for him to think outside of that system', to the extent that it would be 'impossible . . . for him to understand this charge made against him'. This was an exact contradiction of what Muncie had just told the prosecutor – he had said that Ezra 'understands the nature of the charge'. Judge Laws now emphasized, for the benefit of the jury, that all four doctors had signed a joint statement – he asked Muncie to confirm this – and remarked that he did not think 'it was brought out that your examination was in connection with Dr Overholser'. Muncie admitted to this, and said there had been 'no disagreement at all' in the diagnosis. It was now possible to perceive what amounted to the collusion of all four expert witnesses. Certainly Overholser had pulled the rug from under the prosecution by persuading his fellow doctors to agree on a medical judgement favoured by the defence. The prosecution did not appear to mind.

Dr Marion King, medical director of the prison service, was now called, and admitted to Cornell that he had read 'very little' of Ezra's poetry: 'I have seen one of the Cantos, and samples of his poetry that have been reproduced from others.' He had, however, studied some of Ezra's economic tracts, and had seen transcripts of some of the broadcasts. His opinion was that Ezra 'has always been a sensitive, eccentric, cynical person, and these characteristics have been accentuated in the last few years to such an extent that he is afflicted with a paranoid state of psychotic proportions which renders him unfit for trial'.

King was not a specialist in psychiatry. Pressed by Matlack's colleague Donald Anderson to give an example of supposed paranoia, he cited the fact that Ezra had mentioned to him his argument about a visa at the American passport office in Paris in 1919, which Ezra regarded as the start of his campaign against abuses in US Government circles:

> He told a story [said King] of being mistreated or abused by a
> minor consular official . . . and elaborated on that as an example
> of the tyranny of government officials. It may be very true that
> he was mistreated, but that is not sufficient justification for such
> a reaction.

Few psychiatrists would have asserted that this single incident and Ezra's views on bureaucrats conclusively proved paranoia. But Anderson for the prosecution did not press the matter, and allowed King to observe that Ezra had 'never hesitated to criticize, or vilify, or condemn others in no uncertain terms, even without provocation, or without any cause.'

King now ventured into the technicalities of psychiatry – strikingly he, the non-psychiatrist among them, was the only one of the four doctors willing to do so – and asserted that Ezra was suffering from one of those 'paranoid states' which was 'part way between so-called paranoid schizophrenia or dementia praecox, paranoid type, and true paranoia. There are all types or gradations between the extremes, and it is my opinion that he falls in between these two extremes.' This was little more than a display of jargon to impress the jury, and not even very accurate psychiatric jargon (it is not at all clear what King meant to convey by these distinctions, which are not found in psychiatric textbooks); and in any case King was only saying that it was impossible to classify Ezra's supposed paranoia. Moreover, under questioning from the prosecution he admitted that it was 'sometimes' possible to get straight answers from Ezra, and that it would make a difference if an attorney 'skilled in such matters' questioned him carefully. But once again, the prosecution made no attempt to widen this very considerable breach in King's argument.

Overholser was now called. He said he had 'no reason' to change his opinion about the diagnosis that Ezra was unfit to stand trial: 'It is quite obvious that the man has always been unusually eccentric through the years. He has undoubtedly a high regard of his own opinion, and has been extremely vituperative of those who disagree with him.' He asserted that Ezra's 'grandiosity of ideas . . . goes far beyond the normal. From a practical view of his advising with his attorney, there would be the fact that you cannot keep him on a straight line of conversation; he rambles around, and has such a naïve grasp of the situation in which he finds himself, it would not be fair to him or his attorney to put him on trial.'

Under prosecution cross-questioning, Overholser admitted that 'with an infinite amount of patience, and an infinite amount of time, it might be possible sometime in the future to get a lucid answer to a question'; but no more than that. Matlack now touched on the rumour, which had reached him despite Overholser's attempts to suppress it, that not all the St Elizabeths doctors thought Ezra Pound mad. Overholser would only say in reply: 'There has been some discussion about him which has not been formal . . . there has been no formal diagnosis.' Matlack – which would have been astonishing had he been making a serious attempt to conduct the prosecution – let the matter rest there.

Ezra himself had sat silently throughout all these proceedings. Matlack now asked Overholser: 'Did he give you in his general history anything about his belief in Fascism?' Overholser answered: 'I did not discuss that with him particularly.' At this point Ezra jumped to his feet and shouted out: 'I never did believe in Fascism, God damn it; I am opposed to Fascism.' After this, says Cornell, he 'slumped again in his seat'. The *Newsweek* report of the trial adds: 'Quieted by his lawyer, Pound dropped his head dejectedly on the table.'

The incident was likely to give judge and jury the impression of mental instability rather than the opposite. Judge Laws did not reprove Ezra for the outburst, nor address him at all, but simply allowed Cornell's objection to this whole 'line of questioning', telling Matlack: 'Try not to disturb him if you can help it.'

Continuing his cross-examination of Overholser, Matlack asked if Ezra's belief that he had not done anything treasonable was not perfectly normal in the circumstances – 'Isn't it a fact that people charged with crime do that?' Overholser answered: 'Yes.' After further questioning he admitted that the army psychiatrists at Pisa had felt that Ezra was only suffering from 'anxiety neurosis' and 'not . . . from a major mental disease'. But Matlack and his colleagues at the Department of Justice had not bothered to call as witnesses the three army doctors in question. These doctors afterwards averred that nobody ever tried to contact them to ask about their findings, and though Matlack had had access to their reports – had indeed evidently seen them – he did not quote from them in court.

The final witness was Dr Joseph Gilbert, the staff psychiatrist from Gallinger, who gave much the same account of Ezra as had the other three doctors. Anderson cross-questioned him rather languidly for the prosecution, and nothing new was unearthed.

The following conversation then occurred between Cornell, Matlack, and Judge Laws; the trial transcript records that it was 'out of the hearing of the jury':

> *Matlack*: You are not going to call Pound?
> *Cornell*: I don't think so.
> *Matlack*: I was going to ask the Court to call him as the Court's witness. [That is, to give the prosecution an opportunity of demonstrating to the jury that he was, in fact, sane.]
> *Judge Laws*: I don't think so. If we call him he will take two or three hours. [There had already been a lunch recess.] I do not think it is necessary. The Court of Appeals says very plainly you cannot disregard an opinion of the psychiatrists.
> *Cornell*: I am afraid he might blow up. He has been pretty nervous.
> *Judge*: You don't want to argue the case, do you?
> *Cornell*: No.
> *Matlack*: No.

Ezra's fate had hung on how Matlack would answer this last question. If Matlack had chosen to 'argue the case', to conduct further cross-examinations of witnesses with the intention of proving him sane and capable of standing trial, that goal might indeed have been achieved – Matlack and Anderson had come near it again and again during the day. But Matlack said he did not want to. Clearly it was now acceptable enough to him, and to the Attorney General, with whom he must have been in consultation, to see Ezra committed to the asylum, without the risk of losing the prosecution case in a treason trial.

After this private exchange, both counsel returned to their seats, and in the hearing of the jury Cornell asked Judge Laws if he would now direct the jury to return a verdict that Ezra was insane. The judge did not agree to this, but delivered a summing-up which, as Cornell remarks in his book, gave the jury such clear hints that they could be in no doubt as to what verdict they should bring:

> Members of the Jury [said Judge Laws], there is a provision of
> our code . . . to the effect that whenever a person is indicted for

an offense . . . and if the jury shall find the accused to be then insane the Court may then bring about a commitment of the defendant to hospitalization, to remain in hospitalization until or unless there comes a time when it is found that he has recovered from his mental difficulties, and in that event he is certified back into the court for trial . . .

In this particular case the defendant is charged with a serious offense, the offense of treason which, under certain conditions might result, if he is found guilty, in his punishment by electrocution, and when he was arraigned in court there was some suggestion made . . . that he was having mental difficulty . . . We brought him to the point of having him examined by psychiatrists and physicians on mental diseases . . . These doctors . . . filed a written certificate with the Court indicating their unanimous view that Mr Pound under his present state of mind was not in position to stand a trial, to cooperate with his counsel, and go through with a serious charge of this nature . . .

It therefore becomes your duty now to advise me whether in your judgement you find that Mr Pound is in position to cooperate with the counsel, to stand trial without causing him to crack up or break down; whether he is able to testify, if he sees fit, at the trial, to stand cross-examination, and in that regard, of course, you have heard the testimony of all these physicians on the subject, and there is no testimony to the contrary and, of course, these are men who have given a large part of their professional careers to the study of matters of this sort, who have been brought here for your guidance.

Under the state of the law you are not necessarily bound by what they say; you can disregard what they say and bring in a different verdict, but in a case of this type where the Government and the defense representative have united in a clear and unequivocal view with regard to the situation, I presume you will have no difficulty in making up your mind.

The jury then retired. After only three minutes they returned into the court.

The Clerk of the Court: Mr Foreman, has the jury agreed upon its verdict?
The Foreman of the Jury: It has.
The Clerk of the Court: What say you as to the respondent Ezra Pound? Is he of sound or unsound mind?
The Foreman of the Jury: Unsound mind.
The Clerk of the Court: Members of the jury, your foreman

says you find the respondent Ezra Pound of unsound mind, and
that is your verdict so say you each and all?
*(All members of the jury indicated in the affirmative.) (There-
upon, the hearing was concluded.)*

*

Albert Deutsch reported in *PM* next day: 'When the verdict of insanity was
brought in, [Pound] jumped up with alacrity and engaged in affable
conversation with his young lawyer.' James Laughlin, writing to Eliot two
days later, said Ezra seemed very pleased with the verdict and was grateful
to Cornell for having saved his life.

If that is really what he felt, he was clearly unaware of his legal situation.
Perhaps he still assumed that Cornell could get him out on bail and send
him back to Italy a free man. The *New York Herald Tribune* knew better.
The morning after the hearing it observed that this was 'the first time an
accused war criminal has escaped trial because of insanity', and continued:

> The sixty-year-old poet will be confined at the St Elizabeths
> Federal Hospital for the Insane. He may again face trial if he
> recovers from his present 'paranoiac state', government pros-
> ecutors said, pointing out that a treason charge has no limita-
> tion, being valid until the defendant dies.

The newspaper added that the Italian witnesses who were to have given
evidence against him were to be sent home. This indicated that the
Government had no expectation of his 'recovering' in the near future, so
that a trial could take place. Clearly they assumed he would remain in St
Elizabeths indefinitely.

*

Julien Cornell observes in his book on the case: 'Thus Pound found
himself, in effect, under a sentence of life imprisonment despite the fact
that he was innocent in the eyes of the law.' But he was not 'innocent in the
eyes of the law': he had simply not been brought to trial. And what else
could Cornell have expected to be the outcome? He calls the situation 'this
peculiar legal paradox'. It was a paradox solely of his own making, brought
about entirely by his method of conducting the defence.*

*After reading this account of the legal proceedings and his conduct of the defence, Julien
Cornell wrote to the author (3 July 1986): 'It is easy to say by hindsight that the situation
should have been more accurately predicted, but at the time this was impossible. Please
understand that this was the first case of its kind and it aroused something of a furor. There
was no precedents to guide me and the government gave no inkling of what it would do. In
fact, I think the government's lawyers themselves did not have any idea what they were going
to do with Pound if he should be found unfit for trial. In such a situation, it seems to me
unfair to accuse me of lack of foresight.'

If Ezra Pound had been insane, it would have been entirely proper to confine him to hospital as long as he remained in this state and to decide that no trial should take place. The only paradoxical fact was that most people who really knew him, or had bothered to examine his character and history without prejudice, could perceive that he was not insane at all. He could therefore scarcely be expected to 'recover' from a mental disturbance from which he was not suffering. Consequently he could not hope ever to be released from St Elizabeths. And if he were released, it would only be to stand trial all over again.

10

End Of The West

The day after the jury hearing, Dr Muncie wrote to Dr Overholser:

Dear Win:

I don't know how I managed to get in on the Pound case, but however it was I am glad for the opportunity, because not only was it an exceedingly interesting case, but I was glad to have a chance to work with you, Dr King, and Dr Gilbert.

Pound's publisher, who was in the audience, and whom I had met yesterday morning, told me in the intermission it was most interesting to him how three of us who had testified up to that time, while approaching the problem at slightly different angles, arrived at the same answer.

I thought your testimony was very clear and must have had a telling effect with the jury. I hope we can join efforts in this or other directions again some day. Best regards, and thank you again for all your kindnesses and courtesies, and best regards to Mrs Overholser also.

Sincerely yours,
W. Muncie.

'Audience' and 'intermission' were indeed appropriately theatrical terms for the bizarre performance that had been staged in court. Fortunately for the carriage of justice and the interests of defendants, Overholser's method, by which defence and prosecution psychiatrists agreed to 'join efforts', did not become a practice in the American lawcourts.

*

On 14 February, the day after the court hearing, Charles Olson visited Ezra and found him in excellent form, 'with his bounce back', waving fair copies of the typescript of *The Pisan Cantos* which Laughlin had delivered to him that morning. He had already looked through them, and asked Olson to take them back to Laughlin, who was still in Washington. On the way, Olson had his first sight of Canto 74. He wrote that he was 'impressed by the way Pound . . . has all his old power and beauty as a poet'; but this was rather a stilted response by Olson's usual standards of exuberance, and he does not seem to have been much impressed by the first (and most characteristic) of the Pisan Cantos.

At their meeting that day, Ezra told Olson, 'I want to get out into the yard.' He had still not been allowed into the exercise compound at Howard Hall. A few weeks later, the request for exercise was conceded and Olson recorded: 'Healthy. Better. His door is open, he is now let into the moat. He is writing letters and reading Verlaine etc, not whistle stop.' Ezra himself reported the change in his situation in a letter to Arthur Moore on 6 March: 'Conditions better in last 48 hours – let into sort of dry moat of dungeon.' He continued to regard St Elizabeths with the usually uncomplaining and detached interest that Kafka's hero shows to his surroundings in *The Castle*, or Alice towards the creatures of Wonderland. He told his mother he had seen 'one praying mantis inside yard – they say they brought 'em from Australia'.

As soon as the jury hearing was over, Cornell sent Arthur Moore a bill for $2,500, his fee, pointing out that this was a very modest charge in the circumstances. Moore wrote back that he had 'no objection whatever' to paying this on behalf of Ezra and Dorothy, but that there would be a delay of some weeks due to the technicalities involved in transferring the money. (It actually took six months.) Moore added: 'Mrs Pound has ample means to meet the payment of your fees, and I think I know just how grateful she feels for all you have been able to accomplish.' Actually, Dorothy told Douglas Hammond in 1955 that she was not satisfied with the way Cornell had handled the case, and said he 'never tried to understand'. Ezra undoubtedly felt the same way ('Cornell . . . thought I wd/ be back in Italy in six months a free man . . . I admit the incident has since faded from his memory . . .').

Cornell reported the outcome of the trial to Arthur Moore as if it were what he had intended all along:

> Although his family and friends would probably find his condition a normal one, I am inclined to believe that the abnormalities which the doctors found in Mr Pound's mental processes, while they may have been aggravated by recent fear and worry, are deeply rooted and have existed for a long time. I

think it unlikely that there will be any considerable change in
the future.

However, Cornell did put forward to Moore a plan by which he believed it
might be possible to obtain Ezra's release without his having to face a
treason trial.

He explained to Moore that the statute committing people unfit to plead
to psychiatric hospital 'does not expressly prohibit the discharge from a
mental institution of a person under indictment', and wondered whether,
considering that Ezra was not regarded as physically dangerous, the trial
judge might not have 'discretion to order such discharge'. Cornell admitted
that 'there appears to be no precedent for it, and the statute apparently does
not contemplate such an eventuality', but suggested that, quite apart from
the wording of the law, 'I think Mr Pound would have a constitutional
right to be released if we can demonstrate that he is not going to be able
ever to stand trial and that his welfare and public safety do not require
hospitalization'. He suggested, in fact, that a plea of habeas corpus might
be possible, on the grounds that Ezra faced incarceration even though he
had not been found guilty.

Cornell's specific plan was that after 'several months' the opinion of Dr
Overholser be sought, and that if Overholser remained convinced that
Ezra's condition would not change and he would never be fit enough to
stand trial, then 'an application should be made for a writ of habeas corpus
to secure his release'. Cornell imagined that this would require attending a
court of appeal, since Judge Laws would probably not assume responsibility for releasing Ezra, but 'I think the expense of an appeal would be
well worth while, since the prospects for gaining complete freedom would
be favorable. I should like to know whether you and Mrs Pound agree with
these suggestions.'

Moore wrote back on 12 March: 'I confess I am not conversant with the
process of American law, and I find your letter most enlightening.' He told
Cornell he had gathered that Dorothy had booked a passage from Genoa
to the USA, and he was expecting to hear of her departure at any moment;
he could not give an answer on Cornell's proposal until she arrived and
Cornell could talk to her himself, but 'I am of the opinion that we should
not be in too great a hurry to press for the dismissal of the indictment, for I
understand there is still some agitation and a campaign against Mr Pound
going on in the New York paper "P.M."' Dorothy's departure was, in fact,
seriously delayed. Her passport had expired, and it was not until June that
she acquired a new one and set out for America.

Ezra was doing his best to improve his way of life in Howard Hall. On
1 March he wrote to Overholser complaining about the behaviour of some
of the staff:

Dear Dr Overholser,

I have mentioned, I think twice, to Dr Griffin the lack of order on the part of two of the naval pimples – most of the staff is as it should be. – but apparently decency can not be maintained in the case of the exceptions. I should like permission to treat two cads as I would were both they and I outside this institution.

                    E.P.

Two months later, he was complaining of delays in getting purchases of candy and other luxuries from the canteen. Cornell passed on this matter, and received a reply from Dr Samuel Silk, Overholser's deputy:

Investigation reveals that the delay . . . resulted from the fact that Mr Pound did not make his wishes known, concerning purchases, sufficiently in advance so that additional money could be requisitioned from the finance office. We have endeavored to explain this to Mr Pound so that such inconveniences will not be experienced by him in the future. Furthermore, we have increased his allowance so that he will have more money for the purchase of such items.

He bought, and was given, huge amounts of candy. Receipts issued by the hospital for parcels sent by various friends acknowledge, for example, 'Pop Corn Balls & Stuffed Dates', and '1 Box Fudge, 1 Package Chewing Gum' – all sent by his former girlfriend Viola Baxter Jordan. He remarked of visitors bringing food: 'When they don't know what else to do, they poke buns thru the bars.' But he liked the buns. Always the possessor of a sweet tooth, he had been deprived of sugar during food shortages in 1944 and 1945, and now he made up for lost time. Alcohol was not allowed in the hospital (Olson and his wife brought a bottle of wine, but were forbidden to hand it over), but this was no hardship to Ezra.

Cornell proposed to Ezra that he (Cornell) be given power of attorney over Ezra's affairs, since he supposed that any money sent to Ezra at hospital would otherwise be impounded by the authorities. His letter to Ezra outlining this observed that it seemed a sensible measure 'by reason of your mental condition', yet continued: 'Although the doctors found that you were unfit to stand trial, I believe that you are quite capable of taking care of money matters and therefore can properly delegate authority to me.' Ezra's response was cautious; he wrote to Arthur Moore: 'Dear A.V.M., Should I make power of attorney to Cornell? *For limited period?*' Cornell himself could not help observing, in a letter to Overholser, that Ezra was displaying 'an extraordinary clarity of mind, even shrewdness, in his approach to business problems'; he supposed that people could be 'sane on some subjects and insane on others'. Overholser made no comment.

Cornell tried again to get power of attorney, but met with further evasion from Ezra: 're power of atty – not my idea – I haven't any ideas – been too long out of the world to focus on anything nearer than 500 B.C.' (This was a note from Ezra to Arthur Moore.) Cornell told Moore that Ezra was 'apparently a little suspicious of me'. Cornell decided that when Dorothy arrived he would propose instead that she be appointed 'guardian of her husband's estate. Whether he is legally competent to handle his affairs or not, the public generally regard him as insane and he cannot very well do business except through a guardian appointed by a court.'

Ezra began to write letters again in some quantity. One of his earliest from St Elizabeths was sent to Laughlin on 13 January, two weeks before the jury hearing. It read simply:

> haven't
>
> seen
>
> you
>
> E Pound

(To which Laughlin replied that he was very sorry but his father-in-law had just died and the New Directions office was in chaos.) Further notes to Laughlin, handwritten in pencil on rough sheets, poured out from February onwards. Ezra gave constant orders: 'Write to B. Bunting.' 'Get in touch with Rev Henry Swabey' (a Social Creditor in England). 'Mary has gone back to Gais . . . Gornoz'ow. Will you send her seed of sugar maple – if the d—n thing grows from seed. & any Dept. of Ag. circulars. information.' (Laughlin's aunt's house in Connecticut had a large grove of maple trees.)

Charles Olson's visits dropped off. On 30 April, seeing Ezra again after a five-week gap, Olson complained rather hysterically of 'his *use* of me'. He had now come to 'distrust the nice things he says, look upon all his conduct as a wheedling or a blackmail'. Olson came again in June, then paid no further visits for almost two years. After his last journey to St Elizabeths in February 1948 he wrote:

> There is no question he's got the jump – his wit, the speed of his language, the grab of it, the intimidation of his skilfully-wrought career. But he has little power to compel, that is, by his person. He strikes you as brittle – and terribly American, insecure . . . He does not seem . . . to have inhabited his own experience. It is almost as though he converted too fast. The impression persists, that the only life he has lived is, in fact, the literary . . . The verbal brilliance, delightful as it is, leaves the roots dry. One has a strong feeling, coming away from him, of a

lack of the amorous, down there somewhere . . . E.P. is a tennis ball . . .

He's no easy man. He has many devices. And he's large. I'm not sure that, precisely because of the use he has put nostalgia to, and the way he has used himself, he has not made of himself the ultimate image of the end of the West. Which is something.

Ezra's first visitor from the American literary world was H. L. Mencken, who came in April 1946, two months after the jury hearing. Marianne Moore was another early caller, in the face of disapproval by her naval chaplain brother. Theodore Spencer of Harvard came in May; Eliot, briefly in Washington, paid his first call in July. William Carlos Williams did not come for more than a year, nervous of what he might see, but finally he discovered Ezra 'much as I had always found him, the same beard and restless twitching of the hands . . . the half-coughing laugh and short, swift words, no sentence structure worth mentioning'. Before that visit, he and Ezra had exchanged letters, William eloquent in his reproach of all that Ezra had done and said, Ezra replying with semi-legible scrawls. Correspondence was fully permitted by the hospital, Overholser's only form of censorship being a point-blank refusal himself to discuss or divulge anything about Ezra's mental condition; he would answer enquiries merely by intimating that Ezra was 'adjusting' satisfactorily.

Letters from all kinds of people – sympathizers, thesis-writers, university teachers, magazine editors – began to arrive at the hospital as soon as the hearing was over. At first, Overholser fended off the obvious fanatics and those showing signs of too much sympathy with Ezra's political views, writing to them that Ezra was too 'fatigued' to engage in correspondence. But his surveillance gradually dropped off, and Ezra's own letters out of the hospital were not read by the staff.* Meanwhile, he devoured any kind of communication. 'In carcere one lives on postbag,' he told a corrrespondent. By March 1947, a year after the trial, the hospital was beginning to grumble about the excessive cost of his postage stamps. Cornell said that Dorothy would willingly pay.

His letters, like the Cantos, were now in a more fragmented style than they had once been, accompanied by even greater eccentricities of layout, Alan Neame, an early St Elizabeths correspondent of Ezra's, describes them:

> Typed on an erratic machine, the carriage jumping in all directions, no verbs, oblique lines for punctuation, astounding puns and telescoped names, addresses to be contacted, unsigned

---

*After Dorothy had arrived in Washington, the staff had no chance to read them even if they had wanted to, since she mailed them herself from a public box outside the hospital.

(lest he should be further accused of plotting the downfall of the American Republic), short (since almost typed under the bed) . . . the whole, most cryptic, stimulating, elating, like the letter that fell from heaven on Pont Saint-Esprit.

The non-signing of letters was indeed partly for self-protection, lest he wrote anything else that might be construed as 'treasonable'. (In 1953 he was furiously angry when Louis Dudek referred in print to his 'volumin-ous, practical, benevolent correspondence with scores of editors and writers'; Ezra exploded at him: 'God bloody DAMN it . . . SHUT up. You are not supposed to receive ANY letters from E.P. They are UNSIGNED and if one cannot trust one's friends to keep quiet re the supposed source . . .') The absence of signature was also, though, an allusion to his view of himself now as a non-person, an anonymous prisoner, the *Outis* (no-man) of the Pisan Cantos.

The letters betrayed not the faintest trace of self-pity, nor of regret for the actions that had landed him in his present situation. Wyndham Lewis, with whom he began to exchange letters once more, said he thought he 'detected a note of humility in one place. A bad sign I am afraid.' But it was a false alarm; Lewis observed with some relief that really 'he seems much as usual'.

He ordered some printed stationery, just as in Rapallo. This time he chose the motto *J'AYME DONC JE SUIS*, which was printed at the top of the page to form a semicircle, with the words 'ezra pound' in very small type in the top right-hand corner (so much for the ostentatiously unsigned letters) and no address. The phrase was not a quotation but his own invention, a variation of the 'amo ergo sum' found at the end of his 1942 *Carta di Visita*, and in Canto 80, itself suggested by Descartes' 'cogito ergo sum'.

The obscurity of his missives infuriated some correspondents, just as it had always done. E.E. Cummings – who himself wrote in a wonderfully intricate and allusive manner – told him: 'So my letter's obscure. Tiens. Can't compare with your last, I imagine,' and sent it back to Ezra demanding clarification. George Santayana, to whom Ezra was again writing, would on principle only answer every third letter since he said he could barely understand any of them. In England, Auberon Waugh and a schoolfellow at Downside sometimes wrote to him for the sheer comedy of receiving his inimitable, unsigned, and to them utterly nonsensical replies.

By July 1946, five months after his committal to St Elizabeths, Ezra was still complaining of fatigue, but said he now had enough energy to work 'for a few minutes daily'. If he had little desire to tackle literary tasks, he was as full of plans as ever. He told Cornell: 'Next point is to get Jas. [Laughlin] to understand need of pub/ing a nucleus of civilization – more organic than a ' "five foot shelf" & the *tooter* the *suiter*. I don't spose Faber moves in less than a geolog. epoch. or that you can usefully build a fire under Eliot – or that there is any news yet from that ¼er.' Though he was unwilling to grant Cornell power of attorney in financial affairs, he authorized him to be his representative in 'all matters pertaining to publishing' – so that Cornell, who had not offered to do this at all, found himself acting as unpaid literary agent and secretary. Ezra asked him: 'Does anyone attend to Jas' business when he is ski-ing?' (Laughlin now had a financial interest in a ski resort in Utah and spent much of his time there.)

Ezra also asked Cornell to get hold of books for him. For a while, uncharacteristically, he was inclined to read only fiction – it was less strain. 'Anybody who wants to send me *novels*,' he told Cornell, 'not criticism or highbrow tosh can do so & welcome.' But he was soon in search of more typical reading matter, and tried to borrow Chinese texts from the Library of Congress. This proved far from easy, thanks to red tape ('It may be a bitch in the bug-house lieBURY,' he observed), and he found it simpler to get what he wanted from Lester Littlefield, a New York bibliophile and friend of Marianne Moore, who mailed books to him.

He read the newspapers each day, and was as critical as ever of them: 'Waiting for a few simple facts to get by the fog caused by newpaper headlines.' He took a ruthless attitude towards the debate, in the months following Hiroshima, about the atomic bomb. 'Consider which and how MANY of 'em *ought* to be blown to hell,' he told one correspondent, 'and then consider the desirability of leaving a little civilization to be dug out of the eventual ruins. that is to say: step on it, and stop wastin time on irrelevant details.' And a few years later, to MacLeish: 're/ the world not ending in hydrogen, disintegrated. Our problem is that IF it blows up, there COULD be a rebirth, and if it dont blow up, yr grandchildren got to live somewhere.'

His reading of the papers and news magazines gave him all too clear an impression of the character of American life outside the walls of St Elizabeths. He wrote to his mother:

> The dense iggurance of this continent increases daily. Lunacy outside the bug house rising with 10000 x the rapidity that it increases inside. Peasants descend to robot status by the ten million and darkness increases. A land of mooncalves.
>
> Only crime is respected, and even that lacks distinction . . . Everyone known wishes to escape. All except one man on this ward, who knows he is better off. Mr Kerensky got as far as Baltimore but finding sandwiches cost ¢25 returned to this estate.

'Everyone known wishes to escape. All except one man on this ward, who knows he is better off.' Though he meant Mr Kerensky, he was also talking about himself. In none of his letters during the months following the jury hearing – months during which it must have become steadily clearer to him that there was no immediate prospect of freedom – did he give any clear indication that he wanted to be released from a situation that most people would have found intolerable. He rarely alluded to his predicament, and when he did so it was only in the mildest and most oblique terms. A letter to Yeats's widow 'George' some time in 1946 is exceptional in that it does glance for a moment at the possibility of release – but even so, it is scarcely a *cri de coeur*:

> Dear Jarge
>   Shd like nooz of outer – get mind out of this, if not
> body . . . glad to see even printed matter. but wish you cd find
> urge to write. poisnl gnuz v people is max. relief I can get here.

Even in his lachrymose moments with Olson he had not specifically mentioned any desire to be let out of St Elizabeths. He seemed to be accepting his fate with a curious passivity.

Yet this was thoroughly characteristic. For somebody so active, so aggressive, he had always taken a remarkably passive attitude towards his own situation, accepting sudden changes of fortune philosophically – sometimes seeming scarcely to notice them – and showing surprisingly little inclination to control the overall shape of his life. His dramatic failure to make friends at Hamilton in 1903, his sacking from Wabash College in 1908, Dorothy's pregnancy in 1926, his incarceration in the cage in 1945 – such twists of fortune had been met by him with remarkable equanimity, as if he were merely a spectator who could have no influence on the play's plot. Once, he had spoken of this feeling, in his letter to his father immediately after the Wabash dismissal: 'I guess something that one does not see but something very big & white back of the destinies. has the turning & the loading of things . . . ' Making allowances for the jejune phraseology, he would probably have said much the same thing forty years later. Or, as he had put it in 1926 after reporting Omar's birth to his father: 'No expected calamity ever arrives. Them that arrives is onexpected; and usually a blessing in disguise.'

Confinement at St Elizabeths, though undoubtedly a severe ordeal, was not entirely without blessings. It is hard to imagine what way of life, what role, would have remained for him in Rapallo – or elsewhere – if he had been allowed to go free at the conclusion of the war. To play the noble sufferer, the maligned but uncomplaining sage, the wise man in the madhouse, offered far more potential than that of the elderly and not very popular poet still exiled in a Europe that had seen the defeat of his ideas. To have gone back to Italy now would have been a retreat, an attempt to revive an old form of life, a pretence that nothing irrevocable had happened between 1939 and 1945. That was never Ezra's way: throughout his life he moved restlessly if often blindly forward, in search of some new function, some new persona, which would involve him in the drama of the world. It fitted him well enough in 1946 to be a symbol of the ruin of Europe and America, the end of the West itself, and to be sought out by the few remaining 'live minds' of the era.

Meanwhile on a personal level, confinement had one specific convenience. 'And three women waited on the jail steps . . . ' he had remarked wryly of a literary ne'er-do-well in Edwardian London – which now reflected his own situation. Olga, Dorothy and Mary had, whatever his feelings for them individually, collectively become determined rivals for him back in Italy. This had seemed to make free choice less and less possible. It was a conundrum with no solution, and he would have to face it again the moment he emerged from St Elizabeths. From this point of view, the cell in Howard Hall had something to be said for it.

11

Somewhat More Latitude

Certainly he did not seem overjoyed at the prospect of Dorothy's arrival. He wrote coolly about it to Cornell in March 1946: 'If D.P. arrives she might attend to various things.'

Olga was trying to get to Washington too, but had her own passport troubles:

> They wouldn't guarantee that I would be allowed to return . . . I had my job and was living in Siena and the house [in Venice] had been sequestrated . . . If I had been in Washington, I think I could have been more use, at least if they'd allowed me to be there for a few months at the beginning. But they were afraid – they – they didn't – Eliot – Eliot . . .

In this filmed interview, her voice tails off. She realized from the start of Ezra's confinement in St Elizabeths, indeed from the beginning of legal proceedings against him, that the existence of an 'other woman' was thought by Eliot and other friends of Ezra to be better concealed. And, quite apart from this, Olga seems to have felt that now, at least for a while, it was Dorothy's turn once again to take the stage.

Nevertheless it was from Olga and not Dorothy that Cornell received some family news in mid-May 1946, three months after the hearing:

EZRA'S MOTHER 86 FRACTURED LEG CONDITION GRAVE NOT NECESSARY FATAL PRAYING SEE SON UNLIKELY RECOVER SUFFICIENTLY TO TRAVEL RUDGE

Passing this telegram to Ezra, Cornell added: 'If there is anything I can do . . . let me know. I see no possibility of your being able to return to Italy, although I hope that you can be released before long from the hospital. I doubt very much whether you would be allowed to leave the United States.'

Ezra wrote at once to his mother:

> Dearest Mother
>
> Very very sorry to hear of yr accident. Hope it isn't too painful.
>
> Don't know what I can do. Visitors are let in here for ¼ hour – or ½ if they are from out of town.
>
> People who got thru the war seem to be target for present calamities . . .
>
> Pazienza, pazienzaaaa
> > & all good wishes
> > > love
> > > > E.

Isabel Pound decided that as soon as she had recovered sufficiently from the accident, she must travel to Washington and find a place in a home for the elderly; she requested her lawyer in Philadelphia to look for somewhere. He discovered a Presbyterian home in Washington which might suit – except that its waiting list 'might mean one or two years delay'; and he also warned her: 'Living costs in the U.S.A. are very high and your income from . . . investments would be inadequate to support you.' She was at present living in Ezra and Dorothy's old Rapallo flat. Later she went back into hospital, where she wrote to Ezra: 'There is no heat so I remain in bed as leg will not function comfortably when cold.' (This was the bitter winter of 1946 to 1947.) She was still contemplating the journey to Washington, but 'so far no Old Lady's Home seems available tho I have required amount for entrance. Is there such a resort in Washington or near by you might enquire of Miss Mapel.' Ezra continued to write to his mother quite frequently, sending brief notes with good wishes for her recovery: 'Hope you are progressing more rapidly than yr onforchunate product.'

Dorothy arrived in Washington by air early in July 1946. She was met by the Misses Mapel, who put her up in their home until she could find accommodation within walking distance of St Elizabeths. 'Plane trip here O.K. & luggage arrived next day,' she reported to Laughlin, but she felt ill at ease on American soil (she had never before crossed the Atlantic), and long afterwards she said: 'I felt the ground shifting beneath my feet; and it was that way for twelve years.' The Misses Mapel were 'so very kind and helpful', but quite apart from having to accustom herself to American urban life there was the ordeal – and so she clearly found it – of seeing Ezra for the first time in Howard Hall. She went there on 10 July, and reported the next day to Laughlin:

> Saw E.P. yesterday for *one hour special* – & today the usual
> visitors' 15 m[inutes] . . . He seems pretty nervous: I take the
> subject he has uppermost, as visiting time is so short. Yest[er-
> da]y Confucius . . . He seems clear on the subject he has
> arranged to talk about. Says if he can rest 2–3 hrs, one hour is
> clear to him. It *is* a rotten deal.

Their first meeting for nine months was spent in Ezra talking about
Confucius.

Ezra decided that Dorothy's chief function would be to help with his
correspondence. 'He asks me to write certain letters for him each time I go
there and I do my best,' she told Cornell, and went on:

> I do believe we must try to get Ezra *out* of that place. He
> himself says he'll never get well in there and has said so each
> time to me . . . What I am wondering is how E. can be got into a
> private sanatorium, less imprisoned, and if he left St Elizabeths,
> would those four doctors still be in position to testify to his
> mental instability. What can be done as quickly as possible, in
> safety? . . . T.S. Eliot [who was then in Washington] evidently
> feels strongly he should be moved. . . . What places are there?
> Dr Overholser is still away.

Dorothy accepted the notion that there had been some mental deterioration in Ezra – but, then, this was at a period when Ezra was still
complaining of exhaustion, and was saying that he could not talk sensibly
for more than an hour at a time. Dorothy told Cornell after her third visit
to him: 'I find him very nervous and jumpy. I believe his wits are really
very scattered, and he has difficulty in concentrating for more than a few
minutes.' She did not discuss the official diagnosis of him with Cornell, nor
with anyone else, seeming to accept it; she was concerned only to get him
out of Howard Hall. Cornell wrote back to Dorothy to say he did not
think

> that the present is an opportune time to make application to the
> court . . . I discussed this question with Mr Eliot, Mr Laughlin
> and others a few weeks ago and all were agreed that such an
> application should not be made at the present time because of
> public clamor which would rise in opposition. In my opinion
> we should wait . . . at least until the fall, unless, perhaps, Dr
> Overholser could be persuaded to testify that the state of his
> health requires removal to a private sanatorium . . . I suggest
> that you try to see Dr Overholser about this and I shall attempt
> to see him within the next few weeks also.

Dorothy thanked Cornell for this advice, saying that she wanted something to 'reassure' Ezra, who she thought 'feels he is put aside and forgotten'. Shortly afterwards, Cornell did indeed raise with Overholser the question of Ezra's removal to a private sanatorium, but was told bluntly by him (in mid-July 1946): 'As to Mr Pound's going to a sanatorium, I presume that you are aware that I have no authority to release him except back to the Court at such time he is considered to be of sound mind.'

Cornell thought Dorothy's 'devotion' to Ezra, now that she had arrived in Washington, was 'touching'. He particularly noticed how she 'never questioned the rightness of his actions', but would take down and pass on his instructions to friends or correspondents as if they were holy writ. By the winter of 1946 to 1947 she had found herself a room at 3211 10th Place, Washington SW, in the home of a guard at St Elizabeths. Ezra reported to his mother: 'Dorothy is in an unheated attic – for lack of better.' The attic became too hot in summer, but it served her needs. Taken up with her daily visits to Ezra, his correspondence and other tasks he required her to perform, she had no independent existence from him, but she seemed satisfied with this. After the years of contesting for him with Olga, there was quiet relief at having undisputed possession, even though her status was more that of secretary than wife. Her own finances were now satisfactory – her funds had been released by the British Government, and Arthur Moore reported that she had 'a very substantial balance . . . which should relieve her of all further worry' – and Cornell now put into effect his plan of her taking over Ezra's business matters, as guardian or one-person 'Committee' for him. In September 1946 a firm of Washington lawyers prepared documents for Ezra to sign, giving his consent to this arrangement, 'though why,' Dorothy asked Overholser in astonishment, 'an insane person should be asked to sign —?'

Ezra explained the arrangement to a correspondent: 'Money NOT confiscated/ all EP's income is impounded, placed under committee, whose disbursements are supervised by audit.' The income and expenditure of the 'Committee' was indeed audited annually by an accountant appointed by the District Court, who occasionally queried particular items, thereby annoying Ezra, who resented such interference in his affairs. However, his financial position was much better than it had been before the war. With the US Government paying for his board and lodging, such income as he received from his writings could be profitably invested (the auditor gave free advice on this); ten years after his confinement at St Elizabeths had begun he had amassed capital of $15,500 – and this was entirely his own money, Dorothy's capital and income being no business of the auditor.

Laughlin felt that Ezra 'always felt humiliated by the Committee arrangement', and certainly in later years Dorothy was inclined to make autocratic decisions with regard to the control of his published works (which she retained to the end of his life) – in 1970 she refused Laughlin permission to reprint some of Ezra's 'juvenile essays' on the grounds that 'all this raking up of early stuff – almost surely bad – is no contribution'. In the early years of the Committee, though, she merely carried out Ezra's instructions, for example, raising no objection when he wished to send certain royalties or other sums to Mary and Olga, both of whom badly needed the help.

During her first summer in Washington, Dorothy continued to treat Ezra warily. Far from claiming any special understanding of her husband that the doctors might not possess, she would consult them for advice. 'I am most anxious to see Dr Overholser to find out about *which way* to treat him on certain subjects,' she told Cornell. 'He (E.P.) is certainly very nervous and worried.' She added: 'I have been through the pile of doctors' testimony [from the court hearing] – very interesting. I should like to keep it awhile and re-read it when I have a little more leisure.' She and Cornell agreed that there should be no further attempt to get him released 'until after the elections of November 1946' (a Congressional election). They assumed that the Government would not listen sympathetically to such a controversial proposal as his release until a time when public opinion did not matter so much to them.

Ezra continued to display a marked lack of regret about his situation. He told one correspondent that he 'disliked th' heat of a Washtn summer', but brushed aside friends' pity. When he heard that old Professor Ibbotson had had a leg amputated, he wrote to him: 'yr. calamity . . . sounds rather worse than mine'. Basil Bunting wrote to Dorothy in December 1946 apologizing for not being able to help Ezra, but Ezra scrawled in the margin of the letter: 'to hell with the personal angle'. His letters to his mother were as cheerful in tone as ever: 'When ever I get ready to write . . . someone informs D. you are coming over . . . I get various rumours . . . Eliot said to have written something I haven't yet seen.' (Probably *Four Quartets*, which had been published in its entirety in the autumn of 1944.)

Eliot's own visit to Ezra in early July 1946 led him to the same conclusion as Dorothy. 'I am quite sure that Ezra ought to be removed to a private sanatorium as soon as possible,' he wrote to her. 'I thought St Elizabeths was very grim. I was particularly disappointed to miss Overholser, as I have heard so well of him . . . I did not get much out of Dr Griffin whom I saw.' Eliot realized from the outset the necessity of handling Overholser with special tact; it was the only way in which anything would be achieved towards the improvement of Ezra's situation.

During this American visit Eliot wrote to Overholser saying he hoped that they could meet, flattering him by remarking that he must be 'a very

busy man' so that it would obviously be necessary 'to make an appointment in advance'. He himself did not object at all, he said, to the limited
visiting hours he could spend with Ezra: 'From my previous experience of
visiting friends under such conditions, I know that it is usually an
advantage to have the duration of each visit strictly limited.' (Ezra had
corrected Olson when he made a disparaging remark about Eliot: 'Yes, I
know Eliot is now paralyzed . . . But all the years it was Eliot who kept the
lice off my back.') Like the others, Eliot felt that nothing drastic could be
done at present. 'I doubt whether the U.S. Government would allow Ezra
to return to Europe for some time to come,' he wrote to Dorothy after
leaving Washington.

> The first thing is to get him into a proper sanatorium where he
> can get fresh air and grass and trees. Then, probably, some
> remote place in the U.S.A. – there are parts of California and
> Arizona which you might both find tolerable . . . I'll keep
> writing to you from London. As soon as Laughlin lets me have
> a fair text of the [Pisan] cantos to keep . . . I shall urge Faber
> and Faber to publish them.

Eliot and Ezra resumed correspondence of a kind, but not with the same
openness as before – or rather, Ezra played the part of 'Old Ez' so
exclusively in his letters that Eliot tended to become irritated, only
occasionally recovering his former ironical way of handling Ezra. But there
were moments: 'Your postcard,' he told Ezra, 'expressing the first
commendation of Faber & Faber from you within living memory . . . will
probably be framed . . . '

Eliot's letters to Dorothy often devoted some attention to the future of
Omar, who after leaving the US Army went to Hamilton College (where
he was very happy), majoring in Anthropology and French. Later he
studied Islamic History and Persian in London and Tehran, and took an
MA at the Institute of Islamic Studies at McGill in Montreal. When visiting
his mother in Washington he would accompany her on her daily visit to
Ezra, sometimes playing chess with him; he describes Ezra as a 'ratty,
lightning player', sometimes rushing to a quick, brilliant victory, sometimes doing silly things.

At the end of 1946 William Carlos Williams took his own initiative to get
Ezra out of St Elizabeths. He wrote to President Truman asking that 'an
old and honored friend of mine, Ezra Pound, be freed by you from
confinement'. The letter continued:

> Whatever Mr Pound's actual sins against his country may have
> been our history has shown us, by our natures, always to be
> generous towards dissenters from our generally accepted ways

of thinking ... Pound is a writer, a distinguished poet and though in many ways a fool he does not rightly belong in an insane asylum as a criminal.

The White House merely passed the letter to Overholser, who answered Williams:

Mr Pound is certainly not in suitable mental condition to face trial at present time, but we are doing everything we can to make his stay at St Elizabeths Hospital a comfortable one. Your interest in Mr Pound's welfare is deeply appreciated.

In November 1946, after the Congressional election, Cornell proceeded with his own plan, and told Ezra he was making another application for bail, since he believed

that you have a constitutional right to be released if your own health and the interests of society do not require that you be confined. I do not believe that a man can be shut up indefinitely after being indicted when he cannot be tried because of illness.

Cornell claims in his book that by this time Overholser 'did not think his confinement was necessary', but Overholser's letter to Williams shows that, whatever his private opinion, this was not the line he was going to take officially.

Cornell's application for bail was carefully considered by the Department of Justice. An internal memorandum from J. Frank Cunningham to Isaiah Matlack, dated 27 January 1947, shows that the Attorney General's office was prepared to contemplate his transfer to more congenial surroundings:

I think [Cunningham wrote] the psychiatrists who have had this defendant under observation should be interviewed immediately to see whether or not the condition of the defendant is as grave as his attorney states and whether or not his continued confinement at St Elizabeth's Hospital would jeopardize his recovery.

It might be advisable to ascertain whether or not there are other federal mental institutions available to take care of this defendant in an acceptable manner.

It may be argued that the statutes governing the commitment of this accused indicate an intent of Congress that bail should not be allowed.

It may be argued that the defendant has no constitutional right to bail and that the applicable statutes, if construed as precluding that right, are not violative of the Fifth Amendment.

In other words, though moving Ezra to some other hospital was contemplated, it seemed that arguably he had no constitutional right to freedom, and that his continued confinement did not violate the celebrated constitutional amendment which protects personal liberty against infringement without 'due process of law'. Cunningham wrote to Overholser two days later, enclosing a copy of the memorandum, and remarking: 'The problem raised, I think, is an intriguing one, both from the moral and legal point of view.' He said that the memorandum was intended only to suggest 'certain reasons why the motion of bail should be denied'. It was plain that the Department of Justice, like the White House, wished to leave all decisions about Ezra to Overholser himself.

Finding himself under threat of losing Ezra to some other institution – Cunningham's memo had, after all, alluded to the possibility of his being housed in 'other federal mental institutions' – Overholser produced a solution which would keep most parties reasonably happy without in any way loosening his personal grip on Ezra. Howard Hall was, after all, only one of the many departments at St Elizabeths. A more 'acceptable manner' of treating Ezra could be contrived elsewhere in the hospital, on the 'civil' side of the institution, where patients were kept who had not been committed by the courts, while retaining him within the bounds of the hospital and under Overholser's control.

Accordingly, when the motion for bail was heard in the District Court on 31 January 1947, Judge Laws, while 'disclaiming any right to interfere with the internal administration of St Elizabeths Hospital', dismissed the motion but allowed Isaiah Matlack to state 'that the Department of Justice would have no objection if the patient were removed from Howard Hall to another ward in the Saint Elizabeths Hospital with the discretion of the hospital authorities, provided, of course, that reasonable precautions were taken to prevent him from escape.' Overholser then told the court that 'the patient would be removed from Howard Hall to some ward where he would have somewhat more latitude and somewhat more free privileges of receiving visitors'.*

In his book, Cornell describes the decision as a 'compromise' reached after he himself had discussed the matter with Matlack and Overholser. The evidence in the St Elizabeths files, however, is that like every other decision about Ezra it was taken autonomously by Overholser.

*

* Ezra himself had attended the initial hearing on the bail motion, two days earlier. Far from being glad of this short trip out of St Elizabeths he 'expressed great fatigue and received permission to return to the Hospital a short time after arriving in court'.

On 4 February 1947, four days after the bail hearing, Ezra was taken out of Howard Hall and moved to Center Building, initially to Cedar Ward. Dorothy reported to Ronald Duncan a few months later:

> He is now (since Feb. when Cornell got him out of the 'Snake Pit') comparatively comfortable; and Uncle Sam is keeping him . . . He has a little room to himself, where he can type in peace, which is locked by the Guard while E.P. is downstairs in the visitors' compartment, or in the garden. Food dull but satisfying – bar fresh fruit, which I take in.

She was still finding conversation with Ezra a strain. She told Duncan, who had asked her to raise some point with him: 'Can't always get answers – depending on what E.P. has thought up to discuss with me during my visit.'

Cornell was certain that the move from Howard Hall to Center Building was as much as could be achieved at present. He told Eliot that 'a Republican victory in 1948 . . . might result in some relaxation of the autocracy of the State Department, with advantages for Ezra.' Eliot, reporting this to Dorothy, added: 'I don't much understand American politics myself. But I gathered from him that not much more could be attempted before those elections.' He himself still felt that Ezra should be allowed to go to a private sanatorium, but he did not suggest complete release from confinement: 'I am sure that at this stage anything further would be too much responsibility to have to bear.' He saw Ezra again when he was in Washington in June 1947.

A year after he had been taken out of Howard Hall, Ezra was moved from Cedar to Chestnut Ward, one floor above ground level in Center Building. Here he remained for the rest of his stay in St Elizabeths. Again he was given his own room, about 10 feet by 14 feet, with a high ceiling and a view across the lawns below. By the hospital's standards this was special treatment: most patients slept two to a room, and the corridors outside the rooms also contained a number of beds, owing to overcrowding.

Chestnut Ward was next door to Dr Overholser's private apartment, separated from it only by the locked door that led out on to the central stairwell; Ezra soon began to send Overholser casual, friendly notes. For example:

> Thanks for
> photostat.
>
> Have just been given G. S' 'Poets Testament'
> if you haven't seen it. wd. you care to
> have it on loan.
>   Ez. P.

Some time later, when Overholser asked to look over the text of 'Patria Mia', Ezra's 1912 articles about America which he was now checking through for an edition in book form:

> Thanks
> W.O. perfectly welcome to see the xxx book.
> but ought to have better (i.e. more contemporary) ways
> of spending his time.

If Overholser was aware of the cheeky element in such notes, he chose to ignore it. Though he occasionally called on Ezra, he took little personal interest in him; it was enough to have such a well-known figure in the institution, and he clearly felt no need to involve himself in the complexities of the man's character. Many years later, when Charles Norman asked him for his recollections of Ezra, Overholser replied in terms so prim and formal as to border on the absurd:

> As for my personal relationships with Pound, I may say that they were always most pleasant. So far as I am concerned, of course, he, or anyone else who is here as a patient, is entitled to all the respect and sympathy that a sick person deserves. Questions of morals or previous history have no place in a physician's dealings with his patients. I recognized, of course, that Pound was a person of eminent standing in the field of letters and having literary interests myself I visited him not infrequently and we discussed various persons and things of mutual interest. His attitude toward me was always friendly, in spite of the fact that at least technically I was his custodian.

*

In Chestnut Ward, Ezra would usually wake early and, becoming impatient because breakfast always seemed to arrive late, would pass the time with breathing exercises. He enjoyed being able to eat with a knife and fork again; in Howard Hall, for obvious reasons, only spoons had been provided.

Though he had his own room, the noise from the corridor was considerable. The high ceilings and wooden floor outside echoed with the voices of the more disturbed patients, and visitors, who could now come to his room rather than having to see him in a cubicle, found it hard not to be distracted. One of them describes

> EP's ghostly companions, never at rest ... Some of them ... never stopped their aimless walk to come near; but the others ... were often drawn to us ... On several occasions, before EP could get out of his chair, one of them would bend

down in front of me and peer into my face. His hands gripping the arms of my chair cut off any escape . . . Pound would take the intruder by the arm and lead him away.

Ezra's letters occasionally mentioned some of the patients by name or nickname. There was 'pore ole McNeil', with whom he would play checkers when not feeling up to anything else, 'Yo-Yo' (a black man alluded to in Canto 104), and 'Lightfoot'.

Laughlin, visiting him, had the impression that he was undisputed 'king of the ward', and had no difficulty in keeping his more tiresome subjects under control. One day Ezra was having lunch at the end of the ward, and Laughlin watched as an old man came solemnly forward and stood by Ezra's chair, while Ezra fed him a mouthful from his plate before himself beginning the meal. Ezra explained that 'Bernie Baruch' (who had been economic adviser to Roosevelt) was plotting to poison him. The old man was his taster. It was a regal performance: Pirandello's Henry the Fourth.

Visiting regulations were far more relaxed than in Howard Hall. 'Visiting hours 2–4 P.M.,' Ezra told a correspondent, and Dorothy was allowed to see him for these two hours each afternoon instead of the cramped fifteen minutes in the criminal ward. Ezra gave further details in another letter:

> NO visitors Mon/Wed/Fri but Cuchard, the aryan, in charge this wing, had DIScretionary powers/ so might work out more convenient fer the distinguished who do NOT want to run into the indiscriminated younger gen/rtn/ etc. i.e. if they phone for special leniency and PURRmissn precicely on forbidden days. I can't ask for favours, but there is no reason why free citizens of the republic shd/ not do so/ alledging their own convenience (real or feigned).

When visitors arrived they would usually sit with him at the far end of the ward, in the open hallway. William Carlos Williams describes the setting: ' . . . by the big windows adjacent to the old round wooden table with the battered screen making a small room of it at the end of the corridor'. Another acquaintance, David Rattray, recalls how Dorothy (who was invariably present) would sit 'behind a ramshackle old upright piano, so as not to see the people in the hall or be seen by them'.

Rattray describes how on his arrival Ezra

> jumped up . . . 'You'll have tea, won't you?' . . . Immediately he was everywhere at once, in a frenzy of activity, loading himself with jars of various sizes, tin boxes of sugar and tea, spoons and a saucer . . . Suddenly Pound was standing before me, holding out a peanut butter jar filled with hot tea.

It was perhaps a tactic to cover those first awkward moments of conversation, to brush aside any tendency in the visitor to express pity for his situation; and to show that he was in charge, could still do things his own way. Rattray had a look at Ezra's own room, which was

> strewn with wadded papers, bits of envelopes, trampled books, pencils, lengths of string, cardboard files, trunks, old paint cans, jars filled with teabags or scraps of food. The walls were hung with paintings ... The tins ... were filled with doughnuts and bread ... a box filled with boiled eggs and salami ... was marked *Books*, sent by Witter Bynner.

Thanks to all this food he began to have problems with ants: '½ of ONE CRUMB equales 9 ants,' he observed in a letter, 'and only two small containers and the management against installin ice-boxes or other ant-proof apparatus.' And in another letter: 'I tho't paté lasted ferever. instead of which it grows fungus half an inch long/ even on cold window sill/ part UNDER the fungus still tasty.'

The main door of Chestnut Ward was always locked, and though Ezra would have been allowed to go out to eat in the patients' cafeteria, he chose to take all his meals on the ward. As to the fresh air and exercise which the move from Howard Hall had been designed to provide, he was at first only allowed out in 'walking parties' which took place if and when the weather was warm, and usually involved more sitting than walking. Ezra hated this, and made a deliberate nuisance of himself during them. One of the doctors reported: 'When his ward was taken onto the grounds and lawns ... he insisted on keeping apart, refusing to sit on the benches reserved for the group, but instead sprawled on the ground, insisting that he could not remain erect.'

In November 1948, after Ezra had been in Chestnut Ward for nearly a year, Eliot wrote to Cornell asking if it might be possible to get permission 'for him to go out alone in the grounds with his wife, and with her responsible for his returning in due time. This would, incidentally, give a relatively greater degree of privacy than is possible under the conditions in which he can be visited indoors.' Cornell passed on the request; it was eventually granted, and Ezra was thereafter allowed to spend fine afternoons outside with Dorothy and other visitors, Ezra being supposedly under her supervision – he could even play tennis on the hospital court.

Ronald Duncan arrived in Washington soon after Ezra had been granted this outdoor privilege, and describes his own visit to St Elizabeths:

> An attendant or warder led me through miles of inhospitable corridors swarming with noisy inmates. The noise and echoes

reminded me of a public swimming bath. As we approached Ezra's ward we passed a Negro who was comforting a girl who was crying. The Negro turned as we passed him. 'He's out,' he said, indicating Pound's cell. The warder then left me. The Negro . . . led me along another corridor and pointed to a lawn outside. Ezra and Dorothy were sitting there on a couple of deck-chairs.

Ezra got up quickly and erected another chair for me. 'They're very comfortable. One has to go nuts before you have the sense to buy proper chairs,' he announced as an unassailable dictum . . .

I hadn't seen Ezra since 1938. Thirteen years had not aged him particularly. He still looked leonine, big-chested and swarthy. Wearing a yellow sweater that gave him the appearance of a tennis coach . . . Apparently Dorothy was allowed to visit him every afternoon . . . [She] always managed to carry an air of Henley and cucumber sandwiches with her . . . I was relieved when she rose to go . . . Ezra then led me, armed with a deck-chair, to his cell. 'You see why I like deck-chairs,' he said, packing them flat against the wall and indicating the dimensions of his cell . . . The room . . . contained an iron bed, chaos of clothes and a muddle of magazines and paper . . . We had to shout at each other even in his cell because a large television set outside in the corridor blared away. 'They try to reduce us idiots to the level of insanity outside,' Ezra commented . . .

'Have you written any poems in here?' I asked.

'Birds don't sing in cages.' We didn't mention poetry again.

'Any chance of your getting out of here?' I asked, when a very insane old man came and started to look down my ear.

'No,' Ezra replied, 'I'm too big to go down the drain. There'd be comment if they let me slip away. Maybe after the election things may be different – but I don't want to get out to be assassinated.'

This fear of being assassinated was the first and only sign I noticed of Ezra's insanity. But it was not new. He had always imagined himself as the target of some international group of bankers or warmongers . . . 'You see, they know I've tumbled them,' he went on. 'Wars are made solely to create debts.' . . .

Ezra seemed oblivious of . . . a white-headed man beside us who was stroking the radiator and talking to it as if it were a cat. 'Gold is 4 dollars over price,' he went on, venting his obsession with international finance, way above my head, but every remark pertinent. 'Of course that shit Roosevelt was always determined to take the British Empire to pieces. A pander to Stalin: a pity Winnie didn't or couldn't stand up to him.' Then he switched to asking me how Cocteau and Brancusi were and somehow got onto the subject of Vivien Eliot . . . 'You should start *Townsman* again,' he said, getting up and snatching a couple of teacups from a passing trolley. 'Think of it while I go and see if any of my fellow maniacs can supply us with a couple of biscuits.'

I . . . noticed he was still studying Chinese and had a photo of Mary by his bed. 'Try and get Olga out here to see me,' he said, seeing the photo in my hand and passing me a cream cracker . . .

I told him how I had disliked what I had seen of New York. 'The trouble with the U.S.,' he said, 'is they resent finding any other values than money. It's essentially a poor country. How can they understand anything when the function of education here is only to keep the young off the labour market. I see they can now take a Ph.D. in being an usherette.' . . .

I rose to go . . . We shook hands . . . I walked up the long corridor to the door at the end. It was locked. The white haired fellow who'd been trying to make the radiator purr informed me the warder had locked up half an hour ago and, I gathered, he wouldn't be opening the door till the morning. I turned and retraced my steps down the corridor towards Ezra's cell. A man came towards me.

'If you like,' he said, 'I'll clean your watch. I've got some black boot-polish here.'

Then Ezra emerged and observed my predicament. Together we examined the locked door. 'Two bullfinches in the same cage now,' he observed, 'it's really more than Papageno deserves.' We continued to rattle the chain.

'Don't worry,' I said, 'it's much saner inside here . . . Besides, you've got a deck-chair.'

'Yes,' observed the white-haired man, 'and not only has he got a deck-chair but a heart as big as Washington.'

We heard heavy steps coming towards the locked door. It was opened. 'Not so much noise in here,' the warder shouted. The door locked again.

'I want to get out,' I said.

'You don't say!'

'I'm only a visitor.'

'Sure. Next you'll tell me you're sane.'

'No,' said Ezra, 'but he ain't been certified yet.'

12

Bubble-gum

The St Elizabeths staff remained deeply puzzled by him. These are excerpts from the nursing notes in Chestnut Ward:

> Quiet and co-operative . . . Fully oriented. Receives morning paper. Stays in his room most of the time.

> While in room constantly hums.

> At times thru the night will have a light in his room. Appears at times to be singing. Appears to be correctly oriented.

> At times have heard him humming some kind of tuneless chant at night. Appears to be correctly oriented in all spheres.

> Has very good appetite. Nearly every meal he carries some excess food to his room.

> Mr Pound plays chess each evening.

Another more substantial note, dated 16 June 1948 and signed 'Small', reads:

> Patient does no work, causes no trouble, visited by wife every day, has a awful lot of company. writes a lot of letters, receives a lot of mail. does not mix with other patients. stays in his room. neat in dress, clean in habits. keeps his room in a mess.

The untidiness of the room caused some irritation; Overholser observed in a memo to a fellow doctor:

> Mr Langford, the charge nurse of the ward on which Mr Pound is resident, has repeatedly complained to me that he finds it

impossible to properly clean Mr Pound's room, that Mr Pound becomes exceedingly upset and nervous and that it is impossible to get Mr Pound to air out and ventilate the room. It has been suggested that Mr Pound work in one place and sleep in another so that for at least part of the 24 hours he would be in a clean, well-ventilated area. This has not, of course, been feasible so far.

Overholser added: 'I have been thinking of directing that Mr Pound attend the group therapy sessions on Cedar Ward and will do so if you believe that there is no objection.' Nothing was done about this, so the spectacle of Ezra in group therapy must be left to the imagination.

He was given no treatment whatsoever at St Elizabeths: no drugs, no psychotherapy, no occupational therapy, nothing. Overholser left him alone. After all, routine notes by staff doctors invariably indicated that, though eccentric, he was not mentally ill:

No abnormal mental content is elicitable . . . no evidence of hallucinations, delusions . . . appreciates his predicament fully . . . does not exhibit any delusional or other psychotic material . . . his memory is good . . . his insight and judgement do not appear to be impaired.

The only faint suggestion of mental irregularity noted by the doctors was the occasional appearance of 'some paranoid ideas . . . in reference to international banking [and] his attempts to prevent the war'. If Overholser looked at these routine reports, he made no comment about them. He had no wish either to precipitate a treason trial, or deprive the hospital of its most illustrious inmate, a patient whose visitors included T.S. Eliot.

*

A year after Ezra had been incarcerated in Howard Hall, Mary reached her twenty-first birthday, and married a young man to whom she had been introduced by Ezra's friend and fellow-broadcaster in Rome, Princess Troubetzkoi. Half-Russian and half-Italian, Boris Baratti was one of a clan, said Mary, 'with rickety titles, old relics in Capri who hadn't stopped gossiping since they had fled from Petersburg, and old relics in Rome whose only claim to authority was a pair of emerald earrings'. Olga tried to prevent the marriage because Boris was penniless. She 'came posthaste to Rome with Babbo's walking cane and said: "Boris, no need of you." And Boris bowed and said: "Madam, we are going to get married as soon as Mary's papers are ready." And at Cook's, when she said: Two tickets for Rapallo, I said: No, *one*.'

Ezra received the news with pleasure, sending a message of goodwill for

'M. and Boris Ivanovitch or whatever the name is'. On Christmas Eve 1946 the young couple moved into an abandoned castle above Gais, Schloss Neuhaus, where they had permission to live rent-free for a while. Ezra commented to his mother:

> Waal yr g^d darter has a last achieved suitable setting for family portraits   vide enclosure [a photograph of Neuhaus] construzione del mille say 1066   also sd/ to contain stoves. a bit hard to get @ – dunno what they can grow @ this season, or if can get fire wood from under snow.
>   & that's about the news for present, apart from probability of more generations.

Isabel was still in hospital in Rapallo. Although little more than a year earlier the old lady had scarcely acknowledged her granddaughter's existence, Mary now offered her grandmother a home in Neuhaus. Ezra called this a 'magnanimous' gesture, pointing out that even if Isabel could manage the transatlantic journey the USA was now a country fit only 'for millionaires'. Isabel answered that Mary's 'suggestion of the Schloss' was 'most alluring'; Mary had described 'room with balcony & gorgeous view stove & bed'. Writing to Dorothy, Isabel also enquired about Ezra's living conditions in St Elizabeths – this was when he had just been moved out of Howard Hall: 'How does Son like his new quarters or other privileges Red X library & meals does it offer Readers Digest how does society compare with previous . . . ?' She accepted Mary's offer, and Olga – as Mary puts it – 'rose to the occasion; she laid aside old resentments. She drove with the old lady up from Rapallo in a black car.' Thereafter Isabel sat all day in her room in the crumbling *schloss*, 'reading and rereading *Don Quixote*, instructing me how to poach an egg to perfection, how to run a house the American way; planning a canal from Venice to Milan, big enough for big boats to navigate with their cargo'.

Mary gave birth to a baby son. 'I trust you wont start a feud with young Walter,' Ezra wrote to his mother, '& thank god *he* wont read the Readers Digest.' The boy was named Siegfredo Walter Igor Raimondo; the first and last two names were chosen by Boris, after celebrated ancestors, the second by Ezra, in honour of one Walther von der Vogelweide who was supposed to have sung his poetry at Neuhaus. Ezra seemed pleased to have a grandson. 'Young Walter . . . I hear, is far superior to earlier efforts to produce proper variety of the species,' he wrote to his mother. Olga, however, was anxious about the choice of Siegfried as first name, fearing that the ultra-Germanic implications would do Ezra no good.

Ezra was avid for any news from Neuhaus. He sent a wedding-present of $100 – Mary and Boris desperately needed it – and in his imagination, says Mary, he 'immediately set out to populate the vast halls . . . Letters flowed in, seething with ideas.' Mary and Boris themselves dreamed of achieving extraterritoriality for the castle, and thereby rescuing Ezra: 'We would fight for his extradition from the U.S.A., and he could rule over a domain populated with artists.' Boris had his own visions: he would re-establish the Noble Knights of Canossa, a medieval equestrian order founded by one of his forebears. As Mary observed, it was all becoming rather like the Cantos.

Ezra's mother still hoped to go to Washington, but during the Christmas following her arrival at Neuhaus she had a stroke (she was now nearly eighty-eight). 'I had great difficulty in making her eat,' writes Mary. 'No one would come to help me nurse her. The doctor did come, several times, but there was little he could do. Even the priest came once, about a week before she died, and she seemed glad to see him. I left them alone. Next morning she was almost cheerful and said: "Homer came to me last night and told me to give up." And as though she had willed it she went into a coma and never came to again. On the ninth of February [1948] she died . . . She looked very majestic and serene. The tenant helped dig the grave by the chapel. The soil was so frozen we had to be contented with a shallow one . . . Babbo wanted Herr Bacher to do an intaglio for his mother's grave and sent the drawings and wording for it. I was exhausted. Uncle Teddy [Olga's brother] offered hospitality in England and Peter [her cousin] took me and the baby home with him.'

By the time Mary returned to the Tyrol, it had become clear that Neuhaus could never become a permanent home. She and Boris moved to another ruined castle, just outside the village of Tirolo, on the mountain-side above Merano. 'After a few weeks at the village inn we were able to camp in the highest room of the tower. The village carpenter and his son moved into one of the ground-floor rooms with all their tools and set to work . . . Labour was abundant and cheap . . . Our faith and euphoria spread . . . I think all the superstitious peasants were relieved that the place was no longer so sinister and haunted.' So Schloss Brunnenburg now became the focus of Mary's hopes, the Utopia where she was determined her father would make his home when – and if – his present ordeal ended.

Boris was full of further dreams: he obtained the consent of the Vatican for the revival of an old title, granted to a Ghibelline ancestor by the Holy Roman Emperor in the twelfth century, and he took the name Prince de Rachewiltz, so that Mary's identity changed yet again. Once the apparently fatherless and stateless Maria Rudge, she was now Princess de Rachewiltz, inhabiting her own Tyrolean castle. However, on the mundane level Brunnenburg could only be supported by taking in paying guests. One of the first was Olivia Rossetti Agresti, who had broadcast with Ezra in Rome. Soon came a young poet, Mary Barnard, who had corresponded with Ezra and was on a Cantos-itinerary through Europe.

Ezra observed benevolently that Mary's peasant upbringing made 'a good balance with the Rachewiltz lion on the iron crown of the Lombards, plus family hard ware etc.' A second child, Patrizia Barbara Cinzia Flavia, was born to Mary and Boris in 1950, and hereafter Ezra would regularly pass on birthday greetings to 'Walt and Pat'. Charles Olson, visiting him for the last time, observed astutely that 'yet another of his comforts is to see himself in the part of the Old Man, "Grandpa", now that Mary has made him one.'

*

By February 1947, a year after the jury had judged Ezra to be of unsound mind, there was still no sign of *The Pisan Cantos* appearing in print. Ronald Duncan and Ezra himself were inclined to blame Faber and Faber – Duncan called the delay there 'monstrous' – but Eliot put the onus on Laughlin's failure to deliver him a final text: 'I didn't expect,' he wrote to Dorothy, 'that I should have to wait about two years for Cantos without getting any further than uncorrected galley proof with no ideograms . . . and I don't suppose anything more will happen until some time after Laughlin gets back from Switzerland and how much time he intends to put in sliding on the snow I don't know'. Laughlin admits that 'I could have been more attentive . . . but skiing meant a lot to me . . . [and] I saw the ski resort [in Utah], apart from the pleasure of skiing, as an opportunity to make a little money to support the publishing, so that I wouldn't have to keep going begging to my father and my aunt.' In fact, the delay was to prove of no small benefit to Ezra.

In December 1947, Julien Cornell wrote to Dorothy saying that he proposed to resume efforts towards Ezra's release, observing: 'There may be a long struggle ahead of us.' He suggested that Dorothy should decide 'just exactly where you will go' if a release were obtained. Dorothy wrote back on 18 December:

> Ezra should be got out of custody. We have been talking it over. Italy seems very unquiet just now. We should prefer not to go back there for possibly 3–4 months – but we could find somewhere in Virginia or N. Carolina to go on his release . . . There is a possible alternative, of going to Spain. He speaks Spanish well.

During January 1948, Cornell completed a petition for habeas corpus, and this was presented to the District Court on 11 February, in Dorothy's name:

> In view of the fact that my husband appears to be permanently insane and can never be brought to trial . . . I desire that he be

released from St Elizabeths Hospital and placed in my care . . . I am informed by counsel that my husband has the legal and constitutional right to be released from custody, because . . . the Constitution still guarantees to him that his liberty shall not be taken away without due process of law, and . . . it is a fundamental principle of law that every person is presumed to be innocent until he has been found guilty, and also that no person may be imprisoned until his guilt has been determined by due process of law . . . A presumably innocent man is being held in confinement and will be confined for life, merely because . . . he had not sufficient mental capacity to meet the charge.

The District Court refused the petition, but Cornell filed an appeal. He wrote to Dorothy on 4 March 1948 that it might be necessary to take the case as high as the Supreme Court. However on 28 March, Dorothy wrote to him: 'I must ask you to withdraw the appeal for my husband's release. I will write again to Mr Moore.'

Cornell was astonished. Nor did Dorothy give him (or Arthur Moore) any explanation. He surmised that it might have been because he had explained to her that the State Department would probably refuse permission for Ezra to return to Italy or leave the USA at all. Certainly Ezra himself had told him that 'if he had to remain in the United States . . . [he] did not care very much about being released . . . St Elizabeths was probably as good a place for him as any.' At all events Cornell told Dorothy that he regarded her instructions as 'definite and final', and withdrew the appeal, sending in a very modest bill ($225) for expenses in preparing it, and charging nothing at all for his time and work.

Others began to suspect Dorothy of some more private reason for abandoning the habeas corpus appeal. Arthur Moore wrote to Eliot saying he had detected 'some under-current of thought concerning Mrs Pound's attitude to the whole business, and I have felt some difficulty in approaching her on the subject'. Eliot had no such scruples. 'What I want to know is, is anything being DONE?' he asked Dorothy. 'Or if not, why not? What is being waited for?' She gave no answer.

During Mary's visit to England in the spring of 1948, before she moved from Neuhaus to Brunnenburg, she went to see Eliot to discuss her father's predicament:

Tall, thin, stooping, with a sad enigmatic smile, he opened the door and led me into his study: ' . . . you must forgive . . . a better welcome . . . I am just out of the hospital . . . we are alone in the house.' I was struck by the austerity of the room. An imposing desk behind which he sat and behind him a blocked-up fireplace . . . The room and his words felt chilly . . . He talked. Gently, uninterruptedly. Twice I dared put a question, he raised his hand and said: We'll come to it later. We never came to it. It was time to go. For viaticum he handed me, Pandora's box? Gianduia chocolates for my son.

As we moved towards it, a letter was slipped under the door of the study. I promptly picked it up – he had tried – and gave it to him. He blushed and whispered: Is it for you? Did I knot my brows into a question mark? I took leave in a hurry. Alone in the house? . . .

His words lingered: 'I fear your father does not want to accept freedom on any terms that are possible . . .'

Ronald Duncan also saw Mary in London during her visit. He wrote to Ezra:

Her one passion seems to be to create the thing she never knew, a home . . . a place . . . to which you eventually could come. She showed me photographs of her new castle . . . I gather it has seven bathrooms, and I have made her promise to keep one. As for her husband, he has a face as old as the Sforzas, and he seems devoted to his family. They are obviously happy together, and are a couple of children . . . The man wants to do nothing more than found a family and renovate a chateau, and Mary's idea seems to be to cultivate three acres. She said that Olga felt that this was menial and that she would be better employed translating Cantos. You and I know that this is bunk . . . I have had a long letter from Olga. I wish she could get to the States. The situation must be clarified. Nobody but yourself can make the decision . . . What do *you* want to do? You never mention yourself in your letters, but yourself is the only thing that worries your friends.

Ezra wrote often to Olga, but she was disturbed by his letters. In April 1948 she wrote to Overholser from Siena saying that she heard from Ezra 'several times a week', but could not get him to answer important questions. She wondered whether he actually received her replies. She spoke of his 'persistent refusal to face any facts which do not fit into how he would like things to be', and continued:

I have known Mr Pound for 25 years & have always found this tendency very strong, but . . . this now seems stronger . . . Perhaps I should have confined my letters to him entirely to trivial matters but I felt that continually living in an artificially conditioned world would make it harder for him to take up his life in the event of his liberation.

In reply, Olga received a letter from Dr Silk, Overholser's deputy, explaining that Ezra was still complaining of 'great fatigue and weakness', but observing drily that 'this fatiguability is much less evidenced when he is working on his manuscripts in his room alone', and remarking of her own observations: 'As you have noted, it is Mr Pound's mental quirk not to face any facts which are not in conformity with his preconceived beliefs. Because of Mr Pound's intelligence, he is very cleverly able to distort reality to suit his own purpose.' St Elizabeths was beginning to get the measure of Ezra.

Cornell told Laughlin in June 1948: 'I am afraid that Olga will have to give him up. Even if she could get to the States, Dorothy might make it difficult for her to see Ezra ... Overholser is a sympathetic and tolerant person, but I would not predict the attitude in such a triangular situation.' Olga somehow heard of this, and wrote to Ronald Duncan:

> Of course I do not intend 'to give E. up'; not because I have any delusions of any happy ending as far as I am concerned (and it is not Cornell's business anyway) but because I have a feeling of responsibility. I don't think D. would attempt to prevent my seeing him in Washington, or anywhere else ... I think my appearance on the scene would be a thing that might get D. started; bust up her routine. If you knew her life you would realize that she has never had to take any decisions or responsibilities. I think she does pretty well what E. tells her to do – but does *he* know what to do?

Olga decided there were certain measures she could take while remaining in Italy. In October 1948 she organized a petition in Rapallo, signed by the Mayor ('the new Mayor, and not fascist by any means') and more than sixty citizens, in which

> the undersigned having known the American writer Ezra Pound in Rapallo where he lived from 1923, declare that they do not find that he took part in fascist activities in this town. There is no trace of his being present at local meetings nor that he was enrolled in fascist organizations.
>
> He was always considered as an American citizen, friend of Italy, openly sympathizing with certain fascist principles in the branch of social economics and in the struggle against communism which he considered a peril to the U.S. themselves ... It being evident that he never acted with view to lucre he was able to retain the respect of his fellow citizens, even that part of them which disagreed with his political opinions ... He has always behaved correctly and never committed anti-semitic acts.

The petition was sent by Olga via the American Embassy in Rome to the

State Department. She also spent a great deal of time, says Mary, 'writing letters to old friends, often too much in the tone of: Whatever you are doing, stop it and think of Ezra! Which, if it so happened that they were having a fine time, tended to annoy them.' In addition she had the texts of half a dozen of Ezra's Rome Radio broadcasts (chiefly on literary topics) printed under the title *If This Be Treason* . . . , distributing copies during 1949. But this activity tended to worry rather than encourage Ezra's supporters in America. In March 1949 Olga wrote to Hemingway urging him to do something towards Ezra's release, but Hemingway clearly regarded her presence in the case as an obstacle rather than a help. 'The Rudge business is unfortunate,' he wrote to a supporter of Ezra's, 'and I believe is the basis for much of the hysterical thinking about the case.' And to Dorothy, Hemingway observed: 'The person who makes the least sense and most hysteria and trouble in all this is Olga Rudge.' Eliot, as Olga knew, felt much the same.

By now, Arthur Moore in London had come to the conclusion that Ezra would eventually 'float off with the tide', and it was simply a matter of working steadily at public opinion. With this in mind, Moore gave encouragement to Peter Russell, a young man who set up an 'Ezra Pound Circle' which would meet fortnightly in a London pub. Moore told Russell: 'E.P. thinks you might do as he used to half a century ago . . . arrange to be at a given eating place at a given hour each week . . . It must be cheap enough so anyone can afford it, and at a place where such a gathering would be made comfortable. I will undertake to meet the cost of a meal for yourself for this purpose. Then anybody caring to meet other young or intelligent people can turn up . . . only the one person must always be there to make the nucleus.' When Ezra sent the same suggestion to Ronald Duncan in London, he received a blunt rely: 'You say "we" should meet regularly at the same café – my dear Ezra, when we do, we only discuss FOOD. It is now 12 years since I ate a steak. My children aint never seen ½ the worlds delights. I gave my daughter a banana last Christmas & she put it in a candlestick!' On receipt of this, Dorothy sent the Duncans a food parcel.

Peter Russell went to Italy in the summer of 1948, met Olga at Siena, saw John Drummond in Rome, and visited Rapallo, where an American, D. D. Paige, had installed himself in Ezra's and Dorothy's old flat and was working at an edition of Ezra's letters, with Ezra's authority. Paige, a graduate of the University of Pennsylvania who was teaching at Wellesley College, had begun to correspond with Ezra when Theodore Spencer told him that Ezra needed contact with the outside world, and conceived the idea of a book of letters which would help to clear his name. Paige initially thought Laughlin ought to edit it, but Ezra told him to do it himself. 'He thought it would be a help to me . . . in my career, but I have an awful lot of doubt as to how much help a book of that sort was . . . You had to be careful to whom you told the fact that you had done this work on Pound.' Ezra gave him a list of correspondents to approach for letters, and suggested he visit Rapallo and look at carbons in his files. Paige and his wife saved for the trip and went over in 1948. 'The quantity of correspondence was fantastic,' he said. He took almost two years to make the selection, and with his wife's help produced about 4,000 typed pages of transcripts, with Ezra's idiosyncratic spelling, punctuation and layout regularized to some extent. Harcourt Brace agreed to publish, but reduced the selection drastically and further regularized the style. Even in this castrated form, Ezra's explosive correspondence (up to the beginning of the Second World War) still outraged many people when *The Letters of Ezra Pound 1907-1941* appeared in 1950.

Peter Russell's pub group expanded for a time into an Ezra Pound Society, and Russell brought out English translations of six of Ezra's economic tracts, first published in Italian, under the title *Money Pamphlets by £*. This did more harm than good to Ezra's situation, reminding such few readers as the series attracted of the nature of his political opinions. There was also a generally hostile reaction to a *festschrift* assembled by Russell to mark Ezra's sixty-fifth birthday, though the book included some excellent contributions, among them an essay on Ezra by Eliot. However, these efforts seemed but drops in the ocean compared to the consequences of the publication of *The Pisan Cantos*.

*

New Directions published them on 20 July 1948; Faber and Faber did not follow for a further year (the delay seems partly to have resulted from their decision to expurgate some of Ezra's more salacious remarks about contemporary figures). Reviews of the American edition were mixed; there was a general feeling that, as Robert Fitzgerald put it in *New Republic*, these were 'poetic sketch books' rather than finished poetry. William Carlos Williams wrote in the magazine *Imagi*:

> I have not (even yet) read every word of the *Pisan Cantos*, nor deciphered half of those I have read. But I have seen enough to be indifferent to many of them and to find myself wonderfully enlightened by the art of the others . . . The words get a freshness over them that I find in no other lines written in our day. But I will not deny, there's as much trash as excellence . . . incommunicable personal recollections – names, words without color.

On 18 and 19 November 1948, three and a half months after the book had appeared in America, a committee met in Washington to consider the first annual award of a new prize. The Bollingen Foundation had been established a few years earlier by Paul Mellon, banker and art patron, initially to publish in English the collected works of Jung, from whose Swiss home the Foundation took its name (Ezra afterwards referred to it as 'Bubble-Gum'). In 1943 Allen Tate, that year's Poetry Consultant at the Library of Congress, had suggested to the Library that it appoint a body of Fellows in American Literature, who should award an annual poetry prize. The Bollingen Foundation was approached as a likely source of funds, and with the help of Huntington Cairns, an influential figure in Washington artistic circles, this was done. However, not until 1948 was everything ready for the prize to be awarded. Léonie Adams, that year's Poetry Consultant at the Library, was to be ex officio chairman; the other judges (the current Fellows in American Literature) included Conrad Aiken, W. H. Auden, Louise Bogan, Katherine Garrison Chapin (the wife of former Attorney General Francis Biddle who had indicted Ezra for treason), T. S. Eliot, Robert Lowell, Karl Shapiro, and Allen Tate. The November meeting had been arranged to coincide with one of Eliot's visits to America.

Even before the meeting it was assumed that the Fellows were going to choose *The Pisan Cantos* for the prize. On 18 November, Eliot, Aiken, Lowell and Tate were among those who convened at the Library, and Tate observed that 'the choice, now probable of Ezra Pound's *Cantos* [sic] for the award might have political implications embarrassing to the Librarian'. In fact the next day three other nominations were produced, but the only serious contender was William Carlos Williams's *Paterson (Book Two)*, the latest instalment of the long poem generally regarded as Williams's finest work. A ballot was taken: there were eight votes for *The Pisan Cantos*, three for *Paterson (Book Two)*, and two abstentions. Those who voted for Ezra included Auden and Louise Bogan (both apparently by postal vote), Lowell, Tate, Eliot, and Theodore Spencer, who was dead but would have been a Fellow had he lived, and whom everyone said would have voted for Ezra (the business was already assuming a bizarre character). There were votes for *Paterson (Book Two)* from Shapiro, Aiken, and Katherine Garrison Chapin. At one point Shapiro seemed likely to vote for Ezra, but then changed his mind; Allen Tate tried to persuade him that, since he was Jewish, to vote for Ezra would be to 'give anti-Semitism a telling blow'; but Shapiro would not budge. Meanwhile Katherine Garrison Chapin was furious that Ezra should be considered at all, and talked to her husband, who felt similarly and wrote to the Librarian, Luther H. Evans, that he 'recommended strongly against the decision'. It was decided that the Fellows should be asked to vote again, this time by postal ballot, the following February. Léonie Adams meanwhile wrote to Julien Cornell saying that she had been told that publicity for Ezra at this moment would be 'most unfortunate', since it was said that his case was about to be reviewed by the authorities. Cornell replied that he could not see that the prize would do Ezra any harm; on the contrary, it would probably cheer him up.

Robert Lowell was already a friend and correspondent of Ezra's. He had begun to write to him in the autumn of 1947, in block capitals:

> DEAR MR POUND
>   THEY TELL ME THAT ONE HAS TO HAVE
> SPECIAL PERMISSION FROM DR OVERHOLSER TO
> SEE YOU. SO I RETURN HOPE TO SEE YOU WHEN
> ARRANGEMENTS CAN BE MADE. GOOD LUCK.
> > > Robert Lowell.

Aged forty, Lowell had spent some time in prison during the war for refusing the draft. His first book of poems was published in 1944, and he was the 1947 to 1948 Poetry Consultant at the Library of Congress. During his time in Washington he determined to see Ezra, who fascinated him as a man, though he was dubious about the poetry.

They met for the first time in February 1948; Lowell subsequently wrote to Ezra from the Yaddo writers' colony at Saratoga Springs; he was generally thought to be on the edge of a breakdown, and his letter alludes to this:

> Dear Ezra,
>   I've been meaning to write you for weeks, but
> I've been working like hell on my poem . . . Yaddo is a sort of
> St Elizabeth's without bars – regular hours, communal meals,
> grounds, big old buildings . . . I've been reading *The Unwob-
> bling Pivot* slowly and trying to look into my heart.* . . . I was
> much touched by your note to me in Washington, and miss
> seeing you both. I'll see you Friday or Saturday.
> > > Affectionately,
> > > Cal

A year later Lowell experienced a mental storm; after fighting the police in Bloomington, Indiana, and alarming his friends with his violent behaviour, he was put into a padded cell in a Massachusetts hospital, the first of many such incarcerations. He wrote to Dorothy Pound a few months afterwards:

> My 'experiences' that led to the hospital now seem like a
> prolonged dream – and so they were, then almost unbearably

*E.E. Cummings regarded the Confucius translation less reverently, naming it *The Unwob-
bling Pigeon*.

dull and depressing. I have thought of you and Ezra often – the astonishing jolt of having things happen to you, being put somewhere, the surprises you never planned. Of course, the similarities are only external, and my treatment was all for the good.

Ezra took no particular interest in Lowell, speaking of him to MacLeish as 'that LUMP Lowell'. He did not apparently read any of his work, remarking: 'After the age of fifty, one cannot be a telephone directory of younger writers.'

Meanwhile Dr Overholser became concerned about 'the diverse and variegated stream of visitors [to Ezra] procured by Mr Lowell' – several younger poets, including Randall Jarrell, whom Lowell brought with him to St Elizabeths or encouraged to visit Ezra. The concern was not altogether misplaced; a letter from Assistant Attorney General Alexander M. Campbell to Overholser in November 1948 stated that a Dr Rees had called on the Department of Justice to explain that 'his son who is interested in poetry frequently visits Pound', and that father and son both believed Ezra to be 'quite sane'. Campbell asked whether this meant that Ezra could now 'stand trial on the charges against him'. Overholser replied firmly:

> It is my personal opinion that there has been no essential change . . . He is extremely bombastic and opinionated, highly disorganized in his train of thought and possessed of a considerable number of extremely grandiose ideas about himself as well as ideas of persecution directed against others . . . I think it highly unlikely that there will be any substantial improvement in his condition, which is a singularly deep seated one.

The Bollingen Prize judges seemed unlikely to change their minds about *The Pisan Cantos*. Lowell admired William's *Paterson* – he had said of *Book One*: 'It is a sort of anti-Cantos rooted in America, in one city, and in what Williams has known long and seen often . . . It has, along with a few poems of Frost, a richness that makes all other contemporary poetry look a little second-hand.' But his personal affection for Ezra and his sympathy for his predicament made him unshakeably loyal, and Williams himself, when he heard about the Bollingen debate, said Ezra should be awarded the prize. Eliot, naturally, wanted to see Ezra win, and Tate, the inventor of the prize, felt the same. ('Tate is a queer dick with a twisted skull,' wrote Ezra to Archibald MacLeish, 'but he did get in once.') Ezra thought that, had Katherine Garrison Chapin not been married to Francis Biddle, she might have supported him; he told MacLeish: 'Geo Biddle said his sis-in-law was afraid to come in [to St Elizabeths] cause she thought I wd/

be so rude about her legitime.' Of two other judges he observed: 'Aiken and Auden weak reeds.' Aiken had always inclined towards hostility to Ezra, and had intitially voted for Williams, but he had supported Ezra loyally in a 1946 furore – and so, though he had little interest in Ezra's poetry, had Auden. In 1946 Random House had announced that they would not be including any of Ezra's verse in the new edition of their *Anthology of Famous English and American Poetry*, edited by William Rose Benét and Aiken himself. The first edition had included a substantial selection from Ezra's work (twelve pieces in all), but Saxe Commins of Random House announced that the company was 'not going to publish any fascist. As a matter of fact, we don't think that Ezra Pound is good enough, or important enough, to include.' Aiken immediately protested, saying that 'a burning of the books was a kind of intellectual and moral suicide which we might more wisely leave to our enemies', while Auden, who was published by Random House, stepped in and told the company he would withdraw his work from them unless they changed their minds. 'Good for Auden,' Ronald Duncan wrote to Ezra. Bennett Cerf, president of Random House, now admitted publicly that they had made an 'error in judgement', but described himself as 'an angry convert' to the decision to print Ezra's poems after all.

In his regular *Saturday Review of Literature* column (16 March 1946) Cerf said he had received 142 letters opposing the exclusion and 140 approving. Although it appeared that Random House had made a mistake, 'this does not mean that my abhorrence for Ezra Pound the man has abated one iota'. At this point Julien Cornell stepped in, asking Cerf to cease making derogatory statements about Ezra, and pointing out that Random House had not yet requested copyright permission to reprint the poems. Ezra subsequently received $300 in fees from the book.

This episode seemed now like a dress rehearsal for the Bollingen Prize. The postal vote among the Fellows was conducted in early February 1949, three months after their first meeting. Karl Shapiro tried to resign, but in the end simply abstained, saying that he 'did not wish to prejudice' anyone else's vote. Afterwards he explained:

> I voted against Pound in the [original] balloting . . . My first and more crucial reason was that I am a Jew and cannot honor antisemites. My second reason I stated in a report which was circulated among the Fellows: 'I voted against Pound in the belief that the poet's political and moral philosophy ultimately vitiates his poetry and lowers its standards as literary work.'

The postal ballot was conclusively in favour of *The Pisan Cantos*. An announcement of the judges' decision was prepared for release to the Sunday newspapers for printing on the morning of 20 February 1949, though an excited radio station broke the embargo the previous night. A typical headline that Sunday morning was carried by the *New York Times*:

POUND, IN MENTAL CLINIC,

WINS PRIZE FOR POETRY

PENNED IN TREASON CELL.

The *New York Herald Tribune*, carrying its own version a day later, reported that Ezra Pound

> won the $10,000 Bollingen Prize yesterday . . . Pound's work, the jurors held, 'represents the highest achievement of American poetry in the year for which the award is made . . . The Fellows are aware,' the jurors said, 'that objections may be made . . . To permit other considerations than that of poetic achievement to sway the decision would destroy the significance of the award and would in principle deny the validity of that objective perception on which any civilized society must rest.'

The public outcry was, of course, considerable, with predictable attacks from such established anti-Poundians as Albert Deutsch in *PM*, and equally predictable defences of *The Pisan Cantos* from members of the awarding committee and other critics. The ructions reached Radio Moscow, which remarked a month after the announcement: 'One is prompted to ask how low and miserable must be the quality of modern bourgeois poetry in America if even the insane and verified ravings of a confessed madman could win a literary prize?'

The Fellows had anticipated the furore; Allen Tate wrote to the Librarian a month before the announcement saying that they could have decided not to award a prize at all that year, but this would have been 'cowardly', while to give the prize to the second choice (*Paterson (Book Two)*) would be 'disgraceful, as Pound's book has been universally acclaimed as the most distinguished of the year, and nobody would believe we thought it wasn't . . . Hell will no doubt break loose, but I don't see how we can avoid it . . . If we can win this battle, we shall have struck a mighty tough blow for intellectual integrity.'

On the whole they made their point successfully; the Library of Congress files contain almost as many letters supporting the decision as attacking it. The Government was less sympathetic; Auden said he had heard a rumour that the judges were all going to be subpoenaed to explain themselves; and on 19 August the Joint Committee of the House and Senate on the Library of Congress ruled that the Library must abstain in future from giving any prizes or awards. Consequently the Bollingen and other prizes were temporarily abolished; in early 1950 Yale University

Library took over responsibility for the Bollingen, and the next recipient, entirely uncontroversially, was Wallace Stevens.

Ronald Duncan reported that Olga was delighted when he gave her the news of the award. Ezra himself made virtually no comment about it – the money apparently disappeared into his funds without being used for any special purpose – but Huntington Cairns recorded that when he had visited Ezra on the Saturday afternoon before the public announcement, 'Dr Oberholtzer [*sic*] had informed him that he had won the Bollingen Prize, and he was obviously excited by the news. He had prepared a statement for the Press reading: "No comment from the Bug House," but he said he had decided not to give it out. He referred to the Prize as "Bollingen's bid for immortality".'

13

Acolites Etc.

Thanks to the Bollingen, Ezra acquired, for a while, another Boswell; Huntington Cairns became a regular visitor to St Elizabeths and took notes of his conversation. Cairns, who had helped set up the prize, was a senior official of the Smithsonian (National Gallery of Art) in Washington, and the author of various popular works on art and other subjects. Ezra's names for him were variously 'HUNT em down' and 'Hunt and DAMN', a sign of some affection, but he poured scorn on Cairns's learning, and exploded at most of the books of which Cairns spoke highly: 'A man who reads Toynbee INSTEAD of Frobenius DESERVES to waste 12 years of his life . . . why the HELL you read all this Crap and Omit Frobenius/ brit snot and american time lag/.' Cairns said he got 'spiritual refreshment' out of listening to this sort of abuse.

Here are a few selections from Cairns's notes of their conversations:

> I saw Pound Saturday, January 8th [1949], at 2.30 in the afternoon, and was with him until 4.30. When I arrived he had two visitors, Reese and Stites, the latter from the National Gallery of Art. Stites at the moment of my arrival was explaining his criticism of Freud's *Leonardo* to Pound. As usual, Pound was disconcerted by having two people present whose interests did not fully coincide. He pulled out his watch and said that he would give Leonardo 15 more minutes and then would devote himself to my problems. However, the conversation at once became general . . . Stites . . . explained to Pound how much his theory of harmony, as developed in his *Antheil*, had meant to him. Pound said that Stites was only the fifth person who had pointed this out to him . . . Reese had brought

Pound a metronome. Pound made a microscopic adjustment in the rate of the metronome to show what a difference in timing such a minor regulation made.

We discussed the difference between Plato and Aristotle . . . Pound said that he had confronted Aristotle and Confucius in his *Culture*. He admitted that he had not read much of Plato . . . Pound went on to say that some day a publisher would bring out a list of the essential books, and he indicated with his hands that they would fill the space of about two feet. He rattled off some titles, all of which were books Shakespeare had read – Holinshed, North's Plutarch, Montaigne, Ovid, etc . . . He commented on the Hiss case, and asked how could a Carnegie man be innocent.*

Stites asked Pound if he was interested in modern art. Pound replied that he ought to be inasmuch as he had brought Wyndham Lewis and Gaudier-Brzeska to public attention. Stites thereupon asked him, 'Are you interested in children's drawings?' Pound replied, 'I don't know, let me see them.' . . .

Pound handed me a one page memorandum which he had prepared and which described how Blackstone could be edited for the contemporary reader.

During his encounters with Cairns, Ezra talked about publishing a popular edition of Blackstone's *Commentaries on the Laws of England*, first published in the 1760s. He said that 'the basic sections of Blackstone' (whom he sometimes called 'Blackstein') were 'necessary to a well balanced study of the humanities', but he did not explain why.

Cairns's first recorded meeting with Ezra concluded with a discussion of current American policy towards the USSR. Cairns hoped for a settled peace; Ezra's only observation was 'that a war postponed twenty years was no war; that an entirely different group of people would be shot in a war that was twenty years late'. Cairns visited him again the following Saturday afternoon.

I took him a three pound box of chocolates and he proceeded to eat about a third of the box while I was there. He is quite anxious for me to obtain some more apple candy for him, a product which seems to be available only in the Shenandoah Valley or its vicinity. I had sent him two boxes . . . at Christmas. He likes it not only because of its taste but because it fills him up quickly and he does not have to eat so much of it . . .

*Alger Hiss, Nicholas Murray Butler's successor as head of the Carnegie Endowment for Peace, had just been accused of perjury after denying that he was a Communist.

He says he has a new visitor who comes to see him on Wednesday afternoons and who can recite Greek poetry by the hour. Pound says that he himself is not a good Greek student, but that he enjoys the recitations. As usual, we were visited by the inmate who tries to expose himself before any women visitors. Pound, who was sitting in an easy chair in his customary position in a corner by the window, folded a newspaper and threw it at him. The inmate disappeared.

February 5th, 1949 . . . We talked briefly about Blackstone, and he urged me to bring out an abridged edition for two reasons: (a) the job was one that was intellectually necessary today, and (b) I would derive an income from the book which would permit me to live the year round at Kitty Hawk [Cairns's country home].

On January 29th, Mrs Longworth and I paid a visit to Pound. I had given him no notice that she was coming with me, but he had urged me a number of times to bring her again. He had prepared himself to discuss Blackstone with me, and he was plainly disconcerted by her arrival. It took him at least fifteen minutes to get his thoughts in order so that he could talk to her connectedly at all. Driving out, I told Mrs Longworth that I wanted to discuss with Pound his theory of an anthology. As I understood it, Pound would admit to the anthology only the poets who have developed new and striking techniques . . . After we had been with Pound about fifteen minutes Mrs Longworth brought up the topic, but Pound said he had to have notice, and would discuss it with me next week.

March 5th, 1949 . . . He said that American scholarship was 200 years behind Sinology, 40 years behind on Brooks Adams, and 60 years behind on Frobenius.

I saw Pound at 3.0 pm, Saturday April 2nd. He had a little box of clippings and letters on the Bollingen Prize, which he showed me. Most of them were from strangers, and a great majority were favorable . . . Pound spent about ten minutes denouncing our current American criticism . . . I asked him if he detected anything worthwhile in the younger poets and prose writers. He refused to answer the question on the ground that no critic can judge the new generation. I asked him why, and he said because you cannot see your own tail.

May 7th, 1949. I saw Pound for an hour in the hall of St Elizabeth's. We devoted most of the time to discussing Ford Madox Ford's stature as a writer. Pound has a great admiration . . . He had been reading Stella Bowen's . . . autobiography . . .

I asked him what he thought Frobenius' special contribution to anthropology was. He answered me for about ten minutes but the substance of his statement amounted only to praise of Frobenius' method. I pointed this out and he tried again, but with the same result.

It appears that Mrs Pound has approached Mrs Winslow, who is Robert Lowell's aunt or some relation, with an offer of assistance. Lowell is now confined in a mental asylum in Massachusetts. Pound has offered to make room for him at St Elizabeth's in the same ward if Lowell would like to come and stay with him. (All this, of course, is beyond Pound's authority.)

Pound thinks that the Government should at once release him, send him by plane to Rome, where he should be installed without cost to himself in rooms maintained by the American Academy. He should be employed at a compensation by the American Government as a confidential advisor to the American Ambassador in Rome since he, Pound, has an exceptional grasp of European affairs.

July 3rd, 1949. Pound said that he received his education from Ford Madox Ford and Yeats; he spent the days with the former and the evenings with the latter. He had to see them separately because they hated one another . . . Pound discounted Goldring's hint that Ford had Jewish blood from his father's side. Pound said Ford could not have enjoyed digging in the ground the way he did if he had any Jewish blood . . .

He said that the lunatics in the hospital did not get on his nerves. He had never minded crazy people; it was only fools he could not abide. He was dressed in shorts, a shabby old hat pulled over his head, and was sitting in the shade on the lawn in a dilapidated canvas chair which he folded and carried with him.

Ezra involved Cairns in the first new literary project he had tackled since being brought to Washington, a translation of the *Odes* of Confucius, which he made during 1949 with the help of a Chinese student at the Catholic University of Washington, Veronica Sun. During her visits, he would read out to her his proposed English version and she, with the

Chinese in front of her, was supposed to warn him when he was straying too far from it, but she was too much in awe of him to interrupt or criticize very often. His translations included many good passages, but the chief problem with the enterprise was its length. *Cathay* had been a very careful selection, but his version of the *Odes* contains all 300 of the Confucian poems – he alleged that each was essential to the collection as a whole – and was therefore not the product of concentrated energy.

Cairns had the finished translations typed for Ezra over the winter of 1949 to 1950, but the book was then delayed for several years while Ezra battled with Harvard University Press, who had agreed to publish it. He demanded that they include the original Chinese text, which they refused to do. The book eventually appeared without the Chinese, Ezra believing that this would follow in a later volume. Entitled *The Classic Anthology Defined by Confucius*, it had an introduction by Achilles Fang, a Chinese scholar at Harvard (who owed his first name to his father being a classicist); Fang described Ezra as now emerging as 'a Confucian poet'. The promised second volume never appeared – to Ezra's un-Confucian rage.

Achilles Fang began to visit Ezra at St Elizabeths, and wrote to Laughlin asking if he had any idea how the remaining cantos would turn out. Fang wondered if at least part of them should not deal with modern China, and offered any help with this that Ezra might require. For a full four years after writing the Pisan Cantos, Ezra had shown not the slightest inclination to produce any more. Quite apart from his complaint of fatigue, he seems to have felt that to abstain from writing poetry represented a complaint against his incarceration; he often repeated the remark he had made to Ronald Duncan about caged birds not singing. However, around 1950 he discovered the writings of the nineteenth-century American economic historian Alexander del Mar, and began to describe him as America's greatest writer of history, comparing him with Frobenius as a master in the 'art of collecting and arranging a mass of isolated facts, and rising thence, by a process of induction to general ideas'. (As usual with his enthusiasms he did not make it clear what del Mar had actually contributed to knowledge.) This new interest seems to have prompted him to begin work on the Cantos again.

Overholser and his staff now usually said 'yes' to any request to visit him, providing Ezra himself had no objection. Enquirers' letters were passed to Ezra for approval, and he would scrawl 'O.K.' in the margin. Overholser was left to write the reply – was indeed expected to act as Ezra's social secretary.

A regular stream of young writers and academics was now arriving at the hospital, among them Samuel Hynes, A. Alvarez and Malcolm Bradbury. The art historian Kenneth Clark came one April when he was in Washington, and Ezra responded amiably – 'I wanna thank K. Clark fer his book / got impression that he was passing thru/ and ergo failed to suggest he look in again.' Marshall McLuhan, teaching at the University of Toronto, came several times, and wrote in a white heat to Ezra saying he proposed to establish a mimeographed weekly sheet. It would bypass the 'literary cliques' and be sent to '30–40 serious characters' personally known to McLuhan; the object was to open up communications between arts and sciences, and to disseminate 'the grammar and general language of 20 major fields'. This could have been Ezra himself writing thirty years earlier, and later letters from McLuhan began to parrot Ezra's style. McLuhan disappeared as abruptly as he had appeared. He broke off the correspondence violently in a letter to Ezra dated February 1953 with the assertion that the arts were all run by secret societies, and that Ezra, too, was as guilty of such cliquishness.

However, McLuhan brought Ezra one benefit, in the shape of one of his graduate students at Toronto, Hugh Kenner. Initially, Kenner had intended to write his thesis on Joyce, but after seeing *The Pisan Cantos* he began to drift towards Ezra as a subject. By 1950 he was teaching in California and had finished a book which Ezra told him to call *The Rose in the Steel Dust*, but which Kenner, prosaically but more illuminatingly, entitled *The Poetry of Ezra Pound*. By the time it had come out in 1951, Kenner too had caught the infection of Ezra's style in his letters to him.

Robert Lowell, reading Kenner's book, spotted this stylistic influence. He wrote to Ezra that Kenner 'seems to have read no one except you and Eliot and Dr Leavis (his style is barbarous earnest parody of you and Leavis) . . . Be that as it may, I learned something from him, which is perhaps why I'm annoyed.' Ezra himself did not particularly care for Kenner's book, telling a correspondent:

> Certainly the acolites etc. As Hugh, kenners, kennels etc. I usually find my own simple statements more comprehensible than the eggsplantation by flatchested highbrows. H.K. definitely AIMED at Yale grad/ school etc. and frankly said so.

But in another letter he was more complimentary: 'Kenner bk/ . . . gets some of the needed stuff back into print / starts with necessary (I spose necessary) professional wind, but packs a punch in the tail.' And to Huntington Cairns: 'Kenner has read the text and does not talk nonsense, if you MUST get all yr/ information at 2nd. hand.'

*

A twenty-year-old named John Kasper began to write to him in June 1950. Kasper had just graduated from Columbia and intended to work for a doctorate in English and philosophy. Already an admirer of Ezra's work, he had written in an undergraduate essay:

I thrilled at Niccolò Machiavelli, Friedrich Nietzsche and the political Ezra Pound. Hitler and Stalin are clever men and [Woodrow] Wilson a fool. The weak have no justification for living except in service of the strong. What is a little cruelty to the innocuous when it is expedient for the strong ones who have the right to alter the laws of life and death before their natural limits?

Kasper paid his first visit to Ezra in the summer of 1950, and, said friends, came back from Washington to New York 'almost as a person inspired'. Ezra had instantly persuaded him to turn aside from 'fugg of am/ universities' to 'basic stuff' – the dissemination of such writers as he currently considered important. He also put Kasper in touch with another of his admirers, Louis Dudek. Kasper reported to Ezra: 'I'm going to buy a printing press . . . Dudek and I are going to try to get together a loose group in the next few weeks.' Ezra nicknamed him 'Kasp', and, just as the young Laughlin had done in the 1930s, Kasper responded by addressing Ezra as Boss: 'Dear Boss . . . So far as Kasp/ is concerned he will stand on whatever Gramp/ says.'

Kasper's early letters to Ezra show he was at a loose end; he continually asked Ezra what he should do with his life. One of his many embryonic projects was to arrange for Ezra's *Le Testament de Villon* and his Cavalcanti opera to be performed. 'This city gets me down sometimes,' he wrote to Ezra from New York in January 1951. 'I sometimes go over to Yorkville on the East Side just to get a breath of fresh air. That's where the German population of N.Y.C. live . . . There are a few Nazis over there and I enjoy talking to them. They know what is fact and what ain't. Yr. Serv't, der Kasperl.' He and an acquaintance opened a bookshop on Bleecker Street in Greenwich Village which they called Make It New. There was Nazi literature in the window, though at this stage Kasper is said to have had several Negro friends and not to have excluded Jews from his acquaintance.

In June 1951 Kasper contacted yet another Pound admirer, Thomas David Horton, who had been in touch with Ezra since January 1947 when he had written to 'Dr Orelhoser' (*sic*) asking permission to visit, and describing himself as 'a prospective student'. In those days St Elizabeths was still watchful of Ezra's contacts, and permission was refused, but Horton could not be prevented from corresponding, and he eventually managed to join the circle at the hospital. He was then working in a Washington naval laboratory; later he became a student at Hamilton College. He started by writing neat, conventional, civil letters to Ezra, but by 1950 was imitating him and addressing him as 'Gramp'.

Horton and Kasper began to publish a 'Square $' series of booklets, masterminded by Ezra and consisting of texts that he believed every student should read. The series had a nominal editorial board that included Marshall McLuhan and Norman Holmes Pearson of Yale. Booklets were priced at $1, and included the Fenollosa essay on the Chinese Written Character, *The Unwobbling Pivot*, Ezra's translation of the *Analects* of Confucius, and works by Alexander del Mar and Louis Agassiz, the nineteenth-century Harvard naturalist and opponent of Darwin.

Laughlin did his best to prevent publication of the Square $ series, believing that it might harm Ezra's position, but Kasper paid no attention and Ezra was delighted by it. Kasper, meanwhile, took up with a friend's estranged wife, telling Ezra she was 'very Jewish in many respects' but explaining that he was using her simply for

> her pocketbook . . . we ought to have her money for Sq. Dollar . . . the woman is S.O.B. and almost hopelessly rotten . . . So far as I can make out America is entirely in yitt control at the moment. That power must be smashed if anything decent will appear or have a chance to breathe.

In August 1952 Kasper reported to Ezra that he had been heckling a Labor Party street meeting and encouraging bystanders 'to shout the jews and niggers off the platform'. Overholser was aware that people with such views were joining Ezra's circle, but observed blandly that Ezra would not be 'likely to lead many people astray who weren't astray already'.

Another disciple, Eustace Mullins of Staunton, Virginia, called himself Director of the Aryan League of America and had a letterhead printed with the slogan 'Jews are betraying us!!' Mullins was described in print by one of Ezra's friends as seeming 'to have no spine' – it was characteristic of the acolytes to abuse each other – but Ezra raised no objections when Mullins eventually wrote a biography of him, *This Difficult Individual* (1961). Another member of the St Elizabeths circle, Michael Reck, published his own biographical study of Ezra a few years later, in which he – inevitably – abused Mullins's book.

Although males predominated in numbers among the acolytes, one woman was particularly in evidence. Huntington Cairns noted on his last trip to St Elizabeths on 30 May 1952: 'When I arrived he was surrounded by four young couples, to whom he was holding forth on poetry and the importance of Chinese. As he talked, one of the girls made good pencil sketches of him.' This was Sheri Martinelli, a regular visitor from the beginning of 1952. David Rattray describes her, in the usual hostile manner of one disciple writing about another:

> Miss Martinelli . . . with her golden hair falling down around her thin shoulders . . . dressed in blue jeans and a checkered

blouse . . . suggested a frayed and faded survivor of the early bobby-sox days. She had huge eyes like a cat. They bulged in a flushed face that tapered down from an enormous forehead to a tiny chin and tinier double chin. Her lips were tight and pale, but sometimes relaxed and parted into a naïve smile. I assumed that she was a patient from another ward.

Omar Pound, however, calls her 'pretty', and says that Ezra enjoyed her attentions.

Another disciple depicts Ezra greeting Sheri as she came across the lawn at St Elizabeths:

> He jumps out of his chair and hurries to greet La Martinelli with his most affectionate and energetic bear hug. Cookies [brought by Sheri] scatter about them . . . She claim[s]: 'Grampaw is the only man in the world you can bring cookies and before he can eat one of them, he drops them all on the ground; and before you can help him pick them up, he steps on every one.'

'Grampaw' was the persona he now invariably adopted in the presence of visitors. He had developed a special costume for the role. The summer version consisted of 'floppy sandals, walking shorts several sizes too large gathered at the waist with a belt, his shirt thrown off to take in more sun'. Another visitor describes 'tan shorts too big for him, tennis shoes and a loose plaid shirt'. On less warm days he might be found in 'a loose sweatshirt, an old GI overcoat, baggy trousers, heavy white socks, bedroom slippers, long underwear showing at his ankles'. It was a great contrast to such earlier costumes as the dandified Whistler outfit, carefully donned under Richard Aldington's eye at Church Walk in 1912.

Out on the lawn, writes Louis Dudek, he

> continually kept doing little things to make us comfortable: cutting the fruit . . . and passing it around; pouring the tea out of a thermos; offering newspapers to lay on the grass for sitting; bringing out books, magazines, letters from a bag . . . He would also feed the birds . . . Said Mrs Pound: 'he would never do that in the old days; he was always too busy, always doing something.'

Dorothy was supposed to be supervising him during these lawn sessions, but there were rumours that he engaged in some sort of sexual activity with female disciples – if not out of doors, then in his room in Chestnut Ward. E. Fuller Torrey writes in his 1984 book on Ezra:

> By [Sheri] Martinelli's own admission she and Pound were

lovers; she explicitly acknowledged this in a letter to Archibald MacLeish. Descriptions of their relationship by other visitors corroborate this. For example David Rattray records her arrival while he was there: 'Pound embraced her and ran his hands through her hair, and they talked excitedly, each interrupting the other. I turned and talked to Mrs Pound.' When she left, 'Pound threw his arms around her, hugged her, and kissed her goodbye.' A nursing staff member who worked on Pound's ward during these years recalls that Pound was allowed to have certain visitors at any time of the day or evening, that he entertained the visitors in his private room, and that the room was absolutely off limits to the staff. 'None of the staff would have dared to interrupt him when he had visitors.'

Sheri Martinelli wrote to another Pound biographer, David Heymann, in praise of 'guiltless sex of animal desire; pure, simple & uncomplicated'. But though she evidently wished people to believe that she and Ezra were lovers, his room was nothing like as private as Torrey suggests. Even if doctors or nursing staff thought it indecorous to enter while he had visitors (and there is no other evidence of this), the Cedar Ward patients wandered in and out quite unpredictably. Ezra's guests were generally appalled by his lack of privacy. Despite Torrey's assertions, it seems clear that no visitors whatever were permitted to be in the ward after 4.30 p.m., so that evening assignations were out of the question. Sheri Martinelli claimed to be the Undine of Canto 91 ('Thus Undine came to the rock . . . ') but there is nothing else in his writing to suggest that she was a Muse. One of Ezra's circle told Noel Stock: 'Sheri was at first important as a stimulating conversationalist ("dope-dolls"). He later became "interested" in her. Finally she became a bore and he said he was sick of her hippy cans of garbage over him.'

Her letters to Ezra read much like those of his other disciples, and are sometimes anti-Semitic. For a time she was employed at George Washington University, but then lost her job and thereafter largely depended on Ezra for – quite literally – her daily bread. His store of leftovers from the ward meals, and his hoard of what wealthier visitors had brought him, served as a food bank which (though its contents were often none too fresh) now helped to feed the less affluent. His room was described as a confusion of

> jars, bottles, boxes, make-shift containers filled with dainties, exotics, and plain fare of bread, cheese, ham, sweets . . . and all the left-over food he could 'pouch' three times a day from the tables at St Liz . . . The only time in my life I ever had enough caviar was Xmas day at St Elizabeths . . . The main purpose of

his bulging larder was to feed the starving artist; jar after jar of food went off the grounds for 'the noble purpose of nourishing the arts'.

They in return would bring him fudge or jasmine tea, which he drank on nights when he could not sleep.

Though Sheri liked to emphasize the mutual devotion between her and Ezra ('Grandpa loves me,' she told David Rattray, 'it's because I symbolize the spirit of Love to him, I guess'), she was apparently just as fond of Dorothy – or at least took care not to alienate her. Her notes to Dorothy are full of protestations of affection ('I – LUV – U'), and on one occasion Rattray observed her sketching Dorothy:

> Miss Martinelli went on sketching Mrs Pound . . . 'D.P. has a beautiful face . . . but it is so *difficult* . . . Maestro . . .'
>
> 'Yes, Ma'am,' said Pound, jerking around to sit on the edge of his chair.
>
> 'Will you look at this drawing?' Pound looked at it, squinting in the light, then said, 'It's a likeness,' and swung himself violently back into the reclining position.

Ezra made a great fuss of Sheri's supposed talents as an artist, declaring that she was 'reviving the tradition of "Giott and Bott"' (Giotto and Botticelli). She made a portrait of Ezra, saying that he had begged her 'PAINT me out of here, Cara,' so she had 'painted E.P. in Paradise as he had sung me from Purgatory'. In 1956 he got Vanni Scheiwiller of Milan, whose father had published some of his work before the war, to issue a little booklet containing ten colour plates of her work under the title *La Martinelli*. It included her portrait of him (in which his features are unrecognizable) and in the introduction he wrote in praise of her work, calling her 'the first to show a capacity of manifest in paint . . . what is most to be prized in my writing'.

Some of his disciples were taking drugs, and their hallucinations and perceptions briefly interested him; but he soon became concerned about their habits, and wrote to Huntington Cairns about this in March 1952:

> have yu any angles on keeping dope pushers away from young people of talent?
>
> I mean let'em hop up ALL the communists, employees of the late sow bellie's friends etc/
>
> AND the low and average muck/   but there ought to be some means of conveying to the higher ups, that pushing the stuff to sensitive young who might otherwise be capable of doing something of interest ought to be stopped

AND someone ought to pass the word along that special interest may be taken in particular cases / the limited number of same. not such as to greatly diminish the swag of the large dealers.

      y   v   t

           anon.

He does not seem to have raised the subject with the disciples.

He now pretended that he had been against Hitler all along. 'NO, ten thousand times NO/' he wrote to MacLeish in 1956, 'it does NOT depend on view of Hitler/ I take it we are agreed that Adolf should have been STOPPED.' Yet he did nothing whatever to dissuade John Kasper from drifting towards Nazi racial views. When Noel Stock met Kasper years later he thought him 'a poor waif who'd been exploited by Ezra'. Possibly Ezra's encouragement of his disciples' antics was a way of getting his own back at respectable society's treatment of him, but that does not make it the less culpable. And if Ezra should have known better, so should Overholser, who was undoubtedly aware of the atmosphere engendered during their visits to the hospital, but said: 'What goes on at these sessions I do not know.'

14

A National Skeleton

Olga came briefly to Washington in the spring of 1952, telling Overholser before she arrived: 'I represent the interests of Mr Pound's daughter.' Overholser knew who she was and had a talk with her. She did not have an easy time with Ezra himself, saying he was 'a little bit over-excited. You feel you've got a few minutes to – to – anyway – I – I – anyway . . . ' Again in this filmed interview, her voice tails off. But she adds: 'I wasn't able to see him afterwards for years. And it was not the kind of thing that he would have discussed by letter, nor would I. Except indirectly.'

*

A lawyer named Rufus King now interested himself in the case, at the request of Eliot and several of Ezra's friends. He concluded that there were three possibilities for Ezra: to stand trial on the treason charge, to seek a presidential pardon, or to stay where he was. King thought 'we could win an acquittal' if the case went for trial, but gathered that it was widely felt that the strain would be too much for Ezra. He realized that Ezra regarded the idea of asking for a presidential pardon as equivalent to an admission of guilt, and therefore unacceptable. King also observed that Dorothy seemed 'reluctant to move'.

King understood that

> the Department of Justice sends agents to St Elizabeth's Hospital two or three times a year to make sure that Mr Pound is still confined and is not at large, i.e. impliedly recovered. They feel that the Hospital is probably sheltering him when he could in fact be adjudged sane if they pressed the matter.

Certainly the Department wrote to Overholser at frequent intervals to ask

about Ezra's mental state. One such letter, requesting 'a current report on
the present condition and progress of Ezra Pound', together with 'the
diagnosis and prognosis' of his mental illness, was sent by Stanley E.
Krumbiegel, Medical Director, Bureau of Prisons, in June 1953. Overholser replied:

> There has been essentially no difference in Mr Pound's con-
> dition . . . He professes profound weakness and spends the
> largest part of his time in a recumbent position . . . He is
> decidedly disinterested in his personal appearance . . . He is an
> extreme egocentric and, indeed, his egocentricity goes to the
> extreme of a decidedly paranoid attitude . . . He still lacks
> entirely any grasp of the nature of the offense with which he is
> charged and . . . is still mentally incompetent to stand
> trial . . . The exact category in which he should be classified
> diagnostically is difficult to ascertain . . . He does not fit well
> into any of the psychiatric categories. Perhaps the nearest
> approach would be that of Personality Trait Disturbance,
> Narcissistic Personality . . . [He is] without psychosis, but there
> is no doubt . . . that the disturbance of personality
> . . . may properly be said to constitute mental incompetence. In
> our opinion, one may be incompetent without being technically
> psychotic.

Rather surprisingly, this had the right effect, and for the time being there
were no further enquiries about Ezra from the Government.

Rufus King reported to Eliot in October 1953 that (even supposing Ezra
would permit it) a pardon would not be granted. He explained that while
Truman, 'at the end of his term, would have been more approachable
because he was retiring and would not have cared so much about any
adverse reactions to an act such as this', President Eisenhower, who had
just been elected, 'is in a more vulnerable position, and also, I think, a
tougher man'. Moreover, the new Republican administration had changed
the procedure for pardon applications, which now had to be made
publicly, and so attracted attention in the press. 'The old system was
entirely confidential. I think this change seriously affects the remedy from
our point of view. Which leaves the third alternative: it is a horrible thing
to see Mr Pound confined with a ward of depressives and a television set,
yet it is better, perhaps, than the only present escape which would be via a
trial.' King added that 'friends in the Department of Justice' had assured
him that 'there is absolutely no change in the situation, insofar as the
treason prosecution is concerned. They say, as they have said before, that
there is little likelihood that their case will be abandoned, so long as their
witnesses remain alive and available, etc.'

King visited Ezra, who took a dislike to him because he had worked in the Roosevelt Administration, and was (said Arthur Moore) 'most abusive' about him. Ezra himself wrote to Moore:

> WITHOUT telling Possum E.P. has seen Kings twaddle/ AVM [Arthur Moore] might as ON his own knowledge say that the cookie pushers lied to King who is a soft lump / and that he is not having either guts or curiosity accepted the alibi. NO other broadcasters had FREEDOM of microphone to send their own stuff / and Possum ought to be aware of that and not swallow what King swallowed. Naturally a Roosevelt employee wd. lie like his employer. AVM can put that in parliamentary language.

This seems to imply that Ezra still believed he could defend himself in court, on the grounds that he had been given freedom of the microphone and was not a hired propagandist. It would appear, therefore, that he was still prepared to face a trial, and resented that he had not been allowed to.

Eliot concluded, in writing to King in November 1953:

> It does appear at present to be a stalemate. The situation is all the more painful because from time to time Olga Rudge (or someone else) makes a suggestion for action which she would like me to implement, and I have repeatedly the ungrateful task of writing to say that I fear the suggested action would be likely to do more harm than good . . . All that you say tends to confirm my opinion that any steps to be taken, must be taken quietly, and in America, not elsewhere.

Wyndham Lewis suggested to Eliot that a petition could be addressed to President Eisenhower. Eliot raised the idea with King in December 1953, but King wrote back that this would more likely be damaging to Ezra. He now felt, however, that 'our Government may possibly decide to drop the treason charges sooner or later. This is by no means an immediate prospect but it is a possibility which should not be ruled out. Such action would be taken, only if it is felt that Pound has been forgotten by the great mass of the American public. Therefore, anything whatsoever that stirs up . . . interest . . . would be undesirable.'

Mary, who had not seen her father for seven and a half years, came to America in March 1953. 'Mamile took care of the children in Sant' Ambrogio. It was due to her efforts that I was issued an American passport, and it was she who raised the money for the outward journey.' She went 'with the firm intention of taking Babbo . . . home, to Italy'. Olga's latest idea was that Ezra should be persuaded to sign a statement that he was mad, thereby disclaiming responsibility for the supposed treason; Eliot called this 'a travesty' and Mary agreed. 'Even if it were the only way out, I of all people should suggest it?' In New York she saw Laughlin, who told her: 'You are the only person who could influence him – if you can get him to sign certain papers – ' But she would not consider it. She also met Julien Cornell, who took her to lunch with Arthur Garfield Hays of the Civil Liberties Union. To them she expounded her father's belief that he had merely exercised the right of free speech on the radio. She thought she had convinced them, but nothing came of the meeting. Then she went to Washington, staying at first with Caresse Crosby, who took her in a taxi out to St Elizabeths.

'So here we were. For two days he had received no visitors. Waiting. He had not expected me to stop over in New York, was not interested in Cornell and in Garfield Hays. I felt terrible, no excuse, I should have come to him straight off the boat, first things first. "No use being sorry." "Yes, I know." I remembered his lesson and all was well. And he wanted me to fill in the gap: ten years, except for that brief visit to the prison camp in Pisa. I knew he was proud and amused to be a "granpaw", his kindness and curiosity were boundless . . . "Thank God you have taken time to produce a family and lead a sane life." And it never bored him to listen to accounts of Boris and the children and of our efforts with the castle. But whenever I tried to lead the conversation back to "What can we do to get you out of here?" he became tense and impatient: "All you can do is to plant a little decency in Brunnenburg."

'With the passing of days the bleakness of the outlook became clear. I had come armed with letters of introduction from his old friends in Italy, Pellizi, Villari, Signora Agresti, to their friends in the States who might have some influence or advice. But father shook his head: no good. Well then: "If you would sign certain papers – " Did I have a clear notion of what it would involve? "Not clear, but vague – a device which you can repudiate once you are free and back in Italy." But his sharp glance made me feel ashamed. No – for mere impatience pretend guilt or incapacity – not in keeping for a man who harped on responsibility. "Stand trial and you'll be acquitted!" Was Garfield Hays's price exorbitant? "What's the point in my being free if the family has to go bust and one has to pass the bowl around?"

'Caresse Crosby's lawyer obtained an appointment for me at the Department of Justice. I was promptly dismissed. "If you want a piece of good advice you better not insist that the case be reopened; you might land him in the electric chair." . . .

'At social occasions, as long as I was the charming young princess with a fairytale castle in Italy, everything was fine . . . But as soon as I met anyone I thought could help Babbo, I was impatient of trappings and chitchat. An unpardonable breach of etiquette. The prominent lady novelist: "Yes, yes, I know" and impatiently turned to the partner on her other side. And

Francis Biddle, the former Attorney General – as I was thanking the stars for the meeting, the man who surely must know more than anyone else – " – you know at the Bollingen Award – " "Yes, but that was four years ago and he is still – " and he with a disarming smile: "Let me get you a drink." A good thing I was not pining for a drink, for I never saw him again.

'And at St Elizabeths? I went to see the director of the hospital, Dr Overholser, but he was away. A few days later he came, ostensibly to lend father a book, and said: "I am sorry I missed you, come any time you wish." After he had left, Babbo said quietly: "No use bothering him, he is already overworked. There is nothing you can learn from him."

'Every day from his window he watched out for my arrival and was right behind the door when it opened, ready to go out on the lawn or to lead me down the long corridor, leaning on me heavily as he used to for fun in Venice and Sant'Ambrogio. He introduced me with pride to the attendants and if they said something nice he bowed and smiled as though he had heard "*Che bea putea*". Oblivious, it seemed, to the heavy bunch of keys at the end of a chain, to the poor drivelling empty husks rocking with vacant stares in front of blaring televisions, to the frightful leering of younger shades.

'After my second day Dorothy was usually present, sometimes also Omar; and after the first week his regular visitors returned. My role became that of a spectator. I was to be further educated. At first I was intrigued, then indignant, then depressed, then amorphous. I remembered: " – Mr Pound is here as an anthropologist" and thought he was merely appeasing his curiosity. To me, at that time, the young people who came to see him were a new species of human beings in appearance and behaviour: sloppy and ignorant . . . "They all need kindergarten" – but what a waste of his fine mind. It seemed to me no one had read or seen anything, certainly had not read much Pound. There was no conversation. They came with tidbits of political information and racial bias in the nature of what bums might fish out of garbage cans. Vapid jokes. And if father threw a new name at them they ran off with it like crazy dogs with a bone and since it was all they had in their mouths they declared themselves experts: of del Mar, Aggasiz . . . The sad fact was that there was no one else willing or able to keep him company regularly and he needed an outside audience as an antidote to the inmates. The beau monde used that "funny crowd" as an excuse for not visiting more often, but in truth St Elizabeths was a very disagreeable place to go to and Pound was not yet a fashionable topic. Also . . . McCarthyism was in full swing . . . People who might have moved in his defense lay low . . . The only saving element was a group of professors from the Catholic University, foremost among them Craig La Drière and Giovanni Giovannini, who had . . . the patience and the intelligence to acquaint themselves with the facts and circumstances of the broadcasts so that they were able to state the case clearly in print on several occasions . . . They were men with an education and manners . . . But out on the lawn or behind the windscreen in the corridor these gentlemen were outnumbered by the "disciples" who, as often as not, would tease them about their political and racial non-commitment . . .

'Why did he allow this farce to go on in his presence? Why didn't he teach these young people manners! And then I saw the caged panther, the boredom, the weariness of the man hit by history full blast . . . And I was myself so ignorant about America and the new generation sloppily sitting there gobbling up hardboiled eggs which he had saved from his lunch . . . And so I just sat and watched: Babbo had put on weight, but he was very vigorous and his movements swift. His features seemed to have lost their sharp outlines; I did not like the tripartite beard although it gave him a Chinesey old-sage look – it was not his look, the one point suited him better.

'The sense of stagnation increased with the first warm humid days. Inertia and not earning my salt slowly turned my urge for action into depression . . . I lost the courage to mention any practical matters, to talk about ways and means of getting him out. I think it was essential for him to forget about it or he would have gone mad . . . And I had to leave him there. It was time to go home . . . As I left, father seemed concerned primarily about the *Confucian Odes*. I was to stop over in New York only "to put the fear of God into Jas about getting out a proper trilingual edition and fast".'

*

After finishing work on the *Odes* he translated Sophocles' *Trachiniae*, under the title *The Women of Trachis*. He said that the idea 'came from reading the Fenollosa Noh plays for the new edition [in *The Translations of Ezra Pound* (1953)], and from wanting to see what would happen to a Greek play, given that same medium and the hope of its being performed by the Minorou company' (an ancient family of Noh actors). There was an autobiographical element in the plot of the Sophocles play, which describes Herakles transferring his love from his wife Deïanira to Iole, one of the women of Trachis whom he had captured; Deïanira hopes to win him back by smearing his robe with a love charm, which is in fact poison, and he dies in agony. However, Ezra's translation betrays no personal interest in the subject matter, and resembles a comic strip more than a Noh play. Herakles says when dying:

> If only someone would lop my head off and
>   get me out of this loathsome existence, Aaagh . . .
>   A piddling female did it,

not even a man with balls.
Alone and without a sword.

Nor was it an accurate translation; even a sympathetic commentator, S. V. Jankowski, in his preface to the 1969 Faber and Faber edition, admits that Ezra 'refuses to recognize the Greek syntax as a determining factor'.

The first British edition, brought out in 1956 by a supporter of Ezra's, Neville Spearman, carried a foreword by Dennis Goacher, a BBC radio actor and poet, protesting about Ezra's continued detention in St Elizabeths. Peter Whigham, another British supporter, contributed an 'Editorial Declaration' announcing an impending series of Ezra-chosen works – Golding's Ovid, Blackstone, and other familiar names – though this never materialized. *The Women of Trachis* was performed in Britain by the Keele University drama group in November 1962, when the *Times* reviewer described Ezra's text as varying 'from the resolutely conventional, prosodic and involved to terse, not to say banal, colloquialisms'. It was also staged in German in Berlin and Darmstadt in 1959.

By July 1953, Ezra was beginning to talk about future work on the Cantos. That month he told Guy Davenport at St Elizabeths that Canto 100 (sixteen beyond the point he had already reached) would probably not be the end, and remarked: 'The poet looks forward to what is coming next in the poem, not backward to what has been accomplished.' He continued: 'My *Paradiso* will have no St Dominic or Augustine, but it will be a *Paradiso* just the same, moving toward final coherence. I'm getting at the building of the City, that whole tradition. Augustine, he don't amount to a great deal.' Another day, he dictated to Laughlin some thoughts on the structure of the whole work:

A. Dominated by the emotions.
B. Constructive effort – Chinese Emperors and Adams, putting order into things.
C. The domination of benevolence. Theme in Canto 90. Cf. the thrones of Dante's 'Paradiso'.
First 50 cantos are a detective story. Looking around to see what is wrong.
Cantares – the Tale of the Tribe. To give the truth of history. Where Dante mentions a name, EP tries to give the gist of what the man was doing.

He compared the Cantos to the three-tiered frescoes by Francesco del Cossa in the Palazzo Schifanoia in Ferrara, and told Laughlin:

Schifanoia frescoes in three levels.
Top. Allegories of the Virtues. (Cf Petrarch's 'Trionfi') study in values.
Middle. Signs of the Zodiac. Turning of the stars. Cosmology.

Bottom. Particulars of life in the time of Borso d'Este. The contemporary.

a) What is there – permanent – the sea
b) What is recurrent – the voyages
c) What is trivial – the casual – Vasco's troops weary, stupid parts.

'This,' comments Laughlin, 'was the closest I ever got him really to boil down and say what he meant in the architecture of the Cantos.' Actually, it was more a summary of what he had already written than a forecast of how the work might be concluded.

Ezra eventually found a title for the new section of the Cantos. Long ago he had seen Epstein's sculpture 'Rock-Drill', a sinewy human figure astride a mechanical drill that hammers into the rock beneath it. In 1934 he wrote: 'I may frequently want to get a rock-drill in order to make Orage or Douglas SEE something . . .' He told another correspondent in 1957: 'Yes, I saw Epstein's R-D bak in prehistory, but he didn't invent the implement.' He was reminded of it by Wyndham Lewis's review (in the *New Statesman* during 1951) of D. D. Paige's edition of his letters, which was headed 'The Rock Drill'. So, rather oddly for a *Paradiso* or the beginning of one, the new set of cantos (85 to 95) was entitled, when it appeared in 1955, *Section: Rock-Drill De Los Cantares*. Ezra explained that the title was 'intended to imply the necessary resistance in getting a certain main thesis across – hammering'.*

Cantos 85 to 89, the first five of *Rock-Drill*, revert to the manner of the Chinese History Cantos and the American historical cantos. As Donald Davie puts it in his study of Ezra, *Poet as Sculptor* (1965): 'The mere look of Canto 85 on the page . . . announces it as "unreadable" . . . This is at least an advance on the Chinese History and American History cantos, which looked readable but were not.' The style is highly fragmented, as in the Pisan sequence; transitions between subject matter are at best only implied. Ideograms abound, sometimes occupying most of the page. The mood changes in Cantos 90 and 91, a pair that precede the four *Paradiso* cantos that conclude *Rock-Drill*. Canto 90 introduces a beatific vision, but even the best passages are a little mannered and self-conscious, a repetition of an effect already achieved:

> not arrogant from habit,
> but furious from perception,
> Sibylla,

*The choice of Spanish in the second half of the title seems without significance, and recalls Richard Aldington's caustic remark about Ezra's preference for foreign languages in titles. Perhaps he wanted to get away from the Dantean implications of 'Cantos'. He used Spanish again in the title of the next section, calling it *Thrones de los Cantares*.

from under the rubble heap
                    m'elevasti
from the dulled edge beyond pain
                    m'elevasti
out of Erebus, the deep-lying
            from the wind under the earth,
                    m'elevasti
from the dulled air and the dust,
                    m'elevasti
    by the great flight,
            m'elevasti

                    Isia Kuanon
        from the cusp of the moon,
            m'elevasti . . .

Reviewing the new cantos in the *Yale Review* in September 1956, Randall Jarrell felt that a few passages had 'a pure and characteristic beauty' but thought the book chiefly 'indiscriminate notes on books and people'. Jarrell cited Gertrude Stein's celebrated description of Ezra as 'a village explainer', and said this was nonsense, since 'he can hardly ever tell you anything (unless you know it already), much less explain it'. He pointed out that the new cantos included not just Chinese ideograms but Egyptian hieroglyphics, and asked 'next year Minoan B?' *The Pisan Cantos* had been widely judged a writer's notebook; *Rock-Drill*, Jarrell felt, was not even that: 'Aren't good notes, even, more organized than *this*?' A. Alvarez wrote of *Rock-Drill* in the *Observer* that it was 'difficult and uneven . . . With the best will in the world, it is hardly comprehensible.' And Philip Larkin in the *Manchester Guardian* found nothing whatever to praise in it, and judged the Cantos merely a 'long twentieth-century poetic curiosity'.

Ezra himself was now having difficulty in remembering what he had written years earlier in the Cantos, and where. He wrote to Archibald MacLeish of the 'Ecbatan' passage in Cantos 4 and 5: 'I don't merember [*sic*] a damn thing about it.' And to Huntington Cairns: 'cf/ canto. where the hell did I do the Rus/ revl/? ugh XXVII.' While he could still produce superb fragments or phrases – for example the opening of Canto 95, 'LOVE, gone as lightning, / enduring 5000 years' – there was no longer much likelihood that he could make the whole thing cohere.

*

The psychiatrists continued to log their reports on him. A Dr Cruvant noticed that 'an official diagnosis had not been made', and offered his own, in July 1953:

It is my psychiatric opinion that Mr Pound represents an unfortunate parachronism. Born 15 years before the turn of the century, he participated in the industrial revolution of the Victorian era and performed admirably in both an anaclitic and protagonistic fashion to provide a leavening to the crass materialism which in its excess of yeasty ferment applauded and supported him as he went along his histrionic way.

There was much more in this extraordinary vein: Cruvant judged that Ezra was suffering from an excess of Newtonian physics, and criticized him for a failure to appreciate 'the philosophic implications of the quantum theory on the age-old problem of determinism and free will'. Cruvant made one good point: that Ezra approached subjects such as economics with a typically nineteenth-century certainty that precise answers could be achieved. He was a nineteenth-century figure attempting to solve the insoluble dilemmas of the twentieth century. However, Cruvant ended in a welter of psychiatric jargon, declaring him to be a 'passive-aggressive personality' with 'sadistic overtones' that were 'consonant with the narcissistic personality type', and proposing the following formal diagnosis:

51. 3. PERSONALITY TRAIT DISTURBANCE, OTHER. NARCISSISTIC PERSONALITY.

During 1953 Noel Stock, a twenty-four-year-old radio news reporter from Hobart, Tasmania, who had come under Ezra's spell via the Pisan Cantos and Hugh Kenner's book on him, began to correspond with Ezra, and for a time swallowed his credo. Stock arranged for Poundian material – including pseudonymous pieces by Ezra himself – to be published in Australian journals, especially the Social Credit *New Times* of Melbourne, and he also established *Edge*, a magazine which for a time became the nerve centre of what Stock described as 'the international Poundian underground'. Ezra was delighted, telling a correspondent: 'i don't see any Fordies now. except Noel Stock.' And in another letter: 'EDGE . . . the ONLY present means of communication between people with serious AGENDA.' 'Agenda' was a currently favourite word with him, and was chosen as the name of a literary magazine started at his instigation a few years later. William Cookson, its founder, first wrote to Ezra in 1955 when still a pupil at Westminster School in London, and thereafter received many letters from him intended to provide an education. Unlike most Pound-inspired journals, *Agenda* (still in existence) deals exclusively with literature and not exclusively with Ezra Pound.

Faber and Faber produced a volume of Ezra's translations in 1953, with an introduction by Kenner; Ezra was pleased, but said there was still 'need of a COMPLEAT Cavalcanti'. The next year they issued *Literary Essays*, an anthology of his critical writings selected and introduced by Eliot. 'Mr ElYuTT HAS stuck the narsty title of "LITerary essays" on his whatever yu call it/ Ezpurgation of Ez. or Possumation or wotNOT,' Ezra told Huntington Cairns. He also reported, in the spring of 1954: 'one virtuous blockhead and one louse are, (acc/ rumour)/ attempting bibliog/ in TOTAL ignorance of the natr/ of y.v.t. and ergo from my pt/ view unlikely to tell anything valuable'. Meanwhile, Ezra suspected a boycott of his work in New York publishing circles, though Laughlin was faithfully bringing out American editions at a steady rate, and told a London correspondent: 'UNTIL you people hoist the cultural level of this barbary enough to float me off these rocks . . .'

*

The question of a presidential pardon was raised with the Department of Justice early in 1954. They replied that 'although the President is empowered by the Constitution to grant reprieves and pardons . . . there would be no ground [for this] in a case where an individual is not confined as the result of a conviction and sentence'.

He could not be pardoned until he had been found guilty; he could not be found guilty until he had been put on trial: he could not be put on trial until he had been declared sane. All roads, as always, led to Overholser, who refused to discuss Ezra's mental condition. Arthur Moore told Eliot that Overholser had written in February 1954 that 'any material as to his clinical course or diagnosis in this Hospital is privileged, and I am accordingly unable to answer the questions you raise'.

Overholser was not the only obstacle. On 27 January 1955 Douglas Hammond, a Pound admirer from the University of Alabama, telephoned Dorothy, and next day reported his conversation with her to Arthur Moore. The call followed a letter from her, 'the tone of which indicated that she thought we were too much in the dark to undertake the work we contemplate [a campaign for Ezra's release]. I asked her,' continued Hammond,

> if she would see me if I came to Washington, and she replied, no. She said that she has 'led a hell of a life these last sixteen years, first the bloody war, and these nine years here'. She further said that because she is British she would never be able to understand the 'extraordinary Americans'. She thought them 'rather stupid' when it came to understanding Italy, the war, and Mr Pound's activities. She said that her one purpose right now is to keep 'Ezra happy and reasonably well' so that he may complete the cantos on which he is presently working. She said

that he had hardly the physical energy and strength to complete this important task. There is no one in the United States whose opinion she values or would accept, and she said that you [Arthur Moore] are the only man in the United Kingdom whose opinion she values or would accept. She thinks that she would never have any opinion about any attempt to gain Mr Pound's freedom . . . I told her that I would write to you in full . . . She expressed a very keen desire that I do this.

During 1955 the American Committee for Cultural Freedom (affiliated to the Congress for Cultural Freedom, which included Bertrand Russell, Reinhold Niebuhr and Stephen Spender among its active members) considered appealing for Ezra's 'release on probation to a private physician or . . . institution', but was blocked by Overholser. In Italy, Mary tried the tactic of organizing a protest to the US Embassy in Rome, alleging that her father was forced to live in 'intolerable conditions' and had not even been examined properly by psychiatrists. The petition also stated that, quite apart from the 'legalities', Ezra Pound was 'an individual human creature, now in his seventieth year, who has been denied his liberty under Government order for almost ten years'. Like every other appeal, it ended on Overholser's desk, with predictable results.

On 31 May 1955 Overholser instructed a Dr Cushard to record in Ezra's case notes that

> The present approved diagnosis is as follows:
> 24.2. Psychotic Disorder, Undifferentiated.

Overholser now wanted it recorded (just in case anyone managed to see the notes) that Ezra was officially classified as 'psychotic' (mad). It is easy to guess why he preferred 'undifferentiated' as the diagnosis of the supposed disorder to 'narcissistic' – Dr Cruvant's diagnosis two years earlier. If the nature of the patient's insanity was not specified, no one could conclusively argue that he had recovered from it. However, Overholser allowed one small impovement to be made in Ezra's living conditions. In August 1955 special permission was granted for him to sit on the lawn outside Center Building until eight o'clock each evening in summer.

*

Around this time, Archibald MacLeish wrote his first letter to Ezra since the 1930s. He had once tried to visit him at St Elizabeths, but had become snowbound. Ezra had recently sent him a letter about 'service to the arts', and MacLeish replied:

> The service to the arts I should most like to see performed is the service which would give you some peace and quiet in which to

work. You and I differ politically . . . but I have always been . . . of one mind with those who HAVE minds about your work. I have been told by personal friends of yours that . . . no solution would be acceptable to you which did not involve vilification of President Roosevelt and those who served the Republic under him. If that is so it's so – but I'd like to hear it from you before I accept it as the truth.

Somewhat to his surprise, MacLeish got a civil reply from Ezra, and at the end of 1955 paid him a visit.

I should have done it years ago [he wrote afterwards to a friend] but just plain lacked the stomach. I hate asylums and I'd only met Pound once in my life in any case and so I let my conscience sleep . . . He is surrounded by the insane – not dangerous people but horrifyingly abnormal people. What disturbed me most was that he had few books within which to make a life in that place.

MacLeish arranged for the Library of Congress to supply reading matter regularly. But, more important, he met Overholser and talked to him at length about the case.

He scored easily the best result that anyone had so far achieved with Overholser, perhaps because they were Harvard men. In a letter to Hemingway, MacLeish described Overholser, as 'good psycho (Harvard) and good man'. Overholser, speaking off the record, accepted MacLeish's opinion that Ezra was 'quite sane', and said that 'he could perfectly well walk out tomorrow if it weren't for the indictment – couldn't stand the strain of trial but is perfectly all right as long as things don't close in on him'. He told MacLeish he 'would let Ez out in eighteen minutes if the Dept. of Justice would nol pros [quash] the indictment. Said he had never thought Ez's "treason" amounted to much anyway.' MacLeish decided, in consequence, that 'I wouldn't rest till he got out. Not only for his sake but for the good name of the country: after ten years it was beginning to look like persecution and if he died we'd never wash the stain out.' Ten years had been the length of the prison sentence meted out to those pro-Axis American broadcasters who came to trial and were found guilty.

After his visit, MacLeish wrote to Ezra about the possibility of release, saying that it was apparent that 'there was only one way out – to try to persuade the Atty Gen to nol pros the indictment'. Would Ezra accept this legal solution – not a clearing of his name, but simply the deletion of the indictment against him, so that he was no longer under a charge of treason? Ezra in reply sent him, said MacLeish, 'reams of the usual kind of blather', but finally, 'yes – he would. He has stuck to that ever since,' continued

MacLeish, in this account to Hemingway, 'and his solicitor in London whom Tom Eliot got me to write to agrees also.' The method by which Ezra could perhaps be floated off the rocks had been agreed on; but MacLeish felt that it was not quite time yet for an attempt to be made – for a reason that had become all too familiar. 'The consensus of opinion gathered from my Republican friends and political acquaintances,' he wrote to Ezra in April 1956, 'is that it would be unwise as well as useless to approach the Department of Justice before the election. My notion therefore is to prepare for a serious approach to [the] Department in November – not by me, naturally, but by someone who might be *grata* if, as I suspect, the Reps return.'

Ezra seemed to regard his tenth anniversary in St Elizabeths as almost worth celebrating. He sent a chatty note to Overholser, saying it would be pleasant if Overholser were to 'drift down' to his room some time 'for consideration of the bug house as such, the fruits of ten years occasional observation in, and reflection on your REmarkable institution'.

Laughlin marked Ezra's seventieth birthday in October 1955 with the publication of a pamphlet, *Ezra Pound at Seventy*. Hemingway was among the contributors: 'Will gladly pay tribute to Ezra but what I would like to do is get him the hell out of St Elizabeth's.' No one else writing in the pamphlet saw fit to mention the matter, but on 6 February 1956 *Life* magazine came out with a plea for his case to be considered, pointing out that the broadcaster 'Tokyo Rose' (Iva d'Aquino) had just been released from jail, and continuing:

> The Nazi storm trooper responsible for the Malmedy massacre of 1944, General Dietrich, is also out of jail, one of a growing line of commutees and parolees . . . Attention is surely due the case of Ezra Pound . . . Pound's room at St Elizabeths has been called 'a closet which contains a national skeleton' . . . The arguments for quashing the indictment . . . should be publicly considered.

A few months later, *Newsweek* sent Overholser a list of questions they wished to put to Ezra, as part of a symposium on the state of culture in the USA. Ezra's reply to Overholser's office was: 'While confined within the limits of the bughouse, I do not elect to elucidate, let them spring me first.'

Rufus King had observed some time earlier that the Government would only consider quashing the indictment against Ezra if nothing happened to reawaken unfavourable public interest in him and his ideas. During 1956 his St Elizabeths followers began to attract undesired attention. 'Yes Sheri acquitted,' Ezra wrote to MacLeish in January about some unspecified incident, 'jury out 5 minutes.' Another went to jail for drug-peddling; Ezra claimed that 'he had abjured etc/ and was taking to musical composition'.

MacLeish reproved Ezra for mixing with such people, and Ezra snorted back:

> I don't know what the HELL yu mean by 'personal friends of mine'. The blithering idiocy of some denizens has got me buffaloed. And the professions of friendship are sometimes curious.

MacLeish was trying to persuade Ezra to abjure his own worst views, as expressed in the wartime broadcasts. In one letter Ezra told him co-operatively: 'You may say to any shit you meet . . . that Ez considers antisemitism un-Aristotelian and unscientific and that every man shd/ be judged on his own merits.' Yet in his next letter to MacLeish: 'Obviously it is kikes keeping me in here.' MacLeish was going to have an uphill struggle.

15

Our Mood Is Your Mood, Mr Frost

MacLeish asked Robert Frost to join the campaign. Frost was on far better terms with the Eisenhower Administration than MacLeish himself, who was still known as a staunch New Deal Democrat. Also, at this time Frost could claim to be the best-loved American poet in the public eye. Frost thought nothing of Ezra's poetry, and had been outraged by the award of the Bollingen. But a review of Ezra's *Literary Essays* in the *New York Times Book Review* during 1954 had brought it to Frost's attention that Ezra had written enthusiastically of his *North of Boston* in 1914 when Frost was still virtually unknown; Frost presumably felt it would do no harm to lend his name to a campaign that was likely to succeed and was attracting respectable literary support.

MacLeish told Arthur Moore his plan was 'to persuade a few – a very few – writers of position to join in a personal appeal to the Attorney General'. He thought of using 'Tom [Eliot], Frost, Sandburg, Hemingway, Faulkner – something like that'. He would 'also try to stir up a little discreet sympathy in the Senate though Ezra makes this difficult by damning all senators known to him or not. I expect to be hampered personally by the return of the Republican Administration but there are one or two respectable writers who are Republicans and they may be willing to take over.'

Sure enough the Republicans were again voted into office, and in November 1956 MacLeish wrote to Overholser saying that he proposed to get Eliot, Frost, Sandburg, Hemingway and Faulkner to approach the Attorney General on the grounds that Ezra had been detained for almost eleven years, was sane in the opinion of the doctors, and would be driven mad by a trial. But while Overholser had made certain remarks to MacLeish off the record a year earlier, it was a very different matter to ask him to take this attitude officially. He replied to MacLeish on 21 November:

> There are one or two points on which I should like to offer a correction. I agree with you, of course, as to your statement that Pound has undergone nearly 11 years of confinement. I think, however, that we should not bring up the question of his 'insanity'. It is still my opinion, and that of the other doctors here, that Mr Pound is mentally incompetent to advise with counsel and to participate in his own defense, that is, that he is not fit for trial. There is a distinction here between fitness for trial, however, and suitability for release under limited circumstances. I am convinced that we should not bring up the question of release at the present time. That would merely confuse the situation. It is our opinion, however, if this is of help, that it is unlikely that his mental condition will in the future be such that he is competent to stand trial. Indeed, I have already indicated this to the Department of Justice. Since the chances are very much against there being a trial it seems unnecessary at this stage of the proceedings to keep the charges alive any longer.
>
> I am quite ready to be quoted as to my opinion concerning Mr Pound's present unfitness for trial and the prospect that that mental unfitness will continue.

The dog would not, after all, give up its bone. Overholser's only suggestion was that the Department of Justice might cancel the indictment; but clearly they were not going to do this without some assurance from the hospital that Ezra was sane enough to go free, and this Overholser was refusing to give. However, MacLeish, experienced lawyer as he was, pressed Overholser on the only point he had offered for manoeuvre, and replied on 29 November:

> The corrections you suggest in my understanding of the situation are of course most pertinent. I had not realized that it was your opinion and the opinion of your associates that Pound, though unfit to stand trial, is not fit for release.
>
> I take it therefore – and unless I hear from you to the contrary I shall proceed on this assumption – that you feel the charges might well be dropped on the ground that trial is and will be impossible, but that the question of Pound's release should not be raised at this point.

The response was quite promising:

Dear Mr MacLeish,

Your understanding is quite correct. I think that it is high time that charges against Ezra Pound should be dropped, but I think that his release from the Hospital at this time would muddy the waters to an undesirable extent.

MacLeish wrote to Hemingway that he interpreted Overholser to mean that 'with the indictment out of the way, and the pressure off, it might be possible to ease him out into more bearable surroundings . . . I therefore told Tom Eliot, who has been a bit nervous about the whole thing, that this was a two-bites-to-the-cherry case and that we had better take the first bite first.'

Early in December 1956, MacLeish drafted a letter to the then Attorney General, Herbert Brownell, asking for a 'Nol Pros' which would dispose of the charges against Ezra, thus leaving it to the doctors to determine when he might be released. He sent the letter to Eliot, who (MacLeish told Hemingway) 'has agreed to sign. Frost will join him. I have been hoping I could get you to be the third.'

MacLeish then called on Christian Herter, Under Secretary of State. 'Chris heard me out but was obviously worried by the possibility that, once released, Ezra might embarrass the government by shooting his face off in his usual way.' MacLeish gathered that John Foster Dulles, Secretary of State, was opposed to the release plan, and was trying to persuade Herter to have nothing to do with it. MacLeish asked Hemingway to write to Herter, 'making again the point you made so well in your letter to the Atty Gen – that it is the US which will suffer if Pound is allowed to rot in St Elizabeth's.'

*

At the end of 1956, D. G. Bridson, a fellow Social Creditor from pre-Second World War days, came to St Elizabeths to record Ezra reading from the Cantos for the BBC, though it was agreed that the recording would not be broadcast for the time being.* Bridson made the journey because he believed Ezra was in failing health and would probably die in captivity. Overholser made one of the doctors' common rooms available for the recording. Ezra said that the choice of poems must be left entirely to him, and if broadcast at all it must be done *in toto* with no 'selection' from what he had recorded. Bridson describes their first session:

*In the summer of 1952 Barbara Cohen and a colleague from the small Caedmon publishing and record company in New York had come to St Elizabeths to make the first of a series of annual recordings of Ezra reading Provençal poetry and the Cantos. He also made a studio recording for Caedmon in 1958 which included *Hugh Selwyn Mauberley* and several Cantos; this was released in 1960.

Pound . . . chose to give his reading stretched out in an adjustable armchair where he could rest the back of his neck on a cushion. This meant that the book had to be held above the level of his eyes, and I perched myself on the arm of the chair to hold the microphone at the proper angle for him – this despite his initial urge to seize it himself and use it like an old-fashioned upright telephone. He seemed to have forgotten his Roman microphone training . . .

To my amusement, the reading started with some eight of the Alfred Venison poems – the jaunty, satirical squibs which I remembered Pound having contributed to the *New English Weekly*, for which we had both written in Orage's day. In his persona of the rabbit's-meat dealer of Great Titchfield Street in the days of the Depression, he launched out in an Americanized form of Cockney . . . The performance could only be described as *bravura* – as could his reading of 'L'Homme Moyen Sensuel' [his 1915 Byronic satire] with which he followed it up. Some half dozen of the later Cantos – including a splendidly virulent rendition of the 'Usura' – concluded the afternoon's work.

Ezra afterwards explained this eccentric choice of poems to David Rattray: 'I conceived the whole thing more or less as a ribbing for Eliot . . . I just wanted to give the old boy a jolt, some time when he's settling down for a nice cosy evening, if he turns on the Third Programme . . . I chose the ones he likes the least.'

The next afternoon Ezra reluctantly agreed to record Canto I, saying he would do it only as a favour to Bridson, and that it was 'strictly against his principles'; apparently he no longer approved of the poem's resonant opening. He began the session with an impromptu monologue which he called 'Four Steps' – an unscripted summary of the events that had led him to attack the Roosevelt Administration in his Rome broadcasts. Perhaps it was the speech he had been waiting to make in court all these years; if so, it was a discursive, anti-climactic piece of work, more in the nature of reminiscence than rhetoric.

He began it by recalling his disagreement with the American passport official in Paris in 1919, citing this as the immediate cause of his campaign against incompetence in the American Government. His second 'step' towards the Rome microphone was, he said, being told by a Dutch immigrant to America that a judge had told him: 'In this country there ain't nobody has got any goddamned rights whatsoever.' The third was a remark by a prosecuting attorney in an American city: 'All that I'm interested in is . . . seeing what you can put over.' Ezra thought the 'discrepancy' between this and the *mores* of the founding fathers was 'considerable'. The fourth and final step was Senator Wheeler alleging to him in Washington in 1939 that Roosevelt had 'packed the Supreme Court'. Ezra concluded:

> Now that is where I took off from. When the Senator is unable to prevent breaches of the Constitution . . . the duty, as I see it, falls back onto the individual citizen. And that is why, after two years of wrangling, when I got hold of a microphone in Rome, I used it.

However, if the 'Four Steps' were disappointing, they were certainly articulate. Bridson had caught Ezra (so to speak) offstage from his usual performance at St Elizabeths. After the recording session, however, the 'Grampaw' act was immediately resumed. 'We went out together into the hospital grounds,' writes Bridson, 'where a circle of friends and disciples had already gathered to sit at his feet. Once among them, Pound's conversation again became as cryptic and idiosyncratic as he generally chose to make it. Two voices there certainly were . . .'

He thought even worse of the US Government now than he had in 1939. In March 1957 he wrote to a correspondent in London, Patricia Hutchins, who was writing a book about his Kensington days: 'Be assured the present state of the u.s. govt. etc. is 7 times worse/ not only idiocy but pusillanimity, 90 out of 96 senators cowering in abject terror before a few lousy kikes.' It was not a state of mind in which he was likely to be co-operative with tactics for his release.

In early January 1957 MacLeish sent Hemingway a revised text of the letter to the Attorney General that he, Eliot, and Frost were being asked to sign. 'The text,' explained MacLeish, 'is Tom Eliot's based on a draft of mine.' It read as follows:

> We are writing to you about Ezra Pound who has been confined in St Elizabeths Hospital in Washington for eleven years under indictment for treason.
>
> Our interest in this matter is founded in part on our concern for Mr Pound who is one of the most distinguished American writers of his generation, and in part on our concern for the country of our birth. As writers ourselves we cannot but be aware of the effect on writers and lovers of literature throughout the world of Pound's continued incarceration at a time when certain Nazis tried and convicted of the most heinous crimes, have been released and in many cases rehabilitated.
>
> It is our understanding, based on inquiries direct to the

medical personnel at St Elizabeths Hospital, that Pound is now unfit for trial and, in the opinion of the doctors treating him, will continue to be unfit for trial. This opinion, we believe, has already been communicated to the Department of Justice. Under these circumstances the perpetuation of the charges against him seems to us unfortunate and, indeed, indefensible. It provides occasion for criticism of American justice not only at home but abroad and it seems to us, in and of itself, unworthy of the traditions of the Republic. Concerned, as we must be, with the judgements of posterity on this unhappy affair, we cannot but regret the failure of the Department thus far to take steps to nol pros the indictment and remit the case to the medical authorities for disposition on medical grounds.

May we add that this is a personal letter to you and that we have no intention at this time of making a public statement on this matter.

Could we be of service to you, a letter addressed to us in care of the American Academy of Arts and Letters at 633 West 155th Street, New York City, will have our immediate attention.

Herbert Brownell the Attorney General took six weeks to acknowledge the letter. He wrote on 28 February 1957 that he had 'asked that a review of the matter be made, and when it is completed I will communicate further with you'.

On 11 April the Deputy Attorney General, William P. Rogers – soon to replace Brownell, who had announced his impending resignation – wrote to Frost, inviting him and his co-signers to come to Washington and discuss the case. But Frost, whose interest in the matter was still tenuous, did not reply before setting off on a trip to Britain. MacLeish, not to be deterred, took a European vacation himself, and caught up with Frost in London during May, extracting his promise to go to Washington as soon as possible after his return. MacLeish then went to Italy and met Mary at Sirmione. 'A tall gentleman stood in the hotel garden. Beautiful manners and kind voice. I was excited and afraid at the same time. His wife joined us and put me at ease . . . "You know, my husband is a lawyer, and a very good lawyer, too." I hadn't thought of it – I saw only the poet. And the man . . . who had brushed politics aside and stood by his old friend in trouble . . . The strange conviction: here is a man with a golden key in his head.' Mary told MacLeish that if her father were ever permitted to leave America and return to Italy, he expected to live at Brunnenburg. Three years ago he had told her to take to the castle various belongings from the flat in Rapallo, and the family possessions from the little villa where

Homer and Isabel had lived. Brunnenburg had now become 'home' to him.
On 24 June, Frost expressed his current feelings in a letter to MacLeish:

> My purpose holds to help you get Ezra loose though I won't
> say my misgivings in the whole matter haven't been increased
> by my talks with Eliot lately . . . I should hate to see Ezra die
> ignominiously in that wretched place where he is for a crime
> which if proven couldn't have kept him all these years in prison.
> So you go ahead and make an appointment with the Depart-
> ment of Justice. I suppose we might be prepared to answer for
> Ezra's . . . ability to get himself taken care of out in the world.
> Neither you nor I would want to take him into our family or
> even into our neighborhood. I shall be acting largely on your
> judgement.

At this point, Mary's meeting with Arthur Garfield Hays of the Civil
Liberties Union seemed suddenly to have paid off, for Cornell wrote to
Dorothy that the Union was offering to support 'legal steps' in securing
Ezra's release; would she reconsider a habeas corpus writ? In response, he
had a 'very cryptic' letter from Dorothy stating that she 'did not think Ezra
was interested in being financed by anyone'. Cornell, who knew nothing of
MacLeish's clandestine wire-pullings, guessed that 'she prefers the present
situation to the troubles and responsibilities which any change would bring
upon her'.

*

Ezra's position was now seriously jeopardized by John Kasper, the disciple
who had for some years shown racist tendencies. Following the 1954 US
Supreme Court decision on the desegregation of schools throughout the
country, Kasper had organized a 'Seaboard White Citizens' Council' with
the motto 'Save the White' and a slogan beginning

> Now damn all race-mixers
> The stink: Roose, Harry and Ike
> God bless Jeff/ Jax and John Adams . . .

Kasper billed himself as 'Segregation Chief' and began addressing racist
gatherings in the South. He worked with the Ku Klux Klan, and in
Alabama was assisted by George Lincoln Rockwell, later head of the
American Nazi Party. Kasper's message was that the Jews were behind
integration.

Ezra was aware of this; he commented to Peter Whigham in May 1957:
'The Ku Klux is unfortunately illiterate, and the misreports do not mention
ideology.' And in a letter to Patricia Hutchins he spoke of 'KikoRuss
domination and subversion' of American internal affairs. Another letter

indicated his continuing fondness for old attitudes, at least in certain moods:

> A dirty jew has just sent me Jim's [Joyce's] letters edited by his Obesity S. Gilbert, the impertinence of the kike lying in the assumption that I wd be DEElighted to review the book for a parsimonious fee/ etc.

In September 1956 John Kasper participated in riots at a high school in Clinton, Tennessee. The National Guard was called out, and Kasper was arrested on a charge of contempt of court, since he had attempted to interfere with the integration ruling. He was sentenced to a year in prison, but two supporters put up $10,000 and he was released on bail. He then continued his activities in the South, and was back in court in November, this time accused of sedition and inciting a riot, but was found not guilty. Ezra wrote to MacLeish: 'Why pick on Kasp who was NOT on the scene of the riot, and was acquitted by jury in 44 minutes.' He said he himself was 'vurry sceptik re/ K's dislike of Afroamericans', and recalled that Kasper had brought 'an excellent example of their charm and enlightenment to visit me some months ago'. And in another letter to MacLeish: 'I doubt if Kasper hates anyone, his actions in keeping open shack for stray cats and humans seem to indicate a kind heart with no exclusion of nubians.'

However, the press was not interested in such subtleties, and soon made the connection between Kasper and Ezra. On 2 February 1957 the *New York Herald Tribune* carried the headline 'SEGREGATIONIST KASPER IS EZRA POUND DISCIPLE', and also ran a four-part series of articles on Kasper which referred to the friendship with Ezra. This only provoked a mild grumble from Ezra about the 'recent out burst' in the press, while Dorothy took it even more calmly, writing to Arthur Moore: 're Kasper – don't worry – its the kind of thing we are used to – but they will drag in EP's name where he has nothing whatever to do with the subject – its all "smear" by association campaign.' Hemingway was outraged, describing Kasper as one of those 'dangerous fawning jerks' whom Ezra's 'megalomania' had encouraged him to receive at St Elizabeths, and suggesting to MacLeish that his release should be conditional on his giving an 'undertaking on no politics'. Meanwhile, the FBI began to keep a watch on St Elizabeths and to note the names of Ezra's visitors. A memo to Overholser from one of the hospital staff describes how after one visitor had arrived, 'two FBI men came into the Supervisor's Office, flashed their identification, and asked . . . who the man was, what he wanted and what he was out here for'. They were then seen tailing the man.

Kasper continued to keep in touch with Ezra. During 1957 he wrote to him from a Washington DC address on the letterhead of the White Citizens' Council:

We've stopped the Civil Rights Bill for this year . . . We've slowed the entire race-mixing movement a helluvalot . . . Also we've removed 3 jew's pimps from the Anderson County school board, kicked out a jew school principal.

Kasper sent Ezra some Ku Klux Klan material. He had begun to quarrel with David Horton, his fellow publisher of the Square $ series, who demanded payment of $462 Kasper owed him, and threatened to sue; Kasper asked for Ezra's help.

During this period Kasper was in and out of jail. Eventually, following the bombing of a desegregated school in Nashville, he received a lengthy Federal sentence. He was observed carrying a copy of *Mein Kampf* into jail. Ezra did not write to him for a while, but a note of 17 April 1959 advised Kasper: 'Stick to the main points when possible . . . Antisemitism is a card in the enemy program, don't play it. they RELY on your playing it.'

Kasper kept sporadically in touch with Ezra and Dorothy, and in 1962 wrote to Dorothy that her husband was 'certainly the great light of an age, and one day the world will be saved and quickened along intelligent courses through his genius'. Ezra remarked of Kasper to another disciple: 'Well, at least he's a man of action and don't sit around looking at his navel.' And to MacLeish: 'Kasper heard about Confucius and History.'

*

Ezra took little interest in the Kasper affair; he was more concerned to get his book on Gaudier-Brzeska back into print and to 'arrange Gaudier shows in Milano and SZVVizerraaa'. He also observed to Overholser that the English department at Berkeley, California, having established a *Pound Newsletter*, was now the workshop for 'vast INDEX to Cantos . . . 7,500 items, 17,000 references some idiotic, but very good job on the greek by a bloke named Peachey'. The *Annotated Index to the Cantos of Ezra Pound* (edited by John Edwards and William Vasse) finally appeared in 1959.*

In April 1957 the St Elizabeths circle was joined by Marcella Spann, a young Texan graduate. With her serious, rather reserved expression and her hair done neatly in a bun, she made a marked contrast to the ultra-exuberant Sheri Martinelli, who until that time had been undisputed queen of the disciples. Miss Spann came to Washington after working as a secretary in New York, and took a teaching job in a junior college not far from St Elizabeths. Ezra protested at the amount of preparatory work she had to put in there. 'Why M.S. would insist on studying textbooks to teach classes in literature,' she writes, 'when M.S. could come out to St E's and

*It has been superseded by Carroll F. Terrell's *A Companion to the Cantos of Ezra Pound*, in two volumes (1980 and 1984).

"get literature on the hoof" was to him an incomprehensible madness not suited to "a well-grown Texas gal".' Ezra addressed Marcella in the third person, just as he had Olga: 'Marcella not despair. He can take it. She not try and gather *all* the gloom between dark eyelashes.'

She was 'assigned' by him to compile an anthology, to be entitled *Confucius to Cummings*. She protested that he should do it himself; he replied: 'No, no, no, no. E.P. is too highbrow. M.S. has got to make it possible for the whole folk.' The 'Spannthology', he said, would be a 'super Guide to Kulchur', a 'sacred book of the arts'; the aim was 'to show how poetry got the way it was from all its various starts'. He would provide notes and get 'Nude Ructions' to publish it.

*

MacLeish organized the visit he and Frost were to make to Deputy Attorney General William Rogers in Washington, fixing it for Friday 19 July 1957. Hemingway was too unwell to travel, but MacLeish persuaded him to write Frost a letter that could be shown to Rogers, and obtained a similar letter from Eliot, who was in England. With these, he and Frost went to Washington. Three days later, MacLeish wrote Ezra a letter describing the visit:

> Dear Ezra:
>   Robert Frost and I went to see the boys at the Department of Justice last Friday. Hot as it was, Robert came all the way down from Ripton, Vermont.
>   We had with us letters from Tom Eliot and Ernest.
>   What the conversations boiled down to was about what we expected: though maybe a little more hopeful than we feared.
>   For the immediate future and so long as the Kasper mess is boiling and stewing the Department will not move. I have never understood – and neither, incidentally, has your daughter Mary – how you got mixed up with that character.
>   Beyond that, though there are no commitments, the Department does not close the door provided somebody can come forward with a sensible plan for your future. The impression we got was that that future would have to be in the United States.
>   Robert has some ideas about a sensible plan which he would be glad to explore if you approve and which seem promising to me: a sound professional arrangement with your publishers which might work for you as it has for him over many years.
>   All this, you understand, is hypothetical as Hell. No commitments or near commitments were made. But the door wasn't

closed and we were left with the impression that once the
Kasper stink has blown over they would be willing to consider
proposals.

   We ran into one thing you ought to know about. Somebody
has spread the rumor at the Department of Justice (I heard it
also in Italy) that you and your wife would really prefer to stay
on at St Elizabeths. If it is false, as I assume, your wife ought to
make that clear to the Department. But if she does, ask her
please not to quote me.

   Did you ever get my note about our visit with that lovely
Mary?

>   yours faithfully
>   A. MacLeish

Writing to Hemingway, MacLeish added that the plan of sending Ezra to
live with Mary in Italy was not considered 'sound' by the Department of
Justice 'because it would provide a "story" for the papers and because it is
feared that there may be – are – people in Italy who would like to make use
of him, get him talking'. MacLeish added that the association of Ezra's
name with 'that bastard Kasper' might mean a delay of 'as much as a year'.

   Ezra replied to MacLeish on 4 August 1957, beginning his letter: 'Dear
Archie Thanks for yr/ noble efforts/ difficult to comment/,' then pointedly changed the subject. His only further reference to MacLeish's activity
was a sharp comment on Frost: 'As fer energy bein' near to benevolence,
you must have used quite a bit to mobilize the rail fence kurmidgin' (a
nudge at Frost's poem 'Mending Wall', which concludes: 'Good fences
make good neighbors'). However, in another letter to MacLeish three days
later he answered one important question:

>   It is damned nonsense to say that either I or D.P. prefer me to
>   stay in St Eliza. BUT with the press what it is// god DAMN it
>   have you examined any of the current malpractices . . . I am
>   past the state when I can argue for four hours . . . I have offers
>   of housing . . . I have said that there are more IMPORTANT
>   issues than my getting out. I wd/ rather see an honest system of
>   money . . . Have you any suggestions as to HOW to make clear
>   to the Department of ANYTHING that D.P. does NOT prefer
>   me to stay in bughouse? . . . remember I needed 5 years REST/
>   got 15 months endurance test. Only began to move again last
>   year, I mean physically. some muscles limbering up again.

He now wrote to MacLeish very frequently. 'Sorry to keep pestering you,
but whenever I do get a bit ahead physically I get a set back as with the god
DAMNED scirocco yester.' Despite his assurances about his and

Dorothy's feelings, the letters usually showed no interest whatever in liberation from St Elizabeths, and rambled on about the usual 'IMPORTANT issues'.

MacLeish reported to Frost on 22 August that Ezra 'doesn't seem disturbed about not being able to go to Italy'; he said that Eliot had begun to worry that 'the doctors might let Ezra go off and live somewhere down south with nobody but his wife etc. to look after him. He apparently thinks Ezra is nuttier than he is. I've told him that decision will be for the docs to make. Does Eliot strike you as a bit timid?' MacLeish added that Laughlin had promised Ezra an income for life if this would help to persuade the Department of Justice to free him: he would pay him $300 a month as an advance against royalties – enough to cover private sanatorium fees. Laughlin also reported that Frank Lloyd Wright, the architect, was 'very much concerned' with the outcome of the Pound case, and was even willing for Ezra to come and live with him at Taliesin West, the house he had designed for himself near Phoenix, Arizona. This prospect greatly tickled Frost, especially as he had feared the spectacle of Ezra leaning across his own fence. 'I can hardly resist the temptation of putting Ezra and Frank Lloyd Wright in the same gun turret,' he wrote, 'but we must be serious where so much is at stake for poor Ezra. I should think we might accept a house from the great architect for the great poet at a safe distance.'

On 13 August 1957, apparently on his own initiative, Senator Richard L. Neuberger of Oregon asked the Library of Congress to prepare a report on the entire Pound affair, and a week later Representative Usher L. Burdick of North Dakota introduced a resolution which would authorize the House Committee on the Judiciary to conduct 'a full and complete investigation and study of the sanity of Ezra Pound, in order to determine whether there is justification for his continued incarceration'. These two moves led to the compilation during the following months of an official report on 'The Medical, Legal, Literary and Political Status of Ezra Pound', written by H. A. Sieber, a research assistant at the Library of Congress, delivered to Senator Neuberger and Representative Burdick in the spring of 1958, and published in summarized form in the *Congressional Record*. The report had no direct bearing on events, but it indicated an increasing feeling in Government circles that Ezra should be released.

A one-man campaign for his release was being conducted by Harry Meacham, President of the Poetry Society of Virginia, who during 1957 and early 1958 canvassed Ezra's cause by letter, writing, among others, to Dag Hammarskjöld, with whom Meacham raised the possibility of Ezra being nominated for the Nobel Prize for Literature. At one stage even MacLeish believed that a Nobel was on its way to Ezra, and mentioned this to Milton Eisenhower, the President's brother (and himself President of Johns Hopkins University), hoping this might be an additional lever to gain Ezra's freedom; but no Nobel materialized. Ezra described Meacham as 'naïve but benevolent'.*

Ezra mostly refrained from discussing the subject of his release, but in the middle of one of his rambling letters to MacLeish at the end of November 1957, he suddenly observed: 'My feeling is that I have been here about long enough.'

                                           *

In October 1957, Mary wrote from Brunnenburg asking Dr Overholser if her father could not possibly be let out for a holiday, 'on parole', and be allowed to come to Italy, to the castle. Overholser replied politely but firmly that the matter 'is entirely out of my hands'. Robert Frost, however, had begun to realize that exactly the opposite was true: that Overholser, rather than anyone in the Department of Justice, held the key to the final door, and might refuse to turn it. 'I think we can count on Rogers,' Frost told Laughlin. 'If I have any anxiety left it is about meeting Overholser in the right way.'

Frost went to Washington again in the third week of October, but as Overholser was away on vacation nothing was achieved at St Elizabeths. However, he saw William Rogers, who, while remaining annoyingly non-committal, seemed willing to consider Frost's suggestion that, if Ezra could not be released for the time being on account of the Kasper affair, he might be transferred to a private institution until the Civil Rights crisis had quietened down.

During November, Rogers took over as Attorney General, and Frost wrote to him on 19 November:

> I assume people are less busy the higher up they get and the bigger the questions get or I would apologize for taking your time . . . The money seems assured for the private institution and Archie MacLeish tells me this morning that he has Dr Overholser's consent for Pound's transfer the minute he himself is released from holding Pound as a prisoner. I may have to call you on the telephone next. I grow impatient. The amnesty would be a good Christmas present.

There is no evidence that Overholser had said any such thing to MacLeish; Frost was simply citing Overholser's private remarks made in the distant past and off the record. He and MacLeish were now attempting to manipulate Overholser and the Attorney General, playing them off against each other by trying to convince each that the other was waiting for him to

---

*Ezra had hoped for, indeed expected, the Nobel Prize during the 1930s. He told Laughlin he would spend the prize money on hiring a cook.

make the next move. MacLeish wrote to Overholser on 26 November that Rogers had given Frost 'a firm commitment . . . to nol-pros if the doctors at St Elizabeths would advise that Pound could be transferred to a private sanatorium'. No such commitment had been given in writing. It was a risky tactic, but it seemed the only way to keep things moving.

On 5 December 1957, Overholser replied to MacLeish, suggesting, remarkably, that it might be better if Ezra did not go into a private sanatorium, but instead to Italy. This was apparently the result of Mary's long and eloquent plea to him in her October letter that he should be handed over to her care. Overholser wrote to MacLeish:

> It seems to me that nothing much would be gained by moving
> Mr Ezra Pound to a private institution except that, of course,
> the cost would be very considerable . . . I know perfectly well,
> as you do, that he would much prefer to return to Italy . . . I am
> sure that he would be much happier there and would, of course,
> be no menace to any persons or any government. Is there any
> possibility that representations might be made to our State
> Department . . . ?

It was typical of Overholser that he was more willing to unlock the door on terms suggested by himself than to be pressurized into accepting someone else's plan.

MacLeish answered Overholser on 13 December that Frost had reported that Attorney General Rogers had told him that the Department of Justice would 'frown' on Ezra's leaving the USA. On the other hand the Department had said it would 'avert its face' once he had been released to a private sanatorium, so would Overholser approve of his release to such an institution merely as an interim stage in the process? Overholser, having briefly given the impression that he was becoming co-operative, now sent a completely non-committal reply:

> Thank you for your letter of December 13th concerning Mr
> Ezra Pound, and the possibility of his charges being dropped.
>   It is always a pleasure to see you and I shall look forward to a
> chance to talk with you on this matter soon after Christmas.

Ezra and Dorothy now allowed an American lawyer named Furniss, who had handled the administration of the 'Committee for Ezra Pound' to announce to MacLeish that he was 'formally taking over the case', asking precisely what was going on. Understandably MacLeish was furious, and wrote to Ezra on 26 October 1957: 'If you have really authorized him to take over 'the case' I will of course pull out at once leaving the way clear. If, however, as seems probable . . . he has inserted himself I hope you will suggest to him that he hold off at least for the present.' Ezra for once wrote back a clear answer: 'Furniss only wanted enough authorization to be able to ask a few questions. AND he is a damn good guy and honest, and not terrifeid by gobbledegook.' When he understood the situation, Furniss took the matter no further.

Ezra's original lawyer, Julien Cornell, still knew nothing of the moves by Frost and MacLeish with the Government, until one day

> two FBI agents came to my office and questioned me for an hour or more about the Pound case ... They told me the Attorney General was considering the possibility of releasing Pound. I told them that I had not seen Pound for several years but so far as I knew there was no other attorney acting for him.
>
> The FBI men wanted to know in particular why the Department of Justice, at the time of Pound's sanity hearing, had not put up a better fight ... The agents asked: 'Was he really insane, was he really unfit to be tried ...?'

To which Cornell replied: See the testimony of the psychiatrists at the time of the trial. This FBI investigation seems curiously pointless, not to say belated.

Mary wrote to Overholser again on 27 December 1957 that, thanks to an offer of financial help from Norman Holmes Pearson at Yale, she had planned to bring her children over to see her father at Christmas, but Ezra had told her: 'This ward is no fit place for the kids.' She asked if nothing could be done. Overholser wrote back a kindly note saying that if she came, she and the children could see him in a private visiting room. But Ezra made it clear to MacLeish that he did not want such a visit, pointing out 'the chance for sobstuff that it wd/ give the noise makers. I am trying not to hurt Mary's feelings ...'

Meanwhile in a letter to Patricia Hutchins, Ezra observed once more: 'I shd/ like to get OUT. you can, at least, squash rumours to the contrary.' Indeed he was beginning to consider some exotic plans. He wrote to William Cookson:

> Byzantine middle ages, looks like the most fruitful field to dig in. Have just asked Lekakis for a road map of Thressaly [sic] and Aetolia / rails there are not. @ Pisa I got a taste for sleeping in the open/ git me out of quod and one might start an expedition/ dunno if even Fords can get over mule tracks.

*

Around Christmas 1957, MacLeish felt that the approaches to Attorney General Rogers were getting nowhere, so he turned once again to Christian Herter, suggesting to him that whereas the actual decision had to be made by the Department of Justice, 'it was State that was suffering', because Ezra's continued incarceration hurt American prestige abroad. In a letter to Ezra on 18 February 1958, MacLeish reported that Herter

> was interested and impressed, being a decent human being, and said he would make inquiries – which I assume to mean inquiries at Justice and at St Elizabeths . . . However I have relatively little hope for this demarche because Herter has been walled off by Dulles and has relatively little power. Since the Administration as a whole seems to fear to possess power or to use it this means that Herter is not likely to burst from his cell with a hell of a yell. A week or so ago I wrote him again making as strong an appeal as I am capable of making.
>
> We now know that the Administration is aware of l'affaire Pound and would like to resolve it. But we also know that it is afraid of Walter Winchell* et al as it is afraid of almost everything else. I doubt if a more impotent and timid administration ever held office in Washington.

But Herter was made of stronger stuff than MacLeish realized. On 2 January 1958 he wrote to Overholser:

> I do not know whether you remember me from the days when we were associated in Massachusetts, but my recollection of our association then is a very happy one. Archibald MacLeish came to see me in the last few days in regard to the case of Ezra Pound, and he tells me that you can give the whole story insofar as Saint Elizabeths is concerned.
>
> Would it be asking too much if you could drop in some day at your convenience as I would very much like to be fully informed in respect to this difficult individual?

Overholser took no action for a week, then told his secretary to call Herter's secretary 'to say that Dr Overholser had received letter and will be down to see Mr Herter when convenient'. No doubt realizing that the end was near, he was in no hurry, even for the Under Secretary of State.

But eventually he went; after their conversation, Herter discussed the case with Attorney General Rogers, then wrote to MacLeish outlining a proposed plan. MacLeish described it in a letter to Ezra on 16 March:

> I have at last . . . a firm and understandable statement from a responsible member of the present Administration . . . I would rather not name him at this juncture . . . In brief the position is this: a legal way can be found to release you as a kind of

---

*Acerbic columnist in the *New York Mirror*, syndicated throughout the USA.

out-patient of some private sanitarium which means that you would be visited from time to time by a recognized physician, but would live in your own quarters like any body else and would have – I quote – 'a maximum degree of freedom'.

The Government is willing to make use of this legal way if your friends can find a suitable 'inconspicuous place' within reach of the medical attentions described and can raise the necessary money if your own means won't suffice. The locus would have to be in the US.

But all this of course depends on your willingness to accept such an arrangement.

Will you think it over and let me have word as soon as you conveniently can? . . .

Rereading the above, that word 'quarters' seems to me unfortunate. Let me be specific about that. The idea is that you and, I assume, D.P., would live in a house of your own in some quiet town with the kind of climate you like where you could be visited from time to time by a recognized medic . . .

I have told no one about this so far except J. Laughlin who will have to go to work on the money end if you approve the project.

Ezra's reply was sent on 25 March:

Apart from an illegal arrangement with an anonymity, and your own very vague ideas re/ coherence of words and facts, you say nothing about placing my earnings in my own control.

D.P. pestered enough with accounting to Achinson's law office for every ten bucks/ and not allowed to give Walter a Xmas present.

You say 'responsible person' but you do not say it is a person whom you trust,
                              and your large views re/ reliability leave
one rather at sea

I doubt if there IS enough money for me to live on in the U.S. under the present system of taxation, which you refuse to investigate, tho the Manchester Guardian has got round to a few admission re/ England

Do you mean a physician or a quackiatrist?
              appointed by Gene Meyer??
AND I have never heard of a 'private sanitarium' that existed save for profit motive.

The status of unofficial bughouses in this country seems a bit vague.

I spose you mean well.

MacLeish, replying on 30 March, commented of the last sentence: 'Thanks for supposing I mean well. First kind word I've had from you since I started butting my head against this stone wall two years ago.'

He now explained that the anonymous official was Herter, and went on to say that no one thought Ezra would be unable to control his earnings; he suggested Ezra discuss with Overholser the nature of the 'sanitarium'. Ezra answered on 2 April: 'That's better, two men whose word of honour I can accept' (Herter and MacLeish). In fact he had already considered possible places of residence in the USA, remarking in a note to Overholser on 28 December: 'if they WANT me to stay inside the country, they shd/ house me in the stables at Monticello, to stimulate local life.' (Somebody had told him that at Thomas Jefferson's house at Charlottesville, Virginia, there was an unused brick stable.)

Meanwhile Overholser was continuing doggedly with his own independent scheme – the plan he had suggested to MacLeish that Ezra and Dorothy return to Italy. He asked Dorothy to outline her and Ezra's views on this, and she wrote to him on 1 February:

> Dear Dr Overholser -
>
> If Ezra Pound were released, we plan to go to Europe – Financial means are available to live modestly & not be a public charge. Summer quarters are ready in Italy, & he would want mild Mediterranean climate in winter.
>
> My husband has no political views re contemporary Italy, & would take ten years at least to develop any – hardly likely at 82 yrs.
>
> Yours sincerely
> Dorothy Pound.

The last paragraph had clearly been dictated by Ezra.

Frost was carrying on his own negotiations. On 16 January he received a telegram from President Eisenhower congratulating him on winning the Gold Medal of the Poetry Society of America, and on 12 February he wrote to Sherman Adams, White House Chief of Staff, with whom he was on good terms and whom he suspected was the author of the telegram. He suggested to Adams that he might 'meet the President to thank him in person at a meal or something . . . And when I say this half seriously it is not just for myself that I am speaking . . .' Simultaneously Adams was being urged to put Ezra's case before the President by Gabriel Hauge, Eisenhower's economic adviser, who happened to be James Laughlin's brother-in-law.

On 16 February, Frost received a telegram from the President inviting him to an 'informal stag dinner' and 'general chat' at the White House to take place on 27 February, and a letter from Sherman Adams saying he hoped to see him and have a talk before the dinner. Frost telegraphed in reply to Adams: 'WHAT'S ON MY MIND WOULD BE MORE APT TO BE BROUGHT OUT IN TALKS WITH YOU SEPARATELY.' Adams took the hint, and invited Frost to lunch in the White House Mess on the same day as the Presidential dinner. Frost telephoned to accept, and asked Adams if he could persuade Attorney General Rogers to come as well. Adams arranged this, and over lunch Frost raised the Pound matter. Rogers was his usual cautious self, but Frost received the impression that he was at last beginning to lean towards an early release for Ezra. Frost emphasized to Rogers and Adams that it would be a disgrace to the USA if Ezra died in captivity. He may have mentioned this again in the evening to Eisenhower himself at the 'stag dinner'.

Rumours began to circulate: on 16 March the Washington *Sunday Star* reported that

> A decision is near on the twin questions of freeing poet Ezra Pound of treason charges and releasing him from St Elizabeths Hospital . . . One official close to the case . . . said discussions have gone further than ever before. He said the 'whole matter is at boiling point'. An apparently effective pleader . . . has been Robert Frost.

On 1 April the Sieber Report on Ezra's case was released to the press. It was no more than a pedestrian summary of the legal and medical events of the case. That day, however, Attorney General Rogers was holding a routine press conference when someone raised Ezra's case – with striking results. The *New York Times* reported next morning:

> The Justice Department is giving consideration to dropping the treason charges against Ezra Pound, the poet, with a view to letting him return to Italy.
>
> Attorney General William P. Rogers disclosed this today in answer to a question at his news conference. He said Pound's fate depended upon new diagnoses by doctors at Saint Elizabeths . . . The Attorney General then put this rhetorical question: 'Is there any point in keeping him there if he never can be tried?'

It is not clear at which point the Department of Justice had abandoned its assumption that, if released, Ezra must remain in the USA, and had begun to consider allowing him to return to Italy.

Frost and MacLeish waited for further moves but when two weeks after the press conference nothing else had happened, on 14 April, Frost went once again to Washington, at MacLeish's insistence, and called on Rogers. 'I've dropped in to see what your mood is in regard to Ezra Pound,' he said. The delay had probably been because Rogers wanted to see if there would be any adverse public reaction to the prospect of Ezra's release; none had emerged. 'Our mood is your mood, Mr Frost,' Rogers replied. 'Well then,' said Frost, 'let's get him out right away.'

16

The Three Of Us

Rogers told Frost he should go to see William Shafroth, the official Government 'expediter' in legal matters. Frost did so at once, and Shafroth told him that the procedure was to apply to the court for the dismissal of the treason charge. He recommended that a lawyer named Thurman Arnold be engaged to handle the procedure, and arranged an immediate appointment for Frost with him.

Arnold had been a Yale Law School professor and a Court of Appeals judge, and had set up a highly regarded Washington law firm (Arnold, Fortas & Porter). He agreed to take on the case, and requested Frost to write a statement in support of Ezra that could be read in court. Frost went back to his Washington hotel and sat up most of the night composing draft after draft. In the morning he sent it to Arnold by messenger, then left the capital. At some point he had mentioned to a press reporter that Arnold was going to represent Ezra – or rather, represent Dorothy, since as 'Committee' she was obliged to take any legal action on Ezra's behalf. The first Dorothy knew of Arnold's involvement with the case was when she read of it in the newspaper, but she raised no objection.

Arnold needed to arrange a date for a court hearing, and he telephoned Frost in New England to ask if Frost could be in Washington on Friday 18 April, when the motion could be heard. Frost, having worked very hard on Ezra's behalf, now reverted to character and said he could not: he had a poetry reading in New York on the following Saturday and did not 'want to do too much travelling in too short a time'. He asked if the hearing could be arranged for the Monday. No, said Arnold, Friday was the day on which Judge Bolitha Laws sat in the District Court, and since he had been the presiding judge at the original hearings in 1945, Arnold wanted him to hear the case again, to avoid a great deal of explanation and recapitulation to a new judge. Frost then asked if it was really necessary for him to appear in court himself. Arnold thought that after all it would be sufficient if he read Frost's statement for him.

A few days before the hearing, the London *Times* printed an editorial calling for Ezra's release, and the *Nation* in New York similarly declared:

> We believe that Pound should be set free . . . Confinement . . . has not kept Pound from making disciples like John Kasper . . . It will be a triumph of democracy if we set Pound free . . . a sick and vicious old man . . . has his rights too.

No journalistic voices were raised in dissent.

On Friday 18 April in the District Court of Washington DC, Judge Bolitha Laws took his seat. Dorothy and Omar – now a teacher in Boston – were seated on the public benches, as were a group of the St Elizabeths disciples. At the back of the court sat Ezra, let out of St Elizabeths for the first time since the abortive habeas corpus hearing just over ten years earlier. The *New York Times* described him as 'dressed in a shabby blue jacket, a tan sport shirt with the tails not tucked in and blue slacks. His pockets were full of folded envelopes and other scraps of paper.'

Thurman Arnold got to his feet and read his motion for the dismissal of the indictment for treason. It was brisk and to the point:

> Defendant is 72 years old. If the indictment against him is not dismissed he will die in Saint Elizabeths Hospital . . . There can be no benefit to the United States in maintaining him indefinitely in custody as a public charge because that custody cannot contribute to his recovery and defendant's release would not prejudice the interests of the United States . . . Suitable arrangements for the defendant's custody and care are otherwise available . . . Mrs Dorothy Shakespear Pound, committee, proposes to apply for the delivery of the defendant . . . to her restraint and care with bond under such terms and conditions as will be appropriate to the public good and the best interests and peace of mind of the defendant in the remaining years of his life.

Arnold also read out Frost's statement:

> I am here [Frost had written, though of course he was not] to register my admiration for a government that can rouse in conscience to a case like this. Relief seems in sight for many of us besides the Ezra Pound in question and his faithful wife. He has countless admirers the world over who will rejoice in the news that he has hopes of freedom. I append a page or so of what they have been saying lately about him and his predic-

ament . . . There is probably legal precedent to help toward a solution of the problem. But I should think it would have to be reached more by magnanimity than by logic and it is chiefly on magnanimity that I am counting.

Though the general tone of his speech was ingratiating towards the Government, Frost could not resist getting in a characteristic side swipe. He observed of the Department of Justice and its endless delays: 'The bigger the Department the longer it might have to take thinking things through.'

Appended to his speech but not read out in court was a collection of statements in support of Ezra, chiefly culled from existing published remarks by celebrated literati. These included John Dos Passos, Van Wyck Brooks, Marianne Moore, Hemingway, Carl Sandburg, W. H. Auden, MacLeish, Robert Fitzgerald, Allen Tate, and Dag Hammarskjöld. Arnold observed of these testimonials that he himself represented not only Mrs Pound but 'the world community of poets and writers' in seeking the dismissal of the indictment.

Arnold did not call Overholser as a witness – perhaps sensing that, even at the very final moment, he might refuse to co-operate. Instead, he had drafted an affidavit which Overholser signed. It included the following statements:

> Ezra Pound is, and . . . has been, suffering from a paranoid state which has rendered and now renders him unfit . . . for trial . . . The condition . . . is permanent and incurable . . . [and] will not and has not responded to treatment . . . He is permanently and incurably insane.

This was no more than Overholser had been saying for nearly thirteen years. But the affidavit also included the observation that 'further therapeutic attention under hospital conditions would be of no avail and produce no beneficial results', and – at the instigation of Thurman Arnold – the assertion that

> there is a strong probability that the commission of the crime charged was the result of insanity, and I would seriously doubt that the prosecution could show criminal responsibility even if it were hypothetically assumed that Ezra Pound could regain sufficient sanity to be tried.

Then came the most crucial paragraph:

> In the event that the indictment is dismissed, I will recommend the delivery of Ezra Pound from further confinement at Saint Elizabeths Hospital under suitable arrangements for his

custody, care and restraint by his committee, Mrs Dorothy Shakespear Pound. Further confinement can serve no therapeutic purpose. It would be a needless expense and burden upon the public facilities of the hospital. Ezra Pound is not a dangerous person and his release would not endanger the safety of other persons or the officers, the property, or other interests of the United States.

Arnold had taken care that no conditions should be attached to the application for release. He did not read out Overholser's affidavit, but (said the *New York Times*) 'spoke for a few minutes . . . about Dr Overholser's medical findings'.

Arnold then sat down, and Oliver Gasch, an attorney representing the Department of Justice, got to his feet. He said that the Government thought the motion was 'in the interest of justice and should be granted'. At the last stage of negotiations, the Department had sent a memorandum to the President himself stating that it did not intend to oppose the motion for Ezra Pound's release. Eisenhower had initialled the memo, indicating his approval.

Judge Laws asked a few questions, then formally issued an 'Order . . . dismissing Indictment'. It stated that

> upon consideration of the affidavit of Dr Winfred Overholser . . . and it appearing that the Government is not in a position to challenge this medical testimony, and it further appearing that the Government consents to the dismissal of the indictment, it is by the Court this 18th day of April, 1958,
>
> ORDERED that the indictment be and the same is hereby dismissed.
>
> Bolitha J. Laws
> Chief Judge

'Mrs Pound . . . gave her husband a kiss,' reported the *New York Times*. Reporters asked him if he wanted to return to Italy, and he gave a firm 'yes'. Outside the court he 'posed for pictures after putting on a long yellow scarf with Oriental characters on it'. News of his release was carried by the London as well as the New York papers, and Mary heard it at Brunnenburg on an Italian radio bulletin – 'I couldn't believe it'. She was shocked by the statement that he was being released from St Elizabeths not as a free man but to the custody of his 'Committee'. However, the *New York Times* explained: 'He is under no restraint, and in fact he went downtown this afternoon, unattended by anyone from St Elizabeths.' He was in no hurry, though, to leave what had been his home for the past twelve and a half years. Overholser announced to the press that 'Mr Pound would remain in the hospital until his family have made plans for him . . . He has a lot of books and papers to take care of in his room.' He stayed voluntarily in Chestnut Ward for three weeks more.

*

The day after the court hearing, Robert Frost gave his poetry reading in New York. He chose to accept all the credit for Ezra's release, telling his audience that 'though the papers said it had taken him two years to win . . . it had taken him, in fact, only a week'. He made no mention of MacLeish. Ezra himself remarked to a reporter that Frost 'ain't been in much of a hurry' to get him out. Frost answered: 'He ought to have seen me that week.'

*

On 6 May 1958, the afternoon before he had finally arranged to leave St Elizabeths, Ezra sat with Marcella Spann in a car outside the back door of Center Building. She noticed that he was struck by the words of a current pop song, heard from a radio playing nearby:

> Che sarà, sarà,
> Whatever will be, will be
> The future's not ours to see
> Che sarà, sarà.

He was officially discharged next morning. The *Report of Discharge or Death* in the St Elizabeths files, of *Case Number 58,102, Pound, Ezra,* states: '*Condition upon discharge:* unimproved.' Overholser wrote him a brief letter stating 'you were officially discharged . . . today', and adding 'best wishes for your future health and happiness'.

Today, there is a small picture frame outside the room on Chestnut Ward where Ezra lived. It contains a photograph of him and a short newspaper article outlining his career. The room itself, like the rest of the ward, is now used for administrative offices.

*

He moved into 3514 Brothers Place, Washington SE, where Dorothy was now living. He was in an exuberant mood. Before his discharge he had insisted on visiting Thurman Arnold's law office and thanking him personally; Arnold refused to charge anything for his services. Ezra also spent some hours at the home of Representative Burdick who had raised his case in Congress. He was in his Grampaw uniform: 'an open-necked cotton shirt with short sleeves, green cotton trousers and brown shoes only partly laced. Around his neck was a string from which hung a small canvas bag; in it were his two pairs of glasses. He shook Burdick's hand, exclaiming, "This is a historic occasion" . . . [He] sat down in an easy chair. "I can't hold up my head for long . . ." ' He talked without stopping [said a reporter] 'for an hour and a half'. Another day he went with his supporter Harry Meacham down to Meacham's home town of Richmond, Virginia. Other friends took him to Williamsburg and Jamestown. He stayed for a while with Professor Craig La Drière of the Catholic University in Washington.

MacLeish wrote to reprove him for his ungrateful remark about Frost. Ezra replied:

> Naw, me dear aArchie
>   Thanks fer quite a lot, benevolence basic, BUT deploring the corruption in which you have survived,
>   NOT by any means despairing of opening yr/ eyes to the nature of the FILTH you have been surrounded by. The almost impossibility of getting ANY man who came in contact with the great stench of getting back to the smell of clear air.
>
> Alzo, I did speak well of Frost . . . I said Frost paid his debt when he finished writing 'North of Boston'.
>
> I don't know that he yet dares face me and discuss ANY serious issue, philosophical, historical or POlitical,
> God DAMN it neither he nor ELIOT will *look* at undeniable FACTS. I shd/ like some real information re MY debts to various people, contradictory reports on even intimate relationships pullulating . . .
>   ever yrs with that disturbing candour
>   Ez P

Ezra needed a passport to travel to Italy; Overholser wrote to the Passport Division of the State Department: 'In my opinion he is entirely safe to travel here or abroad in the company of his wife.' No difficulties were raised, and on 18 May the *New York Times* reported that he planned 'to return to Italy in June to live with his daughter and grandchildren'. Hemingway sent him $1,000 for 'expenses for you to Italy'. Ezra would not accept it, but framed the cheque. He wrote to Patricia Hutchins on 9 June: 'hell of packing nearly fatal to yr/ correspondent.'

He had been in touch for some time with the present occupant of his family's old house in Wyncote, Mrs Herman L. Gatter, whose son Carl (a Philadelphia schoolteacher) was an enthusiastic collector of local history items relating to Ezra's youth. Mrs Gatter asked if Ezra and Dorothy would like to visit Wyncote and stay a night in the house before they left America. Ezra replied: 'wd/ be delighted . . . wd/ need beds for 3.' The Gatters supposed that the third person must be the driver, but when Ezra wrote to say he would be driven from Washington by David Horton, who would be coming with his wife, and asked if the Hortons could rent a room somewhere for the night 'as five people can scarcely descend on ANY normal household', the mystery deepened as to who the third person might be. Another letter spoke without explanation of 'the three of us'.

Mrs Gatter wrote to say that she could easily put up all five, and the visit was arranged for 18 June. At 9 p.m. that day the party finally appeared, having been lost in the suburban maze that now surrounded Philadelphia. Introductions were made, and the Gatters discovered that the mysterious third person was Marcella Spann; her presence was not explained.

As they came into the house, Horton fussed over Ezra like a nursemaid – 'Grampaw needs a cushion for his head' – but Ezra astonished Carl Gatter by his energy; he 'jumped about like a toad', says Gatter, hurrying round the house, inspecting each room closely and searching the darkening backyard for familiar trees. Dinner was served, Horton fetching a big wicker chair from the back parlour because 'Grandpop's head needs support'. Ezra complimented Mrs Gatter on her roast and on the chlorine-free water; he had hated that supplied to the St Elizabeths' taps. He talked constantly; the other members of his party looked exhausted. After the meal he posed for photographs in the wicker chair, leaning back and shutting his eyes as in the Wyndham Lewis portrait. Dorothy sat silently, without expression; Carl Gatter thought her apprehensive.

The others soon went to bed, but Ezra threw himself down on the sofa in the front parlour and talked exuberantly, answering all Gatter's questions about his childhood; Gatter was struck by how much, and how accurately, he remembered. Eventually Gatter himself thought he should say goodnight, but Ezra indicated that he wanted to stay up for a while; Gatter in his own bedroom soon heard the front door open and shut. Later, Ezra explained that he had gone down the road to Calvary Presbyterian Church; he had wanted to see if an evergreen he and a childhood friend had planted at the back was still standing, but when he got there, had felt it would be wrong to trespass in the church grounds. He thought Wyncote much as he remembered it, except that the houses had been painted different colours.

In the morning, he was up long before anyone else; the Gatters discovered him hunting for oatmeal in the kitchen. After the meal he once more went all over the house and backyard, minutely examining any relic of childhood he could discover. Gatter saw him give Dorothy 'a tender kiss under the apple-tree'.

He searched the telephone directory for names of old Wyncote residents, he tried one or two numbers without success, and began to be upset that no one had called to see him – his visit had been kept secret to avoid reporters – though the previous night he had said he wanted privacy.

Finally, he succeeded in contacting one of his earliest girlfriends, Adele Polk, with whom he had a lengthy conversation. During lunch the Misses Priscilla and Esther Heacock, who had been at their family's dame school with Ezra, arrived under the pretence of having 'just dropped by'.

From Wyncote, Ezra and his party went on to Rutherford, New Jersey, for a brief visit to William Carlos Williams. He was unwell, and had little to say to Ezra; but they were photographed together, Ezra, his shirt hanging loose and open, standing with both hands paternally on Williams's shoulders, Williams displaying no resentment at this implicit statement about their half-century of friendship.

It was now Monday 30 June, and from Rutherford they went straight to the quayside in New York. Tickets had been booked on the Italian liner *Cristoforo Colombo* for Ezra, Dorothy and Marcella: a small stateroom with three bunks.

∗

The liner called at Naples on 9 July, and Italian reporters and photographers came on board. They asked Ezra what it had been like spending twelve years in an American insane asylum. He answered: 'All America is an insane asylum.' The matter of anti-Semitism was raised. He told them: 'The Fascist dictators made a mistake in the way they persecuted the Jews. The mistake was not in fighting the Jews, but the manner in which the Jews were fought. Rather than attack them as a bloc, each case should have been examined individually.' Photographers asked him to pose, and he smilingly obliged. His shirt showing great patches of sweat from the heat, he placed his left hand on his hip, and raised his other arm in the Fascist salute.

∗

At Genoa he disembarked carrying his own suitcases, wearing a shapeless grey felt hat, his shirt open to the navel. There were more photographers, more reporters. They asked him if he was glad to be back on Italian soil. 'I ought to kiss the sacred ground,' he answered, 'but here I see only cement. Give me a meadow, give me some fresh grass.' He repeated the joke about a madhouse being the best place to live in America. The customs officer, astonished by the crowd around this strange figure, chalked his bags without looking inside them. Ezra was delighted: 'No fingerprints, no questionnaires – Italy – free country!'

From Genoa, he, Dorothy and Marcella travelled to Verona, where they stayed overnight and were met next day by Mary, who took them up to the Tyrol in a hired car. The party stopped for lunch in Bolzano; Ezra was in fine form, talking ceaselessly, but Mary began to feel inexplicably uneasy, to sense that 'I was up against something beyond Babbo's control'.

Part Five

1958–72
Personae

1

Trained For A Demigod

The village of Tirolo perches high above the valley of the Adige, half a day's drive from the Brenner Pass. It is nominally Italian territory, but though the traveller from the south pays for his petrol in lire, he may have to speak in German for the pump attendant to understand him. *Lederhosen* are much in evidence, particularly among the visitors. 'A village,' observes the *Blue Guide*, 'given over to tourism, especially favoured by Germans on walking holidays.' The chief tourist attraction is Castel Tirolo – Schloss Tirol – the twelfth-century castle that gave its name to the whole Tyrol, once the home of Margaret Maultasch, the Ugly Duchess. Walking up to it from the village, one looks down the steep slope to another castle; a discreet sign says 'Brunnenburg'.

A narrow lane leads abruptly down, terminating in a yard where chickens peck, and where stands a farmhouse roofed in chalet style. Behind this, entered through massive gates, rises the castle itself. The main tower is Roman, the outside walls eleventh century, dating from a period when Brunnenburg was a watchtower and outer defence for Schloss Tirol itself. At the end of the nineteenth century an eccentric German tried to turn it into a Masonic temple, encrusting it with balconies and turrets in the manner favoured by Ludwig of Bavaria. His money and his sanity ran out, and in 1904 he pushed his wife off one of the balconies. During the First World War the Italian Government confiscated the property, but the crazy old freemason lived on there, the building gradually reverting to ruin around him. The local people feared the place, so that when Boris and Mary de Rachewiltz took it over in 1948 and lights began to shine out once more from the tower, there was a general sense of relief.

At first the young couple and their children occupied just one top room in the tower. Then their domain slowly expanded into twenty rooms, divided into self-contained apartments, each of which occupied one floor. One of these flats was hung with Ezra's Gaudier-Brzeska drawings; it opened out into a small enclosed garden, with the huge stone head of him, brought up laboriously from Rapallo, gazing out valley-ward from under the trees. The communal dining-room was adorned with the Pound and Weston family portraits, and Ezra's papers and books, neatly bundled, had been brought from Sant'Ambrogio.

Brunnenburg had been planned by Mary as the Ezuversity made manifest: 'My vision was that he would be sitting down in that garden, surrounded by really nice students.' While in St Elizabeths Ezra had frequently sent disciples there: 'You shd/ of course stop there if in Woptaly,' he wrote to Patricia Hutchins. By the time of his own arrival in midsummer 1958, the place had inevitably taken on something of the atmosphere of a shrine. Daniel Cory, secretary and assistant to George Santayana, describes it as

> the headquarters of what I might call the 'Pound Club'. The atmosphere . . . was one of unqualified devotion. His bust by Gaudier-Brzeska . . . [in] the large garden . . . seemed to focus in the moonlight the mysteries of initiation. All discussion presupposed that there was only one poet of the 20th century *digne de son nom*: Yeats and Eliot might be respected, but they belonged to a different category. The *Cantos* were the great modern 'classic' . . . Mary de Rachewiltz was the official translator . . . into Italian . . . and Eva Hesse – a close friend and visitor from Munich – was performing a parallel metamorphosis into the German tongue.
>
> Sometimes when we gathered together in the evening the discussion would be enlivened by the tracking-down of elusive references in the *Cantos*: it recalled exciting games of 'treasure-hunt' one used to play around Christmas . . . Occasional visitors like Vanni Scheiwiller (Ezra's publisher from Milan) or Donald Gallup [his bibliographer, from Yale] glided easily into the spirit of the club-room . . . I had never lived in an intellectual closed-shop with either Santayana or [Bertrand] Russell, but then they were philosophers who were accustomed to wrangling with alternative points of view.

Mary is candid about the degree to which Brunnenburg had become a shrine or museum, writing, towards the end of *Discretions*, of

> castles in the air turning into a castle on the rock into which slowly streamed everyone and everything with all the clatter of outlived feelings and discarded belongings and all the papers

tied up and sealed for eternity, tossed and torn and disrupted by
a horde of disciples and publishers scholars secretaries and
collectors – hogs after truffles, greedy widows and fearful
wives, chucked from attic to attic from truck to truck in a
whirlwind . . .

As she arrived back at the castle that afternoon in July 1958 with her
father and his entourage, there was a fresh invasion of reporters and
photographers. Such a public arrival was not, perhaps, an ideal start, and as
soon as the initial euphoria wore off, Ezra relapsed into complete fatigue. 'I
had bad break down at start of July,' he wrote to Huntington Cairns. 'Not
able to finish paragraph, etc.' He observed that while he was in St
Elizabeths, 'Nobody seemed to THINK I was nutsz.' Now that he was
out, he began to feel genuinely unstable. But he was soon 'up' again, and he
wrote to Yeats's widow on 5 August: 'mountain air a pleasant change from
D.C.' Dorothy was equally pleased with the setting: 'The mountains here
are a continual delight,' she wrote to a friend. 'They suggest many Jap. and
Chinese paintings.' And to Mrs Gatter at Wyncote: 'The weight off my
shoulders!! to have got Ezra here . . . Marcella and Ezra send their
Greetings to you.' Marcella was now being described as Ezra's secretary.
Dorothy observed cryptically to Mrs Gatter: 'I hope we have no trouble –
I do not foresee any.'

Ezra continued to complain of exhaustion; Dorothy said he was 'taking
a good deal of repose'. He wrote to Patricia Hutchins a month after his
arrival: 'I SHOULD refrain from all work for another 2 months & receive
only essential correspondence.' And a month later: 'I alternate short bursts
of energy, with total exhaustion.' At first the bursts of energy were
plentifully in evidence. Mary's birthday on 9 July had, over the years,
become the occasion for a village celebration with dancing at the castle.
This year's party had been postponed a few days until Ezra's arrival, and
when it took place he opened the dancing himself with a vigorous polka,
declaring: 'The rhythm of a Tyrolean band gets you going.' A few days
later there was another party, in his own honour, when he read from Canto
81 ('Pull down thy vanity'). Another day he called for tools and began
work building a sturdy refectory table. He climbed some distance up the
7,000-foot mountain that towers over the castle and is known as the 'Mut',
announcing that he would like to build a marble temple on its summit. He
concerned himself with horticulture, making plans for a grove of maple
trees, arranging for 500 white vines to be planted in a section of the castle
vineyard (he had never cared for red wine), and wandering around the
garden with a large pair of shears, trimming indiscriminately. He worked
over Mary's translation of two recent cantos, and was as critical as ever he
had been in Sant'Ambrogio days. He had long talks with Boris, who was

now achieving a reputation as an Egyptologist – hence the hieroglyphics in *Rock-Drill* – and asked him about Egyptian initiation rites and other arcane ceremonies. Boris eventually wrote an article on 'L'Elemento Magico in Ezra Pound'.

On these 'up' days, Ezra would take an interest in the cooking. In the evening he would read to his grandchildren Patrizia and Walter from *Uncle Remus*, and to the adults from the Cantos, from his translations, and from the *Confucius to Cummings* anthology at which he and Marcella were working. (It was eventually published in 1964 by New Directions.) Sometimes he took the children into Merano for the horse-races, making bets himself and celebrating any win with lavish quantities of ice cream all round. He sent a note of thanks to Overholser for 'making possible' the work he had written and published while in St Elizabeths, and also raised the question of whether the Committee could be wound up. Overholser wrote back that this might be allowed; but Ezra's lawyers became anxious that any official moves might disclose his sanity, and so open the way to a possible re-indictment. They recommended that he and Dorothy simply drop the Committee arrangement without legalities; but Ezra does not seem to have understood that this was possible, and Dorothy continued to exercise formal control over all business matters. She agreed to Ezra's request that Marcella be paid $1,200 per annum as 'secretary'.

Ezra prepared another batch of cantos for Laughlin and Eliot. These had been drafted in St Elizabeths, and were numbered 96 to 109. He gave them the title *Thrones de los Cantares*, explaining that

> The thrones in Dante's *Paradiso* are for the spirits of the people who have been responsible for good government. The thrones in the Cantos are an attempt to move out from egoism and to establish some definition of an order possible or at any rate conceivable on earth. One is held up by the low percentage of reason which seems to operate in human affairs. *Thrones* concerns the states of mind of people responsible for something more than their personal conduct.

One such person was Sir Edward Coke, Speaker of the House of Commons under Elizabeth I, and author of *Institutes of the Laws of England*; but all references to him in *Thrones* were apparently made on the assumption that the reader already knew his work intimately.

The texture of the new cantos was much the same as that of *Rock-Drill*:

Coke. Inst. 2.
    to all cathedral churches to be
      read 4 times in the yeare
  20 H. 3

>   that is certainty
> mother and nurse of repose
>   he that holdeth by castle-guard
>   pays no scutage . . .

The only striking change was the impression that Ezra was now bored with writing poetry. Canto 100, dated 1 January 1958, is the mixture very much as before:

> 'Has packed the Supreme Court
>   so that they will declare anything he does constitutional.'
>   Senator Wheeler, 1939.
> – and some Habsburg ploughed his imperial furrow . . .

Noel Stock began to frequent Brunnenburg around this time, and gathered that Ezra now had a 'gnawing feeling that the Cantos did not amount to much'.

✻

Mary knew that beneath the often ebullient surface all was not well with him. At first it had been 'just unbelievably wonderful . . . so much better than any expectations'. Then, as 'the euphoria boiled down, one realized . . . that he had missed out on twenty years of life'. He seemed to feel 'shut in by all these mountains'. He was used to the central heating of St Elizabeths, and Mary was hard put to keep him warm enough, especially as the cold weather began to set in. On 14 November he sent a note to Overholser, breezily asking him to 'drop in and inspect the further developments of the malady'. But two weeks later he was telling Patricia Hutchins: 'NO, dont come out here in cold weather. and DONT send me professors. I thought I had told you that I need time to recuperate.' Soon he was saying bluntly: 'I can't live at this altitude.'

There were also more delicate problems, what Daniel Cory describes as 'the difficulty of accommodating the young Texan lady to an unusual, mixed foreign setting'. As Mary puts it: 'The family had been trained for a demigod, and as such he came. With his wife Dorothy and his secretary Marcella. Committee and bodyguard.' She wished she had given them their own self-contained flat. 'The house no longer contained a family. We were turning into entities who should not have broken bread together.'

He did not like being a demigod. 'Don't keep me up here on this pedestal,' he told Mary, 'it's too damned uncomfortable.' But it was not easy for her to start again. 'Blinded by his glory,' she writes, 'I did not see all his needs.' As winter fell, 'I grew jealous and I grew angry, and I can rattle off a whole string of grievances which are neither here nor there.'

Ezra perceived her discontent and told her sadly: 'I thought you were solid rock I could build on.'

On Christmas morning Mary 'found the Christmas tree lying on the floor. A bad omen, I felt.' Ezra stuck it till March. Then he left, taking Dorothy and Marcella with him to Rapallo.

2

Drammertist

In Rapallo, they took a modern flat in the Albergo Grande Italia, not far from the seafront. 'We got an attic, and an elEvator that works, at least for the present, as that at v[ia] Marsala has NOT for the past 49 years,' Ezra wrote to 'George' Yeats on 1 April 1959. 'Cdn't breathe air in the Tirol / but can that of the Mediterranean basin.'

Daniel Cory, meeting Ezra by chance in Rapallo, was whisked off to the apartment, where he observed Dorothy and Marcella. He writes of Marcella: 'No doubt she had lightened his hours considerably and so helped Dorothy in her thankless task . . . It was obvious that Ezra was fond of her: I think she was the embodiment to him of an almost forgotten springtime.' Noel Stock paid a visit to the triangular ménage, and retains the impression of a carefully organized household, each member sleeping in a separate room. 'Marcella was acting like a nurse, a secretary–nurse. Dorothy just sat in her own room, very upright, reading, and when Marcella was mentioned the atmosphere became distinctly frosty.'

Giuseppe Bacigalupo, whose mother had been the Pounds' doctor before the war and who was now himself a long-established Rapallo medical practitioner, met Ezra on the promenade, 'somewhat aged but apparently the same as ever, and I heard him say straight off: "Why do you pay taxes? Taxes shouldn't be paid" – obviously the influence of Douglas hadn't weakened with the years. He then told me a joke about St Elizabeths that he often repeated in those days: "The only place in America where you could live, because everyone outside was mad."' Daniel Cory, who had not seen Ezra since the war, was 'surprised that he had not altered more'. An American academic, Wallace Martin, who was writing a book on A. R. Orage and the *New Age* circle, came to Rapallo to ask Ezra about those years, and found him very lucid in the daytime but inclined to ramble in the evenings – whereupon Dorothy would make it clear that Martin should leave.

D.G. Bridson was now arranging to make a BBC film about Ezra, and it had been agreed that this should be done at Brunnenburg. During April 1959, the month after Ezra and Dorothy had left the castle, they both returned there briefly for the benefit of the cameras. Bridson was delighted with the results:

> If ever I had doubted that Pound was a natural born actor, watching him before the cameras would certainly have convinced me . . . For four days . . . he took direction as to the manner born. Silhouetted upon the battlements, confronting Gaudier's bust of him that dominated the garden, pacing the stone corridors and climbing the spiral staircases, fingering at his harpsichord or moving silently round his study, writing Chinese ideograms with a brush to prove his points, facing the viewer like Nemesis and lecturing him like an Old Testament prophet, reading his blistering indictment of *Usura* to the world or . . . *Brer Rabbit* to his grandchildren, nobody else could have come up with such a mesmeric performance.

Bridson avoided 'the usual camera interview', knowing how Ezra disliked (and usually ignored) unexpected questions. Instead he merely 'listed the points which ought to be made' and then let Ezra deal with them in his own fashion. For example, Bridson prompted him to explain his very distinctive style of reading his own poetry, with the Scots rolling of the R and a manner strongly resembling Yeats. This is what Ezra said about it:

> My reading style, I believe, has altered a little since we used to meet at that horrible place called 'The Tour Eiffel' with Stulich's protruding stomach and bulbous nose to enhance the flavour of the food. Hulme discovered the place, and Wyndham had credit there. I read the Bloody Sestina one night, and a week later Stulich comes round with a screen and puts it round the table and says, 'Gentlemen, you can make all the noise that you like.' I believe that what Ford called my 'Northumbrian' was more emotional at that period. I suppose one is more emotional at twenty-whatever-it-was. And Yeats' reading – well, in the first place he had Florence Farr who really *could* read – and then Yeats, his means of getting, or *seeing* his rhythm, was pulling out the vowels: 'Made a great peacock in the pri-i-de of his eye' – that kind of thing. I don't know where he got to later.
>
> I think *my* reading now shows more interest in the meaning of what I've got on the page. I know when we were down in

Syracuse [in 1925], out in the Greek theatre there, and Yeats
wanted me to read something – I s'pose he wanted me to read
something of his or recite something – I found that the only
thing one could do in the open like that – the only thing I
remember that you could speak clear enough to get across – was
Sappho's poem 'Poikilothron' – with whatever pronunciation
or mispronunciation I use of it. But I have no idea how he read
after 1920.

In May, Ezra took Dorothy and Marcella on a short tour of Italy. One
of their first stops was on the road north of Pisa where the DTC had stood;
a rose nursery now occupied the site. They also went to Sirmione, and on
the shore of Lake Garda, Ezra asked Marcella to marry him.

Precisely what happened next is not known; perhaps there is a reference
to it in Canto 113: 'Pride, jealousy and possessiveness / 3 pains of hell/ . . .
The hells move in cycles, / No man can see his own end. / The Gods have
not returned.' Dorothy was prepared to put up with almost anything, but
she would never formally surrender him. By the end of the summer
Marcella was on her way back to Texas.

*

' . . . me incapacitated,' Ezra wrote to Archibald MacLeish from the
Albergo Grande Italia in Rapallo on 10 September. ' . . . collapsed. Been no
use to myself or anyone all July and Aug . . . One thing to have Europe fall
on one's head. Another to be set in the ruins of same.'

He did not know where to live. Friends had tried to find him suitable
winter accommodation, but he could think of nowhere other than Rapallo,
'where overhead is too high in hotel, and apartment NOT the perfect
answer. I mean the one I am in. And not in condition to face eight hour
auto ride to Brunnenburg, or the winter there.'

Having regarded his neck as his most vulnerable spot for many years, he
now began to complain of 'calcifications' in the vertebrae there, and even of
'loose' vertebrae. In June he wrote to Overholser in Washington:

Dear W.O.
    Apropos the remarkable calcification or whatever you call it
for my cervical vertebrae, plus one floating bit, a correspondent
(member of far western banking family) asks when they started
fluorinization of Washington D.C. water.
    I spose the annual x ray of thorax missed that level, and that I
have some loose verts/ lower down. (Foto of present condition
if of interest.) i.e. with cartilage in between them . . .
        cordially yrs
        E Pound

Overholser answered that 'the only full sized chest plate which was made of you was in 1947 and no calcification at that time was shown . . . There is no indication . . . that fluorination of water has anything to do with calcification of the sort you mention.' This letter had no effect on Ezra, who continued to complain of the supposed calcification. He wrote to the firm of American lawyers dealing with his business: 'Have grown large amount of superfluous lime or bone in my NEKK hence great fatigue.'

He began to subside into misery and self-pity. 'Plenty of publicity, no support,' he wrote to MacLeish. 'Mass of material to be sorted etc. Work that I have not the strength to do . . . And everybody used to having me the life of the party, and flummoxed by my inertia . . . A nurse, a baby carriage, a really HOT room for the winter, and may be granpaw wd/ rise again.'

Arthur Moore in London reported to Laughlin that

> Dorothy . . . is having a very worrying time indeed, and she feels that he is really too difficult for her alone, and that the young Texan Secretary says she is returning to the U.S.A. I gather E.P. changes his mind so often, and worries – and now says he wants to go back to Brunnenburg to die, and has suicidal spells . . . The calcium growth at the top of his spine . . . worries him considerably.
>
> . . . It looks as if E.P. may make Brunnenburg his home – although he told me he could never return there as the castle was so cold during the winter months.
>
> The reason he left was I think mainly due to the troubles with Mary and the Secretary who could not get on . . .
>
> E.P.'s recent letters to me have been very brief, and he has complained of his 'pore old head'.

On many days he seemed overwhelmed by depression and hypochondria; he wrote to MacLeish that he was 'broken', was suffering 'exhaustion after years of struggle', and was 'yelling for help'. Yet when MacLeish wrote back anxiously, he got this chirpy little note:

> Don't mump, I aint deespaired of savin' yr/ soul,
> slowly perhaps and in fragments, but still –
> > Yrs
> > > EP

In the corner, beneath the large and exuberant initials, he scrawled:

> as one drammertist to another

Laughlin came to Rapallo in September 1959, and grew 'deeply concerned' about him, writing to Overholser three months later:

During all the years in the hospital, when I used to come down to see him, he was always so wonderfully cheerful and optimistic. But now he is at the bottom of the pit of melancholy, and most of his talk was about dying and 'losing his mind'.

I was particularly upset because he wouldn't hear of going to a hospital or a specialist for treatment. But now his daughter Mary writes me that he is a little bit better – they moved back to the castle in Merano in October – and that he has said he would be willing to seek medical help . . . I made some inquiries about doctors in Italy . . . I would like to check out these names with you . . . Mrs Pound is no longer at all strong, and Ezra's daughter is so located that she does not have access to what I would consider first rate medical advice.

Overholser wrote back recommending a Professor Gozzano, whom Laughlin had mentioned, but Ezra did not see him, and the only doctor who seems to have examined him at this stage was a general practitioner who prescribed a tranquillizer (reserpine) and male hormone injections. This treatment, according to a later medical report, was entirely unsuccessful,

the behaviour becoming more retarded and inhibited, the communication more difficult, and the withdrawal increasing; thought was markedly dominated . . . by . . . self-accusation and hypochondriacal contents (he spoke of bodily impurity, and of closed and infected bowels) . . . 'I am covered with microbes.' . . . This was regarded [by the doctor] more as a true delusion than as a phobic fear.

Charles Norman, who had compiled the *PM* report on Ezra in 1945, was now at work on a full-length biography of him, and wished to discuss Overholser's tactics during the 1945 court hearings with Julien Cornell. In view of this, Cornell wrote to Overholser asking if he would mind him revealing that the St Elizabeths staff had always thought Ezra sane. Overholser wrote back to Cornell that this was not strictly true – there had been merely some minor differences of opinion about the degree of mental abnormality – and he continued: 'I have never had any doubts as to the fact that Mr Pound was mentally ill and from what I hear of him since he left the Hospital I am sure that I was right.'

He was still working occasionally at new cantos, and at Christmas 1959 made some 'Notes for 111' (he was now aiming for the round number of 120). It was definitely a *Paradiso*, but, in the words of Canto 74, the paradise could be glimpsed 'only in fragments':

A nice quiet paradise,
         Orage held the basic was pity,
      compassione,
            Amor
Cold mermaid up from black water –
    Night against sea-cliffs
        the low reef of coral –
And the sand grey against undertow
Veritas, by anthesis, from the sea depth
    come burchiello in su la riva
The eyes holding trouble –
      no light
           ex profundis –
naught from feigning.
Soul melts into air,
     anima into aura,
        Serenitas.

On stronger days he would tell everyone at the castle: 'I should have listened to the Possum.' And in consequence, says Mary, 'we all had to read *After Strange Gods*. I wrote to Mr Eliot begging him to come and see Babbo. He sent a birthday telegram saying: "You are the greatest poet alive and I owe everything to you" – or words to that effect. Then he [Ezra] worried that we would not have enough to eat and not enough fuel and Archibald MacLeish sent a check to keep Babbo warm.' Some time after the telegram, Eliot wrote at length trying to cheer Ezra up. Robert Lowell learnt of the state he was in, and sent a note:

> Ezra, I think you should feel happy about your life, and the thousands of kindnesses you have done to your friends, and how you've been a fountain to them. So you've been to me, and I miss the old voice.

At Brunnenburg, Mary and her father 'still talked a lot', but, she adds, 'I suppose it must have been trying for him to have me continually quote the Cantos at him'.

During Christmas 1959, he continued to be restless and self-pitying. Arthur Moore, writing to Laughlin, tells what happened next:

> From a letter dated 3rd Jan. from D.P. she reported that during the night of Jan. 2 E.P. left the Castle, and returned about 8.15 am soaked to the skin, through all sorts of sweaters and a heavy coat, and was put to bed immediately, after a rubbing with alcohol and a dose of brandy, and I understand since he remains rather a handful. His physique is strong, and he is having

injections, and D.P. says he complains his head is slow and hardly works at all – which worries him dreadfully.

There was no role left now except that of King Lear.

Mary decided that he needed male company. He was sent off to Rome to stay with an old friend of Boris's, Ugo Dadone, a retired military attaché, a Second World War veteran who had been injured in the African campaign, and an admirer of d'Annunzio. Ezra arrived during January 1960 and stayed in Dadone's apartment on the Via Angelo Poliziano. Dorothy reported: 'Ezra in Rome with a friend . . . The cold here too much for him – I fled to Rapallo . . .' But Ezra showed little improvement. 'Hope to resume human activity sometime,' he wrote to Mrs Gatter in March, ' . . . six months arrears of correspondence.' Daniel Cory came across him in Rome during February. 'He had changed considerably since I saw him in Rapallo: he was frankly embarrassed by his erratic nervous condition. As he said: "One day I talk like a parrot and the next I can find nothing to say."' On an exuberant day he might speak of the possibility of making a lecture tour of the USA – a prospect that greatly alarmed Laughlin when he heard about it. Next morning he would say something like: 'At seventy I realized that instead of being a lunatic, I was a moron.'

A young American, Donald Hall, contacted him and asked if he might interview him for the *Paris Review*. Ezra agreed, and in March, Hall travelled to Rome from England, where he was then living, feeling 'something like devotion' towards Ezra and his works. Hall was supposed to be writing a review of *Thrones* for the *New Statesman*. He could not really make much of it, but 'I found myself praising it whether I understood it or not'.

Hall describes his first encounter with Ezra at Dadone's apartment: 'Pound answered my knock . . . His eyes . . . were watery, red, weak. "Mr Hall . . . you – find me – in fragments." As he spoke he separated the words into little bunches . . . "You have driven – all the way – from England – to find a man – who is only fragments."' Like Cory, Hall was astonished by the sudden switches in mood. At one moment 'he would walk up and down in the small, bright room, sit in a chair and read to me from manuscript, alternating pairs of spectacles as if he were juggling in a circus; then suddenly his face would sag, his eyes turn glassy like a fish's, and he would collapse onto a sofa and into silence; then he would jump up in five minutes and begin the cycle again, his speech newly vigorous and exact.'

Hall noted that he took the business of being interviewed very seriously, partly because he had let rash remarks slip into print in the past, but also since 'he was not sure that what he said made sense'. He told Hall that there were 'fragments' of new cantos since *Thrones* but said he had 'not written a line' for months. Hall wondered whether he had had a stroke. As he talked, he constantly scratched the back of one hand with the other, obsessively clawing away at his skin.

The interview was recorded on tape over three days, in the apartment, and was characterized, said Hall, by 'incomplete sentences, gaps, great leaps over chasms . . . In all the three days, Pound seldom finished a thought . . . He would begin a long sentence, pause, stumble – and become aware of the rasp of the tape recorder. "No, no, no, no," he would say, and "Turn that damned thing off." . . . When I turned it off and took notes instead, the change didn't seem to help . . . He was beset, he said, by the Jamesian parenthesis . . . Each morning when I returned to him, he had made notes to complete paragraphs abandoned the day before; he worked on the interview all night, between fits of sleep. He worked on the interview after I returned to England, and finished some of his best paragraphs or sentences in letters.'

Hall asked him: 'What are you going to do in the remaining cantos?' The answer, put together in the fashion Hall describes, finally came out like this:

> It is difficult to write a paradiso when all the superficial indications are that you ought to write an apocalypse. It is obviously much easier for an inferno or even a purgatorio. I am trying to collect the record of the top flights of the mind. I might have done better to put Aggasiz on top instead of Confucius.

Hall asked bluntly: 'Are you more or less stuck?'

> Okay, I am stuck. The question is, am I dead, as Messrs. A.B.C. might wish? In case I conk out, this is provisionally what I have to do: I must clarify obscurities; I must make clearer definite ideas or dissociations. I must find a verbal formula to combat the rise of brutality – the principle of order versus the split atom.

Hall was upset by the difficulties Ezra had in putting the answers together. 'But it was the old man's pride that seized me by the throat . . . When he assembled a sharp or clever phrase, he smiled and chuckled and looked at me for approval or confirmation. Sometimes a question . . . provided him opportunity to mimic, and these were his happiest moments . . . He performed Eliot and Hemingway with special finesse and gusto.'

As the interview progressed, 'depression grew thicker in the room . . . Gradually . . . I understood that he doubted the value of everything that he had done in his life . . . To my astonishment, he leapt to take scraps from my hand. I mentioned to him casually that Henry Moore as a young sculptor had taken comfort from his book on Gaudier-Brzeska . . . He was moved almost to tears; it was something he had not known before.'

Yet when he accepted Hall's invitation to dine with him and his wife, a new man appeared. He was asked to choose a restaurant, and 'said in a humorous manner that, well, Crispi's ought to do – as if we should know that Crispi's would do more than *do*; as if he were referring to the Tour d'Argent in Paris . . . As we strolled toward the restaurant door, I looked him over. This was a new Ezra Pound, shirt open at the neck, with a light coat and a great yellow scarf, carrying a stout stick. His large black hat sat back on his head . . . and he walked with his head thrown back, his beard strutting forth at a jaunty angle. He chatted with the head waiter in Italian, holding himself upright like a general, and requested a particular table by pointing at it with his stick. When he had consulted the menu he chose *osso buco* for himself, and recommended it to the rest of us.'

Hall noticed how he paid 'special and even flirtatious attention' to Hall's wife Kirby, 'his eyes glinting as he looked at her, especially if he made her laugh. There were pauses and moments of awkwardness, also, when he would stop in mid sentence forgetting his way, but these lapses were less frequent in Crispi's . . . He told more Eliot stories, mimicking Eliot with an avuncular, mocking, affectionate accuracy . . . He sang stanzas of "The Yiddisher Charleston Band".'

Hall was mildly astonished to learn that he missed America. 'He wanted to return, to see the country outside asylum walls . . . Did we think someone would pay his way over?' They touched on this in the interview, Hall asking if he wanted to go back to the USA:

> I certainly want to. But whether it is nostalgia for an America that isn't there any more or not I don't know . . . I undoubtedly have moments when I should very much like to live in America. There are concrete difficulties . . . Richmond is a beautiful city but you can't live in it unless you drive an automobile. I'd like at least to spend a month or two a year in the US.

He told Hall that he felt more American as time went on:

> One is transplanted and grows, and one is pulled up and taken back to what one had been transplanted from and it is no longer there . . . I suppose one reverts to one's organic nature and finds it merciful.

So had his return to Italy been a disappointment?

> Undoubtedly. Europe was a shock. The shock of no longer feeling oneself in the centre of something is probably a part of

it. Then there is the incomprehension, Europe's incomprehension, of organic America. There are so many things which I, as an American, cannot say to a European with any hope of being understood. Somebody said that I am the last American living the tragedy of Europe.

After dinner at Crispi's he took the Halls sightseeing, winding up at a *gelateria* near Danone's apartment: ' "Stop *here*. I'll buy you an ice cream." . . . Pound stood in the yellow light, his coat flung across his shoulders like a cape . . . He stalked up and down a few feet, smiling as his wooden spoon delivered its mouthfuls, veering back and forth on his toes . . . with youthful gait again for a moment.'

The morning after the dinner, he was elated with his social success – 'I haven't had a relaxed evening like that since I left America . . . Europeans don't understand anything.' But gradually he lapsed into exhaustion. 'The question is – whether I give up now – or have another twenty years to write in.' He asked Hall: 'From what – you see of me – do you think – I will be able to go on writing? Do you think – there is enough of me here – to work?' Hall did not know what to say. Ezra considered the matter, then 'remarked that really, all he needed was two months of relaxation like last night, that would fix him up'.

One day later he announced that he would take the Halls to the Circus Maximus; he wanted to spend the day with them. 'He was pacing, rubbing his hands together, smiling, and looked twenty years younger than . . . when I first saw him.' He showed Hall some fragmentary notes for the ending of the Cantos:

Provisional ending
    re nature of sovereignty
(if I konk out).
nostos.
periplum.
vs. paradiso, difficult
    to find inhabitants for.

to clarify obscurities
    (vers. prosaici
        as note.)

    get clearer
definite ideas or dissociations already expressed.

verbal formula to control rise of brutality
principle of order
    vs. split atom.

Hall learnt that, earlier in the morning, Ezra had been reading over drafts for new cantos.

Showing Hall these notes, 'he spoke with a vigor that made anything seem possible. He settled his hat back on his head, flung his scarf around his neck, and took up his stick. Then he realized, with a short laugh, that he didn't know how to direct me to the Circus Maximus. He sat at the edge of his sofa bed, hat and scarf still on, and studied a map. Then suddenly it happened, horribly in front of my eyes: again I saw vigor and energy drain out of him, like air from a pricked balloon. The strong body visibly sagged into old age; he disintegrated in front of me, smashed into a thousand unconnected and disorderly pieces. He took off his hat slowly and let it drop, his scarf slid to the floor; his stick, which had rested in his lap, thudded to the carpet. His long body slid boneless down, until he lay prone, eyes closed, as if all the lights in a tall building went out in a few seconds, and the building itself disassembled, returning to the stone and water and sand from which it had come.

'For a few minutes he said nothing, only breathing and sighing . . . [Then] he opened his eyes and looked at me. I said nothing but looked back into the eyes that watched me.

'After another two or three minutes, he mumbled. "I can't do anything right." After another pause he added: "I get you to go to the trouble – of bringing a car over here – and then I crump out on you."'

They stayed at the apartment, and at Ezra's suggestion Hall asked more questions for the interview, 'but Pound's depression was heavy. When a question reminded him of the Cantos, he doubted that he would live to complete them. He spoke again of the difficulty of finding inhabitants for a *Paradiso* . . . Maybe he was mistaken after all, he mumbled, to put Confucius at the top; maybe it should have been Agassiz. He looked at me as if I could decide for him.

'Gradually . . . he recovered a little.' He thought about going to the Circus Maximus after all, and then suddenly showed Hall the drafts for new cantos – 'essentially the lines collected in 1968 as *Drafts and Fragments* . . . [though] he worked on them again [a little] in 1960, from March through June . . . There was also a sheet of paper that I remember whenever I think about form in the Cantos: it was a list of quotes and lines from earlier Cantos; it was headed "Things to be Stuck in".'

Hall read the drafts and made enthusiastic comments – 'the best Cantos since the *Pisan*'. He was genuinely 'moved by the poetry of old age, by the acknowledgement of error or failure'. He also felt that they really were 'paradisal, elevated . . . [with] something that persists and survives individual wreckage':

> La Tour, San Carlo gone,
>   and Dieudonné, Voisin . . .

That war is the destruction of restaurants . . .
Bunting and Upward neglected,
          all the resisters blacked out,
From time's wreckage shored,
                    these fragments shored against ruin.

Yet to walk with Mozart, Aggasiz and Linnaeus
          'neath overhanging air under sun-beat
Here take thy mind's space
And to this garden, Marcella, ever seeking by petal, by leaf-vein
                    out of dark, and toward half-light . . .
H.D. once said 'serenitas'
                    (Atthis, etc.)
          at Dieudonné's
                    in pre-history.

This is not vanity, to have had good guys in the family

          Sea, blue under cliffs, or
William murmuring: 'Sligo in heaven' when the mist came
          to Tigullio. And that the truth is in kindness.
The scientists are in terror
          and the European mind stops
Wyndham Lewis chose blindness
          rather than have his mind stop . . .
When one's friends hate each other
          how can there be peace in the world?
Their asperities diverted me in my green time.
A blown husk that is finished
          but the light sings eternal
a pale flare over marshes
          where the salt hay whispers to tide's change
Time, space,
          neither life nor death is the answer.
And of man seeking good,
          doing evil.
In meiner Heimat   ['in my homeland']
          where the dead walked
                    and the living were made of cardboard.

    a nice quiet paradise
          over the shambles . . .
i.e. it coheres all right
                    even if my notes do not cohere.

Many errors,
          a little rightness . . .
But to affirm the gold thread in the pattern . . .
Charity I have had sometimes,
          I cannot make it flow thru.

M'amour, m'amour
          what do I love and
                    where are you?
That I lost my center
          fighting the world.
The dreams clash
          and are shattered –
and that I tried to make a paradiso
                              terrestre.

To be men not destroyers.

I have tried to write Paradise
Do not move
          Let the wind speak
                    that is paradise.

Let the Gods forgive what I
          have made
Let those I love try to forgive
          what I have made.

    Ezra listened to Hall's praise of these fragments, at first excitedly, but
'after a few moments he tired again . . . Horribly his body sagged . . . "The
question is . . . whether to live or die." . . . After a long time he said,
"There – can be such – communication – in silence." . . . Then . . . "well,
maybe nothing – is being communicated – to you," and the fatigue passed
again, and he put on his hat and scarf, "Let's be going," he said.'

3

C'est Autre Chose

They tried to drive to the Circus Maximus but arrived at the Baths of Caracalla instead. Hall took Ezra to lunch with an American friend, where he contributed nothing to the conversation except 'a mysterious line' now and then, or an occasional anecdotal set-piece about Wyndham Lewis, Joyce, or Yeats. That night he dined with the Halls again at Crispi's, and was comparatively steady, with no major ups or downs. He considered once again the possibility of going back to live in America. 'He could not drive a car; was it impossible, as certain Europeans insisted, to live in America without a car? . . . Then in the same tone . . . "How do you feel the influence of the American Communist Party in your daily life?" For a second,' writes Hall, 'I thought he was joking . . . But he was wholly serious.'

On the way home he pointed out 'a huge stone building, and said, "There's the scene of the crime." "Where you made the broadcasts?" He nodded. "Where I handed in the texts." '

They arrived at Dadone's and said an affectionate goodbye. 'The elevator arrived, and Pound – his hat cocked defiantly, his scarf astride his shoulder, his stick poked ahead of him – marched into it . . . and I never saw him again.'

*

Desmond O'Grady, a poet with whom Ezra had corresponded in St Elizabeths and who had met him since his return to Italy, was astonished one morning in Rome when 'there was a great hammering on the door of my family flat in Piazza Mattei in the centre of the Jewish ghetto. I opened it. There was Pound. Alone. "My God, Ezra! What are you doing here?' . . . It seemed he had "run away from home". He immediately moved in.' He stayed with O'Grady for several days, taking over his flat and his life. He said he had decided to make his home in Rome, and they visited various small apartments which could be rented. O'Grady particularly liked one on the via Merulana, but it was on a top floor and Ezra would not take it. 'I might jump off.'

Around mid-May 1960, he left Rome and joined Dorothy in Rapallo; but the summer season had started, and Dorothy complained that the town 'has sorely changed – very tourist-y'. Daniel Cory gathered from Ezra that all attempts to settle down were proving failures. Marcella's enforced departure still upset him: 'A source of stimulation had been taken from him, and after all those years of incarceration it was not encouraging to realize that the future promised little but a succession of grey hours. Ezra made an effort to be cheery which I found quite touching . . . It was obvious that some profound emotional ebb-tide was leaving him stranded and incapable of any sustained concentration. The old trooper had lost all his bravado.'

He told Cory that he might give Brunnenburg 'another chance', and during the summer he and Dorothy went there. Cory himself was now living in a flat in the castle with his wife, and writes that 'we all hoped . . . he would settle down and find some compensation in the clean cool air . . . But he was inconsolable.' Noel Stock was there too, says Cory, 'doing a pretty thorough job' of sorting and filing the manuscripts and books, but Ezra became 'highly agitated over the precise whereabouts of each and every item'. He told Stock one day that his life was 'full of missed opportunities'. And on another occasion, to Cory: 'So much I ought to have read sixty years ago.'

He began to refuse food, and to remain motionless (as Donald Hall had seen him) for hours at a time. Stock noticed that, up to now always a firm and upright figure, he was apparently folding up, becoming bent and shrunken. Eventually it was agreed that he should go into hospital, and a bed was found for him at Martinsbrunn, a private clinic on the outskirts of Merano. Omar, writing to Overholser, described this as 'apparently an unsatisfactory arrangement for all concerned, but no other suitable alternative seems ready to hand'. He came out of the clinic during the autumn and went back to the castle. There were more self-reproaches, more regrets. He now felt that Confucianism was an inadequate creed, telling Stock that it could scarcely provide 'a "Refuge for Sinners" to whom one may appeal'. Stock noticed that he was reading *Four Quartets*, which was surprising, since he had earlier seemed to dislike them. 'He was anxious to assure me, though,' says Stock, 'that he had simply been criticizing *other* aspects of TSE's work.' He added that Eliot 'had already been through his "Purgatory"'.

'Sometimes,' writes Cory, 'he would emerge for a short spell from the seclusion of his study and become more convivial. There was nearby a small reservoir swollen by subterranean streams where we went for a quick plunge on hot days, or after a long hike. On several occasions Ezra amazed us by scrambling down the hillside and leaping at once into the icy water. He would thrash about and spout like a whale before joining the company on the grassy slopes. Only too soon, however, he would return to the castle and for the rest of the day recline on his couch.'

Brief entries in Noel Stock's notebook hint at other crises during this period:

> Attempted burning of Brunnenburg – papers.
>
> Attempted burning of clinic.
>
> Mary and Boris away during 'hunger strike' . . . DP to Cory: 'Dr says he's raving mad'. Patrizia ran screaming down to Gaudier flat where he told them to make Pat. and Walter leave castle, etc. First time he swayed back and forth looking me in eye as 'enemy'. 'Stock and Cory are going to murder me.' Taken away to Martinsbrunn . . .

Suicidal ideas were frequent. He had always mocked the notion in the past. 'When have I ever suggested suicide?' he asked MacLeish in 1956. 'I have always thought the suicide shd/ bump off at least one swine before taking off for parts unknown.' The same notion appears in Canto 93: 'The suicide is not serious from conviction / One should first bump off some nuisance.' But by the time he wrote that, he knew, and added in this canto, 'From sheer physical depression, c'est autre chose.'

Daniel Cory left for England. 'The day before . . . I went to his study again to say goodbye. He stood by the window for a few minutes without speaking, and then coming towards me he said quietly: "I'm sorry I couldn't be brighter this summer." He seemed so shattered in spirit that I felt like crying. "I wish I could do something for you," I mumbled. "What is really the matter with you, Ezra?" He put his arm around my shoulder. "God only knows," he answered in a low, broken voice.'

Leonard Doob, a professor from Yale (who later edited Ezra's wartime broadcasts for publication) was staying in Merano over the winter of 1960 to 1961: his wife Eveline recorded their meetings with Ezra. On 2 February 1961 they endured 'a sad hard 3 hours of more than his usual silences . . . Sometimes he's seemed to enjoy the conversation, contributed a few sentences, much to the point, now and then. No question that he follows our talk and is fully capable of being coherent. But we've seen a steady decline . . . He's terribly thin . . . Today . . . he kept blinking and blinking at every question . . . every effort to bring him into the conversation . . .

it's deep, *deepening* depression. He keeps putting his hands over each other, stares down at them, or suddenly, with rather shocking abruptness, turns around in his chair and stares in my eyes . . . When D.P. thought it was time to leave (it *was*, after 3 hours, actually) she thanked us and said, "Shan't we go now, Ezra?" He stared straight ahead as if she weren't there. So after it was clear that he was not going to get up, she said, "Well, I'll just go ahead to the bus and save seats for you." . . . So Boris asked me, after Mrs P. had gone, if I'd mind walking to the bus with them, which I did, and E.P. came along, with no more trouble, walking between B. and me . . . He finally got on, Boris following, and when I waved as the bus started off, he waved along with the other two, a faint smile, I think, in his eyes.'

On another day, Mrs Doob went up to the castle. She had written Ezra a letter about her excitement in reading his work, and Mary said she thought it had pleased him. 'So . . . when he and M. and I sat down the only thing to talk about was what I was still reading of his . . . Of course E.P. said nothing, but . . . I was feeling inspired. "I think it's time now that we call a halt to your beautiful performance," he said, abruptly.

'It stopped me all right. I fell silent and so did Mary and I felt something like fear at the thought of opening my mouth, fear that he might suddenly explode if I said another word. He did explode once – he was trying to say something to me, and it was as if he couldn't get the words together in his mind. And he grabbed hold of the table where we were standing, gripped it hard and began to shake it. M. and Mrs P. were near and we all stood there, unable to do anything to calm him, and he finally quit.

'But this time, M. and I got up – she was going to find me a paperback of Pound's *Noh* plays I'd asked for earlier. E.P. got up too and followed us through the small room that leads into the study. It took Mary a while to find the book but when she did she handed it to me and Pound snatched it from my hand. "This is the final outrage!" he said, holding it close to his side like an angry child. But M. took it from him. "Here," she said, handing it to me, "it's no outrage at all. It's very beautiful. Besides, it's my book and I have the right to give it to her if I want to."

'Just before I left . . . E.P. said that it was nice of me to say all the things I'd said, even if it *was* "all bunk", and then he grabbed hold of my shoulders, stared straight in my eyes and said: "But don't you see? There was something *rotten* behind it all." There were tears in his eyes and he looked utterly tortured . . . "Do what you can to save innocence! . . . Stop this Pound influence from spreading to the young!" '

*

In the early spring of 1961 he went back to Rome, staying once more with Ugo Dadone. Suddenly he was absurdly 'up'. Dadone was involved with the neo-Fascist Movimento Sociale Italiano and regularly wrote articles about them in right-wing journals. They held a May Day parade, wearing jack-boots and black armbands, displaying the swastika, shouting anti-Semitic slogans, and goose-stepping. Among those photographed at the head of the parade was Ezra.

Then a week later he was badly 'down' again. 'There was a very considerable illness in Rome,' Laughlin wrote to Overholser, 'although I was never able to determine exactly what the diagnosis was. I must say those Italian doctors sound terribly sketchy to me. They had the poor man almost dying, but couldn't seem to come up with a name for it. In any case, there was a great loss of weight and vitality.' On 7 June, Dorothy wrote to Patricia Hutchins from Brunnenburg: 'My husband is in Rome: he is having a sort of rest-cure (we had such a bad winter – cold, snow, ice –) and is not receiving letters, or visitors at present. I cannot tell how long this may last – or when he will be back here.' But one visitor was let in.

All this time Olga had waited. Now she discovered Ezra in a Rome clinic, 'a nursing home for nervous diseases, and as near the atmosphere of St Elizabeths as could have been found. Beautiful place and beautiful villa – but to get out! The gate wasn't unlocked. And when I went to see him, he was in bed and wouldn't eat. Ezra was very silent. He didn't want to drink water, which for a man who was used to drinking litres of water a day –! I thought it was physical, until he said to me: "There's an eye watching me."' But then she found there really was an eye: a nurse keeping guard through the shutters.

Olga talked to the doctors, who 'rather implied that I should mind my own business and who was I? I was just a visitor. I telephoned to Mary, and she telephoned to Dorothy, and Dorothy said to Mary, "I knew he had to be gotten out." They had him transferred to Martinsbrunn.'

He was brought up to the Merano clinic in June by Mary. Mrs Doob recorded: 'He's not taking any fluids, or so little that the skin is peeling off his hands. Of course this has been going on for a long time . . . It's been torture to watch him take a spoonful of something as far as his mouth and then put it down. Or lift a cup of tea – while we all watch hopefully – halfway up, then set it back on the saucer.'

Martinsbrunn, wrote Mrs Doob, was 'informal, and rather homey . . . but he's in terrible shape. He was just lying there, eyes closed, when M. and I went to see him . . . When they'd brought him there in the car, he'd thought he was going back to the castle (they didn't dare tell him otherwise) and a few times on the way up he'd said he was looking forward to making himself some toast . . . Then when they reached the hospital and told him he had to go there for a while and get his strength back, he evidently had a terrible tantrum and they had to have help to get him inside.'

For the first time, a physical abnormality was diagnosed: he was found to be suffering from urinary retention due to an enlarged prostate. It was hoped that this might clear up without surgery, and a catheter was inserted. He remained in bed in the clinic in this condition for several months.

Mrs Doob wrote that the news had come that Hemingway had committed suicide. 'Talked to M. about it and asked if her father knew. "Yes, but it doesn't seem to sink in . . . Maybe," says Mary, "father envies him." . . . Later: Mrs P. had carefully not mentioned that Hemingway had committed suicide. But today one of the nuns (a nurse), thinking he knew, said something to E.P. about it, and he went into a terrible tantrum, said American writers are all doomed and the USA destroys them all, especially the best of them.'

In August, Mary decided that he was dying, and summoned Olga from Sant'Ambrogio, cancelling a farewell party for the Doobs. ' "He's just *dying*," she said . . . "I can't understand how it could be so fast." ' But the next day, 12 August, she reported to Mrs Doob that he was ' "drinking and drinking and drinking" – that is, finally taking fluids. She said he was "cursing", which she believes may be "a sign of health".'

'He began to get quite a bit better,' reported Laughlin to Overholser, 'though there was some sort of little infection in the bladder connected with the prostate, I think. Ezra was running a small daily fever from this.' He continued to improve during September; Dorothy wrote to Overholser on 1 October:

> The last week or 10 days he is much better – now sits up for his midday meal – & eats reasonably well. We have parked him in a clinic near here so Mary & I take it in turns to visit him each day. Being a town for cures (grapes) we have good Drs. & a famous dentist – which is a comfort in ones old age. The other comfort being that one can't live for ever!

Ronald Duncan turned up in Merano and went to see him. He thought Ezra seemed very ill, especially as he lay there in profound silence. But then 'he turned to me after half-an-hour's silence and enigmatically said, "No dogs or Japs admitted." Then he lapsed into silence again. I had no inkling what he meant. I put it down to his delirium.' It was some time later that Duncan remembered the autumn night in London in 1938, and the piece of paper pinned to the wall by the closed restaurant: 'Where it says, No dogs or Japs admitted.'

Ezra remained in Martinsbrunn for the remainder of the year, and the beginning of 1962. 'He had bed sores,' says Olga. 'He had a bar across his bed so that he could lift himself up. Dorothy went down for two hours every other day and Mary went down for two hours the next. But it wasn't what was needed.'

Perdita Schaffner, Hilda Doolittle's daughter, visited him in the clinic early in 1962 while staying with Mary. 'He was lying on the bed, clad in slacks and a tattered red shirt. He gazed back at me. He didn't smile. But there was a fond look of recognition, a lightening in his tragic expression. "Don't get up," I started to say. But it was a matter of pride. He had a sense of occasion. He was on his feet, his hands were on my shoulders. He was inspecting me from top to toe and back again, very grave and yet – no doubt about it – glad too. "Well, well . . . well, well . . ." I thanked him again for his beautiful letter . . . We sat down. Total silence. He seemed to have reached the end of his resources . . . I started babbling of the most inconsequential matters . . . He remained sunken; far, far away. But he never took his eyes off me . . . Then words seemed unnecessary, even intrusive. I held his hand and kissed his shaggy, bristly cheek . . . Back in New York, I received a letter from Mary. Her father was very much better. He had been cheered by my visit. Soon afterwards, he got up, right up, out of his room, and took his first walk in the garden.'

By early spring it was felt that he would benefit from a visit to Rapallo, where he might also find more effective treatment for the prostate and urinary trouble. Mary telephoned Olga saying that her father had 'perked up' and 'wanted to get back to Rapallo'. It was decided, with Dorothy's compliance, that Olga would come and fetch him to Sant'Ambrogio, for a visit. Olga takes up the story: 'In the spring, Dorothy brought him to Rapallo, and what happened then? Oh yes, he went – he came to me, yes! He came to me!'

4

Who Is There Now To Share A Joke With?

Patience had been rewarded: Olga had her prize, and she was not going to give it up again. From now on she was incontrovertibly, ultra-competently, in charge. As Mary had said of her mother's behaviour during the 1945 crisis, 'under dramatic circumstances, she automatically turned into an irresistible force'. Ezra did not return to Brunnenburg. The 'visit' became permanent.

Dorothy told Daniel Cory that she could 'no longer cope with the situation', and to Noel Stock she said: 'Ezra needs a lot of looking after, and Olga's stronger than I am.' (Olga was nearly ten years her junior.) Mary, too, who had borne the brunt of it all, badly needed a respite.

On Ezra's arrival at Sant'Ambrogio, Olga immediately summoned their old friend Dr Bacigalupo to examine him. 'I found a person completely changed,' he writes. 'Thin, considerably aged, he lay on a bed in almost complete silence; only his blue eyes gave a sign of life, shining and taking in everything that was happening around him. His head, once red like a lion's mane, had turned white and his face was hollowed like an ikon. The head of a prophet, in which the years had left their mark, emulating the calm which follows the storm.

'I was upset by this spectacle, and talked at length with Olga about how to tackle the problem. We were undoubtedly facing a serious case of marasmus [wasting], a grave state of depression and a urological situation which was probably at the root of it, and which demanded treatment.

'Decisions were not easy to take because Pound had been "sub conditione", i.e. under the custody of his wife. She was now in Merano and it was difficult to contact her to discuss the problem. What cut short the delay was a serious haemorrhage, which made it imperative he be admitted to hospital without delay.' Olga describes how Ezra suddenly ran 'a very high temperature, and I telephoned them, and they rushed him into the nursing home, and they operated . . . which they should have done years before!'

The operation was carried out in June 1962 at the Villa Chiara private nursing home in Rapallo by a urologist from Genoa, Dr Sacco, who confirmed that there had been serious uraemic poisoning of the blood, due to the retention of urine, and arranged for detoxification to be carried out. The operation itself was not a prostatectomy, but only the insertion of a suprapubic catheter to clear uraemic poisoning, though it was thought that the entire adenoma of the prostate would have to be removed when his condition had improved. 'Ezra recovered well and put on 10 kilos [22 pounds],' writes Dr Bacigalupo. Dorothy reported the success of the operation to Patricia Hutchins, from Brunnenburg, adding: 'Of course [I] am at beck & call, should E.P. need me.'

It was a long time since Ezra had written letters, but now he started to do so again. Jane Lidderdale, a writer, was at work on a biography of Harriet Shaw Weaver, and shortly after his operation Ezra attempted to answer her request for recollections, jotting down various fragments:

> You will, I hope, pardon this scribbling on a bed-table – a sentence or 2 if you can dig one out – better than blockish silence. Wait till I get a good one – shd. be as well cut as those on plain roman incision. Will try again get something clear.

> Incidentally I have only been out of coma (48 hours only as if only part of consciousness worth having that has stood the strain but wd. be grateful if someone wd. anyone particularly ANY live shade of pink has had prevailed à yr highbrow press for 18 months in regard to the many idiocies I have printed.

Eventually he managed to get down a fragment of reminiscence of Harriet Shaw Weaver in her Hampstead garden during an Edwardian summer – a sentence or so in several different versions.

Despite his recovery, writes Dr Bacigalupo, 'he continued to speak very little and answered questions only with effort, as if he could not find the words. The few things which he did say were, however, pertinent and revealed a good memory, even if his underlying frame of mind was decidedly depressive: rejection of his past literary work, sense of guilt, fear of not having enough money to live on.' His responses to visitors' questions were invariably harsh. 'How are you, Mr Pound?' 'Senile.' Or: 'Wrong, wrong, wrong. I've always been wrong. Eighty-seven per cent wrong.'

He came out of hospital at the end of the summer of 1962; the plans for

the follow-up operation were postponed. He went back to Sant'Ambrogio
and resumed life with Olga in Casa 60 – no longer interrupted, as it had
been in the 1930s and 1940s, by the regular return to Dorothy down below
in Rapallo. Hugh Kenner, who came to see him, discovered that 'he could
walk up the *salita* from Rapallo . . . and on up to Sant'Ambrogio without
stopping for breath, visitors half his age panting'.

Noel Stock came one day, and met him and Olga half-way up the *salita*;
they had been out shopping. Stock's notebook entry continues:

> Walked 100 yds. into centre of Sant'Amb: they showed me
> church, the view, and then we sat in cafe garden – and I had
> local bianco, they had espressi. I talked to E.P. while Olga did
> shopping – E.P. and I walked back to the house.

Ezra said little, but Stock gained some response from him:

> When I sd people found W.L[ewis] difficult person – EP 'he
> was, let us say, sometimes difficult' (smiling).
>   Beecham libretto – did not know B. well. Opera never
> performed.
>   Eliot & he went 'around' Excideuil.

When they were all back at the house,

> Olga put on tape in living room . . . [Ezra] reading Cantos,
> including 'Pull down'. EP broke down – depressed – 'harm I
> have done'. I tried to reassure him. As Olga left with me EP
> called out – asking her back: 'I have done enough evil.'

Towards the end of the summer Olga took him off to Venice, where she
still had the 'hidden nest' in Calle Querini. Here again his life resumed
something of the pattern of before the war: long walks through the city,
shopping trips, and now (which had not often been affordable in the 1930s)
restaurant meals, frequently at the Cici, just around the corner from Calle
Querini.

Friends, hearing that he was better, began to look him up. Desmond
O'Grady describes how

> My first morning in Venice (I had never been there before),
> Ezra took me out for walks from the Dogana steps along the
> Zattere. He did not speak at all. As in the old days, he had
> deliberate direction. We walked. We stopped. We looked. Not
> a word spoken. Then it dawned on me that he was taking me on
> a tour of his Venice 1908 and . . . *A Lume Spento*. Later walks
> were through the Venetian Cantos. There was no need for talk
> or explanation. He had written it all down.

Hugh Kenner describes similar walks with him:

> . . . he could set out across Venice, known stone by stone, past
> the window overlooking 'the Squero where Ogni Santi / meets
> San Trovaso' where he had drunk in the Venetian beauty . . .
> past the canal where he had taken lessons from a gondolier,
> across little bridges and through little lanes to the Scuola degli
> Schiavoni, there to sit hunched, contemplating, while friends
> marvelled at the Carpaccios . . . one afternoon to the Biennale,
> where the lady at the American pavilion recognized the great
> revenant and proudly showed off pop sculpture . . . What did
> he think of it? The friend of Gaudier and Brancusi said 'I've
> seen worse' . . . another time by the Giardini Publici, where on
> a plinth adorned with pelican bas-reliefs a stone head of Richard
> Wagner confronted the lagoon: 'Ezra!' (the . . . voice of Miss
> Rudge, custodian of the oracle) 'Why is Wagner's bust here?'
> (In slow remote tones) 'He died here.' 'Ezra! What on earth do
> young pelicans tearing at the old bird's entrails have to do with
> Wagner?' (A short pause. The imperial moment:) 'Toujours les
> tripes.'

He reverted to the style of dress of his 'Ezra' period and persona, the
clothes he had worn in Edwardian London. Out went the baggy 'Grampaw' shirts and shorts, the unlaced shoes, the casual hats. Back came the
broad sombrero, the malacca cane, an elegant overcoat. He always wore a
tie now – the broad, loosely knotted tie of 1909, and the shirt with the
characteristically wide lapels.

'As far as I can learn,' Laughlin wrote to Overholser during Ezra's first
winter back in Venice,

> Ezra isn't doing any writing, or much of it, he doesn't even
> write letters, and from photographs Olga has sent me he looks
> as though he has put on a bit of weight. Although he looks very
> old and somewhat haunted, his face is extremely beautiful . . . I
> don't know whether the increasing physical feebleness has
> diminished the force of the 'upswings', but I rather think so.
> Judge he is a bit calmer, and suffering less, in that respect.

Five months after his seventy-seventh birthday, the Milan magazine
Epoca published an interview with him by Grazia Livi, who met him in the
Venice house:

> His eyes appear glazed, looking straight at faces and objects
> with an aching steadiness . . . There is not a book near him that
> testifies to his past fame: only a 1928 Paris edition of the first 16

Cantos, which he rejects with a moan, 'Oh, it is so ugly! So ugly!' There are no bundles of letters, no manuscripts, no signs of a vital connection with the world.

The interviewer said she had been afraid of coming to see him. 'Afraid? I understand. I spoil everything I touch. I have always blundered . . . All my life I believed I knew something. But then one strange day came when I realized that I knew nothing, yes, I knew nothing. And so words became void of meaning . . . I have arrived too late at ultimate uncertainty.' Miss Livi asked if this realization brought him pain. 'It is a realization I came to with pain. Yes, great pain . . . Man exists only insofar as he becomes increasingly aware of errors . . . And the most foolish are those who believe they know something . . . But lord, these are all such terrible clichés. It's such an effort for me to construct two consecutive sentences that aren't obvious! . . .

'I don't work any more. I don't do anything, I have become illiterate and unread. I simply fall into lethargy . . . and I contemplate.'

She asked if he intended to remain in Italy. 'The Italians have a bizarre vitality, a spontaneity . . . I am living here for the time being. Now they tell me about Sicily; they say I should go there. Yes, but how can you get me there? . . . I have lost the ability to reach the core of my thought with words – I would like to explain. I – I – oh, but it is all so difficult – and all so useless.'

*

Dorothy now spent most of her time in a hotel in Rapallo. Laughlin, who saw her there, realized that she was very lonely; she had no friends in the town other than the cleaning woman from the via Marsala apartment, and rarely went more than twenty paces from the hotel. She spent her days reading – including the whole of Shakespeare – and in writing (with no purpose whatever) a list of all the names of persons who appear in the Cantos. Hugh Kenner met her there and asked where Ezra was living at present. She answered that he was just up the hill with Olga. 'She imparted this information as one imparts the location of a planet.'

She scarcely ever set eyes on them, though Omar says Ezra would send a note or telegram for her birthday, and that communication was not entirely cut off. She was still 'Committee' for Ezra and retained control of his money; Noel Stock believes she was somewhat iron-handed about passing on what was needed to Ezra and Olga. She also controlled matters relating to publication. Julien Cornell, who had now written his book on Ezra's trial, had to submit it to her for approval. She asked him to make a number of changes before she would pass it, and requested that there should be 'no advertising' of it; she asked whether 'any control is possible over sale of copies to "the enemy"?'

Noel Stock is certain that she deeply resented being excluded from Ezra's life. When Stock began work on his biography of Ezra, Laughlin warned him: 'I'm not sure that Olga would mind having her picture in your biography, but I really think Dorothy would be quite upset by it, so better not.' Eliot's second wife Valerie saw Dorothy in the late 1960s, not long after visiting Ezra in Venice. Dorothy asked her: 'Do tell me what he is *thinking* about.'

Omar spent the years 1962 to 1965 in Tangier as headmaster of the American School there. Afterwards he settled with his wife and two daughters in England, and Dorothy would usually visit them at their Cambridge home in the summers. She returned to the Albergo Grande Italia in Rapallo for the winter – though the weather there was often not much better than in England. Laughlin remembers how on some days 'she just sat in her room and looked out of the window'. Occasionally she returned to Brunnenburg, where she was made welcome. She became very deaf, and suffered from cataract, but continued to read a great deal, including much French literature. Omar was certain that she would see Ezra out.

*

In the summer of 1963 Ezra went back into hospital at Rapallo for a total prostatectomy. After the operation he remarked to Laughlin: 'They've made me into a cunt.' Once again he seemed to recover his energy as soon as the surgery was complete; on 17 June he wrote to Laughlin in reply to a letter: 'Yes I think the age of gold & sentir avec ardeur are mine. I dont remember the Langland send me the lines . . . send copies of poems mentioned & I will be able to recognize. Yrs E.P.' He had no further urinary or other physical trouble, but, according to a medical report three years later, he now became 'almost completely silent'. He said, two years later: 'I did not enter into silence; silence captured me.'

Dr Bacigalupo comments of the silence:

> It was a psychological block. He simply couldn't talk. Some-
> times he would come out with the perfect phrase; and every-
> thing he said was fine in itself. And he could read aloud very
> well. In fact he was completely sensible. But when he came to
> dinner with us [in Rapallo] he would look at the maid and be
> unable to ask for what he wanted. And in company he really
> enjoyed – such as Stephen Spender and Isaiah Berlin, at dinner
> here once – he still couldn't speak at all for much of the time.
> There was nothing self-willed about it, nothing affected. It was
> a real psychological or possibly neurological block. And though
> we tried a little treatment of various kinds for it at the beginning

[anti-depressants and male hormones], it soon became apparent that medically nothing could be done.

Isaiah Berlin, spending his summers in that part of Italy, met Ezra

> twice at the Bacigalupos' table. On the first occasion, he certainly said nothing, but nodded his head in agreement or disagreement with whatever was said, and seemed to listen with extreme care . . . His friend, Miss Rudge, later reported that he thought the conversation at table, in which I took part, was remarkably interesting, but that may have been merely her desire to be nice to me, since I might have interpreted his silence as relics of anti-Semitism or whatever. He did look exceedingly tired and tense. On the second occasion, Stephen Spender was also present, and tried to draw Pound: Pound would not be drawn, but did utter some such words as 'Yes, that was H.D.' – but nothing of greater length.
>
> Towards the end of the evening, when Olga Rudge said 'I think, Ezra, we ought to be going home', he said 'We'll never get there'; and ten minutes later, when saying goodbye to his host, he said 'Why is it that one always happens to be where one does not want to be' – not very polite, but perfectly clear and audible.

Asked whether he considered the silence to be an affectation or an involuntary state, Berlin continues:

> My impression was that he was in a state of acute depression. He may have been putting it on a bit, but only a bit, nine-tenths was genuine. However, this is only an unsupported impression on my part. I ought to add that when on the first occasion he nodded or shook his head, it was always in answer to questions from Olga Rudge, who was trying, unsuccessfully, to make him talk.

Of her father's adoption of silence, Mary observes: 'It's not that he didn't say anything. He just didn't say anything trivial. A lot of people came along with silly questions. I guess about the best thing to do is to keep silent.' She calls the silence 'the most wonderful thing that happened to him. Silence is an easy etiquette.' Actually, the opposite is true: the adoption of almost total silence on a social occasion such as Berlin describes requires an iron will and a determination to ignore all etiquette. It is far easier to say something, however trivial, than to remain so aggressively mute.

Olga is not inclined to regard the silence as remarkable: 'Old people become increasingly silent.' She, however, did not as old age approached; always self-confident in conversation, she became, if anything, more loquacious, pouring out unfinished anecdotes and half-explained allusions, punctuated with a characteristic *capito!*, as if she wished single-handed to compensate for Ezra's refusal to speak. Desmond O'Grady noticed that at least on one occasion Ezra's muteness was simply a reaction to this:

> I remember, one day we were having lunch in the Piazza [in Spoleto]. It was a blazing Italian summer's day outside. There must have been thirty of us at table. Ezra sat silently at the head amongst the talking and eating. I sat between Ezra and Olga Rudge. Caresse Crosby sat facing us beside Charles Olson. And Ezra would not eat. No matter how much Olga and Caresse cajoled, Ezra would not eat. 'Tell him to eat,' Olga said to me, 'he only listens to you.' I tried: 'Come on, E.P., eat up. You're always telling me I don't eat enough. Now it's my turn. The kitchen in St Liz's bug house was never as good as this.' And so on. But no go with E.P.
>
> After everybody had finished lunch – and Ezra had not even begun – each went off to their siesta, including Olga. Ezra and I were left alone at the empty table. Immediately he put his walking stick aside and tucked into his lunch with vigour and began complaining about females pushing him around.

When he had eaten the meal,

> he suggested we go over to the Cathedral to look at the Fra Lippo work there. I agreed. So we staunchly stalked out and headed for the church. The Piazza was empty but for the two of us, Ezra upright and striding in his old manner, myself all ears to his intense talk. Suddenly the pitterpatter of feet – female by the step – coming from behind. Immediately Ezra slowed down to an old man's walk, his shoulder drooped and he stopped talking. It was Olga – who had been watching for our emergence from the Trattoria. It was I who got the scolding, and a hot one at that. What did I mean, taking Ezra out in the blazing sun? I should have more concern for his age, be more responsible. Ezra said nothing at all, but dutifully turned round, eyeing me, as if to say 'See what I mean?'

On the other hand he would mumble to O'Grady that he was a burden on Olga, calling himself 'a murderer' because he felt he was exhausting and killing her. Another acquaintance during these years, Richard Stern, observes that

Miss Rudge was clearly the sea in which he floated. She cleaned, she shopped, she stoked the old stove . . . 'I shouldn't have let Olga go,' he said to me once, when she'd left him to go on an errand, and I felt . . . the fear [in him] of even momentary abandonment by her . . . Not, I suppose, that he wasn't sometimes a bit overwhelmed by such extraordinary care. 'Eat your fish.' 'No.' 'It's not good?' 'It's not good.'

There could be unexpected and weird lapses from the silence. Alan Levy, an American journalist, tells this story:

Groping for symbolism, perhaps, when I was first writing about Pound in late 1971, I phoned a friend in Venice and asked her to check with a librarian whether the name of the Giudecca Canal was derived from the Italian word 'giudaico', which means 'Jewish'. She said she thought it was, but the librarian wasn't sure. When he couldn't find an answer readily in his books, he made one phone call and came back in two minutes with this answer: 'No, it derives from the word "giudicati", meaning "the judged" because the island of Giudecca was used as a place of banishment for the murderers of the Doge Pietro Tradonico in the ninth century – and it was used later as a place of confinement, if not a ghetto, for the Jewish, which is why many people think it means "Jewish".' My friend thanked him and asked what his source was. 'Oh,' said the librarian, 'I called the one man in Venice who has such information on the tip of his tongue: Ezra Pound.' My friend was flabbergasted: 'And he spoke to you?' The librarian replied: 'He always does. I just tell Olga Rudge what I want and Mr Pound comes right to the phone with the answer.'

But those who made conventional approaches, even old friends, were almost always disappointed. D.G. Bridson called on Ezra and Olga in Venice during 1963, having some time earlier sent Ezra a tape of his own 1962 BBC Third Programme production of Ezra's opera, *Le Testament de Villon*. 'I only succeeded in coaxing a single remark out of him in the two or three hours we were together,' writes Bridson. 'Suddenly remembering the recording . . . I asked him how he had liked my production. Giving me a steady look, his lips slowly opened at last. "That," he said with infinite candour, "was a considerable MESS."'

Bridson was baffled by this. Afterwards he gathered that Ezra disapproved of the way that Murray Schafer, the editor of the score, had rationalized some of the idiosyncratic rhythms of the music. When Gian-Carlo Menotti produced *Le Testament de Villon* two years later at

Spoleto, Ezra sang the music to him to demonstrate how it should be performed.

When he broke his silence, it was usually to utter such sour remarks as his comment to Bridson. Laughlin recalls only two occasions on which this was not the case. In his poem 'Collage for EP', Laughlin writes:

> you *did* say when I asked you about Djuna [Barnes] in Paris,
> Waal, she waren't eggzackly cuddly,
> and you asked me to tell the Possum that the headache powders
> came
> from a shop back of Chambre des députés
> which must have been circa 1923
> for the mind can bear more easily old things which happened
> before the onset of pain . . .

In letters to Laughlin, too, he occasionally displayed his old spirit. In 1964 an academic from the University of Texas wanted permission to print a variorum text of *Homage to Sextus Propertius*; Laughlin wrote to Ezra about possible financial terms, and Ezra replied:

> Dear Jas
>   Suggest higher fee ($500) more proportionate to greater notoriety of the text. There is still oil in Texas to pay for whims.

During 1962 and 1963, some of the fragments of new cantos that Donald Hall had seen in March 1960 began to appear in magazines. Richard Stern asked him if he was still writing. The answer: 'Five minutes a day.' Stern noticed that 'now and then, the old hand would dart to the table, scrabble up pencil and paper and make a note . . . Even so, he read lots – there were a few American books, new ones, on his table.' He resented people's expectations of more finished cantos. 'Some people think I'm a cocoon spinning out Cantos.'

In January 1964 Olga decided to take him to Switzerland hoping to find a treatment for the depression. They visited a number of clinics, and at one of these, in Basel, a celebrated gerontologist, Dr Walter Pöldinger, gave Olga pills which were supposed to encourage Ezra to eat. At Montreux, Dr Paul Niehans injected animal cells into his bloodstream. These had no more effect on the depression than had the earlier prescription of testosterone – though Ezra remarked to Laughlin of the hormone treatment: 'Ever afterwards, I've never had a head cold.'

While in Switzerland he was drawn by Oskar Kokoschka at his studio in Villeneuve; he sat contentedly while being sketched, though his features were now those of a man much older than his seventy-eight years. And a letter to Laughlin from Sant'Ambrogio six months later, in June 1964, was desperately self-pitying and broken:

Olga
Trying till the last minute to get me to pull my mind together
      and stand up to something.

L̶a̶c̶k̶ ̶o̶f̶
E.P. lack of precise registration of anything from
earliest state / no memory to speak of /
                              no ability to register
either the pitch of a note, or remember sequence
o̶f̶   o̶f̶ notes in a tune.
  tones

complete loss of capacity to
always too slow on uptake.

            non perception of relations
            _____

hen on chalk line.
            _____

failure to learn english, i.e. meaning of words in language, let alone
thoroughness in any foreign tongue. lack parasitic existence.

    weak bladder from the beginning.

    Have not provided Olga with decent umbrella, or warm
    clothing in winter. Or covering for summer.

    [On the back]:
                  If ever any one
                  strove to bring
                  order out of
                  debris Olga did
                  that.

Yet hereafter for some time he wrote occasional notes to Laughlin which
were short and to the point, and showed no overt signs of misery.

Hemingway had died in 1961; Cummings died in 1962, William Carlos
Williams in 1963, and Eliot in January 1965. Ezra decided that he wished to
to to Eliot's memorial service in Westminster Abbey – 'he wanted to go
himself, and not be represented by anybody,' says Olga. Arthur Moore
had intended to stand in for the Pounds at the service, and no one remotely
expected Ezra to turn up. But, says Olga, he 'took a plane and went! As a
matter of fact, he stole the show!'

He had, now and then, tried to persuade the Eliots to come and see him
in Rapallo or Venice, but, says Valerie Eliot, 'Tom wouldn't. He'd had
enough.' Just before the Abbey service, Ezra telephoned her from Rapallo

and said: 'Would you receive me if I came?' He arrived, accompanied, of course, by Olga. After the service she took him round to the Eliots' flat in Kensington, then tactfully disappeared, leaving him alone with Mrs Eliot. He sat there for several hours, went around the flat looking at photographs of Eliot, said little, but gave Mrs Eliot an impression of 'alertness and vigour'. Afterwards she wrote to Dorothy: 'I was very moved by Ezra's visit and know that it would have pleased Tom.'

Eliot's death moved Ezra to write the first piece of prose he had composed for publication since 1959; it appeared in the winter of 1966 number of the *Sewanee Review*, an Eliot memorial issue:

> His was the true Dantescan voice – not honoured enough, and deserving more than I ever gave him. I had hoped to see him in Venice this year for the Dante commemoration at the Giorgio Cini Foundation – instead: Westminster Abbey. But, later, on his own hearth, a flame tended, a presence felt.
>
> Recollections? let some thesis-writer have the satisfaction of 'discovering' whether it was 1920 or '21 that I went from Excideuil to meet a rucksacked Eliot. Days of walking – conversation? le papier Fayard was then the burning topic.* Who is there now to share a joke with?
>
> Am I to write 'about' the poet Thomas Stearns Eliot? or my friend 'the Possum'? Let him rest in peace. I can only repeat, but with the urgency of 50 years ago: READ HIM.

Olga collected him from Kensington and they took a taxi to the airport. But there, says Desmond O'Grady, 'he wouldn't move . . . Olga kept urging that they had to catch their flight. E.P. wouldn't budge. Olga asked him where he *did* want to go. After a silence, he pronounced: "Dublin." ' So they went to Dublin, 'to see Mrs Yeats. The only other literary people he wanted to see were Patrick Kavanagh and Austin Clarke, I'm told. Then he returned to Venice.'

He was in the Rapallo hospital briefly again in the spring of 1965, but there was nothing seriously wrong. From his bed, he wrote to Laughlin:

> Dear Jas
>   I hope you will find some way to print something that will remedy past errors. if you do that I will sign it 200 times.

That summer he made his first of several visits to the Spoleto Festival as the guest of its founder and organizer, the composer Gian-Carlo Menotti. He

---

*Papier Fayard et Blayn was the name of the onion-skin bandage he and Eliot put on their feet during the walking tour.

gave a public reading of poems by Robert Lowell (whose work now seemed to interest him) and Marianne Moore, but would recite none of his own, nor would he go on to the stage, but spoke from Menotti's box, with the aid of a microphone. His voice sounded weak at first, but gained some of its old assurance as he continued. Olga says that the Spoleto people 'were rather inclined to treat Ezra as if he were something very old and brittle. But he was much tougher than they were!'

There were political overtones to the occasion. Uniformed police were in the auditorium to protect him from a Communist demonstration. Outside in the Piazza he was persuaded to read from the Cantos in front of a big crowd and the television cameras. People asked for autographs. He said to Desmond O'Grady: 'It's all wrong, they don't want me here, this is your generation.' But he was back in Spoleto next summer, reading from the stage this time. O'Grady, who saw them both there again, thought that during this period 'Olga grew younger, Ezra stronger . . . every day'.

His eightieth birthday, on 30 October 1965, was marked by articles in newspapers and journals throughout Europe and America. Noel Stock edited a *festschrift* entitled *Perspectives*. A special number of William Cookson's *Agenda* included contributions by Robert Lowell and Marianne Moore, and a poem by Basil Bunting, 'On the Fly-Leaf of Pound's Cantos':

> There are the Alps. What is there to say about them?
> They don't make sense. Fatal glaciers, crags cranks climb,
> jumbled boulder and weed, pasture and boulder, scree,
> *et l'on entend*, maybe, *le refrain joyeux et leger.*
> Who knows what the ice will have scraped on the rock it is
> smoothing?
>
> There they are, you will have to go a long way round
> if you want to avoid them.
> It takes some getting used to. There are the Alps,
> fools! Sit down and wait for them to crumble!

Ezra celebrated the occasion with his first visit to Paris for many years. Natalie Barney, still holding her salons in the rue Jacob as she had for nearly sixty years, gave a party for him. He spoke little, but L'Amazone said she found him 'an eloquent listener'. It was on this occasion that he made the remark to reporters about silence capturing him. Someone decided that he should be taken to see a Samuel Beckett play, *Endgame (Fin de Partie)*. He had already seen *Happy Days* and another Beckett piece in Venice, with Olga. Now, as the play's protagonists spoke their dialogue from dustbins, he muttered to her: 'C'est moi dans la poubelle.' Olga adds: 'You can interpret that how you like.'

When they got back to their hotel, Ezra 'wrote a note to Beckett to say he'd seen the play and enjoyed it, and had heard from Kenner that he was ill, and would come round to see him – thinking that Beckett was a sick man . . . The next day there was a telephone call: "Mr Beckett wishes to speak to Mr Pound."' The two masters of silence conversed for a few moments on the instrument. Then: 'Beckett's coming round in a couple of hours.' Olga describes the meeting as 'very cordial, very nice'. She observes that Beckett 'did the right thing: *he* came to see the old master'.

Ezra had kept loosely in touch with Beckett over the years since their first rather hostile encounter in the company of Joyce in the 1920s; in 1953 Ezra told Patricia Hutchins he had 'seen Beckett once or twice' since then, and recommended him as a reliable source of information on Joyce. They met once again, in Venice around 1970. Beckett afterwards told Richard Ellmann that he had gone to the house in Calle Querini to see Ezra, and that the two of them had sat together in complete silence for a while. Then Beckett, suddenly able to bear it no longer, got to his feet, embraced Ezra, and let himself out of the house.

*

By 1965 it took Olga some time to get him up in the morning, but she kept him on the move. There are records of visits to Greece around 1965, to Zurich in 1967, where he visited Joyce's grave, an Adriatic cruise, and travels within Italy. In June 1967 he went to Paris to mark the publication of French translations of *ABC of Reading*, *How to Read*, and *The Spirit of Romance*; at a meeting with French critics he mostly maintained an 'obstinate silence', but would answer one or two questions with a faraway look. In March 1967 he wrote to Louis Dudek, replying to an invitation to come to Montreal for a World Poetry Conference: 'I am just back from Switzerland, and am due in London and Paris in April, and Spoleto in June for the festival, so why not Montreal in September? . . . Air please . . . am not a sailor.' Neither the Montreal nor the London trip took place, but there were plenty of other journeys.

He wrote to Laughlin just before his eightieth birthday: 'Am alive. Thought I was leaving archives in my will. Mary not discovered that communicating by printed page slows things up. Easier to send postcard.' This refers to prolonged negotiations over the sale of Ezra's papers and books at Brunnenburg to Yale University – a sale that apparently had Ezra's blessing, though as soon as the material had been shipped to Yale in 1966 Dorothy claimed that she, as 'Committee', had not been consulted. A considerable legal wrangle ensued, and continued for the remainder of Ezra's life.*

*See further Donald Gallup, 'The Ezra Pound Archive at Yale', *Yale University Library Gazette*, April 1986.

Attempts continued to diagnose and deal with his depression, and in the spring of 1966 he spent a month in the Clinica delle Malattie Nervose e Mentali at the University of Genoa, where he was examined at length by Professor Cornelio Fazio and his staff. Their report began by summarizing Ezra's recent medical and psychological history, observing that this had been complicated by 'the difficulty in obtaining a thorough history from the patient himself'. It traced the course of the prostate illness up to the two operations, and continued by describing Ezra's state of mind after the second:

> The patient was at this time almost completely silent, uttering only a few words when questioned, impaired physically, often refused food, considered in a delusional way his own conditions and physiologic functions . . . The hypochondriacal contents of thought and the preoccupation with infection and contamination further increased . . . Nevertheless, sometimes a sharp answer, a pertinent observation, a precise and competent recall, attested to a certain degree of concealed liveliness of thought, even though detached and inadequate to reality. Sometimes, prompted by external situations (travels, environmental modification) Mr Pound exhibited again fairly normal activity and interests . . .
>
> Mr Pound was admitted to our Clinica on March 11th, 1966, being discharged on April 16th. We could observe the following picture: a marked retardation and difficulty of movements . . . a general reduction and retardation of psychomotor activity . . . Facial expression was changing, being sometimes proper, brisk and attentive, sometimes blank and inadequate as if the patient were following an inner line of thought.
>
> When addressed he looked perplexed, answering with a marked delay. On the other hand, his answers were correct and coherent, as if the patient, during his silence, had thought over the question, or as if he had difficulty in expressing himself.
>
> The formal verbal expression was therefore reduced, delayed; and a certain degree of slurring of speech could be observed. The contents were limited to strictly necessary topics, and the patient was silent, unless stimulated; sometimes the precision and the correctness of his answers were astonishing; sometimes, they seemed on the contrary inadequate, full of a bizarre humour. The retardation of verbal expression was certainly not paralleled by an analogous slowing of thought, which however seemed to be hyperinclusive and scarcely fluent, following inner pathways without contact with the reality, the link

between thinking and verbal expressions being apparently broken. It could not be ruled out that even when the patient was silent a scarcely coherent pressure of thinking was present, overwhelming everything in an expansive disorder. This could be demonstrated by periods in which the speech became pressing and continuous, accompanied by a chaotic graphic activity, represented by several disordered letters.

Ideas of self-accusation and hypochondriacal delusions were always present . . . blocked bowels, microbic contamination, etc.

These ideas and the general inhibition could probably account for the refusal of food: however, when the food was put near the mouth of the patient, he took it almost automatically with a catatonic-like passivity.

The ideas of self-accusation were the only feature to be ascribed to a melancholic mood, because a full-blown depressive picture was never apparent clinically, being probably overwhelmed by the other symptoms.

A general mental deterioration did exist . . . [but] memory was lively, regarding both retention and recalling. Nor could there be observed troubles in space and time orientation, or specific intellectual defects . . . This deterioration was rather expressed . . . by emotional rigidity, stereotyped attitude, and diminution of emotional availability; in other words by the narrowing and impairment of the emotional attitudes, and by a strong reduction of interests, which were almost exclusively focused on topics regarding his own body.

Then came the most revealing passage of the report:

It seemed as if the personality of the patient had always been on the autistic side, with prevailing phantastic attitudes and insufficient contact with reality, inadequacy of associative structures of thinking . . . so that a psychotic-like situation came out ('borderline patient'), permitting, however, and perhaps encouraging, poetic activity.

The report states that the clinic administered an antidepressant (amitryptiline), but this produced no result, and Ezra's condition when he was discharged remained the same.

5

Prospero

One afternoon in early October 1966, just before Ezra's eighty-first birthday, Daniel Cory, visiting Venice, decided to tackle the old unsolved question of the structure of the Cantos. Finding Ezra apparently 'in the right frame of mind' to talk about it, Cory gave him a number of suggestions as to the possible architecture or purpose: 'Perhaps we might say that the Cantos reflected faithfully the incoherence or fragmentary insights of the contemporary writer in a cosmopolitan milieu?' No answer. Or was it possibly, as Ezra had said to Yeats so long ago, 'the structure of a fugue?' No answer.

And then, 'Ezra scotched all these fashionable hypotheses with one short devastating sentence.

' "It's a botch," he said firmly.

' "Do you mean it didn't come off?" I asked artlessly.

' "Of course it didn't," Ezra mumbled. "That's what I mean when I say I botched it." I was flabbergasted and could find nothing to say. Then he carried on, with many pauses: "I knew too little about so many things. I've read too little and I read very slowly."

' "But you can't know everything," I protested. "It's impossible for a human mind – especially nowadays."

'He was not satisfied. "Ain't it better to know something about a few things if you're trying to do a work like the Cantos? – I picked out this and that thing that interested me, and then jumbled them into a bag. But that's not the way to make" – and he paused for a moment – "a *work of art*." '

Cory revisited him a few days later and asked if he still felt the same. Ezra 'picked his nails for a moment and then answered: "Yop, I botched it." ' Cory reminded him that people's judgement of their own work does not necessarily prove correct: for example, Keats's epitaph for himself,

'Here lies one whose name was writ in water.' In response, 'Ezra looked up and gave a sort of half-chuckle.'

In 'Collage for EP', Laughlin recalls the occasion 'when you asked me to abolish the Cantos because they would not cohere'. He explains: 'Ezra used to get peeved when I asked him about spelling corrections and say "Why don't you *abolish* the Cantos?" He said the same to Peter du Sautoy [of Faber and Faber] at Eliot's funeral and to many scholars who came to Venice to quiz him.'

Yet he surprised Faber and Faber in 1965, some time after Eliot's Westminster Abbey service, by sending them a copy of the Cantos (the 1964 collected edition) with excerpts marked up in his own hand, so that a *Selected Cantos* could be published – which it was in 1967.* He wrote to Laughlin on 1 October 1965:

> Glad you like the selection. I would never have got round to making them. had not Olga kept me at it. Please see that the title page carries the inscription
> To Olga Rudge
> 'Tempus loquendi'†

A year later, he sent New Directions this fragment:

> That her acts
> Olga's acts
> of beauty
> be remembered.

*The selection was intended, he said, 'to provide the best introduction to the whole work for those coming to it for the first time' (this was at least how Faber and Faber worded it). Three notable omissions were Cantos 36 (Donna mi prega), 39 (Circe's bower), and 74 (the first Pisan canto); otherwise it was a fairly representative choice such as a dispassionate editor might have made. The New Directions edition contains a few extra selections.

†Roy Fuller, giving his inaugural lecture as Professor of Poetry at Oxford early in 1969, said: 'The *Cantos* of Ezra Pound are finally, as their author himself has admitted, a failure.' Fuller afterwards explained that Cory's *Encounter* article, which quoted Ezra calling them 'a botch', was his source. G. Singh wrote to Ezra to ask if he really believed the work to be a failure, and received a telegram in reply: 'QUESTION PROF FULLERS SOURCE STATEMENT RE CANTOS NOT MINE SALUTI POUND.' Singh published the telegram in a letter to *The Times Literary Supplement (TLS)* (6 March 1969), and in a later issue (13 March 1969) reported that he had received a letter from Olga which said: 'If he thought they were "a failure" it is hardly likely he would have published a book of *Selections* from them . . . Mr Cory is *not* an intimate friend of Pound. In the past few years he has seen Pound only about three or four times, and never except in the company of Mrs Cory and myself and the conversation was *not* literary.' Cory replied (*TLS*, 10 April 1969) that he had never claimed to be an 'intimate friend', and Olga was wrong: 'I have talked with him [alone] *at Miss Rudge's request*.' Michael Reck (*TLS*, 3 April 1969), wrote to say that 'of course' Pound had made such remarks about the *Cantos*, and 'of course his comment is quite irrelevant . . . Since when does it matter how high or low a poet rates his own work?'

> Her name was Courage
>   ,& is written Olga

These lines are for the
  ultimate CANTO

whatever I may write
  in the interim.

24 August 1966

But when the final volume, *Drafts & Fragments of Cantos CX–CXVII*, was issued by New Directions in 1969 and Faber and Faber in 1970, it concluded with the closing words of 'Notes for CXVII et seq.', which are

> To be men not destroyers.

This is the ending found in the 1975 Faber and Faber *Cantos of Ezra Pound*, but the edition published by New Directions in 1972 adds 'CXX', the eight-line fragment (see page 871) beginning 'I have tried to write Paradise' and ending 'Let those I love try to forgive / what I have made'.*

Olga has claimed that the first of these two endings is the correct one, and has also alleged that the entire work was meant to be dedicated to her. But 'I'm not going to fight with anybody about them!' The disarray of the poem's conclusion, the uncertainty about how Ezra meant it to finish, seems in itself a proper ending.

            *

'Botch' or not, he would sometimes read cantos into Olga's Grundig tape recorder. One morning he got up at five o'clock and announced that he wished to do so. As he spoke into the microphone, his voice sounded ten years younger. That night Olga played the tape back at a dinner party. All were moved, except Ezra, who sat by the machine without a flicker of interest.

Olga told Hugh Kenner that Ezra had marked the quincentenary of Shakespeare's birth, in March 1964, by recording Sonnet 94 – 'They that have power to hurt and will do none.' He also taped Christopher Smart's 'I will consider my Cat Jeoffry'. And the 5 a.m. session had begun with a loud rendering of his own

> Winter is icummen in,
> Lhude sing GODDAMM!!!

- this 'with ferocious emphasis'.

*There are now (1988) three editions available, each with a different ending.

On 2 March 1967 he wrote from Sant'Ambrogio to Archibald MacLeish, apologizing for a rude remark he was supposed to have made, which had been published.

> Dear MacLeish
>   This was published without my knowledge and would never have had my consent. I cant remember what it was all about and no longer feel that kind of thing of importance. What is of importance is an old and tried friendship. I should be sorry to have this brought to your attention by anybody else. I think you know my epistolary habits too well to take it seriously.
>
>   Yours as ever
>   Ezra Pound

Such few letters as he now wrote were succinct, courteous, and neat, in fountain pen or ballpoint. On 10 April 1967 he sent this note to Laughlin about the publication of a limited edition of one of his early poems ('Redondillas', cut from *Canzoni* before publication in 1911):

> Dear Jas.
>   All right, go ahead. It reeks with conceit. It needs punctuation. I want to correct the proofs.
>   I can still sign my own name.
>   yours E.P.
>   Ezra Pound
>   Ezra Pound
>   Ezra Pound
>   Ezra Pound
>   Ezra Pound
>   Ezra Pound
>   Ezra Pound
>   Ezra Pound
>   Ezra Pound
>   Conceit remains.

*

The 'hidden nest' in Venice was nothing like as hidden as it had been in the 1930s. Academics, journalists, and enthusiasts passed the address to each other, and Olga's number was in the telephone book. She and Ezra suffered an increasing number of intrusions. 'We get hippies,' she said, 'coming here and when we're in Rapallo. They have embraced the wisdom of Ezra Pound, but they haven't read him. One of them pitched a tent outside . . . Another was so persistent in his devotion that I told him, "I'll let you in if you can quote one line of Ezra Pound – any line of the thousands he's written" He couldn't . . . Then there are the journalists . . . When I woke up early one morning at our place in Sant'Ambrogio and found one of them had been sleeping all night in a deck chair on our terrace – and was still there! – I flushed him out with a garden hose.'

The worst tormentors, she added, were 'the so-called "biographers". Some of them actually publish "biographies" and one of them, who spent a total of fifteen minutes in our presence before I got rid of him, had the audacity to "acknowledge" my patience and persistent help over a period of years. They ring my bell and announce they are writing books that will "tell both sides". *Both* sides? Both sides! What do they think we are? Ezra Pound is no pancake!'

Among the unexpected callers was Allen Ginsberg. He and an entourage turned up at Sant'Ambrogio in the summer of 1967, and, said Olga, 'made their presence known by performing Hare Krishna' outside Casa 60. Ezra had heard of Ginsberg and was amused by him. Olga's first question to the followers, 'Would you like to wash your hands?', caused looks of horror, but Ginsberg's opening remark to his hosts aroused equal astonishment: 'Do you people need any money?'

Ezra liked Ginsberg enough to tolerate him when he turned up again, in Venice, though Olga now thought him 'like a big lovable dog who gives you a great slovenly kiss and gets lots of hair all over you'. He played Beatles and Bob Dylan records to Ezra and chanted mantras for him, accompanying himself on a portable harmonium. Ezra listened without comment. Then, on the afternoon of 28 October 1967, at the Cici restaurant in Venice, Ginsberg persuaded Ezra to say 'more than a few words' to him. Also present were Michael Reck and his son, and Peter Russell. Reck afterwards wrote up the occasion as 'A Conversation Between Ezra Pound and Allen Ginsberg' and published it in an American journal the next year:

> One fine October day in Venice recently, I saw an apparition that was real: a round face like an apprentice Santa Claus framed by an immense mane of flowing pitch-black hair and beard, its pink nose surmounted by equally black spectacles. From its neck dangled a great silver Buddhist medal. This apparition confronted another real one: a very thin aged face with a minimum of silky fine wispy white hair and beard. Fixed staring eyes of deep aquamarine, now losing their power, seemed to mirror a dreadful sadness. Two long thin hands, the skin of the knuckles raw, rested on the table before him; from time to time he rubbed one against the other. The old man wore a handsome blue wool suit, a tan V-necked sweater, and a bright solid-yellow tie . . .

Russell said,'I have a birthday present for you, E.P. Would you like it?' And he handed him a copy of *It Was the Nightingale*, a long out-of-print autobiography by Pound's dear friend Ford Madox Ford, long since dead. 'Yes, yes,' said Pound. His eyes lit up, and he riffled through the pages with a pleased, almost excited smile. Then he put the book down and was again silent . . .

Ginsberg mentioned to Pound that he had been looking up Venetian places mentioned in the Master's *Pisan Cantos* but had been unable to locate some things . . . In a slow, even voice, looking at his hands, Pound gave precise information . . . Ginsberg asked a number of similar questions, and Pound answered one after the other very painstakingly.

Then Ginsberg leaned over to Pound and said. 'Your thoughts about specific perception and [William Carlos] Williams's 'no ideas but in things' have been a great help to me and to many young poets. And the phrasing of your poems has had a very concrete value for me as reference points for my own perception. Am I making sense?'

'Yes,' said Pound, and after a moment mumbled, 'but my poems don't make sense.'

Ginsberg and I assured him that they made sense to us.

'A lot of double talk,' said Pound. And pursing his lips for a moment as if searching for words, then finding them, the Master said, 'Basil Bunting told me that the Cantos refer, but do not present.'

Ginsberg assured Pound that Bunting had only recently pointed out the Cantos to him as a prime example of economy of language. And I said, 'Presenting means that when someone reads your poetry he is struck with how real the description is, even if he hasn't experienced the thing himself. He says, That's it, that's just how it is. Reading your poetry, I often feel this myself. Your poetry is often shockingly direct.'

Pound was silent, and rubbed the back of one hand with the other. Then a moment later: 'At seventy I realized that instead of being a lunatic, I was a moron.'

Ginsberg said, 'In your work, the sequence of verbal images, phrases like "tin flash in the sun dazzle" and "soap-smooth stone posts" – these have given me, in praxis of perception, ground to walk on.'

'A mess.'

'You or the Cantos or me?'

'My writing. Stupid and ignorant all the way through. Stupid and ignorant.'

And I said, 'In your poetry you have an *ear*. That's the most important thing for writing poetry. So it's hard for you to write a bad line.'

'It's hard for me to write at *all*,' he answered with a dim smile . . .

'You have shown us the way,' Ginsberg said. 'The more I read your poetry, the more I am convinced it is the best of its time. And your economics are *right*. We see it more and more in Vietnam. You showed us who's making a profit out of war . . . '

'Any good I've done has been spoiled by bad intentions – the preoccupation with irrelevant and stupid things,' Pound replied. And then very slowly, with emphasis, surely conscious of Ginsberg's being Jewish: 'But the worst mistake I made was that stupid, suburban prejudice of anti-Semitism.'

'It's lovely to hear you say that,' said Ginsberg. Whereupon he added: 'Well, no, because anyone with any sense can see it as a humour, in that sense part of the drama, a model of your consciousness. Anti-Semitism is your fuck-up . . . but it's part of the model . . . it's a mind like everybody's mind.'

Ginsberg went on to tell Pound, 'Prospero threw away *his* magic staff at the end of the play . . . *Now my charms are all o'er-thrown, / And what strength I have's mine own, – / Which is most faint . . . '*

The Master . . . stared straight ahead.

'But you must go on working,' continued Ginsberg, 'to record the last scenes of the drama. You still have a great deal to say. After all now you have nothing to lose. You *are* working, aren't you?'

Pound was silent, and Ginsberg continued 'Ah well, Prospero, what I came here for was to give you my blessing . . . I'm a Buddhist Jew whose perceptions have been strengthened by the series of practical exact language models scattered through the Cantos like stepping stones, because, whatever your intentions, their practical effect has been to clarify my perceptions. Do you accept my blessing?'

The Master hesitated, opened his mouth a moment, and then the words appeared, 'I do.'

. . . He rose slowly, took his coat, his felt hat, his cane. We all accompanied him and Olga Rudge to their home, along a lapping canal bordered by an iron rail.

*

During September 1968 it was announced in the *Chicago Daily News* that

> Ezra Pound, the 83-year-old American poet, is mustering his strength in a Paris hideout for a long planned trip to his beloved birthplace in Hailey, Idaho, as a film actor. He will be portraying his own life. In an attempt to keep pressure off the enfeebled but still clear-minded poet, neither the film company nor Pound are releasing their plans for the trip. The adventure is prompted by the surprising return of eloquence and agility that Pound demonstrated – after years of taciturnity – before German and Italian television cameras.*
>
> Ever restless, Pound hopes to live up to the epitaph an admirer wrote about him: 'Here he lies, the Idaho Kid, the only time he ever did.'
>
> The poet, accompanied by his second wife [*sic*], Olga, plans to visit his two alma maters, Hamilton College . . . and the University of Pennsylvania. It is not certain whether the film biography will include his postwar period of confinement in St Elizabeth's Hospital . . . Later episodes will be filmed against the background of his wanderings in Spain and Provence, and his sojourns in England . . . Pound . . . is highly photogenic.

A representative of the film company – which was backed by the Ford Foundation and intended to make the programme for educational television – did his best to pin down Ezra and Olga, 'tailing' them between Venice and Rapallo during September. They were supposed to fly to the States on 6 October, and had been invited to Yale for a celebration of Ezra's eighty-third birthday, but a month later they were still in Sant' Ambrogio, and the film company's representative had departed in despair. They moved as they wished, obeying their own inclinations rather than making plans, let alone following the instructions of television companies or of anyone else. They were impervious to 'arrangements', to telephone calls, to business letters.

On 4 June 1969, Valerie Eliot was working in the Berg Collection of the New York Public Library, copying drafts of her husband's most celebrated poem and Ezra's annotations of it for her forthcoming edition of *The Waste Land: a facsimile and transcript*. Distantly, a telephone rang in the inner office, and after a moment the curator, Dr Lola Szladits, hurried out to Mrs Eliot, looking thoroughly nonplussed. 'Ezra Pound has just arrived in New York.' He and Olga were at John F. Kennedy airport, having just

---

*This probably refers to the 1968 television interview with him conducted by the film director Pier Paolo Pasolini, during which Ezra read out prepared answers that Olga had copied for him on to 'idiot boards'. Nothing remarkable was said by either Pasolini or Ezra.

flown in from Italy; Ezra had telephoned the Public Library because either his passport or visa was out of date, and he was having difficulties with officials. He had been invited to New York to attend the opening of an exhibition of the manuscript of *The Waste Land* in the Library (to which it had been sold ten years earlier). He had not replied to the invitation.

Laughlin received an equally sudden announcement that Ezra and Olga had arrived: Olga telephoned him from a hotel on 45th Street which she said she had always used – 'a lovely place'. Laughlin went to collect her and Ezra, and discovered that the hotel was now a brothel from which two policemen were removing one of the occupants. Ezra and Olga were unaware of the change in the nature of the establishment. Laughlin rescued them and took them to his country home in Norfolk, Connecticut, with Walter de Rachewiltz, Ezra's grandson, as driver (Walter was studying at Rutgers University). Laughlin's wife Ann was very impressed by Olga's tireless attention to Ezra, who 'emerged from our guest-room spotless in his white linen suit'.

By chance, Laughlin was to receive an honorary degree from Ezra's old college, Hamilton, two days later, so Ezra and Olga came too. The occasion was an outstanding public success, a marked contrast to Ezra's last appearance there in 1939. The London *Times* reported 'a standing ovation' for him. He sat on stage in cap and gown but did not speak. The head of the English department, Professor Austin Briggs, sat with him at lunch; Mrs Briggs reported that he had 'almost nothing' to say, though he remarked that he hoped to get to his birthplace in Hailey, Idaho.

On the long drive back from Hamilton to the Laughlin home, the party stopped for a late-night hamburger at a roadside fast-food establishment. Laughlin afterwards described it as 'the saddest night . . . I can ever remember'. Ann Laughlin persuaded Ezra to eat some apple pie, but while her husband was paying the bill Ezra disappeared. The Laughlins and Olga hurried out to the car park to look for him, but there was no sign. Laughlin eventually found him 'heading for the woods'. Catching up with him, he heard Ezra say: 'Why don't you discard me here, so that I won't be any more trouble to anyone?'

He and Olga were driven back to New York, and Laughlin settled them into his own apartment on Bank Street in Greenwich Village. They paid a visit to the Public Library, where Valerie Eliot showed Ezra the manuscript with his numerous corrections and suggestions for changes in Eliot's poem. He said he remembered nothing at all about writing them, but 'wept' as he looked at the manuscript.

One night, the critic Forrest Read, who had edited Ezra's correspondence with Joyce, came to dinner at Bank Street and expounded at enormous length his own theory about how the Cantos cohered. (Read later published this theory in his book '76 – *One World*.) After he had gone, Ezra made his only remark of the evening: 'Another one of Forrie's little jokes.'

On the day that Olga went to visit her birthplace of Youngstown, Ohio, Ezra stayed behind in New York. Walter told Noel Stock that Ezra was 'terrified' that Olga would not come back. He refused to eat or get out of bed. The Norwegian maid described him as 'very sick'.

He and Olga saw Marianne Moore; they also made a trip to Philadelphia, visiting the Misses Esther and Priscilla Heacock, now in a Quaker nursing home. The two spinsters later told Carl Gatter that they were 'upset' that Ezra and Olga were 'not married, yet travelling together'. They kept repeating to Gatter: 'They're not married.' But they thought Olga was 'just darling'.

*

Dorothy knew that Ezra had gone to the USA: she sent a message to Laughlin, anxious for his safety, that he was 'not to drive about with Walter'.

On 16 February 1968 she had written to MacLeish on the subject of Harry Meacham's book about Ezra, *The Caged Panther*:

> . . . a very sober, clear vol: I do not know whether Ezra has seen it – I last met him here [Rapallo] in Oct. (Nov.?) & I do not make out how much he follows what is going on everywhere – & I dare not touch it – in case – unless – – He is now in Venice.
>
> 　　Anyway
> 　　　　Thank you –
> 　　Sincerely
> 　　　　Dorothy Pound

In December 1970 she wrote to Meacham saying she had not seen Ezra for eighteen months. Her last sight of him was in the spring of 1972, when she reported to Meacham: 'His voice so soft I can hardly make it out – plenty charm!'

An entry in Noel Stock's notebook: 'D.P. once said to Jas in 1960s: "Nothing really matters, does it, Jas?"'

6

A Bit Of Real Fun

Ezra's eighty-fifth birthday in October 1970 was marked by a special issue of William Cookson's *Agenda*, which contained praise of the *Drafts and Fragments* of the final Cantos by Kenner and others. In 1971 there appeared Mary de Rachewiltz's memoir of her childhood and her parents, *Discretions* – a title that alludes to Ezra's own autobiographical *Indiscretions*. According to Donald Hall, its publication 'shattered Olga, and shattered Ezra as well because of his double devotion to Mary and Olga'.

On 21 August 1970 Ezra sent a note to Cookson, who had proposed editing a selection of his prose for Faber and Faber: 'A great deal too much has already been reprinted, but go ahead . . . In any case you must send me the text you want to use so that I can cross out parts that do not need reprinting or that imply that I still believe I now hold past opinions.'

In May 1971 C. David Heymann, a lecturer from New York State, decided to attempt to meet Ezra and discover whether, as an English critic had recently remarked to him, the old man was still 'a rabid supporter of fascism'. Heymann telephoned the Venice house and was told by Olga that he could call.

> Arriving early at Calle Querini, I sat for a while at a nearby café and watched the gondolas glide smoothly by . . . Then I knocked on Pound's door. Moments later from an open window peeped the head of a lady, who soon stood before me. Olga Rudge was petite and white-haired, with finely honed features; she struck me, in her mid-seventies, as resilient and matter-of-fact. 'Be careful,' she warned me, pointing to a brownish-white, foot-high slab of marble which rose menacingly from the doorway. 'One of these days someone will trip

and break his neck on it. I had it installed after the 1966 floods to keep out the *acqua alta* . . . '

I stepped over the slab and into the house . . . The room downstairs was bright yellow, with painted ocher columns and a shining glass star suspended on thin wire . . . Having seated me, Olga Rudge began to explain what I full well already knew: there was nobody more difficult to converse with than Ezra Pound . . . But one must not lose heart . . . 'Ezra might seem detached and no longer interested, but he follows everything, nothing escapes him. Think of an automobile with its engine idling – it doesn't run but all its parts are moving.' With this introduction, Pound had suddenly come clambering down the stairs, a live wire of energy, bounding up to his visitor, taking the extended hand eagerly in both of his. He smiled slightly, beneath a thin white beard, eyes ablaze, skin starched and deeply lined. He said nothing but led the way back up the stairs, moving quickly, almost jerkily, to his room on the second floor . . .

Couch, chairs, a long bookcase ending in a desk. A marble-topped coffee table . . . a recent portrait of Pound drawn by Kokoschka . . . the bas relief of Ixotta . . . Wyndham Lewis sketches.

Olga 'carried the brunt of the conversation', talking about the disintegration of Venice beneath the waters, and saying it was really no worse than what was happening in the rest of Italy – 'If anything, the whole country was rotting away or was being wrecked by man.' During this,

Pound watched us with piercing eyes, turning his head one way, then the other, as though following the progress of a tennis match, smiling gently whenever a particular volley took an interesting turn. And always he busied himself with his own hands and nails, rubbing the back of one gnarled root against the other, the joints swollen and rheumatic, the knuckles scraped raw. After about ten minutes he still had not uttered a word. There was a break in the conversation, and he said to me, sharply and quite audibly: 'Where are you from?'

Encouraged by this, Heymann began to question him about his conversation with Cory in 1966, when he said he had 'botched' the Cantos. Did he still believe this?

Too soon: Pound ignored the question, turned back to his scarred hands, rubbing nervously. I asked more questions: more silence. I pulled back and waited. Then a flow, the voice parched but strong with a rough edge that corresponded to his visage, the words tumbling out in chunks: 'You ask about my London and Paris friends – Joyce, Hemingway, Brancusi, Eliot. When I was in Zurich in the winter of 1967 I saw Joyce's bare grave – Joyce's name with Nora's sat in a corner of the cemetery, the names nearly illegible on a stone hidden in the grass . . . Hemingway has never disappointed me . . . Brancusi seemed to me a saint . . . I said as much in *Guide to Kulchur* . . . Le Musée d'Art Moderne in Paris contains much of his work, but I would like to see his "Table of Silence" in Rumania . . . The last time I spoke with Eliot was at St Elizabeths, about 1956, I think.'

'Eliot had a lot to do with finally getting you out of St Elizabeths, didn't he?'

'Indirectly, I suppose, as much as anyone. There was a paper to be signed. "No use," I told him. "A travesty," he said. It might have sprung me from the hole a lot sooner.'

'Did Eliot's interest in drama have anything to do with your decision to translate *The Woman of Trachis*?'

'The *Trachiniae* came from reading the noh plays for the new edition and the curiosity of wanting to see a Greek play performed within a new context.'

'Didn't you once attempt a similar adaptation of the *Agamemnon* of Aeschylus?'

'Yes, long ago – I couldn't find the appropriate language. I gave it up.'

'And *Electra*,' said Olga Rudge, breaking into the conversation. 'You began work on the Euripides play during the 'fifties.'

Pound looked up but did not speak. Instead, he returned to his hands, skin wrinkled at the wrists and the back of the hand, an invisible tremor causing a stir of motion in his fingertips. An earnest but impassive expression began to mould the contours of his face.

Olga told Heymann she had 'promised to take Ezra to Rumania next summer'; this year, perhaps they might go to the Joyce Symposium in Trieste, and to Spoleto. Heymann asked Ezra: 'You still manage to do a good deal of travelling?'

'No,' he answered, 'I haven't really done much travelling – in fact I have stayed put for years at a time. I don't see that restlessness is necessary.'

'For artists?'

'For anyone.'

Olga reminded Heymann that the facsimile edition of the *Waste Land* manuscript would soon appear. Heymann asked Ezra if he knew anything about the manuscript's history, and how he felt now that it had been rediscovered. 'But the brittle-boned figure before me had once again retired behind his impenetrable shield of reticence: he said nothing. The hands continued to work away at each other, and the eyes were quiet and far away.'

*

About four months later, Alan Levy, an American journalist, managed to get an invitation to Calle Querini. After waiting in his Venice hotel for some days while Olga kept altering the appointment, Levy was abruptly told by the Swiss friend who was acting as intermediary: 'Get right over . . . before anyone's mind changes.' It was half past seven in the evening; Levy dashed across the city, arriving in twenty minutes, and was ushered by Olga into the presence of Ezra (in bed), who snapped: 'You were supposed to be here at teatime.' Ezra then refused to answer a single question, but eventually produced some snarling remarks: 'Disorder! Disorder! I can't be blamed for all this damned disorder!' And: 'I told [the Swiss] this was not to be one of those interviews.' Levy mentioned a photographer who was to take pictures the next day; Ezra growled: 'I think there have been altogether too many photographs.' Levy gave up.

> I sat in silence and watched the glint of temper fade from his
> face. Then, still saying nothing, I watched him crack and scrape
> and unscrape his knuckles. Then, in the prolonged mutual
> silence, he whistled . . . I laughed, he winked . . . The silence
> resumed.

Olga took Levy up to the top-floor studio to listen to records of Ezra reading; on the way back downstairs they tiptoed past Ezra's bedroom in case he was asleep,

> but he was watching us, so Olga Rudge asked [repeating a
> question Levy had put to her]: 'Well, Pound, did you ever write
> an original play? There are rumors, you know.'
>   He pursed his lips and said: '*Neauouw.*'
>   She said: 'What do you mean, *neauouw?* That's not the same
> as no.'
>   For a moment, he was more sheepish than catlike as he said:
> '*Waaall, I started one and tore it up.*'

Levy returned to the house next morning by appointment, but Ezra would not come downstairs until he heard the voices of friends who had called to see how he was, Then he appeared down the stairs at a jaunty pace. Today he was wearing sharp-creased gray trousers, a blue shirt with the two top buttons open, a grey sleeveless pullover, blue socks, and open-toed slippers. He smiled, but would not chat. The conversation turned to the sculptor Gaudier-Brzeska and his hyphenated name. Olga Rudge asked: 'And wasn't his sister Sophie-Suzanne? Or was it Suzanne-Sophie?'

No answer from Pound.

'I think it was Sophie-Suzanne. Am I right, Pound?'

No response.

'Ezra, don't be impossible! Blink twice if yes.'

Nothing happened.

'Well, then, blink once if no.'

Pound blinked once.*

On Levy's third day Ezra came out to be photographed, and astonished Levy with his energy:

He donned a brown hat, grabbed his walking stick, and put on a reddish-brown checked overcoat over the dark red velvet smoking jacket (with two gold buttons), wide green tie, light brown trousers, and high boots that he was already wearing. Olga Rudge pleaded with him to take an umbrella in case the rain resumed ('*Caro!* Don't be mean'), but he practically skipped over the marble slab in the doorway and was on his way . . . Olga Rudge . . . said . . . 'In the gondola, you *must* sit down. Because I *make* Ezra sit down. But I know he won't do it if he sees you two standing up.'

Then we raced to catch up with Ezra Pound who was striding ahead briskly. We waited briefly for the shuttle gondola . . . that ferries Venetians across the canals for less than a dime a person . . . Pound sat reluctantly, but remained poised to rise even after the photographer and I had obliged Olga Rudge by unchivalrously outracing a lady to the last remaining seat. Olga restrained Pound from giving the lady *his* seat . . .

'Makes no sense traipsin' through this rain,' he muttered . . . 'Makes no sense at all.'

They were joined for lunch by Lotte Frumi, a painter friend of Olga's, 'a marvellously multilingual red-haired widow who knew Kafka in the

*Cf. *The Last Post* (1928), the final volume of Ford Madox Ford's *Parade's End*, in which Mark Tietjens, having voluntarily entered into silence, blinks twice to convey 'yes' to his wife. Mark observes to himself of the silence: 'It was like being dead – or being a God.' (Penguin, 1982, p. 728.)

Prague ghetto ... Pound spoke not a word to Mrs Frumi.' In the restaurant, Olga ordered for Ezra 'a half-portion of *lasagne* and a whole filet of sole - washed down with red wine (which Pound cut with mineral water)'. The pasta course came,

> and Pound was the first to finish.
>
> 'Did you like your *lasagne*?' Olga Rudge asked.
>
> 'Too rich,' said Pound.
>
> 'But you ate it all.'
>
> 'Too rich and too much.'
>
> 'Oh, Ezra! It was only a half-portion.'
>
> 'That was no half-portion.'
>
> 'Oh, go on! Look, Mr Levy ordered a whole portion and he still has more on his plate than you had to begin with.' ...
>
> When the sole came, he devoured it ... 'Full of bones.'

The photographer, Horst Tappe, managed to get some superb pictures; Olga would not agree to be photographed with Ezra 'for reasons of propriety'.

*

In the early months of 1972 Carroll F. Terrell, a professor of English at the University of Maine, founded the quarterly journal *Paideuma*, to be devoted to the study of Ezra's work and life. Terrell also proposed Ezra for an honorary degree at his university. Ezra, informed of this, telegraphed his acceptance – whereupon the university's Trustees turned the nomination down 'for fear', said Terrell, 'of the national press'.

A short time after, the American Academy of Arts and Sciences nominated Ezra for the annual Emerson–Thoreau Medal, an honour that had previously been awarded to Frost, Eliot, and other distinguished poets. Laughlin was on the nominating committee. 'But then,' he wrote to Noel Stock, 'it turned out that the recommendation ... had to be approved by the council of the organization, and they turned us down 13–9. I wish that I had had the sense to conceal a microphone on my person during what I now think of as "the trial" when we, the nominating committee, attempted to defend our choice to the council. To have on tape the slimy mouthings of such as —— and —— ... Just one more kick in the stomach for poor old Ez.'

Two months later, in September 1972, Laughlin told Stock: 'The pot has continued to boil and there have been a great many letters to the editor in various newspapers and even editorials. I would say that the reaction has run about 5 to 1 in favor of Ezra ... One favorable upshot ... is that Dr Hardison, the Director of the Folger Shakespeare Library in Washington, who was a member of the Academy, and resigned in protest ... has now invited Ezra and Olga to come to Washington for a reading at the Library sometime in the next few months, and I understand that Olga has accepted . . . the date . . . is not yet settled.'

In September, David Heymann was back in Venice and visited Ezra again. Heymann had followed the American Academy row, but looking at Ezra in bed he felt that

> it had nothing to do with him now as he lay on his back, lifeless, the classic Grecian head buoyed up by pillows, blue pyjamas draped over his emaciated body. The haunting sapphirine eyes had clouded over. Hands were clenched to the bone. He chipped away with them at dead, eczematous skin. Like his adopted Venezia, he was wasting away . . .
>
> He studied me. After a short while he said: 'You're from New York, aren't you?' The conversation was resumed by him as if, indeed, it had never ceased . . . He pulled himself, with some difficulty, to a half-sitting position. He stared at me openly and candidly. He moved his mouth as though to speak. And then he did . . .: 'I hold no delusions. – What's done cannot be undone. – The error is all in the not done. – I was wrong. – Ninety-per-cent wrong. – I lost my head in a storm.' . . .
>
> One final exchange:
> 'Will you ever return to the United States?'
> A quizzical smile, a long pause before answering:
> 'Anything is possible.'

During the summer, he read over Cookson's selection of his prose for the Faber and Faber volume, and approved it, contributing a short foreword:

> To tread delicately amid the scrapings from the cracker-barrel is no easy job and Mr Cookson has made the best of it.
>
> The volume would be more presentable had it been possible to remove 80% of the sentences beginning with the pronoun 'I' and more especially those with 'we'.
>
> The substitution of 'I' by a comprehensive claim in which 'we' or 'one' is used to indicate a general law may be a pretentious attempt to expand a merely personal view into a universal law.
>
> In sentences referring to groups or races 'they' should be used with great care.
>
> re USURY:
> I was out of focus, taking a symptom for a cause.
> The cause is AVARICE.

Venice, 4th July, 1972   EZRA POUND

*

Laughlin to Stock, 5 October 1972: 'The last word I had from Hardison at the Folger was that he had had no answer at all from Italy since he had proposed the specific dates for Ezra's visit.' And on 20 October: 'I've heard nothing in weeks from Venice or Rapallo and am beginning to worry whether Ezra is all right. I do hope it is just Olga's usual state of overbusyness . . . and not any decline in his condition.'

His eighty-seventh birthday was on Monday 30 October 1972. He was too weak to go downstairs to the party Olga had organized in his honour, so those of her friends who had come to celebrate the occasion walked upstairs to pay their respects to him. One of them said he looked rather frail 'because he hadn't eaten in two days, but otherwise himself. Sitting up in his bed . . . in a pink cover . . .' He talked a little to someone about Monteverdi. A piece of birthday cake was brought up, and a glass of champagne; he had a few nibbles, and complained, in his usual manner: 'I shouldn't have eaten that cake.'

Before the party he had told Olga that he had stomach pains, and in the late evening of the next day she called a doctor, who decided that Ezra must be taken to the municipal hospital of SS. Giovanni e Paolo, in the north of the city. An ambulance boat was summoned, and when the men arrived at midnight they brought a stretcher on which to carry Ezra the twenty-five yards down Calle Querini to the water's edge. He refused; he did not want to go to hospital, but if he must, he would walk to the boat. And so he did, firm and erect. A friend of Olga's, Joan FitzGerald, a sculptor, joined them both at the hospital and sat talking to him for a while. She said he was 'restless, saw no reason to be there'.* After a while, Olga asked her to go back to Calle Querini and fetch Ezra's pyjamas, and to telephone Mary at Brunnenburg, 'just in case, hospitals are hospitals'. While she was away, Ezra 'dozed off and died. One eye, deeply, sapphirically blue, remained open.'

*

Death was recorded at 8 p.m., Wednesday 1 November 1972, the cause being given as 'sudden blockage of the intestine'.

Olga did not want the funeral to be 'a horrid public event' like that some months earlier in Venice for Stravinsky, which had been invaded by tourists with cameras and even transistor radios. Count Cini, whose Foundation now owned the island of San Giorgio Maggiore, arranged for the Benedictines who had charge of the great Palladian church there to hold

---

*Joan FitzGerald's account of Ezra's last hours was given to Richard Stern, in whose words it is recorded here.

a funeral for Ezra with their Catholic rite; a Protestant service would follow at the graveside. The funeral was scheduled with great rapidity, and took place on Friday 3 November, less than forty-eight hours after Ezra's death. Mary and Patrizia just had time to get there from Brunnenburg, but Dorothy was in England and too frail to travel. Omar flew to Venice to represent her, but arrived after the ceremonies were over.

Hugh Kenner says Ezra had wanted to be buried at Hailey, Idaho, with the Gaudier-Brzeska head standing guard over the grave. Instead he was allotted a small plot in the evangelical section of the Venice municipal cemetery, the artificially rectangular island of San Michele half a mile out in the lagoon. His body was carried there by gondola. The grave scarcely looks like a grave: it is a small plot adorned with flowers and a flourishing bay tree; a plain stone tablet carved by Joan FitzGerald has been let into the grass, and bears only the words EZRA POUND.

*

Dorothy cut out the obituaries and pasted them into a scrapbook. 'It's wonderful the way D.P. keeps up,' Laughlin had written to Stock a few weeks before Ezra's death; but eight months after Ezra's funeral, Dorothy broke her hip. She went into a nursing home near Cambridge, and died there on 8 December 1973.

*

In 1940 Ezra had made a will leaving all his property to Mary, but it was not filed with an Italian court at the time of its execution, and was now declared invalid, as was an identical will, re-executed by him in 1964, at a time when he had no legal jurisdiction over his affairs. The lawyers even felt they would have difficulty in deciding which country had been his legal place of residence: not the USA, because he had been brought there compulsorily in 1945; preferably not Italy, because this would involve the interminable proceedings of the Italian legal system.

During the final months of her life, Dorothy frequently insisted that any settlement must 'provide enough for Olga'. But there was a protracted dispute between the two halves of the family about the ownership of papers and other items of value. 'The lawyers are taking forever to get the administration of the Estate set up,' Laughlin wrote to Noel Stock in March 1973. 'I have tried to stay out of all that as much as possible. I want to stay friends with everybody and it's like trying to walk a tightrope.' Eventually a trust was created to pay Olga a pension for life; she stayed on in her little house in Venice, and at Sant'Ambrogio. In October 1985, having passed her own ninetieth birthday, she flew to America to attend celebrations of the centenary of Ezra's birth.

*

Mary, interviewed for a centenary film about her father, *Ezra Pound: American Odyssey*, said of him: 'He wasn't calculating. He should have been more careful, and he wasn't. There's no doubt about that.' Ezra had said much the same about himself to Charles Olson in 1946: 'I've done that all my life, said the wrong things, and brought the whole fucking crockery down around me.' But William Carlos Williams once said he believed that Ezra's mistakes were a crucial part of his achievement: 'He doesn't know a damn thing about China . . . That's what makes him an expert. He knows nothing about music, being tone deaf. That's what makes him a musician . . . And he's batty in the head. That's what makes him a philosopher.'

*

The Cantos are a botch, but they do have unity and coherence, for they are autobiography.*

Eliot, finally, could not enthuse about them. In a letter to F.R. Leavis, written towards the end of his life, he said:

> I agree with you about Pound & the aridity of the Cantos, with the exception of at least one item & a few lines from one of the so-called Pisan Cantos where it seems to me also that a touch of humanity breaks through; I mean the lovely verse of 'Bow [sic] down thy vanity' and the reference to the Negro who knocked him up a table when he was in the cage at Pisa. And of course Pound's incomparable sense of rhythm carries a lot over. But I do find the Cantos, apart from that exceptional moment, quite arid and depressing.

By the end, Ezra himself would probably have agreed with this judgement. As Basil Bunting wrote, too many of the cantos 'don't make sense'. But then, as Bunting says of them in the same poem,

> . . . *l'on entend*, maybe, *le refrain joyeux et leger.*
> Who knows what the ice will have scraped on the rock it is
> smoothing?

And there are also 'The Return' and certain other short early poems, and the whole of *Cathay*, and the fun of *Propertius*, and the poise and rhythm of *Mauberley*, not to mention the brilliant invective of the letters – Ezra is surely the all-time master of insult.

---

*Not as complete an autobiography as they might have been. It is a pity that the Pisan Cantos were not followed by a section inspired by life in Howard Hall and Chestnut Ward.

There they are, you will have to go a long way round
                              if you want to avoid them.

'Of course Ezra is an ass,' said Hemingway, 'but he has written damned lovely poetry.' And Williams again: 'It's the best damned ear ever born to listen to this language!'

*

And the man? Ezra on Sigismundo Malatesta: 'a failure worth all the successes of his age'.

In 1943 Williams said of Ezra, in considering the wartime broadcasts and their likely consequences: 'In a sense I know he's right. If a man doesn't live in this life, if he's always to be just a slave to his contemporaries, always merely trying to improve the general level, to work out a means to exist under uncongenial circumstances . . . if that's all there is to it, then it's a shitty job. Ezra wanted to live, live fully, exquisitely at the peak of feeling, and to feel that he was leading the others into a beautiful world of which he was the disciple. But Jesus, what did it lead him to?'

*

'You have given advice to the young all your life,' said Donald Hall to Ezra. 'Do you have anything to say to them now?'
    'To improve their curiosity and not to fake.'

*

Ezra wrote to Felix Schelling: 'Why the hell dont you have a bit of real fun, before you get tucked under?'

*

To his mother: 'The art of letters will come to an end before A.D. 2000 . . . I shall survive as a curiosity.'

*

Again to his mother: 'The intellect is a very nice whirligig toy. but how people take it seriously is more than I can understand.'

*

During the 1930s, he worked through Horace Rackham's translation of Aristotle's *Nicomachean Ethics*, in preparation for his demolition of the philosopher in *Guide to Kulchur*. In his copy, now at the University of

Texas at Austin, he has made a marginal comment alongside this passage in Rackham's introduction:

> But, strictly speaking, the life of Action has no absolute value: it is not a part of, but only a means to, the End, which is the life of Thought.

Ezra has written: '*Nuts.*'

THE END

Appendix A:

Bibliography

The abbreviations in **bold type** are those used in the notes (Appendix B) which give the sources of quotations.

1 The published writings of Ezra Pound

For a comprehensive list of these, the reader is referred to Donald Gallup, *Ezra Pound, A Bibliography*, University Press of Virginia, second edition, 1983. What follows is merely a handlist of Pound's principal books, with only minimal details of publication.

A Lume Spento, privately printed in Venice, 1908
A Quinzaine for this Yule, privately printed in London, 1908; reprinted for Elkin Mathews, 1908
Personae, Elkin Mathews, 1909
Exultations, Elkin Mathews, 1909
The Spirit of Romance, J. M. Dent, 1910 [**SR**]*
Provença [selections from *Personae* and *Exultations*, and other poems], Small, Maynard, 1910
Canzoni, Elkin Mathews, 1911
Ripostes, Elkin Mathews, 1912
Sonnets and Ballate of Guido Cavalcanti, Small, Maynard/Steven Swift and Co Ltd, 1912
Cathay, Elkin Mathews, 1915
Gaudier-Brzeska: A Memoir, John Lane, 1916 [**G-B**]†
Lustra, Elkin Mathews, 1916
Certain Noble Plays of Japan, Cuala Press, 1916
'Noh' or Accomplishment, Macmillan, 1916
Pavannes and Divisions, Alfred A. Knopf, 1918

*The edition referred to in the notes in this book is that published by Peter Owen in 1952.
†The edition referred to is that published by New Directions in 1970.

Quia Pauper Amavi, Egoist Ltd, 1919
Instigations, Boni & Liveright, 1920
Hugh Selwyn Mauberley, Ovid Press, 1920
Umbra, Elkin Mathews, 1920
Poems 1918-21, Boni & Liveright, 1921
Translation, with Postscript, of Remy de Gourmont, *The Natural Philosophy of Love*, Boni & Liveright, 1922
Indiscretions, Three Mountains Press, 1923 [**Indiscretions**]*
Antheil and the Treatise on Harmony, Three Mountains Press, 1924 [**EP/Antheil**]
A Draft of XVI Cantos, Three Mountains Press, 1925
Personae: the Collected Poems of Ezra Pound, Boni & Liveright, 1926
Translation of Confucius, *Ta Hio*, University of Washington, Seattle, 1928 [**Ta Hio**]
Selected Poems with an introduction by T. S. Eliot, Faber and Gwyer, 1928 [**Sel. Poems 1928**]
A Draft of XXX Cantos, Hours Press, 1930; Farrar and Rinehart/Faber and Faber, 1933
Guido Cavalcanti Rime, Edizioni Marsano SA, 1932
'*How to Read*', Desmond Harmsworth, 1931
ABC of Economics, Faber and Faber, 1933
ABC of Reading, Routledge & Kegan Paul/Yale University Press, 1934 [**ABCR**]†
Make It New, Faber and Faber, 1934; Yale University Press, 1935
Eleven New Cantos: XXXI-XLI, Farrar and Rinehart, 1934
A Draft of Cantos XXXI-XLI, Faber and Faber, 1935
Jefferson and/or Mussolini, Stanley Nott, 1935; Liveright, 1936 [**J/M**]
Polite Essays, Faber and Faber, 1937; New Directions, 1940
The Fifth Decad of Cantos, Faber and Faber/Farrar and Rinehart, 1937
Guide to Kulchur, Faber and Faber, 1938; as *Culture*, New Directions, 1938 [**GK**]‡
Cantos LII-LXXI, Faber and Faber/New Directions, 1940
Translations of Confucius, *The Unwobbling Pivot & the Great Digest*, New Directions, 1947
The Pisan Cantos, New Directions, 1948; Faber and Faber, 1949
The Cantos of Ezra Pound, New Directions, 1948 [containing Cantos 1 to 84]; Faber and Faber, 1950 [excluding the *Pisan Cantos*]; enlarged editions published in 1954, 1964, 1965, 1970, 1975, 1986 [**C**]§
Selected Poems, New Directions, 1949

*The text referred to is that published in Pound's *Pavannes and Divagations*, New Directions, 1958.
†The edition referred to is that published by Faber and Faber in 1961.
‡The edition referred to is that published by Peter Owen in 1952.
§The edition of the Cantos referred to is that published by New Directions in 1970 and Faber and Faber in 1975. (The 1972 New Directions printing adds Canto CXX, which is not in the Faber and Faber edition.) References are given to canto number, then page, as: 'C28/133', i.e. Canto 28, p. 133.

The Letters of Ezra Pound 1907–1941, edited by D. D. Paige, Harcourt Brace, 1950; Faber and Faber, 1951 [**L**]

The Translations of Ezra Pound, Faber and Faber/New Directions, 1953

Literary Essays, edited with an introduction by T. S. Eliot, Faber and Faber/New Directions, 1954 [**LE**]

Translation of *The Classic Anthology Defined by Confucius*, Harvard University Press, 1954; Faber and Faber, 1955

Section: Rock-Drill de los Cantares, Vanni Scheiwiller, 1955; New Directions, 1956; Faber and Faber, 1957

Translation of Sophocles, *Women of Trachis*, Neville Spearman, 1956; New Directions, 1957; Faber and Faber, 1969

Pavannes and Divagations, New Directions, 1958; Peter Owen, 1960

Thrones de los Cantares, Vanni Scheiwiller/New Directions, 1959; Faber and Faber, 1960

Impact: Essays on Ignorance and the Decline of American Civilization, edited with an introduction by Noel Stock, Henry Regnery, 1960

EP to LU: nine letters written to Louis Untermeyer, Indiana University Press, 1963 [**EP to LU**]

Pound/Joyce: the letters of Ezra Pound to James Joyce, edited with commentary by Forrest Read, New Directions, 1967; Faber and Faber, 1969 [**P/J**]

Selected Cantos, Faber and Faber, 1967; New Directions, 1970

Drafts and Fragments of Cantos CX-CXVII, New Directions, 1969; Faber and Faber, 1970

Selected Prose 1909-1965, edited with an introduction by William Cookson, Faber and Faber / New Directions, 1973 [**Sel. Pr.**]

DK/ Some Letters of Ezra Pound . . . [to] Louis Dudek, DC Books, 1975 [**Dudek**]

Selected Poems 1908-1959, Faber and Faber, 1975

Collected Early Poems, edited by Michael John King, New Directions, 1976; Faber and Faber, 1977 [**CEP**]

Ezra Pound and Music: the Complete Criticism, edited with commentary by R. Murray Schafer, New Directions, 1977; Faber and Faber, 1978 [**Schafer**]

'Ezra Pound Speaking': Radio Speeches of World War II, edited by Leonard Doob, Greenwood Press, 1978 [**Doob**]

Pound/Ford: the Story of a Literary Friendship, edited with an introduction by Brita Lindberg-Seyersted, New Directions/Faber and Faber, 1982 [**P/F**]

Letters to Ibbotson, edited by V.I. Mondolfo and M. Hurley, University of Maine, 1979 [**Ibbotson**]

Ezra Pound and the Visual Arts, edited with an introduction by Harriet Zinnes, New Directions, 1980 [**Zinnes**]

Collected Shorter Poems, Faber Paperbacks, 1984. [The most recent and comprehensive edition of the book that was first published as the 1926 *Personae* and the 1928 *Selected Poems*.] [**CSP**]

Ezra Pound and Dorothy Shakespear: their letters, 1909-1914, edited by Omar Pound and A. Walton Litz, New Directions, 1984; Faber and Faber, 1985 [**EP/DS**]

Pound/Lewis: the letters of Ezra Pound and Wyndham Lewis, edited by Timothy Materer, New Directions / Faber and Faber, 1985 [**P/L**]

An important item not reprinted in any of the collections of Ezra Pound's works (though it was included by Noel Stock in *Perspectives*, Henry Regnery, 1965, a *festschrift* in honour of Pound's eightieth birthday) is the essay 'How I Began', first published in *T.P.'s Weekly* (London), 6 June 1913. [**How I Began**]

2 Periodicals containing contributions by Ezra Pound which are frequently cited in this book:

British Union Quarterly, London [**BUQ**]
The *Criterion*, London [**Cri**]
The *Dial*, New York [**D**]
The *Egoist*, London [**E**]
The *Little Review*, Chicago/NewYork/Paris [**LR**]
The *New Age*, London [**NA**]
The *New English Weekly*, London [**NEW**]
Poetry, Chicago [**P**]

3 Letters and other manuscripts by Ezra Pound:

Collections principally used in this book are held in these institutions:

The Beinecke Rare Book and Manuscript Library, Yale University [**Yale**]
The Lilly Library, Indiana University, Bloomington, Indiana [**Lilly**]
The Humanities Research Center, University of Texas at Austin [**HRC**]
Special Collections, Van Pelt Library, University of Pennsylvania [**UP**]

The above are the chief collections of Pound MS material. Others consulted include:

The Berg Collection, New York Public Library [**Berg**]
The Butler Library, Columbia University [**Columbia**]
The Manuscript Division, Library of Congress [**LC**]
National Records Center, Washington DC (Modern Military Field Branch) [**NRC**]
The Ward M. Canaday Center and Special Collections, University of Toledo Library, Toledo, Ohio [**Toledo**]
St Elizabeths Hospital, Washington DC [**St Es**]

Letters exchanged between Pound and W. B. Yeats were kindly shown to me by John Kelly, editor of Yeats's letters for Oxford University Press [**JK**]

The following collections of Ezra Pound's letters are quoted extensively in the text, and are referred to in the notes by the abbreviations given here (the locations of the originals are referred to by abbreviations explained in the above list):

To his father, Homer Pound (Yale) [**HP**]
To his mother, Isabel Pound (Yale) [**IP**]
To Mary Moore (UP) [**MM**]
To Agnes Bedford (Lilly) [**AB**]
To Archibald MacLeish (LC) [**MacL**]
To Huntington Cairns (LC) [**HC**]

To Patricia Hutchins, British Library [**PH**]
Pound's letters to James Laughlin [**JL**] are in the keeping of
    Mr Laughlin, who kindly let me see them.

4 Books and articles containing biographical references to Ezra Pound

This is merely a list of writings which have been cited frequently in this biography. It is arranged alphabetically by the abbreviation I have used for each item in the notes.

A
    Peter Ackroyd, *Ezra Pound and his World,* Thames & Hudson, 1980
Ackroyd/TSE
    Peter Ackroyd, *T. S. Eliot,* Hamish Hamilton, 1984
Agenda 21
    Agenda, Twenty-First Anniversary: Ezra Pound Special Issue, 1979, no. 17
Aldington
    Richard Aldington, *Life for Life's Sake,* Viking, 1941
Anderson
    Margaret Anderson, *My Thirty Years' War,* Alfred A. Knopf, 1930
Antheil
    George Antheil, *Bad Boy of Music,* Hurst & Blackett, 1947
AO
    Ezra Pound: American Odyssey. Unpublished transcripts of interviews with Olga Rudge and Mary de Rachewiltz made during 1981 and 1982 by the New York Center for Visual History, for their film of this title
Bacigalupo
    Giuseppe Bacigalupo, *Ieri a Rapallo,* La Vagabonda, 1980 (English translation made for this book by Roger Griffin)
Barry
    Iris Barry, 'The Ezra Pound Period', *Bookman* (New York), October 1931
Beach
    Sylvia Beach, *Shakespeare & Company,* Harcourt Brace, 1959; Faber and Faber, 1960
Blasting
    Wyndham Lewis, *Blasting and Bombardiering,* 2nd edn, Calder & Boyars, 1967
Boll
    Theophilus E. M. Boll, *Miss May Sinclair,* Associated University Presses, 1973
Bottome
    Phyllis Bottome, *From the Life,* Faber and Faber, 1944
Bowen
    Stella Bowen, *Drawn from Life,* Virago, 1984
Bridson
    D. G. Bridson, *Prospero and Ariel,* Victor Gollancz, 1971

Cairns
Huntington Cairns, interviews with Ezra Pound: typescript in the Manuscript Division, Library of Congress
Case
Charles Norman, *The Case of Ezra Pound*, Bodley Press (New York), 1948
Casebook
A Casebook on Ezra Pound, William Van O'Connor and Edward Stone (eds.), Thomas Y. Crowell, 1959
CH
Ezra Pound: the Critical Heritage, Eric Homberger (ed.), Routledge & Kegan Paul, 1972
Chute
Desmond Chute, 'Poets in Paradise', *The Listener*, 5 January 1956
Cornell
Julien Cornell, *The Trial of Ezra Pound*, John Day, 1966; Faber and Faber, 1967
Cory
Daniel Cory, 'Ezra Pound, a memoir', *Encounter*, May 1968
Death of a Hero
Richard Aldington, *Death of a Hero*, Hogarth Press, 1984
Dis
Mary de Rachewiltz, *Discretions*, Atlantic-Little, Brown/Faber and Faber, 1971
D. P. Williams
David Park Williams, 'The background of the Pisan Cantos', *Poetry* (Chicago), January 1949
Duncan
Ronald Duncan, *All Men Are Islands*, Hart-Davis, 1964
Duncan, *Enemies*
Ronald Duncan, *How to Make Enemies*, Hart-Davis, 1968
Ellmann
Richard Ellmann, *James Joyce*, 2nd edn, Oxford University Press, 1982
Eminent Domain
Richard Ellmann, *Eminent Domain*, Oxford University Press, 1967
Espey
John J. Espey, *Ezra Pound's 'Mauberley': a study in composition*, Faber and Faber, 1955
ETT
H[ilda] D[oolittle], *End to Torment*, Norman Holmes Pearson and Michael King (eds.), New Directions, 1979
E. Williams, *Monroe*
Ellen Williams, *Harriet Monroe and the Poetry Renaissance*, University of Illinois Press, 1977
Fitch
Noel Riley Fitch, *Sylvia Beach and the Lost Generation*, W. W. Norton, 1983; Condor, 1984
Fitzgerald
Robert Fitzgerald, 'Gloom and Gold in Ezra Pound', *Encounter*, July 1956

Fletcher
John Gould Fletcher, *Life is My Song*, Farrar & Rinehart, 1937

Ford, *IWN*
Ford Madox Ford, *It Was the Nightingale*, William Heinemann, 1934

Ford, *Return*
Ford Madox Ford, *Return to Yesterday*, Victor Gollancz, 1931

Gallup
Donald Gallup, *Ezra Pound, A Bibliography*, University Press of Virginia, 2nd edn, 1983

Goldring
Douglas Goldring, *South Lodge*, Constable, 1943

Greenbaum
Leonard Greenbaum, *The Hound and Horn*, Mouton & Co., 1966

H
Patricia Hutchins, *Ezra Pound's Kensington*, Faber and Faber/Henry Regnery, 1965

Hall
Donald Hall, *Remembering Poets*, Harper & Row, 1978

Helix
Ezra Pound in Melbourne: Helix 13/14, edited by Les Harrop and Noel Stock, Ivanhoe, 1983

Hem. Letters
Ernest Hemingway: Selected Letters, edited by Carlos Baker, Scribner, 1981

Heymann
C. David Heymann, *Ezra Pound: the Last Rower*, Viking/Faber and Faber, 1976

HK, *Era*
Hugh Kenner, *The Pound Era*, University of California Press/Faber and Faber, 1972

Hone
Joseph Hone, *W. B. Yeats*, Macmillan, 1942

Izzo
Carlo Izzo, *Civilta Americana*, Edizioni di Storia e Litteratura, Vol. II, 1967

J T–C
Jenkintown Times–Chronicle (Jenkintown, Pennsylvania). Cuttings from this relating to the Pound family are at UP.

Kavka
Psychiatric report on Ezra Pound by Dr Jerome Kavka, dated 14 January 1946, St Elizabeths Hospital

Kimpel
Ben D. Kimpel and T. C. Duncan Eaves, 'More on Pound's Prison Experience', *American Literature*, November 1981

Kutler
Stanley I. Kutler, *The American Inquisition*, Hill & Wang, 1982

Levy
Alan Levy, *Ezra Pound: the Voice of Silence*, Permanent Press, 1983

Longford
Elizabeth Longford, *A Pilgrimage of Passion: the life of Wilfred Scawen Blunt*, Weidenfeld & Nicolson, 1979

McAlmon
Robert McAlmon, *Being Geniuses Together*, revised by Kay Boyle, Michael Joseph, 1970

Meacham
Harry M. Meacham, *The Caged Panther: Ezra Pound at Saint Elizabeths*, Twayne, 1967

Mizener
Arthur Mizener, *The Saddest Story: a biography of Ford Madox Ford*, World Publishing Co., 1971

Monroe
Harriet Monroe, *A Poet's Life*, Macmillan (New York), 1938

Moveable Feast
Ernest Hemingway, *A Moveable Feast*, Scribner, 1964

Myers
Jeffrey Myers, *The Enemy*, Routledge & Kegan Paul, 1980

N
Charles Norman, *Ezra Pound*, Macmillan, 1960

O
Catherine Seelye (ed.), *Charles Olson and Ezra Pound*, Grossman, 1975

Paideuma
Paideuma: a journal devoted to Ezra Pound Scholarship, University of Maine, 1972

Patmore
Brigit Patmore, *My Friends When Young*, William Heinemann, 1968

Peter Brown
Peter Brown, 'Revalued Pound', *New Statesman*, 14 December 1973

PR
'Ezra Pound: an interview' [by Donald Hall], *Paris Review*, 1962, no. 28

Putnam
Samuel Putnam, *Paris Was Our Mistress*, Viking, 1947

Rattray
David Rattray, 'Weekend with Ezra Pound', *Nation*, 16 November 1957

Reid
B. L. Reid, *The Man from New York: John Quinn and his friends*, Oxford University Press, 1968

Russell
Peter Russell (ed.), *Ezra Pound: a collection of essays*, Peter Nevill, 1950

S
Noel Stock, *The Life of Ezra Pound*, Routledge & Kegan Paul/Pantheon, 1970

Selver
Paul Selver, *Orage and the New Age Circle*, Allen & Unwin, 1959

Soft Answers
Richard Aldington, *Soft Answers*, Chatto & Windus, 1932

S/P
Noel Stock & Carl Gatter, *Ezra Pound's Pennsylvania*, Friends of the University of Toledo Libraries, 1976

Steele
Michael King, 'Ezra Pound at Pisa: an interview with John L. Steele', *Texas Quarterly*, Winter 1978

Stern
Richard Stern, 'A Memory or Two of Mr Pound', *Paideuma*, Winter 1972

Stock n/b
Notebook kept during the 1960s by Noel Stock (unpublished)

Surette
Leon Surette, *A Light from Eleusis: a study of Pound's Cantos*, Clarendon Press, 1979

Terrell/Bunting
Carroll F. Terrell (ed.), *Basil Bunting, Man and Poet*, University of Maine, 1981

Thompson & Winnick
Lawrance Thompson & R. H. Winnick, *Robert Frost: the Later Years*, Holt, Rinehart & Winston, 1976

Time
Wyndham Lewis, *Time and Western Man*, Chatto & Windus, 1927

Torrey
E. Fuller Torrey, *The Roots of Treason: Ezra Pound and the Secrets of St Elizabeths*, McGraw Hill/Sidgwick & Jackson, 1984

Wade
Allan Wade (ed.), *Letters of W. B. Yeats*, Hart-Davis, 1954

Wallace
Emily Mitchell Wallace, 'Youthful Days and Costly Hours', in Daniel Hoffman (ed.), *Ezra Pound & William Carlos Williams*, University of Pennsylvania Press, 1983

W/A
William Carlos Williams, *Autobiography*, Random House, 1951

W/L
John C. Thirlwall (ed.), *Selected Letters of William Carlos Williams*, McDowell Obolensky, 1957

Wilhelm
J. J. Wilhelm, *The American Roots of Ezra Pound*, Garland, 1985

Winnick
R. H. Winnick (ed.), *Letters of Archibald MacLeish*, Houghton Mifflin, 1983

WLMS
T. S. Eliot, *The Waste Land: a facsimile and transcript of the original drafts including the annotations of Ezra Pound*, ed. Valerie Eliot, Faber and Faber, 1971

Zapponi
Niccolò Zapponi, *L'Italia de Ezra Pound*, Bulzoni Editore (Rome), 1976 (English translation made for this book by Roger Griffin)

Zinnes
Harriet Zinnes (ed.), *Ezra Pound and the Visual Arts*, New Directions, 1980

Appendix B:

Notes on Sources

The quotations used in the text are identified in this list by the number of the page on which they appear, and by the first words quoted. When two or more quotations from the same source follow each other with little intervening material, I have generally used only the first few words of the first quotation for identification. Abbreviations refer to the Bibliography (Appendix A) where the full title of the work or source is given.

In order to save space, page numbers of articles in periodicals have not been given, but merely the issue number of the periodical. When the date of a letter is given, the digits '18' and '19' indicating the century have been omitted.

At the head of the notes to each chapter will be found a general note in which principal sources for the chapter (if any) are given. Quotations from these sources have *not* been included in the notes themselves, it being assumed that the reader will have no difficulty in tracing them when consulting these sources.

Part One   1885–1908   'Ra'

1. **It Might Go Off And Hurt Someone**
   Principal source: *Indiscretions*. See also Wilhelm.

page
1 'Ezra Loomis Pound was', *Case* 17. 'Born in the', Ford, *Return* 389. 'Ole EZ', to Arnold Gingrich, 30 Oct '34, UP.
2 'a bombastic', *Blasting* 272.
6 'He had ideas', Kavka. 'attacks of viciousness', Wilhelm 39.
   'when it was the thing', EP/DS 337. 'a remote', W/A 64.
7 'stylish New York', Kavka. 'it produces', NA 5 Sept 1912.

---

2. **The Infant Gargantua**
   Principal source: *Indiscretions,* HP, IP.

8 'Violet Hunt', Barry.

9   'I believe I came', Kavka. 'My present position', to Gerhart Münch, 9 Dec '39, Yale. 'Nothing so boring', PH 14 June '58. 'A man who has been', Myers 6. 'You know, Mr Beerbohm' S 3. 'continuous sympathy', Kavka.

10 'my best and', Kavka. 'I send you a few', J T–C 19 Mar 1898. 'That boy', Reid 271.

11 'the philosopher', Putnam 142. 'buncombe', unidentified clipping, Lilly. 'the real Murkhn', HP 10 Jan '19. 'My harmony', Kavka. 'I never', Kavka.

12 'My dear Dorothy', Isabel to DP, 13 Dec '25, Lilly.

14 'the love of adventure', EP/DS 113f.

15 'masculine protest', Kavka. 'a sort of magnetic', Wilhelm 14. 'certain lack', Wilhelm 2. 'Whenever he', *Helix* xiv. (Footnote: 'If I could', HP 23 Aug '17.)

16 'up to the', PR. 'This is my war', Doob 120f.

17 'a candidate', J T–C 12 Apr 1902. 'chief assayer', J T–C 4 Oct 1902. 'miserable salary', MacL, (n.d.). 'an aesthetic perception', PR.

18 'the men half-naked', S 7.

---

3. Suburban Prejudice
    I am greatly indebted to Carl Gatter for his researches into the history of Wyncote, Jenkintown, and the Pounds' life there, most of the fruits of which can be seen at UP; Mr Gatter also showed me his large collection of photographs of Wyncote in Ezra's day, and took me on a tour.

19 'flooded with', NA 15 Jan 1920. 'George W.', *Hatboro Public Spirit*, 22 Mar 1890.

20 'A bear', *Hatboro Public Spirit*, 21 May 1890. 'ole man', 'a very early', to Florence Ridpath, 13 Mar '58, UP. 'friendly and', 'adored', S/P. 'still in loathed', to C. Gatter, 13 Mar '58, UP.

21 'the dashing', S/P. 'announce that', *Hatboro Public Spirit* 18 Apr 1891. 'always round-about', E. H. Parry to C. Gatter, 11 Feb '73, UP. 'suburban', Heymann 298. 'bustuous', S 11.

22 'wd/ Whitcomb', C80/510. 'wasn't quite', A 9. 'I . . . used polysyllables', Kavka.

23 'A man judges', NA 28 Aug 1919. 'to Mr Burrough's', *Hatboro Public Spirit*, 2 Apr 1892. 'Hoss an', to C. Gatter, 11 June '59, UP. 'I was brought up', NA 8 Jan 1930. 'I come from', A 5.

24 'strategic points', to C. Gatter, 18 July '56, UP. 'good food', Doob 122. 'vulgar', GK 89. 'that lolly', IP 19 Feb '10. 'She doesn't', Kavka. 'I am profoundly', IP Jan '13.

25 'I don't know', IP 15 June '14. 'Quite a number', HP 10 Jan '19.

---

4. The Way Poundie Felt
    Principal sources: the Gatter Collection at UP (material collected by Carl Gatter, including letters to him from Pound), *Indiscretions*, HP, IP.

28 'I mean at cookin', Doob 122.

29 'alabaster / Towers', C74/447. 'romantic Colonial', 'backdrop', first sorrow', 'an earnest', Kavka. 'with great seriousness', GK 300.

30 'invented, not a', NA 13 Nov 1919. The cartoon is with Ezra's letters to his parents, Yale. 'too young', Kavka.
31 'too god damn', L 274.
32 'There are, within', NA 12 Sept 1912. 'When Mr Wanamaker's, D Nov 1928.
33 'Though not among', HP 6 Sept '98. 'Comin' from', Doob 137f. 'Every now', to 'Aunt Frank', Oct '12, with letters to his parents, Yale.

---

5. Lily Pound In The Frog Pond

35 'got into college', PR. 'stirred him', Kavka. 'a person aloof', N 7.
36 'Does any', GK 32. 'omnimurkn', HC (n.d.). 'I knew at ', How I Began. 'I have heard', CEP 46.
37 'I am the', poem entitled 'Verbum hominum' in MM (n.d.). 'the "Impulse"', How I Began. 'entered U. Penn', EP to LU 15. 'I began', *Make It New*, Faber and Faber 1934, 8. 'Started in', Doob 137. 'I did have', PR. 'on sheer', G-B 91 'would take out', S/P.
38 'little more', Torrey 24. 'Haven't been', 'wear red', to Ingrid Davies, 28 Apr '55, HRC. 'the lily', N 9. 'Ezra Pound's crazy', ETT 20, 'cut 'em out', Doob 192. 'Will Smith', L 165.
39 'a remarkably', Torrey 36. 'a sort of', N 7. 'asked him', N 8. 'about an hour', N 8f. 'bit one', Torrey 28.
40 'to have made', HP (n.d.) 'Gone while', CEP 39. 'thinking the other', EP/DS 251. 'I remember', W/A 65.
41 'Old Ez', Wallace 18. 'dark Spanish', Wallace 14. 'started to write', William Carlos Williams, *I Wanted to Write a Poem*, Beacon Press, 1958, 5. '& he assuming', MM (n.d.). 'subjects that', W/L 6. 'the livest', W/A 58. 'before meeting', *I Wanted to Write a Poem* (see above) 5.
42 'pore old', to Ford Madox Ford, 7 Aug '24, UP. 'not one person', W/L 6. 'a great blonde', W/A 57. 'impress everyone', *Case* 49. 'I've read', Cory 38. 'It is not necessary', William Carlos Williams, *Kora in Hell*, Four Seas Company, 1920, 13.
43 'In place of', Putnam 152. 'To tell you', *Moveable Feast* 134. 'Tolstoi', HC (n.d.). 'He has tasted', Aldington 104. 'I always said', T.S. Eliot to EP, 23 July '34, Yale. 'With one', C74/427. 'As for your', T. S. Eliot to EP, 23 July '34, Yale. 'He doesn't', *Case* 52. 'the desultory', NA 5 Sept 1912. 'describe precisely', NA 24 Oct 1912. 'from an instinct', LE 324n.
44–5 All quotations are from HP and IP.

---

6. Just So The Mask Shall Fit
Principal sources: HP, IP.

47 'the Idol', N 14. 'UNDER NO', Torrey 28.
48 'hell', Torrey 32.
49 'Kitty's hair', *Paideuma*, vol. 2, no. 1 (spring 1973). 'My first friend', L 95. 'till we are', S 39. The poem 'Scriptor Ignotus', CEP 25.
50 'a painful experience', W/A 56. 'to see me in', EP/DS 337. 'a formidable', Ibbotson 3.

51 'It is nigh on', Ibbotson 114. 'might record', N 356. 'a play about', Ibbotson 114. 'the sort', Timothy Materer, *Vortex*, Cornell, 1979, 72f.
52 'began the Cantos', PR. 'Cantos started', to Peter Whigham (n.d.), Berg. 'Memory faileth', CEP 21. 'For God', CEP 38. 'O Strange face', CEP 34f. 'The real meditation', EP/DS 206.
53 'In the "search for oneself"', G-B 85. 'thru the node', CEP 36. ' . . . 'tis not need', CEP 19. 'Pound is', *Time* 86.

---

7. Not Yet Lost Virginity
Principal sources: HP, IP, ETT, CEP. (I take a more sceptical view of the Pound–Doolittle love affair than do H.D.'s biographers – much more sceptical than that shown by Hilda herself in ETT. My attitude has been shaped by Ezra's conduct of other romantic affairs, and from a close study of the poems in 'Hilda's Book', most of which are reprinted in CEP.)

55 'Really one DON'T', L 93.
56 'I was NOT', H 37. 'temperamental sympathy', SR 22. 'one of the few', Torrey 32.
57 'personal love poetry', L 240. 'Wotcher mean', to May Sinclair, 19 Mar '20, UP. 'respect above all', AO. 'If he ever', W/L 210. 'Dawn light', S 20.
58 'Naow effa', SR 67n. 'clarity and hardness', S 21. 'a thesis on, GK 215f.
59 'Ezra never', W/A 58. 'I was 15', H.D. in *The Cantos of Ezra Pound: Some Testimonies*, Farrar & Rinehart 1933, 17. 'He had a beautifully', William Carlos Williams, *I Wanted to Write a Poem*, Beacon Press, 1958, 6. 'He was not unbeautiful', Bowen 48f. 'I had a friend', H.D. in *The Cantos of Ezra Pound: Some Testimonies* (see above), 17.
60 'She is tall', W/L 8f. 'tall, blond', W/A 67f. 'No one had', W/A 65.
61 'wonderfully in love', W/A 68. 'The america', to Ingrid Davies, 4 April '56, HRC.
62 'She hath some', Wilhelm 104.
63 'Damn it all', MacL 5 Dec '26. 'armloads of books', H.D. in *The Cantos of Ezra Pound: Some Testimonies* (see above), 17. 'our only great', L 10. 'mysticism', Kavka. 'every morning', Cory 31.

---

8. The Athens Of The West
Principal sources: HP, IP, CEP, MM. (This chapter also owes much to Wilhelm.)

64 'go little verse', 'a pittance', S 28.
65 'in the Brit. Museum', GK 219. 'Wyncote has been', J. T–C 9 June 1906. 'the anarchist suspects', N 17. 'Although of the', N 18.
66 'very slippery', 'There must be', GK 53f. 'I've found the lowdown', N 257. 'that nervy little', S 31.
67 'invades the realm', S31.
68 'In 1907', S 34. 'those professors', LE 15. 'I have already', to Felix Schelling, 15 Jan '07, UP. 'no interest', 'He is in', to Wharton Baker, 26 Aug '20, filed with letters to HP and IP, Yale.

69 'I have spatted', S 34. 'a stronghold', Wallace 29. 'NO American', L 99. 'otiose', 'All the U. of P.', L 225. 'the university's', L 100. 'Who is that', Carl Gatter interview with Mary Moore, UP.
70 'In those days', Mary Moore to Carl Gatter, 29 Apr '69, UP. 'People ask', Carl Gatter interview with Mary Moore, UP. 'We were warm', Mary Moore to Carl Gatter, 1 June '70, UP. 'pixyish', Wilhelm 161.
72 'the Athens', 'literary traditions', EP to LU 15. 'From letters', Mary Moore to Carl Gatter, 1 June '70, UP.
73 'Villon never forgets', SR 168f., 176. 'Ezra doesn't', McAlmon 89. 'booze is', PH, Aug '53. 'gingerly', W/L 210. 'most poets', P/F 84. 'exhibitionist', S 42.
74 'Without Pound', *Paideuma*, vol. 13, no. 1 (spring 1984). 'The trace of', N 23.
75 'the poetic', L 3f.
76 'Two stewdents', Wilhelm 171.
77 'Religion, oh,', MM (n.d.).

9. Latin Quarter Type
    Principal sources: HP, IP, MM, Wilhelm, CEP, ETT.

78 'the sixth circle', N 22. 'in middle Indiana', Three Cantos, P, July 1917.
80 'The end came', *Paideuma*, vol. 13, no. 1 (spring 1984). 'She wouldn't', P/J 62f.
81 'told the board', *Paideuma*, vol. 13, no. 1 (spring 1984). 'the Latin', S 43. 'Gee!!', L 7. 'If ever', 'degraded', L 5. 'k-rear as', PH 8 Feb '58.
82 'Pound went', N 5. 'Ye Fellowship', S 44. 'I had exactly', How I Began.

Part Two   1908–20   'Ezra'

1. An Excellent Place To Come to From Crawfordsville
    Principal sources: HP, IP, MM, CEP.

87 'I dunno', L 346. 'It would', NA 14 Nov 1912. 'I don't have', L 322. 'Ezra is', N 69.
88 'Don't expect', L 123. 'Mr Pound', N 26.
89 'an excellent place', *Indiscretions* 5.
90 'by the soap-smooth', C76/460.
91 'Ezra liked', Aldington 137. 'one tremendously', L 4f.
93 'Yeats knew', Zinnes xii. 'to sit', Kavka. 'ripped away', P/J 219. 'chuck the lot', C76/460.
94 'the event of', S 48. 'for days', How I Began. 'bitter, personal', L 4. 'sincere', L 3.
95 'charming', L 4. 'I have been', L 7f. 'A LUME SPENTO', CH 2f. 'Mr Pound is', CH 42. 'Wild and', CH 2. 'stale creampuffs', Gallup 4.
96 'Trovaso', C76/461. 'San Giorgio', typescript at Yale.

2. Deah Old Lunnon
    Principal sources: HP, IP, MM, CEP.

97 'I came to', How I Began. 'the *centre*', British–Italian Bulletin, 4 Apr 1936.

98 'the two peaks', PH 8 Apr '54. 'first little', S 55.
99 'Directions', to Iris Barry (n.d.), Lilly. 'complete with', H 57.
100 'stewing with', C80/502.

---

3. The Most Charming Woman In London
   Principal sources: HP, IP, EP/DS, P/F, CEP.

102 'loudly advertised', S 57. 'From this side', N 33. 'I never have', S/P. 'wrote badly', HP 25 March '19.
103 'So far as', How I Began. 'three teacups', C82/523. 'only miss', C82/523. 'by way of ', L 7.
104 'She had a', W. B. Yeats, *Memoirs*, Macmillan, 1972, 74. 'long passionate' and other quotations about the affair, ib. 85–9. 'Mind and', W. B. Yeats, *Selected Poetry*, Macmillan, 1967, 61.
108 'In attestation', S/P. 'queer', CH 43. 'a thread', CH 44. 'I had had de Born', How I Began.
109 'A complete', Eliot's draft notes for Sel. Poems 1928, Yale. 'a most blood-curdling', to May Sinclair (n.d.), UP.
110 'the greatest', Ford, *Return* 371. 'was himself', Mizener 239f. 'boomed through', N 197. 'The food', Aldington 130f.
111 'Said he never', O 78. 'I don't read', Bowen 114. 'Fordie / never', C82/525. 'never did read', PH 16 Nov '57. 'had all his', Mizener 239. 'see him stopping', N 214. 'When I first', Ford, *Return* 388.
112 'in a magnificent', David Garnett, *The Golden Echo*, Chatto & Windus, 1953, 129.

---

4. Yeats Has At Last Arrived
   Principal sources: HP, IP.

113 'arthritic milieu', P/F 172. 'a horrible', Michael Reck, *Ezra Pound: a Close-Up*, McGraw-Hill, 1967, 14f. 'hear Masefiled', to May Sinclair, 19 Mar '20, UP.
114 'a yahoo', L 71. 'furious likes', CH 287. 'intellectual cheesemite', P/J 51. 'Dear old Shaw', NA 1 Jan 1920. 'old G.B.S.', L 104. 'longest mock', Alun R. Jones, *Life and Opinions of T. E. Hulme*, Gollancz., 1960, 21. 'crap', Cory 32. 'DAMN Bergson', HC (n.d.). 'outward image', H 125.
115 The policeman anecdote, N 49. 'Hulme would', N 48. 'Can't recall', marginal note in typescript by Patricia Hutchins, 'Ezra Pound in Kensington', British Library. 'suave tea-parties', H 126. 'Frank Flint', Fletcher 77. 'never at best', L 247. 'ought to get', PH 17 Nov '57.
116 'a perfect', 'but they didn't', PH 17 Nov '57. 'Mr Pound', CH 97. 'picturesque' etc., *The Review* (Oxford), April 1965. 'Mr Pound is a', CH 46f.
117 'proposed at various', E 1 May 1915. 'If there IZ', JL 28 Dec '35. 'dull enough', CSP 251. 'If young', L 306.
118 'I had been', How I Began. 'Ha' we lost', CEP 112. 'has a much', in EP's *Selected Poems*, Faber and Gwyer, 1928, 21. 'British Empire', SR 95.

119 'become popular', to May Sinclair, 19 Mar '20, UP. 'would read', C80/524. 'Dear Mr Pound', W. B. Yeats to EP, 8 May '09, JK.

120 'destroyed profit', H 57. 'Monsieur Verog', CSP 193. 'that dignified', IP 1 Sept '11. 'I have enjoyed', How I Began.

121 'is only just', CH 48f. 'admirable', CH 53. 'foolish archaisms', CH 58f. 'a very much', CH 60. 'Mr Welkin Mark', CH 6. 'Your book', L 8.

---

5.   Ezra! Ezra!
     Principal sources: HP, IP, H, EP/DS, SR.

122 'White Poppy', CEP 126.

123 'My name but', CEP 214f. 'an interminable', Boll 83.

124 'Oh I do', CH 36f.

125 'It is not maiming', D Mar 1928.

127 'campanolatry', GK 300. 'the act of', NA 12 June 1919. 'Questionings', GK 300.

128 'an extraordinary', Richard Aldington, *Soft Answers*, Chatto & Windus, 1932, 132. 'I find a', L 105. 'should be devoted', to May Sinclair (n.d.), UP. 'He washed', *Death of a Hero* 115.

129 'dread of', N 303. 'my luxurious', L 25. 'a dark blue', *Helix* 47. 'perpetual air', Barry 171.

130 'I hope you', P/J 35. 'Leonardo da', Bottome 71. 'more like', L 85. 'the pale', Doob 66. 'wept copiously', Goldring 42. 'disturbance of', H. G. Wells, *H. G. Wells in Love*, Faber and Faber, 1984, 63.

131 'To the right', P/F 84. 'In a very', Ford, *Return* 388. 'He struck', Goldring 48.

132 'He not only', Goldring 47. 'readier to', Patmore 55. 'sitting down', N 53. 'like playing', P/F 87. 'Violet Hunt had', N 104. 'jumping and', Bottome 71. 'endangered every', Fletcher 59.

133 'a most irritating', Bottome 71. 'a slight', Fletcher 60. 'half swallowing', Patmore 59. 'a velvet', Edgar Jepson, *Memoirs of an Edwardian*, Grant Richards, 1937, 152. 'He is 24', CH 38. 'How exactly', E. Nehls, *D. H. Lawrence: A Composite Biography*, University of Wisconsin Press, 1957, vol. I, 110. 'How would', ib. 125. 'for Lawrence', *Helix* 46.

134 'disagreed', marginal note in typescript by Patricia Hutchins, 'Ezra Pound in Kensington', British Library. 'Though I', NA 25 Feb 1915. 'an awful', to Peter Whigham (n.d.), Berg. 'I think he', L 17. 'may have felt', Ernest Rhys, *Everyman Remembers*, J. M. Dent, 1931, 251f. 'turned to him', *Paideuma*, vol. 3, no. 1 (spring 1974). 'alternately leaning', Aldington 164.

135 'whistled downstairs', Boll 116. 'had no social', Wyndham Lewis, *Tarr*, Penguin, 1982, 13. 'Ezra Pound / And Augustus John', 'Authorship', L 129. 'He introduced', Bottome 73f.

136 'the biology', Bottome 74. 'intellectual', Phyllis Bottome, *The Goal*, Faber and Faber, 1962, 39. 'Dark Eyed', CSP 91. 'Empty are', CSP 112. 'He discussed', *Helix* 47.

137 'the (alleged)', Richard Aldington, *Soft Answers*, Chatto & Windus, 1932, 143f. 'While gallantly', *Death of a Hero* 116. 'W.B.Y. says', MM (n.d.).

138 'This queer', CH 39. 'I have the', P/J 173. 'giving an imitation', Duncan 197. 'Irish brogue', N 366.
139 'dismal', S 73. 'I am aweary', etc., CEP 120, 121, 126. 'those little', CH 40.
140 'if Mr Pound', CH 65. 'turbulent', CH 62. A letter from Manning to EP is among Ezra's letters to his parents, Yale. 'a good deal', *Helix* 13. 'first licherary', *Helix* 15.
142 'Did you come', W/A 113. 'I know hardly', NA 31 Oct 1912. 'all great', L 25. 'all civilization', Cri Jan 1923. 'Not my dish', H 87. 'intense literary', W/A 117.

---

6. Sediment
Principal sources: HP, IP, EP/DS.

143 'the picture', Victor Seroff, *The Real Isadora*, Hutchinson, 1972, 246.
144 'that eminently', EP/DS 38. 'O pleasing shore', SR 230. 'the original', L 210. 'the sun', CEP 150.
145 'Just at present', MM (n.d.). 'I've been about', S 87. 'exact psychology', NA 14 Dec 1911. 'Than Guido', *The Translations of Ezra Pound*, Faber and Faber 1953, 18. 'Because a lady', ib. 133.
146 'my father', ib. 20. 'scholastic', CH 93. 'Either Mr Pound', CH 86–8. 'A. de R.', EP/DS 131. 'I once did', P/J 557. 'obfuscated', LE 193.
147 'was the first', S 86. 'would much rather', *Poetry Review*, Feb 1912. 'at Sirmio', CEP 150. 'What distresses', EP/DS 49.
148 'Obviously the girl', Richard Aldington, *Soft Answers*, Chatto & Windus 1932, 140f. 'Having had', *Helix* 47. 'clear insight', S 89.
149 'The few bits', CH 67. 'negative', CH 69. 'made the proposal', S 93.
150 'sheer bliss', Hilda Doolittle to EP, 28 Oct '48, Lilly.
151 'happily cuckoo', N 25f. 'We began', CH 75f. 'uncouth' etc., 72f. 'any worthy', L 9. 'I met a', S 94f. 'surly', S 95. 'there is', NA 26 Sept 1912. 'college of', NA 17 Oct 1912.
152 'eager, careless', 'The city has', NA 12 Sept 1912. 'botch . . .', 'And New York', NA 18 Sept 1912.
153 'sham fairyland', NA 12 Sept 1912. 'Yeats père', S 90. 'quoting quantities', CH 76.
154 'He seemed always', A 26. 'nomadic', GK 243. 'Ownership is', L 279. 'Ain't got', MM (n.d.). 'he went off', N 90.
155 'Margaret Craven's', S 97. 'deplored', *Helix* 21. 'used more different', Sel. Pr. 42. 'profoundly glad', Gallup 446.
156 'with the artisan's', NA 19 Sept 1912. 'careless ignorance', *Times Literary Supplement*, 25 June 1954. 'He hath not', CSP 65.
157 'Koré my heart', CEP 134. 'lamentable failure' etc., CH 78–85. 'a sort of', EP/DS 38.
158 'Artistically', EP/DS 38. 'I would sing', CEP 216. 'affected by', P/F 8. 'I have gone', CEP 170. 'false starts', N 75. 'moribund', Anderson 172.
159 'There is', L 179.

7. New Age
    Principal sources: HP, IP, EP/DS.

160 'his intense', N 53.
161 'in a sort of medieval', H 115. 'knows anything', N 20.
162 'Ford . . . felt', 'That roll,' P/F 172. 'For myself', P Aug 1913. 'I would rather', P Jan 1913.
163 'making some sort', P/F 9. 'Pre-Raphaelite', P/F 10. 'the best poem', P June 1914. 'ANY dud', to Henry Bamford Parkes, 2 Jan '33, UP. 'fills in the', P/F 9. 'Mr Hueffer is', P/F 10. 'not a poet', P/F 15. 'shall the poet', Sel. Pr. 32. 'The only way', Sel. Pr. 41f.
166 'had filled the gap', ETT 8. 'I think I', ETT 17f. 'Drifting', ETT 18. 'I remember how', ETT 30.
167 'stricter, or more subtle', SR 90f.
168 'whole decades', LR Aug 1918. 'American who', LR 40. 'Old Henry', Doob 143. 'my reminiscence', Boll 83. 'unconscious antipathy', to J. B. Yeats, 4 Feb '18, JK.
169 'excellent friend', ib. 'did more to', H 106. 'I hope you', L 25. 'To this day', Cri Apr 1935. 'found it less', to T. S. Eliot, 14 March '22, Lilly. '2 VERY', PH 12 May '57. 'with his clipped', Selver 33. 'Under this', NA 30 Nov 1911. 'The artist', Sel. Pr. 23.
170 'these rambling,' Sel. Pr. 41. 'something which', Alun R. Jones, *The Life and Opinions of T. E. Hulme*, Gollancz, 1960, 45f. 'poetry which corresponds', 'the trampling', *Poetry Review*, Feb 1912.
171 'Your mind and', CSP 61. 'As we are', LR March 1918. 'When Ezra', Goldring 48f. 'My dear Ezra', W. B. Yeats to EP, 24 Jan '13, JK.
172 'Ezra Pound', W. B. Yeats, *A Packet for Ezra Pound*, Cuala Press 1929, 1f. 'Charge me', W. B. Yeats to EP, 13 Aug '17, JK. 'thrash around', PR. 'a bit wooly', Reid 292. 'gave the impression', PR. 'now muddled', to Peter Whigham (n.d.), Berg.
173 'fires . . . over and spent', CSP 236. 'No, no!', CEP 195. 'See, they return', CSP 74.
174 'the most beautiful', S 153. 'thrill', F. W. Dupee and George Stade (eds.), *Selected Letters of E. E. Cummings*, Harcourt Brace, 1969, 254. 'translating at sight', W. B. Yeats (ed.), *The Oxford Book of Modern Verse*, Clarendon Press 1936, xxvi. 'possessed of', *Case* 49. 'The TOTAL', Izzo 354. 'objective reality', G-B 85.
175 'anarchy', etc., P Aug 1917. 'Beware of the', MacL 5 Dec '26. 'Mr Pound has', 'certain evenings', CSP 251. 'A touch of', CSP 252. 'to our enormous', CH 97.
176 'As for the', CSP 251. 'My own', Aldington 135.

8. Foreign Correspondent
    Principal Sources: HP, IP, EP/DS.

177 'Whenever Ezra', Aldington 135. 'she-poet', to May Sinclair, 19 Sept '11, UP. 'a clever boy', Patmore 60. 'got the idea', N 89. 'a brawnyish', Selver 35.

178 'In the case', *Death of a Hero* 112. 'Of course it's', Ellen Williams, *Harriet Monroe and the Poetry Renaissance*, University of Illinois Press, 1977, 82. 'The Georgians', N 90.

179 'illustrate any', N 82. 'rotten', L 35. 'We used to', Cri July 1932. 'the stupidest', S 182. 'literary hen-coop', L 64. 'the best of', S 182. 'challenged Abercrombie', P/J 48.

180 'singable', 'It is very', LE 264.

181 'had seemed increasingly', *Helix* 21f. 'The old roads', CSP 122f. 'covered with twenty', S 188.

182 'an old woman', 'I have seen', CSP 121. 'the world's best', GK 111. 'climbed rickety', CSP 122. 'The wind came', CSP 119.

183 'Have you seen', CSP 19. 'what the country', LE 95. 'to set here', C76/455, C74/428.

184 'the American mediaeval', NA 12 Sept 1912. 'the imminence', NA 5 Sept 1912. 'look like', L 10. 'Damned mania', HP 10 Jan '19. 'Who bear the brunt', CSP 235.

185 'Dear Madam', L 9f. 'All right', S 121. 'all that I', L 10. 'emphatic resentment', P Feb 1913.

186 'flippant and', Selver 35f. 'They are going', L 10. 'a quiet', S 126f. 'I wasn't allowed', Aldington 109. 'unspeakable', Walter de la Mare to Naomi Royde-Smith, quoted in unpublished biography of de la Mare by Theresa Whistler. 'some of young', N 87. 'Among the very', P Jan 1913.

187 'one of the "Imagistes"', P Nov 1912. '"But Dryad"', ETT 18. 'Ezra was so', Aldington 135. 'In the spring', LE 3. 'the name was', L 213. 'I didn't like', Aldington 135. 'I've had luck', L 11.

188 'a poet and', *Blasting* 253.

189 'I don't know that', L 11. 'Will people', CSP 81. 'Come, my songs', CSP 94. 'The apparition', CSP 109. 'I got out', How I Began.

190 'God knows I', L 15. 'When he tries', *Time* 87. 'your chance to', L 24. 'Morte de', L 18. 'indecencies' etc., CH 100f.

191 'Come my songs', E 15 Jan 1914. The details of the corrections to the Yeats poems, and Ezra's comment ('Oh la . . .'), Ellen Williams, *Harriet Monroe* (see note to p. 178 above) 62f.

192 'I don't think', Monroe 164. 'a fortnight', *Eminent Domain* 66. 'Objectivity and', *Eminent Domain* 67. 'Ezra is', 'In his own work', S 130.

193 'picked up a', Cory 31. 'I find people', MacL 5 Dec '26. 'a chartered', MacL (n.d.). 'The ideal way', MacL 24 Nov '26. 'determination', CH 96. 'no one need', S 130.

194 'one of the', S 131. 'a beautiful and', PH 19 Sept '53. 'A man of', PH 10 Apr '58.

---

9. Our Little Gang
Principal sources: HP, IP, EP/DS.

197 'instructions to', L 18.

198 'The symbolist's', G-B 84. 'expressing emotion', T. S. Eliot, 'Hamlet and his Problems' (1919), quoted in *The Oxford Companion to English Literature*

(ed. Drabble) under 'objective correlative'. 'You know as', L 13. 'Good God!', L 15. 'I'm sick', L 12.

199   'rather violent', N 96. 'These fools', L 16. 'the two hundred', P/F 16. 'The modern artist', E 16 Feb 1914. 'The artist is not', P Oct 1914. 'The voice of', LR Sept 1917.

200   'No poet', Russell 26. 'In his attitude', *Blasting* 280. 'Pound the major', N 275. 'Have just', L 15. 'ju jitsu', N 122. 'I admit he's', Ellen Williams, *Harriet Monroe* (see note to p. 178 above), 67.

201   'Sincere, very', Ezra Pound (ed.), *Profile: An Anthology*, Giovanni Scheiwiller (Milan), 1932, 46. 'Pound . . . took', Ellen Williams, *Harriet Monroe* (see note to p. 178 above), 64. 'feel of some', *New Freewoman*, 1 Sept 1913. 'I don't doubt', L 19. 'Mr Frost . . .', MacL 24 Nov '26.

202   'He makes a', *New Freewoman*, 1 Dec 1913. 'Little Bill', L 67. 'Bill Wms.', L 131. 'I still think', L 28. 'Lawrence has', L 17. 'Lawrence, as you', L 22.

203   'I fetched up', NA 4 Sept 1913. 'able, by question', Fletcher 73f. 'Paris is', NA 16 Oct 1913.

204   'If our writers', P Oct 1913. 'In his eagerness', *The Review* (Oxford), Apr 1965. 'Of course you', *New Freewoman*, 1 Dec 1913. 'Good God', CSP 104. 'O helpless', CSP 92f.

205   'As a bathtub', CSP 100.

206   'no sign', PH 19 Sept '53. 'the lady sitting', Barry 167.

207   'gracious wisdom', EP/DS 242. 'lasting and', LE 42. 'very tiresome', S 268. 'has the good', Ellen Williams, *Harriet Monroe* (see note to p. 178 above), 47.

208   'ten or a', L 22. '*last* obsequies', L 23. 'she had a', *Collected Shorter Poems*, Faber and Faber, 1968 edition, 252. 'I join', CSP 88. 'Much of his', S 153.

209   'the fluid', Aldington 136f. 'When I get', N 106. 'pleasingly intelligent', L 22. 'a sudden', Aldington 136f. 'the Egoist spark', Jane Lidderdale and Mary Nicholson, *Dear Miss Weaver*, Faber and Faber, 1970, 87.

210   'a brief anthology', L 24. 'no particular', Fletcher 77. 'My relations', N 110f. 'What Ezra', Aldington 137. 'We are getting', L 27. 'my school', *New Freewoman*, 15 Sept 1913.

211   'I agree', L 26. 'rotten poetasters', L 35. 'Will you please', 'I don't know', P/F 21. 'All right', L 27. 'won't happen', L 29. 'trying to run', L 35.

212   'Oh gawd!!!' L 64. 'interesting only', L 127. 'Whoop golly-ip', LR Jan 1918. 'the best man', CH 112. 'Sandburg is', L 99. 'represents a tendency', P Dec 1917. 'rank bad', LR Sept 1918.

213   'the wit and', L 157n. 'a fountain', L 157.

---

10.   Orient From All Quarters
      Principal sources: G-B, P/J, HP, IP, EP/DS.

214   'I will keep', Monroe 330. 'because, although', S 145. 'two statuettes', L 27.

215   'the masses of which', H. S. Ede, *Savage Messiah*, Gordon Fraser, 1971, *passim*.

216   'probably the dirtiest', Aldington 165. 'I had over-prepared', CSP 158. 'The jargon', E 15 Feb 1914.

217   'the only person', L 27. 'Jacob is a', L 74. 'It is no use', E 16 Mar 1914.

218 'damn bad', to J. B. Yeats, 21 June '17, JK. 'a man of genius', ib. 4 Feb '18, JK. 'serious intentions', *Dis* 156. 'He has derived', *New Freewoman*, 15 Nov 1913. 'but that he made', L 22f.

220 'and I wasn't content', D. G. Bridson, 'An Interview with Ezra Pound', *New Directions in Prose and Poetry*, 17, 1961. 'after a couple', ib. 'said that Fenollosa', ib. 'There *are* some', Reid 287. 'all old', L 27.

221 'I am taking', Wade 584. 'He is certainly', S 145. 'out in the dampish', to May Sinclair, 31 Dec '14, UP. 'We have four', Wade 584. Miss Welfare's reminiscences were collected by Patricia Hutchins; John Kelly lent me a copy of the typescript.

222 'the noise in', C83/533f. 'Wordsworth . . . was', Ezra Pound, *Pavannes and Divisions*, Alfred A. Knopf, 1918, 139f. 'Yeats is much', L 27. 'O fan of', CSP 108.

223 'will give us', L 30f. 'We ask you', *The Translations of Ezra Pound*, Faber and Faber, 1953, 298. 'read me a great', W. B. Yeats, *Explorations*, Macmillan 1962, 65f. 'With the help', W. B. Yeats, *Essays and Introductions*, Macmillan, 1961, 221.

224 'The Birth of the Dragon' is mentioned in a letter to Homer Pound in Oct '15. 'The phonetic', I.F. 259.

225 'thirty-odd', *Shenandoah*, autumn 1952, 9.

226 'Mr Joyce writes', E 15 July 1914. 'too long', Guy J. Forgue (ed.), *Letters of H. L. Mencken*, Alfred A. Knopf, 1961, 64.

227 'good art however', LE 44. 'very great', W. B. Yeats to EP, 11 Feb '14, JK. 'the two strongest', L 34. 'I can never', Hone 193.

228 'gone your individual', S 150 (a manuscript in the Berg Collection, New York Public Library, identifies the lines as EP's work). 'terribly post-futurist', N 138. 'he wasn't sure', Aldington 168.

229 'with the roast', P March 1914. 'Regarding the roasted', Lady Anne Lytton to Patricia Hutchins, in Hutchins MSS., British Library. 'which in his', Aldington 168. 'Marconis and Jews', Longford 394. 'an American', Longford 397. 'which treasonable', Aldington 168. 'the Blunt stuff', L 34.

230 'I won't stir', L 37. 'so assuredly', P May 1914.

232 'virile . . . biological', Jacob Epstein, *Let There Be Sculpture*, Michael Joseph, 1940, 59. 'much to Violet's', Aldington 166.

---

11. Almost As Intelligent . . .!
    Principal sources: HP, IP, EP/DS.

233 'The Anthology', EP/DS 325. 'columnists parodied', Aldington 138.

234 'It doesn't matter', Torrey 65. 'thousands of prim', E 1 Mar 1916.

235 'bluff based', Sel Pr. 49. 'heroic figure', L 183. 'found for himself', W. B. Yeats to Homer Pound, 30 Mar '14 (among EP's letters to his parents, Yale). 'enough to keep', Kavka.

236 'Nothing written', *Helix* 103. 'I found', ETT 5. 'The Dryad', CSP 110. 'My only real', ETT 8. 'I think mebbe', *Helix* 103.

237 'systematicly obstructed', PH 29 Nov '56. 'an excellent', *Blasting* 277.

238 'deodorized', Longford 398. 'trying to make out', *Paideuma*, vol. 2, no. 3 (winter 1973). 'never understood', Kavka. 'never spoke about', Stock n/b

239 'I got all entangled', *Paideuma*, vol. 2, no. 3 (winter 1973). 'I distrust the', Zinnes xxi. 'Not wildly', NA 1 Aug 1918. 'much more charming', Longford 197. 'just sitting', N 317. 'There is this', Omar Pound in *New York Times Book Review*, 16 Sept 1984, 3. 'Yes, Ez', Barbara Guest, *Herself Defined*, Doubleday, 1984, 64.

240 'A Harvard man', Doob 128. 'I am, with', LR Sept 1917.

241 'The gilded phaloi', CSP 110. 'considerable reluctance', Kavka. 'Mr Hecatomb', CSP 178. 'must have been', Cory 31.

12. Youth Racket.
Principal sources: HP, IP, EP/DS.

242 'an only child', Myers 6. 'in the most', Myers 28.

243 'A face', Myers 30. 'Outwardly, I', *Blasting* 273. 'of an unsuccessful', *Moveable Feast* 109. 'very violent', Myers 29. 'Yes, I vil', LR May 1918. 'a great work', Myers 93.

244 'the weak minded', Jay Martin, *Always Merry and Bright: the Life of Henry Miller,* Capra Press, 1978, 304. 'a sharp blow', Myers 30. 'in 1910', *Blasting* 272. 'his bull-dog', C80/507. 'as one might', *Blasting* 274f. 'in clothes', Myers 32. 'I did not speak', *Blasting* 271f.

245 'Lewis *can*', L 74. 'A volcanic', GK 106. 'Wyndham L/', PH 12 May '57. 'a new Futurist', P/J 26. 'The modern artist', E Feb 1914.

246 'a day of attack', *Blasting* 33. 'Yeats had to', Aldington 108. 'You may get', L 28. 'It was Pound', *Blasting* 252.

247 'The ideal whirl-swirl', Allen Upward, *The New Word*, A.C. Fifield, 1908, 195. 'I am not', Ezra Pound, *Pavannes and Divisions*, Alfred A. Knopf, 1918, 145f. 'It was scarcely', *Blasting* 252. 'a matter of almost', Zinnes 239f. 'brilliant and interesting', E. March 1914. 'I seized', *Blasting* 36.

248 'You Wops', *Blasting* 34. 'a determined', *Blasting* 33. 'impressionism using', G-B 33. 'propaganda that', Doob 194.

249 'Lewis and Ezra', Myers 75. 'Mr Pound cannot', E 15 July 1914. 'cheered things', Myers 66.

250 'young maidens', N 149. 'not nearly', L 45. 'not unintelligible', NA 9 July 1914. 'such a publication', S 162. 'someone who', N 151. 'On two', E 15 July 1914.

13. An American Called Eliot
Principal sources: HP, IP.

253 'probably incompetent', L 38. 'they had to', N 155.

254 'that refined', L 157. 'Ezra is kind', Barbara Guest, *Herself Defined*, Doubleday, 1984, 64. 'a democratic', L 48. 'a navvy', C80/503.

255 'possibly a conflict', L 46f. 'groggy old', J/M 67. 'perhaps the time', to C. F. G. Masterman, 26 June '16, Sotheby's auction catalogue, 17 Dec 1981, 140. 'What I mean', *Death of a Hero* 342.

256 'He was back', G-B 53f. 'Two days', G-B 28. 'contacts with', N 156f.

257 'the God Pan', NA 7 Jan 1915. 'a strange', L 128. 'very fluidly', N 318. 'that rather', MacL 1 Jan '56. 'told me about', Doob 128. 'something DIFFER-ENT', PH 21 Dec '56. 'Oh well', Doob 128. 'A guy', Lyndall Gordon, *Eliot's Early Years*, Oxford University Press, 1977, 66. 'absolutely insane', N 166.

258 'An American', Ellen Williams, *Harriet Monroe* (see note to p. 178 above), 123. 'I was jolly', L 40. 'Here is', L 41. 'I enclose', L 40f.

259 'I confess', D Jan 1928.

260 'I had kept', Russell 26. 'the most dreary', L 44f. '"Mr Prufrock"', L 50.

261 'that unitarian', L 114. 'Eliot has sent', P/L 8. 'I have corresponded', T. S. Eliot to EP (n.d.), Yale. 'King Bolo's', T. S. Eliot to EP, 30 Aug '22, Lilly. 'wrestling with', Stock n/b

262 'If your committee', L 64. 'I have more', WLMS ix. 'Into the restaurant', N 197f.

263 'egotistical meanderings', T. S. Eliot to EP, 22 Oct '22, Lilly. 'rather as', Russell 25. 'Yeats does', T. S. Eliot to EP, 22 Oct '22, Lilly. 'whether TSE', to 'George' Yeats, 21 Nov '57, JK. 'go to any', Russell 26f. 'I don't know', L 49. 'He and Masters', Ellen Williams, *Harriet Monroe* (see note to p. 178 above), 128. 'Eliot has thought', L 114.

264 'Thank God', L 66. 'walked into', L 86. 'I have known', O 88.

---

14. Demon Pantechnicon Driver
Principal sources: HP, IP, EP/DS.

265 'Ezra is doing', N 168. 'The clouds', CSP 142. 'I have constantly', to J. B. Yeats, 21 June 1917, JK.

266 'a form of psychology', *The Translations of Ezra Pound*, Faber and Faber, 1953, 236. 'China is fundamental', L 102. 'unquestionable', 'a tedium', note in the original edition of *Cathay* (see Appendix A). 'he represents', quoted in Peter Brooker, *A Student's Guide to the Selected Poems of Ezra Pound*, Faber and Faber 1979, 130. 'a great compiler', ib. 130f.

267 'Several half-wits', L 347. 'approved by', L 61. 'anybody who', Wai-Lim Yip, *Ezra Pound's Cathay*, Princeton University Press, 1969, 126. 'the ideo-graphs', L 61. 'art of sound', Sel. Pr. 294. 'While my hair', CSP 130f.

269 'My hair was', S 168. 'Soon after', quoted in Brooker (see note to p. 266 above) 136. 'Ezra Pound's', W. B. Yeats (ed.), *The Oxford Book of Modern Verse*, Clarendon Press, 1936, xl. 'out of various', Ezra Pound, *'Noh' or Accomplishment*, Macmillan, 1916, introductory note. 'brilliantly paraphrased', Arthur Waley, *The Poetry and Career of Li Po*, Allen & Unwin, 1950, 12.

270 'I find it', *Future*, Nov 1918. 'a fusilade', Cory 31. 'sharp and precise', S 174. 'things of', CH 108. 'the best and', CH 110. 'Ezra's new', Jean Gould, *Amy: the World of Amy Lowell and the Imagist Movement*, Dodd Mead, 1975, 177. 'the inventor', in EP's *Selected Poems*, Faber and Gwyer, 1928, xvii. 'altered the feel', George Steiner, *After Babel*, Oxford University Press, 1975, 358.

271 'Demon pantechnicon', CH 116. 'I feel', P/J 112. 'ye complete', P/J 146. 'good past', Zinnes 241. 'learned to look', *Paideuma*, vol. 2, no. 3 (winter

1973). 'You really', L 281. 'was so accustomed', G-B 46. 'I had only', Cri July 1938. 'but the adamantine', L 61. 'a study', Ernest Fenollosa, *The Chinese Written Character as a Medium for Poetry*, Stanley Nott, 1936, 7.

272 Besides being printed as a pamphlet (see note to p. 271), the Fenollosa essay appears in Pound's *Instigations*, Boni & Liveright, 1920. 'A new mode', Ezra Pound, *Polite Essays*, Faber and Faber, 1937, 51.

273 'presenting first', GK 51. 'The so-called', *Polite Essays* (see note to p. 272), 106. 'The error of', Doob 115.

274 'I would ask', Hall 137. 'his mental', Cornell 188.

---

15. Get On With Our Renaissance

275 'If a patron', L 51. 'American collectors', NA 21 Jan 1915.

276 'If you are', L 52. 'I think his prices', Zinnes 230. 'You must not corner', Zinnes 234. 'Roughly speaking', Zinnes 236f. 'I am not looking', L 111. 'designed to entrap', P/J 41. 'ancient weekly', Reid 223. 'making something', Reid 249. 'to zero', Lidderdale and Nicholson (see note to p. 209), 118. 'Ezra Pound, MESS', Reid 272.

277 'It seems to me', P/J 39. 'a sloppy sort', HP 6 Apr '17. 'I think you', P/J 145. 'No, Damn it', L 337. 'merely the attempt', P Mar 1918. 'preposterous American', Ann Thwaite, *Edmund Gosse*, Secker & Warburg, 1984, 505, 490. 'Foetid corpse', to May Sinclair, 19 March '20, UP.

278 'almost daily', Nancy Cunard, *These Were the Hours*, Southern Illinois University Press, 1969, 123. 'Miss W/', PH (n.d.). 'But for you', S 210. 'Signore Sterlina', LE 259. 'I suspect your', P/J 85. 'I will see', P/J 35. 'When you are', P/J 47. 'lead off', P/J 68. 'uncouth' etc., LR Mar 1918, Zinnes 297.

279 'far more fecund', S 258. 'Gaudier is getting', IP (n.d.). 'the uncreated', G-B 110. 'Brzeska has', HP (n.d.). 'I went out', Zinnes 291. 'His death', HP (n.d.). 'A great spirit', G-B 118. 'the gravest', G-B 136. 'For eighteen', G-B 140.

280 'Gaudier's death', O 45. 'There are few', G-B 118. 'made me feel', Ede (see note to p. 215). 'Epstein hasn't', Zinnes 237.

281 'When is our', HP (n.d.). 'It's a man's', 'hold down', Reid 204. 'a universal', Reid 248. 'too literary', Reid 253.

282 'Coburn and I', Zinnes 241f. 'funk', L 65.

283 'It was a classic', P/J 87. 'All I can', E June 1917. 'When the Taihaitian', CSP 118. 'months before', L 64f. 'My head is', P/J 44. 'CABLE QUINN', P/J 124f.

284 'First, *we should*', P March 1917.

---

16. Endless Poem

285 'I have walked', CSP 123. 'boom it', L 58. 'Byron's technique', L 90. 'Some men will', CSP 245. 'And timorous', CSP 240. ''Tis of my', CSP 238.

286 'my satires', to J. B. Yeats, 21 June '17, JK. 'for every lady', CSP 151. 'A broken', CSP 157. 'Glad you liked', HP (n.d.). 'Chalais is', CSP 152.

287 'Bewildering spring', CSP 157. 'If you like', HP (n.d.). 'at work on', S 184. 'life work', Reid 248. 'work on a', quoted in Miles Slatin, 'A History of

Pound's Cantos I–XVI, 1915–1925', *American Literature*, vol. 35, 1963–4, 159–83. 'My next', L 81. 'I have begun', P/J 102.

288 'You had six', PR. 'There once', HC 21 July '49. 'is probably', John Pettigrew in his edition of Browning's *Poems*, Yale University Press, 1981, vol. I, 1040. 'the most glorious', ib. 1041.

289ff Quotations from 'Three Cantos' are taken from the text published in *Poetry*, June, July and August 1917.

291 'an approximation', Ronald Bush, *The Genesis of Ezra Pound's Cantos*. Princeton University Press, 1976, 309. 'shouts aloud', L 274.

292 'string it out', L 110. 'After these fireworks', CH 160. 'sorry', 'I can't see ', L 115. 'very shaggy', P/J 112. '*Poetry* is serializing', P/J 121. 'I hope to God', P/J 122.

293 'except for', Reid 452. 'looking forward', Ellmann 661n. 'to the best', P/J 191. 'The sleek head', O 104. 'friendly help', N 274f. 'some American', P/J 191. 'J. J. regarded', PH 19 Sept '53, 'Is it dreadfully', P/J 232.

17. Baser Passions

294 'Anyway my', L 115. 'pulled into', P/J 64. 'These vermin', P/J 65f.

295 'looks terribly', N 155. 'the personal', quoted Gallup 17. 'twistings of', L 62f. 'Can dad', IP (n.d.). 'God buggarin', MacL 7 Jan '34.

296 'mere conversation', MacL 5 Dec '26. 'degree of', MacL '20 something Oct [1927]'. 'I have never', L 111. 'It is more', LR May 1917. 'I've got a', L 13. 'I don't love', Monroe 267. 'Why, why' L 73. 'I AM', PH 17 Nov '57. 'The curse', P/J 176. 'He had rushed', *Blasting* 275. 'Ezra's agitation', Anderson 243.

297 'superior to', *Blasting* 175. 'a rugged', N 133. 'a kinder', *Time* 54. 'your (? negro)', L 62. 'As its glory', LR Oct 1917.

298 'Unfortunately the', LR Sept 1917. 'countless letters', LR Nov 1918. 'His is almost', N 193.

299 'Virgil is', L 87. 'Perhaps one', L 89f. 'Ezra took', Bowen 50. 'no contact', N 362. 'I am down', P/J 62. 'the housekeeping', Reid 215f.

300 'Georgie's face', EP/DS 58. 'NOT one', 'flaming nuissance', Reid 307. 'the best mind', P/J 67. 'a figure', ABCR 187. 'the Fontanelle', IP 9 Apr '16.

301 'the high and', Reid 242. 'I know of', P Jan 1918. 'Yeats thinks', IP 27 Feb '16. 'dominion', HP (n.d.).

302 'very much', IP 25 May '16. 'fanatic', Reid 352. 'There is no', NA 8 Jan 1920. 'unspeakable and', J/M 27. 'largish blank', L 75. 'If more', P/J 90. 'got into a panic', L 81.

303 'Sorry stuff', CH 121. 'Winter is', CSP 116. 'Blasted blasphemy', CH 124. 'O God, O Venus', CSP 117.

304 'Erinna is', CSP 103. 'Bastidides', CSP 100. 'Christianity has', L 97f. 'no plea', E 1 Mar 1916. 'violent', S 194. 'four perfectly', S 195. 'the pretty', L 81. 'in any form', S 195.

305 'Suddenly discovering', CSP 161. 'castrato', L 83. 'any chance', S 196. 'a confused', CH 129. 'no real', CH 127. 'I want to', Reid 280. 'bitch', L 132. 'wrote it', WLMS xiii.

306   'Though Mr', [T. S. Eliot], *Ezra Pound: His Metric and Poetry*, Alfred A. Knopf, 1917, 3f. 'altogether the', L 108. 'Ezzum Pound', T. S. Eliot to EP (n.d.), Yale.

18.   Mr Atheling And Mr Dias

Principal sources: HP, IP. The 'William Atheling' music reviews and the 'B. H. Dias' art criticisms are quoted from NA.

307   'I am bubbling', L 82. 'Cuala weird', Ibbotson 12. 'scattered fragments', L 214. 'I don't like', P/J 102. 'It's all too', L 137. 'the development', Zinnes 240.
308   'Dulac is', Zinnes 239. 'low water', P/J 84. 'because I dared', P/J 89. 'All life's', P/J 82. 'dotted with', 'delighted', P/J 84. 'Joyce is', L 122f. 'sponged stalls', L 95.
309   'It is time', S 201. 'Macmillan affair', Zinnes 240. 'that stinking', Ibbotson 24. 'From that day', LE 18. 'I have absolutely', P/J 61. 'I want a', L 106f.
310   'a jolly place', Ellen Williams (see note to p. 178) 146. 'a damned attractive', Reid 187.
311   'the corpse-like', 'ought to announce', P/J 83. 'filled with pointless', LR Oct 1917. 'DAMN hard', JL (n.d.). 'Your stuff', L 143.
312   'under the dictatorship', LR Nov 1918.
313   'get me a', Reid 320. 'entertaining', L 118. 'Never till', NA 23 Aug 1917. 'Save that', NA 6 Sept 1917.
314   'a *sottisier*', Doob 91. 'the SINEWS', L 259. 'no one writer', Zinnes xxii. 'more a secondary', Bush (see note to p. 291) 166.
315   'an unending series', *Exile*, autumn 1928. 'a frightfully', Schafer 26. 'arrived as', EP/Antheil 27, 34. 'musicians on', Ezra Pound, *An Autobiographical Outline/ Written for Louis Untermeyer*, Ezra Pound Literary Property Trust, 1980.
316   'The protuberance', *Future*, 5 Nov 1918. 'I consider', C Jan 1923. 'my poems', Stock n/b
317   'her relationship', Samuel Levenson, *Maud Gonne*, Cassell, 1976, 323. 'rumours', Nancy Cardozo, *Maud Gonne*, Gollancz, 1979, 321.

19.   Obscene, As Life

318   'I am quite', P/J 105. 'The Egoist is', P/J 125. 'Pages 1–17', P/J 128f.
319   'can never have illumined', *Time* 90. 'no need', PH 12 Mar '55. 'joyous satisfaction', GK 96. 'I read a', W. B. Yeats to EP, 27 July '22, JK. 'obscene', P/J 139, 145. '*Ulysses* is', P/J 251.
320   'I suppose', P/J 129. 'Joyce's new', L 130. 'It's worth', 'Section 4', P/J 131.
321   'I am much', P/J 144.
322   'Whether we', S 217. 'a carefully', CH 142. 'dullness', CH 145. 'a sequence', CH 149. 'a highly', CH 143f. 'finding the', CH 145. 'Your piece', CH 142. 'Baedeker to', Espey 50. 'When he isn't', L 138. 'hater of', Espey 50.
323   'atmospheres', LE 324. 'want to sink', L 132. 'nearly finished', L 127. ' . . . for with', *The Translations of Ezra Pound*, Faber and Faber, 1953, 151. 'They will come', CSP 181. 'drawing of', LE 339.

20. Devirginated Young Ladies
    The text of *Homage to Sextus Propertius* is in CSP. My own Latin is not even
    up to Ezra's standard, and I am heavily indebted to J. P. Sullivan's study of
    the poem (Faber and Faber, 1965). The lists of 'persons of chaRRm' are
    quoted from PH. Other principal sources: HP, IP.

325 'Catullus, Propertius', L 87. 'If you CAN'T', L 91.
326 'the spirit', L 212. 'is colloquial', to May Sinclair, 19 Mar '20, UP.
328 'best work', L 143. 'It is too', LE 347.
329 '. . . there are three', LE 25. 'A great age', LE 232, 235.
330 'composite character', L 150. 'Sextus Propertius Soliloquizes', P/F 55.
     'infinitely valuable', L 178. 'Nobody has', L 264.
331 'seems to imagine', NA 26 Sept 1912. 'pass beyond', to Ingrid Davies, 4 Apr
     '56, HRC. 'The war', *Death of a Hero* 18f. 'a greater', Torrey 75.
332 'bewilderment' etc., CSP 199f. 'After years', CSP 181. 'have nothing', O 78.
333 'I led Eliot', to Henry Bamford Parkes, 2 Jan '33, UP. 'a dance of', O 79.
     'Raymonde Collignon's', NA 16 May 1918.
334 'non-human', NA 15 Apr 1920.
335 'to say good-bye', Bowen 48f. 'rented from', Margaret Cole, *The Life of*
     G. D. H. Cole, Macmillan, 1971, 77.
336 'I [have] had', Kavka. 'shy, untidy', Bowen 53.
337 'agitated the', J. P. Sullivan, *Ezra Pound and Sextus Propertius*, Faber and
     Faber, 1965, 5. 'to observe', L 141. 'We will now', P/J 145f. 'For some', N
     212.
338 'Ezra started', N 214. 'state views', to Henry Bamford Parkes, 2 Jan '33, UP.
     'formidable body', Cory 30. 'Must let', L 148. 'perhaps better', P/J 148.
339 W. G. Hale's attack on *Propertius* is reprinted in CH 155–7.
340 'Cat-piss', Ellen Williams (see note to p. 178) 254. 'a letter', 'Allow me',
     enclosure with letter to May Sinclair, 19 Mar '20, UP.
341 'As a Prof.', L 149f. 'unanswerable', Sullivan (see note to p. 337) 5. 'I did not',
     L 231.
342 'perfectly easy', L 178. 'largely a hoax', LE 239f.
343 'blurred', to May Sinclair, 19 Mar '20, UP. 'I am unable', L 230f. 'I didn't',
     James Laughlin to EP, 11 May '35, JL.
344 'major blunders', CH 161. 'veritable snowstorm', Sullivan (see note to p. 337)
     12. 'an insult', Sullivan (see note to p. 337) viii. 'Be assured', to May Sinclair,
     19 Mar '20, UP.

21. Try This On Your Piano
    The drafts of the Eliot poems with Ezra's corrections are in the Berg
    Collection of the New York Public Library.

345 'as you doubtless', Ellen Williams (see note to p. 178), 258. 'stasis or', P/J
     156. 'Here is a', HP (n.d.). 'imbecilities', to W. B. Yeats, 19 June '24, JK.
     'brute stupidity', NA 18 Dec 1919.
346 'and thus free', to W. B. Yeats, 19 June '24, JK. 'Have been', HP 20 May '19.
     'renew my', P/J 156. 'industriously', Philip Grover (ed.), *Ezra Pound: The*

London Years: 1908–1920, AMS Press, 1978. 'perhaps twenty', 'One *can*', P/J 158. 'A man', NA 21 Aug 1919.

348   'nineteenth century', NA 7 Aug 1919.
349   'I'. has', Grover (see note to p. 346) 'dilutation', Cri July 1932. 'perfectly plain', L 89. 'hard substance', E 285. 'studied Gautier's', Ackroyd/TSE 69.
351   'a crime against', Reid 436.
352   'organ of importance', WLMS xix.

---

22.   Douglas The Real Mind
I would have found it hard to understand Social Credit without the chapter on C. H. Douglas in Hugh Gaitskell's *Four Monetary Heretics*, originally published in 1933 and reissued in 1969 by Lyn Christie of Auckland, New Zealand. My information about American anti-Semitism comes from William M. Chace, *The Political Identities of Ezra Pound and T. S. Eliot*, Stanford University Press, 1973, and from Michael N. Dobkowski, *The Tarnished Dream: the Basis of American Anti-Semitism*, Greenwood Press, 1979.

353   'fired in', L 151. 'a fine', *Athenaeum*, 30 Apr 1920. 'save a general', P/J 174. 'One simply', L 151.
354   'the patchwork', CH 173. 'granite wreaths', L 151. 'You know', CH 182. 'too too', S 228.
355   'bring up', NA 27 Nov 1919. 'inclined to', L 159. 'I don't', *Southern Review*, Jan 1968. 'In the cantos', L 181.
356   'squat and', Selver 28. 'absurd', John Carswell, *Lives and Letters*, Faber and Faber, 1978, 147.
357   'the Einstein', Selver 76. 'very difficult', Gaitskell (see remarks at head of notes to this chapter) 25f. 'great defect', to Peter Whigham (n.d.), Berg. 'managed a', HP 22 Feb '20. 'pseudorasts', Putnam 153.
358   'a fake', NEW 23 Feb 1933. 'out of threatened', C. H. Douglas, *Economic Democracy*, Cecil Palmer, 1920, 153f. 'the nation's', statement dated 9 Mar '34, JL. 'no valid', J. M. Keynes, *The General Theory of Employment*, Macmillan, 1960, 370f. 'not inflationist', *GK's Weekly*, 21 Feb 1932.
359   'absence of', L 339. 'Major C. H.', NA 4 Mar 1920. 'Positions of', Douglas (see note to p. 358) 43f. 'the Jew', NA 6 Nov 1919. 'My last', NA 13 Nov 1919.
360   'Hooked-nose', Dobkowski (see remarks at head of notes to this chapter) 84. 'I don't believe', Reid 597.
361   'rich, stockbroking', EP/DS 261. 'a gleam', James Laughlin, in conversation Mar 1985. 'I am racially', NA 8 Jan 1920. 'Hueffer is', Stock n/b. 'Jews!!!!', HP 1 Nov '27. 'My recollections', HP 11 May '21. 'I will say', AB 17 Dec '21.
362   'There was', O 55.

---

23.   Atmospheres, Nuances
Hugh Selwyn Mauberley is in CSP. I am much indebted to J. J. Espey (see Appendix A).

363   'second-rate', Reid 434. 'European celebrities', L 346. 'Am sending', HP (n.d.).

364 'needlessly obscure', CH 194. 'Yeats appears', HP (n.d.). 'much the', Sel. Poems 1928 xv. 'In *Mauberley*', F. R. Leavis, *New Bearings in English Poetry*, Penguin, 1963, 115. 'The superb', CH 245. 'Propertius/ is', to Henry Bamford Parkes, 19 Jan '33, UP. 'advance', P/F 36. The Yeats letter quoted in the footnote, JK.

365 'Of course', L 180.

367 'partly to oblige', Mizener 305. 'These things', HP 3 Feb '21. 'a lonely', Bowen 63. 'Mr Pound', P/F 38. 'because he facially', Mizener 310.

368 'distinctly a', note in *Personae*, Boni & Liveright, 1926.

370 'definite attempt', PR. 'a study in', L 180. 'atmospheres', LE 324. 'In verse', P/F 35. 'Syncopation from', L 181.

371 'There aren't', L 254.

---

24. Shifting To Paris
     Principal source: P/J 168ff.

372 'one has so', *Indiscretions* 5, 3.

373 'the arrival', C76/456.

374 'Left Italy', AB 19 June '20. 'reckon the', L 153. 'illusion', L 154.

375 'It is difficult', *Athenaeum*, 23 Apr 1920. 'killing off', Reid 437. 'grateful', Zinnes 245. 'the crafty', *Blasting* 293.

376 'There is no', L 158. 'ΗΛΛvud', Reid 437.

377 The Pound/Lewis/Hecht interview, *Agenda*, autumn–winter 1969–70. 'It seems', P/F 49. 'Only question', Reid 437.

378 'a descent', Reid 437. 'Scheduled', IP 20 Dec '20. 'Think it', HP 27 Dec '20. 'perhaps for', CH 199. 'I rather', L 165. 'open any', AB 21 Dec '21. 'difficult to', CH 199f. 'the decay', S 235f. 'I daily', P/F 58.

379 'obliged to', Beach 26. 'I have an', to T. S. Eliot, 14 Mar '22, Lilly. 'the history of', carbon enclosed with same letter.

Part Three   1921–45   'E.P.'

1. 'I Have Made An Opera'.
    Principal sources: HP, IP, AB. Various drafts of the score of *Le Testament de Villon* are at Yale. The opera has been recorded on Philips 9500 927, and I was fortunate in seeing it performed at the 1985 Cambridge Poetry Festival.

384 'the unrealities' etc., P/F 55. 'the BEST', Doob 128. 'When one', S 240. 'go to hell', Reid 491.

385 'a very good', N 256. 'rather on', Reid 492. 'Am taking', P/L 128. 'Some of the best', L 168. 'Brancusi (the beautiful', P/F 61.

386 'acquired pieces', N 248. 'I couldn't', EP/DS 248.

387 'Pound writing', W/A 188. 'the puzzling', Patmore 117, 110.

389 'The HOLE', L 245. 'pounded out', Kavka.

390 'an aid', Rattray. 'The conception', N 154.

391 'Rhythm is', *The Translations of Ezra Pound*, Faber and Faber 1953, 23f. 'greek model', S 255.

392   'I have made', S 255. 'Was it you', S 241. 'Ezra learning', *Moveable Feast* 93.

---

2.   Great Clot Of Genital Fluid

Ezra's essay on sexuality appears as the Translator's Postscript to Remy de Gourmont, *The Natural Philosophy of Love*, Boni & Liveright 1922.

393   'Have been', AB 21 June '21, '25 pages', AB 16 June '21.
394   'every kind', Reid 252. 'Fluids don't', MS by James Laughlin (JL).
395   'the flower', J/M 100. 'unmitigated shit', Torrey 8. 'the vienese', PH 6 Nov '57. Quotations from Eliot on the subject of Freud were kindly supplied by Lyndall Gordon. 'O student', T. S. Eliot to EP, 9 July '22, Lilly. 'Good fucking', ib. 19 July '22, Lilly. 'at all hours', N 259.
396   'without finding', Torrey 112. 'two charrming', PH 26 Mar '57. 'by the time', Noel Stock to the author, 13 July '84. 'immoral', GK 186. 'desperately in', Bride Scratton to EP, 14 Jan '28, Yale. 'With best', ib. 14 Nov '50, Lilly. 'become fairly', Anderson 244.
397   'Where he had', Richard Aldington, *Soft Answers*, Chatto & Windus, 1932, 155f. 'very beautiful', *Moveable Feast* 107.

---

3.   70 *bis*

398   'the erectness', W/A 225f. 'the large', Anderson 243, 'the ladies', Beach 115.
399   'hardy', W/A 229. 'The Dadaists', D Dec 1920. 'provisionally pro', Putnam 154. 'The mere', *Contemporary Poetry & Prose*, Nov 1936. 'like one', N 245. 'your young', L 168. 'It was one', Anderson 246.
400   'Recollection', PH 26 Mar '57. 'start contest', PH 6 Jan '58. 'liked him', N 245. 'Gertie Stein', MacL 13 Feb '27. 'Ezra fell', N 246.
401   'sprawled', W/A 254. 'In conversation', 'I am sorry', N 246. 'an old tub', Fitch 128. 'The Jews', *Exile*, autumn 1928. 'like leaves', P/F 58. 'heard more', to Grandmother Pound, in letters to his parents, Yale. 'The first', Kavka. 'everyman's', A 69.
402   'Ezra was', N 247. 'Please let', F. W. Dupee and George Stade (eds.), *Selected Letters of E. E. Cummings*, Harcourt Brace, 1969, 254. 'bright inimitable', JL 6 Jan '36. 'less in', L 166. 'the intelligent', P/F 58. 'The courtyard', Bowen 88.
403   'We are up', HP 2 Dec '21. 'being on', Bowen 142. 'The rain', AB 29 Oct '22. 'was as poor', *Moveable Feast* 107. 'after 9', HP 2 Dec '21. 'over an alcohol', W/A 226. 'actually . . . cooked', N 259. 'Am having', L 179. 'cleaning, building', HP 2 Dec '21. 'It was enormous', Ford *IWN* 174f.
404   'wondered why', Fitch 59f. 'hideously real', 'a ninth', Ellmann 507. 'great hullabaloo', S 259.

---

4.   Caro Lapino

Many of Eliot's letters to Ezra, which form the basis of this chapter, together with carbons of some of Ezra's to Eliot, Eliot's letters to Dorothy Pound, and Vivien Eliot's letters to Ezra, are in the Lilly Library (see Appendix A); the remainder of the Pound–Eliot correspondence that I was able to see is at Yale. I am especially grateful to Mrs Valerie Eliot for permission to quote from the Eliot letters. WLMS reproduces all Ezra's annotations to *The Waste Land* in manuscript.

405 'Caro mio', L 169. 'I placed', N 250.
406 'superfluities', L 169.
407 'These are the poems', L 170. 'My only', WLMS xxiv. 'the very disappointing', Nicholas Joost, *Scofield Thayer*, Southern Illinois University Press, 1964, 111.
409 'We are saving', AB 18 Mar '22. 'AFTER Eliot', L 173.
410 'Must restart', L 173n. 'Certainly can't', L 176.
411 'Auw shucks!', L 183.
412 'a dismal', S 256n.
413 'Eliot's new', HP 30 Oct '22. 'so heavily', L 187. 'dead and', S 286. 'Criterion has', Greenbaum 111. 'KIRYpes', L 272. 'wasted the', GK 177. 'Not that his', L 240. 'arrived at', Sel. Pr. 53. 'in any sense', Ezra Pound (ed.), *Active Anthology*, Faber and Faber 1933, 10. 'a medium', *Hound & Horn*, Oct–Dec 1930.
414 'Possum's rep', L 202. 'Why do you', O 113.
415 'gorbloody', MacL 8 Jan '34.
416 'wished at that', Donald Gallup, *T. S. Eliot and Ezra Pound: Collaborators in Letters*, H. W. Wenning, 1970, 24. 'Eliot's *Waste Land*', L 180. 'About enough', WLMS xxii. 'It wiped', W/A 174.

---

5. Wise Guy

417 'There is a', AB 17 Feb '22. 'a decent', AB 9 March '22. 'get 'em out', 'I dare say', P/F 67. 'finished the', AB 17 Feb '22.
418 'Having the crust', L 180. 'various materials' etc., Slatin (see note to p. 287) 190. 'a failure', frontispiece caption in GK. '"the wise guy"', ABCR 44. 'No one has', GK 194.
419 'I object', T. S. Eliot to EP (n.d.), Lilly. 'a monumental', GK 159. 'there could be', GK 301.
420 'bhloomin historic', Slatin (see note to p. 287) 194. 'backbone moral', Brooker (see note to p. 266) 157. 'I'm doing', HP 21 June '23. 'very refreshing', HP (n.d.). 'Christianchurchism', HP 21 June '23.
421 'unprintable', AB 29 June '22. 'a portrait', L 191. 'LONDON', L 139. '*other people*', Brooker (see note to p. 266) 262. 'The Cantoes', T. S. Eliot to EP, 21 Sept '33, Yale. 'I dont see', T. S. Eliot to EP 'Michaelmas 1933', Yale.
422 'You have had', L 210. 'revised earlier', HP 14 Aug '23. 'little aid', CH 217. 'The form', CH 182.
423 'half-time', L 189. 'Am plugging', Slatin (see note to p. 287) 190.

---

6. Fiddle Music

424 'kinder . . .' *Moveable Feast* 108. 'He's teaching', Carlos Baker, *Ernest Hemingway*, Collins 1969, 116. 'A splendidly', S 248.
425 'Ezra had not', *Moveable Feast* 108. 'I've been', Hem. Letters 62. 'Pound . . . has', Hem. Letters 65. 'the state of', *Indiscretions* 51. 'the sensitivity', to Arnold Gingrich, 28 Aug '34. UP.

426 'how to write', S 311. 'My income', IP 19 Jan '23. 'our combined', IP 30 Aug
    '23. 'enervation', D Nov 1922. 'in her dotage', *Exile*, autumn 1928. 'the latest',
    D Jan 1923. 'of less', S 256n. 'hard to', Cory 31.

427 'The magic', Ibbotson 34. 'The air', Adrian Stokes, *Inside Out*, Faber and
    Faber, 1947, 30–2. 'Houses mirrored', W. B. Yeats, *A Packet for Ezra Pound*,
    Cuala Press, 1929, 1.

428 'On the broad', W. B. Yeats, *A Packet for Ezra Pound*, Cuala Press, 1929, 1.
    'seems out', Bottome 240. 'As I was', Baker (see note to p. 424) 137. 'Can I',
    Hem. Letters 76. 'the governing', HP 25 Apr '25. 'The sea', Hem. Letters 79.

429 'how and why', Hem. Letters 653f. 'Firenze the', GK 113. 'proper Dante-
    scan', L 200. 'three months', Peter D'Epiro, *A Touch of Rhetoric: Ezra
    Pound's Malatesta Cantos*, University of Michigan Research Press, 1983, 57.
    'The *Dial*', L 186. 'serious financially', P/F 72. 'the last link', L 186. 'Dont for
    Gawds', HP (n.d.).

430 'I was engaged', Ford *IWN* 267. 'to which', Zinnes 294. 'the utmost', Bernard
    J. Poli, *Ford Madox Ford and the Transatlantic Review*, Syracuse University
    Press, 1967, 27. 'if there was', S 283. 'clearing off', Terrell/Bunting 39. 'a
    dark', Terrell/Bunting 40. Bunting's other reminiscences, Terrell/Bunting
    39–42.

431 'one of Ezra's', N 300. 'The young Antheil', AB 23 Aug '23. 'smashed nose',
    Beach 24. 'the mountainous', Antheil 29f. 'a small', Antheil 11. 'the heaviest',
    Ford *IWN* 261. 'a Mephistophelian', Antheil 95.

432 'unusually kind', 'occasionally amused', 'Ezra was', Antheil 96. 'increasingly
    aware', EP/Antheil 20. 'A SOUND', EP/Antheil 3f. 'the whole question',
    GK 73.

433 'From the first', Antheil 98. '*several* violin', Antheil 99. 'I saw Ezra', AO. 'the
    very chair', Schafer 343. 'Don't know', Schafer 345. 'He didn't', AO.

434 'Irish adrenal', Antheil 99. 'I did not', *Dis* 154. 'excellent technique', Schafer
    503. 'well known', Antheil 99. 'fall on', AO. 'I hadn't', AO. 'a new violin',
    Schafer 345. 'great empty', Antheil 100. 'Ezra seemed', Antheil 107.

435 'caused the audience', Schafer 248. 'dug up', Schafer 250. 'After all', AB 8 July
    '24. 'was obviously', N 271. 'Dear Son', Homer Pound to EP, 22 July '24,
    Lilly.

436 'Re opera', AB 21 Feb '24. 'edited 1923', 'I doubt', MS score at Yale. 'so that
    nothing', R. Murray Schafer, 'Ezra Pound and Music', *Canadian Music
    Journal*, vol. 5, no. 4 (summer 1961). 'I DO NOT', to W. B. Yeats, 19 June
    '24, JK. 'propensities', L 187. 'persuaded Mr George', Ford *IWN* 260f.

7. Ez He Lives On The Roof
Principal sources: HP, IP.

437 'cooled down', Kavka.

438 'She fish', to Olga Rudge, 10 May '25 (D. D. Paige carbon, Yale). 'He liked',
    Dis 117. 'I wanted', Olga Rudge, in conversation Apr 1985. 'maelstrom', S
    259. 'We were hefty', P/L 138f.

439 'Yes, ciao', to Olga Rudge, 7 May '25 (D. D. Paige Carbon, Yale). 'the eel/',
    Ibbotson 67. 'By the time', Cory 31. 'Ezra Pound', unidentified newspaper

interview *c.* 1930, transcribed by Cyril Clemens, in Pound MSS, Lilly. 'The, or *a*', AB 11 July '25. 'Marconi's', to Arnold Gingrich, 2 Aug '34, UP.

440   'I had never', Patmore 109. 'Sometimes about', Yeats, *A Packet* (see note to p. 427), 4f.

441   'cucku', Winnick 198, 252. 'without enough', P/F 93. 'my verse', L 213. 'Sorry, I', P/J 226.

442   'Nothing short', L 202. 'that diarrhoea', L 392. 'They belong', P/J 230. 'makes brilliant', P/J 229, 'one evening', Deirdre Bair, *Samuel Beckett*, Jonathan Cape, 1978, 85. 'in that he', Putnam 153. 'the line', P/J 250. 'a bawdy', P/J 256.

443   'a VERY', Doob 141. 'Joyce inflation', P/J 257. 'weakness of', PH 4 Nov '57. 'The more', P/J 234. 'In *Dubliners*', P/J 249. 'editorial function', L 234. 'Eliot's castrated', LE 18.

444   'appropriate to', T. S. Eliot to EP, 1 Dec '51, Lilly.

445   'not merely', Cri Apr 1934.

446   'eccentric, surprising', Conrad Baxter Jordan, *New York Times*, 24 Aug 1985. 'on your bed', James Laughlin, 'Collage for EP' (MS). 'Ezra is', DP to Agnes Bedford, 1 May '40, Lilly.

447   'was very fast', James Laughlin, in conversation Mar 1985. 'a good three-cornered', J/M 29. 'Well, it's all', J/M 31. 'It was an', Bacigalupo 7.

---

8.   Human Complications
Principal sources: HP, IP, AB.

449   'nurse' etc., AO. '*Her* affairs', Heymann 56. 'The impression', Richard Aldington, *Soft Answers*, Chatto & Windus, 1932, 160.

450   'Me & my', T. S. Eliot to EP, 24 Nov and 8 Dec '25, Yale. 'Ezra said', AO.

451   'hanging head', Beach 124. 'Dogs!', P/F 81. 'Ezra Pound answers', *Exile*, autumn 1927. 'possibilities', Schafer 315.

452   'a scandal', W/A 188. 'not quite', Schafer 312. 'one of the best', S 297. 'in the electrician's', 'the variety', GK 366. 'I hear that', N 283.

453   'the taxi', Hem. Letters 742. ' . . .Omar', photostat, Lilly.

455   'the main', T. S. Eliot to EP (n.d.), Yale. 'gone away', Hem. Letters 742. 'Omar-i-bin', Basil Bunting to DP, 14 Sept '32, Lilly. 'Fitzgerald's', L 180. 'Just note', N 284. 'Was it possible', *Soft Answers* (see note to p. 449), 176. 'I divine', N 283.

456   'He jolly', Mary Moore interviewed by Carl Gatter, UP. 'totally indifferent', Omar Pound, in conversation Mar 1985. 'furtively', Duncan 184.

---

9.   Giving 'Em The Medicine

457   'a name', 'Muss prefers', L 208. 'played well', *Sunday Times*, 20 Oct 1985. 'heavy features', Bowen 143. British writers' opinions of Mussolini, Alastair Hamilton, *The Appeal of Fascism*, Anthony Blond, 1971, 257–9.

458   'I personally', L 205. 'with a good', S 265. 'Fascio and', *Exile*, spring 1927, autumn 1928. 'a mess', Sel. Pr. 216. '*Exile* was', L 230.

459   'drear horror', *Exile*, spring 1928. 'the State of Pound', L 219. 'faddle of

passports', *Exile*, spring 1928. 'the lasting', MacL 5 Dec '26. 'invade the', P Dec 1927.

460   'Wot's use', L 214. 'a vain', NEW 6 Oct 1932. 'all his obvious', L 256. 'a particularly', NEW 6 Oct 1932. 'a toady', NEW 23 Feb 1933. 'Butlerism', GK 169. 'You will go', to Nicholas Murray Butler, 27 July '34, Columbia. 'by ref.', *Exile*, autumn 1928. 'wd. not interest', L 212.

461   'The law of', *Ta Hio* 7. The French text is quoted from J. G. Pauthier & G. Brunet (trans.). *Les Livres Sacrés de Toutes les Religions Sauf le Bible*, Paris 1858, vol. I, 155. 'Renouvelle', ib. 156. 'Renovate', *Ta Hio* 12. 'a reaction', Kavka. 'You read a', Zapponi 43. 'penetrating' etc., *Ta Hio* 8f.

462   'should have worn', S 288. 'a sort of', *Time* 54. 'serviceable', *Hound & Horn*, Oct–Dec 1930. 'My dear', Yeats, *A Packet* (see note to p. 427) 33. 'That remark', O 51. 'dear Wyndham's', AB 22 Jan '28. 'the only major', P/J 240. 'very very', Reid 419.

463   'I see', N 300. 'pester', O 114. 'Ezra . . . constantly', Wade 748. 'a great deal', AB 1 Dec '29. 'a monumental', Gallup 153. 'short of cash', N 309. 'care and', CH 273. 'that unbelievable', quoted in Massimo Bacigalupo, *The Forméd Trace*, Columbia University Press, 1980, 84. 'a Bloomsbury', Heymann 142. 'rules out', to the Professor of Romance Languages, University of Pennsylvania, 25 Nov '31, UP. 'an enquiry', HP 22 May '20.

10.   How To Read

465   'How do you', Aldington 104f. 'It is surely', J T–C 19 Sept 1929. 'Wyncote is', J T–C 6 March 1930.

466   'Any attempt', Chute. 'hardly affected', Bacigalupo 7. 'I can't wring', Doob 400. 'that T.C.P.', Sel. Pr. 295. 'two emotions', *Dis* 118.

467   'kill her', *Dis* 20. 'A *Grossvater*', *Dis* 75, 20. 'How To Read' is reprinted in LE.

468   'a little masterpiece', 'Eliot's Five', Winnick 258. 'full list', HP 2 Sept '27.

469   'my conclusions', *Exile*, autumn 1928. 'hap hazard', EP to LU 17. 'an encyclopaedia', Ibbotson 81. 'I cannot', *Agenda* 202f. 'One may quarrel', F. R. Leavis, *How to Teach Reading*, Minority Press, 1932, 1, 5, 39, 49. 'What is Leavis?' L 240. 'looked at', Huntington Cairns interview with EP, 10 Jan '46, LC. 'quite awake', AB 9 Nov '36.

470   'swindle', S 287. 'He is sunk', S 284. 'It began', Sel. Pr. 297. 'without which', GK 352. 'broken', Doob 399.

471   'the tutorial', NEW 3 Sept '36. 'the tangle', GK 57f. 'its creator', S 289. 'stumbled on', O 103. 'no one with', N 322f. 'If I wish', Sel. Pr. 301.

11.   ABCD And Then JKLM
Principal source: *Dis*.

474   'devoted', N 304.

475   'Nancy Cunard's', O 112. 'the intrinsic', CH 266f. 'get all the', L 293. 'Keep what is', *Decision*, Sept 1941.

476   'For Christ's', Winnick 263. 'I wasn't', MacL 27 Sept '33.

477   'I mean release', T. S. Eliot to EP, 16 Jan '34, Yale. 'some scene', Yeats, *A*

Packet (see note to p. 427) 2. 'there is a structure', W. B. Yeats to 'George' Yeats (n.d.), JK. 'CONFOUND uncle', Ibbotson 35. 'He has scribbled', Yeats, *A Packet* (see note to p. 427) 4. 'Your "Cantos"', W. B. Yeats, to EP, 23 Sept '28, JK. 'subject and', L 210.

478 'A. A. Live man', L 210. 'first 2/7ths', to James T. Farrell, 3 Feb '32, UP. 'rhythmic balance', CH 249–52. 'Fitts is', Greenbaum 118. 'a kind of', CH 256–8. 'substituted', CH 255. 'discipline' etc., CH 262f. 'the lost', Edith Sitwell, *Aspects of Modern Poetry*, Duckworth, 1934, 181. 'compromise by', 'WHAT audience', CH 268.

479 'It doesn't', *Dis* 156. 'Waal, perhaps', Cunard (see note to p. 278) 130.

---

12. The Ink Is Mostly Green

480 'what the younger', Torrey 124. 'Poor devil', Winnick 236. 'decade or so', GK 49. 'One of the pleasures', ABCR 26.

481 'Mr Pound should', CH 264. 'You young', L 240. 'the father', CH 294. 'the only intelligent', N 306. 'DON'T work', MacL 27 Jan '27. 'a rather fuzzy', T.S. Eliot to EP, 7 Apr '32, Yale. 'not simple', JL (n.d.). 'this obsessing', Basil Bunting to DP (n.d.), Lilly.

482 'nobody *can*', Basil Bunting to DP, 10 Dec '46, Lilly. 'The broken', *Exile*, spring 1928. 'His verse', T. S. Eliot to EP, 9 Dec '29, Yale. 'As to Z//', JL (n.d.). 'Zuk. understands', to Henry Bamford Parkes, 2 Jan '33, UP. 'an occasional', N 306f. 'when it appeared', Fitzgerald.

483 'Tilius delectus', N 399. 'the master', N 318. 'I personally', L 232. 'This Spender', JL 27 Oct '33. 'the Ezra', Wade 833. 'probably the source', W. B. Yeats (ed.), *The Oxford Book of Modern Verse*, Clarendon Press, 1936, xxvi. 'very few', quoted in *Ezra Pound at Seventy*, New Directions, 1955.

484 'both the communist', Putnam 155. 'too hog', *Front*, Feb 1931. 'more alive', to Arnold Gingrich, 30 Oct '34, UP. 'I will arise', T. S. Eliot to EP, 25 Jan '34, Yale. 'a long', Putnam 89f. 'he had quite', Putnam 151.

485 'I don't see', Greenbaum 110. 'Stinkum', Greenbaum 121. 'in spite', Greenbaum 104. 'Half a loaf', CSP 257.

486 'saluted as', P/F 111. 'a language', Sel. Pr. 305. 'Dear friends', *Helix* 119. 'claims to represent', P/F 115. 'because Ezra', S 304.

487 'Thanks for', P/F 118. 'canter', to Henry Swabey (n.d.), copy in Peter Whigham papers in Berg. 'CIVILISATION WAS', Sel. Pr. 117. 'Right Honourable', T. S. Eliot to EP, 1 Jan '31, Yale. '*longueurs*', N 354. 'conviction that', Winnick 315. 'this is', T. S. Eliot to EP, 8 Oct '34, Yale.

---

13. Me and Muss/

Principal sources: *ABC of Economics* (the text is reprinted in Sel. Pr.); J/M (there is a 1970 reprint by Liveright). The fullest account of Ezra's contacts with Mussolini's office is in Zapponi. Further correspondence between him and Il Duce's departmental officials may be found in Heymann, and carbons of some of his letters to Mussolini are at Yale.

489 'Don't knock', L 239. 'had amiable', N 309f. 'got things', undated fragment, Lilly.

490   'I. Some details', Zapponi 48. 'the swiftness', GK 105. '*divertente*', C41/202.

491   '*Perchè vuol*', GK 105. 'the political', *British–Italian Bulletin*, 4 Apr 1936. 'the town band', Bacigalupo 68. 'Fascism seemed', Bacigalupo 7.

492   'I never was', *Helix* 131. 'he did not', *New Times* (Melbourne), 16 Aug 1955. 'once before', to Olivia Agresti, 2 Mar '54, Berg. 'not dazzled', to Boris de Rachewiltz, 27 Dec '55, Berg. 'a critic', to Victor Ferkiss (n.d.), Lilly. 'As a PERSON', to Arnold Gingrich, 28 Aug '34, UP. 'the only thing', Arthur Moore to T. S. Eliot, 14 Jan '48, Lilly. 'There is no use', to James T. Farrell, 23 Feb '34, UP. 'The Boss', JL 15 Mar '34.

493   'Having been', MacL 9 Jan '34. 'getting ideas', S 397. 'isn't as good', to Arnold Gingrich, 5 Aug '34, UP.

494   'He has taken', W/L 182. 'I asked', 'as if', N 354.

497   'The ABC', MacL 8 Jan '34. 'Pound is really', Winnick 257. 'all wet', S 310–12.

498   'Respected Remus', T. S. Eliot to EP, 8 Nov '33, Yale. 'Britons . . . dont', 12 Jan '34, Yale. 'seller', P/F 125. 'without the full', NEW 29 Mar 1934.

500   'Call me', N 333. 'clearly demonstrate', Heymann 317. 'I will not', P/J 254.

---

14.   Rabbit So Bad

501   'the expression', Myers 189. 'it is conceivable', Chace (see note to Part Two, chapter 22) 144, 146. 'the movement', ib. 166. 'the Reverend', C46/231. 'In virtue', T. S. Eliot to EP, 12 Jan '34, Yale.

502   'constantly ALIVE', Ibbotson 45. 'an irrelevance', NEW 8 Mar 1934. 'scheme of', Ackroyd/TSE 220. 'in sympathy', NEW 3 May 1934. 'It is amusing', Sel. Pr. 291. 'His fragments', *Townsman*, Oct 1938. 'Waal, I heered', JL 6 Jan '36. 'Waal I dont', AB 16 Apr '39. 'We mowed', O 111. 'Possum . . .', JL (n.d.). 'limitation', NEW 9 Feb 1933.

503   'People too', L 253. 'Joyce was', Hem. Letters 550. 'I asked him', W. B. Yeats, preface to *The King of the Great Clock Tower*, Cuala Press, 1934. 'Nobody language', *Eminent Domain* 81. 'that I may', Wade 827. 'So difficult,' L 326.

504   'I tried', PR. 'dead', *Eminent Domain* 82. 'a single', *Letters on Poetry from W.B. Yeats to Dorothy Wellesley*, Oxford University Press, 1964, 23. 'Dear W.B.Y./', to W. B. Yeats, 20 Oct '35, JK. 'There is only', W. B. Yeats to EP, 12 Nov '35, JK.

505   'to chloriform', *Helix* 104. 'quite good', 'George' Yeats to EP (n.d.), JK. ''Neath Ben', *Eminent Domain* 82. 'journalism that', J/M 9. 'sabotage and', L 263. 'into a real', L 266. 'the putrid', *Active Anthology* (see note to p. 413), 22f.

506   'I dont mind', T. S. Eliot to EP, 11 Oct '34, Yale. 'I can't remember', J/M 50. 'The poet's', L 277. 'If the terminology', GK 16f. 'the tone', Fitzgerald. 'fits of', AB 30 Dec '25. 'God I beat', JL 3 Dec '35. 'I seem', AB 14 Sept '33. 'It was not possible', Bacigalupo 68.

507   'There is haste', O 97. 'a diagnosis', *Hound & Horn*, Oct–Dec 1930. 'a vast assortment', 'Damn it', Greenbaum 115. 'Mr Pound's', Greenbaum 122. 'There are more', L 262. 'in that beautiful', N 310. 'quieter in', Fitzgerald. 'Don't work', MacL (n.d.).

508 'It won't wash', to Felix Schelling, 11 Nov '33, UP. 'the rattle', T. S. Eliot to EP, 22 Feb '34, Yale. 'God damn', MacL, 3 Oct '33. 'Your undated', T. S. Eliot to EP, 7 Aug '34, Lilly. 'Owing to', T. S. Eliot to EP, 5 Apr '33, Yale. 'I wonder', T. S. Eliot to DP, 7 Aug '34, Lilly. 'The Economic', MacL 9 Jan '34. 'Am running', JL 20 Nov '34.

15. Casa 60

509 'into cheap', MacL 27 Sept '33. 'the difference', Doob 166.
510 'economics are', L 247. 'Skip anything', L 250. 'solid material', CH 296. 'Great literature', ABCR 28.
511 'Rabbit from', S 342. 'You write', Duncan 160.
512 'is Platonism', LE 159. 'finds Guido', T. S. Eliot, *After Strange Gods*, Faber and Faber, 1934, 42. 'your religion', W. B. Yeats to EP (n.d.), JK.
513 'a whole body', ABCR 104, 141. 'man after man', GK 44, 145. 'The mysteries are', L 327. 'The minute you', L 328f. 'Some sort', GK 45.
514 'I never', AO. 'We climbed', *Dis* 115. 'She warned', Bowen 145. 'Mrs B's', J/M 25.
515 'In twenty', J/M 25. 'awfully good', AO. 'always working', Massimo Bacigalupo to the author, 19 Oct '84. 'The house', *Dis* 115. 'Her home', Bowen 145f.
516 '"MIA"', *Dis* 117. 'used to spend', Duncan 184.
517 'happy enough', Cory 31.

16. Ezuversity
Principal source: the Ezra Pound–James Laughlin correspondence (JL), kindly shown to me by Mr Laughlin.

518 'under the auspices', Schafer 332. 'The charge', *Delphian Quarterly*, Jan 1936. 'came to', AO.
519 'sat thru', P/F 133. 'the Town Hall', Schafer 350f. 'Olga Rudge's', Schafer 369. 'We have not', GK 252. 'Münch plays', to Ronald Duncan, 13 Sept '38, Columbia. 'social suppleness', Ibbotson 47. 'rare and unforgettable', Chute. 'a great deal', ABCR 24.
520 'I am sorry', Ibbotson 73f. 'the enormous "continent"', Schafer 184. 'I want all', to Olga Rudge (n.d.), D. D. Paige carbon, Yale. 'three hundred', *Musical Times*, Dec 1938. 'copying out', Stock n/b. 'desk magnifying', Ibbotson 82.
521 'Shd/ like', AB 6 July '38. 'Have just', AB 19 Aug '38. 'study-workshop', Schafer 384. 'Vivaldi moves', GK 164. 'ole pop', Doob 8. 'too much musical', Ibbotson 40. 'a decent', Ibbotson 81. 'the bourgeoisie', Schafer 356.
522 'at a salary', T. S. Eliot to EP, 25 Jan '34, Yale. 'a whole-time', S 337. 'factual atoms', GK 98. 'is the son-', S 325. 'howled in', GK 54. 'a list', L 267. 'Time Lag', to Roy F. Nichols, 18 June '35, UP. 'With best wishes', N 324.
523 'still a more', Ezra Pound, *Make It New*, Faber and Faber, 1934, 15. 'push me', S 321. 'If Frankie', MacL (n.d.). 'Lest you forget', N 324. 'Are you in', L 276.
524 'goes out of', Silvio Gesell, *The Natural Economic Order*, Neo-Verlag, Berlin-Frohnau, 1929, 213 (I am especially grateful to James Laughlin for

showing me his copy of this rare book.) 'an anti-Marxian', Keynes (see note to p. 358) 357, 373. 'a sane mode', typescript *c.* 1951, Lilly. 'If Douglas', BUQ Apr–July 1937.

525   'dropped soc/', Note in misc. papers (*c.* 1950), Lilly. 'the sort of', Doob 97. 'worthless', N 326. 'a rude postcard', Duncan 131. 'had the sense', L 291. 'Duncan hath', L 290. 'Ezra taught', Duncan 158. 'some shy', *Dis* 100.

526   'ecqn/ conscious', N 326. 'Ezra had', N 327. 'altogether happy', T. S. Eliot to EP, 18 June '34, Yale. 'education by', Bair (see note to p. 442) 183.

527   'Waal, I been' JL (n.d.). 'How his dirty', *Dis* 82. 'It is time', S 358. 'male 100%', P/L 214. 'The tallest', *Dis* 79, 81. 'VISIBILITY', S 323. 'simply could not', *Paris Review*, 89 (1983).

528   'boring Freshman', in conversation, Mar 1983. 'And you accepted', *Paris Review*, 89 (1983).

529   'The movies', *Paris Review*, 89 (1983). 'No, Jas', *Helix* 98. 'raised with 100%', *Helix* 102. 'diffident', L 251.

530   The syphilis story: *Paris Review*, 89 (1983). 'The town', 'the ideological', Sel. Pr. 284. 'Unterguggenberger', Sel. Pr. 262. 'Woergl IS', MacL 22 Nov '34.

531   'exerted a', N 235. 'hard experience', preface to *New Directions in Prose and Poetry*, 1936. 'The foetor', Ibbotson 41. 'how difficult', Laughlin, 'Some Irreverent Literary History' (MS). 'The pubr/' *Helix* 102.

532   'Of course if', *Helix* 104. 'had no flair', O 76. 'the sense of', O 84. 'Nude Erections', P/F 163. 'a second', *Helix* 104.

---

17.   Fighting A Wasp Nest
Principal sources: *Dis*, GK.

534   'this bootshaped', 'the boss', L 265. 'an assembly', S 326f. 'I was in', *British–Italian Bulletin*, 21 Mar 1936. 'The Corporate', ib., 25 Jan 1936. 'You cannot', ib., 28 Mar 1936. 'when it could', ib., 25 Apr 1936. 'Italy needs', ib., 18 Apr 1936.

535   'I am, if', *British–Italian Bulletin*, 14 Mar 1936. 'too jabby/', Ibbotson 48. 'Abyssinian habits', MS headed 'England alias Geneva', JL. 'slave of Coptic', JL (n.d.). 'a bit off', in conversation, Mar 1985.

537   'He didn't like', AO.

538   'very much alike', Mary de Rachewiltz in AO.

539   'That amazin'', JL 23 Sept '35.

540   'a botched', Zapponi 51. 'incomprehensible', Heymann 320. 'It is in', Zapponi 51. 'DUCE!', Zapponi 52.

541   'come Il Duce', *Agenda* 161.

542   'shortly after', *Agenda* 162. 'Broadcast from', AB 22 Jan '35. 'Hell, Eliot', L 279. 'Do I gitt', L 288. 'if your public', L 289.

543   'If only Mr', CH 336. 'fairly alarming', Fitzgerald. 'good writers', ABCR 32.

544   'The Jew', NEW 14 May 1936.

545   Changes in the text of GK are listed in Gallup 62 and S 335. '42–51 are', L 294.

546   'great tracts', CH 309. 'Waaal I have', P/F 141.

547   'nothing like it', CH 316.

18.   First Clawss To Amurika

550   'Rabbit I', T. S. Eliot to EP, 12 Mar '34, Yale. 'Dear Mr', to G. A. Fisher,
      British Union of Fascists (n.d.), Yale.

551   'the only true', Hamilton (see note to p. 457) 267. 'exactly the', Oswald
      Mosley, *My Life*, Nelson, 1968, 226. 'the antics', *Agenda* 74. 'the British',
      Ezra Pound, *Social Credit: an Impact*, Peter Russell, 1951, 19. 'I dont make',
      'much better', Zapponi 209, 'Watch Marse', AB 16 Apr '38. 'You would
      think', BUQ Jan–Apr 1937.

552   'the only English', BUQ Oct–Dec 1937. 'the pinch-penny', 'A race may',
      BUQ Jan–Mar 1938. 'history is', Torrey 144. 'intellectual interest', BUQ
      Apr–June 1939. 'Mr Bunting', BUQ Apr–July 1937.

553   'As to the investors', *Action*, 8 Apr 1939. 'the little kike', JL 1 Dec '35. 'NO/',
      JL 22 Mar '36. 'This is typical', 'The line to', JL 1 Dec '36. 'Fascio', Zapponi
      209. 'What do you', S 351.

554   'Questionnaire', *Authors Take Sides on the Spanish War*, Left Review, 1937.
      'N. incapable', MS fragment, Lilly. 'Europe ENDS', NEW 15 Oct 1936.
      'Spain is', Ibbotson 57. 'the holiday', *Dis* 111.

555   'some Italian', Duncan 196. 'The rooms', Duncan 197. 'missed a phone',
      Doob 397. 'wd. trust', Ibbotson 46. 'bloke who', S 358.

556   'swaggered in', Myers 241. 'Why all this', P/L 220. 'A beautiful', Wyndham
      Lewis to DP, 16 July '39, Lilly. 'substantial means', Arthur Moore to Julien
      Cornell, 4 Dec '45, Lilly. 'We had money', O 63.

557   'I do NOT', P/F 156, 158. 'Your letter . . .' W. B. Yeats to EP, 2 March '33,
      JK. 'You belong', Torrey 151. 'I don't have', L 322. 'COULD with', to Felix
      Schelling, 30 May '38, UP. 'Are you now', L 319. 'Marx and Lenin', Sel. Pr.
      132. 'total democracy', Sel. Pr. 135.

558   'In April', *Dis* 118f. 'I have bin', P/L 206. 'GIVE ECONOMIC', N 357.

559   'The bankers', N 358. 'zoomed into', *Selected Letters of E. E. Cummings* (see
      note to p. 174), 151. 'gargling anti-semitism', Richard Kennedy, *Dreams in
      the Mirror*, Liveright, 1980, 387.

560   'gawd and', P/L 216. 'wandering around', W/L 178. 'just before he', Doob
      25. 'God help', S 363. 'a japanese', P/L 216. '300 sound', *Helix* 104.

561   'If God', N 367. 'but I pointed', 'Whatever you', *Case* 55. 'Father Coughlin',
      British–Italian Bulletin, 14 Mar 1936. 'an absolute', N 371. 'never felt', *Case*
      56.

562   'wrapped in', Torrey 153. 'the fuss', *Dis* 112. 'I found', W/L 184. 'Fascism
      only', S 364. 'No, I, N 367. 'He has made', S 362. 'He seemed', N 363. 'only
      hole', 'an inadequate', P/F 171. 'There passed', P/F 171–3.

563   'one of the', S 363. 'seemed to', N 365. 'magnificent with', N 366. 'sounded as
      if', Hall 139.

564   'My feet', N 367. 'we were refused', N 361. '& they', Ibbotson 99. 'Your
      Alma', N 369. 'It is written', 'Praise God', N 370.

565   'the situation', N 370. 'sought to calm', Ibbotson 3. 'I spent seven', N 370.
      'That was a', to Wyndham Lewis (n.d.), Lilly. 'Kaltenstein', Ibbotson 100.
      'disgruntled', N 371.

19.   Get Hold Of Their Microphone

566   'done (in the main)', L 328. 'inclined to', Ibbotson 99. 'make a li'l', N 373.
      'publicity', Ibbotson 100. 'Mussolini's', *Dis* 128. 'if for any', L 324. 'crying
      need', L 325.

567   'This war is no', S 368. 'Mr Pound', Zapponi 60.

568   'I . . . suggested', *Agenda* 162. 'It took', S 390. 'The war is', S 377. 'Jewry',
      Torrey 156. 'Jewsfeldt', Heymann 97. 'an enormous', S 368. 'The place', L
      340. 'every English', Doob 25. 'infinite harm', S 378.

569   'a progruss', AB 4 Apr '39. 'two advances', Leon Surette, *A Light from
      Eleusis: a Study of Pound's Cantos*, Clarendon Press, 1979, 146f.

570   'getting the Chinese', *Helix* 103.

571   'contain more', *Helix* 53.

572   'John Adams had', GK 254.

573   I am indebted to Frederick K. Sanders, *John Adams Speaking: Pound's
      Sources for the Adams Cantos*, University of Maine Press, 1982, which lays
      bare Ezra's handling of the Adams material.

574   'He thinks', *Helix* 106.

575   'DUCE', Zapponi 53. 'dead matter', L 328. 'there's a final', N 376. 'plungin'
      into', AB 17 Dec '39. 'For heaven's', 'reminded me', 'free to amuse', S 372.

576   'I have', L 331. 'Re Cavalcanti', L 332. 'You must', S 373. 'how elegant', *Dis*
      126. 'I am sorry', L 334. 'Babbo tapped', *Dis* 127.

577   'Had a lot', L 334. 'No philosophy', *Dis* 127f. 'Never met', L 334f. 'less
      romantic', S 373. 'your tendency', S 373f. 'adds just', L 338.

578   'about which', S 374. 'quite a chunk', L 334. 'I don't feel', L 335. 'an analysis',
      L 336. 'Re European', L 339. 'Mass and', L 340f.

579   'the absolute', Zapponi 61. 'Blasted friends', L 342f.

580   'ole Pete', Heymann 97. 'thought of', 'Gornoze', L 346. 'at my time',
      Ibbotson 108.

581   'by simply being', S 386. 'the cold', *Agenda* 161. 'to go into', 'Now sun',
      L 348.

582   'showed me', *Dis* 132f. 'seemed harassed', *Dis* 135. 'come down', *Agenda* 163.

---

20.   Europe Calling! Ezra Speaking!
      Principal source: Doob – the most comprehensive published collection of the
      broadcast scripts, though many still remain unpublished. Among these is the
      Céline broadcast, 'To Be Late', transmitted on 16 May 1942, which I have
      taken as a sample of Ezra's performances at the microphone, transcribing it –
      with phonetic spellings of my own, imitating his broadcasting style – from a
      US monitoring service recording (no. RG 262.28, 486) in the National
      Archives, Washington DC.

583   'It was too', *Dis* 136f. 'ulterior motives', Zapponi 63. 'an Italian', Kavka.

584   'The United States', Heymann 102. 'Europe calling!', William Levy (ed.),
      Certain Radio Speeches of Ezra Pound, Cold Turkey Press, 1975; also Doob
      77, 178. 'I don't so much', JL 18 June '41.

585   'There is no', Heymann 100. 'capitalist reactionaries', Kavka. 'Time, damn',
      Ibbotson 48. 'with a movement', O 80.

586 'young people', *Dis* 164. 'cultural rather', *Dis* 165f. 'so that Pound', quoted in Massimo Bacigalupo to the author, 24 Nov '84. 'I had them', O 80. 'obtained the', N 389. 'no one ever', *Helix* 131.

587 'told me they', N 384. 'quite a good', quoted in Massimo Bacigalupo to the author, 24 Nov '84. 'the shit', O 40. 'listen to', *Agenda* 163. 'I was not sending', Heymann 168.

588 'Nothing solemn', *Agenda* 164.

589 'if Yankee', N 387. 'angry, sardonic', *Dis* 150.

590 'very little', DP to Huntington Cairns (n.d.), LC. 'Hers is just', O 93. 'What I am', Heymann 170.

591 'furious at', *Agenda* 157. 'change a comma', S 396. 'What the hell', W/A 316.

592 '*What about freedom*', *Agenda* 164. The Pound/William Joyce correspondence is at Yale; information about Joyce is taken from J. A. Cole, *Lord Haw-Haw*, Faber and Faber, 1964.

596 'emotionally he', *Dis* 153f., 161. 'teutons', to Wyndham Lewis (n.d.), Lilly. 'exercising the good', Cornell 2.

597 'It was not', *Literary Review* Dec 1984. Statistics on anti-Semitism come from Harold E. Quinley & Charles Y. Glock, *Anti-Semitism in America*, Free Press, 1979, 213. 'an American', Zapponi 55. 'Those in', S 395f.

---

21. Recoming To U/S/
     Principal source: *Dis*.

598 'the only time', Sel. Pr. 188. 'Tom Hardy', Doob 8.

599 'a flying', S 388.

600 'undignified remarks', 'occasionally', *Helix* 127.

601 'pseudo American', N 384. 'Friday', HP (n.d.).

602 'I think he', S 388.

603 'the last American', Doob 26. 'On Arbour', Doob 23–7.

604 'tried at the', *Agenda* 160. 'the principal reason', AO. 'Wot do you', JL 17 Sept '41.

605 'Waaal, as', JL 17 Jan '41. 'Ezra Pound', S 392. 'The day of', Reynolds and Eleanor Packard, *Balcony Empire*, Chatto & Windus, 1943, 179. 'People who', *New Directions in Prose & Poetry*, 1941.

606 'I am a', PR. 'I wish I', AO.

---

22. 8 From US Indicted
     Principal sources: Doob, *Dis*.

607 'even if', 'Damn it', 'It seems', Torrey 160f.

608 'My mistake', O 45. 'Rome Radio', S 393, N 385. 'rather forced', *Helix* 131. 'a form of', Kavka.

609 'You are at war' (transcription service version), FCC Transcript, LC microfilm. 'You are at war' (Norman version), *Case* 38.

610 'when we dialed', *Casebook* 27. 'a vicious tirade', *Helix* 127. 'I told him', W/A 317f.

611 'Lord Ga-Ga', *Decision*, Sept 1941. 'You've printed', Duncan 221. 'The time has', P Apr 1942. 'If Ezra has', Torrey 174.

612   'none of Ezra's', AO. 'I shall make', AO. 'There were no', MacL 30 June '56. 'E.P. did', MacL 17 Jan '57:
613   'said I was', *Paideuma*, vol. 8, no 3 (fall 1979). 'I'm sorry', Torrey 166.
615   'did not like', Sir Isaiah Berlin to the author, 24 Dec '84.
616   'I hope to', T. S. Eliot to DP, 10 Apr '42, Lilly. 'Omar goes', DP to Agnes Bedford, 1 May '40, Lilly. 'recently left', T. S. Eliot to Miss E. A. Madge, 16 Oct '43, Lilly. 'not been very', T. S. Eliot to DP, 13 Aug '45, Lilly.
617   'two testimonies', Zapponi 54. 'prescriptible', Zapponi 55.
618   '-It is an American', Zapponi 55f.
620   'Believe both Chandler', to Arthur Moore, 25 Nov '54, Lilly. 'amend the Articles', *Helix* 125. 'that Ezra Pound', Heymann 135.
621   'the crime of treason', 'Treason against', 'Whoever is convicted', Cornell 150.
622   'via the BBC', N 388.

---

23.   Out Fer The Mountains
      Principal source: *Dis.*

623   'completely surprised', PR. 'to see what', *Helix* 129.
624   'I understand', N 389f.
625   'an application', *Agenda* 169. 'in the event', *Helix* 128.
626   'understandable enough', Winnick 317f. '*badogliare*', *Agenda* 169. 'the confusion', *Dis* 185.
627   '. . . an' Brer Rabbit', *Agenda* 170. 'INCIPIT VITA', typescript at Yale.
628   'On the 10th', Ezra Pound, *Gold and Work*, Peter Russell, 1951, 3. 'the only road', S 401. 'and if they', *Dis* 186. 'with a herd', S 401.

---

24.   Civilized
      Principal sources: *Dis*, Cantos 72 and 73. For long excluded from the canon of Ezra's works, these cantos have been added to the 1987 Fourth Collected Edition of *The Cantos*, but without being translated from Italian. The Mary de Rachewiltz translation on which I have based my own version was shown to me by James Laughlin. I am also indebted to Massimo Bacigalupo, 'The Poet at War: Ezra Pound's Suppressed Italian Cantos', *South Atlantic Quarterly*, winter 1984.

632   'if I could get', *Helix* 129. 'the collaborator', Kutler 62. 'guided by', S 406. 'on a cattle', *Helix* 130.
633   'Give me a bed', 'Nein, ich', 'I see you', 'I've slept', *Agenda* 169. 'towards expenses', *Helix* 130. 'go to Milan', Heymann 151. 'along the same', *Helix* 130. 'created a character', Heymann 150. 'was not on any', 'for services', *Helix* 130.
634   'The live thought', S 403f. 'I am anxious', Heymann 322–4. 'give the Republic', Heymann 145.
635   'main work', *Helix* 132. 'quoted on', 'The archer', S 403. 'We spent a', DP to James Laughlin, 9 Aug '45, JL. 'found a cart', *Paideuma* vol. 2, no. 3 (winter 1973).
636   'Dorothy had', 'The Italians', 'Ezra lost', AO. 'It was a flight', Basil Bunting

to DP, 11 Nov '46, Lilly. 'We were all', in conversation (telephone), Apr 1983.

637 'So the old', typescript at Yale.

640 'radar had won', O 40. 'without radar', to Wyndham Lewis (n.d.), Lilly. 'Ez sez', DP to Ronald Duncan, 5 Sept '47, Columbia.

641 'lots of information', S 407. 'expected to turn', PR. 'to give information', Cornell 52. 'The man of breed', Confucius, translated by Ezra Pound, *The Unwobbling Pivot and the Great Digest*, in *Pharos*, winter 1947. 'came to the front', Cornell 11. 'common thieves!', AO. 'a couple of', Meacham 25.

642 'Slipped into', to Peter Whigham, 23 Sept '53, Berg. 'he didn't know', O 38. 'To the commando', *Dis* 241. 'I came home', Meacham 25.

Part Four   1945–58   'Grampaw'

1. Definitely Not Senile
Principal source: AO

645 'and I thought', PR. 'Communist mob', Kavka. 'tried to report', to Peter Whigham, 23 Sept '53, Berg.

647 'I was not fleeing', Heymann 172. 'Who is this', O 39.

648 'I believe', 'This statement', 'I am willing', *Helix* 131.

649 'ready to testify', *Dis* 143. 'Two pencils', Heymann 157. 'with great care', Heymann 169.

650 'My instinct', Heymann 169. 'but it would', *Death of a Hero* 23. The Edd Johnson interview was taken directly from the *Chicago Sun*, 9 May 1945.

652 'working in centre', HC (n.d.). 'he couldn't walk', O 39.

653 The telegram from MTOUSA, Steele.

---

2. Gorilla Cage
Ezra left no account in connected prose of his imprisonment at Pisa, and this chapter has been pieced together from the material cited below, and of course from *The Pisan Cantos* (Cantos 74–84).

654 'bound for an', Cornell 20. 'nothing gave', *Dis* 237–54 *passim*.

656 'the toughest', A 87. 'rode to the', *Casebook* 33. 'because there wasn't', Steele. 'somebody over-eager', Steele.

657 'extreme precautions', Kimpel. 'really big-time', Peter Brown. 'recognized him', *Casebook* 34. 'was at once', Cornell 20. 'behaved like a', Peter Brown. 'even when the', *Casebook* 37.

658 'Not allowed', N 397. 'Barbed wire', to Peter Whigham, 23 Sept '53, Berg. 'always referred', O 38. 'Ha, I was', Torrey 6.

659 'walked back and', *Casebook* 34. 'Pound's volume', D. P. Williams. 'Bunting / doing', C74/431. 'Spoke only', N 398. 'Stocky and', D. P. Williams.

660 'What heaven', *The Unwobbling Pivot* (see note to p. 641). 'How admirable', Confucius, *Analects* 6.11 (Penguin translation). 'maltreated and', Cornell 184.

661 'hours watching', *Casebook* 35.

662 'making graceful', *Casebook* 35. 'during certain', *Dis* 255.

663   'Placed in confinement', 'His present complaints', Kimpel.

---

3. It Exists Only In Fragments
Principal Source: *The Pisan Cantos* (Cantos 74 to 84).

665   'kissed the earth', C77/470. 'We talked', Steele.
666   'Steele is', Steele.
667   'he had a spring', Steele. 'What's he training', Patricia Hutchins, 'Ezra
        Pound's Pisa', *Southern Review*, Jan 1966.
668   'he would stride', *Casebook* 36. 'strong indications', Kutler 64. 'The pris-
        oner', Kimpel. 'made a satisfactory', Torrey 9.
669   'made a dummy', *Casebook* 36. 'it was felt', Steele. 'it was not unusual',
        Casebook 36. 'had to look', Peter Brown. John Drummond's letters to DP are
        in the Lilly; they are quoted by permission of Mr Drummond.
670   'very sympathetic', Elihu Root to John Drummond, 13 July '45, Lilly. 'the
        constant clanging', *Casebook* 35. 'All Pisans', Kimpel. 'what moved', Louis
        Dudek (ed.), *DK/ Some Letters of Ezra Pound*, DC Books, 1974, 28.
671   'R. D. June', MS at Yale. 'The proper names', Steele.
672   'During the late', *Casebook* 36f.
673   'the strength which', quoted Surette (see note to p. 569) 180f. 'We had a
        large', Steele.
675   'as to POETRY', Ibbotson 56.
680   ' . . . long stretches', Robert Lowell to EP, 12 July '52, Lilly.

---

4. Talk When He Wants You To Talk

681   'anyway yet', DP to John Drummond, 7 Sept '45 (John Drummond). 'a claim
        to see', John Drummond to DP, 30 Aug '45, Lilly. 'He says health', DP to
        James Laughlin, 29 Sept '45, JL. 'the saga of', Meacham 25. 'Tell Uncle', S
        409.
682   'obtain the best', Cornell 5. 'I am not sure', Cornell 7–11.
683   'mitigating', Torrey 12. 'I do not believe', James Laughlin to Arthur Moore,
        30 Sept '45, Lilly. 'as I had always', Cornell 4.
684   'they did not sound', Cornell 1f. 'Counsel for defence', Cornell 6. 'in this
        country', Cornell 15.
685   'Dear Ez', T. S. Eliot to EP (n.d.), Lilly. '[He] is an', T. S. Eliot to Miss E. A.
        Madge, 16 Oct '43, Lilly. 'whether by design', *Dis* 260.
686   'Visit from daughter', N 397. 'were elated', *Dis* 254–6. 'he had grown', AO.
        'One embraced', AO.
687   'heard today', DP to James Laughlin, 31 Oct '45, JL. 'He wanted me', *Dis*
        156. 'I have had', DP to James Laughlin, 31 Oct '45, JL. 'thick batch', DP to
        James Laughlin, 5 Dec '45, JL. 'would have had', Steele. 'overwhelmed . . .',
        Dis 156.
688   'The demand', T. S. Eliot to EP (n.d.), Lilly. 'a new translation', Cornell 10f.
        'If I had only', O 47.
689   'I know how', James Legge, *The Chinese Classics*, Clarendon Press, 1983,
        vol. I, 387. 'read voraciously', *Casebook* 37f. 'If I go down', *Casebook* 38.
        'almost despaired', *Casebook* 37. 'THE F.B.I.', NRC.

690 'Dear Adam', NRC. 'there are no two', Torrey 180.
691 'ready to give', Cornell 12. 'just making the', *Casebook* 37. 'a luxurious vacation', Cornell 35. 'On or about', Heymann 182f. 'THE DEPARTMENT', NRC.
692 'We went', *Dis* 160. 'I hear you', *Dis* 265. 'SECRETARY OF', Heymann 274. 'LEGAL JURISDICTION', NRC.
693 'jurisdiction over', Heymann 174.

---

5. Very Wobbly In His Mind
    Lieut. Col. P. V. Holder's account of the transatlantic flight is in the Pound files, NRC. Other principal source: Cornell.

694 'One evening', *Casebook* 38.
695 'conversed freely', Kimpel (who prints another account by Holder, describing his talk with EP).
696 'kicked out', S 416. 'in dirty shirt', O 119.
697 'Will he inflict', John S. Mayfield, *The Black Badge of Treason*, Park Bookshop, Washington DC, 1944, 15. 'I can't write', *Case* 47–54.
698 'I should prefer', *Case* 55–7. 'crackpot', *Case* 57–9.
699 'less traitor', *Case* 60f. 'all the contributors', *Case* 11. 'He is obviously', Hem. Letters 11. 'even though', Torrey 175. 'He ought', Hem. Letters 549. 'It is pretty', Winnick 315f. 'ANXIOUS DO', Torrey 4. 'not heard a', Torrey 12.
700 'I thought they', James Laughlin, MS written for *American Poetry* (University of Mexico). 'somebody seemed', O 38f.

---

6. Cornered
    Principal source: Cornell.

705 'young Julien Cornell', Winnick 336f. 'There is a curious', T. S. Eliot to Arthur Moore, 3 Dec '45, Lilly.
706 'Cornell thought', Torrey 185.
707 'accepting employment', Heymann 182–5. 'could not properly', Torrey 180.
708 'District of Columbia Jail', IP 22 Nov '45.
709 'The jail at first', O 37. 'Dear Ron', Duncan, *Enemies* 111.
712 'full of pain', O 35f.
715 'At the elevator', O 119.

---

7. He is, In Other Words, Insane
    Sources: Cornell; Julien Cornell's correspondence with Arthur Moore (Lilly); Torrey chapter 7 (my source for much of Overholser's personal history and his observations on mental illness, and for those parts of the doctors' reports on Ezra not quoted in Cornell's book). I have also drawn on *Centennial Papers, St Elizabeths Hospital 1855–1955*, St Elizabeths Hospital, Washington DC, 1956, and on Overholser and Richmond, *Handbook of Psychiatry*, Lippincott, 1947.

8. Hell-hole
    Principal sources: Cornell, O, *Centennial Papers* (see note to previous chapter).

726 'Faustian', Omar Pound, in conversation Mar 1985. '1 Bottle', inventory dated 30 Jan '46, St Es.

727 'normal', 'egotism and belief', Kutler 68. 'very neat and', to Peter Whigham, 23 Sept '53, Berg. 'just plain noise', Kavka.

728 'Ezra will always', Stock n/b. 'cooperated with', Torrey 201. 'The patient does', Kavka.

729 'superior manner', 'His language', Torrey 201. 'denied that he was', Torrey 202. 'I had assumed', Torrey 203. 'quite a bit', 'very cordial', Torrey 204. 'delusions', Torrey 202.

730 'Contrary to', Julien Cornell to Arthur Moore, 24 Dec '45, Lilly. 'They won't believe', Torrey 202. 'No, I don't,' Kutler 69. 'understand how incarcerated', Kavka. 'If I was', MacL 19 Apr '56. 'he didn't think', O 38.

731 Dr Kendig's report, Stock n/b.

732 'Mr Pound has', Julien Cornell to Arthur Moore, 13 Dec '45, Lilly. 'Much as I', Graham Greene to Ronald Duncan, 1 Oct '47, Lilly.

733 'I have received', Julien Cornell to EP, 4 Feb '46, Lilly. 'Can you get', in Julien Cornell to EP, 25 Jan '46, Lilly.

734 'Go around', O xvi. 'My motive', Charles Olson to Winfred Overholser, 5 Jan '46, St Es.

737 'Mr Olson's', to Peter Whigham (n.d.), Berg. 'To see him now', James Laughlin to Winfred Overholser, 9 Jan '46, St Es.

739 A copy of the 'Yiddish Charleston' was kindly shown to me by James Laughlin.

9. Unsound Mind
    Principal source: Cornell.

743 The newspaper quotations are from Torrey 199f.
744 'He said they', O 68.
747 'an impressive', Torrey 218.
749 'Quieted by his', *Casebook* 23.
752 'When the verdict', Torrey 217.

10. End Of The West

754 'Dear Win', Wendell Muncie to Winfred Overholser, 14 Feb '46, St Es.

755 'with his bounce', O 72–5. 'Healthy. Better', O 82. 'Conditions better', Arthur Moore to T. S. Eliot, 18 Mar '46, Lilly. 'one praying', IP (n.d.). 'no objection', Arthur Moore to Julien Cornell, 12 Mar '46, Lilly. 'never tried', in Douglas Hammond to Arthur Moore, 28 Jan '58, Lilly. 'Although his', Cornell 47–9.

756 'I confess', Cornell 50.

757 'Dear Dr', to Winfred Overholser, 1 Mar '46, St Es. 'Investigation reveals', Samuel Silk to Julien Cornell, 14 May '46, St Es. 'Pop Corn', receipt (n.d.), St

Es. 'When they don't', to Ingrid Davies, 4 Apr '56, HRC. 'by reason of', Julien Cornell to EP, 1 Mar '46, Lilly. 'Dear A.V.M.', in Arthur Moore to T. S. Eliot, 18 Mar '46, St Es. 'an extraordinary', Julien Cornell to Winfred Overholser, 2 Apr '46, St Es.

758   're power', in Arthur Moore to Julien Cornell, 26 Apr '46, Lilly. 'apparently a little', 'guardian of', Julien Cornell to Arthur Moore, 16 Apr '46, Lilly. 'haven't seen', JL 30 Jan '46. 'Write to', JL 15 Feb, 28 Feb, 19 Mar '46. 'his *use*', O 86. 'distrust the', O 88. 'There is no', O 99.

759   'much as I', W/A 336. 'In carcere', PH 2 Nov '57. 'Typed on', *Agenda* 194.

760   'God bloody', Torrey 248. 'detected a', *Helix* 153. 'So my letter's', *Selected Letters of E. E. Cummings* (see note to p. 174) 204. 'for a few', Ibbotson 114. 'Next point', Cornell 83.

761   'Does anyone', Cornell 87. 'Anybody who', Cornell 88. 'It may be', MacL 14 Feb '56. 'Waiting for', Ibbotson 114. 'Consider which', HC (n.d.). 're/ the world', MacL (n.d.). 'The dense', IP 5 Oct '47.

762   'Dear Jarge', to 'George' Yeats (n.d.), JK. 'I guess something', HP (n.d.). 'No expected', HP 18 Nov '26.

---

11. Somewhat More Latitude

764   'If D.P.', Cornell 81. 'They wouldn't', AO. 'EZRA'S MOTHER', in Julien Cornell to EP, 22 May '46, St Es.

765   'Dearest Mother', IP (n.d.). 'might mean', J. Henry Warren to Isabel Pound, 29 May '46, Lilly. 'There is no heat', Isabel Pound to DP, 30 Jan '47, Lilly. 'Hope you are', IP 17 July '46. 'Plane trip', DP to James Laughlin, 11 July '46, JL. 'I felt the ground', *Paideuma* vol. 2, no. 3 (winter 1973). 'so very kind', Cornell 52.

766   'Saw E.P.', DP to James Laughlin, 10 July '46, JL. 'He asks me', Cornell 51–3. 'I find him', Cornell 51. 'that the present', Cornell 52.

767   'reassure', Cornell 53. 'As to Mr Pound's', Winfred Overholser to Julien Cornell, 18 July '46, St Es. 'devotion', Cornell 51. 'Dorothy is', IP 12 Feb '47. 'a very substantial', Arthur Moore to T. S. Eliot, 16 Aug '46, Lilly. 'though why', DP to Winfred Overholser, 12 Sept '46, St Es. 'Money NOT', to Peter Whigham, 23 Sept '53, Berg. 'always felt', James Laughlin to Noel Stock, 5 Oct '72, Toledo.

768   'juvenile essays', James Laughlin to Noel Stock, 26 Aug '70, Toledo. 'I am most anxious', Cornell 53. 'until after the', Cornell 54. 'disliked th' heat', HC 11 Aug '49. 'yr. calamity', Ibbotson 122. 'to hell', in Basil Bunting to DP, 10 Dec '46, Lilly. 'When ever', IP 3 Oct '46. 'I am quite', T. S. Eliot to DP, 10 July '46, Lilly. 'a very busy', T. S. Eliot to DP, 22 July '46, Lilly.

769   'Yes, I know, O 85. 'I doubt whether', T. S. Eliot to DP, 22 July '46, Lilly. 'Your postcard', T. S. Eliot to EP, 12 Oct '56, Yale. 'ratty, lightning', Omar Pound, in conversation Mar '85. 'an old and', William Carlos Williams to President Truman, 31 Dec '46, St Es.

770   'Mr Pound is', Winfred Overholser to William Carlos Williams, 10 Jan '47, St Es. 'that you have', 'did not think', Cornell 54. 'I think the psychiatrists', J. F. Cunningham to Isaiah Matlack, 27 Jan '47, St Es.

771 'The problem raised', J. F. Cunningham to Winfred Overholser, 29 Jan '47, St Es. 'disclaiming any', memorandum, 31 Jan '47, St Es.

772 'He is now', Cornell 57. 'Can't always', DP to Ronald Duncan, 22 Oct '47, Columbia. 'a Republican', 'I don't much', in T. S. Eliot to DP, 5 July '47, Lilly. 'I am sure', ib. 27 Feb '47, Lilly. 'Thanks for', to Winfred Overholser (n.d.). LC.

773 'Thanks', to Winfred Overholser (n.d.), LC. 'As for my', Winfred Overholser to Charles Norman, 1 Aug '60, St Es. 'EP's ghostly', *Paideuma*, vol. 13, no. 3 (winter 1984).

774 'Visiting hours', PH 19 Sept '53. 'NO visitors', HC 16 Feb '54. ' . . . by the big', W/A 340. 'behind a ramshackle', Rattray. 'jumped up', *Casebook* 105.

775 'strewn with', *Casebook* 108f. '1/2 of ONE', HC (n.d.). 'I tho't', fragment, Lilly. 'When his ward', Samuel Silk to Olga Rudge, 4 May '48, Lilly. 'for him to go', T. S. Eliot to Julien Cornell, 14 Nov '48, St Es. 'An attendant', Duncan, *Enemies* 320–3.

12. Bubble-gum

778 'Quiet and', Torrey 243. 'Patient does', Ward notes, St Es. 'Mr Langford', Winfred Overholser to Dr Cruvant, 2 Dec '48, St Es.

779 'No abnormal', Torrey 251f. 'with rickety', *Dis* 274f.

780 'M. and Boris', *Dis* 274f. 'Waal yr', IP 7 Jan '47. 'magnanimous', IP 12 Feb '47. 'suggestion of', Isabel Pound to DP, 5 Mar '47, Lilly. 'rose to the', *Dis* 280. 'I trust you', IP 16 Apr '47. 'Young Walter', IP (n.d.). 'immediately set', *Dis* 279.

781 'I had great', *Dis* 282–4.

782 'a good balance', to Mrs Gatter, 9 Mar '58, UP. 'yet another', O 104. 'monstrous', Ronald Duncan to EP, 18 Feb '47, Lilly. 'I didn't expect', T. S. Eliot to DP, 7 Jan '48, Lilly. 'I could have', *Paris Review*, 89 (1983). 'There may be', Cornell 59.

783 'I must ask', DP to Julien Cornell, 30 Mar '48, Lilly. 'if he had', Cornell 61. 'definite and', Julien Cornell to DP, 30 Mar '48, Lilly. 'some under-current', Arthur Moore to T. S. Eliot, 1 Sept '50, Lilly. 'What I want', T. S. Eliot to DP, 7 Feb '48, Lilly. 'Tall, thin', *Dis* 288f.

784 'Her one passion', Ronald Duncan to EP, 15 May '48, Lilly. 'several times', Olga Rudge to Winfred Overholser, 15 April '48, St Es.

785 'great fatigue', Samuel Silk to Olga Rudge, 4 May '48, St Es. 'I am afraid', Julien Cornell to James Laughlin, 29 June '48, transcribed by Olga Rudge, Ronald Duncan papers, Columbia. 'Of course I do', Olga Rudge to Ronald Duncan, 16 July '48, Columbia. 'the new Mayor', AO. 'the undersigned', HC (n.d.).

786 'writing letters', *Dis* 197f. 'The Rudge', Hem. Letters 742. 'The person', Hem. Letters 743. 'E.P. thinks', Arthur Moore to Peter Russell, 23 Dec '48, Lilly. 'You say "we"', Ronald Duncan to EP, 1 Nov '47, Lilly. 'He thought', N 433f.   •

787 'poetic sketch-books', CH 363. 'I have not', CH 371f.

788 'Bubble-Gum', Heymann 221. 'the choice', minutes of the Bollingen Prize

Committee, General Services Division, Library of Congress. 'give anti-Semitism', Allen Tate to Luther H. Evans, 31 Jan '49, Bollingen Prize file, ib. 'recommended strongly', Bollingen Prize file, ib.

789 'most unfortunate', Cornell 117. 'DEAR MR POUND', Robert Lowell to EP (n.d.), Lilly. 'Dear Ezra', ib. (n.d.), Lilly. 'My "experiences"', ib. 13 Aug [1949], Lilly.

790 'that LUMP', MacL 14 Feb '56. 'After the age', in James Breslin, *Something to Say: William Carlos Williams on Younger Poets* (MS shown to me by New Directions). 'the diverse', Winfred Overholser to DP, 26 Apr '48, St Es. 'his son', Alexander M. Campbell to Winfred Overholser, 1 Nov '48, St Es. 'It is my', Winfred Overholser to Alexander M. Campbell, 23 Nov '48, St Es. 'It is a sort', *Sewannee Review*, summer 1947. 'Tate is', MacL 1 Jan '56. 'Geo Biddle', MacL 1 Sept '56.

791 'Aiken and', to Peter Whigham, 23 Sept '53, Berg. 'not going', 'a burning', *Case* 60f. 'Good for Auden', Ronald Duncan to EP, 5 July '46, Lilly. 'this does not', Cornell 114. 'did not wish', Bollingen minutes (see note to p. 788). 'I voted', *Casebook* 61.

792 'One is prompted', Heymann 221. 'cowardly', Allen Tate to Luther H. Evans, 31 Jan '49, Bollingen Prize file, General Services Division, Library of Congress.

793 'Dr Oberholtzer', Cairns interview notes (see note to chapter 13 below).

---

13. Acolites Etc.
Principal sources: Huntington Cairns's interview notes (LC), HC.

795 'necessary to a', S 431.
798 'art of collecting', S 430f. 'I wanna thank', HC 19 Apr '53.
799 'literary cliques', Marshall McLuhan to EP, 5 Jan '51, Lilly. 'seems to have', Robert Lowell to EP, 12 July '52, Lilly. 'Certainly the acolites', PH 27 Aug '56. 'Kenner bk/', Ibbotson 135.
800 'I thrilled', Heymann 227. 'fugg of', Torrey 228. 'I'm going', John Kasper to EP, 6 June '50, Lilly. 'Dear Boss', 'This city', ib. 8 Jan '51, Lilly.
801 'very Jewish', John Kasper to EP, 7 Jan '52, Lilly. 'to shout', ib. 11 Aug '52, Lilly. 'likely to lead', Winfred Overholser to Calvin Drayer, 19 Feb '58, St Es. 'to have no', Michael Reck, *Ezra Pound: A Close-Up*, Hart-Davis, 1968, 102f. 'Miss Martinelli', Rattray.
802 'pretty', Omar Pound, in conversation, Mar 1985. 'He jumps', 'floppy sandals', 'tan shorts', 'a loose', *Paideuma*, vol. 13, no. 3 (winter 1984). 'continually kept', Dudek (see note to p. 670) 30f. 'By Martinelli's', Torrey 241.
803 'guiltless sex', Heymann 226. 'Sheri was', Stock n/b. 'jars, bottles', *Paideuma*, vol. 3, no. 3 (winter 1974).
804 'Grandpa loves', Rattray. 'I – LUV – U', Sheri Martinelli to DP (n.d.), Lilly. 'Miss Martinelli', Rattray. 'reviving the', *Paideuma*, vol. 3, no. 3 (winter 1974). 'PAINT me', Heymann 226. 'the first', *La Martinelli*, Vanni Schei-willer, Milan, 1956.

805 'NO, ten', MacL 17 Jan '56. 'a poor waif', Noel Stock, in conversation Mar 1985. 'What goes', Winfred Overholser to Calvin Drayer, 19 Feb '58, St Es.

---

14. A National Skeleton

806 'I represent', Olga Rudge to Winfred Overholser, 24 March '52, St Es. 'a little bit', AO. 'we could win', Rufus King to T. S. Eliot, 27 Oct '53, Lilly.

807 'a current report', Stanley E. Krumbiegel to Winfred Overholser, 9 June '53, St Es. 'There has been', Winfred Overholser to Stanley E. Krumbiegel, 18 Aug '53, St Es. 'at the end', Rufus King to T. S. Eliot, 27 Oct '53, Lilly.

808 'most abusive', Arthur Moore to T. S. Eliot, 20 Jan '55, Lilly. 'WITHOUT telling', to Arthur Moore, 25 Nov '54, Lilly. 'It does appear', T. S. Eliot to Rufus King, 4 Nov '53, St Es. 'our Government', Rufus King to Wyndham Lewis, 22 Dec '53, Lilly. 'Mamile took', Dis 287–97 passim.

811 'came from reading', PR.

812 'from the resolutely', The Times, 23 Nov '62. 'The poet', Guy Davenport, 'Pound and Frobenius', in Lewis Leary (ed.), Motive and Method in the Cantos of Ezra Pound, Columbia University Press, 1954. 'A. Dominated', Helix 99f.

813 'I may frequently', Heymann 329. 'Yes, I saw', PH 6 June '57. 'intended to imply', PR. 'The mere look', Donald Davie, Poet as Sculptor, Routledge & Kegan Paul, 1965, 204.

814 'a pure and', CH 438–40. 'difficult and', CH 441f. 'long twentieth-century', CH 445. 'I don't merember', MacL 18 Oct '56. 'cf/ canto', HC 11 July '49. 'an official', xerox lent to me by Noel Stock.

815 'I don't see', PH 3 May '57. 'EDGE . . .', circular sent to Ronald Baynes, UP. 'need of a', PH 26 June '53.

816 'Mr ElYuTT', HC (n.d.). 'one virtuous', PH 7 Apr '54. 'UNTIL you', PH 19 Sept '53. 'although the President', 'any material', in Arthur Moore to T. S. Eliot, 26 Nov '54, Lilly. 'the tone of', Douglas Hammond to Arthur Moore, 28 Jan '55, Lilly.

817 'release on probation', American Committee for Cultural Freedom to Winfred Overholser, 11 March '55, St Es. 'intolerable conditions', US Consular Services to Department of Health, 5 and 27 May '55, St Es. 'The present', clinical records, St Es. 'The service', Winnick 377.

818 'I should have', Archibald MacLeish to 'Quincy', 4 Dec '55, Bollingen file, General Services Division, Library of Congress. 'good psycho', Winnick 397. 'quite sane', MacLeish to 'Quincy', 4 Dec '55. 'would let Ez', 'I wouldn't rest', 'there was only', Winnick 397.

819 'The consensus', Winnick 380f. 'drift down', to Winfred Overholser, 23 Nov '55, St Es. 'Will gladly', Ezra Pound at Seventy, New Directions, 1955. 'The Nazi', Cornell 121f. 'While confined', memorandum, 26 Sept '56, St Es. 'Yes Sheri', MacL 17 Jan '56. 'he had abjured', MacL 6 Mar '56.

820 'I don't know', MacL 14 Aug '55. 'You may say', MacL 7 June '56. 'Obviously, MacL 23 June '56.

15. Our Mood Is Your Mood, Mr Frost
Principal sources: Winnick; MacL; MacLeish's letters to Overholser, Over-holser's correspondence, and other papers relating to the case, all of which are at St Elizabeths; Thompson & Winnick pp 250–9.

821 'to persuade', Archibald MacLeish to Arthur Moore, 14 Oct '56, Lilly.
823 Bridson's account of the recording and of 'Four Steps': *Agenda 21*, 131–41.
824 'I conceived', Rattray.
825 'Be assured', PH 26 Mar '57. 'We are writing', Heymann 245f.
826 'asked that a', Heymann 245f. 'A tall gentleman', *Dis* 301.
827 'legal steps', Julien Cornell to Arthur Moore, 23 April and 3 May '57, Lilly. 'The Ku Klux', to Peter Whigham, 20 May '57, Berg. 'KikoRuss', PH 13 Nov '57.
828 'A dirty jew', PH 4 Nov '57. 're Kasper', in Arthur Moore to T. S. Eliot, 10 May '57, Lilly. 'dangerous fawning', Hem. Letters 876.
829 'We've stopped', John Kasper to EP, 11 May '57, Yale. 'Stick to the', to John Kasper, 17 April '59, Yale. 'certainly the great', John Kasper to DP, 27 Dec '62, Lilly. 'Well, at least', S 446. 'arrange Gaudier', PH 5 June '57. 'Why M.S.', *Paideuma*, vol. 13, no. 3 (winter 1984).
830 'Nude Ructions', to 'George' Yeats, 5 Aug '58, JK.
832 'a full and complete', Heymann 242.
833 'naive but', MacL 19 Oct '57.
834 'If you have really', Archibald MacLeish to EP, 26 Oct '57, LC.
835 'two FBI', Cornell 123f. 'I shd/ like', PH 4 Nov '57. 'Byzantine middle', *Agenda 21*, 13.

16. The Three Of Us
Principal sources: Cornell; Thompson & Winnick; *New York Times*, 19 April 1958; Ezra's letters to the Gatters (in UP); Carl Gatter's memoir of the visit (MS at UP).

842 'We believe', *Casebook* 130f.
844 'I couldn't', AO.
845 'Condition upon', clinical records, St Es. 'you were officially', Winfred Overholser to EP, 7 May '58, St Es. 'an open-necked', N 455.
846 'Naw, me dear', MacL 27 May '58. 'In my opinion', Winfred Overholser to Passport Division, 8 May '58, St Es. 'hell of', PH 9 June '58.
848 'All America' and other remarks made on his arrival in Italy, N 459f. 'I was up', *Dis* 305.

Part Five 1958–72 Personae

1. Trained For A Demigod

852 'My vision', AO. 'You shd/', PH 5 June '57. 'the headquarters', Cory 35f. 'castles in', *Dis* 166f.

853 'I had bad', HC 29 Oct '58. 'mountain air', to 'George' Yeats, 5 Aug '58, JK. 'The mountains', DP to Helen Sanders (n.d.), in PH letters. 'The weight', DP to Mrs Gatter, 24 July '58, UP. 'I SHOULD', PH 14 Aug '58. 'I alternate', *Agenda 21*, facsimile reproduction. 'The rhythm', Heymann 262f.

854 'making possible', to Winfred Overholser, 1 Aug '59, LC . 'The thrones', PR.

855 'gnawing feeling', Stock n/b. 'just unbelievably', AO. 'drop in', to Winfred Overholser, 14 Nov '58, St Es. 'NO, don't', PH (n.d.). 'I can't live,' N 464. 'the difficulty', Cory 35. 'The family', *Dis* 305. 'Don't keep', Stock n/b. 'Blinded by', *Dis* 305. 'I grew', AO.

856 'I thought', 'found the Christmas', *Dis* 305.

2. Drammertist
    The second half of this chapter is taken from PR and Hall. The cantos quoted are nos. 110, 113, 114, 115, 116, 'Notes for 117 et seq', and 120.

857 'We got an', to 'George' Yeats, 1 Apr '59, JK. 'No doubt', Cory 34. 'Marcella was', Noel Stock, in conversation Mar 1985. 'somewhat aged', Bacigalupo 75. 'surprised that', Cory 34.

858 'If ever', Bridson 249f. 'My reading', 'An Interview with Ezra Pound', *New Directions in Prose & Poetry* 17, 1961, 165f.

859 ' . . . me incapacitated', 'where overhead', MacL, 10 Sept '59. 'Dear W.O.', to Winfred Overholser, 15 June '59, St Es.

860 'the only', Winfred Overholser to EP, 1 July '59, St Es. 'Have grown', to R. Furniss, 25 May '59, Lilly. 'Plenty of', MacL 10 Sept '59. 'Dorothy . . .' Arthur Moore to James Laughlin, 28 Sept '59, Lilly. 'broken', MacL (n.d.). 'Don't mump', MacL (n.d.).

861 'During all', James Laughlin to Winfred Overholser, 1 Dec '59, St Es. 'the behaviour', report by Clinica delle Malattie Nervose e Mentali dell' Universita di Genova, spring, 1966, St Es. 'I have never', Winfred Overholser to Julien Cornell, 11 Dec '59, St Es.

862 'I should', *Dis* 306. 'Ezra, I think', Robert Lowell to EP, 18 Mar '62, Lilly. 'still talked', *Dis* 306. 'From a letter', Arthur Moore to James Laughlin, 16 Jan '60, Lilly.

863 'Ezra in', DP to Mrs Gatter, 15 Mar '60, UP. 'He had changed', Cory 35. 'At seventy', Michael Reck, 'A Conversation between Ezra Pound and Allen Ginsberg', *Evergreen*, June 1968.

3. C'est Autre Chose
    Principal source: Mrs Doob's reminiscence, which is in *Paideuma*, vol. 8, no. 1 (spring 1972).

870 'He could not drive', Hall 169f. 'there was a great', *Agenda 21*, 189.

871 'has sorely', DP to Mrs Gatter, 26 Jan '61, UP. 'A source of', Cory 35f. 'apparently an', Omar Pound to Winfred Overholser, 11 Dec '60, St Es. 'a "Refuge for sinners"', Stock n/b. 'Sometimes he would', Cory 36.

872 'Attempted burning', Stock n/b. 'When have I', MacL 10 Sept '56. 'The day before', Cory 36.

874 'There was a', James Laughlin to Winfred Overholser, 31 Jan '63, LC. 'My husband', [DP to] PH, 7 June '61. 'a nursing home', AO.

875 'He began', James Laughlin to Winfred Overholser, 31 Jan '63, LC. 'The last week', DP to Winfred Overholser, 1 Oct '61, St Es. 'he turned', Duncan 196. 'He had bed', AO.

876 'He was lying', *Paideuma*, vol. 4, nos. 2–3 (summer–fall 1975), 517f. 'perked up', AO.

4. Who Is There Now To Share A Joke With?

877 'no longer', Cory 37. 'Ezra needs', Stock n/b. 'I found a', Bacigalupo 76f.

878 'Of course', [DP to] PH, 4 July '62. 'You will', Lidderdale papers, MS department, University College, London. 'he continued', Bacigalupo 77. 'How are you', Stern.

879 'he could walk', HK *Era* 559. 'Walked 100 yds', Stock n/b. 'My first', *Agenda* 21, 292.

880 '. . . he could set', HK *Era* 559. 'As far as', James Laughlin to Winfred Overholser, 31 Jan '63, LC. 'His eyes', *Paideuma*, vol. 9, no. 2 (summer 1979).

881 'She imparted', Torrey 279. 'any control', in Julien Cornell to DP, 17 Feb '66, Lilly.

882 'I'm not sure', James Laughlin to Noel Stock, 21 Oct '69, Toledo. 'Do tell me', Valerie Eliot, in conversation July 1985. 'she just sat', 'They've made', James Laughlin, in conversation Mar 1985. 'Yes I think', JL 17 June '63. 'amost completely', Fazio report (see note to p. 891). 'I did not', Torrey 277. 'It was a', Giuseppe Bacigalupo, in conversation Aug 1984.

883 'twice at the', Sir Isaiah Berlin to the author, 17 Sept '84. 'It's not', AO. 'Old people', AO.

884 'I remember', *Agenda 21*, 291f. 'a murderer', *Agenda 21*, 297.

885 'Miss Rudge', Stern. 'Groping for', Levy 17n. 'I only succeeded', Bridson 284f.

886 'you *did* say', James Laughlin, 'Collage for EP' (MS). 'Dear Jas', JL 27 Jan '64. 'Five minutes', Stern. 'Some people'. *Paideuma*, vol. 2, no. 3 (fall 1973). 'Ever afterwards', James Laughlin, in conversation Mar 1985.

887 'Olga', JL 18 June '64. 'he wanted', AO. 'Tom wouldn't', Valerie Eliot, in conversation July 1985.

888 'alertness', Valerie Eliot to Julien Cornell, 17 Sept '65, Lilly. 'I was very', Valerie Eliot to DP, 10 Aug '65, Lilly. 'His was', Heymann 277f. 'he wouldn't', *Agenda 21*, 294. 'Dear Jas', JL 22 May '65.

889 'were rather inclined', AO. 'It's all wrong', October–November 1965 issue of *Agenda*. 'Olga grew', *Agenda 21*, 292. 'There are the', Basil Bunting, *Collected Poems*, Oxford University Press, 1978, 110 (by kind permission of Oxford University Press). 'an eloquent', Heymann 295. 'C'est moi', AO.

890 'wrote a note', AO. 'seen Beckett', PH 4 Dec '53. 'obstinate silence', S 458. 'I am just', Dudek (see note to p. 670) 138. 'Am alive', JL 1 Sept '65.

891 'The patient was', medical report by Prof. Cornelio Fazio of the Clinica delle Malattie Nervose e Mentali dell' Universita di Genova, spring 1966: copy at St Es.

5.   Prospero
     Principal source: Michael Reck, 'A Conversation between Ezra Pound and Allen Ginsberg', *Evergreen*, June 1968.

893   'in the right', Cory 38f.
894   'when you asked', James Laughlin, 'Collage for EP' (MS). 'Ezra used', James Laughlin to the author, 5 Feb '85. 'Glad you like', JL 1 Oct '65. 'That her acts': this has now been printed in the 1987 edition of *The Cantos*, p. 815.
895   'I'm not going', AO. 'with ferocious', *Paideuma*, vol. 2, no. 3 (fall 1963).
896   'Dear MacLeish', MacL 2 Mar '67. 'Dear Jas', JL 10 Apr '67. 'We get hippies', Levy 8–10.
897   'Would you like', Levy 9.
900   'Ezra Pound, the', Stock n/b. 'Ezra Pound has just', Valerie Eliot, in conversation July 1985.
901   'emerged from', Ann Laughlin, in conversation Mar 1985. 'a standing ovation', *The Times*, 10 June 1969. 'the saddest night', James Laughlin, in conversation Mar 1985. 'wept', Valerie Eliot, in conversation July 1985.
902   'Another one', James Laughlin, in conversation Mar 1985. 'terrified', Stock n/b. 'not married', note by Carl Gatter, UP. 'just darling', Stock n/b. ' . . . a very sober', MacL 16 Feb '68. 'His voice', Heymann 301. 'D.P. once', Stock n/b.

6.   A Bit Of Real Fun

903   'shattered Olga', Torrey 280. 'A great deal', *Agenda 21*, facsimile reproduction. 'Arriving early', Heymann 305–9.
906   'Get right over', Levy *passim*.
908   'for fear', Levy 32. 'But then', James Laughlin to Noel Stock, 19 June '72, Toledo.
909   'it had nothing', Heymann 311–13.
910   'The last', James Laughlin to Noel Stock, 5 Oct '72, Toledo. 'I've heard', ib. 20 Oct '72. 'because he hadn't', Levy 37. 'restless, saw no', 'just in case', 'dozed off', Stern. 'sudden blockage', *Washington Star-News*, 2 Nov 1972. 'a horrid', Olga Rudge, in conversation Apr 1985.
911   'It's wonderful', James Laughlin to Noel Stock, 6 Mar '73, Toledo. 'provide enough', Omar Pound, in conversation Mar 1985. 'The lawyers', James Laughlin to Noel Stock, 6 Mar '73, Toledo.
912   'He wasn't', AO. 'I've done that', O 76. 'He doesn't know', *Helix* 106. 'I agree with', *Times Literary Supplement*, 11 Sept 1970.
913   'Of course Ezra', Hem. Letters 331. 'It's the best', O 98. 'In a sense', W/L 213. 'You have given', PR. 'Why the hell', to Felix Schelling, 11 Nov '33, UP. 'The art', IP 1 Jan '10. 'The intellect', IP (n.d.).

Appendix C:

Acknowledgements

Charles Monteith of Faber and Faber invited me to write this book, so my thanks first of all to him. John Bodley was my patient and supportive editor; Craig Raine spared much time to go through the book and make criticisms; Rona Treglown did much of the picture research, and was a valuable critic of the first draft of the typescript; Peter Davison at Houghton Mifflin, the book's American publishers, made useful comments; Juliet Field compiled the index. And I have a very great debt to Hazel Orme; it may be hard to believe that the book was once even longer than it is now, but Hazel, as copy-editor, managed much skilful (and now invisible) pruning which brought it to a more tolerable length.

It is striking that everyone associated with Ezra Pound, with whom I had dealings, and who read the book in MS, was good-natured, kindly, and tolerant of me, whatever their personal feelings about the biography and the portrait it draws. James Laughlin, Ezra's publisher since the 1930s, encouraged and helped me with my research, and gave me hospitality and all kinds of information and assistance. Olga Rudge met me twice, in London and Venice, and was the spirit of courtesy and kindness. Mary de Rachewiltz patiently endured an invasion of Brunnenburg by myself and my family, generously gave me permission to see and quote from her father's letters to his own parents, and lent an abundance of photographs.

Professor A. Walton Litz, both in his capacity as a Trustee of the Ezra Pound Literary Property Trust and as co-editor of Ezra's correspondence with Dorothy Shakespear, gave me wise advice and assistance. Noel Stock, author of the first full-length biography of Ezra, provided extensive and generous help, and much hospitality when I visited him in Toledo, Ohio. Peggy L. Fox of New Directions steered me through the avenues of copyright permissions, and gave encouragement and good cheer.

Carl Gatter, who lives in Ezra's childhood house at Wyncote, gave me a wealth of information about the district and the Pound family's life there in the 1890s, and he and his wife and son were tireless hosts when I visited Wyncote. Julien Cornell, Ezra's defence lawyer in 1945 and 1946, read my account of the legal proceedings, offered some corrections, and generously allowed me to quote from his correspondence and his account of the case.

Lawrence Pitkethly, Mary Dutt, and Elizabeth Kinder of the New York Center for Visual History provided access to uniquely informative filmed interviews with Olga Rudge and Mary de Rachewiltz, made for their film *Ezra Pound: American Odyssey*, and kindly provided still photographs used in the film. Dr Harold Thomas and the staff of St Elizabeths Hospital, Washigngton DC, gave me unrestricted access to the Ezra Pound files there, and provided me with a tour of the hospital.

Without T. S. Eliot's letters to Ezra, the story would frequently be one-sided. It was especially generous of Mrs Valerie Eliot to allow me to quote from them without restriction. Mrs Eliot also kindly gave me her own memories of Ezra.

W. B. Yeats is another indispensable voice in Ezra's story, and John Kelly, editor of Yeats's letters, very kindly let me see and make use of the Yeats–Pound correspondence. Oxford University Press kindly gave permission for quotation from the Yeats letters.

Other literary estates and executors were equally helpful. Briony Lawson and the Ronald Duncan Literary Foundation allowed me to quote from Ronald Duncan's autobiographies and letters. Robert Giroux on behalf of the Estate of Robert Lowell gave permission for the inclusion of passages from Lowell's letters to the Pounds. Richard B. McAdoo and the Houghton Mifflin Company granted leave to quote published and unpublished letters by Archibald MacLeish. George F. Butterick and the Estate of Charles Olson magnanimously gave me *carte blanche* with the Olson material – permission that was granted jointly with the University of Connecticut Library. Donald Hall kindly allowed the inclusion of substantial passages from his *Remembering Poets*.

Many publishers, who are acknowledged in the bibliography, allowed substantial quotation from published material. Special thanks go to Atlantic-Little, Brown for *Discretions* by Mary de Rachewiltz; to Carroll F. Terrell of the National Poetry Foundation, University of Maine at Otono, for permission to quote from *Paideuma*; and to the Permanent Press for allowing the use of excerpts from Alan Levy's *Ezra Pound: the Voice of Silence*.

I must acknowledge the permission granted by those libraries which hold major collections of Ezra Pound manuscripts and letters for me to quote from this material: particularly the Collection of American Literature, the Beinecke Rare Book and Manuscript Library, Yale University; and the Lilly Library, Bloomington, Indiana. The Henry W. and Albert A. Berg Collection, the New York Public Library (Astor, Lenox and Tilden Foundations) also gave permission for quotation.

The staff of these and other libraries provided unfailing assistance and kindness: David Schoonover and his assistants at Yale; William R. Cagle and Saundra Taylor at the Lilly; Dr Lola Szladits at the Berg; also John Wurl, Nancy Burnard and Leslie Sheridan at the William S. Carlson Library, University of Toledo, at Toledo, Ohio (Ward M. Canaday Center for Research and Special Collections); Georgianna Ziegler and her colleagues in the Special Collections, Van Pelt Library, University of Pennsylvania; Charles Kelly of the Manuscript Division and Bobby Dove of the General Services Division, Library of Congress, Washington DC; Cathy Henderson and her colleagues at the Humanities Research Center, University of Texas at Austin; and the staff of the Manuscript and Rare Books Room, University College, London, and the Butler Library, Columbia University, New York. The Bodleian Library, Oxford, as usual provided a highly congenial base for operations. And on the subject of libraries, the Friends of the University of Toledo Libraries at Toledo, Ohio kindly invited me to lecture on Ezra Pound in March 1985, thereby financing my trip to Toledo and making it possible for me to meet Noel Stock.

Many individuals helped me with reminiscences of Ezra, advice, and valuable leads; I hope I have managed to name them all here, and I must apologize to anyone who finds himself or herself inadvertently omitted: Dr Giuseppe Bacigalupo, Sir Isaiah Berlin, George Bornstein, Anna Bujatti, R. W. Burchfield, Clara Cooper, John Drummond, Paul Edwards, the late Richard Ellmann, Dr Cornelio Fazio, Hugh Ford, Lyndall Gordon, Michael Groden, Donald Hall, Sir Stuart Hampshire, Eva Hesse, Caroline Higginbottom, Daniel Hoffman, Patricia Hutchins, Lionello Lanciotti, Roger Lewis (who translated for me from Italian books and articles), Wallace Martin, Julian Mitchell, Michael O'Sullivan, M. R. Perkin, Andrew Rosenheim, Peter Rudge, E. W. F. Tomlin, Jeremy Treglown, and Pat Utechin.

I feel I should include a note of appreciation to all those scholars who have striven patiently to untangle the Cantos and the rest of Ezra Pound's poetry. Though it may not often show it, this book has a very large debt to them, particularly to Peter Brooker's *Student's Guide to the Selected Poems of Ezra Pound* (Faber and Faber, 1979), Christine Froula's *Guide to Ezra Pound's Selected Poems* (New Directions, 1982), and Carroll F. Terrell's two-volume *Companion to the Cantos of Ezra Pound* (University of California Press, 1980, 1984). The journal *Paideuma*, which Professor Terrell edits, is an invaluable compendium of Poundian information, and I have drawn extensively from it.

In search of a guide through the labyrinths of psychiatry and the classification of mental illness, I turned to Anthony Storr, who gave me his own opinion of Ezra Pound, helped me with terminology, and read the manuscript – all greatly to the book's benefit. Another guide was Massimo Bacigalupo, a Pound scholar who proved to be a wonderful Italian contact; he generously shared his knowledge both of Ezra (whom he knew personally) and Rapallo (where he lives), read the manuscript, and lent some splendid photographs.

Edward Mendelson, a faithful ally from my Auden days, read the manuscript, made excellent suggestions, and kept up my spirits marvellously. Mary Jane Mowat, another reader of the text in its early stages, gave useful advice on legal and other matters. My family – my wife Mari Prichard, and my children Clare and Kate – lived uncomplainingly with the shade of Ezra Pound for a number of years (and in the process saw a good deal of Italy). And my American hosts in the spring of 1985, John and Fina Waterston, Ed Mendelson, the Laughlins, and Austin Olney and Marcia Legru, coped with me on my whirlwind research trip when I was at least as mad as Ezra Pound was ever supposed to have been.

Index Of Titles And First Lines

of poems and prose pieces of Ezra Pound

General Index

(The sub-heading 'letters to' refers to a letter of Ezra Pound to the person indicated in the main heading.)

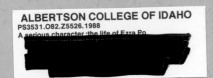